Magill's
Cinema
Annual
2 0 0 8

Magill's Cinema Annual 2008

27th Edition
A Survey of the films of 2007

Hilary White, Editor

**With an Introduction by
Barry Keith Grant**

A VideoHound® Reference

GALE
CENGAGE Learning™

Detroit • New York • San Francisco • New Haven, Conn • Waterville, Maine • London

Magill's Cinema Annual 2008

Hilary White, Editor

Project Editor: Michael J. Tyrkus

Editorial: Laura Avery, Pamela M. Bow, Tom Burns, Jim Craddock, Katherine H. Nemeh, Kathleen Lopez Nolan, Tracie Ratiner

Editorial Support Services: Wayne Fong

Composition and Electronic Prepress: Gary Leach, Evi Seoud

Manufacturing: Rhonda Dover

For product information and technology assistance, contact us at
Gale Customer Support, 1-800-877-4253.
For permission to use material from this text or product,
submit all requests online at **www.cengage.com/permissions**.
Further permissions questions can be emailed to
permissionrequest@cengage.com

Gale
27500 Drake Rd.
Farmington Hills, MI, 48331-3535

ISBN-13: 978-1-55862-611-9
ISBN-10: 1-55862-611-5

ISSN: 0739-2141

Printed in the United States of America
1 2 3 4 5 6 7 12 11 10 09 08

Contents

Contributing Reviewers

Michael Adams
Publishing Professional, Associate Professor, City University of New York Graduate Center

Michael Betzold
Author, Publishing Professional

John Boaz
Publishing Professional

David L. Boxerbaum
Freelance Reviewer

Beverley Bare Buehrer
Educator, Freelance Reviewer

Tom Burns
Publishing Professional

Marisa Carroll
Publishing Professional

David E. Chapple
Freelance Reviewereb

Peter N. Chumo II
Professional Film Critic

Jim Craddock
Publishing Professional

David Flanagin
Educator, Freelance Reviewer

Jill Hamilton
Freelance Reviewer

David Hodgson
Professional Film Critic

Glenn Hopp
Author, Film Critic, Department Head, Howard Payne University

Heather Hughes
Publishing Professional

Chris Lamphear
Author, Filmmaker, Publishing Professional

Eric Monder
Professional Film Critic

James S. O'Neill
Freelance Reviewer

David Metz Roberts
Freelance Reviewer

Brian Tallerico
Professional Film Critic

John C. Tibbetts
Author, Film Critic, Associate Professor, University of Kansas

Christine Tomassini
Publishing Professional

Michael J. Tyrkus
Publishing Professional

James M. Welsh
Author, Film Critic, Professor, Salisbury State University

Michael White
Freelance Reviewer

User's Guide

ALPHABETIZATION

Film titles and reviews are arranged on a word-by-word basis, including articles and prepositions. English leading articles (A, An, The) are ignored, as are foreign leading articles (El, Il, La, Las, Le, Les, Los). Other considerations:

- Acronyms appear alphabetically as if regular words.
- Common abbreviations in titles file as if they are spelled out, so *Mr. Death* will be found as if it was spelled *Mister Death*.
- Proper names in titles are alphabetized beginning with the individual's first name, for instance, *Gloria* will be found under "G."
- Titles with numbers, for instance, *200 Cigarettes,* are alphabetized as if the numbers were spelled out, in this case, "Two-Hundred." When numeric titles gather in close proximity to each other, the titles will be arranged in a low-to-high numeric sequence.

SPECIAL SECTIONS

The following sections that are designed to enhance the reader's examination of film are arranged alphabetically, they include:

- *List of Awards.* An annual list of awards bestowed upon the year's films by the following: Academy of Motion Picture Arts and Sciences, British Academy of Film and Television Arts Awards, Directors Guild of America Awards, Golden Globe Awards, Golden Raspberry Awards, Independent Spirit Awards, the Screen Actors Guild Awards, and the Writer's Guild Awards.
- *Obituaries.* Profiles major contributors to the film industry who died in 2007.
- *Selected Film Books of 2007.* An annotated list of selected film books published in 2007.

INDEXES

Film titles and artists are separated into nine indexes, allowing the reader to effectively approach a film from any one of several directions, including not only its credits but its subject matter.

- *Director, Screenwriter, Cinematographer, Editor, Art Director, Music Director,* and *Performer* indexes are arranged alphabetically according to artists appearing in this volume, followed by a list of the films on which they worked. In the *Performer* index, a (V) beside a movie title indicates voice-only work.

- *Subject Index.* Films may be categorized under several of the subject terms arranged alphabetically in this section.

- *Title Index.* The title index is a cumulative alphabetical list of films covered in the twenty-seven volumes of the *Magill's Cinema Annual,* including the films covered in this volume. Films reviewed in past volumes are cited with the year in which the film appeared in the *Annual;* films reviewed in this volume are cited with the film title in boldface with a bolded Arabic numeral indicating the page number on which the review begins. Original and alternate titles are cross-referenced to the American release title in the Title Index. Titles of retrospective films are followed by the year, in brackets, of their original release.

SAMPLE REVIEW

Each *Magill's* review contains up to sixteen items of information. A fictionalized composite sample review containing all the elements of information that may be included in a full-length review follows the outline on the facing page. The circled number following each element in the sample review designates an item of information that is explained in the outline.

1. **Title:** Film title as it was released in the United States.

2. **Foreign or alternate title(s):** The film's original title or titles as released outside the United States, or alternate film title or titles. Foreign and alternate titles also appear in the Title Index to facilitate user access.

3. **Taglines:** Up to ten publicity taglines for the film from advertisements or reviews.

4. **Box office information:** Year-end or other box office domestic revenues for the film.

5. **Film review:** A signed review of the film, including an analytic overview of the film and its critical reception.

6. **Reviewer byline:** The name of the reviewer who wrote the full-length review. A complete list of this volume's contributors appears in the "Contributing Reviewers" section which follows the Introduction.

7. **Principal characters:** Listings of the film's principal characters and the names of the actors who play them in the film.

8. **Country of origin:** The film's country or countries of origin.

9. **Release date:** The year of the film's first general release.

10. **Production information:** This section typically includes the name(s) of the film's producer(s), production company, and distributor; director(s); screenwriter(s); cinematographer(s) (if the film is animated, this will be replaced with Animation or Animation direction, or it will not be listed); editor(s); art director(s); production designer(s); music composer(s); and other credits such as visual effects, sound, costume design, and song(s) and songwriter(s).

11. **MPAA rating:** The film's rating by the Motion Picture Association of America. If there is no rating given, the line will read, "Unrated."

12. **Running time:** The film's running time in minutes.

13. **Reviews:** A list of brief citations of major newspaper and journal reviews of the film, including publication title, date of review, and page number (when available).

14. **Film quotes:** Memorable dialogue directly from the film, attributed to the character who spoke it, or comment from cast or crew members or reviewers about the film.

15. **Film trivia:** Interesting tidbits about the film, its cast, or production crew.

16. **Awards information:** Awards won by the film, followed by category and name of winning cast or crew member. Listings of the film's nominations follow the wins on a separate line for each award. Awards are arranged alphabetically. Information is listed for films that won or were nominated for the following awards: American Academy Awards®, British Academy of Film and Television Arts Awards, Directors Guild of America Awards, Golden Globes Awards, Golden Raspberry Awards, Independent Spirit Awards, the Screen Actors Guild Awards, and the Writers Guild of America Awards.

THE GUMP DIARIES ①
(Los Diarios del Gump) ②

Love means never having to say you're stupid.
—Movie tagline ③

Box Office: $10 million ④

In writer/director Robert Zemeckis' *Back to the Future* trilogy (1985, 1989, 1990), Marty McFly (Michael J. Fox) and his scientist sidekick Doc Brown (Christopher Lloyd) journey backward and forward in time, attempting to smooth over some rough spots in their personal histories in order to remain true to their individual destinies. Throughout their time-travel adventures, Doc Brown insists that neither he nor Marty influence any major historical events, believing that to do so would result in catastrophic changes in humankind's ultimate destiny. By the end of the trilogy, however, Doc Brown has revised his thinking and tells Marty that, "Your future hasn't been written yet. No one's has. Your future is whatever you make it. So make it a good one."

In *Forrest Gump,* Zemeckis once again explores the theme of personal destiny and how an individual's life affects and is affected by his historical time period. This time, however, Zemeckis and screenwriter Eric Roth chronicle the life of a character who does nothing but meddle in the historical events of his time without even trying to do so. By the film's conclusion, however, it has become apparent that Zemeckis' main concern is something more than merely having fun with four decades of American history. In the process of re-creating significant moments in time, he has captured on celluloid something eternal and timeless—the soul of humanity personified by a nondescript simpleton from the deep South.

The film begins following the flight of a seemingly insignificant feather as it floats down from the sky and brushes against various objects and people before finally coming to rest at the feet of Forrest Gump (Tom Hanks). Forrest, who is sitting on a bus-stop bench, reaches down and picks up the feather, smooths it out, then opens his traveling case and carefully places the feather between the pages of his favorite book, *Curious George.*

In this simple but hauntingly beautiful opening scene, the filmmakers illustrate the film's principal concern: Is life a series of random events over which a person has no control, or is there an underlying order to things that leads to the fulfillment of an individual's destiny? The rest of the film is a humorous and moving

attempt to prove that, underlying the random, chaotic events that make up a person's life, there exists a benign and simple order.

Forrest sits on the bench throughout most of the film, talking about various events of his life to others who happen to sit down next to him. It does not take long, however, for the audience to realize that Forrest's seemingly random chatter to a parade of strangers has a perfect chronological order to it. He tells his first story after looking down at the feet of his first bench partner and observing, "Mama always said that you can tell a lot about a person by the shoes they wear." Then, in a voice-over narration, Forrest begins the story of his life, first by telling about the first pair of shoes he can remember wearing.

The action shifts to the mid-1950s with Forrest as a young boy (Michael Humphreys) being fitted with leg braces to correct a curvature in his spine. Despite this traumatic handicap, Forrest remains unaffected, thanks to his mother (Sally Field) who reminds him on more than one occasion that he is no different from anyone else. Although this and most of Mrs. Gump's other words of advice are in the form of hackneyed cliches, Forrest, whose intelligence quotient is below normal, sincerely believes every one of them, namely because he instinctively knows they are sincere expressions of his mother's love and fierce devotion. ⑤

John Byline ⑥

CREDITS ⑦

Forrest Gump: Tom Hanks
Forrest's Mother: Sally Field
Young Forrest: Michael Humphreys
Origin: United States ⑧
Language: English, Spanish
Released: 1994 ⑨
Production: Liz Heller, John Manulis; New Line Cinema; released by Island Pictures ⑩
Directed by: Robert Zemeckis
Written by: Eric Roth
Cinematography by: David Phillips
Music by: Graeme Revell
Editing: Dana Congdon
Production Design: Danny Nowak
Sound: David Sarnoff
Costumes: David Robinson
MPAA rating: R ⑪
Running time: 102 minutes ⑫

REVIEWS (13)

Entertainment Weekly. July 15, 1994, p. 42.
Hollywood Reporter. June 29, 1994, p. 7.
Los Angeles Times. July 6, 1994, p. F1.
New York Times Online. July 15, 1994.

QUOTES (14)

Forrest Gump (Tom Hanks): "The state of existence may be likened unto a receptacle containing cocoa-based confections, in that one may never predict that which one may receive."

TRIVIA (15)

Hanks was the first actor since Spencer Tracy to win back-to-back Oscars® for Best Actor. Hanks received the award in 1993 for his performance in *Philadelphia.* Tracy won Oscars® in 1937 for *Captains Courageous* and in 1938 for *Boys Town.*

AWARDS (16)

Academy Awards 1994: Film, Actor (Hanks), Special Effects, Cinematography

Nomination:

Golden Globes 1994: Film, Actor (Hanks), Supporting Actress (Field), Music.

A

ACROSS THE UNIVERSE

All you need is love.
—Movie tagline

Within the lyrics of the world's most famous songs, lives a story that has never been told. Until now.
—Movie tagline

They lived without rules. They loved without fear. But as the world changed, so did they.
—Movie tagline

Box Office: $24.3 million

It is surprising no one ever tried the idea before: take the Beatles' songbook, arguably the best known and most popular in the world, and use those recognizable iconic tunes to construct a musical about the tumultuous personal, social, and political upheaval of 1960s. Since the music of Beatles is unquestionably the musical zeitgeist of the era, the possibilities are enormous. Director Julie Taymor, working with screenwriters Dick Clement and Ian La Frenais, took the plunge, and the result, *Across the Universe,* largely infuriated a majority of film reviewers, most of whom argued that the plot and execution failed to fulfill the promise of the movie's undeniably high concept.

In Taymor's defense, perhaps any movie with this ambitious a premise was bound to create unreasonably high expectations. That is not to say, however, that most Beatles fans already came into *Across the Universe* with their own strong opinions about how each song should be depicted visually. Luckily for the generations who have continued to embrace the Beatles, the Fab Four made global waves before the onset of MTV (although the Beatles did create some pioneering music videos for some of their later songs). Their rich, evocative songs largely remain unaccompanied by any preconceived, scripted visuals, so what one would imagine when they hear, say, "I Want to Hold Your Hand," remains, in most cases, the personalized scenario of individual fans. And yet, it is unlikely that most Beatles fans would ever imagine the presentation of "I Want to Hold Your Hand" that Taymor provides—namely, the plaintive cry of desperation from a small-town cheerleader for another member of her squad.

It is one of the film's many wonderfully creative, atypical takes on the Beatles' canon, and Taymor, to her credit, takes the viewer to many unexpected places in her uneven, but almost always fascinating, conceptualizations of those familiar songs. To have "I Want to Hold Your Hand," previously seen by many as an almost chaste anthem of teen love, transformed into a paean of unrequited lesbian desire is brilliant and, just a few minutes into the film, establishes Taymor's credibility with younger audiences. Taymor's movie musical is a 1960s story that is familiar in its themes and plot (much of which is similar to the quintessential 1960s musical *Hair*), but it also bridges the small gap to post-modernity nicely without doing too much damage to its hippie credibility.

Some critics lamented the flimsiness and looseness of the plot, and it is true that the story is rather familiar: a tale of young love set against the backdrop of political tension. But, putting the simplistic story behind, in movie musicals, execution is everything. Narrative is not normally the driving force in the musical genre and, with the root of the film being the stirring Beatles soundtrack, it seems fair to judge the final product also as an interlocked series of music videos. By this standard, *Across the Universe* is a fairly engrossing moviegoing experience. Most of the songs are beautifully performed by the talented cast of largely teenaged performers, most of them unknowns except for the already-veteran Evan Rachel Wood, and it is hard to argue that Taymor's set pieces are anything but innovatively staged and choreographed.

The first part of the film has, by far, the best cohesion between the dual purposes of developing Taymor's characters while using the Beatles songs to advance its plot. The movie opens with a shot from behind of Jude (Jim Sturgess) sitting on the seaside beach of his hometown of Liverpool (where else?) looking out over the ocean. He turns around, singing to the camera, "Is there anybody going to listen to my story / All about the girl who came to stay?" Immediately, the movie's method is established: this is a musical in the traditional sense, where characters burst into song at any time. But Taymor immediately makes a misstep in reminding us in jarring fashion that most early Beatles' love songs were followed by songs of turmoil and conflict. We see images of Jude's love, Lucy (Evan Rachel Wood), seemingly drowning in the waves amid newspaper clippings and protest montages while the song of anarchy, "Helter Skelter," foreshadows the film's later scenes. The whole film is like that—alternating between scenes of quiet beauty and scenes of rampant, almost humorous excess.

Next, we are brilliantly introduced to Jude and Lucy's first loves—in alternating dance scenes set in Liverpool and New Jersey, Jude's girlfriend (Lisa Hogg) and Lucy sing one of the more obscure early Beatles songs, "Hold Me Tight," a perfect evocation of the kind of innocent adolescent love that is about to be shattered. Jude, a dockworker, is leaving his mother behind to go to New York City, while cheerleader Prudence (T.V. Carpio)—yes, all the main characters have names taken from Beatles songs—is leaving Dayton, Ohio, broken-hearted, to hitchhike to New York, where eventually she will join the other characters in a commune.

Jude travels to Princeton to introduce himself to the father he has never met, who works at the university as a janitor, and he meets up with Max (Joe Anderson), an Ivy League misfit, who initiates Jude into his circle of friends, his partners in free-love revelry, with a raucous rendition of "With a Little Help From My Friends." Max is, conveniently, Lucy's brother, and Jude and Lucy fall tentatively in love, with a paired number of slowed-down, falling-in-love songs: "Flying" and "If I Fell" (followed later by a beautiful rendition of "Something"). Eventually the friends end up in an apartment owned by a sexy singer named Sadie (Dana Fuchs), vaguely

reminiscent of Janis Joplin, and they are soon joined by Prudence, who enters through the bathroom window, and Jo Jo (Martin Luther McCoy), a refugee from Detroit's riots, who does a passable evocation of Jimi Hendrix as a guitarist in Sadie's band.

It is not surprising when Vietnam intrudes into the free-love happiness of the era. Max is drafted—this is where the plot seems, at times, to be lifted wholesale from *Hair*—and Lucy becomes an ardent anti-war activist, which drives a wedge between her and Jude, who wants to remain an apolitical artist. The music and situations quickly turn psychedelic, and U2's Bono shows up as Dr. Roberts, a mystical Pied Piper of sorts, singing a menacing rendition of "I Am the Walrus."

The film mostly employs later Beatles material, from the Sergeant Pepper days onward, leaning heavily on numbers from *The White Album* and *Abbey Road*. Much of the fun of the movie is seeing how Taymor, in the service of her plot, employs some of the Beatles' most familiar songs in shocking ways. Many serve multiple purposes—for example, "Strawberry Fields Forever" illustrates both Jude's use of modern art to sublimate his romantic frustrations with Lucy and Max's nightmarish sojourns in Vietnam firefights. "I Want You" deliciously depicts Uncle Sam's desire for Max and other young cannon fodder to join the war effort (the recruits are reduced to mere body parts during a excellently conceived induction sequence), while also serving as a lustful love song for Sadie and Jo Jo. Shoehorning the lyrics of Beatles classics into the services of the plot is a mighty task, which sometimes feels forced. But when Taymor is able to make the exercise work, the effect is powerful. "She's So Heavy," which follows "I Want You" in the *Abbey Road* song suite, is brought to memorable life by Max and his fellow soldiers carrying the Statue of Liberty through the jungles of Vietnam. But the most moving song in the film has to be the rendition of "Let It Be," which bridges two funerals, the services for a young boy cut down in the Detroit riots and Lucy's first boyfriend, killed in the war.

Admittedly, there is one disastrous number, Eddie Izzard's spoken-not-sung rendition of "Being for the Benefit of Mr. Kite," which is, inexplicably, played out in a ridiculously over-the-top and totally egregious circus phantasmagoria, and a few music sequences that border on the predictable. However, these later sequences—for example, Jude singing "Revolution" while he throws a fit in Lucy's political headquarters or Max singing "Hey Jude" to lure his friend back to his sister's arms—are effective in their own right. Still, it is hard to argue that Taymor's vision for *Across the Universe*, a story told through the vocabulary of Beatles songs, is anything but thematically true to the era in which it is set, despite a few hackneyed characters and concepts. Molding Beatles songs into the service of anything other than Beatles songs is risky business, but Taymor cannot be faulted for her admirable ambition, even if the results run the spectrum from weak to brilliant. After watching *Across the Universe*, audiences may be inspired to re-examine the meanings of such tunes as "While My Guitar Gently Weeps" or "Happiness Is a Warm Gun," though, if not, Beatles fans everywhere can continue creating their own interior visuals. If anything, Taymor should be applauded for rejecting the impulse to treat the Beatles canon as if it were sacred text and having some fun with John, Paul, George, and Ringo.

Michael Betzold

CREDITS

Lucy: Evan Rachel Wood
Max: Joe Anderson
Jude: Jim Sturgess
Sadie: Dana Fuchs
Jo-Jo: Martin Luther McCoy
Prudence: T.V. Carpio
Himself: Bono (Cameo)
Origin: USA
Language: English
Released: 2007
Production: Suzanne Todd, Jennifer Todd, Matthew Gross; Revolution Studios, Columbia Pictures; released by Sony Pictures
Directed by: Julie Taymor
Written by: Dick Clement, Ian La Frenais
Cinematography by: Bruno Delbonnel
Music by: Elliot Goldenthal
Sound: Tod A. Maitland
Music Supervisor: Denise Luiso
Editing: Francoise Bonnot
Art Direction: Peter Rogness
Costumes: Albert Wolsky
Production Design: Mark Friedberg
MPAA rating: PG-13
Running time: 133 minutes

REVIEWS

Boston Globe Online. September 14, 2007.
Chicago Sun-Times Online. September 13, 2007.
Entertainment Weekly Online. September 12, 2007.
Hollywood Reporter Online. September 12, 2007.
Los Angeles Times Online. September 14, 2007.
New York Times Online. September 14, 2007.
San Francisco Chronicle. September 14, 2007, p. E1.
Variety Online. September 10, 2007.

Village Voice Online. September 11, 2007.
Washington Post. September 14, 2007, p. C1.

QUOTES

Lucy: "We're in the middle of a revolution Jude. And what are you doing? Doodles and cartoons?"
Jude: "Well I'm sorry I'm not the man with the mega-phone, but this is what I do."

TRIVIA

The film was released in the United States on October 9, which is also John Lennon's birthday.

AWARDS

Nomination:
Oscars 2007: Costume Des.
Golden Globes 2008: Film—Mus./Comedy.

AIR GUITAR NATION

To Air Is Human.
—Movie tagline
The official story of America's unofficial pastime.
—Movie tagline

Kriston Rucker, who along with his friend Cedric Devitt organized the first American Air Guitar Championship, knows that playing air guitar is a joke, but as he puts it, "It's the kind of joke that if you say it 100,000 times, you begin to believe it." While playing the air guitar may be a frivolous pursuit, after seeing this film it becomes clear that air guitar is indeed a skill that can be judged and that some people are more adept at it than others. Despite more than an hour's worth of air guitar playing, *Air Guitar Nation* is a surprisingly enjoyable film. Some viewers may even begin to believe the philosophy of the organizers of the World Air Guitar Championship in Finland who say that when one is holding an air guitar one cannot simultaneously hold a gun. In this way, the film makes a surprisingly convincing argument that playing air guitar can promote world peace.

Air Guitar Nation, however, is not intended as a serious discussion of world issues. Filmmaker Alexandra Lipsitz follows Rucker and Devitt's efforts to bring the first American contestant to the World Air Guitar championship. (To play air guitar is to play along with songs on an imaginary guitar.) Their first contest on the East Coast is surprisingly well-attended. Two contenders rise from the pack. Björn Türoque (Dan Crane), whose name is pronounced "born to rock," is a handsome man who has been in several unsuccessful rock bands. He takes this art form very seriously and has spent long hours in front of the mirror perfecting his moves. His competition comes in the form of C-Diddy (David Jung), the son of Korean immigrants, who is a struggling actor and comedian.

C-Diddy is the breakout star of the film. His charisma and talent make this more than a lightweight documentary on a quirky, marginal subject. C-Diddy, mildly overweight, attacks the stage in a skimpy red kimono and spandex pants accessorized with a Hello Kitty breastplate. He then proceeds to release what he terms his "Asian fury." Whatever it takes to be a world-class air guitarist, C-Diddy has it. He shreds out notes, running his fingers furiously up and down his invisible fret board. He sticks out his tongue and falls to the ground, his eyes popping out with the effort of it all. He is at once funny, skillful, and quite entertaining.

Lipsitz was fortunate in that her story had an excellent rivalry built in. Although Türoque is beaten in the East Coast Championship, he feels that he was robbed of his rightful title and heads to Los Angeles to the West Coast Championship and United States Finals. He is beaten by an upstart in the West Coast competition, but decides that even this loss will not deter him. He starts a collection among his friends and family to send him to Finland for the World Championship. He ends up several hundred dollars short, but comes up with the rest of the money himself. Once in Finland, he gives a surprising performance that earns him rave reviews and the current reigning champion's endorsement as heir to the throne.

The film offers an interesting look at how the art of air guitar is approached in other parts of the world. The World Air Guitar Championship is a popular event and has been around for over a decade. It offers classes on technique and how to work with groupies. Like the rest of the movie, it is all a little frivolous, but that does not negate the fact that it is gratifying to see competitors from all over the world gathering in Finland for this annual salute to this odd sport/art. As the organizers believe, air guitar is indeed a way that people from around the planet can connect peacefully with each other. Perhaps Andrew O'Hehir of *Salon.com* explained the charm of the film best: "In the tradition of the finest forms of American entertainment, both *Air Guitar Nation,* and the geekcraft it chronicles go way beyond shtick and self-parody into some meta-meta-ironic zone, where it's never clear from one moment to the next what is a joke and what is deadly earnest, until the two concepts finally merge into a sort of Buddhist singularity."

Jill Hamilton

CREDITS

Origin: USA

Language: English

Released: 2006

Production: Dan Cutforth, Jane Lipsitz, Anna Barber; Magical Elves; released by Shadow Distribution

Directed by: Alexandra Lipsitz

Cinematography by: Anthony Sacco

Music by: Dan Crane

Sound: Keith Garcia, Douglas Carney

Editing: Conor O'Neil

MPAA rating: R

Running time: 81 minutes

REVIEWS

Austin Chronicle Online. April 13, 2007.
Boston Globe Online. April 20, 2007.
Entertainment Weekly Online. March 28, 2007.
Los Angeles Times Online. March 30, 2007.
New York Times Online. March 22, 2007.
San Francisco Chronicle. May 11, 2007, p. C5.
Variety Online. May 15, 2006.
Village Voice Online. March 30, 2007.

QUOTES

Kriston Rucker: "It sounds like a joke, but it's the kind of joke that when you tell it 100,000 times, you start to forget that it's a joke and you kind of believe it."

ALIENS VS. PREDATOR: REQUIEM

This Christmas there will be no peace on Earth.
—Movie tagline

The last place on Earth we want to be is in the middle.
—Movie tagline

It began on their world. It will end on ours.
—Movie tagline

In space, no one can hear you scream. On Earth, it won't matter.
—Movie tagline

Box Office: $41.8 million

The eighth film to feature either the Alien or Predator creature—made famous largely during the 1980s thanks to the work of Ridley Scott, James Cameron, and Arnold Schwarzenegger—*Aliens vs. Predator: Requiem* is a great example of a franchise that has not only run out of fuel but is on such fumes that it has started to tarnish the legacy of the brilliant films that came before it. Only slightly more creative than the abysmal *Alien vs. Predator* (2004), *Requiem* shows glimpses of B-movie glory but never settles into a style, feeling more like something that should only be caught in a midnight movie marathon and never examined too closely. From a distance, *AvP: Requiem* does have an occasional cheap creature-feature charm and, very wisely, goes for the bloody jugular instead of the neutered PG-13 of the last film, but the complete lack of anything approaching a character will only remind serious filmgoers how far this franchise has tumbled from the heights of *Alien* (1979), *Aliens* (1986), or *Predator* (1987).

Aliens vs. Predator: Requiem opens on a Predator spaceship, where the intergalactic hunter that had been impregnated by a Facehugger and killed by the Alien Queen at the end of the last film gives "birth" to a Chestburster (for those unfamiliar, John Hurt's memorable final scene in the original *Alien* fully explains the gestation and birth cycles of the parasitic Alien race). That creature quickly grows into the Predalien (half-Alien, half-Predator) and starts killing the other Predators on the vessel. The chaos causes the ship, which just happens to be near Earth, to crash in Gunnison, Colorado. The one barely-alive Predator after the Predalien attack launches a distress signal, and the Predalien heads into the Colorado woods to do what his race does best, make duplicates. The distress signal reaches a Predator who heads to Earth to stop the Predalien from turning the human race into a giant incubator.

The poor humans caught in the middle of this sci-fi nightmare include Dallas Howard (Steven Pasquale), an ex-con who picks the worst possible day to come home, Eddie Morales (John Ortiz), the local sheriff, and Kelly O'Brien (Reiko Aylesworth), a soldier returning from Iraq with a set of night-vision goggles that come in handy when your town gets invaded by not one, but two, alien species on the same day. As the Predator chases the Predalien and his offspring, innocent residents of Gunnison start getting in the way, and the carnage piles up. After a few grisly deaths, including that of a child and a homeless woman (*Requiem* has a bizarre motif in which the Aliens seem to only kill the weakest denizens of Gunnison), the townsfolk start to realize that something funny might be going on, and the National Guard gets called in to save the day. The chase between the title creatures ends in a hospital, as the Predalien discovers that pregnant women are the best incubator to expand his species. A new method of replication leads to multiple Chestbursters, and the stage is set for a final battle between the Aliens and the Predator, while the few remaining humans either head into town where they might get killed by their own government or to the hospital roof where the final helicopter in town awaits them.

When the most notable thing about a film is the level of gore, especially when compared to the PG-13 blood level of the last installment, the filmmaking clearly leaves something to be desired. Colin and Greg Strause have taken the directorial reins from Paul Anderson and brought a shallow music video style to a franchise that once thrived on a mixture of relatable humanity in a futuristic world. The *Alien* movies were as much about Ripley (Sigourney Weaver's iconic character) as the creatures that hunted her. The Brothers Strause come from a background of special effects and music videos, and they reduce *Aliens vs. Predator: Requiem* to something just as two-dimensional. Each character has one defining trait—soldier, ex-con, nice guy, cop, hot girl—and the audience is given no reason at all to root for any of them to survive the interspecies war. Sadly enough, the Predator is the most well-drawn character in the entire film.

While both monster franchises were begun with a firm sense of character over carnage, the first *Aliens vs. Predator* film so drained the series of anything three-dimensional that anyone seeking out *Requiem* is probably only interested in the action, which is a notch above the last film, but not enough to recommend the complete product. There are moments—like a sewer battle between Aliens and the Predator and the final showdown on the hospital roof—that have a B-movie energy that was missing from the Anderson film and could be enough for a hardcore sci-fi action junkie. However, for anyone else watching this film any earlier than during a midnight movie marathon, the only joy that *Requiem* will bring is the invocation of the memory of the significantly better films that preceded it.

Brian Tallerico

CREDITS

Kelly: Reiko Aylesworth
Morales: John Ortiz
Ricky: Johnny Lewis
Molly: Ariel Gade
Dallas: Steven Pasquale
Tim: Sam Trammell
Col. Stevens: Robert Joy
Origin: USA
Language: English
Released: 2007
Production: John Davis, David Giler, Walter Hill; Brandywine, Dune Entertainment; released by 20th Century-Fox
Directed by: Colin Strause, Greg Strause

Written by: Shane Salerno
Cinematography by: Daniel Pearl
Music by: Brian Tyler
Sound: Patrick Ramsay
Editing: Dan Zimmerman
Art Direction: Helen Jarvis
Costumes: Angus Strathie
Production Design: Andrew Neskoromny
MPAA rating: R
Running time: 86 minutes

REVIEWS

Austin Chronicle Online. December 28, 2007.
Boston Globe Online. December 27, 2007.
Hollywood Reporter Online. December 25, 2007.
Los Angeles Times Online. December 28, 2007.
New York Times Online. December 26, 2007.
San Francisco Chronicle. December 27, 2007, p. E1.
Variety Online. December 26, 2007.

QUOTES

Dallas: "People are dying…we need guns!"

TRIVIA

This is the first film in either the Predator or AVP franchises to feature a look at the Predators' home world.

AWARDS

Nomination:

Golden Raspberries 2007: Worst Horror Movie, Worst Sequel/Prequel.

ALONE WITH HER

Anytime. Anywhere. He's watching.
—Movie tagline

Shot entirely with hidden cameras, *Alone with Her* is a deeply disturbing, painfully realistic depiction of a stalker-voyeur and his prey. Everything about the film, from plotline to character development to dialogue, is so true to life that it could be a documentary—but only if a stalker's videotapes could be retrieved from a police evidence locker to construct such a chilling narrative.

Written and directed by Eric Nicholas, whose last film was the obscure *River Rats* (1995), *Alone with Her* opens with an unsettling warning from a United States Department of Justice official about how the explosion of readily available, relatively cheap electronic surveillance equipment has been a boon to stalkers and how

prevalent the perversion has become. We then see this disturbing trend being put into practice—through the lens of a hidden camera, we see a man putting his camera into a satchel and, during the course of a day, pointing the camera at various women on the streets of Los Angeles, until he zeroes in on one he considers the most promising prey. Wordlessly, we are placed squirmingly into his world—a nightmarish orgy of constant surveillance.

The stalker, Doug (Colin Hanks), goes to a store, purchasing more sophisticated equipment. When he sees his prey, Amy (Ana Claudia Talancón), leaving her house with a suitcase, he breaks in late at night and installs tiny video devices throughout the house—including in the bedroom and bathroom. Then we watch Doug watching Amy as she returns home and goes through her daily routines, brushing her teeth, taking a shower, walking her dog, eating meals, watching television, and going to bed. When she turns the lights off, the camera switches to a night-vision mode, casting an eerie yellowish light over her body.

All this proceeds as a virtually dialogue-free introduction to the methods and mundane preoccupations of the modern electronic-age stalker. We see Doug in profile in front of his computer screen, watching the feed from her house. His intentions are unclear, but the whole setup is so unnerving and frightening that we are not surprised that, when he sees her masturbating one night in bed, he imitates the same act while watching her.

Doug eventually moves from passive voyeur to an active participant in the life of his prey. First, he meets Amy in a coffee shop, an exchange we watch through a button camera he has in his shirt. Doug is tentative and awkward, and, though the conversations seem normal, he is obviously not accustomed to interacting with the opposite sex. He uses the knowledge he has gained by watching her on camera to insinuate himself into her good graces—having studied her life so closely, he is able to imitate interest in films Amy has seen recently and her own favorite obscure bands.

Doug soon becomes both a director and an actor in his film of Amy's life. But with increasing contact comes his desire for increasing control, especially of her love life. When she makes a date with a potential suitor, Doug begins interfering more directly—he poisons a carton of milk in her refrigerator, causing her to vomit and cancel her date. When another date follows, he resorts to more extreme action, placing a poison ivy-like substance on her pillow, which causes Amy to break into a facial rash that makes her not want to be seen by anyone. The suitor quickly loses interest, thinking she is avoiding going out with him.

Eventually, both victim and stalker are sucked further into the strange narrative Doug is creating, egged on further and further by a fascinating spiral of psychological interdependence. Doug's actions create in Amy the very loneliness he hopes will mirror his own, in effect, driving her into his arms. He also engineers other problems that he can solve and other gifts he can bestow—for example, putting her art work on a web site, convincing a gallery owner to display it, and then buying the paintings himself while she thinks they were bought by a third party.

A girlfriend, Jen (Jordana Spiro), counsels Amy, who senses something is not right about Doug, to give him a chance. Doug initially plays hard to get, mentioning an imaginary girlfriend for reasons that are unclear (aside from his painful shyness). However, after Jen finally meets Doug as the three of them celebrate the sale of Amy's paintings, Jen also becomes suspicious of Doug's motives, particularly when he answers her questions with obviously fabricated answers, and Doug's engineered drama slowly begins to unravel.

Alone with Her is a singularly unique film, not always easy to watch, which many audiences may find repelling. But, to its great credit, it does show the ugly truth about stalking in a completely plausible, convincing way. The acting is awkwardly realistic, so much so that the actors disappear completely into their characters, just as the lack of cinematic embellishment and the use of the hidden cameras make the very narrative itself vanish into what seems like a rough and ugly slice of life. Writer/director Nicholas has created not just a believable but also a highly educational depiction of what it is really like for the incredible number of people who eavesdrop for voyeuristic thrills. And Hanks makes the perpetrator, chalky-hued and nervous, so authentic you can almost feel his sweaty palms. Amy is an ordinary woman, confused, overwhelmed, and slightly naïve, but it is easy to understand how she is able to be sucked in by Doug's strange manipulations. What woman could believe the lengths to which someone might go to gain their attentions/affections?

If *Alone with Her* is demanding of viewers, it is also, despite a few dull stretches, a taut thriller. Unorthodox, haunting, and depressing, this is a film that is not afraid to take chances and has a clear view of its goal. It succeeds brilliantly in turning the larger issue of stalking into a very sad flesh-and-blood story. No moral lesson is given or needed: everything worth knowing is revealed by the hidden cameras. This smart little film is the most powerful evidence you could present about this growing social.

Michael Betzold

CREDITS

Amy: Ana Claudia Talancón
Doug: Colin Hanks
Jen: Jordana Spiro
Matt: John Trent
Origin: USA
Language: English
Released: 2007
Production: Tom Engelman, Bob Engelman; IFC First Take, Weinstein Co.; released by IFC First Take
Directed by: Eric Nicholas
Written by: Eric Nicholas
Cinematography by: Nathan Wilson
Music by: David E. Russo
Sound: Michael Krikorian
Music Supervisor: Peymon Maskan
Editing: Cari Coughlin
Production Design: John Mott
MPAA rating: Unrated
Running time: 78 minutes

REVIEWS

Hollywood Reporter Online. January 19, 2007.
Los Angeles Times Online. February 23, 2007.
New York Times Online. January 27, 2007.
Variety Online. January 22, 2007.
Village Voice Online. January 9, 2007.

ALPHA DOG

> *One crime. 3 days. 38 witnesses.*
> —Movie tagline
>
> *How did a crime with this many witnesses go so far?*
> —Movie tagline
>
> *Inspired by true events.*
> —Movie tagline

Box Office: $15.3 million

Nick Cassavetes has inherited his father John's infatuation with small-time criminals and their idiosyncratic faults, but in his latest film, *Alpha Dog,* very little of the elder Cassavetes's knack for creating appealingly offbeat characters shines through. *Alpha Dog* is populated by a series of unappealing thugs, posers, and egomaniacal delusionals who all seem to be living lives inspired by gangster rap videos. Indeed, one such video is playing on a wide-screen television in an early scene while a throng of young guests of drug lord Johnny Truelove (Emile Hirsch) parties in his mansion. It seems like everyone in the film is trying to imitate the stereotype of the blinged-out rapper, despite the fact that the plot is set in a decidedly white- area of suburban California. The culture of the imitation thug life persists throughout. Whenever there is an interior scene with more than one person, it is almost inevitable they are insulting each other with homophobic and misogynistic comments, smoking marijuana, or groping at scantily clad women.

Cassavetes seems to revel in the profanity-laced, ignorant, halting conversations of these drug-addled young wannabes, as if he has discovered some remarkable species of authentic Americana. Initially he frames the film as a pseudo-documentary, with an unseen interviewer probing Johnny's father Sonny (Bruce Willis), who waxes about the importance of family but bristles when it is suggested that his son went wrong by following in his father's footsteps. Hopefully, this is not meant as a parallel to Cassavetes's film career.

Cassavetes seems to lose interest in this documentary approach, however, as he throws together scenes that introduce us to the main players in this suburban tragedy. The problem is that almost all of the characters are cut from the same cloth—in terms of speech patterns, wardrobes, and attitudes—thus making them barely distinguishable. After a series of introductions, the documentary style suddenly reappears as scenes are labeled with specific times and locations, as if taken from a police dossier, and characters are labeled by name or by their "witness number." Eventually, it becomes clear that they will be witnesses to a crime, namely, the kidnapping of Zack (Anton Yelchin), the fifteen-year-old brother of a lunatic skinhead drug addict named Jake Mazursky (Ben Foster), who owes Johnny $1,200 for a drug deal.

The kidnapping, however, is not planned; it is merely the result of an impulsive move by Johnny, who seems as aimless as the rest of the characters despite being in a position of power. He picks up Zack without rhyme or reason and eventually gives him over to the care of his lieutenant Frankie (Justin Timberlake). Strangely, Zack is not struggling to get free of his captors or return home to the stifling domesticity of his Los Angeles parents—far from it. Zack has been eager to adopt his older brother's lifestyle and emulate his great achievements, and he is more than happy to hang out with Frankie and his friends at parties, especially when drugs are provided and two girls start flirting with him. Zack revels in his imprisonment, and Johnny makes another half-hearted decision. It is illogical and ridiculous, but he decides that the good-natured Zack—who has endeared himself to Johnny's crew of friends—must be killed. Even in what should be a wrenching scene, there is a decided lack of emotion, largely because Cassavetes has allowed us no way to identify with any of these characters. Most are amoral and wretchedly devoid

of redeeming qualities, lacking even the strong personalities that might make them memorable villains.

Why Cassavetes thought there was any virtue in this shallow, unremarkable crime story is hard to fathom. Why he chose to present the story in such a lackluster, impassive fashion is even more difficult to understand. *Alpha Dog* is indeed a dog, but there is no alpha character anywhere in sight. Johnny does not seem to have any leadership characteristics, and the film is uninterested in back-stories, so it is assumed that Johnny has just followed in his father's footsteps for lack of anything better to do. Why anybody follows his orders is unclear. He does not seem to differ from the rest of his posse in any significant way. Hirsch fails to give Johnny any engaging qualities, but then the script does not provide him with many opportunities.

In *Alpha Dog*, Timberlake holds center stage, more so than Hirsch, just by playing a version of his own exaggerated celebrity persona. It seems, in fact, that all the other actors are themselves simply trying to play a parody of Timberlake. There is so little attention to detail that even the matter of why the drugs hold any power over these characters is glossed over. And the sexual interactions are perfunctory as well; since all the females are merely ornaments, they lack any personalities, and the men themselves seem only half-interested. The young women kiss and paw at the men, and at each other, in a sort of daze.

A revelatory film about the upper-middle-class California drug culture of recent years would be welcome, but *Alpha Dog* is not that film, because it neither satirizes nor reveals anything new about the culture and its denizens. In the end, Cassavetes himself seems confused about his purpose. Strangely, audiences only discover that the film is based on a true story at the very end, when we learn that the real Johnny Truelove was finally apprehended for his crimes in Paraguay. John Cassavetes had the knack for spinning gold out of minor characters, letting actors have free rein. But, in *Alpha Dog*, his son confounds that freedom by allowing it to go forward without a compelling story or purpose. None of the characters has clear motivations for any of his actions, so why would any audience be motivated to watch?

Michael Betzold

CREDITS

Johnny Truelove: Emile Hirsch
Frankie: Justin Timberlake
Jake Mazursky: Ben Foster
Zack Mazursky: Anton Yelchin
Elvis: Shawn Hatosy
Sonny Truelove: Bruce Willis

Olivia Mazursky: Sharon Stone
Butch Mazursky: David Thornton
Tiko: Fernando Vargas
Julie: Amanda Seyfried
Susan: Dominique Swain
Angela: Olivia Wilde
Buzz: Lukas Haas
Pick: Vincent Kartheiser
Cosmo: Harry Dean Stanton
Tiffy: Alex Kingston
Wanda: Heather Wahlquist
Origin: USA
Language: English
Released: 2006
Production: Sidney Kimmel, Chuck Pacheco; VIP Medianfonds 2, A-Mark Films; released by Universal Pictures
Directed by: Nick Cassavetes
Written by: Nick Cassavetes
Cinematography by: Robert Fraisse
Music by: Aaron Zigman
Sound: Craig Woods, Ed White
Music Supervisor: Spring Aspers
Editing: Alan Heim
Art Direction: Alan Petherick
Costumes: Sara Jane Slotnick
Production Design: Dominic Watkins
MPAA rating: R
Running time: 117 minutes

REVIEWS

Chicago Sun-Times Online. January 12, 2007.
Entertainment Weekly. January 19, 2007, p. 58.
Los Angeles Times Online. January 12, 2007.
New York Times Online. January 12, 2007.
Rolling Stone Online. January 8, 2007.
San Francisco Chronicle. January 12, 2007, p. E1.
USA Today Online. January 11, 2007.
Variety Online. January 27, 2006.
Village Voice Online. January 31, 2006.
Washington Post. January 12, 2007, p. C1.

QUOTES

Johnny Truelove: "You ever have that dream, the one where you did something…you don't know why, but you can never go back?"

TRIVIA

The defense attorneys for Jesse James Hollywood (who was extradited from Brazil in 2005) tried to prevent the release of the movie as prejudicial to their client's trial.

ALVIN AND THE CHIPMUNKS

Here comes trouble.
—Movie tagline

The original entourage.
—Movie tagline

Box Office: $214.6 million

Despite its familiar premise, *Alvin and the Chipmunks* is a surprisingly fresh take on a familiar theme of child performers thrust into the meat grinder of professional entertainment. There is very little here that has not been done many times over, yet somehow the helium-voiced, computer-generated rodents make an enjoyable ninety-two minutes of family entertainment.

The late songwriter and musician Ross Bagdasarian created Alvin and the Chipmunks in 1958 by recording himself singing at half speed and replaying the takes back at normal speed. The result was a high-pitched vocal that sounded exactly like a childlike singing chipmunk, and Bagdasarian, as the voice of Alvin the Chipmunk, notched chart toppers like "Witch Doctor" and "The Chipmunk Song (Christmas Don't Be Late)." The Three Chipmunks—Alvin, Simon, and Theodore—followed up with the animated *The Alvin Show,* which had a two-season run on CBS beginning in 1961. Over the years, Bagdasarian's creations have recorded more than thirty-five albums and won five Grammy® Awards. Forty-nine years after their inception, Ross Bagdasarian, Jr. is now in charge of the franchise and serves as executive producer of the film.

The film introduces us to struggling songwriter Dave Seville (Jason Lee) who is unable to break into the music business. Dave's old college buddy, Ian Hawke (David Cross), is an executive at Jett Records who scoffs at Dave's efforts, snarkily asking, "Could I take this song to Britney? Could I take it to Justin?" The spurned songwriter leaves with a few stolen muffins and the stowaways Alvin, Simon, and Theodore who have been living in the Jett Records lobby since their home was cut down and brought to Jett as a Christmas tree. Once home, Dave realizes that his rambunctious new roommates have a special talent that goes beyond the systematic dismantling of his domestic bliss. These three chipmunks can sing. Naturally, Dave brings the trio to the attention of the predatory Mr. Hawke. And, with a nod to the legendary animator Chuck Jones, the boys are unable to perform for Hawke, a la Michigan J. Frog in the animated classic *One Froggy Evening* (1955). Once over their stage fright, Alvin (voice of Justin Long), Simon (voice of Matthew Gray Gubler), and Theodore (voice of Jesse McCartney) become a huge success, with Hawke relentlessly driving their public images as Jett Records' latest pop sensations/cash machine. Dave, of course, would rather see the boys allowed a little room to breathe, enjoy their newfound success, and avoid the inevitable meltdown that comes with unrelenting fame.

Jason Lee, from the NBC comedy *My Name is Earl*, was cast as Dave Seville after the role was turned down by the likes of Bill Murray, John Travolta, and Tim Allen, and shows a nice range and knack for character development, becoming more paternal as the film progresses. David Cross brings a nice sense of subversive humor to the hard-driving, conniving Ian, and the two have strong on-screen chemistry. It is interesting to see the two comics play to a younger audience and interact with imaginary co-stars, which they do with a certain charm and ease. Dave's neighbor and sometime girlfriend is Claire (Cameron Richardson), who Dave manages to woo back into his life with a little help from his furry friends. The Chipmunk voices of Justin Long, Matthew Gray Gubler, and singer Jesse McCartney come across as both heartfelt and charming. The computer-generated stars are first rate and look quite natural interacting with their human co-stars. The lone technical criticism of the Chipmunks is that they seem to be nearly identical, with few distinguishing characteristics between the three, and stuck somewhere between full CG characters and 2-dimensional animations.

Alvin and the Chipmunks is, first and foremost, a film for the young and those who remember the Chipmunks from their formative years, though this update does contain more than a fair share of bodily-function humor. For music fans, Alvin and the boys perform no less than sixteen songs for the film, including a hip hop-edged remake of the trio's classic "Witch Doctor," along with covers of "Funkytown" and "I Love Rock & Roll." The film is the latest directorial effort from Tim Hill, who also directed the computer-animated *Garfield: A Tail of Two Kitties* (2006) and *Muppets from Space* (1999). The script was penned by Jon Vitti with Will McRobb and Chris Viscardi, who keep the story's focus on reinforcing good wholesome values between the pop songs and visual gags. The trio have a proven record of generating bankable children's films, and they bring home the goods once again with this outing. With a stellar box office of over $200 million and Ross Bagdasarian, Jr. watching over the family franchise, it seems the Chipmunks will be around for another generation of fans to enjoy.

Michael White

CREDITS

Dave Seville: Jason Lee
Ian Hawke: David Cross
Claire: Cameron Richardson
Gail: Jane Lynch
Alvin: Justin Long (Voice)
Simon: Matthew Gray Gubler (Voice)

Theodore: Jesse McCartney (Voice)
Origin: USA
Language: English
Released: 2007
Production: Janice Karman, Ross Bagdasarian, Jr.; Bagdasarian Productions, Regency Enterprises, Fox 2000 Pictures; released by 20th Century-Fox
Directed by: Tim Hill
Written by: Jon Vitti, Will McRobb, Chris Viscardi
Cinematography by: Peter Lyons Collister
Music by: Christopher Lennertz
Sound: David MacMillan
Music Supervisor: Julianne Jordan
Editing: Peter E. Berger
Art Direction: Charlie Daboub
Production Design: Richard Holland
MPAA rating: PG
Running time: 92 minutes

REVIEWS

Boston Globe Online. December 14, 2007.
Chicago Sun-Times Online. December 14, 2007.
Hollywood Reporter Online. December 14, 2007.
Los Angeles Times Online. December 14, 2007.
New York Times Online. December 14, 2007.
San Francisco Chronicle. December 14, 2007, p. E5.
Variety Online. December 13, 2007.
Washington Post Online. December 14, 2007.

QUOTES

David Seville: "Chipmunks don't talk."
Simon: "Our lips are moving and words are coming out."

TRIVIA

The piano used in the scene during which Dave and the Chipmunks sing "The Chipmunk Song" is the piano Chipmunks creator Ross Bagdasarian used to originally write and perform the song.

AMAZING GRACE

Behind the song you love is a story you will never forget.
—Movie tagline
One voice that changed the lives of millions.
—Movie tagline

Box Office: $21.3 million

Amazing Grace is a pious movie about a pious man—William Wilberforce, the man who led the fight for the abolition of the slave trade in the British House of Commons in the late eighteenth century and early nineteenth century. A name not well known to most, Wilberforce is presented as one of the neglected heroes of modern civilization, not only an abolitionist before such a stance became popular, but also a progressive in every sense: a man ahead of his time. He is even an animal rights activist—in fact, he was the founder of the Society for the Prevention of Cruelty to Animals.

It has been a long time since British director Michael Apted made an impact movie, that being *Coal Miner's Daughter* (1980). Here, from a script by Steven Knight, Apted delivers another underdog saga. While the story of Wilberforce is a long way from that of Loretta Lynn, both movies are about an against-all-odds triumph of spirit and courage over a rigid system of conformity. And, like most such stories, it has easily drawn villains—the sugar companies and their lackeys in the Parliament, personified by the king's nephew, an oily duke (Toby Jones). If there is any doubt he is evil, it is dispelled early on when he is playing cards with Wilberforce (Ioan Gruffudd) and offers to bet his slave ("my nigger," as he calls him—the only time the epithet is uttered in the movie) to meet Wilberforce's raise. High-stakes poker indeed, even if high-stakes poker probably was not played at the time, but the audience gets the point.

One of the problems in this film is that Apted must explain why the unknown hero Wilberforce is so intensely opposed to slavery and why he is such a misfit within his time and rank (though not a proper nobleman, Wilberforce is wealthy). He does not entirely succeed. The protagonist's antipathy is presented as a physical revulsion—when he leaves the aforementioned card game and is pursued by his friend William Pitt (Benedict Cumberbatch), he is almost retching. The pair are young Turks, in their twenties, and they have wild plans to overturn the established social order and make a vaguely "better world." Wilberforce has an idea—and he returns to the parlor where all the lords are drinking, gets up on a table, and belts out "Amazing Grace." He explains that the song was written by a man he knows, the remorseful ex-captain of a slave ship.

That captain turns out to be John Newton (Albert Finney), whose relationship to Pitt is unclear—though he treats him like an uncle or fatherly figure. Newton is now living as a monk. When Wilberforce visits, he is mopping a stone floor, wearing sackcloth, and mournfully wallowing in guilt. He is living, he says, with "20,000 ghosts," representing all the Africans who died during his voyages.

Wilberforce seeks Newton's advice because he is torn between devoting his life to religious solitude or becoming Pitt's point man in a scheme to overturn the established order. Newton tells Wilberforce he is too likable to be a monk—that he is too full of charisma and should use that gift in the political world to advance his moral cause of abolitionism. But there is still a level of uncertainty as to why Wilberforce is so ardent about this cause.

Apted also has difficulty explaining Wilberforce's religious stirrings. He tries to accomplish it with a scene in which Wilberforce begins a direct dialogue with God in the back meadow of his estate, flopping down on wet leaves and contemplating spider webs and the beauty of God's creation. His butler interrupts him, inquiring whether a beggar at the door should be admitted. "Of course," Wilberforce says, because he is the kind of man who feeds all beggars. Wilberforce confesses his problem—his sudden infatuation with God, and how his political schedule keeps frustrating that—and the butler sits down with him on the grass and quotes Beckett to the effect that a great man is not so great if he does not know himself.

The rest of the film does not elaborate on Wilberforce's relationship with God, because Apted does not seem to know how to fit religious conviction into the picture, though he wants very much to emphasize that God is on the side of the abolitionists—thus the title of the film. There is never a satisfactory explanation of the roots of Wilberforce's anti-slavery conviction or how exactly they are tied to his religion. In fact, the idea that there ought to be some kind of conflict between the two is a major theme in the first part of the film. In a key scene, Pitt brings a group of abolitionists to dinner who place on Wilberforce's dinner table the actual chains and shackles used on slaves and suggest to Wilberforce that there is no conflict between serving God and advancing the abolitionist cause—a point that should seem painfully obvious to everyone else in this era. Why that was not clear to Wilberforce is what Apted does not clarify.

In Apted's view, Wilberforce is a miserable misfit, a man ahead of his time in an era and place where religion was allied with pomp and corporate power. Wilberforce is a true iconoclast who decides to use his preacher-level oratorial powers to rail against the slave trade primarily because of his own moral revulsion to it. He is a reluctant politician, signing on to Pitt's scheme, which involves a plan for Pitt to become prime minister—and joining the abolitionists themselves, though clashing with the most radical of them, Thomas Clarkson (Rufus Sewell), when he suggests they make common cause with the French revolutionaries. Clarkson offers that Wilberforce is the "most radical of them all" because he is unwavering and unchanging in his single-minded pursuit of abolition. This is Apted's view, that Wilberforce is right for sticking to his guns, not as a political strategy for taking power or for inciting a broader revolution, but simply because of moral conviction. Yet in the end, Wilberforce only succeeds when he learns to become a political animal and to end the slave trade through legislative cunning.

Apted hinges the movie around a period in the early 1800s when Wilberforce feels utterly defeated, and this makes for a dramatic yet sometimes clumsy backward-and-forward telling of the tale. At this point, Wilberforce has failed for fifteen years in getting Parliament to back his annual bill to end the slave trade. He is suffering both from colitis and from addiction to the opium he takes to cure it, and he is enraged that slavery persists despite his efforts. Enter Barbara Spooner (Romola Garai), a beautiful young admirer who listens to his tale of woe and urges him to return to action. Her love restores his health and political vigor. But Apted's use of Spooner as a way for Wilberforce to tell his story is a bit hackneyed.

Positioning the story at Wilberforce's low ebb allows the necessary character arc a film needs, from despair to hope, and it also seems to fit with Apted's desire to connect to a contemporary audience. The speeches and arguments in Parliament seem intentionally written to resonate with present-day audiences: talk of change is seen as seditious and economically ruinous and the progressive forces seem disheartened and hopeless. In this sense, *Amazing Grace* is a call to arms with the message: "Do not give up. Return to action." Presumably this approach itself is prescribed as curative. Wilberforce frequently clutches his stomach because of his painful colitis, but the ailment is mysteriously resolved by film's end. It is a rather startlingly dropped plot thread.

The film is by turns fascinating, overwrought, and infuriatingly didactic: key arguments come in dialogue dripping with Meaning and Import, and the treatment tries to substitute these broad-brush exchanges for real insight into character. We never understand why Wilberforce is so adamant about the cause or what about his religious conviction drives him to it. Instead, there is a mushy sort of humanism that equates finding God in nature (the spider web) with seeing slavery as wrong and keeping animals that others would kill (the hares) as household pets. Wilberforce is someone contemporary progressives would find recognizable and sympathetic, but he is a fish out of water in the England of his day. Apted is a radical Baby Boomer's kind of director, and his hero in this film shares the Baby Boomer ambivalence about playing the political game. Wilberforce demonstrates he is a modern man as he rarely wears his powdered wig.

Gruffudd does well with this challenging part—he must be believable as a fanatic, a sage, a man of God, a disheartened soul, a reawakened lover, a gentle friend of all creatures, and a reluctant yet principled and eventually savvy politician. It is a heavy load for any actor to carry, and although Gruffudd's appearance and demeanor are too modern, he nonetheless succeeds in channeling the stiffness and stuffiness of the era into a character that modern audiences might appreciate. With dialogue, Knight plays it safely halfway—the language used has been sufficiently modernized to make the conversations passably believable as authentic for their day. The same holds for the other characters: those on the right side of the question all succeed in exhibiting qualities and behaviors that set them apart from the retrograde others. It is a bit of a panache on history—but a sufficiently believable one to make a heartwarming film.

Michael Betzold

CREDITS

William Wilberforce: Ioan Gruffudd
Barbara Spooner: Romola Garai
John Newton: Albert Finney
Lord Charles Fox: Michael Gambon
Thomas Clarkson: Rufus Sewell
Lord Tarleton: Ciarán Hinds
Duke of Clarence: Toby Jones
Henry Thornton: Nicholas Farrell
Marianne Thornton: Sylvestria Le Touzel
James Stephen: Stephan Campbell Moore
William Pitt: Benedict Cumberbatch
Olaudah Equiano: Youssou N'Dour
Origin: Great Britain
Language: English
Released: 2006
Production: Edward B. Pressman, Terrence Malick, David Hunt, Michelle Murdocca; Roadside Attractions, Bristol Bay Prods.; released by Samuel Goldwyn Films
Directed by: Michael Apted
Written by: Steven Knight
Cinematography by: Remi Adefarasin
Music by: David Arnold
Sound: Jim Greenhorn
Music Supervisor: Charles Wood
Editing: Rick Shaine
Art Direction: David Allday
Costumes: Jenny Beavan
Production Design: Lindsay Fellows
MPAA rating: PG
Running time: 111 minutes

REVIEWS

Boxoffice Online. February 23, 2007.
Chicago Sun-Times Online. February 23, 2007.

Detroit News. February 23, 2007, p. 4F.
Entertainment Weekly. March 2, 2007, p. 51.
Hollywood Reporter Online. September 4, 2006.
Los Angeles Times Online. February 23, 2007.
New York Times Online. February 23, 2007.
San Francisco Chronicle. February 23, 2007, p. E1.
Variety Online. September 15, 2006.
Washington Post Online. February 23, 2007.

QUOTES

Lord Fox (referring to William Wilberforce): "When people think of great men, rarely do they think of peaceful men."

TRIVIA

John Newton originally called his 1772 hymn "Faith's Review and Expectation."

AMERICAN GANGSTER

There are two sides to the American dream.
—Movie tagline

Box Office: $130.1 million

Ridley Scott's distinctive film about Harlem drug lord Frank Lucas is an interesting speculation about the nature of ambition, success, and the "American dream," but its title clearly labels it as a gangster film, which brings into play a number of genre expectations. However, Scott not only diverges from the usual crime formula but even ignores some basic components of the genre it presumably represents. The film, although never boring, takes its time and is far more meditative than action-packed, avoiding most of the usual stereotypes one associates with American gangster movies. It is neither *The Godfather* (1972) nor *The French Connection* (1971) (nor *Goodfellas* [1990] nor *Scarface* [1983], for that matter) but, allegedly based upon a true story, it is certainly worth seeing for what it has to suggest about entrepreneurship, business "integrity," family values, success, and ambition in America. Denzel Washington's Frank Lucas believes in the American dream and attempts to live it in his own flawed criminal way. He is less vulgar than Jay Gatsby but more brutal, ruthless, and deceptive than Tom Buchanan. Washington's casting seems perfect for Frank Lucas; his nemesis, Richie Roberts, an honest police detective who aspires to be a lawyer, is played by Russell Crowe, who gives a decidedly superior performance. Another standout in the cast is Ruby Dee, the iconic African American actress, who plays Frank's mother. Frank invites her to bring his whole family up from North Carolina to New Jersey, because he wants to turn his heroin smuggling operation into a

"family" business, a move that is also clearly a matter of control.

Frank is pretty cool and not merely in the vernacular sense. He served an apprenticeship as a driver for a Harlem drug kingpin, Ellsworth ("Bumpy") Johnson (Clarence Williams III), whom he considers his mentor. After Frank's mentor dies of natural causes (more the exception than the rule in this movie), Frank decides to go into the drug business himself, but wants to eliminate the middleman and buy his heroin directly from dealers in Thailand. Through an elaborate and thoroughly corrupt system of bribery, Frank sets up a foolproof infrastructure that enables him to ship the drugs into the United States hidden in the false bottoms of caskets of servicemen killed in action in Vietnam and shipped back to Dover, Delaware. Frank starts his operation in 1968, but his system breaks down after a half-dozen years, as the war effort in Vietnam begins to wind down. By the end of the film, Frank is desperate to get one final shipment delivered, but federal agents are closing in.

Frank succeeds in the drug game because he is selling a superior "product," which he calls "Blue Magic," offering twice the narcotic strength at half the usual price. Typically, drugs sold on the street will be cut by at least fifty percent, but Frank's Blue Magic is unadulterated, and woe to the middleman who tries to dilute the "product" that Frank has branded. Frank eliminates the Mafia middleman (played by Armand Assante) by going directly to the source, a bold move, and stays off the police radar by cutting a low-profile figure. He dresses like a conservative businessman, like an accountant, wearing very ordinary suits, shirts, and ties. He lives a generally tranquil life with his family imported from North Carolina and his Puerto Rican trophy wife, taking his mama to church every Sunday and regularly placing flowers on the grave of his mentor. His strategy works, and the trap does not begin to close on him until 1973. He only slips up when his wife buys him an extravagant fur coat and hat to wear when he attends the prizefight between Muhammad Ali and Joe Frazier, which is exactly the point at which he becomes a person of interest in Robert's investigation of the New York drug trade.

Washington and Scott go to great lengths to convey to the audience that Frank is by no means your stereotyped drug kingpin, which largely explains his unprecedented success. Aside from the Mafia and the inherent racism of the era, his biggest threat comes from New York's finest, a squad of "special" investigators who attempt to blackmail and intimidate him. When the honest detective finally captures Frank with enough evidence to send him away for seventy-five years, Frank is willing to cut a deal to help Roberts get the goods on the corrupt cops. The action is plotted well enough, but the "action" comes in unexpected and bloody spurts. Had the story been fiction, then Scott would have been able to orchestrate it more suspensefully, perhaps. But what the film loses in potential suspense, it gains in verisimilitude.

The question remains—is this story, ripped from yesterday's headlines, true? Presumably what was taken from Mark Jacobson's profile for *New York* magazine ought to be true, but parts of the story were also fictionalized by Ridley Scott's screenwriter, Steven Zaillian, who stretches this relatively thin police procedural into an epic length. *Washington Post* reviewer Stephen Hunter, who praised the film for its "superb feel for time and milieu," was impressed by the way director Ridley Scott "plays the stories of Lucas and Roberts off each other so adroitly that we don't notice that the two antagonists aren't even aware of each other until the movie's second half." *Newsweek*'s David Ansen wrote that as "charismatic as Crowe is, the cop's story can't compete with the crook's," but noted the interesting contrast between the messy personal habits of Richie Roberts and the absolutely well-structured life of Frank Lucas. Ansen claimed that when the two stars finally share a scene, "it seems to belong to another movie."

London Review of Books critic Michael Wood was impressed by *American Gangster* as a genre film, calling it "a little overhaunted by past masterpieces and in the end perhaps dwarfed by them, but gripping and troubling all the way through." Wood complained that the plot goes soft toward the end, when Ridley Scott "loses control of his balancing act, where the fantasy of self forgets about the social reality, and Denzel Washington escapes into pure charm." As noted above, Frank and Richie are parallel characters on opposite sides of the law, though, at the end, we learn that, in real life, Richie later becomes a defense attorney and ends up representing Frank Lucas. Wood reacts to this disclosure by explaining that "it was a buddy movie all along."

New Yorker critic David Denby protested that the film presents Frank's career as "a long-delayed victory of black capitalism" with no irony whatsoever. He thought viewers should demand to know "why it's supposed to be better that hundreds, maybe thousands, of people in Harlem were destroyed by black gangsters rather than by Italians." Yes, Frank's mother slaps his face at the end of the film, but as Denby notes, "that moral judgment comes too late, and it isn't prepared for." Even Washington's infectious, charming smile cannot win viewers over and make Frank likable. His work ethic may be admirable, but his behavior is generally appalling.

James M. Welsh

CREDITS

Frank Lucas: Denzel Washington
Richie Roberts: Russell Crowe
Huey Lucas: Chiwetel Ejiofor
Nicky Barnes: Cuba Gooding, Jr.
Det. Trupo: Josh Brolin
Lou Toback: Ted Levine
Dominic Cattano: Armand Assante
Ellsworth "Bumpy" Johnson: Clarence Williams III
Eva: Lymari Nadal
Javier J. Rivera: John Ortiz
Moses Jones: RZA
Mama Lucas: Ruby Dee
Tango: Idris Elba
Laurie Roberts: Carla Gugino
Turner Lucas: Common
Charlie Williams: Joe Morton
Rossi: Jon Polito
Campzi: Kevin Corrigan
Doc: Ruben Santiago-Hudson
U.S. Attorney: Roger Bart
Richie's Attorney: KaDee Strickland
Origin: USA
Language: English
Released: 2007
Production: Brian Grazer, Ridley Scott; Scott Free, Imagine Films; released by Universal
Directed by: Ridley Scott
Written by: Steven Zaillian
Cinematography by: Harris Savides
Music by: Marc Streitenfeld
Sound: William Sarokin
Music Supervisor: Kathy Nelson
Editing: Pietro Scalia
Art Direction: Nicholas Lundy
Costumes: Janty Yates
Production Design: Arthur Max
MPAA rating: R
Running time: 157 minutes

REVIEWS

Boston Globe Online. November 2, 2007.
Chicago Sun-Times Online. November 2, 2007.
Entertainment Weekly Online. October 30, 2007.
Hollywood Reporter Online. October 22, 2007.
Los Angeles Times Online. November 2, 2007.
New York Times Online. November 2, 2007.
New Yorker Online. November 5, 2007.
Rolling Stone Online. October 18, 2007.
Variety Online. October 21, 2007.

Wall Street Journal. November 2, 2007, p. W1.
Washington Post. November 2, 2007, p. C1.

QUOTES

Frank Lucas: "I sell product better than the competition at prices lower than the competition. I am my own company."

Frank Lucas: "The man I worked for had one of the biggest companies in New York City. He didn't own his company. White man owned it, so they owned him. Nobody owns me, though."

TRIVIA

Director Ridley Scott hired many local villagers while filiming on location in the Chiang Mai province of Thailand (some of whom were actual participants in Frank Lucas' drug-running operation).

AWARDS

Screen Actors Guild 2007: Support. Actress (Dee)

Nomination:

Oscars 2007: Art Dir./Set Dec., Support. Actress (Dee)

British Acad. 2007: Cinematog., Film, Film Editing, Orig. Screenplay, Orig. Score

Golden Globes 2008: Actor—Drama (Washington), Director (Scott), Film—Drama

Screen Actors Guild 2007: Cast.

ANGEL-A

In *Angel-A,* writer/director Luc Besson creates a fairy-tale romance in which a celestial being who looks more like a supermodel than a messenger of God helps a lost soul discover his inner worth. Set in a gorgeous black-and-white Paris courtesy of cinematographer Thierry Arbogast, the film suffers from an uneven screenplay lacking in narrative drive and a plotline that is an uneasy hybrid of a self-discovery story and a gangster tale. Nonetheless, Besson's original spin on *It's a Wonderful Life* (1946) and the interplay of one of the oddest couples in recent cinema make the film a modest delight.

André (Jamel Debbouze), a petty criminal and would-be entrepreneur, is in serious debt to some Parisian mob bosses who are bearing down on him to pay up or face an imminent demise. In one breathtaking shot, his nemesis has the hapless André dangling from atop the Eiffel Tower. Moroccan by birth but possessing a green card and a residence in Brooklyn, André is short and a bit scraggly, certainly not the suave ladies' man he imagines himself to be, but, with big dreams of an olive oil business that have not borne fruit, he feels abandoned by God and is at his wit's end when he climbs over the

rail of a bridge on the Seine. Prepared to end it all, he witnesses a tall, stunning blonde jump first and, acting on instinct, plunges in to save her.

After a comic rescue in which he struggles to carry ashore this woman who towers over him, she introduces herself as Angela (Rie Rasmussen). Feeling indebted to him and dubbing him her "cause," she offers to do whatever he wants. He has her follow him around, figuring that he will be respected by the thugs who are after him if they see him with this woman who is clearly out of his league. On their sojourn to seedy Paris locales, Angela uses her feminine wiles to help André raise the money to pay off his debts, but facing down the bad guys is really only part of her mission. Sent from Heaven, she is an angel determined to help André turn his life around and gain the self-confidence he is so sorely lacking.

The quirky charm of *Angel-A* lies in the exchanges between André and Angela, the self-hating loser and the statuesque beauty who have no business being together and yet somehow make a captivating duo. An unconventional angel who chain-smokes and always seems hungry, Angela may even be a prostitute but, at the very least, gleefully toys with André's expectations. She can create multiple backstories for herself, making one wonder what her life might have been like on earth but, sadly, Angela does not really have a past she can remember, which gives her a poignant undercurrent.

The movie, however, falls short on plot, composed, as it is, of loose ramblings through the streets of Paris with occasional breaks for long conversations. André learns little life lessons along the way, such as the importance of speaking from the heart and not being seduced by flattery, but the screenplay's major flaw is that Angela's mission to help André find himself ultimately feels like vague talk-show psychobabble, especially in the big breakthrough scene in which, standing before a mirror, Angela gets André to look at his reflection and declare that he loves himself. This clichéd, silly climax reduces the mysterious Angela to the role of therapist and the film's message becomes something out of the self-esteem movement. The film is more enjoyable as a light romantic fantasy, and she is more entrancing when shuttling André around town and making him feel like the luckiest man to have found a supermodel to be his guardian angel.

But *Angel-A* beguiles in other ways. The black-and-white cinematography, which is soft and glowing, is not only beautiful, it also gives this fantasy an otherworldly quality that fits the Paris of swanky nightclubs and fancy hotel rooms. And Rasmussen herself is a fantastic sight to behold as the mercurial Angela. Wearing a tight, black minidress that shows off her long legs, she commands attention in every scene. While she is not quite like the eponymous action heroine of Besson's *La Femme Nikita* (1990), Angela's gift for easily subduing villains in original ways is another part of her appeal. And Debbouze, whose André constantly seems on the verge of a nervous breakdown and is often not very likable, lets through glimmers of the character's vulnerability under a desperate, anxious exterior.

Given the wobbly screenplay, the film's arbitrary and disjointed resolution is not surprising. Angela suddenly gets mad at André for asking why she revealed her angelic status to him and then forces him to stand up to Franck (Gilbert Melki), one of the gangsters who have made André's life miserable (which makes no dramatic sense since she has already cleared André's debts). The confrontation with Franck, moreover, feels like another random psychological exercise enabling André to heal by admitting his mistakes and gain a newfound clarity.

Likewise, André's sudden declaration of love for Angela followed by his subsequent battle to bring her down to earth when she sprouts wings and begins to take flight—she is conflicted about having a future with him since she has no past—is a hasty wrap-up to a story that is already thin on plot to begin with. Also, because there is no sense of what she ultimately is giving up in Heaven to stay with him, the happy ending is robbed of the emotional weight it seems to be aiming for.

On a philosophical level, *Angel-A* is fairly simplistic in its lessons about self-esteem, and one wishes that Besson had built a more complex narrative rather than delivering his message in familiar platitudes. But the pleasures of the film lie in its more eccentric accomplishments—namely, a Paris both menacing and lush, a dazzling angel as far from *It's a Wonderful Life*'s Clarence as one can imagine, and an oddball love story that wins the audience over despite its improbability and contrived ending.

Peter N. Chumo II

CREDITS

André: Jamel Debbouze
Angela: Rie Rasmussen
Franck: Gilbert Melki
Pedro: Serge Riaboukine
Origin: France
Language: French
Released: 2005
Production: Luc Besson; Europacorp, TF-1 Films, Apipoulai Productions; released by Sony Pictures Classics
Directed by: Luc Besson
Written by: Luc Besson

Cinematography by: Thierry Arbogast
Sound: Didier Lozahic, Jean Minondo
Music Supervisor: Anja Garbarek
Editing: Frederic Thoraval
Costumes: Martine Rapin
Production Design: Jacques Bufnoir
MPAA rating: R
Running time: 91 minutes

REVIEWS

Guardian Online. July 28, 2006.
New York Times Online. May 25, 2007.
The Observer Online. July 30, 2006.
Rolling Stone Online. May 24, 2007.
San Francisco Chronicle. June 1, 2007, p. E5.
Variety Online. December 21, 2005.
Village Voice Online. May 22, 2007.

QUOTES

André: "My whole life I've been in the s**t. No one ever helped me out. Ever."

ARE WE DONE YET?

New house. New family. What could possibly go wrong?
—Movie tagline
It was the perfect house. Until he decided to fix it.
—Movie tagline
First comes love. Then comes marriage. Then comes suffering.
—Movie tagline

Box Office: $49.7 million

The title of the sub par sequel, *Are We Done Yet?*, more than begs the eponymous question, courting derision from film critics who were more than happy to comply. Director Steve Carr's follow up to Brian Levant's *Are We There Yet?* (2005) purports to take root in *Mr. Blanding Builds His Dream House* (1948), the Cary Grant/Myrna Loy comedy classic based on the novel by Eric Hodgins. *Are We Done Yet?* lacks the literary underpinnings of that film with considerably less thought behind it, feeling more like a hastily constructed *The Money Pit* (1986). The film will, however, assure a place in mainstream family comedies for rap star turned reliable film star Ice Cube who reprises his role as a lovable curmudgeon who must endure yet another humorously disastrous dilemma.

The obviously named *Are We There Yet?* found Nick Persons (Ice Cube) courting divorced mother of two, Suzanne (Nia Long), as well as courting disaster as he was forced to undergo a nightmarish road trip with her impish spawn, Lindsey (Aleisha Allen) and Kevin (Philip Daniel Bolden). *Are We Done Yet?* takes the next logical step, marrying Nick and Suzanne, while exponentially increasing the disaster factor. With the happy little family of four all ready cramped in Nick's bachelor apartment in Portland, Suzanne announces she is pregnant...with twins. They have no choice but to seek a roomier domicile, which they find in rural Oregon. A seemingly gorgeous sprawl, it is soon clear that underneath the glossy exterior lies an endless string of problems.

Providing some much needed good-natured yin to Ice Cube's irascible yang is John C. McGinley who plays the local jack-of-all-trades, Chuck Mitchell, Jr. Universally praised for his performance in the film, McGinley's high energy, unrestrained style nicely balances Ice Cube's more grounded approach, which is exactly what is needed in this slapstick comedy. The perhaps mentally unbalanced Chuck has not only sold the Persons their home and serves as their contractor and building inspector, but boasts a lengthy and unique résumé that includes Polynesian fire dancer and midwife.

Most of the original humor may be credited to McGinley and his chemistry with Ice Cube, as director Carr sees fit to inject nearly every clichéd sight gag a disaster comedy can dream up. Seemingly docile wildlife suddenly become crazed killers when Nick approaches. A chandelier falls to the dinner table exactly on cue after Nick says Grace, thanking God for their beautiful home. When Lindsey remarks that at least they have a sturdy dinner table, Carr ham-handedly goes for the obvious and the dinner table collapses as well. In fact, nearly anything anyone touches breaks, collapses or implodes followed by the film's running joke, Nick's oft repeated, "I can fix that." The one-note nature of the comedy wears as thin as the dry-rotted structure itself. Tellingly, one of the film's better bits involve a group of blind pipe fitters.

A family comedy must also contain elements of drama and, amid the abundance of slapstick and physical comedy, Carr and writer Hank Nelken have Nick bond with his stepchildren through adversity. These scenes add a realistic touch and balance the illogic of the remainder of the film, which has Nick starting up a sports magazine single-handedly, buying what appears to be a multi-million dollar home despite its numerous problems, and continuing to fork over money to the deranged Mitchell whose conflicts of interest are all too obvious.

Despite its lack of originality, the film moves briskly along and most of the characters are likable. The film wisely avoids any raunchy humor, features a soundtrack filled with popular crowd-pleasers, and includes whimsical animation sequences making this familiar, middle-of-the-road comedy family friendly. It is perhaps more interesting, however, to note that the film was reportedly shipped to theaters bearing the moniker, "Needs Work," a double entendre that certainly needs no explanation.

Hilary White

CREDITS

Nick Persons: Ice Cube
Suzanne Persons: Nia Long
Chuck Mitchell, Jr.: John C. McGinley
Lindsey Persons: Aleisha Allen
Kevin Persons: Philip Daniel Bolden
Origin: USA
Language: English
Released: 2007
Production: Ted Hartley, Ice Cube, Matt Alvarez, Todd Garner; Revolution Studios, RKO Pictures, Cube Vision; released by Sony Pictures
Directed by: Steve Carr
Written by: Hank Nelken
Cinematography by: Jack N. Green
Music by: Teddy Castellucci
Sound: David Husby
Music Supervisor: Spring Aspers
Editing: Craig P. Herring
Art Direction: Kevin Humenny
Costumes: Jori Woodman
Production Design: Nina Ruscio
MPAA rating: PG
Running time: 92 minutes

REVIEWS

Chicago Sun-Times Online. April 4, 2007.
Entertainment Weekly Online. April 4, 2007.
Hollywood Reporter Online. April 4, 2007.
Los Angeles Times Online. April 4, 2007.
New York Times Online. April 4, 2007.
San Francisco Chronicle. April 4, 2007, p. E5.
Variety Online. April 3, 2007.
Washington Post Online. April 6, 2007.

QUOTES

Nick Persons: "I can fix that."

TRIVIA

Was shipped to theaters under the title *Needs Work*.

AWARDS

Nomination:
Golden Raspberries 2007: Worst Remake.

ARTHUR AND THE INVISIBLES

(Arthur et les Minimoys)

Adventure awaits in your own backyard.
—Movie tagline

Box Office: $15.1 million

Arthur and the Invisibles was directed by Luc Besson, the French director of *La Femme Nikita* (1990) and *The Fifth Element* (1997), and the film is based on two children's books that Besson penned, *Arthur and the Minimoys* and *Arthur and the Forbidden City.* Besson's film was a hit in France, but it failed miserably in the United States. Although it is questionable that the film warranted such success in France, neither is it deserving of the near universal disinterest it received in the United States.

Part live action and part computer-generated, the live action portion of *Arthur and the Invisibles* takes place in a picturesque old farmhouse, where Arthur (Freddie Highmore) lives with his Granny (Mia Farrow). His parents (Douglas Rand and Penny Balfour) have left him there while they go to the city to seek work. Grandpa (Ron Crawford) is an eccentric inventor and world traveler who has been missing for several years after mysteriously disappearing on one of his adventures. The family is facing problems in the form of a developer, Davido (Adam LeFevre), who wants to foreclose on the farm and build on it. The only hope for the family is for Arthur to find a cache of rubies that his grandfather once buried in the yard.

In order for Arthur to accomplish this, he must decipher a series of clues from his departed grandfather to learn how to enter the world of the Minimoys, a group of elfin creatures who make their home below the turf in Arthur's yard. Through a complicated process featuring several tall African tribesmen and a telescope, Arthur is transported into the world of the Minimoys where he is also rendered in a CGI fashion that looks little like his real-world self. There Arthur discovers that the Minimoys are suffering from problems of their own, particularly from Maltazard (voice of David Bowie), who seeks nothing less than complete dominion over the underground world. Arthur must defeat Maltazard and find the rubies before the farm is lost to Davido.

Arthur and the Invisibles comes with an impressive and eclectic lineup of vocal talent. Arthur's Minimoy love interest Selenia is voiced by Madonna, and her plump and eager younger brother Betameche is voiced by Jimmy Fallon. Also lending voices are Robert De Niro as The King, Harvey Keitel as Miro, Chazz Palminteri as The Travel Agent, and Emilio Estevez, Jason Bateman, Anthony Anderson, and Snoop Dogg. With the exception of Bowie, however, the host of talent are not well used. Bowie's Maltazard is a case where casting, computer rendering, and character mesh well. The character is painfully tall and thin with a dark edge that Bowie effortlessly encapsulates. He is a wounded and embittered villain with a delightfully deliberate and sinister way of moving about his lair. But such synergy between actor and character does not happen elsewhere. Fallon, for example, displays none of the wit and inventiveness he brought to *Saturday Night Live* in his character. Similarly, without checking the credits, it is difficult to recognize Selenia's voice as Madonna's. In both cases, the producers would have been better off hiring professional voice actors over pricey big-names that add little to this ill-conceived affair, and in some cases conspicuously detract from it. Notably, several critics, including Ty Burr of the *Boston Globe,* objected to the implication of a romantic bond between Arthur and Selenia. "Just thinking about the quasi-romantic scenes between the fourteen-year-old Highmore and the forty-eight-year-old Madge makes me feel unclean," wrote Burr. And while boasting a cast list rife with musicians, the film's soundtrack is oddly void of interesting selections.

While in the aboveground world, Highmore's performance is excellent. The talented young actor, who also appeared in *Charlie and the Chocolate Factory* (2005) and *Finding Neverland* (2004), delivers another soulful and nuanced performance. It is a shame that the animated version of Highmore lacks everything that makes the actor's performances so interesting. Where the real Highmore is a small thin boy with a compelling combination of seriousness and hope, his animated self is a spiky-haired blonde pixie. Highmore still brings sincerity to his line readings, but coming from his oddly animated self, it lacks the same gravitas.

Children, luckily, are not as demanding and Besson makes sure that the children are catered to. He keeps the screen filled with action and bright, shiny objects to look at. There are plenty of chases, wild rides, and fight scenes to keep even the squirmiest of children entertained. In the end, the film is a little more charming than the American box office would indicate and a little less charming than it could have been.

Jill Hamilton

CREDITS

Arthur: Freddie Highmore
Grandmother: Mia Farrow
Arthur's Father: Douglass Rand
Arthur's Mother: Penny Balfour
Davido: Adam LeFevre

Maltazard: David Bowie (Voice)

Princess Selenia: Madonna (Voice)

Betameche: Jimmy Fallon (Voice)

The King: Robert De Niro (Voice)

Koolomassai: Anthony Anderson (Voice)

The Travel Agent: Chazz Palminteri (Voice)

Max: Snoop Dogg (Voice)

Darkos: Jason Bateman (Voice)

Miro: Harvey Keitel (Voice)

Ferryman: Emilio Estevez (Voice)

Origin: France

Language: English

Released: 2006

Production: Luc Besson, Emmanuel Prevost; Europacorp, Avalanche Productions, Apipoulai Productions; released by Weinstein Co.

Directed by: Luc Besson

Written by: Luc Besson, Celine Garcia

Cinematography by: Thierry Arbogast

Music by: Eric Serra

Sound: Alexandre Hernandez

Art Direction: Patrice Garcia, Philippe Rouchier

Costumes: Olivier Beriot

Production Design: Hugues Tissandier

MPAA rating: PG

Running time: 102 minutes

REVIEWS

Chicago Sun-Times Online. January 12, 2007.

Entertainment Weekly. January 26, 2007, p. 55.

Hollywood Reporter Online. December 27, 2006.

Los Angeles Times Online. December 29, 2006.

New York Times Online. January 12, 2007.

Premiere Magazine Online. January 11, 2007.

San Francisco Chronicle. January 12, 2007, p. E6.

Variety Online. December 21, 2006.

Washington Post Online. January 12, 2007.

TRIVIA

Director Luc Besson has stated that this film will be his final directorial effort.

THE ASSASSINATION OF JESSE JAMES BY THE COWARD ROBERT FORD

Box Office: $3.9 million

Legendary outlaw Jesse James (1847–1882) has long fascinated filmmakers, inspiring over thirty big-screen treatments of his exploits and numerous television productions. Jesse James, Jr., even played his own father in two 1921 films. The story of Jesse's murder by fellow gang member Robert Ford received its most lavish Hollywood interpretation in Henry King's *Jesse James* (1939), with Tyrone Power as Jesse, Henry Fonda as his brother, Frank, and John Carradine as Ford. Other notable versions of this story include Samuel Fuller's low-budget but stylish *I Shot Jesse James* (1949) and Walter Hill's energetic *The Long Riders* (1980). In comparison, writer/director Andrew Dominik's *The Assassination of Jesse James by the Coward Robert Ford* is vastly superior to its predecessors, resulting in a masterpiece of visual storytelling.

The Assassination of Jesse James by the Coward Robert Ford is less the story of Jesse James (Brad Pitt) than a surprisingly sympathetic account of how Bob Ford (Casey Affleck) came to betray his hero. Dominik, who adapted Ron Hansen's 1983 novel, begins with Bob's joining the James gang in Missouri and telling Frank James (Sam Shepard) of his admiration for the James brothers. Frank is quick to see Bob as a parasite who longs to find glory by associating with the famous as Dominik explores the theme of how celebrity infiltrates the lives of ordinary citizens. The flamboyant Jesse, the opposite of his taciturn brother, has suspicions about Bob yet slowly comes to accept him, even inviting Bob and his older brother, Charley (Sam Rockwell), to live with his family, which includes wife Zee (Mary-Louise Parker) and two small children (Dustin Bollinger and Brooklynn Proulx). Like Bob himself, Dominik is fascinated by how different the public and private Jesses are yet how they overlap at times.

The highlight of the first portion of the film is a train robbery, after which Frank retires from crime and moves to Baltimore, creating a vacuum Jesse is unable to fill. After the gang members scatter, the paranoid Jesse begins tracking them down. Dominik never makes clear exactly why he is doing it, other than his fear that one of them will turn him in or gun him down. *The Assassination of Jesse James by the Coward Robert Ford* shifts from the points of view of Bob, Jesse, and other outlaws as their destinies intersect.

The only previous film by Dominik, *Chopper* (2000), has many similarities to *The Assassination of Jesse James by the Coward Robert Ford*. Both focus on complex, unpredictable real-life criminals, contemporary Australian Mark "Chopper" Read in the first instance. Both deal with such themes as friendship, loyalty, trust, and betrayal. Both also feature unusually long scenes in which the tone and the dynamics of the relationships between characters are constantly shifting.

In the case of *The Assassination of Jesse James by the Coward Robert Ford,* Dominik's style led some reviewers to complain that the film is too long (140 minutes) and too slow. Although the film received mostly positive reviews, including many raves, Warner Brothers did not trust audiences' patience, did not conduct a major advertising campaign, and distributed it to only a few hundred theaters. On a Web site about the history of the James family, Eric James complained about this dilemma, charging that Warner Brothers would not know what to do with a painting by Rembrandt.

The film's style and deliberate pace earned it comparisons to the films of Terrence Malick, especially *Days of Heaven* (1978). Both films are intimate character studies set against sweeping backgrounds, a vast Texas ranch in *Days of Heaven,* the untamed Missouri countryside in *The Assassination of Jesse James by the Coward Robert Ford.* Like Malick, Dominik is fond of cutting away from the action to shots of grass and trees blowing in the wind, as if to comment on the disparity between the order of the natural world and the chaos of what passes for civilization. Both films also have narrators, though Malick's is ironic and Dominik's strives to place the action in a mythic context. Hugh Ross, a prominent reader of audiobooks, gives an outstanding, no-nonsense performance as Dominik's narrator.

Dominik's leisurely approach is especially generous to his cast, with several little-known actors doing excellent work. A significant subplot involves the suspicious nature of James cousin Wood Hite (Jeremy Renner). Wood, who seems not to trust anyone, is particularly annoyed by the prospect that the womanizing Dick Liddil (Paul Schneider) will try to seduce Sarah (Kailin See), his young stepmother. This tension becomes explosive after Sarah seduces Dick before he has a chance to make his advances. Bloodshed ensues.

Renner, See, and, especially, Schneider deliver nicely multi-layered performances. Also noteworthy are Michael Parks as a lawman and famed political consultant James Carville as the Missouri governor who places a bounty on Jesse. The film presents an array of acting styles, with Rockwell, who often calls attention to his technique, admirably subtle for a change and Ted Levine, as another lawman, abandoning his usual underplaying in favorite of Method machinations.

Pitt played villains a few times early in his career and seems to relish the opportunities presented by Jesse. Although Jesse actually appears less often than several of the supporting characters, it is difficult not to focus on him because he is likely to do anything at any time. Robert Duvall also plays Jesse as a psychopath in Philip Kaufman's *The Great Northfield Minnesota Raid* (1972), previously the best James gang film, but Pitt makes the outlaw a greater threat, withering his victims with a penetrating glance. Whether dancing a jig during the train robbery or crying after beating a defenseless child, Pitt's Jesse is riveting.

The real star of the film, however, is Affleck, previously known primarily as Ben's kid brother. Dominik places a great burden on the young actor, with many scenes involving lengthy shots of Bob's face as he contemplates all the possible courses of action. Affleck stands out with Bob's nervous eagerness during his meeting with Frank, his humiliation when Charley shows his precious stash of dime novels about the James gang to others, his self-disgust when he and Charley act out the assassination on stage, his bitter acceptance of the way his infamy clings to him, and his relief at justifying his motivations to his dancer girlfriend (Zooey Deschanel). By nailing the range and complexity of Bob's emotions, Affleck offers what should have been a star-making performance. Both he and Dominik are victims of the studio's lack of faith in their product.

Almost all the technical aspects of *The Assassination of Jesse James by the Coward Robert Ford* are uniformly excellent. These include the unobtrusive editing of Curtiss Clayton and Dylan Tichenor, the production design of Patricia Norris, especially with the muddy village where Jesse meets his end, and the haunting score by Warren Ellis and the Australian rock star Nick Cave, who wrote the screenplay for the quite similar *The Proposition* (2005). Cave appears briefly as a balladeer singing the song that gives the film its title.

Dominik's most significant collaborator, however, is cinematographer Roger Deakins, best know for his work with Joel and Ethan Coen. Deakins uses the austere, forbidding landscapes of Calgary, Edmonton, and Winnipeg as a canvas on which he lashes seemingly endless shades of gray. His washed-out palette helps underscore the film's theme of how moral issues and decisions are rarely black and white. Deakins gives the impression of employing available light in both intimate scenes, as with Dick's conversation with Sarah on a lamp-lit porch, and more dramatic ones, as with the light streaming from the windows of the train during the nighttime robbery. The final portion of the film shifts from gray to brown as the almost sepia tint indicates that Bob has passed from reality to myth. Deakins blurs the edges of several frames to emulate the photographic style of the period. These unforgettable images combined with the performances and Dominik's lyrical, hypnotic approach to storytelling make *The Assassination of Jesse James by the Coward Robert Ford* a magnificent aesthetic and emotional experience.

Michael Adams

CREDITS

Jesse James: Brad Pitt
Robert Ford: Casey Affleck
Frank James: Sam Shepard
Zee James: Mary-Louise Parker
Charley Ford: Sam Rockwell
Dick Liddil: Paul Schneider
Wood Hite: Jeremy Renner
Ed Miller: Garret Dillahunt
Dorothy Evans: Zooey Deschanel
Henry Craig: Michael Parks
Sheriff Timberlake: Ted Levine
Martha Bolton: Alison Elliott
Governor Crittendon: James Carville
Major George Hite: Tom Aldredge
Narrator: Hugh Ross
Origin: USA
Language: English
Released: 2007
Production: Brad Pitt, Dede Gardner, Ridley Scott, David
   Valdes, Jules Daly; Scott Free, Plan B Entertainment,
   Virtual Studios; released by Warner Bros.
Directed by: Andrew Dominik
Written by: Andrew Dominik
Cinematography by: Roger Deakins
Music by: Nick Cave, Warren Ellis
Sound: Bruce Carwardine
Editing: Dylan Tichenor, Curtiss Clayton
Art Direction: Troy Sizemore
Costumes: Patricia Norris
MPAA rating: R
Running time: 152 minutes

REVIEWS

Christian Science Monitor Online. September 21, 2007.
Entertainment Weekly Online. September 19, 2007.
Hollywood Reporter Online. August 31, 2007.
Los Angeles Times Online. September 21, 2007.
New York Times Online. September 21, 2007.
Premiere Online. September 20, 2007.
Rolling Stone Online. October 4, 2007.
Variety Online. August 31, 2007.
Wall Street Journal. September 21, 2007, p. W1.

QUOTES

Jesse James (to Robert Ford): "Can't figure it out: do you want
   to be like me or do you want to be me?"

TRIVIA

When the film begins, the disfigurement of Jesse James' finger
   is revealed to the audience. In subsequent scenes, the top
   half of Brad Pitt's left middle finger is removed using
   computer graphics.

AWARDS

Nomination:

Oscars 2007: Cinematog., Support. Actor (Affleck)

Golden Globes 2008: Support. Actor (Affleck)
Screen Actors Guild 2007: Support. Actor (Affleck).

THE ASTRONAUT FARMER

If we don't have our dreams, we have nothing.
   —Movie tagline
*One small step for man, one giant leap for
   farmers.*
   —Movie tagline

Box Office: $11 million

All movies require some suspension of disbelief. *The Astronaut Farmer* requires more than most. The story of a man who builds a rocket in his barn and plans to have it take him into orbit, the film raises many practical questions. Whether you think they are important or not will determine how much you enjoy the film. The most rewarding way to view this fantasy is to quell cynicism and simply enjoy it as an ode to quirky American individualists. Charlie Farmer (Billy Bob Thornton) falls squarely in a cinematic tradition that includes everything from outlaw cowboys to *One Flew Over the Cuckoo's Nest* (1975) denizens. To most people he seems crazy, but he has a dream. And it is all about the dream.

The plot is hardly original: the iconoclastic genius who is hounded by evil bankers (*It's a Wonderful Life* [1946]) and liberty-suppressing government authorities. He has the requisite devoted wife, Audrey (Virginia Madsen) and a supportive family that includes the obligatory cute little girls (who are played by Jasper and Logan Polish, the daughters of the filmmakers) and the teenage boy genius (Max Thieriot) who sees his dad as a hero. It is about a man who risks everything, including his family, to pursue his impractical ambition.

Filmmakers and twin brothers Michael and Mark Polish's vision of rugged individualism on the high plains is doubled by the conceit that the space program is some sort of sinister government conspiracy to deny the rights of ordinary people to orbit the earth. In the post-9/11 world, this idea actually has some plausibility. Private companies are concocting programs to send people into space, NASA has had its share of high-profile blunders and tragedies, and federal agents have looked foolish and incompetent—when asked by a panel of officials to prove he is not building "some kind of WMD" in his barn, Farmer smugly shoots back a stinging rejoinder: "If I was building a weapon of mass destruction, you certainly couldn't find it." The government—politics and money—is clearly the bad guy.

Farmer decides he is going to build his own "field of dreams," but he does not expect, or desire, anyone to come. Farmer has an intriguing backstory, built to maximize empathy: he was once an astronaut in training, who was discharged from the space program when he left to go back to his father's ranch after his dad shot and killed himself rather than have the bank foreclose on his spread. Farmer is repeating the same journey: his banker friend is going to foreclose on the ranch, but Farmer is planning a more spectacular suicide with a much bigger weapon.

Farmer has quite a spread, too: a huge country home with a barn that looks like a town hall, tall enough to house his rocket, a gleaming phallic means of escape from the pressures of a world run by accountants and bureaucrats. There is a certain charm to the outsized ridiculousness of Farmer's scheme, and it captures the attention of the town. The Polish twins (Michael directed, they co-wrote, and Mark appears as an FBI agent) are not above mixing sexual metaphors, either: a waitress at the place where Audrey works (the wonderfully named Calf-A) is dying to get a glimpse inside the barn, to see how big Charlie's rocket is. The rocket is named "The Other Woman," and there is a ludicrous scene where Charlie crawls into bed at three a.m. with dirty hands and no wedding ring on—it fell off somewhere in the capsule.

Thornton, so adept at playing villains, here has to convince the audience he is a wonderful dad, even if he is the kind of father who takes his kids out of school for a month so they can help him build his spaceship. Thornton pulls it off: he is a combination of Mr. Wizard and Howdy Doody. The main problem with his character, though, is that, for a genius, he is certainly dense. The plot requires him to keep answering the question of how in the world he imagines he is actually going to pull this off. Farmer's only response is to look hurt and shocked: he is not just an oddball with an outsized dream, he seems to be quite stupid as well, as if he is literally living on another planet.

In many stories about men with antisocial ambitions, the protagonists are not only determined but highly aware of the obstacles against them; some are paranoid, others are out-and-out rebels. The way the Polishes have scripted him, however, Farmer (even his wife calls him by his last name) seems thick and unaware, as if he never thought of the idea that anyone might try to stop him from going into outer space. So when the FBI descends on the ranch, having discovered Farmer is trying to buy 10,000 gallons of jet fuel, he acts surprised. He has even sent in an application for the mission, with a flight plan.

As he awakens to the fact that the world is against him, however, Farmer turns angry, like his dad. The final straw is when an old astronaut buddy (an uncredited Bruce Willis) visits and tells him there is no way he will be allowed to do it. The plot against him grows more cynical when a slew of government officials show up to hold a hearing on his application, and afterward the head of the Federal Aviation Administration warns him that the military will shoot him down if he launches. "You're a threat," the FAA boss explains. Now the government looks just as ridiculous as the rebel.

You could go into orbit with all the plot holes in *The Astronaut Farmer*. It is never explained how Farmer manages to own such a handsome spread and how he got into so much debt. And it is somehow all forgiven through the timely death of Audrey's father (Bruce Dern). The entire town sees a rocket launch but the FAA successfully stifles the story, and the media, which had been camped on Farmer's land for months before tiring of the tale, does not even notice.

The film veers crazily in tone between satire, hokum, melodrama, and piousness, but when it soars, it really soars. Thornton's speech, in voiceover at his father-in-law's funeral, about how uncomfortable our society is with the notion of space could be seen as either greeting card-simplistic or quite profound; again, it all depends on how one chooses to approach this film. The cynic will note that the Polishes seem to like to shoot many scenes in silhouette against a setting sun, and pay no regard to continuity (other scenes in the same sequence make it clear it is the middle of the day), but the child-like viewer will merely be awed at the scope of the open scenery.

If one suspends disbelief, there is much delight to be found in the Polish brothers' strange and charming touches: games played at the dinner tables; Lucky Charms cereal that is product placement with a twist (the charms are fine, but the cereal tastes "like wood," one of the kids says); the lost wedding ring reappearing just when all seems lost. They are hokey contrivances, but they work, and make *The Astronaut Farmer* a watchable, and at times quite moving, family film. Its oddities and humanity mesh in a way that makes it the lighter, less profane twin of *Little Miss Sunshine* (2006).

The biggest suspension of disbelief that is required might very well be in fathoming Audrey's character. Madsen gets to have one big scene in which she challenges her husband's priorities, but for the rest of the time she is more supportive than any spouse could be imagined to be. It should be noted that Madsen is making a career out of playing the highly understanding wife or girlfriend of kooks. In this movie she is sweet and cheery as apple pie, and amazingly appealing.

The same can be said for the film itself. *The Astronaut Farmer* is surprisingly entertaining and at times delightful, having fun with the tropes of legendary American cinema and even our most cherished beliefs in rugged individualism, while still honoring them. By out-sizing the dream and challenging our credibility, the Polish brothers stretch the boundaries of imagination. But it is in the small family scenes that the movie really hits home. This may be a dysfunctional family abetting its father's dysfunctional dream, but at least, as Farmer says passionately, it is a family that still has a dream. It is precisely one great purpose of movies to examine such dreams.

Michael Betzold

CREDITS

Charlie Farmer: Billy Bob Thornton
Audrey Farmer: Virginia Madsen
Hal: Bruce Dern
Jacobsen: J.K. Simmons
Kevin Munchak: Tim Blake Nelson
Shepherd Farmer: Max Thieriot
Agent Kilborne: Jon(athan) Gries
Agent Mathis: Mark Polish
Stanley Farmer: Jasper Polish
Sunshine Farmer: Logan Polish
Himself: Bruce Willis (Cameo)
Origin: USA
Language: English
Released: 2007
Production: Mark Polish, Michael Polish, Len Amato, Paula Weinstein; Spring Creek Productions, Polish Brothers Construction; released by Warner Bros.
Directed by: Michael Polish
Written by: Mark Polish, Michael Polish
Cinematography by: M. David Mullen
Music by: Stuart Matthewman
Sound: Matthew Nicolay
Editing: James Haygood
Art Direction: Jim Oberlander
Costumes: Danny Glicker
Production Design: Clark Hunter
MPAA rating: PG
Running time: 104 minutes

REVIEWS

Boxoffice Online. February 23, 2007.
Chicago Sun-Times Online. February 23, 2007.
Entertainment Weekly. March 2, 2007, p. 49.
Hollywood Reporter Online. October 19, 2006.

Los Angeles Times Online. February 23, 2007.
New York Times Online. February 23, 2007.
San Francisco Chronicle. February 23, 2007, p. E5.
Variety Online. October 16, 2006.
Washington Post. February 23, 2007, p. C5.

QUOTES

Charlie Farmer: "Somewhere along the line we stopped believing we could do anything. And if we don't have our dreams, we have nothing."
Charlie Farmer: "When I was a kid, they used to tell me that I could be anything I wanted to be, no matter what…and maybe I am insane, I don't know, but I still believe that."

TRIVIA

While the film is set in Texas, filming was done in and around Santa Fe, New Mexico.

ATONEMENT

You can only imagine the truth.
    —Movie tagline
Torn apart by betrayal. Separated by war. Bound by love.
    —Movie tagline
Joined by love. Separated by fear. Redeemed by hope.
    —Movie tagline

Box Office: $50.6 million

Imagine how much easier life would be if a person possessed the ability to thoroughly and thoughtfully rough draft it or even go back and recraft it, in both cases correctively rewriting and refashioning so that things turn out as one thinks they should. In the critically acclaimed *Atonement*, Briony Tallis desires to do just that concerning an incorrect assertion she uttered in her youth that led to tragic repercussions and endlessly haunting reverberations. By the engrossing film's gut-wrenching end, she has endeavored through the only means left to her to atone for her mistake, setting things right as best she can for those she has so horrifically wronged.

The first moments of *Atonement* tell viewers a great deal about Briony, rivettingly portrayed at thirteen by the blue-eyed Saoirse Ronan. The bright, serious-minded character clearly still has one foot in childhood and the other precociously planted beyond, her bedroom containing little toy figures as well as a typewriter upon which she has just completed her first play. Briony has lined up her tiny playthings just so in a phalanx stretching across the room and toward her desk, as if they must wait with bated breath for her next command.

When the girl rushes to proudly show her mother (Harriet Walter) her premiere opus, Briony has a ramrod-straight, brisk, and purposeful manner of walking. Mrs. Tallis proclaims the work "stupendous," and the girl clearly enjoys being an applauded center of attention.

This first portion of the film takes place at the Tallis family's lovely English countryside manor in 1935, just before both their own meticulously maintained world and the larger world beyond its gates were wrenchingly altered. As yet all is seemingly idyllic as Briony languorously stretches out on the grass in the sweltering summer heat with her brittle, bored, and beautiful older sister, Cecilia (a praiseworthy Keira Knightley). They are awaiting a visit from their brother Leon (Patrick Kennedy) and chocolate magnate Paul Marshall (Benedict Cumberbatch), an occasion that Briony eagerly aims to mark with the first production of her play, aided by some visiting young cousins.

Unfortunately, Briony creates drama of a much more consequential nature after witnessing a series of events that send her active imagination and barely-budding knowledge of amorous interaction in a wholly wrong and destructive direction. How appropriate that the first occasion occurs at a fountain, as everything thereafter springs from this one misconstrued, innocuous event. Briony peers out from her upstairs window and observes Cecilia suddenly and shockingly stripping down to her slip, jumping into the fountain in front of the housekeeper's son, Robbie Turner (James McAvoy), and then stalking off fuming. The younger girl gasps with scandalized astonishment at what she thinks she has witnessed, which she apparently sizes up as an instance of forced degradation. As is repeatedly done in *Atonement*, however, viewers are presented with scenes from multiple perspectives, giving those watching the film a totality of understanding that individual characters do not possess. It is revealed that a peeved Cecilia was simply retrieving a piece of an expensive vase that had broken off when Robbie tried to help her with playful but thoroughly good intentions. Viewers will note how he yelps to make sure she does not step on the broken shards and is even more of a gentleman when he averts his eyes from her soaked and now see-through clothing. One wonders if the shot of Cecilia underwater may reflect the submerged feelings she has for the handsome, good-natured young man, who has been put through college by the Tallises and now promisingly plans to become a doctor. Adding to the day's torrid atmosphere, one certainly perceives a simmering but properly lidded sexual tension between this upper crust young lady and the upstanding servant's son. Briony, with a lack of information and maturity, faultily processes the scene.

While struggling to compose a letter to smooth things over with Cecilia, Robbie impetuously types a version crudely revealing his longing and then sets it aside with a chuckle. He takes the time to express himself honestly and decorously, but then makes the double mistake of handing Briony the wrong draft to take to her sister. Of course, the girl can barely wait to read it herself prior to delivery, and later shares it with her cousin Lola (Juno Temple). Now Robbie is a "sex maniac" who the police ought to know about before poor Cecilia is in any way molested, which is what Briony thinks is happening when she walks in on the couple finally giving in to their passions against the wall of the library. Briony does not hear the bursting forth of "I love you" from both Cecilia and Robbie, to which viewers are privy. She misunderstands it all as a frightening attack and defilement.

After dark, as Briony helps search the grounds for her two smallest relatives, she happens upon a prostrate Lola, and watches the shadowy figure of a man dash off into the night. Lola says she has been accosted but did not see her assailant. Briony feels that all she had previously witnessed makes this sound like Robbie once again running amok, but she had not seen him. In unbridled righteous indignation, she convinces herself to say what is necessary to stop him. "I know it was him," she unwaveringly tells the police who question her story, and then, "I saw him with my own eyes." (A later flashback hints that the hurt feelings and jealousy born of a young girl's unreciprocated crush may have also been a factor in what she does.) As a result, an incredulous Robbie is whisked away by the police to his mother (Brenda Blethyn) and Cecilia's disbelief and horror. There will be a recurring single-noted "pling-pling-pling" that is incorporated into the film's music, representing both the indelibility of that one devastating statement of Briony's, and the fact that it comes to insistently gnaw at her conscience. (The soundtrack also incorporates the sound of typing, the full significance of which is revealed by the film's conclusion.)

Atonement then jumps ahead four years and across the English Channel to France, where Robbie is fighting in World War II. He has been allowed to trade the soul-crushing torment of unjust imprisonment for service to his country, a decision that soon becomes another kind of nightmare. This part of the film is suitably shot with a darker and grittier look. There are some sharp, sobering contrasts here to what went before. The boyish, robust Robbie strolling down the lane in dressy attire for dinner with Cecilia and the other Tallises is now shaken, worn, and utterly exhausted. He encounters a slew of corpses, many of them female, lying in some grass, an ugly, unsettling comedown from his earlier glimpse of Cecilia and Briony luxuriating on the sunny lawn back home. Many critics who viewed *Atonement*, laudably directed by Joe Wright, have taken note of the impressive, carefully choreographed five-and-half minute segment without a single cut, showing the bewildering chaos and carnage Robbie encountered among the multitudes who famously awaited safe transport from the beach at Dunkirk. The shot is accompanied by music that is appropriately dispirited and elegiac. It is surreal to see a Ferris wheel looming above such a hellish sweeping vista. Viewers had previously been shown a chance meeting between Cecilia and Robbie before he shipped out, during which they pledge their undying love. Now Robbie staggers into a theater where a couple is kissing in close-up on the screen. It is too painful for him to watch. Soon looking shockingly debilitated from a wound, Robbie is sustained by a photo of a seaside cottage where Cecilia vowed they would eventually reconnect. This is McAvoy's best performance to date, convincingly conveying a wide range of emotions.

Life is very different for Cecilia and Briony at this point, too. The former is a nurse in London, living in a flat that could probably fit many times over into the Tallis home. Viewers learn that she is not only apart from Robbie but estranged from the parents who believed about him what she has maintained since that fateful night is utterly unbelievable. Briony (now played less memorably as an adult by Romola Garai) is in training to be a nurse, soothing the wounded, one guesses, to help expiate the pain that she herself had inflicted. Those watching will sense that she has become weighted down by remorse, a close-up revealing a far-off look of sadness. Briony is not so sure of herself anymore. She seems to be trying to work through what happened by incorporating it into her writing. Finally, Briony goes to Cecilia to apologize for what the child she once was had done, promising to recant her lie and clear Robbie's name. (Briony reveals that it had actually been Paul atop Lola, an inconvenient fact she had apparently discarded because it did not properly advance the story her imagination had been pursuing.) Robbie is there with Cecilia and uncharacteristically but understandably explodes. Those who read the well-respected 2001 Ian McEwan novel upon which the film is based might recall the line that spoke of human beings being "easily torn, not easily mended."

The film's abruptly appearing final portion peppers those watching with shocking revelations that make emotions ebb and flow like the ocean seen behind a silhouetted Cecilia in a late sublime shot. We learn that the story we have been told is actually an autobiographical novel written by an elderly, successful, and now dying Briony, portrayed by a tremendously effective Vanessa Redgrave. In this final work, the author has yet again chosen to significantly alter what really occurred, but this time she endeavors to create something that might finally, imperfectly, and yet quite movingly give

back to Cecilia and Robbie what she had deprived them of so long ago. Briony had in fact never been able to go to the two and make amends, as Robbie had succumbed to septicemia awaiting help at Dunkirk and Cecilia had been killed during a bombing of London. Thus, she has written for them a permanent happy ending in her novel as a sincerely apologetic parting gift, the film's final images showing the united, elated lovers getting to frolic after all at that yearned-for seaside cottage. Briony's book is titled *Atonement*, also the name of what is unquestionably one of the best and most artistically interesting films of 2007.

David L. Boxerbaum

CREDITS

Robbie Turner: James McAvoy
Cecilia Tallis: Keira Knightley
Briony, age 13: Saoirse Ronan
Briony, age 18: Romola Garai
Older Briony: Vanessa Redgrave
Grace Turner: Brenda Blethyn
Lola Quincey: Juno Temple
Leon Tallis: Patrick Kennedy
Paul Marshall: Benedict Cumberbatch
Emily Tallis: Harriet Walter
Sister Drummond: Gina McKee
Origin: USA, Great Britain
Language: English
Released: 2007
Production: Tim Bevan, Eric Fellner, Paul Webster; Universal Pictures, StudioCanal, Working Title Productions, Relativity; released by Focus Features
Directed by: Joe Wright
Written by: Christopher Hampton
Cinematography by: Seamus McGarvey
Music by: Dario Marianelli
Editing: Paul Tothill
Art Direction: Ian Bailie
Costumes: Jacqueline Durran
Production Design: Sarah Greenwood
MPAA rating: R
Running time: 122 minutes

REVIEWS

Boston Globe Online. December 7, 2007.
Chicago Sun-Times Online. December 7, 2007.
Entertainment Weekly Online. November 28, 2007.
Guardian Online. September 7, 2007.
Los Angeles Times Online. December 7, 2007.
New York Times Online. December 7, 2007.

New Yorker Online. December 10, 2007.
Newsweek Online. December 10, 2007.
The Observer Online. September 9, 2007.
Rolling Stone Online. December 13, 2007.
San Francisco Chronicle. December 7, 2007, p. E1.
Variety Online. August 29, 2007.
Wall Street Journal Online. December 7, 2007.
Washington Post. December 7, 2007, p. C1.

QUOTES

Robbie Turner (voiceover): "Dearest Cecilia, the story can resume. The one I had been planning on that evening walk. I can become again the man who once crossed the surrey park at dusk, in my best suit, swaggering on the promise of life. The man who, with the clarity of passion, made love to you in the library. The story can resume. I will return. Find you, love you, marry you and live without shame."

TRIVIA

The film's herlded five-minute-plus tracking shot was completed in four takes (the third was used) and was conceived because the crew had only a day to film, limited time with the 1,000 extras used in the scene, and needed to wrap before the tide came in and washed away the set.

AWARDS

Oscars 2007: Orig. Score

British Acad. 2007: Film, Production Des.

Golden Globes 2008: Film—Drama, Orig. Score

Nomination:

Oscars 2007: Adapt. Screenplay, Art Dir./Set Dec., Cinematog., Costume Des., Film, Support. Actress (Ronan)

British Acad. 2007: Actor (McAvoy), Actress (Knightley), Adapt. Screenplay, Cinematog., Costume Des., Director (Wright), Film Editing, Makeup, Support. Actress (Ronan), Orig. Score, Sound

Golden Globes 2008: Actor—Drama (McAvoy), Actress—Drama (Knightley), Director (Wright), Screenplay, Support. Actress (Ronan).

AUGUST RUSH

An incredible journey moving at the speed of sound.
—Movie tagline

Box Office: $31.7 million

The decision to cast Freddie Highmore as a magical child was far from a stretch. The most mesmerizing, delightful boy among the moppets in the J.M. Barrie biopic *Finding Neverland* (2004), Highmore is a few years older but no less compelling in the emotionally charged story *August Rush.* Panned by most critics, this film, directed by Kirsten Sheridan, has to be swallowed in one gulp. Suspension of disbelief is required from start to finish, as is a willingness to believe in miracles. But if you go along willingly, the rewards are worth the effort.

Most movies about the power of belief require a leap of faith, from *The Wizard of Oz* (1939) to *E.T.* (1982), and this is no exception. And while *August Rush* will never be confused with such epics, it is a crowd-pleasing, surprisingly well-crafted modern fairy tale about love and wonder. Cynicism will ruin the experience, so leave it at the door. *August Rush* is not a musical, but it is all about music and its power to communicate, awe, and inspire. Like most musicals, it is best experienced without your feet touching the ground too frequently. The script, by Nick Castle and James V. Hart, starts in full-throated volume and stays at a feverish pitch throughout. The tone is one of unabashed wonder at life.

We meet Freddie Highmore's character, whose name is Evan Taylor, at a rural home for orphan boys. There, at age eleven, he pretends to be an orchestra conductor in a field of wheat and listens to the harmonics of the heavens, convinced through and through that he can hear his long-lost parents through the music in the world. He claims he "hears" them all the time, and even when he is throttled by bullies and told to renounce this claim, he refuses to do so.

We see, in flashback, the basis for his belief, during the night of his conception in New York City. His mother, Lyla (Keri Russell), plays the cello in a symphony orchestra; his father, Louis (Jonathan Rhys Meyers), is a singer and guitarist in a rock band. They are each giving a concert at the same time, blocks away from each other, and their music merges in the spirit that creates their son. They meet on a rooftop under a full moon in a shamelessly romantic but refreshingly simplistic scene. By the time this scene is finished, you will either be on board for the story or bailing out, seeking more credible waters.

In some ways, this movie most resembles *The Notebook* (2004), a brave and old-fashioned love story that was denounced for being corny. But there is nothing wrong with genuine movie magic, no matter how implausible and sweeping the story. Here, *August Rush* moves along like a confident piece of music, brushing past our objections with the sheer force of its spirit. At a time when film heroes are increasingly scarce or at least seriously flawed, *August Rush* has a slew of heroic figures, starting with Highmore's boy genius, who is as sunny and open as a spring day. With an infectious smile totally lacking in pretense, and a childish spirit whose innocence brooks no interference from the world around him, Highmore makes for a highly sympathetic protagonist.

His story moves through a world populated by sincere if sometimes confused and thwarted adults. His separated parents do not even know they have created a boy who is looking for them, but they are eventually moved by a longing to recapture their love. A kind and dedicated youth caseworker, played beautifully by Terrence Howard, has the boy's interests at heart. Also figuring into the plot are a young gospel-music prodigy and her minister father and a young streetwise musician who befriends Evan, leading him to the lair of "Wizard" (Robin Williams), a musician and Pied Piper who presides over a colony of runaways in the ruins of the old rock palace, the Fillmore East. With plenty of earrings and short-cropped reddish hair, Williams creates one of his best characters in years. Freed of the actor's penchant for overplaying his role, Wizard is a believable villain with plenty of redeeming qualities: he shares both Evan's passion for music and his belief that it is connected with higher powers, but he has been hurt and corrupted by the hard lessons of the street life and its competitive economy.

By the time the fanciful plot has spun its characters through the magical labyrinth that will lead them to defy time and distance and reconnect, as you know they will in a gloriously happy ending, it is too late to resist. And the score and songs here, though not uniformly excellent, are sufficient to create the necessary wonder and the harmonic threads that tie this tall tale together. All music requires a willingness to put aside objections and be carried away, and so does the music in this film—classical, rock, gospel. It works with the story in a disarmingly shameless appeal to our best instincts. So well crafted is the tale that, for all its lack of surface credibility, it resonates honesty, without contrivance, and it flows with a certain sort of quiet and surprising majesty.

Meyers is a compelling troubadour, a highly sympathetic romantic lost figure regaining his footing after a troublesome decade of uncertainty. Luminous and straightforward, Russell is apple-eyed but determined despite the secrets that have been hidden from her. Howard is thoughtful and compelling, Williams is frighteningly real (perhaps, in fact, this film's most realistic character), and all the minor characters, including the other child actors, are remarkably attractive, each in their way. But at the center of all this power and light is Highmore, believably optimistic and idealistic, a humble prodigy, open to life's harmonic forces. It is another wondrous performance from Highmore, fuller but no less charming than his compelling turn in *Finding Neverland*. He is that rarest of child actors, unspoiled and genuine, and these qualities allow the overreaching

story line of *August Rush* to harmonize and to compel belief in movie magic.

Michael Betzold

CREDITS

Evan Taylor/August Rush: Freddie Highmore
Lyla Novacek: Keri Russell
Louis Connelly: Jonathan Rhys Meyers
Richard Jeffries: Terrence Howard
Wizard: Robin Williams
Thomas Novacek: William Sadler
Arthur: Leon G. Thomas III
Hope: Jamia Simone Nash
Origin: USA
Language: English
Released: 2007
Production: Richard B. Lewis; CJ Entertainment, Odyssey Entertainment, Southpaw Entertainment; released by Warner Bros.
Directed by: Kristen Sheridan
Written by: Nick Castle, James V. Hart
Cinematography by: John Mathieson
Music by: Mark Mancina, Hans Zimmer
Sound: Tom Nelson, Jason Oliver
Editing: William Steinkamp
Art Direction: Mario R. Ventenilla
Costumes: Frank Fleming
Production Design: Michael Shaw
MPAA rating: PG
Running time: 113 minutes

REVIEWS

Boston Globe Online. November 21, 2007.
Chicago Sun-Times Online. November 21, 2007.
Entertainment Weekly. November 30, 2007, p. 117.
Hollywood Reporter Online. November 18, 2007.
Los Angeles Times Online. November 21, 2007.
New York Times Online. November 21, 2007.
San Francisco Chronicle. November 21, 2007, p. E3.
Variety Online. October 22, 2007.
Washington Post Online. November 21, 2007.

QUOTES

Evan/August: "Open yourself up to the music around you."

TRIVIA

Robin Williams' performance as Wizard was supposedly inspired by U2 frontman Bono.

AWARDS

Nomination:

Oscars 2007: Song ("Raise It Up").

AVENUE MONTAIGNE
(Fauteuils d'orchestre)
(Orchestra Seats)

Box Office: $2 million

Danièle Thompson has been writing films, mostly comedies, since 1966 but did not begin directing until 1999. *Avenue Montaigne* (or, *Orchestra Streets* as it is sometimes called), though much better than her previous film, *Jet Lag* (2002), is a slight effort, with a reasonable bit of charm, though no depth or style. Thompson offers a scrubbed-clean, upper-middle-class Paris, much like Woody Allen's Manhattan, with *Avenue Montaigne* resembling minor Allen films such as *Everyone Says I Love You* (1996) and *Anything Else* (2003).

Avenue Montaigne centers around the people encountered by Jessica (Cécile de France), a bright-eyed innocent recently arrived from Mâcon, full of stories of the city relayed by her grandmother (Suzanne Flon), once a maid in Paris hotels. Jessica becomes a waitress at a café across the street from a complex comprising a theater, a concert hall, and an art auction house and makes friends with people associated with each. Catherine Versen (Valérie Lemercier) is appearing in a Georges Feydeau farce she despises, though not as much as she hates her fame as a television soap opera star. She feels her wasted life can be redeemed by playing Simone de Beauvoir in a film by American director Brian Sobinski (Sydney Pollack). Jean-François Lefort (Albert Dupontel) is a successful concert pianist who feels suffocated by his career and dreams of retiring to the country, much to the chagrin of his wife and manager, Valentine (Laura Morante). Jacques Grumberg (Claude Brasseur), an elderly businessman, has reluctantly decided to have his extensive art collection auctioned off. Jacques has a considerably younger mistress, Valérie (Annelise Hesme), unaware that his estranged son, Frédéric (Christopher Thompson), a historian, was once Valérie's lover. Claudie (Dani), a frustrated singer, is about to retire from her post as, apparently, manager of the concert hall.

Danièle Thompson co-wrote the screenplay with her son Christopher Thompson, and their goal was apparently to show how those connected with the arts in Paris suffer for their art, making everyone around them suffer a bit as well. Yet in the end, all the pain is worthwhile, and these self-indulgent neurotics become more lovable—just as in a Woody Allen film.

Thompson lacks a visual style, believing for the most part in simply pointing the camera at the actors and watching them perform, often in close-up. *Avenue Montaigne* opens with a montage of locations Jessica is about to visit, but after that, Paris becomes mere background. *Jet Lag* takes place mostly in an airport

hotel room, an indication that Thompson likes to place her actors in more intimate, even claustrophobic surroundings.

The only visually striking image of the film comes when Jessica, unable to afford a room in the pricey neighborhood, sneaks into Jean-François's rehearsal room to sleep on the sofa. The next morning, she is unable to find a way out of the locked building and ends up on the roof, framed by an angry, overcast sky with the Eiffel Tower looming large in the background. The image perfectly captures Jessica's loneliness and vulnerability.

Though the film is generally low-key, Thompson occasionally strains for effect, showing Jean-François's desperation by having him break down a door between the concert hall and the auction space and by having him remove half his clothing during a performance. Another odd thing about the last scene is that before Jean-François strips, Valentine and Claudie are crying at the passion of his playing. He should be even better after becoming more relaxed, but Thompson does not indicate if this is so. Valentine flees the audience because her husband has proven infantile once again, and Claudie's reaction is not shown. Catherine is also embarrassed in her first meeting with Brian by confusing him with Martin Scorsese, just to get their relationship off to a rocky start.

Thompson does, however, handle her actors well. Unafraid of making Catherine seem ridiculous, Lemercier gives an outstanding comic performance. She excels in Catherine's dinner with Brian as the actress dares to disagree with the director's interpretation of de Beauvoir and again when Catherine abandons the script during the opening night of her play to show Brian her creative side. Lemercier's interaction with Pollack may benefit from her having played a small role in the director's *Sabrina* (1995). Lemercier's performance won her a César, the French Oscar, as best supporting actress. Dupontel is outstanding in the film's most serious role as the pianist who feels his true identity has been stolen by his success. He expertly conveys Jean-François's desperation without making it too pathetic or comic.

Other members of the excellent cast represent the history of film in the second half of the twentieth century. Brasseur's impressive credits include Georges Franju's *Eyes Without a Face* (1960), Jean Renoir's *The Elusive Corporal* (1962), and Jean-Luc Godard's *Band of Outsiders* (1964). Resembling Jean-François, Jacques has discovered that wealth is not enough with the approach of mortality. Dani, who appears in François Truffaut's *Day for Night* (*La Nuit américaine*, 1973) and *Love on the Run* (*L'Amour en fuite*, 1979), makes Claudie, perhaps an older version of Jessica, poignant without becoming sentimental. She was also nominated for a

César. *Avenue Montaigne* was the final film for Flon, who died shortly after completing shooting. Once Édith Piaf's private secretary, Flon made her first film in 1947, with appearances in John Huston's *Moulin Rouge* (1952) and Orson Welles's *Mr. Arkadin* (1955). Flon subtly shows the elderly grandmother's vulnerability without resorting to sentimentality.

Thompson's directing skills falter a bit with de France. Though the young star was nominated for a César for best actress, she is much more limited than her co-stars. Coasting on slight variations of her perkiness, she resembles the young Shirley MacLaine. The Thompsons do not provide much depth for Jessica, whose primary role is to react to the other characters. The others in the cast, however, provide sufficient reasons to overlook the superficiality of *Avenue Montaigne*.

Michael Adams

CREDITS

Jessica: Cécile de France
Catherine Versen: Valérie Lemercier
Jean-François Lefort: Albert Dupontel
Jacques Grumberg: Claude Brasseur
Claudie: Dani
Valentine Lefort: Laura Morante
Brian Sobinski: Sydney Pollack
Valérie: Annelise Hesme
Madame Roux: Suzanne Flon
Origin: France
Language: French
Released: 2006
Production: Christine Gozlan; StudioCanal, TF-1 Films, Thelma Films, Radis Films Production; released by ThinkFilm
Directed by: Danièle Thompson
Written by: Danièle Thompson
Cinematography by: Jean-Marc Fabre
Music by: Nicola Piovani
Sound: Michel Kharat, Vincent Arnardi
Editing: Sylvie Landra
Costumes: Catherine Leterrier
Production Design: Michele Abbe
MPAA rating: PG-13
Running time: 100 minutes

REVIEWS

Entertainment Weekly Online. February 14, 2007.
Hollywood Reporter Online. April 26, 2006.
Los Angeles Times Online. March 2, 2007.

New York Times Online. February 16, 2007.
San Francisco Chronicle. March 16, 2007, p. E5.
Variety Online. February 14, 2006.
Washington Post. March 2, 2007, p. C1.

QUOTES

Director Danièle Thompson: "You can be truthful without being realistic."

TRIVIA

Film is dedicated to actress Suzanne Flon ("Madame Roux") who died June 15, 2005.

AWAKE

Every year, one in 700 people wake up during surgery. When they planned her husband's murder, they never thought he'd be the one.
—Movie tagline

Box Office: $14.4 million

Awake is first-time director and writer Joby Harold's loathsome psychological thriller about a rare but potentially terrifying condition in which a patient is fully conscious during surgery despite being anesthetized. The theme of "anesthetic awareness," an actual medical condition, has never been used as a plot device and offers an intriguing opportunity to explore all sorts of terrifying possibilities. Unfortunately Harold misses the mark with too many subplots and completely unbelievable situations. What should play out as an invigorating thriller ends up being something just short of camp.

Clayton Beresford, Jr. (Hayden Christensen), a twenty-two-year-old billionaire Momma's Boy in need of a heart transplant, falls in love with Sam Lockwood (Jessica Alba) and against his mother's wishes, marries the young social climber on Halloween night. Almost immediately after the ceremony, Clay is contacted by his friend and surgeon, Jack Harper (Terrence Howard), informing him that a suitable donor heart matching his rare blood type has been located and ordering him to get to the hospital immediately for the transplant. This is where things begin to stretch the audience's suspension of disbelief. The Beresford's close family friend is the world-renowned heart transplant surgeon Dr. Jonathan Neyer (Arliss Howard). Against all logic and his mother's wishes (once again), Clayton decides to put his life in the hands of Dr. Harper, a man with no less than four malpractice suits pending against him. Once inside the operating room, which looks more appropriate for a minor veterinary procedure complete with a staff of four, things unsurprisingly begin to go south for the wonder kid. The usual aesthetician is conspicuously missing, replaced by an incompetent hack whose actions put young Clay in this horrifying state of conscious immobilization.

What follows during the gory surgical procedure is a strange, out-of-body experience, complete with a droning, lifeless voiceover, which has Clay moving back and forth in time as he attempts to piece together what has gone wrong before it is too late. What has gone wrong is plainly obvious to anyone who has managed to stay awake to this point in the film. Sam and Dr. Harper are former lovers who have hatched this overly elaborate plan to extract a $100 million settlement upon Clay's death. Fortunately for Clay, and in yet another outrageous plot twist straight out of a bad made-for-television movie, his mother Lilith (Lena Olin) has unraveled the plan and has hatched her own preposterous scheme to save her son. She will commit suicide and have her own heart implanted in her son by the family friend Dr. Neyer. After she fatally overdoses on pills, she is granted an out-of-body experience to wrap up all her unsettled issues with Clay, creating a tidy device for Harold to wrap up some loose plot threads. Lilith also manages to alert the authorities who descend upon the operating room like the proverbial cavalry, just in the nick of time.

Fine performances are turned in by Lena Olin, who manages to give her character a fair bit of depth considering the material she has to work with, as well as Arliss Howard, who shines as Dr. Jonathan Neyer in spite of having to deliver over-the-top lines like, "I've had my hands inside of presidents." Hayden Christensen seems to have taken his character's anesthetized qualities to heart, delivering a listless performance that makes him seem more like the Ambien poster boy than the Barron's Man of the Year the script claims he is. Jessica Alba delivers a truly vapid performance as Sam Lockwood, and while the two visually make a nice couple, they can hardly carry the lead roles.

In the publicity for the film, it is dramatically claimed that anesthetic awareness is experienced by one in 700 patients. The reality is that the condition occurs in only about one in 14,000 patients. The film's depiction of anesthesiologists has also captured the attention of at least one watchdog group that has questioned the science behind the film and the questionable medical practices portrayed by its anesthesiologists.

The film is sparse, barely coming in at eighty minutes but it seems much longer as it plods along from one preposterous subplot to another with little regard for the audience's intelligence. In more capable hands, this could have been a truly watchable and new addition to the genre, but instead it seems destined for obscurity. *Awake* was shot in 2005 and sat around for over a year.

Before its release late in November, in hindsight, it would have been better left to Dr. Kevorkian.

Michael White

CREDITS

Clayton Beresford, Jr.: Hayden Christensen
Sam Lockwood: Jessica Alba
Dr. Jack Harper: Terrence Howard
Lilith Beresford: Lena Olin
Dr. Jonathan Neyer: Arliss Howard
Dr. Larry Lupin: Christopher McDonald
Dr. Puttnam: Fisher Stevens
Clayton Beresford Sr.: Sam Robards
Penny Carver: Georgina Chapman
Origin: USA
Language: English
Released: 2007
Production: Joana Vicente, Jason Kliot, Bob Weinstein, Fisher Stevens; Open City Films, Greenstreet, Weinstein Co.; released by MGM
Directed by: Joby Harold
Written by: Joby Harold
Cinematography by: Russell Carpenter
Music by: Graeme Revell
Sound: Noah Vivekanand Timan
Music Supervisor: Dan Lieberstein
Editing: Craig McKay
Art Direction: Ben Barraud
Costumes: Cynthia Flynt
Production Design: Dina Goldman
MPAA rating: R
Running time: 78 minutes

REVIEWS

Boston Globe Online. December 1, 2007.
Chicago Sun-Times Online. November 30, 2007.
Hollywood Reporter Online. December 3, 2007.
Los Angeles Times Online. December 3, 2007.
New York Times Online. December 1, 2007.
Variety Online. November 30, 2007.
Washington Post. December 1, 2007, p. C1.

QUOTES

Clayton Beresford, Jr.: "Am I supposed to still hear you?"

AWARDS

Nomination:

Golden Raspberries 2007: Worst Actress (Alba), Worst Screen Couple (Alba and Christensen).

AWAY FROM HER

*It's never too late to become what you might have
 been.*
　　—Movie tagline

*Sometimes you have to let go of what you can't
 live without.*
　　—Movie tagline

The ultimate love story.
　　—Movie tagline

Box Office: $4.6 million

It is a rare film that gets nearly unanimous critical approval, but *Away From Her* was one such film. The film was adapted from the Alice Munro story, "The Bear Came Over the Mountain," by twenty-eight-year-old Canadian actress Sarah Polley. Polley, who had a respected career acting in independent films such as *The Sweet Hereafter* (1997) and *My Life Without Me* (2003), was drawn to the story by its portrait of mature love. In an interview on National Public Radio's *Fresh Air*, Polley said that when she first read the story, she was beginning a new relationship of her own and the idea of looking at the end of a long relationship was especially compelling to her. She was also drawn to Munro's strong prose, and commented that the strength of Munro's writing helped make the adaptation for the screen go more smoothly.

Polley, who also directed *Away From Her,* has made a sparse, subtle film, filled with small moments and great tragedy. David Ansen of *Newsweek* called the film "emotionally devastating, but [added that] its insights into the complexities of love and marriage and memory are not the sort you're likely to find on Lifetime. Its tears are earned in more honest, surprising ways." Given that the subject matter is the effect Alzheimer's has on a marriage, it is not difficult to imagine that the film is indeed emotionally devastating. But Polley forgoes sweeping soundtracks and big moments fraught with meaning for smaller moments of truth. Ultimately, such moments are more real and thus more painful.

The story concerns the relationship between Fiona (Julie Christie) and Grant (Gordon Pinsent). The couple has been married for almost fifty years and lives in a charming cottage by a lake in Ontario, Canada. Grant, a retired professor, and his still-gorgeous wife Fiona have settled into a comfortable relationship. They are the sort of educated, companionable couple who spend the day cross-country skiing together, then return home for a fine dinner and a good book.

Fiona's Alzheimer's manifests slowly, as is its nature. She begins to forget words and does odd things such as putting away a pan in the freezer. Even after the disease starts making itself more obvious and Fiona is forced to label the kitchen drawers so that she will know what

they contain, she and Grant try to ignore what might be happening. "Don't worry," Fiona jokes, "I'm just losing my mind."

Eventually, though, it is Fiona who brings up the horrible truth. "I think I may be beginning to disappear," she whispers, both fearfully and matter-of-factly. Against Grant's wishes, she insists on moving to Meadowlake, an assisted living facility nearby that specializes in Alzheimer's. One of the conditions of the facility is that the patients cannot receive visitors for their first month.

One of the rich complexities of the film is that, when Grant returns, Fiona no longer seems to recognize him. She is kind to him, but reserves her interest for a silent fellow patient, Aubrey (Michael Murphy). "My, but you are persistent," she comments kindly and perhaps a bit nervously whenever Grant tries to engage her. The situation is made more interesting by the fact that in flashback it is revealed that Grant was not always such an attentive spouse. In his early days as a professor, he enjoyed an affair with a student. Perhaps Fiona's attentions to Aubrey are a way of paying Grant back for his indiscretions. Or maybe, as Fiona says, Aubrey is a good mate because he does not expect so much from her. For his part, Grant's daily visits and devoted behavior may be a kind of penance for his past bad behavior.

Truly outstanding in the film is Christie's performance. Still as lovely as she was in her career-making films such as *Dr. Zhivago* (1965), Christie gives a rich, layered portrayal of a woman bravely facing a grim future. Fiona's decent into blankness is not a straight path, but rather a meandering one that can double back on itself in odd, off moments. At one point when Fiona and Grant are having a serious discussion about her relocation to Meadowlake, Fiona suddenly looks off into the distance and does not seem to know what Grant is talking about. Grant is alarmed, but Fiona bursts out laughing, revealing that she was only pretending to be confused. Fiona is a lusty, graceful woman who walks toward her fate with the same grace that she has lived her life. Polley's film displays that same sort of grace.

Jill Hamilton

CREDITS

Fiona Anderson: Julie Christie
Grant Anderson: Gordon Pinsent
Marian: Olympia Dukakis
Aubrey: Michael Murphy
Madeleine: Wendy Crewson

Dr. Fischer: Alberta Watson
Kristy: Kristen Thomson
Origin: Canada
Language: English
Released: 2006
Production: Daniel Iron, Simone Urdl, Jennifer Weiss; Foundry Films, Film Farm; released by Lions Gate Films
Directed by: Sarah Polley
Written by: Sarah Polley
Cinematography by: Luc Pontpellier
Music by: Jonathan Goldsmith
Sound: Jane Tattersall
Editing: David Wharnsby
Art Direction: Benno Tutter
Costumes: Debra Hanson
Production Design: Katherine (Kathleen) Climie
MPAA rating: PG-13
Running time: 110 minutes

REVIEWS

Entertainment Weekly. May 11, 2007, p. 57.
Globe and Mail Online. May 4, 2007.
Hollywood Reporter Online. January 18, 2007.
Los Angeles Times Online. May 4, 2007.
Newsweek Online. May 2007.
New York Times Online. May 4, 2007.
Rolling Stone Online. April 18, 2007.
Variety Online. September 11, 2006.
Village Voice Online. May 1, 2007.

QUOTES

Fiona: "I think people are too demanding. People want to be in love every single day. What a liability."
Fiona: "I think I may be beginning to disappear."

TRIVIA

Sarah Polley adapted the short story "The Bear Came Over the Mountain" specifically for Julie Christie.

AWARDS

Golden Globes 2008: Actress—Drama (Christie)
Screen Actors Guild 2007: Actress (Christie)
Nomination:
Oscars 2007: Actress (Christie), Adapt. Screenplay
British Acad. 2007: Actress (Christie).

B

BALLS OF FURY

A huge comedy with tiny balls.
—Movie tagline

Box Office: $32.9 million

In the mythical world the filmmakers have created in *Balls of Fury*, fortunes are won and lost, lives hang in the balance, and one man must achieve redemption, all in the high stakes world of Ping-Pong. Played in seedy back alleys and posh, exotic island hideaways, the imaginative filmmakers have elevated a humble recreation room pastime to the sport of kings in their own brash, ironic manner. Despite all the usual sports film clichés and low-brow humor one would expect from a film with the tagline "A huge comedy with tiny balls," the ridiculous premise works in its favor, tempered by realistic and sympathetic lead performances, even pacing, and many genuinely funny moments.

Balls of Fury stays true to its farcical roots from a long line of sports spoofs that have proliferated in recent years, including *Blades of Glory* (2007), *Talladega Nights: The Ballad of Ricky Bobby* (2006), and *Dodgeball: A True Underdog Story* (2004), and is equally entertaining. One of the main differences is that, although director/writer Robert Ben Garant is a comic veteran who also wrote and directed this year's delicious absurdity *Reno 911!: Miami*, lead actor Dan Fogler is a Broadway actor without the bankability and huge following of such stars as Will Ferrell and Ben Stiller. Fogler will seem familiar to comedy fans, however, seeming like a more low-key and likable Jack Black.

The film centers on Randy Daytona (Dan Fogler), who was a Ping-Pong prodigy who made it to the Olympic finals only to have a freak accident and lose to East Germany's pompous Karl Wolfschtagg (Thomas Lennon). Years later and the washed up wunderkind has traded in his Olympic dreams for the rhinestone-encrusted paddle he uses in his cheesy Las Vegas lounge act. The surreal plot starts in earnest when an agent from the Federal Bureau of Investigation, Ernie Rodriguez (George Lopez), shows up at Randy's act to recruit him for a dangerous mission in which he would have to compete in an illegal and deadly table tennis tournament run by the arms dealer Mr. Feng (Christopher Walken). Rodriguez introduces Randy to a Ping-Pong master who will train him, blind Master Wong (James Hong) and his spunky niece Maggie (Maggie Q).

One amusing scene involves Randy, now deemed "ready" by his trainer, playing the fearsome champion "The Dragon" (Na Shi La). As a muscular, heavily tattooed Asian man enters, Randy nearly faints until he is replaced by a pig-tailed little Asian girl who is indeed, the real Dragon. Not so amusing is the abuse taken by his genitalia when she loses, a tired running gag. Besting The Dragon, Randy is given the Golden Paddle, which is the secret invitation to Feng's tournament where he will go up against the world's best players.

The filmmakers have created a James Bond-style fantasy in Feng's island palace, complete with a host of armed guards, secret chambers, and a femme fatale sidekick Mahogany (Aisha Tyler) who is a crack shot with a deadly blow-dart gun, which she uses each time a player loses. As far-fetched as the plot may be, the mere sight of Walken, dressed as a flamboyant Asian don of sorts, is one the film's main draws. Dressed in his customary Def Leppard t-shirt, Randy bests all the other players but must face Feng in another Bond-style showdown: He is strapped into an electronic Ping-Pong game device that is wired to shock the player who loses each point and eventually kill the loser. Naturally, Randy is victorious and Feng meets with a "shocking" end.

Produced and written by Robert Ben Garant and Thomas Lennon, another *Reno 911!* veteran, *Balls of Fury* certainly reflects the duo's taste for over-the-top situations, some of which work very nicely. Much of the Ping-Pong choreography and effects are quite impressive, especially one scene at Feng's with dozens of synchronized players exactly in step. Maggie Q's balletic martial arts moves are also prominently featured. The film could have been more judiciously edited, however, and should have ended after the gang escape Feng's island lair. The final scene, lasting five minutes or so, is completely unnecessary. And the romantic subplot involving Maggie and Randy simply does not work. While both actors give nice, naturalistic performances, the film gives no reason, other than they both are wonderful Ping-Pong players, for them to fall in love.

As well as fine lead performances, *Balls of Fury* draws on an excellent supporting cast for laughs. Tyler is slyly hilarious as Feng's comely henchwoman. Other familiar *Reno 911!* faces include Kerri Kenney, as a ditsy showgirl, and Jim Rash as an FBI agent, who also add their comic élan. Feng's bevy of male courtesans includes the wonderful and surprising Diedrich Bader (who played Oswald on the *The Drew Carey Show*) who steals each scene he is in, especially one involving rescuing a dead panda.

Hilary White

CREDITS

Randy Dayton: Dan Fogler
Feng: Christopher Walken
Ernie Rodriguez: George Lopez
Master Wong: James Hong
Freddy: Terry Crews
Sgt. Pete Daytona: Robert Patrick
Gary: Diedrich Bader
Mahogany: Aisha Tyler
Karl Wolfschtagg: Thomas Lennon
Maggie: Maggie Q
Origin: USA
Language: English
Released: 2007
Production: Gary Barber, Roger Birnbaum, Jonathan Glickman, Thomas Lennon; Spyglass Entertainment, Intrepid Pictures; released by Rogue Pictures
Directed by: Robert Ben Garant

Written by: Thomas Lennon, Robert Ben Garant
Cinematography by: Thomas Ackerman
Music by: Randy Edelman
Sound: Edward Novick
Editing: John Refoua
Art Direction: Steve Arnold
Costumes: Maryann Bozek
Production Design: Jeff Knipp
MPAA rating: PG-13
Running time: 90 minutes

REVIEWS

Boston Globe Online. August 20, 2007.
Chicago Sun-Times Online. August 28, 2007.
Entertainment Weekly Online. August 28, 2007.
Hollywood Reporter Online. August 24, 2007.
Los Angeles Times Online. August 29, 2007.
New York Times Online. August 29, 2007.
San Francisco Chronicle. August 29, 2007, p. E1.
Variety Online. August 23, 2007.
Washington Post. August 29, 2007, p. C1.

QUOTES

Master Wong: "It is better to die like a tiger, than to live like a pussy."

BECAUSE I SAID SO

She's just your normal, overprotective, overbearing, over-the-top mother.
—Movie tagline

Box Office: $42.7 million

Because I Said So is a romantic comedy aimed squarely at women, also known as a "chick flick," of the decidedly middling variety. The film is superficially pleasing with an attractive and talented cast, which includes Mandy Moore and Piper Perabo, and showcases beautiful sets, taking place in the familiar and charmingly well-appointed homes, apartments, and restaurants inhabited by the well-off denizens of many a romantic comedy. There are a couple of lovely weddings to swoon over, appealing wardrobe choices, and as a whole, the movie is visually satisfying. Venturing beyond the film's glossy veneer is not recommended, however, as the dialogue is trite, the romantic obstacles contrived, and the choice that the heroine must make between men too obvious. Perhaps the most egregious error is the poor use of the talented Diane Keaton. It is especially surprising since this film was directed by Michael Lehmann, who was responsible for the far superior *Heathers* (1989) and *The Truth About Cats and Dogs* (1996).

The story, written by Karen Leigh Hopkins and Jessie Nelson, concerns the romantic life, or lack thereof, of Milly (Mandy Moore). Milly is sweet, pretty, and runs a successful catering business. She lacks self-confidence, largely because her mother Daphne (Diane Keaton) feels it her motherly duty to point out her daughter's flaws. She criticizes everything from Milly's awkward nervous laugh to her bust size. With so many imperfections, Daphne wonders how Milly will ever find a good man like her sisters Maggie (Lauren Graham) and Mae (Piper Perabo). The dysfunctional mother/daughter relationship is so problematic in the film, Carina Chocano of the *Los Angeles Times* was moved to describe the pair as "a mother and daughter bound by a mutual dependence so neurotically obsessive it makes the affair in *Last Tango in Paris* look breezy and wholesome."

In one of her many unlikable maneuvers, Daphne decides to run a personal ad to find a suitor for her daughter. This leads to a predicable montage in which Daphne, at a hotel bar, interviews the rabble that have answered the ad, while the bar's quirky musician, Johnny (Gabriel Macht), looks on with amusement. Finding most of the interviewees shockingly disappointing, Daphne is smitten with the final applicant, Jason (Tom Everett Scott), a well bred, charming, and handsome architect. Daphne scoffs when Johnny steps in, suggesting that he might be a good match for Milly. Citing his tattoo and the fact that he wears a hat as reasons, it is difficult to decipher exactly why Daphne objects to him, other than he is not the stereotypical white collar professional that the stereotypical character of Daphne may approve of. He is also a single father, but Daphne is a single mother.

While it is already painfully clear to viewers that Johnny is the one for Milly, the filmmakers did not want to take any chances, or give the audience any credit, going out of their way to make it plain that Johnny is the right choice for Milly. Milly accidentally breaks something in Jason's flashy high-rise apartment and he erupts in anger. In the very next scene, Milly breaks a dish at Johnny's homey Venice bungalow, where he comforts her and assures her it is all right. Even without all the glass breaking, the real estate alone points to Milly's correct choice.

Keaton gamely tries to keep the train wreck of a film on its rails, but must constantly fight the fact that her character is not merely unlikable and unrelatable, but also poorly fleshed out. Carina Chocano notes that, in *Because I Said So*, Keaton "has been reduced to a set of basic features (neurotic isolation, emotional frigidity, clumsiness) served up in the most infantilizing manner." Daphne's treatment of Milly leans toward psychological abuse, not exactly the stuff of slapstick comedy. In one

scene, she tries to go on the Internet and ends up on a pornography web site. Wackiness ensues as she calls technical support, her computer blaring sexual noises. It all reaches a comedic nadir when her apparently aroused dog starts humping the furniture. Perhaps the worse abuse of Keaton is that her character's catering business is mined for desperate, clichéd physical comedy of the pie-in-the-face variety, with Keaton having to endure disasters involving large cakes on several occasions. While Keaton may not be suited to playing royalty à la Cate Blanchett, a comic actor of her stature surely should be offered more dignified material than she is given in the exploitative comedy *Because I Said So*.

Jill Hamilton

CREDITS

Daphne: Diane Keaton
Milly: Mandy Moore
Maggie: Lauren Graham
Mae: Piper Perabo
Johnny: Gabriel Macht
Jason: Tom Everett Scott
Joe: Stephen Collins
Lionel: Ty Panitz
Derek: Colin Ferguson
Stuart: Tony Hale
Eli: Matt Champagne
Origin: USA
Language: English
Released: 2007
Production: Paul Brooks, Jessie Nelson; Gold Circle Films; released by Universal Pictures
Directed by: Michael Lehmann
Written by: Karen Leigh Hopkins, Jessie Nelson
Cinematography by: Julio Macat
Music by: David Kitay
Sound: Douglas Axtell
Music Supervisor: Dana Sano
Editing: Paul Seydor, Troy Takaki
Art Direction: Christopher Tandon
Costumes: Shay Cunliffe
Production Design: Sharon Seymour
MPAA rating: PG-13
Running time: 102 minutes

REVIEWS

Boxoffice Online. February 2, 2007.
Chicago Sun-Times Online. February 2, 2007.
Entertainment Weekly. February 9, 2007, p. 55.
Hollywood Reporter Online. February 2, 2007.

Los Angeles Times Online. February 2, 2007.
New York Times Online. February 2, 2007.
San Francisco Chronicle. February 2, 2007, p. E5.
Variety Online. February 1, 2007.
Washington Post. February 2, 2007, p. C1.

QUOTES

Daphne (about her 60th birthday): "Why are we celebrating my descent into oblivion?"

TRIVIA

The names of the daughters (Maggie, Milly, and Mae) come from an e.e. cummings poem that starts "Maggie and Milly and Molly and May went to the beach to play one day."

AWARDS

Nomination:

Golden Raspberries 2007: Worst Actress (Keaton).

BECOMING JANE

Her own life is her greatest inspiration.
—Movie tagline

Becoming a woman. Becoming a legend.
—Movie tagline

Between sense and sensibility and pride and prejudice was a life worth writing about.
—Movie tagline

Box Office: $18.8 million

Becoming Jane is a refreshing and satisfying look into the private life of famed English author Jane Austen, focusing on her financial and familial pressures to marry and her frustrated attempt at eloping, which may have led Jane to turn wholeheartedly to a life of writing. Though favorably reviewed on the whole, the film was nonetheless faulted for its speculative treatment of Jane Austen's life. The filmmakers do not present their work as a docudrama or even a factual investigation of an event in the fashion of *JFK* (1991) but as merely a fictionalized account of the author's life, in the tradition of *Shakespeare in Love.* Andrew Sarris, writing in the *New York Observer,* encapsulated a useful approach by saying, "*Becoming Jane* is not as good as the best Austen films, but is much better than most mainstream movies on tap." In an important sense, the film is also about finding one's voice—as an individual and as a writer—as much as it is about the particulars of the life of Jane Austen.

The plot of the movie, like that of a Jane Austen novel, concerns the marriageability of young women,

told from their own point of view. Jane's sister Cassandra (Anna Maxwell Martin) is the first of her sisters to become engaged. The film depicts the social conventions of the world of the parlor, showing us the balls and social gatherings that spawned the matchmaking of the era. As Cassandra becomes affianced, Jane (Anne Hathaway) meets a rusticated young lawyer named Tom Lefroy (James McAvoy) and, in the best tradition of Elizabeth Bennet and Mr. Darcy, their initial friction eventually gives way to deep love. The audience watches the societal complications unfold that threaten and eventually sunder this relationship, while at the same time Jane is developing into a novelist.

The film also takes up a difficult question that other literary-based films have attempted: how to make a believable film about a writer and how to depict convincingly the writing process. The usual tack for filmmakers is to show the writer scribbling away at a desk while, in voice-over narration, the audience hears the famous sentences that resulted. Shots of quill pens scratching across pages of parchment intercut with shots of Jane frowning or smiling from her literary labors do turn up, to be sure, in *Becoming Jane.* However, scriptwriters Kevin Hood and Sarah Williams mostly direct the emphasis away from this movie cliché about writing by dramatizing the trial and errors of the young writer's life and emerging sensibility.

When, for example, Tom Lefroy appears at the country gathering that features Jane reading her own encomium on Cassandra's engagement, he fidgets at her overdrawn sentiments: "Do *both* sides of those pages have writing on them?" Later, a series of jump cuts shows Jane upstairs in response to Lefroy's reaction destroying some of her juvenilia. Some of the most intelligent sentences from Jane Austen in the film emerge in her conversation rather than in the scenes of her writing. It is as if the audience gets to observe Jane editing herself in daily discourse and to follow how her restless intelligence prepares her for the task of novel writing. In one example, Jane compliments Cassandra on her appearance before she sees her intended: "His heart will stop at the very sight of you, or he doesn't deserve to live—and, yes, I'm aware of the contradiction embodied in that sentence." In one of the film's best scenes, Jane dines with the formidable Judge Langlois (Ian Richardson) in an effort to win his approval as Tom's intended. One of Jane's dinner-table observations rankles the stern judge, who coldly interrupts her: "Do I detect you in irony?" he sniffs, calling irony nothing other than "an insult with a smiling face." In the most audience-pleasing moment in the film, Jane instinctively overrules the judge: "No. Irony is the bringing together of contradictory truths to make out of the contradiction a new truth with a laugh or a smile. And I confess that a truth must come with one or the other, or I count it as false and a denial of the very nature of humanity itself." The words spill out as if they are her artistic credo, freshly formed. Though it probably plays a part in costing her a future with Tom, her corrective comment suggests in its spontaneity that Jane's identity as a writer was shaped in the daily stresses and challenges of social life.

Another way of addressing the movie cliché about writers is to make suggestions about the cause/effect of some famous scenes and sentences. Screenwriters Hood and Williams cannot resist wondering how the memorable opening sentence of *Pride and Prejudice* may have come to Jane Austen. In their rendition, Mr. Wisley (Laurence Fox), a rejected suitor of Jane's, consoles her at the end of the film about her missed chances with Tom Lefroy by relying on the phrase "it is a truth universally acknowledged." At that point, the filmmakers cut directly to Jane and her quill at her study window completing and transmuting his locution into one of the most famous opening sentences from any English novel. In addition, Mr. Wisley's cold, disapproving aunt, Lady Gresham (Maggie Smith), seems to be based on the character Lady Catherine de Bourgh from *Pride and Prejudice*. Hunt and Williams may have enjoyed suggesting in one scene that a tense meeting between Jane and Lady Gresham may have been the real-life inspiration for the celebrated final scene between Elizabeth Bennet and Lady Catherine in *Pride and Prejudice*.

The greatest strength of the film, however, is its direction. If good directing mostly involves placing the camera in the perfect spot, then Julian Jarrold, whose professional background is primarily in television, seems already an accomplished hand. Again and again, shots appear that invite and reward the active, attentive viewing of the audience. Jarrold uses space especially well and is able wordlessly to suggest emotional distance or closeness through the proxemics of the screen. When, for example, Jane first meets Tom Lefroy, she is taking a walk in the woods. Going against the current industry fondness for numerous close-ups, Jarrold frames the characters from a greater distance so that body English and negative space pictorialize their mutual wariness. Another scene begins with a panoramic establishing shot of Jane and Cassandra walking on a coastline. Jarrold smartly allows the dynamics of a scene to dictate the photographic style, so that the stately dinners and balls are done with lengthier shots and smoother, slower camera movements while impromptu boxing matches and rowdy scenes at outdoor fairs are rapidly cut and done with shaky, handheld shots often infused with reds, the color of aggression.

Two noticeable matching shots from different moments in the film also illustrate Jarrold's visual care. In the first, Jane leaves Tom Lefroy after his patron has, in effect, forced Tom to break his engagement with Jane. She glumly enters a coach to return to her family. Jarrold shoots her face through the tiny back window of the coach, framed in the larger black of the carriage fabric, which, when the coach begins to move away from the stationary camera, becomes smaller and smaller. The frame-within-the-frame of the tiny window and the rapidly receding size suggest pictorially the crushed hopes and reduced emotions of the sad young woman. Later, a matching shot frames Tom outside from a similar coach window. After Jane has decided against eloping with him, the camera shoots Tom from the inside of Jane's coach. We see him in the distance suddenly grow smaller as the coach starts away. The two low points of Jane's romantic life with Tom are thus rendered visually in parallel fashion, suggesting that the only emotion remaining between them is their helpless frustration.

Jarrold's use of selective focusing also conveys meaning wordlessly by showing the relation between thought (and by implication a writer's deep inner life) and the events around her. In a scene set at a long, crowded dinner table at Lady Gresham's estate, the camera shoots Jane in a pensive close-up through a window from outside the house. Even as she dines with others, she seems in thought. Without a cut, the focus suddenly alters to the foreground windowpane as a drop of rain falls on it, and Jane's face in the background goes out of focus. The rain intensifies as a messenger rides up with tragic news. The racking focus has signaled pictorially the way events will impinge on Jane's thoughts. A subsequent scene begins with a close-up of Jane's hand holding a quill pen as she works on her novel. In the background out of focus is Cassandra in bed watching her sister. The focus then changes from the foregrounded quill to the girl in the background as she desperately questions her sister about her book. The dialogue about the novel becomes a distraction from the tragic news just delivered. The giant close-up of the moving quill, like so much of the movie, suggests the power of art to shape human life and to minister to heartache. It reminds its viewers that in addition to being a pleasing biographical film about Jane Austen, *Becoming Jane* is also a compelling movie about writing and the driving need to find one's own voice.

Glenn Hopp

CREDITS

Jane Austen: Anne Hathaway
Tom Lefroy: James McAvoy
Mrs. Austen: Julie Walters
Reverend Austen: James Cromwell
Mr. Wisley: Laurence Fox

Lady Gresham: Maggie Smith
Judge Langlois: Ian Richardson
Cassandra Austen: Anna Maxwell Martin
Henry Austen: Joe Anderson
Mrs. Radcliffe: Helen McCrory
John Warren: Leo Bill
Origin: USA, Great Britain
Language: English
Released: 2007
Production: Graham Broadbent, Douglas Rae, Robert Bernstein; Ecosse Films, Scion Films, Blueprint Films, Octagan Films; released by Miramax Films
Directed by: Julian Jarrold
Written by: Kevin Hood, Sarah Williams
Cinematography by: Eigil Bryld
Music by: Adrian Johnston
Sound: Nick Adams, Tom Johnson, Peter Blayney
Editing: Emma E. Hickox
Art Direction: David McHenry
Costumes: Eimer Ni Mhaoldomhnaigh
Production Design: Eve Stewart
MPAA rating: PG
Running time: 120 minutes

REVIEWS

Boston Globe Online. August 3, 2007.
Chicago Sun-Times Online. August 3, 2007.
Entertainment Weekly Online. August 2, 2007.
Guardian Online. March 9, 2007.
Los Angeles Times Online. August 3, 2007.
New York Times Online. August 3, 2007.
The Observer Online. March 11, 2007.
Variety Online. March 8, 2007.
Washington Post. August 3, 2007, p. C5.

QUOTES

Mrs. Austen (on marriage): "Affection is desirable; money is absolutely indispensable."

TRIVIA

Anne Hathaway learned to play the piano and worked with a dialect coach for the preparation of this movie.

BEE MOVIE

Born to bee wild.
—Movie tagline
Honey just got funny.
—Movie tagline

Box Office: $126.6 million

The absurdist humor of Jerry Seinfeld made his eponymous show one of television's most beloved comedies, but the "show about nothing" does not translate into anything more than a minor amusement on the big screen in Seinfeld's debut film *Bee Movie.* Much hyped for nearly a year before its release, *Bee Movie* plays like a minor idea that got way overblown. According to early trailers Seinfeld originally wanted to make this a live-action comedy, but in reality it was a DreamWorks Animation project from the start. If nothing else, the result proves that a star of Seinfeld's magnitude can get the money and backing he needs to do whatever movie he wants—at least once.

Compared to similar recent movies from the insect perspective such as *Antz* (1998) and *A Bug's Life* (1998), *Bee Movie* is a lightweight in both plot and execution. Co-directed by Steve Hickner and Simon J. Smith, and co-written by Seinfeld and three other screenwriters, *Bee Movie* feels cobbled together, with a story line that buzzes this way and that. It is more like an extended series of skits than a coherent movie. Its amusing lines are inconsistent, and the movie veers from silly to flat.

The film certainly does not begin with a punch. Seinfeld voices the character of Barry B. Benson, who lives in a hive that looks more like something imagined by a manufacturer of plastic toys than anything organic or naturalistic. The look of the movie is all bright colors and artificial surfaces, a cartoon world short on realistic animation that is quite uninteresting compared to the complex palettes of most Pixar, DreamWorks or Disney competitors. It is as if advanced animation techniques have been used way too overbearingly in the service of rather simplistic visual concepts.

We meet Barry on the day he graduates from college (the joke here is that high school took three days and college three more). It is also the day he and his friend Adam Flayman (voice of Matthew Broderick) are supposed to start work for the corporation that runs the hive, Honex. Adam is typically beelike, that is, rather dense and agreeable, but Barry, a ready-made rebel, quickly catches on that the job description of a worker bee is repetitive, long and hard, and dangerous. He longs to escape by flying with the "pollen jocks," the bees that bring the nectar to the hive and get the admiration of all the girls. And with surprising ease, he is able to do so. (It would have been far more dramatic if Barry had to overcome more obstacles to get his wish, but in this film any ideas that pop into the protagonist's head instantly materialize. Seinfeld is not much interested in the process of developing tension to advance a plot point; in this you can tell he is a veteran of quick television sketches.)

Once outside, Barry witnesses how the pollen jocks pollinate flowers, but through a series of slapstick incidents he ends up almost being killed in an apartment by Ken (voice of Patrick Warburton), a shallow, self-possessed idiot. He is rescued by Ken's girlfriend, Vanessa (voice of Renée Zellweger), who opines that his life is as valuable as Ken's. Grateful and smitten, Barry then breaks the cardinal rule of the bees—"Don't talk to humans!"— and strikes up a rather ridiculous romance with Vanessa.

Seinfeld soon tires of the romantic plot and concocts a new one. While visiting a supermarket with Vanessa, Barry is enraged to find that human beings sell and eat honey. Outraged at the injustice of humans profiting from the hard work of his fellow bees, Barry turns from free spirit to crusader for the little guy. Seinfeld's absurd idea is that Barry sues the human race for its honey pilfering. Well, at first it is the human race and then it is five major corporations who make honey.

While the idea of the lawsuit seems weak and preposterous, the trial is actually one of the film's high points, thanks largely to the pompous behavior of the corporate defense attorney, as voiced by John Goodman in a wonderful display of verbal gymnastics. The antics of the attorneys on both sides range from silly to sharp, and the wordplay flows thick and anarchic. This part of the film works much better than the third act, in which the consequences of Barry's legal victory play out badly, resulting in the bees being able to quit their jobs and live a purposeless life of loafing; as a result, plants start dying off everywhere. Not only does the script set up a rather contrived problem, the solution—which involves hijacking a float from the Tournament of Roses parade in California and flying it to New York—seem both poorly conceived and overheated.

Seinfeld's humor is mostly verbal and his concepts absurdist, and the result is hit-and-miss. When the jokes work—as they do in a brief scene with Chris Rock voicing a mosquito smashed against a windshield—they are mildly amusing, but Seinfeld seems to be working way too hard at desperately pumping humor into situations that are less than brilliantly conceived or executed. There is simply not enough material here to make a full-length feature film, and it is doubtful that children will get most of the jokes. At its best, *Bee Movie* has a few scenes of rapid-fire patter and mayhem that are enjoyable, but they are squished between long dull stretches.

Perhaps there is hidden social satire in the film's skewering of corporate greed and pomposity, but if so, it is undercut by the film's ultimately silly take on even its own pretensions. And strangely enough, the real-world issue of colony collapse disorder, which affected the beekeeping industry seriously in 2007, makes the entire last third of the movie not really about nothing, but more like a silly riff on something serious and meaningful. That seems more of an accident than anything, because Seinfeld is committed to inconsequence. As a result, *Bee Movie* lacks sting. The best kind of humor, even absurdist humor, is the kind that pokes fun at society's pretensions. It is great that *Bee Movie* steers clear of the heavy-handed moralism that plagues most children's animated features, but it fails to grab the audience at any point and hold on. Instead, the humor seems random and disconnected. The mind of Seinfeld can be delightfully wacky, and his take on the commonplace is often pleasantly skewed, but it is not enough to sustain a feature film.

Michael Betzold

CREDITS

Barry B. Benson: Jerry Seinfeld (Voice)
Vanessa Bloome: Renée Zellweger (Voice)
Adam Flayman: Matthew Broderick (Voice)
Layton T. Montgomery: John Goodman (Voice)
Ken: Patrick Warburton (Voice)
Mooseblood: Chris Rock (Voice)
Janet Benson: Kathy Bates (Voice)
Martin Benson: Barry Levinson (Voice)
Judge Bumbleton: Oprah Winfrey (Voice)
Buzzwell: Larry Miller (Voice)
Trudy: Megan Mullally (Voice)
Lou Lo Duca: Rip Torn (Voice)
Bud Ditchwater: Michael Richards (Voice)
Himself: Larry King (Cameo)
Himself: Ray Liotta (Cameo)
Himself: Sting (Cameo)
Origin: USA
Language: English
Released: 2007
Production: Jerry Seinfeld, Christina Steinberg; Columbus 81 Productions, DreamWorks Animation; released by Paramount
Directed by: Simon J. Smith, Steve Hickner
Written by: Jerry Seinfeld, Spike Feresten, Barry Marder, Andy Robin
Music by: Rupert Gregson-Williams
Sound: Andy Nelson, Anna Behlmer
Editing: Nick Fletcher
Art Direction: Christophe Lautrette
Production Design: Alex McDowell
MPAA rating: PG
Running time: 90 minutes

REVIEWS

Boston Globe Online. November 2, 2007.
Chicago Sun-Times Online. November 2, 2007.

Entertainment Weekly Online. October 31, 2007.
Hollywood Reporter Online. October 29, 2007.
Los Angeles Times Online. November 2, 2007.
New York Times Online. November 2, 2007.
Rolling Stone Online. November 1, 2007.
Variety Online. October 28, 2007.
Wall Street Journal. November 2, 2007, p. W1.
Washington Post. November 2, 2007, p. C1.

QUOTES

Vanessa: "Why don't you just fly everywhere? Isn't it faster?"

Barry B. Benson: "Because flying gets very tiring. Why don't you humans just run everywhere, isn't that faster?"

Vanessa: "I see your point."

TRIVIA

Jerry Seinfeld has said that his character, Barry B. Benson, is named in tribute to the 1979 sitcom *Benson* (1979) in which he got one of his first TV roles playing the character "Frankie."

AWARDS

Nomination:

Golden Globes 2008: Animated Film.

BEFORE THE DEVIL KNOWS YOU'RE DEAD

> *Loyalty. It's all relative.*
> —Movie tagline

> *No one was supposed to get hurt.*
> —Movie tagline

Box Office: $7.1 million

Sidney Lumet's *Before the Devil Knows You're Dead.* from a masterful script by first-time screenwriter Kelly Masterson, is a dazzling thriller that may prove to be one of the high points of a directorial career that has already seen so many. What is amazing is that Lumet, at the age of eighty-three, has made a movie that, in its complex, time-shifting structure, rivals the experimental movies made by much younger filmmakers. But what sets this work apart from other suspense films that demand the audience follow multiple time strands is that it does not skimp on developing the principal characters. On the contrary, these are real, flawed people who destroy not only their own lives but the lives of those who are supposedly closest to them. And as their backstories are gradually revealed, we see that their ultimate tragedy is rooted in the relationships themselves.

In a film loaded with stellar performances, Philip Seymour Hoffman is a standout as Andy Hanson, someone who is successful enough to have climbed the corporate ladder to a six-figure salary at a real estate company but whose life is nevertheless always on the verge of imploding. He has an uneasy marriage to Gina (Marisa Tomei in one of her finest performances) and a less than satisfying sex life. A generally disappointed man, he has a drug habit and cannot help but feel that he has never fit in with his family and was never loved the way his little brother, Hank (Ethan Hawke), was.

But Hank has his own set of problems. Estranged from his wife, Martha (Amy Ryan), and owing child support for their little girl, he is the weak little brother, referred to as a "baby" by both his brother and father. In love with Gina, he meets her every Thursday for sex but does not have the means to take her away from Andy.

When Andy approaches Hank with a scheme that will solve all of their financial problems, he goes along despite his reservations. Andy wants to rob a mom-and-pop jewelry store, fence the merchandise, and have each of them collect $60,000. The hitch is that the target is not just any mom-and-pop operation but the one owned by their very own mom and dad. Hank at first balks, but it is not long before the imposing Andy has persuaded him to go along with his plan.

Of course, this supposedly victimless crime, as Andy refers to it—he figures no one will get hurt and their parents will collect the insurance on the stolen diamonds—turns out to be anything but. Instead of doing the job himself, Hank brings in a lowlife named Bobby (Brian F. O'Byrne) to do the actual robbery while Hank drives the getaway car. And, instead of the usual employee working that morning, the boys' mom, Nanette (Rosemary Harris), is there. When she is able to pull a gun on Bobby and shoot him, he shoots back. Bobby ends up dead, and Nanette ends up in a coma.

Like Lumet's *Dog Day Afternoon* (1975), *Devil* is about a crime gone horribly wrong, but whereas that Al Pacino classic compresses the action into one long day, Masterson's brilliant script plays out in nonlinear fashion, which allows us to see the story unfold from different points of view. After a pre-credits sequence of Andy and Gina having sex on vacation in Rio, an idyllic moment that they wish they could live out all the time, the film presents the botched robbery and then cuts to events before the robbery to show us what led up to it. Chapter titles cue us in to the time frame as well as to the point of view we are seeing. Only by gradually putting the pieces together and seeing how each character experiences the same events do we get a complete picture of the story. It is a great device that promotes suspense and facilitates character development. We may see, for example, one side of a phone call only to see the other side later. But the fractured narrative never feels like a gimmick or a pretentious way to organize the plot but rather a way to delve into the story from multiple angles and to feel more deeply the tragedy when the family begins to unravel.

At the center of the maelstrom is Hoffman, who gives one of the most complex performances of the year and of his career as a man who is slowly coming undone. Contrasting his sloppy life to the neatness of an accountant's book, Andy reflects that his "life, it doesn't add up. Nothing connects to anything else. I'm not the sum of my parts. All of my parts don't add up to one me, I guess." And in this one moment, Hoffman makes us feel a glimmer of sympathy for a character we may otherwise hate. Moreover, in Andy's messiness, Hoffman reveals many facets of the character—the bully who can manipulate his brother into doing just about anything, the insecure husband desperate to prove his worth to his wife, the failed son who never felt valued by his father. Whether Andy is breaking down on the drive home after having a run-in with his father or simply allowing his wife to leave him because he is too numb and disconnected to do anything about it, he is a man constantly on the edge.

Hawke is impressive as well, but Hank does not have as many nuances as Andy. Browbeaten by his older brother, demanding father, and shrewish wife, Hank is always hanging by a thread and is in a perpetual state of panic, at times no more than a wounded animal trying his best to survive. Hoffman's Andy may be a loser as well, but he has more self-awareness; he knows how bad things are but somehow continues down the path his plans have led him, even if that road leads to his destruction.

While Hoffman dominates the film as a whole, as the story progresses, Albert Finney takes command as Charles, the patriarch of this troubled clan. Once he is left no choice but to pull the plug on his comatose wife, he makes it his mission to get to the bottom of the crime that took her from him. Finney is marvelous as a man who is simultaneously in a constant daze from the unbearable grief he is in and yet determined to make sense of the most senseless thing that could happen. There is a tenderness and a ferocity in his performance, chilling in its rawness. When he stumbles upon the final piece of the puzzle he needs, when he discovers that his own son Andy is responsible for Nanette's death, when, as another character tells him, "The world is an evil place," it is a devastating moment, as if his eyes were being opened for the first time.

The final act of the film is an inexorable descent for just about everyone. Eschewing the time shifts, the film lunges to its climax. Andy learns of Hank's affair with Gina, and the brothers face a blackmail scheme from Bobby's girlfriend, Chris (Aleksa Palladino), and her brother, Dex (Michael Shannon). Committing robbery and murder before squaring off with his brother, Andy essentially spirals out of control. But a bullet from Chris sends Andy to the hospital and Hank fleeing for his life. And in the hospital, in one of the most chilling endings in any movie this year, Charles kills his son by smothering him with a pillow. What is most disturbing is that it is not the act of a man out of control but rather the methodical, premeditated plan of a man avenging his wife's death and somehow feeling that he is setting things right. The way Charles takes the electrodes off Andy's chest and attaches them to his own so that the machine will not alert the nurses is an unsettling, shocking sight; we are witnessing a father momentarily assuming his own son's heartbeat while snuffing out the life he gave him. It is the final tragedy for a family that has torn itself apart.

In the film's first scene, after an intense session of lovemaking, Andy's heart is racing from ecstasy, and he has Gina put her hand on his chest. In the last scene, Charles makes the same gesture to ensure that his son is dead. The repetition suggests how far Andy has fallen—from experiencing one of his few blissful moments to being destroyed by his own foolhardiness and selfishness, his lack of heart for everyone else.

Before the Devil Knows You're Dead is the familiar story of a supposedly foolproof crime that should have been easy and made everyone a fortune if only everything had gone as planned. But the brilliance in using the heist plot as a means to explore a family at war—brother versus brother, son pitted against father, husband against wife—lends a heft and gravity lacking in most caper films. Moreover, despite a certain exhilaration inherent in its dynamic style, the film offers a sobering, even pessimistic, view of human nature—an examination of pettiness, cruelty, guilt, and vengeance, in essence a cycle of evil that cannot be contained once it is unleashed. Vital as ever in the twilight of his career, Sidney Lumet once again has brought out the best in his actors and told a story whose freshness and fierceness leave us gasping as much as its merciless exposure of the bleak landscape of the human heart.

Peter N. Chumo II

CREDITS

Andy Hanson: Philip Seymour Hoffman
Hank Hanson: Ethan Hawke
Gina: Marisa Tomei
Charles: Albert Finney

Nanette: Rosemary Harris
Bobby: Brian F. O'Byrne
Martha: Amy Ryan
Dex: Michael Shannon
Chris: Aleksa Palladino
Origin: USA
Language: English
Released: 2007
Production: Michael Cerenzie, William S. Gilmore, Brian Linse, Paul Parmar; Capitol Films, Unity Productions, Funky Buddha Group, Linsefilm; released by ThinkFilm
Directed by: Sidney Lumet
Written by: Kelly Masterson
Cinematography by: Ron Fortunato
Music by: Carter Burwell
Sound: Chris Newman
Editing: Tom Swartwout
Art Direction: Wing Lee
Costumes: Tina Nigro
Production Design: Christopher Nowak
MPAA rating: R
Running time: 117 minutes

REVIEWS

Christian Science Monitor Online. October 26, 2007.
Entertainment Weekly Online. October 23, 2007.
Hollywood Reporter Online. September 7, 2007.
New York Times Online. October 26, 2007.
New Yorker Online. October 29, 2007.
Rolling Stone Online. October 18, 2007.
Variety Online. September 7, 2007.
Village Voice Online. October 23, 2007.

TRIVIA

Title comes from the Irish toast: "May you be a half an hour in heaven before the devil knows you're dead."

AWARDS

Nomination:
Ind. Spirit 2008: Support. Actress (Tomei), First Screenplay.

BEOWULF

Pride is the curse.
—Movie tagline

Box Office: $82.2 million

When the most difficult and ancient piece of literature in English can be smoothly adapted to the cinematic equivalent of a video game, it is clear that technology can conquer even the most formidable assignments. But certainly not gracefully, if Robert Zemeckis's extraordinary *Beowulf* is any indication. Perhaps this film's computer-assisted live action-animation hybrid is a revolutionary breakthrough of sorts, but it looks and plays awkwardly.

Zemeckis has a history of pioneering visual techniques. In the classic, *Who Framed Roger Rabbit?* (1988), he was one of the first directors to successfully marry animation with live action, as real actors played opposite cartoon characters. His *The Polar Express* (2006), a children's fantasy adventure, made landmark use of motion-capture technology in a feature film. Now Zemeckis has taken that technology another step.

Beowulf was released as a three-dimensional feature, and there is no doubt its three dimensions are more involving than the old 3-D movies of the 1950s. Do not see it in an IMAX version, however, because the curvature of the screen will make everything but the central image fuzzy. Once you adjust your visual expectations, take a closer look and judge for yourself whether the technology is a triumph—or a step backward or sideways.

Motion-capture technology allows actors, such as Ray Winstone's Beowulf, to perform in front of cameras, as always. But their bodies are bedecked with sensors that allow computers to subsequently mold and shape those performances. It is not the same technique as the labor-intensive Rotoscoping that Richard Linklater has used in the recent films *Waking Life* (2001) and *A Scanner Darkly* (2006) and the Charles Schwab Company has used in television commercials, which involves drawing on computer screens from a live-action video. That process produces a painterly effect, whereas motion-capture results in video-game-style characters and images. In *Beowulf,* especially for the background figures in group scenes, the characters resemble the animated creations in *Shrek* (2001) more than anything, so it is not clear the technique has provided a visual breakthrough.

Strangely enough, Zemeckis and his hydra-headed crew of special-effects technicians and animators have more success with making men look realistic than they do with women. Certainly, Winstone's visage as Beowulf, as well as Anthony Hopkins (even with an enlarged head) as Hrothgar, appears more nuanced and human than what happens to Robin Wright Penn as Wealthow and to the other female faces in the film. Perhaps it is because their female skin has been rendered smooth and featureless; the women's countenances look uniformly too round, smooth, puffy, and fat. A sexualized variant of this is Angelina Jolie as Grendel's mother, who resembles nothing more than a bronzed Hugh

Hefner sex toy, with impossibly smooth statue-like skin, perfectly round breasts, and the obligatory bunny tail, here lengthened to a serpentine appearance. She even has built-in high heels as part of her physique—a pretty absurdly anachronistic touch in the sixth century, but Zemeckis does not worry about that.

Crispin Glover's turn as Grendel, a drooling man-monster whose body surface makes uneasy compromises between inside and outside, is more compelling. Certainly he is a gruesome figure, though also rather childlike in his temper tantrums, and he will inevitably remind you of Gollum/Smeagol of the *The Lord of the Rings* trilogy. No doubt Zemeckis riffing off Peter Jackson is excusable, since J.R.R. Tolkien counted *Beowulf,* the epic poem, as among his inspirations. John Malkovich as Unferth, a lurking naysayer in King Hrothgar's court, also seems directly modeled after a similar character in Jackson's trilogy.

If only the rest of *Beowulf* were even worthy of being called a knockoff of Jackson's fantasy masterpiece. It is not. For one thing, there are very few sets: most of the action takes place in Hrothgar's legendary mead hall, Heorot, or in Grendel's mother's cave. The last act, in which an aging Beowulf fights an avenging dragon, finally involves intriguing landscapes and a protracted fight across a wide sweep of cinematic territory, and it is by far the best part of the film. Everything up until then, however, is disappointingly unimaginative. Worse yet, Zemeckis cannot resist the impulse to literally throw body parts, weapons, and blood into the audience's lap, over and over and over again. At first it is exciting, but soon it grows tiresome.

Perhaps a future 3-D motion-capture film could engage an audience more deeply, but in *Beowulf* that is not the case. That is largely because the dumbed-down plot and ridiculously juvenile dialogue combine with the visual effects to create something much more like a video-game experience than a movie experience. The epic poem becomes a downsized bore, with plenty of anachronistic and just plain stupid screenwriting by Neil Gaiman and Roger Avary. Aboard a ship in a storm, Beowulf says he cannot see the shoreline, "I can only see the wind and the rain." When Beowulf's comrades-in-arms sing a song in a mead hall, it is like a parody of a fraternity party, and they actually do say that the women in Iceland are "hot." Beowulf strips naked to fight Grendel, causing a shock to poor Wealthow. Hopkins patters around, saying repetitive lines as if he were reciting Shakespeare, when in fact it appears he is reciting *CliffsNotes.* "We need a hero to fight Grendel," he intones. And then Beowulf appears, and he exclaims "We have our hero!" just in case you were not following.

While contorting this legend into the confines of twenty-first century mainstream entertainment, you cannot blame the filmmakers for taking liberties with the story. *Beowulf* as a poem seems rather disjointed and disconnected, so they smooth it all out with the help of Jolie. Whoever got the clever notion of making Grendel's mother into a bewitching siren, instead of a standard monster, should get all the credit for improving the plot. Now, we end up not with a disconnected dragon-slayer battle in the third act, but with an endlessly recycled motif that plays to the favorite contemporary notion of the sexy mother-goddess-seducer as the source of all evil. Jolie is so enticing that she can literally melt Beowulf's big sword, and even a threesome back in the castle (with queen and mistress, who both end up getting along splendidly) is no match for the temptress in the cave. She gets to bring down Hopkins, Brendan Gleeson, and Winstone in one movie.

This *Beowulf* resembles nothing more than a college paper written by a fraternity boy hot-shot with a desire to catch the interest of his sexy female teacher. And it plays out like a neatly packaged dream script for the eternally adolescent male. Watch out for those power-sapping liaisons with the babes in the cozy lairs—they will ruin your chances for a happy family life. Who would have thought that is what this dreary epic poem was really all about? Apparently the same people who believe that it is an advance to make movies look like video games.

Michael Betzold

CREDITS

Beowulf: Ray Winstone (Voice)
Grendel's Mother: Angelina Jolie (Voice)
Grendel: Crispin Glover (Voice)
King Hrothgar: Anthony Hopkins (Voice)
Wealthrow: Robin Wright Penn (Voice)
Unferth: John Malkovich (Voice)
Ursula: Alison Lohman (Voice)
Origin: USA
Language: English
Released: 2007
Production: Steve Starkey, Robert Zemeckis, Jack Rapke; Shangri-La Entertainment, Imagemovers; released by Paramount
Directed by: Robert Zemeckis
Written by: Neil Gaiman, Roger Avary
Cinematography by: Robert Presley
Music by: Alan Silvestri
Sound: William B. Kaplan
Editing: Jeremiah O'Driscoll

Art Direction: Norman Newberry, Greg Papalia
Costumes: Gabriella Pescucci
Production Design: Doug Chiang
MPAA rating: PG-13
Running time: 114 minutes

REVIEWS

Boston Globe Online. November 16, 2007.
Chicago Sun-Times Online. November 16, 2007.
Entertainment Weekly Online. November 14, 2007.
Hollywood Reporter Online. November 12, 2007.
Los Angeles Times Online. November 16, 2007.
New York Times Online. November 16, 2007.
Rolling Stone Online. November 15, 2007.
San Francisco Chronicle. November 16, 2007, p. E1.
Variety Online. November 11, 2007.
Wall Street Journal. November 16, 2007, p. W1.
Washington Post. November 16, 2007, p. C1.

QUOTES

Beowulf: "I am Ripper...Tearer...Slasher...Gouger. I am the Teeth in the Darkness, the Talons in the Night. Mine is Strength...and Lust...and Power! I am Beowulf!"

BEYOND THE GATES
(Shooting Dogs)

> *What would you risk to make a difference?*
> —Movie tagline

Beyond the Gates (originally released under the title *Shooting Dogs*), directed by Michael Caton-Jones, revisits the tribal violence and genocide that also served as a background for *Hotel Rwanda* (2004). It is therefore not only difficult, but excruciatingly painful to watch. Its premiere for an audience of 5,000 on an inflatable screen set up in a the main football stadium in Kigali, the capital of Rwanda, got international attention when it was covered by reporter Xan Rice Nairobi for *The Guardian* in Britain on March 27, 2006. Rwandan President Paul Kagame attended the premiere, along with thousands of extras who had worked on the film, which was criticized by others for having distressed survivors of the genocide.

The framework of the story will be familiar to anyone who has already seen *Hotel Rwanda,* a far more expensive film that for many viewers will still be the last word on the Rwandan genocide involving tribal warfare between the Hutus and the Tutsis that led to the slaughter of 800,000 Tutsis in just over a three-month period. In *Beyond the Gates,* which was also based upon

actual events, 2,000 Tutsis seek refuge at a secondary school, the École Technique Officielle, during the beginning days of the 1994 genocide, where a small force of Belgian United Nations peacekeepers happen to be stationed, under strict orders not to fire upon the rioting Hutu mobs that threaten the compound unless fired upon.

The film was criticized by the British-based Rwandan charity Survivors Fund and by Ibuka, the main Rwandan genocide survivors' association, which as a matter of principle condemned all films dealing with the massacre of the Tutsis. *Hotel Rwanda* is the most famous of these, but there are others besides the BBC-funded *Beyond the Gates,* notably *Sometimes in April,* made for United States television in 2004, and *Un dimanche a Kigali* based on Gil Courtemanche's novel, *A Sunday at the Pool in Kigali,* filmed in Rwanda and released in 2006. The latter film led to panic when it reconstructed an attack on a convent. *Beyond the Gates* inspired panic during filming a reconstruction of Hutu thugs chanting and whistling as they prepare to attack the Tutsis after the UN peacekeepers have left the school compound. "The noise triggered flashbacks and panic among girls in a nearby school dormitory," according to *The Guardian* newspaper. "Several children had to be taken to hospital the following morning." Michael Caton-Jones told *The Guardian* that "People have taken one small incident during the filming and blown it out of proportion. The Rwandans have to live with the trauma of what they went through every day," Caton-Jones added. "The idea that a film can reawaken this is wrong." Joseph Habineza, the Rwandan Minister of Culture, agreed with Caton-Jones, and claimed that the film should "help in the process of reconciliation."

The film begins with shots of a teenaged girl, Marie (Clare-Hope Ashitey) running a footrace to the missionary school, where she is awaited by her classmates and a European teacher, Joe Connor (Hugh Dancy). Marie is a Tutsi, and later Hutu boys will throw stones at her, calling her a cockroach, which is the way the Hutus dehumanize and demean their tribal enemies. The story begins on April 5, 1994, and continues through the week, during which the country falls into a state of reactionary chaos following the news that the president's plane has been shot down. During the night, news comes that "there are people at the gate," desperate Tutsis, seeking refuge within the school compound. "My orders are not to allow this school to become a safe haven," Captain Delon (Dominique Horwitz) of the United Nations peacekeeping force explains to Father Christopher (John Hurt), who is in charge of the school. Nonetheless, Father Christopher opens the gates to these refugees. Eventually only the armed UN peacekeepers will stand between the howling mob of murderous Hutus and the

Tutsis inside the compound. This standoff dominates the film.

The next day, April 7, Joe drives the school truck into Kigale, looking for Marie and her father, Roland. No one is at their home, except for a guard dog. When Joe returns to the school, he finds Roland and Marie, who managed to get to the compound safely by carefully choosing back streets. Joe also brings with him a BBC camera crew, comprised of a cameraman and a woman reporter, Rachel Watson (Nicola Walker). Joe only manages to drive the truck past the Hutu rioters because one of them, François (David Gyasi), who worked at the school until the previous week but left the compound out of tribal loyalty to the Hutus, influences the soldiers to let the truck pass.

Back at the compound, news comes that missing UN soldiers, believed to have been kidnapped, were found, executed and butchered. When asked why, Captain Delon explains to Father Christopher that "In Somalia, eighteen soldiers died, and that was enough to cause a complete withdrawal" of occupying troops. If the French and Belgian peacekeeping force is withdrawn, there would be no protection for the Tutsis from the armed Hutus, lusting for blood. The situation is hellish. The Hutus, armed with machetes, are mobbed "beyond the gates," awaiting an opportunity to kill Tutsis. A small group of Tutsis attempts to escape and is hacked to pieces, "beyond the gates." Later, when dogs are seen feeding on the corpses, the UN commander orders his soldiers to shoot the dogs (hence the British title of the film, *Shooting Dogs*). Father Christopher demands to know how, if the dogs have not fired upon them, the Captain could give such an order. The point he is making is that such an order against the Hutus might have brought an end to the slaughter to begin with.

Finally, the United Nations send trucks to evacuate, but only white people. A Tutsi leader begs the UN soldiers to shoot the Tutsis, since that would be an easier death than being hacked to death by machetes, but of course the soldiers cannot grant this request. Joe decides to evacuate, but Father Christopher chooses to stay with his congregation, knowing he will surely be killed. At the final hour, Father Christopher loads Tutsi children into the bed of the school truck and covers them with a tarp. As he attempts to drive the truck to safety, he is stopped by the Hutus. The leader recognizes Father Christopher, who argues with him over whether the priest or the state owns the truck, but this soldier shows neither respect nor pity and shoots him dead. This dispute creates a useful diversion, however, enabling Marie to escape with the other children. Shots of Marie running away through the night match the running shots seen at the opening of the film.

The film concludes with an epilogue, five years later, when Marie, now grown, finds Joe in England at the school where Father Christopher was trained, and asks him "Why did you leave us?" All he can do is to tell the truth and admit, "I was afraid to die." But that should have been obvious five years earlier. The film ends with an epigraph written by Elie Wiesel: "The opposite of faith is not heresy but indifference." But Joe's moral failure was not simply a matter of indifference. The scriptwriters might have found a better and more coherent and satisfactory conclusion. The greatest strength of this film is surely in the characters, wronged Marie, who has to run for her life, Captain Delon, who attempts to deal with the impossible frustrations of his assigned peacekeeping mission, and, especially, Father Christopher, who tells a very frightened Marie late in the film: "Terrible things happen in this world, but you are in my heart, and you will be there until I die," knowing full well that his days, if not his very hours, may be numbered. This is a man of moral and spiritual courage, and John Hurt plays him perfectly.

The film was produced and co-written by BBC journalist David Belton, who had lived through and personally witnessed the slaughter of the Tutsis by the Hutus while he was on assignment in Rwanda; he was assisted by Richard Alwyn with the story and David Wolstencroft, who wrote the screenplay. One shortcoming of the screenplay is its failure to provide a context and an explanation for the tribal hostilities that exist between the Hutus and the Tutsis. *New York Times* reviewer Stephen Holden criticized the screenplay for ignoring "the role of Belgian colonists in stimulating simmering tribal hatred," and for suggesting simplistically that "the Hutus are fiends and the slaughtered Tutsis martyred saints." Holden speculates that the Joe Connor character might be "the fictional alter ego of David Belton" and that the film might be considered "as a belated act of contrition." The events portrayed in this film put humanity to shame, and simply watching it and having to think about the consequences felt like doing penance for having watched the trivial entertainments typically served up by Hollywood during any banal year. Though flawed structurally and historically incomplete, the film is worthwhile and sincerely acted and made. That it is also so disturbing will no doubt limit its viewership.

James M. Welsh

CREDITS

Father Christopher: John Hurt
Joe Connor: Hugh Dancy
Captain Delon: Dominique Horwitz

Rachel: Nicola Walker
Sibomana: Louis Mahoney
Roland: Steve Toussaint
Origin: Great Britain, Germany
Language: English
Released: 2005
Production: Pippa Cross, Jens Meurer, David Belton; BBC Films, Filmstiftung NRW, Invicta Capital; released by IFC Films
Directed by: Michael Caton-Jones
Written by: Richard Wolstencroft
Cinematography by: Ivan Strasburg
Music by: Dario Marianelli
Sound: Rosie Straker
Editing: Christian Lonk
Art Direction: Astrid Sieben
Costumes: Dinah Collin
Production Design: Bertram Strauss
MPAA rating: R
Running time: 115 minutes

REVIEWS

Boston Globe Online. March 30, 2007.
Entertainment Weekly Online. March 7, 2007.
Hollywood Reporter Online. March 6, 2007.
Los Angeles Times Online. March 16, 2007.
New York Times Online. March 9, 2007.
San Francisco Chronicle. March 23, 2007, p. E1.
Variety Online. September 28, 2005.
Washington Post Online. March 16, 2007.

TRIVIA

Producer David Belton was a BBC news cameraman on location in Rwanda in 1994.

BLACK BOOK

(Zwartboek)

> *To fight the enemy, she must become one of them.*
> —Movie tagline

Box Office: $4.4 million

Though best known for such Hollywood films as *RoboCop* (1987) and *Basic Instinct* (1992), writer/director Paul Verhoeven had his breakthrough in his native Holland with such films as the World War II drama *Solider of Orange* (1977) and the psychosexual thriller *The Fourth Man* (1983). With *Black Book,* (*Zwartboek*) Verhoeven returns to World War II, mixing the Dutch resistance movement, the Holocaust, and an unlikely

romance into a thick stew that works better than it perhaps should most of the time.

Rachel Stein (Carice van Houten) is a Jewish singer hiding in the Nazi-occupied Netherlands near the end of World War II. After her parents (Jacqueline Blom and Jack Vecht) and brother (Seth Kamphuijs) are killed in an attempt to escape the country, Rachel is rescued by the Dutch resistance. Under the name Ellis de Vries, she dyes her hair blonde, goes undercover to work at Nazi headquarters, and becomes the mistress of German officer Ludwig Müntze (Sebastian Koch). Although Müntze soon guesses that Rachel is Jewish, he continues their affair and allows her to work at Gestapo headquarters. The remainder of *Black Book* focuses on the efforts of the resistance to rescue captured colleagues and Rachel's spying on the enemy while avoiding discovery. All this is complicated by the growing belief that someone in the resistance is betraying the group, with Rachel herself coming under suspicion.

Black Book may lack the gritty realism of Jean-Pierre Melville's French resistance classic *Army of Shadows* (1969), but Verhoeven is clearly knowledgeable about World War II. In addition to *Soldier of Orange,* he has also made *Portrait of Anton Adriaan Mussert* (*Portret van Anton Adriaan Mussert,* 1968), a documentary about the head of the Dutch fascist party. *Black Book* at first seems conventional, resembling the way Hollywood portrayed World War II during the 1960s in such films as *Von Ryan's Express* (1965) and *Where Eagles Dare* (1968), with narrow escapes, frequent bursts of violence, and humor in the face of adversity. Anne Dudley's rousing score also harkens back to an earlier era.

Despite its similarities to *Soldier of Orange, Black Book* initially seems unlike a typical Verhoeven film. The director is best known for his treatment of sex and violence. There are plenty of shootouts in *Black Book,* including a lengthy battle during a botched attempt to rescue the imprisoned resistance fighters. While there is a fair amount of nudity, including a scene of Rachel dying her pubic hair, the sexual content is rather tame for Verhoeven. The director is both ridiculed and admired for his excesses, especially in the lurid melodrama *Basic Instinct* and the camp classic *Showgirls* (1995). This tendency dominates the final half hour of *Black Book,* as revelations of duplicity lead to extreme acts. The most Verhoeven-like moment comes at the end of the war when a naked Rachel is punished for collaborating with the Nazis by having a vat of excrement dumped on her.

Black Book is engrossing throughout, even when Verhoeven tempts the boundaries of credibility. The liberating Canadian forces, for example, inexplicably allow a German general (Christian Berkel) to retain his authority, but the revelation of the treachery within the resistance, while convoluted, seems logical. Verhoeven, who co-wrote the screenplay with longtime collaborator Gerard Soeteman, is a natural storyteller who revels in moral ambiguity. He elicits considerable dramatic tension through desire to have the resistance's Rachel prostitute herself while simultaneously being repulsed at her willingness and through her performance of musical duets with the man (Waldemar Kobus) who murdered her family.

Verhoeven also excels with his actors. Derek de Lint, one of the stars of *Soldier of Orange,* brings his usual sensitivity to the role of an intellectual worried about the fate of his son. Thom Hoffman, from *The Fourth Man,* stands out as the most dynamic member of the resistance. Best known as the playwright in *The Lives of Others (Das Leben der Anderen,* 2006), Koch makes Müntze almost credible. Some reviewers complained that this good German is the least believable aspect of *Black Book,* yet the goodness of seemingly good people and the reverse have always been Verhoeven's favorite themes. Van Houten should be given much of the credit for the film working as well as it does. She must maintain two distinct personalities, the smart, determined Rachel and the compliant, unintelligent Ellis and be convincing in both. Dominating each of her scenes, van Houten delivers a true star-making performance.

Many foreign filmmakers lose their zest after spending time in Hollywood. Verhoeven, however, reinvents himself with *Black Book,* combining his insight into the European character with the action skills he developed in America to produce an entertaining epic with just enough psychological nuances to make it respectable for those who prefer a little art with their action.

Michael Adams

CREDITS

Ludwig Müntze: Sebastian Koch
Hans Akkermans: Thom Hoffman
Ronnie: Halina Reijn
Gerben Kuipers: Derek de Lint
Rachel Stein/Ellis de Vries: Carice van Houten
Guenther Franken: Waldemar Kobus
Gen. Kaeutner: Christian Berkel
Van Gein: Peter Blok
Origin: Great Britain, Belgium, Germany, Netherlands
Language: English, Dutch, German, Hebrew
Released: 2006
Production: San Fu Maltha, Jens Meurer, Teun Hilte, Jos van der Linden; Fu Works; released by Sony Pictures Classics
Directed by: Paul Verhoeven
Written by: Paul Verhoeven, Gerard Soeteman
Cinematography by: Karl Walter Lindenlaub

Music by: Anne Dudley
Sound: Georges Bossaers
Editing: Jobter Burg, James Herbert
Costumes: Yan Tax
Production Design: Wilbert van Dorp
MPAA rating: R
Running time: 145 minutes

REVIEWS

Boxoffice Online. March 2, 2007.
Entertainment Weekly Online. April 4, 2007.
Hollywood Reporter Online. September 5, 2006.
Los Angeles Times Online. April 4, 2007.
New York Times Online. April 4, 2007.
The Observer Online. January 21, 2007.
Premiere Online. March 21, 2007.
Rolling Stone Online. March 7, 2007.
Variety Online. September 1, 2006.
Village Voice Online. April 3, 2007.

QUOTES

Rachel: "I never thought I'd dread liberation."

TRIVIA

Paul Verhoeven and screenwriter Gerard Soeteman also worked together on *Turkish Delight* (1973), *Katie Tippel* (1975), *Soldier of Orange* (1978), *The 4th Man* (1979), *Spetters* (1980), and *Flesh and Blood* (1985).

BLACK SNAKE MOAN

Everything is hotter down south.
—Movie tagline

Box Office: $9.4 million

Hollywood often comes out with films that make it quite obvious how the audience should react: overbearing soundtracks, telegraphed plot turns, and heavy-handed storytelling let viewers know exactly when and what they should be thinking and feeling. What is unusual about *Black Snake Moan,* the second feature by *Hustle & Flow* (2005) writer/director Craig Brewer, is that the viewer is allowed to interpret the film individually in spite of its inflammatory events. For example, the film's protagonist Rae (Christina Ricci) spends much of the movie half-naked and chained to the radiator in the home of the other main character, Lazarus (Samuel L. Jackson). That alone might be the basis for a strong reaction, but it is not as simple as that. Perhaps intended as a religious metaphor or a film with a serious message, the overheated Southern drama is also probably a bit of a joke. Lou Lumenick of the *New York Post* wrote that Brewer was "obviously out to push some politically incorrect buttons with this ludicrous—yet, in the end, sweetly involving—Southern Gothic pulp yarn."

When Rae's boyfriend Ronnie (Justin Timberlake) is shipped overseas with his Army unit, Rae immediately falls to the ground, writhing with "the fever." She is a nymphomaniac and is able to find a plethora of men in her small Southern town who are willing to help her out with her problem. She is less successful in finding men who are also kind. After a drug-fueled night on the town, she is raped and beaten by Ronnie's best friend and left for dead by the side of the road.

Meanwhile, Lazarus has also had an eventful night. After learning that his wife finds him too staid and is planning to run off with his younger brother, Lazarus spends the night drinking and trashing his small house. When he spots the sickly, barely dressed Rae the next morning in front of his home, he decides that it is his mission to cure her of her "sickness." Her sickness consists of both a lingering cough as well as her nymphomania. Lazarus treats the former ailment with special cough syrup purloined for him by Angela (S. Epatha Merkerson), the local pharmacist who is sweet on him. He treats the latter affliction with a more unconventional method. He chains Rae to a radiator, intending to give her some intensive Bible study. "I aim to cure you of your wickedness. You sick," he explains.

After this startling setup, the movie begins to flounder. Lazarus finally locates some clothes for Rae and the two misfits slowly develop a friendship. Then, abruptly—and for no particularly well-stated reason—Lazarus decides to unchain Rae. She likes him well enough to stay around and eventually inspires him to return to his love of performing the blues. (Oddly, Jackson's blues-singing voice is not nearly as good as one would expect given his melodic speaking voice.) In the end it is difficult to see what all the melodrama was leading up to. According to Andrew O'Hehir of *Salon.com*, Brewer was aiming for "a drive-in aesthetic and deep mythological roots." Brewer partially achieves this, but it does not coalesce in any meaningful way.

The performances are universally strong. Jackson, as always, is a commanding presence. He proves, once again, that no one else can curse with the same flair. Ricci uses her slight yet womanly physicality to convey much about Rae. The cause of, and temporary answer to, all of her problems is her shapely body, and she wields it as such. Timberlake brings a natural style to his role as the anxiety-plagued Ronnie. And veteran actress Merkerson brings more sweetness and life to her character than was provided by the script.

By combining the combustible issues of race, gender, and sex in *Black Snake Moan*, Brewer proves that he knows how to incite, yet he seems unclear about what to do with the strong emotions he has aroused. In the end, all the lurid imagery and fervent situations do not add up to much more than an overheated romp.

Jill Hamilton

CREDITS

Lazarus: Samuel L. Jackson
Rae: Christina Ricci
Ronnie: Justin Timberlake
Angela: S. Epatha Merkerson
R.L.: John Cothran, Jr.
Rae's Mother: Kim Richards
Tehronne: David Banner
Origin: USA
Language: English
Released: 2007
Production: John Singleton, Stephanie Allain; New Deal Productions, Southern Cross the Dog Productions; released by Paramont Vantage
Directed by: Craig Brewer
Written by: Craig Brewer
Cinematography by: Amy Vincent
Music by: Scott Bomar
Sound: Andy Black
Editing: Billy Fox
Art Direction: Liba Daniels
Costumes: Paul Sims
Production Design: Keith Brian Burns
MPAA rating: R
Running time: 115 minutes

REVIEWS

Boxoffice Online. February 23, 2007.
Chicago Sun-Times Online. March 2, 2007.
Entertainment Weekly. March 9, 2007, p. 86.
Hollywood Reporter Online. January 29, 2007.
Los Angeles Times Online. March 2, 2007.
New York Times Online. March 2, 2007.
Premiere Magazine Online. February 16, 2007.
Salon.com. January 26, 2007.
San Francisco Chronicle. March 2, 2007, p. E4.
Variety Online. January 28, 2007.
Washington Post. March 2, 2007, p. C5.

QUOTES

Lazarus (to Rae): "I aim to cure you of your wickedness."

TRIVIA

The title of the film derives from the Blind Lemon Jefferson song recorded in 1927.

BLADES OF GLORY

Kick Some Ice.
　　—Movie tagline

Box Office: $118.6 million

The plot summary of *Blades of Glory* is almost certainly how DreamWorks was able to assemble its top-flight cast: Two male skaters, banned for life from professional singles competition, are forced to team up and skate as a pair. The bombast and pageantry of figure skating is definitely fertile ground for comedy—*Blades of Glory* looks like a slightly exaggerated incarnation of actual professional competitive figure skating—and though the film has a bit of difficulty sustaining itself, it boasts some good performances and some genuinely funny moments. The thin premise strains noticeably under the crushing pressure of constantly having to point out that figure skating is ridiculous, but the ridiculousness is wonderful.

Blades of Glory centers on the fortunes and missteps of the (fictional) skating world's two greatest male singles stars: the textbook-perfect, effeminate wunderkind Jimmy MacElroy (Jon Heder) and the improvisational, fiery, and ultra-macho (if such a thing exists in figure skating) Chazz Michael Michaels (Will Ferrell). The two are banned from professional singles competition for life as the result of a winner's podium brawl following their tie for first place. Three-and-a-half years later, Chazz hits bottom skating with The Grublets on Ice (an Ice Capades-style show for children), including a moment of drinking and vomiting while skating. Jimmy is working in a ski and skate apparel shop when his number one stalker/fan Hector (Nick Swardson) drops by to tell him, after much obsessive research, he has discovered that Jimmy can only be banned from his division: Men's singles. Jimmy goes to the Grublets to try to find a female doubles partner, bumps into Chazz and the two get into a very acrobatic fight. Jimmy's old coach sees the two of them on the news and realizes that the two men would make an excellent team, the first male-male doubles team ever. Though they chafe at the idea, and at the thought of working together, Jimmy and Chazz realize that they have no other options.

The standard sports film clichés apply in *Blades of Glory.* Jimmy and Chazz go through training montages, including one for an impossible move called the Iron Lotus that usually ends in one skating partner being decapitated. Their comeback attempts are subjected to the schemes of rival brother-and-sister pairs skaters Stranz and Fairchild Van Waldenberg (Will Arnett and Amy Poehler). Jimmy falls for the younger Van Waldenberg sister, Katie (Jenna Fischer), who also happens to be Stranz's and Fairchild's unwilling lackey (the Van Waldenberg parents were killed in a car crash on the way to one of Katie's skating lessons—Stranz and Fairchild manipulate her guilt over this to force her to do their bidding). Katie also falls for Jimmy, and the elder Van Waldenbergs try to use Katie's relationship with Jimmy to break up Michaels/MacElroy team, which almost succeeds when Jimmy catches Chazz, who is a sex addict, in Katie's room. Chazz and Katie have done nothing, but Jimmy runs off the night before the big competition. Jimmy and Chazz reunite just as they are about to be disqualified for being absent when called to take the ice. They successfully perform the Iron Lotus, win the competition, and then, as if to underscore all of the preceding bravura and silliness, they raise their arms super-hero style into the air and literally soar out of the stadium.

Directors Josh Gordon and Will Speck, veterans of directing commercials, helm their first feature with mixed results. *Blades of Glory* is ably put together—the film is good-looking, fairly well paced, the casting is excellent, and the movie is reasonably entertaining and funny. Behind the veneer of good production value and performances that clearly seek to make the most of every silly situation, however, lurk unseemly blemishes. Four different screenwriters scripted *Blades of Glory* and the film certainly gives the impression that it would take as many people as possible to string together the various permutations of "figure skating is funny," essentially a one-joke premise, into a feature-length film.

This is not to say that *Blades of Glory* is not funny. As with many such comedies that have ridiculousness as a cornerstone of the plot, the movie is, in parts, quite hilarious. The skating scenes are all very humorous, whether featuring Jimmy in a peacock outfit, or Chazz in a flaming red one-piece (shooting fire from his hands, no less). In fact, the various over-the-top ensembles of MacElroy and Michaels sort of invoke an enormous, traveling, ice-dancing drag show. In the realm of costumes and concepts for routines, though, it is difficult to top the Van Waldenbergs, who go from an incredibly white-bread vision of hip-hop culture to an audacious number that features Stranz as John F. Kennedy and Fairchild as Marilyn Monroe.

What saves *Blades of Glory* from being an exercise in simply concocting as many skating and latent homophobia jokes as possible, is the power of its ensemble. Ferrell and Heder are not only funny, the growth of their relationship from bitter rivals to partners and friends is actually touching. Ferrell's fearlessness with his body, often on display in his films, fits in so perfectly with his character that it is impossible to imagine anyone else as Chazz Michael Michaels (Chazz's personal philosophy is "Clothing optional"). Will Arnett and Amy Poehler are brilliant as the Van Waldenbergs. Even the extended supporting ensemble lends prodigious talent to the proceedings, especially the scene-stealing Nick Swardson as Jimmy MacElroy's stalker, Hector. Just to hear Hector say, "I totally want to cut off your skin and wear it to my birthday… It's coming up…" is absolutely worth the price of admission. Ultimately, *Blades of Glory* may not be the funniest movie ever made, but it is an enjoyable bit of light, goofy entertainment—much like figure skating.

John Boaz

CREDITS

Chazz Michael Michaels: Will Ferrell
Jimmy MacElroy: Jon Heder
Fairchild Van Waldenberg: Amy Poehler
Stranz Van Waldenberg: Will Arnett
Katie Van Waldenberg: Jenna Fischer
Coach: Craig T. Nelson
Darren MacElroy: William Fichtner
Hector: Nick Swardson
Origin: USA
Language: English
Released: 2007
Production: Ben Stiller, Stuart Cornfeld, John Jacobs; DreamWorks, Red Hour, Smart Entertainment; released by Paramount
Directed by: Will Speck, Josh Gordon
Written by: Jeff Cox, Craig Cox, John Altschuler, Dave Krinsky
Cinematography by: Stefan Czapsky
Music by: Theodore Shapiro
Sound: David McMillan, Peter Hliddal
Music Supervisor: George Drakoulias
Editing: Richard Pearson
Art Direction: Seth Reed
Costumes: Julie Weiss
Production Design: Steven Lineweaver
MPAA rating: PG-13
Running time: 93 minutes

REVIEWS

Boxoffice Online. March 30, 2007.
Chicago Sun-Times Online. March 30, 2007.
Entertainment Weekly Online. March 28, 2007.
Hollywood Reporter Online. March 30, 2007.
Los Angeles Times Online. March 30, 2007.
New York Times Online. March 30, 2007.
San Francisco Chronicle. March 30, 2007, p. E1.
Variety Online. March 29, 2007.
Washington Post. March 30, 2007, p. C1.

QUOTES

Jimmy: "Get out of my face."
Chazz: "I'll get inside your face."

TRIVIA

Jon Heder broke his ankle while training to ice-skate.

BLOOD AND CHOCOLATE

Temptation comes in many forms.
    —Movie tagline

Everyone has two lives. The one we show the world. And the one that was never meant to be seen.
    —Movie tagline

Box Office: $3.5 million

Fictional young people in love have faced all sorts of problems over the centuries. Class, economic status, ethnicity, and recalcitrant parents are the most time-tested obstacles. *Blood and Chocolate,* however, goes for a new slant. While family objections do threaten to keep Vivian (Agnes Bruckner) and Aiden (Hugh Dancy) apart, there is a bigger problem. He is a human. She is a werewolf.

When Vivian is a child in Colorado, her family is massacred by hunters for reasons not made clear, and then not entirely clear, until late in the film. *Blood and Chocolate* then jumps ten years to her uneasy existence in Romania, where she lives with her aunt, Astrid (Katja Riemann), in Bucharest. Astrid is the former lover of Gabriel (Olivier Martinez), leader of the local pack of werewolves. (The film implies that almost everyone in Bucharest, including the police, is a werewolf.) Their son, Rafe (Bryan Dick), resents Gabriel's abandonment of his mother and his attentions to cousin Vivian, whom the leader is trying to force to become his new queen. Rafe longs to be Gabriel's successor, but his father realizes the youth, who violates protocol by hunting alone, is hotheaded and impulsive. While Astrid dreams of being taken back by Gabriel, Vivian hopes to find a way out of becoming his consort. This is not a happy family.

The complicated situation becomes even more intense when Vivian reluctantly falls for Aiden, an American graphic novelist in Romania doing research on werewolves for his next book. Though *Blood and Chocolate,* adapted by Ehren Kruger and Christopher B. Landon from a popular young-adult novel by Annette Curtis Klause, has little humor—and could have used some—there is irony when the unsuspecting Aiden explains werewolf lore to Vivian. Though he assures her that the legendary werewolf vulnerability to silver is merely a myth, he thankfully discovers that this is not the case.

Once the basic conflicts have been established, *Blood and Chocolate* develops into an action film, with Aiden and Rafe doing battle, followed by Gabriel and his followers chasing Aiden through a forest. Unlike the immortal Lawrence Talbot of Lon Chaney, Jr., in the series of films beginning with *The Wolf Man* (1941), these creatures are not human-wolf hybrids but conventional wolves. (Klause has said she grew up with her father telling her the plots of the Universal horror films as if they were children's stories.) This approach actually heightens the drama because the werewolves closely resemble German shepherds and seem benign, at least to dog lovers, until they bear their fangs and become even more frightening than some mythical monster. Director Katja von Garnier and special effects director Nick Allder, whose credits include *Braveheart* (1995) and *Hellboy* (2004), handle the transformation by having the humans run and then jump, spiraling through air in slow motion, before morphing into wolves.

The morphing bodies are covered in twinkling lights, as is appropriate for what is more a fairy tale than a true horror film. Rather than have the hero rescue the damsel, though, the traditional roles are reversed in *Blood and Chocolate,* one of several clues that the film tries to be true to its young-adult roots and appeal to young female viewers. In keeping with this quest, the violence in the PG-13 film is subdued. When Rafe kills a young woman (Maria Dinulescu) who has snubbed him, the attack occurs off-camera.

Although *Blood and Chocolate* received almost unanimously negative reviews, with Jeannette Catsoulis of the *New York Times* calling it "uninvolving and cliché-ridden," the film has modest charms, moving smoothly, with one exception, from one plot point to the next. Some reviewers objected to the changes from Klause's novel, such as the shift in setting from suburban Maryland. While its romantic angle may satisfy some viewers, the blending of teen romance and horror genres do not merge that easily. The film needs, in other words, more bite. Vivian should be a tortured soul but comes off, especially in Bruckner's bland performance, as someone pouting because she has not been invited to the prom by the boy she likes the most. Then there is the exception mentioned above, a truly laughable interlude with Vivian and Aiden frolicking in a park while an innocuous pop tune plays on the soundtrack. Such a spectacle was out of date thirty years ago.

Dancy, with his puppy-dog eagerness, makes Aiden likeable, and few films give a writer or artist a shot at being an action hero. With his feral looks, Dick makes a good werewolf antagonist. Riemann, impressive in the Holocaust drama *Rosenstrasse* (2003), gives Astrid more emotional weight than any of the other characters. Martinez has done well in some of his English-language roles, most notably as Diane Lane's lover in *Unfaithful* (2002), but he has trouble enunciating the mostly clunky dialogue. Of the two screenwriters, Landon has a special qualification as the son of Michael Landon, star of the low-budget classic *I Was a Teenage Werewolf* (1957).

Blood and Chocolate is an attractive film. Garnier and production designer Kevin Phipps do an excellent job of using the Bucharest architecture, alternately imposing and crumbling, to create a strong sense of place. Brendan Galvin provides some beautiful images, especially in the forest scenes, making the landscape both fearsome and enchanted. An additional element to make *Blood and Chocolate* appealing to some viewers is that it is loosely based on William Shakespeare's *Romeo and Juliet* (1597). Although the film departs considerably from Shakespeare's version, the basic premise is the same, and there are a few direct parallels, especially with Rafe as a stand-in for Tybalt. The re-imagining of the double suicide scene is cleverly handled.

Michael Adams

CREDITS

Vivian: Agnes Bruckner
Gabriel: Olivier Martinez
Aiden: Hugh Dancy
Rafe: Bryan Dick
Astrid: Katja Riemann
Origin: Great Britain, Germany, Romania
Language: English
Released: 2007
Production: Richard Wright, Tom Rosenberg, Hawk Koch, Wolfgang Esenwein; Lakeshore Entertainment, Berrick Filmproducktion; released by MGM
Directed by: Katja von Garnier
Written by: Ehren Kruger, Christopher B. Landon
Cinematography by: Brendan Galvin
Music by: Johnny Klimek, Reinhold Heil
Sound: Mervyn Moore
Editing: Martin Walsh, Emma Hickcox
Art Direction: Adam O'Neill
Costumes: Marco Scotti
Production Design: Kevin Phipps
MPAA rating: PG-13
Running time: 96 minutes

REVIEWS

Boston Globe Online. January 27, 2007.
Boxoffice Online. January 26, 2007.

Hollywood Reporter Online. January 29, 2007.
New York Times Online. January 27, 2007.
San Francisco Chronicle. January 26, 2007, p. E1.
Variety Online. January 26, 2007.

QUOTES

Aiden: "Is that a threat?"
Rafe: "No…[headbutts him] this is a threat."

THE BOURNE ULTIMATUM

This summer Jason Bourne comes home.
—Movie tagline

Box Office: $227.5 million

The Bourne Ultimatum, third in a trilogy loosely based on Robert Ludlum's Jason Bourne novels, speeds along at a near-dizzying pace yet manages to succeed on every level as a skillfully constructed action thriller with intriguing character development adding depth to its suspenseful story. Both *The Bourne Identity* (2002) and *The Bourne Supremacy* (2004) were better-than-average, polished films that took the "secret agent" genre away from the over-the-top plotlines that tend to plague many of the James Bond films and also explored a complex psychological struggle in the character of Jason Bourne, who lost all knowledge of his true identity but knows that he does not like the killing machine that he has become. *The Bourne Ultimatum* is in the minority when it comes to sequels, because the film manages the feat of equaling if not in some cases surpassing its predecessors in terms of both character development and suspense and action.

The film centers on the quest of Jason Bourne (Matt Damon) to learn, once and for all, the complete truth about his identity and find out who was ultimately responsible for "programming" him to be the ruthless, unstoppable agent he is. He has begun to have flashbacks that come in piecemeal, revealing vague memories of having been taken before an old man who asked him, "Are you committed to this program?" He also remembers being submerged and held down in water as some kind of conditioning or behavior modification. Meanwhile, as Jason determines to track down the masterminds behind the program that robbed him of his identity, a British journalist named Simon Ross (Paddy Considine) comes into contact with a CIA chief stationed in Madrid, later revealed to be Neal Daniels (Colin Stinton), a man who witnessed the beginnings of the Treadstone project that "created" Jason Bourne and evidently has had second thoughts about the direction

the program has gone. He informs Ross that Bourne was just the beginning and mentions something called Blackbriar, which he calls a Treadstone upgrade. Without revealing his source, Ross writes an article about Bourne. When Jason reads the article, he sets out to find Ross and track down the CIA source, hoping it will lead him to the answers he seeks. Unfortunately, Ross winds up getting killed in an operation staged by CIA Deputy Director Noah Vosen (David Strathairn).

Vosen claims that Bourne is still a threat and that it is crucial the agency track down the leak who has betrayed the CIA, but he meets resistance in Pamela Landy (Joan Allen), who does not believe Jason is dangerous but suspects that he is just looking for answers. She also soon begins to question Vosen's motives. The bulk of the movie details Jason's search for the truth, all the while hunted by Vosen's agents. Along the way, Jason encounters agent Nicky Parsons (Julia Stiles), whom he last saw in Berlin (in the second movie). Nicky chooses to help him and eventually finds herself on the run with him as she becomes a target for one of Noah's "assets," specially programmed agents who are as deadly as Bourne can be. Nicky does not say much but it is clear that she has feelings for Jason, and at one point she hints that at some point in the past they had a relationship, but Jason cannot remember anything.

Eventually the hunt takes Jason to New York, where Pamela—now convinced that Noah and CIA Director Ezra Kramer (Scott Glenn) are corrupt and covering up the truth about the Treadstone and Blackbriar projects—decides to help him break into Vosen's office to find incriminating documentation. She also tells him that his real name is David Webb. In the climactic scenes of the film, Jason heads to the facility where "assets" are trained and where his identity as Jason Bourne began. Finally he confronts Dr. Albert Hirsch (Albert Finney), the man who oversaw his conditioning and training. Hirsch (the man Jason had been seeing in his flashbacks) claims that David Webb chose to become Jason Bourne of his own will and tells him that he joined the program to "help save American lives." The reality is, though, that Bourne became an agent who took as many innocent American lives as he saved, just as is the case with all the other special "assets" out there. Defiantly, Jason informs Hirsch that he is no longer Bourne, that he is in fact David Webb.

The Bourne Ultimatum is dynamically and often frantically paced, a constantly moving ride from start to finish, much in keeping with the plot itself. Just as Jason is eager to uncover the truth and as he is constantly on the run, the film itself is edited so that the images on-screen rarely give the viewer time to rest. Yet, rather than growing tiresome or exhausting, this pacing works to keep the viewer emotionally involved in the story and facilitates a kind of identification with Bourne. The kinetic nature of the film functions to seamlessly correspond with the dramatic course of the plot. For example, the scene in which Jason attempts to meet with Simon Ross and guide him to a safe place away from the threats of the CIA agents is constructed with such urgency and a sense of impending danger that one can almost sense Ross's panic when he begins to imagine every bystander who sees him is an agent. The sense of danger and the reality that the threat is real comes painfully home when Ross makes a split-second decision that leads to his death.

What elevates the story above an average thriller, however, is the more complex psychological underpinning of Bourne's character. He is a man who does not like what he has become, but he is forced to fight and to kill in order to save his life or that of people he cares about. He struggles with the knowledge of terrible things he has done and wants to know how and why he became this man. As such, he is both hero and anti-hero, a character with a tarnished past who is forced to resort to ruthless behavior even though it tears at his conscience, yet a character who knows that his true identity is not bound by how he was conditioned and programmed by others. After a very destructive and violent chase by one of Vosen's assets, the assassin is trapped in a vehicle, giving Jason a perfect opportunity to dispose of him. However, Jason cannot bring himself to kill the man. In fitting fashion, this good deed is rewarded later in the film when the assassin gets a second chance to kill Jason but chooses not to do so.

The story also addresses thought-provoking questions about the appropriate lengths a democracy will go to in the name of protecting itself. Hirsch, Kramer, and Vosen advocate the position that almost anything seems permissible in the name of "saving American lives," but they seem unable to realize that they are undermining democracy itself as they place themselves outside the law and as they authorize the killing of American citizens to protect their interests. The issues are timely and relevant, of course, prompting one to consider the age-old question of whether we are really any better than our enemies if we undermine our own values and choose to employ "defenses" that are no better than the terrorism we struggle against.

David Flanagin

CREDITS

Jason Bourne: Matt Damon
Nicky Parsons: Julia Stiles
Pamela Landy: Joan Allen
Noah Vosen: David Strathairn
Simon Ross: Paddy Considine
Paz: Edgar Ramirez
Ezra Kramer: Scott Glenn
Dr. Albert Hirsch: Albert Finney
Tom Cronin: Tom Gallop
Wills: Corey Johnson
Martin Kreutz: Daniel Bruhl
Neal Daniels: Colin Stinton
Desh Bouksani: Joey Ansah
Origin: USA
Released: 2007
Production: Frank Marshall, Patrick Crowley, Paul L. Sandberg; Ludlum Entertainment; released by Universal
Directed by: Paul Greengrass
Written by: Tony Gilroy, Scott Burns, George Nolfi
Cinematography by: Oliver Wood
Music by: John Powell
Sound: Kirk Francis
Editing: Christopher Rouse
Art Direction: Andy Nicholson, Jason Knox-Johnston, Robert Cowper
Costumes: Shay Cunliffe
Production Design: Peter Wenham
MPAA rating: PG-13
Running time: 111 minutes

REVIEWS

Boston Globe Online. August 2, 2007.
Chicago Sun-Times Online. August 3, 2007.
Entertainment Weekly Online. August 1, 2007.
Los Angeles Times Online. August 3, 2007.
New York Times Online. August 3, 2007.

QUOTES

Pamela Landy: "This is Jason Bourne, the toughest target that you have ever tracked. He is really good at staying alive, and trying to kill him and failing…just pisses him off."

TRIVIA

In a scene in the C.I.A. deep-cover New York City office, an image of Donald Rumsfeld is visible on a computer monitor.

AWARDS

Oscars 2007: Film Editing, Sound, Sound FX Editing
British Acad. 2007: Film Editing, Sound
Screen Actors Guild 2008: Outstanding Performance by a Stunt Ensemble in a Motion Picture
Nomination:
British Acad. 2007: Cinematog., Director (Greengrass), Visual FX.

BRAND UPON THE BRAIN!

If the American Western has been proclaimed dead, then silent film must be a long forgotten ghost. It is this now-specter of a genre that Canadian film director Guy Maddin has chosen to revive with his outrageously delightful black-and-white, silent spectacle, *Brand Upon the Brain!* As one critic noted, an exclamation point in a Maddin film is not to be taken lightly and the experimental auteur mixes a wildly shocking blend of character, storyline, and filming techniques within a plot, written by Maddin and his usual collaborator George Toles, loosely based around Maddin's own childhood memories. Filmed on Puget Sound it is, oddly enough, Maddin's first film shot in the United States.

Film aficionados love Maddin's imaginative, surrealistic approach to filmmaking and storyline. His is a truly unique brand of film that is virtually indescribable and must be viewed in order to fully appreciate. Shot in eight millimeter, Maddin uses elements of Grand Guignol (late nineteenth/early twentieth-century Parisian horror/shock theatre), teen detective stories à la Nancy Drew/Hardy Boys, science fiction, and classic silent cinema with narration provided by Isabella Rossellini to tell a "twelve-chapter remembrance" he claims is rooted in the conflict between his mother and his rapidly maturing young sister.

The film is told in flashback, the heated titles signifying "The past! The past!" as a now older Guy Maddin (Erik Steffen Maahs), a housepainter, rows back to the island to help his dying mother (Susan Corzatte) and instead journeys into his melodrama-filled childhood.

The young Guy Maddin (Sullivan Brown) and his teenage sister (Maya Lawson) live on Black Notch Island in a lighthouse that also houses an orphanage. Their domineering, over-protective mother (Gretchen Krich) sits atop the lighthouse with a searchlight and bullhorn-like device dubbed the "Horn of Chastity" in hand, so as to better oversee and control her children's goings-on. In the basement below, their mad-scientist father (Todd Moore) spends his days and nights obsessively engaged in a secret experiment. The brother and sister team of teenage detectives, Wendy and Chance Hale (both played by Katherine E. Scharhon), known as the Lightbulb Kids, come to the island to investigate the case of the mysterious holes in the heads of orphans newly adopted from the island's orphanage. They provide both the isolated Guy and "Sis" with their first love interests, the knowledge of which must naturally be kept from Mother.

"As the investigation progresses," the press kit states, "it leads the kids into the darkest regions of revelation and repression and spins dangerously out of control as the terrible secrets of Guy's family are laid bare…" Such inflammatory language also echoes the silent film's intertitles, which scream provocative pronouncements, such as "Jealous Guy!" and Mother's frightening and judgmental assertions: "You look like you just got out of the bed of a seducer!" Utilizing less agitated punctuation, the titles also convey the mood in the lighthouse: "Dinner as usual. Grim." Not unusual for a family whose matriarch bathes in turpentine and whose father may be involved in harvesting bodily fluids from the orphans in a subplot involving turning back the clock on aging. There are also Satanic Masses, Oedipal desires, and feral children running amok amid the usual stifled, adolescent longings of Guy and Sis. The duo, as it turns out, both long for the same Lightbulb, as in fine Shakespearean comedy tradition, Wendy is actually Chance in disguise, as a traumatized Guy discovers.

It turns out that all the island's children bear the dreaded "brand upon the brain," a circular mark that actually may be found on the back on their necks. Just as the lighthouse is a fitting metaphor for the isolation and loneliness of adolescence, so the "brand upon brain" is the permanent impression on the psyche left by one's parents.

However disturbing the subject matter (which usually approaches the unthinkable), Maddin is somehow, always able to incorporate humor. Even *The Saddest Music in the World* (2003), Maddin's last feature-length production, managed a healthy dose of absurd wit amid the dark proceedings. That film also utilized haunting cello pieces, which he has incorporated into this dreamlike childhood redux that also features a crashing orchestra score by Jason Staczek that one would expect to punctuate the melodrama of a silent film.

Unlike his previous effort, Maddin uses relatively unknown, theatre-based actors to bring his exquisitely tortured characters to life who, in some cases, are made-up to resemble actual silent film stars—although, finely nuanced performances are certainly not the focus of *Brand Upon the Brain!*, which has been hailed as a tour de force. At once capturing a nightmarish journey back to adolescence and a loving childhood remembrance, the film is the perfectly moody, purely cinematic expression of both.

Fittingly enough, the film opened at festivals and some theaters with a live orchestra, a variety of celebrity narrators, live sound effects from Foley artists, and a singing castrato. There is little lost in the gradual transition to taped effects and the inspired narration of Rossellini.

Hilary White

CREDITS

Guy Maddin: Erik Steffen Maahs
Young Guy: Sullivan Brown
Mother: Gretchen Krich
Sis: Maya Lawson
Father: Todd Moore
Wendy/Chance: Katherine E. Scharhon
Narrator: Isabella Rossellini
Origin: Canada, USA
Language: English
Released: 2006
Production: Amy E. Jacobson, Gregg Lachow; Film Co.;
 released by Vitagraph
Directed by: Guy Maddin
Written by: Guy Maddin, George Toles
Cinematography by: Benjamin Kasulke
Music by: Jason Staczek
Editing: John Gurdebeke
Costumes: Nina Moser
Production Design: Tania Kupczak
MPAA rating: R
Running time: 95 minutes

REVIEWS

Chicago Sun-Times Online. May 18, 2007.
Hollywood Reporter Online. September 15, 2006.
New York Times Online. May 9, 2007.
San Francisco Chronicle. June 15, 2007, p. E7.
Variety Online. May 15, 2007.
Village Voice Online. May 8, 2007.

QUOTES

Narrator: "What's a suicide attempt without a wedding?"

BRATZ

Out of the box.
 —Movie tagline
Get ready. Get glam. Get real.
 —Movie tagline

Box Office: $10 million

Squarely aimed at a preteen female audience, *Bratz* is this millennium's *Clueless* (1995). A veritable testimonial to the benefits of better living through fashion, the film lacks the prestigious Jane Austen literary pedigree of the latter, and is instead based on a line of fashion dolls that also spawned an animated television series. Unlike their toy incarnations, the Bratz have been stripped of sexuality for the big screen with the filmmakers careful not to introduce anything remotely male into the Bratz's clique,

playing up the female empowerment message, albeit with a healthy dose of lip gloss. What passes for a plot is the director simply placing the girls in every conceivable circumstance, keeping the energy high and the music loud, making for a frenetic but at least passably entertaining film.

The four eponymous heroines attend Carry (sic) Nation High School where their close bond of friendship rooted in shopping is broken when the girls split off into distinct cliques based on their non-consumer-related interests/talents. Sasha (Logan Browning) joins the cheerleading squad, Cloe (Skyler Shaye) takes up with the soccer team, and Jade (Janel Parrish) finds kindred spirits in the geeky school brains while also studying fashion design. The filmmakers establish a role model for individuality with Yasmin (Nathalia Ramos), the only Bratz who does not join a clique but instead harbors a secret dream to become a singer. Although the girls are forced apart, by the time the freshman Bratz become juniors, a common enemy will unite them once again.

All family comedies must impart morality amid the hijinks and here the lesson the girls must learn is that although being in a clique may be a high school necessity, you also must remain loyal to your true friends. The film tackles other serious topics in a perfunctory manner with a plot that deals with the girls overcoming their own fears and rising above peer pressure. Yasmin learns a lesson in prejudice when she scolds the deaf Dylan (Ian Nelson) for being blind when she literally has a run-in with him in the hall. Cloe has a single parent and is not as well off as the other students. Sasha's parents are bitterly divorced. And Yasmin suffers from stage fright.

The majority of the film's clichéd comedy is of the slapstick and physical variety. The most entertaining character is the school bully, the impossibly spoiled and arrogant Meredith (Chelsea Staub), who actually resembles a bona fide teenager. As Ruthe Stein noted in her review in the *San Francisco Chronicle*: "Staub seems to be channeling Reese Witherspoon in *Election*. As inspirations go, that one is awfully good…" Her hilariously horrible attitude and sense of entitlement is only made worse by the fact that the toadying Principal Dimly (Jon Voight) is her father, who lets her run amuck at school where she personally assigns students to cliques and they must obey…or else. One of the film's highlights is her sweet sixteen party, which she amusingly enters riding an elephant. With a film referencing anything that may remotely resonate teenage pop culture, the party is naturally being filmed for MTV's *My Super Sweet 16*.

Joining Voight in the serious actors over eighteen category is Lainie Kazan, who plays Yasmin's grandmother. Both are chameleons, with Voight able to pull off a fine performance behind a very bad prosthetic nose and Kazan convincingly portraying a Latino character.

Most all the situations have been sanitized for the protection of the intended audience and the famously trashy fashions sported by the Bratz doll line have been seriously toned down, with the costumers still managing to keep the young girls looking stylish and up-to-date. The dialogue is similarly tame, with one of the raunchier lines referencing a video game controller ("Hey ladies, have you seen my joystick?"). Typical teenage expressions and slang are peppered throughout as the girls chat in the hallways, text message, and instant message on all the latest tech gadgetry.

The film was directed with little inspiration by Sean McNamara and unimaginatively written by Susan Estelle Jansen from a story by Adam De La Peña and David Eilenberg. Paula Abdul was originally signed on as *Bratz*'s executive producer, fashion designer, and dance choreographer but was famously very publicly fired via Blackberry on an episode of her reality television series *Hey Paula* (2007). Abdul's absence just may have saved *Bratz* from a far worse fate.

Hilary White

CREDITS

Cloe: Skyler Shaye
Avery: Anneliese van der Pol
Principal Dimly: Jon Voight
Bubbie: Lainie Kazan
Yasmin: Nathalia Ramos
Jade: Janel Parrish
Sasha: Logan Browning
Meredith: Chelsea Staub
Cameron: Stephen Lunsford
Dylan: Ian Nelson
Origin: USA
Language: English
Released: 2007
Production: Avi Arad, Steven Paul, Isaac Larian; Crystal Sky Pictures; released by Lions Gate
Directed by: Sean McNamara
Written by: Susan Estelle Jansen
Cinematography by: Christian Sebaldt
Music by: John Coda
Sound: David Chornow
Editing: Jeff W. Canavan
Costumes: Bernadene Morgan

Production Design: Rusty Smith, Rosario Provenza
MPAA rating: PG
Running time: 100 minutes

REVIEWS

Boston Globe Online. August 3, 2007.
Chicago Sun-Times Online. August 3, 2007.
Entertainment Weekly Online. August 2, 2007.
Hollywood Reporter Online. July 31, 2007.
Los Angeles Times Online. August 3, 2007.
New York Times Online. August 3, 2007.
San Francisco Chronicle. August 3, 2007.
Variety Online. July 30, 2007.
Washington Post Online. August 3, 2007.

TRIVIA

Paula Abdul was originally hired as the movie's Executive Producer, Fashion Designer, and Dance Choreographer. During an episode of her reality TV series *Hey Paula* (2007), she found out that she had been fired from the movie through an e-mail message on her Blackberry.

AWARDS

Nomination:

Golden Raspberries 2007: Worst Picture, Worst Actress (Ramos, Shaye, Parrish, Browning), Worst Screen Couple (any combination of two characters), Worst Support. Actor (Voight), Worst Remake.

THE BRAVE ONE

How many wrongs to make it right?
—Movie tagline

Box Office: $36.8 million

The makers of *The Brave One* repeatedly utilized what they dubbed a "wobbly-cam" to create images that unsettlingly teeter this way and that like an intoxicated sailor struggling to get his sea legs. The shots are meant to reflect a reeling woman's out-of-kilter, topsy-turvy mindset, unable to right herself after her world has been suddenly, savagely, and irreparably turned upside down by a random act of senseless violence. Blithe as can be before entering a shadowy Central Park tunnel during an evening stroll with her adored fiancé and their dog, the lady emerges physically battered and emotionally crushed into a very different person.

After lying unconscious in a hospital bed for weeks, this victim, at once terrifically pained and numb, finally comes to life with a vengeance, finding herself navigating through life anew with no one on her arm but a gun in her hand. Increasingly seduced by the powerful and empowering weapon—which—she initially grasped with a shaky hand for protection this reedy woman blossoms into a bold, avenging vigilante, blowing holes through the hearts of the kind of scum who left a cavernous, unfillable one in her own. The film will satisfy viewers who thrill to such retribution, with its dramatic eyefuls of eye-for-an-eye carnage like a distaff *Death Wish* (1974). One can understand what producer Joel Silver saw in this scenario, having been responsible for such action-packed, bloodstained potency as the *Lethal Weapon* franchise and the first two *Die Hard* films. Silver and director Neil Jordan insisted on keeping the project's robust but unadvisedly laudatory-sounding title despite the discomfiture of their star, Jodie Foster, who stressed that there was something deeper, more complex, and decidedly cautionary to be communicated here.

The Brave One is unlikely to be touted by the New York City Chamber of Commerce, with enough mournful talk of urban decay and anxiety-inducing depictions of seemingly omnipresent menace during its running time to make many feel like running the other way. One cannot help but wonder if having Foster's lead character, Erica Bain, chomp away on a nice "Big Apple" at the outset is perhaps further biting commentary. Erica is known to the city's dwellers—and, initially, to viewers through a voice-over narration—as a smooth, clearly enunciated, National Public Radio-type of voice delivering contemplative radio essays on life in the concrete jungle. At this point in the film, an effort is made to stress Erica's cheerful, carefree contentment. She seems easygoing and smiles a lot. She giggles on her cell phone with the handsome doctor she is set to marry (Naveen Andrews). As she chats breezily, Erica glides along the city's sidewalks feeling precious little need to heed her surrounding. With her white top, perky blond haircut, and lighthearted manner, she is the embodiment of as-yet-unscathed, buoyant bliss. The film is clearly setting her up for quite a fall, and like Eve in Eden, things quickly sour after she devours the fruit.

Everything possible is done to graphically accentuate the fiendish ferocity of the two lovers' subsequent nightmarish assault. The pair is initially presented in a tightly framed two-shot as they kiss, visually underscoring a harmonious unity that is about to be permanently ripped apart. The ensuing chaotically photographed, nervously cut images are painfully potent. Jordan rather distastefully chooses to further emphasize matters by juxtaposing shots of the prone, ravaged bodies being handled in the emergency room with those of the couple recently ravishing each other in bed.

Foster, who is thoroughly compelling throughout the film, skillfully conveys Erica's at-a-loss dispiritedness and new, bottomless vulnerability. The aforementioned wobbly-cam especially comes into play in getting across how dizzyingly difficult it is for Erica to even attempt leaving the safety of her home. When she does, her face is pinched, she proceeds gingerly and with a jittery, hyper-awareness that is in stark contrast to her earlier vivacious, unencumbered strides. As a man walks innocently behind her, his footsteps are amplified so that viewers hear them the way Erica does, ominous sounds that seem to portend something dreadful approaching.

Perhaps Erica might feel more secure if she learns the police are making headway in finding the perpetrators, but she waits in vain at the station for someone to speak with and leaves feeling even more hopeless, alone, and afraid. While so many people have listened to her on the radio, she cannot seem to get a single soul on the right side of the law to hear how badly she needs their help. "I need something now," she plaintively stresses, unable to budge a gun shop owner from his adherence to the legally mandated waiting period. "I won't survive thirty days!" So, unable to retrieve some sense of security from those on the up-and-up, Erica, fast unraveling and now hanging by a fragile emotional thread, begins her descent with the purchase of an illegal handgun. She cannot even tell if the weapon is prepared to fire. It seems clear, however, that Erica is.

By coincidence (one of many in *The Brave One*), Erica soon finds herself in a convenience store as an irate, armed husband puts an end to some nagging custody issues by doing the same to his estranged wife. Realizing there is a witness present, he begins suspensefully stalking the aisles for her. As Erica's heart audibly pounds, she blows him away, and one senses the pent-up feelings of powerlessness and retributive rage that are bursting forth along with the bullets. Erica's face registers horrified disbelief but also something else, an assuaging, steadying, and even emboldening sense of the upper hand that can be gained when there is a loaded weapon in it. When confronted on a nearly-deserted subway car by two thuggish thieves who also have rape on their minds, she wonders afterward why she did not even attempt to scare them off by brandishing her weapon before simply mowing them down.

As the media is awash with speculation about this mysterious (and assumed male) vigilante, Erica audaciously goes on to free a young woman she encounters from a pimp (with bloody results), and an unrepentant, wife-beating pig who had repeatedly utilized high-priced lawyers to avoid justice fails to escape Erica's own brand. It is alarming to watch this escalation of mettle—born of that concealed metal, her brazenness—and the way she now walks as if she has nothing to fear. Erica's clothes now get darker, her toned arms exposed. Her narration fully recognizes that an unstoppable domino effect began in that tunnel that has since created a primal "stranger," further removed from her old self each time the wronged woman succumbs to that increasingly addictive pull to set something right by swift, unfettered force. If such a transformation is possible for an amiable, intelligent, thoroughly-civilized liberal woman, the film clearly asserts, it can happen to any pained individual who, tiring of legal ineffectuality and frustratedly feeling without recourse, refuses to be one of society's pushovers and opts to push back—hard.

Erica's foil and unexpected friend as the film progresses is Sean Mercer (Terrence Howard), the by-the-book detective investigating her crimes. He is a man who has not only seen it all but seen too much. Due to a divorce, Sean has, like Erica, found himself unexpectedly and forlornly alone, a wounded survivor. Tension builds as the world-weary cop gradually realizes that this kindred spirit with whom he has gotten personally close during her thoughtful radio coverage of his investigation is the very person upon which it is now closing in. Providing some welcome comic relief is Nicky Katt as Sean's partner working the case. Although Sean's faith in mankind in general and the legal system's efficacy in particular has been sorely tested, he still cannot condone what Erica is doing and will, upon obtaining sufficient evidence, follow through with his duty. She says she would hope for nothing less from him, expressing esteem for his moral/ethical steadfastness with a wistfulness that seems to mourn the unwanted unmooring of her own.

While *The Brave One* successfully blew away its competition during the film's opening weekend, it only garnered mixed reviews. How unfortunately appropriate that a film in which so many meet a bad end should end so badly. When Sean rushes on the scene to catch Erica exacting revenge on the murderous thugs who initially shoved her down this slippery slope, he takes the weapon he has drawn on her...and, unbelievably, hands it to her to use. (After some brief trepidation, she accepts it.) He then concocts a convoluted plan (which includes her wounding him), a web of lies that enables Erica to walk off toward the closing credits legally free and clear. It is not only difficult to buy this negating of all Sean stood for and spoke of earlier, but also that Erica would participate in the destruction of the integrity she had admired most about him. She has certainly paid a price for her assailants' actions, but what about for her own? The film gives Erica a rather appalling pass, even for her slaying of those who only gave her trouble when she herself went looking for it. Silver defended the appropriateness of the heroic-sounding title by saying that Erica found "the courage to overcome the fear and take back her life in whatever way she can. That's what makes her '*The Brave One*.'" That statement may disturb many as much as the gripping but troubling film itself.

David L. Boxerbaum

CREDITS

Erica Bain: Jodie Foster
David Kirmani: Terrence Howard
Jackie: Naveen Andrews
Jackie: Carmen Ejogo
Det. Vitale: Nicky Katt
Carol: Mary Steenburgen
Mortell: Lenny Venito
Chloe: Lenny Kravitz
Origin: USA
Language: English
Released: 2007
Production: Joel Silver, Susan Downey; Silver Pictures, Village Roadshow Pictures; released by Warner Bros.
Directed by: Neil Jordan
Written by: Roderick Taylor, Bruce Taylor, Cynthia Mort
Cinematography by: Philippe Rousselot
Music by: Dario Marianelli
Sound: Tom Nelson
Editing: Tony Lawson
Art Direction: Robert Guerra
Costumes: Catherine Thomas
Production Design: Kristi Zea
MPAA rating: R
Running time: 119 minutes

REVIEWS

Boston Globe Online. September 14, 2007.
Chicago Sun-Times Online. September 13, 2007.
Entertainment Weekly Online. September 12, 2007.
Hollywood Reporter Online. August 30, 2007.
Los Angeles Times Online. September 14, 2007.
New York Times Online. September 14, 2007.
San Francisco Chronicle. September 14, 2007, p. E4.
Variety Online. August 27, 2007.
Wall Street Journal. September 14, 2007, p. W1.
Washington Post. September 14, 2007, p. C1.

QUOTES

Detective Vitale: "I'd say it was probably the fall that killed this guy...or it could be the crowbar embedded in his skull. I'd say it's about 50-50."

AWARDS

Nomination:

Golden Globes 2008: Actress—Drama (Foster).

BREACH

Inspired by the true story of the greatest security breach in U.S. history.
—Movie tagline

Box Office: $33.2 million

As he sits for the rest of his life in solitary confinement, allowed out of his cell for only a single hour per day, Robert Hanssen, an enigmatic, twisted tangle of contradictions, remains a psychoanalyst's dream. He was also the FBI's worst nightmare, an agent who had solemnly sworn to serve and protect his country but proceeded to sell it out for twenty-two of his twenty-five-year career, a stunning, damaging betrayal referred to as "the worst breach of U.S. intelligence" in the Bureau's history. Until his arrest on February 18, 2001, Hanssen sold thousands of pages and numerous computer files brimming with extremely vital classified information to the Soviet Union and then Russia thereafter, military and intelligence secrets that even included details about precisely where the president, vice president, members of the cabinet, and the Congress would be hidden during an attack. His treasonous treachery cost the nation billions of dollars and more than one operative's life, the exact extent of the damage caused by Hanssen's hit to the nation's security currently as tightly under wraps as the ignominious man himself.

Even more interesting than knowing all the ramifications would be some clarification of why Hanssen did it. Perhaps this cold, arrogant, often irritable and abrasive man with the deadpan face and the steel-trap brilliant mind was straining for a singular way to feel superior as those he deemed beneath him rose above him at the Bureau. Maybe he was still trying to prove his worth to an oppressive, self-esteem-stunting cop father. Then again, as he is shown having characterized himself as "insanely loyal," could he have actually thought himself a patriot (as he insinuated upon his arrest), taking extraordinary, extremely misguided measures to call attention to dangerously lax security? No one may ever learn what motivated the man, but *Breach*, a tense, absorbing, well-acted, and fact-hugging retelling of how Hanssen was halted, serves up at least a few tantalizing morsels of food for thought that are sure to be gobbled up by audiences filled with armchair analysts.

The film, which shows Hanssen sitting for a portrait honoring his quarter century of service, provides its own riveting likeness of the man. As masterfully, intriguingly played by Chris Cooper (whose work most critics lauded), Hanssen simultaneously draws viewers in and repels them as they struggle to size up this extraordinarily paradoxical, thoroughly curious, and unsettlingly creepy creature. On the one hand, Hanssen is a senior FBI agent whose skills are so admired that he had been

put in charge of the unit hell-bent on uncovering the suspected mole. He is a devoutly religious Opus Dei Roman Catholic, attending Mass regularly and never straying far from a cross or rosary. He is a devoted husband to comely wife Bonnie (Kathleen Quinlan), the rock who grounded him with that faith, and seems to sincerely value the loving family atmosphere enjoyed with their children and grandchildren. Hanssen is the picture of concrete conservatism, from his patriotic derision of Soviet "godlessness" to his being thoroughly peeved by women who wear pants. Advising against drink, he is seemingly the straightest of straight arrows. Yet Hanssen is now known to also have been the towering turncoat who doled out sensitive material to those atheistic enemies. He was also something of a pervert, sharing lurid stories about his sex life on the Internet and mailing surreptitiously videotaped bedroom encounters with Bonnie for his pals' pleasure. Besides the destructive betrayal of his homeland, one can only imagine the acute devastation these last revelations of deceit caused at home.

It is a daunting task to spy on a noteworthily skillful spy, but that was the job given to promising agent-in-training Eric O'Neill (a solid Ryan Phillippe), called upon to (in every sense of the word) act as Hanssen's assistant. However, O'Neill is initially only informed that his boss is reportedly a "sexual deviant," in need of someone to keep an eye on him lest he cause embarrassing problems for the Bureau. Viewers can tell that this is not an assignment for which the ambitious young man would have bucked. It certainly is not a very pleasant post, especially with a supervisor whose odd, frosty stare is constantly, searchingly scanning him, intently taking his measure with an ever-vigilant, wary paranoia. "Tell me five things about yourself, four of them true," he says upon first laying eyes on O'Neill. After the younger man asserts that he is not especially good at bluffing, Hanssen's processing of the response is palpable before his dry retort: "That would have counted as your lie right there." As Hanssen senses correctly that O'Neill had been casually looking around his office, he icily warns, "If I ever catch you in my office again, I'll have you pissin' purple for a week." When O'Neill tries to formally introduce himself, Hanssen sourly, belittlingly stipulates, "Your name is 'Clerk' and my name is 'Sir' or 'Boss.'"

In short order, the man O'Neill is monitoring somewhat softens and becomes a kind of mentor, not only advising the assistant on the Bureau's ins-and-outs but encouraging the wayward Catholic to pray more and attend church with him. Hanssen also invites O'Neill to his home to spend time with his family. Viewers are likely to feel a sense of uneasiness as the neophyte agent appears to be getting sidetracked, thinking his boss is merely an admittedly different but nonetheless decent man who has somehow been misunderstood. O'Neill chafes at what he thinks of as "perversion detail," deeming it a waste of both his time and talents. Complaining about this to his actual boss, the potently determined, nobody's-fool Special Agent Kate Burroughs (always dependable Laura Linney), he is let in on the full, true, stunning nature of both his job and Hanssen. It is clear that O'Neill is sobered by the grave responsibility of somehow bringing to a head a case to which Burroughs and hundreds of others had already devoted years: "the biggest case we've ever seen."

Even those who have retained knowledge of the case will find themselves watching anxiously as a green but game David must repeatedly think and act with maximum nimbleness in attempting to best a Goliath armed with powers of discernment as formidable and dangerous as the guns that fill the trunk of his car. Especially gripping is the scene in which an increasingly unnerved Hanssen, his keen antennae warning of impending entrapment, takes O'Neill to a snowy, night-enshrouded Rock Creek Park and confronts him with questions and a loaded gun, all intimidatingly pointed and insistently firing in his direction. "I need to know if I can trust you," the spy asks repeatedly, and it is nerve-wracking to watch as O'Neill, with his cover, the entire case, and his very life on the line, deftly handles Hanssen. He not only talks the spy back down into a false sense of security, but, by tweaking the man's sizable but fragile ego, subliminally goads Hanssen on to make the final, all-important drop, where an arrest can—and is—at last made.

Like surgeons who must call upon every bit of knowledge, skill, focus and fortitude in the race to locate a hemorrhage's source and stanch the deleterious flow, those endeavoring to pinpoint the mole and stop the steady, potentially-disastrous seepage of secrets were also entrusted with an urgent, vital task demanding a great deal of them. *Breach* makes a point of showing the personal costs of such meticulous, all-encompassing dedication, as friction gradually develops between a distracted, often absent O'Neill and his lovely Juliana (Caroline Dhavernas), with whom he shares a happy life but cannot, to her frustration, share everything. (This is on top of the East German-born, Protestant being made by her husband's boss to feel un-American, untrustworthy, or simply unacceptable.) As for Burroughs, the woman's single-minded, time-consuming devotion to her job has kept her single, too dogged, she notes, to even look after a cat.

Breach was directed and co-written by Billy Ray, who previously dealt in *Shattered Glass* (2003) with another true, Washington-based story about serial deception eventually exposed. In fact, it was admiration for that similarly themed film, about fabulist Stephen Glass's fabulous rise and fantastic fall at the *New Republic*, which led producer Bobby Newmyer to bring in Ray to rework an initial script by Adam Mazer and William Rotko that fell short of the mark. Ray's earlier film was able to be more illuminating as far as the reasons for the central character's deceit, showing him to have clearly been neurotically needy of approbation. Viewers were likely to have found themselves sympathizing with pathetic young Glass as people began to see through him, something they are unlikely to feel for sinister Hanssen as O'Neill's work finally cages the cagey spy.

David L. Boxerbaum

CREDITS

Robert Hanssen: Chris Cooper
Eric O'Neill: Ryan Phillippe
Kate Burroughs: Laura Linney
Dean Plesac: Dennis Haysbert
Juliana O'Neill: Caroline Dhavernas
Rich Garces: Gary Cole
John O'Neill: Bruce Davison
Bonnie Hanssen: Kathleen Quinlan
Origin: USA
Language: English
Released: 2007
Production: Robert Newmyer, Scott Kroopf, Scott Strauss; Outlaw Productions, Intermedia, Sidney Kimmell Entertainment; released by Universal Pictures
Directed by: Billy Ray
Written by: Billy Ray, Adam Mazer, William Rotko
Cinematography by: Tak Fujimoto
Music by: Mychael Danna
Sound: John J. Thomson
Editing: Jeffrey Ford
Art Direction: Andrew Stearn
Costumes: Luis Sequeira
Production Design: Wynn Thomas
MPAA rating: PG-13
Running time: 110 minutes

REVIEWS

Chicago Sun-Times Online. February 16, 2007.
Entertainment Weekly. February 23, 2007, p. 82.
Hollywood Reporter Online. February 9, 2007.
Los Angeles Times Online. February 16, 2007.
New York Times Online. February 16, 2007.
San Francisco Chronicle. February 16, 2007, p. E7.
Variety Online. February 8, 2007.
Washington Post. February 16, 2007, p. C1.

QUOTES

Kate Burroughs: "A couple of years ago, the bureau put together a task force. Lots of assets had been disappearing.

So this task force was formed to find the mole who was giving them up. Our best analysts poring over data for years looking for the guy, and they could never quite find him. Guess who was put in charge of the task force? He was smarter than all of us. Actually, I can live with that part. It's the idea that my entire career has been a waste of time, that's the part I hate. Everything I've done since I got to this office, everything we've all been paid to do, he was undoing it. We all coulda just stayed home."

BREAKING AND ENTERING

Love is no ordinary crime.
　—Movie tagline
Lie. Cheat. Steal. Love.
　—Movie tagline

Anthony Minghella gained a reputation as a thoughtful director in critically acclaimed films such as *The English Patient* (1996) and *Cold Mountain* (2003)—richly detailed movies with compelling characters and intricate plots. In *Breaking and Entering,* he had a talented cast to work with, but unlike his other successful scripts, he was not adapting a story from another source. Minghella's weaknesses as a screenwriter are spotlighted in *Breaking and Entering,* with a plot so contrived and clunky that it hardly seems worthy of being filmed.

Minghella tries to distract us from the paltriness of the story with an overabundance of artistic camera work. Characters are often filmed through glass, in mirrors, or in reflections. While some of these shots are beautifully constructed and executed, their artistry seems cold and distancing. That is because Minghella has not filled his movie with people we could care about.

His protagonist is Will (Jude Law), a chic and visionary (but somewhat phony) architect who has a grand scheme to remake the Kings Cross neighborhood of London's North End into an urban landscape that capitalizes on natural assets. His biggest critic in the film turns out to be a prostitute, Oana (Vera Farmiga), who shows up out of nowhere and dispenses the opinion that the plan will only drive the street people to another neighborhood. So much for the merits of gentrification.

Will's bigger problems are not self-appointed critics, but the issues in his family and work life. For ten years he has been living with Liv (Robin Wright Penn) and helping her raise her daughter Bea (Poppy Rogers), an unusual child indeed. She spends most of her time doing somersaults and other gymnastics, has been diagnosed as autistic, and has trouble sleeping at night. With this central struggle, and for other unexplained reasons, Will and Liv have grown distant. She will not marry him, and he feels excluded from her tight relationship with Bea. From their few scenes together, it is also obvious that Will is less indulgent with Bea than her mother is.

At his firm, which is in the rundown Kings Cross neighborhood, Will loses his laptop computer and much of his work, along with other company computers and equipment, in a break-in. The cleaning woman is suspected, but we soon see that a boy on a rooftop has been using binoculars to steal the cleaning woman's alarm code when she leaves the building at night. We learn this during a second break-in. The thieves are teenage boys working for a man who sells the stolen electronic equipment. Apparently they do not heed the accepted taboo against returning to the scene of a crime. The police seem disinterested, or more accurately, almost nonexistent, so Will and his boss start staking out their own building at night. That is when the hooker, Oana, jumps in the car with them. When she fails to interest them in her body, she starts having talks about architecture with Will. So much for even an effort at plausibility.

We see that the boy who has been breaking into the architectural firm through the roof is the troubled son of a Bosnian immigrant, Amira (Juliette Binoche). Fifteen-year-old Miro (Rafi Gavron) is actually working for his dead father's brother in the heists. Amira's husband, Miro's father, was a Serbian killed during the Balkan wars. Amira is trying unsuccessfully to keep her son in school and out of trouble while working as a tailor.

After a slowly moving hour-plus that barely advances the plot, Will catches Miro trying to break into his office for a third time, an act that itself strains credulity. He takes off after the boy and finds out where his apartment is. Trying to find out more about him, he brings a suit for Amira to repair, so that he can get into her apartment. There he discovers his missing computer files in the boy's room. Instead of exposing the boy, however, he suddenly and inexplicably falls for Amira. Her own motives are mixed; after he falls asleep, she invites her friend to take photographs. She plans to use these to blackmail Will to prevent her son from being prosecuted for the thefts.

Jude Law, who is at his best playing a cad, here portrays a character who is seemingly shallow, self-centered, and careless, but rather purposelessly so, and it is hard to take much interest in his plight. Through his neglect Bea gets in an accident (in a scene that is telegraphed way in advance) and is hospitalized. He then turns on Amira, rejecting her plea not to testify against Miro after the police finally catch him. At the end, Will reverses course again and redeems himself, but in a very contrived fashion. He tells the court that they have arrested the wrong boy, and the reason he knows this is that he has been having an affair with the boy's mother. The odd thing is that he certainly does not have to confess to the affair to save the boy.

Nearly as bizarre as the plot is the script itself. Most of the actors seem to be mumbling their lines as if in embarrassment. Liv is supposed to be Swedish, so Penn affects an accent; Binoche is supposed to be Bosnian, though she has a French accent; and Law just reprises his customary rapid-fire, double-talking character. Throughout, the characters have to say lines about how breaking hearts is more of a crime than breaking into buildings, as Minghella belabors his obvious points. When Will and Liv fight at the end and Will wonders why she refuses to marry him, she says, "I don't want a husband, I want a good night's sleep!"

None of the characters or their situations rings true, and the entire film seems strange and completely unnatural. Will is an entirely unsympathetic protagonist, Binoche just plays Amira as a lost soul with little affect, and Penn's Liv is carelessly drawn—perhaps her own emotional problems have affected her daughter, but it is all rather murky. The characters are like pieces on a game board that get moved around by the unseen writer's hand without regard to coherence. And what is the point of it all? Apparently, some softhearted message about emotional crimes being more salient than property crimes. Clearly, Minghella should stick to adaptations.

Michael Betzold

CREDITS

Will Francis: Jude Law
Amira: Juliette Binoche
Liv: Robin Wright Penn
Sandy: Martin Freeman
Bruno: Ray Winstone
Oana: Vera Farmiga
Rosemary: Juliet Stevenson
Miro: Rafi Gavron
Bea: Poppy Rogers
Origin: Great Britain
Language: English
Released: 2006
Production: Sydney Pollack, Anthony Minghella, Timothy Bricknell; Weinstein Co., Mirage Enterprises, Miramax Films; released by MGM
Directed by: Anthony Minghella
Written by: Anthony Minghella
Cinematography by: Benoit Delhomme
Music by: Gabriel Yared
Sound: Jim Greenhorn
Music Supervisor: Mike Gillespie
Editing: Lisa Gunning

Art Direction: Andy Nicholson
Costumes: Natalie Ward
Production Design: Alex McDowell
MPAA rating: R
Running time: 116 minutes

REVIEWS

Boxoffice Online. December 15, 2006.
Guardian Online. November 10, 2006.
Hollywood Reporter Online. September 14, 2006.
Los Angeles Times Online. December 15, 2006.
The Observer Online. November 12, 2006.
Time Magazine Online. December 18, 2006.
Variety Online. September 13, 2006.

QUOTES

Will: "I don't know how to be honest, that's why I'm so fond of metaphors."

TRIVIA

The techniques used to burgle Green Effect come from parkour, a physical discipline and recreational activity of French origin whose practitioners are called traceurs. Sometimes confused with free running, a related discipline derived from parkour, the art, as it is called by some practitioners, has gained popularity in urban areas, particularly in Europe, during the early 21st century.

BRIDGE TO TERABITHIA

Discover a place that will never leave you, and a friendship that will change you forever.
—Movie tagline
Close your eyes, but keep your mind wide open.
—Movie tagline

Box Office: $82.3 million

Based on the Newbery Award-winning novel of the same name, *Bridge to Terabithia* focuses on young artistic outcasts Jess Aarons (Josh Hutcherson) and Leslie Burke (AnnaSophia Robb) who create their own world in order to transcend the limitations of their real lives at home and school, and to explore their friendship with one another. Though the previews and other promotional materials for *Bridge to Terabithia* showcased the film's fantasy elements, perhaps in an attempt to attract moviegoers who have not read the book but have enjoyed other popular film adaptations of children's literature such as the *Harry Potter* films or *The Chronicles of Narnia* (2005), this is a bit misleading as the fantasy component of the film is minor. They do not actually stumble upon some magical gateway that leads them into an otherworldly realm. Terabithia is a place that exists only in their imaginations but, for Jess and Leslie, the kingdom of their own creation not only helps them connect with one another and other people, but also provides a creative outlet that is otherwise lacking in their daily lives (especially for Jess). The result is a charming and moving tale whose magic lies not in spells, flying broomsticks, or talking animals, but in the creative power of the imagination to bridge differences and to turn the sometimes harsh realities of day-to-day existence into stories and lessons of strength and beauty.

At its most basic, *Bridge to Terabithia* is about children whose circumstances and sensibilities make them outcasts, which their creative strengths enable them to transcend. Jesse (Jess) Aarons is the middle child and only son in a poor farming family—Jess's mother and father are clearly worried about money constantly, which makes for a tense home environment. Jess's only outlet is through drawing. On his first day back at school, he encounters new girl Leslie Burke. Leslie attempts to connect with Jess, but Jess shuns her when she beats him in a race. It is only after Leslie reads a story of hers in front of the class and is derided for not owning a television that Jess sympathizes with and takes an interest in her. They go exploring the nearby woods together and come upon a rope swing that connects the opposite banks of a creek. They swing across and Leslie proposes that they create a magical kingdom that can be entered only by swinging across the "enchanted rope." They find an abandoned tree house, and Jess and Leslie spend a lot of time there and in the surrounding woods building their kingdom, which they call Terabithia. The children use their imaginary lives to work out their problems in ways they cannot in reality—as Leslie puts it, "We rule Terabithia, and nothing crushes us."

One day, Jess's music teacher, Ms. Edmunds, played winningly by Zooey Deschanel, asks if Jess would like to go on a field trip to a museum with her. Jess asks his half-asleep mother if he can go and, in his excitement, mistakes a groggy moan for a "yes." Jess has had a crush on Ms. Edmunds for some time and opts not to invite Leslie. When Jess returns from the museum, his family is clearly upset. Jess's father, Mr. Aarons, played by Robert Patrick, says that they did not know where Jess was and thought he was dead. It turns out that Leslie tried to take the rope swing to Terabithia by herself but the rope broke—she fell into the creek, hit her head on something, and drowned. Jess does not want to believe the news at first. In fact, he wakes up the next day and seems not to remember that it happened at all until his parents suggest that they go pay their respects to Leslie's parents. Jess is utterly consumed by grief and guilt over Leslie's death. He blames himself because he did not

invite her to the museum and was not there to help her when she went to Terabithia alone. Mr. Aarons tells Jess that what happened is not his fault, that it is no one's fault, but that Leslie gave Jess something special and that he should keep that spirit alive. Jess uses his artistic skill to transform a fallen tree that stretches across the creek into an ornate bridge into Terabithia—above the bridge, Jess hangs a sign which reads, "Nothing Crushes Us." He leads his little sister, May Belle (Bailee Madison), who had always been curious about where Jess and Leslie went, across the bridge and crowns her Princess of Terabithia, and they begin to imagine the kingdom anew.

Bridge to Terabithia is a delightful surprise of ingenuous filmmaking. First-time feature director, Gabor Csupo, whose background is mostly as a writer and producer of animation, obviously has strong source material from which to work, but his handling of that material shows a keen depth of feeling and skill. Not only does he elicit excellent performances from his actors, but he manages to convey the difficulties of growing up in a way that is lighthearted (it is easy to be swept up in the obvious joy the children feel in Terabithia), but that also manages to show the complexity and evokes the weight of formative childhood experiences.

What makes *Bridge to Terabithia* such a compelling piece of filmmaking lies in the totality and depth of its storytelling, and in its determination not to shy away from difficult issues. This is a film about the power of the imagination to overcome preconceived notions and real-world limitations—and the film's plot, characters, and visual storytelling elements all work in conjunction to achieve that end. Jess and Leslie come together because they are outcasts and because they both share a penchant for the artistic. Leslie begins to show Jess that the imagination can transform reality, and that keeping one's mind wide open allows for greater vision than the naked eye allows. Indeed, Jess and Leslie use their imaginary kingdom to confront the troubles they face at school and home—and they begin to see that by facing their fears and challenges in the imaginary world gives them the strength to use those victories to change their real lives. For instance, at school, they are both tormented by an eighth grade girl, Janice Avery—one of the great girl-bully characters of all time, brought to life in a fantastic performance by Lauren Clinton—who is the inspiration for a Terabithian troll due to her practice of charging younger kids a toll to use the bathroom. Confronting the imaginary troll gives Jess and Leslie the strength to take on Janice in real life. When Janice is ostracized herself, Leslie's status as outcast makes her recognize Janice's need for connection and help, and is able to comfort her. Indeed, one of the most affecting dimensions of *Bridge to Terabithia* is its call for tolerance and its imperative for people to reach out and make connections with one another (it is no coincidence that a bridge connects the imaginary realm of Terabithia to the real world). Even Jess's family's poverty, clearly something that weighs heavily on Jess, is alleviated by his friendship with Leslie and their exploration of Terabithia. When Jess's father accuses Jess of losing his work keys (which Mr. Aarons needs for his job to support the family), he commands Jess to get his head out of the clouds, and ridicules his son's pastime of drawing with the harsh admonishment, "Why don't you draw me some damn money?", the search for the keys is transformed into a triumphant quest in Terabithia, and Jess returns to the real world with the keys.

What truly makes *Bridge to Terabithia* a cut above other fantasy fare about and aimed at children is its fearless engagement of difficult issues. Conflict, whether in the form of facing off against bullies, or in the tension cause by financial hardship, is part of the world of children as much as that of adults. *Bridge to Terabithia* does not stop there, though—it goes on to address (a bit too controversially for some, perhaps) the metaphysical question of whether God would condemn an otherwise good person to hell simply for not believing in the Bible. This question (as well as the issue of mortality itself) is brought into stark relief when Leslie dies. Jess, in his guilt and sadness, is terrified that God will send Leslie to hell because she was not a churchgoer (her first visit to a church is with Jess's family). Mr. Aarons assures Jess that God would not send Leslie to hell, and Jess's re-imagining of Terabithia after Leslie's death is, in a way, his willing into existence the heaven that Leslie deserves—indeed it is the place that saved his life from the drab concerns of daily life. The experience of the film's wonderful story, excellent performances, and transporting (yet not overwhelming) special effects does the same thing for it audience, allowing it to recall and re-experience the power and joy of the imagination, and encouraging it to be brave enough to keep an open mind.

John Boaz

CREDITS

Jess Aarons: Josh Hutcherson
Leslie Burke: AnnaSophia Robb
Jack Aarons: Robert Patrick
Ms. Edmonds: Zooey Deschanel
May Belle Aarons: Bailee Madison
Nancy Aarons: Kate Butler
Janice Avery: Lauren Clinton
Origin: USA

Language: English
Released: 2007
Production: Hal Lieberman, Lauren Levine, David Paterson; Walden Media, Walter Disney Pictures; released by Buena Vista
Directed by: Gabor Csupo
Written by: Jeff Stockwell, David Paterson
Cinematography by: Michael Chapman
Music by: Aaron Zigman
Sound: Tony Johnson
Music Supervisor: George Acogny
Editing: John Gilbert
Art Direction: Jennifer Ward
Costumes: Barbara Darragh
Production Design: Robert Gillies
MPAA rating: PG
Running time: 94 minutes

REVIEWS

Boxoffice Online. February 16, 2007.
Chicago Sun-Times Online. February 16, 2007.
Entertainment Weekly. February 23, 2007, p. 81.
Hollywood Reporter Online. February 12, 2007.
Los Angeles Times Online. February 16, 2007.
New York Times Online. February 16, 2007.
San Francisco Chronicle. February 16, 2007, p. E1.
Variety Online. February 11, 2007.
Washington Post. February 16, 2007, p. C1.

QUOTES

Leslie Burke: "Just close your eyes and keep your mind wide open."

TRIVIA

Screenwriter David Paterson is the son of novelist Katherine Paterson.

THE BROTHERS SOLOMON

They want to put a baby in you.
—Movie tagline

The losers-make-good comedy written by *Saturday Night Live*'s Will Forte, *The Brothers Solomon*, plays like one of that television show's bad skits during an off season, with a one-note premise, paper-thin characters, and the feeling that it has gone on far too long. Director Bob Odenkirk's second feature film showcases oddball slapstick in some of the most extended gags ever captured on film. *The Brothers Solomon* is so derivative, from the same old idiot routine to the worn out and tired music, (St. Elmo's Fire's "Man in Motion" is oft heard), it is essentially a bizarre twist on such comedy misfires as *A Night at the Roxbury* (1998) or better low-brow fare like *Dumb & Dumber* (1994) and *The Jerk* (1979) but lacking the heart or soul. The film's thoughtful, polished look, solid casting, and a few inspired segments hint at the filmmakers creativity and intelligence, but it is ultimately lost amid the dross.

The inane plot revolves around the thirty-something bachelor brothers John and Dean Solomon who were raised in the Arctic by their father Ed (Lee Majors). They are, implausibly, brilliant scientists who are also utterly dim-witted and completely socially inept. An example of this is John very publicly proposing to one hapless female (Jenna Fischer) in the middle of dinner on their first date. So when their father lapses into a coma and his last words include regretting that he has no grandchild, the boys will doubtless run into a variety of obstacles while trying to honor that wish.

They soon realize that no woman is willing to bear their child in the traditional way but find one on the Internet site Craigslist who would be willing to host their spawn for $12,000. Janine (Kristen Wiig) is a good-hearted, well-intentioned surrogate who is inexplicably patient with the clueless Solomons, explaining the insemination process will not involve intercourse. Another *Saturday Night Live* regular, Wiig's comic genius is completely squelched here, playing the straight man, as does the very funny *The Office* favorite Fischer in her tiny role. Janine's imposing, African American boyfriend James (Chi McBride) is a mystifyingly odd mix, spewing profanity and prone to outbursts of rage one minute and on his knees, overcome with emotion in a crying jag, the next.

The Solomon's neighbor, Tara (Malin Akerman) is the final main character, who merely serves as an object for John to futilely lust after. The boys have moved their coma-stricken father into their bachelor pad and being a nursing student, Tara keeps an eye on Ed when they are away. One of the film's bizarre running gags is that she is always seen unexpectedly emerging from their bathroom.

With deliberate pacing, the film then proceeds to the progressing pregnancy. The narration includes the disembodied heads of the brothers spinning across the screen while intoning, "First Trimester," "Second Trimester," and so on. The mandatory father training montage features ridiculous bits like one of boys dropping a doll from several stories up and seeing if the other can catch it, but it also includes the film's best segment. The truly original and highly creative scene has the brothers engaging in a delightfully mad diaper changing drill that has one brother filling the diaper with a fun variety of assorted ingredients, which comes as a surprise each time to the other brother opening the diaper. Popcorn happily tumbles out of the dolls undergarment in one cut, chicken fingers the next, and even quarters fill the overflowing diaper to one Solomon's surprise. It is nearly brilliant, but like all the other jokes in the film, it goes too far when a dead bird appears.

The script throws in some rote obstacles in the third reel that involve Janine disappearing after she decides she wants to keep the baby. The boys utilize a unique method of mass communication in order to find her: using an aerial banner. The extended scene is the film's set piece and pays homage to a similar scene in *Austin Powers: International Man of Mystery* (1997) as a variety of people spy Dr. Evil's phallus-shaped space craft. It is also another extended gag that starts promisingly but loses its punch as the banner's message goes on and on, humorously at first as various people on the street read it, then milking the increasingly tedious and tiresome joke beyond all reason.

It almost seems that Odenkirk is, in some weird fashion, paying homage to Wes Anderson. He includes several of that director's signature quirky touches found in some of the tinkling music; subtitles; narration; exotic, far-flung locales; the artificial, staged feel to the scenes; and assorted peculiar details like the way the brothers hunker down to bed in sleeping bags. Odenkirk uses a palette of pastel hues and includes some of Anderson's penchant for showcasing odd artifacts. But, unlike Anderson, he fails to create dimensional, sympathetic characters, fresh humor, or a semi-believable plot.

James S. O'Neill

CREDITS

John Solomon: Will Arnett
Dean Solomon: Will Forte
James: Chi McBride
Michelle: Jenna Fischer
Janine: Kristen Wiig
Tara: Malin Akerman
Ed Solomon: Lee Majors
Origin: USA
Language: English
Released: 2007
Production: Matt Berenson, Tom Werner; Revolution Studios, TriStar Pictures, Casey-Werner Films; released by Sony Pictures
Directed by: Bob Odenkirk
Written by: Will Forte
Cinematography by: Tim Suhrstedt

Music by: John Swihart
Sound: Stephen Halbert
Music Supervisor: G. Marq Roswell, Adam Swart
Editing: Tracey Wadmore-Smith
Art Direction: Marc Dabe
Costumes: Melina Root
Production Design: John Paino
MPAA rating: R
Running time: 93 minutes

REVIEWS

Boston Globe Online. September 7, 2007.
Chicago Sun-Times Online. September 7, 2007.
Entertainment Weekly Online. September 5, 2007.
Hollywood Reporter Online. September 6, 2007.
Los Angeles Times Online. September 7, 2007.
New York Times Online. September 7, 2007.
San Francisco Chronicle. September 7, 2007, p. E7.
Variety Online. September 5, 2007.

QUOTES

John Solomon: "I literally cannot wait to feel myself inside you!"

Janine: "Woah! The only thing you're going to feel yourself inside of is a cold Dixie cup."

John Solomon: "Well that certainly doesn't make your vagina sound very appealing."

BUG

> *First they send in their drone…then they find their queen.*
> —Movie tagline
>
> *Paranoia is contagious.*
> —Movie tagline

Box Office: $7 million

Imagine Ashley Judd, her scarred body clad only in a shabby shift, her arms upraised in an ecstatic gesture, shouting: "I am the supermother bug!" It is an apotheosis, perhaps, of sorts. But it is also absolutely insane. Shortly after that she and her companion take off their clothes, douse each other with kerosene, declare their mutual love, light a match, and go up in a pillar of flame, framing a spectacular conclusion.

Agnes (Ashley Judd) works as a part-time waitress in a local lesbian club, somewhere in rural America. One night her girl friend R.C. (Lynn Collins) introduces her to Peter Evans (Michael Shannon), who is in need of a place to stay. The next morning, it is not Peter who greets Agnes, but her abusive ex-husband, Jerry Goss

(Harry Connick, Jr.) who was just released from prison. After slapping her around, he leaves. Peter returns and tells Agnes he has not had a woman in years. Within seconds, she draws him into her bedroom for a night of love, a night, later to be interrupted by his warning that her apartment is full of bugs…aphids, to be exact. Life is like that in *Bug,* based on an off-Broadway play by Tracy Letts introduced in 2004.

Peter is certainly complicated, and potentially dangerous, it turns out. He is a loner, apparently a drifter. He explains to Agnes that he is able to "pick up on things not apparent to other people." He "picks up" on the fact that Agnes is lonely. Peter confides that he wants a friend, but not necessarily for sex. Peter gradually initiates a relationship with Agnes, as he becomes more intimate and personal. "You lied to me about having children," he says, for example, adding again his mantra, "I pick up on things." Even Peter's seduction is roundabout and indirect: "I haven't been in bed with a woman for a long time," he says, "but I think I could go to bed with you." After they make love, he finds a bug in the bed, "truly small, like an aphid," adding, significantly, "there might be more." Of course, the bug is too small for the viewer to actually see.

Thereafter, Peter's behavior—and his backstory—gets increasingly bizarre. "I got into some trouble with the army," he explains. "The doctors gave us pills. I was having some weird thoughts. They put me in a hospital and ran tests. Those f**king doctors were experimenting on me! I went A.W.O.L. and [now] they are after me. I shouldn't have told you that, but I had to tell somebody. I don't want to go!" he says. Peter gets crazier and crazier as his obsession with the imagined "blood-sucking, burrowing aphids" grows. He begins to show gruesome signs of self-mutilation, while trying to rid himself of the burrowing aphids.

From this point forward, the story takes off on a murderous, insane trajectory for the rest of the film. Peter turns out to be an escapee from a veteran's hospital, where he confesses he has been the subject of experiments that have implanted sacs of bug eggs inside his skin or beneath the fillings in his teeth. Nonplussed, Agnes decides she sees bugs everywhere, too. They both get out a microscope to inspect drops of his blood. Soon, Peter and Agnes have covered the furniture, the walls, and the ceiling with aluminum foil to ward off the "coded signals" the bugs are emitting. By the time Agnes's unwelcome ex returns, the whole room resembles the inside of a refrigerator freezer. It looks like an arctic wasteland, frozen to a chilly blue, illuminated by bug zappers. Viewers, however, have yet to see a single insect. Understandably, the ex-husband leaves, as Agnes and Peter slump further into a nasty, shared paranoia. Both their bodies are now covered in bites. The room is a mess. Then, a stranger appears, announcing that he is Peter's doctor.

When Dr. Sweet (Brian F. O'Byrne) comes calling on Agnes, he gives an apparently rational explanation for Peter's behavior. Peter was confined for four years in an army hospital, the doctor says, diagnosed as a delusional paranoid schizophrenic, not sought by the army and by the C.I.A. Agnes shows little or no surprise at this announcement, as Dr. Sweet tells Agnes that if she will cooperate, he will help her locate her missing son, Lloyd. This gets her attention, but then Peter appears, attacks Dr. Sweet with a syringe and a butcher knife, and kills him. "He's a replicant, a robot, sent here by the leaders of the conspiracy," Peter confides to Agnes. And they both fall to more microscope gazing in nothing short of a sexual frenzy.

Agnes is convinced they are both infected by "rapidly-multiplying, brainwashing bugs." Together, they remember the details leading to the first discovery of the aphids, and, together, they seem to make sense of it, as they approach a cathartic moment of shared insanity at the dramatic core of the play and film. Director William Friedkin, famous as the director of the supernaturally repulsive *The Exorcist* (1971), claims in his DVD interview that *Bug* is "the most profoundly disturbing film I've made." Suffice it to say, that claim is believable. It is not a film one would look forward to seeing a second or third time, or maybe ever again.

Bug is a far cry from Friedkin's most critically acclaimed film, *The French Connection* (1971), famous for arguably the most exciting car chase ever captured on film. Friedkin's *The Exorcist* (1973), on the other hand, was famous for its malevolent atmosphere and set a new standard for horror filmmaking, his gift to mass culture. In fact, the alleged "danger" of mass hysteria became a marketing tool for the film. The horror of *The Exorcist* depends on whether viewers believe in supernatural events. The horror of *Bug* is, by contrast, purely psychological, and some would argue, therefore more effective.

The action is well adapted to the claustrophobic setting (most of it taking place in Agnes's motel apartment) and the actors are truly astonishing. A key scene of the film involves a virtuosic display by Ashley Judd, as she delivers a truly amazing monologue to Peter. For nearly five minutes, she rages and rants in fine lunatic fashion, citing "evidence" to support her interpretation of Peter's conspiracy theory involving the army and the C.I.A. Bloodied and scarred, her face a scarlet, twisted mask, she displays remarkable inventiveness, providing a superb correlative to Peter's enthralled paranoid responses. The insects that fester beneath their skins are like the chips Peter says were implanted in him, as their now shared fantasies spiral out of control.

In the director's commentary for the DVD release, William Friedkin mentions that the thin line between good and evil is a recurrent motif that occurs in his cinema. In *Bug* the line is more likely between sanity and insanity. It would be easy enough to dismiss all this anguish as merely the projections of the paranoia of Peter and Agnes. There are no tiny bugs in sight, after all, but too many things, like the insect bites, are all too real. Why does Agnes so readily buy into Peter's fantasy? Or has she been harboring her own parallel fantasies already? And there is the hinted (but never fully explained) backstory involving Agnes's "lost" son. Apparently, years before she had "lost" her son in a supermarket, when he disappeared from her shopping cart. Images of an empty shopping cart haunt her. Perhaps in her mind the child's disappearance links up somehow with the bugs and the microchips.

Friedkin's treatment of this psychodrama is generally way over the top. For some viewers, *Bug* might seem hilarious at times because of the way it skirts absurdity and defies plot logic. But if in William Friedkin's hands the play's intensity and bizarre situations cross over the line, the director's excesses only make the whole nightmare all the more disturbing. There is no gainsaying the performances of Ashley Judd and Michael Shannon as Agnes and Peter. This play adaptation is the closest Friedkin has come in years to matching the brilliance of his earlier films, but its scenes of mutilation and mayhem, leading to an ultimate suicide pact between two disturbed and demented characters, will certainly be too toxic for some viewers.

Any artist will be defined by the choices he or she makes, and this is just as true of Ashley Judd as it is of director William Friedkin in the present instance. A film director may make "bad" choices in order to keep afloat in the movie marketplace. Friedkin has taken chances in the past with difficult projects such as *Cruising* (1980), which was also too brutal and realistic for many viewers; but most of his pictures have leaned toward the popular and the entertaining. The film Friedkin made before *Cruising*, after all, was *The Brinks Job* (1978), which was little more than an entertaining romp. *Bug* is not especially entertaining, not is it likely to be popular; but it was a brave choice for a director to make some thirty-five years into a faltering career.

James M. Welsh and John C. Tibbetts

CREDITS

Agnes: Ashley Judd
Peter: Michael Shannon

Jerry Goss: Harry Connick, Jr.
R.C.: Lynn Collins
Dr. Sweet: Brian F. O'Byrne
Origin: USA
Language: English
Released: 2006
Production: Michael Burns, Malcolm Petal, Holly Wiersma, Kimberly Anderson, Gary Huckabay; Lift Productions; released by Lions Gate
Directed by: William Friedkin
Written by: Tracy Letts
Cinematography by: Michael Grady
Music by: Brian Tyler
Sound: Jeffrey Haupt
Music Supervisor: Jay Faires
Editing: Darrin Navarro
Art Direction: Frank Zito
Costumes: Peggy Anita Schnitzer
Production Design: Franco-Giacomo Carbone
MPAA rating: R
Running time: 101 minutes

REVIEWS

Chicago Sun-Times Online. May 25, 2007.
Entertainment Weekly Online. May 22, 2007.
Hollywood Reporter Online. May 20, 2006.
Los Angeles Times Online. May 25, 2007.
New York Times Online. May 25, 2007.
Variety Online. May 19, 2006.
Village Voice Online. May 22, 2007.
Washington Post Online. May 25, 2007.

QUOTES

Agnes White: "You don't sound like you're from Oklahoma."
Peter Evans: "I'm from Beaver."
Agnes White: "Well, we're all from beaver, ain't we?"

TRIVIA

The film was shot in July and August of 2005 in Southern Louisiana, and wrapped up only a week before Hurricane Katrina hit the area; the cast and crew narrowly escaped the disaster by only a few days.

C

EL CANTANTE

Based on the true story of the King of Salsa, Héctor Lavoe.
—Movie tagline

Box Office: $7.6 million

Leon Ichaso's *El Cantante,* from a script by Ichaso, David Darmstaedter, and Todd Anthony Bello, tells the story of Héctor Lavoe (Marc Anthony), a singer who apparently had a profound impact on the development of salsa before destroying himself with drugs and ultimately succumbing to complications from AIDS in 1993 at the age of forty-six. But this biopic charting his rise and fall is so scant on details regarding his music, why it was important to him, and his place in history that it is possible to watch the film and still not know why we should care about this tortured figure.

Jennifer Lopez, who is credited as a producer on *El Cantante* and is married to Anthony in real life, costars as Puchi, Héctor's long-suffering wife, who enables his toxic lifestyle and participates in it more than she tries to help get him clean. The film opens in 2002 with an older Puchi being interviewed about her husband's life, a framing device that Ichaso will cut back to many times to provide running commentary but which, unfortunately, does not add much insight to the story.

Héctor begins his singing career in his native Puerto Rico before making the leap to New York City in 1963, a move that his father (Ismael Miranda) disapproves of. Their conflict is revisited later but never fleshed out, leaving us to wonder how his father's lack of support affected the young Héctor. He partners with Willie Colón (John Ortiz) and has a meteoric rise, but we do not learn what made the pair distinctive and what they contributed to salsa. Interspersed throughout the film are energetic musical performances, but the frenetic cutting and odd placement of the lyrics all over the screen for the Spanish songs make these interludes more of a chore to watch than a joyful celebration of Héctor's music. And yet, while the hyperkinetic editing is annoying, at least it keeps our attention. Without these musical numbers, the film would be very boring.

There is no explanation for why Héctor descends into a world of drug addiction, but, once he does, that becomes the story's main focus as he gradually destroys his family life and himself and engages in countless bitter arguments with his wife along the way. Lopez at least brings a certain passion to the role of Puchi and some range to this limited character. Anthony, however, exhibits very little emotional depth and, as a result, we never know what the music means to Héctor or what demons drive him to an early death. Anthony does not build a character. He just plays the familiar self-destructive star yielding to the temptations that often accompany showbiz success.

Along the way, subplots are glossed over, and musical montages are relied upon to convey the passage of time without delving into the story behind the music. It is clear that neither Héctor nor Puchi is a very attentive parent, but, since we understand so very little of their son's troubles, the tragedy of his accidental shooting death does not resonate as it should. Héctor's uneasy relationship with his sister, who seems to take an instant dislike to Puchi, and his alienation from his father are likewise given short shrift. Even Héctor's professional partnership with Willie is sketchy at best—a series of conflicts based on Héctor's irresponsibility and culminating in Willie leaving to pursue a musical career on his own. After the breakup, we are treated to a Lavoe song about going solo, as if we were getting some grand statement on how life influences art. In short, any plot point or character that does not touch on Héctor's descent into a drug-fueled existence and his tempestuous relationship with his wife—their fights are intense but redundant—does not seem to matter to the filmmakers.

Indeed, while *El Cantante* gives us brief glimpses into the music itself, such as an encounter with Ruben Blades (Victor Manuelle), who writes what would become Lavoe's signature song, "El Cantante" ("The Singer"), the screenplay only skims the surface of the creative part of his story, which is, presumably, why we should care about him in the first place.

And the ending simply fizzles. Héctor survives jumping from a building in a botched suicide attempt, but we are left in limbo about his final years. Puchi's claim that she wants to remember him as he was is supposed to spare us from seeing him in his diminished condition, but the portrait we have been given is so unflattering that it is almost laughable to think that is really how his wife would want him to be remembered.

Musical biopics are a tricky genre because they can devolve into simply showing a series of highs and lows that do not necessarily lend themselves to a compelling dramatic arc. *Ray* (2004), the Ray Charles biopic, employs a fairly straightforward narrative that succeeds largely because of Jamie Foxx's performance, while *La Vie en Rose* (2007), a more impressionistic look at the life of Edith Piaf, is anchored by the riveting Marion Cotillard. But both movies, in their own way, communicate their protagonist's connection to and passion for music, something that neither *El Cantante*'s thin script nor Anthony's lackluster performance comes close to doing.

And *El Cantante* has a bigger challenge at the outset than those films since Lavoe's work is largely unknown to mainstream American audiences. The movie never persuades us that Lavoe is someone whose work we should care about, let alone a man we should feel sympathy for as his life spirals out of control. Since Lopez and Anthony share a Puerto Rican ancestry, one would think that the film is a labor of love for them. Unfortunately, it turns into a vanity project in which Anthony gets to do a few stylish musical numbers and Lopez gets to chew the scenery as the shrewish wife.

Peter N. Chumo II

CREDITS

Héctor Lavoe: Marc Anthony
Nilda "Puchi" Rosado: Jennifer Lopez

Willie Colón: John Ortiz
Eddie: Manny Perez
Ralph: Vincent Laresca
Jerry Masucci: Federico Castelluccio
Johnny Pacheco: Nelson Vasquez
Origin: USA
Language: English, Spanish
Released: 2006
Production: Julio Caro, Jennifer Lopez, Simon Fields, David Maldonado; Nuyorican Productions, R-Caro Productions, Union Square Works; released by Picturehouse
Directed by: Leon Ichaso
Written by: Leon Ichaso, David Darmstaedter, Todd Anthony Bello
Cinematography by: Claudio Chea
Music by: Andres Levin
Sound: Jeff Pullman
Music Supervisor: Tracy McKnight
Editing: David Tedeschi
Art Direction: Nicholas Lundy
Costumes: Sandra Hernandez
Production Design: Sharon Lomofsky
MPAA rating: R
Running time: 116 minutes

REVIEWS

Boston Globe Online. August 3, 2007.
Chicago Sun-Times Online. August 3, 2007.
Entertainment Weekly Online. August 2, 2007.
Hollywood Reporter Online. September 18, 2006.
Los Angeles Times Online. August 3, 2007.
New York Times Online. August 3, 2007.
Variety Online. August 19, 2006.
Washington Post Online. August 3, 2007.

QUOTES

Puchi: "It was good. It was bad. It was beautiful."

TRIVIA

The title translates in English as "The Singer."

CAPTIVITY

Abduction. Confinement. Torture. Termination.
—Movie tagline

Box Office: $2.6 million

Captivity continues the sub-genre of horror films that have come to be known as "torture porn." Opinions vary as to whether this label, first used by writer David

Edelstein in *New York* magazine, has yet moved from a pejorative term to a neutral one. Staples of this genre include director Eli Roth's *Cabin Fever* (2003) and *Hostel* (2005) and director James Wan's *Saw* (2004). *Captivity* seems to find its inspiration more from *Saw* than from the other forerunners in the genre. It is mostly predictable and derivative, but it does have a few interesting touches of style from the established director, Roland Joffé. The film received an extremely negative reception both critically and commercially.

Captivity reveals the extent to which video games and graphic novels now exert a strong influence on the film industry. The film rejects character development in favor of a looping series of plot situations in which a beautiful model, Jennifer Tree (Elisha Cuthbert), is psychologically and physically tortured in a dark basement cell between her attempts to escape. In the first two-thirds of the film, a few moments of real torture (though less graphically rendered than one might expect, given the genre) mix with red herrings in a mostly static series of scenes. Jennifer's captor communicates with her through sliding drawers and the contents of four numbered lockers. Eventually, Jennifer discovers a thick, frosted-over glass that divides her cell from another in which a young man named Gary (Daniel Gillies) is a captive in similar circumstances. Snippets from video interviews that Jennifer gave before her kidnapping play on monitors throughout the killer's house. In them, she mentions her phobias, which her captor utilizes in tormenting her, or talks about the power of fame and beauty. The plot twists toward the end are predictable, and the resolution, in which the motive for the villain's actions is revealed, is probably the most mundane and disappointing aspect of the movie.

Rumors about the film at the time of its release raised the possibility that the first cut of the movie turned in by Roland Joffé may have been altered by others with new scenes added. The added material has been referred to as the directorial work of Courtney Solomon, the founder and head of After Dark Films, the horror production company that was associated with *Captivity* and with distributor Lionsgate. One likely continuity lapse appears in the film when the villain in a dual torture scene of Gary and Jennifer brutally extracts one or more of Gary's teeth with a pair of pliers only to have Gary appear unhurt in the next scene. Joffé, however, receives the only director's credit, and he has also participated in some publicity interviews for the film, talking about the way that celebrity appeal can lead to the darker side of desire. For clarity and simplicity, he will be referred to in this essay as the director.

Joffé manages to generate some visual interest. For example, he uses the moving camera—tracking or panning—at times to add nuance to the story materials. In

one shot shortly after the kidnapping, the camera follows the limp legs of Jennifer being dragged across a floor. A shoe comes off as the camera continues to follow the model's legs into a room and up onto a bed. Such a depersonalizing shot stimulates the audience's curiosity by excluding Jennifer's face and any glimpse of her captor. The longer duration of the shot both creates suspense about the final destination of Jennifer's drugged body and emphasizes the anonymous power of the villain.

Another moving-camera shot is more elaborate and darkly witty. Jennifer is tightly strapped in a chair with a gun barrel next to her head and a triggering device next to her hand. In a single shot, the camera slowly follows the intricate wires, cords, and connections from her hand up and around the space over her head to an elaborate contraption with an elongated rifle barrel that fits into a cage holding Jennifer's frightened dog, a pampered and blow-dried bichon frise. The camera settles on a timer that begins to count down the number of seconds that Jennifer has to decide whether she will pull the trigger next to her hand or do nothing and spare her dog but allow herself to be shot by the other gun pointed at her head. This slow-moving shot, making the audience curious about the final destination of the camera, visually suggests the ingenuity and inexorable control of her captor. The audience puts together the cause-effect of the torture devices and realizes that Jennifer has been outsmarted at roughly the same time that she does—and while the counter is ticking down—so that the shot fosters identification with the victim at the same time that it builds suspense.

Joffé also at times uses *mise en scene* to add visual richness. The most interesting shot in the film comes toward the middle and includes many viewing options for the audience. Jennifer has been given the key to another locker and has found in it the clothes she was wearing when kidnapped, along with her makeup kit. Joffé and director of photography Daniel C. Pearl shoot her discovery and decision to take a chance that she will be released in a long shot from the far side of her cell. The audience sees her arrange her clothes on the bed and begin to dress while in the background of the shot through the exposed glass of the other cell Gary tries to warn her about the danger of a possible trap. The frame is filled with important information in the foreground, midground, and background so that a dramatic point in the film is nicely emphasized by Joffé's rich packaging of the cinema frame. The final shot of the film presents another such visual contrast. The camera reveals a survivor from the captivity in a long shot as the former victim staggers out onto a bright but deserted city street. The character turns a corner and walks away toward safety but is dwarfed by a giant billboard of Jennifer on the side of a building next to the word "dare," a stark visual reminder of the danger just concluded.

Other key shots also emphasize the art of *mise en scene*. When Jennifer and Gary talk from their separate cells, Joffé photographs them in the same wider, full shot. They are both shown sitting on the same stone slab and inches apart but separated by the thick glass that divides their cells. This framing conveys both the physical proximity of the two victims and the likely impossibility of their reaching each other. It is a visual way of suggesting their frustration over their plight. Nearly all of the visual elements of the film are geared at having the audience feel what Jennifer must be feeling as a victim.

Because close-ups do not seem overused in the film, when Joffé does employ them they assume greater force. They, too, illustrate in graphic fashion the power of the captor and the frailty of the victim. The torture scenes of the film often rely on close-ups. In a pre-credit sequence, for example, close-ups of a container of plaster of Paris and the shot-by-shot mixing of ingredients forecast the final fate of the killer's victim before Jennifer. In another scene, close-ups of body parts being dropped in a blender—an eye ball with the socket still attached, an ear—are followed by a funnel being fitted into Jennifer's mouth, a grisly cause-effect of images that have the exaggerated effect of the panels in a graphic novel. After the opening credits, the initial shots of Jennifer are also often done in close-up (such as a very tight close-up of her mouth as she applies lipstick right after the killer has assembled, in words cut from a magazine, "Selecting the Victim"). Other early shots of Jennifer at her photo shoot often reveal her through the viewfinder of the photographer's cameras, which like the use of close-ups, depersonalize her right before her capture.

These examples of visual style correctly suggest that the film is more a vehicle for the director than for the actors. The plot does not emphasize character development, so the actors are not asked to register many emotions other than fear, anger, or duplicity. The film in many ways could even be taken as a film-school exercise—how a confined setting can be made visually interesting through the use of the elements of film. Until Jennifer discovers Gary in the adjoining cell, for example, the film has very little dialogue and almost seems like an attempt in the modern era to make a silent film.

Part of the film's negative reception probably grew out of the controversy connected with a graphic poster publicizing the film in June 2007, which After Dark Films withdrew after public complaints. The film was one of the most negatively reviewed motion pictures of 2007, earning, for example, only four favorable reviews out of sixty-one, as measured by the Web site Rottentomatoes.com. This comment by Ty Burr in the *Boston Globe* is representative of the scorn aimed at the movie: "*Captivity* is stylish in a low-budget way, but it's wholly pointless. There's a twist fans of the genre will see coming a mile away, not to mention plot holes the characters could escape through. More bothersome is that Cuthbert's character's so bland …that it's tough to care what happens to her."

Glenn Hopp

CREDITS

Jennifer: Elisha Cuthbert
Gary: Daniel Gillies
Disantos: Laz Alonso
Ben: Pruitt Taylor Vince
Bettiger: Michael Harney
Origin: USA, Russia
Language: English
Released: 2007
Production: Mark Damon, Sergei Konov, Gary Mehman, Leonid Minkovski; After Dark Films, Foresight Unlimited, Ramco; released by Lions Gate
Directed by: Roland Joffé
Written by: Larry Cohen, Joseph Tura
Cinematography by: Daniel Pearl
Music by: Marco Beltrami
Sound: Scott Sanders
Music Supervisor: Frankie Pine, Allison Wright Clark
Editing: Richard Nord
Production Design: Addis Gadzhiev
MPAA rating: R
Running time: 85 minutes

REVIEWS

Boston Globe Online. July 13, 2007.
Entertainment Weekly. July 27, 2007, p. 52.
Guardian Online. June 22, 2007.
Hollywood Reporter Online. July 16, 2007.
Los Angeles Times Online. July 16, 2007.
New York Times Online. July 14, 2007.
The Observer Online. June 24, 2007.
Variety Online. July 13, 2007.

QUOTES

Ben: "Why do good things happen to bad people? That's the mystery."

AWARDS

Nomination:

Golden Raspberries 2007: Worst Actress (Cuthbert), Worst Director (Joffé), Worst Horror Movie.

CATCH AND RELEASE

Life is messy…love is messier.
—Movie tagline

Box Office: $15.5 million

Although *Catch and Release* is set against the scenic Colorado mountains, little else about the film seems natural or organic. The behavior of the main characters strains believability, the mood shifts wildly from scene to scene, and the story is riddled with too many subplots that fail to resonate. Writer/director Susannah Grant ambitiously attempts to juggle romance, comedy, and drama, but drops the ball on all counts. Unfortunately she is handicapped from the start by her film's rather queasy premise: Girl meets boy, boy dies…girl quickly falls for dead boy's best friend.

When *Catch and Release* begins, Gray (Jennifer Garner) is having a bad day. She is supposed to be celebrating her wedding, but instead she has just buried her fiancé, Grady, who was killed in an accident the weekend before their nuptials. No longer able to afford their new house, Gray moves in with Grady's roommates, Sam (a manic Kevin Smith) and Dennis (Sam Jaeger). Also crashing there is Los Angeles director Fritz (Timothy Olyphant), Grady's childhood friend. While settling Grady's estate, Gray soon learns he had a $1 million cache that supported a West Coast mistress, Maureen (Juliette Lewis), and their four-year-old son, Mattie (Joshua Friesen). As Gray copes with the knowledge of her fiancé's secret life, she reevaluates her own choices and finds herself falling for the roguish Fritz.

Simply by virtue of her dimpled cheeks and painfully swollen lips, Garner is at first sympathetic as the young widow. Gray is twice granted voice-over narration—at the beginning of the film and the conclusion—and in these brief moments, she comes alive as a unique, credible character. At her fiancé's funeral, she addresses him in her thoughts: "How could you leave me alone with all these people? You know I hate crowds. And high heels. I'm wearing high heels. I don't know what I'm doing. I would if you were here." In the intervening scenes, however, the character gets lost as Grant bombards Gray with obstacle after obstacle. Not only must she deal with her fiancé's death, mistress, and son, but she is also required to fend off the advances of the lovesick Dennis, tussle with Grady's mother (Fiona Shaw) over her fiancé's estate, tend to Sam after his suicide attempt, and begin a romantic relationship with Fritz. There is barely a moment for Gray to catch her breath, much less the audience's sympathy. Compounding the frantic pace is the overwhelming alternative pop soundtrack, which bridges nearly every scene. The pac-

ing of a film that takes place after a sudden death would have benefited from moments of silence.

In addition to jumping through myriad emotional hoops, Gray is shuttled from one sitcomish situation to the next. *Catch and Release* is chockfull of well-worn romantic-comedy tropes, like the scenes when Gray drinks too much, Gray gets caught dressing up in her wedding gown ("It's a girl thing," she explains), and Gray slaps Fritz before she swoops in for a kiss. By favoring these pratfalls over true pathos, Grant makes her heroine seem bewildered, not grieved. With the exception of the framing voice-overs, no evidence of Gray's internal turmoil is presented; as a result, the character is shallow and nondescript, and neither of the love relationships carries much weight. Though Olyphant is at times tender and sexy as Garner's romantic foil (the kiss after that slap generates considerable heat), he is given little to do here but find his costar adorable and "surprising." Indeed, he is so detached in his scenes with the other actors (especially Smith), he almost seems unaware of their presence.

The story's chronology is also problematic. It is never clear how much time has passed between Grady's funeral and Gray's new relationship with Fritz. This ambiguity may be a result of sloppy editing, but it seems more likely that Grant is deliberately being coy—lest Gray seem too cold. Based on her own set-up, Grant is fighting a losing battle. By the film's logic, Gray would not have found her true love (Fritz) unless her fiancé had died first. *Catch and Release* may have aimed to be a lesson about the human spirit triumphing over tragedy, but instead it is a distasteful twist on the facile philosophy that "everything happens for a reason."

The film does boast a few bright spots, however. The mountainous backdrop of Colorado is ravishing, and the detailed production design makes the characters' Boulder home look realistically lived-in and overflowing. In addition, Juliette Lewis delivers a truly winning performance as Grady's mistress, Maureen. Even as the other woman, she endears herself to the audience with a combination of warmth, quirkiness, and pluck. True, she has played this type of role before, but no other actress does "kooky" so well. The scenes between Sam, Maureen, and her son, Mattie, are among the movie's best. In fact, young Friesen nearly steals the film with a single line. When Sam tells the boy that his father was a great fisherman, Mattie lights up, then clarifies, "My dad was a superhero!" Here, Grant gracefully illustrates how Mattie fails to comprehend the gravity of his loss, and it is a truly poignant moment. It is a shame there are not more like it in the film.

In the hands of a highly competent director, a film can combine romance, comedy, and drama, but first-timer Grant lacks skills and focus necessary to coherently balance these elements. She has commented that she wanted *Catch and Release* "to be something that doesn't feel the same as what you've seen before." While her intentions are admirable, she has failed to pull off this feat. Ultimately the film comes across as muddled rather than multifaceted.

Marisa Carroll

CREDITS

Gray Wheeler: Jennifer Garner
Fritz: Timothy Olyphant
Sam: Kevin Smith
Maureen: Juliette Lewis
Dennis: Sam Jaeger
Mrs. Douglas: Fiona Shaw
Mattie: Joshua Friesen
Origin: USA
Language: English
Released: 2007
Production: Jenno Topping; Columbia Pictures, Relativity; released by Sony Pictures
Directed by: Susannah Grant
Written by: Susannah Grant
Cinematography by: John Lindley
Music by: BT (Brian Transeau), Tommy Stinson
Sound: Larry Sutton
Editing: Anne Coates
Art Direction: Shannon Grover
Costumes: Tish Monaghan
Production Design: Brent Thomas
MPAA rating: PG-13
Running time: 110 minutes

REVIEWS

Boston Globe Online. January 25, 2007.
Boxoffice Online. January 26, 2007.
Chicago Sun-Times Online. January 26, 2007.
Detroit Free Press Online. January 26, 2007.
Los Angeles Times Online. January 26, 2007.
New York Times Online. January 26, 2007.
Rolling Stone Online. January 24, 2007.
San Francisco Chronicle. January 26, 2007, p. E6.
Variety Online. January 24, 2007.
Washington Post. January 26, 2007, p. C5.

QUOTES

Fritz (to Gray, who's wearing her wedding dress): "Nice dress."
Gray: "I never got a chance to wear it. It's a girl thing."

TRIVIA

Jennifer Garner was pregnant while filming this movie.

CHARLIE WILSON'S WAR

A stiff drink. A little mascara. A lot of nerve. Who said they couldn't bring down the Soviet empire?
—Movie tagline

Based on a true story. You think we could make all this up?
—Movie tagline

Box Office: $66.7 million

Of all the movies about Iran and Afghanistan to come out of Hollywood in 2007, the most frivolous and puzzling is surely *Charlie Wilson's War*. With a cast headed by megastars Tom Hanks and Julia Roberts, this film, directed by the veteran Mike Nichols and released for the Christmas season, is a big-ticket excursion into a hall of mirrors.

Nichols, a Hollywood liberal, has taken on the story of a 1980s Congressman who supposedly engineered and bankrolled the CIA's covert war in Afghanistan, in which the United States secretly helped the mujahideen defeat the Soviet invaders. *Charlie Wilson's War* is "based on a true story" in the form of a book about Wilson by George Crile, but that does not mean it is automatically credible. The screenplay was written by *The West Wing* producer Aaron Sorkin, and it plays like a lightweight television satire. But no matter how close to the facts this version of history comes, it is impossible to take the film seriously. It is a cheap and unfunny comedy joined with unconvincing and expedient political sentiment.

During the Reagan presidency, folks like Nichols were not cheering on the covert war against the Soviets. But in this film, the characters continue to gush about how much they want to kill Russians, and the film spends plenty of time on the atrocities committed by the Soviets against Afghan civilians, painting the rebels as heroic freedom fighters (and completely ignoring the fact that the mujahideen were the breeding grounds for the Taliban and Al Qaeda). Wilson, played by Hanks, is portrayed as a savior of American security and values, simply because he had the clout to increase the Congressional "black" budget (the secret appropriations for special operations) from $5 million to $500 million and because he helped arrange to funnel weapons to the Afghan resistance. Not only does *Charlie Wilson's War* blatantly cheer on its protagonist and his secret war, it blames Congress for not "finishing the job" by funding education and reconstruction. Then it leaves the unenlightened viewer hanging as to what the consequences were of not finishing the job—namely, the subsequent mess in Afghanistan.

The film wants us to believe, contrary to documented evidence, that were it not for two cowboys, Wilson (Tom Hanks) and crusty CIA journeyman Gust Avrakotos (Philip Seymour Hoffman), and the help of a rich Texan right-wing Christian zealot, Joanne Herring (Julia Roberts), the CIA establishment would not have given the mujahideen enough help and the Soviets would have won in Afghanistan and extended their influence southward toward the Persian Gulf. In other words, the Reagan administration was not hawkish enough about the Cold War, according to this revisionist history from the director who during the 1980s was directing films like *Silkwood* (1983).

In this muddle of a morality play, the filmmakers lionize the principals' politics and then try to humanize them by making them men and women of loose morals. Hanks as Wilson is a boozing philanderer whose staff (dubbed in the credits as "Charlie's Angels") is a bunch of brainy sexpots headed by chief of staff Bonnie Bach (Amy Adams, a little less provocative and cleavage-revealing than the others). Wilson is a Texan of little accomplishment but apparently pays only lip service to his Christian constituents. Nichols takes pains to include a scene in which Wilson tells a local bigwig not to worry about the ACLU fighting a Nativity scene at the local firehouse; there are plenty of churches the crèche could be moved to, he says. And he blurts out to Gust that all his major funding sources are Jews who back him because he is such a major supporter of Israel. These seem like calculated tactics to bring audiences along who might not automatically cheer for the likes of Wilson.

Roberts, dolled up in frighteningly intense makeup and a hairdo that itself resembles a jet fighter, is apparently having fun playing a bedrock conservative whose special interest in the Afghanistan crisis is never sufficiently explained. She stands accused of hypocrisy simply because she beds down Charlie, though in this film all male-female relationships seem to follow the rules of the Playboy mansion. And in fact, the thesis of the film is that U.S. foreign policy was saved because Julia Roberts played Domme to a sex-addicted Tom Hanks.

Hoffman's Gust is the true locus of liberal conscience in the film: though firmly anti-Communist, he is profane and hardheaded, stands up for descendants of immigrants like himself against bigotry, and is fervently anti-religious. (The real Gust was expelled from Greece after abetting government thugs.) His worry, points out Wilson, is that sometime soon God will be on both sides—one of several easy digs at the coming war on terror.

Hoffman provides all the laughable lines in a furiously sarcastic interpretation of a career maverick who finally gets his day in the sun. The rest of the film is an awful mess. The tone verges from unrepentant Hugh Hefner (the opening scene offers a *Playboy* model and some strippers cavorting in a hot tub in Las Vegas with the congressman) to cheap humanitarian posing (the film includes not one, but two, visits to an Afghan refugee camp in which limbless children talk about picking up land mines, and Bonnie asks one "What do you want to be when you grow up?" and Ned Beatty bloviates about freedom) to laughably amateur war scenes (a couple of Afghan resistance fighters shooting down a Soviet helicopter look buffoonish, and there are seemingly endless superimposed stats about planes downed that make the war seem like a sporting event). The tone is just a step short of Mel Brooks—at any moment you expect the heroic Afghan troops to break out into song—yet we are supposed to take this seriously. But there are no characters, scenes, dialogue, or plot that any intelligent person could take seriously.

Charlie Wilson's War is embarrassingly amateurish, incredibly tacky, politically hypocritical, and very rarely funny. It is a pointless exercise in Monday-morning quarterbacking, history rewritten to make it look like the heartland Americans that Hollywood rarely speaks for were the true heroes, and that their only resistance was some fuzzy-headed bureaucrats whose motivations are completely opaque. It is an elaborate setup for a few halfhearted pokes at current foreign policy, most of which fall flat either for lack of substance or lack of clarity. What are big stars like Hanks and Roberts doing in this dog-and-pony show of a movie? Well, Hanks is doing a lot of earnest mumbling, and his portrayal is utterly unconvincing, but it is still more plausible than Roberts as a vampish version of Tammy Faye Bakker. *Charlie Wilson's War* is Mike Nichols's folly.

Michael Betzold

CREDITS

Charlie Wilson: Tom Hanks
Joanne Herring: Julia Roberts
Gust Arrakotos: Philip Seymour Hoffman
Bonnie Bach: Amy Adams
Doc Long: Ned Beatty
Jane Liddle: Emily Blunt
President Zia: Om Puri
Zvi: Ken Stott
Henry Cravely: John Slattery
Harold Holt: Denis O'Hare
Larry Liddle: Peter Gerety

Paul Brown Brian Markinson
Origin: USA
Language: English
Released: 2007
Production: Tom Hanks, Gary Goetzman; Playtone Picture, Participant Production, Relativity; released by Universal
Directed by: Mike Nichols
Written by: Aaron Sorkin
Cinematography by: Stephen Goldblatt
Music by: James Newton Howard
Sound: Peter Hliddal
Editing: John Bloom, Antonia Van Drimmelen
Art Direction: Bradford Ricker, Marco Trentini
Costumes: Albert Wolsky
Production Design: Victor Kempster
MPAA rating: R
Running time: 97 minutes

REVIEWS

Boston Globe Online. December 21, 2007.
Chicago Sun-Times Online. December 21, 2007.
Entertainment Weekly Online. December 12, 2007.
Hollywood Reporter Online. November 28, 2007.
Los Angeles Times Online. December 21, 2007.
New York Times Online. December 21, 2007.
New Yorker Online. December 24, 2007.
Rolling Stone Online. December 13, 2007.
San Francisco Chronicle. December 21, 2007, p. E1.
Variety Online. November 28, 2007.
Washington Post. December 21, 2007, p. C1.

QUOTES

Charlie Wilson: "You know you've reached rock bottom when you're told you have character flaws by a man who hanged his predecessor in a military coup."

AWARDS

Nomination:

Oscars 2007: Support. Actor (Hoffman)
British Acad. 2007: Support. Actor (Hoffman)
Golden Globes 2008: Actor—Mus./Comedy (Hanks), Film—Mus./Comedy, Screenplay, Support. Actor (Hoffman), Support. Actress (Roberts).

CODE NAME: THE CLEANER

In a dirty world, he's our only hope.
—Movie tagline

Box Office: $8.1 million

Director Les Mayfield and his writing team of Robert Adetuyi and George Gallo have crafted an action-comedy that frenetically whiplashes between action and comedy, never finding an acceptable rhythm and ending up a film that does not work in either genre. A prime example of this dichotomy may be found in the middle of one particularly suspenseful sequence when the hero, Jake Rodgers (Cedric the Entertainer), halts the action to engage in a session of clog dancing. As Scott Tobias of the *A.V. Club* wrote, "though it's labeled as a comedy, in the majority of the scenes, it's like a straight-to-video action thriller, albeit with Cedric feebly trying to assert himself whenever he gets the opportunity."

The film was not without promise. The concept is an engaging one—a man suffering from amnesia has to guess his own identity based on the clues around him. Jake wakes up in a hotel room next to a dead man and has no memory of who he is or how he got there. This setup offers hope of a humorous twist on *The Bourne Identity* (2002). Jake staggers out to the hotel lobby where he meets a beautiful woman, Diane (Nicollette Sheridan), who claims to be his wife. She takes him to a mansion that she says is his. The house and his alleged wife are unfamiliar to Jake, but he goes along with the ruse until he can decide upon his next move. Predictable fish-out-of-water comedy ensues as Jake orders a servant to fetch him the latest copy of *Jet* and some Skittles.

Jake eventually becomes suspicious and escapes to a local diner where an attractive waitress, Gina (Lucy Liu), claims to be his girlfriend. He learns that his nickname is "The Cleaner" and assumes that he must be some sort of secret agent. Demonstrating some martial arts moves, he deduces that he must be a very dangerous man until the amused Gina informs him that his nickname actually refers to his career as a janitor at the computer game company across the street. His "moves," she tells him, come from a video game he particularly enjoys. Although Jake is willing to accept the less glamorous version of himself, odd things keep happening to make him believe that perhaps he is some sort of spy. Is it possible he saw something he should not have when he was sweeping up at the computer game company? Again, such ideas are intriguing, but the writers do not bother to explore them beyond the surface level.

Cedric the Entertainer does not have the energy or acting ability that the role requires. He gamely attempts a few of the comedic bits, but the majority of his performance seems phoned-in. The highlight of the film is watching him test out his new life in the mansion, but, unfortunately, the action portion of the action-comedy moves the plot along to far less humorous territory.

Liu and Sheridan serve only as attractive visual diversions, marking time within the plodding script. The one bit of actual comedic spark among the supporting cast comes from a short scene with Jacuzzi (Niecy Nash), the sassy parking attendant at Jake's building. When he arrives to park his car, she informs him that they had a romantic interlude at the office party and that she would like to claim the dinner he promised her, and a nice dinner at that. "I don't want no damn nine piece!" she barks indignantly. Still, such brief moments of humor are not nearly enough to elevate *Code Name: The Cleaner*. Brian Lowry, in a prescient review for *Variety*, wrote that the film "is an especially limp star vehicle that delivers a few widely spaced moments of frivolity before what should be a quick mop-up trip to the DVD aisles."

Jill Hamilton

CREDITS

Jake Rodgers: Cedric the Entertainer
Gina: Lucy Liu
Diane: Nicolette Sheridan
Eric Hauck: Mark Dacascos
Shaw: Callum Keith Rennie
Jacuzzi: Niecy Nash
Riley: Will Patton
Ronnie: DeRay David
Origin: USA
Language: English
Released: 2007
Production: Jay Stern, Eric C. Rhone, Cedric the Entertainer, Brett Ratner; Rat Entertainment, FilmEngine, A Bird & a Bear; released by New Line Cinema
Directed by: Les Mayfield
Written by: Robert Adetuyi, George Gallo
Cinematography by: David Franco
Music by: George S. Clinton
Sound: Eric J. Batut
Music Supervisor: Kevin J. Edelman
Editing: Ariel Galvan
Art Direction: Ross Dempster
Costumes: Jenni Gullett
Production Design: Doug Higgins
MPAA rating: PG-13
Running time: 91 minutes

REVIEWS

A.V. Club Online. January 5, 2007.
Entertainment Weekly. January 19, 2007, p. 60.
Hollywood Reporter Online. January 1, 2007.
Los Angeles Times Online. January 5, 2007.
New York Times Online. January 5, 2007.
San Francisco Chronicle. January 5, 2007, p. E6.
Variety Online. January 4, 2007.
Washington Post. January 5, 2007, p. C1.

QUOTES

Jake: "I'm rich. I live in a big house and I'm married to a white woman. Am I Lionel Richie?"

AWARDS

Nomination:

Golden Raspberries 2007: Worst Support. Actress (Sheridan).

COLOR ME KUBRICK

They wanted something for nothing. He gave them nothing for something.
—Movie tagline

A True...ish Story.
—Movie tagline

Anyone considering impersonating a celebrity would do well to choose a genius. After all, what is the challenge of pretending to be just the average singer or actor or football star? It also helps if said genius is reclusive, reducing the chance of bumping into the double and spoiling the charade. *Color Me Kubrick* (also known as *Colour Me Kubrick: A True...ish Story*) never explains why the British con man Alan Conway (John Malkovich) chose legendary American film director Stanley Kubrick, but pretending to be the man who made *Dr. Strangelove or; How I Learned to Stop Worrying and Love the Bomb* (1964), *2001: A Space Odyssey* (1968), and *A Clockwork Orange* (1971) surely worked. Though looking, acting, and speaking nothing like the real Kubrick, Conway was able to obtain food, drinks, sex, and money simply by promising to help the careers of aspiring young actors, musicians, and restaurateurs. Made by Kubrick's colleagues, *Color Me Kubrick* is both a character study and an examination of the mischief created by the cult of celebrity.

The film consists of a series of encounters between Conway and his victims, mostly working-class young men with whom he hopes to have sex. Screenwriter Anthony Frewin works slight variations on these encounters, though several are somewhat repetitious. The objects of Conway's attentions are wary at first because of his scruffy appearance, only to perk up once they discover who he claims to be, all seemingly having heard of Kubrick or, at least, his films. Conway takes matters as far as possible until suspicions set in and he must move on to another target.

Conway's success is especially amazing since he does not actually know that much about Kubrick. Attempting to pick up someone in a bar, he is flattered by an impressed young man (Marc Warren) who begins listing all of Kubrick's films. Conway does not blink when Stanley Kramer's *Judgment at Nuremberg* (1961) is included to trap him in his lie. Conway also claims to have directed Greta Garbo, who made her last film over a decade before Kubrick's first, and to have played the young Pip in David Lean's *Great Expectations* (1946). Kubrick was reportedly less annoyed by Conway's audacity than by learning that his doppelganger had seen only portions of his films and did not like what he saw. Conway continues to succeed in his deception because his victims want to believe him, needing to elevate themselves through their association with a celebrity. Matters begin unraveling when a drunken Conway encounters, in a London restaurant, a skeptical Frank Rich (William Hootkins) of the *New York Times*. Rich's subsequent article helped unmask Conway.

There are several "in-jokes" that are scattered throughout the film. In one of these instances, Conway claims to be considering Malkovich for his next film. That his listener is not sure who Malkovich is continues the actor's self-mockery begun in *Being John Malkovich* (1999), in which no one can quite remember exactly what films he has been in. Also, when sent to a mental institution, Conway encounters a patient played by Ken Russell, director of *Women in Love* (1969), whose daughter, Victoria, is the costume designer for *Color Me Kubrick*. Another patient is played by Peter Sallis, best known as the voice of Gromit's friend Wallace, whose son, Crispian, is the film's production designer.

Additional in-jokes come courtesy of Frewin, Kubrick's assistant from the late 1960s until the director's death in 1999, and director Brian W. Cook, Kubrick's assistant director on *Barry Lyndon* (1975), *The Shining* (1980), and *Eyes Wide Shut* (1999). Marisa Berenson, who plays a small role, starred in *Barry Lyndon*. (Many of the in-jokes are explained in the excellent making-of documentary included in the DVD of *Color Me Kubrick,* which appeared a few days after the film opened in New York and Los Angeles.)

Malkovich approaches the part as a variation of Peter Sellers's method of playing multiple roles in *Dr. Strangelove.* He adjusts Conway's personality from scene to scene, toning down or turning up the con man's camp histrionics. Conway's effeminate side is accented by Russell's sometimes flamboyant costumes, dressing the character in semi-drag at times. Malkovich also uses different voices and accents, including a southern one to charm a trusting restaurateur (Richard E. Grant). Malkovich comes close to losing control at times but gives the film an undeniable energy and panache. Although

Color Me Kubrick is essentially a series of sketches, all the pieces flow smoothly together. Cook's understated style is reminiscent of Bruce Robinson's *Withnail & I* (1987), with the presence of one of that film's stars, Grant, being a possible acknowledgement of the filmmakers' debt.

Conway, unfortunately, did not live to see this tribute to his guile. The bumbling impersonator died in 1998, just months before the real Kubrick.

Michael Adams

CREDITS

Alan Conway: John Malkovich
Lee Pratt: James Davidson
Jasper: Richard E. Grant
Rupert Rodnight: Luke Mably
Norman: Terence Rigby
Melvyn: James Dreyfus
Cyril: Peter Bowles
Freddie: Leslie Phillips
Frank Rich: William Hootkins
Origin: Great Britain, France
Language: English
Released: 2005
Production: Michael Fitzgerald, Brian Cook; Europacorp, Isle of Man, First Choice Films; released by Magnolia Pictures
Directed by: Brian Cook
Written by: Anthony Frewin
Cinematography by: Howard Atherton
Music by: Bryan Adams
Sound: Peter Glossop, Ed Colyer
Editing: Alan Strachan
Art Direction: Paul Ghirardani
Costumes: Victoria Russell
Production Design: Crispian Sallis
MPAA rating: Unrated
Running time: 86 minutes

REVIEWS

Boxoffice Online. March 23, 2007.
Chicago Sun-Times Online. March 23, 2007.
Entertainment Weekly. March 30, 2007, p. 54.
Hollywood Reporter Online. March 23, 2007.
Los Angeles Times Online. March 23, 2007.
New York Times Online. March 23, 2007.
San Francisco Chronicle. March 23, 2007, p. E5.
Variety Online. November 21, 2005.
Washington Post Online. March 23, 2007.

TRIVIA

The UK heavy metal band Head-On, which is featured in the movie, was hand-picked from 400 other bands.

THE COMEBACKS

Keep your eye on the ball.
—Movie tagline

Box Office: $13.3 million

The Comebacks in no way remedies the recent precipitous slide in the quality of genre spoofs, epitomized by the *Movie* films: *Scary Movie* (2000) and its sequels, *Date Movie* (2006), and *Epic Movie* (2007). The filmmakers might as well have called it *Sports Movie*. It is indeed a long descent from the heyday of lampoon, epitomized by such classics as *Airplane!* (1980) and *The Naked Gun: From the Files of Police Squad!* (1988).

In a send-up of recent inspirational sports films, such as *Rudy* (1993), *Radio* (2003), and *Remember the Titans* (2000), down-on-his-luck former coach Lambeau Fields (David Koechner) receives one last chance at Heartland State University, in Plain Folks, Texas. The film's one semi-clever sequence shows why Fields needs this last gasp. The montage shows him helping to cause some of sports more famous gaffes, such as Bill Buckner's error in the 1986 World Series and Zinedine Zidane's head-butt incident in the 2006 World Cup.

The Comebacks gets the structure of the sports film right, even adding the rebellious, bad-girl gymnast. Of course, that is the easy part. The difficulty lies in creating something unique and funny within that timeworn structure. This is a genre ripe for satire, because, as Wesley Morris points out in the *Boston Globe,* while watching *The Comebacks* "you realize not only how many of these inspirational films get cranked out and how bad they are, but how indistinguishable their scenes are from each other." The "recruiting and building the team" sequence is where director Tom Brady uses that fact to make most of his hit-and-run references to other sports films, dropping in a Mark Wahlberg look-alike to get *Invincible* (2006) out of the way, and bringing in a soccer-playing Indian girl to kick, for a *Bend it Like Beckham* (2002) moment.

The problem remains that the movie spends too much time name-checking and refilming scenes from other movies and simply adding pratfalls, fart jokes, or raunchy language. It even stoops to spoofing the already-existing satires of the genre, such as *Dodgeball: A True Underdog Story* (2004), with an aping of the scene in which Rip Torn throws tools at his charges. Here, they up the ante by using firearms, to less-than-hilarious effect. The jokes, while showing small flashes of passing wit, come off as labored, obvious, or flat. In one such joke, the name of the star running back destined for injury, Aseel Tare (Robert Ri'chard) is pronounced "ACL Tear" by the coach. Unfortunately, the gag is repeated so much that it becomes tiresome.

The Comebacks ultimately fails in its attempt to spoof a genre worthy of a little poking by not providing enough inspired lunacy, and, ironically, playing many of the scenes too broadly. David Koechner tries vainly to prop up the film, but that effort shows up too obviously on screen as overly manic. While it is not as execrable as, say, *Epic Movie,* it is also nowhere near as good as it could have been.

Jim Craddock

CREDITS

Coach Lambeau Fields: David Koechner
Barb Fields: Melora Hardin
Michelle Fields: Brooke Nevin
Freddie Wiseman: Carl Weathers
Lance Truman: Matthew Lawrence
Mr. Truman: Nick Searcy
I-Pod: Jermaine Williams
Jorge: Jesse Garcia
Buddy Boy: George Back
Foreign Exchange Student: Eric Christian Olsen
Mailman: Will Arnett
Cowboy: Bradley Cooper
Sheriff: Dax Shepard
Trotter: Jackie Long
Aseel Tare: Robert Ri'chard
Randy Randinger: Martin Spanjers
Barber: Jon(athan) Gries
Toilet Bowl ref: Andy Dick
Sports Judge: Kerri Kenney
Warden: Dennis Rodman
Chip Imitation: Frank Caliendo
Titans coach: Finesse Mitchell
Jizminder Featherfoot: Noureen DeWulf
Himself: John Salley (Cameo)
Himself: Lawrence Taylor (Cameo)
Himself: Eric Dickerson (Cameo)
Himself: Michael Irvin (Cameo)
Origin: USA
Language: English
Released: 2007
Production: Peter Abrams, Andrew Panay, Robert Levy; Tapestry Films; released by Fox Atomic
Directed by: Tom Brady
Written by: Ed Yeager, Joey Gutierrez
Cinematography by: Anthony B. Richmond
Music by: Christopher Lennertz
Sound: Walter Anderson
Music Supervisor: Buck Damon
Editing: Alan Edward Bell
Art Direction: Douglas Cumming

Costumes: Salvador Perez
Production Design: Marc Fisichella
MPAA rating: PG-13
Running time: 84 minutes

REVIEWS

Boston Globe Online. October 20, 2007.
Entertainment Weekly Online. October 24, 2007.
Hollywood Reporter Online. October 23, 2007.
Los Angeles Times Online. October 22, 2007.
New York Times Online. October 20, 2007.
Variety Online. October 19, 2007.

QUOTES

Michelle Fields: "I want to have what you and mom have."
Coach Lambeau Fields: "Herpes?"

COMEDY OF POWER
(L'ivresse du pouvoir)

Director Claude Chabrol's latest film to be released in the U.S., *Comedy of Power* (also known as *L'ivresse du pouvoir*), is an exacting and ruthless study of...ruthlessness. This sophisticated dark comedy/drama will not satisfy everyone, but discriminating audiences will have a rewarding time.

Though based on an actual event—the so-called "Affaire Elf" scandal of the 1990s—*Comedy of Power* should be accessible to viewers who have never heard of the French political imbroglio that involved oil company executives in an Enron-styled setup. The goal of the film is not so much to recreate history as it is to unveil how power affects the human condition on a variety of levels. Even some of the details become less important as the narrative takes unexpected and intriguing turns.

On its surface, *Comedy of Power* (which really should be called *Folly of Power*) is one of Chabrol's most plot-driven films. In his screenplay (co-written with Odile Barski), Isabelle Huppert plays Jeanne Charmant-Killman, an examining magistrate, who holds a prestigious position in French government. Jeanne, known as "the Piranha," is currently setting her sights on the corrupt businessman Humeau (François Berléand), who has embezzled funds, in part to provide for his high maintenance mistress. Meanwhile, at home, Jeanne's zealous focus on her work is taking its toll on her marriage to Philippe (Robin Renucci), and Jeanne finds more sympathy and solace in her nephew (Thomas Chabrol, the director's son) than in her husband.

As Jeanne's investigation evolves, she discovers a wider and wider web of lies and corruption. What she does not know is that her own boss is involved with the bad guys as they plot to distract and dissuade her from her mission. One ploy includes "kicking her upstairs" with a promotion. Another ruse forces Jeanne to accept a female judge (Marilyne Canto) as a coworker, on the flawed theory that two women will destroy each other (instead of the boys' club they are scrutinizing).

After she is hurt in a car accident, Jeanne suspects she has been targeted by her enemies. Even having bodyguards assigned to her does not reassure Jeanne. As Jeanne's home life is overwhelmed by her work life, Philippe feels displaced and unwanted and decides to leave Jeanne. Later, Philippe is nearly killed in yet another suspicious "accident," but Jeanne soldiers on. In the end, she realizes her pursuit will never end nor will it be completely realized: the powers that be are just too well entrenched and all encompassing. Jeanne may still be "the Piranha," but she will always be surrounded by larger, sneakier sharks.

Claude Chabrol's prodigious and fascinating oeuvre often concerns crime and criminals. The difference in this minor masterwork is that the focus is much less psychopathological—at least on the surface (Huppert herself usually plays the "bad guy" in her earlier, more Hitchcockian collaborations with the director).

Much of the time, *Comedy of Power* appears to be a straightforward melodrama about a dedicated detective (Jeanne, the judge) and the cohort of white-collar crooks who try to elude her. In Chabrol's hands, however, the literal is transformed into something far more ambiguous, unexpected, and ultimately tragic. Yet, the tragedy is not individual—no one dies and the characters never lose their hubris—instead, it is a societal tragedy, no matter what political party happens to be in charge. Power is so inherently abused, it makes one wonder if justice (or the French Revolution mantra, "Liberté, Égalité, Fraternité") will ever be possible. Thus, quite subtly, *Comedy of Power* represents Chabrol's most pessimistic, downbeat, and anarchic film.

If *Comedy of Power* had been made in Hollywood, Jeanne at least would have been a crusading heroine—something like Meryl Streep's *Silkwood* (1983), Sissy Spacek's *Marie* (1985), or Julia Roberts's *Erin Brockovich* (2000). As played by Huppert (and written by Chabrol and Barski), Jeanne is a much more complicated figure, not terribly likable at times, particularly in how she treats her husband, but also a victim of class (her rise-from-the-bottom background plays a minor but interesting role in the story). Of course, in a European film, the issue of class is often more pronounced. Since Jeanne finds herself caught up in the sweep of power, even her steely integrity comes into question, not a twist a mainstream American film would have included.

The production is impeccably well done. Chabrol directs each scene with great purpose—nothing seems extraneous, even when we are not sure why certain elements are present (for example, the emphasis on the nephew at the beginning of the story). During the best part of the film, Chabrol uses what can only be described as black leader (a completely dark screen for an extended period) and shocking jump cuts to juxtapose the disintegrating marriage with the increasingly devious deceptions. Here, the editing by Monique Fardoulis and the camerawork by Chabrol favorite Eduardo Serra deserve special mention for their almost Godardian style of self-reflexivity.

At the same time, the richly detailed sets, from the judge's stuffy chamber to her "tasteful" middle-class apartment, help give the film a naturalistic, documentary feel, and Matthieu Chabrol's score is low-key, never obtrusive (quite unlike some early Chabrol films, including *Les Biches* [1968] and *La Femme Infidèle* [1969], where the music deliberately called attention to itself). It is as though Chabrol wishes to draw us into a "real" narrative, then remind us on occasion it is only a story. This is also the case from the start, during the pre-credit sequence, when the following is stated: "Any resemblance to persons living or dead is, as they say, coincidental."

Best of all are the performances, particularly of the superb Huppert in her seventh film (over a three-decade period) with Chabrol. It is quite amazing how this actress has been able for so many years to maintain a consistent star persona while playing so many different roles. Huppert also portrayed a much more vulnerable and sympathetic woman in Joachim Lafosse's *Private Property* (2006). Compare these two parts with the psychopathic one she daringly depicted in Michael Haneke's *Piano Teacher* (2001), and you have an idea of her range. Like the best actors, Huppert suggests a great deal by doing very little, and she contrasts nicely with the purposefully more colorful performances by Patrick Bruel, Jean-François Balmer, and François Berléand, as just three of the pompous baddies. Thomas Chabrol also makes a very fine impression in the key role of Jeanne's nephew and closest confidante.

Comedy of Power received mostly high praise from the reviewers, although there were a few dissenters. *Variety's* Lisa Nesselson called the film, "enjoyable as a sardonic glimpse of unspoken codes at the intersection of politics and business," while the *Village Voice's* Jim Ridley also called it "enjoyable" but also a "curiously weightless trifle...."

By the end of *Comedy of Power*, we have more questions than answers, but that is how it should be in a film as dense and mature as this unassuming jewel.

Eric Monder

CREDITS

Jeanne Charmant-Killman: Isabelle Huppert
Michel Humeau: François Berléand
Felix: Thomas Chabrol
Philippe: Robin Renucci
Jacques: Patrick Bruel
Erika: Marilyne Canto
Boldi: Jean-François Balmer
Origin: France, Germany
Language: French
Released: 2006
Production: Patrick Godeau; Alicelio, France 2 Cinema, Ajoz Films, Integral Film; released by Koch Lorber Films
Directed by: Claude Chabrol
Written by: Claude Chabrol, Odile Barski
Cinematography by: Eduardo Serra
Music by: Matthieu Chabrol
Sound: Thierry Lebon, Pierre Lenoir
Editing: Monique Fardoulis
Art Direction: Catherine Pierrat
Costumes: Mic Cheminal
Production Design: Francoise Benoit-Fresco
MPAA rating: Unrated
Running time: 110 minutes

REVIEWS

Boston Globe Online. February 16, 2007.
Entertainment Weekly Online. January 17, 2007.
Hollywood Reporter Online. February 21, 2006.
New York Times Online. January 5, 2007.
Variety Online. February 16, 2006.
Village Voice Online. January 2, 2007.

TRIVIA

The scenario is based on a true story, the "Affaire Elf" political and financial scandal in France.

CONTROL

Ian Curtis's gravestone is inscribed with the title of one of his best-loved songs, "Love Will Tear Us Apart." Originally released in April 1980, after Curtis's suicide by hanging that May, the heartbreakingly beautiful song became his band Joy Division's only chart hit that remains popular to this day. After his death, the band from Manchester broke up and reformed as New Order. *Control* is Anton Corbijn's beautifully crafted and emotionally rich black-and-white biographical film about the late Ian Curtis (1956–1980), singer and songwriter with the post-punk band he formed in 1976, Joy

Division. With a screenplay written by Matt Green-halgh, the film is based on the book *Touching from a Distance*, by Curtis's wife, Deborah Curtis, who also co-produced the film.

Sam Riley gives a sincere and moving performance as the troubled young Curtis in a film that details his life in 1970s Britain. Together with musicians Peter Hook (Joe Anderson) Bernard Sumner (James Anthony Pearson) and Stephen Morris (Harry Treadaway), Curtis formed Joy Division (originally dubbed Warsaw) where he created a new sound stemming from the punk rock scene. Signed by Tony Wilson (Craig Parkinson) and manager Rob Gretton (Toby Kebbell) to the Factory Records label, Joy Division had only two albums to their credit, *Unknown Pleasures* (1979) and *Closer* (1980), and while the band never found mainstream fame, they quickly became a highly revered cult sensation in their native England. Possibly poised on the brink of worldwide renown, they were about to embark on their first tour of the United States when Curtis tragically took his own life.

At the height of Joy Division's fame, Curtis was diagnosed with epilepsy. His stage style, which incorporated spasmodic dancing movements, led people to wonder if he was actually having a seizure or if, perhaps, the violent stage movements were triggering his epileptic seizures. He attempted to control the disease with a range of drugs that had varying success and erratic side effects. His depression over his increasing seizures were thought to have contributed to his suicide at age twenty-three.

Showing a knack for poetry at a young age, Curtis was an avid writer interested in art and literature, which eventually led him to music. Singing in his signature baritone voice, his songs spoke of melancholy, loneliness, sorrow, pain, darkness, death, loss of control, isolation, and disintegration. Joy Division's dark, gloomy lyrics were balanced by producer Martin Hannett (Ben Naylor), who played up the danceable music aspect, resulting in a unique sound that influenced not only the gothic rock bands who came after, but a wide range of mainstream groups such as U2 and The Cure. Corbijn employs Riley and his actor bandmates as musicians, their uncanny renditions of the songs virtually indistinguishable from those of the real group.

Control, whose title references another song by Curtis, "She's Lost Control," which deals with epilepsy, also chronicles his volatile marriage. Already wed when he formed the band, Curtis was nineteen when he married eighteen-year-old Deborah (Samantha Morton). The couple had one daughter, Natalie, in 1979. Morton excels as the long-suffering wife, dealing with her husband's physical affliction and mental distress that

often caused him to become quiet, depressed, and moody. Curtis became involved and fell in love with Belgian journalist Annik Honoré (Alexandra Maria Lara), who interviewed him after one of his concerts. The affair and resulting strain on his marriage may have been another factor in his decision to kill himself.

Successful rock photographer and sometime music videographer from Holland, Corbijn's sophisticated debut feature combines his knowledge and love of music and cinematography. Given the dark nature of Curtis and his band, Corbijn's decision to film in black-and-white, simply and beautifully photographed and lit by cinematographer Martin Ruhe, is at once both obvious and brilliant. Corbijn also has similarities with Curtis: born within a year of each other, Corbijn moved to England in 1979, a year before Curtis's death, and his photographs of the band are some of the most highly regarded. Michael Winterbottom's *24 Hour Party People* (2002) (in which Riley also appeared, playing another rock singer) chronicled the Manchester music scene but dealt with Joy Division and Ian Curtis as a subplot. Here, Corbijn puts the young cult icon front and center in a biographical film that, despite its grim and well-known outcome, still manages to inject radiance and a sense of optimism along the way.

Critically acclaimed, *Control* garnered a host of awards at the British Independent Film Awards, including Best British Independent Film, Best Director of an Independent Film for Corbijn, Best Supporting Actor for Kebbell, and Most Promising Newcomer Award for Sam Riley. While the film will appeal to fans of the band and music in general, the well-told and moving story, interesting and well-written characters, aesthetic brilliance, and pitch-perfect performances transcends its genre as a mere music biopic. As Corbijn said of the film in a interview, "It's basically the story of a young boy finding his way, and getting lost."

Hilary White

CREDITS

Debbie Curtis: Samantha Morton
Annik Honoré: Alexandra Maria Lara
Peter Hook: Joe Anderson
Bernard Summer: James Anthony Pearson
Ian Curtis: Sam Riley
Tony Wilson: Craig Parkinson
Rob Gretton: Toby Kebbell
Stephen Morris: Harry Treadway
Terry: Andrew Sheridan
Twinny: Robert Shelly
Origin: Great Britain, Australia, Japan

Language: English

Released: 2007

Production: Orian Williams, Anton Corbijn, Todd Eckart; Northsee Ltd., 3 Dogs and A Pony, Warner Music, Becker Films International; released by Weinstein Company

Directed by: Anton Corbijn

Written by: Deborah Curtis, Matt Greenhalgh

Cinematography by: Martin Ruhe

Music by: New Order

Sound: Peter Baldock

Editing: Andrew Hulme

Production Design: Chris Richmond

MPAA rating: R

Running time: 121 minutes

REVIEWS

Entertainment Weekly Online. October 3, 2007.

Guardian Online. October 5, 2007.

New York Times Online. October 10, 2007.

New Yorker Online. October 15, 2007.

The Observer Online. October 7, 2007.

Rolling Stone Online. October 18, 2007.

The Times of London Online. May 17, 2007.

Variety Online. June 8, 2007.

Village Voice Online. October 9, 2007.

TRIVIA

As a celebrity still photographer, Anton Corbijn worked with Joy Division in 1979, shortly before Ian Curtis committed suicide.

AWARDS

Nomination:

British Acad. 2007: Support. Actress (Morton).

CRAZY LOVE

> *He had to have her.*
> —Movie tagline

As the title suggests, it is lurid subject matter that is at the heart of writer/director Dan Klores's and co-director Fisher Stevens's documentary *Crazy Love.* Klores originally thought of making the bizarre, well-publicized story of Burt and Linda Pugach a drama, but theirs is a classic case of the truth being far stranger than fiction, and so wisely decided on the documentary format, winning a nomination for the Grand Jury Prize at the Sundance Film Festival. While the tale is extremely well-researched and gives an accurate portrait of the couple's Greek tragedy-like forty-year saga, the film's made-for-television feel—utilizing static interviews mixed with old newspaper clippings, black-and-white photos, and grainy home movie clips—and bouncy soundtrack whose lyrics match the action undercut the drama and the filmmakers ultimately mine the story for comedy.

In September 1957, undersized and bespectacled Burt Pugach was a highly successful New York negligence lawyer in his early thirties who drove a Cadillac convertible and owned a nightclub and a private plane. He was just back from London, where he had a hand in producing a film, when he spied beautiful, twenty-one-year-old working girl Linda Riss on a park bench. It would begin a lifelong obsession for Pugach, who used his success and charm to date the virginal Riss. Although Riss found him "very weird" when she met him, he swept her off her feet with weekly dates in his celebrity-filled nightclub and outings on his plane which quickly had her dreaming of an engagement. Her dreams were dashed when months later, she learned of his wife and severely disabled child. When Pugach claimed he had filed for divorce, Linda found out that too was a lie and broke it off with Pugach. On a trip to Florida with a girlfriend, Linda met and fell in love with the handsome Larry Schwartz.

The increasingly deranged Pugach stalked Linda, and when he learned she was engaged to Schwartz, vowed that if he could not have her, no one would. In 1959, Pugach hired three thugs who threw lye in Linda's face as she answered the door. Partially blinded and mildly disfigured, the attack became a media sensation. Pugach, acting as his own lawyer, was arrested and sentenced to thirty years in prison. Linda's attempts at a normal life were dashed time and time again, as Schwartz called off the engagement and later, another serious suitor turned and ran the first time he saw her without her trademark glamorous, dark eyeglasses. Riss became depressed and reclusive. When Pugach is released from prison after serving eleven years, he is as obsessed with Linda as ever but barred from seeing her. The policewoman hired to guard Linda after the attack and now her good friend is the most unlikely matchmaker who sets up a meeting with Pugach and Linda to see if there is a chance they could make it work. In a most bizarre turn, the two marry.

The film builds to its first highlight with the lye attack, with friends echoing the fateful words of Pugach and the song "Release Me and Let Me Love Again" playing forebodingly in the background. However, the grotesquely compelling crux of the story is what happens afterward and what exactly is involved in bringing the star-crossed couple back together again. The film suggests their dysfunctional relationship perhaps stemmed from their troubled childhoods—Pugach was abused by his mother and Riss was given to her aunt's family at a young age—but the film does not delve too deeply into the psychological aspects of their relationship other than to put its dysfunction on full display. Revenge is given as another possibility as to why Riss would reunite with the man who blinded her. Never admitting she actually loved Pugach, Linda certainly needed money and the care that he was more than willing to supply her. Seeing the bickering couple as they are today, the film humorously suggests that marrying Pugach was the best retribution of all.

Burt and Linda's first-person recollections miraculously sound as fresh today as in countless previous interviews on such programs as *Geraldo* and *The Mike Douglas Show*. In addition to the eccentric Pugachs, the film is littered with colorful characters. Burt's secretary, Janet Pomerantz, with whom he had an affair, muses on the reason he hired her. "I think he probably hired me because he like the way I looked," she says definitively, before adding, "not that I was a bad secretary…but…maybe I was bad, I didn't really like being a secretary." Other interesting interviews include Pugach's friend Bob Janoff, who weighs in humorously about the attack. Journalist Jimmy Breslin is also prominently featured, offering some of the film's most poignant and witty observations.

Hilary White

CREDITS

Origin: USA
Language: English
Released: 2007
Production: Fisher Stevens, Dan Klores; Shoot the Moon, Stevens/Zieff Films; released by Magnolia Pictures
Directed by: Dan Klores
Cinematography by: Wolfgang Held
Music by: Douglas J. Cuomo
Sound: Ira Spiegle, Marlena Graszlewicz
Editing: David Zieff
MPAA rating: PG-13
Running time: 92 minutes

REVIEWS

Hollywood Reporter Online. January 20, 2007.
Los Angeles Times Online. June 8, 2007.
New York Times Online. June 1, 2007.
Rolling Stone Online. May 30, 2007.
San Francisco Chronicle. June 8, 2007, p. E5.
Variety Online. January 23, 2007.
Village Voice Online. May 29, 2007.

AWARDS

Ind. Spirit 2008: Feature Doc.

D

DADDY DAY CAMP

This summer is going to be in tents.
—Movie tagline

Box Office: $13.2 million

Former child star Fred Savage makes his directorial debut with *Daddy Day Camp,* the sequel to the Eddie Murphy-starring box office success *Daddy Day Care* (2003), which grossed more than $100 million. Critically trounced, *Daddy Day Camp* could still be considered a triumph of sorts for Savage, with the film earning $16 million on a budget of only $6 million. Cuba Gooding, Jr., steps into Eddie Murphy's role of Charlie Hinton with his usual unbridled enthusiasm and casting the Oscar®-winning star is one of the film's strong points. Gooding's gusto alone, however, is unable to save the film from its idiotic premise and crass, scatological humor liberally littered throughout.

Already running a successful children's daycare business, Hinton makes the bold leap to running a children's camp, taking over the decaying Camp Driftwood, which he attended as a youngster. Although his reasons include spending more time with his son Ben (Spencir Bridges), his ulterior motive is to finally get revenge against his old Camp Driftwood rival, Lance Warner (Lochlyn Munro) who now runs the posh, competing Camp Canola. Paul Rae plays Phil Ryerson, Jeff Garlin's part in the original, Charlie's lovable but goofy partner and sidekick.

Much of the slapstick, physical comedy springs from the mishaps that occur while fixing up the dilapidated camp. A central gag is an outhouse that regularly belches methane gas and eventually explodes. Classic camp calamities, such as poison ivy, regurgitation, and bed-wetting are readily employed, along with the standard genre flatulence and bodily function humor. Similar to this year's *Are We Done Yet?*, the put-upon heroes and their family members fall prey to remodeling disasters of various proportion, which are usually unsuccessful in producing much in the way of laughs.

Charlie enlists the help of his estranged father, Marine Colonel Buck (Richard Gant), which serves to strengthen the film's central message of the importance and ritual of father and son bonding, a typical morality espoused in PG-rated family comedies. Naturally, competition factors largely in this theme, and the rivalry is ratcheted up when Charlie's nemesis Lance goads his camp into participating in the Summer Camp Olympiad. This reopens old wounds, as it was the very competition where Lance humiliated Charlie in 1977.

To prepare for the contest, Buck leads the kids through military style drills, both inspiring them and bringing out the best of each young camper. He also offers the children the chance at creating some controlled mayhem, something grandfathers in film are charmingly wont to do, and he leads covert raids aimed at Lance's camp. His father's popularity among the campers, especially Ben, causes Charlie some chagrin. As a father, Buck was a strict, by-the-book disciplinarian but has mellowed with time, and eventually Charlie comes to terms with his father and his need to be a better father to Ben. This plotline does not work as well as it was intended as we only are shown the kinder, gentler Buck, making the disgruntled Charlie less sympathetic and their reconciliation much less potent.

Gooding and Rae are well-cast and able to play well against each other, but cannot live up to the verve of comedy veterans Eddie Murphy and Jeff Garlin, and the earlier film casts a pall over its lesser sequel. Savage picked a project that would seem tailor made for him, working with child actors, and his child-wrangling skills with his cast of stock kid characters is evident. The rest, however, is a simple, by-the-numbers affair that will in no way distinguish Savage as a director. The film was so unremarkable, in fact, that Disney originally designated a straight-to-video release but decided in would play in theaters only to heighten interest for the DVD.

Most interesting to note is that this seemingly innocuous, family-friendly comedy may actually contain a more serious subtext. Matt Zoller Seitz noted in his *New York Times* review that "Mr. Gant's charming characterization—Norman Schwarzkopf by way of Captain Kangaroo" may actually lead one to believe that "Like *The Pacifier* and *Transformers, Daddy Day Camp,...* is a recruiting poster for kids, insisting that there's no domestic problem that military values can't solve."

James S. O'Neill

CREDITS

Charlie Hinton: Cuba Gooding, Jr.
Lance Warner: Lochlyn Munro
Col. Buck Hinton: Richard Gant
Ben Hinton: Spencir Bridges
Phil Ryerson: Paul Rae
Dale: Josh McLerran
Kim Hinton: Tamala Jones
Uncle Monty: Brian Doyle-Murray
Jack Mayhoffer: Talon G. Ackerman
Origin: USA
Language: English
Released: 2007
Production: William Sherak, Jason Shuman; Davis Entertainment Company, Blue Star Entertainment; released by Sony Pictures
Directed by: Fred Savage
Written by: David N. Weiss, Geoff Rodkey, J. David Stern
Cinematography by: Geno Salvatori
Music by: James Dooley
Sound: Les Udy
Music Supervisor: Manish Raval, Tom Wolfe
Editing: Michael Aller
Art Direction: Mark J. Mullins
Costumes: Carolyn Leone
Production Design: Eric Weiler
MPAA rating: PG
Running time: 93 minutes

REVIEWS

Boston Globe Online. August 8, 2007.
Chicago Sun-Times Online. August 8, 2007.
Entertainment Weekly Online. August 8, 2007.
Hollywood Reporter Online. August 6, 2007.
Los Angeles Times Online. August 8, 2007.
New York Times Online. August 8, 2007.
San Francisco Chronicle. August 8, 2007, p. E1.
Variety Online. August 3, 2007.
Washington Post Online. August 19, 2007.

TRIVIA

Originally intended as a straight-to-DVD sequel, the film tested so well with the target audience that the studio decided to release it in theaters.

AWARDS

Golden Raspberries 2007: Worst Sequel/Prequel
Nomination:
Golden Raspberries 2007: Worst Picture, Worst Actor (Gooding), Worst Director (Savage), Worst Screenplay.

DADDY'S LITTLE GIRLS
(Tyler Perry's Daddy's Little Girls)

Give life. Teach love.
—Movie tagline
Having children made him a father. Taking care of them made him a man.
—Movie tagline
Family Comes First.
—Movie tagline

Box Office: $31.4 million

Tyler Perry is a filmmaker who has created a lucrative brand identity. His *Diary of a Mad Black Woman* (2005) and *Madea's Family Reunion* (2006) were successful theatrical presentations that he turned into even more successful films. Perry's films preach the gospel of "doing the right thing," being a good black man and, if not, receiving swift punishment. In the process, there is a plethora of melodrama, slapstick comedy, and at least one romance. The familiar Perry brand is instantly recognizable in his latest effort, *Daddy's Little Girls* (also known as *Tyler Perry's Daddy's Little Girls*). Perry strays from his formula here in several important ways, however, as the film is his first to be written directly for the screen and the first not to include Madea, the smart-mouthed, rotund grandmother character played by Perry in drag. Another first is that the popular producer, writer, director Perry does not appear onscreen at all in his latest film, which may have freed him up to create an ultimately more polished product.

Perry's underdog hero is Monty (Idris Elba), a big-hearted mechanic and single father raising three adorable daughters (real-life sisters Sierra Aylina McClain, China Anne McClain and Lauryn Alisa McClain). While the virtuous Monty is clearly the film's moral compass, Monty's ex-wife is the polar opposite: the film's one-dimensional villain Jennifer (Tasha Smith), who is too busy cavorting with her drug-dealing gang overlord boyfriend (Gary Anthony Sturgis) to bother with caring for her daughters. While at work, the girls are left in the care of Monty's mother-in-law, but when she dies and entrusts the care of the girls to Monty, Jennifer sues Monty for custody, backed by all the money and power afforded to her by her association with her seedy boyfriend.

Monty enlists of the aid of the attractive, tightly wound Julia (Gabrielle Union), a high-powered lawyer whom he has served as a driver. The two so loathe one another that it is certain they will eventually fall in love. But first Julia must suffer through a series of bad dates, not realizing that her dream man is none other than the blue-collar Monty. Julia's friends must disapprove of what they see as her unsuitable suitor. Jennifer must get temporary custody of the sweet girls and treat them shabbily. And to throw a wrench into the budding romance, Monty must reveal some shocking events in his past to Julia.

Perry does a fine job of creating characters that represent all aspects of African American culture and rejecting popular stereotypes. Black drug dealers live alongside black lawyers and upstanding working men who are also good single fathers. Elba's Monty echoes other Perry protagonists as a stoic martyr who quietly endures as the world heaps more problems upon him. He has an untapped power as a big man forced to keep his physicality in check. Union is well-cast as the uptight, overachieving lawyer. She yearns for the love that Monty can give her, but she has been raised to believe that only a financially successful man will be suitable for her. And Smith is suitably hiss-worthy as one of the worst mothers to hit theater screens in 2007.

Despite Tyler's expressed belief in being a good Christian, his film's characters frequently use violence to resolve their problems, which seems morally questionable. Tyler's Madea was quick to administer corporal punishment and, in *Madea's Family Reunion*, essentially beats the will of the good Lord into a young foster girl living with her. This old-fashioned brand of discipline was played as necessary and even humorous. In *Daddy's Little Girls*, the virtuous Monty solves his problems by ramming his car into one carrying his ex-wife and her drug-dealing beau. His actions are portrayed as righteous because his victims are the evil villains and Monty is the Everyman hero. Although a simplistic view of morality, Perry has proved that it is nonetheless popular. Also problematic and confusing is the fact that the heretofore righteous hero reveals his involvement in a rape in his past.

Despite the films drawbacks, *Daddy's Little Girls* marks a milestone for the filmmaker in that it is certainly the most professionally made of his films to date. It shows a maturity, with even pacing and a greater understanding of staging his work for the screen. Mark Olsen of the *Los Angeles Times* wrote, "Whether by design or default, Perry has no use for conventional notions of filmic story structure or characterization, which is what gives his films, even at their most annoying, an oddball and idiosyncratic charm."

Jill Hamilton

CREDITS

Monty: Idris Elba
Julia: Gabrielle Union
Willie: Louis Gossett, Jr.
Jennifer: Tasha Smith
Maya: Malinda Williams
Cynthia: Tracee Ellis Ross
Joseph: Gary Sturgis
Sierra: Sierra Aylina McClain
China: China Anne McClain
Lauryn: Lauryn Alisa McClain
Origin: USA
Language: English
Released: 2007
Production: Tyler Perry, Reuben Cannon; Tyler Perry Studios, Reuben Cannon Productions; released by Lionsgate
Directed by: Tyler Perry
Written by: Tyler Perry
Cinematography by: Toyomichi Jurita
Music by: Brian McKnight
Sound: Jim Hawkins
Music Supervisor: Joel High
Editing: Maysie Hoy
Costumes: Keith Lewis
Production Design: Ina Mayhew
MPAA rating: PG-13
Running time: 95 minutes

REVIEWS

Chicago Sun-Times Online. February 16, 2007.
Entertainment Weekly. March 2, 2007, p. 52.
Hollywood Reporter Online. February 15, 2007.
Los Angeles Times Online. February 16, 2007.
New York Times Online. February 15, 2007.

San Francisco Chronicle. February 15, 2007, p. E7.
Variety Online. February 14, 2007.

TRIVIA

Monty's daughters' first names in the movie are their first names in real life. They are also actual sisters.

DAN IN REAL LIFE

Something's happening to Dan. It's confusing. It's awkward. It's family.
—Movie tagline

Box Office: $47.6 million

Dan in Real Life is not a bad movie, but it is not an especially good one either. It is, on the whole, rather pleasant and revolves around a likable Everyman we want to root for. But, in its uneasy blend of family drama and romantic comedy, the screenplay by Pierce Gardner and director Peter Hedges is at odds with itself, never certain whether it should mine the serious themes of a widower in a complicated love triangle or go for broad laughs in the best screwball tradition. Either option would have been preferable to the fuzzy middle ground the film occupies. Whatever charm *Dan in Real Life* musters stems from the talented cast, especially Steve Carell, who walks a delicate line between pathos and humor as Dan Burns, a widower trying to raise three daughters and facing an unexpected new love.

Dan is a decent guy who dispenses advice to strangers in a newspaper column but can barely handle his own fragile home life. It is a variation on the timeworn cliché of the therapist who is himself in need of healing. Dan is still mourning the death of his wife after four years and struggling to raise three daughters on his own. He has an especially contentious time with his teenagers—Jane's (Alison Pill) big problem is that, against her father's wishes, she desperately wants to drive, while Cara's (Brittany Robertson) burgeoning interest in a boyfriend is a constant source of anxiety for her father. Little Lilly (Marlene Lawston), who is in the fourth grade, is the most manageable of the three and has a great rapport with her father.

On a trip to his parents' country home for a big family gathering, Dan runs into a woman named Marie (Juliette Binoche), and, after pretending to be an employee at the local bookstore and recommending a slew of books in a typical meet-cute scene, he strikes up a conversation with her. After visiting for some time, Dan is completely smitten. Even though the viewer might take this chance meeting as the possible starting point of a relationship rather than an instantaneous, life-changing moment, the film insists that this is love at first sight. But we never see a real conversation, just snippets of Dan telling his life story, and the fact that the whole movie hinges on this meeting makes everything that follows hard to believe since we do not see what Dan loves about her.

No sooner does Dan tell his family that he has met this great new woman than he discovers that Marie is his brother Mitch's (Dane Cook) new girlfriend, leaving Dan to feel uncomfortable and awkward just being around her. Carell does a fine job of showing Dan's inner conflict; the problem is that the conflict itself feels rather contrived, as if one morning together could produce such certitude after he has avoided relationships ever since his wife's passing. Indeed, exploring the very issue of how Dan feels about discovering new love after so long could have deepened the thin screenplay if the filmmakers had chosen to go in that direction.

In the film's funniest scene, Dan goes out on a blind date with a girl named Ruthie (Emily Blunt), who used to be called "Pigface." But now she is brilliant and beautiful. With Mitch and Marie joining them at the local bar, Dan goes out of his way to show an interest in Ruthie to make Marie jealous and shows off some wild dance moves. But Ruthie is such a great gal in her own right that most men would take a legitimate interest in her and not merely use her as a prop. Despite being a plastic surgeon who treats burn victims and children with facial deformities as well as being a fan of Dan's column (which, incidentally, is a lot more than we know about Marie), Ruthie is portrayed as being just a bit flaky, as if this were automatically a deal breaker when, in other romantic comedies, such a woman would be just what the lonely hero needs to bring him out of his shell. Blunt gives the movie's freest, most engaging performance, which, unfortunately, is an extended cameo. Still, the way Dan cuts loose in this scene suggests the film aiming for a comic tone that, while very entertaining, does not fit with the movie's more serious themes.

Most of Dan's extended family barely register as individuals—indeed, we never get a clear sense of who everyone is—but John Mahoney and Dianne Wiest offer reliable support as the parents of the clan. What is worth noting is how amazingly well adjusted this whole group is, even to the point of incredulity. They compete in a crossword puzzle contest, play charades, do aerobics together on the front lawn, play football, and even hold a talent show for each other. There is not a trace of dysfunction in the bunch, which, admittedly, is refreshing in its own way but is also a cliché replacing the more familiar convention of nonstop bickering. There is even, in a clumsy nod to political correctness, a little Asian girl in the family, who must have been adopted since none of the adults are Asian. And, of course, everyone takes an interest in Dan's love life and wants him to find happiness.

But if *Dan in Real Life* is a generally amiable film, it does not rise above a certain genial take on family life and the predictability of its story. In fact, it is so genial and Mitch such a nice guy (despite being a tad dumb and having a reputation as a playboy) that the film struggles for an excuse for Marie to leave him. She reads Dan's one book and discovers that Mitch has stolen his best lines from his brother—a shorthand way of highlighting Mitch's shallowness and unsuitability for Marie.

It is only a matter of time before Dan and Marie admit their love for each other and Mitch hits his brother. By the end, however, the brothers are reconciled, and, in this idealized world, their rivalry for the same woman does not have any lasting repercussions. Dan learns to be a better father and, with his daughters' blessing, wins Marie before it is too late. A lighthouse, seen early in the film and brought back in a piece of art by little Lilly, even serves as an obvious symbol guiding Dan. All of this is well executed but very mechanical, as if each plot point were preordained to fit neatly into place. Compare this vision of family life with Hedges's previous effort, the indie hit *Pieces of April* (2003), which embraced the messiness of family relationships at a Thanksgiving gathering. This is not to suggest that each of his films needs to have this point of view, but the mainstream *Dan in Real life* could have benefited from more of this sensibility.

And, interestingly enough, there are moments when the movie seems like it could go in that direction. Carell brings a soulfulness, even a world-weariness, to Dan as a man trying to appear okay but constantly suffering on the inside. At times, despite the big family around him, he seems very lonely, often isolated in a hallway or in the small room where, in a great comic touch, he has been relegated to sleep with the washer and dryer. The sadness at his center really is heartfelt, but the formula will not let him work out his problems honestly. There is a hint, for example, that Dan is a failed fiction writer whose one effort went unappreciated. There is also the sense that he is at least slightly out of place at this family reunion, as if his good cheer required effort and he is enduring all of this fun merely for the sake of his girls. But the screenplay just hints at these ideas without taking them further. Moreover, in flirting with stale bits of comedy—Dan falling off the roof, Dan wisecracking with a policeman—the filmmakers only undercut their serious treatment of the character.

The movie is so insistent on tying up loose ends that, at the end, Mitch is dating Ruthie, almost as if she were the consolation prize for losing Marie to his brother. The irony, though, is that Ruthie may actually be the more interesting love interest—not as mature or polished as Marie but almost certainly more fun. This is a possibility that a more fully realized script would have at least toyed with instead of treating Ruthie as a mere narrative device.

Perhaps what is most disappointing about *Dan in Real Life* is its schizophrenia, the tension between the filmmakers' seeming impulse to tell a grown-up story and their indulgence in broad comedy. Despite its title, this film is not interested in exploring family life and middle-aged love in a realistic way, and ultimately we find ourselves in an idyllic world populated by an extended family that seems to come from another age. This is a story of healing, new beginnings, and lessons learned. It goes down easily with some amusing moments along the way, but it does not do as much with the drama inherent in the material as it could have.

Peter N. Chumo II

CREDITS

Dan Burns: Steve Carell
Marie: Juliette Binoche
Mitch: Dane Cook
Nana: Dianne Wiest
Poppy: John Mahoney
Ruthie Draper: Emily Blunt
Jane: Alison Pill
Cara: Brittany Robertson
Lilly: Marlene Lawston
Clay: Norbert Lee Butz
Eileen: Amy Ryan
Marty Barasco: Felipe Dieppa
Origin: USA
Language: English
Released: 2007
Production: Jonathan Shestack; Focus Features; released by Touchstone Pictures
Directed by: Peter Hedges
Written by: Peter Hedges, Pierce Gardner
Cinematography by: Lawrence Sher
Music by: Sondre Lerche
Sound: John Pritchett
Music Supervisor: Dana Sano
Editing: Sarah Flack
Art Direction: Mark Garner
Costumes: Alix Friedberg
Production Design: Sarah Knowles
MPAA rating: PG-13
Running time: 98 minutes

REVIEWS

Boston Globe Online. October 26, 2007.
Chicago Sun-Times Online. October 26, 2007.

Entertainment Weekly Online. October 24, 2007.
Hollywood Reporter Online. October 22, 2007.
Los Angeles Times Online. October 26, 2007.
New York Times Online. October 26, 2007.
Rolling Stone Online. October 18, 2007.
Variety Online. October 21, 2007.
Washington Post. October 26, 2007, p. C1.

QUOTES

Marty Barasco: "Love is not a feeling, Mr. Burns. It's an ability."

DARFUR NOW

> *Six Stories. One Hope.*
> —Movie tagline

Despite having high-profile movie star George Clooney loudly advocating for the cause in the United States, garnering support in any part of the world to stop the genocide in Darfur has proved to be no easy feat. An impoverished western region of Africa's Sudan, Darfur has seen nearly a quarter million people killed and two and a half million survivors displaced by the thuggish Janjaweed militias unofficially employed by the government since 2003. The problem is extremely complex and long ranging, dating back centuries, and thus far, it has received little aid from the global community.

Darfur Now attempts to change that, as this documentary is essentially a call to action. Writer/director Ted Braun also clarifies some of the factors involved in bringing about the mass killings that target both peaceful civilians and rebels. While rooted in religious and tribal conflict wrought by uniting the two formerly independent regions of Darfur and the Sudan by the Egyptian government in the 1800s, it has also been fueled by the fact that sixty percent of the region's oil is imported by China. Braun also points out that support to end the Darfur crisis has been lost with most of the world focused instead on the war in Iraq.

Braun shows us six people who are committed to the cause, both inside and outside of Africa. His approach echoes the complexity of the problem itself, using this diverse group of involved individuals in an effort to view the problem from a variety of angles. The film's effort to appeal to as many people as possible is also its fault, and dispersing the focus among so many lessens the potency of the most compelling of Braun's subjects and prevents delving into any one too deeply.

One of the most chilling and heartbreaking of these stories is told by villager Hejewa Adam, who appears at both the beginning and end of the film. After her three-month-old child was brutally murdered by the Janjaweed and her village destroyed, Adam armed herself with an automatic rifle and joined the rebels, taking up fighting so readily and easily, she compared it to drinking water. World Food Program head Pablo Recalde risks his life running food and supplies to refugees amid gunfire. The stories of the rebels and a look inside the refugee camps are where the film is most effective. *Los Angeles Times's* Kenneth Turan noted that "the best material is the result of the rare opportunity to shoot inside those refugee camps: hearing firsthand testimony from victims about the catastrophic horrors inflicted on their villages is forceful and persuasive."

Another campaigner in the fight to bring justice to the troubled region is Luis Moreno-Ocampo, the chief prosecutor of the International Criminal Court in The Hague. Moreno-Ocampo grew up in Argentina when a military dictatorship caused the torture and death of thousands but ended when those responsible were eventually prosecuted for their crimes. Frustrated by the excruciatingly slow pace in punishing those in the Sudan government responsible for the crimes, he is also confident the same could happen in Darfur. Moreno-Ocampo's court has issued arrest warrants for Sudan's interior minister, Ahmad Harun, and Janjaweed militia leader Ali Kushayb, although they have been ignored by the Sudanese government.

American actor Don Cheadle first became aware of the crisis while filming the highly-acclaimed *Hotel Rwanda* (2004) in Africa. Along with the aforementioned Clooney, Cheadle spearheads a movement to bring American and European intervention to Darfur. University of California–Los Angeles student Adam Sterling works on getting a bill passed that would divest the Golden State of any business interests in the Sudan. While Governor Arnold Schwarzenegger readily signs the bill, it is rendered nearly impotent as the United States federal government assiduously avoids any official involvement. In Kenneth Turan's view, "Though they are completely committed and doing difficult, meaningful work, the Americans in the film just do not hold the screen with the same force and power."

The provocative stance taken by Sudan's government is also illuminated. Abdalmahmood Abdalhaleem Mohamad, Sudan's United Nations ambassador, denies that genocide is in fact taking place in Darfur. Preferring to see the matter as internal, he refuses to comply with the actions of the International Criminal Court.

Generally well-received, *Darfur Now* is educational, timely, and well-intentioned but suffers some shortcomings in its presentation. Roger Ebert of the *Chicago Sun-Times* praised it as "instructive and disturbing" but added, "it is not a compelling documentary" with "too much exposition, not enough on-the-spot reality." Although other critics echoed these sentiments, all acknowledged the laudable effort of Braun and the nearly impossible task of bringing awareness and insight into Darfur's little-known plight.

Hilary White

CREDITS

Origin: USA

Language: English

Released: 2007

Production: Don Cheadle, Cathy Shulman, Mark Jonathan Harris; Participant Productions, Mandalay Independent Pictures, Crescendo; released by Warner Independent Pictures

Directed by: Theodore Braun

Written by: Theodore Braun

Cinematography by: Kirsten Johnson

Music by: Graeme Revell

Sound: Wellington Bowler

Editing: Edgar Burcken, Leonard Feinstein

MPAA rating: PG

Running time: 99 minutes

REVIEWS

Chicago Sun-Times Online. November 8, 2007.

Entertainment Weekly Online. October 31, 2007.

Hollywood Reporter Online. October 5, 2007.

Los Angeles Times Online. November 2, 2007.

New York Times Online. November 2, 2007.

San Francisco Chronicle. November 9, 2007, p. E9.

Variety Online. September 13, 2007.

Washington Post Online. November 9, 2007.

THE DARJEELING LIMITED

Box Office: $11.9 million

Writer/director Wes Anderson's road trip comedy-drama, *The Darjeeling Limited,* is as carefully constructed and whimsical as his previous four feature films and bear all of the director's signature stylistic hallmarks. Echoing his previous efforts, the film deals with a quirky family's strained relations and features children's storybook-like settings. The exquisitely framed shots reveal the director's deliberate, painstakingly-detailed choices from wardrobe, props, and accessories to the careful selection and choreography of background actors. Often dubbed a

miniaturist, the world Anderson creates in *The Darjeeling Limited*—the fanciful, eponymous train and the exotic world of India—are especially suited to his particular talents. In *Rushmore* (1998), Anderson built the singular world of the private school and distinct meta-theatrical productions, while *The Life Aquatic with Steve Zissou* (2004) saw the auteur expanding his repertoire to include computer-animated underwater sea life and fashioning the unique interiors of the vessel. But perhaps *The Darjeeling Limited* has the most in common with his *The Royal Tenenbaums* (2001), where he explored the dysfunctional workings of the titular family and created the quaint Gypsy Cab Co. that most closely resembles this film's Orient Express-like train.

The Darjeeling Limited serves as Part Two, following the director's thirteen-minute prologue, *Hotel Chevalier,* starring Jason Schwartzman and Natalie Portman, that explains Schwartzman's character's heartbreak. Taking place in a lavish Paris hotel room, the short is gratingly slow-paced and comes across as too deliberately staged. The characters exhibit little chemistry and the short lacks the good spiritedness and heart of the main film.

Citing Jean Renoir's India-set, *The River* (1951), as inspiration, Anderson and co-writers Jason Schwartzman and Roman Coppola fashioned the humorous and touching script for *The Darjeeling Limited* while they traveled through the Indian subcontinent. The film stars the frequent Anderson collaborator Owen Wilson as Francis, a man who convinces his younger brothers Peter (Adrien Brody) and Jack (Jason Schwartzman) to board a train and embark on a spiritual journey to India in order to bring them closer as a family and heal the wounds from their father's recent death. Francis—his face and head heavily bandaged from a motorcycle accident that may have been intentional—is compulsive and controlling, with his personal assistant, Brendan, (Wallace Wolodarsky) in tow to attend to the printing and laminating of the detailed daily schedule for the brothers. Though happily married to Alice (Camilla Rutherford), Peter is unusually morose and clings to his dead father's belongings, wearing his sunglasses and using his razor, while Jack neurotically checks his ex-girlfriend's answering machine messages. While Francis demands that they must be completely honest with each other, each one has secrets they wish to keep from one or more of each other. Constantly swigging Indian cough syrup and ingesting a variety of painkillers for their various mental and physical ailments, the proboscis-endowed threesome give the impression of "a contemporary, depressive version of the Three Stooges," according to Carina Chocano of the *Los Angeles Times.* Anderson wisely and humorously makes it a point not to sublimate his visual metaphors, with the boys carrying a prodigious amount of custom-made, safari-themed Louis Vuitton luggage with them throughout the long journey.

The filmmakers expand the notion of traditional Indian characters and create unique and modern ethnic portrayals. Jack finds comfort in the arms of the Indian stewardess, Rita, who brings them sweet lime drinks (Francis endearingly dubs her "Sweet Lime"). Though she dresses and initially seems completely traditional, Rita (Amara Karan) is actually quite modern, and after they share a cigarette, meets Jack in the bathroom for an impulsive tryst. The brothers' reckless behavior, including bringing a poisonous snake on board that manages to get loose, gets them kicked off the train and they find themselves wandering the countryside. They engage in several farcical attempts at spirituality, but meaning comically eludes them time and time again until they come upon some boys drowning while trying to cross a river. They are able to save all but one and they are regaled in the boys' village and invited to attend the boy's funeral. The humanity of the traditional Indian village contrasts with the inanity of the brother's attempts at pseudo-spiritualism, and they are finally able to achieve some sort of understanding.

Francis also has the hidden agenda (that he has nonetheless designated as "TBD" on the laminated schedule) of reuniting with their mother Patricia (Anjelica Huston), who fled to a convent in India after their father's death. Patricia is the antithesis of the conventional mother stereotype and quite unsympathetic as she cares for the locals she claims need her much more than her own children who crave her attention and support. She disappears the day after the boys arrive, leaving them to pack up and head home. The boys have grown much closer during their adventure, bonding even in their mother's rejection, and the metaphor is complete as the boys leave their luggage behind as they run to board their train out.

It has been suggested that Francis is the most autobiographical of Anderson's brothers, although each one has autobiographical characteristics. Jack is a writer who insists the characters in his stories are purely fictional but which his brothers nonetheless recognize as themselves. By the film's end, Jack also acknowledges that fact. Francis's revelation also comes in the third reel as he literally strips the bandages away from his head and face to reveal still unsightly, large scars. When his brother remarks that he still has a lot of healing to do, it is both literal and metaphorical. As they depart India, Peter finally accepts that his wife is pregnant and calls to tell her where he has disappeared to. The characters' growth is subtle, but distinct.

Always a unique and innovative feature of his films, in *The Darjeeling Limited* Anderson made use of original music from Indian films, including those of Indian director Satyajit Ray, to lend an authentic feel. Also in keeping with his other films, Anderson's visuals are magical, aided by longtime cinematographer Robert Yeoman.

Hilary White

CREDITS

Francis: Owen Wilson
Peter: Adrien Brody
Jack: Jason Schwartzman
Rita: Amara Karan
Brendan: Wallace Wolodarsky
Patricia: Anjelica Huston
Alice: Camilla Rutherford
Origin: USA
Language: English
Released: 2007
Production: Wes Anderson, Scott Rudin, Lydia Dean Pilcher, Roman Coppola; American Empirical Pictures, Collage; released by Fox Searchlight Pictures
Directed by: Wes Anderson
Written by: Jason Schwartzman, Wes Anderson, Roman Coppola
Cinematography by: Robert Yeoman
Sound: Pavel Wdowczak
Music Supervisor: Randall Poster
Editing: Andrew Weisblum
Art Direction: Adam Stockhausen
Costumes: Milena Canonero
Production Design: Mark Friedberg
MPAA rating: R
Running time: 91 minutes

REVIEWS

Boston Globe Online. October 5, 2007.
Chicago Sun-Times Online. October 5, 2007.
Entertainment Weekly Online. September 26, 2007.
Los Angeles Times Online. October 5, 2007.
New York Times Online. September 28, 2007.
Rolling Stone Online. October 18, 2007.
San Francisco Chronicle. October 5, 2007, p. E6.
Variety Online. September 3, 2007.
Village Voice Online. September 25, 2007.
Washington Post. October 5, 2007, p. C1.

QUOTES

Jack: "I wonder if the three of us would've been friends in real life, not as brothers, but as people."

DAYS OF GLORY
(Indigènes)

The true story of World War II's forgotten heroes.
—Movie tagline

The true story so controversial, it couldn't be told until now.
—Movie tagline

With some of the most impressively staged battle sequences since *Saving Private Ryan* (1998) and featuring a story of World War II that has rarely been told in any form, *Days of Glory* (also known as *Indigènes*) stands above most of its recent genre peers. Directed by Rachid Bouchareb, *Days of Glory* was nominated for the Academy Award® for Best Foreign Language Film but was swept away by the wave of popularity for *Pan's Labyrinth* (2006) and the category winner, *The Lives of Others* (2006). In many other years, *Days of Glory* would have easily walked away with the Oscar®. The unusually graceful war film dramatizes the final days of World War II in France and, more specifically, the position of French Africans who served in De Gaulle's Army but were discriminated against before, during, and after combat. With stunning cinematography and heartfelt, believable performances, *Days of Glory* builds slowly towards a final conflict as memorable as anything in recent war movie memory.

The French First Army, which was formed to liberate France after the Nazis were defeated at the end of World War II, featured many soldiers from Algeria, Tunisia, and other French-occupied countries of Africa. *Days of Glory* highlights several of the soldiers from these areas who were recruited to fight alongside native Frenchmen but never treated with the same respect. The film focuses primarily on four of the "Indigènes," the original French name for the film and a word that was used to describe French Africans, and their different responses to the campaign to liberate France from the Nazis. In Morocco, we meet Yassir (Samy Naceri), the most hardened of the Indigènes, a man who goes to war seemingly just to collect trophies from the men he kills. Messaoud (Roschdy Zem) is a North African marksman who thinks he has no luck until he meets the most beautiful French girl he has ever seen and finally has something to fight for. The most ambitious of the featured soldiers, Abdelkader (Sami Bouajila) fights for

equality for his fellow North Africans, who have to dodge the same German bullets but are not even allowed the same food. Finally, we meet Saïd (Jamel Debbouze), a quiet man who believes he is doing something greater by serving France than he ever could have in his Algerian town. Each man fights for a different reason but are all treated as second-class citizens by the French soldiers they serve alongside in the liberation of France.

As the paths of these characters intertwine and build toward a violent climax in Alsace, Bouchareb maintains an incredible sense of dignity and grace with his heroes. Without too many patriotic speeches, it becomes easy to root for the heroes of *Days of Glory* and be saddened when they fall because of the humanity given them by Bouchareb and the actors he cast. At one point, Saïd says to a French girl he is trying to woo, "I free a country, it's my country. Even if I never saw it before." *Days of Glory* is a film about people fighting for ideas, trying to defend a motherland that they never even laid eyes on until they were asked to possibly give their lives for it. And yet, *Days of Glory* never feels melodramatic or clichéd, as it easily would have in a lesser director's hands. Bouchareb wisely avoids too many of the "war is hell" pitfalls of the genre, instead portraying the more noble idea of serving your country in whatever way you know how, even if your country fails to serve you. Bouchareb is helped by an excellent ensemble, most notably popular comic actor Debouzze, who has an expressive face that makes him easy to identify with and root for, and Bouajila, who struggles between his sense of duty and his keen awareness that his duty may never be rewarded.

The performances and the screenplay of *Days of Glory* are better than average, but it is the cinematography from Patrick Blossier and the design of the battle sequences that are most effective and memorable. The final gunfight, as our heroes try to survive an attack in Alsace, is one of the most impressive of the war genre. Bouchareb does an amazing job of utilizing the space of this small French town without allowing his audience to get overwhelmed. War films often descend into chaos, but Bouchareb always makes clear where his heroes are, what they are doing, and how much danger they are in at every moment. Like the rest of the film and the people it eulogizes, *Days of Glory* remains graceful and dignified, even during battle.

Brian Tallerico

CREDITS
Saïd: Jamel Debbouze
Messaoud: Roschdy Zem
Abdelkader: Sami Bouajila

Leroux: Mathieu Simonet
Yassir: Samy Naceri
Martinez: Bernard Blancan
Captain Durieux: Benoit Giros
Origin: Algeria, Belgium, France
Language: Arabic, French
Released: 2006
Production: Jean Brehat; Tessalit Productions, Kissfilms; released by IFC Films
Directed by: Rachid Bouchareb
Written by: Rachid Bouchareb, Olivier Morelle
Cinematography by: Patrick Blossier
Music by: Armand Amar
Sound: Olivier Hespel, Olivier Walczak
Editing: Yannick Kergoat
Costumes: Michele Richer
Production Design: Dominique Douret
MPAA rating: R
Running time: 123 minutes

REVIEWS

Entertainment Weekly Online. December 13, 2006.
Hollywood Reporter Online. May 26, 2006.
Los Angeles Times Online. December 6, 2006.
New York Times Online. December 6, 2006.
Variety Online. May 25, 2006.
Village Voice Online. December 5, 2006.

TRIVIA

The French title means "natives," referring to France's colonies in North Africa.

DEAD SILENCE

You scream. You die.
—Movie tagline

Box Office: $16.8 million

"Beware the stare of Mary Shaw / She had no children, only dolls/And if you see her in your dreams / Be sure you never, ever scream."

This haunting children's rhyme bubbles to surface as Jamie Ashen (Ryan Kwanten) receives a ventriloquist's dummy at the doorstep of his metropolitan apartment where he lives with his wife, Lisa (Laura Regan). The memory is a portentous one; the rhyme was one based on an urban legend in the couple's hometown of Raven's Fair. As with many Grimm's fairy tales, this eerie chant was used by parents to keep their children complacent. The dummy is a foreboding gift for good reason. As Jamie returns home the same evening with a takeout

dinner for the two, he finds his beloved wife now a corpse staring blankly at him with her tongue and lips ripped from her face.

As the prime suspect (there is no evidence of forced entry, and he was last one to see the deceased), Jamie is subjected to the film's source of comic relief, Detective Jim Lipton (Donnie Wahlberg, bearing no resemblance in presence or manner to that of James Lipton, the oft parodied interviewer of *The Actor's Studio*). When Jamie imparts his theory to Lipton that he believes the doll might have a part in his wife's murder, the sardonic detective (complete with a Columbo overcoat and donut) snidely remarks, "The mystery toy department is down the hall. This is the homicide department." Still a free man while the investigation puts together a case against him, Jamie jumps in his candy apple red 1970s muscle car and returns to Raven's Fair to bury his bride.

Dead Silence is an atypical entry in the modern film horror genre. Directed by James Wan and written by Leigh Whannell (the creative duo of the *Saw* series) the film pays tribute to old school horror techniques such as an atmospheric set complete with cobwebs and a perpetual rolling fog. An aging dilapidated mansion complete with a creaky ivy-covered main gate and stone gargoyles make up the Ashen manor, which could be described as a page from Edgar Allen Poe's classic tale, "The Fall of the House of Usher." Similarly, Raven's Fair is a decrepit Victorian-styled town that lost its vibrant pulse long ago. Mary Shaw (eerily played by Judith Roberts) resides in the antiquated Guignol Theater (named after the famous horror playhouse in Paris, The Grand Guignol). Raven's Fair's golden age was in the 1930s and 1940s, but it has long ago been overcast with a dark secret. Ironically, the dying town's shabby unattended condition reflects the state of the lion's share of today's box office-driven horror, which too often replaces substance and style with gimmicks, awash with gore, torture, and an escalating body count. Deviating from their *Saw* franchise, Wan and Whannell provide an intelligently written script rife with suspense and creepiness and layered with an abundant amount of fright-provoking scenes that prove the terror chord may strike in a film with a mere four murders.

The movie's disappointing box office yield could possibly be due to modern audiences being so numbed by an array of violent splatter films that any work with content that is both fresh as well as nostalgic goes unnoticed. However, one contributing factor is the film's star, Ryan Kwanten, whose narrow range fails to convey shock, anger, or terror. There is absolutely nothing convincing about his portrayal (the shock is how Kwanten won the role). Conversely, the performance of Bob Gunton, whose talent was highlighted in *The Shawshank Redemption* (1994), is remarkable. As Jamie's invalid father, Gunton's character, Edward Ashen, has recently suffered from a stroke and is being cared for by his nubile third wife Ella (Amber Valletta). The introduction of this character is a key element to the picture's surprise ending, giving the first *Saw* (2004) installment a critical nod, by rendering him the true dummy of the story. At the film's climax, Jamie thunders to his father's house in order to destroy Mary Shaw's last remaining dummy, through which she is able to channel her spirit. (The doll was given the name Billy as an homage to the tricycle riding *Saw* dummy who is also seen in the movie as one of Mary Shaw's 101 "children.") Jamie's horror at realizing his father was turned into one of Mary Shaw's dummies is artfully delivered through a pastiche of shots that snap together in a blurring black-and-white flashback.

Interestingly, horror rarely has a crossover into the field of ventriloquism. To date, 1977's *Magic* with Anthony Hopkins is at the forefront. Yet as an artistic ghost story successful in fear-invoking intrigue, perhaps Wan and Whannell could diversify with a how-to-book of genre filmmaking: *Horror for Dummies*.

David M. Roberts

CREDITS

Jamie Ashen: Ryan Kwanten
Det. Jim Lipton: Donnie Wahlberg
Ella Ashen: Amber Valletta
Henry Walker: Michael Fairman
Edward Ashen: Bob Gunton
Mary Shaw: Judith Roberts
Lisa Ashen: Laura Regan
Marion Walker: Joan Heney
Origin: USA
Language: English
Released: 2007
Production: Gregg Hoffman, Oren Koules, Mark Burg; released by Universal Pictures
Directed by: James Wan
Written by: Leigh Whannell
Cinematography by: John R. Leonetti
Music by: Charlie Clouser
Sound: Kelly Cabral
Editing: Michael N. Knue
Art Direction: Anastasia Masaro
Costumes: Denise Cronenberg
Production Design: Julie Berghoff
MPAA rating: R
Running time: 90 minutes

REVIEWS

Boston Globe Online. March 16, 2007.
Entertainment Weekly. March 30, 2007, p. 54.
Hollywood Reporter Online. March 19, 2007.
Los Angeles Times Online. March 19, 2007.
New York Times Online. March 17, 2007.
Variety Online. March 16, 2007.

QUOTES

Det. Jim Lipton (to Jamie): "You are forcing me to use the word 'perplexed.'"

TRIVIA

There are two different versions of the "Mary Shaw" poem. In the movie the poem goes, "Beware the stare of Mary Shaw. She had no children only dolls. And if you see her in your dreams, do not ever, ever scream." In the trailer it goes, "Beware the stare of Mary Shaw. She had no children, only dolls. And if you see her do not scream, she'll rip your tongue out at the seam."

DEATH AT A FUNERAL

Last rites...and wrongs.
—Movie tagline

Box Office: $8.6 million

George Bernard Shaw once said, "England and America are two countries separated by a common language." After a viewing of Frank Oz's *Death at a Funeral*, it would appear that the language is comedy. A number of American directors have successfully crossed the pond to craft effective dramas (Woody Allen's *Match Point* [2005] being a recent example) and British directors travel stateside for both comedy and drama all the time, but a comedy director from the United States trying his hand at British whimsy is a much rarer occurrence. *Death at a Funeral* makes clear that even a talented comedy director like Oz, who was born in England but moved to California at the age of five, can stumble when trying to capture the dry, British deadpan sense of humor that serves as the foundation for most comedies from the United Kingdom. From first scene to last, *Death at a Funeral* feels like a filmmaker trying to work in a country where he barely knows the language, much less what makes it funny.

Death at a Funeral opens with Daniel (Matthew Macfadyen) waiting at his parents' house for the casket that bears the body of his father. Immediately flashing neon signs that the film will take no prisoners in its attempts at British bad taste, the undertaker brings the wrong casket. After the mix-up is corrected, Daniel works on his eulogy with his wife Jane (Keeley Hawes) and the two complain about their family. Jane does not get along with Daniel's mother, Sandra (Jane Asher). Other friends and family are on their way to Daniel's house for the funeral, including Howard (Andy Nyman), a sniveling hypochondriac; Justin (Ewen Bremner), a man hoping to recapture his one-night stand at a funeral; Martha (Daisy Donovan), the aforementioned stand; and her fiancé Simon (Alan Tudyk). Simon and Martha pick up her brother Troy (Kris Marshall), who happens to manufacture illegal drugs, some of which Simon accidentally ingests, thinking that they are Valium to calm his nerves before dealing with his future father-in-law, who dislikes him for no other reason than the necessary conflict for comedy to ensue. Finally, Daniel's older brother, Robert (Rupert Graves), is on his way from New York and unprepared to deal with the responsibility of possibly tending for his now-widowed mother.

After the gaggle of personality disorders arrive at the funeral, writer Dean Craig throws them a variety of curveballs. Simon trips on the acid he thought was Valium, which inevitably ends up with him knocking over the casket during the eulogy, stripping down, and climbing to the top of the house. In a plotline with a little less male nudity, Daniel is approached by Peter (Peter Dinklage), who turns out to have been his father's lover with the pictures to prove it. While Daniel is being blackmailed by Peter to keep the photos under wraps, another miscommunication about the Valium bottle ends up killing the nefarious dwarf. The gang of incompetents have to bury one body and hide another, while Simon is busy showing off his own on the roof and declaring his love for Martha.

The cast of *Death at a Funeral* do their best with the material to lift a surprisingly unfunny script off the page, but effort only goes so far. Macfadyen has a face that was designed to play the straight man and character actors Peter Dinklage and Alan Tudyk can brighten up any film. The women do not fare quite as well, although they are given significantly less to do than their male counterparts.

Comic timing is a delicate, hard-to-pinpoint thing and British wit contains some of the most complicated beats in the history of the genre. If a joke is pushed too hard or a reaction shot held too long, it can easily fall apart. Knowing when to hit the punchline and how long to hold the awkward beat afterward is essential to a film like *Death at a Funeral*. A script with this many ridiculous twists and turns would never feel traditionally believable, but we need to think that the characters believe it for the comedy to work. Oz mistakes self-awareness for whimsy. He and his undeniably talented group of actors are constantly winking at the camera, as if even they cannot believe the ridiculous behavior they are acting out under the guise of wacky comedy. There is a fine line between whimsical and ridiculous and the best British comedy walks it delicately. *Death at a Funeral*

starts off ridiculous and never crosses back over that line, proving that perhaps a British sense of humor is something that comes from living in England, not just being born there.

Brian Tallerico

CREDITS

Robert: Rupert Graves
Peter: Peter Dinklage
Simon: Alan Tudyk
Martha: Daisy Donovan
Daniel: Matthew Macfayden
Justin: Ewen Bremner
Uncle Alfie: Peter Vaughan
Jane: Keeley Hawes
Howard: Andy Nyman
Sandra: Jane Asher
Troy: Kris Marshall
Victor: Peter Egan
Origin: USA, Netherlands, Germany
Language: English
Released: 2007
Production: Diana Phillips, Sidney Kimmel, Share Stallings, Laurence Malkin; VIP Medienfonds 1 & 2, Parabolic Pictures, Stable Way Entertainment; released by MGM
Directed by: Frank Oz
Written by: Dean Craig
Cinematography by: Oliver Curtis
Music by: Murray Gold
Sound: John Midgely
Editing: Beverley Mills
Art Direction: Lynne Huitson
Costumes: Natalie Ward
Production Design: Michael Howells
MPAA rating: R
Running time: 90 minutes

REVIEWS

Boston Globe Online. August 17, 2007.
Chicago Sun-Times Online. August 17, 2007.
Entertainment Weekly Online. August 15, 2007.
Hollywood Reporter Online. June 11, 2007.
Los Angeles Times Online. August 17, 2007.
New York Times Online. August 17, 2007.
San Francisco Chronicle. August 17, 2007, p. E5.
Variety Online. June 5, 2007.
Washington Post Online. August 17, 2007.

QUOTES

Sandra: "Tea can do many things, Jane, but it can't bring back the dead."

TRIVIA

The movie was filmed in seven weeks.

DEATH SENTENCE

Protect What's Yours.
—Movie tagline

Box Office: $9.5 million

Death Sentence is an action-adventure revenge thriller from *Saw* (2004) co-creator and director James Wan, starring Kevin Bacon as the patriarch of the Hume clan. When his son is killed in a gang initiation ritual, Nick Hume pursues a quest for revenge that ultimately costs him much more than he bargained for. Though the film boasts some genuine technical savvy, its weak plot, thin characterizations, and misguided attempts to elevate film's content via allegory and direct references to director Martin Scorsese's vastly superior *Taxi Driver* (1976) ultimately only serve to emphasize exactly how hollow *Death Sentence* is as a piece of storytelling. All of the film's elements combine to make what could have been a compelling thriller with parallels to the war on terror into a cinematic train wreck.

Nick Hume's son Brendan (Stuart Lafferty) is killed at a gas station as part of a gang initiation. Realizing that the murderer is going to get only a brief jail sentence, Nick opts not to testify against the killer, who walks. Nick later pursues the gang member and kills him. Instead of bringing Nick a sense of justified vengeance, Nick feels remorse. The gang member Nick killed, however, happened to be the brother of the gang leader, Billy Darley (Garrett Hedlund). The gang hunts Nick down, on the street, in his office. One of the thugs delivers a package to him—it is a briefcase containing a photo of the surviving members of Nick's family with their faces crossed out and a phone number on the back. Nick calls the number, and Billy informs him that his family has been given a death sentence. The gang members break into Hume's home that night, kill his wife (Kelly Preston), gravely wound his other son, Lucas (Jordan Garrett), and nearly kill Nick. Nick does some time in the hospital, sees his wounded son, and then escapes and goes on the offensive. He buys guns, he shaves his head, and starts hunting down the gangsters, culminating in a bloodbath straight out of *Taxi Driver,* complete with Nick finally sitting on a sofa as the authorities surround him.

Death Sentence is a case study in bombastic storytelling. Subtlety is completely out the window. Only Kevin Bacon's character is allowed anything remotely approaching nuance, and even this is eventually chucked in favor of a one-dimensional quest for vengeance. Some of the filmmaking shows adept technical proficiency, such as the scene in which the gang members chase Nick down streets and through a parking garage, but the scene has no real dramatic power—its only excitement is derived from wondering how its many long takes were accomplished (through the use of a special camera rig that allowed the camera to be passed between various operators on dollies and cranes). The film goes from being a merely bad curiosity to truly horrible during the scene in which the gang attempts to execute Nick and his family. After killing the police officers sitting in a car just outside the Hume home, and coming inside and (apparently) murdering Nick's entire family, Billy is content to deliver what may or may not be a fatal shot to Nick's side. Given all of the violence that has led up to this moment, and after going to such great lengths, one would think that Billy would accept nothing less than flaying Nick alive, or at least emptying several clips into him. Other elements of *Death Sentence* stretch plausibility to the breaking point, to be sure, but this failure to be truly brutal in a moment that seems to call for brutality is egregiously sloppy.

The film painfully tries to make the occasional stab at social consciousness—a scene in which Nick's lawyer explains that a jury will be sympathetic to a troubled youth who has only known violence and Billy Darley's observation that thugs are always being killed but it takes the death of the son of a corporate vice president to make the newspaper are prime examples. In this way, *Death Sentence* puts forth a little cursory commentary about class war—but this, like so much else in the movie, is paper thin. That the film implicitly and so completely seeks to reaffirm the moral superiority of the mainstream social order by aligning its sympathies with the wronged, rich white man undercuts any pretension of interest in genuine analysis of any of the ills plaguing society.

Death Sentence none too subtly tries to shift into an allegory for the war on terror in a speech about how everybody thinks they are right in a war, but nobody wins—violence begets violence, and the equation is just chaos. What makes this so disappointing is not the message itself, but its delivery—the word choice of "everybody thinks they are right in a war," is an instance of a filmmaker not trusting his audience at all and beating them over their collective head with the metaphor stick to make sure that there is no way the intended message slips by. Similar messages about retribution and the cycle of violence abound (commenting on Nick's shaved head and street clothes, Billy says, "You look like one of us. Look what I made you"). The carnage at the end is clearly meant to be an homage to director Martin Scorsese's *Taxi Driver,* but the reference is so brazen that it threatens to cross the thin line that separates homage from plagiarism, especially given that the two films are so tonally and thematically different. Whereas *Taxi Driver* uses violence as a component of redemption, the violence in *Death Sentence* is purely tied to vengeance. By invoking *Taxi Driver* at all, director James Wan seems not to trust the efficacy or mission of his own filmmaking and attempts to elevate his subject at the eleventh hour by cribbing from a much greater film. When the credits finally roll, it is clear that this movie's very existence is all the evidence needed for its own death sentence.

John Boaz

CREDITS

Nick Hume: Kevin Bacon
Billy Darly: Garrett Hedlund
Helen Hume: Kelly Preston
Det. Wallis: Aisha Tyler
Bones Darly: John Goodman
Joe Darly: Matt O'Leary
Lucas Hume: Jordan Garrett
Brendan Hume: Stuart Lafferty
Origin: USA
Language: English
Released: 2007
Production: Ashok Amritraj, Howard Baldwin, Karen Baldwin; Hyde Park Entertainment; released by 20th Century-Fox
Directed by: James Wan
Written by: Ian Mackenzie Jeffers
Cinematography by: John R. Leonetti
Music by: Charlie Clouser
Sound: Jonathan S. Gaynor
Music Supervisor: Michelle Silverman
Editing: Michael N. Knue
Art Direction: Rosa Palomo
Costumes: Kristen M. Burke
Production Design: Julie Berghoff
MPAA rating: R
Running time: 105 minutes

REVIEWS

Boston Globe Online. August 31, 2007.
Chicago Sun-Times Online. August 31, 2007.
Hollywood Reporter Online. August 31, 2007.
Los Angeles Times Online. August 31, 2007.
New York Times Online. August 30, 2007.
San Francisco Chronicle. August 31, 2007, p. E5.
Variety Online. August 30, 2007.
Washington Post. August 31, 2007, p. C1.

TRIVIA

Based on the book, *Death Sentence*—the direct sequel novel to *Death Wish*, which itself was made into a movie in 1974 starring Charles Bronson, and spawning four sequels, none of which were influenced by the novel series.

DELTA FARCE

A funny thing happened on the way to Iraq.
    —Movie tagline

In this war the wind doesn't blow it hurls.
    —Movie tagline

War isn't funny…but this movie is.
    —Movie tagline

Box Office: $8.1 million

Veteran television director C.B. Harding makes his big screen debut in another abysmal Larry the Cable Guy vehicle, the war comedy *Delta Farce*. Screenwriting neophytes Bear Aderhold and Tom Sullivan concoct a mildly amusing premise and manage to insert some on-target one-liners amidst the glut of misguided racial slurs, homophobia, scatological humor, and generally tired sophomoric absurdity, but the film as a whole misfires so badly, only a single film critic gave *Delta Farce* a semi-favorable review. *Variety*'s John Anderson notes that the film contains, "a subcutaneous wit that has a lot to do with Iraq war fatigue." Indeed, turning the Iraq war into a utterly absurd mockery within this film may well be its sole saving grace.

The plot marries various aspects of far superior but decidedly dated 1980s comedies such as *Stripes* (1981), *Private Benjamin* (1980), and *Three Amigos* (1986) with the redneck flavor of *Blue Collar TV,* Larry the Cable Guy's television milieu. Essentially playing himself, Larry stars as Larry, a waiter who is humiliated after his girlfriend Karen (Christina Moore) reveals she is pregnant by another man. Larry's other friends are similarly down-and-out: Bill (Bill Engvall) is unhappily married to Connie (Lisa Lampanelli), and Everett (DJ Qualls), a former police officer, lives in a storage garage with a blow-up doll. Fate intervenes in their dreary lives when the three Army Reservists are deployed to Fallujah but inadvertently dropped in Mexico. The boys' Sergeant Kilgore (Keith David), whose name is a reference to *Apocalypse Now*'s (1979) Lieutenant Colonel Kilgore, is a typically hard-nosed, loudly barking military tyrant who has hardened the film's "heroes" in the requisite basic training montage. Found unconscious and mistaken for dead, Kilgore is buried alive in the desert by the hapless "weekend warriors."

The soldiers spend most of the first half of the film mistaking Mexico for Iraq, with Larry commenting, "We are in the most dangerous city in the world, except maybe for Detroit." They eventually make their way to the tiny village of La Miranda, devoid of most modern amenities. The town is beleaguered by an evil band of banditos, led by the conveniently named Carlos Santana (Danny Trejo), whom the boys have chased off after mistaking them for Iraqi insurgents. When the trio realize they are not actually in the Middle East, Bill, served a cerveza by a sexy senorita, convinces Larry they must stay with the now-familiar line, "If we leave now, the terrorists win." Comedic drama ensues as Santana plots his revenge, leading to one of the film's funnier exchanges: "Looks like we've got ourselves a Mexican standoff," a soldier says. "Down here we just call it a standoff," Santana replies.

The film's trio of stars are certainly likable in a Three Stooges vein, with Larry likely to draw viewers from his solid core of fans. Trejo and David suffer equally at the hands of their two-dimensional, sketchily conceived and badly written characters. And almost as deplorable as the crude Arab jokes (the boys inquire of the locals whether they are "Turds or Shi'tites") and Mexican stereotypes that populate the village are the highly implausible romances between the stout, crude Larry and the beautiful senorita Maria (Marisol Nichols) and glamorous ex-girlfriend Karen. The film does possess a few brief highlights, including the rail-thin Everett enjoying an improbable wrestling ring triumph and Carlos Santana's unexpected karaoke rendition of "I Will Survive."

At one point Bill declares, "One man's international incident is another man's preemptive strike in the war on terror." While *Delta Farce* may not exactly qualify as an international incident, with "more problems than a Cub Scout at Neverland Ranch," to quote one of the film's funnier lines, the film may be a preemptive strike on war comedies for some time to come.

Hilary White

CREDITS

Larry: Larry the Cable Guy
Everett: DJ Qualls
Maria Garcia: Marisol Nichols
Carlos: Danny Trejo
Bill: Bill Engvall
Sgt. Kilgore: Keith David
General Walker: Glenn Morshower
Karen: Christina Moore
Connie: Lisa Lampanelli
Victor: Ed O'Ross
Origin: USA
Language: English
Released: 2007
Production: Alan C. Blomquist, J.P. Williams; Parallel Entertainment Pictures, Samwilla; released by Lions Gate
Directed by: C.B. Harding
Written by: Bear Aderhold, Thomas F.X. Sullivan
Cinematography by: Tom Priestley
Music by: James Levine
Editing: Mark Conte
Art Direction: Dins W.W. Danielsen
Costumes: Louise de Teliga

Production Design: Cabot McMullen
MPAA rating: PG-13
Running time: 89 minutes

REVIEWS

Boston Globe Online. May 12, 2007.
Entertainment Weekly. May 25, 2007, p. 63.
Hollywood Reporter Online. May 14, 2007.
Los Angeles Times Online. May 14, 2007.
New York Times Online. May 12, 2007.
San Francisco Chronicle. May 14, 2007, p. C1.
Variety Online. May 11, 2007.

QUOTES

Larry (when Everett wakes up wearing a dress): "Everett, that's another reason you shouldn't drink tequilla."
Everett (sees the dress): "Damn, this always happens when I eat the worm."

TRIVIA

The airplanes in the hanger were done using CGI because of the lack of Department of Defense support.

DISTURBIA

Every killer lives next door to someone.
—Movie tagline

Box Office: $80.2 million

While *Disturbia* may aspire to Hitchcockian grandeur, it ultimately assumes the traits of the now stale slasher film. The film has some things to recommend it, but its shortcomings slightly outweigh the positives. The most horrifying scene in *Disturbia* happens within the first ten minutes. Good-natured, seventeen-year-old Kale (Shia LaBeouf) and his dad are returning home from a fly fishing trip when their car is passed by a reckless SUV driver. This leads to the first of two crashes involving Kale and his father, and while both survive the first accident, Kale's father doesn't survive the second. It is something the audience only experiences through Kale's facial expressions, and it is heartbreaking.

One year later, we meet up with Kale in his Spanish class on the last day before summer break. The once good-natured youth is now angry and withdrawn. When the teacher unwisely taunts Kale with the memory of his father, Kale's immediate response is to punch him. This earns Kale a sentence of three months house arrest complete with an ankle bracelet that notifies the police should he wander one hundred feet from the main monitor.

To reinforce the fact that his behavior is self-destructive and house arrest is supposed to be a punishment, Kale's mother Julie (Carrie-Anne Moss) cancels his live Xbox, revokes his iTunes privileges, and cuts the cord to his bedroom television. Angry and withdrawn before, Kale's incarceration makes him incredibly self-centered and downright unpleasant. With little else to occupy his time, Kale begins spying on his neighbors. Across the street, after the wife has gone off to play tennis, her husband comes home to play with the maid. Next door are three malicious little boys who watch cable pornography when their mother is not looking. And the new family that has just moved in has a most comely daughter, Ashley (Sarah Roemer), who likes to dress in skimpy shorts and tube tops, practice yoga in front of an open window, and parade around in a bikini in the backyard pool.

Although Kale notices Mr. Turner (David Morse), the single man obsessed with mowing his lawn, there seems little of interest there…until Kale hears the news about a missing woman and the search for a blue 1960s Ford Mustang with a dent on the left side. Mr. Turner drives a blue Mustang, which Kale now notices has a dent on the left side. Mr. Turner becomes an object of Kale's attention on the same level as Ashley but for quite a different reason.

Soon it becomes apparent that Ashley knows she is being watched—Kale seems to be too self-absorbed to realize he would be more secretive in his spying if he turned his lights off—and it is not long before the teen seductress is knocking on Kale's door and inviting herself in, much to Kale's consternation and his loopy buddy Ronnie's (Aaron Yoo) delight.

One night Kale sees Turner bring home a date. He watches the seduction, then thinks he sees the young woman running through the house in fear but later observes her leaving the house and driving away. However, Kale is still convinced Turner is a murderer and is horrified when Turner is conveniently present to give his mother a ride home after her car mysteriously gets a flat tire. Kale enlists the help of his friends and begins to obsessively watch Turner. He even tries to leave his house to continue his surveillance when his ankle bracelet summons the police and Kale is now seen as a disturbed kid stalking an innocent man.

One of the film's main shortcomings is that Turner is never portrayed as anything other than guilty. Morse has played the soft-spoken sociopath so often that perhaps he is simply typecast and so the writers, Christopher Landon and Carl Ellsworth, never bothered to give Morse any scenes in which he is anything other than menacing. There are several other problems with this *Rear Window* (1954) wannabe. While some may argue that the movie's leisurely pace allows for character development and the creation of suspense, it nonetheless takes far too long for anything really interesting to happen after the unsettling opening car accident.

LaBeouf uses his nerdy charm to create a intelligent, complex character but he is short-changed by the fact that the writers do not allow any self-doubt to creep into his homicidal imaginings about his neighbor. What made James Stewart's character so compelling in the Hitchcock original was that the character's actions were always tempered by self-doubt. This makes Kale a far less interesting protagonist in a similarly less interesting film.

Disturbia finally degenerates to the level of slasher film, which is curiously when the plot holes also begin to manifest. Until this point, it is a believable enough thriller that makes one wonder what Hitchcock and Stewart might have done with *Rear Window* if they had had access to a video cell phone, a laptop, the Internet, and a digital video camera.

Beverley Bare Buehrer

CREDITS

Kale: Shia LaBeouf
Mr. Turner: David Morse
Julie: Carrie-Anne Moss
Officer Gutierrez: Jose Pablo Cantillo
Ashley: Sarah Roemer
Ronnie: Aaron Yoo
Origin: USA
Language: English
Released: 2007
Production: Joe Medjuck, E. Bennett Walsh, Jackie Marcus; Montecito Picture Co., DreamWorks, Cold Spring Pictures; released by Paramount
Directed by: D.J. Caruso
Written by: Christopher Landon, Carl Ellsworth
Cinematography by: Rogier Stoffers
Music by: Geoff Zanelli
Sound: Mark Ulano
Music Supervisor: Jennifer Hawks
Editing: Jim Page
Art Direction: Douglas Cumming
Costumes: Marie-Sylvie Deveau
Production Design: Tom Southwell
MPAA rating: PG-13
Running time: 105 minutes

REVIEWS

Boxoffice Online. April 13, 2007.
Chicago Sun-Times Online. April 13, 2007.

Entertainment Weekly Online. April 11, 2007.
Hollywood Reporter Online. March 12, 2007.
Los Angeles Times Online. April 13, 2007.
New York Times Online. April 13, 2007.
San Francisco Chronicle. April 13, 2007, p. E1.
Variety Online. March 21, 2007.
Washington Post Online. April 13, 2007.

QUOTES

Ashley (to Ronnie and Kale): "What took you so long?"
Kale: "We were upstairs playing."
Ronnie: "Video games!"

TRIVIA

The title *Disturbia* is a play on the words "disturb" and "suburbia."

THE DIVING BELL AND THE BUTTERFLY

(Le Scaphandre et le papillon)

Let your imagination set you free.
—Movie tagline

Box Office: $5.7 million

The Diving Bell and the Butterfly (*Le scaphandre et le papillion*) is based on the extraordinary true story of Jean-Dominique Bauby, who suffered a debilitating stroke that left him completely paralyzed and yet able to dictate his eponymous memoir using the only organ that was still functional, his left eye. The film is the third feature of director Julian Schnabel, whose background as a highly influential Neo-expressionist artist has informed his previous work in *Basquiat* (1996) and *Before Night Falls* (2000). Schnabel uses his artistic sensibility to the fullest extent in *The Diving Bell and the Butterfly,* which combines dreams, fantasy, altered reality, and brutal actuality to bring Bauby's remarkably unique account to stunning life on the silver screen, a feat that many thought improbable if not impossible.

The film is mainly told from Bauby's point of view and opens as the man is waking from his coma after suffering a massive stroke. The viewer experiences the fuzzy images of doctors and nurses in a hospital that Bauby (Mathieu Amalric) is just starting to recognize as his eyes slowly open. We hear in his voiceover that he is cognizant of his situation and is able to correctly respond to each question that the doctors ask; except that they cannot hear him. The use of his mind's voice as the nar-

rator recalls another acclaimed film featuring a protagonist that cannot verbally communicate, Jane Campion's *The Piano* (1993). When Bauby is informed by his doctor (Patrick Chesnais) that he is, in fact, in a hospital in Berck-sur-Mer suffering from "locked-in syndrome," his brain functioning normally but unable to communicate, he imagines himself sinking to the bottom of the sea in a diving bell, also echoing an image from *The Piano* when Campion's mute Ada sinks to the bottom of the ocean tethered to her beloved piano.

The audience only sees forty-three-year-old Bauby's post-stroke visage for the first time when he does, catching a glimpses of his now nearly unrecognizable face in glass windows while being wheeled down the hospital hallway. His right eye sewn shut by doctors who feared sepsis and his mouth frozen in a half-downturned grimace, Bauby is a far cry from the handsome, vibrant father of three, womanizer, and editor-in-chief of French *Elle* shown in frequent flashbacks.

Schnabel and screenwriter Ronald Harwood (*The Pianist,* 2002) do not dwell on Bauby's initial self-pity, which is brief, but rather quickly introduce him to therapist Henriette (Marie-Josée Croze) that develops the system of communication via blinking his left eye as she reads off a list of most-used letters. He blinks when she has reached the letter he wants and then the process starts over again, forming letter by letter, word by word in this excruciatingly slow manner. He informs his publisher, with whom he already has a book deal, that he still wants to proceed with the book, albeit in a very different way and with new subject matter. She reluctantly agrees, sending over the comely Claude (Anne Consigny) to take his unusual dictation.

Both his female therapists, Henriette and speech therapist Marie (Olatz López Garmendia, Schnabel's wife), are also beauties, something that does not go unnoticed by Jean-Do, as he is affectionately called, who finds irony in the ridiculous situation. His lust and sense of humor are still intact, and much of the first half of the film highlights Jean-Do's enviable wit and imagination in the face of his unbearable circumstances. His good friend Laurent (Isaach de Bankolé) comes to visit and the well-meaning man places a large fur hat on his head as a gift. Jean-Do's internal response is laced with sarcasm, thinking he looks like an overgrown rabbit. Laurent expresses his outrage that he has overheard acquaintances saying that Jean-Do is now a vegetable, causing Jean-Do to idly wonder what kind of vegetable he now was. "A carrot?" he muses. Fantasy sequences taking place in his mind have him engaging in a Bacchanalian feast complete with oysters with Henriette and in various other dreamy escapes with characters both living and dead—the imagination his butterfly.

A more poignant moment is also one of the film's highlights, featuring the legendary Max von Sydow who masterfully plays Bauby's father Papinou. The scene is a flashback, depicting Bauby tenderly shaving his elderly, frail, and housebound father. The elder Bauby scolds him for leaving his wife and children for his young mistress but the scene ends with the forgetful old gentleman tenderly telling his son that he is proud of him; something that Bauby says comforted him then and even more after his stroke. A later scene has Papinou call his son in the hospital, overcome with emotion and tears, but able to relate to his son that, in a way, they are in the same predicament—Papinou bound within the four walls of his apartment and Bauby bound within his own body. It is an extremely touching moment for the audience and for Bauby, the camera lens blurring as his eye wells with tears.

Bauby's female relationships in the film are not as clear cut. His ex-wife Celine (Emmanuelle Seigner) lovingly and dutifully visits and brings their adorable children when he requests. She is clearly still in love with him but he is in love with another woman (Marina Hands) who does not want to see him in his current condition. Another heart-wrenching scene comes as Celine is visiting and the woman finally calls. Bauby's caretakers are off that day and an emotionally wrecked Celine is forced to translate the call, with Bauby professing he wishes she was there every day. The filmmakers underscore the fact that his life as an invalid is no less messy than his previous life.

Harwood's script was originally in English but Schnabel was able to convince producers to translate it into Bauby's native French, a language that Schnabel then learned in order to do the film as he intended. Beautifully photographed by cinematographer Janusz Kaminski, *The Diving Bell and the Butterfly* is filled with touching images, both beautiful and tragic, and is neither wholly uplifting nor completely devastating, but a satisfying mix of both.

Hilary White

CREDITS

Jean-Domnique Bauby: Mathieu Amalric
Celine: Emmanuelle Seigner
Henriette: Marie-Josée Croze
Dr. Lepage: Patrick Chesnais
Papinou: Max von Sydow
Claude: Anne Consigny
Laurent: Isaach de Bankolé
Roussin: Niels Arestrup
Marie Lopez: Olatz López Garmendia
Josephine: Marina Hands
Origin: France
Language: English, French
Released: 2007
Production: Kathleen Kennedy, Jon Kilik; Pathe Renn, France 3 Cinema; released by Miramax Films
Directed by: Julian Schnabel
Written by: Ronald Harwood
Cinematography by: Janusz Kaminski
Sound: Jean-Paul Mugel, Paul Cantelon
Music Supervisor: Julian Schnabel
Editing: Juliette Welfing
Costumes: Olivier Beriot
MPAA rating: PG-13
Running time: 112 minutes

REVIEWS

Christian Science Monitor Online. November 30, 2007.
Entertainment Weekly Online. November 28, 2007.
Los Angeles Times Online. November 30, 2007.
New York Times Online. November 30, 2007.
New Yorker Online. December 3, 2007.
Newsweek Online. December 3, 2007.
Premiere Online. November 29, 2007.
Rolling Stone Online. December 13, 2007.
Variety Online. May 22, 2007.
Wall Street Journal. November 30, 2007, p. W1.

QUOTES

Jean-Dominique Bauby: "I decided to stop pitying myself. Other than my eye, two things aren't paralyzed, my imagination and my memory."

TRIVIA

The script, written by Ron Harwood, was originally in English. Director Julian Schnabel convinced the studio, Pathé, to change the language to French to stay true to Bauby's life and story.

AWARDS

British Acad. 2007: Adapt. Screenplay
Golden Globes 2008: Director (Schnabel), Foreign Film
Ind. Spirit 2008: Cinematog., Director (Schnabel)
Nomination:
Oscars 2007: Adapt. Screenplay, Cinematog., Director (Schnabel), Film Editing
British Acad. 2007: Foreign Film
Directors Guild 2007: Director (Schnabel)
Golden Globes 2008: Screenplay
Ind. Spirit 2008: Film, Screenplay
Writers Guild 2007: Adapt. Screenplay.

DOA: DEAD OR ALIVE

Alone they are unbeatable...together they are invincible.
—Movie tagline

Killer looks are nothing without the right moves.
—Movie tagline

They're the ultimate fighters. They've got the looks. They've got the moves. And men fall at their feet.
—Movie tagline

If you want an idea of what to expect from *DOA: Dead or Alive,* one of several recent video game adaptations to hit the big screen, it is worth noting that one of its screenwriters, J.F. Lawton, penned eighty-seven episodes of buxom pin-up star Pamela Anderson's syndicated action television show, *V.I.P.* (1998–2002). And while film critics tend to err on the side of snobbery when it comes to films based on video game properties—though, in their defense, there has yet to be a truly great (and some would argue, even good) video game-based film ever produced—when examining a film like *DOA* is hard not to enter into a discussion about expectations. What should critics and audiences expect from a movie based on a video game about an *Enter the Dragon*-esque fighting tournament where the contestants (seemingly designed by the ghost of Russ Meyer) take frequent breaks to engage in bikini-clad volleyball tournaments? Perhaps it is unfair to fault a film for staying true to its source material. This is a film about sexy women fighting each other, and it rarely purports to be anything else. There is no subtext. There is barely even text. However, to his credit, director Corey Yuen does a decent job of convincing us that he is in on the joke too, which goes a long way toward making this goofy arcade throwback much more digestible.

To be fair, when a movie opens with a Japanese ninja princess escaping past 400 guards, diving off her cliff-top palace, tossing off her kimono to reveal a hi-tech hang-glider, and, mid-air, receiving a remote-controlled, throwing-star invitation to an ultimate fighting tournament in its first four minutes, it basically renders your suspension of disbelief completely useless. The plot is classic arcade fodder, as simple as they come. Fighters from around the world find themselves invited to the DOA tournament, competing for ten million dollars. The main players are the aforementioned Princess Kasumi (Devon Aoki) and her bodyguard Hayabusa (Kane Kosugi), American wrestling diva Tina Armstrong (Jaime Pressly), British cat burglar Christie (Holly Valance), and the young Helena (Sarah Carter), whose late father started the DOA tournament and passed the reins over to his partner Donovan (Eric Roberts). While everyone else just wants the money and bragging rights,

Kasumi wants to find out what happened to her brother Hayate (Collin Chou), who allegedly died in the competition the previous year.

But just like reality, logic, and physics, story means nothing in the world of *DOA*. The entire film is essentially just one fight scene after another for eighty minutes, and, if you edited out all the dialogue, you would probably only shorten the movie by five minutes. Yuen obviously wants us to feel like we are watching a live-action video game—the costumes, sets, and music are straight out of a *Mortal Kombat* (1995) theme park attraction—so can we blame him for wanting to skip past the boring, overly expository cut scenes? However, the question remains: Did Yuen deliver enough action and softcore titillation to satisfy his prepubescent target audience?

The answer is—almost. The ladies in *DOA* are undeniably attractive, though some male fans will be heartbroken to find that the PG-13 heroines fail to show as much skin as their video game counterparts. Devon Aoki and Sarah Carter do the best job of selling themselves as convincing martial arts experts, while the undeniably fit Jaime Pressly, Holly Valance, and Natassia Malthe all look like they chose to leave their fighting scenes up to the editing team. (Valance does, however, get the film's most creative and revealing action scene, assaulting a roomful of police officers while topless as she slides into her bra in slow motion.) The martial arts sequences range from boring to near-creative, but if you are not a fan of "wire-fu," beware. The women spend half their time floating around the screen like Peter Pan before they kick someone.

While the pacing of *DOA* moves along at a decent clip, it hits some major problems toward the end. It is hard to warn about spoilers in a movie with almost no story, but there is a part in the third act where we are asked to believe that Eric Roberts, the third-tier, gravelly-voiced American character actor, has become the best fighter in the world. And that is simply an act of faith that no audience will be willing to embrace. When the aging Roberts, clad in his flowing, green silk karate outfit, steps up to fight the amazingly muscular Collin Chou, accompanied by same kind of editing that tried to turn an apathetic Sir Ben Kingsley into a sword-fighting vampire in *BloodRayne* (2005, another game-based movie), and he starts to win, the film's sense of cheesy fun goes out the window and we start resenting the movie for insulting our intelligence.

Given the film's origins and premise, the fact that one's intelligence is insulted late in the film, in *DOA's* third act, speaks volumes about Yuen's directorial talents. Although Yuen makes the most of what he has to work with, it cannot be ignored that *DOA* exists almost solely for the benefit of thirteen-year-old boys. If you have already made it through puberty, there is really no reason to seek out *DOA: Dead or Alive*.

Tom Burns

CREDITS

Princess Kasumi: Devon Aoki
Helena Douglas: Sarah Carter
Ayane: Natassia Malthe
Tina Armstrong: Jaime Pressly
Donovan: Eric Roberts
Weatherby: Steve Howey
Maximillian Marsh: Matthew Marsden
Hayate: Collin Chou
Christie Allen: Holly Valance
Ryu Hayabusa: Kane (Takeshi) Kosugi
Bass: Kevin Nash
Zack: Brian J. White
Pirate Leader: Robin Shou
Bayman: Derek Boyer
Leon: Silvio Simac
Origin: Great Britain, Germany, USA
Language: English
Released: 2006

Production: Paul W.S. Anderson, Jeremy Bolt, Bernd Eichinger, Robert Kulzer, Mark A. Altman; Constantin Film, VIP 4 Production, Impact Pictures; released by Weinstein Company
Directed by: Corey Yuen
Written by: J.F. Lawton, Adam Gross, Seth Gross
Cinematography by: Chi Ying Chan, Kwok-Man Keung
Editing: Eddie Hamilton, Angie Lam, Ka-Fai Cheung
Art Direction: Wong Ching
Costumes: Frank Helmer
Production Design: Choo Sung-pong
MPAA rating: PG-13
Running time: 87 minutes

REVIEWS

Entertainment Weekly. June 29, 2007, p. 117.
Guardian Online. September 15, 2006.
Hollywood Reporter Online. June 18, 2007.
New York Times Online. June 16, 2007.
Variety Online. June 15, 2007.
Village Voice Online. October 17, 2006.

TRIVIA

During the first fight scenes the screen layout and voice announcer are lifted straight from the game.

E

EAGLE VS. SHARK

Opposites. Unattractive.
—Movie tagline

Finding love was never so…awkward.
—Movie tagline

There's someone for everyone…apparently.
—Movie tagline

Written and directed by New Zealander Taika Waititi (also known as Taika Cohen), *Eagle vs. Shark* is a quirky romantic comedy about two twenty-something oddballs: Jarrod (Jemaine Clement), a self-deluded video store clerk, and Lily (Loren Horsley), a shy fast food cashier. With its low-budget aesthetic, absurdist humor, and cast of misfits, *Eagle vs. Shark* was dismissed by many critics as a retread of *Napoleon Dynamite* (2004) upon its release. While these comparisons are somewhat apt, *Eagle vs. Shark* distinguishes itself from *Napoleon Dynamite* with revelatory moments of genuine heartbreak and regret, at times achieving the pathos of *Muriel's Wedding* (1995), another eccentric, melancholy-tinged comedy from Down Under.

Each day from her cashier's station at Meaty Boy, Lily awaits the arrival of her crush, Jarrod, a strapping lad with unfortunate bangs—and even more unfortunate tinted glasses. One afternoon, he delivers a party invitation to another Meaty Boy cashier, and Lily takes the initiative, crashing the party with her beloved older brother, Damien (Joel Tobeck), in tow. The guests are dressed as their favorite animals, and Lily's shark costume impresses Jarrod, the self-styled Eagle Lord. He is further wowed by her gaming skills, declaring her "the best female Fight Man player he has ever seen." Two minutes

of tepid sex ensues, after which Jarrod crank calls his high school tormentor, Eric (David Fane). Soon Lily and Damien are accompanying Jarrod on a trip to his hometown, where he intends to see justice served by fighting Eric to the death. As Jarrod trains for the impending showdown, Lily grapples with her new boyfriend's self-absorption as well as his father's depression and her own loneliness.

As the two lovers, Horsley and Clement deliver slyly funny and sympathetic performances. Socially awkward and naive, Lily is endearing from the start. Although both her parents are dead ("like Oliver Twist['s]," Jarrod explains) and she eventually loses her job at Meaty Boy, Lily remains upbeat. As she says to Jarrod's father (Brian Sergent), "Life is full of hard bits, I think, but in between the hard bits, there are really lovely bits too." On the other hand, Jarrod—an immature pathological liar with a penchant for melodrama—is not immediately likable. Similar to Napoleon Dynamite, he takes prides in his "skillz," and he fancies himself an action hero-cum-soulful artiste. He can also be a total jerk, like when he scoffs at Lily and Damien's car-ride game of counting horses they spot along the way. But Waititi and Clement show that Jarrod's insensitivity is an outgrowth of his insecurities and desperate need for approval. After he returns home to find his family laughing at a joke told by Lily, Jarrod replies that he and his friend Tracy "have been pretty much laughing the whole day. Like this, but about ten times more laughing." Even more poignant, when he and Lily nestle in their sleeping bags at bedtime, he tells her, "You can hold my hand if you want to."

Because Jarrod and Lily often behave like stuttering adolescents (sometimes younger), it is easy to see why some critics have accused *Eagle vs. Shark* of being corny,, and why others, like John Anderson of *Newsday*, claim the film laughs at its characters instead of with them. While Jarrod's obsession with his high school bully is, indeed, ridiculous, the film does not offer it up merely as fodder for giggles; Waititi takes pains to show why Jarrod is fixated on this moment in his past, and the reasons are more complex than Jarrod himself realizes. When the day of the fight arrives, it is clear that Eric has become the repository for all of Jarrod's disappointments, like his favored brother's suicide, his mother's abandonment, and his father's neglect. The audience understands that Jarrod's regressive behavior is the result of his frustration and despair. That Lily recognizes his vulnerability and is empathetic to it illustrates that she is more mature than was initially apparent.

These sensitively drawn characterizations of Jarrod and Lily add a dimension of sadness and regret to *Eagle vs. Shark*, but the film remains humorous and fanciful throughout. Waititi has an eye and ear for the absurd, and he includes a few laugh-out-loud visual jokes, like when he reveals the surprising source of a presumably nondiegetic guitar solo. Animated sequences about two apples (analogues of Jarrod and Lily) who also find each other give the film a magical flavor all its own.

Although *Eagle vs. Shark* may seem derivative of other recent independent comedies, this sad, sweet film should be seen by a wider audience. With its touching performances, unexpected depth, and unique visual flair, Waititi's first feature-length effort has much to offer. At the film's conclusion, Jarrod ends up counting horses on the ride back to town, embracing what looked silly from the start. *Eagle vs. Shark* deserves to be embraced by viewers in much the same way.

Marisa Carroll

CREDITS

Jonah: Brian Sergent
Doug: Craig Hall
Damon: Joel Tobeck
Jarrod: Jemaine Clement
Lily: Loren Horsley
Nancy: Rachel House
Eric: David Fane
Origin: New Zealand
Language: English
Released: 2007
Production: Ainsley Gardiner, Cliff Curtis; New Zealand Film Commission, Wheuna Fioms, Unison Films; released by Miramax Films

Directed by: Taika Waititi
Written by: Taika Waititi
Cinematography by: Adam Clark
Music by: Phoenix Foundation
Sound: Nic McGowan
Editing: Jono Woodford-Robinson
Costumes: Amanda Neale
Production Design: Joseph Bleakley
MPAA rating: R
Running time: 94 minutes

REVIEWS

Boston Globe Online. June 22, 2007.
Christian Science Monitor Online. June 15, 2007.
Entertainment Weekly. June 22, 2007, p. 53.
Hollywood Reporter Online. February 6, 2007.
Los Angeles Times Online. June 15, 2007.
New York Times Online. June 15, 2007.
Variety Online. May 16, 2007.
Washington Post Online. June 22, 2007.

TRIVIA

The script was workshopped at the exclusive Sundance Director's and Screenwriter's Labs.

EASTERN PROMISES

Every sin leaves a mark.
—Movie tagline

Box Office: $17.3 million

Eastern Promises, so named for the promises made to young girls in Russia and former Eastern bloc countries about opportunities in the West, is from the same director/leading actor combination (David Cronenberg and Viggo Mortensen) that produced the much less effective *A History of Violence* (2005). As with the rest of his filmography, Cronenberg's use of on-screen violence is a major component of the storytelling in *Eastern Promises* and, as in *A History of Violence*, Cronenberg again explores familial themes, as well as the knotted relationship between appearance and reality, using a unique subculture, in this case the expatriate Russian underworld in London. What emerges from this odd and complex jumble of cinematic elements is a rich and intelligent film-going experience replete with excellent performances and challenging material, all wrapped in the guise of a crowd-pleasing, if extremely violent, thriller.

Eastern Promises opens with a bloody one-two punch: first, a throat-slashing in a barbershop; then, a young girl hemorrhages in a grocery/drug store. The girl is rushed to a London hospital where midwife Anna Khitrova (Naomi Watts) is able to rescue the baby before the mother dies. The girl has no identification on her—just a diary written in Russian and business card for the Trans-Siberian restaurant. Anna goes to the restaurant to see if she can find out anything about the girl. There, she meets Semyon (Armin Mueller-Stahl), the owner of the Trans-Siberian, who denies knowing the girl, but offers to translate the diary for her. As she leaves the restaurant, she has a brief encounter with Nikolai Luzhin, played to understated perfection by Viggo Mortensen, who is a chauffer for Semyon's unstable son, Kirill (Vincent Cassell). Nikolai and Kirill are dispatched to Azim's barbershop, the site of the film's opening grizzly murder, to help dispose of the body—Nikolai, Kirill, Azim, and Semyon are all involved in the Russian mafia—which Nikolai almost single-handedly chops up and dumps in the Thames River. The body is later discovered by the police, and is revealed to be covered in tattoos, indicating his position as a captain in the Russian mob—the stars tattooed on his knees indicate that he will never kneel before anyone. Anna returns to the Trans-Siberian with photocopies of the diary pages, but Semyon is persistent about acquiring the original diary. Anna refuses to hand over the diary and will not divulge her address. The next day, Semyon shows up at the hospital where Anna works and says that he will give Anna the address of the baby's family in Russia if she gives him the original diary. He also says that the diary contains information about his son, Kirill, that could cause trouble if the diary were to wind up with the police, and he makes a subtle threat on the baby's safety. Shortly after this encounter, Anna's Russian uncle Stepan (Jerzy Skolimowski) translates the section of the diary that reveals it was actually Semyon who raped the girl, leading Anna to believe, correctly, that he is the father of the baby. Fearing for the safety of the baby and her family members, Anna agrees to turn over the diary. Nikolai is sent to pick it up and when Anna asks for the address of the baby's family in Russia, Nikolai says, "What address?" Nikolai takes the diary and turns it over to Semyon, who burns it, but Nikolai reads enough of it first to realize, as Anna did, that Semyon is the father of the baby.

Meanwhile, Semyon has learned that Kirill ordered the killing of the rival Russian mobster, a Chechen, at Azim's barbershop. Chechens arrive in London to avenge the death of their brother. They start by killing Azim's nephew who had helped in the murder. Azim goes to Semyon and says that he must hand Kirill over to the Chechens or they will kill him as well. When Semyon learns that they do not know what Kirill looks like, he hatches a plan to send Nikolai in Kirill's place. Semyon

promotes Nikolai to a captain and gives him the star tattoos that indicate his rank. Shortly thereafter, Nikolai and Azim go to a bathhouse steam room to discuss business, and Azim excuses himself—the Chechens may not know what Kirill looks like, but they know he is a captain and so they attack the man with the tattoos of a captain, Nikolai. Though naked and unarmed, Nikolai manages to kill both of the Chechens. Nikolai is admitted to the hospital for his injuries, and there he is visited by detectives from Scotland Yard—it is revealed that Nikolai himself is actually a Russian agent working with Scotland Yard to investigate the Russian mob in London. The baby, he says, is the key. Ultimately, he brings down Semyon for statutory rape using the DNA evidence from the baby to link Semyon to the underage dead girl, and then uses his newly elevated rank to become a mob boss himself, whether simply to advance his own ambitions or to penetrate the Russian mob at higher levels is an open question. The orphaned baby is raised by Anna and her family.

It must be emphasized that *Eastern Promises* is a remarkable bit of filmmaking, and no simple summary can adequately capture the surprises (both visually and in terms of plot and character) that await the viewer. More than anything else, the film is about complexity itself, about the complicated structures (social and otherwise) that underlie surface reality. Whereas Cronenberg's 2005 effort *A History of Violence* was somewhat marred by a fanciful, comic book story (the film's graphic novel origins are all too apparent in its penchant for coincidence and in its operatic treatment of the power of the criminal underworld) and scattershot performances (William Hurt's Philadelphia dialect being the chief culprit), *Eastern Promises* resonates with a sense of specificity and authenticity. Although it takes place within a world that is about as far removed as possible from the average person's everyday experience, and though many of the situations are certainly stretched to the limits of plausibility for dramatic effect, the film never throws itself out of balance. The very alien world of the Russian mafia provides a context for the exploration of certain values (such as the meaning of family, loyalty, and honor), and Anna's alienation from her own heritage and the world of Nikolai and Semyon allows the audience entrée into that world through Anna's eyes. She provides a context for the viewer and serves as a touchstone for normalcy. Whether the movie turns its attention briefly to human trafficking, or the lengths to which parents will go for their children, or to moments of shockingly brutal violence, *Eastern Promises* is genuine in its exploration of the darker aspects of humanity and provides the audience with Anna as a companion in the labyrinth and a reminder that there is some good in the world.

The truly outstanding feature of *Eastern Promises* though, is actor Viggo Mortensen's portrayal of chauffeur/mob soldier/Russian agent Nikolai Luzhin. Mortensen, known for his obsessive research, not only traveled throughout Russia to gear up for the role, but also helped bring the much talked-about tattoo culture of the Russian underworld and prison system to the fore of the movie. By bringing his discovery of *The Russian Criminal Tattoo Encyclopedia* and the film *The Mark of Caïn* (2000), a documentary about Russian criminal tattooing, to the attention of director Cronenberg and screenwriter Steven Knight, Mortensen not only helped give the film some of its signature moments (such as Nikolai's interrogation by Russian mob bosses and the nude bathhouse fight), but also contributed immensely to the thematic thrust of the story: Nikolai's life is written on his body, but he is more than his tattoos and appearance suggest. So it is with *Eastern Promises* as a whole, a rich, complex, and unexpected bit of storytelling.

John Boaz

CREDITS

Nikolai: Viggo Mortensen
Anna: Naomi Watts
Kirill: Vincent Cassel
Semyon: Armin Mueller-Stahl
Helen: Sinead Cusack
Stepan: Jerzy Skolimowski
Yuri: Donald (Don) Sumpter
Azim: Mina E. Mina
Origin: Great Britain, Canada
Language: English
Released: 2007
Production: Paul Webster, Robert Lantos; BBC Films, Serendipity Point Films, Kudos Production; released by Focus Features
Directed by: David Cronenberg
Written by: Steven Knight
Cinematography by: Peter Suschitzsky
Music by: Howard Shore
Sound: Stuart Wilson
Editing: Ronald Sanders
Art Direction: Rebecca Holmes
Costumes: Denise Cronenberg
Production Design: Carol Spier
MPAA rating: R
Running time: 95 minutes

REVIEWS

Boston Globe Online. September 14, 2007.
Chicago Sun-Times Online. September 13, 2007.

Entertainment Weekly Online. September 12, 2007.
Hollywood Reporter Online. September 10, 2007.
Los Angeles Times Online. September 14, 2007.
New Yorker Online. September 17, 2007.
Rolling Stone Online. September 4, 2007.
San Francisco Chronicle. September 14, 2007, p. E4.
Variety Online. August 8, 2007.
Wall Street Journal. September 14, 2007, p. W1.
Washington Post. September 14, 2007, p. C5.

QUOTES

Nikolai (to Anna): "Forget any of this happened. Stay away from people like me."

TRIVIA

The film, shot in England, marked the first time director David Cronenberg shot a movie entirely outside of Canada.

AWARDS

Nomination:

Oscars 2007: Actor (Mortensen)
British Acad. 2007: Actor (Mortensen)
Golden Globes 2008: Actor—Drama (Mortensen), Film—Drama, Orig. Score
Screen Actors Guild 2007: Actor (Mortensen).

ELIZABETH: THE GOLDEN AGE

Woman. Warrior. Queen.
—Movie tagline

Box Office: $16.4 million

Cate Blanchett was little known when she starred in Shekhar Kapur's *Elizabeth* (1998). Her performance earned her an Academy Award® nomination and began her ascent to stardom. Soon after this critical and commercial success, Kapur began encouraging Blanchett to consider doing a sequel, especially since the earlier film dealt with only the early years of the reign of Elizabeth I (1533–1603). The result, alas, has not met with the same acclaim.

Elizabeth: The Golden Age focuses on the British monarch at the height of her power and during her biggest crisis. While much of *Elizabeth* is devoted to the queen's matrimonial prospects, such is essentially forgotten in the second film. She has bigger issues, mainly Spain's efforts to install Mary, Queen of Scots (Samantha Morton), on the English throne. Spain's King Philip

II (Jordi Mollà) wants to see England a Catholic kingdom again and is willing to sacrifice the lives of as many of his subjects as possible to achieve his goal.

Enter Sir Walter Raleigh (Clive Owen), who dazzles Elizabeth with his charm and charisma and promises to defeat the Spanish. The screenplay by Michael Hirst, who wrote *Elizabeth,* and William Nicholson takes several liberties with history, essentially giving Raleigh the role played by Sir Francis Drake in the battle against the Spanish Armada. In *Elizabeth,* Hirst has the queen cut Robert Dudley (Joseph Fiennes) out of her life, though he continued to be a trusted advisor until his death. This time Raleigh also fills Dudley's role as the potential suitor whose attentions to Elizabeth Throckmorton (Abbie Cornish), Elizabeth's principal lady-in-waiting, provoke the queen's jealousy.

Historical inaccuracy is not, however, the problem with *Elizabeth: The Golden Age.* The first film is a fascinating account of how Elizabeth uncovered the treachery in her court and dealt with it accordingly. The lengthy scene in which traitors are dispatched, with Kapur cutting back and forth between the praying queen and the dispatching of her enemies, is obviously modeled after one of the classic scenes in *The Godfather* (1972). The entire film actually has a structure similar to that of Francis Ford Coppola's masterpiece. With *Elizabeth: The Golden Age,* Hirst and Nicholson provide no such dramatic impetus, and the film plods its weary way from one obligatory plot point to another, eliciting yawns from reviewers along the way. The film's studied conventionality is surprising since Nicholson also co-wrote *Gladiator* (2000), one of the most intelligent epics of all time, and Hirst is the creator and writer of the lusty Henry VIII television series *The Tudors* (2007).

Geoffrey Rush is still around as Sir Francis Walsingham, the queen's main advisor, but he lacks the sly mischievousness Walsingham possesses in the first film, a combination of Rasputin and Henry Kissinger. Neither does *Elizabeth: The Golden Age* have a villain to match the vibrancy of Christopher Eccleston's Duke of Norfolk in the original film. Owen has done period pieces before: *King Arthur* (2004). But he seems uncomfortable and unfocused as Raleigh.

The story of Mary, Queen of Scots, seems to be a curse for filmmakers. The great John Ford's *Mary of Scotland* (1936), with Katharine Hepburn as the Scottish queen, is arguably his dullest, least interesting film. Despite the casting of Vanessa Redgrave as Mary and Glenda Jackson as Elizabeth, *Mary, Queen of Scots* (1972) is almost as boring as Ford's version. *Mary, Queen of Scots* is only notable for imagining not one but two meetings between the battling monarchs, artistic license resisted by the makers of *Elizabeth: The Golden Age.*

Elizabeth: The Golden Age, nevertheless, remains watchable because of the efforts of Blanchett, Kapur, and cinematographer Remi Adefarasin. One of the most arresting presences in films, Blanchett finds layers of playfulness and sadness in the screenplay. While her earlier Elizabeth takes tentative steps toward power, the more mature Elizabeth of 1588–1589 exults in her authority. Blanchett looks every bit a queen and seemingly alters the structure of her face at will to convey Elizabeth's latest emotion. Clad in armor, Elizabeth exhorts her troops into battle, with Blanchett roaring like a lioness.

The later scene is one of several handled brilliantly by Kapur, who provides a visual energy missing from the script. He knows how to compose shots, filling frames with details, evoking both the vastness and the intimacy of Elizabeth's court, as her castle becomes her fortress and her prison. Kapur allows himself to fall in love with certain bits of business, repeating a scene of Elizabeth nervously practicing a speech from the earlier film.

As with *Elizabeth,* Adefarasin achieves some striking visual effects: an overhead shot of Elizabeth standing on a map of Europe, a 360-degree shot of Elizabeth in an elaborate, winged gown, creating the image of an avenging angel, a beautiful nighttime shot of Elizabeth, wearing only a nightdress, stealing away from her army's camp to stare wonderingly at the sea. As with Kapur, Adefarasin allows himself indulgences. A shot of Elizabeth holding Raleigh's infant is lit to make her seem like a Madonna. The cinematographer even bathes Elizabeth and Raleigh with a golden glow. The visual style of *Elizabeth: The Golden Age* exhibits a sense of fun and adventure missing from its comparatively inert screenplay.

Michael Adams

CREDITS

Queen Elizabeth I: Cate Blanchett
Sir Francis Walsingham: Geoffrey Rush
Sir Walter Raleigh: Clive Owen
Bess Throckmorton: Abbie Cornish
Robert Reston: Rhys Ifans
King Phillip II: Jordi Mollà
Mary Stuart: Samantha Morton
Sir Amyas Paulet: Tom Hollander
Dr. John Dee: David Threlfall
Thomas Babington: Eddie Redmayne
Lord Howard: John Shrapnel
Spanish Archbishop: Antony Carrick
Origin: Great Britain

Language: English
Released: 2007
Production: Tim Bevan, Eric Fellner, Jonathan Cavendish; StudioCanal, Working Title Productions, MP Zeta; released by Universal
Directed by: Shekhar Kapur
Written by: Michael Hirst, William Nicholason
Cinematography by: Remi Adefarasin
Music by: Craig Armstrong
Sound: David Stephenson
Music Supervisor: Nick Angel
Editing: Jill Bilcock
Art Direction: Frank Walsh
Costumes: Alexandra Byrne
Production Design: Guy Hendrix Dyas
MPAA rating: PG-13
Running time: 114 minutes

REVIEWS

Boston Globe Online. October 12, 2007.
Chicago Sun-Times Online. October 12, 2007.
Entertainment Weekly Online. October 10, 2007.
Los Angeles Times Online. October 12, 2007.
New York Times Online. October 12, 2007.
Rolling Stone Online. October 18, 2007.
San Francisco Chronicle. October 12, 2007, p. E1.
Variety Online. September 9, 2007.
Wall Street Journal. October 12, 2007, p. W1.
Washington Post. October 12, 2007, p. C1.

QUOTES

Queen Elizabeth I: "Go back to your rathole! Tell Philip I fear neither him, nor his priests, nor his armies. Tell him if he wants to shake his little fist at us, we're ready to give him such a bite he'll wish he'd kept his hands in his pockets!"

TRIVIA

The words Mary, Queen of Scots, mouths before being executed are "I forgive you with all my heart," said to be her last words, spoken to the executioner when he asked her forgiveness.

AWARDS

Oscars 2007: Costume Des.
Nomination:
Oscars 2007: Actress (Blanchett)
British Acad. 2007: Actress (Blanchett), Costume Des., Makeup, Production Des.
Golden Globes 2008: Actress—Drama (Blanchett)
Screen Actors Guild 2007: Actress (Blanchett).

ENCHANTED

The real world and the animated world collide.
—Movie tagline

This fairytale princess is about to meet a real Prince Charming.
—Movie tagline

Box Office: $127.7 million

Seldom does a film come along that not only has an original idea but executes it so magnificently that one wonders why no one ever thought of it before. Such is the case with Disney's *Enchanted,* which also boasts one of the great performances of the year. Directed by Kevin Lima from a script by Bill Kelly, *Enchanted* imagines a world where the animated fairy-tale universe that Disney is famous for is able to break into the real world and thereby foster a clash of sensibilities regarding romance and the search for true love. It is at once a gentle spoof of the Disney tradition and a glowing love letter to it.

The movie opens in the fairy-tale kingdom of Andalasia with a sequence evocative of the studio's classic 2-D animation. Giselle (voice of Amy Adams) instantly falls in love with the handsome Prince Edward (voice of James Marsden) when he rescues her from a gigantic troll, but their impending marriage poses a threat to his stepmother, the evil Queen Narissa (voice of Susan Sarandon), who would lose her throne if he should marry. Giselle is an amalgam of many Disney princesses. Facially she probably most resembles Ariel from *The Little Mermaid* (1989), but her character, from the way she communes with her animal friends to the way she is a rival to the Queen, aligns her more closely with the heroine of *Snow White and the Seven Dwarfs* (1937). To stop the marriage, Narissa, who resembles the evil Queen from *Snow White* and can take on the form of the witch figure as well, tosses Giselle down a well, which sends her to modern-day New York City, where the film moves from animation to live action and Amy Adams emerges in her human form (the other actors from the animated opening will later follow). Here, too, begins the film's innovation of transporting Giselle's fairy-tale mind-set to a big, bad city where relationships are fraught with complications and happily ever after is as foreign as the beautiful ball gown that Giselle wears through a bustling Times Square crowd.

At the center of this fantasy is Amy Adams, who does something that is not easy—she makes innocence and wide-eyed wonder not only appealing but credible in a cynical world. Giselle is such a positive creature that even anger is a strange concept to her. The only friend she makes in the city is Robert (Patrick Dempsey), a single father raising a little girl named Morgan (Rachel Covey). He is set to propose to his girlfriend of five years, Nancy (Idina Menzel), which seems like an eternity to Giselle, who, of course, fell in love with her prince during their first meeting. And Robert's profession of divorce lawyer, a repudiation of everlasting love, is simply unfathomable to Giselle, who cries at the very notion.

Adams brings to the role a sense of openness, which seems odd, to say the least, in New York City. And she never breaks from her fairy-tale persona, even in body language; she sleeps with her hands tucked under her head and seemingly glides as she walks, as if animated. She also imbues Giselle with a strength and fortitude, an unyielding belief that she will find her prince no matter what. Adams first gained attention for playing a different kind of innocent in the art-house darling *Junebug* (2005), but her role in *Enchanted* should solidify her place as a great actress to watch in the future.

Enchanted is unique in that it parodies a longstanding tradition while being firmly in that tradition. Indeed, Alan Menken, the composer of the music for many Disney animated musicals, most notably *The Little Mermaid* and *Beauty and the Beast* (1991), and Steven Schwartz, the lyricist who collaborated with Menken on *Pocahontas* (1995) and *The Hunchback of Notre Dame* (1996), wrote new songs for this work. The first, "True Love's Kiss," introduced in the animated opening, gently pokes fun at the ease of two people instantaneously falling for each other at first kiss and then singing a duet to celebrate their union.

The funniest tune is "Happy Working Song," which plays off "Whistle While You Work" from *Snow White*. The twist is that it is, quite literally, a gritty take on the original. In cleaning up Robert's apartment, Giselle enlists the help of animals that turn out to be rats, pigeons, and cockroaches. But while this urban menagerie is a far cry from the woodland creatures she is used to, the plucky Giselle adapts to the situation and rallies her new friends to tidy everything up. The actual cleaning means scrubbing a toilet and vacuuming, then cleaning out the vacuum. It is a darling number, not least because, as is the case with Snow White, Giselle maintains her cheeriness throughout the cleanup. The sequence ends with a pigeon eating a cockroach—a great, unexpected capper.

The biggest musical number espouses Giselle's philosophy of love. Called "That's How You Know," it takes place in Central Park, beginning on a small scale as Giselle sings with a small calypso band (a sly reference to *The Little Mermaid*'s "Under the Sea") and then growing until she soon has the whole park joining her in a lavish production celebrating all the little ways two people show their love. In essence, she makes simple what the jaded Robert thinks is a complicated subject.

Adams and Dempsey play off each other wonderfully. His Robert is the cynical divorce lawyer whose life experience makes him skeptical of the triumph of true love, especially since his wife left him. He does

not want his daughter to grow up with fairy-tale illusions about life, but he cannot help but gravitate to Giselle's romanticism. Thus, much of the comedic conflict results from his and Giselle's opposing philosophies.

Another source of enjoyment is the way familiar conventions from *Snow White* are reinvented. When Narissa grows more threatened by Giselle, she sends her henchman, Nathaniel (Timothy Spall), to kill her with a poisoned apple, which takes on such modern-day incarnations as a caramel apple and an apple martini. And Giselle's most loyal woodland friend, a CGI-animated chipmunk named Pip (voiced by Jeff Bennett in animation and Kevin Lima in live action), is constantly tagging along to try to save Giselle. But the twist is that, while Pip can talk in Andalasia, he can only squeak in New York City and so must pantomime his warnings of peril.

Enchanted's take on the handsome prince is also original. Edward is a bit vain and dumb. He has some of the swagger of Gaston in *Beauty and the Beast* but is not a villain. Nonetheless, Edward's efforts to adapt to human ways are not successful like Giselle's. He attempts to slay a bus because he thinks it is a beast, and he mistakes a TV for a magic mirror.

When Edward finally finds Giselle, she and Robert have already fallen in love, and it is only a matter of time before they admit their feelings for each other. Just as Giselle tempers Robert's cynicism and reawakens his belief in love, he offers her the benefit of a worldlier, even down-to-earth, perspective. He explains the concepts of dating and getting to know a person, which are alien to Giselle but which are precisely how she and Robert fall in love. And when she suggests to Edward that they go on a date, it becomes apparent how little they have in common. She does not lose her optimism, but she grows up and finds that a mature, informed perspective is the real path to happiness.

True to its fairy-tale origins, the story climaxes at a grand ball where Narissa finally succeeds in poisoning Giselle, and only a kiss from her true love can awaken her. Giselle's true love, of course, turns out to be Robert. (Edward actually wins Nancy, and they end up returning to Andalasia.) If the film has a fault, it is that the conclusion relies too heavily on an action sequence in which Narissa takes on the form of a dragon that must be vanquished. For a story that works so well on a human level, it is disappointing that the resolution is so laden with CGI. And the fact that Robert is in danger and Giselle must rescue him at the climax—an obvious reversal of expectations—suggests an awkward, forced stab at political correctness in a film that, up to this point, has been cheerily traditional in its gender roles.

But one thing remains constant—Giselle's vision of happily ever after is vindicated.

Enchanted is one of those rare films for which it is impossible to imagine anyone else playing the leading part. Amy Adams takes what seems like a simple role and makes Giselle a fully realized, utterly charming character we can easily fall in love with. And the screenplay, direction, and music support her completely, making this modern-day fairy tale not only a worthy addition to the Disney canon but a film that lives up to its title.

Peter N. Chumo II

CREDITS

Giselle: Amy Adams
Robert Philip: Patrick Dempsey
Prince Edward: James Marsden
Nathaniel: Timothy Spall
Nancy Tremaine: Idina Menzel
Queen Narissa: Susan Sarandon
Morgan Philip: Rachel Covey
Narrator: Julie Andrews
Origin: USA
Language: English
Released: 2007
Production: Barry Josephson, Barry Sonnenfeld; Walt Disney Pictures; released by Walt Disney Studios
Directed by: Kevin Lima
Written by: Bill Kelly
Cinematography by: Don Burgess
Music by: Alan Menken
Sound: Tod A. Maitland
Music Supervisor: Dawn Soler
Editing: Stephen A. Rotter, Gregory Perer
Art Direction: John J. Kasarda
Costumes: Mona May
Production Design: Stuart Wurtzel
MPAA rating: PG
Running time: 107 minutes

REVIEWS

Boston Globe Online. November 21, 2007.
Chicago Sun-Times Online. November 21, 2007.
Entertainment Weekly. November 30, 2007, p. 115.
Hollywood Reporter Online. November 19, 2007.
Los Angeles Times Online. November 21, 2007.
New York Times Online. November 21, 2007.
Rolling Stone Online. November 15, 2007.
San Francisco Chronicle. November 21, 2007, p. E1.

Variety Online. November 18, 2007.
Washington Post. November 21, 2007, p. C1.

QUOTES

Prince Edward (talking to a TV): "Magic Mirror. I beg you. Tell me where she is!"
Mary Ilene Caselotti (on TV): "Reporting from 116th and Broadway."
Prince Edward (hugs the TV): "One hundred and sixteen and Broadway!"
Prince Edward (kisses TV and runs off): "Thank you mirror!"

TRIVIA

The bus driver's hair is shaped like Mickey Mouse's ears.

AWARDS

Nomination:

Oscars 2007: Song ("That's How You Know"), Song ("Happy Working Song"), Song ("So Close")
Golden Globes 2008: Actress—Mus./Comedy (Adams), Song ("That's How You Know").

EPIC MOVIE

We know it's big. We measured.
—Movie tagline

Box Office: $39.7 million

In the golden days of cinema lampooning, the genre-pioneering team of David Zucker, Jim Abrahams, and Jerry Zucker, either collectively or separately, brought audiences the side-splittingly funny *Airplane!* (1980), the police-squad send-up *The Naked Gun* (1988), and the Ramboesque *Hot Shots!* (1991). With the exception of a few of the *Scary Movie* entries, most of the current attempts at sending up certain cinema trends fail miserably and do not even come close to the bar that Zucker/Abrahams/Zucker films set. *Epic Movie* is no exception.

The creative team—if one may use that term—behind *Epic Movie* consists of two of the six writers from the original *Scary Movie* (2000), Jason Friedberg and Aaron Seltzer. Friedberg and Seltzer's first solo writing venture produced the spectacularly unfunny *Date Movie* (2006). Adding directing to their list of credits, the result is a film that is just as humorless.

Epic Movie begins with the story of four twenty-something orphans. Lucy (Jayma Mays) has been raised by a museum curator (David Carradine) who has been murdered by an albino monk (Kevin Hard), who also menaces Lucy until she finds a golden ticket to visit a chocolate factory. Edward (Kal Penn) lives in a Mexican orphanage and wants to wrestle his way out of there, but cannot defeat even his fellow orphans. But then he finds a golden ticket, too. Susan (Faune Chambers) is on her way to Namibia to meet her new parents when the snakes on her plane cause her to confront a Samuel L. Jackson look-alike who throws her out of the plane, only to have her land on Paris Hilton, in whose purse Susan finds a golden ticket. Peter (Adam Campbell) attends a mutant high school, where he has a crush on shape-shifting Mystique (Carmen Electra), who is part of the cool crowd that will have nothing to do with him. When he runs into an open locker door, it should come as no surprise that he finds a golden ticket.

Sending up an odd mish-mash of 2006 films including *The Da Vinci Code, Nacho Libre, Snakes on a Plane,* and *X-Men: The Last Stand,* the movie then turns to *Charlie and the Chocolate Factory* (2005), with its Willy (Crispin Glover) channeling Johnny Depp channeling Michael Jackson. Willy, it appears, has invited the children to his factory because he uses bits of them in his candy, and now they are his captives. But then Lucy finds a wardrobe and eventually the four are off to the land of *The Chronicles of Narnia* (2006), redubbed "Gnarnia."

In Gnarnia they meet Mr. Tumnus (Héctor Jiménez), a randy faun whose life partner is a beaver named Harry and whose digs are displayed à la *MTV's Cribs.* Threatening Gnarnia is the White Bitch (Jennifer Coolidge). One of the film's funniest scenes involves a nod to Coolidge's role in *American Pie* (1999), when she is greeted by Edward with "Whoa, Stifler's Mom." Penn's role as the titular Kumar in *Harold & Kumar Go To White Castle* (2004) is also given due tribute as the White Bitch leads him to her own white castle.

Aided by a diminutive sidekick, Bink (Tony Cox), the White Bitch seeks to eliminate her major competitor, another over-sexed character, the half-man, half-lion Aslo (Fred Willard), who enlists the four orphans' aid. Along the way they are trained by a very old Harry Potter (Kevin McDonald), who insists he is still fourteen, and meet up with Capt. Jack Swallows (Darrell Hammond) and his merry band of pirates.

The only worthwhile pursuit while viewing a spoof that screams straight-to-video may be to count the number of movies referenced, but that is hardly worth sitting through the sea of sophomoric humor. With its deceptive title, at a brief eighty-six minutes, a "relieved" A. O. Scott remarked in his *New York Times* review that "unlike the movies it sends up, *Epic Movie* is short." It's chief asset being brevity, *Epic Movie* nonetheless takes time to revel in the lowest and most vulgar humor possible, and instead of witty dialogue and any sort of challenging comedy, the filmmakers resort to a host of the worst kind of scatological jokes, titillating imagery, and broad physical humor. Grossing nearly $40 million at the box office, *Epic Movie* profited perhaps by catering to the lowest common denominator.

Overblown epics are ripe for lampooning, and *Epic Movie* certainly has good cause to take a stab at blockbuster franchises such as *Harry Potter* and *Pirates of the Caribbean.* Some of the filmmakers' curious other choices, including *Nacho Libre* and *Charlie and the Chocolate Factory,* much more outré and nearly spoofs themselves, are more difficult to lampoon. Putting them all together with no cohesive storyline, *Epic Movie* feels like it was written by a roomful of teenage boys.

Beverley Bare Buehrer

CREDITS

Edward: Kal Penn
Peter: Adam Campbell
The White Bitch: Jennifer Coolidge
Susan: Faune A. Chambers
Lucy: Jayma Mays
Willy: Crispin Glover
Aslo: Fred Willard
Mr. Tunmus: Héctor Jiménez
Capt. Jack Swallows: Darrell Hammond
Mystique: Carmen Electra
Museum Curator: David Carradine
Narrator: Roscoe Lee Browne
Origin: USA
Language: English
Released: 2007
Production: Paul Schiff; Regency Enterprises; released by 20th Century-Fox
Directed by: Jason Friedberg, Aaron Seltzer
Written by: Jason Friedberg, Aaron Seltzer
Cinematography by: Shawn Maurer
Music by: Ed Shearmur
Sound: David Wyman
Music Supervisor: Dave Jordan, JoJo Villanueva
Editing: Peck Prior
Art Direction: Daniel A. Lomino
Costumes: Frank Helmer
Production Design: William A. "Bill" Elliott
MPAA rating: PG-13
Running time: 86 minutes

REVIEWS

Boston Globe Online. January 27, 2007.
Chicago Sun-Times Online. January 27, 2007.
Los Angeles Times Online. January 29, 2007.

New York Times Online. January 27, 2007.
Variety Online. January 26, 2007.

QUOTES

Peter: "I want flabby grandma arms!"

TRIVIA

This was Roscoe Lee Browne's last film.

AWARDS

Nomination:

Golden Raspberries 2007: Worst Support. Actress (Electra), Worst Screenplay, Worst Remake.

EVAN ALMIGHTY

A comedy of biblical proportions.
—Movie tagline

Box Office: $100.2 million

Steve Carell's breakthrough performance occurred in *Bruce Almighty* (2003), playing the news-anchor rival whom Bruce (Jim Carrey) literally tongue ties. Carell's scenes as the babbling broadcaster were among the film's funniest. Perhaps Carell felt a degree of indebtedness to director Tom Shadyac and writer Steve Oedekerk, which may explain why he starred in *Bruce Almighty*'s sub-par sequel *Evan Almighty* despite the fact that Carell's popularity has skyrocketed with the success of the American version of *The Office.*

As Carell is transformed from playing a background character to being the center of a film, Evan Baxter (Steve Carell) has moved from being a news anchorman to being Buffalo, New York's representative to Congress. Evan, his wife Joan (Lauren Graham), and their three sons have relocated to a posh Virginia subdivision where "McMansions" have destroyed an idyllic valley, just as the oblivious denizens' Hummers are destroying the environment.

Elected on the slogan "Think Big, Think Baxter, and Change the World," Evan may not take his political promises to heart, but there is someone who does: God (Morgan Freeman). God tells the freshman congressman that he must build an ark by midday September 22. Of course, Evan panics every time God visits or he spots a reference to Genesis 6:14 (Noah's story), but eventually Evan's reluctance fades and the ark gets built. Needless to say, this happens concurrently with Evan's attempts to fit in as a politician, with the requisite comedic results.

Evan Almighty is a predictable movie. No global flood wipes out mankind by the film's end; the bluster-

ing, arrogant Congressman Long (John Goodman) receives his just desserts; and Evan's actions are ultimately vindicated. Evan's wife, who leaves him, later returns and gives him her full support. It is a cookie-cutter, feel-good type of film. That is also why the God in this film cannot be the vengeful God of the Old Testament (Noah's God). This God is not even particularly demanding. Shadyac and Oedekerk's God is more of a practical joker and magician whose only desire is for us to be nicer to each other and take better care of our world. Evan is told to build an ark not to avoid the wrath of God, but to learn about performing Acts of Random Kindness (ARK) and perhaps to have some quality time with his family.

Carell excels at the humor the film requires: physical gags, big reaction shots, and portraying the put-upon everyman. Perpetually confused campaign manager Marty (John Michael Higgins), Evan's one-liner slinging assistant Rita (Wanda Sykes), idiot-savant intern Eugene (Jonah Hill), and even realtor Eve Adams (Molly Shannon) all provide a solid comic canvas against which Carell's Evan performs. Perhaps only Graham's comic ability is underused, in the thankless role of Evan's wife.

With its estimated $175 million price tag, *Evan Almighty* is one of the most expensive comedies Hollywood has produced to date. It appears that most of that money went on the animal handlers and CGI effects needed to create and populate the ark. What *Evan Almighty* lacks, however, is a sufficiently witty screenplay. There are a few good gags, including a local theater marquee displaying *The 40 Year Old Virgin Mary* (a reference to Carell's 2005 hit *The 40 Year Old Virgin*), and when Joan meets God in a fast-food restaurant and his nametag reads "Al Mighty." But as the reviewer for the *New York Daily News* wrote: "Somewhere between the first and second films, director Tom Shadyac and writer Steve Oedekerk either lost their edge or found religion."

While *Evan Almighty* is a charming family film, it is also very Christian-friendly, perhaps at a cost of being dull and unmemorable. Universal has been actively wooing churchgoers to see this "comedy of biblical proportions." According to Michael Phillips of the *Chicago Tribune*, *Evan Almighty* is "the most identifiably biblical mainstream picture since the Mel Gibson project with all the bleeding and hacking."

The way the film mixes its Christian message with an environmentally conscious plot is also a bit confusing politically. The filmmakers seem to be courting both the Right and the Left, but with such a costly film, they certainly needed to sell as many tickets as possible. *Variety*'s Brian Lowrey wrote that the film "entices religious conservatives...with talk of God and nothing racier than bird-poop gags, while still stroking the political left with a 'save the planet' message." The *New York Times*'s A. O. Scott described the film as combining "bland religiosity and timid environmentalism into a soothing Sunday-school homily about the importance of being nice." The result is a one-joke movie that is not likely to offend a soul; a lightweight entertainment for the whole family.

Beverley Bare Buehrer

CREDITS

Evan Baxter: Steve Carell
God: Morgan Freeman
Mrs. Baxter: Lauren Graham
Congressman Long: John Goodman
Marty: John Michael Higgins
Rita: Wanda Sykes
Ryan Baxter: Jimmy Bennett
Dylan Baxter: Johnny (John W.) Simmons
Eugene: Jonah Hill
Eve Adams: Molly Shannon
Jordan Baxter: Graham Phillips
Origin: USA
Language: English
Released: 2007
Production: Tom Shadyac, Gary Barber, Roger Birnbaum, Neal H. Moritz, Michael Bostick; Spyglass Entertainment, Relativity Media, Shady Acres Entertainment, Original Film; released by Universal
Directed by: Tom Shadyac
Written by: Steve Oedekerk, Joel Cohen, Alec Sokolow
Cinematography by: Ian Baker
Music by: John Debney
Sound: Jose Antonio Garcia
Music Supervisor: Kathy Nelson
Editing: Scott Hill
Art Direction: Jim Nedza
Costumes: Judy Ruskin Howell
Production Design: Linda DeScenna
MPAA rating: PG
Running time: 95 minutes

REVIEWS

Boston Globe Online. June 22, 2007.
Chicago Sun-Times Online. June 22, 2007.
Entertainment Weekly. June 29, 2007, p. 118.
Hollywood Reporter Online. June 18, 2007.
Los Angeles Times Online. June 22, 2007.
New York Times Online. June 22, 2007.
Rolling Stone Online. June 20, 2007.

San Francisco Chronicle. June 22, 2007, p. E1.
Variety Online. June 15, 2007.
Washington Post. June 22, 2007, p. C1.

QUOTES

Joan Baxter (to her husband): "Maybe God meant a flood of awareness?"
Evan replies: "If that's true, I'm going to be so pissed."

TRIVIA

Evan's wife's name is Joan, as in Joan of Arc (Ark).

AWARDS

Nomination:
Golden Raspberries 2007: Worst Sequel/Prequel.

EVENING

Her greatest secret was her greatest gift.
—Movie tagline

Box Office: $12.4 million

The way things transpire in life tends to diverge at least to some degree from what had once been envisioned or initially desired. Few pristine plans escape alteration, and many a high hope about how things will wind up has been deflated by some letdown. This truth about the process of living also pertains to the process of adapting a literary work for the screen. Just ask Susan Minot about *Evening*, the admirable but flawed cinematic adaptation of her respected 1998 novel.

Having previously lent her pen to the screenplay for Bernardo Bertolucci's *Stealing Beauty* (1996), Minot took several stabs at the difficult task of adapting her own story, which takes place largely within the ever-drifting, morphine-muddled mind of an elderly woman on her deathbed. When producer Jeffrey Sharp found Minot's attempts wanting, he placed the screenplay in the hands of Michael Cunningham, whose Pulitzer Prize-winning words were brought to the screen by David Hare in 2002's much-heralded *The Hours*. Cunningham proceeded to mold Minot's book, altering her work in ways that not only chagrined the writer but also, more importantly, fundamentally weakened the resulting film. Perhaps now Minot feels even more connected to the characters she created, pondering wistfully along with them about different and perhaps brighter outcomes down roads not taken.

About to meet her fate, the thoughts of Ann Lord (Vanessa Redgrave) are repeatedly drawn back in particular to a fateful weekend some fifty years before, when a brief, entrancing entanglement with the love of her life led to tragedy. It is the source of profound reverberations of promise and pain that apparently never have quieted within her. Back then, she was brimming with life, a bohemian and an aspiring singer and therefore a breath of fresh air amidst the much tonier class gathering for the wedding of her college best friend, Lila Wittenborn (Mamie Gummer). (In these flashbacks to the early 1950s, Ann is portrayed by Claire Danes.) Gentle, sweet-natured Lila not only has asked her close confidant to be her maid of honor, but also has requested that Ann grace the reception that follows with her promising vocal talent. The bride-to-be's mother (Glenn Close) conceals her disapproval behind a rigidly maintained, genteel smile upon hearing that Ann will croon a contemporary popular song instead of something grand and classical by a long-dead composer.

At once hopeful and doubtful, Ann's chum is wavering on the brink of settling for a wholly suitable but not exactly swoon-inducing suitor, offering herself up at the eleventh hour to Dr. Harris Arden (Patrick Wilson). He declines, which leaves her feeling both crushed and humiliated. However, Lila's eyes are not the only ones fixed in adoration upon Harris. Her ebullient, alcoholic brother Buddy (Hugh Dancy) imperfectly hides a general inner turmoil and an attraction to both Ann and the good doctor. (He eventually professes a long-standing secret veneration for Ann right after placing an awkward, drunken smooch on Harris's lips.) After Buddy introduces Harris to Ann, Ann's own passionate and ultimately unshakeable feelings for Harris alone are born.

Once Lila has found her way out of her quandary and down the aisle, the film is free to focus in the flashbacks on this central and ultimately disastrous triangle involving Ann, Harris, and Buddy. It is a creation of Cunningham, who has ballooned the character of Buddy into a boozy, possibly bisexual lead. Numerous ominous lines and what initially looks like a death-inducing dive into the Atlantic provide layer upon exceedingly thick layer of impossible-to-miss foreshadowing of his ultimate doom. Soon after Ann exasperatedly turns her back on Buddy and dashes off with Harris, the inebriated wreck stumbles after them and into the path of an oncoming car. Buddy, now broken physically as well as emotionally, lies bleeding and in need of the absent pair who consistently had saved him from himself during the weekend, but Ann and Harris are shown lying intertwined in a secluded shack, unaware of anything but each other. This helps explain Ann's guilt-ridden mumblings about how "Harris and I killed Buddy."

What is not sufficiently conveyed to viewers of *Evening*, however, is what Minot described as "the great emotion" that powerfully overtook young Ann like a sudden tidal wave, which can hardly be felt or understood from what has made it to the screen. Furthermore, one must guess that the pall created by Buddy's demise aborted the great love, as there is no mention whatsoever about the significant revelation that Harris had a pregnant fiancé back home. Lastly, as portrayed by Wilson, Harris is handsome but rather blank and subdued, certainly not the magnetic dreamboat radiating charismatic allure who could cast a spell over so many for so long.

A clear contrast is drawn through the incessant zigzagging between the hushed, shadow-enshrouded confinement of the bedridden, spent figure and the vibrant, sun-drenched, color-laden flashback scenes from the wedding weekend, back when Ann's life had yet to begin and she was as breezy as her breathtaking seaside surroundings. The hallucinating old woman, who at one point in the darkness asks her night nurse (Eileen Atkins) "where did my life go?" is shown years before twirling blithely and nimbly with Buddy to the strains of "I've Got the World on a String." The mise-en-scène of many memory sequences includes broad expanses of clear blue sky and unobstructed panoramic ocean views, visually underscoring how Ann's world once seemed full of limitless possibility. When a heavy-hearted Ann goes down to the water after Buddy's death, the camera is angled so that much of the sky is blotted out, the top of the frame seeming to bear down on her like her cares. Chronologically later flashbacks are interior shots of the dimly lit joint from which her singing career never progressed, a claustrophobic and an unhappy kitchen scene giving a glimpse of how her marriages did not work out, and an awkward, muted run-in with Harris in the rain on a New York City street.

A la the utterance "Rosebud" in *Citizen Kane* (1941), Ann's daughters Constance (Natasha Richardson), a contented wife and mother, and Nina (Toni Collette), still drifting in life and neurotically unsure about how best to proceed, hear their mother's mumblings about a man they have never heard of and wonder what it all means. Of course, their mother is also struggling to come to grips with what it all means, mulling over choices and chances, strivings and stumblings pertaining to romance, motherhood, and career. As Constance and Nina have meaningful talks with each other and their mother, the two take stock of their own lives. What is said both about life in general and about the losses and gains involved in a woman's often confounding navigation towards true fulfillment will be relevant but not eye-opening to most female viewers. Supporting the theme of mothers and daughters, Meryl Streep, real-life mother of newcomer Gummer, arrives on the scene late in the film to play an elderly Lila, who makes a final visit to her old friend and helps assuage everyone's angst.

"At the end," she says soothingly, "so much of it turns out not to matter." Her scene with Redgrave, their characters curled up in bed together as they appraise the past, is perhaps the film's best.

Made on a budget of $14 million, *Evening* received tepid reviews. Advertisements trumpeted it as "This Summer's Must See Film Starring the Greatest Actresses of Our Time"—not an idle boast considering it features Redgrave, Streep, and Close, who are all excellent here. Also noteworthy are the truly lovely images of the New England coast that remind one of paintings by Fitz Hugh Lane and the other luminists. This is not surprising, as the film was directed by a veteran cinematographer, Lajos Koltai, who previously mixed pain, death, and beauty in *Fateless* (2005), the Hungarian's Oscar-nominated directorial debut about the Holocaust. However, despite no shortage of acting excellence, stirring visuals, affliction and tears, and wise words about living one's life, it all somehow fails to draw viewers strongly enough to make hearts flutter and eyes well up along with those on the screen. The film drifts along at a distance, like Harris's boat that Ann dreams about, admittedly and admirably beautiful and true, yet somehow managing to leave one almost as cold as the dreamer herself at *Evening*'s end. Before her death, Ann comes to the comforting conclusion that one does the best one can, and that there is "no such thing as a mistake." Minot, and those filmgoers who loved the way she told the tale, might not completely agree.

David L. Boxerbaum

CREDITS

Ann Grant Lord: Vanessa Redgrave
Constance Lord: Natasha Richardson
Nina Mars: Toni Collette
Lila Wittenborn Ross: Meryl Streep
Young Ann: Claire Danes
Harris Arden: Patrick Wilson
Buddy Wittenborn: Hugh Dancy
Luc: Ebon Moss-Bachrach

Young Lila: Mamie Gummer
Night Nurse: Eileen Atkins
Mrs. Winterborn: Glenn Close
Mr. Winterborn: Barry Bostwick
Origin: USA
Language: English
Released: 2007
Production: Jeffrey Sharp; Hart-Sharp Entertainment, Twins Financing; released by Focus Features
Directed by: Lajos Koltai
Written by: Susan Minot, Michael Cunningham
Cinematography by: Gyula Pados
Music by: Jan A.P. Kaczmarek
Sound: Tom Williams
Music Supervisor: Linda Cohen
Editing: Allyson C. Johnson
Art Direction: Jordan Jacobs
Costumes: Ann Roth
Production Design: Caroline Hanania
MPAA rating: PG-13
Running time: 117 minutes

REVIEWS

Boston Globe Online. June 29, 2007.
Chicago Sun-Times Online. June 29, 2007.
Hollywood Reporter Online. June 22, 2007.
Los Angeles Times Online. June 29, 2007.
New York Times Online. June 29, 2007.
San Francisco Chronicle. June 29, 2007, p. E7.
Variety Online. June 21, 2007.
Village Voice Online. June 29, 2007.
Washington Post. June 29, 2007, p. C6.

QUOTES

Harris Arden: "I have to tell you something…I still know what stars are ours."

TRIVIA

Mamie Gummer plays the younger version of her real-life mother, Meryl Streep, while Natasha Richardson plays daughter to her real-life mother, Vanessa Redgrave.

F

FACTORY GIRL

When Andy met Edie, life imitated art.
—Movie tagline

Box Office: $1.6 million

The 1960s "It Girl" and Andy Warhol superstar Edie Sedgwick never managed to cross over into mainstream fame. Similarly, *Factory Girl's* Sienna Miller, an independent movie actress and London's latest "It Girl," was not destined to pass into mainstream movie stardom with her riveting and canny performance in the choice role of the notorious underground icon known simply as Edie. There are several reasons why Miller's breakout performance was overlooked, chief among them the scant release the of the film, legal woes over the original screenplay's suggestion of a relationship between Edie and Bob Dylan, and most importantly, the film's overall lack of substance.

Sedgwick is the subject of more than a few biographies and popular rock songs, and featured in several Warhol films, notably *Poor Little Rich Girl* (1965), but George Hickenlooper's *Factory Girl* is the first mainstream film about the life of the actress/model/socialite. Hickenlooper is no stranger to biographical films, with several short documentaries to his credit, including *Picture This: The Times of Peter Bogdanovich in Archer City, Texas* (1997), *Monte Hellman: American Auteur* (1991), and the feature-length *Mayor of the Sunset Strip* (2005). But the director, along with screenwriter Captain Mauzner (*Wonderland,* 2003) mines all-too-familiar territory with *Factory Girl*, merely skimming the surface of Edie's tortured psyche and the chaotic, drug-filled New York underworld that she inhabited. An infinitely more imaginative picture of Edie's life in Andy Warhol's tinfoil-walled Factory is *Ciao! Manhattan* (1972), a gritty, bizarre, and arguably exploitative film that starred the doomed Sedgwick herself in the days before her barbiturate overdose in 1971 at age twenty-eight.

Factory Girl begins with a fresh-faced, drug-free Edie's visit to a Santa Barbara therapist. Hickenlooper then flashes back to her famed life in New York. Sedgwick, who hailed from a prominent Massachusetts family, traveled from her native Santa Barbara to New York City after a brief stint at a Boston art school. There, her mentor Chuck Wein (Jimmy Fallon) introduces her to Andy Warhol (Guy Pearce), who is immediately smitten by the free-spirited and gorgeous young heiress and invites her to appear in one of his films. Edie becomes the pop impresario's new muse and Factory favorite until her increasing drug use and dwindling fortune become problems that Warhol cannot ignore.

Although Miller herself is just as lovely as the incandescent Edie was, in true Hollywood tradition Pearce's Warhol is quite a bit prettier than the real-life Warhol was. The filmic Warhol is every bit as chillingly superficial and self-absorbed, however, and the script is certainly not sympathetic to the eccentric pop artist. Despite his more commercially attractive appearance, Pearce disappears into Warhol's emotionless artiste persona and is the perfect foil for Miller's increasingly fragile and vulnerable Edie. Infinitely less convincing is the seriously miscast Fallon as Edie's flamboyantly gay companion Wein. Although the multitalented Fallon is an actor, musician, and member of New York's hip downtown scene, he is the antithesis of Wein, and seems hopelessly lost onscreen.

Hayden Christensen in the role of "Musician" fares better than Fallon, but is not entirely convincing as the converse of Warhol's character. Christensen possesses neither the acting chops nor the depth of character to portray a legendary folk poet based on Bob Dylan, but in his few scenes he is sufficiently representative of the more admirable model of celebrity with a soul that Edie should emulate. Although Dylan and Edie certainly knew each other—Dylan's "Just Like a Woman," "Like a Rolling Stone," and "Leopard-Skin Pill-box Hat" supposedly were written about Edie—the exact nature of their relationship is unknown. The film posits that Edie fell in love with the singer, who abhorred all Warhol stood for, but that she could not bear to turn against the vapid artist. She realizes her mistake in choosing Warhol much too late, after all her money and most of her sanity are gone and the Musician has married. Dylan's fears of being portrayed in the film as having driven Edie to suicide seem unfounded, as *Factory Girl* puts the blame squarely on Warhol.

Aside from the joy of watching Miller's Edie don one fashionable outfit after another while gorgeously unraveling, the film contains few memorable scenes. The sequences at the Factory are sterile and contrived. In a more revealing scene, Edie's eccentric parents invite Warhol to dinner to find out what kind of person their daughter is cavorting with. Her arrogant father, known as Fuzzy (James Naughton), quickly surmises that Warhol is homosexual, and declares it loudly and in derogatory terms at the start of dinner. While Edie is mortified, Warhol is typically unresponsive, and Edie's mother (Peggy Walton-Walker) unfazed. Although the film briefly addresses the long-term sexual abuse of Edie by her father, her stint in a mental institution, and the deaths of two of her beloved brothers, the dinner party is the only scene that glimpses the dysfunctional interaction with her family. Conversely, a mirroring scene has Edie dining with Andy's Old-World mother, the Slovak-speaking, grandmotherly Julia (Beth Grant), who is encouraged that her effeminate boy is with someone as beautiful and glamorous as Edie.

The film's period details are exceptional. The costumes and sets are dead-on, down to Edie's own stuffed leather rhinoceros, which was featured in an iconic *Vogue* shot of her posed atop it in arabesque, in her customary black tights. Among the supporting roles, which include Mena Suvari as Factory denizen Richie Berlin, Illeana Douglas is a standout as *Vogue*'s Diana Vreeland. Mary-Kate Olsen—for the first time onscreen sans twin—has a cameo as an art gallery patron.

For a film set in one of the most fertile periods of musical creativity, the soundtrack is surprisingly pedestrian and, perhaps not surprisingly, contains no Dylan songs.

The *Los Angeles Times*'s Kevin Crust summed up what is most disappointing about the film: "Fans well-schooled in the lore of Warhol in general and all things Edie in particular will come away with no deeper understanding of the principals, while newcomers will wonder what the fuss was all about in the first place."

Hilary White

CREDITS

Edie Sedgwick: Sienna Miller
Andy Warhol: Guy Pearce
Musician: Hayden Christensen
Chuck Wein: Jimmy Fallon
Richie Berlin: Mena Suvari
Syd Pepperman: Shawn Hatosy
Diana Vreeland: Illeana Douglas
Fuzzy Sedgwick: James Naughton
Julia Warhol: Beth Grant
Gerald Malanga: Jack Huston
Origin: USA
Language: English
Released: 2007
Production: Kimberly C. Anderson, Morris Bart, Holly Wiersma, Aaron Richard Golub, Malcolm Petal; Weinstein Company, LIFT Productions; released by MGM
Directed by: George Hickenlooper
Written by: Captain Mauzner
Cinematography by: Michael Grady
Music by: Ed Shearmur
Sound: Jeffrey Haupt
Music Supervisor: Matt Aberle
Editing: Dana E. Glauberman, Michael Levine
Art Direction: James A. Gelarden
Costumes: John Dunn
Production Design: Jeremy Reed
MPAA rating: R
Running time: 90 minutes

REVIEWS

Boxoffice Online. December 29, 2006.
Hollywood Reporter Online. December 29, 2006.
Los Angeles Times Online. December 29, 2006.
Variety Online. December 28, 2006.

QUOTES

Edie Sedgwick: "I went to a party once, and there was a palm reader there and when she looked at my hand, she just froze. And I said to her 'I know. My lifeline is broken. I know I won't live past thirty.'"

TRIVIA

Bob Dylan threatened to sue the producers for defamation, claiming that the film portrayed him as responsible for

Sedgwick's death. Thus, any mention of Dylan was omitted from the script and Hayden Christensen is billed only as "musician."

FANTASTIC FOUR: RISE OF THE SILVER SURFER

Rise.
    —Movie tagline
Discover the secret of the surfer.
    —Movie tagline

Box Office: $131.9 million

A film with the moniker Fantastic Four in its title has a lot to live up to. Fortunately for this sequel it does not take much to surpass the quality of the original. The hypnotic baritone of Laurence Fishburne, who provides the voice of the laconic alien the Silver Surfer (acted by Doug Jones), automatically improves the film over its predecessor. Fishburne delivers each line with the embittered authority of Shakespeare's Othello, a role he played in the 1995 film of the same name. Unlike other films in the superhero genre flooding the box office for the past decade, *Fantastic Four: The Rise of the Silver Surfer* lacks the character development, crisp dialogue, and seamless scene flow that may be seen in the *X-Men* franchise, *Batman Begins* (2005), and the first two *Spider-Man* films. Also absent from this ensemble is chemistry among the actors, which was so apparent between Hugh Jackman as Wolverine and Famke Janssen as Jean Grey in the *X-Men* trilogy. And although director Tim Story and writers Don Payne and Mark Frost raise the bar on this sequel's script, most of the cast cannot pull off the plethora of corny one-liners and tasteless dialogue.

One notable exception is Chris Evans, who plays Johnny Storm (a.k.a. the Human Torch) like an irascible Ricky Nelson. Johnny is the team's resident narcissist who wallows in his newly attained celebrity status as an X-games bad boy of sorts and sports more sponsor patches on his latex costume than a NASCAR driver. Evans delivers his often insipid lines with the wry grin of a sophomoric frat boy as he courts both the paparazzi and a bevy of supermodels. The cheesy dialogue works for the Torch, who oozes it.

The movie begins two years after the end of its predecessor, *Fantastic Four* (2005), when Dr. Reed Richards (Ioan Gruffudd) has proposed to Johnny's older sister Sue Storm (Jessica Alba). Reed is the soft-spoken, stereotypical scientist who is the leader of the group, and he has the ability to stretch his body to great lengths as well as to freakishly contort it, ergo his anonym Mr. Fantastic. Sue has the ability to bend light in such a way as to render her invisible to most organisms, thus her

moniker Invisible Woman. She can also generate psionic force fields around herself or other objects. The couple is heading for the altar despite numerous postponements due to their world-saving antics, and the media is embracing it as the "Wedding of the Century" on par with the televised ceremony of Prince Charles and Lady Diana.

As depicted in the Marvel Comics publication, Johnny and Ben Grimm, the bulky Thing (Michael Chiklis), resemble typical squabbling siblings, albeit siblings whose altercations result in massive property damage. Chiklis as the grumbling, blue-eyed Thing shows the greatest breadth of character subtext. The Thing serves as the crew's muscle due to his great strength, rivaling that of Superman, and near invulnerability. But he is also a tortured soul with a monstrous epidermis, causing him to resemble an orange-colored fissured rock formation. While Sue and Johnny are siblings and Sue is engaged to Reed, the film depicts Ben as the solitary loner.

Aside from the couple's nuptials, another story getting top press is a series of anomalies erupting all over the Earth. A portion of the ocean off the coast of Japan seems to have solidified into a petrified state, and it is snowing in Egypt. A silver blur is witnessed soaring over these aberrations. While scientists assure the populace that these mysterious events are not due to global warming, the United States government sends Army General Hager (Andre Braugher) to obtain Reed's assistance in tracking down this aerial object. After an initial refusal, the brilliant Dr. Richards develops a device capable of tracking down the cause of these geographical alterations.

As the wedding begins, the mysterious silver object descends on New York City and causes a blackout that results in a series of mishaps that Sue, Reed, and Ben contend with while Johnny ignites into an egomaniacal blaze and pursues the agitator. He quickly discovers the UFO to be a shiny silver bald man soaring through the skies on a long board. "Cool!" he says admiringly. Annoyed by Johnny's pursuit, the Surfer yanks him into the upper stratosphere by the neck, hence cutting off his oxygen supply enough to extinguish his thermogenically produced flame. He plunges back to Earth as a fallen Icarus. Johnny's encounter with the alien has rendered his molecular structure unstable, and he learns that physical contact of any kind with his partners causes a power exchange. Thus Johnny inadvertently trades abilities with Sue, Ben, and Reed in some of film's more amusing moments.

Meanwhile, the Surfer's "Power Cosmic," the ability to harness cosmic power to almost any end, resurrects the dictatorial Victor Von Doom (Julian McMahon) from a stasis as a metal figure stored away in his native

Latveria. A colleague of Richards and a genius in his own right, Von Doom tracks down the Surfer to the Arctic and extends a Mephistophelean offer to him to be co-conquerors of the world. The apathetic extraterrestrial snubs him and blasts him through snow and ice when a scorned Von Doom attacks him. This return fire of cosmic energy unintentionally restores Von Doom to his formidable state before he was defeated in the original film.

In his brilliance, Von Doom theorizes that the Surfer's power is derived from his board, and that once separated from it, that power can be usurped, allowing the military to contend with him. He offers his service to General Hager, who determines that the two adversaries should combine their respective resources to thwart their mutual threat. While setting up the trap for the sky rider with an impulse generator they constructed, General Hager and Reed get into an argument straight out of an after-school special when Hager ridicules Reed for not having played high school football. Reed admits he was a nerd who, rather than engage in sports, hit the books and became one of the most brilliant men in the world. They are successful in draining the Surfer's power, and the military detain him in Siberia, where they question him utilizing torture and abuse reminiscent of the Abu Ghraib prison scandal.

During his rescue by the Fantastic Four, it is learned that the Surfer is nothing more than a pawn for an immensely destructive entity known as Galactus. The Surfer was once a human named Norrin Radd, an astronomer on a world known as Zenn-La who offered himself as herald if Galactus would spare his home planet. Galactus conceded and imbued him with the Power Cosmic. Here the film is faithful to the Surfer's story as presented in the pages of *Fantastic Four,* volume I, number 48. Joining forces against Von Doom, who has now harnessed the Power Cosmic emanating from Norrin's board, Johnny uses his new ability of flux to absorb the powers of his colleagues and becomes a parallel of the magazine's Superskrull, a villain of the Fantastic Four who wields the same powers. Johnny manages to return the board to the Surfer, who soars into the pit of Galactus (who resembles a massive vacuous cosmic cloud) and unleashes his Power Cosmic to a level that proves destructive to both Galactus and the Surfer himself.

Full of CGI effects and dealing with a literally world-shattering catastrophic premise, the *Fantastic Four: Rise of the Silver Surfer* is a movie clearly crafted for the typical prepubescent boy who seals his comics in plastic bags and treats them like the Ark of the Covenant. Soaring high above filmic calamities such as *Hulk* (2003), *Daredevil* (2003), and *Elektra* (2005), the *Silver Surfer's* succeeds in its seeming intention of providing an afternoon of escapist entertainment for the whole family.

As Scott Bowles sums the film up in *USA Today*: "Surfer, the family learns, is a herald sent to scout out edible planets for the evil Galactus, and the Earth apparently is paté de foie gras. Yes, that's stupid. But so is a kid who can shoot webs from his hands, a playboy who thinks he's a bat, or an alien from Krypton who lands a low-paying job. And once you accept that *Fantastic Four* is not trying to be anything deeper than popcorn fare, the ride can be fun—with an ending more satisfying than *Spider-Man 3*."

David Metz Roberts

CREDITS

Reed Richards/Mr. Fantastic: Ioan Gruffudd
Susan Storm/Invisible Woman: Jessica Alba
Johnny Storm/Human Torch: Chris Evans
Ben Grimm/The Thing: Michael Chiklis
Victor Von Doom/Dr. Doom: Julian McMahon
Norrin Radd/Silver Surfer: Doug Jones
General Hager: Andre Braugher
Alicia Masters: Kerry Washington
Lieutenant: Gonzalo Menendez
Silver Surfer (Voice): Laurence Fishburne
Origin: USA
Language: English
Released: 2007
Production: Bernd Eichinger, Avi Arad, Ralph Winter; Constantin Film Produktion, Marvel Enterprises, 1492 Pictures; released by 20th Century-Fox
Directed by: Tim Story
Written by: Don Payne, Mark Frost
Cinematography by: Larry Blanford
Music by: John Ottman
Sound: Craig Henighan
Editing: William Hoy, Peter S. Elliot
Art Direction: Sandra Tanaka
Costumes: Mary Vogt
Production Design: Kirk M. Petruccelli
MPAA rating: PG
Running time: 92 minutes

REVIEWS

Boston Globe Online. June 15, 2007.
Chicago Sun-Times Online. June 14, 2007.
Entertainment Weekly. June 29, 2007, p. 117.
Hollywood Reporter Online. June 15, 2007.
Los Angeles Times Online. June 15, 2007.
New York Times Online. June 15, 2007.
San Francisco Chronicle. June 14, 2007, p. E1.

Variety Online. June 14, 2007.
Washington Post. June 15, 2007, p. C1.

QUOTES

Johnny Storm: "How do you fight something that can eat planets?"

TRIVIA

Given a PG rating by the MPAA, the first Marvel film since *Howard the Duck* (1986) to earn this rating.

AWARDS

Nomination:

Golden Raspberries 2008: Worst Actress (Alba), Worst Screen Couple (Alba and Gruffudd).

FAY GRIM

Featuring the continuing adventures of Henry Fool.
—Movie tagline

Iconoclastic independent film director Hal Hartley has a talent for intricate spoofs that proceed with deadpan seriousness. *Fay Grim* fits comfortably into his unique style, though in a puzzling fashion. The film is a sequel to *Henry Fool,* released in 1997, which was one of Hartley's most popular and accessible films. In *Henry Fool* the protagonist (Thomas Jay Ryan) is a novelist of little talent who teaches his brother-in-law, Simon (James Urbaniak), a garbage man, how to write poetry. When Simon inexplicably becomes a famous poet, Henry descends into drinking, but then he gets in trouble with the law for his involvement in a long-ago death, and Simon helps him escape from the country.

Fay Grim picks up the story ten years later, as Fay (Parker Posey), Henry's wife, struggles with raising their fourteen-year-old son Ned (Liam Aiken), who is always getting into trouble at school. Like his father, he seems to have an uncivilized, misfit streak. Simon is serving a jail sentence for his role in helping Henry escape, and his publisher wants to capitalize on Simon's fame by publishing Henry's long-lost notebooks, which have gained a certain value not for the quality of their writing but simply because they are associated with the famous Simon.

But the publisher is not the only one seeking the notebooks, which contain Henry's mysterious confessions. Soon a CIA agent, Fulbright (Jeff Goldblum), asks Fay to help him retrieve the notebooks, saying that they are associated with an important national security issue. He wants to send her to Paris on a mission to retrieve them. Fay says she will go only if her brother is released from prison.

It is gradually revealed that Henry, unbeknownst to Fay, has been involved in secret United States government operations in Chile, Afghanistan, and elsewhere. He may be a spy, and it turns out his confessions implicate the CIA in dirty tricks. When Fay arrives in Paris, she discovers that several different people and organizations are after the notebooks, and the battle soon turns deadly.

Fay Grim starts out as an outlandish farce, with the unseen Henry something of a Forrest Gump of U.S. foreign policy, turning up in unusual places at crucial times, a shadowy figure who seems to serve as a shorthand for a larger critique of American government meddling and ineptitude. It then turns into a spy spoof of increasing complexity without losing its goofy sense of humor. Stereotypical musical riffs introduce various tropes, all played a little off-kilter.

Hartley's screenplay is entertaining, full of small jokes and intricate storytelling, but then again the film shifts, this time into a more serious mode, and the jokes begin to turn grim. The effect is surpassingly odd, as if a screwball comedy suddenly turned into a thriller. Hartley begins taking his cleverly concocted plot way too seriously, and the overall intent of the film becomes puzzling.

Hartley's directorial style is not as multifaceted as his writing. It quickly becomes tiresomely "indie." Almost every scene in the movie is shot at an angle, with the image tilted up to either the left or right. It is as if Hartley is so afraid of shooting anything in conventional fashion that his lack of convention itself becomes its own convention. Another overused device is that Fay's cell phone rings at the most inopportune moments. The story starts to sprawl as well, introducing a bevy of insufficiently developed and murkily plotted characters. It remains an intelligent but bizarre mix of the comic and the pretentious. The film lurches back and forth from ambitious satire to many moments of taking itself far too seriously.

Henry Fool himself eventually turns up, in the hideout of an Islamic terrorist in Istanbul. Henry is defiant and arrogant but is warned, "Your past is catching up with you." And it is a past crammed full of betrayals and misdeeds. It turns out that Henry is more than a lout—he is an immoral trader of political favors.

For much of the film, Fay grimaces when others say that she must love and miss Henry. It seems she is happier with him gone. But all this evidence of her superficiality and the problematic nature of their marriage is then contradicted when Fay places herself in great danger in order to find her husband. Fay quickly turns from a selfish, unenlightened lightweight, who seems to care more about how likeable she is than about the fate of humankind, into a cunning player in an international game of terrorism. And their relationship becomes deadly serious, worth more than the lives of others.

For much of the film, Posey, the queen of indie comedies, plays her role perfectly, a modern update on the heroines of old screwball comedies of the 1940s. She has that half-knowing, "are-you-kidding" look down pat, and is an expert at the guileless comeback. Others in the film seem like comic caricatures until they, too, turn into more serious players.

It is not clear what Hartley is trying for as the film becomes increasingly complicated and tense. Characters involved in various types of conspiracies and with various unexplained loyalties come and go, including mysterious femme fatales such as Juliet (Saffron Burrows) and a Chechnyan girlfriend of Henry's named Bebe (Elina Löwensohn). Hartley's writing is sophisticated and his plot at times fascinating, but he has undermined it from the start with his spoofing set-up. It is hard to believe Fay's character transformation from frivolous to formidable, though Posey gives it a game try (comedy is more her forte than drama, however). *Fay Grim* moves from riveting drama to silly send-up to an inexplicable pastiche, back and forth and around, in frustrating circles. Hartley's downfall is that he cannot seem to commit himself to the consistently serious movie he wants to make; he wants always to remain quirky and self-consciously indie, and the hallmark of that style is to present everything with irony, so when he does try to be serious it is hard to take it seriously.

Fay Grim is a movie that never tires of its quirkiness. It makes for entertainingly smart viewing, but it just does not fit comfortably into any genre. Unclassifiable and always a bit off kilter, *Fay Grim* fails to involve us in its title heroine or in its other characters because it initially presents them as not worthy of being taken seriously. Hartley will always have a cult following, however, and both this film and its predecessor, *Henry Fool,* will be considered as some of his most intriguing work. Perhaps this film is the prelude to the movie some Hartley fans might be dying for him to make—one that uses his enormous talents in a straightforward, gripping drama.

Michael Betzold

CREDITS

Fay Grim: Parker Posey
Agent Fulbright: Jeff Goldblum

Simon Grim: James Urbaniak
Ned Grim: Liam Aiken
Juliet: Saffron Burrows
Bebe: Elina Löwensohn
Carl Fogg: Leo Fitzpatrick
Angus James: Chuck Montgomery
Henry Fool: Thomas Jay Ryan
Origin: USA, Germany
Language: English
Released: 2006
Production: Jason Kliot, Joana Vicente, Hal Hartley, Michael S. Ryan, Martin Hagemann; This Is That Productions, HDNet Films, Possible Films, Zero Film GmbH; released by Magnolia Pictures
Directed by: Hal Hartley
Written by: Hal Hartley
Cinematography by: Sarah Crawley Cabiya
Music by: Hal Hartley
Sound: Paul Oberle
Editing: Hal Hartley
Art Direction: Susanne Hopf, Natalja Meier
Costumes: Anette Guther, Daniela Selig
Production Design: Richard Sylvarnes
MPAA rating: R
Running time: 118 minutes

REVIEWS

Boston Globe Online. May 18, 2007.
Chicago Sun-Times Online. May 18, 2007.
Entertainment Weekly. May 25, 2007, p. 63.
Hollywood Reporter Online. September 15, 2006.
Los Angeles Times Online. May 18, 2007.
New York Times Online. May 18, 2007.
San Francisco Chronicle. May 18, 2007, p. E5.
Variety Online. September 25, 2006.
Village Voice Online. May 15, 2007.

QUOTES

Fay Grim: "Why is it, when someone starts talking about civilization, I hear the sound of machine guns?"

FEAST OF LOVE

A story for anyone with an appetite for love.
—Movie tagline

Box Office: $3.5 million

Would anyone really be surprised if God turned out to sound like Morgan Freeman? The makers of *Bruce Almighty* (2003) and this year's sequel, *Evan Almighty,* certainly would not, having cast him as their cinematic version of the Creator for the authoritative quality of that wonderful, uncommonly sonorous voice. Although in *Feast of Love* Freeman is not called upon to play that ultimate possessor and purveyor of wisdom who speaks from on high, he does begin the film with a richly toned, sagacious voice-over narration, commenting on the heady passion and crushing pain, the deep steadfastness, and the thoroughly discombobulating shifts of the human heart. Indeed, he even speaks of powers up above, relating how bored Greek gods first created mortals and then gave them the ability to love, providing the deities with a thoroughly engrossing spectacle to observe. After giving in to temptation and trying love for themselves, the gods quickly felt the need to also invent laughter— "so they could stand it."

The voice attempting to impart insightful words of deep meaning here belongs to Harry Stevenson, a college professor who is currently on leave and spending much of his time acting as a kindly, coffee-sipping oracle. Harry is able to recognize where relationships are headed even when those involved are proceeding blithely and blindly toward sharp detours or ominous cliffs. However, it actually does not take any great powers of discernment to see where anything is going in *Feast of Love*; the film has an obviousness, coupled with an irksome excess of foreshadowing, that makes eventual outcomes seem like old news.

The polar opposite of this solid, steadying counselor with the keen antennae is his friend Bradley (Greg Kinnear), the owner of the appropriately named Jitters Coffee Shop who is too busy buoyantly yapping to recognize that he has precious little to be buoyant about. Everything is clearly on the verge of slipping through his fingers when an aggressive lesbian softball player named Jenny (Stana Katic) boldly puts her fingers on the leg of Bradley's equally athletic wife, Kathryn (Selma Blair), who seems open to switching teams. At first appearing to be signs of discomfiture, Kathryn's faint smiles and awkward, flitting glances actually signal a diffident reciprocity of feeling. While both Harry and Bradley are present as this occurs, the former notices the ladies' budding bond while the latter, prattling on, remains oblivious.

Many viewers may be turned off by how ludicrously little Bradley is tuned in to his supposedly valued mate, particularly when he excitedly presents the thoroughly canine-phobic woman with a dog for her birthday. He had ridiculously assumed that a single, brief, and unwanted trip to the Humane Society, during which Kathryn endeavored to gamely look around while churning internally, had not only cured her fear of hounds but also fostered a desire to adopt one. Harry had gently cautioned Bradley to perhaps think things through a tad further before proceeding, but to no avail. While Jenny

zeroes in on Kathryn like a photographer fascinatedly capturing every detail of her subject, Bradley is hard-pressed to remember the color of his wife's eyes. Few watching will blame her for exasperatedly stalking out to find contentment elsewhere, wherever it may lie. As Kathryn departs Bradley's life, the camera holds on the utterly dumbfounded look upon his face, both for emphasis and, it seems, to engender sympathy. However, it is rather hard to muster. The character may have a wide-eyed stare, but precious little insight.

Lonely Bradley next stumbles into a relationship with cynical Diana (Radha Mitchell) after the icy but thoroughly hot-looking blond real-estate agent ducks into Jitters to escape a downpour. In short order, she is showing him everything she has to offer—as well as some houses. Diana finds Bradley lovable but never falls in love, seeing him as more of a lighthearted, positive influence who at least is free to give her his heart, along with his other organs, unlike her married, hunky soul mate David (Billy Burke). Even after accepting Bradley's marriage proposal, Diana continues to clandestinely pursue torrid but seemingly dead-end sex with David. (The scorching slapfest that ensues when Diana tells David she is engaged is one of the film's more memorable scenes.) At least this time, Bradley pays enough attention to notice Diana's far-off, inappropriately dismal expression and odd hesitancy when called upon to say "I do," but once again, he is elatedly and deeply in love by himself.

When Diana's wholly apparent misgivings are combined with talk of the newlyweds' home being a cursed, habitual crusher of matrimonial bliss, no one could be surprised in the least when Diana succumbs to that passionate pull toward David after his wife cuts him loose. This paves the way for another one of the film's many coincidental romantic intersections, in which Bradley finds what appears (at least for now) to be true love with the sweet doctor (Sherilyn Lawson) who reattaches the portion of his finger that he has purposely chopped off in despair. Why she seems to have no qualms about becoming attached to someone who has just violently detached one of his digits is a real puzzler.

Feast of Love interweaves the story of Bradley and his women with tales of two other relationships, one a deep-rooted, abiding, mature love, and the other exhibiting the intoxicating thrill, unspoiled beauty, and beguiling tenderness of amour shared by those of a much more tender age. The first involves Harry and his wife Esther (Jane Alexander), who are grappling below the surface with grief over their son's heroin-related death. This is actually the most likeable couple, but their life together is unfortunately only sketchily explored. Freeman and Alexander's scenes together are more intriguing in their quiet way than the melodrama of those involving young lovers Chloe (Alexa Davalos) and Oscar (Toby Hemingway), whose eyes meet and souls meld after a chance glance through the coffee house's front window. Oscar has struggled with drugs, lost his mother when he was about eight, and has had to deal with a volatile father, Bat (Fred Ward), who carries on, drenched in bitterness and booze. Chloe and Oscar have a sweet scene in which they daydream about a glowing future together and all it will entail. However, with a crazed, drunken, knife-wielding dad named Bat lurking about, and a psychic who gets such funereal feelings about Oscar that she assumes he must already be dead, the young man's eventual tragic demise while playing football (from a previously undetected congenital heart defect) comes off as sad but anticlimactic.

Wise old Papa Harry is on hand for it all, continually, contrivedly intermingling with all these problem children so the character can shine his warm, soothing, clarifying light upon their troubles. (When he is not busy guiding or comforting, Harry is shaking his head and gently chuckling while filling in Esther on the latest complications and tribulations, perhaps to help keep the couple's minds off their own difficulties.) He is even ambling by at just the right time to glimpse a weapon-wielding, inebriated Bat in the bushes outside Chloe's home, and he disarms the man with brute strength and, of course, what he hopes are some epiphany-inducing words. By the film's end, however, with Harry despairing that "God is either dead or he despises us," it is Bradley who is held up as the film's unlikely paragon to emulate. He is meant to be admired as an adorable, resolute Energizer Bunny of Love, one of life's most pathetically hopeless of hopeless romantics who nonetheless perseveres because love is "everything—the only meaning there is to this crazy dream." To many, including *Los Angeles Times* critic Carina Chocano, he will instead come off as more "dumb and desperate."

Neither the movie-going public nor most critics fell head over heels in love with what was offered up in the middling *Feast of Love*. One of the changes made in adapting Charles Baxter's 2000 novel was the westward relocation of the story's setting from Ann Arbor, Michigan to Portland, Oregon, and the film wonderfully presents the latter's verdant picturesqueness. However, no discussion of natural beauty on display in *Feast of Love* would be anywhere near complete without mentioning the abundance of nudity, particularly female, during the film's numerous and often graphic scenes of lovemaking. (Viewers even get an eyeful of the home-made porn film made by Chloe and Oscar.) As veteran director Robert Benton offers up such a feast of bare bosoms, one wonders if perhaps *Feast of Love*'s end-of-September release might have been timed to help enthusiastically kick off the following month's national

awareness campaign devoted to the preservation of healthy breasts.

David L. Boxerbaum

CREDITS

Harry Stevenson: Morgan Freeman
Bradley Smith: Greg Kinnear
Esther Stevenson: Jane Alexander
Diana: Radha Mitchell
David Watson: Billy Burke
Kathryn: Selma Blair
Chloe: Alexa Davalos
Oscar: Toby Hemingway
Bat: Fred Ward
Jenny: Stana Katic
Origin: USA
Language: English
Released: 2007
Production: Tom Rosenberg, Gary Lucchesi, Richard S. Wright; GreeneStreet Films, Revelations Entertainment, Lakeshore Entertainment; released by MGM
Directed by: Robert Benton
Written by: Allison Burnett
Cinematography by: Kramer Morgenthau
Music by: Stephen Trask
Sound: Steve Morrow
Editing: Andrew Mondshein
Art Direction: John Chichester
Costumes: Renee Ehrlich Kalfus
Production Design: Missy Stewart
MPAA rating: R
Running time: 101 minutes

REVIEWS

Boston Globe Online. September 28, 2007.
Chicago Sun-Times Online. September 28, 2007.
Entertainment Weekly Online. September 26, 2007.
Hollywood Reporter Online. September 24, 2007.
Los Angeles Times Online. September 28, 2007.
New York Times Online. September 28, 2007.
San Francisco Chronicle. September 28, 2007, p. E6.
Variety Online. September 21, 2007.

QUOTES

Harry Stevenson: "Sometimes you don't know you've crossed a line until you're already on the other side."

FIDO

Laugh your head off.
    —Movie tagline
Good dead are hard to find.
    —Movie tagline

It now seems that the zombie comedy has evolved to the point where there is a specialized subgenre for every taste, be it splatter punk (*Return of the Living Dead* [1985]), Three Stooges-style slapstick (*Evil Dead II* [1987]), or bittersweet family tale (*Shaun of the Dead* [2004]). Andrew Currie's *Fido* offers a new spin on the genre: an alternate universe version of 1950s suburban America following the Zombie Wars, in which radioactive cosmic dust began reanimating the dead, necessitating a novel corporate solution by the Zomcon conglomerate—collars that tame zombies, allowing them to be used as domestic servants and manual laborers. Examining the same creepy flipside of post-World War II American salad days as Bob Balaban's *Parents* (1989), Currie's funny and original tale also features a proto-feminist heroine and a sardonic but surprisingly cuddly examination of the dangers of keeping up with the Joneses. Though it might be slightly dry for serious gore fans, *Fido*'s big heart could win over non-horror indie film fans looking for a something different.

A portrait of cleanliness, order, and success, the town of Willard is rife with manicured lawns, pastel-colored houses, and shiny new cars. It also has zombies—delivering milk, pushing lawnmowers, and gardening. Zomcon, the corporation whose familiar "Z" logo appears on everything from hood ornaments to milk bottles to "head coffins" (in which a corpse's severed head is buried to prevent the body from coming back to life), has made it possible for the living and the reanimated to live side by side. When Zomcon executive John Bottoms (Henry Czerny), a new resident of Willard, makes a visit to his daughter Cindy's (Alexia Fast) elementary school classroom, Timmy Robinson (K'Sun Ray) is not impressed. Distrustful of the all-encompassing corporation, his vocal dissent makes him the target of two bullying classmates, conformists right down to their matching scout uniforms. Timmy's mother Helen (Carrie-Anne Moss), however, fearful of being the only zombie-less house on the block, purchases Fido (Billy Connolly) to help with the housework. Patriarch Bill (Dylan Baker) is unhappy about the idea, but goes along. The unthinkable happens, though, when Fido's collar comes off as he attempts to protect Timmy from his tormentors in the park, and his bloodlust leads him to bite neighborhood crone Mrs. Henderson (Mary Black), causing a chain reaction of rogue zombie feedings. Once Fido's collar is reattached, however, he becomes not only a "pet" and friend for Timmy, but also something of a stand-in for absentee father Bill, who would rather be fishing. As the outbreak of wild zombies is discovered, they are traced back to Fido, and the Hendersons must fight for their right to keep their faithful servant. In the end, *Fido* seems to be saying that once the hunger for human flesh is eliminated, some

zombies are better than people, and some people are better off as zombies.

With Helen, Carrie-Anne Moss is given her most rewarding role since the *Matrix* films. A true liberated woman before the movement existed, Helen makes her own decisions and refuses to bow down to her inattentive husband. The developing relationship between Helen and Fido even strikes some surprisingly tender notes, as when she dances with the zombie after Bill refuses, and she tells Fido "I wish I would've known you before you died." As Fido, Connolly has little to do but grunt and grit his teeth, but he wrings palpable pathos from the character. This could be considered a perverse role to take after his acclaimed work in *Mrs. Brown* (1997), but it somehow suits the idiosyncratic Scottish comedian.

Director Currie, who cowrote the Leo©-nominated script with Robert Chomiak from a story by Dennis Heaton, has obvious reverence for zombie lore in the films that preceded this one. *Fido*'s zombies lumber along like the dead things in the films of George Romero, not like the late-model sprinters of 2003's *Dawn of the Dead* remake. His tamed zombies even seem to reflect the same science that produced Bub, the Walkman-listening zombie mascot of Romero's *Day of the Dead* (1985). The "Zombie War" detailed in the wonderful Zomcon-produced educational film shown to Timmy's class could even act as a companion piece to Max Brooks's best-selling 2003 tome *The Zombie Survival Guide*.

Currie keeps the humor sly and dry, rarely resorting to easy slapstick. But as Peter Travers notes in *Rolling Stone*, "Currie is better at laughs than scares, but he can't sustain either as *Fido* runs out of steam in the final stretch," when it appears he feels obligated to stage a climactic action set piece at Zomcon headquarters. As the name may suggest, the heart of the film is a sweet riff on the classic boy-and-his-dog (or zombie) story, resulting in "a beautifully slow-to-build joke that demands a familiarity with the typical story arc and climactic dialogue from the old *Lassie* television series," as noted by Manohla Dargis in the *New York Times*.

Made for a modest $9 million, *Fido* never looks less than impressive. Production designer Rob Gray has created a vivid reimagining of suburban 1950s America, right down to the smallest detail—including Timmy's "Zombie War" bed sheets. The zombie makeup may be a bit mild and uninventive for the seasoned genre fan, but it is not likely to gross out those less inclined toward splatter, and it never threatens to overwhelm the actors' performances.

Cinematically speaking, suburban conformity, evil corporations, and zombies are well-trodden comedic and dramatic territories in and of themselves. Somehow, though, *Fido* modestly combines these elements into an unassuming but visually exciting entertainment that is slanted enough to appeal to fans of the offbeat and just sick enough to hold the attention of zombie aficionados. Currie's strongest trick, though, is giving his film such a surprisingly large and beating heart for something so preoccupied with the dead.

David Hodgson

CREDITS

Fido: Billy Connolly
Helen Robinson: Carrie-Anne Moss
Bill Robinson: Dylan Baker
Mr. Bottoms: Henry Czerny
Mr. Theopolis: Tim Blake Nelson
Timmy Robinson: K'Sun Ray
Tammy: Sonja Bennett
Origin: Canada
Language: English
Released: 2007
Production: Blake Corbet, Mary Anne Waterhouse; Lionsgate, Anagram Pictures, Astral Media, Téléfilm Canada; released by Roadside Attractions, Lionsgate
Directed by: Andrew Currie
Written by: Andrew Currie, Robert Chomiak, Dennis Heaton
Cinematography by: Jan Kiesser
Music by: Don Macdonald
Music Supervisor: Sarah Webster
Editing: Roger Mattiussi
Art Direction: Michael Norman Wong
Costumes: Mary E. McLeod
Production Design: Rob Gray
MPAA rating: R
Running time: 91 minutes

REVIEWS

Los Angeles Times Online. June 15, 2007.
New York Times Online. June 15, 2007.
Premiere Online. June 15, 2007.
Rolling Stone Online. June 14, 2007.
Variety Online. September 10, 2006.
Village Voice Online. June 13, 2007.

QUOTES

Bill Robinson: "I'd say I'm a pretty darn good father. My father tried to eat me. I don't remember trying to eat Timmy."

TRIVIA

Director Currie used his own 1996 short, *Night of the Living*, as the B&W classroom instructional film.

THE FINAL SEASON

How do you want to be remembered?
—Movie tagline

Box Office: $1.1 million

The Final Season means to be a feel-good, inspiring sports movie in the vein of *Hoosiers* (1986), which set the standard by which this kind of film is inevitably measured. Although *The Final Season* is apt to please those who enjoy such movies, regardless of how formulaic they tend to be, the film attempts to be more than it is, resulting in a story that is muddled with too many narrative layers and that strives too hard for sentimentality. It is an adequate movie that is often engaging, but it fails to stand out among its many peers because it never really offers anything more than what has been seen before in similar films. Put succinctly, it is just another "underdog challenges the odds and defies expectations to achieve victory" story.

The story, based on actual events, is set in 1991 in the very small town of Norway, Iowa, where the townspeople have been devoted, faithful supporters of the high school baseball team, the Norway Tigers, who had an amazing record of winning nineteen state championships in a row. Baseball is so rooted in the town's culture that coach Jim Van Scoyoc (Powers Boothe) proclaims, "We grow baseball players like corn." Unfortunately, it appears the team may not get a chance to win a twentieth championship. The powers-that-be decide to merge Norway with another school (Norway has only one hundred students), which comes as a crushing blow to the students as well as the townspeople. Beloved coach Van Scoyoc is fired—forced out by the school board, led by villainous Harvey Makepeace (Marshall Bell)—and his assistant Kent Stock (Sean Astin) is brought in to replace him. Bell doubts Stock has what it takes to lead the team to a winning season (thus, by his logic, making the merger more palatable), and evidently the townspeople and students share the sentiment.

Thus the primary conflict in the film revolves around Kent's quest to lead the team to one final victory and to re-inspire the town. A secondary plot involves one of the players, Mitch Akers (Michael Angarano), a troubled youth who has just moved to Norway from Chicago. His involvement with the team indirectly helps him deal with several of his issues, including a distant father (Tom Arnold). Another level of the story explores Kent's budding relationship with a school board lawyer, Polly Hudson (Rachael Leigh Cook).

It is in fact the multiple layers of narrative that ends up being one of the film's significant weaknesses. The film attempts to tell several intertwined stories, but the plotlines often seem rushed and underdeveloped, resulting in a movie that comes across as splintered and unsure of its own focus. Ironically, the lack of strong development within the subplots contributes to a sense that the film runs too long. The relationship between Kent and Polly, for example, suffers from poor execution and insufficient depth, making it seem rushed and inexplicable.

The performances in the film are more than adequate, and both Astin and Angarano play their parts convincingly, but at times the writing is weak and dialogue suffers from heavy-handed appeals to sentiment. The film overplays its themes with too many obvious attempts to tug on heartstrings, whether it is with the motivational words of coaches and family members or a nearly impossible catch during a game. Even the musical score is overbearing, unmatched to the action onscreen and more in keeping with a grandiose epic, creating a kind of narrative dissonance that only serves to underscore how hard the film tries to work on the emotions of the audience. The unfortunate side effect is that, even though the filmmakers' love for baseball is evidenced throughout the film, too often the sentimentality comes across as gimmicky.

In short, *The Final Season* is an enjoyable film, particularly for those who enjoy sports movies of its kind, but its self-importance is not substantiated by the plot, performances, or script. It is a rather small, adequate film that thinks it is an epic.

David Flanagin

CREDITS

Kent Stock: Sean Astin
Coach Jim Van Scoyoc: Powers Boothe
Polly Hudson: Rachael Leigh Cook
Jared Akers: James Gammon
Roger Dempsey: Larry Miller
Harvey Makepeace: Marshall Bell
Burt Akers: Tom Arnold
Mitch Akers: Michael Angarano
Ann Akers: Angela Paton
Origin: USA
Language: English
Released: 2007
Production: Herschel Weingrod, Michael Wasserman, Steven Schott, Tony Wilson, Parker Widemire; Fobia Films, Final Partners, TRMC Productions; released by Yari Film Group
Directed by: David Mickey Evans
Written by: Art D'Alessandro, James Grayford
Cinematography by: Daniel Stoloff
Music by: Nathan Wang
Sound: Mary Jo Devenney

Editing: Harry Keramidas
Art Direction: Barry Gelber
Costumes: Lynn Brannelly-Newman
Production Design: Chester Kaczenski
MPAA rating: PG
Running time: 123 minutes

REVIEWS

Austin Chronicle Online. October 12, 2007.
Boston Globe Online. October 12, 2007.
Hollywood Reporter Online. October 9, 2007.
Los Angeles Times Online. October 12, 2007.
Variety Online. October 7, 2007.
Washington Post Online. October 12, 2007.

TRIVIA

Eliza Dushku was originally cast as "Polly Hudson" in this film, but dropped out. She was later replaced by Rachael Leigh Cook.

THE FLYING SCOTSMAN

Hope made him a dreamer. Heart made him a hero.
—Movie tagline

The true story of the unlikely champion that inspired a nation.
—Movie tagline

In July 1993 Scotsman Graeme Obree broke the distance record for cycling by riding 51.596 kilometers (32.06 miles) in only sixty minutes. Just a week later, Englishman Chris Boardman stole the title of the fastest cyclist from the Scotsman, and it would be almost another year before Obree refined his bicycle and riding mechanics to vie for it again. According to his autobiography, Obree was a revolutionary in design, taking the issues of the reduction of wind resistance and instability to levels that had never been seen in the sport before. He moved the handlebars, changed the seat location, and even mastered new styles of sitting to maximize his speed. He became "the Flying Scotsman." If the film of the same name by Douglas Mackinnon is to be believed, he accomplished all of this while dealing with intense and sometimes deadly depression. A tragic hero, an establishment that tried to keep him down, a new world record—*The Flying Scotsman* has all the ingredients for a successful, feelgood sports story, but a clichéd script and pedestrian direction keep *Scotsman* frustratingly grounded.

As portrayed in *The Flying Scotsman*, Obree (Jonny Lee Miller) was a quiet, unassuming man who was driven, almost to a fault, to break the world speed record for cycling. Obree looked at the cycles being ridden in races and in record-breaking attempts and saw countless flaws. He noticed that, lying with one's back on the ground and legs in the air, the natural human instinct would be to leave one banana's worth of space between his appendages, but that most bikes were designed with two. He noticed how the ball bearings in his washing machine helped the wheels of that device reach higher speeds. Obree took all of these ingredients and built a better bike, whose impact is still felt in cycling today, but he could never fix the demons in himself. Haunted by continuous bullying as a child and never able to enjoy his cycling victories, Obree flirts with suicide throughout *The Flying Scotsman*—in fact, the film opens with a scene of the hero trying to hang himself and then works forward to that point through flashbacks. Obree broke the rules of cycling, but even the undying support of his wife Anne (Laura Fraser), his manager/friend Malky McGovern (Billy Boyd), and local minister Douglas Baxter (Brian Cox) would not make him a winner in his own mind.

The devotion to character by Miller—he spent time with Obree as early as 2002 to try and pick up some of the speech patterns and behavior of the character he would be playing—is evident in the performance, but authenticity does not necessarily make for riveting storytelling. As written by John Brown, Declan Hughes, and Simon Rose, Obree was an often morose loner, making him a hard hero to build an inspirational sports movie around. *The Flying Scotsman* edges into dramatic territory around the issue of depression, but also wallows in too many sports movie clichés for the dark material to be emotionally effective.

Part of the problem with *The Flying Scotsman* is the lack of cinematic material in the story that Mackinnon has been given to film. Working with a strong cinematographer in Gavin Finney, Mackinnon does his best to make trying to break the cycling speed record exciting, but watching a man ride around a track as fast as possible for an hour (the record is determined by how many laps can be ridden in sixty minutes) just does not have the inherent excitement of a lot of other sports on film.

The subject matter of *The Flying Scotsman* may have hindered the filmmaker's ability to turn the film into a rousing, inspirational sports story, but it certainly does not stop him from trying. On the contrary, *The Flying Scotsman* hits far too many familiar notes in the genre, including a very traditional structure and a group of authoritarian villains who might as well be curling handlebar mustaches they are so two-dimensionally written. From the very beginning, the beats of *The Flying Scotsman* can be seen coming around every corner—a (relatively) likable hero, a comic partner, a supportive wife, a set-back or two, and an inevitable victory. It can

be hard to criticize a film for following too predictable a structure when it uses a true story as its subject matter, but the trio behind *The Flying Scotsman* never finds the life to give the viewer the impression that, despite his undeniable accomplishments, Obree's story was worth telling in the first place.

Brian Tallerico

CREDITS

Graeme Obree: Johnny Lee Miller
Young Graeme Obree: Sean Brown
Graeme's Mother: Julie Austin
Malky: Billy Boyd
Anne Obree: Laura Fraser
Douglas Baxter: Brian Cox
Scobie: Ron Donachie
Katie: Morven Christie
Ernst Hagemann: Steven Berkoff
Francesco Moser: Philip Wright
Chris Boardman: Adrian Smith
Child Gang Leader: Joseph Carney
Graeme's Father: Niall Macgregor
Baby Ewan: Christopher Anderson
Armstrong: Moray Hunter
Adult Gang Leader: Niall Greig Fulton
French Mayor: Daniel André Pageon
Mayor's Wife: Gudrun Mangel
President: Muzaffer Cakar
Origin: Great Britain
Language: English
Released: 2006
Production: Peter Broughan, Peter Gallagher, Sara Giles, Damita Nikapota; ContentFilm International, Scion Films, Scottish Screen; released by MGM
Directed by: Douglas Mackinnon
Written by: John Brown, Declan Hughes, Simon Rose
Cinematography by: Gavin Finney
Music by: Martin Phipps
Editing: Colin Monie
Art Direction: Ursula Cleary
Costumes: Alexandra Caulfield
Production Design: Mike Gunn
MPAA rating: PG-13
Running time: 96 minutes

REVIEWS

Boston Globe Online. May 4, 2007.
Chicago Sun-Times Online. May 4, 2007.
Los Angeles Times Online. January 1, 2007.
New York Times Online. May 4, 2007.

San Francisco Chronicle. May 4, 2007, p. E5.
The Scotsman Online. August 15, 2006.
Variety Online. August 15, 2006.
Washington Post. May 4, 2007, p. C6.

1408

*The Dolphin Hotel invites you to stay in any of
its stunning rooms. Except one.*
—Movie tagline

Box Office: $71.9 million

Michael Enslin (John Cusack) plays a renowned best-selling author who has forged a career in debunking haunted rooms in various inns and hotels throughout the country and then detailing his experiences in books. Although journaling as an apparition skeptic is his forte, his real passion is writing fiction, though he has achieved only marginal success, as shown when an avid fan asks him to sign an obscure novel he wrote years ago. As the story unfolds, the film delves into Enslin's troubled past, which began when his daughter, Katie (Jasmine Jessica Anthony), became terminally ill. Before she eventually succumbed to her illness, this Doubting Thomas attempted to quell his daughter's fears by assuring her that there is indeed an afterlife. After the marriage to his wife Lily (Mary McCormack) fails, Enslin leads a lonely life; a semi-vagabond, he is invited to spend evenings in rooms bewitched by the paranormal. Although a prosperous writer, Enslin lives out of a suitcase and yields to the seductive whims of John Barleycorn.

Following a surfing accident (when not traveling, Enslin resides in California) he is given a mysterious anonymous postcard of the Dolphin Hotel in New York City with a warning for him not to enter room 1408. Intrigued, Enslin decides to accept the challenge. Armed with the knowledge that hotels must rent out unoccupied rooms in accordance with the Fair Housing Act, Enslin insists that the staff allow him to pay for a night in the infamous room. The smooth, rational Dolphin Hotel manager, Gerald Olin (Samuel L. Jackson), attempts to dissuade the author by enticing him into an upgrade to the penthouse suite, accompanied by an extremely expensive bottle of cognac, to no avail. Refusing to enter the thirteenth floor, where 1408 is located, Olin sees Michael off at the elevator.

Once inside room 1408, all manner of necromancy ensues. It begins with the benign sounds of the Carpenters's "We've Only Just Begun" emanating from a clock radio that snaps on of its own accord. For the next hour, Enslin is plagued by what can be described as hell unleashed in a room he cannot escape (echoing the Eagles's tune, "Hotel California"). It is as if by unlocking the room with its big brass key, he has opened a personal Pandora's Box. Preying upon his deep-rooted fears that ultimately involve his deceased daughter, who appears to him as a revenant, and his ex-wife, whom he still loves, it appears that he is truly insane or is being gaslighted by cabalistic phenomena. Once the hour passes, the clock radio digits back to 60:00 and another hour's countdown begins with the resumption of the Carpenters's familiar song. Enslin realizes he is caught in a nightmarish temporal loop; a hellish Mephistophelean "Groundhog Day".

Enslin escapes by setting the room ablaze and creating a backdraft, upon which the NYFD rescue him. Reunited with Lily, he is unable to convince her that he saw their daughter. It is not until he finds his mini recorder, which he left running during his encounter, and replays it that they both, chillingly, hear Katie's unmistakable voice.

Directed by Mikael Håfström, *1408* is a blend of horror and psychological thriller, and swerves from the bloody carnage dominating contemporary horror film productions of recent years. The last scene of the film version released on June 22, 2007, is not the original Håfström shot. In the first ending filmed, Enslin dies in the room's fire and is briefly seen by Olin as a badly burnt apparition. Enslin, apparently consigned to haunt room 1408, is called away by Katie's beckoning voice. Both endings are available on DVD (the director's cut has the original).

1408 is based upon the short story by Stephen King of the same name and can be found in the collection *Everything's Eventual: 14 Dark Tales.* Among these stories is a gem called "The Man in the Black Suit," for which King won the World Fantasy Award in 1995 and the O. Henry Award the following year. A short film was made of the tale involving a boy's encounter with the devil, but *1408* was the only full-length film adaptation made thus far from the compilation.

David M. Roberts

CREDITS

Mike Enslin: John Cusack
Mr. Olin: Samuel L. Jackson
Lily: Mary McCormack
Katie Enslin: Jasmine Jessica Anthony
Origin: USA
Language: English
Released: 2007
Production: Lorenzo di Bonaventura; Dimension Films, Di Bonaventura Pictures; released by the Weinstein Company
Directed by: Mikael Håfström

Written by: Matt Greenberg, Scott Alexander, Larry Karaszewski

Cinematography by: Benoit Delhomme

Music by: Gabriel Yared

Sound: Brian Simmons

Editing: Peter Boyle

Costumes: Natalie Ward

Production Design: Andrew Laws

MPAA rating: PG-13

Running time: 104 minutes

REVIEWS

Boston Globe Online. June 22, 2007.

Chicago Sun-Times Online. June 22, 2007.

Entertainment Weekly. June 22, 2007, p. 52.

Hollywood Reporter Online. June 18, 2007.

Los Angeles Times Online. June 22, 2007.

New York Times Online. June 21, 2007.

San Francisco Chronicle. June 22, 2007, p. E1.

Variety Online. June 15, 2007.

Washington Post Online. June 22, 2007.

QUOTES

Mike: "Hotels are unusually creepy places. How many people have slept here before me? How many of them were sick? How many lost their minds? How many died?"

TRIVIA

There are many references to the number "13" throughout the movie. The room is numbered "1408," add each number together equals 13. The room is on the 14th floor, and the Hotel skips the 13th floor, so the room is technically on the 13th floor. The room's key lock also has "6214" etched into it, which adds up to 13. And the first death was in the year 1912, which adds to 13.

FRACTURE

> *If you look closely enough, you'll find everyone has a weak spot.*
> —Movie tagline

Box Office: $39 million

One is a coldly calculating old cuckold who is arrogantly sure he can blow away his cheating wife, provide the police with both the murder weapon and a confession, and still walk away scot-free. The other is a young hotshot Los Angeles assistant district attorney who comes to the case with a 97 percent conviction rate and 100 percent confidence. At the outset of *Fracture*, a thoroughly entertaining, crafty thriller that prevails over its implausibilities, it will be a tough call for viewers to

decide which is the more cocksure character. What at first appears to be an open-and-shut case turns into a battle royal of wits and wills that is likely to keep those watching enjoyably absorbed until the final, satisfying triumphant trumping.

Ted Crawford (Anthony Hopkins) is a wealthy, brilliant structure-failure analyst for the airline industry who once prided himself on an ability to spot even the faintest flaw while candling eggs. He has now hatched a plan to commit the perfect murder, which has him oozing odious, smirking smugness. Ted is certain that the precise attention to detail that has always served him so well will prevent him from serving any time for his crime. Quite telling about the man is the fact that his home is filled with intricate kinetic sculptures, featuring marbles that can only successfully proceed down complex, twisting turns if everything has been meticulously, methodically (or is it obsessively?) calibrated just so. Ted feels compelled to shoot Jennifer (Embeth Davidtz), December having found out about May's love affair with someone warmer and much closer to her time of life. Having carefully premeditated his devious plan, a perverted sense of self-satisfaction assuaging his intolerably wounded ego, he proceeds to purposefully deface her face with a bullet that tears on into her brain. After Ted washes up and changes clothes, burning those he had on, everything seems to be going as planned when one of the responding officers is indeed the woman's policeman paramour, Lieutenant Rob Nunally (merely adequate Billy Burke), aghast to recognize his lover lying comatose in a widening pool of blood. The pain and horror viewers see in his eyes is in stark contrast to the glint of devilish, retributive delight eerily visible in Ted's as he is hauled off to jail.

As this is occurring, Willy Beachum (Ryan Gosling), legal eagle on the rise, is poised to soar up out of public service toward a loftier and more lucrative perch at a prestigious private law firm. It is a golden opportunity made all the more attractive by Nikki Gardner (Rosamund Pike), the blond stunner of a new boss who has already acquainted Willy with both the company's offices and her bed. It is all enough to give a young man who originally hails from a working-class neighborhood a big head, although there is even more concern that choosing the cushy corporate world over working for the people may diminish his soul. Willy's current boss, District Attorney Joe Lobruto (David Strathairn), is aptly described by *Fracture*'s cowriter Glenn Gers as the self-centered young lawyer's "conscience waiting to be found," pulling Willy in one direction while Nikki yanks him toward the other. Joe thinks Willy "belongs" where he is, doing something truly "important," but his striving subordinate is clearly impatient to fly. ("I didn't work this hard to stay where I 'belong'" is his reply.)

Already enthusiastically planning his new digs' décor, Willy will only tarry long enough to handle what has all the appearances of being an open-and-shut case.

On his way to this final slam-dunk, however, Willy is unexpectedly blocked by Ted and sent reeling. Suddenly the latter man is pleading not guilty to the attempted murder, and will represent himself at trial. Inexplicably and unsettlingly, Ted is lighthearted and seems profoundly unconcerned. Then the astonishing lab results come back on the murder weapon: it had not been fired. Willy brusquely demands that the police comb the spacious home again and again for the vital piece of evidence, to no avail. "He's screwing with us!" says the habitual winner who has no intention of going out on a sour note. It is obvious that Willy has never been thrown before, and does not like it one bit.

"I'm not going to play games with you," Willy says during his first face-to-face encounter with this unanticipated, unpredictable nemesis. "I'm afraid you have to, old sport," Ted replies, sounding ominous yet creepily casual. While Hopkins said he did not want Ted to tend toward Hannibal Lecter redux, one cannot help but recall that earlier and indelible character to some extent as this acutely clever killer relishes playing manipulative mind games with Willy, smoothly, disconcertingly certain every step of the way that he is in control of the situation. With a slight cock of an eyebrow, a flare of the nostrils, or an icy leer capable of making one's blood run as cold, the actor capably conveys that there is much more going on in that head than is being revealed, and the state of not knowing what it is makes one shudder perhaps even more than if one knew exactly what lurked there.

Similar to his egg candling expertise, Ted asserts that he can find weaknesses in people that he can exploit to his advantage. He apparently thinks that, with Willy being so accustomed to success and having one foot out the door, he will be overconfidently unprepared, which turns out to be the case. There is unexpected but entirely welcome humor in the scene where Ted effectively, thoroughly flummoxes Willy during the courtroom hearing. While the old saying goes that a man who chooses to represent himself has a fool for a client, Ted quickly makes clear to everyone that he knows all too well what he is doing. After the man gets Rob to angrily lunge at him in open court upon revealing the policeman's romantic connection to Jennifer in purposely vulgar terms, Ted is more easily able to convince the judge to throw out his confession, now known to have been extracted in the threatening presence of his wife's badged lover. Willy sputters that things are "getting out of hand," but actually they are being precisely controlled by reins held firmly in Ted's clutches, and engrossed

viewers will eagerly anticipate learning how the lawyer will be able to grab them back.

Willy's poor showing not only puts him in hot water with Joe, but also nearly causes a revocation of his invitation to greener pastures. In effect, Nikki is perched upon one shoulder, a peeved siren impatiently calling out for him to simply cut and run from a mess that is making not only him but also her and her firm look bad, and Joe, concerned with doing good, on the other. The lesser scenes focusing on this tug-of-war contention for Willy's soul will make viewers want what he wants—to get back to the pursuit of Ted. Those watching will sense not only Willy's nagging frustration and humiliation over the way things have been playing out (how could he be losing in court to that old coot?), but also a growing moral outrage and sense of responsibility that fuse into a determination to make things right. He will do it the right way, too, refusing (after brief but suspenseful deliberation) to use fake evidence manufactured by Rob. An acquittal results, and the despondent cop shockingly commits suicide outside the courtroom, having lost all faith in justice being served. Willy, however, has not.

What follows is high-stakes one-upmanship that is quite involving, an exceedingly consequential chess match in which each endeavors to thwart the other's progress and ultimate victory. In a particularly riveting sequence, tenacious Willy and wily Ted slap each other with restraining orders, the former trying to prevent the latter from fiendishly shutting off unconscious Jennifer's life-support system, and the latter trying to ensure the former does not hinder him from doing just that with glee. It is after Ted cannot help himself from overreaching, finishing off a woman who would have died anyway, that acumen he had not appreciated and persistence he had not counted on enables his adversary to figure out how to nail the miscreant—now not for attempted murder, but for murder itself.

Fracture, which many critics and moviegoers enjoyed, was described by its director, Gregory Hoblit, as a "popcorn thriller." It is reminiscent of his *Primal Fear* (1996), which put Edward Norton on the map. This film is likely to help continue the rise of promising actor Gosling. Just as his up-and-coming character was able to successfully go toe-to-toe with Ted's long-honed skills, Gosling is admirably able to do the same in his scenes with the oft-hailed Hopkins.

David L. Boxerbaum

CREDITS

Ted Crawford: Anthony Hopkins
Willy Beachum: Ryan Gosling

Joe Lobruto: David Strathairn
Nikki Gardner: Rosamund Pike
Jennifer Crawford: Embeth Davidtz
Rob Nunally: Billy Burke
Detective Flores: Cliff Curtis
Judge Robinson: Fiona Shaw
Judge Gardner: Bob Gunton
Judge Moran: Xander Berkeley
Norman Foster: Josh Stamberg
Mona: Zoe Kazan
Origin: USA
Language: English
Released: 2007
Production: Charles Weinstock; New Line Cinema, Castle Rock Entertainment; released by New Line Cinema
Directed by: Gregory Hoblit
Written by: Daniel Pyne, Glenn Gers
Cinematography by: Kramer Morgenthau
Music by: Mychael Danna, Jeff Danna
Sound: David Ronne
Editing: David Rosenbloom
Art Direction: Mindy Roffman
Costumes: Elisabetta Beraldo
Production Design: Paul Eads
MPAA rating: R
Running time: 113 minutes

REVIEWS

Chicago Sun-Times Online. April 10, 2007.
Entertainment Weekly. April 27, 2007, p. 121.
Hollywood Reporter Online. April 12, 2007.
Los Angeles Times Online. April 20, 2007.
New York Times Online. April 20, 2007.
Rolling Stone Online. April 18, 2007.
San Francisco Chronicle. April 20, 2007, p. E1.
Variety Online. April 10, 2007.
Washington Post. April 20, 2007, p. C5.

QUOTES

Ted (to Willy): "If you look closely enough you can find everything has a big spot where it can break."

TRIVIA

When Anthony Hopkins' character is being arraigned, a directory of judges is seen over his shoulder with the names Eads and Vacarro. Those are the last names of the production designer and set designer, respectively.

FRED CLAUS

Santa's brother is coming to town.
—Movie tagline

Everybody has that one relative who can't help but cause problems over the holidays. Even Santa.
—Movie tagline
You're invited to a very unusual family reunion.
—Movie tagline

Box Office: $72 million

Like many Christmas stories, *Fred Claus,* directed by David Dobkin from a screenplay by Dan Fogelman, revolves around a grumpy character who learns to appreciate the spirit of the season. That this character just happens to be Santa's black sheep of a brother gives this familiar premise a unique twist. A whimsical prologue shows the rivalry beginning in childhood as young Fred, despite his best intentions, cannot stand the sheer goodness of his brother, Nick, who is, of course, Mom's (Kathy Bates) favorite. Vince Vaughn plays the adult Fred, an underachiever who lives a pedestrian life in Chicago, while Santa (Paul Giamatti) lives at the North Pole and is loved the world over. At this point in his career, comedic Vince Vaughn performances are fairly interchangeable; he once again plays an irreverent, fast-talking smoothie getting himself into various scrapes. But putting him in this tale of sibling rivalry gives this familiar character type the new wrinkle of having to live in his famous brother's shadow. It is too soon to tell if *Fred Claus* will become a Christmas classic, but it is a very entertaining movie that utilizes its talents to tell a delightful and surprisingly touching story of fraternal love.

Fred is the ne'er-do-well of the Claus family. While his brother is famous for giving presents and making children happy, Fred's job is that of a repo man, someone who takes things away and makes people miserable. He also forgets his long-suffering girlfriend Wanda's (Rachel Weisz) birthday and criticizes Santa to Slam (Bobb'e J. Thompson), a poor neighborhood kid who comes from an unfit family and is taken to an orphanage. In this Christmas tale, he is the obligatory orphan figure whose bad behavior ultimately will help Fred see the error of his ways.

Fred's attempt to start a gambling business is going nowhere. In a desperate effort to raise $50,000, he dons a Santa suit and tries to horn in on the legitimate Salvation Army Santas with a generic-sounding, phony charity hilariously called People Help the People, a con job that leads to real Salvation Army Santas chasing him down the street and his ending up in jail. Despite his reluctance, Fred nonetheless calls his little brother for help, and good-hearted Santa, because he is a saint, cannot help but say yes. However, Santa attaches a string to bailing Fred out—because Santa is behind schedule and needs help getting through the busy season, he makes

Fred come to the North Pole for an extended visit. Fred is forced to agree, and, of course, his maverick style complicates things at the North Pole.

Fred's attitude is especially problematic given the fact that a steely efficiency expert named Clyde (Kevin Spacey) has arrived at the North Pole to see if the operation needs to be shut down. After all, children's wish lists have grown, and Santa may no longer be up to the task of meeting the demand. The notion of Santa being beholden to a board of directors is a hilarious idea, and Spacey is perfect as the corporate drone who even sabotages Santa's efforts. Spelling more trouble for his brother is Fred's nonconformity. He leads the elves in spontaneous dancing and is unable to brand any child as naughty because he believes all kids, like himself, are basically good.

The plot is clever, but the real joys of *Fred Claus* lie in the comic bits that pepper the film, such as tall Fred doing his best to sleep in an elf-size bunk bed that is clearly too small for him; a North Pole disc jockey named DJ Donnie (Chris "Ludacris" Bridges) constantly playing "Here Comes Santa Claus" (to Fred's chagrin); and Fred showing the head elf, Willie (John Michael Higgins), how to dance so he can win the heart of Charlene (Elizabeth Banks), a very comely Santa's Little Helper.

And Giamatti's take on the iconic character of Santa is a fresh one. He plays him as a harried boss trying his best to please everyone—after all, that is Santa's nature—but finding it increasingly difficult. The children of the world want more toys, his wife, Annette (Miranda Richardson), is constantly nagging him about his weight and encouraging a "tough love" approach with his brother, and Clyde is breathing down his neck. Giamatti, with masterful expressions of world-weariness, makes us think how hard it really would be to shoulder Santa's global responsibilities.

Once Fred ruins everything and the North Pole operation is shut down, he returns home and opens a gift from his brother, a birdhouse to replace one that Santa accidentally destroyed as a child, along with an apology. This prompts Fred to attend a meeting of Siblings Anonymous for the less successful siblings of famous people, where he finds himself sitting in a support-group circle with Frank Stallone, Roger Clinton, and Stephen Baldwin. It is a classic little sequence—not only very funny but completely unexpected.

While its many charming touches distinguish *Fred Claus*, the denouement is, unfortunately, rather predictable. Fred returns to the North Pole and saves Christmas by reopening the factory, getting the toys made, and delivering the presents himself. He redeems little Slam's faith in Santa, just as Santa renews Clyde's

belief in Christmas; it turns out that he was bearing a grudge from a childhood Christmas when he did not receive a Superman cape. Fred's view that there are no bad children, just misunderstood kids, is happily validated all around. It is a bit of a cliché, to be sure, and the extended race to get all the presents delivered in time makes the film too long, but there is also one quite beautiful scene in the closing minutes. The North Pole has a giant snow globe that allows the elves to monitor the naughty-or-nice status of children, and, at the end, to Sinéad O'Connor's haunting version of "Silent Night," the elves gather around to see the children of the world opening their presents. It is a subtle, touching moment that, in its simplicity, captures the spirit of the season.

Peter N. Chumo II

CREDITS

Fred Claus: Vince Vaughn
Nick (Santa) Claus: Paul Giamatti
Annette Claus: Miranda Richardson
Wanda: Rachel Weisz
Willie: John Michael Higgins
Mother Claus: Kathy Bates
Papa Claus: Trevor Peacock
DJ Donnie: Chris "Ludacris" Bridges
Charlene: Elizabeth Banks
Bob Elf: Jeremy Swift
Linda Elf: Elizabeth Berrington
Clyde: Kevin Spacey
Origin: USA
Language: English
Released: 2007
Production: David Dobkin, Jessie Nelson, Joel Silver; Silver Pictures; released by Warner Bros.
Directed by: David Dobkin
Written by: Dan Fogelman
Cinematography by: Remi Adefarasin
Music by: Christophe Beck
Sound: Tim Chau
Editing: Mark Livolsi
Art Direction: Giles Masters
Costumes: Anna Sheppard
Production Design: Allan Cameron
MPAA rating: PG
Running time: 116 minutes

REVIEWS

Boston Globe Online. November 9, 2007.
Chicago Sun-Times Online. November 8, 2007.

Entertainment Weekly Online. November 5, 2007.
Hollywood Reporter Online. November 6, 2007.
Los Angeles Times Online. November 9, 2007.
New York Times Online. November 9, 2007.
San Francisco Chronicle. November 9, 2007, p. E5.
Variety Online. November 5, 2007.
Washington Post. November 9, 2007, p. C5.

QUOTES

Clyde: "You're all fired, in the morning you'll all be on a bus back to Elfistan!"

TRIVIA

Kevin Spacey's character Clyde asks for (and later receives) a Superman cape from Santa Claus. Spacey played Lex Luthor in *Superman Returns* (2006).

FREEDOM WRITERS

Our story. Our words.
—Movie tagline

Box Office: $36.5 million

Invariably and periodically there are movies about teachers, not your average, run-of-the-mill, burnt-out, cynical drudges of the kind all too often protected by tenure and unions at schools everywhere, but fresh, smart, dedicated optimists capable of reaching and inspiring the disadvantaged, the threatened, and the brutalized. This genre can be traced back to *Blackboard Jungle* (1955), with Glenn Ford trying to tame the recalcitrant to the tune of "Rock Around the Clock," or, some forty years later, to *Dangerous Minds* (1995), with Michelle Pfeiffer at the blackboard. "Yo, Daddy-O" was the insolent tagline of *Blackboard Jungle*. With Hilary Swank at the blackboard in *Freedom Writers* the more cynical tagline is, "I give this bitch about a week."

Though maybe not exactly "ripped from the headlines" in the way Swank's breakthrough performance in *Boys Don't Cry* (1999) was, the Swank character in *Freedom Writers* is based upon the real-life experiences of an inspired inner-city Southern California schoolteacher named Erin Gruwell, who realized she would have to vamp mightily if she expected to survive classroom boot camp. It turns out she was up to the challenge and was able to adjust her lesson plans to the "reality" her students knew, whereas some teachers simply constructed their own "reality" and pretended it worked for their students as well, engaging in a mere pretense of teaching, as Gruwell was advised to do by her superior. At first, wearing a string of pearls her father gave her and a huge smile, Erin seems awkward, artificial, out of place,

and hopeless. The students simply ignore her, until she decides to meet them on their own turf. When Gruwell asks her students if any of them has heard of the Holocaust, not a single hand goes up. When she then asks how many of them have been shot at, almost all of the hands go up.

It is Long Beach, California, in 1994, two years after the Rodney King riots, when Gruwell is assigned a remedial English class made up of whites, blacks, Asians, and Latinos, who are all tribalized, hateful, and mistrustful. The community has not forgotten that the riots resulted in 120 murders. In addition, the high school has been marginalized as a result of forced integration. As minority students were brought in, the school lost 75 percent of its top students. Because she is the "new girl" on the faculty, Erin gets assigned the hard-case remedial students in classroom 203, students with low expectations that the system prefers to simply process and move on. The problem is, Erin takes her charge of teaching them seriously.

Erin believes that writing is important, so she asks her students to keep journals and to become "freedom writers," echoing the "freedom riders" of the civil rights movement (who were idealists of different races, all working toward the same goal). In reality, Gruwell's educational approach and reforms involved a great deal more, but the Freedom Writers are the focal point of the story for writer/director Richard LaGravenese. In truth, it is not a bad hook. By the time they graduated, the students even managed to get a collection of their diary excerpts published. According to *Washington Post* feature writer Christina Talcott, when the Freedom Writers "sold the rights to their book for the movie, proceeds went directly to scholarships for underprivileged kids."

Gruwell achieved these remarkable results at no small personal cost. First, there was a problem with the school administrators who preferred warehousing books bought with tax money rather than using them in classes. Thwarted on this front, Gruwell takes a second job as a sales clerk, then a third job as concierge at a local hotel in order to provide for her students, but by doing so, she is not providing for her husband Scott (Patrick Dempsey), who, it turns out, does not share her optimism and resents being neglected. After four semesters, he leaves her. She is disappointed but not deterred. Dempsey as the long-suffering and, frankly, dull and unimaginative Scott, is adequate but hardly more than background furniture.

Among Gruwell's remarkable achievements was getting her students to read *The Diary of Anne Frank*, multiple copies of which she purchased with her own money. Then, as an assignment, she asks her students to write a letter to the woman who protected Anne Frank's family from the Nazis. She sends those letters to the Netherlands, with an invitation for the lady to visit her class and, counter to all expectations, the visitation takes place. At the end of their sophomore year, the students are angry and frustrated when they learn that Ms. Gruwell will not be teaching them during their junior and senior years. They petition the Board of Education so that she may be retained as their teacher. They are strongly opposed by the woman responsible for assigning classes (Imelda Staunton) and by the school principal, but the students ultimately win out. A note at the end of the film indicates that Gruwell was later able to follow her students to the University of California, Long Beach, where she was given a teaching job. The film's final image is a still photograph of the real Erin Gruwell at the center of a group picture with all of her students.

If all of this sounds a bit saccharine and unrealistic, that is because, at times, it is. But if the teacher's home life is made difficult by her workaholic dedication, that is almost trivial in comparison to what her students have lived through. Fragments of their life stories are dramatized as they write in their journals. A ghetto boy watches in horror as his friend accidentally shoots himself. Another young man takes to living on the streets after his mother drives him away from home. A young Latino student is urged to give false witness in order to protect her criminal father, who will otherwise be sent to prison. Another student, Eva (April Lee Hernandez) witnesses a shooting and is forced to testify in court; because she tells the truth, she is made a pariah by members of her "gang." Still another young woman is beaten and abused at home. The teaching in this film seems to cut two ways, and certainly the journal writing becomes therapeutic. The class bonds together, like a family.

There is a one-dimensional quality that tends to flaw all films about heroic and dedicated teachers. The focus of *Freedom Writers* is entirely on Gruwell's single remedial English class, as if she taught no others and had no other obligations. She is simply always there for her students. While that is certainly admirable, it is also a bit obsessive and unbelievable. Which is not exactly to be cynical, or to sneer at this movie or its noble intentions, but the film is capable of straining credulity. No doubt teachers like Erin Gruwell do exist and have done wonderful things for all the right reasons. The film is remarkably inspiring for a January release, since January is usually the dumping ground for failed motion pictures that were not deemed good enough for the holiday marketplace. Swank takes the improbable and brings it convincingly to life. *Freedom Writers* not only provided

Swank with a role worthy of her talents but also gives encouragement to good teachers everywhere.

James M. Welsh

CREDITS

Erin Gruwell: Hilary Swank
Scott Casey: Patrick Dempsey
Steve: Scott Glenn
Margaret Campbell: Imelda Staunton
Brian Gelford: John Benjamin Hickey
Miep Gies: Pat Carroll
Eva: April Lee Hernandez
Jamal: Deance Wyatt
Andre: Mario
Brandy: Vanetta Smith
Origin: USA
Language: English
Released: 2007
Production: Michael Shamberg, Stacey Sher, Danny DeVito; Jersey Films, Double Feature Films, MTV Films; released by Paramount
Directed by: Richard LaGravenese
Written by: Richard LaGravenese
Cinematography by: Jim Denault
Music by: Mark Isham
Sound: David Parker
Music Supervisor: Mary Ramos
Editing: David Moritz
Art Direction: Peter Borck
Costumes: Cindy Evans
Production Design: Laurence Bennett
MPAA rating: PG-13
Running time: 123 minutes

REVIEWS

Chicago Sun-Times Online. January 5, 2007.
Entertainment Weekly. January 19, 2007, p. 59.
Hollywood Reporter Online. January 4, 2007.
Los Angeles Times Online. January 5, 2007.
San Francisco Chronicle. January 5, 2007, p. E6.
Variety Online. January 3, 2007.
Washington Post. January 5, 2007, p. C1.

QUOTES

Andre: "Justice doesn't mean the bad guy goes to jail, it just means that someone pays for the crime."

TRIVIA

At the hotel dinner for the kids, after their trip to the Holocaust museum, all of the Holocaust survivor characters are played by actual Holocaust survivors.

FULL OF IT

The truth is all that counts.
    —Movie tagline

He couldn't make it big, so he made it up.
    —Movie tagline

With a title like *Full of It,* a movie is bound to tempt viewers and critics alike to comment on the irony if the film turns out to be a bad one. Unfortunately (for the film, at least), that is exactly the case with this less-than-mediocre teen comedy. Although there are a few amusing moments in the movie, it is largely an uninspired, unremarkable, and unmemorable venture down a path that has been trod too many times before—a shallow, often silly story about awkward teenagers and the importance of being one's self.

The main character in *Full of It* is Sam Leonard (Ryan Pinkston), a high school senior who seems to have several things working against him as the new kid in school, having just moved to town. Sam, a mathematics whiz who is planning on getting an academic scholarship to college, is short for his age. His parents make a scene when they drop him off for school directly in front of the main entrance, hugging him and essentially treating him like a younger child. Very quickly he finds himself either ignored or teased by almost everyone—all except the book-smart Annie (Kate Mara), who befriends him and sympathizes with him. After a visit with the school counselor ends with Sam receiving some bad advice, Sam decides that the only way he can be popular is to lie. Subsequently he begins twisting the truth and telling outrageous lies. He is a great basketball player who never misses a shot. His father is a rock star. He drives a Porsche. He loves brussels sprouts so much he would eat them all the time if he could. His English teacher has the hots for him.

After he slams his bedroom door and breaks the mirror attached to it, Sam begins discovering an amazing development: his lies are coming true. He *does* have a Porsche. His English teacher seems obsessed with him. He finds himself eating brussels sprouts at every meal. He becomes a star player on the basketball team, and the most popular girl in the class invites him to the homecoming dance. Predictably, though, he eventually discovers that all these wonderful things are not so wonderful, and he realizes his life is unraveling around him. He ultimately learns that he is happier being himself, even if that means being teased by others.

The film's message may be nice, but it has been told many times before, and in better movies. *Full of It* suffers from lack of creativity, from stale dialogue, and from an inexplicable, clumsy plot device that sets in motion the "magical" turn of events driving the story. The broken mirror is simply added with no relevance or explanation, as if it were inserted as an afterthought. The teasing Sam experiences, the fascination with a popular girl while the best friend is clearly the better choice, and the conflict with the bullying jock are all cookie-cutter scenarios, and the movie offers nothing new to elevate the story above others like it.

Another weakness is character development. Sam is not even a very likeable character. He comes across as immature, shallow, and impulsive, making up foolish, outlandish lies that are obviously untrue, and he is unlikely to elicit much sympathy from an audience. It is also surprising that he does not recognize how fortunate he is to have a friend like Annie, who is actually a very attractive girl (in fact, it is difficult to perceive what she sees in Sam), a strange dynamic that hurts the credibility of their relationship. Annie may be the most interesting character in the story and, as such, does not get enough time onscreen. She is the only character who seems to have some depth and maturity, though viewers may wonder why she bothers with Sam; evidently it is her innate kindness and ability to empathize with him that draws her to him, even though she initially projects an "I'm above it all" attitude. None of the other characters are drawn very well; they are stock characters and stereotypes, and the movie seems content to expect the audience to recognize them from other films.

Full of It could easily be one of the most forgettable films of the year, and for good reason.

David Flanagin

CREDITS

Sam Leonard: Ryan Pinkston
Annie Dray: Kate Mara
Mike Hanbo: Craig Kilborn
Mr. Leonard: John Carroll Lynch
Mrs. Leonard: Cynthia Stevenson
Vicki Sanders: Amanda Walsh
Prinicipal Hayes: Derek McGrath
Mrs. Moran: Teri Polo
Kyle Plunkett: Joshua Close
Herself: Carmen Electra (Cameo)
Origin: USA
Language: English
Released: 2007
Production: Mark Canton, Steve Barnett; Relativity Media, Atmosphere Entertainment; released by New Line Cinema
Directed by: Christian Charles
Written by: Jon Lucas, Scott Moore
Cinematography by: Kramer Morgenthau
Music by: John Swihart

Sound: Paul Germann

Music Supervisor: Dave Hnatiuk

Editing: Susan Shipton

Art Direction: Rejean Labrie

Costumes: Abram Waterhouse

Production Design: Kathleen Climie

MPAA rating: PG-13

Running time: 93 minutes

REVIEWS

Hollywood Reporter Online. March 1, 2007.
Los Angeles Times Online. March 2, 2007.
San Francisco Chronicle. March 2, 2007, p. E4.
Variety Online. March 1, 2007.

QUOTES

Mr. Hanbo (to Sam): "Winners always lie and liars always win."

G

THE GAME PLAN

Joe Kingman had the perfect game plan to win the championship...but first, he has to tackle one little problem.
—Movie tagline

Box Office: $90.6 million

Dwayne Johnson, the actor and former World Wrestling Federation (WWF) standout once known simply as "the Rock," plays a professional football player in Disney's family comedy, *The Game Plan*. This film is the last in which Johnson will use the "Rock" moniker, as he makes the final break with his WWF past and moves solely into film. Johnson's character Joe "the King" Kingman is an exceedingly narcissistic, confirmed bachelor who seems to have it all. He is the star quarterback of the fictional Boston Rebels, who are on the verge of winning football's biggest prize. With Kingman and his team on the brink of filling the one remaining hole in his professional resumé, it looks as though the sweet life is about to get even sweeter.

Predictably, everything is turned upside down when Peyton (Madison Pettis), Kingman's long-lost eight-year-old daughter, shows up on his doorstep for a month-long stay while mom is away in Africa doing charity work. In the blink of an eye, his nights on the town are replaced by evenings at children's ballet rehearsals. The gags that follow are the overly familiar collection of exploding kitchen appliances, tutu-wearing dogs, and the feminization of the King's bachelor pad. The Rebel players take to Peyton, immediately sensing that this really is the one thing missing from Kingman's resumé, even if he does not quite "get it." This is the template

used in so many Disney films of yesteryear, good wholesome family fun, and while the film is a bit long and predictable, it is still entirely watchable.

The Rock is likeable and charismatic in his role as Kingman, an Elvis fan who lifted his "King" moniker from Presley and is not afraid to warble through an Elvis song for comedic effect. His performance can appear a bit one-dimensional and wooden, but the Rock knows how to turn on the charm in front of the camera and use his athleticism (in addition to his WWF exploits, he was a college football player) to help get him over most of the rough patches. The good-natured Johnson even allows himself to take on a bit role in Peyton's ballet recital—not as a rock but as a tree.

The gifted Madison Pettis, in her film debut, has her Peyton alternate between cutesy childlike charm and heartstring-pulling manipulation, while delivering some dubiously mature dialogue and too-keen observations. When she is introduced to one of her father's lady friends, she proclaims, "To think you walked out on my mom just to hang out with the likes of that."

The highly regarded Kyra Sedgwick completely misses the mark with her performance as Stella Peck, Kingman's agent. She overplays the part, which seems like a caricature of the nasty, overbearing conniving super agent. She sees the young and innocent Peyton as just another marketing opportunity for her client. Kingman's fellow players come across much better, with likeable performances by Morris Chestnut as Travis Sanders, the sage-like wide receiver, and Hayes MacArthur as the simple-minded Kyle Cooper.

The film is set in Boston, and the filmmakers give the audience all the expected sights and sounds, from

Custom House Tower to the now-defunct Foxborough Stadium, which serves as the Rebels's home field. Peyton's ballet classes take place at the Boston Ballet School, allowing some the students to be included in the filming. It all gives the film an genuine sense of place and an authenticity that is conspicuously lacking in the football action. There is no reference to the National Football League or the Super Bowl (the Rebels are playing for "the championship"), whose trademarks and marketing rights are vigorously protected by the league, an unusual twist in this era of cross-marketing and overexposure.

At a surprisingly long 110 minutes, *The Game Plan* travels the well worn path of so many family comedies, but delivers good wholesome fun without the kicks to the groin or gross-out humor that seem so prevalent today. The writers, Nichole Millard and Kathryn Price, take the story predictably down the middle but avoid the temptation to venture into romantic comedy, which is about the only predictable turn the film passes on.

Mike White

CREDITS

Joe Kingman: Dwayne "The Rock" Johnson
Stella Peck: Kyra Sedgwick
Monique Vasquez: Roselyn Sanchez
Travis Sanders: Morris Chestnut
Peyton Kelly: Madison Pettis
Jamal Webber: Brian J. White
Karen Kelly: Paige Turco
Coach Mark Maddox: Gordon Clapp
Kyle Cooper: Hayes MacArthur
Clarence Monroe: Jamal Duff
Larry the Doorman: Jackie Flynn
Origin: USA
Language: English
Released: 2007
Production: Gordon Gray, Mark Ciardi; Mayhem Pictures, Walt Disney Pictures; released by Buena Vista
Directed by: Andy Fickman
Written by: Nichole Millard, Kathryn Price
Cinematography by: Greg Gardiner
Music by: Nathan Wang
Sound: Pud Cusack
Music Supervisor: Jennifer Hawks
Editing: Michael Jablow
Art Direction: John R. Jensen
Costumes: Genevieve Tyrrell
Production Design: David J. Bomba
MPAA rating: PG
Running time: 110 minutes

REVIEWS

Boston Globe Online. September 28, 2007.
Chicago Sun-Times Online. September 28, 2007.
Entertainment Weekly Online. September 26, 2007.
Hollywood Reporter Online. September 24, 2007.
Los Angeles Times Online. September 28, 2007.
New York Times Online. September 28, 2007.
San Francisco Chronicle. September 28, 2007, p. E6.
Variety Online. September 23, 2007.
Washington Post Online. September 28, 2007.

QUOTES

Monique Vasquez (to Joe): "Ballerinas can jump just as high as you but when they come down they come down in plies, and then they stand pointe, and they stand like that for hours. If ballet was easy, it would be called football."

TRIVIA

Dwayne "The Rock" Johnson's character, Joe Kingman, suffers a separated shoulder that temporarily knocks him out of the big game. In real life, The Rock actually did suffer a season-ending shoulder separation while playing defensive tackle as a freshman at the University of Miami.

GEORGIA RULE

Mother. Daughter. Grandmother. In this family, attitude doesn't skip a generation.
—Movie tagline

Sometimes you have to lose your way to find your family.
—Movie tagline

Box Office: $18.8 million

Georgia Rule is one of director Garry Marshall's weaker films. Marshall has tackled subjects from the prostitute with the heart of gold in *Pretty Woman* (1990) to the sweet, awkward girl who learns she has royal blood in *The Princess Diaries* (2001), but most of his films have a comic edge that is appropriate for the subject matter. The chief problem with *Georgia Rule* is that the film tackles a very serious subject and never seems quite sure what to do with it, often veering into comedy where comedy may not be the most appropriate tone to take. Consequently, many elements of the film are awkward and seemingly mismatched. Given that the film ends up dealing largely with a family's response to the sexual abuse of a minor, *Georgia Rule* may have been better suited as a more serious drama. As it is, it teeters awkwardly on a fence, suffering from a kind of narrative identity crisis.

The movie begins by introducing the strained relationship between a mother, Lilly (Felicity Huffman), and her teenage daughter, Rachel (Lindsay Lohan), as they are on the way to Lilly's mother's house in the small town of Hull, Idaho. Rachel is a headstrong, rebellious girl who has disappointed her mother and stepfather, Arnold (Cary Elwes), by botching her admission to Vassar. Lilly leaves Rachel with her mother, Georgia (Jane Fonda), thinking that perhaps a summer with her tough grandmother will do the girl some good. Ironically, Lilly apparently does not have a close relationship with her own mother, as they have not seen each other for years. After an awkward meeting between Lilly and Georgia, Lilly takes off for a vacation with Arnold, leaving Rachel behind.

Not surprisingly, Rachel and Georgia do not get along too well at first, mainly because Georgia is a very organized and strict woman who will not bend her rules for anyone. For example, dinner is served at a specific, announced time, and anyone who is late does not get to eat until the next meal. Thanks to Georgia, Rachel starts a summer job working for Dr. Simon Ward (Dermot Mulroney), a veterinarian who actually seems to treat more humans than animals. And it just so happens that Simon once dated Lilly when they were in high school. Rachel also befriends and flirts with a young man named Harlan (Garrett Hedlund), a devout Mormon—and, Rachel is baffled to discover, a virgin—who plans to go on a mission trip in the near future. Harlan's rather insulated world is given quite a shock as he is exposed to, and ultimately attracted by, Rachel's uninhibited behavior.

For some reason Rachel trusts Simon enough that she reveals a terrible secret to him—that she has been sexually molested by her stepfather since she was twelve. Apparently she does not think Simon will tell anyone, because when Georgia finds out and asks her about it, Rachel initially denies it, claiming she was just trying to help Simon realize that he was not the only one who had experienced tragedy. Georgia, unconvinced, contacts Lilly, who leaves Arnold and returns at once to demand the truth, horrified by the story—and devastatingly confused because she does not know who to believe. This sets up the primary crisis in the film, the relationship between the three women and in particular the strain between Lilly and Rachel. The mother becomes overwhelmed with self-pity and tries to drown her sorrows with alcohol, while Rachel attempts to seduce Simon out of a misdirected need for male affection. She also attempts to relieve her mother's despair by claiming, once again, that the molestation did not happen. In the end, however, the truth does come out, and Lilly finally leaves Arnold behind to embrace her daughter.

There are numerous problems with the film, but most spring from the movie's lack of clear purpose and theme as well as the insufficiently credible behaviors of the characters. Up until Rachel reveals her secret to Simon, *Georgia Rule* seems to be a typical movie dealing with relationships between women, leaning to the less dramatic end of the spectrum and often injecting humor into the interplay between characters—especially between Rachel and her grandmother and between Rachel and Harlan. Yet it seems odd that this tone does not significantly change once the secret is out. The focus shifts somewhat as Lilly comes back into the story and becomes a more central character, torn over whether to believe Rachel and wondering how she missed so much if the accusations are true. Even Lilly's despair is not handled with much depth; she immediately turns to alcohol and winds up having a brief, introspective conversation with her mother, yet the film misses many opportunities to explore the psychological depth of such a painful situation. Even more so, the film attempts to make many implications about the effects of the molestation on Rachel's personality and behavior, but none of that is explored directly. Consequently, it is difficult to know whether Rachel is simply a spoiled girl who blatantly flaunts her sexuality and enjoys seducing men, or she is expressing a confused need for male affection that was tragically twisted and distorted by the abuse she suffered.

The ambiguity in tone and lack of depth results in several very awkward scenes that are handled rather clumsily. In one, Rachel discovers Harlan is a virgin and invites him to look under her skirt, then encourages him to touch her there. Subsequent scenes reveal that Rachel, in fact, ended up performing oral sex on Harlan. Later in the movie, several other awkward moments occur when Rachel stays for a few days at Simon's house. In one scene, the two are watching television, and Rachel asks if she can lean on Simon because it makes her feel safe. Simon is not comfortable and gets up to leave. Later, another night, Rachel gets into bed with Simon (and again, Simon refuses her advances). These situations could have led to a revealing, significant discussion of how Rachel's past has distorted her view of love and her need for attention from men, but that does not happen. The scenes simply leave the audience wondering and speculating about Rachel's behavior and the help she obviously needs.

Similarly, character behavior and depth is not consistent, resulting in a sense that much of the story is contrived and superficial. Georgia is supposed to be a "tough" woman with a very strict lifestyle, yet this is depicted in only a few rather shallow ways, and ironically, she begins to get along with Rachel fairly quickly. Although Rachel initially balks at some of Georgia's expectations and throws a childish fit or two, her rebellion does not seem that sincere, and before long the two are managing each other reasonably well. A similar situation occurs with Simon. Although Rachel meets Simon early in the film, it does not really make sense that

Rachel tells Simon about her past, particularly since she knows Simon is a good friend of Georgia's. Simon comes across as a rather bland character at times—although he is supposed to be a sad, hurting man, he seems more annoyed and stiff in his initial scenes with Rachel. If the two have grown closer, the film fails to explore that until later in the movie, when Rachel eventually spends several nights at the veterinarian's house. Even Rachel's relationship with Harlan suffers from this lack of believable development. Harlan obviously finds himself attracted to Rachel because she is outgoing, attractive, and willing to break the rules, yet the film does not explore their relationship enough to convince the audience that Harlan really has fallen in love with Rachel by the end of the story. The full extent of their interaction onscreen could just as easily suggest Harlan is merely motivated by hormones.

Ultimately, *Georgia Rule* may have had the potential, at the concept stage, to be a dramatically engaging and thoughtful film exploring not only strained family relationships but also the pain and consequences of sexual abuse. However, instead of weaving a powerful, contemplative, and meaningful story with something significant to say about important issues, the movie settles for superficial development and seemingly attempts to cover its lack of depth and credibility with humor, resulting in a film that often stumbles in its good intentions.

David Flanagin

CREDITS

Georgia: Jane Fonda
Rachel: Lindsay Lohan
Lilly: Felicity Huffman
Simon: Dermot Mulroney
Arnold: Cary Elwes
Harlan: Garrett Hedlund
Paula: Laurie Metcalf
Izzy: Hector Elizondo
Origin: USA
Language: English
Released: 2007
Production: James G. Robinson, David Robinson; Morgan Creek Productions, Trust Me; released by Universal Pictures
Directed by: Garry Marshall
Written by: Mark Andrus
Cinematography by: Karl Walter Lindenlaub
Music by: John Debney
Sound: Thomas Causey
Music Supervisor: Dawn Solér
Editing: Bruce Green, Tara Timpone

Art Direction: Norman Newberry
Costumes: Gary Jones
Production Design: Albert Brenner
MPAA rating: R
Running time: 113 minutes

REVIEWS

Boston Globe Online. May 11, 2007.
Chicago Sun-Times Online. May 11, 2007.
Entertainment Weekly. May 18, 2007, p. 50.
Hollywood Reporter Online. May 9, 2007.
Los Angeles Times Online. May 11, 2007.
New York Times Online. May 11, 2007.
Premiere Online. May 9, 2007.
San Francisco Chronicle. May 11, 2007, p. C5.
Variety Online. May 8, 2007.
Washington Post. May 11, 2007, p. C5.

QUOTES

Georgia: "For a smart girl, you do stupid well."

TRIVIA

Felicity Huffman got so physical in her car fight scene with Cary Elwes that she broke the windshield, so when the car pulled over they filmed it from behind as they both get out.

GHOST RIDER

> *Hell is about to be unleashed.*
> —Movie tagline
> *His curse will become his power.*
> —Movie tagline

Box Office: $115.8 million

It probably will not be long before every comic-book character in history has its own movie. *Ghost Rider* is based on an old, somewhat obscure Marvel Comics series, and it has been brought to the screen by writer/director Mark Steven Johnson. Like many movies of its ilk, it is a heavily visual, caricatured effort, and the plot is cobbled together from various storylines in the life of the comic-book series.

A voice-over narrator begins the film by informing viewers that every culture has its legends, that legends serve a purpose, and that some legends are real, and then recounts the old Western saga of "ghost riders in the sky" who sold their souls to the devil and spent their lives—and sometimes their afterlives—doing Satan's work. In particular, we are told, there is an outstanding contract for 1,000 souls that one particular ghost rider has hidden from the devil.

We next meet a young Johnny Blaze (Matt Long) and his father, Barton (Brett Cullen), partners in a circus act in which they ride motorcycles up opposing ramps and through a blazing ring of fire. Johnny wants a better future than performing in small-town circuses. That future is unfocused, but includes his hope of running off with his girlfriend, Roxanne (Raquel Alessi). Barton opposes this plan, calling his son a hotshot and reminding him that choices have consequences, even as he lights up another cigarette and coughs violently. Johnny discovers his dad has lung cancer, and that night Mephistopheles (Peter Fonda) visits and offers young Johnny a deal—he will cure his dad of cancer in exchange for Johnny's soul.

The boy snaps up the deal with little hesitation. The next morning, his father is healthy and fully recovered. His son announces that he is leaving, and this time his father gives him his blessing. But as Johnny is leaving the circus, his dad crashes and dies doing the motorcycle act alone. On the road out of town, the devil appears again, nearly causing Johnny to crash his bike, and reminds the boy about the contract. The smirking Satan says he did what he promised: he cured the cancer. But he never promised to keep his father from dying.

The film flashes forward to the performance of an older Johnny (Nicolas Cage), whose death-defying motorcycle feats keep getting more and more outlandish because he knows his life, pledged to Mephistopheles, is doomed. Roxanne (Eva Mendes) reappears as a television reporter assigned to interview Johnny, who doesn't have much to say except to ask about getting a second chance and to repeat his mantra "you can't live in fear." The dialogue in the film is just as unsubtle as a comic book, and the plot is also merely at the service of the standard comic-book central motif: the transformation of the central character into his superhuman or outsized alter ego.

But in this case, a rather creaky and contrived plot is needed to effect the transformation of Johnny Blaze. It seems Mephistopheles has a rebellious son, Blackheart (Wes Bentley), who is bent on seizing that outstanding contract for 1,000 souls. Blackheart comes to earth with a plan and resurrects three dead souls to join him. Mephistopheles enlists Johnny to become his Ghost Rider mercenary, promising to free his soul if he kills Blackheart. After he carries out his killing spree in spectacular fashion, Johnny finds a cemetery caretaker who turns out to be the original Ghost Rider with the contract that both the devils, father and son, want.

It is hard cheering for Johnny when the stakes seem to be so compromised—whether one amoral and vicious devil triumphs over an even more hellacious one. But if you care about such matters and other niceties, you are watching the wrong movie. The devil-on-devil plot is all just an excuse to have the Ghost Rider set off all over the countryside with his skull flaming and his wheels on fire. Johnny has one hell of a bike—and that is all that really matters in this movie.

With its B-grade, comic book-style special effects, *Ghost Rider* is fun in a cheesy sort of hellfire way—visually arresting but not technically awe-inspiring. Compared to the intricacies and nuances of *Sin City* (2005), this film is much less ambitious and complex—a comic book, not a graphic novel. Still, it is entertaining to see the fiery visuals and to hear bystanders pronounce campy judgments about how well the Ghost Rider's costume and act work together. *Ghost Rider* achieves the look it is aiming for—lowbrow comic-book visuals, with lots of color and splash, and a few striking vistas and landscapes.

If you take the whole movie as the genre romp it is meant to be, the lumpy, leaden dialogue and the corny plot work together with the visuals to produce the cinematic equivalent of a comic book: light, unapologetic escapism with no pretensions. There is not much more that the film has to offer. Cage plays his central role as usual, with low-key, deadpan straightforwardness. This movie does not reach for the kind of arch, self-mocking tone that many other comic-book adaptations have. Johnson offers more of a take-it-or-leave-it approach: the movie is what it is, a movie about a motorcyclist selling his soul to the devil. That was enough for the film to score big at the box office and continue to rake in money in video release. The trick is to pretend you are at a drive-in theater a half-century ago.

It is nice to see Fonda back, doing his best to make the devil deeply creepy, but in a way that still commands respect. Mendes does not seem to know how to make her ridiculous part credible, and there is absolutely no chemistry between her and Cage. It is not all her fault: Cage is so sullen he is semi-somnolent and lacks much sex appeal. His Ghost Rider would be a lot more interesting if Cage had more passion and energy for his role. A younger Cage might have brought his wackier, more anarchic characterizations to bear, but this fine actor seems to have fallen back into a default mode, relying too much on an antihero lack of affect.

The success of the film immediately spun off a video game and sparked plans for a sequel, a rather dreary prospect, for it does not seem like the character or the material has enough complexity and depth to merit a return engagement. It hardly matters, however, as long as the look is compatible with video games and the action violent in a cartoonish way. If characters can shapeshift and materialize and dematerialize, that is sufficient.

Lots of real-looking flames, rather than painted-on flames, on fast-moving vehicles help too. It may not be cinema at its finest, but it hits its mark squarely as a cheaply entertaining joyride. That, and a comic-book hero to build a story around, is all that is needed today to make a hit movie.

Michael Betzold

CREDITS

Johnny Blaze/Ghost Rider: Nicolas Cage
Roxanne Simpson: Eva Mendes
Blackheart: Wes Bentley
Caretaker: Sam Elliott
Mack: Donal Logue
Mephistopheles: Peter Fonda
Barton Blaze: Brett Cullen
Young Johnny: Matt Long
Young Roxanne: Raquel Alessi
Origin: USA
Language: English
Released: 2007
Production: Avi Arad, Steven Paul, Michael De Luca, Gary Foster; Relativity Media, Columbia Pictures, Crystal Sky Pictures; released by Sony Pictures Entertainment
Directed by: Mark Steven Johnson
Written by: Mark Steven Johnson
Cinematography by: Russell Boyd
Music by: Christopher Young
Sound: Gary Wilkins
Music Supervisor: Dave Jordan
Editing: Richard Francis-Bruce
Art Direction: Richard Hobbs, Peter Russell
Costumes: Lizzy Gardiner
Production Design: Kirk M. Petrucelli
MPAA rating: PG-13
Running time: 114 minutes

REVIEWS

Boston Globe Online. February 16, 2007.
Boxoffice Online. February 16, 2007.
Entertainment Weekly. March 2, 2007, p. 51.
Hollywood Reporter Online. February 19, 2007.
Los Angeles Times Online. February 17, 2007.
New York Times Online. February 17, 2007.
San Francisco Chronicle. February 16, 2007, p. F1.
Variety Online. February 16, 2007.

QUOTES

Caretaker: "You alright?"

Johnny (replies): "Yeah, I'm good. I feel like my skull's on fire, but I'm good."

TRIVIA

Nicolas Cage's computer generated skull was made from a three dimensional x-ray taken of his actual skull.

AWARDS

Nomination:

Golden Raspberries 2007: Worst Actor (Cage).

GOD GREW TIRED OF US
(God Grew Tired of Us: The Story of the Lost Boys of Sudan)

God Grew Tired of Us (also known as *God Grew Tired of Us: The Story of the Lost Boys of Sudan*) won the Grand Jury Prize and the Audience Award at the 2006 Sundance Film Festival. It is easy to see why. The film manages to be inspirational, melancholy, socially relevant, thought-provoking, and even funny within its brief ninety-minute running time. Ty Burr of the *Boston Globe* wrote, "Seesawing between despair and soul-affirming inspiration, *God Grew Tired of Us* is a documentary to make you proud of what America offers to the rest of the world and worried that it can't keep its promises."

The movie concerns the plight of the so-called "Lost Boys" of Sudan. These boys, ranging from age three to thirteen, were victims of the 1980s civil war in Sudan. When northern Sudanese came to the southern villages with the intention of sterilizing or killing all the boys, the boys fled. At first, there were 25,000 of these Lost Boys, trekking across Sudan to safety in Ethiopia. It was an arduous 1,000-mile journey. The boys' homeland had been lush and tropical; their trek took them through barren, arid desert. Starving and thirsty, they drank urine to help them keep going. The older boys, who were children themselves, took care of the younger ones, and had the duty of burying the ones who could not make it. The journey took five years.

Finally, they found safe haven at a refugee camp in Ethiopia, but after a few years they were forced to leave and take another dangerous journey across the desert. They finally arrived at a refugee camp in Kenya, where they lived for ten years. Conditions in the camp were deplorable. Rations were sporadic, and they were stuck there with little idea of what their futures might hold. And, of course, there were the ever-present memories of the hideous things they had witnessed and lived through. Still, they made the best of their situation. One of the more charismatic members of the group, Daniel Abol Pach, formed a group called Parliament, in which the boys could gather together to sing, tell stories, dance, and do just about whatever else they could think of to get their minds off of their hunger and misery.

Filmmaker Christopher Quinn began filming the boys just weeks before some of them were set to journey to America as part of a relocation program. They are put into small groups and sent to various cities, such as Syracuse, New York, and Pittsburgh, Pennsylvania, where they will be given food and shelter for few months while they find steady work. And, in what seems like embarrassing stinginess on the part of America, the boys will then be required to pay back their airfare.

The humor (and some of the pathos) in the film comes from seeing the boys' culture shock upon encountering the western world. They eat airplane food, and even though they literally have been starving, they declare it to be very bad. This might have something to do with the fact that they eat the condiments straight from the packets. In their new apartments they are amazed by the shower, the refrigerator, and the green dishwashing liquid. They are instructed to throw their garbage in the trashcan, instead of out the window. A trip to a supermarket offers them an almost overwhelming view of consumer abundance. They stare quizzically at some brightly colored doughnuts and ask, "This is food?"

But life in the United States does not immediately deliver the bright future they had once expected. They take (sometimes more than one) low-level, minimum-wage jobs. They are lonely in their apartments with only a few roommates. And they are isolated. In one of the towns, the locals view the boys as threatening, and ask them not to travel in groups. For the boys, who have lived their entire lives in groups, this is a particularly devastating request.

They struggle to make sense of the Americans' Christmas (how exactly does Santa tie in with Jesus?), try to find enough money to send back to the boys still in Kenya, and wonder if their relatives are still alive.

The story itself is highly engaging, but what makes this film extraordinary are the boys themselves. Carina Chocano of the *Los Angeles Times* likened them to "spiritually evolved visitor(s) from another planet." The extremely tall Dau is especially appealing. He was a leader among the boys back home, and keeps that responsibility in his heart. He saves every penny to send to the boys back home, but he realizes that it is not going to be enough. He forms an organization that offers aid to the Lost Boys and makes sure that the relocated

Lost Boys stay in touch with each other. Touchingly, he frets that some of the younger Lost Boys are adopting a hip-hop style and forgetting their own culture.

God Grew Tired of Us is an ambitious film with its heart in the right place. Its only fault may be that it attempts to tackle too many important issues—including religious war, racism, and cultural difference—in too short a space. Ultimately, however, it is a triumph. Stephen Holden of the *New York Times* wrote, "Handsomely photographed and inspirational, but not cloyingly so, it is the rare contemporary documentary that doesn't leave a residue of cynicism and outrage." Andrew O'Hehir of *Salon.com* wrote, "This is an important film. It's amazing that it exists, and the events it recounts are still more amazing. Everybody should see it."

Jill Hamilton

CREDITS

Himself: John Bul Dau
Himself: Panther Bior
Himself: Daniel Abol Pach
Origin: USA
Language: English
Released: 2006
Production: Christopher Quinn, Molly Bradford, Tommy Walker; National Geographic Films, Silver Nitrate Pictures; released by Newmarket Films
Directed by: Christopher Quinn
Cinematography by: Paul Daley, Bunt Young
Music by: Jamie Saft
Editing: Geoffrey Richman, Johanna Giebelhaus
MPAA rating: PG
Running time: 89 minutes

REVIEWS

Austin Chronicle Online. February 2, 2007.
Hollywood Reporter Online. January 26, 2006.
Los Angeles Times Online. January 12, 2007.
New York Times Online. January 12, 2007.
San Francisco Chronicle. January 19, 2007, p. E5.
Variety Online. January 27, 2006.

QUOTES

John Bul Dau: "People come at night with guns, and if you are not Muslim, they can kill you."

THE GOLDEN COMPASS

There are worlds beyond our own—the compass will show the way.
—Movie tagline

Box Office: $69.9 million

The Golden Compass, based on *Northern Lights* (as it was called in Britain), the first novel in Philip Pullman's renowned *His Dark Materials* trilogy of fantasy novels, must have been a challenging adaptation. The novel takes place over a wide variety of locations and is both dense and expansive in its array of ideas, characters, and conflicts. Written and directed by Chris Weitz, the movie touches on many of the key elements, but despite several impressive set pieces, fails to give the novel a coherent shape on screen or construct a consistent through line. Colorful characters are briefly introduced and pop in and out of the action but are never fully developed.

A little girl named Lyra Belacqua (Dakota Blue Richards), a ward of Jordan College, is at the center of the story, which takes place in a variation on our world but with many parallel universes surrounding it. Freethinkers are in conflict with a centralized authority known as the Magisterium. Lyra's uncle, Lord Asriel (Daniel Craig), is a scholar exploring those universes and specifically the significance of "Dust," a mysterious substance that seems to connect them. In Pullman's world, human beings have daemons—animal embodiments of their souls. The animals follow them around and take on the emotional states of their human counterparts, a special effect that translates quite well to the screen. A child's daemon, such as Lyra's Pantalaimon (voice of Freddie Highmore), is unsettled, meaning that it can take on many different animal shapes.

Lyra falls under the tutelage of the beautiful and mysterious Mrs. Coulter (Nicole Kidman), who takes a special interest in the little girl and whisks her away from Jordan College to be her personal assistant. Before she leaves with Mrs. Coulter, however, Lyra receives a gift from the Master of the college (Jack Shepherd). It is an alethiometer (also known as a golden compass), the last one remaining in the world, which can divine "secrets at the heart of things." Unbeknownst to her, Lyra is believed to be a crucial player in an upcoming war, as foretold in a prophecy, and has a special ability to use the compass. The movie, unfortunately, makes the compass into a kind of parlor trick, a crystal ball of sorts, whereas in the novel, we get a better sense of the little girl gradually learning to use it and the almost spiritual connection between her and the instrument.

The big problem with Weitz's adaptation is that the story's main thread is never made compelling enough. A group called the Gobblers is stealing children and transporting them to the North for some mysterious purpose. When Lyra discovers that Mrs. Coulter is the power behind this group, Lyra flees from her and joins up with the Gyptians, a Gypsy-like boat people, to embark on an expedition to bring back the kids.

Along the way, the movie loses its energy and sense of pacing, and devolves into a series of episodes featuring odd characters, elaborate battles, and daring rescues, too many of which feel random. Moreover, we do not get a firm sense of why those helping Lyra get involved in such a dangerous mission in the first place. Eva Green drops in, literally, as Serafina Pekkala, a sympathetic witch. In the novel, she is a fairly important character, but she appears so briefly in the film that, when she reappears later with a whole brigade of witches during a decisive battle, we are left to wonder why they are fighting. Sam Elliott appears as Lee Scoresby, a Texan who joins up to help Lyra. Elliott is actually quite entertaining in this bit of comic relief because his Western character is so out of place in the film's eccentric world. His drawl and laconic manner cannot help but make one smile, especially since he seems to be channeling his character from 1998's *The Big Lebowski.* Lyra also enlists the aid of a proud, exiled bear from the North named Iorek Byrnison (voice of Ian McKellen).

But the sequence with Iorek is emblematic of the larger problem—a randomness borne, probably, of trying to squeeze the highlights of the novel into the length of a feature film and having to discard so much connective tissue. Iorek's rescue of Lyra after she is captured and brought to the bear king, Ragnar Sturlusson (voice of Ian McShane), as a prisoner feels more like a distraction from the main story than an integral part of it. Nonetheless, the fight between Iorek and Ragnar in which Iorek reclaims his rightful place as the king of the bears is the visual highlight of the film, which is, overall, quite successful in its blending of CGI with the real world.

It is understandable that a novel as complex as *Northern Lights* would have to be streamlined and its more disturbing moments softened for a general, family-friendly audience. For example, "intercision," the horrendous procedure of splitting a child from his daemon (a practice meant to keep the populace in line and prevent it from questioning authority), is much more graphically depicted, along with its tragic consequences, in the novel. The bigger problem, though, is not Weitz's timidity but the fact that if we do not have a sense of the danger and terror in store for the kidnapped children, then we do not know what is really at stake in their rescue.

The film concludes on a happier note than the novel, in which Lyra's mission to save her friend Roger fails in a strange way at the hands of Lord Asriel. The film ends with Lyra and Roger (Ben Walker) determined to "set things right," but the ending is murky, setting up a sequel while trying to make us feel that this tale has resolved itself relatively well, with just some unfinished business ahead.

For the most part, the actors do not have much of a chance to bring nuance to their characters, although some make more of an impression than others. Daniel Craig has very little screen time to establish much beyond the fact that Lord Asriel is a rebel who believes in free inquiry and is opposed to repression. But newcomer Dakota Blue Richards has pluck and spirit as Lyra, and is not conventionally cute like other child actors. We can believe that she has the fortitude to carry out a destiny she does not fully understand. Her complex rapport with Mrs. Coulter and friendship with Iorek are both compelling. And Kidman nicely balances Mrs. Coulter's icy menace with the empathy and sense of class that would make her attractive to a little girl.

It would be impossible to discuss *The Golden Compass* without briefly mentioning the religious issues surrounding it. Pullman is an avowed atheist, and his fiction is interpreted as a critique of organized religion, specifically the Catholic Church. While the oppressive body in the film retains the Catholic term "Magisterium," the religious themes are downplayed. The conflict is still free will versus oppression, free inquiry versus suppression, but the villains, though they look vaguely like clerics and speak of stopping heresy, could really stand in for any kind of authoritarianism that seeks to control people's minds and behavior. Some might see this as a betrayal of Pullman's point of view, and certainly a case could be made that the film at least partly retreats from what the novel is really about. But it is also true that to introduce the complex religious ideas from the novel—"Dust," for example, is associated with Original Sin in the final pages—would risk making more confusing a movie that already has a convoluted narrative.

As sheer spectacle and rousing adventure, *The Golden Compass* is often successful, but as narrative, it is very fractured and even choppy. The film desperately needs a unifying framework to straighten out the vast array of characters, locations, interpersonal conflicts, and abstract ideas that underpin this universe.

Peter N. Chumo II

CREDITS

Mrs. Coulter: Nicole Kidman
Lord Asriel: Daniel Craig
Serafina Pekkala: Eva Green
First High Councilor: Christopher Lee
Lyra: Dakota Blue Richards
Lee Scoresby: Sam Elliot
Roger: Ben Walker
Farder Coram: Tom Courtenay
Magisterial Emissary: Derek Jacobi
Hester: Kathy Bates (Voice)
Stelmaria: Kristin Scott Thomas (Voice)
Pantalaimon: Freddie Highmore (Voice)
Iorek Byrnison: Ian McKellen (Voice)
Ragnar Sturlusson: Ian McShane (Voice)
Origin: USA
Language: English
Released: 2007
Production: Deborah Forte, William C. Carraro; Scholastic Productions, Depth of Field, Ingenious Film Partners; released by New Line Cinema
Directed by: Chris Weitz
Written by: Chris Weitz
Cinematography by: Henry Braham
Music by: Alexandre Desplat
Sound: Tony Dawe
Editing: Peter Honess, Anne V. Coates, Kevin Tent
Art Direction: Chris Lowe, Andy Nicholson
Costumes: Ruth Myers
Production Design: Dennis Gassner
MPAA rating: PG-13
Running time: 113 minutes

REVIEWS

Boston Globe Online. December 6, 2007.
Chicago Sun-Times Online. December 7, 2007.
Entertainment Weekly Online. December 4, 2007.
Hollywood Reporter Online. November 30, 2007.
Los Angeles Times Online. December 7, 2007.
New York Times Online. December 7, 2007.
San Francisco Chronicle. December 7, 2007, p. E1.
Variety Online. November 29, 2007.
Wall Street Journal Online. December 7, 2007.
Washington Post. December 7, 2007, p. C1.

TRIVIA

The name "Serafina Pekkala" originated when author Philip Pullman browsed through a Finnish telephone directory.

AWARDS

Oscars 2007: Visual FX
British Acad. 2007: Visual FX
Nomination:
Oscars 2007: Art Dir./Set Dec.

GONE BABY GONE

Everyone wants the truth...until they find it.
—Movie tagline

Box Office: $20.3 million

Ben Affleck makes an admirable directorial debut with *Gone Baby Gone*, based on a Dennis Lehane crime novel that Affleck adapted with Aaron Stockard. Set in Boston and revolving around the abduction of a four-year-old girl, the movie is a suspenseful tale that compresses the expansive novel while maintaining its essential elements. The plot is, however, often unwieldy, and the screenplay leans too heavily on flashbacks to spell out major plot revelations, one of which hurts the credibility of the entire story. These problems are endemic to the novel itself, which was probably difficult to adapt, but even on such a rudimentary level as untangling the connections between the many low-life characters, the screenplay is often too convoluted for the viewer to digest.

Casey Affleck, the director's brother, stars as Patrick Kenzie, a private investigator who, along with his partner and girlfriend Angie Gennaro (Michelle Monaghan), is hired to look into the disappearance of a little girl named Amanda McCready (Madeline O'Brien). The little girl's mother, Helene (Amy Ryan), is a loser with a cocaine habit. She hangs out with criminals, runs drugs, and generally does not take care of her daughter. Helene's sister-in-law Bea (Amy Madigan) calls upon Patrick because she believes that the Boston police are not doing enough to find Amanda and that Patrick's neighborhood connections may yield some answers.

Patrick receives reluctant cooperation from the police, most notably Captain Jack Doyle (Morgan Freeman), whose loss of his own child inspired him to set up a special unit to look for missing children, and Detective Remy Bressant (Ed Harris), a tough cop who begrudgingly befriends Patrick but gives him lots of attitude.

The deeper Patrick investigates, the more he enters the Boston underworld, specifically the tough Dorchester neighborhood that he is familiar with but still has trouble navigating. Helene, it turns out, was part of a drug deal in which she and a partner stole $130,000 from a crime lord named Cheese (Edi Gathegi). When it is believed that Cheese kidnapped Amanda to get his money back, the police set up a meeting at a quarry (outside of proper police procedure) to trade the money for the child. But the plan goes awry, leaving Cheese dead and Amanda most likely at the bottom of the quarry. Unfortunately, Affleck's inexperience as a director reveals itself with the muddled plot mechanics and the ambiguous geography of the scenes. Granted, the dense plot had to be condensed, but the key meeting at the quarry is shot so haphazardly that it is impossible to tell what is happening, even after we learn that the supposed exchange was really a sham engineered by the cops and we see flashbacks that are meant to clarify this plot twist but end up promoting more confusion.

More important, the setup, which loosely follows the novel in overall conception even if the novel is much more detailed, proves to be the linchpin that most damages the movie's credibility. The upper brass in the police department have essentially been playing Patrick for a fool to cover their own misdeeds. Helene's brother Lionel (Titus Welliver) and the police conspired to kidnap Amanda themselves to give her a shot at a decent life, the prospect of which seemed increasingly unlikely with the irresponsible Helene, and the child now lives with Captain Doyle and his wife.

But the major flaw of the novel as well as the movie is that it is hard to believe that a group of police officers would conspire to steal a child and then think that such a high-profile figure as a police captain could raise the girl out in the country without anyone finding out or ever noticing that something is odd. First of all, the little girl was the subject of massive media coverage. Secondly, she is being raised by a couple old enough to be her grandparents. These hackneyed plot machinations not only make the resolution far-fetched, but what is worse, they undercut the film's gritty realism, naturalistic performances, and supposed serious theme of what happens to missing children. After all, children are kidnapped for a variety of unsavory reasons every day, but hardly ever for the noble intention of giving the child a better life.

When Patrick puts the plot together and decides to turn Doyle in because Helene is, even with all of her faults, Amanda's mother, Angie objects because the little girl looks so happy with her new parents and Helene is so bad. But it is hard to swallow that a woman dedicated to solving crimes would suddenly side with breaking the law and ultimately choose to leave Patrick over his decision to return Amanda to Helene.

No matter how questionable the plot turns may be, the acting from the whole cast is first-rate, but special mention must be made of Ryan's performance as Helene. She is not a very likeable character, and Ryan fearlessly embraces Helene in all of her messiness. There is a rawness to Ryan's portrayal of a woman who has experienced a tremendous loss and yet stubbornly will not change her heedless ways. She lives in her own world, self-deluded that she is a decent person no matter how much her negligence and criminality have cost her. And though we do see glimmers of vulnerability when Helene weeps for her missing daughter, she can also be apathetic about the case and downright combative with the people trying to help her. Ryan never softens Helene's rough edges and vulgar manner or pleads for us to like her, making it a gripping, realistic portrait of a woman perpetually sinking into an abyss of her own making but never willing to acknowledge it.

And Casey Affleck provides a moral center to the proceedings as a man who knows the world is a bad place but somehow will do what is right no matter what the personal risks may be. His boyish looks are disarming, and Affleck uses them to his advantage against people who underestimate him. One truly riveting scene in a bar where he defuses a dangerous situation hints at the quiet strength underlying his character.

As wobbly as the narrative is and as confusing as some details are—there may be just too much plot from the novel, including an ugly detour into the home of a child molester—Ben Affleck succeeds in other areas, most notably in evoking a mood of almost constant danger and immersing us in the tough, working-class milieu. Affleck made a decision to cast local Bostonians in the background roles to give the film an authentic feel. And the performances he elicits from his actors, especially Ryan's indelible turn, are excellent. Despite its often disjointed script, *Gone Baby Gone* is an impressive if very uneven first effort that may signal the start of a promising directorial career.

Peter N. Chumo II

CREDITS

Patrick Kenzie: Casey Affleck
Angie Gennaro: Michelle Monaghan
Jack Doyle: Morgan Freeman
Remy Bressant: Ed Harris
Nick Poole: John Ashton
Helene McCready: Amy Ryan
Bea McCready: Amy Madigan
Lionel McCready: Titus Welliver
Devin: Michael K. Williams
Cheese: Edi Gathegi
Dottie: Jill Quigg
Origin: USA
Language: English
Released: 2007
Production: Ben Affleck, Alan Ladd, Jr., Danton Rissner, Sean Bailey; Ladd Company, LivePlanet; released by Miramax Films
Directed by: Ben Affleck
Written by: Ben Affleck, Aaron Stockard
Cinematography by: John Toll
Music by: Harry Gregson-Williams
Sound: Alan Rankin, Jim Stuebe
Editing: William Goldenberg
Art Direction: Chris Cornwell
Costumes: Alix Friedberg
Production Design: Sharon Seymour

MPAA rating: R
Running time: 115 minutes

REVIEWS

Boston Globe Online. October 18, 2007.
Chicago Sun-Times Online. October 19, 2007.
Entertainment Weekly Online. October 17, 2007.
Hollywood Reporter Online. September 5, 2007.
Los Angeles Times Online. October 19, 2007.
New York Times Online. October 19, 2007.
Rolling Stone Online. October 18, 2007.
San Francisco Chronicle. October 19, 2007, p. E1.
Variety Online. September 5, 2007.
Washington Post. October 19, 2007, p. C5.

QUOTES

Patrick Kenzie: "He lied to me. Now I can't think of one reason big enough for him to lie about that's small enough not to matter."

TRIVIA

Amy Ryan was so convincing with her Boston accent in her audition that director Ben Affleck asked her what part of Boston she was from.

AWARDS

Nomination:

Oscars 2007: Support. Actress (Ryan)
Golden Globes 2008: Support. Actress (Ryan)
Screen Actors Guild 2007: Support. Actress (Ryan).

GOOD LUCK CHUCK

He has to break his curse before she breaks his heart.
—Movie tagline

True love is a blessing and a curse. She's the blessing. He's the curse.
—Movie tagline

Box Office: $34.9 million

At its core, Mark Helfrich's *Good Luck Chuck* has a terrific, original premise—what if a man thinks that the only way he can win the woman he loves is to refrain from having sex with her? The comedic possibilities seem endless. In an age of movie romances in which almost anything goes sexually, abstinence could be the last barrier facing the romantic couple. Unfortunately, almost from the beginning, this idea is squandered horribly, and the film rapidly devolves into one of the worst movies of the year.

Charlie Logan (Dane Cook), a dentist unable to find true love, believes that he has been cursed. During a childhood game of Spin the Bottle, young Charlie (Connor Price) resists the amorous advances of a little Goth girl (Sasha Pieterse) who gets revenge by placing a hex on him. Flash-forward to the present day, and Charlie finds that every woman he sleeps with ends up finding true love with the very next man she dates. As he develops a reputation as a lucky charm, beautiful women desperate to have a one-night stand with him overrun his office. Only in the warped logic of this movie, however, could these women with model looks have a hard time finding husbands. While Charlie initially has moral qualms, he is egged on by his friend, the lecherous Stu (Dan Fogler), a cosmetic surgeon specializing in breast augmentation.

Good Luck Chuck essentially becomes an extended dirty joke, and the script by Josh Stolberg is lacking in wit and empathy for its characters. Charlie is nothing more than an emotional blank who cannot believe his good fortune in being able to bed so many gorgeous babes, and Cook, who is utterly charmless as a romantic lead, does nothing to make him an intriguing or even an especially sympathetic character. Moreover, the actual episodes of lovemaking are not handled very imaginatively. They are neither funny nor sexy, and most are encapsulated in a montage that is more pornographic than hysterical. Fogler, who won a Tony© for his smart, memorable portrayal of an adolescent nerd in *The 25th Annual Putnam County Spelling Bee,* is just plain obnoxious as the sex-crazed Stu, whose boast of masturbating with a warmed-up grapefruit is supposed to be funny but fails to amuse. His loudmouth shtick grows old very fast.

When Cam (Jessica Alba) enters Charlie's life, he believes that he has finally found true love, and pursues her even as she initially resists him. Cam is given two main qualities. The first is that she works with penguins, a feature that gives Stolberg the opportunity to treat penguin mating rituals as heavy-handed metaphors for the human world. And the second is that she is clumsy to such an extent that she poses a minor threat to herself and others. Perhaps it is supposed to be endearing that the beautiful love interest is a klutz, but this characteristic is more tiresome than cute, and ends up feeling like a cheap way to give Cam some kind of distinguishing quality since she is otherwise so dull. And her ne'er-do-well stoner brother Joe (Lonny Ross) is yet another stock character.

Making the movie worse is downright cruelty. When Reba (Ellia English), Charlie's heavyset black receptionist, demands sex from Charlie so that she can have a shot at getting married and pounces on him, breaking the table under them, the screenplay is straining to find humor in the most offensive way, as if a lonely, fat, black woman wanting sex were automatically funny. But the hideousness really comes to the fore when Charlie, determined to test his validity as a lucky charm, sleeps with the crudest woman possible, Eleanor Skipple (Jodie Stewart), morbidly obese, acne-ridden, dirty, and foulmouthed, to see if even she can find true love. It is not funny that Charlie is willing to sleep with her; rather, it is a grotesque episode in a movie constantly straining for fresh comic ideas.

After he has sex with Cam and learns that Eleanor has indeed found a man, Charlie tries hard to keep Cam since he is now afraid of losing her, but she grows wary of him as he smothers her with attention and acts like a stalker. No character's behavior makes any emotional sense or is grounded in any kind of reality (unlike, for example, the vulgar but sweet situations in Judd Apatow's *Knocked Up*). One honest conversation between Charlie and Cam could easily smooth everything out, but that, of course, would end the story. Instead, *Good Luck Chuck* takes a labored, contrived route to get them together, climaxing in Charlie mistakenly thinking that Cam is in love with someone else and racing to the airport to win her back before she flies off to Antarctica. It is a romantic comedy cliché that makes the screenplay as hackneyed as it is unfunny.

But perhaps the pedestrian romantic comedy conventions and tired characters are the least of the screenplay's problems. Whenever *Good Luck Chuck* tries to do something seemingly daring in its outlandish humor, it just comes across as ugly and ham-handed. Stu, for example, finally finds love with a woman, but she has three breasts, as if this freak were a godsend for him. If the film serves any purpose, it may be to shed light on what makes the Judd Apatow school of risqué comedies so appealing. This year's *Knocked Up* and *Superbad* push the envelope of good taste but are also smart, clever, and touching, and do not stoop to lazy mean-spiritedness to get laughs. Even more important, Apatow and his protégés understand something that director Helfrich does not: Genuine humor and conflict come out of characters facing real choices, even if they are in the context of a light comedy. We do not need silly pratfalls, acrobatic sex, and freakish and obnoxious characters. In short, even an outrageous, edgy romantic comedy needs to have a heart, one of the few organs that the humor-impaired *Good Luck Chuck* is missing.

Peter N. Chumo II

CREDITS

Charlie: Dane Cook
Cam: Jessica Alba

Stu: Dan Fogler
Reba: Ellia English
Carol: Chelan Simmons
Joe: Lonny Ross
Origin: USA
Language: English
Released: 2007
Production: Tracey E. Edmonds, Mike Karz, Barry Katz, Brian Volk-Weiss; Karz Entertainment; released by Lionsgate
Directed by: Mark Helfrich
Written by: Josh Stolberg
Cinematography by: Anthony B. Richmond
Music by: Aaron Zigman
Sound: Darren Brisker
Music Supervisor: Jay Faires
Editing: Julia Wong
Art Direction: Tony Wohlgemuth
Costumes: Trish Keating
Production Design: Mark Freeborn
MPAA rating: R
Running time: 96 minutes

REVIEWS

Boston Globe Online. September 21, 2007.
Chicago Sun-Times Online. September 21, 2007.
Hollywood Reporter Online. September 21, 2007.
Los Angeles Times Online. September 21, 2007.
New York Times Online. September 21, 2007.
San Francisco Chronicle. September 21, 2007, p. E6.
Variety Online. September 20, 2007.
Washington Post Online. September 21, 2007.

QUOTES

Charlie: "Don't look at me in that tone of voice."

TRIVIA

In the movie, the building where Chuck and Stu work at is named the Seltaeb building. Backwards, "seltaeb" is "beatles". Seltaeb was also the name of the corporation which, in 1964, oversaw product licensing arrangements for The Beatles.

AWARDS

Nomination:

Golden Raspberries 2008: Worst Actress (Alba), Worst Screen Couple (Alba and Cook).

GRACE IS GONE

Grace Is Gone stands apart from other Iraq war dramas in the fact that it involves a female soldier being killed

and her husband and children having to come to terms with her death in combat. With John Cusack cast as that husband and two bright young newcomers playing his daughters, it features exceptional and sensitive lead performances that resonate with genuine emotion, elevating the otherwise mediocre movie to one of the better genre films of the year.

Writer/director James C. Strouse's debut film clearly takes an antiwar stance while managing to also give due reverence to the troops and poke gentle fun at antiwar liberals. The politics of the war are conspicuously played down, focusing on the personal, family drama it has generated on the homefront. *Grace Is Gone* is, at heart, a film about a crisis that forces a father to discover what is really important in life, his children, and growing closer to them in shared grief. It is also the coming-of-age story of a young girl forced into early maturity by the death of her mother.

An opening scene foreshadows Stanley Phillips's (John Cusack) alienation, as the only male at a support group for soldiers' wives. When an Army captain and a chaplain show up at his Minnesota home, he senses what they quickly confirm, that his wife Grace (Dana Lynne Gilhooley) has been killed in battle. While he waits for his daughters, twelve-year-old Heidi (Shélan O'Keefe) and eight-year-old Dawn (Grace Bednarczyk), to come home from school, he wracks his brain to find a way to break the unthinkable news.

But Stanley has yet to come to terms with the news himself, so rather than face his greatest fear and break his daughters' hearts, he opts for taking them on a road trip to one of their favorite amusement parks, a fictional Disney World stand-in called Enchanted Gardens. The film's road trip conceit allows father and daughters, who were much closer to their mother, to do some much-needed bonding during the long drive.

We learn that Stanley, a gung-ho patriot freshly minted after 9/11, met Grace in the Army, where he served until he was ejected for having poor eyesight, a fact he had concealed when he enlisted. Stanley's politics also play a part in his reluctance to tell the girls of their mother's fate, his blind support of the war and the Bush administration now clearly at odds with his personal predicament.

On the way to the Florida theme park, they stop at Stanley's parents home, where his brother also lives. As well as providing some much-needed comic relief and sarcasm, John (Alessandro Nivola) also serves as Stanley's political counterpoint, a staunch and vocal antiwar liberal distrustful of the government. Although John's arguments are likely closer to that of the filmmakers, they winkingly portray John as a thirty-two-year-old still living with his parents while contemplating graduate school. But John is sympathetic when his brother tells him about Grace, and agrees not to reveal anything to the girls.

Strouse does an admirable job eliciting nuanced performances from his young thespians, especially O'Keefe. On the verge of becoming a teenager, Heidi is old enough to know that something seems amiss, with her father suddenly pulling her and her sister out of school for a spur-of-the-moment family vacation targeted specifically for them. She is alternately suspicious, elated, sullen, and withdrawn, and plays each convincingly. Bednarczyk is mainly called upon for unbridled enthusiasm, which she aptly musters.

After reaching their destination, Stanley finally tells his daughters what he has kept stifled within him for days and what the audience has been waiting for since the film's opening. Set on a beach, the scene is too long in coming, inexpertly shot, and poorly edited, but the moment is appropriately filled with pathos, and the much-needed catharsis a welcome relief for the characters and audience alike.

Cusack's career has spanned three decades and he has embodied a range of roles that shows he is equally adept at playing cool and sarcastic (*Grosse Pointe Blank* [1997], *High Fidelity* [2000]) as well as sensitive (*Say Anything* [1989], *Being John Malkovich* [1999], *Martian Child* [2007]). He plays Stanley without a trace of irony, seeming every bit the tortured and suddenly lost widower. The screenplay paints Stanley as a curious and complicated mix of thwarted champion, unable to serve his country while his wife does her patriotic duty, and mild-mannered Everyman, working as a manager of a big-box retailer. Strouse provides a satisfying conclusion when Stanley is ultimately allowed to fulfill his destiny by becoming a real hero to his daughters.

Hilary White

CREDITS

Stanley: John Cusack
John: Alessandro Nivola
Grace: Dana Gilhooley
Heidi: Shélan O'Keefe
Dawn: Grace Bednarczyk
Origin: USA
Language: English
Released: 2007
Production: Galt Niederhoffer, Daniela Taplin Lundberg, Celine Rattray, John Cusack, Grace Loh; Plum Pictures, New Crime Productions; released by the Weinstein Company
Directed by: James C. Strouse

Written by: James C. Strouse
Cinematography by: Jean-Louis Bompoint
Music by: Clint Eastwood
Sound: David Obermeyer
Editing: Joe Klotz
Art Direction: Lissette Schettini
Costumes: Ha Nguyen
Production Design: Susan Block
MPAA rating: PG-13
Running time: 85 minutes

REVIEWS

Entertainment Weekly Online. December 5, 2007.
Los Angeles Times Online. December 7, 2007.
New York Times Online. December 7, 2007.
Premiere Online. December 6, 2007.
Rolling Stone Online. October 18, 2007.
Variety Online. January 22, 2007.
Village Voice Online. December 4, 2007.

TRIVIA

The original score was replaced after Clint Eastwood saw the film at Sundance and offered to write a new one.

AWARDS

Nomination:

Golden Globes 2008: Song ("Grace is Gone"), Orig. Score.

GRACIE

Inspired by one family's real story.
—Movie tagline
The rules of the game are about to change.
—Movie tagline

Box Office: $2.9 million

In many ways, *Gracie* is a typical female soccer film in the vein of *She's the Man* (2006) and *Bend It Like Beckham* (2002), but its semi-autobiographical roots, realistic performances, and sober approach are ultimately what sets *Gracie* apart. The film also bears the sports drama genre's standard "you can do it" message which, under Oscar©-winning director Davis Guggenheim (*An Inconvenient Truth* [2006]), leans toward the heavy-handed at times. Produced by Guggenheim, his wife Elisabeth Shue and her brother Andrew Shue, the story is based on the experiences of Elizabeth Shue as an aspiring athlete who faced sexist policies in the 1970s, and it touches on the tragic death of Elisabeth and Andrew's brother, William.

Written by Lisa Marie Peterson and Karen Janszen from a story by Andrew Shue, Davis Guggenheim, and Ken Himmelman, *Gracie* is also the story of a young woman's struggle to be accepted by her father Bryan, played by Dermot Mulroney in one of his finest dramatic portrayals. Set in South Orange, New Jersey in 1978, an excellent Carly Schroeder stars as the title character Grace Bowen, whose older brother Johnny (Jesse Lee Soffer) dies in a car accident. The high school soccer team's star player, Johnny was also Grace's only ally supporting her dream of playing soccer. The brief scene concerning Johnny's death comes very early on in the film and is quite underplayed. The event itself is not shown, and few details are given surrounding what actually happened; the effects of his passing are viewed mainly through Grace's eyes.

Meeting with Johnny's teammates, Bryan suggests they honor Johnny's memory by defeating their rival team, Kingston. Grace takes the message to heart and trains to join the boys' soccer team to aid in the victory, but is met by scorn from everyone, including the coach, her younger brothers Mike (Hunter Schroeder) and Daniel (Trevor Heins), and both her parents, who all believe that a girl cannot play soccer with boys. She responds by defying authority—cutting classes to sneak cigarettes with her rebellious best friend Jena (Julia Garro) and flirting with the bad-boy soccer captain Kyle (Christopher Shand). When she fails her classes and is caught in the back seat of her parent's car with a college student, Bryan awakens from his grief to realize he has another child he can save. He begins training Grace in earnest to win a place with the boys on the team.

One of the challenges regularly faced in sports films is making an actor look like an actual athlete. Although she is a talented actress, the pale, delicate Schroeder is not entirely convincing as an accomplished athlete. In the usual inspirational training montages and game scenes, most of which are ably choreographed, Schroeder could have benefited from an experienced stunt double. The predictable game-winning final scene offers little in the way of surprises, other than that Grace misses the all-important free kick against Kingston, just as her brother had done against the same team, but she goes on to score the game-winning goal nonetheless.

The film's real strength lies in the chemistry of Mulroney and Schroeder as the believable father and daughter who are finally able to connect and gain each other's respect. Elisabeth Shue as Grace's mother Lindsay turns in a quiet but powerful performance in the well-written role of a woman forced to subdue her own dreams due to social convention. One of the film's highlights is a short scene with Shue finally speaking out to the school board in support of her daughter's aspirations. Andrew Shue, once a professional soccer player, also has a small but memorable part as the assistant soccer coach.

The film makes great use of period details and boasts an excellent soundtrack that features quintessential 1970s bands such as Boston, the James Gang, and Sweet. Bruce Springsteen's "Growin' Up" plays during the film's lighthearted opening scene, which shows Grace and Johnny in happier times. Although some of the editing is abrupt and a little disjointed, the cinematography and sound are first-rate. In an afterword, the film notes that since the Title IX law that called for equal opportunity in education was reinterpreted in 1979 to include athletics, some five million girls now play soccer in the United States. The closing credits offer an even more poignant, personal touch, featuring photos and home movies of the Shues playing soccer as children.

Hilary White

CREDITS

Gracie Bowen: Carly Schroeder
Lindsay Bowen: Elisabeth Shue
Bryan Bowen: Dermot Mulroney
Coach Clark: Andrew Shue
Jena Walpen: Julia Garro
Coach Colasanti: John Doman
Johnny Bowen: Jesse Lee Stoffer
Peter: Joshua Caras
Kyle Rhodes: Christopher Shand
Origin: USA
Language: English
Released: 2007
Production: Lemore Syvan, Andrew Shue, Elisabeth Shue, Davis Guggenheim; Elevation Filmworks, Ursa Major Films; released by Picturehouse Entertainment
Directed by: Davis Guggenheim
Written by: Karen Janszen
Cinematography by: Chris Manley
Music by: Mark Isham
Sound: Jeff Pullman
Music Supervisor: John Houlihan
Editing: Elizabeth King
Art Direction: Jennifer Dehghan
Costumes: Caitlin Ward
Production Design: Dina Goldman
MPAA rating: PG-13
Running time: 95 minutes

REVIEWS

Boston Globe Online. June 1, 2007.
Chicago Sun-Times Online. June 1, 2007.

Entertainment Weekly. June 8, 2007, p. 63.
Hollywood Reporter Online. May 30, 2007.
Los Angeles Times Online. June 1, 2007.
New York Times Online. June 1, 2007.
San Francisco Chronicle. June 1, 2007, p. E5.
Variety Online. May 29, 2007.
Washington Post Online. June 1, 2007.

TRIVIA

The female lead was to be cast as part of a nationwide search for an unknown. After two months they went with *Lizzie McGuire* star Carly Schroeder.

GRAY MATTERS

*A romantic comedy about a brother, a sister and
the girl of their dreams.*
—Movie tagline

Gray Matters is a hybrid of an independent film and a big Hollywood romantic comedy that combines the worst elements from each genre. The film has the risqué material, awkward rhythms, and not-quite-fleshed-out plotline of a low-budget independent film, along with the glossy veneer and superficial emotional depth of a big-budget Hollywood romance. The result is uninspired, derivative fare that fails to engage the viewer on any level. Sam Adams of the *Los Angeles Times* found the movie so unoriginal, he wrote that director Sue Kramer "piles on tried-and-true tropes as if she's just come from Nora Ephron's garage sale...As the camera tracks down trendy TriBeCa streets, you half-expect it to turn a corner and reveal another crew shooting an identical movie."

Heather Graham plays the wide-eyed and well-dressed title character, Gray, an advertising copywriter. She lives with her equally attractive brother Sam (Tom Cavanagh), a prominent heart surgeon, in a well-appointed New York City apartment. The brother and sister prefer each other's company to anyone else's and are often mistaken for a couple, which they seem to encourage as they banter gleefully about old movies and perform for friends à la Fred and Ginger. While implying that their relationship is somewhat disturbing, first-time screenwriter and director Sue Kramer ultimately seems reluctant to delve too deeply into the subject.

Gray decides that it is time they meet other people, and forces Sam into taking a walk at a local dog park. After a brief and not particularly subtle interview, she introduces Sam to Charlotte (Bridget Moynahan), a new arrival in town who has the stunning good looks of a European model. Sam and Charlotte, also known as Charlie, hit it off immediately. So well, in fact, that after one date, they decide to go to Las Vegas and get married.

Gray is not too happy about the abrupt plan, but begrudgingly heads to Vegas to be the maid of honor.

The night before the wedding, Gray and Charlie have a girls night on the town. After a drunken rendition of Gloria Gaynor's "I Will Survive," the two stumble back to their hotel room and end up in an intoxicated lip lock. While Charlie passes out, with no memory of the event the next day, Gray spends the night pacing nervously. In the course of one evening, Gray has betrayed her brother and discovered that she is a lesbian. Kramer inappropriately makes light of Gray's rather important revelation by condensing it to this brief scene, which on the surface seems interesting enough, but does not allow the viewer to experience any kind of emotional involvement with the character. The fault also lies in Graham's oddly desperate performance as she tries too hard to make Gray lovable. She comes across as a cute puppy dog with about just as much emotional depth. Stephen Holden of the *New York Times* wrote, "Ms. Graham's Gray may be fetching, but she tries so strenuously to charm that her ditziness begins to pall." Kramer's heavy-handed touches only make matters worse: Charlie works in an aquarium and studies the behavior of homosexual fish.

The other lead performances in the film are equally uninspired. Cavanagh is solid, if not a little dull, as the newly in love brother. And Moynahan convincingly portrays her character's complete unawareness that Sam's little sister is desperately in love with her. The film's saving grace lies in the canny performances of the heavy-hitting supporting cast. Molly Shannon is unattractive-best-friend perfect as the heroine's requisite zany sidekick. Alan Cumming is sweet and a bit sad as a Scottish cab driver with an unrequited crush on Gray. Even Sissy Spacek shows up, as a therapist with untraditional methods—she leads one of Gray's sessions at a bowling alley—who does not seem to have the tools to help her patient.

Kramer sets the action against a backdrop of 1940s musicals and screwball comedies. The characters banter about old movies and share a love for them. At one point, Gray and Charlie recreate the "I Won't Dance" number from *Till The Clouds Roll By* (1946). In doing this, Kramer seems to imply that *Gray Matters* is another entry in the venerable genre. But references alone cannot magically inject the grace, humor, and light touch needed to be included in such classics.

Jill Hamilton

CREDITS

Gray: Heather Graham
Sam: Tom Cavanagh

Charlie: Bridget Moynahan

Gordy: Alan Cumming

Carrie: Molly Shannon

Dr. Sydney: Sissy Spacek

Julia Barlett: Rachel Shelley

Herself: Gloria Gaynor (Cameo)

Origin: USA

Language: English

Released: 2006

Production: Bob Yari, Jill Footlick, John Hermansen, Sue Kramer; El Camino Pictures, Archer Entertainment; released by Yari Film Group

Directed by: Sue Kramer

Written by: Sue Kramer

Cinematography by: John Bartley

Music by: Andrew Hollander

Sound: Eric Lamontagne

Editing: Wendey Stanzler

Costumes: Shelia Bingham

Production Design: Linda Del Rosario, Richard Paris

MPAA rating: PG-13

Running time: 96 minutes

REVIEWS

Hollywood Reporter Online. November 27, 2006.

Los Angeles Times Online. February 23, 2007.

New York Times Online. February 23, 2007.

San Francisco Chronicle. February 23, 2007, p. E5.

Variety Online. October 25, 2006.

QUOTES

Charlie Kelsey: "I spend more money on lingerie than I do on rent."

THE GREAT DEBATERS

*When the nation was in need, he inspired them
to give us hope.*
—Movie tagline

Box Office: $30 million

Set in Marshall, Texas in 1935, *The Great Debaters,* from a screenplay by Robert Eisele, tells the inspiring story of the Wiley College debate team. At a time when Jim Crow laws denied blacks their rights and lynchings were still occurring in the South, this team from a black college earned respect and found glory as a competitor with other black schools and eventually as a challenger to the best white debate teams as well. Directed by and starring Denzel Washington as Melvin B. Tolson, the charismatic professor who leads his team to victory, the

film hews closely to two tried-and-true formulas—the inspiring teacher who changes lives and brings out more in his students than they thought they had, and the sports team that takes everyone by surprise and rises to glory in the big game (or in this case, the big debate). And yet, despite the very familiar genre trappings, *The Great Debaters* delivers an emotional journey with fine characterizations, particularly of the students on the squad, and superb acting. What may be even more important, it effectively provides a window into the times by depicting not only the virulent racism that made the Wiley triumph all the more remarkable but also the labor-organizing activities that made the leftist Tolson a controversial figure, even within his school.

Tolson, who also gained recognition as an organizer of the Southern Tenant Farmers' Union and a poet, is a fierce, no-nonsense teacher who expects nothing short of greatness from his students. The four he chooses for his team represent a cross-section of personalities: Hamilton Burgess (Jermaine Williams), a returning debater from the previous year; Henry Lowe (Nate Parker), a handsome, smart kid with great potential but also a bit of a ne'er-do-well who needs to keep his anger in check and learn self-discipline; Samantha Booke (Jurnee Smollett), the school's first female debater; and James Farmer, Jr. (Denzel Whitaker), a precocious fourteen-year-old who also happens to be the son of the college president, James Farmer Sr. (Forest Whitaker, no relation).

As a film about debate, it succeeds beautifully. The script succinctly communicates what it takes to be an effective debater, and the classroom scenes distill what the preparation is like and how the coach whips his charges into mental shape. Without ever being heavy-handed about it, this is the rare film that celebrates learning and the hard work of education. At the same time, it gives a sense of how these bright students endure the pervasive racism of the times, which could result in violence and even death at any moment. In one riveting scene, James Farmer, Jr. has to witness his father humbling himself to white sharecroppers after he accidentally runs over a pig with his car. It is a tough lesson that shapes the boy's worldview. And there is a strong scene later in which Tolson and his charges witness the aftermath of a lynching. The film does not shy away from the harsh realities, and these incidents shape the final, climactic debate, which is as much about the students' life experiences as it is about forming a coherent argument.

At the same time, the more personal interactions are also rather engaging. James Farmer, Jr. develops a boyhood crush on the pretty Samantha but, because of his age, really has no chance with her. When she becomes involved with Henry, it brings out all the hurt and confusion in the young boy's adolescent longings. And Henry must ultimately learn to be a leader, to mature, and to commit himself to debate and to his relationship with Samantha.

Tolson's efforts to unite whites and blacks into a sharecroppers' union takes a toll on the team. Burgess quits because his father suspects that Tolson might be a Communist, and Tolson's arrest for his activism by the racist sheriff (John Heard) leads to a rousing scene in which a throng of people rally for Tolson's release outside the jail. Such a scene may be questionable; while we want to see the sheriff get his comeuppance, it may be too pat to think that a black demonstration could elicit Tolson's release. It works dramatically, nonetheless, in allowing James Farmer, Jr. to see his father take a stand against the corrupt lawman. This complex father-son relationship, built on love, admiration, and respect but also clouded by a young boy not fully understanding why his father must do some of the things he does, is one of the film's richest subplots.

The screenplay does a fine job of tracking the progress of the team. In their first debate with a white college, Samantha gradually improves her style, so it feels like a natural progression. While there is one major setback, a loss against Howard University in which James fumbles badly, the film shows restraint in not depicting the actual defeat; we witness the aftermath, which effectively makes the point.

All of the team's hard work leads to a climactic finish when Harvard invites Wiley to debate. (In real life, Wiley debated USC, not Harvard, a change that suggests that the filmmakers are trying too hard to ratchet up the stakes in having the team compete against the most prestigious university in America when facing USC is, of course, also impressive.) Because Tolson is unable to join them—he cannot leave the state as a condition of his bail—the three teammates must do it on their own. Even though he himself is clearly the most seasoned debater and should be participating, Henry, who is now the designated captain, has Samantha and James debate. In a film that is not afraid to tug at our heartstrings, the screenplay has the two students with the most to prove compete in the big debate. Since an earlier debate with a white school revolved around blacks' access to higher education, it feels a bit contrived that this debate revolves around the morality of nonviolent civil disobedience, a subject that will, of course, shape the future civil rights movement. On an intellectual level, the fact that Wiley twice debates issues that are so personal strains credulity, but on a purely emotional level, these scenes work; even if we are being manipulated, the screenplay is entitled to look forward and, in essence, to place the students' victory at the forefront of the struggles yet to come. And when James, in the last argument of the debate with Harvard, quotes his father, declaring that "An unjust law

is no law at all," it ties their personal relationship to the competition and larger life lessons.

The Great Debaters is a rare kind of film—a studio product that celebrates education, intellect, and the drive for academic excellence. When Tolson refers to the bond between a teacher and his students as "a sacred trust," it may seem quaint and old-fashioned, but it should be a universal standard. Rousing and uplifting, with a message about never giving up, the screenplay shies away from the sentimental and the mawkish. The emotions are earned, and an important chapter of history is brought to light without it feeling like a dull history lesson. Washington's direction is assured, and he garners excellent performances from his young cast members. The movie may not transcend the conventions of the sports-movie genre, but it hits all the right notes so well that it is hard not to be moved and even a bit awed that everything comes together so effectively.

Peter N. Chumo II

CREDITS

Melvin B. Tolson: Denzel Washington
James Farmer Sr.: Forest Whitaker
Henry Lowe: Nate Parker
Samantha Booke: Jurnee Smollett
James Farmer, Jr.: Denzel Whitaker
Hamilton Burgess: Jermaine Williams
Ruth Tolson: Gina Ravera
Sheriff Dozier: John Heard
Pearl Farmer: Kimberly Elise
Origin: USA
Language: English
Released: 2007
Production: Todd Black, Oprah Winfrey, Joe Roth, Kate Forte; Harpo Films, the Weinstein Company; released by MGM
Directed by: Denzel Washington
Written by: Robert Eisele
Cinematography by: Philippe Rousselot
Music by: James Newton Howard, Peter Golub
Sound: Willie D. Burton
Music Supervisor: G. Marq Roswell
Editing: Hughes Winborne
Art Direction: John R. Jensen
Costumes: Sharen Davis
Production Design: David J. Bomba
MPAA rating: PG-13
Running time: 123 minutes

REVIEWS

Boston Globe Online. December 25, 2007.
Chicago Sun-Times Online. December 24, 2007.

Hollywood Reporter Online. December 19, 2007.
Los Angeles Times Online. December 25, 2007.
New York Times Online. December 25, 2007.
San Francisco Chronicle. December 25, 2007, p. D1.
Variety Online. December 18, 2007.
Washington Post. December 25, 2007, p. C1.

QUOTES

Tolson: "Debate is blood sport."

TRIVIA

The diploma hanging in Dr. James Farmer's study is an authentic copy provided to the art department by Boston University archivist Kara Jackman.

AWARDS

Nomination:

Golden Globes 2008: Film—Drama.

GRINDHOUSE
(Planet Terror)
(Death Proof)

The sleaze-filled saga of an exploitation double feature.
—Movie tagline

Box Office: $25 million

Grindhouse is an intriguing artifact of moviemaking, not only as a piece of cinema in itself, but also as a chronicle of the fickle nature of the movie business, from the people who make movies to moviegoers themselves. The concept underlying *Grindhouse* is both simple and subversive: create an homage to the double-feature exploitation-style "grindhouse" experience of the 1970s for a twenty-first-century audience. Helmed by two of the greatest auteurs of ultra-cool pulp genre/schlock cinema, Robert Rodriguez and Quentin Tarantino, the two films that make up *Grindhouse* (Rodriguez's *Planet Terror* and Tarantino's *Death Proof*) are innovative expressions of classic grindhouse genres (horror/zombie films and chase/muscle-car/lone-man-against-society films of the 1970s, respectively) and also cinematic in-jokes, referencing an arcane movie-going experience, but they lack the broad appeal necessary to attract a wide audience and to be commercially successful. The Weinstein Company, the fledgling namesake production company of the team that created Miramax (which is now a part of the Walt Disney Company), Bob and Harvey Weinstein, banked on the proven success of Rodriguez and

Tarantino to deliver an audience for *Grindhouse*—an audience that did not materialize. The result is a well-made, critically well-received romp that tanked at the box office and led to an unusual DVD and international release strategy.

The theatrical release of *Grindhouse* consists of a double feature in the grindhouse tradition of the 1970s, and each feature is preceded by "fake" previews ("trailers") for films that do not actually exist (though at least one of the trailers, Robert Rodriguez's *Machete*, may actually be made into a feature film). The order of the trailers is rumored to vary depending on the theater playing *Grindhouse*, but in general, the most widely reported order of the trailers is that *Machete* precedes Rodriguez's feature, *Planet Terror*, and *Don't, Werewolf Women of the S.S.*, and *Thanksgiving* appear before Tarantino's *Death Proof.* Like the features themselves, each trailer embodies particular grindhouse genres and subgenres, with horror being the clear favorite (*Don't* captures the sensibility of the British Hammer horror films of the 1960s, *Thanksgiving* emulates the slasher films of the 1970s and early 1980s, particularly *Halloween* [1978], *Friday the 13th* [1980], and their many sequels, and the supremely unusual *Werewolf Women of the S.S.* embraces a sort of horror/sci-fi hybrid). The action-adventure-revenge genre is represented by Rodriguez's *Machete*, featuring Danny Trejo as a sort of Mexican Charles Bronson à la *Death Wish* (1974) or *The Mechanic* (1972). Just as these trailers are meant to provide the proper grindhouse atmosphere, so is the aged appearance of the trailers and the films themselves—the films have all been digitally weathered with scratches, burns, and "missing reels" that are meant to give the impression that the prints of these films have been in circulation for a long time.

The first full-length feature on *Grindhouse*'s double bill is Robert Rodriguez's *Planet Terror*, a very tongue-in-cheek zombie picture similar in sensibility if not tone or execution to the zombie films of George A. Romero, especially *Dawn of the Dead* (1978). Shortly after a brief sequence that introduces the audience to Rose McGowan as Cherry, *Planet Terror*'s reluctant heroine-to-be, a shadowy group of soldiers led by Lieutenant Muldoon, played by Bruce Willis, and Abby, an ethically dubious scientist played by Naveen Andrews (Sayid from the television series *Lost*), drive to an army base to negotiate the acquisition of a mysterious gas. During the exchange all hell breaks loose, and the gas is released and begins to infect people in the neighboring town (though, strangely, not the soldiers, or so it seems), turning them into zombies. After walking out on her stripping gig, Cherry bumps into El Wray (Freddy Rodríguez), who offers to give her a ride. The film cuts to Dr. Block, played by the wonderfully menacing Josh Brolin, and his anesthesiologist wife, Dakota (Marley Shelton). She is clearly planning to leave her husband for her lesbian lover but, of course, the zombie epidemic intervenes. El Wray and Cherry are attacked by zombies, who run off with Cherry's right leg. El Wray gets Cherry to the hospital, only to be detained by Sheriff Hague (Michael Biehn), apparently for past crimes. Eventually, El Wray is able to escape with the sheriff as the zombies overrun the jail. El Wray and the sheriff make their way back to the hospital in time to rescue Cherry and Dakota from the hospital patients and staff, most of whom, including Dr. Block, have become zombies. They rush back to the restaurant seen at the beginning of the film, the Bone Shack, where they regroup. They then try to leave town, but are captured by Lt. Muldoon and put into quarantine. There the survivors meet Abby, who informs them that the soldiers are infected with the gas, that the only known treatment is constant inhalation of more gas to stave off the zombie transformation, and that a small percentage of the population is immune, which is why the survivors are quarantined—in the hope of finding a cure. El Wray and Abby break out of quarantine to destroy the large stockpiles of the gas hidden beneath the base—there, they encounter Muldoon, who explains that he and his men were infected during the assassination of Osama bin Laden, and that Muldoon promised his men that he would do everything in his power to find a cure. Abby and El Wray kill Muldoon and stage a breakout from the base, during which many of the characters are killed, including Abby and El Wray. Cherry leads the survivors to Mexico, where they begin a new society with Cherry as their chief defender, thanks in large part to her mini-gun leg (in place of the leg taken by the zombies). In the final moments of the film, it is revealed that Cherry has given birth to El Wray's daughter.

This outlandish plot and its down-and-dirty presentation are characteristic of grindhouse films, and *Planet Terror* captures the experience well, right down to a "missing reel" notice at one point in the action (just as a sex scene really starts to heat up, naturally). That the film is also an excellent expression of an archetypal zombie movie is a wonderful surprise. Like most good zombie (or science-fiction) films, *Planet Terror* creates a fictional world that comments upon and examines the real, empirical world (the film's title is no coincidence—it is a direct reference to the war on terror). Rodriguez is very aware of the fact that his audience is led to believe every day that it lives under the constant threat of a terror attack. The plot device of a small group of survivors set against an entire planet turned to zombies expresses the position of the sane person in a world gone mad—something has turned the populace into mindless creatures, and the fear that anyone could be next is

palpable. That Muldoon directly references actions in Afghanistan only serves to put the film's parallel universe in stark relief with objective reality. Never mind that these ideas come wrapped in a package of gore and guts—somehow the lowest-common-denominator appeal of the action, which would fit right in with any Reagan-era orgy of violence starring the likes of Sylvester Stallone or Arnold Schwarzenegger, helps drive home the point that the audience, simply by watching, may also be among the infected. *Planet Terror* offers the careful viewer plenty to consider, though Tarantino's *Death Proof* is generally credited with being the more aesthetically pleasing and cerebral half of *Grindhouse*.

Quentin Tarantino's half of *Grindhouse* is in fact about as far removed from *Planet Terror* as can be imagined. *Death Proof* is a hybrid of a serial-killer movie and a muscle-car/race/chase/stunt film in the mold of 1971's *Vanishing Point* (which is often referenced in the dialogue of the second half of *Death Proof*). In the first half of the movie, three friends—Shanna (Jordan Ladd), Arlene (Vanessa Ferlito), and "Jungle Julia" (Sydney Tamiia Poitier)—go on a drinking spree to celebrate Jungle Julia's birthday. They engage in petty banter about men and drugs as they drive through Austin, Texas and while they drink at Guero's Taco Bar. A mysterious figure known as Stuntman Mike (Kurt Russell) has been following them almost all afternoon and shows up at the bar. There, he engages in conversation with a woman at the bar, Pam (Rose McGowan), mostly about his work as a Hollywood stuntman. After he flirts with the women and presumably manipulates Arlene into giving him a lap-dance (as with *Planet Terror*, this would-be steamy scene is gone and a "reel missing" notice pops up in its place), the women decide to leave with their pot dealer in tow for a cabin by the lake to continue the birthday celebration. Stuntman Mike leaves too, and offers Pam a ride. Pam gets into the passenger's side of Mike's car, which has only a temporary seat and no seatbelt, but Mike assures her that the car is designed to be "death proof." Once inside the car, Mike explains that to take advantage of the car's safety features, one must be sitting in the driver's seat—he reveals his cruel nature and dispatches Pam by driving wildly and slamming on the brakes, driving her head into the dashboard and killing her. Mike eventually catches up to the car full of women and kills them by driving his death-proof car into them head-on. As Stuntman Mike recovers in the hospital, the sheriff, played by Tarantino and Rodriguez veteran Michael Parks, intimates that he is sure that Stuntman Mike deliberately killed the women, but Mike is cleared of charges because the women were intoxicated and Mike was not—the stage is set for Mike to strike again.

The film cuts to fourteen months later in a different state (Tennessee) and to a different group of women—Abernathy (Rosario Dawson), Kim Mathis (Tracie Thoms), and Lee (Mary Elizabeth Winstead)—who are all involved in the entertainment industry. They are on their way to the airport to pick up their friend Zoë Bell (an actual stuntwoman—in fact, she was Uma Thurman's stunt double in Tarantino's *Kill Bill* movies). A shady-looking 1969 Dodge Charger seems to follow the women wherever they go, and it is obvious to the audience that it is driven by Stuntman Mike. When the friends pick up Zoë at the airport, she announces that she has found a white 1970 Dodge Challenger for sale in the area, the same car used in one of her favorite movies, *Vanishing Point*. Her plan is to talk the owner into letting her test-drive the car (leaving one of the friends behind as collateral) while she plays a game called "ship's mast" (in which she rides on the hood of the moving car while holding on to two belts). The women pick up the car, Lee is left behind as collateral, and the other three women drive off to perform Zoë's "ship's mast" stunt. As the ladies barrel down country roads with Zoë strapped to the Challenger's hood, Stuntman Mike comes out of nowhere and begins to attack them. Inside the car, Abernathy and Kim get bounced around as they try to evade Mike, while Zoë hangs on for dear life. Eventually, both cars are run off the road, and Zoë goes flying into some bushes. Thrilled to have met worthy prey, Mike exits his car to thank the women for the exciting ride, and is promptly shot in the arm by Kim (who carries a pistol for protection). Mike scrambles back into his car and hurriedly drives off before he can fasten his safety restraints. Once the women retrieve a miraculously uninjured Zoë, they speed off in hot pursuit of Mike. In what must be one of the greatest cinematic car chases of all time, the ladies turn the tables on Mike—they stalk and ram him, ultimately flushing him from the relative safety of his cockpit, and then proceed to beat him to the ground. Abernathy delivers the fatal blow to Stuntman Mike's head with the heel of her shoe.

Just as Rodriguez's *Planet Terror* had embedded layers of meaning beyond the spectacle of its carnage, so too does *Death Proof,* though its message is not so concrete. *Death Proof* often references the content of *Vanishing Point,* as well as that film's central theme—the existential journey of the thrill-seeker against an oppressive society—but it does so with a twist: in the case of *Death Proof,* the thrill-seeker has become a sadistic perversion of the free spirit, and in his choice of women as targets for his violence, he embodies the horror of the patriarchal status quo. In the end, he chooses victims who turn out to be more than a match for him, and who hark back to the purity of the thrill-seeking spirit. Abernathy, Kim, and Zoë are able to reclaim from Stuntman Mike the true spirit of the rebel adrenaline junkie:

the defeat of institutional masculine authoritarianism through a defiant act of rebellion—in this case, the unexpected murder of their would-be killer. In this way, both the features that comprise *Grindhouse,* in their own bizarre ways, carry on Tarantino's apparent veneration of the power of women (as evidenced in 1997's *Jackie Brown* and the *Kill Bill* films), though Cherry in *Planet Terror* must be put on her path to destiny by a man, and the women of *Death Proof* idolize the masculine.

Unfortunately, all of this innovative storytelling and fascinating manipulation of cinematic form did not translate into box-office success. Many factors have been blamed, including the choice to release the film on Easter weekend, hardly the most opportune time to premiere an exploitation double feature, no matter how high-minded. In fact, it seems that the Weinsteins considered the double-feature format of *Grindhouse* to be a key factor in its failure. The film was split into its two separate features for release on DVD in the United States and for theatrical release abroad. Neither Rodriguez nor Tarantino have protested this turn of events, which seems unusual given that the double-feature format was part of the *Grindhouse* idea from its inception (the idea came from Tarantino's home screening of exploitation films, which Rodriguez attended). Tarantino has hinted that splitting the features makes sense for overseas distribution since the exploitation double feature is a uniquely American tradition. Splitting the film for DVD release in the U.S., however, is an unusual move given that it could alienate fans of the theatrical version, the people most likely to purchase the film on DVD. Indeed, many fans called for a boycott of the DVD, saying that the release of the individual features on DVD without offering the entire *Grindhouse* experience as it appeared in theaters was merely a business ploy by the Weinstein Company to recoup some of its investment. Whatever the reasoning behind the release of *Grindhouse* as separate features, the move was clearly influenced by the extremely disappointing box-office performance. Perhaps the concept was too obscure to attract a mainstream audience, or perhaps the prospect of sitting through a high-concept exploitation double feature proved too daunting for the average American moviegoer. The result of this joint Rodriguez/Tarantino venture is a film that is slightly bloated and laden with obscure references, but *Grindhouse* is a well-made and ultimately rewarding bit of pulp.

John Boaz

CREDITS

Cherry Darling (Planet Terror)/Pam (Death Proof): Rose McGowan

El Wray (Planet Terror): Freddy Rodríguez
Dakota Block (Planet Terror): Marley Shelton
Dr. Block (Planet Terror): Josh Brolin
Sheriff Hague (Planet Terror): Michael Biehn
J.T. (Planet Terror)/The Senator (Machete): Jeff Fahey
Abby (Planet Terror): Naveen Andrews
Lt. Muldoon (Planet Terror): Bruce Willis
Tammy (Planet Terror): Stacy Ferguson
Earl McGraw (Planet Terror/Death Proof): Michael Parks
Joe (Planet Terror): Nicky Katt
Romey (Planet Terror): Julio Oscar Mechoso
Deputy Carlos (Planet Terror): Carlos Gallardo
Deputy Tolo (Planet Terror): Tom Savini
Stuntman Mike (Death Proof): Kurt Russell
Abernathy (Death Proof): Rosario Dawson
Arlene (Death Proof): Vanessa Ferlito
Shanna (Death Proof)/Judy ("Thanksgiving" trailer): Jordan Ladd
Jungle Julia (Death Proof): Sydney Tamiia Poitier
Kim (Death Proof): Tracie Thoms
Lee (Death Proof): Mary Elizabeth Winstead
Zoe (Death Proof): Zoë Bell
Dov (Death Proof)/Tucker ("Thanksgiving" trailer): Eli Roth
Nate (Death Proof): Omar Doom
Venus Envy (Death Proof): Melissa Arcaro
Omar (Death Proof): Michael Bacall
Jasper (Death Proof): Jonathan Loughran
Edgar McGraw (Death Proof): James Parks
The Rapist (Planet Terror)/Warren (Death Proof): Quentin Tarantino
Fu Manchu ("Werewolf Women of the S.S." trailer): Nicolas Cage
Gretchen Krupp ("Werewolf Women of the S.S." trailer): Sybil Danning
Franz Hess ("Werewolf Women of the S.S." trailer): Udo Kier
Eva Krupp ("Werewolf Women of the S.S." trailer): Sheri Moon
Dr. Heinrich von Strasser ("Werewolf Women of the S.S." trailer): Bill Moseley
Bobby ("Thanksgiving" trailer): Jay Hernandez
Machete ("Machete" trailer): Danny Trejo
Priest ("Machete" trailer): Richard "Cheech" Marin
Origin: USA
Language: English
Released: 2007
Directed by: Robert Rodriguez, Quentin Tarantino
Written by: Quentin Tarantino, Robert Rodriguez, Eli Roth, Jeff Rendell, Edgar Wright, Rob Zombie
Cinematography by: Quentin Tarantino, Robert Rodriguez, Milan Chadima, Phil Parmet
Music by: Robert Rodriguez, Graeme Revell, David Arnold, Nathan Barr, Tyler Bates, Carl Thiel

Editing: Robert Rodriguez, Ethan Maniquis, Sally Menke
MPAA rating: R
Running time: 192 minutes

REVIEWS

Austin Chronicle Online. April 6, 2007.
Boston Globe Online. April 6, 2007.
Chicago Sun-Times Online. April 6, 2007.
Entertainment Weekly Online. April 4, 2007.
Hollywood Reporter Online. April 2, 2007.
Los Angeles Times Online. April 6, 2007.
New York Times Online. April 6, 2007.
Rolling Stone Online. April 3, 2007.
Variety Online. April 1, 2007.
Washington Post. April 6, 2007, p. C1.

QUOTES

Stuntman Mike: "There are few things fetching as a bruised ego on a beautiful angel."

TRIVIA

Robert Rodriguez, Eli Roth, Edgar Wright, and Rob Zombie are the directors of the fake trailers.

THE GROUND TRUTH

A brutal war film featuring only a modicum of actual battle footage, *The Ground Truth* exposes the lies behind the American armed forces's recruiting campaign. The physical and psychological damage inflicted upon the soldiers who sign up for duty are vividly on display in this sharply focused though often flawed documentary.

"Your purpose is to kill," matter-of-factly states one ex-veteran of the ongoing and seemingly endless Iraq conflict. Despite the government's patriotic rationales for joining the army, the real aim of the military is to turn young men and women into killing machines, says *The Ground Truth.* Writer/director Patricia Foulkrod's interviews with veterans of this most recent war are more powerful than any violent scenes would have been.

The Ground Truth is composed primarily of the sit-down, "talking head" interviews with the vets, though Foulkrod weaves in the slick and seductive army recruiting commercials, scenes from recruiting camps, family homecomings and antiwar marches, and even a little of the underreported violence against Iraqi civilians (apparently taken from the Internet).

In an instructive, methodical manner, Foulkrod takes the viewer from recruitment to the induction ceremony, from basic training to the first mission, from a year of hell to the return home. The subjects who share their experiences include Specialist Robert Acosta, Sergeant Kelly Dougherty, Demond Mullins, First Lieutenant Paul Rieckhoff, First Lieutenant Melissa Stockwell (the lone female), Sergeant Rob Sarra, Specialist Aidan Delgado, Staff Sergeant Jimmy Massey, and Corporal Sean Huze.

Foulkrod makes her antiwar position clear, but she also shows compassion for the individuals who fight in war. One issue she stresses—the postwar effects—is not completely uncharted territory since the Walter Reed scandal of 2006, but then *The Ground Truth* wrapped production in 2005 and has not been updated to include more recent newsworthy revelations about the Iraq War. Still, Foulkrod could have disclosed that Paul Rieckhoff, the founder of Iraq Veterans Against the War, was one of the financial backers of her film.

A more serious defect in *The Ground Truth* is the film's lack of larger historical context. One might well wonder how soldiers were affected differently in earlier wars (interviews with older vets would have helped provide the answer, although the single Vietnam soldier who appears briefly does not address this issue). It also would be interesting to hear the contemporary subjects' views on the controversial use of better-paid private contractors, their changes (if any) in political allegiance, and their feelings about the necessity of war.

But the most pronounced problem with Foulkrod's approach is her decision not to interview any government or military representatives. It is possible that no one on "the other side" wanted to be included, but then Foulkrod should have included that information—or chased them down à la Michael Moore. After all, why shouldn't the secretary of defense (Donald Rumsfeld or Robert Gates) or President George W. Bush himself answer to the charges that the military has short-changed the very people they have hired to do their dirty work?

Several critics pounced on this latter issue. *Variety's* reviewer noted, "Had [Foulkrod] obtained some counterarguments from the military, the film would have had more balance and more heft." Stephen Holden of the *New York Times* echoed, "No one from the government or the military is trotted out to give an opposing view." And speaking of imbalance, Foulkrod barely acknowledges how poor minorities are unfairly targeted by recruiters, and only secures one major interview with an African American, one with a Latino, and none at all from the Iraqis' perspective.

Still, there remains a lot to absorb and appreciate about this informal, anecdotal study. Foremost are the heartfelt testimonies by the veterans, most of whom suffer from depression and PTSD (post-traumatic stress disorder), a misunderstood and under-researched diagnosis. In one particularly poignant story, a Marine (Jimmy Massey) relates how a psychologist in Veterans' Affairs tells him, "I can't help you. We don't treat conscientious objectors here." In another, even more disturbing recounting, a soldier talks about killing an Iraqi woman approaching his tank, then later discovering she was carrying a white flag. Demond Mullins, a National Guardsman, remembers being promised he would not see combat, only to see plenty. The family members of an army suicide mourn their loss in another moving sequence.

Of course, it would have been difficult for Foulkrod to criticize her interviewees, but it is hard to reconcile the thoughtful intelligence of those speaking with their professions of naiveté when they were duped into recruitment. This is not to doubt their stories or their sincerity, but some of the vets sound more like college professors than individuals who saw the light of pacificism during combat.

Apart from the stories, Foulkrod provides a fair amount of supplemental material—the misleading but seductive government ads, the Internet downloads, the insider training-camp footage, the photos from the battlefield. The director keeps things simple, and most critics responded well (overall) to *The Ground Truth*: *Variety* said, "the substance of the movie is potent"; the *New York Times* declared, "on its own terms...[it is] devastating"; and the *Chicago Tribune* added that the film is "compelling and intensely provocative."

With so many powerful Iraq war documentaries released over the years, *The Ground Truth* does not stand out as much as it might. Yet it succeeds far better than the dramatic fictional film *Badland* (2007), about one soldier's difficulty readjusting to civilian life while suffering from post-traumatic stress disorder.

The Ground Truth does not present a whole picture, but then what film could? If seen along with some other cinematic reportage, this documentary fills a gap by offering an important message in a forceful way.

Eric Monder

CREDITS

Origin: USA

Language: English

Released: 2006

Production: Patricia Foulkrod, Daniela Taplin Lundberg; Plum Pictures, Radioaktive Film; released by Focus Features

Directed by: Patricia Foulkrod

Cinematography by: Reuben Aaronson

Music by: Dave Hodge

Sound: Sam Lehmer

Music Supervisor: Kevin Dowling, Robert Adams
Editing: Rob Hall
MPAA rating: R
Running time: 72 minutes

REVIEWS

Boston Globe Online. September 15, 2006.
Hollywood Reporter Online. January 21, 2006.
Los Angeles Times Online. September 15, 2006.

New York Times Online. September 15, 2006.
San Francisco Chronicle. September 15, 2006, p. E9.
Time Online. September 17, 2006.
Variety Online. January 24, 2006.
Village Voice Online. September 12, 2006.
Washington Post Online. September 15, 2006.

QUOTES

National Guardsman Demond Mullins: "Your world is gone and you have no world to replace it with."

H

HAIRSPRAY

Who's who behind the do?
— Movie tagline

Box Office: $118.8 million

In 1988 John Waters released what is probably his sweetest and least offensive movie, *Hairspray*. In 2002 it was adapted for the stage as a musical, and by the time *Hairspray: The Musical* received a Tony Award©, it was assured new life as a movie musical. Some may think this would be one incarnation too many, but surprisingly it works.

Set in 1963 Baltimore, *Hairspray* starts on a high note with the heroine, Tracy Turnblad (Nikki Blonsky), singing the compulsively upbeat "Good Morning, Baltimore" as she heads off for school. It is a catchy song that will disarm even the more skeptical viewers, and it separates the film from the typical tiresome musical. The movie merrily continues to spin its web of musical good-naturedness and high-energy dancing until its conclusion.

Plump and perpetually perky Tracy has two goals in life. One of her dreams is to dance on the Baltimore version of *American Bandstand, The Corny Collins Show*. But the dancing teens who appear on the show are all good-looking, thin, and popular. Tracy is none of those things. The show is segregated, but one day a month is "Negro Day," hosted by Motormouth Maybelle (Queen Latifah), who also just happens to be the mother of Seaweed (Elijah Kelley), one of the best black dancers in Tracy's high school. Tracy is "color-blind," and when she is sent to detention (because her hair is of an immoral height!) she meets Seaweed and learns a few sexy dance moves.

When an opportunity arises to audition for Corny's show, Tracy tries out with the blessing of her father Wilbur (Christopher Walken) but against the wishes of her mother Edna (John Travolta). Almost immediately, station manager and one-time Miss Baltimore Crab Velma Von Tussle (Michelle Pfeiffer) dismisses her, but the show's star, Corny (James Marsden), appreciates Tracy's dancing ability and signs her on. When Tracy's popularity on the show skyrockets, the ever-intolerant Velma is even more enraged as Tracy upstages her own daughter Amber (Brittany Snow).

Being on the show affords Tracy a chance at her other dream, winning the love of heartthrob Link Larkin (Zac Efron), Amber's boyfriend and dance partner. In addition to attaining her lifelong dream, Tracy's participation on the show inspires her in a larger sense as she fights to win a permanent place for the black dancers on the show and, by default, champions civil rights in 1960s Baltimore. Tackling the topic of prejudice, the filmmakers, and originally John Waters, present the view that all types of discrimination are equally undesirable. The America of the 1960s treats overweight Tracy badly, just as it treats African Americans badly. Not to the same degree or in the same manner, obviously, but Tracy is a likeable poster girl for acceptance, and the music helps to celebrate our differences.

The fact that this presentation of social commentary with an upbeat tempo works is as surprising as it is entertaining. Director Adam Shankman's early career as a dancer and choreographer certainly serves him well here, and the score by Marc Shaiman, with its catchy, sometimes wicked lyrics keeps the film perfectly on track. Credit also goes to the wonderful ensemble cast. The role of Edna has always been played by a man in drag (Divine in the original film and Harvey Fierstein in the musical), but Travolta avoids playing the part like a scenery-chewing drag queen and treats Edna like any other character. Although he does appear to have an inordinately good time dancing in his fat suit, Travolta seems equally concerned with realistically portraying a caring mother. Much like the quintessential 1950s father he portrayed in *Blast from the Past* (1999), Christopher Walken is cast against type as a character who is sweet, tender, and even innocently wise. Pfeiffer snarls her way through a Cruella De Vil impersonation, and Allison Janney hits just the right note as a religious prude appropriately named Prudy Pingleton. There are also fun cameos by John Waters as a flasher and by Jerry Stiller, who played the original Wilbur Turnblad and now plays Mr. Pinky.

The film is incredibly good-natured, exuberant, and engagingly goofy. According to Carina Chocano of the *L.A. Times,* the film is "a buoyant fantasy of once-upon-a-time innocence." According to the *New York Times*'s A. O. Scott, "*Hairspray* is fundamentally a story about being young—about the triumph of youth culture, about the optimistic, possibly dated belief that the future will improve on the present—and its heart is very much with its teenage heroes and the fresh-faced actors who play them." The whole experience of the film and its place in the summer of 2007 may be summed up best by the review of Roger Moore of the *Orlando Sentinal* as it appeared in the *Chicago Tribune*: "*Hairspray* is a musical for people who love them. Big, flamboyant, brimming over with giggles, goodwill and PG-rated wit…it's a toe-tapper to make you forget sashaying pirates, comic-book heroes, robot Camaros and cartoons. This is the movie event of the summer."

Beverley Bare Buehrer

CREDITS

Edna Turnblad: John Travolta
Wilbur Turnblad: Christopher Walken
Velma Von Tussle: Michelle Pfeiffer
Motormouth Maybelle: Queen Latifah
Tracy Turnblad: Nikki Blonsky
Penny Pingleton: Amanda Bynes
Corny Collins: James Marsden
Link Larkin: Zac Efron
Amber Von Tussle: Brittany Snow
Prudy Pingleton: Allison Janney

Seaweed J. Stubbs: Elijah Kelley
Mr. Pinky: Jerry Stiller
Mr. Spritzer: Paul Dooley
Little Inez: Taylor Parks
Origin: USA
Language: English
Released: 2007
Production: Craig Zadan, Neil Meron; Ingenious Film Partners, Storyline Entertainment; released by New Line Cinema
Directed by: Adam Shankman
Written by: Leslie Dixon
Cinematography by: Bojan Bazelli
Music by: Marc Shaiman
Sound: David MacMillan
Music Supervisor: Matt Sullivan
Editing: Michael Tronick
Art Direction: Dennis Davenport
Costumes: Rita Ryack
Production Design: David Gropman
MPAA rating: PG
Running time: 117 minutes

REVIEWS

Boston Globe Online. July 20, 2007.
Chicago Sun-Times Online. July 20, 2007.
Christian Science Monitor Online. July 20, 2007.
Entertainment Weekly. July 27, 2007, p. 48.
Hollywood Reporter Online. July 2, 2007.
Los Angeles Times Online. July 20, 2007.
New York Times Online. July 19, 2007.
Premiere Online. July 12, 2007.
Rolling Stone Online. July 18, 2007.
San Francisco Chronicle. July 20, 2007, p. E1.
Variety Online. June 29, 2007.
Wall Street Journal Online. July 20, 2007.
Washington Post. July 20, 2007, p. C1.

QUOTES

Edna Turnblad (singing): "You can't stop my happiness, 'cuz I like the way I am. And you just can't stop my knife and fork when I see a Christmas ham! And if you don't like the way I look, then I just don't give a damn!"

TRIVIA

John Waters, creator of the 1988 film, cameos as the neighborhood flasher.

AWARDS

Nomination:

British Acad. 2007: Makeup

HALLOWEEN

Evil has a destiny.
   —Movie tagline
When darkness fell, HE arrived.
   —Movie tagline
The face behind the mask.
   —Movie tagline

Box Office: $58.2 million

Rob Zombie's ambitious (if not misguided) re-imagining of John Carpenter's *Halloween* (1978) lends credibility to the maxim "less is more." It is not for lack of substance, point in fact, it is an abundance of substance and excessive gore in *Halloween* that snuff out what all horror films strive to do: instill fear. With a $15 million budget (compared with the $325,000 allotted the original) this renovation simply does not measure up to the compelling horror classic helmed by master craftsman John Carpenter. Carpenter's *Halloween* has been cited as the impetus for the barrage of teen splatter flicks that hit the box office in subsequent decades. Although the killer Michael Myers could be heralded as the cinematic godfather of similar characters, such as Jason Voorhees and Freddy Krueger (spawned from the *Friday the 13th* and *A Nightmare on Elm Street* franchises, respectively), he has become almost a neutered, household name. Zombie disclosed it was for this reason that he wished to revamp the iconic character in an effort to restore the terror the masked killer once elicited.

Zombie decides to flesh out Michael's childhood. In his version, we hear young Myers (creepily played by Daeg Faerch) speak out for the first time. It is significant because in the previous series, the character never uttered a syllable. The film begins on the morning of October 31 at the Myers's household, where a disturbing paradigm of severe white-trash dysfunction unfolds. In the first ten minutes, several elements of Michael's troubled home life are presented. He is psychologically tormented by Ronnie (William Forsythe), the alcoholic boyfriend of his strip-dancing mother Deborah (Sheri Moon Zombie), as well by his vitriolic and promiscuous older sister. The wounds inflicted upon Michael's psyche manifest themselves in his torturing and killing of animals. Once he's at school, it is quickly apparent that the boy's disturbing family milieu is simply one component of his living nightmare. In the boy's restroom he is taunted by his peers, who shove a flyer of his scantily clothed mother in his face.

Dr. Samuel Loomis (Malcolm McDowell) is brought in to reason with Mrs. Myers when a dead cat is found in her son's backpack. Although he is depicted as a virtuoso in the field of psychopathology, the doctor's motives are later found to be less than altruistic, as he is driven to gain fame as an author profiling the boy. Following the day's emotional trauma, Michael stalks one of his tormentors on his way home from school and bludgeons him to death with a heavy branch. His psychotic break complete, Michael returns home and duct tapes Ronnie to a living room chair once he goes into a beer-induced coma in front of the television set. After bludgeoning his sister's boyfriend to death in the kitchen, Michael dons the same clown mask seen in the classic film as he climbs up the staircase and butchers his cruel sister with a large kitchen knife. Zombie gives a nod to the original by having a portrait of John F. Kennedy in the scene (Kennedy was assassinated in 1963, the year the original six-year-old Michael killed his sister).

In the original's 1981 sequel, we learned that the heroine Laurie (played by Jamie Lee Curtis with an innocence and presence that overshadows Scout Taylor-Compton's portrayal here) is in fact Michael's little sister. This retroactive continuity, as well as other plot elements from *Halloween II* (1981) such as using the Chordettes hit "Mr. Sandman," were spliced into Zombie's version. Zombie's screenplay gives the story a heavy 1970s atmosphere that the writer/director has an obvious affection for, and the soundtrack is full of classic songs by rock groups such as KISS, Blue Oyster Cult, and Nazareth. Aside from reverence for the decade, also abundant in Zombie's *House of 1000 Corpses* (2003) and *The Devil's Rejects* (2005), his musical choices seem random and discordant in many of the scenes.

Once young Myers escapes from Smith's Grove Sanitarium, he returns to Haddonfield on a mass murder spree. The body count mounts in this rendition, with the formidable Michael (played by the six-foot-eight Tyler Mane) wearing the familiar distorted William Shatner mask used throughout the franchise. This analogue racks up four to five times the victims with a preternatural verve that resembles an Eli Roth film in that it capitalizes on the violent gore rather than the escalation of fear. The film repeats some of the original's climactic scenes before it strays by having Myers kill his psychiatrist. He then grabs Laurie's wrist, seeming to place her aim at his own head as she repeatedly shoots her brother in the head with Dr. Loomis's gun.

What started out as an homage quickly turns into splatter porn; this *Halloween* would fit nicely in a DVD box set with Zombie's previous films. The improvements made here were an increase in exposition at the expense of mystery. In Carpenter's tale, the reason for Michael's descent into a psychotic abyss is an enigma. In the opening scene, it appears as though he was raised in a normal, suburban, middle-class home. His parents were shocked to find him walking out of their home with a knife half his size in his grip after slashing his sister. He remains silent from that night on. The only thing that is known is that he feels compelled to kill. In Carpenter's script (cowritten by Debra Hill), Myers was known simply as "the Shape." Carpenter heightened his story by dramatically building up tension that preceded a slaying. He often placed the audience in the know with a portentous foreshadowing of an oblivious character's expeditious demise. He utilized suspense and buildup, whereas Zombie uses neither. These three main components—mystery, suspense, and buildup—were abundant in Carpenter's film and completely absent in Zombie's retinkering, rendering this work predictable and inert.

David M. Roberts

CREDITS

Dr. Sam Loomis: Malcolm McDowell
Michael Myers: Tyler Mane
Laurie Strode: Scout Taylor-Compton
Sheriff Brackett: Brad Dourif
Ismael: Danny Trejo
Ronnie: William Forsythe
Annie: Danielle Harris
Judith Myers: Hanna Hall
Deborah Myers: Sheri Moon Zombie
Origin: USA
Language: English
Released: 2007
Production: Andy Gould, Rob Zombie, Malek Akkad; Dimension Films; released by MGM
Directed by: Rob Zombie
Written by: Rob Zombie
Cinematography by: Phil Parmet
Music by: Tyler Bates
Sound: Buck Robinson
Editing: Glenn Garland
Art Direction: T. K. Kirkpatrick
Costumes: Mary McLeod
Production Design: Anthony Tremblay
MPAA rating: R
Running time: 110 minutes

REVIEWS

Boston Globe Online. September 1, 2007.
Hollywood Reporter Online. September 3, 2007.
Los Angeles Times Online. September 1, 2007.
New York Times Online. September 1, 2007.
Premiere Online. August 31, 2007.
San Francisco Chronicle. September 1, 2007, p. E1.
Variety Online. August 27, 2007.

QUOTES

Dr. Loomis: "These eyes will deceive you, they will destroy you. They will take from you your innocence, your pride, and eventually your soul. These eyes do not see what you and I see. Behind these eyes one finds only blackness, the absence of light, these are of a psychopath."

TRIVIA

Film is dedicated to Moustapha Akkad, the producer of the previous films in the franchise, who died in 2005.

HANNIBAL RISING

It started with revenge.
—Movie tagline

Box Office: $27.6 million

One of the most compelling aspects of the Hannibal Lecter character is his mystery, so to create an origin story for the infamous cannibal was, perhaps, an unwise premise for his latest cinematic incarnation. Director Peter Webber (*Girl with a Pearl Earring* [2003]) crafts an interesting-looking film overshadowed by stiff performances, laughable dialogue, and an overly long running time. The story plods along, never pulling the audience in. Even worse, it substitutes graphic violence for what could have been suspense and genuine horror.

In this installment, author/screenwriter Thomas Harris recounts Hannibal's childhood in Lithuania. It is 1944 and the Lecters are an aristocratic family who are forced out of their castle and into a hunting lodge during World War II. A Russian tank is attacked by a German plane right in the lodge's front yard and while nine-year-old Hannibal Lecter (Aaran Thomas) and his younger sister Mischa (Helena-Lia Tachovská) watch, the rest of their entire family is killed in the ensuing battle.

The two children try to survive as best they can in the winter isolation of the lodge, but their situation becomes even more precarious with the arrival of a band of Lithuanian Nazi-collaborators led by the especially nasty Grutas (Rhys Ifans). They set about looting the countryside while wearing Red Cross armbands and piling their booty into a stolen Red Cross ambulance. To escape retribution, they take over the Lecter's lodge. Hannibal tries to protect his sister from these felons, but as the food runs out, Grutas makes a decision that will be fatal to Hannibal's psyche: they kill and eat Mischa.

Eight years later, the teenage Hannibal (Gaspard Ulliel), a psychologically damaged mute, is back in Lecter castle, which is now a Soviet orphanage. When he finally stands up to the orphanage bully, Hannibal finds himself locked in the castle's cellar. The cellar, however, has a hidden exit and Hannibal sneaks into his mother's old bedroom and extracts some letters from a secret drawer. From the letters he learns the address of his uncle in Paris. That night he escapes from the castle, over the Berlin Wall, and into France.

Once in France he discovers that his uncle is dead but is survived by a beautiful widow, Lady Murasaki (Gong Li), who takes Hannibal in. In Lady Murasaki, Hannibal finds not only a safe haven, but also someone who instructs him in the ways of the samurai. Her chef also hones Hannibal's culinary skills. These early lessons come in handy when Hannibal must teach a loutish butcher (Charles Maquignon) some manners after he insults Lady Murasaki. However, the butcher's gruesome death brings Hannibal to the attention of Inspector Popil (Dominic West). The investigation forces Lady Murasaki and Hannibal to move to Paris, where he enrolls in medical school and becomes quite adept at autopsies.

With his first taste of vengeful murder, Hannibal now decides to avenge his sister. In Lithuania he finds the first of the looters, who tells him that most of the gang is, conveniently, back in France. Hannibal proceeds to make a tasty brochette out of the looter's cheeks and some wild mushrooms. Back in France, Hannibal continues on his mission, eliminating his childhood tormentors one by one, with a special revenge waiting for the ringleader Grutas, who is now a white-slave trader living on a houseboat on the canals of France.

Hannibal Rising is the fifth filmic appearance of author Thomas Harris's Hannibal Lecter. The first, *Manhunter* (1986), featured Brian Cox in the role, but it was Anthony Hopkins's mesmerizing turns in *The Silence of the Lambs* (1991), *Hannibal* (2001), and *Red Dragon* (2002) that have defined the franchise. Although *Hannibal Rising* is the first of the series' screenplays to be written by the character's creator Harris, the 2006 novel of the same name on which it was based was poorly received by critics.

There are several problems with this latest Lecter, the most minor of which is that it is virtually impossible to imagine Anthony Hopkins evolving from Gaspard Ulliel. Despite the satanic smile, a sense of culture, and a chilling unflappability, they look nothing alike. Whereas Hopkins's Lecter had an essence of sly mystery, Ulliel's Lecter just seems empty. That calm, unflappable demeanor makes him more like an evil robot than a damaged human being. There is little of the wit or intelligence that characterized Hopkins's portrayals.

A bigger problem for the audience is in trying to identify with a main character who is a soulless serial killer. As a child and even a teenager, Hannibal might elicit sympathy. As an adult, his vengeance seems justified, but certainly not his methods. The fact that he is a sociopath who has no qualms about murdering, then delightedly eating his victims puts the character far beyond any lingering sympathy. But *Hannibal Rising* does not spend time analyzing the ethics or psychology of the serial killer; instead it focuses on the lovingly gruesome detail of the many murders committed by Lecter.

Beverley Bare Buehrer

CREDITS

Hannibal Lecter: Gaspard Ulliel
Lady Murasaki: Gong Li
Grutas: Rhys Ifans
Kolnas: Kevin McKidd
Inspector Popil: Dominic West
Young Hannibal: Aaran Thomas
Mischa: Helena-Lia Tachovská
Origin: USA, Great Britain, France
Language: English
Released: 2007
Production: Dino De Laurentiis, Martha De Laurentiis, Tarak Ben Ammar; Quinta Communications, Ingenious Film Partners; released by MGM
Directed by: Peter Webber
Written by: Thomas Harris
Cinematography by: Benjamin Davis
Music by: Ilan Eshkeri, Shigeru Umebayashi
Sound: Eddy Joseph, Oliver Tarney
Editing: Pietro Scalia, Valerio Bonelli
Art Direction: Nenad Pecur
Costumes: Anna Sheppard
Production Design: Allan Starski
MPAA rating: R
Running time: 117 minutes

REVIEWS

Chicago Sun-Times Online. February 9, 2007.
Entertainment Weekly. February 23, 2007, p. 80.
Hollywood Reporter Online. February 9, 2007.
Los Angeles Times Online. February 9, 2007.
New York Times Online. February 9, 2007.
Premiere Magazine Online. February 8, 2007.
San Francisco Chronicle. February 9, 2007, p. E1.

Variety Online. February 8, 2007.
Washington Post. February 9, 2007, p. C5.

QUOTES

Hannibal Lecter: "I've come to collect a head."

TRIVIA

Actors who tested for the role of Hannibal include: Hayden Christensen, Macaulay Culkin, Hugh Dancy, Rupert Friend, Dominic Cooper, Tom Sturridge, and Tom Payne.

AWARDS

Nomination:

Golden Raspberries 2007: Worst Horror Movie, Worst Sequel/Prequel.

HAPPILY N'EVER AFTER

The future looks Grimm.
—Movie tagline

Fairytale endings aren't what they used to be.
—Movie tagline

Box Office: $15.5 million

Advertisements for *Happily N'Ever After* were aiming for comparisons to *Shrek* (2001) when they boasted that the film was "from the producer of *Shrek* and *Shrek 2*." What they did not mention was that producer John H. Williams was only one of five credited for the far superior Dreamworks comedy and that, truthfully, it is not as though one-fifth of the producers are the primary creative force behind a film. The ads worked, in a sense. Many critics did indeed compare the film to *Shrek*—just not favorably. Wrote Matt Zoller Seitz of the *New York Times*: "Anyone who dismisses the *Shrek* movies as lowbrow junk should see *Happily N'Ever After*, a cartoon feature that apes those films' visuals, soundtrack choices, and rude jokes, while throwing away their sweetness and conviction."

This postmodern fairy story shares *Shrek*'s idea of taking familiar fairy-tale creatures and tweaking their images. The story takes place in a fairy-tale land presided over by a wizard (voice of George Carlin). The wizard is in charge of overseeing the fairy tales and making sure that the balance between good and evil stays at the proper level to ensure the expected happy ending. When the wizard sets off for a golfing vacation, he puts his annoying lackeys in charge of the machinery that controls the stories. Munk (voice of Wallace Shawn) is an obedient helper with good sense. Mambo (voice of Andy Dick) is the rascally, irresponsible one who finds happy endings boring and wants to stir things up.

Soon the wizard's machinery is in the hands of Cinderella's (voice of Sarah Michelle Gellar) malicious stepmother Frieda (voice of Sigourney Weaver). Frieda starts tinkering with the machine and, for a few moments, *Happily N'Ever After* is at its most entertaining. While watching the giant capture Jack from the beanstalk and Rumpelstiltskin get custody of the child, Frieda chuckles happily. But her ultimate goal is to alter the ending of Cinderella's story, aiming for a resolution in which she gets a royal title or, at the very least, becomes very rich.

But Cinderella, or Ella, as she is called in the story, is a feisty woman. She is determined to marry the dim-witted Prince Humperdink (voice of Patrick Warburton). And there is another twist. The narrator of the story, Rick (voice of Freddie Prinze, Jr., Gellar's real-life husband), is in love with Ella. Rick is a dishwasher in the castle and Ella's best friend. Blinded by her quest to marry the prince, Ella fails to realize that Rick is the man she should marry.

Predictable and increasingly tiresome, *Happily N'Ever After* does offer a few unexpected delights. There is a creative moment in which Rick comes to a stop in his storytelling and the film correspondingingly bucks and stops, as though it were getting stuck in the projector. And, as in *Shrek*, it is entertaining to see familiar characters caught in unfamiliar circumstances. But by the time the credits roll, *Happily N'Ever After* is just a handful of good ideas that never come together in a wholly entertaining or cohesive fashion.

Perhaps the most unpleasant thing about the film is its visual style. The film was started in the old-fashioned 2-D style but was changed during production by producer Williams and codirector Paul J. Bolger to 3-D. The result is an awkward mix, with characters animated in an off-putting, eerie fashion who move through their computer-created world unnaturally—not in a cartoonish way, but in a disturbingly unreal and unsettling manner. Several critics commented on the animation. Ty Burr of the *Boston Globe* bluntly called it "one ugly sucker" and Lou Lumenick of the *New Post* called it "an ugly, unfunny, headache-inducing fairy-tale spoof."

Prinze does a surprisingly nice job as the dryly embittered Rick. Gellar does not fare as well, and as a disembodied voice, she cannot hold her own in an arena with several old pros. The talented Weaver gives an over-the-top performance as the evil stepmother with an equally exaggerated hourglass figure. Aforementioned seasoned voice professionals Shawn, Dick, and Warburton do their best to spice up the proceedings in supporting roles, but are doomed by the film's overall blandness.

Though possessing moments of originality and wit, *Happily N'Ever After* is unable to sustain those moments long enough to turn it from a middling film into a good one.

Jill Hamilton

CREDITS

Fairy Godmother: Lisa Kaplan
Ella: Sarah Michelle Gellar (Voice)
Rick: Freddie Prinze, Jr. (Voice)
Frieda: Sigourney Weaver (Voice)
Mambo: Andy Dick (Voice)
Munk: Wallace Shawn (Voice)
Prince Humperdink: Patrick Warburton (Voice)
The Wizard: George Carlin (Voice)
Rumplestiltskin: Michael McShane (Voice)
Stepsister #1/Baby/Red Riding Hood: Kath Soucie (Voice)
Origin: USA, Germany
Language: English
Released: 2007
Production: John H. Williams; Vanguard Films, Odyssey Entertainment, BAF Berlin Animation Film, BFC Berliner Film Companie; released by Lionsgate
Directed by: Paul J. Bolger
Written by: Rob Moreland
Cinematography by: David Dulac
Music by: Paul Buckley
Sound: Robert Shoup
Music Supervisor: Liz Gallacher
Editing: Ringo Waldenburger
MPAA rating: PG
Running time: 87 minutes

REVIEWS

Chicago Sun-Times Online. January 5, 2007.
Los Angeles Times Online. January 5, 2007.
New York Times Online. January 5, 2007.
San Francisco Chronicle. January 5, 2007, p. E6.
Variety Online. December 17, 2006.
Washington Post. January 5, 2007, p. C1.

QUOTES

Rick: "Munk's the guy who looks at the glass as half-empty. Mambo's the guy who…probably peed in the glass."

HARRY POTTER AND THE ORDER OF THE PHOENIX

The rebellion begins.
—Movie tagline

Box Office: $292 million

The fifth in the series of Harry Potter films, *Harry Potter and the Order of the Phoenix* is something of a paradox. *Order of the Phoenix* is the shortest film of the series, though the novel on which it is based is the longest of the Potter novels, and the film was well-received by critics but coolly welcomed by fans of the books (who have, by and large, embraced the previous four Potter films). It is also the first of the Harry Potter movies to be directed by a relative newcomer to feature films, David Yates, a British television director. The story has been stripped to its bare essentials (even more so than in the previous Potter films) for the sake of keeping the movie from spiraling out of control (the novel is more than 890 pages, the movie clocks in at a manageable two hours and eighteen minutes), and this threatens to make *Harry Potter and the Order of the Phoenix* somewhat less enchanting than audiences have come to expect—but deft filmmaking and simply remarkable acting help emphasize a darker view of Harry's world. Though this is the least satisfying of the Potter films to date, *Harry Potter and the Order of the Phoenix* manages to take the characters where they need to be in order to continue the series (while ingeniously commenting on the workings of the real world), and the truly wonderful performances (all the more amazing for the scant material provided to the actors) prevent the by-the-numbers plot from draining all of the magic out of the franchise.

At the beginning of the film, Harry (Daniel Radcliffe), after repelling two Dementors (creatures that drain the happiness out of people, and can steal human souls), quickly finds himself at the headquarters of the Order of the Phoenix awaiting trial for illegally using magic in front of a Muggle (a nonmagical human). The Order is a group of wizards dedicated to fighting the dark wizard Lord Voldemort (Ralph Fiennes), composed of several of Harry's teachers, mentors, and friends. At Order headquarters, Harry learns that the trial is part of an attempt by Cornelius Fudge, the Minister of Magic himself, to silence Harry—the minister is terrified that Dumbledore (Michael Gambon), the headmaster of Hogwarts, is out to become Minister of Magic, and proof of Voldemort's return would go a long way toward that end. Harry is acquitted largely due to the intervention of Dumbledore, who mysteriously leaves once the trial is over without saying a word directly to Harry.

Harry leaves for school to find that the mark of the Ministry is there as well: Fudge has appointed one of his devotees and the most vocal prosecutor of Harry during the trial, Dolores Umbridge (Imelda Staunton) as professor of Defense Against the Dark Arts. Umbridge immediately begins teaching a "Ministry-approved" version of the course that emphasizes theory over the actual use of magic: Fudge fears that Dumbledore might use the Hogwarts students against him. Umbridge's refusal to teach the students defensive magic and her draconian rule-making throughout Hogwarts leads the other students to ask Harry, the only student wizard among them who has fought Dark Wizards, to form a secret Defense Against the Dark Arts club, which the students come to call Dumbledore's Army out of reverence and allegiance to the headmaster.

Professor Umbridge's regime, however, is only one of many challenges that besets Harry in his fifth year at Hogwarts: Since Voldemort's return, the link between Harry and Voldemort that has allowed Harry to see into Voldemort's thoughts has become much stronger. In one vision, Harry sees Ron Weasley's father, Arthur (Mark Williams), attacked within the Ministry—agents of the Order of the Phoenix are dispatched to the place Harry describes, and Arthur is found dying. Once Arthur is taken to safety, and the link between Voldemort and Harry is proven, Dumbledore assigns Harry Occlumency (the ability to withstand a magical attack on the mind) lessons with Professor Snape (Alan Rickman). The lessons are mentally and physically demanding, Harry is a poor study, and Snape is a harsh taskmaster. Ultimately, Snape cancels the lessons after a session in which Harry manages to gain access to Snape's memories. Many months after the Occlumency lessons end, Harry has a vision of his godfather, Sirius Black (Gary Oldman), being tortured by Voldemort in the Department of Mysteries at the Ministry. Convinced the vision is genuine, Harry and his friends rush to the Ministry, where Harry finds a small crystal ball with his name on it on a shelf in the Hall of Prophecy. He removes the orb from its place, and he and his companions are immediately surrounded by Lucius Malfoy (Jason Isaacs), the father of Harry's nemesis at school, Draco Malfoy, and various other Death Eaters (followers of Lord Voldemort). Malfoy explains that Voldemort wanted the prophecy for himself and needed Harry to retrieve it. A brief battle ensues, as does a chase through the Department of Mysteries. Just when Harry and his friends are surrounded, Sirius Black and other Order members arrive to help. Sirius is killed in the battle and the orb containing the prophecy is accidentally destroyed. Voldemort arrives to collect the prophecy himself, only to be defeated by Dumbledore. Fudge and other Ministry officials arrive and see Voldemort before he retreats. Unable to continue to deny Voldemort's return, Fudge lifts his control over Hogwarts. Dumbledore reveals to Harry that he was, in fact, ignoring Harry over the course of the year, thinking that Voldemort would use the connection with Harry's mind to attack Dumbledore—his goal, Dumbledore explains, was to protect Harry from the possibility that Voldemort might be tempted to use Harry to attack him. The film ends with the students

preparing to leave the school for the summer, the future uncertain.

The plot, not coincidentally, emphasizes the reaction of a government to the threat of constant attack. *Order of the Phoenix* received a good amount of critical praise for its deft concision, though Potter fans will certainly wince at the deep cuts. True, the through-line of action has been preserved: Harry must navigate life at Hogwarts with its new draconian headmistress, Dolores Umbridge, who is installed by the Minister of Magic to try to undermine him at every turn. J.K. Rowling's book was released in the summer of 2003 and, being the first post-9/11 Potter book, it was certainly informed by world events or, at the very least, by the obsession with conformity and the desire to control information that has since permeated western society, made manifest in the Patriot Act, secret wiretaps, and the use of torture in interrogation.

These elements of the book are emphasized in the film and find their greatest expression in the oppressive regime of Dolores Umbridge. Imelda Staunton is wonderfully detestable as Professor Umbridge, replete with her (former British Prime Minister) Margaret Thatcher-like hair-do and wardrobe, and deeply conservative Thatcherite sensibility. Though younger viewers will not pick up on the references to the ultra-conservative 1980s political figure (Britain's corollary to Ronald Reagan), a conscious choice obviously has been made to invoke her and her politics, and the specificity of that choice lends the character and her actions a certain universality— whether enhanced by the Thatcher reference or not, Umbridge is a power-hungry rule-maker and a cruel dictator who is convinced that she is making the world a better place. Staunton brilliantly captures the essence of Umbridge, and is able to project the character's shocking capacity for sadism, whether in her detentions (she has Harry write out lines with a special quill that etches the phrase "I must not tell lies" into his skin) or in the threat to use a torture curse on Harry to determine Dumbledore's whereabouts. She is the embodiment of an all-too-familiar dynamic of the War on Terror—abusing the power of authority to the point of becoming just like (or worse than) the enemy, and doing so in the name of security and freedom.

All of the things that audiences have come to expect from the Harry Potter films are certainly present in *Order of the Phoenix*—the special effects are top-notch, new obstacles are faced and overcome, Harry is introduced to new creatures—but the most welcome and stalwart feature of these movies is the quality of the supporting performances (fortunately, Staunton's is not the only one). The characters of *Order of the Phoenix* are brought to life by some of the finest actors of all time. It cannot be overstated that all of the actors have created indelible screen characterizations of their literary counterparts, but there are some standouts in *Order of the Phoenix*, including: David Thewlis as the bedraggled Professor Lupin; Gary Oldman as the brooding Sirius Black, Harry's godfather; Helena Bonham Carter as the deranged and wicked Bellatrix Lestrange; and Ralph Fiennes as the menacing Lord Voldemort. The most impressive performance across the series, however, is still that of Alan Rickman. Charged with the task of portraying arguably the most complex and mysterious of all of the characters in the Potter universe, Rickman is once again the embodiment of potion-master Professor Severus Snape. Confronted by Umbridge at one point about his attempt to become the Defense Against the Dark Arts teacher, she asks, "You were unsuccessful?", and Snape replies, "Obviously," in the driest manner possible, and that one word speaks volumes about the character and about acting technique: Rickman's Snape can say a thousand things with one word and a glance. Snape remains as inscrutable as ever, his loyalties unknown, and his capacity for loathing Harry apparently bottomless. Watching Rickman navigate the twists and turns of Severus Snape is reason enough to follow the Potter series, and he helps make *Order of the Phoenix* worth the price of admission.

Overall, *Harry Potter and the Order of the Phoenix* is not as rich and varied as the other films in the series, but it is not meant to be. Harry is entering into particularly dark times, and the film, aided by subtle references to current events and informed by extraordinary performances, transitions Harry from the cares of his school days to the greater concerns of the world beyond.

John Boaz

CREDITS

Harry Potter: Daniel Radcliffe
Hermione Granger: Emma Watson
Ron Weasley: Rupert Grint
Albus Dumbledore: Michael Gambon
Severus Snape: Alan Rickman
Sirius Black: Gary Oldman
Dolores Umbridge: Imelda Staunton
Lucius Malfoy: Jason Isaacs
Lord Voldemort: Ralph Fiennes
Bellatrix Lestrange: Helena Bonham Carter
Remus Lupin: David Thewlis
Rubeus Hagrid: Robbie Coltrane
Aunt Petunia: Fiona Shaw
Minerva McGonagall: Maggie Smith
Sybil Trelawney: Emma Thompson

Alastor Moody: Brendan Gleeson
Draco Malfoy: Tom Felton
Cho Chang: Katie Leung
Uncle Vernon: Richard Griffiths
Molly Weasley: Julie Walters
Luna Lovegood: Evanna Lynch
Arthur Weasley: Mark Williams
Ginny Weasley: Bonnie Wright
Filius Flitwick: Warwick Davis
Cornelius Fudge: Robert Hardy
Argus Filch: David Bradley
Origin: USA
Language: English
Released: 2007
Production: David Heyman, David Barron; Heyday Films; released by Warner Bros.
Directed by: David Yates
Written by: Michael Goldberg
Cinematography by: Slawomir Idziak
Music by: Nicholas Hooper
Sound: Stuart Wilson
Editing: Mark Day
Art Direction: Neil Lamont
Costumes: Jany Temime
Production Design: Stuart Craig
MPAA rating: PG-13
Running time: 139 minutes

REVIEWS

Boston Globe Online. July 9, 2007.
Chicago Sun-Times Online. July 10, 2007.
Entertainment Weekly. July 20, 2007, p. 55.
Hollywood Reporter Online. June 30, 2007.
Los Angeles Times Online. July 10, 2007.
New York Times Online. July 10, 2007.
Rolling Stone Online. June 29, 2007.
San Francisco Chronicle. July 10, 2007, p. B1.
Time Online. July 5, 2007.
Variety Online. June 29, 2007.
Washington Post. July 11, 2007, p. C1.

QUOTES

Kingsley Shacklebolt: "You may not like him, Minister, but you can't deny: Dumbledore's got style."

TRIVIA

In the scene where Harry, Ron, and Hermione are discussing Harry's kiss with Cho, the three begin to crack up near the end of the scene. This was all real laughter from the three actors. The director thought it was good for the scene and kept rolling.

AWARDS

Nomination:
British Acad. 2007: Production Des., Visual FX.

THE HEARTBREAK KID

It seemed like a good idea...at the time.
—Movie tagline

Box Office: $36.7 million

The Heartbreak Kid was touted as being in the same vein as *There's Something About Mary* (1998), also directed by the Farrelly brothers (Bobby and Peter) and starring Ben Stiller. The Farrelly brothers are known for their often crude and sometimes socially insensitive comedy, and *The Heartbreak Kid* definitely fits into that category. The movie, loosely based on a 1972 film with a screenplay by Neil Simon, has its humorous moments, and many of them are blatantly crude, but unfortunately the story itself fails to provide a meaningful plot, misses the opportunity to explore a worthwhile theme, and lacks sympathetic characters. Overall, the movie comes across largely as an exercise in bad taste featuring confused, impulsive characters. There is little to remember about the film other than its crudity and its off-the-wall humor.

Ben Stiller plays Eddie Cantrow, a forty-year-old bachelor who has never found the right woman to settle down with. When one of his ex-girlfriends gets married, Eddie's friend Mac (Rob Corddry) and his father Doc (Jerry Stiller) insist that it is time for him to find someone. A chance encounter introduces Eddie to beautiful Lila (Malin Akerman), and after a whirlwind romance, Eddie decides to pop the question and the two are married. However, on the way to their honeymoon in Mexico, Eddie begins to wonder if he made the right decision as he learns more about his new bride.

Eddie's dilemma worsens in Mexico when he meets Miranda (Michelle Monaghan), an attractive, funny woman with whom he establishes an immediate rapport. While Lila seems to be crazier by the minute, Miranda appears to be well-grounded, intelligent, and sensitive. Fortunately for Eddie, Lila ends up with a ridiculous sunburn that keeps her indoors for a few days, affording him the opportunity to spend time with Miranda. Eventually, of course, everything comes out in the open, Miranda and her family discover Eddie is married, and Lila leaves Eddie. Several months later, when Eddie tries to track Miranda down to explain what happened and tell her how he really feels, he discovers she has married. The movie then jumps forward eighteen months. Eddie is now living in Mexico, operating a water-sports rental business on the beach. One day he is surprised to see Miranda walking up to him; it turns out that she and her husband have split up. Eddie makes plans to see Miranda later, but the final moment in the film reveals that Eddie had married again...and is now willing to give up his wife for another chance with Miranda.

While one is likely to sympathize with Eddie to some degree as he discovers the reality about Lila, it is difficult to empathize with him or feel sorry for him when he meets Miranda and falls for her. Eddie's behavior, as a character, is not consistent or credible. The beginning of the film paints him as a man who has been extremely picky when it comes to women, an indecisive person who has been unable to commit because of his fear of marriage. After he meets Lila, he spends quite a bit of time with her; a montage of shots shows the two in various locales and enjoying numerous activities together (where they always wind up kissing). Even if the two did not know each other long, it is difficult to believe that Eddie shared those various moments with Lila and never discovered that she did not actually have a "real" paying job, or that she had a deviated septum that often resulted in food getting stuck in her nose (or flying out of it). The fact that Eddie missed all these outrageous aspects of Lila undermines his character. It is also curious that, when Eddie mistakenly believes Miranda's family knows he is married, he is not puzzled or confused by their apparent acceptance of his situation (the truth is they think his wife was killed). Logically, Eddie should wonder how they found out and what they know, but he does not...again, making him appear foolish.

Though the filmmakers obviously intend to go for laughs with the low-brow humor associated with Lila's character, the extent to which they go to portray her as wacky and unappealing is a bit extreme. Perhaps they felt that, after introducing a very attractive woman, they had to do everything they could think of to make her no longer desirable. She demonstrates that she is emotionally unstable; she admits to having used drugs in the past; she is less intelligent than she first appeared (somehow); she enjoys only violent lovemaking; she sings incessantly when in the car; she has an obese mother; and she urinates on Eddie—in public—when he suffers a wound from a man o' war. Considering this is a Farrelly brothers film, it is not surprising to see the ways in which she is used for humorous effect, but again, it does not make sense that Eddie would have failed to discover some of these issues. More significantly, the dramatic effect would have been more interesting and relevant had she not turned out to be such an oddball and had Eddie's growing discomfort with her been based on more realistic character traits. It seems the filmmakers have taken the seemingly easy road and simply attempted to paint Lila in as poor a light as possible, but the result actually backfires, because Eddie ultimately appears to be a fool for marrying her to begin with.

By the end of the film, one is tempted to wonder whether there is a point to the movie. Eddie apparently has not learned much, judging from the last scene (which undermines his character to an even greater degree). At this point, no one—except, perhaps, Miranda—is very likeable, and even though it is meant to be funny, the fact that Eddie has married again and is so quick to abandon his wife just taints the character and weakens any meaningful theme the movie might have been trying to convey. Essentially, *The Heartbreak Kid* exists primarily for the humor, but the humor itself is not sophisticated or strong enough to elevate the movie out of the depths to which it has sunk.

David Flanagin

CREDITS

Eddie Cantrow: Ben Stiller
Miranda: Michelle Monaghan
Lila: Malin Akerman
Doc: Jerry Stiller
Mac: Rob Corddry
Martin: Danny McBride
Boo: Scott Wilson
Uncle Tito: Carlos Mencia
Origin: USA
Language: English
Released: 2007
Production: Ted Field, Bradley Thomas; Dreamworks Pictures, Radar Pictures, Davis Entertainment, Conundrum Entertainment; released by Paramount Pictures
Directed by: Bobby Farrelly, Peter Farrelly
Written by: Bobby Farrelly, Peter Farrelly, Scot Armstrong, Leslie Dixon, Kevin Barnett
Cinematography by: Matthew F. Leonetti
Music by: Bill Ryan, Brendan Ryan
Editing: Alan Baumgarten, Sam Seig
Costumes: Louise Mingenbach
Production Design: Sydney J. Bartholomew, Jr., Arlan Jay Vetter
MPAA rating: R
Running time: 115 minutes

REVIEWS

Boston Globe Online. October 5, 2007.
Chicago Sun-Times Online. October 5, 2007.
Hollywood Reporter Online. October 2, 2007.
Los Angeles Times Online. October 5, 2007.
New York Times Online. October 5, 2007.
Rolling Stone Online. October 4, 2007.
San Francisco Chronicle. October 5, 2007, p. E5.
Variety Online. September 8, 2007.
Washington Post. October 5, 2007, p. C1.

QUOTES

Lila: "Oh Grouchy Marx, calm down."

TRIVIA

Release prints were shipped to some theaters under the fake title "Hansel." Hansel is a character in *Zoolander* (2001), another Ben Stiller movie.

THE HILLS HAVE EYES II

The lucky ones die fast.
    —Movie tagline

Box Office: $20.8 million

The Hills Have Eyes II is derivative in so many ways— not the least of which is the fact that one of its writers, Jonathan Craven, comes from an established horror film tradition—his father, horror master Wes Craven. The two Craven men wrote the film together as a sequel to *The Hills Have Eyes* (2006), which in turn was a remake of the elder Craven's 1977 film of the same name. At this level of banality, even the writers, the director (music-video auteur Martin Weisz), and the bland cast seem to have grown tired of the idea. Peter Hartlaub of the *San Francisco Chronicle*, who enjoyed the 2006 version of *The Hills Have Eyes*, wrote, "There's almost nothing original or surprising in the dialogue or action. This is exactly the kind of predictable horror detritus that Craven made fun of more than a decade ago when he directed *Scream*."

The movie follows the lives and deaths of a group of new National Guard recruits set to be shipped off to Kandahar. The group fails so badly during a training exercise that one can imagine that they will not fare very well against the conniving mutants that await them later in the movie. Their mission is changed when they get an alarm call from the mysterious "Sector 15," a military site in New Mexico. When they arrive, they discover that all the military technicians are missing. They deal with this in the clichéd horror-movie manner of splitting up so that the mutants can attack their victims one by one in a gorily efficient manner. One such repugnant attack results in a Porta Potti erupting with a man who appears to have died in a particularly unpleasant fashion.

The group soon discovers that there is an enclave of violent beings living in an elaborate system of caves in the hills. These partially human beings were harmed by nuclear testing and have become disfigured and violent mutants. They seek to extend their family line by breeding with some of the female humans. This means that the audience has to bear the sight of a randy mutant thrusting his excessively long tongue lasciviously over the face of one of the female guards.

Besides the unsettling concept and accompanying visuals of mutant sexual life, the rest of the film is of little note and surprisingly dull for a horror film. It follows the usual pattern of death that is typical of the genre, that is, characters tend to die in reverse order of their physical attractiveness. No one in this film behaves in an intelligent fashion. The mutant cannibals do not seem terribly bright, but perhaps they do not need to be. Their intended prey is constantly splitting up and leaving guns lying around. These predictable plot devices do not seem meant to pay homage to earlier films, or even to add humor, though humor might have been what this film needed. Scott Tobias of *The A.V. Club* wrote, "Humorlessness is probably the least of the film's problems, lagging behind amateur-night performances from the no-name cast, a homogenous video palette (and from a music-video director, no less!), and lots of pointless sadism."

In this film, death becomes less an earth-shattering event than a plot device, and not a particularly interesting one. The deaths are not creative or gory enough to arouse any feeling about them other than a vague depression and boredom. And since the characters are so ill defined and bland, it is hard to care when one of them is killed. There are some attractive women, Amber and Missy (Jessica Stroup and Daniella Alonso, respectively), an amiable soldier, Napoleon (Michael McMillian), and a fiery-tempered soldier, the aptly named Private Crank (Jacob Vargas) who is always searching for a fight. The mutants are suitably hideous, but their elaborate and obvious special-effects make-up renders them unrealistic and therefore not truly threatening.

The Hills Have Eyes II is a sequel that is light years away from its 1977 progenitor and, indeed, hardly compares to its recent predecessor, of which Peter Hartlaub wrote, "Sure, the movie had nothing to say that wasn't covered in Wes Craven's 1977 original, but it still came through with stylishly gruesome directing, quality actors who could sell the dark humor and buckets and buckets of gore."

Jill Hamilton

CREDITS

Sgt. Jeffrey Millstone: Flex Alexander
Pvt. Crank Medina: Jacob Vargas
Hades: Michael Bailey Smith
Pvt. Delmar Reed: Lee Thompson Young
Pvt. Napoleon Napoli: Michael McMillian
Pvt. Amber Johnson: Jessica Stroup
Pvt. Missy Martinez: Daniella Alonso
Cpl. Spitter Cole: Eric Edelstein
Origin: USA
Language: English
Released: 2007

Production: Wes Craven, Peter Locke, Marianne Maddalena; released by Fox Atomic
Directed by: Martin Weisz
Written by: Wes Craven, Jonathan Craven
Cinematography by: Sam McCurdy
Music by: Trevor Morris
Sound: Jonathan Miller
Music Supervisor: David Franco
Editing: Kirk Morri, Sue Blainey
Art Direction: Alistair Kay
Costumes: Katherine Jane Bryant
Production Design: Keith Wilson
MPAA rating: R
Running time: 89 minutes

REVIEWS

Boston Globe Online. March 24, 2007.
Hollywood Reporter Online. March 25, 2007.
Los Angeles Times Online. March 26, 2007.
New York Times Online. March 24, 2007.
Premiere Online. March 23, 2007.
Variety Online. March 25, 2007.

QUOTES

PFC Delmar: "I'm not sure God knows anything about this place."

THE HITCHER

Never pick up strangers.
—Movie tagline

Box Office: $16.3 million

The Hitcher, a remake of a 1986 film starring Rutger Hauer and C. Thomas Howell, is a horror film for the wrong era. A poorly made movie about hitchhiker who turns out to be a psychopathic killer may have been frightening subject matter in a decade when hitchhiking was more prevalent, but today it simply comes across like the dated retread it is. Ty Burr of the *Boston Globe* wrote, "I don't think I've seen a movie with less reason to exist."

The hitcher of the title is the appropriately named John Ryder (Sean Bean). The plot concerns Ryder's unexplained and unprovoked desire to kill a particular couple—Jim Halsey (Zachary Knighton) and his girlfriend Grace Andrews (Sophia Bush)—who are driving to their spring break destination. In typical slasher-film fashion, Ryder's efforts to do away with the pair take an excessively long time, although the killer seems to have no trouble wiping out entire families, fleets of police, and various other perceived dangers.

At first, Jim and Grace find Ryder to be well-spoken and polite. But after they offer him a ride, he starts making off-color remarks about Grace. Then he begins the first of his many attempts to kill them. After a tense fight, the couple are finally able to kick Ryder out the car door and leave him by the side of the road, believing he is dead. Unfortunately for them, and the audience, this is not the case, and the rest of the film simply repeats variations of this same scenario. John attacks Jim and/or Grace, a fight ensues, and Ryder seems to be dead. This makes for an exceedingly simple job for writers Eric Red, Jake Wade Wall, and Eric Bernt, but an exceedingly unrewarding experience for the audience. So obviously boiled down to these basic elements, the film loses all the suspense and novelty of its cult-classic predecessor. Mark Olsen of the *Los Angeles Times* wrote that the film "bleaches out the existential psychosis that made the original more than just another nasty little cheapie and instead just makes everything bigger and louder." Perhaps to make the plot repetition less obvious, there are slight tangents from the basic pattern. Ryder kills an evangelical family, then a police officer. The police suspect Grace and Jim in the killings, so now the couple are not only fleeing a homicidal maniac, they are running from the law, too.

One of the primary flaws of the film is that it requires excessive suspension of disbelief. Ryder, for example, is the sort of villain who apparently has superhuman powers. Though he cannot kill them, he is quite good at showing up wherever Grace and Jim are. He mysteriously—almost magically—finds their hotel, spots their car among many on the interstate, and breaks into the police station right after they are jailed. To get into the jail, Ryder must kill several armed police officers, but once again, he cannot manage to eradicate the unarmed couple. The subplot about the police suspecting Grace and Jim in the killings is also troublesome. The situation does not ring true because it is the kind of misunderstanding that could easily be cleared up with one calm phone call.

Director Dave Meyers, a music-video director making his film debut, enlivens the moments between the killings with smatterings of gore both big and small. Thrown in for good measure are a rabbit and a realistically computer-generated bug that meet their respective demises on the front of Grace and Jim's car. Later, an important character is tied between a truck and trailer and graphically ripped in half. The violence is gratuitous, but the film remains remarkably bland despite all the action, gore, and violence packed into its eighty-four-minute running time.

That this remake is so easily forgettable is not only the fault of the writing and directing, but also due in large part to the poor quality of the acting and utter lack of chemistry between the lead characters. The stand-out performance in the film comes from Neal McDonough, who plays Lieutenant Esteridge. He brings a level of skill to his role as the quick-witted, tough cop that is more than what is required in this B-movie affair. Bean is fine enough, though his role does not involve much beyond looking menacing while killing people. Knighton does a believable job of seeming bland and insipid. But poor Bush fares the worst, forced to wear skimpy clothing while simultaneously trying to serve as a one-woman S.W.A.T. team.

Jill Hamilton

CREDITS

John Ryder: Sean Bean
Grace Andrews: Sophia Bush
Jim Halsey: Zachary Knighton
Lt. Esterbridge: Neal McDonough
Origin: USA
Language: English
Released: 2007
Production: Michael Bay, Andrew Form, Brad Fuller, Charles Meeker, Alfred Haber; Focus Features, Intrepid Pictures, Platinum Dunes; released by Rogue Pictures
Directed by: Dave Meyers
Written by: Eric Red, Jake Wade Wall, Eric Bernt
Cinematography by: James Hawkinson
Music by: Steve Jablonsky
Sound: Alan Rankin
Music Supervisor: JoJo Villanueva
Editing: Jim May
Costumes: Leeann Radeka
Production Design: David Lazan
MPAA rating: R
Running time: 83 minutes

REVIEWS

Boston Globe Online. January 19, 2007.
Hollywood Reporter Online. January 22, 2007.
New York Times Online. January 20, 2007.
Premiere Magazine Online. January 19, 2007.
San Francisco Chronicle. January 20, 2007, p. E1.
Variety Online. January 19, 2007.

QUOTES

John Ryder: "Strangers think I'm trustworthy."

TRIVIA

The movies that Grace is watching in the hotel near the end are *North by Northwest* (1959) and *The Birds* (1963).

HITMAN

Box Office: $39.6 million

While not every video game cries out for film immortality, the Danish-created *Hitman* may be an exception. The game was inspired by films to begin with: Hong Kong action films generally, and Luc Besson's *La Femme Nikita* (1990) and *The Professional* (1994) particularly. Fittingly, Besson is one of the producers of the film *Hitman*. Despite being greeted by American reviewers as one of the vilest creations ever to reach the big screen, *Hitman* is actually modestly entertaining.

The unnamed hero (Timothy Olyphant) was raised in some secret government facility and trained to be an assassin. Like his fellow killers, he sports a shaved head with a barcode on the back of his skull. The purpose of the barcode is never explained, nor does anyone ever call attention to it. There is some confusion when he is confronted by three sword-wielding colleagues, at least one of whom does not appear to have a barcode. Then there are other, completely bald men not associated with "the organization." It is hard to discern whether director Xavier Gens and screenwriter Skip Woods are being deliberately ambiguous, playful, or just plain sloppy. The film alternates between well-done scenes and carelessness.

Hitman opens with the man eventually revealed to be "Agent 47" carrying out an especially gruesome hit in Niger. Then he is off to St. Petersburg to assassinate the newly elected Russian president, Mikhail Belicoff (Ulrich Thomsen). No sooner has 47 blown Belicoff's head to bits than the president appears on television with a bandage on his head. Has 47 killed a double, or the real Belicoff? If a double, what is going on? A film inspired by a video game can be accused of trying to appeal to the lowest common denominator, yet *Hitman* strives for a level of sophisticated complexity, sometimes muddled, that is bound to confuse some viewers.

Ordered to kill Nika Boronina (Olga Kurylenko), Belicoff's mistress, Agent 47 instead enlists her as a reluctant sidekick. Their relationship has slightly discordant echoes of Robert Redford and Faye Dunaway in *Three Days of the Condor* (1975). While luscious Nika does her best to seduce 47, he is oddly resistant. It is not clear whether the assassin must remain pure for his work—sex being much more distracting than murder—or the filmmakers are offering absolution to their sex-fearing fanboy audience base.

Agent 47's exploits take him from St. Petersburg to Istanbul and back, and include a bloody showdown with Belicoff's sleazy brother, Udre (Henry Ian Cusick), a purveyor of drugs, prostitutes, and weapons. All the while 47 is pursued by Mike Whittier (Dougray Scott) and Jenkins (Michael Offei) of Interpol. Their efforts are hindered by turf wars with Yuri Marklov (Robert Knepper) of the Russian secret police and Smith Jamison (James Faulkner) of the CIA. Almost as much screen time is devoted to jurisdictional issues as to mayhem.

Typical of reviewers' overreactions was that of Manohla Dargis of the *New York Times:* "It's bang, boom, blah—action movies for bored dummies." As mentioned previously, *Hitman* does require a certain degree of concentration. Its double and triple twists are amusing. Others complained about the gratuitous nudity, of which there is very little. The violence is primarily of the acrobatic variety, though the film does get nasty occasionally. Agent 47 tells a wounded opponent (Jean-Marc Bellu) to stay put and then shoots him in the shoulder to make sure—rough, manly humor in the tradition of James Bond and Dirty Harry.

In keeping with its video origins, *Hitman* is less stylized than unrealistic. Hundreds, perhaps thousands of bullets fly by the unharmed Agent 47, while he kills dozens effortlessly. His winning a swordfight with three assailants depends on their taking turns rather than ganging up on him at once. On another level is a title announcing the setting as "London—England," as if the viewers do not know where London is. Another reads "Russian Border—Turkey," though Turkey abuts Azerbaijan and Georgia, not Russia. At a train station, Agent 47 says he is following someone to track 9, but the sign reads track 6.

All this nonsense is kept going by a cast that does not condescend to the pulpy material. An exception is the stolid Scott, whose range consists of two types of befuddlement. One of the stars of *Lost* (begun in 2005), Cusick is frighteningly grubby as the most despicable character. Another television veteran, Knepper, of *Prison Break* (begun in 2005), looks and sounds Russian, his eyes hinting at conflicted motivations. Thomsen, a villain in *The World Is Not Enough* (1999), gives Belicoff the arrogant authority of the self-important politician. Unusual for a model, Kurylenko has an engaging twinkle in her eye, giving her stereotyped role some needed humanity.

Some reviewers called Olyphant miscast and robotic, but like some of the other cast members, he uses his expressive eyes to elevate Agent 47 beyond the mechanical qualities the role requires. Despite his profession, 47 is almost an innocent. He knows killing and does not stop to think about the ramifications of his acts. Until he meets Nika and begins experiencing new emotions, that is. One of the best touches provided by Woods and Gens comes when Agent 47 rejects the advances of an attractive woman (Anca Radici) in a bar and then resorts to reading a slick magazine article professing to be a man's guide to women. Far from robotic, Olyphant, one of the stars of *Deadwood* (2004–2006), gives Agent 47 a degree of sad sensitivity. He also speaks in a subtly cocky whisper reminiscent of Clint Eastwood's. Such a film would be monotonous without a likeable hero, and Olyphant makes the audience pull for Agent 47.

Hitman represents an improvement for Woods over his previous screenplay, *Swordfish* (2001), which is too complicated for its own good and often demeaning to its characters. Though a meager effort, *Hitman* is easier to take than 2007's previous assassination films *Smokin' Aces* and *Shoot 'Em Up*.

Michael Adams

CREDITS

Agent 47: Timothy Olyphant
Nika Boronina: Olga Kurylenko
Mike Whittier: Dougray Scott
Yuri Marklov: Robert Knepper
Mikhail Belicoff: Ulrich Thomsen
Udre Belicoff: Henry Ian Cusick
Jenkins: Michael Offei
Origin: France/USA
Language: English
Released: 2007
Production: Luc Besson, Chuck Gordon, Adrian Askarieh, Pierre-Ange Le Pogam; Anka Film, Daybreak Productions, Europa, Dune Entertainment, Prime Universe Productions; released by 20th Century-Fox
Directed by: Xavier Gens
Written by: Skip Woods
Cinematography by: Laurent Bares
Music by: Geoff Zanelli
Sound: Frederic Dubois
Editing: Carlo Rizzo, Antoine Vareille
Art Direction: Johann George
Costumes: Olivier Beriot
Production Design: Jacques Bufnoir
MPAA rating: R
Running time: 100 minutes

REVIEWS

Boston Globe Online. November 21, 2007.
Chicago Sun-Times Online. November 21, 2007.
Entertainment Weekly. November 30, 2007, p. 117.
Hollywood Reporter Online. November 20, 2007.
Los Angeles Times Online. November 21, 2007.
New York Times Online. November 21, 2007.
San Francisco Chronicle. November 21, 2007, p. E3.
Variety Online. November 20, 2007.
Washington Post Online. November 21, 2007.

QUOTES

Nika (to 47): "You know, you're really quite charming when you're not killing people."

TRIVIA

When the project was first announced, Vin Diesel was going to star as Agent 47. Despite the fact that Timothy Olyphant took over the role, Diesel is still credited as executive producer.

THE HOAX

Never let the truth get in the way of a good story.
    —Movie tagline
Based on a true story. Would we lie to you?
    —Movie tagline

Box Office: $7.1 million

The setting for Lasse Hallström's adaptation of Clifford Irving's memoir is significant: America in time of dissent, with a corrupt government in near collapse as the result of a disastrous war in Southeast Asia, and a paranoid President Nixon who apparently believes Howard Hughes intends to destroy him by releasing information to Clifford Irving concerning the president's brother Donald and his close advisor and friend, Bebe Robozo. This is an uncertain world where nothing is quite what it seems and where the truth is stretched and manipulated. In other words, it is the perfect sort of world for a rogue con man to bustle in, and Clifford Irving is clearly up to the challenge. *The Hoax* begins with writer Irving (Richard Gere) trying to close a deal with his publisher. The deal looks like a sure thing, but at the last minute it collapses, and Irving goes into an emotional meltdown. Desperate to find a high-profile subject for a book, Irving claims that the eccentric and reclusive billionaire tycoon Howard Hughes has entrusted him with writing his autobiography. This is not merely an unauthorized biography, mind you, but an autobiography, said to have Hughes's authorization and cooperation.

Irving cooked up this bizarre deception with his pal Richard Suskind (Alfred Molina), who is presented as a sort of historian-hack and researcher who wants to write a book about the homosexual King Richard the Lionhearted. The book is complicated by one serious biographical glitch, which causes Suskind to think of the project as "a study in medieval pederasty," making it a hard sell as a children's book. An "Author's Note" to the print edition makes clear that Suskind was far more than "Irving's researcher," as reported in the press. Irving admitted in 1981 that Suskind was "an author in his own right, and many of the passages in this book which deal with shared experiences have been written by him from my point of view." In fact, the movie tie-in edition of *The Hoax* is dedicated to Richard Suskind, who died in 1998.

Suskind should have a moderating influence on Irving, but no one could contain the runaway hubris that defines the perpetrator of this "Hoax." Of Hughes, Irving says: "He'll never come out of hiding long enough to denounce me because he's a lunatic hermit. And I am the spokesman for the lunatic hermit. So the more outrageous I sound, the more convincing I am." Screenwriter William Wheeler exploits the unknown here, making it the gimmick on which the plot turns. It is clear that eventually the scheme will collapse, and the audience waits for the other shoe to fall, as the band plays on. At first, McGraw-Hill senior editor Andrea Tate (Hope Davis) is skeptical, but Clifford's building confidence makes a believer out of her and her employer, the company president, played by Stanley Tucci. He is even able to figure out a way to have his wife (Marcia Gay Harden, with a German accent and wigs) set up a Swiss bank account and deposit the million-dollar check made out to "H.R. Hughes."

But, to be sure, Irving is the star here, the one who was actually able to sell the idea of the fake autobiography to McGraw-Hill and fool some of the smartest people in the publishing industry. Irving's previous book, *Fake!*, had been based on tape-recorded interviews with Elmyr de Hory, the art forger, as Irving describes it. What better preparation for his Hughes project and his next book, *The Hoax*, written just before he went to prison? The film shows Irving dressing up like Hughes, getting in "character," then dictating the faux "memoirs" into a tape recorder. Better than most, perhaps, Irving understood the process of forgery. The irony, of course, was that just as Irving and Suskind were attempting to exploit Howard Hughes, Hughes later exploited them, the movie insinuates, by using the fraudulent biography (informed by a box of documents mysteriously sent to Irving from Las Vegas) to put pressure on the Nixon administration and to save TWA, which was in danger of going under. What the movie shows is the story of the con man conned. In his preface to the movie tie-in edition of the book, Irving predicts that the producer, director, and screenwriter will have their way with his story: "They had every right to do that," Irving notes, "but I think it's important to realize that the movie doesn't tell the story of what actually happened. It never intended to do that." So the movie is a "hoax" of *The Hoax*? Or is Irving slyly planting at the top of his preface a reason for readers wanting to know the truth to buy the book? Further question: Is Clifford Irving capable of telling the truth? Consider the source.

The Hoax, then, is about deception and betrayal and truth and abuse on many levels. Clifford Irving is a philanderer who betrays his wife, repeatedly, by carrying on an affair with celebrity mistress Nina van Pallandt (Julie Delpy); more than simply a Paris Hilton figure, Van Pallandt was an actress who worked with Elliott Gould in Robert Altman's 1973 film *The Long Goodbye*. Throughout the narrative he betrays just about everyone with whom he comes into contact, McGraw-Hill most spectacularly and expensively, but also Richard Suskind in smaller and more subtle ways. Later on, Suskind betrays himself. After Irving is released from prison, he walks past a bookstore window in New York and sees Suskind autographing his book *Richard the Lion-Hearted* for youngsters, no doubt written as a partial truth, with the sodomy removed. Irving's moment of triumph in the film comes when a journalist who had actually interviewed Howard Hughes is brought in to evaluate the Irving manuscript and proclaims it to be authentic. But what can be said for an author whose best-known books are entitled *Fake!* and *The Hoax*? Irving seems to be a perfect cynic when he writes: "I believe that the past is fiction, the future is fantasy, and the present for the most part is an on-going hoax." That is simply pathetic.

The film conveys a rather different impression. Irving seems touched by madness, just as earlier he had been touched by inspiration, perhaps even genius, when he imagined that he had been visited by the ex-CIA goons of Howard Hughes, thrown out of a high-rise resort hotel's window only to land conveniently in the swimming pool below without injury, and then, having learned his lesson, had been returned to his home. Later, we see him having an imaginary conversation with Hughes's personal lawyer. This is a surreal stretch, but it is in keeping with the improbability of the story. *New Yorker* critic Anthony Lane saw this late-coming development as a mistake, however: As viewers are "plunged into talk of Watergate and airline-industry deals," he wrote, "the joy starts to drip from the movie, which cannot quite bear such reality."

Performances are quite strong throughout the movie, and Richard Gere, disguised with a prosthetic nose, is certainly convincing. One reviewer wondered if viewers could "swallow a Jewish Richard Gere," because of the nose? Arguably, in this instance, the film is probably better than the book, which suffers from the dominance of its unreliable narrator. The film is more detached and therefore more amusing and entertaining. Irving touts his project as "the greatest book of the century" in his pitch to the publisher. Suskind says to him a bit later, "you might have said 'of the decade,'" but, no, that would not have been consistent with Irving's overconfident style.

Opening reviews were typically overstated in a spring market starved for quality. *Rolling Stone* reviewer Peter Travers considered *The Hoax* a "devilish satire with mischievous wit." In *USA Today* Claudie Puig praised Richard Gere's "Oscar©-calibre performance" and also proclaimed Albert Molina's performance to be "excellent." In the *Wall Street Journal* Joe Morgenstern concurred that Molina was "sensationally funny." While such praise may seem extravagant, *The Hoax* might well be Richard Gere's career-defining performance. Several reviewers wrote that the film was uncommonly "smart," and David Ansen found it the "most surprising American movie so far this year," meaning merely the "most surprising" movie up to the Easter season. *Boston Globe* reviewer Wesley Morris, who compared *The Hoax* with the late Orson Welles's film *F for Fake* (1974), described the film as a "farce about how people, in their need to be wowed, simply see what they want to see." Certainly Morris has a point there, but the film is more than merely a "farce." Rather, it is a moral allegory for our times, touching upon corrupt government, a dangerous and devious president, and the malleability of truth. Anthony Lane's *New Yorker* review also mentioned Welles, "who took one look at Clifford Irving and pulled him out of the hat in *F for Fake* (1974)." Lane then quoted Welles, musing: "Does it say something for this age of ours that he could only make it big by fakery?" And that, presumably, was a rhetorical question. Lasse Hallström could hardly do better than to have his work compared to that of Orson Welles.

James M. Welsh

CREDITS

Clifford Irving: Richard Gere
Richard Suskind: Alfred Molina
Andrea Tate: Hope Davis
Edith Irving: Marcia Gay Harden
Shelton Fisher: Stanley Tucci
Nina Van Pallandt: Julie Delpy
Origin: USA
Language: English
Released: 2006
Production: Leslie Holleran, Betsy Beers, Joshua D. Maurer; Bob Yari Production, Mark Gordon Company, City Entertainment, Mutual Film, Stratus Film; released by Miramax Films
Directed by: Lasse Hallström
Written by: William Wheeler
Cinematography by: Oliver Stapleton
Music by: Carter Burwell
Sound: Allan Byer
Music Supervisor: Tracy McKnight
Editing: Andrew Mondshein
Costumes: David Robinson
Production Design: Mark Ricker
MPAA rating: R
Running time: 115 minutes

REVIEWS

Boxoffice Online. April 6, 2007.
Chicago Sun-Times Online. April 6, 2007.
Entertainment Weekly Online. April 4, 2007.
Hollywood Reporter Online. October 17, 2006.
Los Angeles Times Online. April 6, 2007.
New York Times Online. April 6, 2007.
San Francisco Chronicle. April 6, 2007, p. E1.
Variety Online. October 16, 2006.
Washington Post. April 6, 2007, p. C5.

QUOTES

Clifford Irving: "The more outrageous I sound, the more convincing I am."

TRIVIA

Richard Gere appeared with the real Nina Van Pallandt (played here by Julie Delpy) in *American Gigolo* (1980).

HONEYDRIPPER

This better be SOME Saturday night.
—Movie tagline

When John Sayles makes a movie, even one that is not based on a true story, you can count it on being richly authentic in terms of the place, the era, and the characters. His sixteenth film, *Honeydripper,* is no exception, but it is sweeter and less contentious than many of his recent efforts. It is also less preachy.

According to Sayles, he got the idea to make *Honeydripper* from growing up in the South in the 1950s and hearing all types of music, including gospel, blues, swing, and eventually rock. Later, he began to wonder what it must have been like when the first rural communities were introduced to the strange new sound and look of the electric guitar. And that is how he came to concoct a time and place for his story, rural Alabama in 1950.

His central character, Tyrone "Pinecone" Purvis (Danny Glover), is a musician who once played in New Orleans, but has settled in his middle age for running an out-of-the-way club, the Honeydripper Lounge, that is decidedly old-fashioned and therefore about to go out of business. Unlike his competitor down the road, who attracts young people simply by playing the jukebox, Pinecone sticks to playing the piano to accompany an old

Ma Rainey-style blues singer, Bertha Mae (Mable John). But when he is faced with the prospect of losing his business to his landlord, this proud black man bites the bullet and books the young traveling sensation Guitar Sam, hoping that one very successful Saturday night will provide him the funds he needs to stay in business. It is his first concession to musical modernity.

When Sonny (Gary Clark, Jr.), a young man with a guitar case, steps off the train, having ridden a boxcar and landed in the town by accident, it is not hard to imagine how he might figure in the plot. *Honeydripper* lacks the complexity of some recent Sayles movies such as *Silver City* (2004), but it still has richly drawn characters and plenty of insights into human relations of its era. Pinecone's wife Delilah (Lisa Gay Hamilton) is a religious person who cannot quite take the step to give herself completely to a tent-revival preacher and his fundamentalist sermons, but she is tempted to do so, to save her soul from the influences of her sinful, drinking husband if for nothing else. Their daughter China Doll (Yaya DaCosta) is a bright-eyed girl who suffers from a congenitally weak heart and plans to go to beauty college because the brochures say it is a portable skill that would allow her to travel the world. Of course, she falls for the charms of the vagabond guitarist.

Sayles gives us glimpses into the brutal white power structure that still runs the town, especially in the person of the sheriff (Stacy Keach), who wants a take of the action in exchange for overlooking some of the transgressions in the music clubs. He also can be charming, threatening, or downright brutal. When he finds Sonny walking down the road in search of a job in the next town, he arrests him for vagrancy and takes him to the judge, who without a trial immediately sentences him to work in the cotton fields. On the other side of the coin, Mary Steenburgen plays the genteel wife of the mayor for whom Delilah works as a maid; she is well-intentioned but patronizing.

With its keen insights into social relationships in the mid-twentieth-century racist South, at bottom, *Honeydripper* is a movie about the coming of the modern age, as represented by the precursors of rock-and-roll music and a newly rebellious attitude. It is a fascinating glimpse of people caught between the old ways and the new. As a business owner, Pinecone has something precious, his dignity, even though he brings in less income than his wife does being a servant to the white folks. To him, it is worth the struggles because it is a step out of oppression and servitude. Most black folks in the area are still picking cotton, and they still get cheated by their bosses; an upstart from Memphis questions why they put up with it. It is the beginnings of the stirrings of the civil rights era.

But the most startling symbol of the coming change is in young Sonny's guitar case, and the turning point of the movie is when Pinecone and his partner Maceo (Charles S. Dutton) pull it out of the case and examine it. It is a guitar with no holes in the body, just a trapezoidal box, with a wire attached to what looks like a radio set mounted on a board, which is actually an amplifier. Pinecone initially thinks the electric guitar is ludicrous, but he soon changes his mind about that.

Infectiously appealing and low-key, *Honeydripper* shines as a typically insightful, well-researched Sayles saga, a glimpse of a receding time when the century turned from rural culture and backwoods music to something more audacious and modern. The film's characters are both fully human and charmingly sympathetic, and there is even a devilish muse, Possum (Keb' Mo'), a blind guitar player who knows the dark secrets of Pinecone's past.

With plenty of foreshadowing, it looks like Sayles is setting up one of his complex tragic endings. But intimations of a coming disastrous showdown do not materialize, and even the girl's disease has no consequence. Sayles opts for a feel-good ending that is pleasant but a little sappy. And he includes a lecture by Pinecone about the need to end black-on-black violence that seems like more of a stab at political correctness than a logical consequence of the plot. It is the only didactic moment in an otherwise appealing film that is unique both in its casting and perspective. The music is also wonderful, including a couple of songs written by the talented director himself.

The hallmark of a John Sayles movie is that it is securely grounded in its setting. From the presence of a nearby army base and references to the new war (the Korean War), to the knowing riffs on a variety of musical genres, to the way the characters speak and behave, there is abundant authenticity and a wise perspective about the underlying issues of the day, including those of race, class, and gender. Sayles even researched how to pick cotton, ferreting out the few locals who were still willing to talk about it.

The acting is also rich and nuanced, as is usually the case in a Sayles film. The casting is pitch-perfect, with Glover balancing his character perfectly between old-fashioned values and a begrudging awareness of the coming changes. Gary Clark, Jr. is fresh and intriguing as the new guitar hero, and even the small roles are played with gusto and full appreciation; they are all written carefully and respectfully.

Sayles and his longtime partner, producer Maggie Renzi, financed the film and distributed it on their own. That gave them total control, but necessarily limited the film's exposure. It is a truly independent film, with an honest perspective and a smart, sharp script by the veteran Sayles.

Michael Betzold

CREDITS

Tyrone Purvis: Danny Glover
Delilah: Lisa Gay Hamilton
China Doll: Yaya DaCosta
Maceo: Charles S. Dutton
Sonny Blake: Gary Clark, Jr.
Slick: Vondie Curtis-Hall
Sheriff: Stacy Keach
Bertha Mae: Mable John
Origin: USA
Language: English
Released: 2007
Production: Maggie Renzi; Honeydripper Films, Anarchist's Convention Films; released by Emerging Pictures
Directed by: John Sayles
Written by: John Sayles
Cinematography by: Dick Pope
Music by: Mason Daring
Sound: Judy Karp
Music Supervisor: Tim Bernett
Editing: John Sayles
Art Direction: Eloise Stammerjohn
Costumes: Hope Hanafin
Production Design: Toby Corbett
MPAA rating: PG-13
Running time: 123 minutes

REVIEWS

Hollywood Reporter Online. September 12, 2007.
Los Angeles Times Online. December 28, 2007.
New York Times Online. December 28, 2007.
Variety Online. September 11, 2007.
Village Voice Online. December 26, 2007.

TRIVIA

Singer Mable John is the sister of legendary blues performer Little Willie John.

THE HOST
(Gwoemul)

It is lurking behind you.
—Movie tagline

Box Office: $2.2 million

When it comes to pan-Asian cinema, the longtime (and rarely challenged) king of the monster movie has been Japan, home of Godzilla and Rodan. The nation essentially invented the *kaiju*, man-in-suit monster genre—through the works of film studios such as Toho, among others—and few modern monster films (the 2008 Paramount release *Cloverfield* comes to mind) escape comparisons to the early Japanese masters. But in 2006 South Korea came blasting onto the monster landscape with *The Host* (*Gwoemul*), a groundbreaking creature feature that became the highest grossing film in the country's history. (It was released theatrically in the United States in 2007.) To his great credit, director Joon-ho Bong, already popular in South Korea thanks to 2003's *Memories of Murder* (a *Zodiac*-esque serial-killer investigation drama), delivered one of the most effective and affecting monster movies in decades, drawing frequent comparisons to such genre staples as Steven Spielberg's *Jaws* (1975).

The Host succeeds largely due to Bong's skillful ability to both embrace and reject what some consider the defining characteristics of the modern monster movie. The film assembles such disparate elements as family drama, bureaucratic satire, class struggle, and political commentary, marries them with a cracking, fast-paced monster thriller, and somehow the finished product works brilliantly. There is nothing heavy-handed or clumsy about any aspect of *The Host*. Every thematic and plot element is balanced with a juggler's grace, delivering a much more satisfying and emotional pay-off than your average Godzilla movie. Logan Hill from *New York* magazine raved that "*The Host* is the ultimate monster movie," commenting further that the film "scrambles small-scale storytelling, big-time effects, laughs, and startling scares in just the right amounts."

The film opens with an American military scientist instructing his South Korean assistant to dump voluminous bottles of noxious chemicals into Seoul's Han River, simply because the bottles are dusty. This scene is the most overt of the moments of anti-American sentiment throughout the film, a recurring political theme that Bong handles deftly, never allowing it to become oppressive or didactic. America has long played a major (and some would argue, intrusive) role in South Korean politics, and *The Host* reflects a South Korea where, despite the frustrations of the average citizen, the local government is more than willing to hand over control of their internal affairs to the United States. We move several years into the future and are introduced to the Park family, a lower-class clan whose patriarch Hie-bong (Hie-bong Byeon) owns a small refreshment stand on the shores of the Han River. His eldest son, Park Gang-Du (Kang-ho Song), is an oafish slacker who hangs around the kiosk all day, waiting for his clever daughter, Hyun-seo (Ah-sung Ko), to return from school. Gang-Du's younger brother, Nam-il (Hae-il Park), is a former student radical (now an alcoholic, unemployed college graduate), and his younger sister, Nam-Joo (Du-na Bae), is an Olympic-class archer who always seems to choke in the final round of competitions. The siblings struggle to get along with each other, and a subtle sense of failure seems to hang over the family.

One morning, Gang-Du and a crowd of onlookers notice something strange hanging off the Han River-spanning Wonhyo Bridge, and that is when all hell begins to break loose. Perhaps Bong's most bold choice in *The Host* is his insistence on showing us the monster within the first ten minutes of the film. Traditionally, monster movies tease their audiences with brief glimpses of their terrifying creatures until the third act, when the protagonists finally witness exactly what they are facing. (This is probably most famously embodied by Roy Scheider's famous "You're going to need a bigger boat" moment in *Jaws*.) However, in *The Host*, Bong never hides what the Park family is facing, a shocking rejection of monster movie tradition that works ridiculously well. Barely after the opening credits have ended, we are shown the full glory of the mutated Han River behemoth—presumably created by the American-dumped toxic chemicals—as he swims toward the shores and begins plowing through crowds of terrified passersby. The creature, designed by New Zealand's Weta Workshop, among others, is an evolutionary throwback: part-fish, part-dinosaur, with a gaping, teeth-filled maw and a vicious series of victim-grabbing tentacles.

After the monster's initial rampage, it retreats back into the Han River, grabbing Gang-Du's daughter Hyun-seo at the last moment and dragging her away from her father. A military quarantine of the area soon follows, and the despondent Park family, assuming that Hyun-seo is dead, is taken to a hospital for further study of their exposure to the monster. Both the South Korean and the now-involved American governments believe (or, at least "claim") that the monster is the host of a powerful virus that potentially could kill anyone exposed to it. Throughout the rest of the film, the veracity of the virus claim is constantly challenged, and it appears that the disease is a myth created to control access to the Han River and those who witnessed the monster attack. During his forced quarantine, Gang-Du receives a faint cell-phone call from Hyun-seo, who is alive and trapped in the creature's nesting grounds in a local sewer. When the Park family tries to inform the authorities, they are met with a ceaseless series of bureaucratic denials. Realizing that no one is going to help them, the Park family escapes from the military hospital (becoming fugitives in the process) and sneaks into the Han River quarantine zone, desperate to save Hyun-seo before her time runs out.

The Park family's almost fanatical devotion to Hyun-seo springs from both familial love and what the young girl represents. While all of the other Park siblings seem to have failed lives, Hyun-seo is a beacon of goodwill and affection. The family doesn't want to rescue her as much as they *need* to, which makes the resulting hunt for her underground prison all the more exciting and vital. After several aborted attempts to find and kill the monster—involving the family bribing their way into the quarantine zone—Hie-bong falls prey to the creature, Gang-Du falls back into military custody, and Nam-il and Nam-Joo are separated. Meanwhile, trapped in the monster's sewer lair, Hyun-seo tries to escape on her own, while protecting a poor orphan boy who also was captured by the creature. The rest of the film revolves around the Park siblings' fight to regroup and re-attack the monster, Hyun-seo's increasingly desperate escape attempts, and the looming threat of the United States government's plans for confronting the monster with an ominous chemical bioweapon called Agent Yellow.

While *The Host* succeeds brilliantly as simply a superior monster movie—providing some of the most thrilling, nail-biting action sequences in recent memory—it is also amazingly effective in its portrayal of the idiosyncrasies of the struggling Park family. If Hyun-seo represents the best of the Park family, then the Park siblings' quest to rescue her brings out the best in themselves. Gang-Du is a listless slacker, but his sense of parental responsibility reawakens his sense of purpose and drive. Nam-il had gone from being a cause-driven radical to an over-educated corporate reject, and his skills with skirting the law and violently opposing his enemies re-emerge during his final battle with the creature. Similarly, Nam-Joo, an archer who is constantly criticized for not knowing when to let go, finds in her quest to save Hyun-seo that she can act when the time is right. This model of a dysfunctional family having their best qualities reborn due to the aspirations of one of their youngest members caused *The Host* to be compared to Jonathan Dayton and Valerie Faris's award-winning *Little Miss Sunshine* (2006) almost as frequently as *Jaws*, and it is an apt comparison.

In the end, Joon-ho Bong's *The Host* works so well because the director rejected the urge to make the film "just" a monster movie, approaching the traditional Godzilla scenario from an atypical perspective and infusing this genre tale with the drama, comedy, and thrills of the best that cinema has to offer. Move over, Japan. South Korea is now a serious contender for the monster-movie crown of the twenty-first century.

Tom Burns

CREDITS

Nam-Joo: Du-na Bae
Gang-Du: Kang-ho Song
Hie-bong: Hie-bong Byeon
Nam-il: Hae-il Park
Hyun-seo: Ah-sung Ko
Origin: South Korea
Released: 2006
Production: Yong-bae Choi; Showbox/Mediaplex,
  Chungeorahm Film; released by Magnolia Pictures
Directed by: Joon-ho Bong
Written by: Joon-ho Bong, Chul-hyun Baek, Jun-won Ha
Cinematography by: Hyung-ku Kim
Music by: Byung-woo Lee
Sound: Tae-young Choi
Editing: Seon Min Kim
Costumes: Sang-gyeong Jo
Production Design: Seong-hie Ryu
MPAA rating: R
Running time: 119 minutes

REVIEWS

New York Times Online. March 9, 2007.
San Francisco Chronicle Online. March 9, 2007.
Seattle Post-Intelligencer. March 8, 2007.

QUOTES

Park Hie-bong: "Have any of you heard it? The heartbreak of a parent who's lost a child…When a parent's heart breaks, the sound can travel for miles. So I really need to say this to you. Be as nice to Gang-du as you can. Don't scold him, okay?"

TRIVIA

Director Joon-ho Bong and the designer of the creature nicknamed it Steve Buscemi, based on the actor's screen persona and the way he acted in the movie *Fargo* (1996).

HOSTEL: PART II

Box Office: $17.5 million

Horror films often serve as a podium for social commentary. This arguably can be said of the exploitative *Hostel* series as written and directed by Eli Roth. The first installment, in 2005, was a satire of the "ugly American," acting in a brash, smug manner and treating the rest of the world as its doormat, strutting through foreign countries with a grandiose sense of entitlement. It mocked the zeitgeist of arrogant immunity held by stereotypical Americans traveling abroad, while question-

ing the wisdom of such a temperament in a post-9/11 world where this ostentatious sense of bravado has proven to be a grave mistake. It also mirrored the torture tactics undertaken by United States military personnel at the Abu Ghraib prison in Iraq. In *Hostel: Part II*, Roth takes the premise of the original film to another level. The sequel continues to unfold the depraved, malevolent undertakings of the organization Elite Hunting, which caters to the sadistic murderous fantasies held by certain members of the haut monde.

The film begins by snipping the lone loose end from the original. The sole survivor, Paxton (Jay Hernandez) is plagued by nightmares stemming from his ghoulish experiences of mutilation. Missing two fingers severed from him at Elite Hunting's torture factory, Paxton is in hiding at the house of his girlfriend's grandmother, paranoid that the extensive network of the "Splatterati" will find him. To paraphrase the famous Henry Kissinger: "Just because you're paranoid doesn't mean they're not after you;" this is true for Paxton. His head is delivered in a box to Elite's CEO, Sasha (Milan Knazko), who maintains in his mansion a macabre, hidden boardroom adorned with several previous victims' heads perched on spikes. (Eli Roth had a replica of his own head crafted and placed on a stick).

Remaining true to the abundant amount of torture porn in the first installment, Roth strays a bit by fleshing out the main characters in this film. The three American college coeds profiled here evoke greater sympathy and present as more refined. The protagonist males in the original were merely insipid, prurient frat boys determined to inseminate Europe. Whitney (Bijou Phillips), Beth (Lauren German), and Lorna (Heather Matarazzo) are far more likeable, so the audience grieves all the more the trio's naiveté that leads them into a horrific situation.

Another development is an additional story line paralleling the girls' that provides a sketchily drawn biography of the lives of two of the grisly organization's clientele. Todd (Richard Burgi) is a slick entrepreneurial mogul who has won an online global auction for his chance to become a murdering tormentor. He appropriates a victim for his beta male buddy, Stuart (Roger Bart). The duo often has talked about killing another human being in order to obtain an ineffable, dominating vibe that they believe others will sense in them as animals sense fear. The pair hypothesize that killing victims that are bound and gagged for them and presented like food at a smorgasbord will transform them into übermenschen, a hostile conceit. In a sense, Stuart and Todd are analogous to the testosterone-driven college boys in the first *Hostel* film. Disturbingly, the duo provides most of the movie's few comedic moments.

They are cast as the Laurel and Hardy of antisocial misogynists.

What makes *Hostel: Part II* a compelling addition to the horror film industry is the fact that the evil afflicting the antagonists is not preternatural—it is a twisted submerged nook found in human nature. The audience can identify with suburban, white-collar guys like Stuart and Todd. They also can identify with the normality of the girls, who are usually sequestered safely within the system of academia. Most of the genre's monsters are either consorts or products of factors rooted in the realm of the supernatural. Roth' accomplishment is in holding a mirror to the audience, showing the dark corners of its own society. In a time where the top stories are all too often about serial killers or mass murderers, Roth perpetrates the notion that the real horror is not Michael Myers, but the quiet man walking by with a briefcase and a Starbucks cup, who happens to live next door.

Roth adds a few more creative touches, including a surprise ending that is foreshadowed in the script when we learn that Beth, the main character in the film, is an extremely wealthy heiress. In another nice touch, Roth's avowed favorite director, Ruggero Deodato (director of the 1980 Italian horror classic *Cannibal Holocaust*) makes a cameo as a human flesh-eating client of Elite Hunting.

David M. Roberts

CREDITS

Beth: Lauren German
Whitney: Bijou Phillips
Lorna: Heather Matarazzo
Axelle: Vera Jordanova
Stuart: Roger Bart
Todd: Richard Burgi
Miroslav: Stanislav Ianevski
Paxton: Jay Hernandez
Stephanie: Jordan Ladd
The Professor: Edwige Fenech
Sasha: Milan Knazko
Origin: USA
Language: English
Released: 2007
Production: Mike Fleiss, Eli Roth, Chris Briggs; Screen Gems, Raw Nerve, Next Entertainment; released by Lionsgate
Directed by: Eli Roth
Written by: Eli Roth
Cinematography by: Milan Chadima
Music by: Nathan Barr
Sound: Tomas Belohradsky
Editing: George Folsey, Jr., Brad E. Wilhite

Art Direction: David Baxa
Costumes: Susanna Puisto
Production Design: Robb Wilson King
MPAA rating: R
Running time: 94 minutes

REVIEWS

Austin Chronicle Online. June 8, 2007.
Boston Globe Online. June 8, 2007.
Chicago Sun-Times Online. June 8, 2007.
Entertainment Weekly. June 22, 2007, p. 52.
Hollywood Reporter Online. June 8, 2007.
Los Angeles Times Online. June 8, 2007.
New York Times Online. June 8, 2007.
Premiere Online. June 8, 2007.
San Francisco Chronicle. June 11, 2007, p. D2.
Variety Online. June 7, 2007.

QUOTES

Whitney (on rich pal Beth): "She could pretty much buy Slovakia if she wanted to."

TRIVIA

In the full trailer, you can clearly see in the background on television that two girls are watching *Pulp Fiction*, directed by Quentin Tarantino, executive producer of the Hostel films.

AWARDS

Nomination:

Golden Raspberries 2007: Worst Horror Movie, Worst Sequel/Prequel.

HOT FUZZ

Big cops. Small town. Moderate violence.
—Movie tagline
They're bad boys. They're die hards. They're lethal weapons. They are…Hot Fuzz.
—Movie tagline

Box Office: $23.6 million

Edgar Wright, Simon Pegg, and Nick Frost scored a surprise critical and commercial hit with *Shaun of the Dead* (2004), their affectionate parody of zombie films. With a bigger budget for *Hot Fuzz*, they tackle the action genre associated with producer Jerry Bruckheimer, director Michael Bay, and actors like Bruce Willis. The comedy comes from juxtaposing explosions and car chases with the banality of everyday life in a sleepy Gloucestershire village.

Nicholas Angel (Simon Pegg) is the best police constable in London. Because his colleagues are jealous that his arrest rate is 400 percent higher than that of anyone else, his boss (Bill Nighy) dispatches Nick to Sanford, where the biggest problems appear to be under-age drinking and a swan on the loose. Even before reporting for duty, Nick arrests several miscreants, including a drunk driver that he is shocked to discover the next morning is his new partner, Danny Butterman (Nick Frost). Nick's new boss, Inspector Frank Butterman (Jim Broadbent), Danny's father, assures him that Sanford is crime-free.

With the notable exception of the elusive swan, Butterman's assessment of the village seems accurate. Everyone is friendly, not too eccentric, and the village prides itself on being a perfect example of its type. Then lawyer Martin Blower (David Threlfall) and his mistress, Eve Draper (Lucy Punch), are killed in a horrendous traffic mishap. When more deaths follow, Nick becomes suspicious, especially of supermarket owner Simon Skinner (Timothy Dalton), who always seems to be near the scene. Nick's suspicions are mocked by detectives Andy Cartwright (Rafe Spall) and Andy Wainwright (Paddy Considine), who call the newcomer and his partner "Crockett and Tubby."

While most reviewers of *Hot Fuzz* have emphasized its satire of action-film conventions, much of the film is a spoof of British cozy mysteries, exemplified by Agatha Christie's Miss Marple novels and stories. In this genre, life in a small village seems boringly normal until one or more deaths reveal a dark secret or two. In the case of Christie in particular, the obvious solution to the crime turns out to be a red herring, with the real culprit or culprits having an unexpected motivation. Such is the case with *Hot Fuzz,* when the key to the mystery proves to be both more complex than Nick has assumed and, in another sense, simpler, with a possible nod to Christie's Hercule Poirot classic *Murder on the Orient Express* (1934).

Hot Fuzz also owes a debt to the long-running British television series *Midsomer Murders* (begun in 1997), which carries on the Miss Marple tradition, though more darkly and with a tad more sex. Several *Hot Fuzz* cast members have appeared on *Midsomer Murders,* with Punch in one episode suffering a violent murder almost as gruesome as the one here. The film pokes fun at a frequent theme of mainstream British fiction and films: that progress will somehow destroy the essence of tranquil village life. According to *Hot Fuzz,* those who want to preserve the status quo pose as much danger as those who hope to alter it.

Yet the focus of *Hot Fuzz* is American action films. Wright, the director and cowriter, employs the tech-

niques of this genre long before guns are drawn. Simply showing Nick hanging and unhanging his jacket involves the kinds of close-ups and quick cuts associated with Michael Bay in films such as *The Rock* (1996). Danny is obsessed with action films, especially Bay and Bruckheimer's *Bad Boys II* (2003) and Kathryn Bigelow's *Point Break* (1991). Danny treats Nick to DVD screenings of these two films, and the experience brings the partners even closer. As with *Shaun of the Dead, Hot Fuzz* sends up the implicit homoerotic connection between the protagonists of buddy movies, but does so without any "nudge nudge, wink wink" smirking. Wright and cowriter Pegg have genuine affection for action films and never condescend to them, making their satire all the more appealing.

Shaun of the Dead is funny because of the juxtaposition of horrific events with the domestic travails Pegg's character experiences with his girlfriend, roommates, mother, and stepfather. In *Hot Fuzz,* when the guns come out and the cars are revved up, the experience is all the more amusing for occurring in the idyllic setting the filmmakers have so painstakingly established. The score by David Arnold, whose credits include three James Bond films, provides non-ironic action music throughout the film.

Some of the verbal humor flops, but most of it is hilarious. Inspector Butterman punishes his underlings for foul-ups by making them eat cake and other sweets. His response to Danny's drunk driving arrest is "Well, let's just say we won't be running out of Chunky Monkey for the next month." Danny is disappointed when Nick passes up a chance for an easy one-liner after depositing a criminal in a freezer. Pegg contributes to the hilarity by underplaying his role, making Nick laconic and expressionless in the tradition of Clint Eastwood.

Dalton gives an especially lively performance, having fun at sending up his James Bond persona. Edward Woodward is good as a citizen appointed to make certain nothing disrupts the village's self-image. The denouement of *Hot Fuzz* acknowledges Woodward's best-known film, *The Wicker Man* (1973). The cast also includes such excellent British character actors as David Bradley, Ron Cook, Kenneth Cranham, Paul Freeman, Karl Johnson, Anne Reid, Billie Whitelaw, and Stuart Wilson, a veteran of *Lethal Weapon II* (1989). As with spoofs such as *Airplane!* (1980), these performers play their roles as straight as possible in the circumstances, making the jokes all the funnier.

Shaun of the Dead won Wright, Pegg, and Frost many fans in the film industry. When a journalist asked Pegg what his next role would be, the actor replied *Mission: Impossible III* (2006), only for Tom Cruise to give him a part. Quentin Tarantino and Robert Rodriguez asked Wright to direct one of the trailers, "Don't," that appeared in *Grindhouse* (2007). An almost unrecognizable Steve Coogan plays a small role as one of Nick's London superiors, and Peter Jackson, dressed as Santa, stabs Nick in the hand. The best of the *Hot Fuzz* cameo performances however, is Cate Blanchett's as Jeanine, Nick's London girlfriend, a crime-scene technician. Only the masked Jeanine's eyes are visible as she tells Nick she is dumping him for a coworker.

It is not necessary to catch all the in-jokes, which include verbal and visual references to numerous films, to enjoy *Hot Fuzz.* A more wide-ranging and sophisticated achievement than *Shaun of the Dead,* it delights on many levels.

Michael Adams

CREDITS

Sgt. Nicholas Angel: Simon Pegg
PC Danny Butterman: Nick Frost
Inspector Frank Butterman: Jim Broadbent
DS Andy Wainwright: Paddy Considine
Simon Skinner: Timothy Dalton
Joyce Cooper: Billie Whitelaw
Tom Weaver: Edward Woodward
DS Cartwright: Rafe Spall
PC Doris Thatcher: Olivia Colman
Rev. Philip Shooter: Paul Freeman
Metropolitan Sergeant: Martin Freeman
Metropolitan Chief Inspector Kenneth: Bill Nighy
Metropolitan Police Inspector: Steve Coogan
Jeanine: Cate Blanchett
Thief dressed as Santa: Peter Jackson
Sgt. Tony Fisher: Kevin Eldon
Dr. Robin Hatcher: Stuart Wilson
Origin: Great Britain, USA, France
Language: English
Released: 2007
Production: Nira Park, Tim Bevan, Eric Fellner; Working Title Films, Big Talk Productions, Ingenious Film Partners, StudioCanal; released by Rogue Pictures
Directed by: Edgar Wright
Written by: Simon Pegg, Edgar Wright
Cinematography by: Jess Hall
Music by: David Arnold
Sound: Richard Flynn, Julian Slater
Editing: Chris Dickens
Costumes: Annie Hardinge
Production Design: Marcus Rowland
MPAA rating: R
Running time: 121 minutes

REVIEWS

Boxoffice Online. April 20, 2007.
Chicago Sun-Times Online. April 20, 2007.

Entertainment Weekly. April 27, 2007, p. 116.
Guardian Online. February 16, 2007.
Hollywood Reporter Online. April 20, 2007.
Los Angeles Times Online. April 20, 2007.
New York Times Online. April 20, 2007.
The Observer Online. February 18, 2007.
San Francisco Chronicle. April 20, 2007, p. E1.
Variety Online. February 20, 2007.
Washington Post. April 20, 2007, p. C5.

QUOTES

Nicholas Angel (shouting): "Have you ever wondered why, why the crime rate in Sandford is so low, yet the accident rate is so high?"

TRIVIA

Lead character "Nicholas Angel" was named in homage to Nick Angel who worked as music supervisor for this film as well as *Shaun of the Dead* (2004).

HOT ROD

Smack destiny in the face.
—Movie tagline

Box Office: $13.9 million

Rod Kimble, played by *Saturday Night Live* comic Andy Samberg, is a socially awkward, overly sincere teenage stuntman wannabe convinced that no matter the odds, he will succeed. When faced with the prospect of raising $50,000 for his stepfather's life-saving heart operation, Rod dreams up a most unusual way to raise the money—he will jump his moped over fifteen school buses. His cause seems noble, but the reality is he wants to save his stepfather Frank so that he can get one more shot at beating the old man in hand-to-hand combat and complete this rite of passage as defined by Frank. Like so many recent teenage film characters, Rod is the bumbling, loveable, stuck-in-the-1980s kid who seems oblivious to his overt nerdiness—he actually thinks he is one of the cool kids, destined for greatness and the hand of the girl he covets.

Hot Rod is the first feature film for Samberg, Jorma Taccone, and Akiva Schaffer, who parlayed the success of their Internet digital short *Lazy Sunday* into *Saturday Night Live* stardom, with Andy Samberg performing in front of the camera and Taccone and Schaffer working as writers. Like so many *Saturday Night Live* veterans before them, the trio, dubbed the Lonely Island Comedy Troupe, attempt the final leap to the silver screen via the Lorne Michaels-produced *Hot Rod.* However, it is a big jump from a three-minute digital short on YouTube to an eighty-eight-minute feature, and *Hot Rod* is not quite able to make it over the final bus. The film attempts to be a quaint, hand-crafted, almost deconstructed comedy, with its lack of punch line set-ups and its '80s pop culture references, but it merely comes across as a sloppy collection of lowbrow one-liners and individual skits.

The film is directed by Schaffer and written by Pam Brady, a longtime *South Park* contributor whose two film credits are *South Park: Bigger Longer & Uncut* (1999) and *Team America: World Police* (2004). While Brady gets the writing credit, much of the blame should fall on the ad-lib comedy of Samberg and Taccone, which only serves to enforce the film's already disjointed quality.

The cast includes the Academy Award©-winner Sissy Spacek, who plays it straight as Rod's mother Marie Powell, and Isla Fisher as Denise, the object of Rod's infatuation, who is conspicuously denied any opportunity to demonstrate her comic skills. Samberg's longtime collaborator Taccone plays Kevin Powell, Rod's stepbrother, and the two exhibit the type of chemistry that comes with such familiarity. Rod's stepfather Frank Powell is played by *Deadwood*'s excellent Ian McShane, who shows off his physical comedy skills in the over-the-top fistfights he and Samberg engage in throughout the film, including in the grand finale, a rollicking collection of tried-and-true bits, including use of Chinese throwing stars and bricks to the face, crashing through windows, and a Tai Chi move that results in a most embarrassing climax. Naturally, *SNL* alumni may be seen in supporting roles, including Chris Parnell and Bill Hader.

The film is set in modern-day Anytown, USA but was shot in British Columbia, Canada. Most of the characters and jokes revolve around 1980s pop culture references that run the gamut from *Footloose* (1984) to AM disc jockeys and big, 1980s-style mustaches. The filmmakers even include a parody training sequence as Rod prepares for the movie's climactic stunt, his attempt to jump fifteen school buses—exactly one more than the late pop icon Evel Knievel successfully navigated. Standout scenes include the aforementioned training montage and a truly imaginative scenario involving Rod's vision of a grilled cheese sandwich and a taco in a battle royal that ends with the triumphant taco pummeling the sandwich with a folding chair. These scenes aside, the creators of *Lazy Sunday* should be able to do so much better.

The homage to the 1980s is continued on the soundtrack, which includes no less than eight songs by 1980s Swedish supergroup Europe (including the nearly ubiquitous "The Final Countdown"), with a dose of George Michael's "One More Try," and MC Hammer's "Too Legit to Quit" thrown in for good measure.

Hot Rod does have some funny moments, but they are far too infrequent and random, and the film lacks the structure and craftsmanship necessary to make this series of gags work as a feature-length movie.

Michael White

CREDITS

Denise: Isla Fisher
Rod Kimble: Andy Samberg
Kevin Powell: Jorma Taccone
Dave: Bill Hader
Marie Powell: Sissy Spacek
Frank Powell: Ian McShane
Jonathan: Will Arnett
Barry Pasternak: Chris Parnell
Cathy: Brittney Irvin
Rico: Danny McBride
Origin: USA
Language: English
Released: 2007
Production: Lorne Michaels, John Goldwyn; Lonely Island; released by Paramount
Directed by: Akiva Shaffer
Written by: Pam Brady
Cinematography by: Andrew Dunn
Music by: Trevor Rabin
Sound: Michael McGee
Music Supervisor: Stephen Baker
Editing: Malcolm Campbell
Art Direction: Chris August, Catherine Ircha
Costumes: Tish Monaghan
Production Design: Stephen Altman
MPAA rating: PG-13
Running time: 88 minutes

REVIEWS

Boston Globe Online. August 3, 2007.
Chicago Sun-Times Online. August 3, 2007.
Entertainment Weekly Online. August 2, 2007.
Hollywood Reporter Online. August 2, 2007.
Los Angeles Times Online. August 3, 2007.
New York Times Online. August 3, 2007.
Rolling Stone Online. August 2, 2007.
Variety Online. June 29, 2007.
Washington Post Online. August 3, 2007.

QUOTES

Rod Kimble: "The front of his face exploded out the back of his skull. He died instantly, the next day."

THE HOTTEST STATE

Ethan Hawke's second feature film as a director is slightly more successful than his previous attempt, helming the poorly received *Chelsea Walls* (2001), a film about struggling artists living at the Chelsea Hotel. Criticized for being pretentious and immature, *Chelsea Walls* was based on Nicole Burdette's play and written by the playwright. Hawke wrote the screenplay for *The Hottest State,* based on his semiautobiographical novel, and while it, too, is pretentious and immature, it is more authentic than *Chelsea Walls* in that the characters are more believable but no less likable or sympathetic.

The minimal yet disjointed plot involves struggling actor William (Mark Webber) and aspiring singer Sara (Catalina Sandino Moreno), lovers bridging the gulf over a number of clichéd obstacles. She is wealthy and well-bred from Connecticut. He is a poor boy from Texas whose young parents parted early and badly. She is Latina; he is white. Begging comparisons to *Romeo and Juliet* does not help Hawke's already long-winded and long-running film, with William spouting soliloquies from Shakespeare's play about young star-crossed lovers under Sara's window after their affair has soured. Hawke employs a full range of well-worn cinematic techniques in an attempt to achieve the sort of poetic and inspired film he craves but cannot manage to achieve, and the audience is subjected to many slow-motion segments, a plethora of flashbacks, voice-overs, and an insistent jazz soundtrack.

What Hawke does manage to deliver are attractive lead characters who are nonetheless unbaked and unsympathetic. After meeting in a New York bar, William and Sara appear to fall madly in love, bonding over their shared love of the arts, and move in together. Things are not always as they appear, however, and because they are artists, Hawke suggests that they are more in love with being in love than with each other. They take a romantic trip to Mexico, where they couple for the first time and nearly wed. Upon the return to New York, Sara abruptly breaks it off with William for no apparent reason, driving William to become a desperate, half-crazed stalker.

This plot twist—Sara's unfeeling, cold rejection of William—renders her unlikable to the audience, which thus far has been given only their relationship to invest in. The same is true for the character William, who becomes so unglued that the audience deems him equally unworthy of caring about in any meaningful way. Both characters already are sketchily drawn, with few character traits highlighted, save their artistic natures. Being Hawke's alter ego, the character of William is allowed more range and depth, displaying deep emotion and humor, and a growing mania resulting in answering-machine messages to Sara that are sadly funny in their utter desperation.

Flashbacks of William's childhood in Texas (the state, along with the emotional state of young love, that is referenced by the title) attempt to explain his bizarre behavior. The opening scenes show his father (Daniel Ross) as a teenager meeting his mother (Anne Clark), then later leaving her to raise their eight-year-old son alone, intimating that this abandonment is at the root of William's romantic problems. Hawke and Laura Linney appear as the older incarnations of William's parents. The film's highlights are scenes with these actors, including a truly affecting scene in which William confronts his father, and every scene with the excellent Linney, who convincingly conveys her character's bitterness and enmity while still managing to be likeable.

In much smaller roles but also stealing scenes are Sonia Braga as Sara's disapproving mother and Michelle Williams playing an ex-girlfriend of William's.

Variety's Leslie Felperin notes that the film's "semi-improvised" feel may be Hawke taking a cue from a more talented director, Richard Linklater, who briefly appears in cameo in the film and who directed Hawke and Julie Delpy in the similar romantic dramas *Before Sunrise* (1995) and *Before Sunset* (2004). Except Hawke is unable to elicit performances from his actors that equal those in Linklater's films; Felperin calls the young leads "stiffer and more self-conscious."

Hawke perhaps is attempting to illustrate the age-old adage that heartbreak and suffering contribute to the legitimacy of an artist and, in fact, almost is deemed necessary in order to succeed. If this is the case, he nearly accomplishes his goal, giving the audience a character who truly has suffered but, like Hawke's film, has yet to succeed.

Hilary White

CREDITS

William Harding: Mark Webber
Sara Garcia: Catalina Sandino Moreno
Jesse: Laura Linney
Samantha: Michelle Williams
Mrs. Garcia: Sonia Braga
Dave Afton: Jesse Harris
Vince: Ethan Hawke
Origin: USA
Language: English
Released: 2006
Production: Yukie Kito, Alexis Alexanian; Barracuda Films, Elixir Films, Under the Influence Films; released by ThinkFilm
Directed by: Ethan Hawke
Written by: Ethan Hawke

Cinematography by: Christopher Norr
Music by: Jesse Harris
Sound: Griffin Richardson
Music Supervisor: Linda Cohen
Editing: Adriana Pacheco
Costumes: Catherine Thomas
Production Design: Rick Butler
MPAA rating: R
Running time: 117 minutes

REVIEWS

Los Angeles Times Online. August 24, 2007.
New York Times Online. August 24, 2007.
Premiere Online. August 23, 2007.
Variety Online. September 2, 2006.
Village Voice Online. August 21, 2007.

QUOTES

Jesse (to William) "Your whole life, people are gonna ask you to be weak. They're gonna practically beg you. But all anyone really wants is for you to be strong."

THE HUNTING PARTY

How can they find the world's most wanted war criminal when the CIA can't? By actually looking.
—Movie tagline

One of the problems with making a film about war correspondents is finding the right approach and tone. Alfred Hitchcock came close with his blend of comedy and propaganda in *Foreign Correspondent* (1940), as the reporter played by Joel McCrea advances from naïve indifference to world affairs to a firm grasp of the dangers facing Europe at the beginning of World War II. Writer/director Richard Shepard tries for a similarly jaunty style in *The Hunting Party*, mixing satire and low comedy with the horrors of the 1990s conflict in Bosnia. While parts of the film are effective, for the most part *The Hunting Party* is neither funny nor gritty enough.

Based on "What I Did on My Summer Vacation," an *Esquire* article by Scott Anderson, *The Hunting Party* depicts the bloodshed of the 1992–1995 Bosnian War and the resulting consequences. Television reporter Simon Hunt (Richard Gere) witnesses the atrocities along with his longtime cameraman, Duck (Terrence Howard). Simon loses his network job when he attacks the smug complacency of anchor Franklin Harris (James Brolin) during a live broadcast. After Simon is fired, Duck goes to New York as Harris's personal cameraman.

In 2000 Duck accompanies Harris to Bosnia, along with Benjamin (Jesse Eisenberg), a recent Harvard graduate whose parents are network vice presidents. Duck, who narrates the film, is reunited with Simon, who is struggling to make a living as a freelancer selling the same footage to outlets in multiple countries. Simon tells Duck he has a source who knows where Bosnia's most notorious war criminal, known as the Fox (Ljubomir Kerekes), can be found. If Simon can track down the Fox, he will get his old job back, as well as a $5 million reward for the capture. Simon, Duck, and the naïve Benjamin head deep into the mountains in pursuit of the story of their lives.

Shepard balances comic and serious themes in his offbeat hitman film *The Matador* (2005), but with *The Hunting Party*, he cannot seem to decide whether to emphasize the American government's indifference to Bosnia or simply to satirize television journalists. At times Shepard seems to want to follow the lead of Robert Altman's over-the-top satire *MASH* (1970), but he constantly eases up on the wackiness. The film, originally entitled *Spring Break in Bosnia*, ends up being neither edgy nor ironic enough, diverting but not captivating.

The Hunting Party opens with the boast that "Only the most ridiculous parts of this story are true," but it is not ridiculous enough. Shepard indicts the United Nations police for only pretending to search for war criminals, adding humor by having a U.N. officer (Nitin Ganatra) eat Dunkin' Donuts just like an American cop. At least this cliché is given some reverse spin, unlike such tired jokes as having a dwarf kick Simon in the gonads.

Shepard loves having the unrealistic, war-glorifying Chuck Norris film *Missing in Action* (1984) appear on a hotel television—so much that he repeats it to make sure the audience grasps this too easy irony. Similarly, during a chase scene, Shepard cuts between shots of the Fox and those of a real fox. Other clumsiness includes an unimaginative score by Rolfe Kent that announces too obviously when danger lies ahead.

The best scene involves the three journalists having to pretend to be CIA agents to save their lives, with the always frightened Benjamin finally finding his courage. Shepard also devises a clever cell-phone joke to save the protagonists' lives on another occasion. Gere is appropriately grizzled and world-weary, and Howard's likeability contributes greatly to caring about the fates of the characters.

Before the closing credits, Shepard offers notes about the real-life people and events behind *The Hunting Party*. These comments, which question whether the American government really wants to find not just Bosnian war criminals but Osama bin Laden as well, are much more biting than the rest of the film, and suggest what *The Hunting Party* could have been.

Michael Adams

CREDITS

Simon Hunt: Richard Gere
Duck: Terrence Howard
Benjamin: Jesse Eisenberg
Mirjana: Diane Kruger
Franklin Harris: James Brolin
Chet: Dylan Baker
The Fox: Ljubomir Kerekes
Origin: USA
Language: English
Released: 2007
Production: Mark Johnson, Scott Kroopf, Paul Hanson; Intermedia, QED International, Cherry Road Films, Jadran Film; released by the Weinstein Company
Directed by: Richard Shepard
Written by: Richard Shepard
Cinematography by: David Tattersall
Music by: Rolfe Kent

Sound: Reinhard Stergar
Music Supervisor: Liza Richardson
Editing: Carole Kravetz
Art Direction: Mario Ivezic
Costumes: Beatrix Aruna Pasztor
Production Design: Jan Roelfs
MPAA rating: R
Running time: 101 minutes

REVIEWS

Christian Science Monitor Online. September 7, 2007.
Entertainment Weekly Online. September 5, 2007.
Hollywood Reporter Online. August 31, 2007.
Los Angeles Times Online. September 7, 2007.
New York Times Online. September 7, 2007.
Premiere Online. September 7, 2007.
Variety Online. August 30, 2007.
Village Voice Online. September 4, 2007.

QUOTES

Duck: "One time in Rwanda, Simon decided he was gonna assassinate the leader of the Hutus and end the war. Three days later, he was in Morocco getting a massage from a hooker named Gladys."

I

I AM LEGEND

The last man on earth is not alone.
—Movie tagline

Box Office: $255.2 million

I Am Legend opens with a television interview with a doctor (an uncredited Emma Thompson) recalling how the measles virus has been genetically altered and used on cancer test patients. The exciting news is that it is 100 percent effective. Unfortunately the genetically engineered viral cure also turns out to be a more than a little unpredictable, and has mutated into an airborne, end-of-the-world catastrophe. The mutated virus now has a 90 percent kill rate, but the immune survivors soon found themselves faced with another problem: the Dark Seekers. Those who are infected but do not die become albino, light-sensitive cannibals with superhuman strength and quickness. They feed on the immune survivors at night, when they are most vulnerable.

By 2012 there seems to be only one human survivor in New York City, ground zero for the plague. He is Robert Neville (Will Smith), a military scientist and doctor who is working on a cure based on his own blood. In flashbacks we learn how his wife Zoe (Salli Richardson) and daughter Marley (Willow Smith) were evacuated with tragic results, and how Neville was left with his only living companion, a German shepherd named Sam (Abby).

Sam and Robert drive through the deserted, overgrown, abandoned car-clogged streets of New York City looking for supplies and hunting the packs of deer that run through Central Park. But they must be home

before nightfall or they will become prey for the Dark Seekers.

It is this desolate landscape that captures the eye and the imagination in *I Am Legend*. It is disorienting to see the normally bustling city so abandoned. A city where oversized ads for Broadway hits *Wicked* and *Hairspray* look down on streets populated only with weeds, where only wildlife roam. A city in which Neville spends his days talking to mannequins that he has given names and placed around the city in a desperate attempt to alleviate the loneliness. A city in which Neville must live in a fortress, the walls of which are decorated with priceless works of art rescued from museums, in which supplies are stacked in every space, and in which every opening can be sealed with metal plates. In the basement of Neville's house is his lab where he tests his serum on Dark-Seeker rats and the occasional human Dark Seeker that he has captured.

None of this would be believable if it were not for Will Smith's credible portrayal of Robert Neville. Smith is an Everyman actor in the vein of Tom Hanks. No matter what the role, we identify with him, we root for him, and most importantly, we like him. As with Hanks in *Cast Away* (2000), whose costar was a soccer ball, Smith's costar, the German shepherd Abby who plays Sam, is the perfect counterpart. In a pivotal scene in the movie, Neville is faced with a terrible task—he must kill the infected Sam. Thankfully, the entire act is played out only on Smith's face, but still it is heart-wrenching. Similarly, when Neville finally meets two other immune survivors, Anna (Alice Braga) and a young boy Ethan (Charlie Tahan), Smith plays the scene in a most unusual way. Instead of being overjoyed at finally having human companionship, it almost drives him over the edge. It is at first a puzzling reaction, and yet it becomes quite powerful. It is becoming more obvious with every film that not only does the likeable Smith have an appealing charm, but also he is becoming quite an accomplished actor.

I Am Legend is the latest incarnation of Richard Matheson's 1954 science-fiction novel of the same name. It was first adapted for the screen in 1964 with Vincent Price in *The Last Man on Earth*, and more famously in 1971's *The Omega Man* with Charlton Heston. The current remake is one Warner Bros. Pictures has been planning to make for ten years. Originally, it was to have been directed by Ridley Scott and starred Arnold Schwarzenegger, but as time went on, other directors (Michael Bay) and other actors (Tom Cruise and Michael Douglas) were attached to it. The version that finally has reached the screen was written by Mark Protosevich and Akiva Goldsman, and while not exactly true to the original story—the ending seems especially out of place—it is still a potent expression of what it must be like to be the last person on the face of the earth. Viewers experience the deep sense of loneliness and even hopelessness that Neville fights with his desperate search for a cure, and the almost unnecessary normalcy—he borrows DVDs from a rental store and bothers to return them—that comes from establishing a routine. But the adrenaline comes just from his daily need for survival.

The Dark Seekers are a villains who make this survival most difficult. While they seem to have a leader and even demonstrate a pack mentality, they are portrayed as a primal and highly efficient killing machine. They can only just be outrun. As if the mutant virus were not enough, the Dark Seekers are a most horrifying enemy for the humans that remain.

It is the unimaginably chilling monsters, the desolation of the city, the emotional highs and lows of survival, the imaginative art direction, and ultimately, Smith's powerful acting, that create a powerful and memorable sci-fi thriller.

Beverley Bare Buehrer

CREDITS

Robert Neville: Will Smith
Alpha Male: Dash Mihok
Zoe: Salli Richardson
Anna: Alice Braga
Ethan: Charlie Tahan
Marley: Willow Smith
Origin: USA

Language: English
Released: 2007
Production: Akiva Goldsman, James Lassiter, David Heyman, Neal H. Moritz, Erwin Stoff; Weed Road Pictures, Overbrook Entertainment, Village Roadshow Pictures; released by Warner Bros.
Directed by: Francis Lawrence
Written by: Mark Protosevich, Akiva Goldsman
Cinematography by: Andrew Lesnie
Music by: James Newton Howard
Sound: Tod A. Maitland
Editing: Wayne Wahrman
Art Direction: Patricia Woodbridge, Howard Cummings, Bill Skinner
Costumes: Michael Kaplan
Production Design: Naomi Shohan
MPAA rating: PG-13
Running time: 101 minutes

REVIEWS

Boston Globe Online. December 14, 2007.
Chicago Sun-Times Online. December 14, 2007.
Entertainment Weekly Online. December 12, 2007.
Hollywood Reporter Online. December 10, 2007.
Los Angeles Times Online. December 14, 2007.
New York Times Online. December 14, 2007.
San Francisco Chronicle. December 14, 2007, p. E1.
Variety Online. December 7, 2007.
Wall Street Journal. December 14, 2007, p. W1.
Washington Post. December 14, 2007, p. C1.

QUOTES

Anna: "The world is quieter now. We just have to listen. If we listen, we can hear God's plan."

TRIVIA

Will Smith grew so enamored of his canine co-star, Abby, that he tried to adopt her when the shooting was finished, but the dog's trainer could not be persuaded to give her up.

AWARDS

Nomination:

Screen Actors Guild 2008: Outstanding Performance by a Stunt Ensemble in a Motion Picture.

I KNOW WHO KILLED ME

If you think you know the secret...think again.
—Movie tagline

Box Office: $7.2 million

Filmmakers reveal what is important to them by what they devote their attention to in developing a story. In *I Know Who Killed Me*, a scene appears in which a high school girl (Lindsay Lohan) returns home after a lengthy hospital recuperation. She had disappeared one night following a high school football game and had been missing for seventeen days. Her parents and the small-town community feared that she had become another mutilated and murdered victim like another girl who had disappeared some weeks before. But one night a motorist finds the Lohan character with a partly severed right leg and arm, yet still alive. Now the girl, who was known as Aubrey Fleming when she disappeared, insists that she is really Dakota Moss, an exotic dancer who dances at a "gentleman's club." After being interrogated at the hospital by police and by a psychologist, the maimed girl returns home with Aubrey's parents (Julia Ormond and Neal McDonough), still maintaining that she is Dakota. Soon Aubrey's boyfriend Jerrod (Brian Geraghty), a star on the high school football team, arrives for a visit.

The scene revealing the filmmakers' intentions is the living room meeting between Dakota and Jerrod. Dakota hobbles in on crutches, and Jerrod timidly introduces himself and offers her flowers. Inferring that Jerrod is Aubrey's boyfriend, Dakota tells him that she is not Aubrey. Jerrod immediately crosses the room and kisses her. Dakota kisses back. As the film cuts to an extreme close-up of their mouths, Dakota bites into his underlip and says, "Aubrey wouldn't kiss you like that, would she?" Jerrod, presumably kept at a distance by Aubrey, now hungrily reaches out for Dakota. They are kissing passionately when Aubrey's mother walks in on them. Dakota boldly announces, "We're going to go upstairs." For the next few moments, the film intercuts between the copulating, moaning teens upstairs and the mother downstairs scouring the kitchen sink in frustration.

Again and again, *I Know Who Killed Me* rejects the human and emotional element (as seen in the moment when Dakota and Jerrod are about to converse and confront the question of identity) in favor of the more shocking and gratuitous. The frankness and audacity of the Jerrod/Dakota scene reflect the filmmakers' unapologetic aims at exploitation. Other moments in the film show in a less obvious way the same priority. When Aubrey's mother talks to Dakota at the hospital, for example, she takes with her Aubrey's teddy bear and pictures of Aubrey as a little girl. But a scene that could have been dramatic and revealing of personality instead has no force because no relationship between Aubrey and her mother has been established or even suggested. The characters remain strangers to one another and to the audience. Consequently, the film becomes an example of how to crassly exploit the popularity of Lindsay Lohan and to manipulate an audience, rather than develop a story meaningfully. *I Know Who Killed Me* was one of the most negatively reviewed films of 2007 (receiving only five favorable reviews out of the sixty documented at rottentomatoes.com).

A list of the set pieces in the film bears out the emphasis on the sensational and shocking. A surprising early scene shows Aubrey returning home from school and pausing to watch a muscle-bound yardworker peel off his sweaty shirt while he gestures to her provocatively. Aubrey, whom the movie seems to want to present as the opposite of Dakota, slowly climbs out of her car and poses for him in flirtatious reciprocity before walking off and flipping him an obscene gesture of her own. Three extended montages, including the opening-credits sequence, show Dakota contorting at the strip club. At least two scenes of torture delineate Dakota's mutilations during her captivity, and some nightmarish flashbacks recall these scenes after her rescue. The initial scene of Dakota's treatment in the hospital also recalls in its color scheme and camera placement the earlier torture scenes. The framework of the story invites a contrasting development of the personalities of Aubrey and Dakota, but the film ignores all chances to explore personality.

Marginalizing the human element as drastically as the movie does means that the revelations that fill the final thirty minutes of the film—twists involving stigmatic twins, a withheld secret, and a premature burial, among other implausible elements—do more to confuse than to resolve a complicated story with no believable characters.

Glenn Hopp

CREDITS

Aubrey Fleming/Dakota: Lindsay Lohan
Susan Fleming: Julia Ormond
Daniel Fleming: Neal McDonough
Julie Bascome: Garcelle Beauvais
Jerrod Pointer: Brian Geraghty
Phil Lazarus: Spencer Garrett
Dr. Greg Jameson: Gregory Itzin
Kenny Scaife: Rodney Rowland
Marnie Toland: Paula Marshall
Saeed: Eddie Steeples
Jazmin: Kenya Moore
Sheriff Leon Cardero: Donovan Scott
Fat Teena: Bonnie Aarons
Douglas Norquist: Thomas Tofel
Lanny Rierden: David Figlioli
Jacob K./Joseph K.: Michael Papajohn

Origin: USA
Language: English
Released: 2007
Production: Frank Mancuso, Jr.; 360 Pictures; released by TriStar Pictures
Directed by: Chris Sivertson
Written by: Jeffrey Hammond
Cinematography by: John R. Leonetti
Music by: Joel McNeely
Sound: Ed White
Editing: Lawrence Jordan
Costumes: Rachel Sage
Production Design: Jerry Fleming
MPAA rating: R
Running time: 105 minutes

REVIEWS

Boston Globe Online. July 28, 2007.
Chicago Sun-Times Online. July 28, 2007.
Hollywood Reporter Online. July 30, 2007.
New York Times Online. July 28, 2007.
Premiere Online. July 27, 2007.
Variety Online. July 27, 2007.

QUOTES

Dakota Moss: "So my finger got cut off. But nobody did it. Who's going to believe that? Look at you. You don't even believe it."

AWARDS

Golden Raspberries 2007: Worst Picture, Worst Actress (Lohan), Worst Director (Sivertson), Worst Horror Movie, Worst Screenplay, Worst Remake
Nomination:
Golden Raspberries 2007: Worst Screen Couple (Lohan and Lohan), Worst Support. Actress (Ormond).

I NOW PRONOUNCE YOU CHUCK AND LARRY

They're straight as can be, but don't tell anyone.
—Movie tagline
How far would you go for a friend.
—Movie tagline

Box Office: $120 million

As President Clinton's "don't ask, don't tell" policy regarding gay men and women in the military was an uneasy compromise between promoting acceptance of gays and appeasing his conservative constituents, *I Now Pronounce You Chuck and Larry* is an awkward balancing act between making fun of and advocating acceptance of gay men and women. As Wesley Morris of the *Boston Globe* wrote, the film "is torn between shouting down homophobia and asserting its own hetero urges." Stephanie Zacharek of *Salon* echoed this opinion: "The picture creeps along in a way that feels both forced and tentative, as if director Dennis Dugan, his cast, and writers (Barry Fanaro, Alexander Payne, and Jim Taylor, from a treatment by Lew Gallo) couldn't decide if they wanted to make a mainstream movie with a progressive message, or a progressive movie that would play safely to the mainstream. The picture they've made seesaws uncertainly between the two."

That the film comes from Payne and Taylor, the duo who wrote *Sideways* (2004), *About Schmidt* (2002), and *Election* (1999), is particularly surprising. Those films showed a deft touch for subtle adult humor. It scarcely seems possible that the same team was behind *I Now Pronounce You Chuck and Larry*, which has a markedly lower level of sophistication. Given the premise—that two heterosexual men must pretend to be gay—there are several obvious beats that the script may hit, and *Chuck and Larry* dutifully hits them all. As one might expect, the two men will be forced to share a kiss. One can also surmise that the men will share a bed at some point, and again, that event happens as expected.

Due to the city's arcane bureaucracy, New York City firefighter Larry Valentine (Kevin James), a widower and father of two, stands to lose his pension. Larry determines that the only way to retain his benefits is to register in a domestic partnership with his best friend and fellow firefighter Chuck Levine (Adam Sandler). Chuck is initially against the idea—after all, he is the sort of committed heterosexual who routinely beds down a variety of women. He also openly disdains gay men. But as Chuck and Larry try to pass as a gay couple, they realize the kind of discrimination gay people face. In its grandest and best sense, *Chuck and Larry* is about the transformation of one man from small-minded bigot to one who literally would testify in a courtroom on behalf of homosexuals. Such sentiments fit uneasily in a film that also manages to use derogatory terms several times for humorous effect. While the film eventually declares its tolerance of gay people, it is also a film that portrays homosexuals as people who dress outrageously and spend much of their time attending AIDS benefits and dancing to disco songs.

Although one would not expect such a film to be a paragon of good taste, the baseness of some of the comedy is galling. Particularly crass is a cameo by Rob Schneider, a veteran of *Saturday Night Live* and many low-level movie comedies, playing an Asian minister at a gay wedding chapel in Canada. Schneider's portrayal is such an offensive stereotype that it recalls Mickey Rooney's regrettable turn as Mr. Yunioshi in *Breakfast at Tiffany's* (1961). He squints his eyes behind thick glasses, replaces his *r*'s with *l*'s, and sports buck teeth. He does not even keep his stereotypes straight. His liberal use of *l*'s might be associated with a Chinese-speaking person, yet he also frequently barks the Japanese salutation "Hai." There is also a scene in which a character is pinned underneath an obese man stricken with a case of flatulence. As Manohla Dargis of the *New York Times* wrote: "It's next to impossible to reconcile Mr. Payne and Mr. Taylor, who excel in sharply honed, intelligent satire, with the crude laughs and nyuck-nyuck high jinks that characterize *Chuck and Larry*, much less the relentless barrage of idiotic jokes about gay men, most of which hinge on sex, or rather straight male fear of such sex, and involve groaning puns about backdoors and the like."

As if to balance its supposedly gay-friendly message, *Chuck and Larry* also has an aggressive heterosexuality bordering on misogyny. When Chuck is hospitalized he has an attractive female doctor whom he insists upon addressing as "honey" or, alternately, "Doctor Honey." She takes great offense and reprimands him, but a few scenes later, she is part of a giggly entourage of women waiting to romp in Chuck's bedroom. And Chuck and Larry's attractive lawyer Alex (Jessica Biel) ends a "girl's day out" with Chuck by undressing in front of him and insisting that he touch her breasts. Such a circumstance is not only absurdly false but as corny and contrived as anything found in an episode of television's *Three's Company* (1977–1984). Any progressive ideas that *Chuck and Larry* posits are canceled out by its overall attitude of boorishness, immaturity, and one-note comedy.

Jill Hamilton

CREDITS

Chuck Levine: Adam Sandler
Larry Valentine: Kevin James
Alex McDonough: Jessica Biel
Duncan: Ving Rhames
Clint Fitzer: Steve Buscemi
Capt. P. Tucker: Dan Aykroyd
Renaldo: Nicholas Turturro
Cabbie: Dennis Dugan
Steve: Allen Covert
Councilman Banks: Richard Chamberlain
Asian Minister: Rob Schneider
Benefits Supervisor: Rachel Dratch
Teresa: Mary Pat Gleason
Jim the Protestor: Rob Corddry

Kevin McDonough: Nick Swardson
David Nootzie: Jonathan Loughran
Dr. Honey: Chandra West
Homeless Man: Blake Clark
Mr. Auerbach: Richard Kline
Origin: USA
Language: English
Released: 2007
Production: Adam Sandler, Jack Giarraputo, Tom Shadyac, Michael Bostick; Happy Madison Productions, Shady Acres Entertainment, Relativity Media; released by Universal
Directed by: Dennis Dugan
Written by: Barry Fanaro, Alexander Payne, Jim Taylor
Cinematography by: Dean Semler
Music by: Rupert Gregson-Williams
Sound: Thomas Causey
Music Supervisor: Michael Dilbeck
Editing: Jeff Gourson
Art Direction: Alan Au, David Swayze
Costumes: Ellen Lutter
Production Design: Perry Andelin Blake
MPAA rating: PG-13
Running time: 110 minutes

REVIEWS

Boston Globe Online. July 20, 2007.
Entertainment Weekly. July 27, 2007, p. 50.
Hollywood Reporter Online. July 16, 2007.
Los Angeles Times Online. July 20, 2007.
New York Times Online. July 20, 2007.
Rolling Stone Online. July 19, 2007.
San Francisco Chronicle. July 19, 2007, p. E1.
Variety Online. July 13, 2007.
Village Voice Online. July 17, 2007.
Washington Post. July 20, 2007, p. C5.

QUOTES

Chuck Levine: "The only thing I'm doing with my eyes is putting a bag over your head, you toothless moron!"

TRIVIA

During the parade when Chuck and Larry are quizzing each other on different aspects of each other's personalities, Adam Sandler and Kevin James each give their real birthdays when asked.

AWARDS

Nomination:

Golden Raspberries 2007: Worst Picture, Worst Actor (Sandler), Worst Support. Actor (James, Schneider), Worst

Support. Actress (Biel), Worst Director (Dugan), Worst Screen Couple (Biel and either Sandler, James), Worst Screenplay.

I THINK I LOVE MY WIFE

In marriage no one can hear you scream.
—Movie tagline

Box Office: $12.5 million

The source material for writer/director/star Chris Rock's *I Think I Love My Wife* was the Eric Rohmer film *Chloe in the Afternoon*. The first was a French movie made in the early 1970s and Rock's is an urban movie set in New York City in the 2000s. Both concern issues of fidelity within a marriage, and the effect of temptation on that fidelity. How well the film honored its source material was a point of contention among critics. Lisa Schwarzbaum of *Entertainment Weekly* compared Rock's film unfavorably with Rohmer's original, writing, "Rock…has taken Rohmer's marvelously probing, psychologically refined, exquisitely yakky, and deeply French movie and turned it into a coarse-talking, race-conscious, tonally challenged life-crisis comedy." But Scott Tobias of *The A.V. Club* felt quite differently, and wrote, "Though hampered at times by Rock's limitations as an actor and a director, *I Think I Love My Wife* stays faithful to the spirit of Rohmer's original, grappling honestly with the uncertainties of settling down and the temptations that lurk outside even the most stable marriages."

Richard Cooper (Chris Rock) has settled into a version of the American dream. He has a well-paying job at a high-powered Manhattan banking firm. He has a lovely house, two cute kids, and a gorgeous, loving wife, Brenda (Gina Torres). The problem is that his wife no longer wants to have sex with him. "My face hurts," is one of her particularly poor excuses for avoiding intimacy. As he states in voice-over, Richard also has grown weary with the predictability his marriage offers and has accepted that his sex life will consist of ogling good-looking women on the train. That is, until sultry Nikki (Kerry Washington) shows up at his office.

Nikki, the ex-girlfriend of a friend, is the kind of bad girl who smokes indoors and would seduce Richard for the sport of it. Such a woman is nearly irresistible to a bored married man like Richard. When Nikki first visits Richard, she innocently asks him for a job reference. Later, her needs increase. Could Richard take her apartment hunting? Could Richard provide her a shoulder to cry on? Could Richard fly to Washington, D.C. for the day to help her pick up some of her belongings? Richard and Nikki are not technically having a sexual affair, but the line is fairly tenuous. His office-mates take note of Nikki's frequent visits, and her risqué attire, and assume Richard is having an affair. They glare pointedly at him, making sure Richard registers their disapproval, while Richard finds himself lying to his wife about his whereabouts.

While *I Think I Love My Wife* is not nearly as bad as earlier Rock films (which sadly include such fare as *Beverly Hills Ninja* [1997]) it is unfortunate that Rock has yet to make a film that even comes close to the brilliance of his standup comedy. It is difficult to understand why his onstage comedy genius disappears when he tries to apply it to moviemaking. Wesley Morris of the *Boston Globe* took note of the disparity between Rock's comic talent and the quality of films that he has made. "Rock could be making movies as culturally sharp about love's vicissitudes as Woody Allen or Albert Brooks," he wrote. "Lord knows he has Allen's same knack for whimsy and Brooks's exasperated wit."

As a vehicle for Rock's comedy, *I Think I Love My Wife* is middling. But as a modern Hollywood romantic comedy, it is better than most. Unlike many in this genre, the film at least gives some thought to mature topics such as marriage and fidelity. It is unusual for a Hollywood film to deal with the subject of romance after marriage. However, this film does not always treat said topics with a great degree of maturity. In one over-the-top comic scene, Richard has an adverse reaction to Viagra and ends up in the hospital with a severe case of priapism. While Rock and his frequent writing partner Louis C.K. aspire to make a philosophical film about modern marriage, when the two get together, it seems they cannot resist such low-brow humor.

Jill Hamilton

CREDITS

Richard Cooper: Chris Rock
Nikki Tru: Kerry Washington
Brenda Coooper: Gina Torres
George: Steve Buscemi
Mr. Landis: Edward Herrmann
Teddy: Michael K. Williams
Sean: Wendell Pierce
Jennifer: Cassandra Freeman
Mary: Welker White
Origin: USA
Language: English
Released: 2007
Production: Chris Rock, Lisa Stewart; Fox Searchlight Pictures, Zahrlo Productions, UTV Motion Pictures; released by Fox Searchlight Pictures

Directed by: Chris Rock
Written by: Chris Rock, Louis C.K.
Cinematography by: William Rexer
Music by: Marcus Miller
Sound: Richard Murphy
Music Supervisor: Dave Jordan
Editing: Wendy Greene Bricmont
Art Direction: Adam Scher, Toni Barton, Alicia Maccarone
Costumes: Suzanne McCabe
Production Design: Sharon Lomofsky
MPAA rating: R
Running time: 94 minutes

REVIEWS

Boxoffice Online. March 16, 2007.
Chicago Sun-Times Online. March 16, 2007.
Entertainment Weekly. March 23, 2007, p. 42.
Hollywood Reporter Online. March 7, 2007.
Los Angeles Times Online. March 16, 2007.
New York Times Online. March 16, 2007.
San Francisco Chronicle. March 16, 2007, p. E1.
Variety Online. March 7, 2007.
Washington Post. March 16, 2007, p. C1.

QUOTES

Mr. Landis: "You can lose lots of money chasing women, but you will NEVER lose women by chasing money."

I WANT SOMEONE TO EAT CHEESE WITH

Sometimes love is just a big bowl of wrong.
        —Movie tagline

As its quirky title suggests, *I Want Someone to Eat Cheese With* is indeed offbeat, but it is also a very funny and touching independent film from producer/director/writer/star Jeff Garlin. Garlin is a veteran of Chicago's Second City improvisational comedy troupe but is best known for playing the sidekick on HBO's *Curb Your Enthusiasm* (which he also executive produces), and both have a major impact on Garlin's debut feature. The film is set in Chicago, where Garlin works as a struggling actor with Second City, and a host of talented Second City alumnus inhabit various roles. The film has the same improvisational feel of *Curb Your Enthusiasm*, down to the jangly accordion music heard throughout. The portly Garlin is the star here, with a slim, Larry David-type sidekick, and he gets to show a different side of himself as a overweight, middle-aged man still living with his mother and unable to find love.

The comedy springs from the daily life of the increasingly downtrodden James Aaron (Jeff Garlin). Although he has worked steadily for many years with Second City, he takes a second job on a third-rate television hidden-camera show that plays reprehensible practical jokes on unsuspecting citizens. After one particularly nasty stunt, James quits, much to the chagrin of his agent, who decides to drop him as a client on the same day. His agent Herb (Richard Kind), like a host of others in James's life, says "I'm sorry," to which James's standard reply is a matter-of-fact "No you're not." The sad fact is that most of the time they are not sorry, and James deals with the rejection by overeating, and regularly vents while trading sarcastic comments with best friend Luca (David Pasquesi).

James also has a special relationship with convenience-store owner Dick (Dan Castellaneta), who reluctantly supplies him with the junk food he regularly washes down with a pint of milk while lying on the hood of his car, parked outside Wrigley Field to hide from his disapproving mother (Mina Kolb). It seems that James's prospects are improving when a flirty young ice-cream parlor clerk named Beth (Sarah Silverman) offers him a free sundae and a veiled, dirty proposition involving what she calls a "hoagie shack." Although smitten by the impetuous Beth, he also meets the more age-appropriate schoolteacher Stella (Bonnie Hunt) while the two are both looking for the same jazz record. Beth sleeps with James for sport, saying she had never been with a fat guy before, and nothing comes of James and Stella's flirtation.

The crux of the film's plot involves James learning about the Chicago casting call for a remake of the film version of Paddy Chayefsy's *Marty* (1955). It is James's favorite film, and Marty is a role he believes he was born to play. First, though, he must suffer the indignity of dressing as a pirate and hawking free hot dogs on the street, standing in for his friend Larry (Joey Slotnick), who is going to the audition. James finally decides to make a stand, and courageously goes to the audition anyway, refusing to leave until he is seen. The hilarious result is that he is told by the casting director that the part of Marty, originally played by Ernest Borgnine, has already been cast, and is being played by Aaron Carter (playing himself), the nineteen-year-old pop singer and teen idol.

While indignities suffered by James are quite humorous, the film frequently shows its heart, as well. James's speech to an elementary school classroom full of children on career day is a raw, poignant, and bitter stream-of-consciousness rant about how hard it is to find love and success in the world. Although James never achieves many of his goals—finding a girlfriend, losing weight, success in acting—the character's growth may be seen in the sweetly satisfying final scene showing James performing a stage version of *Marty* in a retirement home.

To simply say that the film is low-key is perhaps to do it a disservice. The performances, script, and premise of the comedy that comes from the everyday suffering of the Everyman are exactly on-key. The jokes are not forced, and the cast of seasoned comedy professionals make it look so realistic and easy, one may easily miss its sly wisdom and effortless hilarity.

Hilary White

CREDITS

James Aaron: Jeff Garlin
Beth: Sarah Silverman
Stella Lewis: Bonnie Hunt
Ms. Clark: Amy Sedaris
Claude Cochet: Wallace Langham
Larry: Joey Slotnick
Herb Hope: Richard King
Mrs. Piletti: Gina Gershon
Mrs. Aaron: Mina Kolb
Luca: David Pasquesi
Origin: USA
Language: English
Released: 2006
Production: Jeff Garlin, Erin O'Malley, Steve Pink; Sawin' and Puddin' Productions, 3 Art Entertainment, the Weinstein Company; released by IFC Films
Directed by: Jeff Garlin
Written by: Jeff Garlin
Cinematography by: Pete Biagi
Music by: Rob Kolson
Sound: Scott Stolz
Editing: Steve Rasch
Art Direction: Michael Levinson
Production Design: Margaret M. Miles
MPAA rating: R
Running time: 80 minutes

REVIEWS

Boston Globe Online. September 14, 2007.
Entertainment Weekly Online. September 5, 2007.
Los Angeles Times Online. September 14, 2007.
New York Times Online. September 5, 2007.
Variety Online. June 5, 2006.
Village Voice Online. September 4, 2007.
Washington Post Online. September 14, 2007.

I'M NOT THERE

The lives and time of Bob Dylan.
—Movie tagline

Box Office: $4 million

Cinematic character point of view has rarely been more complex than it is in *I'm Not There,* just one of the many recent projects honoring the renaissance of singer Bob Dylan. Todd Haynes's challenging, self-reflexive, richly intricate film will delight some and frustrate others.

Eschewing most of the conventions of the typical Hollywood biopic, Haynes provocatively challenges the very idea of truth in cinema. Nevertheless, his boldly alinear, Chinese box of a movie is more enjoyable to pick apart during a postscreening bull session than to actually view.

During 2007 alone, there were several homages to Bob Dylan, including D.A. Pennebaker's traditional cinema veritédocumentary released on DVD, *65 Revisited,* a reconstruction of outtakes from Pennebaker's legendary 1967 film *Don't Look Back,* about Dylan's tour through Great Britain in 1965. There was also the iTunes debut of the original *Don't Look Back* and the cable television airing of *No Direction Home,* Martin Scorsese's 2005 Dylan documentary.

I'm Not There is the only enterprise of the many to call into question Dylan's career and achievements. Todd Haynes makes a concerted aesthetic and thematic effort to deconstruct the mythology of Dylan, from the vocalist's personal life to his professional standing and cultural significance. The big irony here is that Bob Dylan himself actually cooperated in the making of this, less flattering, portrait, rather than in the more celebratory projects.

Haynes's primary approaches to revising and reinventing are to scramble the storyline and use the six separate characters to portray different aspects of Dylan's life and persona. By questioning who Dylan is in this fashion, Haynes makes the statement that we never really know other people, least of all a media-constructed celebrity. Here, Haynes echoes two classics: Orson Welles's *Citizen Kane* (1941), a thinly veiled biography of William Randolph Hearst told in shuffled order; and Luis Buñuel's *That Obscure Object of Desire* (1977), with its two actresses (Carole Bouquet and Angela Molina) alternating scenes to play the same character (with no explanation for the switching and no change in reaction from the other characters).

The different incarnations of Dylan in *I'm Not There* include a folk singer named Jack who becomes born again as Pastor John (Christian Bale); an African American youngster who claims to be Woody Guthrie (Marcus Carl Franklin); a movie star named Robbie who flees Hollywood (Heath Ledger); a rock legend named Jude who dismisses his folk music past (Cate Blanchett); a poet named Arthur Rimbaud who argues with an interviewer about his career (Ben Whishaw);

and an older actor appearing in a Western about Billy the Kid (Richard Gere). Finally and startlingly, the real Dylan appears at the end of the film—but is he real?

Blanchett gives by far the best literal impersonation of Bob Dylan (ironically, since she is the only female actor of the bunch); she captures the look and mannerisms of Dylan during his career peak and the start of his decline in the late 1960s, yet her performance is never campy or insulting. If anything, it is the most haunting. Most of the other actors try to depict a single aspect of the Dylan persona (or, more accurately, various audience perceptions of the artist), though Richard Gere seems totally unfit to even attempt the Dylan of some odd twilight period. Christian Bale stands out as the singer claimed by religious fervor, and proves to be the most accomplished in the lip-synching department.

It would take intense study to catch all the Dylan references—Haynes hurls them at the viewer as if he were creating a gestural abstract-expressionist painting from the 60s rather than trying to slot them into an "and then he wrote, and then he sang" narrative. The supporting characters just add more ambiguity (as opposed to definition and understanding). There is Alice Fabian (Julianne Moore, who starred in Haynes's more accessible *Safe* [1995] and *Far From Heaven* [2002]), a variation of a jaded, older Joan Baez; and Claire (Charlotte Gainsbourg), resembling Dylan's wide-eyed first wife, Sara. Yet, just to mix things up and be deliberately inconsistent, there is Allen Ginsberg (David Cross) being Allen Ginsberg. Also, the songs are Dylan's, and you hear him sing them in his signature style.

Possibly, Haynes is playing off of Dylan's own epic mockumentary-cum-home movie, *Renaldo and Clara* (1978), though he stops short of calling Dylan a complete fraud. That was the theme of the 2000 documentary *The Ballad of Ramblin' Jack,* which revealed that Dylan was born Robert Zimmerman in Minnesota, but appropriated the name of the Welsh poet Dylan Thomas and the look and sound of Woody Guthrie's mentor, Ramblin' Jack Elliott. The more recent *The Killing of John Lennon* (2006) implies that another music god, Lennon, was also a phony, but in a very different way (and from the point of view of Lennon's assassin, not Lennon himself).

Though difficult to follow at times, the production is a dazzling kaleidoscope of styles and looks (Edward Lachman's cinematography, Jay Rabinowitz's editing, and Judy Becker's production design merit special praise). The use of Dylan's music is excellent, from "I Want You" accompanying a love-making scene between Ledger and Gainsbourg to Christian Bale's riff on "The Times They Are a-Changin'."

Haynes has come a long way since the days of the amateurishly made *Poison* (1991), though even then his storytelling was iterative and his ideas interesting. If anything, *I'm Not There* recalls Haynes's earlier documentary about Karen Carpenter, *Superstar* (1987), more than his better-known streamlined features, though he proved with *Safe* that he could produce a conventional melodrama quite brilliantly.

Like the film itself, the reviews for *I'm Not There* were all over the place. Todd McCarthy's piece in *Variety* slammed it as "a film a precocious grad student in musicology might make about a creative hero. Stylistically audacious in the way it employs six different actors and assorted visuals to depict various aspects of the troubadour's life and career, the film nevertheless lacks a narrative and a center, much like the 'ghost' at its core." But A.O. Scott was enthusiastic in his piece: "…*I'm Not There* is a profoundly, movingly personal film, passionate in its engagement with the mysteries of the recent past." And Roger Ebert was somewhere in between in his review in the *Chicago Sun-Times:* "No effort is made to explain how these Dylans are connected, which is the point, I think…we are left not one step closer to comprehending Bob Dylan, which is as it should be."

As the title indicates, *I'm Not There* negates its subject. You may feel after seeing the film that you know less about Bob Dylan than you did before, but there is no doubt you will be stirred, either positively or negatively or both.

Eric Monder

CREDITS

Jack/Pastor John: Christian Bale
Robbie: Heath Ledger
Jude: Cate Blanchett
Arthur: Ben Whishaw
Woody: Marcus Carl Franklin
Billy: Richard Gere
Claire: Charlotte Gainsbourg
Alice Fabian: Julianne Moore
Coco Rivington: Michelle Williams
Allen Ginsberg: David Cross
Keenan Jones/Pat Garrett: Bruce Greenwood
Origin: Germany, USA
Language: English
Released: 2007
Production: James Stern, John Sloss, John Goldwyn, Jeff Rosen, Christine Vachon; Endgame Entertainment, Killer Films, VIP Medienfonds 4; released by the Weinstein Company
Directed by: Todd Haynes

Written by: Todd Haynes, Oren Moverman
Cinematography by: Edward Lachman
Sound: Leslie Shatz
Music Supervisor: Randall Poster, Jim Dunbar
Editing: Jay Rabinowitz
Art Direction: Pierre Perrault
Costumes: John Dunn
Production Design: Judy Becker
MPAA rating: R
Running time: 135 minutes

REVIEWS

Boston Globe Online. November 21, 2007.
Chicago Sun-Times Online. November 21, 2007.
Entertainment Weekly. November 30, 2007, p. 112.
Hollywood Reporter Online. September 3, 2007.
Los Angeles Times Online. November 21, 2007.
New York Times Online. November 21, 2007.
New Yorker Online. November 26, 2007.
Rolling Stone Online. November 15, 2007.
San Francisco Chronicle. November 21, 2007, p. E1.
Variety Online. September 4, 2007.
Washington Post. November 21, 2007, p. C12.

QUOTES

Arthur: "I accept chaos. I don't know whether it accepts me."

AWARDS

Golden Globes 2008: Support. Actress (Blanchett)
Ind. Spirit 2008: Support. Actress (Blanchett)

Nomination:

Oscars 2007: Support. Actress (Blanchett)
British Acad. 2007: Support. Actress (Blanchett)
Ind. Spirit 2008: Director (Haynes), Film, Support. Actor (Franklin)
Screen Actors Guild 2007: Support. Actress (Blanchett).

IN THE LAND OF WOMEN

Get ready to fall.
—Movie tagline

Box Office: $11 million

In the comedy-drama *In the Land of Women,* the protagonist is a young Hollywood screenwriter with family roots in Michigan who wonders when he is going to write a legitimate feature film. The movie is written and directed by Jonathan Kasdan, the thirty-something son of Michigan-bred Lawrence Kasdan (writer and director of *The Big Chill* [1983], *Body Heat* [1981], and *The Accidental Tourist* [1988]). The younger Kasdan has nothing of significance on his resume, so it is fair to say the character he has created bears a striking resemblance to himself.

Carter Webb (Adam Brody) is searching for a way to write something meaningful about his experience at a privileged private high school in Los Angeles and, in the wake of being spurned by the beautiful young actress Sofia (Elena Anaya), to improve his relationship record. He seeks to accomplish these goals by moving back to "suburban Michigan" and looking after his grandmother (Olympia Dukakis) who, despite no discernible physical ailments, insists she is dying.

The script does not provide a plausible explanation for this move. Carter simply declares that he has a feeling that getting away from L.A. is just what he needs to clear his head. That would not fly in most screenwriting workshops, but neither would the entire set-up for the film. After all, his grandmother lives right across the street from two women who immediately fall for him: teen Lucy (Kristen Stewart) and her mother Sarah (Meg Ryan). It does not take long to grasp that Carter not only will be learning about life and love from his neighbors, he also will be simultaneously providing them with the answers they need to straighten out their own problems. This is a movie where the characters teach each other lots of life lessons.

Carter's mother, Agnes (JoBeth Williams), who appears briefly in an early scene, notes that for some inexplicable reason women have always been attracted to Carter. As played by Brody, he is a coolly huggable combination of neediness and self-assurance. He is outwardly unflappable, always taking even the most difficult developments with a shrug and a smile. Inside, however, he is a mess, heartsick over Sofia—distraught enough to run into a tree while jogging and being overwhelmed by a flashback of their passionate love scenes. But he is also more than a little smug. Kasdan lampoons Carter's self-centeredness in a scene where he brags to Sarah about what a good listener he is, even though he seems to find himself doing all the talking. She says, "Maybe you're not really a good listener," he says "what?", and then she has to repeat herself. As an attempt at humor, it is a groaner. Aside from this one dig, however, Carter seems to float magically through the movie on the implausible wings provided by his screenwriter/director alter ego, unaware of how self-absorbed he is.

There is really no good reason, either, for why Sarah asks him to help walk her dog, and why they open up to each other immediately. It is definitely Hollywood-style interaction with her daughter Lucy, too, as she immediately approaches him in confidence: trust if not exactly lust at first sight. Only in a screenplay this immature can a protagonist be immediately thrust into the middle of several domestic crises just by taking out the garbage. Here are the crises Kasdan has concocted to serve as lessons for Carter: Sarah discovers she has breast cancer; her husband is having an affair; Lucy hates her mother and feels abandoned; Lucy is confused about which boy in her high school she really likes. Her younger sister, Paige (Makenzie Vega), provides precocious-child comic relief. Dukakis provides senile-old-lady laughs, though of a rather disturbingly tone-deaf sort (in her, Kasdan has concocted a stereotypical character who veers wildly and inconsistently from lucidity to dementia). Brody, for his part, just shakes his head and takes everything in stride.

Whenever Kasdan gets near some serious business, he backs off. The movie jumps around from scene to scene and illogically across gaps in time. Though Carter is living right across the street and doing little besides attempting to occasionally write on his laptop, he only encounters Lucy and Sarah at points where it is convenient for the plot, with unaccountable hiatuses in between.

The characters aren't fully developed either. When Lucy decries Sarah as a self-absorbed housewife who cares only about whether her house looks like a store catalogue, it does not seem to agree with what we know of her mother. Why Sarah does not have a job is similarly unclear. Her husband (and the few other male characters in the film) are only sketchy bit players. Kasdan does not give us enough for us to care about either Lucy or Sarah. Lucy seems shallow, and Sarah is a victim of disease, a bad marriage, and the ennui of a housewife's life. Her longing to break free from her chains is illustrated in clumsily obvious ways: She and Carter visit the nearby woods that she pretends could be a gateway to another planet, and she divulges a memory of a magic moment in a Manhattan supermarket (only in Hollywood movies do people have intense conversations while pushing shopping carts down the aisles). Sometimes the dialogue is so on-the-nose that it is as if Kasdan is channeling Woody Allen, but without Allen's facility for deft wordplay.

Even so, Kasdan has a fair ear for contemporary dialogue, especially of the halting, superficial kind that is interlaced with sudden awkward bursts of great meaning. *In the Land of Women* unfolds like a film-school thesis screenplay. The script touches all the bases, but with noticeable lapses in smoothness and judgment, and frequently resorts to the land of faux-indie cliché (Lucy pours out her anger by painting self-portraits on the basement wall, a clown gets out of a parked car while Sarah and Carter are walking). His protagonist is not

very appealing, though that is not entirely Kasdan's fault: Brody's acting range is pretty limited.

The women fare better. As Lucy, Stewart nails a certain kind of contemporary teen on the nose: jittery, awkward, but gutsy and determined. Yet she does not vary her style and tone enough to make her character multidimensional. The movie belongs, hands down, to Ryan, who has matured as an actress by taking on more challenging parts. Here, she has graduated from the girl next door to the mother next door. She is so radiant and vital that at first she does not seem old enough to be Lucy's mother. Her Sarah oozes a self-effacing but audacious combination of strength and vulnerability. She is a warm and intriguing mother who is searching for nurturance of her own. Though the scene where she reveals her disease to Carter is literally drenched in cliché (they meet in pouring rain on the street), her portrayal of deep fear at facing death is genuinely moving. Even as a chemotherapy patient with a bald head, Ryan is luminous. It is too bad, however, that Kasdan does not seem to know what to do with the romance he has created between Sarah and Carter, other than tone it down to make it unthreatening by lapsing at the end into unsatisfying exchanges of thanks. The love letter Carter ends up writing to Sarah is disappointingly pedestrian.

In the Land of Women seems more like an exercise in writing and making a movie than an actual movie. At any point where the plot threatens to become plausible or dangerous, Kasdan yanks it back to sanctimonious middle-brow entertainment by doling out another unsurprising scene. The movie plays sweet and cute and traffics in mundane life lessons and easily digestible morality. In short, it seems exactly like the yearnings of a young scriptwriter from Los Angeles trying desperately to discover what the real world is like, but not succeeding in overcoming the handicaps of his La-La Land upbringing.

Michael Betzold

CREDITS

Carter Webb: Adam Brody
Lucy Hardwicke: Kristen Stewart
Sarah Hardwicke: Meg Ryan
Phyllis: Olympia Dukakis
Paige Hardwicke: Makenzie Vega
Sofia: Elena Anaya
Agnes Webb: JoBeth Williams
Eric Watts: Dustin Milligan
Janey: Ginnifer Goodwin
Nelson Hardwicke: Clark Gregg
Teenage Girl #3: Gina Mantegna

Origin: USA

Language: English

Released: 2006

Production: Steve Golin, David Kanter; Castle Rock Entertainment, Land Films, Anonymous Content; released by Warner Bros.

Directed by: Jonathan Kasdan

Written by: Jonathan Kasdan

Cinematography by: Paul Cameron

Music by: Stephen Trask

Sound: David Husby

Editing: Carol Littleton, Marty Levenstein

Art Direction: Margot Ready

Costumes: Trish Keating

Production Design: Sandy Cochrane

MPAA rating: PG-13

Running time: 97 minutes

REVIEWS

Boxoffice Online. April 20, 2007.

Chicago Sun-Times Online. April 20, 2007.

Entertainment Weekly. April 27, 2007, p. 119.

Los Angeles Times Online. April 20, 2007.

New York Times Online. April 20, 2007.

Premiere Online. April 19, 2007.

San Francisco Chronicle. April 20, 2007, p. E5.

Variety Online. May 21, 2006.

Washington Post Online. April 20, 2007.

QUOTES

Carter: "Hey grandma, not okay to answer the door when you're not wearing clothes."

Grandma Phyllis (to Carter): "I'll be dead soon and you'll still be alive, so stop complaining."

IN THE SHADOW OF THE MOON

Remember when the whole world looked up.
—Movie tagline

Box Office: $1.1 million

"Tomorrow, we, the crew of Apollo 11, are privileged to represent the United States in our first attempt to take man to another heavenly body." —Neil Armstrong.

And so began one of the most astonishing chapters of human exploration, a journey that pushed the boundaries of man's physical, mental, emotional, and creative capabilities. To not only send a man to the moon, but to return him safely to Earth. *In the Shadow of the Moon,* a documentary by David Sington, retraces the amazing accomplishments and tragic setbacks of the Apollo missions of the 1960s and early 1970s.

From 1969 to 1972 the NASA Apollo missions visited the lunar surface with an almost matter-of-fact regularity, the exception being the near-tragic Apollo 13 mission in NASA's third attempt, the subject of Ron Howard's *Apollo 13* (1995). Rather than focusing on the technical and scientific aspects of the missions, British filmmaker David Sington focuses on the human aspect. He achieves this through interviews with nearly all the surviving Apollo astronauts (the glaring exception being the reclusive Neil Armstrong) interspliced with archival footage. These interviews and archival audio tracks serve as the film's narration.

The astronauts, now in their seventies, recall the missions, the training, and the times with great clarity, a true sense of perspective, and sage-like wisdom. Michael Collins of the Apollo 11 crew notes, "We did something the whole world appreciated, participated in. Everyone felt, we, the human race, did it." This optimism is echoed throughout the film and in the film's tagline, "Remember when the whole world looked up."

The film focuses on the manned Apollo missions, but no film about the American space program could be complete without John F. Kennedy's famous speech declaring the moon to be the space program's ultimate goal, or the tragedy of the Apollo 1 fire that claimed the lives of Virgil I. "Gus" Grissom, Ed White, and Roger B. Chaffee, three of NASA's finest men. The tenuous nature of the work was known by the men but rarely, if ever, spoken of. Gus Grissom, a victim of the January 1967 Apollo 1 fire, had expressed some concern to his fellow astronauts about the potential fire hazards of working in an oxygen-rich environment, but did not dare go on record for fear of being dismissed. The tragedy and uncertainty was summed up best by Eugene Cernan, "I wasn't sure if we were burying the entire Apollo program or three of our buddies."

The program did go forward, and by Christmas 1968, Apollo 8 (manned by Frank Borman, James Lovell, and William Anders) had orbited the moon. It seemed that putting a man on the moon was within our grasp, and on July 16, 1969, Neil Armstrong became the first human to set foot on another world. The surviving astronauts express the utmost respect and admiration for Armstrong, recounting his zen-like ability to remain calm regardless of the situation, even his own near-death experience in a training accident.

Almost four years to the day after the first lunar orbit, the Apollo program was over. All told, NASA sent seven rockets to the moon, landing six, the lone exception being the aborted Apollo 13 mission.

The film's creators were given access to the NASA archive at the Johnson Space Center in Houston, Texas, and what they discovered there was a treasure trove of historical data. NASA had documented nearly every detail of the missions. The thousands of miles of film sat in their original canisters, much of it untouched, for nearly forty years. Coproducer and assistant director Chris Riley tirelessly began pulling together footage from the vaults in 2005 and transferring it to high-definition tape. The result is a visually stunning viewing experience ideally suited to the dramatic vistas of space, and much of the footage is seen for the first time.

Sington, formerly a producer for PBS's *Nova,* eschews traditional narration and allows the interviews and archival footage to tell the story. The result is extremely insightful but oftentimes confusing narration, considering the ten on-camera interviews interspliced throughout.

The original score was composed by Philip Sheppard of the Royal Academy of Music, who wrote music "that I'd want to hear," not the large, bombastic score that typically accompanies such a film. Playing on the film's frontier mentality, Sheppard drew inspiration from American string music, using the sound's simplicity as a foil against the cold, technological isolation of the moon. The effect supports the film; in the launch sequence, for example, he utilizes a piece that starts small and builds as the slowly diminishing craft hurtles into space, a direct contrast to the onscreen drama.

The movie does touch on some of the Vietnam-era struggles of the pilots and the guilt associated with not serving in combat. But it does not dwell on the conflict, but rather uses it to frame the mood of the times. Almost to a man, the men speak of how fragile the Earth seems from space and the wispy atmosphere that protects us. Sington wraps up the film with the astronauts giving their frank responses to the many conspiracy theories surrounding the missions.

Michael White

CREDITS

Origin: Great Britain, USA
Language: English
Released: 2007
Production: Duncan Copp; Passion Pictures, Discovery Films, FilmFour; released by ThinkFilm
Directed by: David Sington
Cinematography by: Clive North
Music by: Philip Sheppard
Sound: Kevin Meredith
Editing: David Fairhead

MPAA rating: PG
Running time: 100 minutes

REVIEWS

Entertainment Weekly. September 7, 2007, p. 60.
Los Angeles Times Online. September 7, 2007.
New York Times Online. September 7, 2007.
Rolling Stone Online. September 4, 2007.
Variety Online. January 31, 2007.
Wall Street Journal. September 7, 2007, p. W1.

QUOTES

Charlie Duke: "My father was born shortly after the Wright Brothers. He could barely believe that I went to the Moon. But my son, Tom, was five. And he didn't think it was any big deal."

IN THE VALLEY OF ELAH

Sometimes finding the truth is easier than facing it.
—Movie tagline

Box Office: $6.7 million

In the Valley of Elah purposefully informs viewers that running up a flag so that it flies upside down is an internationally recognized sign of distress, declaring that something has gone horribly wrong and calling urgently for someone to help make things right again. Almost half a decade after the United States invaded Iraq, and with more young lives being sunk into a quagmire that seems to continuously reveal new and horrifying depths, a genuinely concerned Paul Haggis attempted to send up just such a compelling signal with *Elah.* Perhaps too many in the country were suffering from battle fatigue, or critically saw the flag as a white one, because the film struggled at the box office despite good reviews that glowingly praised its star, Tommy Lee Jones.

In his screenplay for Clint Eastwood's *Flags of our Fathers* (2006), Haggis dealt with the agonizing psychological reverberations of war suffered by an earlier generation of Americans, showing how harrowing, emotionally indigestible experiences can linger on to painfully twist and turn within the soul for decades after the combat zone has been left behind physically. Decompression and reintegration into everyday life surely has always been challenging for those primed to kill or be killed, and one needs to find an effective, healthy shut-off valve for the full-steam-ahead aggression and hair-trigger nerves when the fighting is through. However, as Haggis illustrates, the startling number and severity of Iraq War-related post-traumatic stress syndrome (PTSS) flare-ups and meltdowns should perhaps give us pause, raising questions about the advisability of daunting urban warfare in which it is often impossible to swiftly distinguish innocents from insidious enemies devoid of identifying uniforms one can target. *In the Valley of Elah* is based primarily on a PTSS case that was chronicled in *Playboy* under the title "Death and Dishonor." The article provided a thoroughly unsettling account of a young soldier just back from Iraq who was repeatedly stabbed and then carved into pieces, his father's determined push to find those responsible, and the shocking revelation of his platoonmates' guilt that shed an eerie new light on the disorder's capacity to short-circuit judgment with nightmarish results.

The battle-torn inverted Old Glory waving atop its pole is definitely an attention-grabbing representation of American disquietude. Far less conspicuous but infinitely more powerful and affecting, however, is the sorrow imperfectly hidden behind the eyes of Hank Deerfield (Tommy Lee Jones), the patriotic common man of few words who feels the need to have the flag raised in distress by the film's final scene. The character is played with Oscar©-worthy gruff gravitas by Jones, who here gives a master class in minimalism, skillfully conveying everything from the smallest thought to the most seismic, surging emotion in a manner that creates a potent, magnetic draw through its economy of expression. Watch the carefully calibrated movements of Jones's body and furrowed face as the man he portrays fights to keep himself in check while dealing both with his son's ghastly murder by comrades who returned safe but unsound from Iraq and with a frustratingly self-serving investigation by the very institution he and his son had so selflessly served.

The film begins with Hank being notified that his son, Mike (Jonathan Tucker, seen in flashbacks), has gone AWOL upon returning stateside and should rejoin his unit in New Mexico—pronto. Hank is now a hauler of gravel in Tennessee, but once proudly served as a military policeman (MP) in Vietnam. Looking at the photos and other framed objects in the home he shares with his wife Joan (vocal Iraq War opponent Susan Sarandon), it is quickly made clear to viewers that the two sons who grew up there must surely have been imbued—by osmosis and then some—with a bedrock sense of patriotism, honor and duty. (The older boy died some years back while serving his country.) Hank leaves messages via phone and email for Mike, but there is no response. The man feels he knows his son, and his MP training kicks in. Something is not right here. Hank races cross-country in his truck to get to the bottom of things. Behind those baggy eyes peering out of that

world-weary face, one senses his own wheels turning swiftly, and in a direction he does not want to go.

Upon reaching the base, Mike's fellow soldiers are surprisingly unfazed by his disappearance, as if he has probably gone off to unwind with a bottle of booze, a prostitute, or both. Hank presses on, however, looking around his son's quarters and flashing Mike's photo around a topless joint popular with the young enlisted men. Repeated shots of Hank back in his motel room—purposefully buffing his shoes, meticulously smoothing wrinkles out of his trousers—get across with effective succinctness a lingering, regimented military mindset, a discipline that is also reflected in the terseness of his speech and the tightly reined-in nature of his emotions. Especially moving is the scene in which a soldier shows up to inform him that the charred, chopped-up body parts found scattered in a nearby field are believed to be the remains of his son. Before the young man can relate this information, Hank briefly retreats to the bathroom to staunch the blood from a shaving nick on his neck with a bit of tissue, giving himself a few more precious moments of not knowing. Braced, he reappears, crisply returns the soldier's salute, and gets hit with the shattering confirmation of his worst fears. Hank keeps his body oh-so-rigid, but his watery, horrified eyes show he is crushed.

For a stretch, *Elah* becomes an absorbing whodunit, complete with ups and downs, red-herring dead ends, and stunning disclosures. As the investigation gets underway, the police hand things off to the Army, and the Army's fervent interest seems to materialize only out of fear of how public knowledge of the soldiers' bloody abomination could stain the military itself. Teaming up with the dogged, sharp (and sometimes sharp-tongued), grieving father is local police detective Emily Sanders, played by a dark-haired Charlize Theron marvelously disappearing into character. The department's lone female cop endures belittlement and crude sexual innuendo from various boors with badges, but her guts and gray matter eventually shut them up. Haggis gives devoted single mom Emily a cute little boy (Devin Brochu) to help explain what drives her to see the case solved. As she curls up next to the sleeping child, gently laying his hanging arm back up onto the bed, one senses that she is sympathetically thinking of another parent and that other cherished son reduced to burnt parts gnawed upon by animals.

Even before Hank forcefully pleads for Emily's assistance ("My son spent the last eighteen months bringing democracy to a s***hole. He deserves better than this!"), Haggis begins sowing seeds that will eventually make this murder mystery blossom into the Academy Award©-winning writer/director/producer's message movie. Emily is seen dismissing a plea for help from the wife of a recently returned soldier because he drowned only a dog in the bathtub and not a human being. Soon the distraught lady suffers the same fate, and the tearful policewoman clearly wishes she had been able to do something to head off such a tragic outcome.

It is appropriate that Hank keeps viewing broken images from corrupted files stored upon Mike's cell phone, as each one gives a glimpse of how both those adjectives can apply to soldiers in an immensely perilous, pressure-cooker atmosphere. In the first, his son is seen playing ball with some Iraqi children. ("That's Mike," Hank says with unmistakable paternal pride.) Later ones depict the soldier eliciting guffaws from his buddies by jokily jabbing his hand over and over again into a writhing man's wounds. One soldier laughingly passes it off as doing "stupid things," levity to help one cope. However, it certainly appears to disturb Hank. He cannot shake the memory of what Mike had said with a quavering voice in a phone call from Iraq, now understanding it better: "Dad? I gotta get out of here."

Elah has a number of especially gut-wrenching scenes, two of the most poignant involving Sarandon. The first is the telephone conversation in which her character dissolves upon learning that now both her sons, having marched off in their father's footsteps, have met tragic ends. "Hank, you could've left me one!" she cries. The second is the visit she insists on making to see what little is left of her boy. "Is that everything?" she inquires with heartbreaking, numb incredulity.

The chilling scene in which Hank absorbs the details of his son's demise, related with an alarming, cool detachment by Mike's cohort and killer Corporal Steve Penning (real-life Iraq War veteran Wes Chatham), is followed by a brief image that is one of the most haunting *Elah* offers up. As Hank tries to reconcile a previously simplistic view of the military—as the good guys—with all he has now learned, his eyes now jerked open to a rather blind patriotism, an exceedingly boyish-looking new recruit passes him on the way in to who knows what. He looks like he just stepped out of a Norman Rockwell portrait of nostalgic Americana. As Hank gazes after him, the melancholy look on the man's face reveals a reflective concern. Haggis's film possesses enough power to make many walk away at its end with that very same look.

David L. Boxerbaum

CREDITS

Hank Deerfield: Tommy Lee Jones
Det. Emily Sanders: Charlize Theron
Joan Deerfield: Susan Sarandon

Lt. Kirklander: Jason Patric
Mike Deerfield: Jonathan Tucker
Sgt. Dan Carnelli: James Franco
Arnold Bickman: Barry Corbin
Chief Buchwald: Josh Brolin
Evie: Frances Fisher
Cpl. Steve Penning: Wes Chatham
Spc. Gordon Bonner: Jake McLaughlin
Pvt. Robert Ortiez: Victor Wolf
Origin: USA
Language: English
Released: 2007
Production: Laurence Becsey, Patrick Wachsberger, Paul Haggis, Patrick Wachsberger, Steven Samuels, Darlene Caamano; Summit Entertainment, Blackfriar's Bridge, Nala Films; released by Warner Independent Pictures
Directed by: Paul Haggis
Written by: Paul Haggis
Cinematography by: Roger Deakins
Music by: Mark Isham
Sound: William Sarokin
Editing: Jo Francis
Art Direction: Greg Hooper
Costumes: Lisa Jensen
Production Design: Laurence Bennett
MPAA rating: R
Running time: 121 minutes

REVIEWS

Boston Globe Online. September 14, 2007.
Chicago Sun-Times Online. September 13, 2007.
Entertainment Weekly Online. September 5, 2007.
Hollywood Reporter Online. August 31, 2007.
Los Angeles Times Online. September 14, 2007.
New York Times Online. September 14, 2007.
Newsweek Online. September 6, 2007.
San Francisco Chronicle. September 14, 2007, p. E1.
Variety Online. August 30, 2007.
Wall Street Journal. September 14, 2007, p. W1.
Washington Post. September 14, 2007, p. C4.

QUOTES

Hank Deerfield: "Why don't you come over here! I'll show you what the devil looks like!"

TRIVIA

The film takes its title from the Bible—Elah was the valley where David met Goliath.

AWARDS

Nomination:

Oscars 2007: Actor (Jones).

INTERVIEW

Everything you say can and will be used against you.
   —Movie tagline

A journalist and a starlet take on media, truth and celebrity.
   —Movie tagline

The Dutch auteur Theo van Gogh, great-grandson of Vincent van Gogh's brother Theo, intended to remake three of his films in English and set in New York, and had already chosen stars Steve Buscemi and Sienna Miller for *Interview*. After van Gogh's murder by an Islamic extremist in 2004, Buscemi, who also directed *Trees Lounge* (1996) and *Lonesome Jim* (2005), took over as cowriter and director. Using van Gogh's preference for three hand-held video cameras to create an intimate character study stripped bare of the usual filmic devices, Buscemi's *Interview* reads more like a stage adaptation. Buscemi, with his animated visage, and Miller, with her striking blonde beauty, are unusually well-suited for the low-budget, heavy-on-close-ups style, and the two share an electric chemistry that holds the audience captive despite a time-worn premise that has the duo engaging in a feature-length battle of wits.

A Washington journalist and war correspondent for a weekly news magazine, Pierre Peders (Steve Buscemi) has been relegated to a puff-piece, tabloid assignment and impatiently waits at a restaurant for his intended interviewee, the popular television and movie actress Katya (Sienna Miller). When she arrives an hour late despite openly admitting she lives just around the block, and insists upon her favorite table even though it is already occupied, the disgusted Pierre is unable to hide his contempt, smugly revealing that he has done absolutely no research on his subject and knows nothing about her. Offended by his utter lack of professionalism, Katya quickly walks out on Pierre. Swarmed by the paparazzi outside, Katya also causes a taxi carrying Pierre to crash and, feeling somewhat responsible, invites the bleeding reporter to recover at her spacious loft.

The extended scene at the loft comprises nearly the entire rest of the film, which was shot in a mere nine days. While imbibing, snorting illegal drugs, and intermittently chatting on the phone to her boyfriend (voice of James Franco), Katya offers Pierre a much different kind of interview than he had bargained for. While outwardly displaying all the vapid and superficial trappings of celebrity and fame, Katya proves she is actually quite savvy and very aware of the games of seduction she and those of her ilk are often required to play. Armed with a video camera, Pierre asks insultingly mundane questions which are waved away by the media-weary young actress. She demands he do his job, just as she proves she can do hers—seducing the testy reporter into an impassioned kiss before telling him she despises him. The love-hate dynamic is woven into nearly every exchange. He reminds her of her father, and she reminds him of his daughter who overdosed on heroin at nineteen. While Katya is busy in another room handling calls from her persistent puppy dog of a boyfriend, Pierre alternately pouts as he watches footage on television of a White House scandal he would rather be covering and snoops around on her computer reading her diary. In between the plethora of lies, they both reveal something truthful about themselves to the other while simultaneously jockeying to gain superiority and victory. Pierre feels he has won when he captures a videotaped "confession" by Katya admitting she secretly has cancer, which he swears will be "off the record." She demands he do the same, and Pierre also confesses his dark secrets on tape.

Victory is both concrete and something more vague. Pierre wants to brings his editor a sensational interview that will help get his career back on track. Katya wants to prove to Pierre than she is more than just a dumb blonde bombshell. They both seek some sort of psychological dominance as well. Ultimately, Katya wins on both fronts. What Peter thinks is Katya's diary is actually a script from her television show. The videotaped confession that Pierre thinks he has cleverly captured is straight from the script. The confession she elicits from Pierre, however, is the gritty truth that got him exiled from Washington—that he lied and made up sources for stories, and, more shockingly, that he passively let his wife die. Katya also has cleverly switched the tapes, leaving Pierre with nothing. In an ironic turn, it is clear that not only has she proven to him she is someone to be reckoned with, she also has proven she is by far the better journalist. After he has left empty-handed and she is alone watching his confession, one may imagine she is contemplating another career as the next Barbara Walters.

With its ruminations on media, fame, and truth, both of the film's accomplished actors are more than equipped to inhabit their characters. A more mature Buscemi is especially appealing in this film, his usually manic persona more subdued. With her fierce, indomitable performance, Miller, who also had a star-making turn in the little seen *Factory Girl* (2007), proves her mettle once again. While it is their undeniable chemistry, familiarity, and ease that makes the film watchable even as the story begins to flag midway through, Buscemi also injects canny, insider details. The amusing ringtone on Katya's cell phone is the annoying sound of a tiny barking dog (the ever-present accessory of many a Hollywood ingénue). Pierre's brother is played by Michael Buscemi, the director's real-life brother. And paying homage to van Gogh, the woman who exits a limosine in front of Katya's apartment and bumps into Pierre is Katja Schuurman, who played Katya in the original 2003 Dutch version of the film.

Hilary White

CREDITS

Pierre Penders: Steve Buscemi
Katya: Sienna Miller
Origin: USA
Language: English
Released: 2007
Production: Bruce Weiss, Gijs van de Westelaken; Ironworks Productions, Column Productions, Cinemavault; released by Sony Pictures
Directed by: Steve Buscemi
Written by: Steve Buscemi, David Schechter
Cinematography by: Thomas Kist
Music by: Evan Lurie
Sound: Mary Ellen Porto
Editing: Kate Williams
Costumes: Victoria Farrell
Production Design: Loren Weeks
MPAA rating: R
Running time: 83 minutes

REVIEWS

Boston Globe Online. July 20, 2007.
Chicago Sun-Times Online. July 20, 2007.
Entertainment Weekly. July 20, 2007, p. 58.
Los Angeles Times Online. July 13, 2007.
New York Times Online. July 13, 2007.
San Francisco Chronicle. July 20, 2007, p. E5.
Variety Online. January 23, 2007.
Village Voice Online. July 10, 2007.
Wall Street Journal. July 13, 2007, p. W1.

QUOTES

Katya (angry): "It's been very nice wasting time with you, Peter Peders."

TRIVIA

The woman who steps out of the limo at the end of the movie, almost walking into the distracted Pierre, is played by Katja Schuurman. She played Katya in the original 2003 Dutch version of the movie by Theo van Gogh.

AWARDS

Nomination:
Ind. Spirit 2006: Actress (Miller).

INTO THE WILD

Your large adventure on Alaska.
—Movie tagline

Box Office: $18.3 million

Sean Penn's fourth directorial effort, *Into the Wild*, is a compelling, fascinating film exploring a young man's quest for meaning through embarking on a dangerous—and some might say foolhardy—journey into the wilderness of Alaska. Based on the book by Jon Krakauer, the film chronicles the adventures of Christopher McCandless (Emile Hirsch), who left his home and family and headed across the country and then north to Alaska to break away from the vices of modern civilization. The story has a tragic ending, and the film (like the book) does not glorify Chris or all the decisions he made, but there is a thread of sympathy for his underlying motives as well as the courage he displayed, even though it was tainted by a certain degree of selfishness and arrogance. The film is a carefully, artistically constructed study of the human drama at the core of this unusual journey.

After graduating from Emory University, Chris Mc-Candless decides to abandon the life he knows, seeking enlightenment that has, to date, escaped him. Partially as a rebellious act against the unhappy, disingenuous life of his parents (played by William Hurt and Marcia Gay Harden) and mostly because of a general disillusionment with the world around him, Chris donates the $24,000 left from his law school fund to Oxfam, burns the rest of his money, and heads west, working odd jobs and meeting many different people along the way. He begins calling himself "Alexander Supertramp" and believes he is above the life he left behind. Among those he meets on the road is a kind, middle-aged hippie couple, Rainey and Jan (Brian Dierker and Catherine Keener), a friendly farmer named Wayne (Vince Vaughn), an amorous young singer (Kristen Stewart), and an elderly widower, Ron (Hal Holbrook), who comes to see Chris as a wandering grandson. Eventually, Chris makes it to Alaska, where he is determined to survive alone in the wilderness and therein find the enlightenment he seeks. Unfortunately, he is not as capable of surviving as he thinks he is, and ultimately he dies of starvation.

Penn does not construct the story linearly, which works to the film's advantage. When the movie begins, Chris has already arrived in Alaska. His "present," in which he struggles to survive in the beautiful but very dangerous wild, alternates with flashbacks that tell the story of how he got where he is. The structure works well as it contrasts Chris's lonely quest and ultimately ill-fated attempt to survive the wilderness with the adventures he experienced over the course of the journey that brought him to this place. Ironically, it is the enrichment of his life gained from those he encounters along the way that provides the most valuable enlightenment, rather than the fatal solitude of the wild. Unfortunately he does not realize that until it is too late.

Chris is not a completely likeable character, as he often comes across as self-seeking, proud, and foolishly idealistic. When he leaves home, he does not even bother to tell his family—not even his sister Carine (Jena Malone)—where he is going. And although he appears to be well-read, his references to writers of the past tend to be self-aggrandizing. Yet, especially as played by Hirsch, the character demonstrates a genuine sincerity and hope for finding the answers he knows cannot be found in the corrupted society he renounced. Hence, the film strikes a thoughtful balance in weighing the merits of his motives—the sincerity of his quest—against the often extreme choices he makes. The characters he encounters along his journey are crucial to the development of the story, in terms of the themes in particular, and the actors give credible, engaging performances. Hal Holbrook especially imbues Ron Franz with a depth and warmth that stand out as one of the highlights of the film.

Visually, the film features some beautiful cinematography, and Penn employs a variety of shots, angles, and editing choices that correspond thematically to the drama that unfolds. One weakness of the movie is the over-use of original songs by Eddie Vedder that tend to sound like blatant commentary. The film would have been better served by more understated music.

Into the Wild is easily one of the most engaging and interesting films released in 2007, and a mature, sophisticated effort by director Penn, telling an unconventional story about the pursuit of a dream, a story that is in some sense tragic but also challenging, courageous, and thought-provoking.

David Flanagin

CREDITS

Christopher McCandless: Emile Hirsch
Billie McCandless: Marcia Gay Harden
Walt McCandless: William Hurt
Carine McCandless: Jena Malone
Jan Burres: Catherine Keener
Wayne: Vince Vaughn
Tracy: Kristen Stewart
Ron Franz: Hal Holbrook
Rainey: Brian Dierker
Origin: USA
Language: English
Released: 2007
Production: Sean Penn, Art Linson, William Pohlad; Art Linson Productions, River Road Entertainment, Square One C1H; released by Paramont Vantage
Directed by: Sean Penn
Written by: Sean Penn
Cinematography by: Eric Gautier
Music by: Michael Brook, Edward Vedder, Kaki King

Sound: Edward Tise
Music Supervisor: John Kelly
Editing: Jay Cassidy
Art Direction: Domenic Silvestri, John Richardson
Costumes: Mary Claire Hannan
Production Design: Derek R. Hill
MPAA rating: R
Running time: 148 minutes

REVIEWS

Christian Science Monitor Online. September 21, 2007.
Entertainment Weekly Online. September 19, 2007.
Hollywood Reporter Online. August 31, 2007.
Los Angeles Times Online. September 21, 2007.
New York Times Online. September 21, 2007.
Premiere Online. September 20, 2007.
Rolling Stone Online. October 4, 2007.
Variety Online. September 1, 2007.
Village Voice Online. September 18, 2007.
Wall Street Journal. September 21, 2007, p. W1.

QUOTES

Christopher McCandless: "I read somewhere…how important it is in life not necessarily to be strong…but to feel strong."

TRIVIA

Sean Penn waited ten years to make the film to make sure he had the approval from the McCandless family.

AWARDS

Golden Globes 2008: Song ("Guaranteed")
Nomination:
Oscars 2007: Film Editing, Support. Actor (Holbrook)
Directors Guild 2007: Director (Penn)
Golden Globes 2008: Orig. Score
Screen Actors Guild 2007: Actor (Hirsch), Support. Actor (Holbrook), Support. Actress (Keener), Cast
Writers Guild 2007: Adapt. Screenplay.

THE INVASION

Do not trust anyone. Do not show emotion. Do not fall asleep.
—Movie tagline

Box Office: $15 million

The Invasion suffered from a host of production woes and resulted in the least successful of the four movies based on the 1955 novel *The Body Snatchers*. With little in the way of suspense or compelling characters, the

2007 version of Jack Finney's science-fiction classic also lacks a modern allegorical context, what made the other three adaptations so effective and relevant.

The basic premise followed in all four films is that alien pods have landed on earth, invaded human hosts, and taken over their very beings. Don Siegel's *Invasion of the Body Snatchers* (1956) became a classic B-movie, playing on the rampant communist paranoia of the day. More than two decades later, Philip Kaufman gave his remake, *Invasion of the Body Snatchers* (1978), a timely Watergate/Vietnam slant. Abel Ferrara's San Francisco-set *Body Snatchers* (1993) features a highly sympathetic lead character with a military twist and suggests an AIDS metaphor. The current version lacks any such subtext, vague references to Iraq and Darfur aside, and the film falls flat, relying on action over character.

The English-language debut for German director Oliver Hirschbiegel was written by David Kajganich, but they cannot shoulder all the blame for this slick but unsubstantial and lackluster effort. The two originally envisioned an innovative documentary approach laced with political commentary, but it failed to make the cut with studio executives. They hired the Wachowski brothers, Andy and Larry, for an extensive rewrite and subsequently reshot a majority of the film using James McTeigue; all are three veterans of *The Matrix* films. This bland commercialization of the movie not only ruined it artistically but also failed to produce audiences and box office, recouping a dismal $15 million of its bloated $80 million budget.

The Invasion has the pods that infect humans upon contact finding their way to earth on a downed space shuttle and adds the disgusting twist that the infection is spread through vomit. Very creative, and often projectile, regurgitation scenes follow ad nauseum.

The best the film has to offer is its reputable stars. Nicole Kidman stars as Carol Bennell, a Washington, D.C. psychiatrist privy to the fact that something is seriously amiss. She spends much of the film popping uppers, as the infection occurs during sleep. Her costar Daniel Craig, unfortunately absent from many scenes as doctor Ben Driscoll, is impotently miscast as Carol's best friend who pines for her in vain. Carol's distant ex-husband Tucker Kaufman is played by Jeremy Northam, who is conveniently a higher up at the Centers for Disease Control who gets infected and then is able to spread the infection by offering inoculations for a made-up flu epidemic. Despite the talent of these three actors, who make a valiant effort here, and the star power of Kidman and Craig, they cannot rise above the stock characters, leaden dialogue, and all-too-familiar situations of this pulp fiction. While a nice piece of casting is Veronica Cartwright's clever cameo as a patient of

Carol's—a nod to the 1978 film in which she starred as Nancy Bellicec—it also will draw negative comparisons to that earlier, better film.

Other than trying to subvert the alien pandemic, much of the plot involves Carol, with Ben and biologist Dr. Stephen Galeano (Jeffrey Wright) in tow, chasing down her young son Oliver (Jackson Bond), who was kidnapped by his alien father but is happily immune to the infection. Forced to act like one of the replicants in order to move about undetected, Kidman's immobile, mannequin-like demeanor is completely believable.

The replicants themselves are certainly no reason to see the film. They are clichéd, zombie-like incarnations we have seen countless times, and there is little explanation for why they are invading Earth. They claim if humans were more like them there would be no war, but their message of world peace is uneasily mingled with their desire to cause as many problems as possible for earthlings. The audience will hardly be on the edge of their seats, frantically worrying about the fate of the human race. The aliens are easily killed, while the movie coolly assures us that a cure for the easily identified infection is fast in the making.

An illogical and inane epilogue suggests that humans may be the real monsters as war, famine, and the usual disasters of the world continue unabated. Perhaps alien invasion is actually the answer to the human dilemma after all.

Hilary White

CREDITS

Carol: Nicole Kidman
Ben: Daniel Craig
Tucker: Jeremy Northam
Oliver: Jackson Bond
Dr. Galeano: Jeffrey Wright
Wendy: Veronica Cartwright
Autumn: Malin Akerman
President: John M. Jackson
Dr. Belicec: Josef Sommer
Mrs. Belicec: Celia Weston
Schuster: Jeff Wincott
Danila: Alexis Raben
Yorish: Roger Rees
Origin: USA
Language: English
Released: 2007
Production: Joel Silver; Silver Pictures, Vertigo Entertainment, Village Roadshow Pictures; released by Warner Bros.
Directed by: Oliver Hirschbiegel

Written by: David Kajganich
Cinematography by: Rainer Klausmann
Music by: John Ottman
Sound: David M. Kelson, Mary H. Ellis
Editing: Hans Funck, Joel Negron
Art Direction: James F. Truesdale, Caty Maxey
Costumes: Jacqueline West
Production Design: Jack Fisk
MPAA rating: PG-13
Running time: 99 minutes

REVIEWS

Boston Globe Online. August 17, 2007.
Chicago Sun-Times Online. August 17, 2007.
Entertainment Weekly Online. August 15, 2007.
Hollywood Reporter Online. August 16, 2007.
Los Angeles Times Online. August 17, 2007.
New York Times Online. August 17, 2007.
San Francisco Chronicle. August 17, 2007, p. E1.
Variety Online. August 15, 2007.
Washington Post. August 17, 2007, p. C1.

QUOTES

Carol: "Something's happening. I don't know what it is, but I can feel it. Have you noticed anything?"

TRIVIA

While filming in Baltimore, Daniel Craig got the call from Barbara Broccoli informing him he won the role of James Bond. He had to take a short period off shooting to fly back to London for the *Casino Royale* (2006) press release.

THE INVISIBLE

Life, death and something in between.
—Movie tagline

How do you solve a murder when the victim is you?
—Movie tagline

Box Office: $20.5 million

While adaptations of Japanese horror films may be quite common to American audiences, *The Invisible* is an adaptation of the Swedish film *Den Osynlige* (2002), which itself is based on the novel by Mats Wahl. The result is a movie that is not so much a horror film as a minimally interesting tale of psychology and redemption.

The surreal dream sequence that begins the American version of *The Invisible* is designed to immediately throw the viewer off balance. It is Nick Powell's (Justin Chatwin) high school graduation party, and while some

of the guests are seated normally at the dinner table, others mill around aimlessly, seeming out of place. Nick's mother, Diane Powell (Marcia Gay Harden), the picture of suburban perfection, prattles on endlessly in a toast to her ideal son. Without saying a word, Nick leaves the table and makes his way to the basement, and taking a rifle from a wall rack, shoots himself.

The following breakfast scene shows Nick's mother hiding behind her morning paper, coldly refusing to engage her son in a meaningful conversation. A budding poet, Nick tries desperately to get her to agree to send him to London to study writing. In the face of her adamant refusal, the self-reliant Nick finds a way to fund the trip himself by writing and selling term papers. He uses the proceeds to purchase his ticket to London and is scheduled to leave in just a few days.

Nick reveals his plan to his best friend, Pete Egan (Chris Marquette), who has money woes of his own—his parents will not give him any. Consequently, the cash-strapped Pete resorts to buying teenage necessities such as a cell phone from the school's own black marketeer, Annie Newton (Margarita Levieva). When Pete is unable to pay Annie the money he owes her, a clichéd bathroom-confrontation scene ensues when Annie and her gang corner Pete. She puts her ever-ready knife blade under his fingernail as a warning to come up with the money he owes her, or suffer a most painful "manicure."

Annie is a juvenile delinquent and a minor felon-in-training. Her boyfriend Marcus (Alex O'Loughlin) is on parole, but that does not keep the two from frequently engaging in criminal activity, including car theft. The high Annie gets from their illegal activities soon leads to an impulsive jewelry-store display heist, and Annie stashes the stolen goods in her school locker.

When an anonymous caller leads the police to Annie, she assumes the tipster is Pete. When Annie is released on bail, she and her cohorts find Pete and torture him to try to force a confession. Pete was not, in fact, the one who called the police; it was her boyfriend Marcus. But Annie is relentless in her interrogation of Pete, and under extreme duress, Pete implicates Nick, believing he has flown safely off to London. Nick, however, has had second thoughts about the trip and is still in town. Annie quickly finds Nick and administers a savage beating. So savage, in fact, she thinks she has killed him, and she and her posse, along with Pete, dump Nick's body down a manhole in the forest.

When Nick goes to school the next day and no one can see him he assumes he is dead and in some sort of spiritual limbo. Eventually he realizes he is not dead but in a coma, and his body has not yet been found. From his unique position of invisibility, Nick learns all that he needs to help heal himself. He watches as the search for him unfolds and while Detective Larson (Callum Keith Rennie) and Detective Tunney (Michelle Harrison) question his mother and Annie. He learns more about Annie and her abusive home life; how she tries to protect her little brother. He sees his friend Pete try to commit suicide due to his guilt over what he has done. And eventually, he sees his mother's hard veneer crack and he realizes, much to his surprise, how much she loves him.

It becomes a race against the clock as Nick persuades the hard-hearted Annie (who somehow manages to "hear" him on the other side) to develop a conscience and finally tell the police where his body is. It is clear that Annie will eventually find redemption and, therefore, Nick will be found.

In keeping with the film's pared-down aesthetic, Nick is portrayed as a more traditional paranormal entity, devoid of computer-generated imagery and gimmicky special effects. He interacts with his environment—getting jostled by crowds, being hit by cars, throwing books—but in reality, his surroundings are actually unaffected by his presence. There are no clichéd ghost activities, such as walking through walls or playing cheap tricks on the visible, merely Nick's frantic attempts to be rescued from a slow but certain death.

The Invisible is visually appealing, with a rough-around-the-edges noir quality that helps support this story of redemption. Levieva's Annie proves to be a butterfly when she finally takes off her moth-eaten knit cap and emerges from her tough-girl cocoon. But Nick as played by the sad-eyed Chatwin is so nonplussed and unfeeling throughout his journey that he is completely compassionless. Despite its filmic merits, the lack of tension and mystery, along with poorly drawn characters, has *The Invisible* fade from memory as soon as the end credits start to roll.

Beverley Bare Buehrer

CREDITS
Nick Powell: Justin Chatwin
Diane Powell: Marcia Gay Harden
Pete Egan: Christopher Marquette
Marcus Bohem: Alex O'Loughlin
Annie Newton: Margarita Levieva
Det. Brian Larson: Callum Keith Rennie
Det. Kate Tunney: Michelle Harrison
Matty: Ryan Kennedy
Martin Egan: Serge Houde
Origin: USA
Language: English
Released: 2007
Production: Roger Birnbaum, Gary Barber, Neal Edelstein, Mike Macari, Jonathan Glickman; Spyglass Entertainment, Hollywood Pictures, Limbo Productions; released by Buena Vista
Directed by: David S. Goyer
Written by: Mick Davis, Christine Roum
Cinematography by: Gabriel Beristain
Music by: Marco Beltrami
Sound: Aaron Glascock
Music Supervisor: Alexandra Patsavas
Editing: Conrad Smart
Production Design: Carlos Barbosa
MPAA rating: PG-13
Running time: 97 minutes

REVIEWS

Boston Globe Online. April 28, 2007.
Boxoffice Online. April 27, 2007.
Los Angeles Times Online. April 30, 2007.
New York Times Online. April 28, 2007.
Variety Online. April 27, 2007.

QUOTES

Nick Powell: "Pete! This isn't the way out! If you die, I die! God, Pete, you're my last hope!"

TRIVIA

A subplot was removed involving drug smugglers. It was feared this would give it an R-rating and wasn't necessary to the plot.

J

THE JANE AUSTEN BOOK CLUB

You don't have to know the books to be in the club.
—Movie tagline

Box Office: $3.5 million

Countless highly acclaimed films have been based on the six novels written by Jane Austen and feature some of Hollywood's biggest stars as her popular heroines. Some of the more recent entries are literal and classically set, including Gwyneth Paltrow's *Emma* (1996) and Keira Knightley's *Pride & Prejudice* (2005). Some are loosely based, modern updates, including Alicia Silverstone's *Clueless* (1996) and Renée Zellweger's *Bridget Jones' Diary* (2001). There is even a Bollywood version featuring Aishwarya Rai, *Bride & Prejudice* (2004). And a biographical film about Austen made this year, *Becoming Jane,* starred Anne Hathaway.

While entry into this not-so-exclusive club may require an original premise, it would seem to ensure a built-in audience of eager, mostly female fans. Based on the novel by Karen Joy Fowler, Robin Swicord's *The Jane Austen Book Club* certainly boasts a unique plot, based on six Sacramento women who gather to discuss Jane Austen and discover that their lives parallel aspects of the novels. The limited-release independent film was harder pressed to find an audience, however, and with a budget of under $6 million, garnered only $3.5 million domestically.

The number six resonates throughout the film. Just as Austen wrote six novels, the club boasts six members, who meet over six months to discuss the books. All Austen's heroines must overcome various obstacles to find love, including social and economic differences, rival love interests, and misunderstandings, and the *Jane Austen Book Club* heroines are no different. While Swicord's directorial debut feature lacks a certain cinematic style—with uneven pacing and lacking clarity in some of the relationships—the writer/director, who penned the screenplay for *Little Women* (1994), has no trouble creating compelling situations and convincing characters.

While the conceit is somewhat contrived and predictable—that each member would find parallels in their own lives within the novels—it is also half the fun. The audience knows what to expect and can simply enjoy the good-natured ride. The characters are interesting, and the talented and animated cast work well together. Bernadette (Kathy Baker), the club's founder, is somewhere in her sixth decade and has been divorced six times. Her friend Jocelyn (Maria Bello) is a dog breeder who stages an overly elaborate funeral for her deceased Rhodesian Ridgeback that more than hints at loneliness. After years of a seemingly happy marriage, Sylvia (Amy Brenneman) finds that her husband Daniel (Jimmy Smits) is cheating on her and wants a divorce. Unbeknownst to Sylvia, her daughter Allegra (Maggie Grace) is a lesbian with relationship problems of her own. Prudie (Emily Blunt) is a rigid, uptight high school French teacher in a troubled marriage with husband Dean (Marc Blucas).

The club's sole male member, Grigg (Hugh Dancy), is a science-fiction aficionado seeking to branch out in the world of literature. The independent Jocelyn, serving as the Emma of the club, is a matchmaker who tries to fix up Grigg and Sylvia, but in true Austen style, he is interested in Jocelyn, who is naturally as clueless about his intentions as he is about Austen's works (Jocelyn is forced to explain to him that the books are not sequels).

The film cuts between the book discussions and scenes from the members' lives, which they also discuss during the meetings. This serves both to illuminate themes from the books and to allow the women to gain insight from Austen's words. The characters' discussions of the books reflect the intelligence of both the script and the actors. It is a rare film that is a tribute to reading and literature, and although it is a difficult task to dramatize such a sedentary activity, Swicord is able to find a pleasing middle ground where quiet reading shots are interspersed throughout the action.

Many scenes naturally involve love and heartbreak. One of Prudie's handsome students (Kevin Zegers) takes an unwholesome interest in her. "He looks at me like he's the spoon and I'm the dish of ice cream," she sighs wistfully. The film also boasts a savvy sense of humor. Allegra is exasperated with Prudie's pretentiousness: "If only she'd stop speaking French!" Jocelyn quips, "Or at least go to France, where it would be less noticeable." Blunt delivers Prudie's posturing lines with hilarious deadpan. When asked which Austen book she would be interested in, she chooses *Persuasion*, saying she is "increasingly drawn to its elegiac tone."

Roger Ebert, proving yet again he is both witty and wise, summed up the timelessness of Austen in his review of the film. "You could say that Austen created Chick Lit and therefore Chick Flicks. You could, but I would not, because I despise those terms as sexist and ignorant. As a man, I would hate to have my tastes condescended to by the opposite of Chick Lit, which, according to Gloria Steinem, is Prick Lit. I read Jane Austen for a simple reason, not gender-related: I cannot put her down and often return to her in times of trouble."

Hilary White

CREDITS

Bernadette: Kathy Baker
Jocelyn: Maria Bello
Prudie: Emily Blunt
Sylvia: Amy Brenneman
Allegra: Maggie Grace
Grigg: Hugh Dancy
Sky: Lynn Redgrave
Daniel: Jimmy Smits
Dean: Marc Blucas
Trey: Kevin Zegers
Cat: Nancy Travis

Corinne: Parisa Fitz-Henley
Origin: USA
Language: English
Released: 2007
Production: John Calley, Julie Lynn, Diana Napper; Mockingbird Pictures; released by Sony Pictures Classics
Directed by: Robin Swicord
Written by: Robin Swicord
Cinematography by: John Toon
Music by: Aaron Zigman
Sound: Peter J. Devlin
Music Supervisor: Barklie Griggs
Editing: Maryanne Brandon
Art Direction: Sebastian Schroeder
Costumes: Johnetta Boone
Production Design: Rusty Smith
MPAA rating: PG-13
Running time: 106 minutes

REVIEWS

Boston Globe Online. September 21, 2007.
Chicago Sun-Times Online. September 21, 2007.
Entertainment Weekly Online. September 19, 2007.
Hollywood Reporter Online. September 10, 2007.
Los Angeles Times Online. September 21, 2007.
New York Times Online. September 21, 2007.
San Francisco Chronicle. September 21, 2007, p. E1.
Variety Online. September 9, 2007.
Village Voice Online. September 18, 2007.

QUOTES

Prudie Drummond: "Being the only child of a woman who gave birth in a commune after changing her name to Skygirl, I've come to loath hippie-handie crafts."

TRIVIA

Each cast member was required to read the said book they had to discuss in the film.

JINDABYNE

Under the surface of every life lies a mystery.
—Movie tagline

In the 1970s the Australian New Wave brought a unique kind of cinema to international audiences. In films like *Picnic at Hanging Rock* (1975), *The Last Wave* (1977), and *Walkabout* (1971), the mystical powers of the land and the belief systems of aboriginal culture were major characters, often formidable obstacles to the life journeys and goals of white Australians. Ray Lawrence attempts to do something similar with *Jindabyne,* a quiet, quirky film that uses water as a symbol for danger, challenge, freedom, and rebirth.

Lawrence's previously best-known work was the thriller *Lantana* (2001). In *Jindabyne* he attempts an unusual combination of murder mystery, marital character study, and magical tale, and it is quite intriguing, even if ultimately it lacks the coherence and forcefulness of many of the 1970s Aussie classics. The film was written by Beatrix Christian, based on Raymond Carver's short story "So Much Water So Close to Home." Indeed, the tale is immersed in watery mysteries.

The film set in the town of Jindabyne, an odd place in a corner of New South Wales. When a river was dammed in the 1960s, the entire town was moved to higher ground. In an early scene, Stewart Kane (Gabriel Byrne) takes his young son Tom (Sean Rees-Wemyss) fishing along the shore of the lake created by the dam, and the boy reels in an old clock. His father gives him a spooky talk about the old submerged town, saying that sometimes you can still hear church bells ringing under the water.

The odd, disturbing tone of the film is set by an opening scene in which an old man in a truck traps a young aboriginal woman driving down a bleak road; it is not long before we learn he has raped and killed her. But even everyday life in the town is spooky—Tom and a schoolmate are fond of killing small animals, for instance, for unexplained reasons. Stewart, a former champion race-car driver, owns an automobile garage, and he and his buddies have an obsession with fly fishing that embodies their male rebellion against civilized norms. Domestic difficulties are revealed when Stewart's mother visits and tries to take over household chores from Claire (Laura Linney); it turns out that, though now seemingly stable, Claire was so disturbed that she left home for eighteen months after their son was born.

When Stewart and his three fishing buddies finally take their epic weekend trip to a river so remote and magical it is almost legendary, they find the body of the murder victim in the river. Unwilling to trek out immediately, and rendered irrational by the lure of their fishing expedition and the bounty of the river, they decide to stay the weekend anyway, and Stewart ties a leg of the corpse to a tree branch in the river to keep it from floating downstream and being destroyed in the rapids below.

When the men return to town, they are greeted with stern rebukes from the local authorities and with unwanted attention from the media. Since the victim was nonwhite, the incident immediately takes on a racial hue, and rock throwing and graffiti spraying is the response from nearby aborigines. In the town, most of the fishing party's womenfolk are forgiving, but not Claire, who unbeknownst to Stewart is carrying another child. She is incensed and determined to show that this time she is the good parent. She organizes a drive to collect money for the victim's funeral and travels to her town, where she unknowingly has two encounters with the murderer.

Water is a locus of menace throughout the film. In one scene, we are hooked into Tom's fear as he watches Claire swim far out into the lake and disappear for many anxious seconds underwater, only to resurface. Later, his friend runs off to the swimming hole with him and tricks him into trying to rescue her; the boy almost drowns but learns how to swim on his own in a frightening life-or-death trial.

Lawrence shoots the film in short episodes that fade out quickly to a blank screen or the next scene. There are no musical cues to direct an audience's emotions— except for the swelling choruses that accompany the many vistas of the lake, the land, and the river valley of the fishing expedition. The music obviously conveys both a magic and a danger, as if warning the principals that the spirits of the land are restless and potentially vengeful. Something very similar occurs in *The Proposition* (2006), the brilliant Australian western, but there the spooky music and landscapes worked together to add to the tension. In *Jindabyne,* however, the motif is overused, and you feel like Lawrence is trying to concoct additional drama that is not in the story itself. The tale is simple, unique, and compelling, but Lawrence is so intent on trying to make the landscape such a mysterious and monumental character that he ends up detracting from the story.

Byrne is bumbling, opaque, and slippery in his characterization of an alpha male under siege domestically, and except for one explosion of rage it is hard to get a handle on the source of his character's discontent—it seems a rather free-floating anger. Linney, however, is brilliant doing a quiet slow burn, rock-steady and principled and, despite her past, seemingly the only sane woman in town. Lawrence lays on the high-minded message way too thickly in the end, however, with a hopeful reconciliation that seems hard to believe after the fissures that have occurred. It is as if all that has to happen is for everyone to hear a love song, and everything is solved. There is a subtle and nasty little postscript regarding the consequences for the murderer—it seems he gets away with it, but Nature may be exacting revenge.

In style, subject matter, and theme, *Jindabyne* is quirky and intelligent, but it is also a bit lightweight. Lawrence's deftness in many scenes is canceled out by his heavy-handedness in the sweeping suggestions of the land as spirit ruler. The land, in fact, seems fairly passive and inconsequential, and much of the way the townsfolk interact seems just mildly ludicrous and petty rather than fated or sinister. Had its two-hour length been trimmed by about thirty minutes and the story told more directly and compactly, *Jindabyne* would have made a dandy, disturbing little oddball tale. Instead, it seems more than a bit forced.

Michael Betzold

CREDITS

Stewart: Gabriel Byrne
Claire: Laura Linney
Carl: John Howard
Rocco: Stelios Yiakmis
Jude: Deborra-Lee Furness
Carmel: Leah Purcell
Gregory: Chris Haywood
Elissa: Alice Garner
Billy: Simon Stone
Tom: Sean Rees-Memyss
Caylin-Calandria: Eva Lazzaro
Susan: Tatea Reilly
Origin: Australia
Language: English
Released: 2006
Production: Catherine Jarman; April Films, Australian Film Finance Corporation, Babcock & Brown, Redchair Films; released by Sony Pictures Classics
Directed by: Ray Lawrence
Written by: Beatrix Christian
Cinematography by: David Williamson
Music by: Paul Kelly, Dan Luscombe
Sound: Peter Grace
Editing: Karl Sodersten
Costumes: Margot Wilson
Production Design: Margot Wilson
MPAA rating: R
Running time: 123 minutes

REVIEWS

Boxoffice Online. April 27, 2007.
Entertainment Weekly. April 27, 2007, p. 122.
Hollywood Reporter Online. July 20, 2006.
Los Angeles Times Online. April 27, 2007.
New York Times Online. April 27, 2007.
Variety Online. May 24, 2006.
Village Voice Online. April 24, 2007.

TRIVIA

The screenplay is based on the short story "So Much Water So Close to Home" by American writer Raymond Carver. The

song "Everything's Turning to White" by Australian singer-songwriter Paul Kelly was also inspired by Carver's story.

JOSHUA

The story of a perfect boy who had a perfect plan.
—Movie tagline

A meditation on the cruelty of children and a virtual public service announcement warning of the dangers of procreation, *Joshua* is an unnerving and spookily comic thriller that fits nicely alongside *The Omen* (1976), *Rosemary's Baby* (1968), and *The Bad Seed* (1956) in the "murderous children" genre. Free of supernatural elements, George Ratliff's film gives us a young villain who feels completely misunderstood by his parents and will stop at nothing to get what he wants, even if that involves practicing ancient Egyptian mummification methods on his pet guinea pig or purposefully creating violent crayon drawings that warn the authorities of parental abuse.

The Cairns are a Manhattan family who appear to have everything. Patriarch Brad Cairn (Sam Rockwell) is a hedge fund manager and wife Abby (Vera Farmiga) does not need to work for them to keep their cavernous Upper East Side apartment. Everything appears rosy upon the arrival of their second child, Lily, including the lack of postpartum depression that plagued Abby after the birth of their first child, Joshua. Now nine, Joshua (Jacob Kogan) is preternaturally smart, a piano prodigy specializing in atonal compositions who favors jackets and ties, keeps his prodigious head of hair conservatively combed into a side-parted helmet, and speaks with a detached cool that calls to mind a primary-school version of Patrick Bateman in *American Psycho* (2000).

Early in the film, shortly after Brad picks Joshua up from a soccer game to go to the hospital to see his new sister, Joshua announces that he does not want to play the game anymore, establishing his desire to stick strictly to intellectual and artistic pursuits. Upon Abby's return home with baby Lily, Abby's brother Ned (Dallas Roberts) and Brad's fundamentalist Christian mother Hazel (Celia Weston) are visiting. As Joshua is performing a piano piece for the guests, Abby asks him to stop playing for the baby's sake. Joshua promptly vomits, a physical reaction to his being pushed aside in favor of the newborn and the first sign that things are going to get worse.

Joshua's affinity for Uncle Ned, a gay musical-theater composer and the relative most understanding and encouraging of his musical endeavors, is evident early on. When Joshua performs at his exclusive private school a rendition of "Twinkle Twinkle Little Star" that quickly descends in to avant-garde territory, only Ned appreciates the result. On the other hand, when Brad goes to meet Joshua's teacher for a conference, she tells him the boy is so far ahead that he could benefit from skipping two grades. Brad responds by telling her "I'd probably be the kid in the class who picked on him because he was different."

Soon, it is implied that Joshua is a serial killer in training when several of Joshua's classroom pets die on the same day, and Buster, the family dog, is found dead on the kitchen floor. Abby's severe mood swings and Lily's nonstop crying also seem rather suspicious, but the first major red flag is raised for Brad when he finds an eerie night-vision videotape that Joshua has made of a nocturnal visit to his new sister's nursery. Brad promptly installs a lock on his door and keeps the baby in his own bedroom. Joshua's scheming escalates to the point of casualties, and it becomes clear that his intention is a complete familial restructuring.

Joshua is a lean, tight, and modest thriller that clearly models itself on the cinema of the 1970s. Though it often evokes *The Omen* in that a father is alone in recognizing that his child is evil, and *Rosemary's Baby* both for thematic reasons and for its wonderful use of New York locations, unlike those films, *Joshua* never introduces the supernatural. In fact, Joshua even dispels antichrist notions by attending a revival meeting with Hazel and telling his parents upon returning home that he wants to be born again. (Ratliff, whose first feature was the documentary *Hell House* [2001], about a church-sanctioned Halloween funhouse in Texas, seems to be making another statement about organized religion.) The script, by Ratliff and David Gilbert, chooses to have us believe that Joshua is simply evil. At times, the proceedings are so exaggerated that they veer into the uncomfortably comedic, creating a tonal unevenness. At the same time, Abby's bipolar downslide is genuinely nerve-wracking, and the sight of her sobbing uncontrollably while trying to use a breast pump is both bizarre and harrowing.

At its root, the film is about Brad's perfect life being completely torn asunder. Rockwell, always an incredibly watchable performer, creates Brad as a laid-back overachiever who, through the course of the film, becomes increasingly unhinged. It is a strong and reserved performance. Farmiga has more of an opportunity to create fireworks, and she does virtually explode as Abby's chemical imbalance overcomes her. A scene in which she cuts her foot on a piece of glass in the kitchen, only to smear blood up and down her legs while describing to Joshua a pair of red boots that made her feel sexy in her dating days, is particularly

uncomfortable. When Abby's condition eventually merits her visit to a mental hospital, *The Onion*'s Nathan Rabin believes it "heralds the film's fall from a classy psychological thriller suffused with atmosphere and dread into one of those silly fright flicks about a child whose angelic visage masks a heart of pure evil."

Kogan is a talented young actor, and though his Joshua's robotic, businessman-in-training demeanor is often funny, it never comes off as parody. As Todd McCarthy notes in *Variety*, "with his abundant dark hair, steady gaze, and defiant serenity, Kogan resembles the child actor Buddy Swan, who played the young Charles Foster Kane in *Citizen Kane,* and commands center stage in every scene he's in." Kogan also deserves commendation for learning the piano and playing some visibly complex compositions on his own, and for singing a song, written for the film by Dave Matthews, that strikes a perfect note of obsessive creepiness. The Matthews version, which appears over the end credits, is a deviation from the performer's usual style.

Though *Joshua* does not really bring anything new or incredibly inventive to the table, a great cast and a clever ambiguity elevates the material. As the *Village Voice*'s J. Hoberman notes, "for all the craziness, *Joshua* is still based largely on the power of suggestion and caginess as to which character is actually having the breakdown." Reactions to the film's bizarre moments of humor are likely to differ from viewer to viewer. Funny bits aside, there are moments of true helplessness and despair in *Joshua,* and Kogan's sharp turn is sure to have the blood of more than a few new or expecting parents running cold in their veins, even as they giggle uncomfortably.

David Hodgson

CREDITS

Brad Cairn: Sam Rockwell
Abby Cairn: Vera Farmiga
Ned Davidoff: Dallas Roberts
Hazel Cairn: Celia Weston
Chester Jenkins: Michael McKean
Joshua Cairn: Jacob Kogan
Origin: USA
Language: English
Released: 2007
Production: Johnathan Dorfman; ATO Pictures; released by Fox Searchlight
Directed by: George Ratliff
Written by: George Ratliff, David Gilbert
Cinematography by: Benoit Debie
Music by: Nico Muhly

Sound: Ken Ishii
Editing: Jacob Craycroft
Art Direction: Katya DeBear
Costumes: Astrid Brucker
Production Design: Roshelle Berliner
MPAA rating: R
Running time: 105 minutes

REVIEWS

Boston Globe Online. July 13, 2007.
Entertainment Weekly. July 20, 2007, p. 58.
Hollywood Reporter Online. January 26, 2007.
Los Angeles Times Online. July 6, 2007.
New York Times Online. July 6, 2007.
Premiere Online. July 6, 2007.
San Francisco Chronicle. July 13, 2007, p. E1.
Variety Online. January 24, 2007.
Washington Post. July 13, 2007, p. C5.

QUOTES

Joshua (to his dad): "You don't have to love me."

JUNO

> *A comedy about growing up…and the bumps along the way.*
> —Movie tagline

Box Office: $135 million

The eponymous heroine of *Juno,* from a breakthrough script by first-time screenwriter Diablo Cody, is a bright, sarcastic teen the likes of which we so seldom see in movies. Quick-witted, ever ready with a sharp retort, sometimes a bit hard-edged but ultimately good-hearted, Juno MacGuff stands as one of the most memorable characters in movies this year. Imagine a teen comedy with a heroine who is more self-aware than everyone in the room and yet still has a lot of growing up to do. Indeed, Juno herself is such an original creation that it engenders the rare perfect marriage of character to actress. Ellen Page stars as a teenager facing an unplanned pregnancy in the kind of role that many fine actors never get to play in a lifetime, but at the age of twenty, Page has made an indelible impression in a standout role.

Directed by Jason Reitman, *Juno* is more than a sparkling showcase for Page—it is also one of the funniest, most heartfelt comedies to emerge in quite some time, and a coming-of-age tale that eschews traditional teen angst for something more sophisticated. Every character who orbits Juno is a distinct person who is more complex than we would at first suspect. While everyone tries his or her best to respond to Juno's crisis, oddly enough, the film rarely feels like it is about a crisis. It maintains an offbeat tone so that we can laugh uproariously to a stinger of a wisecrack and then find ourselves startled by a touching moment that reveals an unexpected side of a character.

From the moment she suspects that she is pregnant and takes several home-pregnancy tests, it is clear that Juno will not be felled by this turn of events. She can engage in witty repartee with the drugstore employee and then be sardonic as she tells her best friend, Leah (Olivia Thirlby), about her situation. Juno is a product of a hip teenage world—using a hamburger-shaped telephone, peppering her speech with pop-culture references and odd bits of slang, downing huge slushies—and yet rises above it with a show of smarts and verbal dexterity. Juno dashes off funny lines such as "I'm just calling to procure a hasty abortion" when calling a clinic. And she chooses a clinic called Women Now because, as she deadpans, "they help out women now."

But when a classmate picketing out front tells Juno that the baby already has fingernails, Juno changes her mind. That the film contains a sympathetic pro-life character who is not a religious nutcase and an abortion clinic that looks like a small nightmare is just one sign that *Juno* will not play it safe. Such is the unpredictability of Cody's screenplay that it cheekily toys with liberal orthodoxy. After all, Reitman, as he showed in *Thank You for Smoking* (2006), is one director in Hollywood willing to be politically incorrect.

Deciding against the abortion, Juno tells her parents the news. Her dad, Mac (J.K. Simmons), and stepmother, Bren (Allison Janney), take the announcement rather well, probably because they feared Juno had something worse to announce, such as a drug habit. Resolving to give the baby up for adoption, she finds an ad placed by a yuppie couple, Vanessa (Jennifer Garner) and Mark (Jason Bateman), who have tried in vain to conceive and now want to adopt. While Juno's family is clearly middle class, Mark and Vanessa live in an upwardly mobile neighborhood in a beautiful, albeit sterile, house that the anal-retentive Vanessa strives to make perfect.

The surprising treatment of this couple is actually one of the nicest touches in *Juno.* It turns out that Vanessa is desperate for a child, while Mark is not as sure. A composer of commercial jingles, he forges a bond with Juno over punk music, which gradually drives a wedge between him and Vanessa. While his work has made him a good living (one deodorant commercial bought them their kitchen, he wryly observes), it becomes increasingly apparent that he considers himself a sellout

(Juno's astute perception) and still harbors dreams of rock stardom. When Juno discovers Mark's room—his wife has allotted him a small space for his musical passions—and Vanessa catches them doing a spontaneous jam to a Courtney Love song, it might as well be that she has caught them having sex.

Mark, we come to understand, does not really want to take on the responsibilities of adulthood (meaning the responsibilities of parenthood), and his connection to Juno reawakens these doubts. On some emotional level, he is a good match for Juno, but obviously he cannot take up with a pregnant sixteen-year-old, even though he is clearly intrigued by her. Bateman gives a spot-on portrayal of a certain creative type who cannot quite face the reality that his time has passed him by. And Garner does a fine job as well; it would have been easy to turn Vanessa into a shrewish, controlling wife belittling her husband, but instead we understand her yearnings for a child and realize it is her misfortune that her husband is not on the same page with her. In one surprising scene in a mall, she runs into Juno, who has Vanessa touch her stomach and talk to the unborn child. It is an unexpected development that reveals Vanessa's vulnerability, a side of her we do not see with her husband. And Page, in a subtly magical moment, shows a softer side of Juno as she sees what the baby means to a woman she may have stereotyped as a materialistic yuppie.

Everyone else in the cast is excellent as well. Michael Cera plays Paulie Bleeker, a likeable geek and the father of Juno's baby. He is obviously scared but does not know what to do and looks like he would rather stay out of the way and just hope that Juno can take care of everything without involving him. But in playing this typically uncommunicative male who, despite his generally well-meaning intentions, cannot quite show his feelings or offer the support she needs, Cera gradually shows that Paulie does care deeply about Juno. In his own adolescent way, he does not know how to show it, and his tongue-tied demeanor is no match for Juno's hyperactive mouth.

The movie takes a bold turn when Mark tells Juno that he is going to leave Vanessa. At this point, it is pretty obvious that Juno has a crush on him, but when he suggests that he will soon be available, she is shocked back into reality. A fantasy of an ideal guy who shares her love of music is one thing, but she knows that she cannot be with a man more than twice her age, especially one whose own fantasies have taken an irresponsible turn.

For Juno, Mark's surprise decision is critical. She must face the reality that the adult world will let her down and that her best laid plans will not necessarily go

the way she wants them to. It forces her to reevaluate everything, and we come to see that the brilliance of Page's performance is that a snarky, tough-talking façade does indeed mask a little girl dealing with issues that are, as Juno puts it, "way beyond my maturity level." She sees all too clearly the precariousness of a seemingly perfect marriage—the sadness at the core of this couple she genuinely likes.

At this key moment, Juno looks to her father. Conveying the essence of a man who has probably experienced so much in life that he will not be undone by his daughter's dilemma, Simmons proves unflappable as Mac. Of all the people in Juno's life, he is the one who "gets" her the best and understands her arch sense of humor (indeed, we see hints that she inherited it from him) when others might be shocked. It is a genuinely touching moment when he gives her advice about finding the right person, one "who loves you for exactly what you are."

Vanessa's dream of motherhood is fulfilled when Juno gives birth to a baby boy. And, in the end, Juno and Paulie get together. In a truly moving scene, Juno sheds the ironic posturing that she so often adopts, and bares her soul to him. It is just one more amazing wrinkle in this remarkable performance that this wiseacre girl could also be so credible in declaring that she loves him.

If the story and characters were not reason enough to celebrate this screenplay, the dialogue itself is the most distinctive of the year, heralding a fresh voice in Diablo Cody. It is filled with one-liners and quips and is that rare and strange combination of being artificial—after all, no one in real life talks in this stylized way, blending pop-culture sassiness and sly rejoinders—and realistic-sounding at the same time. Maybe it is fun to imagine living in a world where people such as Juno are always ready with a cutting remark or crackling line to disarm everyone else.

In addition to the dialogue, Cody rounds out this world with many bright details, such as the ever-present track team jogging around the school to signal the change of seasons and an ongoing joke about Leah's seemingly unfathomable crush on a teacher who is not even handsome. Even in the throwaway jokes and odd character quirks, the screenplay creates an eccentric world similar to ours but, like Juno herself, just a little cooler.

Indeed, rare is a movie that is hip and clever without sacrificing its humanity or love of its characters. *Juno* is as brainy as the young woman whose name it bears, but also has an enormous heart. It is almost impossible not to fall in love with her and the film. In explaining her odd name, Juno says that it came from mythology; while

Zeus had many women, Juno was his wife. The implication is that she had something a little extra special, just like this modern-day girl and the movie that bears her name.

Peter N. Chumo II

CREDITS

Juno MacGuff: Ellen Page
Paulie Bleeker: Michael Cera
Vanessa Loring: Jennifer Garner
Mark Loring: Jason Bateman
Bren MacGuff: Allison Janney
Mac MacGuff: J.K. Simmons
Leah: Olivia Thirlby
Origin: USA
Language: English
Released: 2007
Production: Lianne Halfon, John Malkovich, Russell Smith, Mason Novick; Mandate Pictures, Mr. Mudd; released by Fox Searchlight
Directed by: Jason Reitman
Written by: Diablo Cody
Cinematography by: Eric Steelberg
Music by: Mateo Messina
Sound: James Kusan
Music Supervisor: Peter Afterman, Margaret Yen
Editing: Dana E. Glauberman
Art Direction: Michael Diner, Catherine Schroer
Costumes: Monique Prudhomme
Production Design: Steve Saklad
MPAA rating: PG-13
Running time: 96 minutes

REVIEWS

Boston Globe Online. December 14, 2007.
Chicago Sun-Times Online. December 14, 2007.
Christian Science Monitor Online. December 14, 2007.
Entertainment Weekly Online. November 28, 2007.
Hollywood Reporter Online. September 10, 2007.
Los Angeles Times Online. December 5, 2007.
New York Times Online. December 5, 2007.
New Yorker Online. December 17, 2007.
Rolling Stone Online. December 13, 2007.
San Francisco Chronicle. December 14, 2007, p. E1.
Variety Online. September 2, 2007.
Washington Post. December 14, 2007, p. C1.

QUOTES

Juno MacGuff: "You should've gone to China, you know, 'cause I hear they give away babies like free iPods. You know, they pretty much just put them in those t-shirt guns and shoot them out at sporting events."

TRIVIA

Ellen Page suggested that her character Juno would be a fan of the music by Kimya Dawson and The Moldy Peaches.

AWARDS

Oscars 2007: Orig. Screenplay
British Acad. 2007: Orig. Screenplay
Ind. Spirit 2008: Actress, Film, First Screenplay
Writers Guild 2007: Orig. Screenplay

Nomination:

Oscars 2007: Actress (Page), Director (Reitman), Film
British Acad. 2007: Actress (Page)
Golden Globes 2008: Actress—Mus./Comedy (Page), Film—Mus./Comedy, Screenplay
Ind. Spirit 2008: Director (Reitman)
Screen Actors Guild 2007: Actress (Page).

K

KICKIN' IT OLD SKOOL

Breakdancing isn't dead. It's been in a coma.
—Movie tagline

Box Office: 4.5 million

Kickin' It Old Skool is another unwelcome entry in the man-child/low-brow comedy genre. The fanciful twist here is that the hero, Justin Schumacher (Jamie Kennedy), is more than just a man who acts like he has the maturity of a preteen, he actually is a man with the maturity of a preteen.

In the 1980s, twelve-year-old Justin (Alexander Calvert) was a popular boy who was known for his break-dancing prowess. But while participating in a school-wide dance-off with his break-dancing team, the Funky Fresh Boyz, Justin leaps off the stage and hurts himself so badly that he falls into a coma. He stays in his coma for twenty years, but just as his parents, Sylvia (Debra Jo Rupp) and Marty (Christopher McDonald), are about to turn off the machines that are keeping him alive, he wakes up. Oddly, director Harvey Glazer spends quite a long time on the sequences in which Justin's parents agonize over having to pull the plug. It is not played for comedy, and the strange decision to linger on a subject that is not known for its comedic qualities takes the film on an unexpected—and unsuccessful—detour.

Glazer, aided by writers Trace Slobotkin, Josh Siegal, and Dylan Morgan, shows similarly bad taste elsewhere in the film. Justin, now in his thirties but with the mind of a twelve-year-old, returns home. His father, financially ruined by medical bills, decides not to spring for physical therapy, declaring it just another way the hospital is trying to extract money from patients. Marty is eager to make up for having done twenty years of Justin's chores and sends his son outside to get to work. Justin, who lacks control of his limbs, wobbles hideously on his nearly useless legs. Not only is it in poor taste—which could be forgiven in such a comedy—but it is not at all funny, and in a comedy, that is not forgivable.

The plot concerns the efforts of Justin to find a way to repay his parents for his medical bills. He is thrilled when a dance contest, sponsored by a video channel similar to MTV, comes to town. Hoping to win the top prize of $100,000, Justin attempts to reunite the Funky Fresh Boyz. Darnell (Miguel A. Núñez, Jr.) has become a security guard at a mall. Aki (Bobby Lee) works in a cubicle at a bank. And Hector (Aris Alvarado) is an overweight meter maid. Typically, the film treats the situation as a chance to make a fat joke. "Is that Hector?" Justin asks when he and Darnell first spot Hector. Darnell replies, "Or some dude that ate Hector?"

The various plot permutations serve as the setup for jokes about 1980s culture. Perhaps that could have been enough on which to rest a film like this, but the writers never quite find the humor in their cultural references. Despite a good gag where Justin tries to kill himself using Pop Rocks and cola, the filmmakers apparently think dressing Justin in a series of bad parachute pants is high cultural satire. The film is entirely lackluster, and even the very funny Bobby Lee from *Mad TV* doing the robot dance is not enough to interrupt the audience ennui.

The movie was not a hit with audiences or critics. Audiences largely ignored the film and, in general, critics agreed that *Kickin' It Old Skool* was a bad movie, only disagreeing on the extent of its awfulness. Mark Olsen of the *Los Angeles Times* called the film, "a witless, mind-numbingly inert comedy," while Lou Lumenick of the *New York Post* dubbed it merely "a pathetically unfunny comedy."

The weak link in this film is Kennedy. The twelve-year-old Justin was a sweet boy with a shy charm, but Kennedy plays the adult Justin as someone who is so idiotic and naïve that he could easily be mistaken for someone suffering from brain damage. Kennedy talks in a slow, cloyingly cutesy voice and sounds more like a four-year-old than the preteen he is supposed to be. It is hard to gain audience enthusiasm for a character that is so far from possessing identifiable human traits.

But perhaps the hardest thing to believe about the film is that such a man has a chance of rekindling a romance with the likes of the lovely Jennifer Stone (Maria Menounos), Justin's former girlfriend and a dance teacher. Jennifer dates Justin's old nemesis (Michael Rosenbaum), now the arrogant host of the dance show. Even though Justin seems barely able to function appropriately in the world, the movie insists that Jennifer is attracted to him because he is so innocent. And that is harder to believe than the idea that all of Justin's old 1980s parachute pants still somehow manage to fit him.

Jill Hamilton

CREDITS

Justin Schumacher: Jamie Kennedy
Darnell Jackson: Miguel A. Núñez, Jr.
Jennifer Stone: Maria Menounos
Kip Unger: Michael Rosenbaum
Sylvia Schumacher: Debra Jo Rupp
Marty Schumacher: Christopher McDonald
Roxanne: Vivica A. Fox
Dr. Fry: Alan Ruck
Aki Terasaki: Bobby Lee
Hector Jiminez: Aris Alvarado
Young Justin: Alexander Calvert
Kim: Michelle Trachtenberg
Yun: Kira Clavell
Young Jennifer: Alexia Fast
Himself: David Hasselhoff (Cameo)
Himself: Erik Estrada (Cameo)
Himself: Roddy Piper (Cameo)
Origin: USA
Language: English
Released: 2007
Production: John Hermansen, Bob Yari, Philip Glasser, Jamie Kennedy; Jizzy Entertainment, Hi-Def Entertainment; released by Yari Film Group
Directed by: Harvey Glazer
Written by: Trace Slobotkin, Josh Siegal, Dylan Morgan

Cinematography by: Robert M. Stevens
Music by: James A. Venable
Sound: John Boyle
Editing: Sandy Solowitz
Art Direction: Chelsea Yusep
Costumes: Maria Livingstone
Production Design: Tink
MPAA rating: PG-13
Running time: 108 minutes

REVIEWS

Boston Globe Online. April 28, 2007.
Hollywood Reporter Online. April 30, 2007.
Los Angeles Times Online. April 30, 2007.
New York Times Online. April 28, 2007.
Variety Online. April 27, 2007.

TRIVIA

In Justin's hospital room you can see he is hooked up to a flux capacitor, which in *Back to the Future* (1985) is what makes time travel possible.

KILLER OF SHEEP

Charles Burnett's 1977 feature debut, *Killer of Sheep* finally received a major theatrical run in 2007, but this highly vaunted, hitherto little-seen effort may have been a bit oversold by establishment critics. Without question, *Killer of Sheep* represents something different from Hollywood films and even most independent films of its era. Charles Burnett's conscious break from the blaxploitation genre and most films involving African American issues was significant for even if few people actually saw this effort, the reverberations were and are real (witness the work of Julie Dash, David Gordon Green, and Billy Woodbury, among others). The question today is this: For not being shown widely, did *Killer of Sheep* gain an over-inflated reputation?

The minimalist narrative is certainly part of what makes this film different from others of the time. In Burnett's original story, Stan (Henry G. Sanders) works in a south-central Los Angeles slaughterhouse by day and comes home to his family at night—his wife (Kaycee Moore) and small children (Jack Drummond and Angela Burnett). Between mopping up the sheep's blood on the slaughterhouse floor and after-hours sparring with friends and neighbors, Stan is too tired to romance his wife, which causes friction in their marriage. Meanwhile, despite their sad and impoverished existence, the children create their own world of play. Desperate to make more money, Stan considers committing a criminal act; yet in the end, he only reconfirms the futility of his life and demonstrates how little he differs from the sheep he slaughters.

The genesis of *Killer of Sheep* is much more complicated than the deliberately simple film plotline might suggest. As writer, director, producer, cameraman, and editor, Burnett shot much of the film in the Watts district of Los Angeles while a graduate student at the University of California Los Angeles in the early 1970s. He finally completed this $10,000 production in 1977, but he then faced a distribution problem: Not only was the subject oft-putting to most exhibitors, Burnett had failed to acquire the music rights to much of the soundtrack. Thus, the release was limited largely to film festivals. Nevertheless, over the years a number of critics discovered the film at festivals around the world and declared it an overlooked gem. By 1990 the Library of Congress had placed it on its prestigious National Film Registry list. The director restored the film in 2000 and subsequently acquired rights to the music used in the soundtrack.

Thirty years after its initial release, *Killer of Sheep* appeared in theaters and on DVD to great acclaim. Yet the question still remains as to whether or not reviewers have accurately accessed the film. Writing in the *New York Times,* Manohla Dargis declared it "an American masterpiece," and other reviewers followed suit. This masterpiece label needs to be qualified, however. Unlike many of the blaxploitation films of the 1970s, *Killer of Sheep* fits into the earlier tradition of independent "race films" of the 1920s, 1930s and 1940s, particularly those produced and directed by African American filmmakers, including Oscar Micheaux and Spencer Williams. Scholars and critics have realized that the previously dismissed "race film" genre must be judged by standards appropriate to the genre, one that is quite different from the polished Hollywood filmmaking of the era. Like these mostly forgotten (some lost) films made specifically for African American audiences, *Killer of Sheep* is amateurishly acted and technically unpolished. Yet in the context of these anti-Hollywood, independent productions, *Killer of Sheep* provides a powerful vision, one that is at least as good as the best of Micheaux's surviving work (*The Symbol of the Unconquered* [1920], *Body and Soul* [1925], *Murder in Harlem* [1935]) and less problematic in its filmic representation of race. *Killer of Sheep* also seems to be loosely tied to the New American avant garde film movement by combining neorealism with expressionism, thereby creating vividly poetic black-and-white imagery. When judged by the Hollywood standards, however, the film seems lacking, not just in plot and pacing, but also in production value and traditional performance style.

Kenneth Turan summed up the originality of Burnett's treatment of race in *Killer of Sheep* in his review for the *Los Angeles Times* by saying that it is a "film that is more episodic than plot driven, that offers a character-centered portrait of a community rarely seen on film to this day: people of color who are part of the working poor, living from check to check and trying to make ends meet and get ahead." In his *Village Voice* review, J. Hoberman wrote, "*Sui generis, Killer of Sheep* is an urban pastoral—an episodic series of scenes that are sweet, sardonic, deeply sad, and very funny. It's a movie of enigmatic antics, odd juxtapositions, disorienting close-ups, and visual gags…" The single most lauded aspect of *Killer of Sheep* has always been its extraordinary soundtrack, what Burnett wanted to be an aural history of African American popular music, which encompasses everything from Dinah Washington's "This Bitter Earth" (accompanying a memorable slow dance by the husband and wife characters) to Paul Robeson's classic, "The House I Live In," to the contemporary edge of Earth, Wind & Fire.

Thus, action movie fans (or those horror enthusiasts expecting another *Silence of the Lambs* [1991], based on the title) may feel bored by a movie in which so little happens narratively and in which sounds and images dominate. On the other hand, dedicated, well-meaning cineastes might treat the film as an "object d'art," as the Europeans did during its original festival showings. To do so, however, would be to ignore some of the historical and ethnographic realities the film presents. Even in the *New York Times,* Dargis continued this line of criticism by comparing the film to "the work of such photographers as Helen Levitt and Robert Frank…". As Hoberman keenly observed, Burnett never quite repeated the organic beauty of his debut in his subsequent films, although he approached this level with the television movie *Nightjohn* (1996) and movie *To Sleep with Anger* (1990).

Killer of Sheep deserves recognition as a major work, though viewers will not fully appreciate it until they understand it better. Perhaps watching the film will inspire them to learn more about it; nevertheless, even without the background information, viewers will likely be moved by its quiet strength and heartfelt portrayals.

Eric Monder

CREDITS

Stan: Henry Sanders
Stan's Wife: Kaycee Moore
Eugene: Eugene Cherry
Bracy: Charles Bracy
Origin: USA

Language: English

Released: 1977

Production: Charles Burnett; released by Milestone Film and Video

Directed by: Charles Burnett

Written by: Charles Burnett

Cinematography by: Charles Burnett

Sound: Charles Bracy

Editing: Charles Burnett

MPAA rating: Unrated

Running time: 80 minutes

REVIEWS

Boston Globe Online. June 8, 2007.
Entertainment Weekly Online. March 28, 2007.
Los Angeles Times Online. April 6, 2007.
New York Times Online. November 14, 1978.
New York Times. March 30, 2007, p. E12.
Premiere Online. March 28, 2007.
San Francisco Chronicle. May 18, 2007, p. E5.
Village Voice Online. May 27, 2007.
Washington Post. June 1, 2007, p. C5.

TRIVIA

No permits were obtained in the filming of the movie.

AWARDS

Natl. Film Reg. 1990
New York Film Critics Circle Awards 2007: Special Award.

THE KING OF KONG: A FISTFUL OF QUARTERS

Don't get chumpatized.
    —Movie tagline

The King of Kong: A Fistful of Quarters, a documentary by Seth Gordon about the rivalry between two die-hard video game players, might at first seem like a movie for a niche audience. It is, after all, set in a milieu most people do not think much about and are probably not interested in exploring. Yet in the eccentric personalities who populate this subculture and in a classic showdown between two very different competitors, this film ends up being very insightful about success and failure, group dynamics, and the basic desire to make one's mark in the world. It is also a very funny movie, one of the most entertaining of the year.

A hot sauce businessman from Hollywood, Florida, Billy Mitchell is such a fantastic creation, one would think that only the most talented screenwriter could invent him. The fact that he is real and has spent a good portion of his life crafting his own persona makes him all the more incredible. A champion video game player as a teenager, he has been hailed as the "Gamer of the Century," a title he has parlayed into an entire lifestyle. Holder of the world record score in Donkey Kong, considered the most difficult of all classic arcade games, Billy Mitchell is driven to be the best and speaks in grandiose terms about his achievement: "When you want to attach your name to a world record, when you want your name written into history, you have to pay the price." From his carefully combed long hair and patriotic neckties to his pronouncement that "No matter what I say, it draws controversy, sort of like the abortion issue," uttered without even a hint of irony, Billy may be forever playing out his teenage heyday but is nonetheless a man of singular purpose.

On the other hand Steve Wiebe, from Redmond, Washington is just an ordinary family man who, unlike Billy, has experienced one disappointment after another dating from high school. After being laid off, he channels his downtime into a new obsession that gives meaning to his life, breaking the Donkey Kong record, and becomes adept at navigating the highest levels of the game. When he surpasses Billy's mark, representatives from Twin Galaxies, the organization that monitors and arbitrates video game records, come to Steve's home to inspect his machine. Discovering that he received a suspicious replacement part, they call into question the veracity of Steve's record. However, the controversy feels like an excuse for Twin Galaxies to nullify the record of a newbie who dares to challenge the legendary Billy Mitchell.

While all of the video game minutiae about hand-eye coordination and pattern recognition and the politics of Twin Galaxies might seem to interest only the gamers in the audience, the portrait of these two very different men who each need to find validation has universal appeal and wider implications. Ultimately this wacky subculture populated by an assortment of eccentrics is driven by the basic human motivation to compete and be recognized as the best, which makes this community more similar to mainstream culture than viewers may initially realize.

Moreover, the film is similarly illuminating about group behavior in the way that all of the authorities at Twin Galaxies rally around Billy and make it difficult for Steve to win recognition. From Walter Day, who has spent much of his adult life managing Twin Galaxies, to Robert Mruczek, who has devoted countless hours to reviewing videotapes to verify world records, to Brian Kuh, a video game expert who has retired at age thirty and acts like Billy's protégé, everyone is protective of the champion because he is essentially the commercial face of Twin Galaxies. Thus, it would be bad business to acknowledge a new champion regardless of his gaming prowess.

No sooner does Steve, determined to redeem himself, break Billy's world record at a tournament in a famed New Hampshire arcade improbably called Funspot than Billy's friends produce a videotape chronicling a game in which Billy surpasses Steve's new mark. It is typical of Steve's luck that his success is short-lived and that Billy can steal his thunder without even showing up at the tournament.

It is clear that director Gordon supports Steve or at least does what he can to make Billy seem as sinister as possible, including using Leonard Cohen's cynical "Everybody Knows" song to make it clear that such a guileless man as Steve stands no chance against Billy's cunning and the support of his minions. Indeed, Steve, who eventually finds work as a middle school science teacher, ends up making cross-country trips, first to Funspot and then to Billy's hometown to compete in live tournaments. Although Billy maintains that this is the best way to authenticate a record-breaking score, he steers clear of putting himself on the line publicly.

Steve falls short in his attempt to set a world record in public, but he maintains a positive attitude and, in a satisfying development, gradually gains the respect of the gaming community, garnering an apology from Walter for the way Twin Galaxies has treated him. The film ends on a note of triumph for Steve. We learn in an epilogue that, at home, he eventually breaks Billy's world record, meaning that Steve eventually holds the top scores in public and private play. Treating this plot turn in a coda, however, and not as a major part of the story is the film's biggest flaw. After all, it would have been satisfying to see Billy's reaction when he gets his comeuppance.

Hearing about her father's attempt to earn a spot in the *Guinness Book of World Records*, Steve's young daughter declares, "Some people sort of ruin their lives to get in there." It is an out-of-the-mouths-of-babes moment and one that succinctly encapsulates the mania of the true gamer in pursuit of a goal most people would undoubtedly find unimportant.

Peter N. Chumo II

CREDITS

Origin: USA
Language: English
Released: 2007
Production: Ed Cunningham; Launch Pad; released by Picturehouse

Directed by: Seth Gordon
Cinematography by: Seth Gordon
Music by: Craig Richey
Editing: Seth Gordon
MPAA rating: PG-13
Running time: 79 minutes

REVIEWS

Boston Globe Online. August 24, 2007.
Chicago Sun-Times Online. August 24, 2007.
Entertainment Weekly Online. August 15, 2007.
Los Angeles Times Online. August 17, 2007.
New York Times Online. August 17, 2007.
Rolling Stone Online. August 7, 2007.
San Francisco Chronicle. August 24, 2007, p. E1.
Variety Online. August 15, 2007.
Washington Post Online. August 24, 2007.

QUOTES

Walter Day: "I wanted to be a hero. I wanted to be the center of attention. I wanted the glory. I wanted the fame. I wanted the pretty girls to come up and say, 'Hi, I see that you're good at Centipede.'"

THE KINGDOM

Under fire. Under pressure. Out of time.
—Movie tagline

How do you stop an enemy who isn't afraid to die?
—Movie tagline

An elite FBI team sent to find a killer in Saudi Arabia. Now they have become the target.
—Movie tagline

Box Office: $47.5 million

Director Peter Berg's *The Kingdom* begins with a quick rundown of America's involvement in Saudi Arabia, told in a montage of archival footage, the upshot of which is essentially that America and Saudi Arabia are inextricably linked through oil. The sequence shows at confounding speed the tension caused by the Saudi Kingdom's dependence on both Islamic fundamentalists (the Wahabbis) and American corporations and military protection not only to maintain control of the country's population but also to ensure the Saudi Royal family's massive wealth, although fifteen of the nineteen September 11, 2001 hijackers were Saudis. The film maintains a similar tenuous balance of content and tone throughout: it is a meditative think-piece on American-Saudi relations told in the confused context of an international crime-thriller centered on a joint FBI-Saudi investigation of the bombing of an American oil company's civilian compound on Saudi soil. This dichotomy constantly threatens to drag *The Kingdom* into either banal stereotype (which does occasionally happen) or pseudo-intellectuality, but the movie manages to walk this precarious tightrope fairly well. Though it stumbles along the way, *The Kingdom* packs a punch at its conclusion, which makes its seeming missteps appear to be well-laid traps for viewers who wish to see nothing more than what they are expecting to find.

From the opening credits sequence, *The Kingdom* maintains a furious pace. During a softball game held at an American oil company's housing compound in Riyadh, Saudi Arabia, a group of terrorists dressed as Saudi State Police shoot at and kill American civilians, and a suicide bomber, also posing as a policeman, detonates a bomb in the midst of those fleeing the scene. Later, as investigators and medical personnel gather at the site of the attack, another enormous explosion occurs killing American officers and several American and Saudi civilians. As the film makes clear, the Federal Bureau of Investigation is the agency called in to investigate when Americans are killed on foreign soil. Back in the United States, FBI Special Agent Ronald Fleury (Jamie Foxx), briefs other agents on the situation. One of them, agent Janet Mayes (Jennifer Garner), is visibly shaken by the news, and agent Fleury whispers something in her ear to calm her down. Initially, the Attorney General and State Department heads are reluctant to send his team to Riyadh for fear that "more foreign boots on Saudi soil will make an already combustible situation more combustible," but Fleury is able to manipulate the Saudi ambassador into letting his team investigate the incident. Fleury's team consists of agent Mays, agent Grant Sykes (Chris Cooper), and agent Adam Leavitt (Jason Bateman). Once in Saudi Arabia, the team finds itself stymied at every turn by Saudi National Guard members, who consider the bombing to be a local matter. Agents Mayes and Leavitt in particular are treated with suspicion—Mayes for being a woman and Leavitt for his Jewish heritage (his passport indicates that he has even been to Israel).

Not until Fleury convinces one of the local Saudi princes to allow Saudi State Police Colonel Faris al Ghazi (Ashraf Barhom, in an excellent performance), head of security at the compound and recognized by Fleury as a natural detective, to assist does the investigation begin to make headway. After several false starts, an examination of the explosion site reveals that the bomb was hidden inside an ambulance and that the bomb itself used marbles as projectiles. As a result, the police track down and shoot a group of men who had access to state police uniforms and ambulances. The U.S. Ambassador consid-

ers the case closed at this point and demands that the team return to America. Fleury's convoy is attacked, however, and Leavitt is captured by terrorists. Fleury's team and the Saudi police pursue the terrorists to a very poor neighborhood and begin looking for Leavitt in the various apartment buildings the terrorists use as a refuge. They are able to rescue Leavitt just as he is about to be beheaded. As the team is leaving the apartment complex, they stop in a particular apartment so that agent Mays can check on a little girl and her family that she had earlier frightened. Mays offers the girl a lollipop and the girl offers Mays a marble—the same kind of marble that was found at the bomb crater. In short order, the grandfather of the family is revealed to be noted terrorist mastermind and bomb maker Abu Hamza, one of his grandsons shoots Colonel al Ghazi in the neck, Fleury kills that grandson, Abu Hamza points a gun at Fleury, and Abu Hamza himself is gunned down. Colonel al Ghazi dies in Fleury's arms as Abu Hamza whispers something into another (younger) grandson's ear in order to calm the boy, and dies shortly thereafter. At the end of the film, it is revealed to the audience that what Fleury had whispered to agent Mayes and what Abu Hamza whispered to his grandson was essentially the same, to paraphrase: "Don't worry. We're going to kill them all."

While it is true that *The Kingdom* relies heavily on the elements of a cliché action-adventure thriller, several of its components point to and argue strongly for, its more high-minded aspirations. The central event in *The Kingdom* was clearly inspired by the 1996 Khobar Towers bombing in Saudi Arabia in which a fuel truck exploded near housing for U.S. Air Force personnel, and possibly by the 2003 Riyadh Compound bombing, and the surrounding circumstances (a foreign force trying to function within an indigenous populace) are resonant of the U.S.-led war in Iraq. The moment when it is revealed that both Fleury and Abu Hamza independently of one another make the statement, "we will kill them all" is both compelling and surprising, even shocking. It seems designed to destroy the preconceptions of anyone who has come to see the film—both the Americans and the Islamic fundamentalists are denied ultimate moral superiority. It is a moment that undercuts audience expectation with great effect. Also, the relationship between al Ghazi and Fleury may be trite (both men are professionals and fathers from different cultures united by a sense of expertise, a love of family, and a desire for the truth), but the charisma and focus of the actors allows their performances to transcend the material. A genuine connection between the characters shines through and brings a much-needed touch of humanity, however maudlin, to *The Kingdom*.

Though the film was a box office success, the schizophrenic nature of *The Kingdom* (its attempt to be high-concept while sticking to the rather formulaic trappings of a crime thriller) earned it a split critical response. The following views are typical of the schism among critics: Stephanie Zacharek of *Salon.com* said that, "The picture is made with a degree of care, and what's surprising about it is the way [director Peter] Berg actually resists making rah-rah jingoistic proclamations instead of relying on them"; yet Kenneth Turan of the *Los Angeles Times* complained that the movie wants the audience to feel as though it is "watching something relevant when what's really going on is a slick excuse for efficient mayhem that's not half as smart as it would like to be." Even so, there is definitely something to be said for *The Kingdom*'s bombast other than its technical proficiency or its ability to provide moviegoers with a thrill. Its completely overwhelming effect seems to be the result of a conscious effort to portray the confusion and brutality of that combat that has taken place daily in Iraq. Such a dizzying array of violence and confusion can wreak havoc on the human psyche.

Although *The Kingdom,* may be billed as entertainment and use stereotypes to draw in the audience, its point of view and surprising plot turns indicate that the seemingly mindless violence and stock characterizations have a point. If nothing else, they force viewers to question their own preconceptions.

John Boaz

CREDITS

Ronald Fleury: Jamie Foxx
Grant Sykes: Chris Cooper
Janet Mayes: Jennifer Garner
Adam Leavitt: Jason Bateman
Col. Faris Al Ghazi: Ashraf Barhoum
Sgt. Haytham: Ali Suliman
Damon Schmidt: Jeremy Piven
Origin: USA
Language: English
Released: 2007
Production: Michael Mann, Scott Stuber; Forward Pass Productions, Relativity; released by Universal
Directed by: Peter Berg
Written by: Matthew Carnahan
Cinematography by: Mauro Fiore
Music by: Danny Elfman
Sound: Willis D. Burton
Music Supervisor: Kathy Nelson
Editing: Kevin Stitt, Colby Parker, Jr.
Art Direction: A. Todd Holland

Costumes: Susan Matheson
Production Design: Tom Duffield
MPAA rating: R
Running time: 110 minutes

REVIEWS

Boston Globe Online. September 28, 2007.
Chicago Sun-Times Online. September 28, 2007.
Entertainment Weekly Online. September 26, 2007.
Hollywood Reporter Online. September 12, 2007.
Los Angeles Times Online. September 28, 2007.
New York Times Online. September 28, 2007.
Rolling Stone Online. October 4, 2007.
San Francisco Chronicle. September 28, 2007, p. E1.
Variety Online. September 11, 2007.
Washington Post. September 28, 2007, p. C6.

QUOTES

Ronald Fleury (before breaking open a door in terrorist apartment): "Which side do you think Allah's on?"
Colonel Faris Al Ghazi: "We are about to find out!"

TRIVIA

Ronald Fleury (Jamie Foxx) mentions the *Terrell Tribune* newspaper when discussing the terrorist attacks. Terrell, Texas, also happens to be Jamie Foxx's hometown.

AWARDS

Nomination:

Screen Actors Guild 2008: Outstanding Performance by a Stunt Ensemble in a Motion Picture.

THE KITE RUNNER

There is a way to be good again.
—Movie tagline

Box Office: $15.4 million

Khaled Hosseini's bestselling novel *The Kite Runner* was both a heart-warming and harrowing story that captured the attention of readers for its carefully detailed description of a boyhood friendship ruined on the shoals of political intolerance, class bias, and war. The lengthy book was adapted for the screen by writer David Benioff and captained by Marc Forster, who directed *Finding Neverland* (2004). Because of the novel's popularity and critical acclaim, expectations for the movie were high. Even before its release, the film made news when two of the young children used as actors in the movie had to flee Afghanistan because they were endangered by the

Taliban for their performance in a rape scene that is a key part of the story.

The child actors who played the two young friends are the compelling soul of the story, but the script struggles with conveying the key issues of the book, and some unfortunate directorial choices expose some of the contrivances of the plot. The protagonist of the story—who in the book, but not the movie, is also the narrator—is a privileged Pushtan boy, Amir (Khalid Abdalla), living in Kabul in the late 1970s. His father, Baba (Homayoun Ershadi), is a wealthy progressive capitalist who has made money in construction. Baba despises both the fundamentalist mullahs and the communist radicals who are struggling to overturn the government. An intriguing man who straddles the traditional Muslim culture and modern humanist values, Baba is ashamed of his son because he backs away from every fight. For his part, Amir feels ashamed and guilty because his mother died giving birth to him.

Amir's best friend is Hassan (Ahmad Khan Mahmoodzada), a member of the lower-class Hazara tribe that is disdained by the Pushtans. Hassan's father is Baba's most long-serving and devoted servant. Hassan is devoted to Amir, admiring his intelligence and the stories he writes. By a fruit tree on the outskirts of Kabul, Amir reads to Hassan, who is illiterate. Hassan and Amir also engage in the city's traditional kite-flying competitions, and Hassan is an uncannily adept kite "runner"—without even looking at the sky, he always seems to know where an opponent's captured kite will land.

Despite being bullied by an older, overtly prejudiced Pushtan boy, Assef (Elham Ehsas), the two friends are victors in the annual kite contest. When Hassan chases down a kite, he is cornered by Assef and friends, and Assef rapes him. Hiding, Amir sees the event but does not intervene. Then he turns against his friend, setting him up on a phony charge of theft and driving both Hassan and his father to quit their jobs as Baba's servants, much to the dismay of Baba.

The Russians invade, Baba flees with Amir to Pakistan, and eventually he moves to California. Along the way, there is an incident at a border crossing where Baba risks his life by standing up to an armed Russian soldier who wants to rape one of the women fleeing with them. This drives home, none too subtly, the point that Amir does not have the integrity and honor to defend even his best friend, whereas his father will risk everything for the honor of a stranger.

The middle act of the film has Amir marrying the daughter of a former Afghan general, and Baba dying. Because Benioff and Forster have chosen not to have Amir narrate, there is no tension and little of interest during this part of the story. It is not clear why Amir

drives Hassan away, whether he is indifferent to his old friend, whether he is angry or ashamed, and whether he cares at all about the war in his homeland. There is no reference to what happened in the past, and little connection to the initial part of the story.

Thus, when the final act of the drama unfolds, it is like a bolt from the blue. Amir's father's old friend, Ali (Nabi Tanha), who was a confidante of Amir as a child, calls him up and tells him to come to Pakistan. Ali too is dying, and he reveals to Amir that Hassan is dead, shot down for resisting the Taliban, who are now in control of Afghanistan. His wife was killed too, and their son is an orphan. Not only that, but Ali reveals that Hassan's son is Amir's nephew, because Hassan was the child of Baba and a servant. Amir has a chance to redeem himself by going to Kabul to rescue his nephew from an orphanage. Kabul is devastated by war and ruled ruthlessly by the Taliban, and Amir's son has become a plaything for powerful warlords, including a grown-up Assef, his childhood tormentor.

Although there are undeniably heart-wrenching scenes in the devastated Kabul, including the stoning of an adulterer in a soccer stadium and an orphanage full of children missing various limbs, the redemption of Amir—especially the way Assef is defeated—is too obviously contrived. When the head of the orphanage asks Amir why he wants to rescue only one child and give him a good life in America while ignoring the plight of the others, the question goes unanswered. Indeed, in a terribly sappy ending, the nephew gets his own suburban bedroom and a presumed middle-class American life, and he learns the art of kite flying.

Because we do not sufficiently understand why Amir rejected Hassan to begin with (it has to do with the role of shame and honor in his culture), and we do not see that he ever cares about him again, the transformation of Amir is not satisfyingly motivated. Everything in the story is too neat and tidy, including the fact that Amir and his wife want children but have not conceived any. Audiences will grapple with the question of whether or not the protagonist really deserves redemption. Morover, is his redemption really convincing, or is it really just another selfish act, a way of making Amir feel he has set things to right when during his entire life he has turned his back not only on his childhood friend but on his entire country? It is a peculiarly American sentiment to believe that adopting an orphan is an act of supreme charity.

The melodramatic setup of the plot is made more maudlin by Forster, who does not seem to understand how to strengthen the story. The sympathies and emotions inspired by the film are due not to well-developed characters and a strong plot but rather to obvious plays for emotion, most of them involving the plight of children.

The use of nonprofessional child actors was either inspired or a huge mistake, depending on your reaction to their one-dimensional performances. Mahmoodzada is undeniably sympathetic and credible as Hassan, but as Amir the young Abdalla seems remote and expressionless. It does not help that the translation of the children's speech is rendered in extremely stilted and formal English. It appears as if the subtitles were concocted by someone living in London 150 years ago. In fact, none of the film's dialogue is realistic; rather, it sounds contrived, just like the story itself.

Michael Betzold

CREDITS

Amir: Khalid Abdalla
Baba: Homayoun Ershadi
Rahim Khan: Shaun Toub
Young Amir: Zekiria Ebrahimi
Young Hassan: Ahmad Khan Mahmoodzada
Assef: Elham Ehsas
Ali: Nabi Tanha
Origin: USA
Language: English
Released: 2007
Production: William Horberg, Walter F. Parkes, E. Bennett Walsh, Sidney Kimmell Entertainment, Rebecca Yeldham; Participant Production, Dreamworks Pictures; released by Paramount Classics
Directed by: Marc Forster
Written by: David Benioff
Cinematography by: Roberto Schaefer
Music by: Alberto Iglesias
Sound: Chris Munro
Editing: Matt Chesse
Art Direction: Karen Murphy
Costumes: Frank Fleming
Production Design: Carlos Conti
MPAA rating: PG-13
Running time: 122 minutes

REVIEWS

Boston Globe Online. December 14, 2007.
Chicago Sun-Times Online. December 14, 2007.
Entertainment Weekly Online. December 12, 2007.
Los Angeles Times Online. December 12, 2007.
New York Times Online. December 14, 2007.
New Yorker Online. December 17, 2007.
Rolling Stone Online. December 13, 2007.

San Francisco Chronicle. December 14, 2007, p. E1.
Variety Online. October 4, 2007.
Wall Street Journal. December 14, 2007, p. W1.
Washington Post. December 14, 2007, p. C1.

QUOTES

Older Hassan: "I dream that my son will grow up to be a good person, a free person. I dream that someday you will return to revisit the land of our childhood. I dream that flowers will bloom in the streets again…and kites will fly in the skies!"

TRIVIA

In many of the kite-flying shots, the children were pulling balloons and the kites were added in post-production.

AWARDS

Nomination:

Oscars 2007: Orig. Score
British Acad. 2007: Adapt. Screenplay, Foreign Film, Orig. Score
Golden Globes 2008: Foreign Film, Orig. Score.

KNOCKED UP

What if this guy got you pregnant?
  —Movie tagline
Save the due date.
  —Movie tagline

Box Office: $148.7 million

Writer/director Judd Apatow has a talent for blending the vulgar and the sweet, for finding that delicate balance between frat-house-style high jinks and romantic comedy. Delighted by the depth of emotion that can be found in the unlikeliest and even crudest of the situations he concocts, as was seen in his directorial debut, *The 40 Year Old Virgin* (2005), critics seem to be in a rush to declare Apatow the voice of his generation and to place *Knocked Up,* in the pantheon of great romantic comedies. If Apatow does indeed end up acclaimed as the Preston Sturges or Woody Allen of his era, which might happen given his ear for great dialogue and memorable one-liners, then this very funny film about relationships will certainly be seen as a major step in the right direction, but it is not the masterpiece that many claim.

Ben Stone (Seth Rogen) and Alison Scott (Katherine Heigl) have no business being together. He is a boorish, unemployed, overweight slacker with no ambition beyond hanging out with his equally lazy stoner buddies; their dream is to start a Web site pinpointing the exact moments of female nudity in movies, a service that guys like themselves will appreciate. Alison, a pretty blond on the rise at the E! cable network, is making the leap to being an on-air personality when she is out celebrating her promotion with her older sister, Debbie (Leslie Mann), and meets Ben. After a few drinks and some dancing, Ben and Alison are stumbling back to her place and end up having a one-night stand. These early scenes are among the film's funniest, especially an uncomfortable, cringe-worthy morning-after scene in which Alison slowly comes to realize what a loser Ben is as he gradually comes to see how little she thinks of him.

Eight weeks later, when Alison comes to the terrifying conclusion that she is pregnant, she knows immediately who the father is. Once she contacts him, their meeting is a reminder of why she was so horrified earlier. Ben may be amiable enough, but he is not remotely close to what she had pictured for her future, and the looks on Heigl's face are hilarious as she registers Alison's realization of how bad this situation could be. Surprisingly, however, once Alison chooses to have the baby, Ben, virtually a child himself, decides to make an effort, and this mismatched couple tries to get to know each other and plan for their child's arrival. A scene of them holding hands as they stroll through the mall after visiting the baby store and buying books on pregnancy exemplifies the film at its best—the sweetness nudging itself out of an improbable and outlandish beginning.

In just two films, Apatow has already created a distinctive character type; his protagonists are child-men who live in an extended adolescence they can shed only with the help of a good woman and the demands of family. In *The 40 Year Old Virgin* Andy may be an innocent, while Ben is a wizened, would-be player, but neither has a clue as to how to deal with women. The charm of these films and the fantasy underpinning them is that hope is not lost for a guy who finds a more sophisticated woman willing to invest the extra time and energy to make him into a man.

Surrounding Alison and Ben are a host of oddballs, including Ben's unmotivated roommates, a foursome whose names are identical to their real-life first names—Jason (Jason Segel), Jay (Jay Baruchel), Jonah (Jonah Hill), and Martin (Martin Starr)—and whose repetitive, silly antics and marijuana-fueled shtick make their scenes incredibly tedious. In addition to their poor business model (it turns out that another Web site detailing cinematic female nudity already exists), their big running joke, which grows old quickly, concerns a bet as to whether or not Martin can grow a beard for a whole year. Much more engaging are Debbie and her husband

Pete (Paul Rudd), who have a tense, even strained home life. Her shrewishness plays like a constant warning to Ben of what his life might become, and yet there is a realism at the core of their marriage, of a woman who loves her husband so much that he chafes from being under her constant scrutiny. The fact that Mann is Apatow's real-world wife and their two daughters (Iris and Maude Apatow) play Pete and Debbie's children probably contributes to the lived-in, natural feeling of the household. Harold Ramis has a funny cameo dispensing advice as Ben's good-natured dad, who may have too optimistic a picture of his son's situation but whose support is nonetheless a big boost.

Best of all are Alison's bosses, Jack (Alan Tudyk) and Jill (Kristen Wiig), who, in just two scenes, nail corporate culture and all of its phoniness. When Alison gets her promotion, the bosses tell her to lose weight but, for legal reasons, are careful not to say exactly what they mean. Jill is clearly jealous of Alison's rise in the company but expertly masks her feelings behind proper corporate etiquette while quietly slipping in what she truly thinks. These scenes are the funniest in the film, and, like the screenplay's best moments, have the ring of truth.

Apatow's great achievement is balancing the raunchy humor with heartfelt empathy for his characters, which makes us root for them despite the seemingly long odds against them. When Ben, trying in his own way to do the right thing, proposes to Alison and presents her with an empty ring box that he hopes one day to fill, it may be pathetic and sad, but it is also earnest and well meaning at the same time. The film also gives its supporting characters more dimension than we might expect. Debbie, for example, is overly critical of her husband and thinks that this is the path to a successful marriage, but she also has the poignancy of a woman desperately clinging to her youth when she knows it is slipping away. When she is denied entrance into a trendy nightclub because she would, at her age, spoil the youthful atmosphere, it is a stinging moment that leads to an unexpected emotional connection with the doorman.

For all of its virtues, however, *Knocked Up* is far from perfect, and, at over two hours, cannot sustain its initial energy. There is a misshapen, meandering quality to the story, and it is not the randomness of real life but rather that of a film in need of some judicious editing. Ben's stoner milieu, for example, grows tiresome since the roommates do not have distinctive enough personalities to make their clownish behavior very entertaining. The film ambles toward the conclusion. After Pete and Ben hit a rough patch with the women in their lives—Debbie feels betrayed when she discovers Pete sneaking off to spend some fun time without her, and Alison grows disillusioned with Ben for a host of reasons—the boys take a road trip to Las Vegas. It is a digression that is largely clichéd (getting a lap dance at a strip club) and not very funny (getting high on mushrooms while watching a Cirque du Soleil show) and exemplifies Apatow's lack of discipline as he stretches out a story that does not need such padding.

Moreover, after the return from Vegas, the resolutions feel too neat. Pete and Debbie reconcile, although we never see how their conflicts are handled. Perhaps the point is that their marital problems will never completely go away, or maybe Apatow simply did not know how to bring this subplot to a satisfying conclusion. Having been shunned by Alison and realizing that he has to get his act together, Ben suddenly turns into a model citizen—getting a job, moving out on his own, and earnestly preparing for the baby. Because the comedy is broad and Ben has a good-heartedness about him, we can welcome his sudden transformation, but, for a movie that wastes time on other digressions, it would have been more effective to show a gradual transition in his character and not an abrupt, wholesale rejection of childish ways just because the script demands that he finally grow up.

If Apatow fumbles on basic plot mechanics, he comes through with the laughs in a delivery room scene that is hilarious, shocking, and even touching as Ben takes charge and becomes the man Alison needs him to be. Similarly, Rogen, who is effective as the befuddled guy out of his depth for most of the story, makes the change believable. After so much tension between Alison and Ben, the film returns to its exuberant, raucous humor leavened with humanity.

If there is a temptation to be nitpicky about a comedy that is so entertaining, that is because the declaration of Apatow's genius seems premature, but this enthusiasm may have been the result of critics not expecting much from what at first looked like a routine sex comedy and being pleasantly surprised by Apatow's unique stamp on the genre. When it comes to the fundamentals of character, plot, and pacing, the screenplay needs more shape to be dubbed a classic, but *Knocked Up* nonetheless shines as one of the brightest comedies of the year.

Peter N. Chumo II

CREDITS

Alison Scott: Katherine Heigl
Ben Stone: Seth Rogen
Debbie: Leslie Mann
Pete: Paul Rudd
Dr. Pellagrino: Tim Bagley

Jay: Jay Baruchel
Jonah: Jonah Hill
Jack: Alan Tudyk
Jason: Jason Segal
Dr. Angelo: J.P. Manoux
Young Doctor: B.J. Novak
Jill: Kristen Wiig
Ben's Dad: Harold Ramis
Martin: Martin Starr
Origin: USA
Language: English
Released: 2007
Production: Judd Apatow, Shauna Robertson, Clayton Townsend; released by Universal
Directed by: Judd Apatow
Written by: Judd Apatow
Cinematography by: Eric Alan Edwards
Music by: Loudon Wainwright III, Joe Henry
Sound: David MacMillan
Music Supervisor: Jonathan Karp
MPAA rating: R
Running time: 132 minutes

REVIEWS

Boston Globe Online. June 1, 2007.
Chicago Sun-Times Online. June 1, 2007.
Entertainment Weekly. June 8, 2007, p. 60.
Hollywood Reporter Online. May 31, 2007.
Los Angeles Times Online. June 1, 2007.
New York Times Online. June 1, 2007.
Rolling Stone Online. May 30, 2007.
San Francisco Chronicle. June 1, 2007, p. E1.
Variety Online. March 13, 2007.
Washington Post. June 1, 2007, p. C5.

QUOTES

Debbie: "I'm not gonna go to the end of the f***ing line, who the f**k are you? I have just as much of a right to be here as any of these little skanky girls. What, am I not skanky enough for you, you want me to hike up my f***ing skirt? What the f**k is your problem? I'm not going anywhere, you're just some roided out freak with a f***ing clipboard. And your stupid little f***ing rope! You know what, you may have power now but you are not god. You're a doorman, okay. You're a doorman, doorman, doorman, doorman, doorman, so…F**k You! You f***ing fag with your f***ing little faggy gloves."

Doorman: "I know…you're right. I'm so sorry, I f***in' hate this job. I don't want to be the one to pass judgement, decide who gets in. Sh** makes me sick to my stomach, I get the runs from the stress. It's not cause you're not hot, I would love to tap that ass. I would tear that ass up. I can't let you in cause you're old as f**k. For this club, you know, not for the earth."

Debbie: "What?"

Doorman: "You old, she pregnant. Can't have a bunch of old pregnant bitches running around. That's crazy, I'm only allowed to let in five percent black people. He said that, that means if there's 25 people here I get to let in one and a quarter black people. So I gotta hope there's a midget in the crowd."

TRIVIA

The film's translation in Russian is "A little bit pregnant."

AWARDS

Nomination:
Writers Guild 2007: Orig. Screenplay.

L

LADY CHATTERLEY

Lady Chatterley's Lover (1928) is D. H. Lawrence's best-known novel and one of the most notorious in literary history. Because it features graphic, for its time, sexual content, Lawrence initially had the novel published privately, and expurgated editions followed. When unexpurgated editions finally appeared in the 1950s, court cases resulted, with the United States ruling in favor of the book's publication in 1959 and the British doing the same the following year. The drama of the latter case is captured wonderfully in the television film *The Chatterley Affair* (2006), as two jurors have an adulterous relationship similar to that in the novel.

Lawrence revised the novel several times. Earlier versions were published as *The First Lady Chatterley* (1944) and *John Thomas and Lady Jane* (1972). The latter, whose title comes from the characters' nicknames for each other's genitals, is the basis of *Lady Chatterley*, written by Pascale Ferran, Roger Bohbot, Pierre Trividic and directed by Ferran.

Film versions of Lawrence's infamous story have had a spotty history. *Young Lady Chatterley* (1977) and Just Jaeckin's *Lady Chatterley's Lover* (1981) are soft-core interpretations. Marc Allégret's *L'Amant de lady Chatterley* (1955), with Danielle Darrieux, offers a rather tame approach typical of its era. More faithful is Ken Russell's *Lady Chatterley* (1993), made for British television. Russell, whose *Women in Love* (1969) is generally considered the best Lawrence film adaptation, and who also made *The Rainbow* (1989) from another Lawrence novel, chose to emphasize the class-difference theme, also central to Ferran's interpretation.

Sir Clifford Chatterley (Hippolyte Girardot) has been left crippled and impotent by the Great War, and his young wife, Constance (Marina Hands), is somewhat at a loss. To get exercise—and to have something to do—she begins walking about the vast Chatterley estate, while Sir Clifford tends to matters related to the coal mine he owns. Because she is a bit run down, Constance begins taking rest breaks at the hut of the estate's gamekeeper, Oliver Parkin (Jean-Louis Coullo'ch). Parkin is also unhappily married, his wife having left him for another man. A friendship with the taciturn Parkin slowly develops and eventually leads to a sexual relationship.

Ferran spends considerable time looking at plants, trees, birds, and running water to connect the natural world with Constance's dilemma. Life with a remote, bitter husband with whom sex is impossible is an unnatural state of affairs. Sex with the burly Parkin may be against the rules of society—not only for the adultery but the class differences as well—but it is definitely natural. Such acts of nonconformity and celebrations of natural behavior occur throughout Lawrence's works.

Constance and Parkin are initially timid and awkward, having intercourse while fully clothed. Eventually, some garments are loosened and shed. Only when Constance asks to see Parkin's erect penis are both naked. Lawrence considered calling his novel *Tenderness,* and it is the intimate side of the affair that Ferran accentuates. While the nude wrestling match between Alan Bates and Oliver Reed in Russell's *Women in Love* is meant to shock, the nudity here is presented as matter of fact, even with the erection.

An exception is the film's big scene, as Constance and Parkin run naked, except for boots, through the woods in a pouring rain. The scene expresses their joy not only in their love for each other but the sense of freedom given them by both the romantic and carnal sides of their relationship. Their affair is a way of thumbing their noses at a restrictive society. Clifford has given Constance permission to have an affair so that he can have an heir, with the proviso that her lover must be "of good stock." Their society condones adultery to a degree but would be appalled by a woman like Constance having sex with a mere gamekeeper.

Ferran has been writing and directing films since 1983, but *Lady Chatterley* is her first effort to receive much American exposure. Her film is slowly, deliberately paced, with lengthy scenes and little camera movement, beyond the forest romp. There is little cutting in the sex scenes, creating the impression that the audience is spying on the couple, which is Ferran's method of drawing the viewer into the intimacy of the act. *Lady Chatterley* has a studied artlessness and Ferran seems to be striving to keep matters as simple as possible to avoid sensationalizing the story of Constance and Parkin.

The same simplicity applies to the actors as well, with Hands and, especially, Coullo'ch underplaying their roles. The daughter of French actress Ludmila Mikaël and British stage director Terry Hands, Hands resembles the young Mariel Hemingway, while Coullo'ch looks like a boxer or rugby player. In casting these actors, Ferran departed from what might be expected. Rather than going with glamorous or sexy, as with Joely Richardson and Sean Bean in the Russell interpretation, she calls attention to Hands's fresh-faced innocence and Coullo'ch's beefy earthiness. This Lady Chatterley is looking for meaning in her life and approaches sex as would a virginal teenager, while the hesitant Parkin is confused about what he is getting into.

Ferran provided little dialogue for the lovers. She focused instead on their faces as the characters struggle to understand what is happening to them and what the consequences will be. Hands's very expressive face conveys Constance's curiosity, bewilderment, and, eventually, joy. Coullo'ch's best moment comes when Parkin thinks, wrongly, that Constance is interested in him only as someone who can make her pregnant, and the actor displays the gamekeeper's pain, bordering on simmering rage. Lawrence's class concerns are not diminished by the French cast and the director's Gallic sensibility.

Cinematographer Julien Hirsch lights the film to suggest a daguerreotype, with soft browns and greens and slightly washed-out colors, making clear that *Lady Chatterley* is a look at social conditions in the distant past. The look of the film, which some reviewers described as unfortunate, resembles that of Christopher Miles' *The Virgin and the Gypsy* (1970), another deliberately paced interpretation of Lawrence's view of sexual awakening and class difference. Ferran has cited *Blissfully Yours* (2002) by the Thai director Apichatpong Weerasethakul as an influence for both its depiction of sex in outdoor settings and the Buddhist serenity of its approach to sex.

Lady Chatterley was a huge success in France, named the fourth best film of 2006 by the influential film journal *Cahiers du Cinéma*. Nominated for nine Césars, the French equivalent of the Academy Award®, it won five, including best film, best adapted screenplay, best actress, best cinematography, and best costume design (Marie-Claude Altot). Hands was also named best actress at the 2007 Tribeca Film Festival.

Lady Chatterley is not perfect. The slow pacing may annoy some; knowing too little about the characters may concern others. What, for example, drew Constance to Sir Clifford to begin with, and how long have they been married? The film is also much less erotic than some may expect because Ferran cares less about sex itself than how her characters use it to communicate their feelings. While *Lady Chatterley* may not be very Lawrentian, downplaying the animal instincts central to his fiction, Ferran's personal, idiosyncratic approach distinguishes it from the previous interpretations of the novel.

Michael Adams

CREDITS

Lady Constance Chatterley: Marina Hands
Sir Clifford Chatterley: Hippolyte Girardot
Oliver Parkin: Jean-Louis Coullo'ch
Mrs. Bolton: Hélène Alexandridis
Origin: Belgium, France
Language: French
Released: 2006
Production: Gilles Sandoz; Arte France Cinéma, Saga Films, Maia Films, Les Films de Lendemain; released by Kino International
Directed by: Pascal Ferran
Written by: Roger Bohbot, Pascale Ferran, Pierre Trividic
Cinematography by: Julien Hirsch
Music by: Béatrice Thiriet
Sound: Jean-Pierre Laforce
Editing: Yann Dedet, Mathilde Muyard
Art Direction: Alan Leonis
Costumes: Marie-Claude Altot
MPAA rating: Unrated
Running time: 168 minutes

REVIEWS

Boston Globe Online. July 13, 2007.
Chicago Sun-Times Online. July 6, 2007.
Entertainment Weekly Online. June 20, 2007.
Hollywood Reporter Online. February 8, 2007.
Los Angeles Times Online. July 13, 2007.
New York Times Online. June 22, 2007.
Rolling Stone Online. June 13, 2007.
Variety Online. November 17, 2006.
Washington Post. July 13, 2007, p. C5.

TRIVIA

Director Pascale Ferran scheduled six weeks of intensive
rehearsal to help put the actors at ease with each other in
preparation for the explicit scenes.

AWARDS

Nomination:
Ind. Spirit 2008: Foreign Film.

LARS AND THE REAL GIRL

The search for true love begins outside the box.
—Movie tagline

Box Office: $5.9 million

Lars Lindstrom (Ryan Gosling) is the lonely man of his
community. He lives in the small garage apartment on
the property that he and his brother, Gus (Paul
Schneider), inherited from their parents. His big brother
and good-hearted sister-in-law, Karin (Emily Mortimer),
who are expecting a child, live in the main house, but
Lars is fine with the arrangement; even if he were not,
he would not say anything. The painfully shy Lars keeps
to himself and does his best to avoid human contact.
Karin literally has to tackle him to try to get him to
come to dinner. One day Lars learns about a Web site
that sells life-size, anatomically correct female dolls, and
he orders one. When the doll arrives, however, he does
not use it as other men would. Instead, he treats her as a
girlfriend and introduces her to everyone as Bianca, a
missionary of Brazilian and Danish descent. Strange as
his behavior is, what is stranger is the townspeople's
reaction. Everybody goes along with the delusion for
Lars's benefit and makes the plastic Bianca an integral
part of the community.

Directed by Craig Gillespie from a script by Nancy
Oliver, *Lars and the Real Girl* begins with a strange
premise—what seems like the recipe for an extended
dirty joke, really—but takes it in an unexpected direction, one that magically walks the fine line between
pathos and whimsy while exploring the big themes of
dealing with loss and making the leap from childhood
to adulthood.

Lars and the Real Girl is a funny movie, with humor
derived from the incongruity of Bianca sitting in church
and holding a hymnal or visiting the doctor or, as she
becomes an accepted part of the community, doing
volunteer work and even going off to attend a school
board meeting. While the way everyone joins in humor-
ing Lars may seem farfetched, the kindness of the
townspeople is genuine. Indeed, this closely knit town,
where people regularly attend church and care about
each other, feels like a throwback to Frank Capra's
universe.

There is, however, something much deeper at the
heart of the movie, a serious side that gives the film its
heart. Lars craves not sex from his doll; he even has Bianca stay in the big house while he maintains his usual
residence since they are religious and any other arrangement would not be proper. What Lars really wants is a
sense of permanency in his life, of a relationship that
can never change, wither away, or die. It is a need that
stems from his own sense of loss when his mother died
giving birth to him, a trauma that has defined his life
and made him afraid to be emotionally intimate with
anyone, but especially women.

Lars projects this trauma on Bianca's backstory as
well, and, in time, we see that his fixation on her is the
way for him to work out his personal issues, take the
first steps toward female companionship, and ready
himself for adult relationships. At the same time, the
smart screenplay also hints that Bianca is a surrogate
mother, and the symbolism is fairly obvious. She stays
in his late mother's room, known as the "pink room,"
connoting femininity and perhaps even a return to the
womb. At the very least, Lars seems to be searching for
something he has never experienced—the unconditional
love that a mother can offer.

One of the great qualities of Oliver's screenplay is
how these issues are brought to light. The local doctor,
Dagmar (Patricia Clarkson), is not only a physician but
a psychologist and, under the guise of treating Bianca
for some serious mysterious ailment, arranges sessions
with Lars that become de facto therapy. These scenes in
which Lars opens up about his fear of being touched
and the trauma of his mother's death are among the
most poignant in any film this year. Dagmar herself has
experienced her share of pain, which makes her well
suited to understanding Lars. The interplay between
Gosling and Clarkson is perfect; they never go for some
big, artificially inflated revelation but rather embrace the

humanity of the characters and let them subtly reveal themselves to us and to each other.

Gosling also has some fine moments with Schneider. Skeptical at first of going along with his brother's delusion, Gus feels a certain amount of guilt over having left home as soon as he could and leaving Lars with their emotionally distant father. The family dynamics are fairly complex—even Lars' living in the garage is a source of guilt for Gus and Karin—and, in an unexpected way, Bianca's presence makes Gus reflect on his own relationship with his brother and what it means to be an adult.

As time progresses and a coworker named Margo (Kelli Garner) takes an increasing interest in Lars, he gradually begins to reciprocate her feelings. His need for Bianca begins to wane, and he even claims that Bianca turned down his marriage proposal—a sign that he is preparing himself for a real relationship. In the final act, as his attraction to Margo grows, Lars orchestrates Bianca's fatal illness and death. Signaling an end of childhood for Lars and his entry into adulthood, the events are at once sad and uplifting. Bianca's funeral, which is attended by the caring townsfolk and includes pictures of her surrounding the casket, is, of course, absurd on some level but ultimately quite moving, almost as if a real human being did pass away.

Ryan Gosling's performance is masterful. In every tight gesture or blink of an eye, he registers social discomfort and perfectly conveys a young man uncomfortable in his own skin. Lars' stiff, guarded body language is a wary response to a world in which emotional attachment is fraught with the possibility of loss. Another actor might have turned Lars into a caricature or allowed the movie's tone to become farcical, but Gosling commits both physically and psychologically to a man scarred by his upbringing but trying, ever so slowly, to come out of his shell.

Lars and the Real Girl is one of the biggest movie gambles of the year. To make a film about a sex doll without any sex and to fashion a story around a man so tightly reined in that he can barely express himself are challenges enough. Yet to take what could have been a seemingly ludicrous premise and turn it into a sweet, heartfelt tale of self-discovery, healing, and maturation make the movie a small marvel.

Peter N. Chumo II

CREDITS

Lars: Ryan Gosling
Gus: Paul Schneider
Karin: Emily Mortimer
Dagmar: Patricia Clarkson

Margo: Kelli Garner
Mrs. Gruner: Nancy Beatty
Cindy: Karen Robinson
Origin: USA
Language: English
Released: 2007
Production: Sidney Kimmel, John Cameron, Sarah Aubrey; released by MGM
Directed by: Craig Gillespie
Written by: Nancy Oliver
Cinematography by: Adam Kimmel
Music by: David Torn
Sound: Perry Robertson
Editing: Tatiana S. Riegel
Art Direction: Joshu de Cartier
Costumes: Gerri Gillan, Kirston Mann
Production Design: Arvinder Grewal
MPAA rating: PG-13
Running time: 106 minutes

REVIEWS

Christian Science Monitor Online. October 12, 2007.
Entertainment Weekly Online. October 10, 2007.
Hollywood Reporter Online. September 12, 2007.
Los Angeles Times Online. October 12, 2007.
New York Times Online. October 12, 2007.
Variety Online. September 11, 2007.
Wall Street Journal. October 12, 2007, p. W1.

TRIVIA

To help Ryan Gosling stay in character, the real doll was treated like an actual person, as is done by the characters in the movie. She was dressed privately in her own trailer and was only present for scenes that she was in.

AWARDS

Nomination:

Oscars 2007: Orig. Screenplay
Golden Globes 2008: Actor—Mus./Comedy (Gosling)
Screen Actors Guild 2007: Actor (Gosling)
Writers Guild 2007: Orig. Screenplay.

THE LAST LEGION

Before King Arthur, there was Excalibur.
—Movie tagline

The end of an empire... the beginning of a legend.
—Movie tagline

The untold beginning of the King Arthur legend.
    —Movie tagline

Box Office: $5.9 million

It is 460 A.D. and the Goths have invaded Rome. Their leader, Odoacer (Peter Mullan), controls the city but wants more. He also wants to control the last of the Caesars. Twelve-year-old Romulus (Thomas Sangster) is the last of the Caesars, the last descendent in whom the blood of Julius Caesar himself runs. To take custody of the boy Odoacer sends out his blood-thirsty lieutenant, Wulfila (Kevin McKidd).

Wulfila attacks the villa of Romulus' parents, kills them and takes possession of the boy and his teacher, Ambrosinus (Ben Kingsley). Odoacer imprisons Romulus and Ambrosinus on the island of Capri, where their warden is the spiteful Wulfila, who would just as soon kill the boy. Since Romulus is the embodiment of the glory and power of Rome, his personal bodyguard, Aurelius (Colin Firth), is sent to rescue him. He is accompanied in this mission by his three Roman cohorts and a mysterious Byzantine warrior, Mira (Aishwarya Rai).

They do free Romulus, but returning him to the throne will be no easy task with the Goths controlling the city. With Wulfila in hot pursuit, they head off to the island of Britannia to take command of the Ninth Legion, the last legion left standing that is loyal to the emperor. With its help, they will return to Rome and take on Odoacer.

Had the filmmakers adhered to this basic plot, it might have made historians wince, but at least the film would have stood on its own. Nothing if not ambitious, *The Last Legion* incorporates numerous lesser story fragments that confuse matters. There is the thread of friendship betrayed regarding Aurelius' friend and Senator, Nestor (John Hannah) and another thread concerning a ruthless Britannic leader named Vortgyn (Harry Van Gorkum), who colludes with Wulfila and who has a mysterious past with Ambrosinus. There is a romance between Aurelius and Mira and a subplot involving a pentangle and, incorporating Arthurian legend, a renowned sword of Caesar that will become a legendary sword of Britain. Despite the film's epic scope, "nothing, however, is to be taken seriously, not the story, not the acting and certainly not the history," said John Anderson in the *Los Angeles Times*.

Based on Valerio Massimo Manfredi's novel, the story passes itself off as history, then strays into legend. *The Last Legion* was marketed to appeal to audiences that flocked to the similarly heroic, sword-and-sandal movie *300* (2007), but the film falls far short of that visually enticing epic. Even viewed as a simple adventure story, the characters are so sketchily drawn that it is dif-ficult to care about them or their quest. There is no romantic chemistry between Firth and the undeniably beautiful Rai, and as an action picture it lacks rousing, well-choreographed fighting and battle sequences. Even the uninspiring computer-generated imagery sequences are overly conspicuous and draw attention away from the story.

What little comic relief may be found in the film is groan-inducing and heavy-handed. If the filmmakers are going to play with history to the point of making it fantasy, they should allow the characters to play as well, as if they are in on the joke. The quartet of heroes is forced to joylessly trudge along after one another without so much as a clever quip or titter to break up the monotony. As Neil Genzlinger wrote in the *New York Times*, "Its few attempts at humorous camaraderie fall flat, leaving you wondering why this grim group wants to keep living at all."

The Last Legion is the feature film directing debut of Doug Lefler who is known primarily for his work on the television shows *Xena: Warrior Princess* and *Hercules* and, although he undoubtedly had a larger budget and better-known cast, the film has much the same cable television feel as those shows. The plot of *The Last Legion* is clichéd and predictable, relying on a surprise ending for impact. Its unengaging characters speak stilted and mundane dialogue, and the special effects seem to be low-budget and gimmicky.

Somewhere within the film lie the seeds of a truly interesting story. In more competent hands—from director to screenwriter and from special effects supervisor to action coordinator—*The Last Legion* could have been an entertaining summer diversion. As presented by the legendary Dino De Laurentiis and co-produced by his wife Martha and daughter Raffaella, however, the film is a puffed up spectacle that Genzlinger wrote "might have made a good children's film."

Beverley Bare Buehrer

CREDITS

Aurelius: Colin Firth
Ambrosinus: Ben Kingsley
Romulus Augustus: Thomas Sangster
Wulfida: Kevin McKidd
Nestor: John Hannah
Orestes: Iain Glen
Mira: Aishwarya Rai
Demetrius: Rupert Friend
Odoacer: Peter Mullan
Theodorus: Alexander Siddig
Kustennin: Robert Pugh

Hrothgar: James Cosmo

Vatrenus: Owen Teale

Origin: France, Great Britain, Italy

Language: English

Released: 2007

Production: Dino De Laurentiis, Martha De Laurentiis, Raffaella De Laurentiis, Tarak Ben Ammar; Quinta Communications, Ingenious Film Partners; released by Weinstein Company

Directed by: Doug Lefler

Written by: Jez Butterworth, Tom Butterworth

Cinematography by: Marco Pontecorvo

Music by: Patrick Doyle

Sound: Martin Trevis

Editing: Simon Cozens

Art Direction: Roberto Caruso

Costumes: Paolo Scalabrino

Production Design: Carmelo Argate

MPAA rating: PG-13

Running time: 110 minutes

REVIEWS

Boston Globe Online. August 18, 2007.
Entertainment Weekly Online. August 22, 2007.
Hollywood Reporter Online. August 20, 2007.
Los Angeles Times Online. August 20, 2007.
New York Times Online. August 20, 2007.
Variety Online. August 17, 2007.

THE LAST MIMZY

The future is trying to tell us something.
—Movie tagline

Box Office: $21.4 million

Scenes from *The Last Mimzy*, adapted from Lewis Padgett's short story "Mimsy Were the Borogoves," have a certain charmingly whimsical feel. A rabbit purrs instructions, visible molecules whiz about, and rocks glow hypnotically. As Nathan Rabin wrote in *The A.V. Club*, "It's hard to describe the details of *The Last Mimzy*'s plot without sounding like someone recounting a crazy dream." These strange and unreal moments are the best parts of the film for they give it a spark and a splashy visual impact while paying appropriate tribute to the source material. It is the more mundane elements of the plot that ultimately drag the film down. Teresa Budasi, writing in the *Chicago Sun-Times,* echoed the sentiments of many film critics who were not charmed by the film: "*Mimzy* is an emotionless empty shell."

The story revolves around a summer in the lives of two Seattle siblings, Noah Wilder (Chris O'Neil), and his younger sister, Emma (Rhiannon Leigh Wryn). They live a comfortable life with their attentive mother, Jo (Joely Richardson), and their always busy father, David (Timothy Hutton). The children and their mother set off to the family's charming lake cottage for the summer. Chris and Emma find a mysterious box of objects they decide to call "toys." Emma's favorite is a stuffed rabbit that she calls Mimzy. Mimzy makes little cooing sounds and Emma reports that she is talking to her. Noah would probably not be too apt to believe her except for the fact that the rest of the toys are very odd as well. There are some crystals that glow and give Noah telekinetic powers. There are also other rocks, which they call spinners, that when arranged in the proper fashion, twirl around into a vortex that can make objects disappear.

The Last Mimzy shines when the children are discovering the objects. These items are mysterious and magical, and it is enjoyable to speculate about what they might do. At one point, Noah uses one of the toys and can hear the language of bugs. He stares at a caterpillar and can hear each of its tiny feet as it shuffles across the ground.

Whenever the action veers away from the toys themselves, however, the movie becomes instantly less interesting. Magical toys are a fascinating concept—ordinary people reacting to the objects are less fascinating. The children agree to keep the toys a secret, but Emma cannot help showing some of the spinners to their babysitter (Randi Lynne). The hysterical babysitter shares the news with Jo, who refuses to believe something of that sort could be going on in her well-ordered family. Noah's teacher, Mr. White (Rainn Wilson), gets involved when he notices that Noah is absentmindedly sketching ancient mandalas. Mr. White excitedly enlists the help of his girlfriend, Naomi (Kathryn Hahn), who studies palm reading and other New Age pursuits.

The tiresome elements enter the plot when it is revealed that Mimzy and the rest of the toys were sent from the future and that it is up to little Emma to save this future civilization. She discovers that other Mimzys had been sent out before. One of them was sent to little Alice of the Lewis Carroll stories. The Mimzys were on a rescue mission of sorts. Apparently these future beings need to collect some human DNA or their world will cease to exist. Why the highly intelligent Mimzy does not just grab a snippet of Emma's hair right away and end his mission in a timely fashion is never made quite clear.

The movie starts falling apart completely when, in a parallel to *E.T.* (1982), wholly evil government agents get involved. The Homeland Security Department, led by Nathanial Boardman (Michael Clarke Duncan), chases the family down after Noah inadvertently causes a major power outage. The whimsy of the first part of the film is replaced by routine "children-race-the-clock-to-save-the-world" action. The suspension of disbelief required in the first acts pays off because it is delightful to imagine magical toys, but ignoring the plethora of senseless plot machinations merely becomes dreary in the final act.

The Last Mimzy did not make much of an impact at the box office, although it was somewhat well received by critics. In the *Boston Globe* Ty Burr wrote, "You can't really argue that this is a well-made movie, but it is a good one—true to the emotional reality of its young characters and young audience and flattering the latter into thinking way outside the box."

Jill Hamilton

CREDITS

Jo Wilder: Joely Richardson
David Wilder: Timothy Hutton
Larry White: Rainn Wilson
Naomi Schwartz: Kathryn Hahn
Chris O'Neil: Noah Wilder
Emma Wilder: Rhiannon Leigh Wyn
Nathaniel Boardman: Michael Clarke Duncan
Origin: USA
Language: English
Released: 2007
Production: Michael Phillips; released by New Line Cinema
Directed by: Robert Shaye
Written by: Bruce Joel Rubin, Toby Emmerich
Cinematography by: J. Michael Muro
Music by: Howard Shore
Sound: Dane A. Darvis
Editing: Alan Heim
Art Direction: Ross Dempster
Costumes: Karen Matthews
Production Design: Barry Chusid
MPAA rating: PG
Running time: 90 minutes

REVIEWS

Boxoffice Online. March 23, 2007.
Chicago Sun-Times Online. March 23, 2007.
Entertainment Weekly. March 30, 2007, p. 54.
Hollywood Reporter Online. January 31, 2007.
Los Angeles Times Online. March 23, 2007.
New York Times Online. March 22, 2007.
San Francisco Chronicle. March 23, 2007.
Variety Online. February 5, 2007.
Washington Post Online. March 23, 2007.

QUOTES

Naomi Schwartz: "What are you doing? We're talking about miracles here! The whole Universe is trying to communicate

with you, and you're worried about something as earth-bound as kidnapping? God I love you, but you drive me crazy!"

LICENSE TO WED

First came love...then came Reverend Frank.
    —Movie tagline

Box Office: $43.7 million

License to Wed is a weak, often flat romantic comedy about a reverend who requires engaged couples to attend and pass his unconventional marriage preparation program before he will marry them. The thought behind the film—that, given the failure rate of marriages in the world today, couples should be more prepared for the realities of marriage than they often are—is a worthwhile one, but the execution and the plot (and often the characters) do not successfully address the theme in a significantly meaningful way. Much of the humor in the film is below par or only mildly funny, and the character of the reverend employs questionable methods in his program that should actually make any couple highly suspicious of him, thereby undermining the credibility of much of the plot.

Other than Reverend Frank (Robin Williams), the main characters in the film are Sadie (Mandy Moore) and Ben (John Krasinski), a young man and woman who meet in the beginning of the film and quickly fall in love. Their courtship is only portrayed briefly for the plot of the movie concerns their premarital "counseling," provided by the reverend. Sadie has her heart set on getting married in Frank's church, so she and Ben must attend the minister's mandatory course. Reverend Frank explains several rules that every couple must follow to pass the course, including the requirement that they write their own vows and the prohibition from having sex until after the wedding. It soon becomes clear that the minister intends to become closely involved in monitoring their progress. He (along with his young minister-in-training) bugs their apartment and often follows them on their assignments, such as when he tests their abilities as parents by giving them two robotic babies to tend. Other sessions and tests include a group meeting in which couples explore how to fight fairly, a game of word association that results in Ben inadvertently insulting Sadie's family, and a "communication test" in which Ben is supposed to guide a blindfolded Sadie as she drives a car.

Predictably, Ben and Sadie ultimately encounter problems, and Ben begins resenting the reverend's intrusion in their lives. When he tries to discredit Reverend

Frank and winds up embarrassing himself, Sadie calls off the wedding and goes on their planned honeymoon trip to Jamaica, accompanied by her family. Of course Ben realizes that Sadie really is the one he wants to spend his life with, so he goes after her and they reconcile. Reverend Frank just happens to be in Jamaica as well, and the movie ends with the wedding taking place there in Jamaica.

While Robin Williams manages to draw some laughs with his portrayal of Reverend Frank, the movie is not as funny as it attempts to be. The minister is drawn as a comic character even though he is to be taken seriously, and there are times when Williams's delivery elicits a chuckle or two (such as when Frank reviews the Ten Commandments with a group of youngsters), but one of the most significant problems with the film is that many of the reverend's actions, meant to amuse, are apt to raise eyebrows as much as provoke laughter. The character comes across as deceptive and sneaky when he sits in a van outside the couple's apartment building and listens in on their private conversation via the listening devices his assistant has planted. This kind of behavior is meant to be humorous, but it also leads the viewer to question the minister's ethics, if not more. Consequently, when the ending of the movie basically affirms Frank's actions throughout the film, the story loses some credibility, even if it is supposed to be a comedy.

Another weakness of the film is that the reverend's assignments and tests seem contrived and unlikely to really reveal anything of consequence about a relationship. The group meeting where Frank encourages couples to practice getting angry is probably the most "useful" scenario, but the other tasks just seem designed to cause problems, not to uncover real issues. Of course, this is not a dramatic film and to expect depth here would be to expect too much, but even as a romantic comedy, the situations simply fail to ring true and seem designed to create superficial conflict. The conflicts that do occur between Ben and Sadie do not clearly speak to specific issues all couples face—or, if they do, those issues are not clearly defined.

The word "superficial" is a good adjective to describe the film as a whole, from the plot to the characters. It is possible that a funny and insightful story could have been told about a couple enduring a difficult, challenging premarital program, but unfortunately *License to Wed* is neither very amusing nor insightful. There is no more substance to the theme behind the film than its observation that couples should be very careful and as realistic as possible going into a marriage.

David Flanagin

CREDITS

Father Frank: Robin Williams
Sadie Jones: Mandy Moore
Ben Murphy: John Krasinski
Carlisle: Eric Christian Olsen
Lindsay: Christine Taylor
Mr. Jones: Peter Strauss
Janine: Rachael Harris
Joel: DeRay Davis
Judith: Angela Kinsey
Shelley: Mindy Kaling
Jim: Brian Baumgartner
Choir Boy: Josh Flitter
Origin: USA
Language: English
Released: 2007
Production: Mike Medavoy, Arnold W. Messer, Robert Simonds, Nick Osborne; Phoenix Pictures, Village Roadshow Pictures; released by Warner Bros.
Directed by: Ken Kwapis
Written by: Kim Barker, Tim Rasmussen, Vince DeMeglio
Cinematography by: John Bailey
Music by: Christophe Beck
Sound: Craig Woods
Music Supervisor: Spring Aspers
Editing: Kathryn Himoff
Art Direction: Sue Henzel
Costumes: Deena Appel
Production Design: Gae Buckley
MPAA rating: PG-13
Running time: 91 minutes

REVIEWS

Boston Globe Online. July 3, 2007.
Chicago Sun-Times Online. July 3, 2007.
Entertainment Weekly. July 13, 2007, p. 49.
Hollywood Reporter Online. July 2, 2007.
Los Angeles Times Online. July 3, 2007.
New York Times Online. July 3, 2007.
Premiere Online. July 3, 2007.
San Francisco Chronicle. July 3, 2007, p. E1.
Variety Online. June 29, 2007.
Washington Post. July 3, 2007, p. C1.

QUOTES

Reverend Frank: "I'm gonna have to heal you. We have got to pray! We have got to pray! We have got to pray to make it through the day!"
Ben Murphy: "Was that M.C. Hammer?"

TRIVIA

Ben Murphy's parents are played by John Krasinski's real life parents.

LIONS FOR LAMBS

*If you don't stand for something, you might fall
   for anything.*
   —Movie tagline

What do you: live...die...fight...stand for?
   —Movie tagline

Box Office: $15 million

Lions for Lambs is a dialogue-heavy political film with
which its makers take a look at three differing points of
view about the United States' involvement in Iraq. If a
film can become an acquired taste, this one may just be
it, with a payoff of multiple endings for repeat viewings.

Lions for Lambs intertwines three stories involving
the war on terror. Meryl Streep plays Janine Roth, a
journalist who receives an exclusive interview with
Republican Senator Jasper Irving (Tom Cruise). Irving
plans to reveal a new plan that will help win the war on
terror in Afghanistan, and he wants Roth to promote his
new plan. Roth supported Irving before the war on terror, but her new liberal views make her skeptical of
Irving's plan. California Professor Stephen Malley
(Robert Redford) reviles the war on terror. Malley reveals
to brilliant but failing student Todd Hayes (Andrew
Garfield) one of the professor's big regrets: his failure to
prevent former students Ernest Rodriguez (Michael
Peña) and Arian Finch (Derek Luke) from joining the
army. Meanwhile, Rodriguez and Finch find themselves
stranded at an Afghan post, looking for ways to survive.

As it happens, they are involved in the very military
strategy that the senator is touting to the journalist. It
involves seizing the high ground in Afghanistan earlier
in the season before the Taliban can get there, to control
mountain passes and therefore prevent Taliban troop
movements. Senator Jasper presents this as a strategic
breakthrough on a level that is tantamount to Nelson's
rout of Napoleon.

In Los Angeles, the promising student has just
stopped caring, and the talk with his professor is
designed to reignite his passion. He should become
involved in his nation's politics—take an interest, take a
stand. A flashback sequence shows the two soldiers winning a classroom debate by calling the other side's bluff:
they have enlisted in the military.

The movie seems to take an anti-Bush stance
because the journalist makes better points than the
senator. However, what the professor and his student
think is hard to say, although they are very adept at
muddying the waters. As for the two enlistees, it is safe
to assume that at the end of the film, they are wondering whether their debate strategy was the right one.

There is a long stretch toward the beginning of the
film that draws interest, under the delusion that it is going somewhere. This new Robert Redford film even
contains some laughs, perhaps, though, unintentionally.
For instance, there is a scene in which Roth uncovers
photographs of fictional Republican Jasper Irving with
real politicians, varying from Colin Powell to George W.
Bush. The photos look so fake and awkward that it is
unintentionally funny to witness Cruise with such
famous politicians. The serious tone of the film veers
toward the self-consciously artificial because of some
overdone moments. From the musical score to symbolic
images (particularly during the final credits), Redford
accentuates the sheer pretentiousness of the film, and
the end result seems campy occasionally.

Many reviewers criticized *Lions of Lambs* for
containing seemingly endless preachy dialogue, but the
topic treated by *Lions for Lambs* warrants such
preachiness. Unlike recent political pieces of Oscar®
bait like *In the Valley of Elah* (2007), *Lions for Lambs*
intends to inform, not entertain. It is hard to entertain
and inform without creating a fatally preachy motion
picture, so Robert Redford and Matthew Michael Carnahan (*The Kingdom* [2007]) turn *Lions for Lambs* into
an admirable ninety-minute lecture. Obviously, *Lions for
Lambs* will only appeal to moviegoers who find politics
to be fascinating, but Redford's movie successfully
fascinates as an engaging political drama. In fact, *Lions
for Lambs* works at its best with its long speeches on
politics, war, and hypocrisy since the film happens to be
at its weakest whenever it focuses on battle sequences.
Nevertheless, *Lions for Lambs* rarely bores and frequently
intrigues, so Redford deserves kudos for turning a
preachy lecture into an absorbing film.

Lions for Lambs contains one significant flaw that
nearly negates the film's many strengths: the ending.
Robert Redford does not seem to know where to end
the film, so he concludes his political drama with what
seem to be twenty endings. About four of the endings
stand the chance of leaving a powerful impact on the
viewer (particularly an image depicting the fates of Rodriguez and Finch), but the rest of the endings stand as
conclusions that are preachy in a tedious manner.

Lions for Lambs contains some terrific performances.
Redford reminds viewers that he knows how to deliver
an excellent whiff of charisma. Although Streep gives a
solid performance as another politically conflicted
character, the most impressive performance belongs to
Cruise, who took advantage of the media's tendency to
depic him as a charmless figure in real life. As Senator
Jasper Irving, Cruise delivers his best performance since
Collateral (2004). *Lions for Lambs* will not appeal to
everyone; yet political thriller enthusiasts will be satisfied.

Despite its flaws, the film deserves a mild recommendation.

Kent Rogers and David Flanagin

CREDITS

Dr. Stephen Malley: Robert Redford
Janine Roth: Meryl Streep
Sen. Jasper Irving: Tom Cruise
Ernest Rodriguez: Michael Pena
Wirey Pink: Peter Berg
Howard: Kevin Dunn
Arian Finch: Derek Luke
Todd Hayes: Andrew Garfield
Origin: USA
Language: English
Released: 2007
Production: Robert Redford, Andrew Hauptman, Matthew Michael Carnahan, Tracy Falco; Wildwood Enterprises, United Artists, Brat Na Pont Productions, Andell Entertainment; released by MGM
Directed by: Robert Redford
Written by: Matthew Carnahan
Cinematography by: Philippe Rousselot
Music by: Mark Isham
Sound: Peter Hliddal, Richard Hymns
Editing: Joe Hutshing
Art Direction: Francois Audouy
Costumes: Mary Zophres
Production Design: Jan Roelfs
MPAA rating: R
Running time: 92 minutes

REVIEWS

Boston Globe Online. November 9, 2007.
Chicago Sun-Times Online. November 8, 2007.
Entertainment Weekly Online. November 7, 2007.
Hollywood Reporter Online. October 23, 2007.
Los Angeles Times Online. November 9, 2007.
New York Times Online. November 9, 2007.
New Yorker Online. November 12, 2007.
San Francisco Chronicle. November 9, 2007, p. E1.
Variety Online. October 22, 2007.
Wall Street Journal. November 9, 2007, p. W1.
Washington Post. November 9, 2007, p. C5.

QUOTES

Senator Jasper Irving: "Do you want to win the War on Terror? Yes or no?"

LIVE FREE OR DIE HARD

Yippee Ki Yay Mo... - John 6:27
—Movie tagline

Box Office: $134.5 million

It has been twelve years since the last *Die Hard* film, which may leave audiences to wonder why the time is right for yet another adventure in this popular franchise. While the first movie, *Die Hard* (1988), is a classic action film and made Bruce Willis a bona fide star as John McClane, the tough, wisecracking New York detective who finds himself in one outlandish scrape after another, the two sequels that followed—*Die Hard 2* (1990) and *Die Hard: With a Vengeance* (1995)—represented a steady decline in the quality of the storytelling. Yet reviving the series in 2007 turned out to be a smart move. *Live Free or Die Hard* is not only a superlative action film in its own right, but it uses the passage of time wisely as McClane must now face a new challenge, a crime based in computer technology with which he is not familiar. While in abundant supply, brawn and firepower are not enough to defeat the villain, a computer hacker operating on a grand scale, so McClane is given a young sidekick named Matt Farrell (Justin Long), who helps him navigate and ultimately triumph in this new world of cyber crime.

Directed by Len Wiseman from a screenplay by Mark Bomback, *Live Free or Die Hard* is based on an article that appeared in *Wired* (May 1997) called "A Farewell to Arms," in which John Carlin wrote about the increasing vulnerability of our information technology and the chilling implications for a new kind of warfare that the United States is unprepared to wage. This thesis is the blueprint for villain Thomas Gabriel's (Timothy Olyphant) plan to show the powers that be the devastating consequences of a cyber attack. Of course, he wants to collect a huge payoff for himself as well.

Farrell was one of Gabriel's unwitting henchmen, part of a team of hackers who did his dirty work but did not know the full scope of what they were involved in. After using them, Gabriel has had them systematically killed, but Farrell escapes with the aid of McClane, who is charged with bringing him to FBI headquarters. As McClane tries to fathom the larger picture, Gabriel's minions are on a mission to hunt them down.

McClane and Farrell make a great team, and the screenplay uses the generational divide not only as a source of humor but also as a smart way to allow the viewer into the story. If McClane himself is off balance in this world and needs help understanding cyber terrorism, then so does the audience, which makes it necessary to have a character who can explain all the technical issues in an easy-to-understand way that makes us care about the action, not slow it down.

But if Willis and Long nicely humanize the tech warfare, *Live Free or Die Hard* really excels in the action arena. The movie features some incredible set pieces,

Unlike some films directed by experienced screen-writers, *The Lookout* has considerable visual style. Frank and cinematographer Alar Kivilo shoot Chris in cramped spaces to emphasize his claustrophobic life and frame him in doorways and windows to underscore his need to move from one type of existence to another. Kivilo is also an expert in desolate, snowy landscapes, having shot *A Simple Plan* (1998) and *The Ice Harvest* (2005). Editor Jill Savitt helps make the complicated action during the bungled robbery easy to follow and skillfully accentuates the tension during the final showdown between Chris and Spargo.

Gordon-Levitt makes Chris a sympathetic protagonist. Going well beyond the blank veneer he adopts in the similar *Brick* (2005), Gordon-Levitt does not settle for any of the clichéd mannerisms usually associated with mentally challenged characters. He plays Chris as a normal person with a remarkably bad memory and makes the young man's eagerness to deal with his problem appealing without resorting to sentimentality. Daniels does the same for his character, making Lewis belligerent, never asking for pity. The performance is one of the most distinctive in Daniels' long career. Fisher ably conveys Luvlee's regret at duping Chris. Goode is masterful as Spargo progresses from friendly to helpful to vicious and offers, as well, an exceptional credible American accent.

The Lookout is too violent for those who like art films and too understated, for the most part, for those who like more action. It is a small film with modest goals but achieves them quite well, especially in delineating the friendship of Chris and Lewis and their acceptance of their co-dependency.

Michael Adams

CREDITS

Chris Pratt: Joseph Gordon-Levitt
Lewis: Jeff Daniels
Gary Spargo: Matthew Goode
Luvlee Lemons: Isla Fisher
Janet: Carla Gugino
Robert Pratt: Bruce McGill
Barbara Pratt: Alberta Watson
Mrs. Lange: Alex Borstein
Deputy Ted: Sergio Di Zio
Bone: Greg Dunham
Origin: USA
Language: English
Released: 2007
Production: Roger Birnbaum, Gary Barber; Spyglass Entertainment; released by Miramax

Directed by: Scott Frank
Written by: Scott Frank
Cinematography by: Alar Kivilo
Music by: James Newton Howard
Sound: Leon Johnson
Editing: Jill Savitt
Art Direction: Dennis Davenport
Costumes: Abram Waterhouse
Production Design: David Brisbin
MPAA rating: R
Running time: 99 minutes

REVIEWS

Boxoffice Online. March 30, 2007.
Chicago Sun-Times Online. March 30, 2007.
Entertainment Weekly Online. March 28, 2007.
Los Angeles Times Online. March 30, 2007.
New York Times Online. March 30, 2007.
Rolling Stone Online. March 21, 2007.
San Francisco Chronicle. March 30, 2007, p. E5.
Variety Online. March 11, 2007.
Village Voice Online. March 27, 2007.
Washington Post Online. March 30, 2007.

TRIVIA

To be more convincing as a blind man, Jeff Daniels spent time at the Michigan Commission for the Blind Training Center in Kalamazoo, observing and learning some basic skills used by blind people on a daily basis.

AWARDS

Ind. Spirit 2008: First Feature.

LOVE IN THE TIME OF CHOLERA

How long would you wait for love?
—Movie tagline

Box Office: $4.6 million

Gabriel García Márquez is one of the world's greatest writers, winner of the Nobel Prize for Literature in 1982. *Love in the Time of Cholera* (1985) is one of his most highly regarded novels, but those whose first exposure to García Márquez is the film adaptation may be wondering what all the fuss is about. Despite a few good performances and some lush scenery, *Love in the Time of Cholera* comes off as little more than a tepid romance.

Set in Cartagena, Colombia, from 1879 to 1932, the film tells the story of the unrequited love of Florentino Ariza (Javier Bardem) for Fermina Daza Urbino (Giovanna Mezzogiorno). The young Florentiono (Unax Ugalde) falls for Fermina the first time he sees her, but her socially ambitious father, Lorenzo Daza (John Leguizamo), refuses to allow her to see a mere clerk at a telegraph office. Instead she marries the older, well-to-do Dr. Juvenal Urbino (Benjamin Bratt). Fermina does not love Dr. Urbino, but she submits to her father's wishes.

Love in the Time of Cholera opens with the death of the elderly Urbino and then flashes back to the beginning of Florentino's infatuation with Fermina. After being rejected, the young man finds himself seduced on a riverboat by a woman whose face he cannot see. This experience prompts Florentino to drown his sorrows by seducing women and keeping meticulous notes in a journal. The number of affairs reaches 662 by the time of Urbino's death, with only two of these relationships lasting any length of time. Florentino gives his body to others, but his heart remains Fermina's for fifty-three years.

The film cuts back and forth between Florentino's life and Fermina's relationship with her husband and family, principally her vivacious cousin, Hildebranda (Catalina Sandino Moreno). In addition to his love affairs, Florentino is shown trying to cheer his long-suffering mother, Tránsito (Fernanda Montenegro), who has raised him on her own after her lover ran away. Florentino is hired by his uncle, Don Leo (Hector Elizondo), and eventually takes over the family's shipping business. All this is told against the background of revolution and cholera epidemics.

Cholera becomes a metaphor for love, passion, and the instability of life, but it is an unsteady metaphor as screenwriter Ronald Harwood seems to be more concerned with condensing Gabriel García Márquez's tale than in exploring any of its themes. To say that the source is reduced to the level of a Harlequin romance is not quite fair but accurate nevertheless. Fermina and Urbino's characters are poorly developed. It is a surprise to see her, near the end of the film, suddenly confronted by middle-aged children who have seemingly sprung from nowhere. Because Fermina is more of a conceit than a fully realized character, it is difficult to see why Florentino is obsessed by her.

Many reviewers complained about the casting of Mezzogiorno, saying that Moreno, Oscar® nominated for *Maria Full of Grace* (2004), would have been a better choice. Yet Mezzogiorno has given nuanced performances in *Facing Windows* (2003) and *Don't Tell* (2005), so the fault cannot all be hers. Someone else might have been equally bland and passive because the role is so poorly written, but it would have been interesting to see

what Moreno or the spunky Marcel Mar, as Florentino's final, much younger lover, could have done as Fermina.

During his four years on *Law and Order* (begun in 1990), Bratt had a sophisticated presence, but he has not fared as well in the transition to the big screen. Urbino is even more of a cipher than Fermina, and it is shocking to hear him profess his love for his wife because neither Bratt nor Harwood has given any indication of much depth of emotion in the doctor. The only truly disastrous performance, though, is Leguizamo's. Delivering his lines in something between a mumble and a growl, he seems to be doing a third-rate Marlon Brando imitation.

The best supporting performance is by Ugalde, recommended for the part by Bardem. The young actor looks as if he could grow up to be Bardem and ably conveys Florentino's sense of wonder over Fermina. Though some reviewers, most of whom savaged the film, felt Bardem is miscast, he brings a sense of style to his performance. Adopting a stiff-legged walk and a goofy grin, Bardem seems like a silent-film comedian.

García Márquez's novels, especially *One Hundred Years of Solitude* (1967), his masterpiece and arguably the greatest Latin American novel, are known for their so-called magic realism, the appearance of unusual events in everyday settings. While there is no such magic in *Love in the Time of Cholera*, beyond the aged Florentino's continued sexual prowess, Bardem's offbeat performance gives the film a needed layer of eccentricity. His work here can be appreciated better by comparing it to *No Country for Old Men* (2007), which he had just finished filming before embarking on *Love in the Time of Cholera*. His face, body, voice, and manner are so different that it is hard to believe it is the same person.

Love in the Time of Cholera looks beautiful, thanks to production designer Wolf Kroeger and cinematographer Affonso Beato. All the houses look lived in, with rooms crammed with details, and Beato gives it all a lush look, with deep greens and reds. Mike Newell, however, provides rather pedestrian direction, as the film lurches from one plot point to another without giving the audience a reason to care. A craftsman more than an artist, Newell has made several good films, notably *Dance with a Stranger* (1985), *The Good Father* (1985), *Four Weddings and a Funeral* (1994), and *Donnie Brasco* (1997), which demonstrate his storytelling skills and his admirable handing of actors. Given their plodding approach, he and Harwood, who won an Oscar® for *The Pianist* (2002), were the wrong people to bring *Love in the Time of Cholera* to the screen.

Reviewers were almost universal in saying the film should have been made in Spanish and directed by Pedro Almodóvar, Alfonso Cuarón, or any of the many other Spanish or Latin American directors who have come to prominence since the 1990s. Producer Scott Steindorff claims García Márquez rejected over fifty other offers to adapt the novel and that he called the novelist almost daily for three years, proving that he was as obsessed as Florentino himself. Like Fermina, García Márquez should have made him wait fifty-three years.

Michael Adams

CREDITS

Florentino Ariza: Javier Bardem
Fermina Daza Urbino: Giovanna Mezzogiorno
Dr. Juvenal Urbino: Benjamin Bratt
Hildebranda: Catalina Sandino Moreno
Don Leo: Hector Elizondo
Lotario Thugut: Liev Schreiber
Olimpia Zuleta: Ana Claudia Talancon
Lorenzo Daza: John Leguizamo
Origin: USA
Language: English
Released: 2007
Production: Scott Steindorff; Stone Village, Grosvenor Park; released by New Line Cinema
Directed by: Mike Newell
Written by: Ronald Harwood
Cinematography by: Alfonso Beato
Music by: Antonio Pinto
Sound: Mark Auguste
Editing: Mick Audsley
Art Direction: Roberto Bonelli, Paul Kirby
Costumes: Marit Allen
Production Design: Wolf Kroeger
MPAA rating: R
Running time: 138 minutes

REVIEWS

Boston Globe Online. November 16, 2007.
Chicago Sun-Times Online. November 16, 2007.
Entertainment Weekly Online. November 14, 2007.
Hollywood Reporter Online. November 12, 2007.
Los Angeles Times Online. November 16, 2007.
New York Times Online. November 16, 2007.
New Yorker Online. November 19, 2007.
San Francisco Chronicle. November 16, 2007, p. E5.
Variety Online. November 12, 2007.
Washington Post. November 16, 2007, p. C1.

QUOTES

Florentino Ariza: "Shoot me. There is no greater glory than to die for love."

TRIVIA

Producer Scott Steindorff spent more than three years courting Gabriel García Márquez for the rights to the book telling him that he was Florentino and wouldn't give up until he got the rights.

AWARDS

Nomination:
Golden Globes 2008: Song ("Despedida").

LUCKY YOU

Change your game. Change your life.
—Movie tagline
Take a chance.
—Movie tagline

Box Office: $5.7

Writer/director Curtis Hanson's *Lucky You* is a character study set in the world of professional poker in 2003. This year signaled the entry of professional poker into popular consciousness for the private world of backroom high-stakes poker became a televised pseudo-sport for the curious masses, much to the chagrin of many veteran players.

Many professional players lament 2003 as the year the game was corrupted, and private play between professional players was violated by the introduction of the intrusive "hole-card" cameras allow spectators to see each player's hand and allow them to play along. It was also the year that Chris Moneymaker, an amateur Internet poker player, won the World Series of Poker without ever playing in a live game. What could have been an interesting plotline is just background, however, as the filmmakers instead crafted a clichéd father and son melodrama that only provides viewers with a feeling of déjà vu.

Eric Bana is Huck Cheever, a professional poker player living on the Las Vegas strip and under the shadow of his estranged father, L.C. Cheever (Robert Duvall), a two-time World Series of Poker champion. Unlike his father, Huck is impulsive and given to losing his cool when challenged, which usually costs him in poker and in his relationships as well. He plays poker the way he should live his life, and he lives his life the way he should play poker.

Huck's goal is to prove to his father that without his father's help he can win the $10,000 entrance fee needed for a seat at the table in the World Series of Poker. Yet before he can do that, he must first beat the demons in his past and his own ego.

Huck's life consists of nothing but poker. In the workforce he would be considered a workaholic, earning triple-overtime. Gambling consumes his every move and every thought. Viewers are shown that this is not uncommon for most professional players, as players often make side bets. Whether it is a bet that involves walking across a floor on chair legs or running five miles and then finishing eighteen holes of golf in less than three hours, gambling dominates their lives. Director Hanson and writer Eric Roth are interested in examining these obsessed people.

Unfortunately, their examination is superficial, and shallow Hollywood stereotypes of players populate the film even amidst real-life professional players who would seem to be more interesting. Instead of truly examining the diverse personalities and reasons that cause people to give up their day jobs to take up professional poker, the filmmakers use snippets culled from conversations with real-life players to create one-off character bits that are used solely as comic relief.

As Huck, Bana's constant monotone delivery throughout the film mirrors Huck's poker face but does nothing to let the audience in on his emotions. Thus it makes it difficult for the audience to root for him, which clearly it is meant to do. More reliable in that area is Duvall, who as Huck's father, steals the show and audience interest. Through his humanity, he becomes a more accessible character than Bana's and inadvertently becomes more likeable as a result. He is the only character that the audience gets to know and because of this, the audience has no choice but to grasp onto him. Clearly this is not what the filmmakers intended.

Adding to the narrative confusion is Drew Barrymore as Billie Offer, a naïve girl from Bakersfield, who comes to Vegas to pursue her dream of becoming a lounge singer. She meets Huck and immediately and inextricably falls for him. She knows nothing about the game of poker, and through her we get a crash course in the rules and strategy of the game from Huck. Her purpose in the screenplay is to fall in love with the main character and stick with him no matter what, even after he steals money from her purse after sleeping with her so he can gamble. She is in the film to allow Huck to explain poker rules to viewers and fullfil a Hollywood cliché: the love story.

After that the audience is treated to scene after scene of Huck winning big, only to recklessly lose it all. This plotline reinforces the fact that he is a serious addict who needs help. It is unclear if the filmmakers care about this aspect, or if they were even aware of it, because they move on from this topic quickly in order to show the well-researched ins and outs of card play.

Adding to this pretentious story, Roth and Hanson fill their meandering screenplay with superficial and uninspired pabulum masquerading as dialogue, further

alienating viewers from a world that the filmmakers think they want to know more about. In doing so, the filmmakers lose the one hole-card that could win audiences over. Ultimately, the father and son face off in the big game, and the climax loses all drama. The audience has already lost interest in both them and the game, and their reconciliation feels as hollow as the entire proceedings.

David E. Chapple

CREDITS

Huck Cheever: Eric Bana
L.C. Cheever: Robert Duvall
Billie Offer: Drew Barrymore
Suzanne: Debra Messing
Ready Eddie: Horatio Sanz
Michelle Carson: Jean Smart
Roy DeRuscher: Charles Martin Smith
Telephone Jack: Robert Downey, Jr.
Chico Banh: Kelvin Han Yee
Jason Keyes: Evan Jones
Ray Zumbro: Michael Shannon
Origin: USA
Language: English
Released: 2007
Directed by: Curtis Hanson
Written by: Curtis Hanson, Eric Roth
Cinematography by: Peter Deming
Music by: Christopher Young
MPAA rating: PG-13
Running time: 123 minutes

REVIEWS

Boston Globe Online. May 4, 2007.
Chicago Sun-Times Online. May 4, 2007.
Entertainment Weekly. May 11, 2007, p. 56.
Hollywood Reporter Online. May 3, 2007.
Los Angeles Times Online. May 4, 2007.
New York Times Online. May 4, 2007.
San Francisco Chronicle. May 4, 2007, p. E5.
Variety Online. May 2, 2007.

QUOTES

L.C. (to Huck): "Don't chase what you can't catch."

LUST, CAUTION
(Se, jie)

Box Office: $4.6 million

After the controversial *Brokeback Mountain* (2005) Ang Lee might be expected to make a less controversial film.

Yet the director has followed his gay cowboy drama with another look at passion and betrayal, this time during the World War II Japanese occupation of Shanghai. The illicit love affair depicted in *Lust, Caution* (also known as *Se, jie*) is set against an epic background and features unusually graphic sex for a mainstream film.

As a Shanghai student in 1938, Wong Chia Chi (Tang Wei) becomes involved with a theater group, led by Kuang Yu Min (Lee-Hom Wang), that stages patriotic, anti-Japanese plays. Impressed by Wong's inspired acting, Kuang invites her to become involved in even more patriotic duties as a spy. Pretending to be Mrs. Mak, the wife of a businessman (Johnson Yuen), actually another student, Wong ingratiates herself with Mrs. Yee (Joan Chen), whose husband (Tony Leung Chiu Wai) is a pro-Japanese government official. Wong is asked to have an affair with Yee and set him up for an assassination, but events take another course before Yee can be killed.

Three years later in Hong Kong, Wong meets Kuang again and is convinced to return to Shanghai for more intrigue involving Yee. By the time their affair begins, Yee is a powerful collaborator who tortures prisoners. Yee's first sexual encounter with Wong is almost like a rape, displaying the brutality typical, viewers are invited to speculate, of his unseen interrogations. Later encounters, if not exactly tender, are at least passionate on the part of both lovers, as Wong moves from victim to participant. A variety of sexual positions are on display, an effort, Lee has explained, to convey the tortured nature of their relationship. The affair is especially confusing for Wong, a romantic who cries as such Hollywood films as *Intermezzo* (1939) and *Penny Serenade* (1941).

Lust, Caution is based on a short story by Eileen Chang who was married to Shanghai's propaganda minister in the Japanese-controlled government and went into hiding after the war. The series of stories she wrote about occupied Shanghai all deal with male-female relationships, with their emphasis on the painful side of love earning them the description anti-romantic. As Larry McMurtry and Diana Ossana did in expanding Annie Proulx's story into Lee's *Brokeback Mountain*, James Schamus, collaborating with Lee for the eighth time, and Hui-Ling Wang, veteran of two previous Lee films, including *Crouching Tiger, Hidden Dragon* (2000), treat Chang's story as a starting point and add more political and sexual content.

This sexual side has made *Lust, Caution* almost as controversial as *Brokeback Mountain*. The explicit sex earned the film an NC-17 rating, the first for a widely distributed film since *Showgirls* (1995). As a result, some newspapers refused to carry advertising for *Lust, Caution*, and many theaters were reluctant to show it. That the film was distributed in only a few hundred American theaters may also have been the result of its being set against unfamiliar history.

Though the sex scenes are the center of the film, Lee takes over an hour and a half to get to them, slowly establishing the characters and their situations. At a time when few American films address sexual issues, many reviewers were shocked by the sexual content of *Lust, Caution*. The sex does not seem to be simulated, and Lee has declined to clarify this possibility in interviews. Regardless, Wei and Leung are courageous, not to say athletic, to have created the vivid impressions left by these scenes. The sexual content of *Lust, Caution* is most notable not because it is graphic but for how it works thematically. Both Wong, who is left behind when her father flees to England, and Yee are essentially loners. Their affair begins as merely physical but slowly evolves into something else. They are not exactly in love or dependent upon each other, but they communicate through sex, find a sort of peace absent elsewhere in their lives. In this regard *Lust, Caution* echoes Bernardo Bertolucci's *Last Tango in Paris* (1972) and Nagisa Oshima's *In the Realm of the Senses* (1976). Communication and the failure to communicate seem to be major themes throughout Lee's work.

Production designer Lai Pan does an outstanding job of recreating wartime Shanghai. As he did with *Brokeback Mountain*, cinematographer Rodrigo Prieto provides both beautiful and bleak images, especially during Wong's long walk through Shanghai during a particularly chaotic moment. Mixing both Western and Eastern sounds, Alexandre Desplat provides any even grander, more lushly romantic score than he did for the similar *The Painted Veil* (2006).

In her first film, Wei captures Wong's innocence and growing maturity. Leung, whose impressive credits include *Flowers of Shanghai* (1998), also based on a work by Chang, usually plays admirable characters yet finds the darker recesses of Yee as well as his unexpected softness. The American-born Wang, a popular singer in Asia, subtly conveys Kuang's distant affection for Wong.

Many reviewers, including Anthony Lane of the *New Yorker* and Manohla Dargis of the *New York Times*, strongly objected to the pacing and length of *Lust, Caution*, seemingly a common complaint of critics toward several 2007 releases. Reviewers especially objected to the attention given Mrs. Yee's endless mahjong games. Lee and his screenwriters, however, are to be applauded for taking the necessary time to establish this very specific milieu and the intricacy of the characters' complicated relationships. A tragic decision is made near the end of the film. Without the slow buildup, it would make little sense. As it is, it is heartbreaking.

Despite its tepid reception in the United States, *Lust, Caution* was a huge critical and box-office hit in Hong Kong and Lee's native Taiwan. Even though the Chinese, who have no film ratings system, cut thirty minutes of sexual and political content, the film was also successful on the mainland. It was so popular in Hong Kong that *Lust, Caution* tours of the sites depicted in the film began a few weeks after its release.

Michael Adams

CREDITS

Mr. Yee: Tony Leung Chiu-Wai
Mrs. Mak/Wang Jiazhi: Tang Wei
Mrs. Yee: Joan Chen
Kuang Yu Min: Lee-Hom Wang
Lai Shu Jin: Chih-ying Chu
Origin: USA, Hong Kong, China
Language: English, Chinese, Japanese
Released: 2007
Production: Bill Kong, Ang Lee, James Schamus; River Road Entertainment, Shanghai Film Group Corp, Haishang Films, Sil-Metropole Organisation; released by Focus Features

Directed by: Ang Lee
Written by: James Schamus, Wang Hui-ling
Cinematography by: Rodrigo Prieto
Music by: Alexandre Desplat
Sound: Drew Kunin, Philip Stockton, Eugene Gearty
Editing: Tim Squayres
Art Direction: Sai-Wan Lau
Production Design: Lai Pan
MPAA rating: NC-17
Running time: 158 minutes

REVIEWS

Entertainment Weekly Online. September 26, 2007.
Hollywood Reporter Online. August 31, 2007.
New York Times Online. September 28, 2007.
Premiere Online. September 26, 2007.
Variety Online. August 30, 2007.
Village Voice Online. September 25, 2007.

AWARDS

Nomination:

British Acad. 2007: Costume Des., Foreign Film
Golden Globes 2008: Foreign Film
Ind. Spirit 2008: Actor (Leung Chiu-Wai), Actress (Wei), Cinematog.

M

MARGOT AT THE WEDDING

One family. Infinite degrees of separation.
—Movie tagline

Box Office: $1.9 million

Noah Baumbach's brilliant 2005 drama *The Squid and the Whale* proved that this promising young writer/director had an amazing ear for the way fathers and sons speak to each other and an understanding that the sins of the parent are only going to be amplified in the behavior of the child. His follow-up, the even darker *Margot at the Wedding*, works with similar themes of parent and child and the evil that people can do to their most beloved, but it ends up an artistic misfire due to Baumbach's inability to write for women and his hatred for the characters he puts through the ringer for the sake of comedy, drama, and pathos. *Margot at the Wedding* features excellent performances from Nicole Kidman and Jennifer Jason Leigh but they are wasted by a filmmaker who seems less interested in examining anything about the human condition than defiling it for the sake of comedy or drama.

Margot Zeller (Nicole Kidman) is a neurotic writer in the middle of her own relationship problems and on her way to the wedding of her semi-estranged sister Pauline (Jennifer Jason Leigh, Baumbach's real-life wife). Margot brings her troubled son Claude (Zane Pais) to the intimate weekend with her sister and soon-to-be brother-in-law Malcolm (Jack Black). Margot spits venom at everyone around her, openly disapproves of her sister's choice of groom, and tries and sabotage their

nuptials. A writer who has always used her family as fodder for her short stories, Margot seems to be purposefully tormenting her loved ones just to spark an idea to revive her writing career.

Margot at the Wedding tries to be about honest human relationships but Baumbach keeps staging bizarre complications for the characters to bicker about instead of giving viewers anything to relate to or understand. The neighbors of the Zellers seem to be insane and cause problems for the wedding party when they argue over a beloved tree. Margot's own marriage is falling apart as she has an affair with an old family friend (Ciarán Hinds), whose flirtatious underage daughter proves to be a downfall for Malcolm. Despite the fact that some of the awkward situations in *Margot at the Wedding* feel straight out of a soap opera, Baumbach could have written a tale about family being the one final refuge when the world spins out of control. Instead, he seems to be saying that loved ones will not support other family members when life goes off the rails but contributed to the derailment and laugh about it afterward.

Kidman tackles the icy role of Margot with her typical fearlessness, and none of the film' flaws revolve around her performance or that of Leigh. From the minute she appears on-screen, Leigh appears as believable as her husband's script allows, reminding viewers that she makes every project she chooses to film better.

One of several problems with the misanthropic *Margot at the Wedding* is the complete lack of believability in the dialogue between Margot and Pauline. Both characters sound more like the product of a writer who watched movie women from John Cassavetes or Woody

Allen movies to craft his sisters instead of actually listening to the way women speak to each other in the real world. They sound written. The awful behavior in *Margot at the Wedding* and the filmmaker's clear hatred for the characters in it only works if the dialogue rings true. The fact that it never does only draws attention to the complete lack of likable characters or verisimilitude.

Everything about *Margot at the Wedding* feels ugly, from the characters who become impossible to root for, to the darkly lit cinematography that relies far too heavily on natural light. There have been many masterpieces made about vile interactions between man and woman, even (or maybe especially) if they are family members, but the lack of believability sinks *Margot at the Wedding,* placing the spotlight more on the creator than the characters. After a while, the behavior of Margot and Pauline becomes far less interesting than the decisions made by the man behind the camera.

Brian Tallerico

CREDITS

Margot: Nicole Kidman
Pauline: Jennifer Jason Leigh
Malcolm: Jack Black
Jim: John Turturro
Dick: Ciarán Hinds
Ingrid: Flora Cross
Maisy: Halley Feiffer
Claude: Zane Pais
Origin: USA
Language: English
Released: 2007
Production: Scott Rudin; released by Paramount Vantage
Directed by: Noah Baumbach
Written by: Noah Baumbach
Cinematography by: Harris Savides
Sound: Drew Kunin
Editing: Carol Littleton
Art Direction: Adam Stockhausen
Costumes: Ann Roth
Production Design: Anne Ross
MPAA rating: R
Running time: 92 minutes

REVIEWS

Christian Science Monitor Online. November 16, 2007.
Entertainment Weekly Online. November 14, 2007.
Hollywood Reporter Online. September 1, 2007.
New York Times Online. November 16, 2007.
New Yorker Online. November 19, 2007.
Premiere Online. November 15, 2007.
Variety Online. September 2, 2007.
Village Voice Online. November 13, 2007.

TRIVIA

Nicole Kidman, Jennifer Jason Leigh, and Jack Black moved in together during filming, because they wanted to perfect their roles as a dysfunctional family.

TRIVIA

The cinematographer, Harris Savides, used old lenses and shot mostly in natural light to get the dim, ominous look of the film.

AWARDS

Nomination:

Ind. Spirit 2008: Support. Actress (Leigh).

MARTIAN CHILD

The story of a man becoming a father...and a boy becoming a son.
—Movie tagline

Box Office: $7.5 million

Quirky and heartwarming are the dangerously paired adjectives that most easily describe the plot of *Martian Child.* A young widower with a heart still full of love takes a shot at adopting a disturbed, formerly abused and abandoned boy who thinks he is from Mars. The danger should be obvious: This film promises to be an affected postmodern melodrama that lacks originality because it features two misfits who forge a bond despite all odds.

In fact, this is movie therapy by the numbers. A the man who had an unhappy childhood rescues an actual unhappy child, freeing himself from his own past, while teaching the child how to pretend to fit in and thereby cope in a society that does not understand them. To make such a plot work requires outstanding writing and forceful characters. Unfortunately, *Martian Child* has neither. The script, by Seth Bass and Jonathan Tolins from a book by David Gerrold (itself a fictionalized account of his own attempt as a gay man to adopt a child), has all the subtlety of a flying saucer. Menno Meyjes' direction ranges from cloying to sappy.

Meyjes has worked with John Cusack before, in the forgettable *Max* (2002), in which Cusack played Hitler's art teacher. Although a fine actor, Cusack never fully inhabits the character of David because he has been given so little to work with. David is little more than a

256

MAGILL'S CINEMA ANNUAL

cliché: a successful science fiction writer who has channeled the fantasies that got him through a lonely childhood into a series of best-selling novels that have become a book-to-movie franchise. Before his wife died, the couple had planned to adopt a child, and now he has decided to explore this process on his own.

Somehow he is connected with Sophie (Sophie Okonedo, wasted here in a minor role), who runs a large foster home of some sort. Dennis (Bobby Coleman) is the misfit among the misfits at the home. He spends his days on the sidewalk in a box, ostensibly because he is afraid of sunlight. David brings him sunscreen and sunglasses and eventually coaxes the boy out of the box. Nevertheless, he cannot convince him to part with the weighted belt made of old batteries that Dennis believes keeps him from flying off into space, "Earth gravity being much less powerful than that of Mars."

David convinces the requisite authorities to allow him to take Dennis home for a trial adoption, explaining that he understands fantasies because he has written so many of them. It is not easy warming up to Dennis, whose way of getting to know people is to steal their precious things and take Polaroids snapshots of them and everything else in sight. He is on a mission, and part of his mission is to collect and catalogue this evidence of Earthling behavior.

To help us understand David's own painful past, there is a role for his real-life sister, Joan Cusack, playing David's sister Liz. Meyjes gives her the opportunity to play a familiarly offbeat, blunt-spoken character, but the comedy in Liz's part is a little strained and even scary. Her harried mother role is so overdone that it creates a sneaking suspicion that she truly hates her children. Harlee (Amanda Peet), the best friend of David's deceased wife, is the romantic interest. The film takes intermittent and rather desultory interest in their budding romance, and Harlee is apparently useful only to counter Liz, who thinks Dennis is crazy, by suggesting the child is an "old soul" and perhaps some kind of wise mystic.

The film moves along uninterestingly and predictably down the path of moralisms and clichés. David teaches Dennis about baseball and how to cope with failure by never giving up; Dennis tries to go to school but does not fit in; David is under pressure to finish his next novel, and Dennis interrupts him; they fight Hollywood-cute (breaking dishes and spraying each other with ketchup), but they are caught by the man in charge of the case. The plot is simple and straightforward, and its scriptwriter was clearly desperate for ideas when he killed off a beloved pet mid-story. The case is finally reviewed, and Dennis inexplicably becomes

articulate enough to carry the day. Then, predictably, David loses faith in the boy's fantasy, and Dennis runs away, setting up an ending that is so obviously melodramatic that it would have fit squarely into a silent movie from the 1920s.

If David and Dennis were more compelling, at least there would be more response when the movie tries to jerk the tears (the soundtrack is annoyingly sentimental right from the start). Cusack plays David's awkwardness unconvincingly, as if he is trying to dumb down an obvious intelligence. When David screws up and reverts to anger or intolerance, it is a shock; Cusack is too sensitive a man to make these lapses believable.

A more significant flaw is the movie's indecisive portrayal of Dennis. Is this a child with serious emotional problems, or is he actually a visionary of some sort? A therapist who rejects prescribing medication in favor of attention from David is certainly welcome relief, but it is not very plausible because Dennis seems at times to be almost catatonic. The movie conflates all kinds of behavior—from hanging upside down to stealing—and them all as equal manifestations of Dennis's weirdness, without distinguishing what is delusional from what is merely different. At other times, Dennis is just ridiculously cute, as when having shown no previous signs of coordination, he suddenly breaks into a Martian dance, and David joins in. His is definitely a Hollywood sort of madness.

There is a superficiality to the child's character and the movie's depiction of his problems that is troublesome. In the film's earnestness to make David a brave rescuer, there is a shying away from exploring the true depths of the child's possible mania and the seriousness of it. The far-out possibility that the kid really is from another planet is treated merely as metaphor for the strange wisdom that children might provide. In the final analysis, Dennis becomes a pathetic figure who provides no insight. He is not a magical child, just a kid in need of a big hug. That is a perfectly fine story to tell but rather disappointingly down-to-earth for a movie that bills itself as *Martian Child*.

Michael Betzold

CREDITS
David: John Cusack
Dennis: Bobby Coleman
Harlee: Amanda Peet
Sophie: Sophie Okonedo
Jeff: Oliver Platt
Liz: Joan Cusack
Mimi: Anjelica Huston

Origin: USA
Language: English
Released: 2007
Production: David Kirschner, Corey Sienega, Ed Elbert; released by New Line Cinema
Directed by: Menno Meyjes
Written by: Seth Bass, Jonathan Tolins
Cinematography by: Robert Yeoman
Music by: Aaron Zigman
Sound: Michael Williamson, Robert C. Jackson
Editing: Bruce Green
Costumes: Michael Dennison
Production Design: Hugo Luczyc-Wyhowski
MPAA rating: PG
Running time: 106 minutes

REVIEWS

Boston Globe Online. November 2, 2007.
Chicago Sun-Times Online. November 2, 2007.
Entertainment Weekly Online. October 31, 2007.
Hollywood Reporter Online. October 29, 2007.
Los Angeles Times Online. November 2, 2007.
New York Times Online. November 2, 2007.
Variety Online. October 23, 2007.
Washington Post Online. November 2, 2007.

QUOTES

David: "I don't want to bring another kid into this world. But how do you argue against loving one that's already here?"

MEET THE ROBINSONS

If you think your family's different, wait 'til you meet the family of the future.
—Movie tagline

Box Office: $97.8 million

Meet the Robinsons is the first film to come out of Disney's animation wing since Pixar's John Lasseter took over. Reflecting a studio that has not really found its voice yet, *Meet the Robinsons* uneasily combines the lump-in-the-throat childhood trauma of a Disney film (in this case, a mother abandoning her baby) with the zaniness and modern references that are the hallmarks of Pixar. Coupled with the fact that seven writers are credited on the film, *Meet the Robinsons* comes off as somewhat of a hodgepodge, albeit a mindlessly entertaining one.

The film's highlight is its unique, futuristic look; think the *The Jetsons* with a anachronistic twist, the future of suburban America as envisioned in the 1950s.

In the *Boston Globe* Ty Burr wrote, "Almost as funny as it is hyperactive, the new computer-animated family comedy is luscious to look at and as fizzy as a can of soda popped open in your face." There are vast, manicured lawns, talking plants, and time-traveling spacecraft of gleaming and rounded stainless steel all rendered in glorious 3-D, another "futuristic" invention of 1950s. The film is notable as it marks the first wide release of an animated film in digital 3-D, dubbed Real D technology, used in conjunction with polarized glasses. Disney's pioneering use of Technicolor in its animated feature *Snow White* (1937) had a lasting impact upon the genre, although it is unlikely that Real D technology will become mainstream in animation, as Disney has hoped.

The movie, whose plot is loosely based on the William Joyce children's book, *A Day with Wilbur Robinson*, concerns the fate of Lewis (voice of Jordan Fry and Daniel Lewis). Lewis is an orphan, sporting large glasses on his over-sized cranium, who spends his time tinkering (mostly unsuccessfully) with his scientific inventions. One such invention, a peanut-butter-and-jelly-dispensing system, explodes on a man who is highly allergic to peanuts and Lewis drives away yet another couple who might have been interested in adopting him.

Lewis hopes to find some inner peace with his greatest invention yet, a memory retrieval device. He wants to use it to return to the moment his mother dropped him off at the orphanage. If he can watch the event and see her face, perhaps he can figure out why she left him. Yet before Lewis gets a chance to try out the device at the school science fair, he is whisked three decades into the future in a time machine by a fast-talking teenager, Wilbur Robinson (voice of Wesley Singerman).

Lewis finds himself oddly comfortable with Wilbur's large, eccentric family, which includes a talking robot (voice of Harland Williams), a superhero uncle who delivers pizzas (voice of Adam West) and an odd grandfather (voice of director Stephen Anderson) who wears his pants backwards. The group of misfits accepts him as one of their own, and for the first time in his life, he feels like he is part of a family. Lewis is content in the sprawling Robinson mansion, with its octopus butler and a collection of frogs who play in a band, until Wilbur insists that Lewis fix the broken time machine and return to the school science fair. He runs into further problems with a clichéd villain (voice of Stephen Anderson), who literally twirls his moustache, and his remarkably intelligent sidekick, a bowler hat, who both seem quite intent on stealing Lewis' memory retrieval machine.

The plot is not of major importance. *Meet the Robinsons* works best as a sheer visceral experience. While marveling at the superbly rendered futuristic landscape, there are some charming details to note. The evil villain, for example, writes his to-do list of evil deeds on a little unicorn spiral notebook. A T-Rex hampered by short arms that was featured prominently in television advertisements for the film is a favorite of younger viewers.

Some viewers will not appreciate the film's overly brisk, if not frantic, pace. Writing in the *San Francisco Chronicle*, Peter Hartlaub suggested that at least four of the writers "must have had advanced cases of attention deficit disorder. There's so much going on with the film that the plot becomes secondary to the constant motion and often pointless jabbering." In the end, the success of the film rests with an individual viewer's tolerance for sitting through ninety-three minutes of unrelenting visual stimuli.

Jill Hamilton

CREDITS

Lewis: Jordan Fry (Voice)
Mildred: Angela Bassett (Voice)
Cornelius Robinson: Tom Selleck (Voice)
Carl: Harland Williams (Voice)
Lewis: Daniel Hansen (Voice)
Wilbur: Wesley Singerman (Voice)
Lucille Krunklehorn: Laurie Metcalf (Voice)
Uncle Art: Adam West (Voice)
Franny: Nicole Sullivan (Voice)
Bowler Hat Guy: Stephen John Anderson (Voice)
Origin: USA
Language: English
Released: 2007
Production: Dorothy McKim; Walt Disney Pictures; released by Buena Vista
Directed by: Stephen John Anderson
Written by: Jon Bernstein, Donald Hall, Stephen John Anderson, Michelle Bochner Spitz, Nathan Greno, Aurian Redson, Joe Mateo
Music by: Danny Elfman
Sound: Todd Toon
Music Supervisor: Tom MacDougall
Editing: Ellen Keneshea
Art Direction: Robh Ruppel
MPAA rating: G
Running time: 102 minutes

REVIEWS

Boston Globe Online. March 30, 2007.
Chicago Sun-Times Online. March 30, 2007.
Entertainment Weekly Online. March 28, 2007.
Hollywood Reporter Online. March 30, 2007.
Los Angeles Times Online. March 30, 2007.
New York Times Online. March 30, 2007.
Premiere Online. March 28, 2007.
San Francisco Chronicle. March 30, 2007, p. E5.
Variety Online. March 29, 2007.
Washington Post. March 30, 2007, p. C1.

THE MESSENGERS

> There is evidence to suggest that children are highly susceptible to paranormal phenomena. They see what adults cannot. They believe what adults deny. And they are trying to warn us.
> —Movie tagline

Box Office: $35.3

The Messengers is the much-hyped English language directorial debut of twin brothers Danny Pang and Oxide Pang Chun, the auteurs of Hong Kong ghost stories, including *The Eye* (2002), which they both wrote and directed. Although *The Messengers* retains many of the brothers' visual trademarks and style, the script they have chosen is woefully bad. The screenplay written by Mark Wheaton from a story by Todd Farmer is, at best, derivative and predictable, and at worst, unthinkingly illogical. Derivative of previous horror films, such as *The Amityville Horror* (1979), *The Shining* (1980), and another Asian remake, *Dark Water* (2005), *The Messengers* offers nothing new and is a pale imitation of its predecessors.

The Solomon family, escaping some unnamed family problem which has something to do with their sullen teen daughter Jess (Kristen Stewart), has moved from Chicago to grow sunflowers in the North Dakota countryside near where father Roy (Dylan McDermott) grew up. Why they would pick this incredibly ramshackle farmhouse in which to start a new life is perhaps the deepest mystery in the film.

The isolated and dilapidated house is straight out of central casting by way of *The Amityville Horror*. A murder of crows also haunts the farm in a manner most reminiscent of Alfred Hitchcock's *The Birds* (1963). There are fingernail scratch marks on the floor, a growing black stain on the master bedroom wall that just will not be washed away, doors that lock and unlock at will, and the obligatory dark and cobweb-filled basement. The house's rotten exterior reflects its horrendous past, and the film opens in the house with the black-and-white story of the brutal murder of two women and a little boy by an unknown murderer. Since then the house has been abandoned...until the Solomons arrive, that is.

The local banker, Colby Price (William B. Davis), has the spooky habit of appearing out of thin air, offering to buy Roy's farm back for more than the original price. For unknown reasons, however, the financially-strapped Roy never entertains the thought of selling to make a quick profit. Even after events become nasty, he continues to turn down the generous offers from the mysteriously reappearing banker.

While the family struggles to get its finances in order, it also strives to sort out its damaged family dynamics, but these takes are difficult to achieve. A mysterious stranger, John Burwell (John Corbett), shows up to lend a hand. With his long greasy hair, unknown origins, over-friendly ways, and willingness to work for free, it is clear he is not what he appears to be.

Meanwhile, the tightly wound Denise Solomon (Penelope Ann Miller), busies herself by trying to turn the hovel into a home while also trying to cope with her three-year-old Benny (Evan and Theodore Turner). Benny has not said a word since the mysterious, traumatic event that put the family in crisis. However, what Benny lacks in vocal abilities he makes up for with a supernatural ability to sense the demons lurking in the home. Benny sees shadows move across the room and watches as things skitter across the walls and ceilings. Unfortunately, he cannot tell anyone about them.

The film then focuses on the couple's other child, the troubled Jess, who begins to become aware of the malevolent spirits that infest the house. Every time she tries to warn her parents, they dismiss it as a part of her rebellious past. The horror cliché at work here is that children can sense things adults cannot. Disturbing events escalate, Jess becomes more panicked, and her parents become even more angry and distrustful of her to the point where Jess is forced to confide in the mysterious, shotgun-toting hired hand. Even as Jess is rushed to the emergency room with mysterious wounds, her parents cannot see that the house, and not their daughter, is to blame.

Relying more on cheap thrills than on legitimate suspense and shock, *The Messengers* favors atmospheric imagery over an intelligible storyline; inane dialogue over character development; and out-of-the-blue plot devices and twists over a coherent plot. The result is a mess that is barely capable of sustaining interest, let alone building any kind of suspense, until its awful ending.

The final reel poses more questions than it answers. Jess finds a pocket watch under the floorboards with a woman's picture in it, obviously a clue to the murdered prior occupants, but a pocket watch seems anachronistic based on the time that has elapsed since the previous murders. It is also implausible that such a thick watch

could end up under the floor. Moreover, the motive of the ghosts is unclear. If they were innocent victims in life, why are they so malevolent in death? The film also fails to delineate exactly who "the messengers" of the title are. If it is the crows, which is what the press kit suggests, then they are not doing a very good job. They do not warn; they attack. The real message of this stylish but generic film is one the Solomons should have heeded when they first saw the farmhouse: Stay away.

Beverley Bare Buehrer

CREDITS

Jess: Kristen Stewart
Roy: Dylan McDermott
Denise: Penelope Ann Miller
John: John Corbett
Ben: Evan Turner
Ben: Theodore Turner
Bobby: Dustin Milligan
Colby: William B. Davis
Origin: USA
Language: English
Released: 2007
Production: Sam Raimi, Robert Tapert, William Sherak, Jason Shuman; Blue Star Pictures, Screen Gems, Ghost House Pictures, Columbia Pictures; released by Sony Pictures
Directed by: Danny Pang, Oxide Pang Chun
Written by: Mark Wheaton
Cinematography by: David Geddes
Music by: Joseph LoDuca
Sound: Garrell Clark
Editing: John Axelrad, Armen Minasian
Art Direction: Ken Watkins
Costumes: Mary Hyde-Kerr
Production Design: Alicia Keywan
MPAA rating: PG-13
Running time: 84 minutes

REVIEWS

Boston Globe Online. February 2, 2007.
Entertainment Weekly. February 16, 2007, p. 60.
Hollywood Reporter Online. February 5, 2007.
Los Angeles Times Online. February 3, 2007.
New York Times Online. February 3, 2007.
Variety Online. February 2, 2007.

MICHAEL CLAYTON

The truth can be adjusted.
—Movie tagline

Box Office: $48.9

Even if the malfunctioning screen of his in-car navigation system were working perfectly, the title character in the engrossing thriller *Michael Clayton* knows full well that he would still find himself profoundly lost. Hailing from a working-class family of policemen and at one time an idealistic assistant district attorney, Michael (George Clooney) has gone from making the rules stick to helping finesse people out of sticky situations as the fixer for a prominent Manhattan law firm. Any time of the day or night, when Kenner, Bach and Ledeen's tony clients get themselves into unseemly messes, the handsome, charismatic and thoroughly capable Michael is called upon to determine the best way to extricate them, tidying things back up with well-placed phone calls and the affable handing out of discretion-ensuring cash. Michael's impressive efforts have been at the expense of an important portion of his soul, the man's exceptional aptitude getting him stuck for fifteen years in a narrow, ethically-questionable niche far below what he had once hoped to be doing by the time his hair started to gray. The firm bosses do not want this increasingly frustrated man as a partner, nor even as a litigator. They unfortunately see Michael as indispensable and trapped in a role he would very much like to dispense with.

Michael probably also did not expect to be a divorced father of a son (Austin Williams) he loves but too infrequently sees, nor a problem gambler, nor someone scrambling to get within mere days the $75,000 owed to some shady characters, as a result of an ill-advised restaurant venture entered into with his drug-addicted brother (David Lansbury). As Michael grimly speaks about limited options to an excuse-spouting, privileged man who had failed to even slow down his expensive car to verify that he had run someone down in the fog, the words could double as a painfully realistic assessment of his own situation. Michael dismisses the label of "miracle worker," soberly offering up the prosaic "janitor" as more apt. There is a burned-out world-weariness in his eyes, and a corrosive cynicism has for some time been eating away at his core. Damage control has clearly taken its toll.

Once one finally recognizes that he or she has gone too far, traveled down the wrong road, or advanced in the wrong direction, will a corrective, redemptive U-turn be attempted, or even still be possible? For Michael's longtime friend and colleague, Kenner, Bach and Ledeen's star litigator Arthur Edens (Tom Wilkinson), that decisive moment of clarity ironically manifests itself as a shocking, volcanic eruption of seemingly mad incoherence. For six years, Arthur has devoted his life to defending agrichemical colossus U/North against a potentially crippling, multi-billion dollar class action lawsuit concerning a chemical it purportedly knew would eliminate people along with their pesky weeds. A

document has now come into Arthur's possession that horrifically proves he has in fact been expertly holding decent folk like dear, sweet Anna (Merritt Wever) at bay while protecting a callous, unconscionable killer. Overwhelmed with guilt and undermedicated for his manic depression, Arthur goes spectacularly berserk in a Milwaukee deposition room, repentantly ranting things that could jeopardize U/North's defense as he strips naked and dashes out into a snowy parking lot after a thoroughly stunned Anna. As a result, the firm's authoritative founding partner, Marty Bach (well-cast Sydney Pollack), especially eager to divert disaster in the midst of potentially lucrative merger negotiations, orders Michael to rein Arthur in posthaste. It proves to be an impossible assignment.

Also wanting to shut Arthur up is Karen Crowder (the increasingly noteworthy Tilda Swinton), who has barely settled into her new position as U/North's in-house counsel. Karen, pale, pearl-draped, eminently presentable, and acutely in command, is an especially fascinating character, a great white shark when others' eyes are upon her but a panic-attack-ridden jellyfish when by herself. It is obvious that she is straining mightily to prove herself worthy, desperate to show that she can successfully swim with the male barracudas around her. During one of Karen's polished public performances, telling shots are inserted which contrastingly show how she had anxiously, endlessly rehearsed in front of a mirror. Viewers also watch her seek relieved refuge at one point in a bathroom stall, where she can have a gasping, sweat-stained meltdown in private. Terrified that the all-important case that has inched along for so long has now taken a precipitous downturn on her nascent watch, Karen goes out on a limb and chooses to hire a couple of shadowy figures to spy on the loose cannon litigator, following him and bugging his phone. Learning that Arthur has the damning document and is preparing to catastrophically turn the tables, using it against the company he is supposed to be defending, Karen does not go to her boss and mentor, Don Jefferies (Ken Howard), nor anyone else to ask for guidance or assistance in managing the rapidly unraveling situation. Instead, goaded forward by her insecurities, she gives a green light to her surveillance team to have Arthur silenced—permanently.

Before Arthur's murder, Michael had attempted to get him back in line, not just to make yet another brilliant save for KLB but also to try with sincere compassion to save the troubled man from himself. "I'm not the enemy!" the frustrated fixer had said, to which Arthur, looking him straight in the eyes, had pointedly replied, "Then who are you?" The response is simple and at the same time tremendously profound and thoroughly arresting, meaningfully, hauntingly hanging in the air for the remainder of the film. Its echoes obviously reverberate insistently in Michael's ears when, questioning the ruling of his friend's death as a suicide, he uncovers the memorandum that instantly transforms Arthur's seemingly outrageous paranoid rants into something monstrously, terrifyingly real. He is now convinced that Arthur, a man who knew too much, had been slain.

One can tell that Arthur's question is working on Michael's conscience when the firm agrees to loan him the money so desperately needed to pay off his debts—if he signs a confidentiality clause to a new contract that would prohibit him from rocking the boat with anything he has learned. There is a powerful shot of Michael lost in thought at the most crucial crossroad of his life, the damning U/North document in one hand, what he has been asked to consent to in the other, and a fundamental choice to make. This is when *Michael Clayton* truly begins to most firmly grip its audience. Who, indeed, will Michael be: someone who selfishly keeps quiet, or someone who will finally, defiantly reclaim principles ditched by the side of the road at a past, pivotal fork and press on anew to make sure those at U/North are nailed for every bit of their malevolence?

Most of *Michael Clayton* is an extended flashback, showing what led up to the booming dawn destruction of Michael's car by the side of a country road seen early on. He had pulled over and walked up a hill to gaze at a sight eerily identical to an illustration in a fantasy book both his son and Arthur had been reading. Viewers will have heard tell of a story concerning things that may initially seem "crazy" and illusory but turn out to be real, and about the recognition of things larger than oneself. When the scene's extended tranquility is jarringly broken by the explosion of a bomb planted by Karen's deadly duo, it is like a powerfully meaningful wake-up call, a clarion blast that once and for all jolts Michael's eyes fully open, shattering any lingering illusions about his situation and obliterating any doubts about how he must proceed.

The film's satisfying climactic scene is a showdown in which Karen's in-command façade dissolves into quaking desperation, barely knowing what hit her when she is decisively, determinedly trumped by someone seemingly back from the dead. As members of New York's Finest cart off some of the business world's worst from a U/North meeting, a high-angle shot holds on Michael riding an escalator next to another one heading in the opposite direction, seemingly emphasizing that there are always two ways that a person can choose to go in life. Michael has now changed course.

Held all the way through the credits is a final shot of Michael sitting in the back seat of a cab after telling the driver to just drive around a while. Clooney, excellent throughout as the afflicted, conflicted man motivated by events to at last reclaim his cobwebbed integrity, here has many emotions cross his face, including relief, pain, exhaustion, uncertainty, and, perhaps, a sense of accomplishment. Exactly what will happen next for Michael is as unclear to him just then as it is to the audience. He is free, however, to begin afresh. This time, in the long run, the fixer may have fixed himself.

Dark, intriguing, and intelligent, demanding of one's patience and careful attention but uncommonly rewarding for those efforts, *Michael Clayton* is the promising directorial debut of successful screenwriter Tony Gilroy, who also penned this film's script. Gilroy, best known in recent years for the *Bourne* trilogy (2002, 2004, 2007), works in a classical style markedly different from the visual freneticism evident in those films. Gilroy has stated his love of the look, mood, and attitude of 1970s works by directors like Sidney Lumet (*Serpico* [1973], *Network* [1976]), Alan J. Pakula (*The Parallax View* [1974], *All the President's Men* [1976]), and Pollack (*Three Days of the Condor* [1975]), influences clearly in evidence here. *Michael Clayton*, widely praised by critics, had a respectable showing at the box office. Numerous reviewers mentioned the possibility of Oscar® consideration for Clooney. However, all of the film's main characters are brought to life with an admirable, interesting complexity—sometimes potent, at other times poignant. While the film features such thrilling elements as a car chase at breakneck speeds, a murder committed with horrifying, swift precision, and a sudden, fiery explosion, what is most gripping about *Michael Clayton* is the grappling going on within those characters.

David L. Boxerbaum

CREDITS

Michael Clayton: George Clooney
Arthur Edens: Tom Wilkinson
Karen Crowder: Tilda Swinton
Marty Bach: Sydney Pollack
Barry Grissom: Michael O'Keefe
Ivy: Jennifer Van Dyck
Don Jefferies: Ken Howard
Mr. Verne: Robert Prescott
Origin: USA
Language: English
Released: 2007
Production: Sydney Pollack, Jennifer Fox, Steven Samuels, Kerry Orent; Castle Rock Entertainment, Mirage Enterprises, Section Eight, Samuels Media; released by Warner Bros.
Directed by: Tony Gilroy

Written by: Tony Gilroy
Cinematography by: Robert Elswit
Music by: James Newton Howard
Sound: Michael Barosky
Music Supervisor: Brian Ross
Editing: John Gilroy
Art Direction: Clay Brown
Costumes: Sarah Edwards
Production Design: Kevin Thompson
MPAA rating: R
Running time: 119 minutes

REVIEWS

Boston Globe Online. October 5, 2007.
Chicago Sun-Times Online. October 5, 2007.
Entertainment Weekly Online. October 3, 2007.
Hollywood Reporter Online. August 31, 2007.
Los Angeles Times Online. October 5, 2007.
New York Times Online. October 5, 2007.
Rolling Stone Online. October 18, 2007.
San Francisco Chronicle. October 5, 2007, p. E5.
Variety Online. August 31, 2007.
Washington Post. October 5, 2007, p. C5.

QUOTES

Michael Clayton: "I'm not the man you kill. I'm the man you buy."

AWARDS

Oscars 2007: Support. Actress (Swinton)
British Acad. 2007: Support. Actress (Swinton)

Nomination:

Oscars 2007: Actor (Clooney), Director (Gilroy), Film, Orig. Screenplay, Support. Actor (Wilkinson), Orig. Score
British Acad. 2007: Actor (Clooney), Film Editing, Orig. Screenplay, Support. Actor (Wilkinson)
Directors Guild 2007: Director (Gilroy)
Golden Globes 2008: Actor—Drama (Clooney), Film—Drama, Support. Actor (Wilkinson), Support. Actress (Swinton)
Screen Actors Guild 2007: Actor (Clooney), Support. Actor (Wilkinson), Support. Actress (Swinton)
Writers Guild 2007: Orig. Screenplay.

A MIGHTY HEART

It was an event that shocked the world. This is the story you haven't heard.
—Movie tagline

Box Office: $9.1 million

When Angelina Jolie embraces a cause, she does so with a singular dedication. The favorite subject of tabloid cover stories, the actress is a celebrity with strong convictions, and her worldwide humanitarian work is no mere pastime. With superstar Brad Pitt, she has adopted children from other countries, making her politics very personal. For all these reasons, she is a perfect choice to play Mariane Pearl, the wife of journalist Daniel Pearl, who was taken hostage in Iraq in 2002 and, after weeks of anguish, beheaded and brutalized by members of an obscure terrorist cell.

It is a role many actresses would shy away from, but Jolie embraces it with obvious relish. Over her career, Jolie has played a number of rather trivial characters in fantasy and lightweight films, but Pearl is someone more in keeping with Jolie's humanitarian, activist persona. It is her chance to play an authentic heroine. In this film adaptation of Pearl's published biography of the same name, Jolie is the main drawing card for a difficult, wrenching movie, directed by Michael Winterbottom with his customary love for confusing narrative and chaotic visuals.

Dan Futterman plays Daniel Pearl, a *Wall Street Journal* reporter covering the tensions in the Middle East and Central Asia in tandem with Mariane, who is a reporter for French public radio. Several months after 9/11, they are staying in a house in Karachi, Pakistan with a native Indian journalist, a woman named Archie (Asra Nomani), who is apparently a colleague (it is never exactly clear what their connection is). One evening, Daniel arranges to meet a sheikh who has rumored ties to jihadists. It is a dangerous assignment, so he consults several knowledgeable people first, who tell him a meeting is safe as long as it is in public. Instead, eager for an interview and a good story, he agrees to be picked up outside a restaurant and never returns.

The identity of the kidnappers is uncertain, and their demands are similarly unclear. Soon an obscure group claims responsibility and asks that the United States alter its policies toward detainees at Guantanamo Bay, Cuba, where allegations of torture are widespread. The Bush administration refuses to negotiate. Meanwhile, both Pakistani and American authorities, including the FBI, investigate the case, and two *Wall Street Journal* staffers fly to Karachi to help pursue leads.

The Karachi home becomes a round-the-clock nerve center for the operation, with journalists tracing leads and the authorities often stopping by to share new information. Mariane, shaken but steadfast, insists that the parties openly discuss all their theories and investigations, but it is not always clear whether the authorities are sometimes ignoring her request and operating independently. With the backdrop of the political tensions in Pakistan—a U.S. ally in the "war against terrorism" yet also a haven for the Taliban, Al-Qaida, and its sympathizers who have fled the war in Afghanistan—it is also uncertain that the host country is going all out to catch the kidnappers. In a tense meeting with a high-ranking government official, Mariane is lectured on the risks journalists should not take, namely, meeting with dangerous people. She replies adamantly that this is exactly the business of journalism.

It is a difficult story to tell cinematically. Most people who see the movie already know the outcome, so building tension is not easy. The pursuit of the kidnappers is also frustrating, full of blind alleys, false leads, and massive confusion. Winterbottom, known for wallowing in obscurity, seems to relish the opportunity that the story presents for constructing a film that is almost entirely a frantic rush of unfathomable or vaguely meaningful events. Characters rush in and out of scenes, with the barest of identifications, and it is often unclear who is chasing whom, and why.

Compounding the frustration is the way the characters get communications—almost entirely by cellphones and over the Internet. In fact, *A Mighty Heart* is, among other things, a nightmare about the breakdown of modern communications. Mariane, her husband, and everyone else in the film from police to jihadists are accustomed to connecting with one another by cellphones and electronic mail. She finds out he is missing because her calls to him will not go through. Calls are constantly being dropped, people cannot be reached, and dependence on this technology is made abundantly clear. Then, in the middle of the night, Mariane's cellphone rings, with the message displayed: "Danny calling." It is the kidnappers, but they speak in Urdu, so Mariane cannot understand them. It is just like everyday modern life, suddenly turned horrific. When the kidnappers issue their demands, it is through e-mails, accompanied by photographs of the hostage, bound and with a gun to his head; instantly these photos are being printed and passed about.

Mariane does not have much privacy. She is immersed in the whirlwind of the investigation and perhaps maintained by the adrenaline of the chase. It is as if she is working with colleagues on another story, the biggest story of her life. In sleep she is besieged by flashbacks of her husband and her marriage, and in one of the film's most powerful yet subtle scenes, she awakens from dreams of them together and looks behind her to find the other side of the bed empty.

Winterbottom's direction is long on mood and woefully short on exposition. The film certainly creates a vivid picture of a woman's world spun out of control, of a stranger in a strange land negotiating a labyrinth that yields no easy secrets. Shots of Karachi's crowded, chaotic streets fill every possible seam in the story. Inside the heavily guarded compound where Mariane paces, directs the investigation, and awaits word of the results, there is continuous frustration. Unfortunately, the screenwriter does not seem interested in portraying how police and journalistic investigations work, and Mariane and her friends sketch the possible connections in marker on a large dry-erase board—as hackneyed a device as exists in cinema. Unfortunately viewers do not know enough about the people whose names are on that board, or the connections among them. It is as if Winterbottom is throwing up his hands and saying no one can make sense of all this, instead of trying to shed more light on the politics behind the kidnapping. Perhaps that is how it really happened, but it does not make for good cinema.

Jolie's rock-solid performance as Mariane helps the viewers keep their heads above the swirling water of the film's opaque exposition. Her character believes in journalism ardently, she believes in teamwork, and she trusts that the pursuit of truth and solid information will break the case. When it does not, she blames no one; in fact, she thanks everyone for trying. For this role, Jolie's skin was darkened as Pearl has a French mother and a Cuban father. She wears her hair in a big, tangled mass of dark curls in a style that seems outdated. Jolie's passion for the character infuses every scene. When she finally gets the word that her husband has died, she lets out a blood-curdling scream of grief. It is one of those iconic cinematic moments: her keening can stand for all the anguish of all the loved ones of those whose lives have been snuffed out in this confusing, modern, global conflict that has no rules and from which there is never adequate refuge. Her ardent declaration afterward that "I am not terrorized" is also a rallying cry of sanity and hope in the most extreme of circumstances. In a final flourish of emotional impact, Jolie's Mariane declares to her newborn baby, Adam: "This film is for you." It is a notable breaking down of the third wall that separates actors and entertainment from the reality of the story they are depicting.

It is an easy enough task for an actress to make audiences care about Mariane Pearl. The more difficult task, which Jolie handles masterfully, is to portray her character's remarkable strength. Mariane is a Buddhist, and her religious philosophy infuses her entire approach to crisis, but her faith is wisely downplayed. Jolie steers the treacherous course of making Mariane both sympathetic and courageous without her seeming too sanctimonious or unbelievably unflappable. Whatever the attributes of the real Mariane Pearl, Jolie's work is a convincing portrait of a heroic woman, whose attitudes and actions can serve as a model for everyone.

Though Jolie assiduously avoided overplaying her role, there is one problem. While it is true that her celebrity status will entice many people to watch this film, which otherwise might be too daunting and difficult a movie for most audiences, that very stardom also makes it impossible her to disappear into her character. The viewer never loses sight of the fact that s/he is watching Jolie do a star turn in perhaps the choicest role of her career. Even Winterbottom's herky-jerky, attention-deficit-disorder-style filmmaking cannot leave her alone; in fact, she is almost constantly in close-up, her face a touchstone and a refuge for a movie that threatens at all times, like the story it tells, to completely unravel. Mariane is barely holding it together, that is clear, but at least Jolie lets us see the effort she puts into doing so; we see fear constantly defeated by resolve, a marvelous sight to behold. On the other hand, the director seems uninterested in keeping tight control of the film for he is too entranced with how life falls apart. Overall, it is an inspiring movie, but not a pretty picture.

Michael Betzold

CREDITS

Mariane Pearl: Angelina Jolie
Daniel Pearl: Dan Futterman
Randall Bennett: Will Patton
Asra Q. Nomani: Archie Panjabi
Captain: Irrfan Khan
John Bussey: Denis O'Hare
Zafir: Sajid Hasan
Steve LeVine: Gary Wilmes
Origin: USA
Language: English
Released: 2007
Production: Brad Pitt, Dede Gardner, Andrew Eaton; Revolution Films, Plan B Entertainment; released by Paramont Vantage
Directed by: Michael Winterbottom
Written by: Michael Winterbottom, Laurence Coriat, John Orloff
Cinematography by: Marcel Zyskind
Music by: Molly Nyman, Harry Escott
Sound: Joachim Sundstrom
Editing: Peter Christelis
Art Direction: David Bryan
Costumes: Charlotte Walter
Production Design: Mark Digby
MPAA rating: R
Running time: 103 minutes

REVIEWS

Boston Globe Online. June 22, 2007.
Chicago Sun-Times Online. June 22, 2007.
Christian Science Monitor Online. June 22, 2007.
Entertainment Weekly. June 22, 2007, p. 50.
Hollywood Reporter Online. May 22, 2007.
Los Angeles Times Online. June 22, 2007.
New York Times Online. June 22, 2007.
Rolling Stone Online. June 15, 2007.
San Francisco Chronicle. June 22, 2007, p. E7.
Variety Online. May 21, 2007.
Washington Post. June 22, 2007, p. C1.

AWARDS

Nomination:

Golden Globes 2008: Actress—Drama (Jolie)
Ind. Spirit 2008: Film, First Screenplay, Actress (Jolie)
Screen Actors Guild 2007: Actress (Jolie).

MISS POTTER

The life of Beatrix Potter was the most enchanting of all.
—Movie tagline

Box Office: $3 million

An early feminist and environmentalist, Beatrix Potter was also one of the best-selling children's book authors of all time, her twenty-three books bringing to life such lovable and enduring characters as Peter Rabbit. Australian director Chris Noonan (*Babe* [1995]), brings his knack for nature to this family-friendly biographical film and injects a fanciful, some say kitchy, lovability with its charming animated illustrations. With a sweetness and light that decidedly leans toward the precious, *Miss Potter* is as innocent and whimsical as the English author's adorably-named Flopsy, Mopsy, and Cotton-tail bunnies, so those looking for a more realistic and weighty biopic will be disappointed.

In the role of Miss Potter, Renée Zellweger dusts off the British accent that carried her through the successful *Bridget Jones' Diary* (2001) and its sequel, but it loses something in translation to the more proper Victorian England of Potter's time. Successfully reteaming with actor Ewan McGregor (*Down with Love,* 2003), who portrays her publisher and fiancée Norman Warne, Zellweger gives another award-nominated performance in a plum title role of yet another plucky spinster determined to succeed against the constraints of society.

The film covers a relatively short period in Potter's life, circumscribing the time she published her first book in 1902. Flashbacks show a young Beatrix (Lucy Boynton) so engrossed in a fantasy world of her own construct that she imagines her pet bunny talks to her. Her utter fascination with the live animals that surround her in the family's country abode in the Lake District, as well as her beloved pets in town, leads her to endlessly sketch the creatures, making up stories about them in the process. Little had changed for the thirty-two-year-old Beatrix (Renée Zellweger), who still lived at home and still imagined her drawings coming to life off the pages. After completing her first story, Beatrix is determined to find a publisher.

Brothers Harold (Anton Lesser) and Fruing Warne (David Bamber) of Frederick Warne & Company are dismissive of what they term Beatrix's "bunny book" but decide it would be a good starter project for their younger brother, Norman (Ewan McGregor), who wants to break into the family business. McGregor is at his mannered and charming best as the chaste and conservative publishing novice in a bygone era, displaying amazing adaptability as the actor seamlessly moves from drama to comedy to musicals.

Norman takes his job to heart and becomes Beatrix's most avid supporter in the detailed process of making the little book a success. The film concentrates on this period, following the enthusiastic publisher and strong-willed author as they bond through their work and eventually fall in love. Beatrix's parents initially object to her marrying Norman, whom they consider below their rank, and despite much protestation from Beatrix, persuade her to agree to postpone their engagement until the end of summer.

Despite her parents' stipulations, Beatrix and Norman become secretly engaged. Potter also forms a close bond with Norman's confirmed spinster sister, Millie (Emily Watson), as they share a similar feminist credo that women are able to get along fine without a man. The film takes a gentle approach to the Sapphic undertones surrounding their bond, dancing around that fact that Millie's feelings toward her brother's fiancée may not be entirely innocent. Watson and Zellweger have as much on-screen spark as the two leads and are entirely believable as sisterly kindred spirits. Furthering the film's women's rights message, Potter is able to realize her dreams of financial independence when her book, "The Tale of Peter Rabbit," becomes a surprise bestseller and leads to numerous other books.

There is little in the way of actual drama, as the tale spins merrily along until the tragic and sudden death of Norman during their brief engagement. The film does not dwell on Potter's loss and after a minor breakdown, Beatrix is quickly able to move on after a little help from Millie. The only antagonistic character in the movie is Potter's mother Helen (Barbara Flynn), an unreasonably harsh matriarch who inexplicably refuses to acknowledge her daughter's talent and ambition.

While it may have been understandable in that era that a mother might be dismayed that her thirty-something unmarried daughter be more interested in doodling silly animals than finding a suitable husband, it seems unusually stubborn for Helen to continue her attitude long after Beatrix's considerable financial and creative success. Although her father Rupert (Bill Paterson) had been Potter's long-term ally, he nonetheless takes instructions from his ill-tempered, old-fashioned wife. While Helen serves as the film's only foil, the character also fits neatly into the film's depiction of women as strong-willed and powerful.

After the loss of her fiancé, Beatrix buys Hill Top farm in 1905 and begins an idyllic and lengthy pastoral period, buying up surrounding farms—eventually amassing some 4,000 acres, which she bequeathed to the U.K. National Trust—breeding and raising Herdwick sheep, and lobbying for the preservation of land. In this effort, she enlists the help of lawyer William Heelis (Lloyd Owen), whom she eventually married in 1913 at age forty-seven.

In his first screenplay, Broadway denizen Richard Maltby, Jr. is for the most part historically accurate, taking some dramatic license surrounding her parents' strong disapproval of Norman, however. Maltby's concentrating on such a brief period in Beatrix's long life (1866–1943) may have undermined the importance of her later achievements. Still, the film succeeds wonderfully in conveying the arguably eccentric Beatrix's creative process, with her creations leaping off the page and taking on a life of their own.

Hilary White

CREDITS

Beatrix Potter: Renée Zellweger
Norman Warne: Ewan McGregor
Millie Warne: Emily Watson
Mrs. Potter: Barbara Flynn
Rupert Potter: Bill Paterson
Miss Wiggin: Matyclock Gibbs
Harold Warne: Anton Lesser
Fruing Warne: David Bamber
Mrs. Warne: Phyllida Law
William Heelis: Lloyd Owen
Origin: Great Britain, USA
Language: English
Released: 2006
Production: Mike Medavoy, David Kirschner, Corey Sienega; Isle of Man, Phoenix Pictures, Weinstein Co.; released by MGM
Directed by: Chris Noonan

Written by: Richard Maltby, Jr.
Cinematography by: Andrew Dunn
Music by: Nigel Westlake
Sound: Peter Lindsay
Music Supervisor: Maggie Rodford
Editing: Robin Sales
Art Direction: Grant Armstrong
Costumes: Anthony Powell
Production Design: Martin Childs
MPAA rating: PG
Running time: 92 minutes

REVIEWS

Boxoffice Online. December 29, 2006.
Hollywood Reporter Online. December 20, 2006.
Los Angeles Times Online. December 29, 2006.
Time Magazine Online. December 18, 2006.
USA Today Online. December 28, 2006.
Variety Online. December 19, 2006.

QUOTES

Rupert Potter: "Our daughter is famous, Helen. You're the only person who doesn't know it."

TRIVIA

Renée Zellweger and Ewan McGregor previously co-starred in 2003's *Down with Love.*

AWARDS

Nomination:

Golden Globes 2007: Actress—Mus./Comedy (Zellweger).

THE MIST

Fear Changes Everything.
—Movie tagline
Stephen King's Legendary Tale of Terror.
—Movie tagline

Box Office: $25.5

"There's something in the mist." As a herald of horrors to come, that line may fall more than a little flat, or draw a snort of derision from viewers accustomed to creaky horror-movie dialogue of the show-and-tell variety. Yet there is indeed something in the mist as well as something to *The Mist,* (also known as *Stephen King's The Mist*) a mainstream horror movie that manages to transcend its own clunky dialogue and lurching plot.

Adapted from the Stephen King novella of the same name, *The Mist* begins with what appears to be a freak storm, one that causes damage to the home of artist David Drayton (Thomas Jane). Accompanied by his young son, Brent (Nathan Gamble), and his disgruntled neighbor, and non-local Norton (Andre Braugher), Drayton heads to the supermarket for supplies, but not before having a conversation with his wife (Kelly Collins Lintz) that signals plot developments to come: Heavy mist rolling off the mountains is definitely unusual, and heavy mist rolling off the mountains where the top-secret military Arrowhead Project is located is even more unusual.

As *The Mist* is set in a small Maine town, of the type immortalized by King, a cross-section of the towns-folk has descended on the supermarket as well. There are the inevitable horror movie archetypes (stalwart, handsome leader; arrogant trial lawyer; cowardly store manager; foolhardy, and therefore doomed, adolescent; nebbish underling who emerges as an unlikely hero; competent and comely schoolteacher; feisty elderly schoolteacher, etc.), but Darabont and his talented cast, including Jane, Gamble, Braugher, Marcia Gay Harden, Toby Jones, Frances Sternhagen, and William Sadler, manage to individualize the characters. They are also blessedly unburdened with the hokey accents that actors in Maine-set movies often adopt in what is apparently a misguided attempt to establish "authenticity."

After a perfunctory setting of the stage, *The Mist* unleashes what the audience has really come to see: computer-generated creatures that cause bloody and protracted deaths. Visual effects supervisor Everett Bur-rell ensures that the large, winged insects and featherless, prehistoric-looking birds are of appropriately grotesque and squirm-inducing appearance. As the terrified crowd huddles within the market, they grasp for any logical explanation of what is happening—a pollution-spewing mill, an earthquake—and some not-so-logical explana-tions (judgment day). When the beast is finally glimpsed in its entirety, however, it does not possess the startling grace and horrific beauty of the monster in *The Host* (1996), another multi-tentacled creature that results from human arrogance.

The movie's human villain emerges as Mrs. Car-mody (Marcia Gay Harden), a Bible-thumping, verse-spouting local who appoints herself as God's conduit and uses the fear of others to manipulate them into do-ing her bidding. As Carmody's self-righteous mania grows and her hair comes undone to fall messily about her shoulders, Harden seems to be channeling—not entirely successfully—Piper Laurie as Mrs. White (*Car-rie* 1976), another of King's religious fanatics.

When the explanation for the mist and the creatures that have emerged from it finally comes, it is rushed, unconvincing, and seems primarily to serve as an opportunity to showcase more computer-generated critters, which is especially disappointing after the skillful escalation of tension. "It's our fault," gurgles an MP connected with the Arrowhead Project—just before his pustule-riddled skin bursts and spills deadly, flesh-eating beetles to the floor.

The war in Iraq is obliquely referenced when three young soldiers talk about being sent "over there." Long before the movie's final scene, as contamination-suited and gas-masked members of the military move through the landscape they have laid waste to, it is clear that larger, more earthly matters are driving director and screenwriter Frank Darabont. Like Joe Dante's excoriating *The Homecoming* (2005), *The Mist* belongs to the genre of socially conscious horror films. Class, race, and outsiders-versus-locals tensions are all touched upon, without any blatant or ham-handed signaling that "messages" are being addressed. When was the last time a mainstream and generously budgeted horror movie referenced Fidel Castro?

The understated score by Mark Isham never overwhelms the horrors that lurk without—and within—the market. It serves, as few horror movie soundtracks do, to emphasize and heighten the tension without assaulting the viewer.

Darabont is no newcomer to adapting King's material for the screen. He both wrote and directed *The Shawshank Redemption* (1994) and *The Green Mile*. Yet the endings of these films appear to be almost friendly compared to that of *The Mist* in which no hope—easy or hard-won— is offered, only the suggestion that for those who survive the horror will never stop.

Heather L. Hughes

CREDITS

David Drayton: Thomas Jane
Mrs. Carmody: Marcia Gay Harden
Amanda Dunfrey: Laurie Holden
Brent Norton: Andre Braugher
Billy Drayton: Nathan Gamble
Ollie: Toby Jones
Jim: William Sadler
Dan: Jeffrey DeMunn
Sally: Alexa Davalos
Origin: USA
Language: English
Released: 2007
Production: Frank Darabont, Liz Glotzer; Darkwoods, Dimension Films; released by MGM
Directed by: Frank Darabont
Written by: Frank Darabont

Cinematography by: Ronn Schmidt
Music by: Mark Isham
Sound: Paul Ledford
Editing: Hunter M. Via
Art Direction: Alex Hajdu
Costumes: Giovanna Ottobre-Melton
Production Design: Gregory Melton
MPAA rating: R
Running time: 125 minutes

REVIEWS

Boston Globe Online. November 21, 2007.
Chicago Sun-Times Online. November 21, 2007.
Entertainment Weekly Online. November 14, 2007.
Hollywood Reporter Online. November 13, 2007.
Los Angeles Times Online. November 21, 2007.
New York Times Online. November 21, 2007.
New Yorker Online. November 26, 2007.
San Francisco Chronicle. November 21, 2007, p. E1.
Variety Online. November 12, 2007.
Washington Post. November 21, 2007, p. C1.

MR. BEAN'S HOLIDAY

Disaster has a passport.
　—Movie tagline
France doesn't stand a chance.
　—Movie tagline
Disaster is a small step away.
　—Movie tagline

Box Office: $33.3

Rowan Atkinson's oddball creation Mr. Bean is the soccer of comedy, incredibly popular around the world, but only moderately successful in the United States. His second film, the strangely sweet family comedy *Mr. Bean's Holiday* had one of the biggest openings of 2007 in the United Kingdom and made an amazing $225 million globally, but only $33 million of that was stateside. With the tagline, "Disaster has a passport," *Mr. Bean's Holiday* struck a family comedy nerve around the world, but, besides being an interesting cultural commentary in its worldwide success, it is also proof that this character works better in brief installments than in feature-length films. What was once endearing and charming on the television series *Mr. Bean* (1990) and even had a little edge in *Bean* (1997), wears out its welcome at eighty-six minutes. Moreover, the G rating does not entice viewers over the age of ten.

Following his last film by a decade, *Mr. Bean's Holiday* opens with the title character winning a trip to

Cannes, France, some money, and a Sony video camera in a raffle. After a misunderstanding on his way to the Gare de Lyon train station in Paris, Bean finds himself at a fancy restaurant where the bizarre hero samples seafood for the first time. After poor Bean eats some shrimp with the shells intact and discards his mussels in his neighbor's purse, he is off to the waiting train. This early scene is the first of many moments in *Mr. Bean's Holiday* when it becomes a little unclear what exactly is wrong with our odd hero. The physical comedy of errors that made up the series and even most of the first film seems to have been replaced by ridiculous behavior that makes one wonder if he might actually be developmentally disabled.

Before such troubling questions can be answered, Mr. Bean finds his way to the train station, where he asks a man (Karel Roden) to take the camera he won and record him getting on board. The problem is that the man then watches the doors close and realizes his son Stepan (Max Baldry) is still on board. Mr. Bean spends the rest of the film trying to take care of Stepan and reunite him with his father, who happens to be a jury member at the Cannes Film Festival. Mr. Bean and Stepan beg for money, try to steal a bicycle, and Bean even ends up as an extra in a commercial being filmed by legendary director Carson Clay (Willem Dafoe). On the set, which Bean blows up, of course, he meets the lovely actress Sabine (Emma de Caunes), who is also heading to Cannes, and our trio of awkward heroes speeds down the road in a lime green Mini, heading for the French Riviera.

Following a long legacy that includes everyone from Charlie Chaplin to Leslie Nielsen, Rowan Atkinson's Mr. Bean is an icon of physical comedy. Double takes, pratfalls, and the kind of funny faces that mothers warn "will freeze that way" are his weapons of choice, and they combine to create a character that could have thrived in the era of silent film. In fact, Atkinson only has about a page of dialogue in *Mr. Bean's Holiday*, and half of that consists of his character saying "Gracias" to the French people he encounters.

The show *Mr. Bean* had a dark edge, and the first film, *Bean* (1997), was rated PG-13, but *Mr. Bean's Holiday* takes the hero to what was probably an inevitable arena, the family film. Pitched straight at eight-year-old boys who will find a grown man dancing to Shaggy hilarious, *Mr. Bean's Holiday* only occasionally works for anyone old enough to have been alive when the last adventure hit screens a decade ago. Atkinson's commitment to the character remains the strength of the franchise, but even that goodwill wears off after the halfway mark when it becomes clear that *Mr. Bean's Holiday* aspires to be nothing more than a live-action cartoon for youngsters.

Rowan Atkinson has said that *Mr. Bean's Holiday* will be his last big-screen adventure for a character that he has been playing for almost two decades. The edge that once defined Atkinson's style on the brilliant televison show *The Black Adder* (1983) and even on the series *Mr. Bean* has been dulled by time and perhaps the mellowing of a comedian who now looks to appeal to the children of the adults who used to love him. However, considering the international success of *Mr. Bean's Holiday*, maybe the relative failure of the film stateside both commercially and critically is an indication of cultural differences more than any aspect of quality.

Brian Tallerico

CREDITS

Mr. Bean: Rowan Atkinson
Sabine: Emma de Caunes
Carson Clay: Willem Dafoe
Maitre d': Jean Rochefort
Stepan: Max Baldry
Emil: Karel Roden
Vicar: Steve Pemberton
Origin: Great Britain, USA
Language: English
Released: 2007
Production: Tim Bevan, Eric Fellner, Peter Bennett-Jones; Working Title Productions, Tiger Aspect Pictures; released by Universal
Directed by: Steve Bendelack
Written by: Robin Driscoll, Hamish McColl
Cinematography by: Baz Irvine
Music by: Howard Goodall
Sound: Jean-Marie Blondel, Bernard O'Reilly, Andrew Stirk
Music Supervisor: Nick Angel
Editing: Tony Cranstoun
Costumes: Pierre-Yves Gayraud
Production Design: Michael Carlin
MPAA rating: PG
Running time: 90 minutes

REVIEWS

Boston Globe Online. August 24, 2007.
Chicago Sun-Times Online. August 24, 2007.
Entertainment Weekly Online. August 22, 2007.
Guardian Online. March 30, 2007.
Hollywood Reporter Online. May 27, 2007.
Los Angeles Times Online. August 24, 2007.
New York Times Online. August 24, 2007.
The Observer Online. April 1, 2007.
San Francisco Chronicle. August 24, 2007, p. E7.

Variety Online. March 21, 2007.
Washington Post Online. August 24, 2007.

QUOTES

Waitress on train: "Un café?"
Mr. Bean: "Oui."
Waitress on train: "Du sucre?"
Mr. Bean: "Non."
Waitress on train: "You speak very good French."
Mr. Bean: "Gracias!"

TRIVIA

Rowan Atkinson has stated that this movie would be the last story of the character, Mr. Bean.

MR. BROOKS

The man who has everything has everything to hide.
—Movie tagline

There's something about "Mr. Brooks."
—Movie tagline

Box Office: $28.5

"The fever has returned to Mr. Brooks's brain. It never really left." That is what viewers are told at the very beginning of this preposterous thriller, *Mr. Brooks,* just before we see Kevin Costner, as Earl Brooks, reciting the "Serenity Prayer" before receiving the Portland Chamber of Commerce's Man of the Year Award for being such a successful businessman. Not only is he head of the Brooks Box Company, but Earl Brooks is himself in a box.

That "fever" explanation is the only one viewers get over the course of a film that keeps asking the audience to suspend so much disbelief that it becomes a two-hour exercise in escalating disbelief-suspension. Brooks is reciting the favorite prayer of twelve-step program adherents because, as we are reminded frequently, he is "addicted to killing." The movie treats this problem as if it were any other addiction, with Earl believing he can handle it by going to Alcoholics Anonymous meetings.

In real cases of addiction, there is a reason that someone achieves two years of sobriety, as Brooks has, and there is also a trigger that would make someone fall off the wagon. In this film no explanation is given for either. Viewers are left to wonder why Brooks has not killed lately and why he wants to kill again after earning the award. All viewers know is that Brooks is seemingly an ordinary man, except that he has this "addiction."

The addiction is embodied by Marshall (William Hurt), who plays the unseen devil in Brooks's brain.

Marshall, who is often in the backseat of the car when Brooks is driving, or sometimes in the room when he is having a conversation with a non-ghost, is a fine if somewhat hackneyed literary device. Visible and audible only to Brooks, he allows the protagonist to be literally of two minds and thus have constant debates with himself. "That's the addiction talking," might be the twelve-step shorthand for this tempter. Yet even this hallucinatory partner in crime is easy to swallow compared to the rest of the film.

Undistinguished writer/director Bruce A. Evans (*Kuffs* 1992) wants us to belived that after Brooks sneaks into a copulating couple's room and mows them down with his gun, he must agonize over the act and then complete a ritual burning of photographs he has taken of them, and that he does so naked in his secret basement studio with candles burning. It appears that there is some sort of perverse sexual hook to Brooks' compulsion, except we later learn that he has killed many people for many reasons. So there is no real explanation.

Brooks is not the only psychopath in the film. There is "Mister Smith" (Dane Cook), a man who lives in the apartment across from where the murders were committed who liked to take photographs of the couple while they were making love (of course) with their curtains open. Smith has photos of Brooks at the murder scene; as careful as the killer is, he forgot to close the blinds (this is explained by Brooks to Marshall with the line "It's almost as if I want to get caught, isn't it?"). Smith's blackmail terms are unusual, to say the least: he is a wannabe serial killer who admires "The Thumbprint Killer" (the police and media name for Brooks) and wants to learn from the master. Brooks agrees to take him along on his next murder in exchange for his silence about the incriminating photos. For the rest of the film, Smith functions as an annoying obligation to Brooks, who soon has other issues to keep him occupied and thus keeps standing up Smith on their killing dates. It seems that the only reason Brooks does not simply kill Smith is because he will come in handy for a final absurd plot twist at the end.

First, however, there are other unbelievable or irrelevant subplots and characters to introduce, foremost among them Demi Moore as Tracy Atwood, a police detective who has caught a remarkable number of villains, including a serial killer named Meeker, who has just escaped from prison and is out to get revenge. This Meeker and his scary girlfriend are not really necessary to the larger plot, but they provide a few pumped-up action sequences to keep bloodthirsty viewers attentive: one an aborted kidnapping and fight in a van, and later a shootout, conducted to some pulsing rock music, in a tenement hallway.

Atwood has her own distractions as she attempts to catch the Thumbprint Killer. She is being blackmailed during divorce proceedings. Atwood is a rich heiress who has rejected her father and devoted herself to law enforcement because she is her own woman. She has a supervisor who will order her to a desk job if she does not resolve the divorce conflict, for reasons that do not add up. Atwood's problem, according to her boss is "You don't know how to ask for help." Whether Moore is believable as a detective is debatable, but this potential flaw is overshadowed by the plot's more major credibility issues.

Brooks has a loving, beautiful and otherwise un-scripted wife, Emma (Marg Helgenberger), and a daughter, Jane (Danielle Panabaker), who has just dropped out of college. Jane has some good reasons for leaving school: she says she is pregnant, but then the police show up and question her about a murder on campus. During an extended conversation with Mar-shall, Earl puzzles out this development. It turns into a case of "like father, like daughter." Jane has the gene, if there is a gene that carries an addiction to murder, if there is such an addiction. Moreover, Jane wants to take over her father's business, so perhaps she might plot to kill him, viewers are lead to speculate.

Brooks loves his daughter almost as much as he loves killing innocent people, and he concludes that he has to save his daughter by going to her campus and killing another student in the same way that the original suspect did, with a hatchet. Since Jane is at home when the second killing occurs, this deflects any suspicion that might have fell on her.

Yet Brooks still has the Mr. Smith problem. He has misled his protégé into thinking he will agree to kill the driver of a truck that cut them off on a highway, but then he loses interest. He tries to explain that selecting a murder victim is "a bit like falling in love" in that there are a lot of candidates, but the killer must keep search-ing until he finds that "special one" who makes his "heart beat faster." Although thick as a block of wood, Smith cannot be put off forever.

Then there is the Tracy Atwood problem. The detec-tive announces, "I have all the pieces, I'm just not look-ing at it right" and tells her partner she has a hunch that Mr. Smith might be worth following. This must be just the kind of hunch she used to catch all those other vil-lains, except that it might occur to anyone at all that a creepy guy with camera equipment who lives across the street from the fornicating-in-the-windows couple might know something. Smith is curious about Atwood but not worried about her. He knows that if she gets too hot on his trail, a convenient plot device will throw her off, namely, the fact that Smith has suddenly moved out of

his apartment and into the building where Meeker and his girlfriend are hiding.

The plot deteriorates further. Brooks has a plan to deal with his addiction that involves taking Smith with him to kill someone and then figuring Smith will kill him afterward. If viewers guess that the murder victim turns out to be Atwood's ex-husband and his lawyer, they must be in telepathic contact with Bruce A. Evans, who with Raynold Gideon wrote this shameless script.

What is frightening about this movie is not Mister Brooks himself, and certainly not Kevin Costner, who makes his typical deadpan delivery extra bland. As Brooks, Costner discusses each murderous idea and confronts every threat as if he were issuing an order for one of his boxes. He is not just detached or disturbed, he seems completely disinterested. He is humorless, pas-sionate, and even pedantic—the kind of villain who does not so much as make a person's blood curdle as tire it out. No, what is extremely terrifying is that since both Brooks and Atwood survive in the end, and she knows the killer is still at large, there is the awful threat of a sequel.

Michael Betzold

CREDITS

Mr. Brooks: Kevin Costner
Marshall: William Hurt
Emma Brooks: Marg Helgenberger
Det. Tracy Atwood: Demi Moore
Mr. Smith: Dane Cook
Jane Brooks: Danielle Panabaker
Hawkins: Ruben Santiago-Hudson
Capt. Lister: Lindsay Crouse
Jesse Vialo: Jason Lewis
Jesse's Lawyer: Reiko Aylesworth
Nancy Hart: Aisha Hinds
Thorton Meeks: Matt Schulze
Atwood's Lawyer: Michael Cole
Origin: USA
Language: English
Released: 2007
Production: Jim Wilson, Kevin Costner, Raynold Gideon; Element Films, Eden Rock Media, TIG Productions, Relativity; released by MGM
Directed by: Bruce A. Evans
Written by: Bruce A. Evans, Raynold Gideon
Cinematography by: John Lindley
Music by: Ramin Djawadi
Sound: Steve Aaron
Editing: Miklos Wright
Art Direction: William Ladd (Bill) Skinner

Costumes: Judianna Makovsky
Production Design: Jeffrey Beecroft
MPAA rating: R
Running time: 120 minutes

REVIEWS

Boston Globe Online. June 1, 2007.
Chicago Sun-Times Online. June 1, 2007.
Entertainment Weekly. June 8, 2007, p. 63.
Hollywood Reporter Online. May 29, 2007.
Los Angeles Times Online. June 1, 2007.
New York Times Online. June 1, 2007.
San Francisco Chronicle. June 1, 2007, p. E1.
Variety Online. May 30, 2007.
Washington Post. June 1, 2007, p. C1.

MR. MAGORIUM'S WONDER EMPORIUM

You have to believe it to see it.
—Movie tagline

Box Office: $32 million

It is largely true that family films are not what they used to be, as even G-rated fare often is riddled with flatulence and potty humor. Not so for *Mr. Magorium's Wonder Emporium,* which looks and feels like something from the early 1960s. Writer/director Zach Helm makes no nods to topical humor of any sort, as his characters apparently live in a world before computers and video games. All the adults and children are enchanted by old-fashioned toys and games in a magical toy store that has been around for longer than anyone can remember.

Not a single suggestive line, not even an innocent kiss mar the childlike innocence of this film. There is nothing scary in it either, unless you get upset at the idea of a 243-year-old man deciding it is time to die. The prospect is certainly wrenching, however, for Molly Mahoney (Natalie Portman), who will inherit the store owned for so long by Mr. Magorium (Dustin Hoffman). Magorium, with the gentle whimsy typical of this film, decides it is time to leave because he has worn out the last of his beloved pairs of Italian shoes. It is certainly not because he has lost any of his silliness or optimism.

Magorium is more than just a throwback; he is like a walking dream of every naïve child's favorite indulgent, imaginative grandfather. He is mostly elf, part sage, and part buffoon, as well as a magician and creative genius. Eccentric, of course, is an adjective that also applies—after all, Magorium keeps a zebra as a pet, and at a business meeting he will have various stuffed animals in at-

tendance, seating at chairs around a conference table. Hoffman plays him as a gentle pixie with a puckered mouth, a lisp that comes and goes, and an utter lack of the real mystery and wonder you would expect from a great magician.

His toy store is an odd-looking building on a downtown street (the city is not identified in the story, but the film was shot in Toronto), and inside it is filled with every imaginable toy, including all the classics from the Baby Boomer era, like Slinkies and Lincoln Logs. Some of the toys come to life in various ways, and there are mobiles with live fish—and a dead one with fish sticks. Behind one big door is either a stairway to the second level, or a room full of balls or hoops, depending on how you set the wheel that opens the door. When a customer cannot find an item, Mahoney, working the cash register, opens the "big book," a musty old tome that is more than a catalogue. If something is in stock, it will magically appear from the pages of the book.

Mahoney is a former child prodigy on the piano, but she has not taken the next step toward becoming a great composer, though she has got a symphony almost at her fingertips. At twenty-three year old, she is at an impasse, unable to figure out how to realize her talents and unhappy at being Magorium's store manager, though she does have the right attitude (one reviewer noted Portman was in "full pixie mode" in this movie, and that is an understatement). We do not need eleven-year-old Eric (Zach Mills), the film's narrator, to tell us that Molly's problem is that she needs to believe in herself, but we get the message anyway, over and over. Eric narrates the tale episodically, with the conceit that it is written by someone named Bellini, who lives in the store's basement, looks like a circus strongman, and is an odd candidate to be Magorium's chronicler.

Each character has a problem that will be an easy one for audiences to help solve; virtually nothing is demanded of the viewer. Mahoney needs to believe in herself, Eric needs to stop being a loner, and Henry (Jason Bateman, an accountant hired by Magorium to take stock before he turns over the store to Mahoney, needs to loosen up and believe in magic too. Magorium's problem is how to exit without ruining the store. When the store learns of his plans, it throws a temper tantrum, and Mahoney lapses into a long, whiny refusal to accept what is being offered her.

Having set up an easy plot, Helms (who succeeded in 2006 with the inventive *Stranger than Fiction*) seems not to know how to develop it. Mahoney makes Magorium go to the hospital, where of course the doctors find nothing wrong, and then she spends a day trying to convince him life has much more to offer him than the store, but he already knows that, and so do the viewers.

In fact, there are no surprises at all in this film as the viewers always understand everything the characters do not. Eric's inability to make friends is mirrored by Henry's grown-up version of the same problem, so it is no shock when the two become buddies.

There is some clever but predictable banter between Henry and Molly, and a hint of possible romance, but Helms, keeping the story extremely safe, does not take this thread too far. Eric's problem is undermined by Mills' extreme gregariousness; he is not believable as a friendless introvert because he is probably the most personable character in the movie, bright and smart, but also understanding. Morevover, he has already made friends with Magorium and Mahoney, so adding Henry, another adult, is not really much of an accomplishment. Perhaps another child character for Eric to play off would have helped round out the story.

Portman plays Molly with her characteristic earnestness, and seems to be trying to summon up depths to her character that simply are not provided by the script. She gives the impression of trying too hard all the time, so what should be a light, engaging character becomes a burden for viewers to watch. When she summons her belief in herself and orchestrates a revival of the store, her performance looks incredibly awkward.

The story, too, seems extremely stiff and rote. The idea of a magical store is not realized in the plot. Just because there are toys that can do magic things does not make for wonder, and for a film that purports to be about wonder, this is an awfully pedestrian undertaking. Helms cannot summon up any real awe or deep magic; everything that purports to be magical is really quite superficial. It is a flat and uninvolving tale, and it goes entirely as expected from start to finish. *Mr. Magorium's Wonder Emporium* provides mild amusement, but it does not dazzle. A quantity of amusing toys adds up to mere merchandise, and when very early in the film Kermit the Frog wanders through the store, chattering about nothing of consequence, you already sense Helms's desperation. This is supposed to be a tale of magic, but the writer needs crutches to summon up the wonder he is trying to invoke.

Michael Betzold

CREDITS

Mr. Magorium: Dustin Hoffman
Molly Mahoney: Natalie Portman
Henry Weston: Jason Bateman
Eric Applebaum: Zach Mills
Origin: USA
Language: English

Released: 2007
Production: Richard N. Gladstein, James Garavente; FilmColony, Gang of Two, Mandate Pictures, Walden Media; released by 20th Century-Fox
Directed by: Zach Helm
Written by: Zach Helm
Cinematography by: Roman Osin
Music by: Aaron Zigman, Alexandre Desplat
Sound: Glen Gauthier
Editing: Steven Weisberg, Sabrina Plisco
Art Direction: Brandt Gordon
Costumes: Christopher Hargadon
Production Design: Therese DePrez
MPAA rating: G
Running time: 94 minutes

REVIEWS

Boston Globe Online. November 16, 2007.
Chicago Sun-Times Online. November 16, 2007.
Entertainment Weekly Online. November 14, 2007.
Hollywood Reporter Online. November 15, 2007.
Los Angeles Times Online. November 16, 2007.
New York Times Online. November 16, 2007.
San Francisco Chronicle. November 16, 2007, p. E1.
Variety Online. November 11, 2007.
Washington Post Online. November 16, 2007.

QUOTES

Mr. Edward Magorium: "Your life is an occasion, rise to it."

MR. WOODCOCK

Letting go of your past is hard...especially when it's dating your mom.
—Movie tagline

Box Office: $25.7 million

It is the stuff of which nightmares are made: You return to your hometown as a young adult to find that the gym teacher who made your life miserable in middle school is dating your mother. That is the idea behind *Mr. Woodcock,* and it must have sounded like a promising comic premise. The problem is, it is the only idea in the movie.

Woodcock is played by Billy Bob Thornton, a perfect choice for the role of a conceited, no-nonsense drill sergeant who takes delight in humiliating his students, whether they are fat, asthmatic, or simply wimpy. Thornton does sneering well, and he does one-screw-loose uptightness well too, and he has made a successful career out of playing such comic villains. In this case, however, his portrayal is very seldom funny. It not entirely his fault, however—the script has a tin ear for comedy, and Thornton has to make do with plenty of lines that are clunkers.

His nemesis is John Farley, whom we first meet as the pudgy seventh-grader who is the recipient of Woodcock's sarcasm and wrath for failing to show up to class in gym shorts, failing to wear a protective athletic cup, and failing to make any kind of impression at all. Farley has grown up to be the successful author of a self-help book, *Letting Go,* and he has been invited back to his fictional Nebraska hometown to receive the "corn-cob key" to the city. It is only after he returns that he discovers his mother, Beverly (Susan Sarandon), is smitten with the autocratic bane of young Farley's existence. In no short order she announces her plans to marry him, so he learns that the gym teacher who once reviled and tortured Farley is going to become his stepfather.

As played by the talented but rarely seen Seann William Scott, Farley is a regular guy who has forged a hard-won self-confidence after overcoming a childhood and adolescence fraught with unpopularity. Scott plays him with a deer-in-the-headlights sincerity, reaching for comic riches that simply have not been written for him. Farley's own book is shallow enough to be the inspiration for many of his former classmates, and one of the film's few tolerably humorous running gags is that lots of losers in his hometown claim it has changed their lives, even though they are still losers. Farley, of course, is caught in a massive contradiction. He has written a book about how to overcome the troubles of the past, and now the nemesis of his past is staring him in the face, having sex with his mother, and bragging about it even.

Where can this plot go? Nowhere, as it turns out. Farley and Woodcock engage in a film-long series of sparring matches, verbal and physical, most of which result in Farley's further humiliation and enragement. Desperately, Farley launches a scheme with a former friend, Nedderman (Ethan Suplee), to discredit Woodcock in the eyes of his mother, unmasking his true malicious nature, but that idea founders on a lack of evidence and inspiration. Just as desperately, first-time screenwriters Michael Carnes and Josh Gilbert attempt a few thin subplots: Farley meets the wholesome, pretty Tracy (Melissa Sagemiller) who was his former crush, and she likes him because now he is thin and successful. He gets so angry he starts to leave town, then returns. His agent (Amy Poehler) summons him to meet with a staffer from *Oprah,* but he is too embroiled in his troubles to accommodate him, so later Tyra Banks interviews him, sending in a crew to film him in Nebraska.

Viewers would expect this kind of movie to be crude and inane, but it is not even entertainingly so. It is not clever enough to be laughably stupid, even. The script has no sense of comic timing, and the writing is deadly dull and redundant. When Farley asks the bulky Nedderman to loan him some underwear, the friend warns him it might be too big. Then when Nedderman gives him the underwear, he says: "I'm sorry if it's too big."

The direction by Craig Gillespie is not much better, though to be fair he is saddled with a plot that goes nowhere and a script to match. Gillespie likes to have us hear Woodcock's words echoing in Farley's head, as he lies in bed at night, for instance, but sometimes the words are ones that have just been spoken a few seconds earlier. Gillespie, who spent sixteen years directing television commercials before making his film debut with *Mr. Woodcock,* also lacks comic timing, and his few sight gags fall flat.

In Woodcock's gym class, there is little action, either. The cruelty consists of Woodcock verbally harassing the students, making them do laps, and then throwing balls at them. They never are seen playing any actual sports or doing any real activities. The plot continues to spin out ridiculous and un-engaging contests between Woodcock and Farley—a corn-eating contest, one-upmanship on a running machine—until it is time, mercifully, for a climax. At that point, for insufficient reasons Beverly turns on Woodcock; Farley inexplicably beats Woodcock in a wrestling match; and afterward Farley decides Woodcock is a decent guy. All are highly improbable events.

It is a wonder that a movie with a script this poorly written could have been made at all, much less released, but with the salaries commanded by and paid to Thornton and Sarandon, there was likely not much choice but to proceed. Thornton has been in awful movies previously, and this one might have looked to him like a variation of *Bad Santa* (2003), a scathing but funny movie that allowed him to play a similar role. What Sarandon is doing in this picture is a real mystery; she is an actress who usually chooses her infrequent roles judiciously, and here she is given an uninspired part. She has no opportunity to display her comic talents and must instead play a kindhearted woman who is obviously also a little dense, if not desperate. Although it is great to see Scott in any movie, this one will not help his career much. As for the agent Maggie, Poehler tries her best to make her role interesting, but she cannot pull comic lines out of thin air.

Mr. Woodcock could have gone over the top in depicting the lengths to which its title character's cruelty could go; instead, it just keeps repeating the same non-jokes over and over. The result is a real dud: a limp comedy with no laughs.

Michael Betzold

CREDITS

Mr. Woodcock: Billy Bob Thornton
John Farley: Seann William Scott
Beverly: Susan Sarandon
Young John: Kyley Baldridge
Tracy: Melissa Sagemiller
Maggie: Amy Poehler
Sally: Melissa Leo
Dad Woodcock: Bill Macy
Nedderman: Ethan Suplee
Origin: USA
Language: English
Released: 2007
Production: Bob Cooper, David Dobkin; Landscape Entertainment; released by New Line Cinema
Directed by: Craig Gillespie
Written by: Michael Carnes, Josh Gilbert
Cinematography by: Tami Reiker
Music by: Theodore Shapiro
Sound: Steve Cantamessa
Editing: Alan Baumgarten, Kevin Tent
Art Direction: James F. Truesdale
Costumes: Wendy Chuck
Production Design: Alison Sadler
MPAA rating: PG-13
Running time: 87 minutes

REVIEWS

Boston Globe Online. September 14, 2007.
Chicago Sun-Times Online. September 13, 2007.
Entertainment Weekly Online. September 12, 2007.
Hollywood Reporter Online. September 13, 2007.
Los Angeles Times Online. September 14, 2007.
New York Times Online. September 14, 2007.
San Francisco Chronicle. September 14, 2007, p. E4.
Variety Online. September 12, 2007.
Washington Post Online. September 14, 2007.

TRIVIA

Billy Bob Thorton broke his foot during filming, while wrestling in a scene with Seann William Scott.

MUSIC AND LYRICS

Box Office: $50.5 million

Hugh Grant and Drew Barrymore make such a winning team in *Music and Lyrics,* a charming romantic comedy written and directed by Marc Lawrence, that it would be easy to overlook how bright and bubbly the script is. Full of sharp one-liners, goofy nostalgia for 1980s pop music, and a wry take on the recording business that never sinks to mean-spiritedness or withering satire, *Music and Lyrics* is one of the most enjoyable and well-made light comedies in quite some time.

The movie opens on a hilarious note with a music video starring an 1980s group called PoP, a segment that gently mocks over-the-top videos from the period, complete with period hair, hip-swinging dance moves, and a corny story line, while also embracing the silliness of the era. Grant's Alex Fletcher is the second man in the band, who took a back seat to star Colin Thompson (Scott Porter)—think of Andrew Ridgeley's relationship to George Michael in Wham!—and is now the subject of where-are-they-now speculation. Alex currently plays gigs at such modest venues as Knott's Berry Farm, fairs, and high school reunions, where middle-aged women swoon over him, but now he has to struggle to keep even these meager bookings.

When his manager, Chris Riley (Brad Garrett), brings him the opportunity to write in the space of just a few days a song for young, hot pop star Cora Corman (Haley Bennett), who initially comes across as a parody of Britney Spears, Alex knows it is a great chance for him but balks at the short deadline. She has a title already picked out, "Way Back Into Love"; she just needs the song itself. Alex writes music but is not skilled with lyrics, and, in a bit of serendipity, his substitute plant-watering lady, Barrymore's Sophie Fisher, just happens to have a knack for words and putting rhymes together. While she is reluctant at first, they soon form a partnership.

It is not hard to anticipate the trajectory of this plot. We know that Alex and Sophie will move from wary collaborators to potential lovers, but Grant and Barrymore, like the best screwball couples, are such a natural combination that they make the formula work. In roles that suit the stars perfectly and draw on the audience's fondness for their unique screen personae, Grant is expert at the snide putdown and self-deprecating remark, as when Alex calls himself "a happy has-been," and Barrymore is adorable playing off his sarcastic wit. The plot gives each character just enough backstory and something to overcome from the past without weighing down the film. Sophie was dumped by a heartless writing professor, Sloan Cates (Campbell Scott), who used their relationship as grist for his new novel, while Alex has to come to terms with his failed solo career and maintain some semblance of success and dignity as a nostalgia act.

Under Sophie's influence, Alex sees the value of making people happy and begins to appreciate his life entertaining the women who come to see him shake his hips at an amusement park and sing the old hits. Their scenes as songwriting partners are humorous give-and-take sessions in which his pragmatism and her perfectionism are cheerfully at odds, and even details such as the way she rearranges his furniture to aid the creative process become cute bits of character development. He just wants to write a hit tune, while she wants to set the proper mood so they can create a gratifying work.

Adding to the enjoyment are the supporting characters, especially Sophie's older sister, Rhonda (Kristen Johnston), who is not just her confidante but a huge fan of Alex and cannot contain her excitement over Sophie's good fortune. Cora is a more nuanced character than she at first appears. Coming across as an airheaded pop princess who pretentiously injects a faux Eastern spirituality into her stage performance, she also exhibits an endearing ditziness when she utters such lines as, "I want to show you the roof. It's upstairs." She becomes an obstacle to Alex and Sophie's happiness when, after initially liking the song they write, she decides to alter the tune to suit her sexy dancing style.

This conflict with Cora sets the stage for the crucial test of the couple's fledgling relationship—Sophie wants to fight, while Alex, desperate for a hit song, lacks the backbone to stand up for their creation. The film climaxes at the Madison Square Garden concert, but, given that Sophie and Alex have had a falling-out, Sophie is uncomfortable being there. However, in a dramatic flourish, Alex wins her back with a sweet tune called "Don't Write Me Off," penned especially for her, which he sings to a packed auditorium. It is a satisfying, upbeat ending, one that is punctuated by Cora and Alex debuting "Way Back Into Love."

While the resolution may be fairly conventional, the treatment of Cora is actually surprising. At first set up to be a shallow, crass, commercial pop star, in the end, she turns out to be a romantic at heart, someone willing to return to the original version of the song so that Alex can win back Sophie. It may seem like a small detail, but it demonstrates that Lawrence did not take the easy route in creating a stock comic villain.

Indeed, aside from the pompous Sloan, there really are no villains in *Music and Lyrics*. It is too good-hearted to cast anyone as being really villainous in this romanticized view of the cutthroat music business. Instead, Alex and Sophie have only to overcome their own anxieties about their failed pasts so that they can fall in love and craft something beautiful together. Adding to the fun is the screenplay's genuine affection for the 1980s and its musical styles. PoP's big hit song, "PoP Goes My Heart,"

written by Andrew Wyatt and Josh Deutsch, as well as "Don't Write Me Off" and "Way Back Into Love," both penned by Adam Schlesinger, are not mere throwaways but catchy melodies that really feel like they could top the charts.

Peter N. Chumo II

CREDITS

Alex Fletcher: Hugh Grant
Sophie Fisher: Drew Barrymore
Chris Riley: Brad Garrett
Rhonda: Kristen Johnston
Khan: Aasif Mandvi
Sloan Cates: Campbell Scott
Cora Corman: Haley Bennett
Colin Thompson: Scott Porter
Origin: USA
Language: English
Released: 2007
Production: Martin Shafer, Liz Glotzer; Village Roadshow Pictures, Castle Rock Entertainment, Reserve Room; released by Warner Bros.
Directed by: Marc Lawrence
Written by: Marc Lawrence
Cinematography by: Xavier Perez Grobet
Music by: Adam Schlesinger
Sound: Danny Michael
Editing: Susan E. Morse
Art Direction: Patricia Woodbridge
Costumes: Susan Lyall
Production Design: Jane Musky
MPAA rating: PG-13
Running time: 106 minutes

REVIEWS

Chicago Sun-Times Online. February 14, 2007.
Entertainment Weekly. February 23, 2007, p. 78.
Hollywood Reporter Online. February 9, 2007.
Los Angeles Times Online. February 14, 2007.
New York Times Online. February 14, 2007.
San Francisco Chronicle. February 14, 2007, p. E1.
USA Today Online. February 14, 2007.
Variety Online. February 9, 2007.
Washington Post. February 14, 2007, p. C1.

QUOTES

Sophie: "That's wonderfully sensitive, especially from a man that wears such tight pants."
Alex: "It forces all the blood to my heart."

MY BEST FRIEND
(Mon meilleur ami)

> *It takes a lifetime to learn the meaning of friendship...Francois has 10 days.*
> —Movie tagline

Box Office: $1.4 million

Director Patrice Leconte has an affinity for exploring offbeat relationships. In *The Girl on the Bridge* (1999), a man recruits a would-be suicide for his knife-throwing act only to become dependent upon his assistant. *The Widow of Saint-Pierre* (2000) finds a prison warden's wife making a protégé of a man awaiting execution. In *The Man on the Train* (2002), a thief and a teacher are united by their concerns with aging. A woman mistakes the office of an attorney for that of her therapist in *Intimate Strangers* (2004) and begins telling him all her secrets.

While *The Man on the Train* takes a serious look at male friendship, with several comic moments, *My Best Friend* (also known as *Mon meilleur ami*) approaches similar material with a lighter touch. François Coste (Daniel Auteuil) is co-owner of a Paris antiques firm but cares for nothing beyond his business. He neglects his daughter, Louise (Julie Durand), takes his mistress, Julia (Élisabeth Bourgine), for granted, and has not even noticed that his business partner, Catherine (Julie Gayet), is a lesbian. After François uses the firm's money to impulsively buy an expensive Greek vase for himself, Catherine ridicules him as a friendless soul who cares more for things than people. She challenges him to find a friend in ten days, forfeiting the vase if he fails. Ironically, the vase depicts the friendship between Achilles and Patroclus from Homer's *The Illiad.*

After several fumbling attempts to have strangers explain how they became friends, François notices that Bruno Bouley (Dany Boon), a cab driver, gets along well with everyone and asks Bruno to teach him how to make friends. Slowly, as François struggles with Bruno's philosophy of being sociable, smiling, and sincere, the two men realize that they have become friends, only for the socially clumsy François to betray Bruno. He also learns that Bruno's easygoing veneer hides considerable pain. Bruno's best friend has run away with his wife, and his lifelong dream of appearing on a television quiz show remains unfulfilled because he has nervously flubbed several auditions. François must find a way to set things right.

Leconte has been attacked by French critics for lacking a consistent style, yet his films constantly display his compassion for characters bumbling their way through a chaotic world. His head crammed with miscellaneous facts learned from quiz shows, Bruno mistakes the ad-

dress of painter Auguste Renoir for that of his son, Jean, the director. Leconte's films demonstrate the humane treatment of human foibles as seen in such Jean Renoir films as *The Rules of the Game* (1939) and *The Human Beast* (1938). Leconte also resembles Renoir in his refusal to be didactic. The director told the *Los Angeles Times,* "I don't need to feel like I need to teach anybody anything or give lessons or any kind of morals." His treatment of friendship "is more about exploration."

Leconte and co-writer Jérôme Tonnerre, who also wrote *Intimate Strangers,* take material that could easily have degenerated into slapstick farce or maudlin sentimentality and avoid the excesses of both. The somber lighting of Jean-Marie Dreujou's cinematography adds a slightly ironic tint to the film's comedic aspects. With its distinctive blending of the silly and the sad, *My Best Friend* closely resembles Leconte's sublime comedy *The Hairdresser's Husband* (1990).

As always, Leconte handles his actors quite well. Boon, the title character's roommate in *The Valet* (2006), ably conveys Bruno's attempts to use trivia to mask his sensitivity. As with *A Heart in Winter* (1992), Auteuil excels at uncovering the humanity within a repressed character. When François watches Bruno desperately try to come up with the right answer on a game show, Auteuil is a master of displaying deep emotions using minimal effects.

Michael Adams

CREDITS

François: Daniel Auteuil
Bruno: Dany Boon
Catherine: Julie Gayet
Louise: Julie Durand
Origin: France
Language: French
Released: 2006
Production: Olivier Delbosc, Marc Missonnier; Fideline Films, TF-1 Films, Lucky Red; released by IFC Films
Directed by: Patrice Leconte
Written by: Patrice Leconte, Jérôme Tonnerre
Cinematography by: Jean-Marie Dreujou
Music by: Xavier Demerliac
Sound: Paul Laine
Editing: Joëlle Hache
Art Direction: Ivan Maussion
Costumes: Annie Périer Bertaux
MPAA rating: PG-13
Running time: 94 minutes

REVIEWS

Entertainment Weekly. July 27, 2007, p. 52.
Guardian Online. May 11, 2007.
Hollywood Reporter Online. September 15, 2006.

Los Angeles Times Online. July 13, 2007.
New York Times Online. July 13, 2007.
The Observer Online. May 13, 2007.
Variety Online. September 14, 2006.
Village Voice Online. July 10, 2007.

QUOTES

Bruno: "Isn't there anybody you can call at 3 a.m. in case you have a big problem?"

Francois: "I don't have any big problem."

Bruno: "Yes, you have one, you can't call anybody at 3 a.m.!"

N

THE NAMESAKE

Two Worlds. One Journey.
—Movie tagline

Box Office: $13.5 million

There are certain tricks and techniques the novelist has that the filmmaker may be unable to approximate. Take for example Mira Nair's *The Namesake,* adapted from the Pulitzer Prize-winning novel by Jhumpa Lahiri, mainly about a displaced family and cultural identity, while telling the story of a Bengali-American boy, Gogol Ganguli, named for the Russian novelist Nikolai Gogol, who had simplified his surname from Gogol-Yanovsky to simply Gogol at the age of twenty-two. This is more than the film tells you, though the novel explains all this, and more, about the Russian author of the short story, "The Overcoat" and, more significantly, perhaps, *Dead Souls,* considered to be his masterpiece.

Lahiri's novel begins in 1968, just before Gogol was born; following a different narrative design, the film begins with a train wreck in India years earlier. The film later shows, however, what the novel describes on its first page, Gogol's mother "combining Rice Krispies and Planters peanuts and chopped red onion in a bowl," but the film never bothers to explain that she is trying to approximate a snack sold in Calcutta "and on railway platforms across India," the one food this pregnant mother craves.

If the source novel is richer in context than the film adaptation written by Sooni Taraporevala and directed by Mira Nair, that is as expected, though *The Namesake* remains reasonably close to its source and generally more "faithful" than the usual adaptation. According to Jhumpa Lahiri, *The Namesake* started with a simple phrase she jotted down in her notebook: "a boy named Gogol." Five years were to pass before she started her first draft in 1997, and the novel was not completed until 2002. Two years later director Nair contacted Lahiri about making a film adaptation. "People talk about immigrants as being displaced," Lahiri wrote in 2006. "I prefer the word 'transposed,' used in music to describe shifting to a different key. That is what happens when a person leaves one homeland for another, and that is what happened as *The Namesake* made its voyage from paper to film."

The film's prologue establishes the importance of the name Gogol, a favored author for the young Ashoke Ganguli (Irrfan Khan), who survives a train wreck in India in 1974 as he is going to visit his grandfather. Ashoke survives and is rescued from the wreckage after his Gogol book is noticed by rescue workers and brings Ashoke to their attention as well. This accident therefore represents a turning point for Ashoke, who prior to the accident had been sharing a compartment on the train with an agreeable stranger who had advised him to go abroad and see the world. Feeling lucky to be alive, Ashoke will later follow that advice. After many difficult months of rest and recuperation following the train wreck, the young man goes on to become an engineer who brings his wife, Ashima (Tabu) to America, where they raise their children, Gogol (Kal Penn) and Sonia (Sahira Nair). The film follows the events of the lives of Ashoke and Ashima, then of Gogol in chronological order, as the story of the father gradually turns into the story of the son. Russian writer Nikolai Gogol becomes the "namesake" for this displaced Bengali boy, named

Gogol by his father in a moment of whimsy when he discovered that his wife and son would not be allowed to leave the hospital unless the baby was named. The boy's name was supposed to be temporary, but it became permanent, becoming as well the perfect metaphor for the complex issues of identity confusion the story raises.

Interviewed by Nick James for *Sight & Sound,* the magazine of the British Film Institute, Nair indicated that she preferred to focus upon Gogol's "two major relationships: with Maxine [Jacinda Barrett], the American girlfriend he lives with, and, later, with Moushumi [Zuleikha Robinson], a would-be sophisticate who wants to be French." The later character enters the film earlier as an awkward, gangly pre-teenager, and then later he re-enters Gogol's life after the death of his father as a "slick, re-invented immigrant." What Nair found most appealing about the source novel was that "the laughter allows the sorrow to be sweeter and the sorrow welcomes the laughter all the more." If the story has a flaw, it comes from the sentimental subtext of this family melodrama, which is generally well contained and effective.

As critic Caryn James noted in the *New York Times,* Nair was a perfect match for Lahiri's 2003 novel. The novelist was born in London to Indian parents, raised in Rhode Island, and educated at Barnard College, earning advanced degrees from Boston University. Nair was born in India, educated at Harvard University, and later settled in New York City. She also maintains homes in New Delhi and Kampala, Uganda, where her husband, Mahmood Mamdani, was born, and where the story of her first film, *Salaam Bombay!* (1988) begins in 1972, when Idi Amin expelled Indians from the country. While at Harvard during the 1970s, Nair met Sooni Tarapor-evala, who later collaborated with Nair on the screenplay of *Mississippi Masala* (1991), before writing the adapted screenplay for *The Namesake.* All of the artists involved in the making of this film understand problems of cultural assimilation and identity. British reviewer Philip Kemp claimed in his *Sight & Sound* review that *Monsoon Wedding* (2001), which he considered Nair's best film to date, could almost be considered a prequel to *The Namesake* for both films deal with alienation "from other cultures and from one's own."

The cast, too, is perfectly matched to the challenge of adapting *The Namesake.* The actress who plays Gogol's mother, Ashima Ganguli, was born in Hyderabad, in central India, Tabassum Fatima Hashmi, but she became a Bollywood icon using her childhood nickname, Tabu. In India, this thirty-five- year-old actress is as famous as Meryl Streep is in America. *The Namesake* is her first international starring role. In his *Sight & Sound* review, Philip Kemp was enchanted by Tabu's performance: "If *The Namesake* remains engaging for most of its two-

hour running time," he wrote, "it's largely thanks to the casting. Bollywood star Tabu, making her American screen debut, convincingly ages from playful girl of 20 to careworn forty-something mother." Reviewing the film for *The Nation,* Stuart Klawans also praised the casting: "Best of all," he wrote, "the main characters are played by Irrfan Khan as the sweet, gentle father; Tabu as the game but dislocated mother; and the irrepressible Kal Penn as Gogol. You will be happy to spend two hours in such good company." Kal Penn is an American actor of Indian descent, whose given name is Kalpen Modi, who was one of the leads in *Harold & Kumar Go to White Castle* (2004). Nair's fifteen-year-old son first suggested that she cast Penn for the role of the Americanized Gogol rather than a Bollywood talent. He gave her good advice.

The film's dominant metaphor is captured by the phrase "We all come out of Gogol's overcoat," suggesting, of course, that Gogol was the precursor both of Dostoevsky and Chekhov in Russian literature, but Gogol has a deeper meaning for Ashoke, the father, who "tells his son that they are all there because he was saved by Gogol's book in the train crash." Clearly, both the novel and film were shaken out of Gogol's overcoat. Appropriately, the novel begins with the following quotation from Nikolai Gogol's "The Overcoat": "The reader should realize himself that it could not have happened otherwise, and that to give him any other name was quite out of the question." Indeed, the novel ends with Gogol Ganguli wrapped metaphorically in "The Overcoat" his father had once given him, in a collection of *The Short Stories of Nikolai Gogol* inscribed "For Gogol Ganguli," adding "The man who gave you his name, from the man who gave you your name." There is a wonderful coherence and consistence in that passage that will ring true to anyone who has seen this remarkable film adaptation.

James M. Welsh

CREDITS

Gogol: Kal Penn
Ashima: Tabu
Ashoke: Irfan Khan
Maxine: Jacinda Barrett
Moushumi Mazumdar: Zuleikha Robinson
Origin: USA
Language: English
Released: 2006
Production: Lydia Dean Pilcher, Mira Nair; Mirabai Films, Fox Searchlight, Entertainment Farm, UTV Motion Pictures, Cine Mosaic; released by 20th Century-Fox
Directed by: Mira Nair

Written by: Sooni Taraporevala
Cinematography by: Frederick Elmes
Music by: Nitin Sawhney
Sound: Edward Novick
Music Supervisor: Linda Cohen
Editing: Allyson C. Johnson
Art Direction: Suttirat Larlarb
Costumes: Arjun Bhasin
Production Design: Stephanie Carroll
MPAA rating: PG-13
Running time: 122 minutes

REVIEWS

Boston Globe Online. March 16, 2007.
Boxoffice Online. March 9, 2007.
Chicago Sun-Times Online. March 16, 2007.
Entertainment Weekly. March 15, 2007, p. 48.
Hollywood Reporter Online. September 12, 2006.
Los Angeles Times Online. March 9, 2007.
New York Times Online. March 9, 2007.
Premiere Online. February 16, 2007.
Rolling Stone Online. March 7, 2007.
San Francisco Chronicle. March 9, 2007, p. E5.
Sight & Sound. March 27, 2007.
Variety Online. September 6, 2006.
Washington Post. March 16, 2007, p. C1.

AWARDS

Nomination:

Ind. Spirit 2008: Support. Actor (Khan).

NANCY DREW

Small town girl. Big time adventure.
—Movie tagline

Get a clue.
—Movie tagline

Box Office: $25.6 million

The beloved girl detective and literary icon created in the 1930s mystery-novel series has been given a pseudo-modern update by director Andrew Fleming in his muddled, lackluster *Nancy Drew.* Written by Fleming and Tiffany Paulsen, the character of Nancy Drew retains many of her appealing 1930s qualities but is placed in modern-day Los Angeles, and in trying to have it both ways the filmmakers have turned her into a mere curiosity instead of a vital, contemporary, and three-dimensional character. While it is refreshing to see a teenage girl eschew belly-baring tank tops, too-tight

jeans, and a "Whatever!" attitude, Nancy's knee socks, demure plaid skirts, and impeccable manners are too conservative and seem highly anachronistic within the present-day Hollywood context of the film.

The casting of Emma Roberts—daughter of actor Eric Roberts and niece of actress Julia Roberts—as the spunky sleuth was certainly a natural fit, and she injects the role with all the youthful vigor necessary to the character but is undermined at every turn by direction and script. Even with her keen powers of observation and mental prowess, it seems Nancy cannot figure out how to fit in at her new school. Busy underscoring her fish-out-of-water status with the stereotypical teenagers who populate her high school, the filmmakers most egregiously leave the mystery she must solve as an afterthought in their quest to pander to the pre-teen and teenage target audience expecting the next *Mean Girls* (2004).

Nancy starts out fighting crime in her hometown of River Heights, painted as broadly as possible as quaint, "Anytown U.S.A." of a bygone era. She bids her friends adieu, promises to give up sleuthing, which her father, lawyer Carson Drew (Tate Donovan) believes is an unhealthy addiction, and heads to Hollywood where Mr. Drew has business. They wind up staying at the Draycott Mansion, formerly owned by screen siren Dehlia Draycott (Laura Elena Harring) who was found murdered there decades ago. In addition to Harring playing a similar role in *Mulholland Drive* (2001), other David Lynch similarities turn up along the way, including a stop at the Twin Palms resort.

The much-loved supporting characters Bess (Amy Bruckner) and George (Kay Panabaker) of River Heights are replaced in Los Angeles by obnoxious sidekick Corky (Josh Flitter) and watered-down love interest Ned (Max Thieriot) to aid Nancy in solving the vintage crime. Driving in her late model convertible and wearing dresses sewn from patterns left to her by her late mother, everything, including the crime, seems dated and stale despite the modern electronic devices Nancy uses being on constant display. She receives anonymous threats and narrowly avoids cars careening in her direction but remains undeterred, finding Draycott's rightful heir Jane Brighton (Rachel Leigh Cook), who is the beneficiary of the movie star's missing will. The predictable plot involves Nancy cleverly piecing together clues found in Dehlia's old films, finding the missing will, and being kidnapped by villainous henchmen before escaping and restoring order to all.

Donovan gives a fine performance as Nancy's earnest father, while Barry Bostwick injects some spark into his role as evil lawyer Dashiel Biedermeyer. Marshall Bell is given the thankless role of the menacing estate groundskeeper Leshing, who turns out to be Jane's real father and an unlikely hero when he saves Nancy from the henchmen.

The Nancy Drew mystery series was created by Edward Stratemeyer, with the first twenty-two books written by Mildred A. Wirt Benson under the pseudonym Carolyn Keene and edited by Stratemeyer's daughter, Harriet Stratemeyer Adams. Not new to the big screen, the series spawned several movie adaptations in the 1930s starring the Oscar®-nominated Bonita Granville and directed by William Clemens, as well as a 1970s television series, *The Hardy Boys/Nancy Drew Mysteries* starring Pamela Sue Martin. While those productions retained the spirit of the novels and relied more heavily on plot and the machinations of detective work, Fleming's adaptation creates humdrum characters in clichéd situations and puts little emphasis on the intricacies of mystery solving. As A.O. Scott noted in his *New York Times* review, "Worse, *Nancy Drew* corrupts the clean, functional, grown-up style of the books with the kind of cute, pseudo-smart self-consciousness that has sadly become the default setting for contemporary juvenile popular culture produced by insecure, immature adults."

Hilary White

CREDITS

Nancy Drew: Emma Roberts
Carson Drew: Tate Donovan
Corky: Josh Flitter
Ned Nickerson: Max Thieriot
Jane Brighton: Rachael Leigh Cook
Bess: Amy Bruckner
George: Kay Panabaker
Dahlia Draycott: Laura Elena Harring
Trish: Kelly Vitz
Leshing: Marshall Bell
Barbara Barbara: Caroline Aaron
Father Murphy: David Doty
George: Kay Panabaker
Inga: Daniella Monet
Dashiel Biedermeyer: Barry Bostwick
Origin: USA
Language: English
Released: 2007
Production: Jerry Weintraub; Virtual Studios; released by Warner Bros.
Directed by: Andrew Fleming
Written by: Andrew Fleming, Tiffany Paulsen
Cinematography by: Alexander Gruszynski
Music by: Ralph Sall

Sound: Ron Bartlett
Editing: Jeff Freeman
Art Direction: Todd Cherniawsky
Costumes: Jeffrey Kurland
Production Design: Tony Fanning
MPAA rating: PG
Running time: 98 minutes

REVIEWS

Boston Globe Online. June 15, 2007.
Chicago Sun-Times Online. June 15, 2007.
Christian Science Monitor Online. June 15, 2007.
Entertainment Weekly. June 22, 2007, p. 53.
Hollywood Reporter Online. June 11, 2007.
Los Angeles Times Online. June 15, 2007.
New York Times Online. June 15, 2007.
Variety Online. June 8, 2007.
Washington Post. June 15, 2007, p. C1.

THE NANNY DIARIES

A comedy about life at the top, as seen from the bottom.
—Movie tagline

Box Office: $25.9

From a best-selling book with pretensions to social insights, *The Nanny Diaries* is a throwback American movie in this sense: its subject is class, and its moral thrust is about following your heart, not the money. In most other ways, it is typical and formulaic in its portrait of a young woman thrust into adulthood without a plan for success who has to learn how to love, be loved, and trust her instincts.

This fluffy tale with few surprises features a college graduate documenting the previous summer as an application essay for a graduate program in anthropology. Annie Braddock (Scarlett Johansson) has graduated from college uncertain about her future. Her mother, a nurse (Donna Murphy), wants her to improve her social class by getting a job at a financial firm rather than pursuing anthropology. On her first interview at a firm where she is told there are 8,000 applicants for ten positions, Annie cannot answer the open-ended question about who is Annie Braddock, and she rushes out in tears. It is the standard opening for a "chick flick"—the search for identity by a young woman on the verge of maturity.

What is immediately interesting about what otherwise seems like a rather typical coming-of-age story is that it attaches specific price tags to Annie's choices, and it is rooted in the social strata of New York City. To fully appreciate the message, the viewer must understand the topography. Annie is from New Jersey, which means she is common and middle-class in the eyes of Manhattanites. As a prospective anthropologist, she considers the various species of Manhattan womanhood and despairs that she may end up a Central Park bag lady. In true movie fashion an opportunity then descends upon her when she saves a little boy from being run over by a man riding on a Segway who is distracted by a sexy woman. The boy happens to be the son of a mother who is looking for a new nanny.

More than a little naively, Annie enters the world of rich and spoiled Upper East Side matrons. Even though her new job pays well, she is slumming. In the eyes of her best friend (Alicia Keys), she is betraying her intelligence and integrity. In fact, Annie is so ashamed of what she is doing that she hides it from her mother, pretending she is working at a big financial firm like her mother wants. Annie is apparently the only native-born white American who is working as a nanny in Manhattan. She has thrust herself below her social class, and below its aspirations to a higher status, by taking a job as a servant.

The tension that centers along class lines is something that is more reminiscent of a 1930s or 1940s Hollywood screwball comedy than it is of more modern fare. In fact, few essentials would have to be changed about *The Nanny Diaries* to make it a film of that era. At its center point, Johansson displays many of the qualities of a typical screwball heroine—she is smart but naïve, sexy but tomboyish, sweet but capable of meanness. Most essentially, though, she is confused, and needs to find out about herself from looking at who she is not.

The targets of this satire are easy pickings. The archetypal Mrs. X (Laura Linney) is a pampered egotist who views her son Grayer (Nicholas Reese Art) as an impediment to her freedom. She is married to an arrogant businessman (Paul Giamatti), who loves nothing more than money and his own self-aggrandizement. These characters are such broad caricatures that they are barely believable, but Linney, who is game for anything, makes Mrs. X an entertaining ogress—she is an amazingly adept and versatile actress. Giamatti, however, seems badly miscast; it is difficult to believe that he belongs to the upper class, though he does succeed in portraying a truly loathsome pig of a man, if not a rich tycoon.

What transpires is just what one would expect, complete with the broad and easy moral lessons this kind of movie loves to convey. Annie learns what it is like to be one of the accessories of the rich and arrogant, her freedom is taken away, and she is plunged into a problematic relationship with Grayer. She makes them into buddies who secretly break the rules together, and she learns what it is like to love someone she cannot commit to. For a little romantic interest, a handsome young Harvard man (Chris Evans) living in the building enters the story, but the premise that he is off-limits because of her job seems very strained. They meet in awkward circumstances after Grayer pulls down Annie's pants in the apartment lobby during her first day on the job, and they travel the usual Hollywood dating arc, including a quarrel (also based on class) and then a quick reconciliation during a steamy first date.

Nothing in *The Nanny Diaries* is very subtle. The comedy gives way to maudlin stretches as Annie discovers the ugly secrets in her employers' relationship. The story is overlong and the sequence of events that leads to Annie's dismissal murky and insufficient, giving the heroine an easy way out of her relationship with Grayer, who has fallen in love with her—it is not her fault in the end that she leaves, though it is something she had planned to do all along. It all leads up to a revenge climax when she scolds Mr. and Mrs. X and shows her moral superiority, which is not a difficult feat since they have the parental morals of garden slugs. In the end, Mrs. X is portrayed as a victim herself—it is all the fault of Mr. X—and she is redeemed. However, since Mr. X is, like Annie's boyfriend and Grayer, the product of a nanny upbringing, the easy critique of the habits of the very rich is complete.

It is all very smug and rather facile, but suitably entertaining. Johansson gets to show off her wide range of talent, while remaining that fantastic paradox of womanhood that only cinema can provide a starlet—the always-sexy beauty who is nonetheless believable as a regular girl. In pigtails, knockabout casual outfits, and occasional fancier wear, Johansson is all over the screen, and the camera loves her so much you want it to linger more before it goes on to the next necessary bit of silliness. Like the heroines of the screwball comedies of the past, Johansson's Annie has plenty of moxie and a sweet heart, and it is that combination of courage and tenderness that will see her through life's trials, including being trapped in a totally predictable plot.

Michael Betzold

CREDITS

Annie Braddock: Scarlett Johansson
Mrs. X: Laura Linney
Mr. X: Paul Giamatti
Harvard Hottie: Chris Evans
Grayer: Nicholas Reese Art
Lynette: Alicia Keys

Judy Braddock: Donna Murphy
Milicent: Judith Anna Roberts
Calvin: Nathan Corddry
Origin: USA
Language: English
Released: 2007
Production: Richard N. Gladstein, Dany Wolf; Film Colony; released by Weinstein Co.
Directed by: Shari Springer Berman
Written by: Shari Springer Berman, Robert Pulcini
Cinematography by: Terry Stacey
Music by: Mark Suozzo
Sound: Allan Byer
Music Supervisor: Randall Poster
Art Direction: Ben Barraud
Costumes: Michael Wilkinson
Production Design: Mark Ricker
MPAA rating: PG-13
Running time: 105 minutes

REVIEWS

Boston Globe Online. August 24, 2007.
Chicago Sun-Times Online. August 24, 2007.
Entertainment Weekly Online. August 22, 2007.
Hollywood Reporter Online. August 20, 2007.
Los Angeles Times Online. August 24, 2007.
New York Times Online. August 24, 2007.
San Francisco Chronicle Online. August 24, 2007.
Variety Online. August 17, 2007.
Washington Post. August 24, 2007, p. C1.

NATIONAL TREASURE: BOOK OF SECRETS

Box Office: $216.5 million

National Treasure: Book of Secrets follows the path of many other sequels before it, existing primarily as a means of capitalizing on its predecessor's success and accomplishing little in the way of further character exploration or dramatic development. The film presumes audience familiarity with the characters and plot of the first story (*National Treasure* [2004]) and consequently comes up short in its potential to function as a stand-alone narrative. Additionally, the film's plot suffers from several obvious coincidences and contrivances that weaken the its credibility. Still, even with these flaws, *Book of Secrets* is an enjoyable film to watch, an agreeable "popcorn flick" that is short on real substance but adequate for pure entertainment.

When a lost page from John Wilkes Booth's diary surfaces in the hands of Mitch Wilkinson (Ed Harris),

the descendent of a Confederate, historian and adventurer Benjamin (Ben) Franklin Gates (Nicolas Cage) finds himself facing a familial dilemma. The page seems to implicate Ben's great-great grandfather, Thomas Gates, in the assassination of Abraham Lincoln. According to the story passed down to Ben and his father Patrick (Jon Voight), Thomas had burned one of the diary pages to prevent the revelation of the location of a vast treasure that could have enabled the Confederacy to win the Civil War. Determined to clear the family name, Ben and Patrick conclude that they must find the treasure and prove their ancestor's story. Aided by ex-girlfriend Abigail (Diane Kruger) and technology-savvy friend Riley (Justin Bartha), Ben embarks on a quest to follow the trail of the secret code found in the diary. Not surprisingly, Wilkinson (aided by a group of henchmen) follows Ben's every move, intending to claim the treasure for himself.

The hunt first takes Ben to the scale model of the Statue of Liberty in Paris, where he and Riley find a clue indicating the answers they are looking for may be found in the (famous two desks), one located in Buckingham Palace and the other in the White House. So of course the next stop along their journey is London, where Ben, Riley, and Abigail carry out a plot to sneak into the Queen's home and search the desk. In the desk, Ben finds a piece of wood with ancient Native American inscriptions carved into its surface. The inscription is written in an ancient language very few scholars can read—but, luckily, Ben's mother Emily (Helen Mirren) happens to be one of them. Patrick is very reluctant to see Emily, as he has not seen his former wife in more than thirty years, but nevertheless he accompanies Ben to the university where Emily teaches. Emily confirms Ben's suspicions that the inscription refers to the legendary ancient City of Gold. Unfortunately, the rest of the information is evidently found on another, matching piece of wood...likely to be found in the President's desk in the Oval Office.

Thus, Ben's next stop is the White House, where he and Abigail manage to get into the Oval Office (thanks to a gullible friend of Abigail's). When Ben finds the hidden compartment in the desk, he discovers that the piece of wood is gone. He does, however, discover a special presidential symbol—a symbol that Riley identifies as a link to a legendary "Book of Secrets," a book supposedly passed down from president to president, the content of which supposedly contains all the nation's biggest secrets, from the mystery of Area Fifty-One to the truth behind the Kennedy assassination. Since the answers Ben and company are looking for may be found in the Book of Secrets, the next logical step seems to be locating the Book of Secrets. The problem, Ben says, is that access to the book can only be gained two ways: to become President, or to kidnap the President. So naturally he decides to do the latter.

Ben's plan to kidnap the President (Bruce Greenwood) actually plays out rather smoothly (one of the more implausible elements of the plot), and the President, intrigued by Ben's story, actually winds up being amiably cooperative about revealing the existence and location of the Book of Secrets, though he warns Ben that he will only be able to clear Ben of kidnapping charges if he actually finds the City of Gold and proves his claims. Ultimately, after finding the book, Ben and company learn that the City of Gold is located somewhere under Mount Rushmore. As the story moves toward its conclusion, the paths of protagonists and antagonists converge as Wilkinson kidnaps Emily and shows up on the scene at Mount Rushmore. After discovering the City of Gold under the mountain, and following an inevitable final confrontation between Ben and Wilkinson, the heroes emerge victorious and Thomas Gates' name is cleared.

As mentioned previously, many turns of the plot tend to be implausible or over-the-top, from the ease with which Ben figures out the meaning of the clue on the Statue of Liberty to the coincidence that his own mother is one of only a few people who can read the ancient inscriptions, from the ease with which Ben breaks into Buckingham Palace and the White House, to the circumstances of his successfully "kidnapping" of the President. One might say that even though a film like this may be expected to have such an implausible element or two, *Book of Secrets* tends to have too many, particularly since most of the crucial plot points are like this. On the other hand, it can also be argued that these unlikely events are intended to be part of the fun of the movie. Still, the pattern of one coincidence after another does eventually undermine the credibility of the story, no matter how fantastic it is supposed to be.

As far as character development is concerned, the main characters—Ben, Riley, Patrick, and Abigail—do not really grow much from the characters they were in the first film. This is not necessarily a negative quality because the characters are all interesting to watch and are played well by the actors, but in a significant sense, the mostly static characters are, at the end of this film, the same people they were at the end of the first movie, although the filmmakers added several twists to attempt some character development. The two main complications are Ben's relationship with Abigail and Patrick's relationship with Emily. In the beginning of the story, Ben and Abigail have broken up, but by the time the story concludes, the adventure predictably draws them back together. Yet the film never really explores why they broke up to begin with; the brief explanations that are given seem contrived and are not really supported by the behaviors of the two characters on-screen. In other words, it seems the filmmakers simply inserted the tension between the two for the sake of tension itself, not because it is a logical outgrowth of the characters or their interactions. The relationship between Patrick and Emily is actually more interesting, mainly since Emily is a new character and her appearance does enable the introduction of a new facet of Patrick's personality—primarily, he fumbles around nervously and uncertainly and is easily shaken by her, obviously intimidated and also still in love with her. Emily is a strong-willed character, a woman who apparently could not put up with Patrick's adventuresome spirit and evidently a tendency to neglect responsibilities at home. Once again, though, the script predictably leads the two back together. Their reuniting happens too easily, perhaps, occurring rather quickly as they share their own adventure together under Mount Rushmore. It is a crowd-pleasing moment when they kiss, but it is a moment that has not really had sufficient build-up or credible development.

The movie's pacing may help to keep the viewer's mind off of some of the plot contrivances. It moves quickly and includes enough action and humor to keep it from becoming boring, yet the pacing also betrays the lack of depth and development alluded to previously. The story launches directly into the history of the Booth diary and immediately turns to the problem that sends Ben on his journey. During the first half of the film, the story advances so rapidly that there is little time to think about the logic of what is happening on-screen.

Performances in the film are more than adequate, though none of the characters really break significant new ground. Cage seems to walk through his performance of Ben without much effort, but he keeps the character an interesting one to watch. Bartha injects Riley with most of the humor of the film, while Mirren provides one of the movie's most well rounded performances as Ben's mother, though she unfortunately does not have much screen time until the end of the movie. Like the film itself, the performances accomplish what they set out to do—help tell a fun yet insignificant story—but do not go beyond what is necessary to serve the plot.

Ultimately that is the nature of almost every element of *National Treasure: Book of Secrets*. The filmmakers seem content to simply create a fun sequel that takes no risk with a formula that proved successful in its predecessor.

David Flanagin

CREDITS

Ben Gates: Nicolas Cage
Patrick Gates: Jon Voight
Abigail Chase: Diane Kruger
Riley Poole: Justin Bartha
Emily Appleton: Helen Mirren
Sadusky: Harvey Keitel
Mitch Wilkinson: Ed Harris
The President: Bruce Greenwood
FBI Agent Spellman: Alicia Coppola
Daniel: Michael Maize
Seth: Timothy Murphy
Thomas Gates: Joel Gretsch
Origin: USA
Language: English
Released: 2007
Production: Jerry Bruckheimer, Jon Turtletaub; Saturn Films, Junction Entertainment; released by Walt Disney Pictures
Directed by: Jon Turteltaub
Written by: Cormac Wibberley, Marianne S. Wibberley
Cinematography by: John Schwartzman, Amir M. Mokri
Music by: Trevor Rabin
Sound: Peter J. Devlin
Music Supervisor: Bob Badami
Editing: William Goldenberg, David Rennie
Art Direction: Drew Boughton
Costumes: Judianna Makovsky
Production Design: Dominic Watkins
MPAA rating: PG
Running time: 124 minutes

REVIEWS

Boston Globe Online. December 21, 2007.
Chicago Sun-Times Online. December 19, 2007.
Hollywood Reporter Online. December 21, 2007.
Los Angeles Times Online. December 21, 2007.
New York Times Online. December 21, 2007.
San Francisco Chronicle. December 21, 2007, p. E1.
Variety Online. December 20, 2007.

QUOTES

Riley Poole: "So let's recap: We've broken into Buckingham Palace, and the Oval Office, stolen a page from the President's super-secret book, and actually kidnapped the President of the United States. What are we gonna do next, short-sheet the Pope's bed?"
Ben Gates: "Well, you never know."

AWARDS

Nomination:

Golden Raspberries 2008: Actor (Cage), Supporting Actor (Voight).

NEXT

If you can see the future, you can save it.
—Movie tagline

Box Office: $18.2 million

For the prescient protagonist in utterly negligible *Next*, decisions on how best to proceed are informed by an ability to first take mental trial runs down each possible course of action, seeing which leads to Easy Street and which to a very dead end. Both those who chose to adapt Philip K. Dick's 1954 short story "The Golden Man" in such a regrettable and exceedingly loose manner and those who paid hard-earned money to see what resulted must surely wish that they too had been able to clairvoyantly avoid such a calamity. *Next* is a gimmick masquerading as a film, and there were multiple reports of boos emanating from disgusted moviegoers who felt they had been had instead of entertained. No wonder it was not pre-screened for critics.

Most reviewers and moviegoers agreed that Nicolas Cage, lately laying enough eggs to make an omelet, added another ovum to his oeuvre by playing Cris Johnson, a.k.a. Frank Cadillac, a low-end Las Vegas nightclub magician. He is able to sufficiently please his martini-marinated audiences by making safely camouflaged use of real precognitive powers, ESP disguised as mere delightful trickery out of fear that scientists who knew the truth would want to get their hands on him. Cris also uses his gift while gambling in the casinos, hoping to increase his income as much as he can without also raising suspicions.

Unfortunately for Cris, few people have ever been as hell-bent in following up on their suspicions as FBI counterterrorism agent Callie Ferris (Julianne Moore), and she has them about him. It seems that a powerful Russian nuclear weapon, capable of causing a cataclysm, is ominously unaccounted for and may have already been smuggled into the United States by some shadowy, sinister villains. (In one of the film's many deficiencies, exactly who these European terrorists are and what their specific gripes might be are never elucidated.) Every second counts in the scramble to find the fiends and stop them, and supremely serious Callie is a bulldozer in hot pursuit. It makes one fear for the nation's security if, in the event of such monumentally dire circumstances, anyone would fritter away precious time desiring to pick the brain of a lounge act. Admittedly, Callie's hunch is correct that Cris is keeping more hidden than just a dove up his sleeve, but, as viewers learn at the very outset, his abilities only let him peer a mere two minutes into his own future and no one else's. So no matter how much punch Moore puts into her portrayal, those watching will find her character's resolution to collar Cris risible. As her Callie begins searching for him, barging in on a character played by Peter Falk, one cannot help wishing that Falk's highly entertaining Columbo were on the case instead. The veteran actor's appearance is exceedingly brief, the remainder presumably lying on the cutting room floor where the rest of *Next* should also have landed.

Nobody would want to be dragged off to a lab to be strapped to a special chair with painful-looking devices attached to one's eyes, and Cris is no exception. So one would think he would make use of his perpetual head start to immediately go into hiding. However, Cris cannot get the lovely Liz (Jessica Biel) out of his head, repeatedly haunted by visions of an intriguingly shaped vision. Inexplicably, Cris can suddenly see into her future too, and for more than just two minutes. He does not know her nor why she keeps flashing through his brain, but Cris is not going anywhere until he meets her to find out. When she finally shows up in a diner he has been casing, the lady's allure is further accentuated by being bathed in a golden, glowing light. In the film's sole genuinely enjoyable use of its gimmick, viewers see the various ways Cris ponders approaching her before he proceeds with one foreseen to have maximum effectiveness.

Amazingly, far from telling Cris to get lost, Liz, a teacher on a Native American reservation, is soon headed out of town with a strange man after a laughably cursory query about whether or not he is a "psycho." Hearing as they travel toward Flagstaff that Cris's stage name is a combination of Frankenstein and Cadillac and finding him "charming—but odd," most women would likely be clutching the door handle with a misgiving-induced sweaty palm. Liz, however, snuggles up to him as he drives, becoming a dozing, drooling easy mark.

This startlingly quick, trusting familiarity only grows as a plot-necessitated road washout forces the two to stop at a motel, closely followed by the FBI and consequently also by the curious evildoers. This pit stop sets up the showcasing of Biel's barely-concealed form, wrapped in a towel that is soon discarded for some coupling. The entire episode is unbelievably forced. Whether or not the two challenged advisable speed limits on the road, the pair's lightning-fast bonding certainly has. Even those who can detect some chemistry between Cage and Biel would surely balk at the swoony assertion in the production notes that "at its heart" the film is "a beautiful love story."

The plot, dialogue, and special effects increasingly compete to see which can become less convincing. There is the scene in which Liz, warned by Callie that Cris is a thoroughly dangerous man, initially agrees to concoct his morning orange juice pick-me-up into something that will knock him flat before predictably yelping at the very last second for him not to down it. "I don't know what I'm doing," she whines about the acute quandary in which she finds herself, complaining to Cris about how tough it is to decide whether or not he is indeed a sociopath. Then follows a visually humorous sequence in which Cris, knowing exactly what to expect, is able to sidestep bullets, boulders, a steam locomotive, a car, enough logs to dam a river, and all sorts of other debris that is smashing down all around him as he tries to outrun Callie down a steep hillside. Another unintentional mirth-maker is the scene in which Cris, having seen that Liz (now the villains' hostage) will end up being blown up by a bomb if he fails to assist Callie in testing a multitude of ways to proceed as they attempt to navigate the terrorists' lair. What viewers see is a screen absolutely crawling with crises, a veritable Nicolas Cage infestation that demands a licensed exterminator, or at least a sizeable can of Raid.

Unnerving, catastrophic occurrences lose the power to unnerve each time they are quickly revealed to be merely scenes of aborted catastrophe, depictions of things that never had the chance to happen thanks to Cris's precognition. With each use of this device, viewers will stay further and further back from the edge of their seats, disengaged because there is no point in getting worked-up about something when there is likely another rewind to safety ahead. This gimmick ends up not only neutering *Next* but effectively nullifying it entirely when the filmmakers go so far as to retract everything those watching had been shown for a sizeable portion of the film. The cacophonous showdown with the terrorists and all the action leading up to it that was purposefully propelled forward by dramatic music never actually occurred outside of Cris' head. Just when his and Callie's efforts to save not only Liz but all of Los Angeles culminate in nuclear annihilation, Cris decides that he certainly does not like the plot resolution, so he simply rewinds back to the serenity of the motel room, from whence he will try another tack. "I made a mistake," he has come to realize, a conclusion surely shared by many who felt their time had been wasted in watching *Next*.

David L. Boxerbaum

CREDITS

Cris Johnson: Nicolas Cage
Liz Cooper: Jessica Biel
Callie Ferris: Julianne Moore
Mr. Smith: Thomas Kretschmann
Cavanaugh: Tory Kittles
Irv: Peter Falk
Security Chief Roybal: José Zúñiga
Wisdom: Jim Beaver

Kendall: Michael Trucco

Jeff Baines: Jason Butler Harner

Origin: USA

Language: English

Released: 2007

Production: Nicolas Cage, Norm Golightly, Todd Garner, Arne L. Schmidt; Revolution Studios, Saturn Films, IEG Virtual Studios, Broken Road; released by Paramount

Directed by: Lee Tamahori

Written by: Gary Goldman, Jonathan Hensleigh, Paul Bernbaum

Cinematography by: David Tattersall

Music by: Mark Isham

Sound: William B. Kaplan

Editing: Christian Wagner

Art Direction: Kevin Ishioka

Costumes: Sanja Milkovic Hays

Production Design: William Sandell

MPAA rating: PG-13

Running time: 96 minutes

REVIEWS

Chicago Sun-Times Online. April 27, 2007.
Hollywood Reporter Online. April 27, 2007.
Los Angeles Times Online. April 27, 2007.
New York Times Online. April 27, 2007.
San Francisco Chronicle. April 27, 2007, p. E5.
Variety Online. April 26, 2007.

QUOTES

Cris Johnson: "Here is the thing about the future. Every time you look at, it changes, because you looked at it, and that changes everything else."

AWARDS

Nomination:

Golden Raspberries 2008: Actor (Cage), Supporting Actress (Biel).

NO COUNTRY FOR OLD MEN

> *There are no clean getaways.*
> —Movie tagline
>
> *One discovery can change your life. One mistake can destroy it.*
> —Movie tagline

Box Office: $72.6

No Country for Old Men is notable for several reasons beyond simply being an excellent, philosophical thriller.

Although co-writers and directors Joel and Ethan Coen have claimed in interviews that their main inspiration has always been literature, not films, this is their first film based on a novel. Except for *The Ladykillers* (2004), a remake of the 1955 Alexander Mackendrick film, the Coens' previous eleven films have been original screenplays. *No Country for Old Men* also represents a comeback for the filmmaking brothers who had not had a critical and commercial hit since *Fargo* (1996), though *The Big Lebowski* (1998) has gone on to achieve cult status and is considered by many to be their best film. Finally, it is a cliché of the film business that good novels make bad films, while adaptations of lesser books are often more successful. For example, the film versions of Herman Melville's *Moby-Dick* (1851) and F. Scott Fitzgerald's *The Great Gatsby* (1925) have been disappointing, yet Francis Ford Coppola turned Mario Puzo's 1969 potboiler into the masterpiece *The Godfather* (1972).

Though Cormac McCarthy's 2005 novel has all the trappings of a thriller, the novelist was long established as a major American literary figure before its publication. Because McCarthy uses the conventions of a thriller to explore larger issues, another surprising aspect of *No Country for Old Men* is how seriously the Coens take these concerns and how much depth the film provides for McCarthy's protagonists. In their previous films, the Coens are often condescending to their characters and treat their circumstances with irony. *No Country for Old Men* manages to be faithful to McCarthy's intentions while retaining distinctive Coen touches in its treatment of violence and flashes of dark humor.

No Country for Old Men is the story of three men in southwestern Texas of 1980. Since he was twenty-five year old, Ed Tom Bell (Tommy Lee Jones) has been a sheriff, like his father and grandfather. The world-weary, laconic Bell thinks he has seen everything in his time and ponders retirement. Llewelyn Moss (Josh Brolin) is a Vietnam veteran struggling to make a living for himself and his young wife, Carla Jean (Kelly Macdonald). One day while hunting antelopes, Moss stumbles into a drug deal gone wrong. Two criminal groups have had a shootout, leaving all dead but for two men wounded and dying. Moss ignores the pickup truck loaded with heroin but takes a satchel containing two million dollars. When Anton Chigurh (Javier Bardem) is hired to recover the money, the film becomes an extended chase, with Moss trying to find a safe place to hide the loot, Chigurh searching for him, and Bell looking for them both.

No Country for Old Men focuses on Moss' struggle for survival after being wounded by the men who hire Chigurh and on Chigurh's capacity for evil as Bell follows the bodies left behind by the relentless killer. Moss and Bell are both of the Everyman sort: Moss an essentially good person compelled by circumstances to extreme acts, Bell a philosophical type still trying after all his years as a lawman to understand the nature of depravity. Bell meets his match in the cold-blooded Chigurh. Chigurh is fascinating because neither McCarthy nor the Coens do anything to explain him or his actions. *No Country for Old Men* is a psychological thriller without a hint of Freudianism.

Chigurh is a true enigma. According to Ethan Coen, in an interview on *Charlie Rose,* McCarthy intended the character's name to suggest an untraceable ethnic origin. Bardem adds to the mystery by using a subtle, indeterminable accent. Chigurh's strangeness is accentuated by a hairstyle recalling the British rock groups of the mid-1960s. *No Country for Old Men* opens with Chigurh being arrested for a crime never explained. He seems less compelled by greed in his pursuit of the satchel than by simply seeing a job through to the end. His professionalism does not keep him from tormenting those he casually encounters, making the life of a gas station owner (Gene Jones) hinge on a coin toss.

Chigurh carries an instrument attached to an air cylinder that he uses to blow the locks out of doors, but he also uses it on some of his victims. The sight of Chigurh with this weapon is truly terrifying. Unlike Anthony Hopkins' Hannibal Lecter, Bardem never makes Chigurh a caricature. The way Bardem exhales after saying "Call it" in his confrontation with the gas station owner is chilling for making clear how little human life means to him. When the man says he has nothing to put up for a coin toss, Chigurh replies, "You've been putting it up your whole life. You just didn't know."

This being a Coen Brothers film, there is occasional humor. Bell's deputy, Wendell (Garret Dillahunt), not attuned to nuances, constantly points out the obvious. The scenes between the taciturn Bell and the loquacious Wendell have the rhythm of a comic routine, regardless of what they are saying. Despite his ferocity, even Chigurh provokes humor, as when he tries to learn Moss' whereabouts from the uncooperative manager (Kathy Lamkin) of a trailer park. When Chigurh tries to intimidate her with his deadly stare, the overweight, middle-aged woman squares her shoulders to prove she is not frightened. This simple scene is beautifully edited by Roderick Jaynes (a pseudonym for the Coens) to underscore the humor lurking within what could have become a violent situation.

Gene Jones, Lamkin, and other members of the cast, especially Beth Grant as Carla Jean's whining mother, appear so natural that they could easily be nonprofessionals, though all are experienced performers well cast by Ellen Chenoweth. Grant looks and talks like the amateur playing Bonnie Parker's mother in *Bonnie and*

Clyde (1967), subtle foreshadowing by the Coens. The casting of the accomplished Macdonald at first seems odd because Carla Jean has so little to do. Then comes her confrontation with Chigurh. How Macdonald handles Carla Jean's absolute refusal to be afraid is remarkable. As Carson Wells, hired by another side in the aborted drug transaction, Woody Harrelson shines by underplaying his role. Wells is initially cocky about his ability to find the money, but when Chigurh finds him first, Harrelson, with just slight changes in his expression and body language, conveys the character's heartbreaking resignation to his fate.

To put it mildly, Brolin, who made his first film as a teenager in 1985, has had an undistinguished career, with his bisexual FBI agent in *Flirting with Disaster* (1996) the only standout performance. But 2007 changed all that, with significant roles in *Grindhouse, In the Valley of Elah,* and, especially, *American Gangster.* Best of all is his Llewelyn Moss, a role for which he created an audition reel, photographed by Robert Rodriguez and directed by Quentin Tarantino, while on a *Grindhouse* lunch break. (The Coens did not give him the part, however, until they interviewed him.)

Brolin creates a memorable portrait of a man disappointed by everything in his life except his love for Carla Jean. This point, like almost everything else about the film, is not spelled out. Moss is not motivated by greed; he would simply be foolish not to take the opportunity presented him. Brolin excels in the matter-of-fact way he delivers lines, as when Carla Jean asks, "What's in the satchel?" and he replies, over his shoulder, "Full of money." Almost every shot in the film is perfectly composed, with one of the best being the decision to shoot Moss from behind during a telephone conversation with Chigurh. Brolin leans his head against a wall and slumps his shoulders to convey his acceptance that something very bad must happen.

As good as all the other actors are, Tommy Lee Jones is even better, painstakingly deciding the most effective way to deliver each line, some quickly, some drawn out, stressing each syllable perfectly. This seemingly naturalistic yet stylized approach is most obvious in the two longest scenes in *No Country for Old Men*: a meeting with a disabled lawman (Barry Corbin, matching Jones pause for pause) and Bell's dream about his father recounted to his wife (Tess Harper). Bell serves as an unusual moral spokesman because he knows there are no easy answers to the issues posed by the film.

The Coens' longtime cinematographer Roger Deakins shot many scenes near dawn or in twilight to underscore the film's ethical grayness. Deakins makes the West Texas landscape look painfully lonely and desolate. The skills of Deakins and the Coens become especially evident when a wounded Moss flees across a river pursued by a furious, large dog, one of the filmmakers' few additions to McCarthy's text. The beauty of the fading light gleaming off the water acts as a counterpoint to the violence of the scene, made quite credible in the Coens' staging. Another of the film's most compelling images features another dog, wounded, looking forlornly back over its shoulder at Moss. The film is crammed with indelible images: a bloody body floating in a motel pool, a driver slumped over his steering wheel after a collision, Chigurh limping away from a car as it explodes.

Despite considerable bloodletting, the Coens choose not to show two significant deaths. This admirable restraint puzzled viewers wanting something more visceral, but it helps establish the more contemplative tone of the final portion of the film. Ironically, the lack of expected violence proved to be highly controversial, with many viewers disappointed by the film's not-with-a-bang-but-a-whimper ending. The Coens, taking McCarthy's lead, provide greater emotional impact by showing that good does not always triumph over evil. Resolution of all issues is too conventional. Examining the absence of humanity is more haunting. The Coens achieve poetry through understatement.

Michael Adams

CREDITS

Ed Tom Bell: Tommy Lee Jones
Anton Chigurh: Javier Bardem
Llewelyn Moss: Josh Brolin
Carson Wells: Woody Harrelson
Carla Jean Moss: Kelly Macdonald
Loretta Bell: Tess Harper
Wendell: Garret Dillahunt
Ellis: Barry Corbin
Origin: USA
Language: English
Released: 2007
Production: Scott Rudin, Ethan Coen, Joel Coen; Paramount Vantage; released by Miramax
Directed by: Joel Coen, Ethan Coen
Written by: Joel Coen, Ethan Coen
Cinematography by: Roger Deakins
Music by: Carter Burwell
Sound: Peter Kurland
Editing: Roderick Jaynes
Art Direction: John P. Goldsmith
Costumes: Mary Zophres
Production Design: Jess Gonchor
MPAA rating: R
Running time: 122 minutes

REVIEWS

Boston Globe Online. November 9, 2007.
Chicago Sun-Times Online. November 8, 2007.
Christian Science Monitor Online. November 9, 2007.
Entertainment Weekly Online. November 7, 2007.
Los Angeles Times Online. November 9, 2007.
New York Times Online. November 9, 2007.
New Yorker Online. November 12, 2007.
Rolling Stone Online. November 1, 2007.
San Francisco Chronicle. November 9, 2007, p. E5.
Variety Online. May 18, 2007.
Wall Street Journal. November 9, 2007, p. W1.
Washington Post. November 9, 2007, p. C1.

QUOTES

Sheriff Ed Tom Bell: "You have to be willing to die to do this job."

TRIVIA

The Coen brothers purchased specially made fake blood that they shipped from London to their location for $800 a gallon. This was done so the extras that were lying in the sand for hours wouldn't be attacked by bugs and animals that might otherwise be attracted to the sugar from the more commonly used fake blood which is typically made with corn syrup.

AWARDS

Oscars 2007: Adapt. Screenplay, Director (Coen, Coen), Film, Support. Actor (Bardem)
British Acad. 2007: Cinematog., Director (Coen, Coen), Support. Actor (Bardem)
Directors Guild 2007: Director (Coen, Coen)
Golden Globes 2008: Screenplay, Support. Actor (Bardem)
Screen Actors Guild 2007: Support. Actor (Bardem), Cast
Writers Guild 2007: Adapt. Screenplay
Nomination:
Oscars 2007: Cinematog., Film Editing, Sound, Sound FX Editing
British Acad. 2007: Adapt. Screenplay, Film, Film Editing, Sound, Support. Actor (Jones), Support. Actress (Macdonald)
Golden Globes 2008: Director (Coen, Coen), Film—Drama
Screen Actors Guild 2007: Support. Actor (Jones).

NO END IN SIGHT

The American occupation of Iraq: The inside story from the ultimate insiders.
—Movie tagline

Box Office: $1.4 million

After the fall of Saddam Hussein, as the looting continued non-stop in Baghdad, Secretary of Defense Donald Rumsfeld said to the press at one of his many conferences, "Stuff happens." Even the most die-hard Rumsfeld supporter would call that an understatement, especially given the privilege of hindsight. A few years later, a growing number of documentarians have tried to detail exactly what took place in Iraq. *No End in Sight* is the best of the lot. With this brilliant documentary, director Charles Ferguson gives viewers the most comprehensive look yet filmed at how we got from the morning of September 11, 2001 to the middle of a war from which there are no easy exit strategies. In a mostly non-partisan way, Ferguson interviews many architects of the current conflict in Iraq and paints a complete picture of what went wrong in the Middle East just by using archival footage and the memories of the people involved. *No End in Sight* is the rare documentary that is both enlightening for political aficionados completely familiar with every maneuver of the war and still accessible enough for viewers unaware of the decisions that led the United States to the condition so accurately described by the title.

Ferguson makes a number of smart decisions in his construction of *No End in Sight,* including laying out the events of the war chronologically, focusing on a few key mistakes by the Bush administration in that time, and not using a mouthpiece who might make the film easily dismissed by the more politically polarized. *No End in Sight* is narrated by Campbell Scott in a tone that is consistently interesting but free from the kind of political animosity that would have been brought to the project by someone like Michael Moore or possibly even Ferguson himself. Scott remains calm and collected, which gives the film a more frightening tone than it would have had with a more passionate narrator. Wisely, Ferguson only becomes part of the film when asking questions of its incredible subjects, letting his perfect mix of Scott's narration, archival footage, and new interviews tell the story of Iraq.

Using the people behind the Iraq War to detail not just what happened but what went wrong was another brilliant decision made in the early construction of *No End in Sight.* When people like Paul Hughes, a one-time employee of ORHA (the Office for Reconstruction and Humanitarian Assistance) and a man who was in the Pentagon when it was hit on 9/11, and General Jay Garner, who actually ran the reconstruction of Iraq until he was replaced by L. Paul Bremer, to describe their own personal experiences frees *No End in Sight* from political animosity and allows the more basic human truths of the situation to surface. Ferguson is not that interested in the political maneuverings of the Bush administration (although he is naturally fascinated by

the continued hiring of the inexperienced by them), yet focuses *No End in Sight* on some of the undeniable consequences of politically motivated decisions. *No End in Sight* could have easily turned into a political diatribe if Ferguson had focused on the "why" of Iraq, but his film is far more concerned with merely the "what," letting viewers come to their own conclusions about what has happened in that war-torn country over the last half-decade.

No End in Sight details three major mistakes made by Bremer, who headed the Coalition Provisional Authority (CPA), and the ripple effect they have had over subsequent years. In the early stages of the occupation, the CPA moved toward "De-Ba'thification" and discarded many skilled government workers who might have helped guide the country. With the Ba'th Party employees ousted, Bremer and the CPA then made the baffling decision to disband the Iraqi Army, taking half a million soldiers, many of them breadwinners and most of them fully aware of the location of the country's weapon stockpiles, and sending them right into the arms of the resistance. Finally, the choice not to declare martial law in the days after Hussein fell was a crucial one. Museums were looted, libraries were burned, and arms depots were raided because the average Iraqi realized that the Americans were not there to protect them. As Rumsfeld said, "Stuff happens." *No End in Sight* is the best documentary yet produced about the nightmare that stuff has created in Iraq.

Brian Tallerico

CREDITS

Origin: USA

Language: English

Released: 2007

Production: Charles Ferguson, Jennie Amias, Jessie Vogelson; Representation Pictures; released by Magnolia Pictures

Directed by: Charles Ferguson

Written by: Charles Ferguson

Cinematography by: Antonio Rossi

Music by: Peter Nashel

Sound: David Hocs

Music Supervisor: Tracy McKnight

Editing: Chad Beck, Cindy Lee

MPAA rating: Unrated

Running time: 102 minutes

REVIEWS

Boston Globe Online. August 10, 2007.
Chicago Sun-Times Online. August 10, 2007.

Entertainment Weekly Online. August 2, 2007.
Hollywood Reporter Online. July 27, 2007.
Los Angeles Times Online. August 3, 2007.
New York Times Online. July 27, 2007.
New Yorker Online. August 6, 2007.
San Francisco Chronicle. August 10, 2007, p. E5.
Time Online. July 27, 2007.
Variety Online. January 24, 2007.
Washington Post. July 27, 2007, p. C4.

QUOTES

Secretary of State Donald Rumsfeld: "Quagmire? I don't do quagmires."

AWARDS

Nomination:

Oscars 2007: Feature Doc.
Writers Guild 2008: Screenplay.

NO RESERVATIONS

Life isn't always made to order.
—Movie tagline

Box Office: $43.1 million

No Reservations features a slew of sumptuously presented and utterly scrumptious-looking culinary creations that illicit a strong response from one's salivary glands. Unfortunately, the film also contains a pleasant but pallid love story that is unlikely to stir any other glands nor quicken hearts even. The film is simply *Mostly Martha* (also known as *Bella Martha* 2001), the German film upon which *No Reservations* is based, served up American style and far gloomier than the comedic moments spotlighted in advertisements suggested. This pall, along with the aforementioned lack of palpable feeling and a huge dollop of predictability, make *No Reservations* an easily digested but strangely zestless entrée.

Despite an attempt to mute her usual sexy sauciness, the loveliness of Catherine Zeta-Jones unquestionably rivals that of any of the film's other showcased dishes. She plays Kate, a brilliant, ferociously perfectionistic, and decidedly serious head chef at a top Manhattan restaurant who is infinitely better at crafting marvelously satisfying hot meals than warm relationships. A powerful lady of formidable skills, Kate meticulously prepares artistically presented gastronomic wonders that consistently enrapture the upscale establishment's clientele. When occasional dissatisfaction is voiced, her hackles immediately rise. Her frosty disdain quickly becomes prickly confrontation, and the less-than-

decorous scenes that result when this pressure cooker boils over would surely lead to Kate's dismissals if it were not for her exceptional ability.

It is quickly made clear that Kate expresses herself best through cuisine, and that her identity and self-worth are not just inexorably intertwined but wholly synonymous with what she so painstakingly prepares. It is a telling moment when she is at least briefly thrown from her high horse upon hearing herself referred to as "one of the best" chefs in the city instead of its finest by her sorely-tested boss, Paula (Patricia Clarkson). Kate's reaction gives viewers a glimpse of an underlying insecurity beneath a stiff outer layer of utter certitude. This revelation adds a much-needed degree of softness and likeability to a character who would otherwise seem too cold for many to comfortably embrace.

No Reservations does an excellent job of capturing a restaurant's high-pressure, fast-paced kitchen choreography, the breakneck crisscrossing of staff as they cooperatively blend varied talents and ingredients. A sharp contrast is drawn between the bustling camaraderie and rewarding sense of accomplishment found in Kate's work world and how empty the rest of her plate is once she is done for the day filling those of her patrons. While the kitchen is filled with bright, exquisite concoctions, her apartment's décor is almost devoid of color. There are no messages waiting for her on her answering machine, and Kate tells the therapist (Bob Balaban) she sees upon Paula's insistence that she has not had a romantic connection in years. The woman wakes up early and alone, heading out at the crack of dawn and coming alive once again while carefully selecting key items for that day's fare. If anyone ever cut Kate's apron strings, it is quite evident that she would be at a complete loss.

The film's screenplay sets out to rectify this unhealthy imbalance in Kate's existence by abruptly forcing her to take on the responsibility of preteen niece, Zoe (Abigail Breslin), who survives a car crash which kills rigid, dark-haired Kate's sunny blond sister. Viewers are informed that the sweet but traumatized youngster's name means "life," lest they not recognize her as an agent of change who will gradually grant her aunt a new lease on just that. The peacock feathers, multi-hued scarves, and stuffed animals that the girl brings with her into Kate's home are offered up as immediate, hard-to-miss visual cues indicating that the enlivening and eventual brightening of Kate's life away from the restaurant has been set in motion.

Before that is actually accomplished, however, there are the wholly expected stumblings of a grieving, single and single-minded career woman, both ill-prepared and ill-equipped to place a child whose entire world has been shattered anywhere near the center of her own. Kate returns too quickly to work, in effect retreating to reassuringly comfortable surroundings where she feels in control. At one point, she ill-advisedly leaves Zoe in the care of a peculiar, Goth babysitter who may very well be interested in rapidly-mutating deadly viruses because she is one herself. On another occasion, she hands the child a cellphone and leaves her to fend for herself. Kate obliviously dishes up kid-unfriendly meals (including a school lunch bag full of duck), making Zoe opt for hunger while yearning for frozen fish sticks and other basic fare that Kate barely recognizes as edible. Trying to juggle responsibilities, Kate brings Zoe to work late into the evenings, resulting in the child falling asleep during the school day and officials there threatening to call child protective services. Despite all these predictable parenting misfires, everyone watching *No Reservations* will be assured that all the complications and crying are just bumps in the road toward Kate and Zoe's satisfactory unification, emphasized by an eventual contented two-shot of them sweetly curled up in bed together.

Providing some much-needed levity is handsome, easygoing Nick (Aaron Eckhart), a talented sous-chef hired to work in Kate's kitchen. He is seen dancing around playfully with food and enthusiastically singing along to recordings of Italian opera, garnering delighted approval and instantaneous acceptance from the staff—except Kate. *No Reservations* does not miss an ingredient in meticulously following the recipe of countless other films in which a rather hard, icy, tightly-wound career lady is thawed, humanized, and guided to the realization that there is more to life by a man whom she initially loathes but ultimately loves. Thus, Kate feels threatened by, and jealous of, Nick, seeing him as a threat to her reign. She expresses profound horror at his informal behavior, certain that no one so silly belongs anywhere near foie gras. Kate wants nothing to do with Nick and gives him the coldest shoulder she can muster. When she makes him feel so uncomfortably unwelcome that he quits, leaving Paula precariously short-staffed, Kate grudgingly agrees to withdraw her objections and asks Nick back. He is pleased, sensing a promising crack in the ice. Nick smiles warmly at Kate, and in turn her outfit instantaneously catches on fire. No one will miss the significance of this less than subtle bit of symbolism and foreshadowing. Neither will they fail to note the contrast between the tense scenes of Kate and Nick arguing in the kitchen's dimly-lit walk-in refrigerator and the later, clichéd image of the two enjoying each other's company with a bright, roaring fire seen in the background of the shot. However, despite all these flames, *No Reservations* could definitely stand a lot more heat when it gets out of the kitchen. As critic Roger

Ebert wrote, "the characters seem to feel more passion for food than for each other."

At various times during the film, Kate and poor Zoe fail to be heartened when they gaze at photo albums and vacation videos depicting care-free, happy times, finding it hard to shake off the weighty cloak of melancholy that envelopes them. It will be somewhat the same for many watching *No Reservations*, as it is often hard to get into the lighter and more romantic moments of the film when lost, lonely and heartbroken Zoe is crying pitifully for her dead mother (her father has never been in her life) or running away to the cemetery filled with terror that her memories of mom will fade. (Many will be astonished that Kate never thinks to have her therapist recommend a good child psychologist for the suffering girl.) So even though the film's main characters overcome obstacles to fuse over food, delight in board games and pillow fights, cram together into cramped photo booths, and have an epiphany or two, all while the soundtrack shifts from spare and somber to opera to rock with upbeat lyrics like "you'll never be rejected," there is still always an inescapable drag on the proceedings.

Made on a budget of $28 million, *No Reservations* was able to surpass that at the box office despite generally unenthusiastic reviews. Offered here among the gloominess are some very familiar cinematic meat and potatoes, but with precious little seasoning or distinctive, savory flavor to make them any more than merely passable fare.

David L. Boxerbaum

CREDITS

Kate Armstrong: Catherine Zeta-Jones
Nick Palmer: Aaron Eckhart
Zoe: Abigail Breslin
Paula: Patricia Clarkson
Leah: Jenny Wade
Therapist: Bob Balaban
Sean: Brian F. O'Byrne
Bernadette: Lily Rabe
Mrs. Peterson: Celia Weston
Mr. Peterson: John McMartin
Ellen Parker: Stephanie Barry
Origin: USA
Language: English
Released: 2007
Production: Kerry Heysen, Sergio Aguero; Castle Rock Entertainment, Village Roadshow Pictures; released by Warner Bros.
Directed by: Scott Hicks

Written by: Carol Fuchs
Cinematography by: Stuart Dryburgh
Music by: Philip Glass
Sound: T.J. O'Mara
Music Supervisor: John Bissell
Editing: Pip Karmel
Art Direction: W. Steven Graham
Costumes: Melissa Toth
Production Design: Barbara C. Ling
MPAA rating: PG
Running time: 105 minutes

REVIEWS

Boston Globe Online. July 27, 2007.
Chicago Sun-Times Online. July 27, 2007.
Christian Science Monitor Online. Jul 27, 2007.
Hollywood Reporter Online. July 23, 2007.
Los Angeles Times Online. July 27, 2007.
New York Times Online. July 27, 2007.
Premiere Online. July 27, 2007.
Variety Online. July 27, 2007.
Washington Post. July 27, 2007, p. C5.

TRIVIA

The film's score composer, Philip Glass, can be seen sitting at an outdoor table at the Bistro near the end of the film.

NORBIT

Have you ever made a really big mistake?
—Movie tagline

Box Office: $95.6 million

Norbit arrived in theaters as if from a freshly-opened time capsule from the early 1990s. Directed by Brian Robbins, the film is little more than a broad comedic vehicle for star Eddie Murphy, who plays three different roles, and a case study in special effects make-up, courtesy of Rick Baker who was also the wizard behind Murphy's latex in *Nutty Professor* (1996) and *Nutty Professor II: The Klumps* (2000). The strident humor, essentially a string of fat jokes with a few ethnic jokes woven in, is tired and dated. What is worse, *Norbit* was released on the heels of Murphy's Oscar®-nominated turn in *Dreamgirls* (2006), the award-winning musical that set the stage for what looked like a bold new direction for Murphy's career. Instead, audiences were subjected to Murphy donning yet another fat suit in a lesser version of *The Nutty Professor.*

The problem is not with Murphy's ability to play characters. *Norbit* again proves that Murphy is a master of disappearing into characters; he is so adept as the elderly Chinese Mr. Wong, that it is impossible to determine whether it is, in fact, Murphy without taking a peek at the credits. However, the script dooms the entire proceedings, failing to provide the multitude of characters with either interesting situations or funny dialogue. Written by Murphy and his brother Charles (along with Jay Scherick and David Ronn), there were probably few people involved with the production brave enough to criticize it. In the *Minneapolis Star-Tribune* Colin Covert wrote, "*Norbit* is a movie at the top of the bottom rank of comedies," adding, "It's a shame to see performing talent like this squandered, even on a vehicle he created himself." Criticism was mixed, however, and in the *San Francisco Chronicle* Mick LaSalle praised the film: "This is Murphy doing what he does best, genial cruelty and good-natured nastiness...You've heard of rapier wit. This is sledgehammer wit, wielded with sledgehammer precision."

Also dooming the film is the lead character Norbit (Eddie Murphy). Meek and not particularly intelligent, he is far from a romantic lead and is not remotely engaging enough to command the screen and carry the film. Baby Norbit is abandoned in front of an orphanage/Chinese restaurant run by the grouchy Mr. Wong (Eddie Murphy). Despite Mr. Wong's aversion to Norbit's appearance ("You ugry brack baby!"), Mr. Wong takes him in. Norbit (Khamani Griffen, age five, Austin Reid, age ten) is able to survive life in the orphanage with the love of his friend Kate (China Anderson). Devastated when Kate is adopted, Norbit is left to fend for himself. When the rotund Rasputia (Lindsey Sims-Lewis) decides that she is going to be Norbit's new girlfriend, he blindly accepts this. She is mean and pushy, but she gives him protection from bullies.

As an adult, the wonderfully named Rasputia (Eddie Murphy) grows even more corpulent and cares only about her personal comfort. When she insists that Norbit marry her, he is too passive to say no, and is given a job working for Rasputia's three tough, mob-connected brothers. Norbit is content being dominated by the demanding Rasputia until Kate (Thandie Newton) suddenly returns. She and her fiancé, Deion Hughes (Cuba Gooding, Jr.), are looking into buying the orphanage and running it themselves. What Kate does not know is that Deion has no intention of running an orphanage. He is only interested in buying it for its liquor license. Norbit, for his part, is madly in love with Kate, but unsure how to proceed.

The main message of the film is "Rasputia is fat...and mean!" The majority of the film's jokes concern Rasputia's girth, some of which are mildly entertaining. When Rasputia goes to a water park, she is stopped at the door by a man demanding to know if she is wearing bottoms. She huffily hoists up her tremendous belly to reveal that, indeed, she is wearing bikini bottoms. Mostly, though, the filmmakers fall back on cartoonish and tired fat gags. The bit where all the water splashes out when Rasputia plops into a pool will not be amusing to any viewer over the age of three.

Although the humor may be lacking, the makeup work of Rick Baker is impeccable. Rasputia may not be the most original character, but she is certainly unrecognizable as being Murphy. Even when her face is projected hugely onto a movie screen, it is impossible to recognize Murphy's features in hers. The body make-up is similarly amazing. In the aforementioned water park scene, Rasputia's body jiggles and shakes like natural human flesh. But make-up alone, no matter how ingenious, cannot carry the enormously heavy load of this second-rate comedy.

Jill Hamilton

CREDITS

Norbit/Rasputia/Mr. Wong: Eddie Murphy
Kate: Thandie Newton
Big Jack: Terry Crews
Earl: Clifton Powell
Deion Hughes: Cuba Gooding, Jr.
Pope Sweet Jesus: Eddie Griffin
Lord Have Mercy: Katt Micah Williams
Buster: Marlon Wayans
Blue: Lester "Rasta" Speight
Origin: USA
Language: English
Released: 2007
Production: John Davis, Eddie Murphy; DreamWorks; released by Paramount
Directed by: Brian Robbins
Written by: Charles Murphy, Jay Scherick, David Ronn
Cinematography by: Clark Mathis
Music by: David Newman
Sound: Steve Nelson
Editing: Ned Bastille
Art Direction: Jay Pelissier
Costumes: Molly Maginnis
Production Design: Clay A. Griffith
MPAA rating: PG-13
Running time: 95 minutes

REVIEWS

Chicago Sun-Times Online. February 9, 2007.
Entertainment Weekly. February 16, 2007, p. 56.
Hollywood Reporter Online. February 9, 2007.
Los Angeles Times Online. February 9, 2007.
Miineapolis Star-Tribune Online. February 8, 2007.
New York Times Online. February 9, 2007.
San Francisco Chronicle. February 9, 2007, p. E1.
Variety Online. February 8, 2007.
Washington Post. February 9, 2007, p. C1.

TRIVIA

Rick Baker also did Murphy's special effects makeup for *The Nutty Professor* and its sequel.

AWARDS

Golden Raspberries 2007: Worst Actor (Murphy), Worst Support. Actor (Murphy), Worst Support. Actress (Murphy)

Nomination:

Oscars 2007: Makeup
Golden Raspberries 2007: Worst Picture, Worst Director (Robbins), Worst Screen Couple (Murphy and Murphy), Worst Screenplay.

THE NUMBER 23

> *The truth will find you.*
> —Movie tagline
> *First it takes hold of your mind...then it takes hold of your life.*
> —Movie tagline

Box Office: $35.1 million

The Number 23, a thriller directed by Joel Schumacher and starring Jim Carrey, does a decent job of building suspense early on, and then manages to undercut all of its most powerful elements as the film progresses. The title refers to a peculiar numerological phenomenon, both in the real world and in the context of the film: the number twenty-three has an uncanny way of cropping up in unexpected places, often foreshadowing tragedy. Such is the case with this film. A good-looking, atmospheric movie, *The Number 23* showcases an excellent example of content and form working against one another to render the ideal function of the movie, in this case providing the audience with stimulating and tense film-going experience, utterly moot.

The Number 23 tells the story of Walter Sparrow (Jim Carrey), unassuming animal control worker and family man who, through seeming coincidence, comes into possession of a book titled "The Number 23." The book tells an altered version of Walter's life, or so he maintains. Several details of Walter's life match up with some experiences of the book's main character, who calls himself Fingerling. His wife, Agatha (Virginia Madsen) keeps pointing out that, though there may be a few similarities between his life and Fingerling's, Walter is choosing the ones he wants and is disregarding the differences, which are significant. She encourages Walter to keep reading. Walter does but only becomes more deeply obsessed.

Fearing that the number twenty-three phenomenon described in the book may hold some bizarre dominion over his life, he begins to have nightmares about killing his wife (Fingerling kills his lover in the book). He becomes so obsessed, in fact, that, after an evening of polishing off the book, which ends abruptly at the end of chapter twenty-two, he stumbles across the grave of a woman named Laura Tollins (Rhona Mitra) who died on her twenty-third birthday, and he becomes convinced that the author must be the killer. Sparrow is ultimately revealed to be the author of the book, as well as Laura Tollins' murderer (though she manipulated him into killing her). The book, it turns out, was intended to be a suicide note but came to be a fictionalized account of his own life and the effect that the number twenty-three enigma had on his life and the lives of his parents (his mother and father were both suicides). Walter tried to kill himself by jumping out of a window but instead wound up in a hospital with memory loss. When all of this is revealed to him, Walter ponders suicide again, but instead he chooses to spend time in prison for the murder he tried to run away from years ago.

Normally, part of the delight in this sort of film is the anticipation built into the structure. Odd things might be happening on screen, yet they are somehow familiar. It may not be difficult to figure out some pieces of the puzzle (perhaps even some large ones), but it is the hope of the engaged audience that the filmmakers, as craftspeople, as artists (albeit beholden to certain commercial interests and constraints) have adeptly built a genuinely interesting and surprising turn into the movie—something that makes the familiar elements pay off without being a horrible, incredulous cheat. Unfortunately, it is in this area that *The Number 23* fails most egregiously. The surprise ending is somewhat prepared for, but it is unequal to all that has come before it. By the end of the film, the audience is left with the sense that a genuinely compelling mathematical enigma (not to mention decent actors) has been wasted on a poorly constructed story.

The brilliantly tantalizing, seemingly mystical enigma of the number twenty-three, the device that has drawn the audience in, evaporates as psychobabble and some proselytizing about choice, free will, and accepting responsibility. This "what I have seen, what I have done, was so horrible, I blocked it out" approach coupled with the notion that "there's no such thing as fate—only different choices" is so utterly disingenuous, so unequal to

the possibilities invoked by the number twenty-three phenomenon, that it is almost impossible to consider the last twenty to thirty minutes of the film as anything but a cheat. Perhaps the horrible pseudonym of the book's author, "Topsy Kretts" (a clunky homophone for "Top Secrets") should be a signal to the audience not to expect too much.

To call any film derivative in the twenty-first century belies a bit of wistful optimism about the nature of originality for the modern audience has, most likely, seen it all before. The cinematic roots of *The Number 23,* however, can almost certainly be traced to the films of director David Fincher (*The Game* [1997], *Fight Club* [1999], and *Zodiac* [2007]), especially in the design of the opening title sequence. The title sequence features a typewriter-like typeface popping on and off a stained, off-white background clearly intended to evoke book pages in the mind of the viewer (and the careful observer will note several factoids regarding the number twenty-three enigma embedded in the opening credits). Unfortunately, this excellent sequence misleads the viewer into thinking that the entire film will be treated with the same cleverness and attention to detail. While it should set the film up to be a wonderfully satisfying thriller, it instead promises well beyond what the actual content of the film is capable of delivering. It feels throughout like *The Number 23* aspires to be a Fincher film, with the upshot being that one comes away wishing it had been directed by the more adept (especially where stories of obsession and alienation are concerned) Fincher. That *The Number 23* is helmed by Joel Schumacher, director of some of the most reviled movies of the last fifteen years, including *Batman and Robin* (1997) and *Falling Down* (1993), goes a long way toward explaining its colossal failure.

Perhaps the greatest problem with *The Number 23,* however, is its failure to answer satisfactorily its central contention—that the number twenty-three phenomenon is a uniquely powerful and engrossing mathematical conundrum that may have some influence on the physical world. Used more as a device to hook the audience than as an organic piece of the rest of the movie, it simply falls away into half-hearted, eleventh-hour musings about choice and free will, which utterly deflate any sense of suspense and destroy whatever audience good will may remain before the closing credits roll.

John Boaz

CREDITS

Walter Sparrow/Fingerling: Jim Carrey
Agatha Sparrow/Fabrizia: Virginia Madsen
Robin Sparrow: Logan Lerman

Isaac French/Dr. Miles Phoenix: Danny Huston
Laura: Rhona Mitra
Suicide Blonde: Lynn Collins
Kyle: Mark Pellegrino
Father Sebastian: Ed Lauter
Origin: USA
Language: English
Released: 2007
Production: Beau Flynn, Tripp Vinson; Contrafilm/Firm Films; released by New Line Cinema
Directed by: Joel Schumacher
Written by: Fernley Phillips
Cinematography by: Matthew Libatique
Music by: Harry Gregson-Williams
Sound: Jay Meager
Editing: Mark Stevens
Art Direction: Jon Billington, David Sandefur
Costumes: Daniel Orlandi
Production Design: Andrew Laws

MPAA rating: R
Running time: 95 minutes

REVIEWS

Boxoffice Online. February 23, 2007.
Chicago Sun-Times Online. February 23, 2007.
Entertainment Weekly. March 2, 2007, p. 47.
Hollywood Reporter Online. February 21, 2007.
Los Angeles Times Online. February 23, 2007.
New York Times Online. February 23, 2007.
San Francisco Chronicle. February 23, 2007, p. E1.
Variety Online. February 20, 2007.
Washington Post. February 23, 2007, p. C5.

AWARDS

Nomination:
Golden Raspberries 2007: Worst Actor (Carrey).

O

OCEAN'S THIRTEEN

What are the odds of getting even? 13 to 1.
    —Movie tagline

Revenge is a funny thing.
    —Movie tagline

Box Office: $117 million

Ocean's Thirteen reportedly came about because star George Clooney was disappointed with *Ocean's Twelve* (2004) and did not want the con-man/heist series to end on a sour note. Most reviewers were lukewarm to *Ocean's Eleven* (2001), the first film in the series, wondering why someone of director Steven Soderbergh's talent was wasting his time on a remake of the mediocre 1960 Frank Sinatra-Dean Martin vehicle. Critics were even more hostile to *Ocean's Twelve,* dismissing it as lazy and meandering. The critical and public reception to *Ocean's Thirteen* has been much more positive, with some reviewers perhaps predisposed, because of Clooney's honesty about the previous effort, to view it as better than it actually is.

Ocean's Thirteen is essentially a remake of the first film, minus the love interest. In *Ocean's Eleven,* Danny Ocean (Clooney) is motivated by revenge against Las Vegas casino owner Terry Benedict (Andy Garcia) for stealing his wife, Tess (Julia Roberts), as well as running his friend Reuben Tishkoff (Elliott Gould) out of business, by robbing Benedict's casino. *Ocean's Thirteen* centers around a sting against Willy Bank (Al Pacino), owner of The Bank, an elaborate, even for Las Vegas, new hotel and casino. Bank has cheated Reuben out of his interest in the enterprise, leaving him in catatonic despair. The resulting scheme, hatched by Danny, Rusty

Ryan (Brad Pitt), and Linus Caldwell (Matt Damon), involves using loaded dice, rigged slot machines, and other means to allow Bank's gamblers to win huge sums. Colleague Basher Tarr (Don Cheadle) also uses a huge drill beneath the hotel to simulate an earthquake.

The film is both too hectic and too insubstantial, even for a popcorn movie. Con-artist films such as *The Sting* (1973), an obvious influence on the screenplay by Brian Koppelman and David Levien, are fun because of the way the plot is laid out one step at a time. The steps in *Ocean's Thirteen* are not so clear and how each of the pieces fits into the whole is difficult to follow. For example, Basher brags that the drill was used to make the Chunnel between France and England, yet how it was obtained, transported, and gotten into place without anyone noticing is a mystery. When the drill breaks, another one has to be purchased for $36 million. This development serves merely as an excuse to get Danny's old antagonist Benedict involved, when the casino owner reluctantly agrees to finance the rest of the scheme. Miraculously, the new drill appears immediately. Lighthearted entertainments cannot be held to the same standards as more serious fare, but there should be some degree of logic. Topping off this matter, the drill creates only a mild diversion and hardly seems essential.

Ocean's Thirteen is not, however, totally without merit. It is amusing when Virgil Malloy (Casey Affleck) is sent to work in the Mexican dice factory where he must tamper with the production process only to instigate a workers' strike over wages. Danny also wants to control the review of the hotel, which Bank desperately needs to be a rave. Bank is convinced that a disguised Saul Bloom (Carl Reiner) is the critic, while

Danny and Rusty sabotage the visit of the real critic (David Paymer). All this is mildly amusing. A rare high-point comes when Danny and Rusty get teary-eyed watching *Oprah*, poking fun at the actors' macho image. There are also several in-jokes as when Danny advises Rusty to settle down and have a couple of kids, a reference to Pitt's massively publicized relationship with Angelina Jolie.

One of the problems with *Ocean's Twelve* was that characters disappeared for long stretches for no apparent reason, and the same occurs here, though not as obviously. Because so much is going on and it is not easy to keep up, viewers may not realize until the end that Clooney, Pitt, and Damon have not actually had much to do. Pacino's part is much larger but lacks any depth, leaving this great actor with little to do but dash about looking worried. Paymer, a specialist in put-upon ordinary men, comes closest to giving a performance with any texture. As a mastermind Danny and Rusty consult, Eddie Izzard also makes an impression in a small role.

The notable absence of Roberts' Tess is filled by Ellen Barkin as Abigail Sponder, Bank's top assistant, the only significant female character. Barkin has not had a good role in a good film in a long time, and it is gratifying to see her in a major production, though the part is not all it could have been. At first, Abigail is a clichéd hard-edged executive, but when Linus shows up disguised behind a fake nose to divert her attention during the sting, she turns to love-starved mush. A line about her being susceptible as a woman of a certain age seems unnecessarily cruel. It is an achievement for Barkin to carry off the role with a degree of dignity.

Ocean's Eleven is slick and efficient, a vast improvement on its source, though still not watchable a second time. *Ocean's Twelve* has some good scenes but seems a bit sluggish. *Ocean's Thirteen* is the weakest of the three, seemingly aiming to trample its viewers into submission by bombarding them with plot developments and images and hoping that they do not notice that it all adds up to very little.

Michael Adams

CREDITS

Danny Ocean: George Clooney
Rusty Ryan: Brad Pitt
Linus Caldwell: Matt Damon
Terry Benedict: Andy Garcia
Willie Banks: Al Pacino
Frank Catton: Bernie Mac
Abigail Sponder: Ellen Barkin
Virgil Malloy: Casey Affleck
Turk Malloy: Scott Caan
Reuben Tishkoff: Elliott Gould
Yen: Shaobo Qin
Basher Tarr: Don Cheadle
Livingston Dell: Eddie Jemison
Saul Bloom: Carl Reiner
Roman Nagel: Eddie Izzard
Dr. Stan: Michael Mantell
The V.U.P.: David Paymer
Francois Toulour: Vincent Cassel
Greco Montgomery: Julian Sands
Agent Caldwell: Bob Einstein
Nuff Said expo girl: Noureen DeWulf
Origin: USA
Language: English
Released: 2007
Production: Jerry Weintraub; Weintraub Productions, Section Eight, Village Roadshow Pictures; released by Warner Bros.
Directed by: Steven Soderbergh
Written by: Brian Koppelman, David Levien
Cinematography by: Steven Soderbergh
Music by: David Holmes
Sound: Paul Ledford
Editing: Stephen Mirrione
Art Direction: Tony Fanning
Costumes: Louise Frogley
Production Design: Philip Messina
MPAA rating: PG-13
Running time: 122 minutes

REVIEWS

Boston Globe Online. June 8, 2007.
Chicago Sun-Times Online. June 7, 2007.
Entertainment Weekly. June 15, 2007, p. 58.
Hollywood Reporter Online. May 25, 2007.
Los Angeles Times Online. June 8, 2007.
New York Times Online. June 7, 2007.
Rolling Stone Online. June 7, 2007.
San Francisco Chronicle. June 7, 2007, p. E1.
Variety Online. May 24, 2007.
Washington Post. June 8, 2007, p. C1.

ONCE

How often do you find the right person?
—Movie tagline

Box Office: $9.4 million

Once, the humble Irish musical with a big heart, garnered nearly universal praise and, despite such lofty expectations, does not disappoint. This independent film with a budget of $150,000 and a small release earned more than $9 million in the United States, garnered high-profile fans, including Steven Spielberg, and won over audiences primarily due to its enviable word-of-mouth publicity. The title not only conveys the notion that true love rarely comes around but also implies the idea of a fairy tale, and indeed *Once,* a simple and affecting boy-meets-girl story, plays much like a modern version of one. Director-writer John Carney practically reinvents a genre most often overflowing with unabashed pageantry with the low-key, naturalistic way in which he weaves the music in to the point where it simply becomes the plot instead of distracting from it in any way. The music is the point, the songs that convey the characters' inner emotions seemingly written on the spot by the two lead actors who are musicians and play musicians who fall in love. While the film does not have a fairy-tale ending, the journey itself fully satisfies.

After actor Cillian Murphy backed out, Carney wisely cast his former The Frames band mate, Glen Hansard, in the lead as the nameless musician. Hansard's only previous acting credit was a small role in another Irish musical, *The Commitments* (1991), although his performance certainly does not betray that fact. With his large, expressive eyes and method acting naturalness, not to mention his winning song writing and singing, Hansard is surprisingly effective as a romantic lead. As a busker (street musician) with a beat-up old guitar playing for spare change, the worst that may be said of his performance is that he may seem a bit too good for a street musician, his plaintive wailing and polished presentation betraying his professional background. Although performing covers during the day, at night he plays his own songs, which attracts the attention of an inquisitive young Czechoslovakian immigrant girl, also nameless, played by Markéta Irglová. The impressive Irglová, only seventeen when she made the film, had collaborated musically with Hansard in the past and contributed her considerable songwriting and singing talent to the film.

As we follow the two around modern-day Dublin on their romantic journey, it is a refreshing change to see actual working-class people in a working-class environment. They both live in small, dingy flats, wear drab, workaday clothing, and work at menial jobs while also pursuing their creative outlets. This only adds to the transcendence of their dreamy romantic flight while at the same time acknowledging the reality that most people are poor, or at least not the giant loft-dwelling, Prada-wearing denizens that inhabit most Hollywood romances. Irglová's character sells flowers and cleans houses to support her young daughter and mother with whom she lives. The thirty-something Hansard lives

with his father and works in his vacuum cleaner repair shop. Like a dog on a leash, she rolls her broken vacuum up to where the singer is plying his trade, and he reluctantly agrees to take her to the shop to fix it. On the bus, via his "Brokenhearted Hoover Fixer Sucker Guy" snippet of a song composed on the spot, he reveals he has had his heart broken by his ex-girlfriend, who now lives in London.

The next day the flower seller takes the singer to a piano showroom, where the manager allows her to play the unsold models during lunchtime. Sitting together, the two compose the hauntingly beautiful, "Falling Slowly" whose lyrics describe their budding relationship: "I don't know you / But I want you / All the more for that / Words fall through me / Always fool me / And I can't react / And games that never amount / To more than they're meant / Will play themselves out." It is one of the most moving scenes in a film filled with many such intimate, lovely moments.

The singer and pianist collaborate on other songs and he asks her to play with him on a demo tape he plans to record. Hungry for a creative outlet, she quickly agrees and dives eagerly into the task, listening to the music he has written on her old personal CD player. Another one of the film's best scenes shows her frustration as the batteries die just as she is jotting down the lyrics she has composed, and in her pajamas she shuffles to the store in the middle of the night to buy fresh ones, finishing her composition on the way home.

The film shows an admirable restraint where the couple's romance in concerned. Early on, the singer extends an awkward invitation to the girl to stay the night when they are in his room. She is utterly disgusted at the suggestion as their connection is so much more to her than mere sex. She later reveals another reason for the refusal: She is married with a husband still living in Czechoslovakia. Although she admits she no longer loves him—he is much older and they have nothing in common—she has no plans to leave him because of their daughter. Typical of the film's low-key surprises, in the scene where the singer asks her if she still loves her husband, her response in Czech (which the singer does not understand) is, "No. I love you." The audience is also left unaware of her true feelings toward him as the comment is not subtitled. Although it is clear they have a connection, she continually encourages him to win back his old girlfriend, bearing no trace of selfishness. Unlike the singer, she realizes he needs to heal and go back to his girlfriend and she must stay in her loveless marriage. Although tragic, she never betrays her sadness at this fact.

The two assemble a ragtag group of musicians willing to record their demo with them. A rather predictable and clichéd setup has the neophyte band fumbling cluelessly around in the studio for awhile as the seasoned mixing professional included in the studio fee looks on disgustedly, preparing for an amateur hour that will last the entire weekend they have the studio booked. He quickly changes his tune as they perform powerful song after song, and soon he is on board as their biggest ally. This typical plot convention may be forgiven, though, because of the quality and originality of the rest of the film and its first-rate compositions.

Once is a love story firmly grounded in reality, and the chemistry between the two actors is palpable. The chief reason, however, to see the film is the music, which ranges from melancholy and moving with "If You Want Me," written and performed by Irglová, to sweetly funny with "Brokenhearted Hoover Fixer Sucker Guy," to several affecting duets, including "When Your Mind's Made Up".

Hilary White

CREDITS

Guy: Glen Hansard
Girl: Markéta Irglová
Origin: Ireland
Language: English
Released: 2006
Production: Martina Niland; Samson Film, Irish Film Board; released by Fox Searchlight

Directed by: John Carney
Written by: John Carney
Cinematography by: Tim Fleming
Music by: Glen Hansard, Markéta Irglová
Editing: Paul Mullen
Production Design: Tamara Conboy
MPAA rating: R
Running time: 86 minutes

REVIEWS

Boston Globe Online. May 25, 2007.
Entertainment Weekly Online. May 15, 2007.
Hollywood Reporter Online. January 30, 2007.
Los Angeles Times Online. May 16, 2007.
New York Times Online. May 16, 2007.
Premiere Online. May 16, 2007.
Rolling Stone Online. May 17, 2007.
San Francisco Chronicle. May 27, 2007, p. E5.
Variety Online. January 29, 2007.

TRIVIA

Writer/director John Carney played bass for the Frames until 1993.

TRIVIA

It was shot in 17 days.

AWARDS

Oscars 2007: Song ("Falling Slowly")
Ind. Spirit 2008: Foreign Film.

P

THE PAINTED VEIL

Sometimes the greatest journey is the distance between two people.
—Movie tagline

Box Office: $8 million

This film by director John Curran is a remake of one of W. Somerset Maugham's most exotic and beautifully tragic stories. A 1934 version starred Greta Garbo. Lead actor Edward Norton reportedly recruited Naomi Watts to star opposite him in this intriguing film, which was lost in the shuffle of award-worthy films released at the end of 2006 and the beginning of 2007.

Maugham sets his tale, also titled *The Painted Veil,* in the early 1920s. Watts stars as Kitty, a fetching but bored socialite who is tired of her mother's efforts to marry her off to some suitable but lackluster upper-class suitor. At a party, she catches the eye of a young doctor, Walter Fane (Edward Norton), who falls in love with her immediately. Fane is a hardworking scientist specializing in infectious diseases who has little interest in frivolity. When he succumbs to the beauty of Kitty, it is a match made in hell. Walter is blinded by her beauty and wit. Kitty sees him as her ticket to escape the suffocation of her parents and English society, for Walter's marriage proposal comes with a catch: He is soon to go to China. Out of rebellion and vanity, Kitty impulsively agrees, while Walter as a serious and earnest man adores her.

It soon becomes clear that she does not really love him. Once in China, Kitty is separated from her usual pleasures and the comforts of familiar companions. She finds her husband to be a stern man more interested in a staid domestic life than in the social whirl and entertainment that she still craves. She has an affair with an equally self-absorbed pleasure seeker, Charlie Townsend (Liev Schreiber), but they are too careless. Walter discovers the adultery just as he receives word of an opportunity to help out at a clinic in a remote, cholera-stricken rural area. He gives Kitty a choice of two unappealing alternatives: a divorce that will leave her destitute and alone, or once again to uproot herself and travel with him.

Maugham's deftly executed plot leaves a story about two bitter spouses plunged into the turbulence of not only a terrifying epidemic but also intense political unrest among the peasants in the village to which they are assigned. Kitty is sullen and withdrawn, uninterested in her surroundings and angry with her husband. Walter is seething with rage at Kitty's betrayal but determined to do everything in his power to save lives while punishing his wife with indifference and exile.

In the village they find a veteran British minor diplomat, Waddington (Toby Jones), who has settled into a life of exotic freedom, complete with a Chinese mistress and plenty of alcohol and secrets. On an opposite moral pole is a convent of nuns led by a Mother Superior (Diana Rigg), who proves herself eventually to be more humanitarian than doctrinaire.

The lushly photographed film, with a screenplay by Ron Nyswaner, unfolds slowly as the characters steep in their own juices for awhile. The tedium and isolation and meaninglessness of Kitty's life contrast vividly with her husband's dedication to his humanitarian work. Walter discovers that the source of the cholera is a polluted well and launches a scheme to deliver water from an uncontaminated location upstream, but he meets with resistance from many locals who see him as nothing more than an extension of colonial rule. Waddington illustrates the dissipation of that rule, while the nuns carry out their own missionary agenda.

As the situation continues to unravel, Curran cooks the tension to a delicious boiling point. Kitty eventually makes her own discoveries and breaks painfully out of her own self-absorption. Walter, too, is challenged to become more human and forgiving. As all hell breaks loose, the estranged couple meets each other anew, this time without blinders of immaturity and compulsion.

Maugham has no use for mawkish sentimentality, and Curran's film also avoids the trap of giving the story a standard love-conquers-all motif. The camera is observant of domestic disharmony, throwing Kitty and Walter into close quarters made all the more claustrophobic because of the rift between them, while setting their ongoing icy squabble against the backdrop of an untamed frontier. They have ventured to the ends of their known universe and are forced to come face to face with each other, but still they hide. The interior scenes are full of shadows and darkness, the exteriors lush with brilliant light. Rarely has the contrast between the inner torment of wretched souls and the outer beauty of a wretched land been more apparent, and that landscape also conceals volcanic political and social upheavals.

What gives this film its greatest resonance, however, is the remarkable performances of its leads. Norton has played this sort of role before: that of a man tightly constricted by circumstances, cornered emotionally, yet carrying on. Yet never has he fit the character so well, and never has he delivered the intensity of such a tortured and principled soul so compellingly. Norton makes Walter's pettiness and vindictiveness, his refusal to forgive Kitty, as compelling as his large-hearted attitude toward humanity, and the conflict between his two selves, personally unforgiving but socially embracing, is vivid and excruciating. Norton, whose character is much more the sympathetic of the two, wisely refuses not to make Walter saintly: his heroism, then, in the end, is more admirable because he achieves it despite his flaws.

Watts, whose role choices seem almost calculated to challenge herself and to display her versatility, has an even more difficult task: To take a vain, shallow woman and make her transformation to altruism believable. Again, the temptation to downplay the character's moral flaws is wisely resisted. Instead, Watts makes Kitty supremely disagreeable, an egotistical, pampered brat, and it is hard not to feel her comeuppance is well deserved. Slowly, however, Watts lets us see how frightened and confused Kitty is, and when she displays unexpected strengths of character, they are thrilling to

see but do not emerge out of nowhere. Watts has carefully laid the foundation by letting us see the woman emerging from the overindulged girl.

Riggs, whose reappearance after so many years is startling but welcome, and Jones, a stalwart, are also very skillful in providing their minor but important characters with resonance and depth. The result is that *The Painted Veil* is something of a dramatic and cinematic tour de force. But it is not everyone's cup of tea. Slow and thoughtful, the movie seems almost determined to underplay even the most explosive scenes. Yet that gives them all the more impact in the end. It is a fine and fearful excursion into the heart of darkness, and the darkness of the heart, but in essence it is optimistic, for it illustrates the power of the human capacity to overcome even the most daunting challenges.

Michael Betzold

CREDITS

Kitty Fane: Naomi Watts
Walter Fane: Edward Norton
Charlie Townsend: Liev Schreiber
Waddington: Toby Jones
Mother Superior: Diana Rigg
Colonel Yu: Anthony Wong
Origin: China, USA
Language: English
Released: 2006
Production: Sara Colleton, Jean-Francois Fonlupt, Bob Yari, Edward Norton; Colleton Company, Class 5 Fims, Dragon Studios; released by Warner Independent Pictures
Directed by: John Curran
Written by: Ron Nyswaner
Cinematography by: Stuart Dryburgh
Music by: Alexandre Desplat
Sound: David Lee
Editing: Alexandre De Francheschi
Art Direction: Peta Lawson, Tu Xinran
Costumes: Ruth Myers
Production Design: Tu Juhua
MPAA rating: PG-13
Running time: 125 minutes

REVIEWS

Boxoffice Online. December 20, 2006.
Hollywood Reporter Online. December 14, 2006.
Los Angeles Times Online. December 20, 2006.
New York Times Online. December 20, 2006.
Rolling Stone Online. December 12, 2006.
USA Today Online. December 20, 2006.
Variety Online. December 14, 2006.

PAPRIKA

> *This is your brain on anime.*
> —Movie tagline

Following in the footsteps of such Japanese animation pioneers as directors Hayao Miyazaki (*Spirited Away,* 2001) and Mamoru Oshii (*Ghost in the Shell 2: Innocence*, 2004), director Satoshi Kon takes animation in a decidedly adult direction in *Paprika,* with fantastical, sophisticated visuals and a chilling, complex, and inventive premise that explores the border between dreams and reality. Based on the novel by one of Japan's major science-fiction writers, Yasutaka Tsutsui, and written by Kon and Seishi Minakami, this disorienting saga is essentially a man-versus-machine cautionary tale in the vein of science fiction master Ray Bradbury.

The completely unrestrained and somewhat convoluted plot centers around the DC-Mini. This experimental device developed by a psychiatric institute and used to record and analyze patients' dreams for therapeutic purposes. Nonetheless, the brilliant young research psychologist Dr. Atsuko Chiba (voice of Megumi Hayashibara) uses it to treat patients outside the clinic, actually entering her patients' dreams in the form of a delightful and fearless red-headed pixie named Paprika.

While commenting on technology and dreams, Kon also makes clever and humorous use of film allusions to comment on the escapist nature of movies and the blending of truth and fiction. One of the patients Atsuko is treating is a macho police detective by the name of Konakawa (voice of Akio Ôtsuka), who suspiciously resembles the *Spider-Man* film's J. Jonah Jameson with his distinctive flat-top haircut and mustache. He abhors movies but his elaborate recurring nightmare includes an elevator whose stops represent different genres of film—action, romance, adventure—and feature Konakawa as the star of each film. *Paprika*'s opening scene also chronicles his John Malkovich-esque circus nightmare where all the performers morph into facsimiles of him.

When four of the DC-Minis go missing, along with the research assistant Himuro (voice of Daisuke Sakagu-chi), someone starts using the devices for their own nefarious purposes, namely entering the dreams of Atsuko's colleagues and trapping them in implanted dreams and nightmares that carry over into their waking state. Accompanying Atsuko in the search for the missing devices is the inventor of the DC-Mini, the morbidly obese genius, Dr. Kosaku Tokita (voice of Tôru Furuya) and the wise department chief Dr. Torataro Shima (voice of Katsunosuke Hori). The chief also brings in his old friend Konakawa to investigate. Looming ominously in the background are the shady corporate chairman Inui (voice of Toru Emori) and his handsome right hand man, Osanai (voice of Kôichi Yamadera).

Kon's point is to illustrate and question how technology and machines have affected the human experience. As both the detective and Atsuko chase down the missing devices, reality starts to blur with dreams, with the barriers eventually completely disappearing. Kon also gives more than a passing nod to animation legend Disney, when Atsuko looks for clues to the missing DC-Minis by entering people's dreams, she morphs into versions of Tinkerbell, Pinocchio, and the Little Mermaid. While being transported to an unnatural amusement park, Paprika is nearly killed by a mysterious, giant geisha doll-like creature that keeps appearing throughout the dreams. The detective uses a surreal Internet site called the Radio Club that eerily reveals his own past. In one dream, he is sitting at the bar with Paprika who says, "Don't you think dreams and the Internet are similar? They are both where the repressed conscious mind vents."

Atsuko and Paprika splinter more and more into distinct personas and the dream world they inhabit, while Konakawa similarly becomes more engrossed in his own alternate reality. It initially seems as if Himuro is behind the chaos, but when Tokita enters the dangerous dream world to get some answers from his former assistant, he is soon taken hostage by the madness of the dream, as are all who dare enter. It is revealed that Himuro is not the mastermind controlling the dream, but the chairman and Osanai.

Aided by Shima, Paprika attempts to rescue Himuro and Tokita but is pinned down like a butterfly by Osanai, who reveals he is in love with her alter ego, Atsuko. Konakawa is able to save Paprika from Osanai, finally discovering the root of his recurring nightmare in the process. Eventually, their dreams, along with the dreams of everyone else, begin to merge into one. The result of all the reality tampering that is being effected is a disaster of Godzilla-like proportions, threatening all of Tokyo itself. In a stunning finale, the superhero-like Paprika is ultimately able to defeat the chairman and save the world.

While the myriad plot twists and turns, including an unlikely romance, coupled with the surreal quality of the plot may prove overly challenging. Visually the film offers all manner of charming, bizarre, and enchanting images from a master craftsman. The nonstop, over-the-top dream sequences are especially suited to the three-dimensional and hand-drawn animation that portrays anthropomorphized household appliances assembled in a giant parade: flute-playing frogs, Maneki Neko-beckoning cats, dolls, teddy bears, robots, and the Statue of Liberty sweep by, taking victims into its collective madness of the dream as the parade moves constantly forward. Kon's use of the delightful, original music by Susumu Hirasawa, is judicious and effective.

Kon uses the character of the chairman, who was against the creation of the DC-Mini, to comment upon where technology is ultimately taking the human race. "Science is nothing but a piece of trash before a profound dream."

Hilary White

CREDITS

Paprika: Akio Ohtsuka (Voice)
Tokita Kohsaku: Toru Furuya (Voice)
Jin-nai: Satoshi Kon (Voice)
Origin: Japan
Language: Japanese
Released: 2006
Production: Maruta Jungo, Takiyama Masao; Madhouse; released by Sony Pictures
Directed by: Seishi Minakimi
Written by: Seishi Minakimi, Seishi Minakimi
Cinematography by: Michiya Kato
Music by: Susumu Hirasawa
Sound: Masafumi Mima
Editing: Seyama Takeshi
Art Direction: Nobutaka Ike
MPAA rating: R
Running time: 90 minutes

REVIEWS

Hollywood Reporter Online. October 10, 2006.
Los Angeles Times Online. June 1, 2007.
New York Times Online. May 25, 2007.
San Francisco Chronicle. June 8, 2007, p. E1.
Variety Online. September 5, 2006.
Village Voice Online. May 22, 2007.

QUOTES

Paprika: "Don't you think dreams and the Internet are similar? They are both areas where the repressed conscious mind vents."

TRIVIA

The tall and short bartenders in Paprika's Web site are voiced by director Satoshi Kon, and the original author of the *Paprika* novel, Yasutaka Tsutsui, respectively.

PARIS, JE T'AIME
(Paris, I Love You)

Stories of Love. From the City of Love.
   —Movie tagline
One City. 10 Million Hearts. One Love Story. One Film.
   —Movie tagline
Stories of love from the heart of the city.
   —Movie tagline

Box Office: $4.8 million

Eighteen of Paris' twenty arrondissements, or boroughs, form the setting of *Paris, je t'aime.* As the title suggests, both the city and the vagaries of love are the subjects for the eighteen short films, in French and English, by filmmakers from around the world, each working on a limited budget and shooting schedule. Working from an idea by television director Tristan Carné, producer Emmanuel Benbihy assembled a diverse group of unconventional writers and directors, who see the city, as well as love, quite differently. As with any such anthology, the films, each around five minutes long, range widely in their quality and tone.

Paris, je t'aime begins with Bruno Podalydès's "Montmartre," one of several films in which couples "meet cute." In this case, a young woman (Florence Muller) collapses beside a parked car whose driver (Podalydès himself) comes to her aid. In the second film, "Quais de Seine" by Gurinder Chadha, another young woman (Leïla Bekhti) falls, but the young man (Cyril Descours) hesitates before helping her because she is a Muslim and his loutish friends would not approve. "Quais de Seine" is the most subtle and least didactic of several considerations of the problems facing immigrants or ethnic minorities.

Different varieties of love are treated. Homoerotic love is featured in Gus Van Sant's "Le Marais," one of several entries with trick endings in the manner of O. Henry short stories. A philandering husband (Sergio Castellitto) rediscovers his love for his wife (Miranda Richardson) in Isabel Coixet's "Bastille." Mother love is the focus of Nobuhiro Suwa's "Place de Victories," in which a mother (Juliet Binoche) mourning the death of her young son (Martin Combes) is reunited with him thanks to the supernatural appearance of a cowboy (Willem Dafoe). There are even young vampires (Olga

Kurylenko and Elijah Wood) in love in Vincenzo Natali's charming and funny "Quartier de la Madeleine" and love between mimes (Paul Putner and Yolande Moreau) in Sylvain Chomet's slapstick "Tour Eiffel." A blind French student (Melchior Beslon) and an American actress have a rocky romance in Tom Tykwer's "Faubourg Saint-Denis." The director of *Run, Lola, Run* (1998) uses a speeded-up montage to come close to giving the sense of a complete story.

An American movie star (Maggie Gyllenhaal) loves her drugs in Olivier Assayas' downbeat "Quartier des Enfants Rouges." This seemingly pointless exercise is the weakest entry by far. Also disappointing is Alfonso Cuarón's "Parc Monceau," with a father (Nick Nolte) and daughter (Ludivine Sagnier) strolling toward an unknown destination. Michael Seresin's nighttime cinematography is so dim that the actors are almost unrecognizable. Christopher Doyle is one of the world's greatest cinematographers, but his "Porte de Choisy" is merely stylish with no wit or substance, depicting a salesman (Barbet Schroeder) who caters to hair salons for Asian women. What it is saying about love or Paris is unclear. Barbet, the director of such films as *Reversal of Fortune* (1990), is the only cast member to have appeared in the previous arrondissements anthology, *Six in Paris* (1965), whose contributors included Claude Chabrol, Jean-Luc Godard, and Eric Rohmer.

The most satisfying film in *Paris, je t'aime* is Richard LaGravenese's "Pigalle." Fanny Ardant and Bob Hoskins are apparent strangers who meet and flirt in a bar only for her to follow him to a house of prostitution. LaGravenese keeps the viewer guessing about the nature of their relationship right up to the end—one of the few trick endings that works. It is also amusing to hear Hoskins speak French in his distinctively gruff voice. Though Wes Craven is best known for his horror films (and plays a vampire's victim in "Quartier de la Madeleine"), his "Père-Lachaise" is one of the lightest entries. The ghost of Oscar Wilde (Alexander Payne, who directed the anthology's finale segment) saves the romance of bickering British tourists (Emily Mortimer and Rufus Sewell). Craven wrote his script in two hours and filmed it in two days.

The film most accessible for American audiences is probably Ethan and Joel Coen's slapstick comedy "Tuileries," with a completely silent tourist (Steve Buscemi) waiting for a train in the Metro. In "Quartier Latin," co-directed by Frédéric Auburtin and Gérard Depardieu, a longtime couple (Ben Gazzara and Gena Rowlands) meet in a restaurant to discuss their divorce. While French films are crammed with café scenes, this is the only one in *Paris, je t'aime*. Rowlands, who wrote the "Quartier Latin" script, gives perhaps her least mannered performance since she was a starlet in the 1950s. In

Payne's "14ème Arrondissement," Margo Martindale, as a Denver mail carrier, narrates in amusing, deliberately bad French about her visit to Paris. As in his *Sideways* (2004), Payne has genuine, unforced sympathy for the disappointments experienced by working-class Americans.

Some may complain that *Paris, je t'aime* does not give enough of a sense of Paris as a physical place, despite sumptuous shots of the city, by Auburtin and Benbihy, as transitions between the segments. A sense of the French character, however, as well as the effect of Paris on visitors and expatriates, is clearly conveyed. The idea that almost everyone in Paris knows about films and reads serious books comes across. In "Bastille," the narrating husband says that he read *Sputnik Sweetheart* (2001) to his wife, implying that this Haruki Murakami novel is one with which everyone is familiar.

The consensus of reviewers was that "14ème Arrondissement" is the best segment of *Paris, je t'aime*. Together with the bittersweet emotions of "Quartier Latin," the penultimate entry, it provides a fitting conclusion to this anthology about the joys and sorrows of life and love in Paris.

Michael Adams

CREDITS

Zarka: Leila Bekhti
Marianne: Marianne Faithfull
Elie: Elias McConnell
Gaspard: Gaspard Ulliel
The Tourist: Steve Buscemi
Ana: Catalina Sandino Moreno
Monsieur Henny: Barbet Schroeder
The Husband: Sergio Castellitto
The Wife: Miranda Richardson
The Mistress: Leonor Watling
Suzanne: Juliette Binoche
The Cowboy: Willem Dafoe
The Father: Hippolyte Girardot
Female Mime: Yolanda Moreau
Vincent: Nick Nolte
Claire: Ludivine Sagnier
Bob Leander: Bob Hoskins
Fanny Forestier: Fanny Ardant
Liz: Maggie Gyllenhaal
Sophie: Aissa Maiga
The Tourist: Elijah Wood
Frances: Emily Mortimer
William: Rufus Sewell
Francine: Natalie Portman

Thomas: Melchior Beslon
Cafe Owner: Gerard Depardieu
Ben: Ben Gazzara
Gena: Gena Rowlands
Carol: Margo Martindale
Driver: Bruno Podalydes
Young Woman: Florence Muller
Francois: Cyril Descours
Julie: Julie Bataille
Axel: Axel Kiener
Madame Li: Li Xin
Male Mimie: Paul Putner
Ken: Lionel Dray
Sophie: Seydou Boro
The Vampire: Olga Kurylenko
Origin: France, Liechenstein
Language: English, French
Released: 2006
Production: Claudie Ossard, Emmanuel Benbihy; Victoires International, Pirol Film Productions; released by First Look International
Directed by: Gerard Depardieu, Gurinder Chadha, Gus Van Sant, Joel Coen, Ethan Coen, Walter Salles, Daniela Thomas, Christopher Doyle, Isabel Coixet, Sylvain Chomet, Alfonso Cuaron, Richard LaGravenese, Olivier Assayas, Oliver Schmitz, Vincenzo Natali, Wes Craven, Alexander Payne, Tom Tykwer, Noburhiro Suwa
Written by: Gurinder Chadha, Gus Van Sant, Joel Coen, Ethan Coen, Walter Salles, Daniela Thomas, Christopher Doyle, Isabel Coixet, Sylvain Chomet, Alfonso Cuaron, Richard LaGravenese, Olivier Assayas, Oliver Schmitz, Vincenzo Natali, Wes Craven, Alexander Payne, Tom Tykwer, Noburhiro Suwa
Cinematography by: Christopher Doyle, Mathieu Poirot-Delpech, Pascal Rabaud, Bruno Delbonnel, Eric Gautier, Jean-Claude Larrieu, Pascal Marti, Eric Guichard, Gerard Sterin, Michel Amathieu, Michael Seresin, Pierre Aim, J. Eddie Peck, Tetsuo Nagata, David Quesemand, Frank Greibe
Music by: Tom Tykwer, Michael Andrews, Reinhold Heil, Johnny Klimek
Sound: Capucine Courau
Editing: Luc Barnier, Alex Rodriguez, Anne Klotz, Simon Jacquet, Hisako Suwa, Isabel Meier, Matthias Bonnefoy
Costumes: Olivier Beriot
Production Design: Bettina von den Steinen
MPAA rating: R
Running time: 120 minutes

REVIEWS

Entertainment Weekly. May 18, 2007, p. 51.
Hollywood Reporter Online. May 18, 2006.
New York Times Online. May 4, 2007.
Variety Online. May 18, 2006.
Village Voice Online. May 1, 2007.

QUOTES

Carol: "Sitting there, alone in a foreign country, far from my job and everyone I know, a feeling came over me. It was like remembering something I'd never known before or had always been waiting for, but I didn't know what. Maybe it was something I'd forgotten or something I've been missing all my life. All I can say is that I felt, at the same time, joy and sadness. But not too much sadness, because I felt alive. Yes, alive. That was the moment I fell in love with Paris. And I felt Paris fall in love with me."

TRIVIA

The segment "Parc Monceau" directed by Alfonso Cuarón was shot in a single continuous shot.

PATHFINDER

Two Worlds, One War. The Ultimate Battle Begins.
—Movie tagline
An Untold Legend.
—Movie tagline

Box Office: $10.2 million

Pathfinder is a movie about the clash of civilizations before there is any historical record that such a clash took place, sometime during the muddle that was the Middle Ages, near the tenth century AD, between American Indians and the Viking hoards, who were not so very civilized after all and were at the time developing a negative reputation throughout Europe as barbarian invaders and marauders. The picture was directed by Marcus Nispel, who was earlier involved in the remake of *The Texas Chainsaw Massacre* (2003), and written by Laeta Kalogridis. The Norsemen were famous for their epic sagas, but viewers should not be misled by that assumption. This picture, which, be warned, has nothing at all to do with James Fenimore Cooper and classic American literature, has all the epic grandeur of a comic book that some might call a graphic novel. It was originally scheduled for a much earlier release, twice, in fact, in 2006, but the release date kept being delayed and postponed, never a good sign that the distributor has faith in the picture.

The film is verbally impeded, but there is a hero of sorts, played by Karl Urban, a Norseman who had been abandoned to the Indians and lived among them for fifteen years. His name is "Ghost," though no one in the film actually refers to him as "Ghost." He does come and go like a ghostly (if not ghastly) apparition. His genetic background and racial memory works to the advantage of the tribe that raised him, since he is therefore able to prepare and help them to fight newly arrived Viking invaders. As a boy, Ghost is rescued by an Indian woman of the Wampanoag tribe, who raises him as if he were her own offspring. The film begins with her walking through the snow along the treeline toward the coast and into the wreckage of a Viking longship, littered with corpses; there she finds a survivor, a boy, who clutches a Viking sword. Later, in a dream flashback, viewers are treated to the boy's memory of being ordered to use the sword to kill an Indian, but he refuses, and is whipped and punished, this apparently before the ship was mysteriously reduced to rubble. This revulsion against violence would seem to indicate that he is different from his ancestors, more respectful of human life. The racist assumption here seems to be that the Vikings can only be defeated by one of their own. At any rate, the woman takes the boy to her village, where a pow-wow is held to decide whether to kill him or let him live. These noble Indians have mercy, however, and the woman's husband tells the boy: "You were born to the dragonmen, but you are ours." (It may come as a surprise to learn that these Indians have heard of dragons and to hear Norse barbarians quoting from the Old Testament, for example, "An eye for an eye.")

Thus the boy is adopted by "The People of the Dawn." Cut to fifteen years later, and the boy has grown into young manhood. Pathfinder (Russell Means), the spiritual leader and shaman of the "People of the Dawn," comes calling on a trading mission to the village where the boy has grown up. Pathfinder's successor, he informs his followers, was killed in an avalanche and so he needs to select a new successor, but the Viking boy clearly does not qualify as a candidate. The Pathfinder arrives just ahead of another, more menacing crisis: a new flotilla of Viking longships is about to arrive. The Viking boy's village is razed and his parents slaughtered, providing a powerful motive for revenge, the engine that drives the rest of the film.

The adopted "Ghost" quickly assumes a leadership position. Pathfinder has told him (in Medieval psychobabble) that he needs to "confront the demons of his past," and so he sets of with a single sidekick to intercept the Norse army. The Vikings are more valorous than smart, however, and they are oddly prone to announce their coming by strange trumpeting on animal horns. This gives Ghost an edge in stopping these Norsemen hellbent on genocide. He wages guerilla warfare with some success, barely escaping with his life after a chase scene that looks like a primitive sledding competition from the Winter Olympics. The Pathfinder finds a wounded boy, patches him up, faces down a grizzly bear by outgrowling him, and then uses a mumbling spell to heal the young warrior, who eventually will set out again on his revenge quest, followed by the Pathfinder's daughter Starfire (Moon Bloodgood), who has taken a fancy to

the young Norseman. Despite getting in the way, she is feisty, and in the end, she presides over a conflict between the young warrior and a Norse captain that can only be described as a "cliffhanger."

Despite the scenic beauty of British Columbia where this movie was filmed, reviewers were not kind. *Entertainment Weekly* reviewer Lisa Schwarzbaum complained, for example, that "music-video director Marcus Nispel" could not "distinguish between people and tree trunks when it comes to emotional content," a complaint that is supported by the grunting, barking, monosyllabic dialogue, some of it sounding Germanic and explained by subtitles. (All native Canadian dialogue seems conveniently to be in English.) In the *New York Times* Manohla Dargis dismissed this gory "splatterfest" as a "witless action flick." The best he could say is that director Marcus Nispel "takes his butchery very seriously." Noting that this film fantasy allows "no time for accuracy, credibility, or characterization," Anna Smith wrote in her *Sight & Sound* review that *Pathfinder* "has all the emotional depth of a three-minute music video, and the excitable camerawork to match."

From start to finish, Nispel delivers a bloody, bad, and repulsive spectacle, rather like *Apocalypto* (2006) on ice, with shades of Sergei Eisenstein's Teutonic knights at the end of his World War II propaganda epic *Alexander Nevsky* (1938). In Eisenstein's film the brutal and barbaric invaders killed women and children and advanced against the noble Russians like faceless machines of death and destruction. The Vikings of *Pathfinder* are also hairy, faceless beasts, wrapped in fur and chain mail, and wearing absurdly horned helmets that wrap around where their faces should be, showing only hostile eyes and menacing teeth. Not that there is much that is visually original here, though maybe there is something new in the terrible conclusion, when Ghost leads the Vikings over a mountain pass and into an avalanche, that ultimately wipes them out.

At the end, the Norse invaders are all dead and the Viking menace resolved, at least for the time being. The Pathfinder has also been killed, but the young warrior passes the totemic rabbit's foot he wore around his neck on to his daughter, who is then acknowledged as the new "Pathfinder." The film ends in peace and harmony with a glorious Canadian sunset. All of this happened 600 years before the coming of Christopher Columbus to the New World (though several reviewers pegged it at 500 years, despite the film's inter-title). Of all the films having to do with the European discoveries of America, Terence Malick's *The New World* (2005) is the only one worth notice, but that picture could boast a cast that included Colin Farrell, Christian Bale, Christopher Plummer, and Wes Studi. The only recognizable actor in the cast of *Pathfinder* is Native American Russell Means, demonstrating that this Viking horror show was outclassed by acting talent and budget, and a sense of history rather than "legend." Too bad the screenwriter could not have turned to an epic source, such as Snorri Sturlason's *Edda* or Saemund's *Poetic Edda*, rather than an earlier film (acknowledged in the credits) written and directed in 1987 by Nils Gaup, apparently based on an ancient Lapp fable, and also entitled *Pathfinder*. That one was good enough for an Academy Award nomination. Despite a soundtrack that apparently attempts to echo the "Carmina Burana," this remake does not even come close. It deserves the ridicule some critics gave it. In the *Washington Post* Stephen Hunter wrote that this movie made *Conan the Barbarian* (1982) "seem like Dostoyevsky in its complexity." Many others wisely chose simply to ignore it.

James M. Welsh

CREDITS

Ghost: Karl Urban
Pathfinder: Russell Means
Starfire: Moon Bloodgood
Gunnar: Clancy Brown
Ulfar: Ralph (Ralf) Moeller
Blackwing: Jay Tavare
Gunnar: Clancy Brown
Origin: USA
Language: English
Released: 2007
Production: Mike Medavoy, Arnold W. Messer, Marcus Nispel; Dune Entertainment, Phoenix Pictures, Major Entertainment Partners; released by 20th Century-Fox
Directed by: Marcus Nispel
Written by: Laeta Kalogridis
Cinematography by: Daniel Pearl
Music by: Jonathan Elias
Sound: Trevor Jolly
Editing: Glen Scantlebury, Jay Friedkin
Costumes: Renee April
Production Design: Gregory Blair
MPAA rating: R
Running time: 99 minutes

REVIEWS

Boxoffice Online. April 13, 2007.
Detroit News. April 13, 2007, p. 3F.
Entertainment Weekly. April 18, 2007.
Los Angeles Times Online. April 13, 2007.
New York Times Online. April 13, 2007.
San Francisco Chronicle. April 13, 2007, p. E5.

Variety Online. April 12, 2007.
Washington Post. April 13, 2007, p. C5.

TRIVIA

Actors wore hockey shoulder pads underneath their viking costume to make them appear larger and fiercer.

PERFECT STRANGER

How far will you go to keep a secret?
—Movie tagline

Box Office: $23.9 million

Halle Berry is regularly positioned near the top on lists of the world's most beautiful women, and *Perfect Stranger* seems dedicated to capitalizing on that fact. Ostensibly a movie about the intersection of rich, powerful, potentially murderous men and their victims, it is really an opportunity to capitalize on Berry's beauty. Director James Foley's murder-mystery film seems focused only when his camera is closing in on Berry, which is often. Otherwise, it seems a bit lost in its own overcooked and under-compelling sociopolitical potboiler.

Berry plays Rowena Price, a postmodern Lois Lane who is out not to woo supermen, but to topple them. As a reporter for the "New York Courier," she specializes in nailing her powerful prey by exposing their scandalous underbellies. To aid in her undercover operations, she writes under a male pseudonym and partners with a fellow reporter, techie genius, Miles Haley (Giovanni Ribisi). As the film begins, their clever sting operation to nail a powerful Republican senator in a sex scandal with a male intern is aborted when her newspaper pulls the plug on the story for political reasons. Rowena is outraged and quits the paper.

However, she does not end her partnership with Miles nor her quest to right wrongs, especially those perpetrated by big-shot white men. When a mysterious longtime friend, Grace Clayton (Nicki Aycox), is murdered after confiding in her about a fling with a powerful ad agency head, Harrison Hill (Bruce Willis), Rowena and Miles decide to independently go after Harrison. He is the prime suspect in their minds, so they leave the police to fend for themselves without a bit of key information Rowena gleaned from her last conversation with Grace. The film then slides into a slow, slippery, and sleazy cat-and-mouse game in which Miles persuades Rowena to act as bait to catch Harrison. Not surprisingly, since this movie's main attraction is Berry, her methods consist of salacious online chats while posing as one of Harrison's former love interests and getting a position as a head-turning temp at Harrison's agency.

These twin strategies to flush out Harrison allow Foley to play with viewers' presumed desire to see Berry flirt verbally and physically, using her feminine wiles to pin down Harrison as a kinky adulterer with the means, the motive, and the intent to have murdered Grace. While Berry seductively goes after her target, incriminating evidence keeps piling up incrementally, mostly in breathless telephone calls from Miles, who is also working the story: Grace was poisoned with belladonna, which Harrison's artist wife has an interest in and knowledge of; Grace was pregnant; and Grace was connected with Harrison through a trail of online contacts.

So if viewers must endure a brutal number of Rowena's instant-message computer chats with Harrison, monitored and helped along by Miles, who sees himself as Rowena's computer instructor (Berry presumably never having had to resort to such a means to romance a man). As usual in films, the chat boxes seem to take up the entire computer monitor (and the screen), and the conversation is both laughably lame and bawdy, like snippets of dialogue from a porn movie.

Only slightly less ridiculous is Rowena's sojourn in the advertising agency. Soon taken in tow by an office gossip who tells her everything about Harrison's extramarital excursions, Rowena immerses herself in a land of seductively dressed female employees all preening for the boss. We learn that his wife has reined in Harrison after a couple of embarrassing sexual harassment lawsuits. His affairs are now guarded by an Amazonian lesbian gatekeeper (an extremely stereotypical character) who shadows him every second (except when it is convenient for the plot that she does not). Naturally, the boss takes an immediate interest in his new hire.

All this takes up the bulk of the movie, during which viewers see Berry in various cleavage-enhancing dresses, flashing numerous audacious and flirty glances, and moving her lips provocatively as she types naughty come-ons. Just for diversion, they also watch her clutching and groping at the end of a real date with an actual boyfriend. The camera is a slave to Berry's desire, teasing the viewer with a variety of sexy poses and a seemingly endless number of close-ups of Berry's face and, often, just her mouth. Foley loves close-ups, which work well with Berry, but not so well with Willis, whose face in close-up looks bloated and almost bovine.

Probably the most remarkable thing about *Perfect Stranger* is that Berry survives this treatment with her dignity intact. It is one of the actress' many talents that she can completely inhabit such a blatantly exploitative role yet manage to be believable as a woman of integrity. Berry can be adorably cute, sizzlingly seductive, and powerfully intelligent and forceful not just by turns, but sometimes all in the same take. She has never been more appealing. Yet the film is so tawdry (despite its veneer of glamour) and her character so unconvincingly contradictory (seemingly savvy and naïve at the same time) that her performance is sunk by the script. Viewers get the impression that Berry is simply enjoying herself playing with a role that shows off all her talents to maximum effect, withoug asking her to stretch herself.

Meanwhile, the plot's bloated red herrings pile up on the shoreline of the film. Obviously Harrison cannot really be everything he seems—the damning evidence is too obvious. It is also quite clear that Miles is not everything he seems to be, either, as the dialogue reminds viewers at several points that appearances are misleading. Unfortunately, these machinations set up a plot twist that has to be revealed unexpectedly in a lengthy dump of exposition exactly where the climax should be. Viewers may find satisfaction in the final shot of this clever, convoluted, and largely unsatisfying film.

In fact, the economy of the film's beginning and closing scenes would have served the entire movie well. As it is, however, viewers are so bogged down in shots of Berry's lips mouthing salacious teasing phrases that *Perfect Stranger* ends up being laughably bad, pseudo-sophisticated soft porn packaged lumpily within a couple snippets of a taut psychological thriller. Pairing squinty-eyed and bland-faced Willis with Berry was unfortunate. Their interplay has all the chemistry promised by the clumsy "hey baby" online banter of their characters—that of a doltish predator and his enticingly packaged prey. Ribisi is better, however, as he is both amusing and creepy. Willis is neither.

Berry does not exactly rise above this material; she supercedes it. It is almost immaterial to her star turn here. To her credit, Berry has often chosen more challenging parts, so she deserves a film where the camera simply laps her up and she gets to play cute and sassy and sexy. After all, that is all that Hollywood usually expects of a leading lady. Yet Berry can, and should, do better.

Michael Betzold

CREDITS

Rowena Price: Halle Berry
Harrison Hill: Bruce Willis
Miles: Giovanni Ribisi
Narron: Richard Portnow
Grace: Nicki Aycox
Cameron: Gary Dourdan
Elizabeth Clayton: Kathleen Chalfant
Lt. Tejada: Florencia Lozano

Origin: USA
Language: English
Released: 2007
Production: Elaine Goldsmith-Thomas; Revolution Studios; released by Sony Pictures
Directed by: James Foley
Written by: Todd Komarnicki
Cinematography by: Anastas Michos
Music by: Antonio Pinto
Sound: Allan Byer
Music Supervisor: Denise Luiso
Editing: Christopher Tellefsen
Art Direction: Charley Beal
Costumes: Renee Ehrlich Kalfus
Production Design: Bill Groom
MPAA rating: R
Running time: 109 minutes

REVIEWS

Chicago Sun-Times Online. April 13, 2007.
Entertainment Weekly Online. April 11, 2007.
Hollywood Reporter Online. April 12, 2007.
Los Angeles Times Online. April 13, 2007.
New York Times Online. April 13, 2007.
San Francisco Chronicle. April 13, 2007, p. E1.
Variety Online. April 12, 2007.
Washington Post. April 13, 2007, p. C1.

QUOTES

Rowena: "All it takes to commit a murder are the right ingredients at the right time."

TRIVIA

The filmmakers filmed three different endings to the film, each with a different character as the killer.

PERFUME: THE STORY OF A MURDERER

He lived to find beauty. He killed to possess it.
—Movie tagline

Box Office: $2.2 million

Tom Tykwer's *Perfume: The Story of a Murderer* is an adaptation of what movie-making giants Stanley Kubrick and Martin Scorsese deemed to be utterly unfilmable, the novel by German writer Patrick Süskind originally published in Germany as *Das Parfum*. *Perfume* attempts to present the book's olfactory prose in panoramic visualization, where the camera leans on the

viewer's memory of various smells as it scans over a set depicting the filthy rat-infested streets of eighteenth-century Paris. The dilemma is an understandable one. How does one describe the ineffable sensory realm of scents?

Not straying far from the novel's plot, Tykwer's film opens near the story's climax when it is learned that the protagonist, Jean-Baptiste Grenouille (Ben Whishaw), is due to be executed for the murders of thirteen young women. It is significant that the character's name translates to "frog." Like that amphibian, Grenouille's inner world is a simple one confined to stimulus and response. Similar to a person demonstrating the signature traits of a true schizoid, Grenouille is detached from humanity, socially inept, and completely indifferent to praise and criticism. His personality seems completely bereft of any emotional construction. Ben Whishaw convincingly conveys this oddity with his vacuous expressions and flattened affect.

Grenouille's sole interest is to capture and preserve the essence of the perfect scent derived from beautiful women in the prime of their lives. This obsession leads him on a serial killing spree. However, unlike most serial killers who take pathological pleasure in the hunting and/or killing of their victims, Grenouille is incapable of this sick euphoria. His goal is simply to create the most seductive fragrance. Dustin Hoffman eccentrically plays Grenouille's mentor, Giuseppe Baldini, as a master craftsman in the field of perfume making. Baldini likens the process to composing music and the search for the perfectly resonating note. Grenouille quickly surpasses this odd man, whose perfume shop is nestled on an overcrowded bridge overlooking the Seine. What makes Grenouille such a prodigy is that he was bestowed from birth with a supernatural sense of smell that would cause a bloodhound to resemble an anosmatic by comparison. Mimicking nature's odd imbalance, Grenouille's uncanny ability is coupled with a strange condition: he exudes no personal scent whatsoever. This deficit set him up as an outcast among the wet nurses in the orphanage he was raised in prior to being sold to a tanner, where he endured more cruelty and hardships as he lived a slave's existence.

Once Baldini gives him his journeyman papers, Grenouille sets of for Grasse, where he wishes to learn the science of enfleurage, the extraction of aromas from flowers. It is here that Grenouille begins his ghastly carnage, holding to Baldini's musical model to procure the perfect scent. He is able to complete his perfect creation by murdering the daughter of a prominent aristocrat (superbly played by Alan Rickman). This also leads the authorities to him. Thus far they have been baffled by the murders as none of the naked corpses display any sign of rape or other sexual violation. The perfume he has developed evokes euphoria and feelings of amorous regard for those who smell it. A tiny amount not only causes the French court to reverse its decision to execute him, but the entire crowd assembled for his hanging is subject to a pheromonal event, as the perfume in larger quantities serves as a maddening aphrodisiac, causing the gathered villagers to be caught up in a frenzied orgy. Grenouille remains largely unaffected by its potent effect. Yet the screenplay allows for a single display of emotion, when from the gallows platform as he witnesses romp below a tear rolls down his cheek.

John Hurt narrates Grenouille's story due to the young man's isolation and his penchant for monosyllabic responses. Exonerated, Grenouille returns to Paris in despondency as he realizes that harnessing the properties of the perfect scent has failed to generate a capacity to love or cause others to love him authentically. He pours the remainder of the perfume over himself in front of group representing the dross of Parisian society. The effect is that of a powerful hallucinogenic, which causes the crowd to consume both his flesh and essence, leaving nothing more of him save his clothing and, poignantly, an empty bottle of perfume.

Roger Ebert of the *Chicago Sun-Times* was especially engrossed with all versions of this tale from the novel and audiobook to the film. Of it he wrote, "There is nothing fun about this story, except the way it ventures so fearlessly down one limited, terrifying, seductive dead end, and finds there a solution both sublime and horrifying. It took imagination to tell it, courage to film it, and act it, and from the audience it requires a brave curiosity about the peculiarity of obsession."

David M. Roberts

CREDITS

Jean-Baptiste Grenouille: Ben Whishaw
Giuseppe Baldini: Dustin Hoffman
Antoine Richis: Alan Rickman
Laura Richis: Rachel Hurd-Wood
Mme. Arnulfi: Corinna Harfouch
Narrator: John Hurt
Origin: Spain, France, Germany
Language: English
Released: 2006
Production: Bernd Eichinger; Constantin Film, Nouvelles Editions de Films, Castelao Proucciones, Rising Star; released by Paramount
Directed by: Tom Tykwer
Written by: Tom Tykwer, Andrew Birkin, Bernd Eichinger
Cinematography by: Frank Griebe
Music by: Tom Tykwer, Johnny Klimek, Reinhold Heil

Sound: Roland Winke, Matthias Lempert
Editing: Alexander Berner
Art Direction: Laia Colet
Costumes: Pierre-Yves Gayraud
Production Design: Uli Hanisch
MPAA rating: R
Running time: 145 minutes

REVIEWS

Boxoffice Online. December 27, 2006.
Chicago Sun-Times Online. January 5, 2007.
Hollywood Reporter Online. October 19, 2006.
Los Angeles Times Online. December 27, 2006.
New York Times Online. December 27, 2006.
Premiere Magazine Online. December 27, 2006.
Variety Online. October 4, 2006.
Village Voice Online. December 26, 2006.

TRIVIA

As of 2006, this is the most expensive German film ever made.

PIRATES OF THE CARIBBEAN: AT WORLD'S END

At the End of the World, the Adventure Begins.
   —Movie tagline

Box Office: $309.4 million

Historians have said that nothing unites a people better than a common enemy. In *Pirates of the Caribbean: At World's End* the common enemy is the conniving Lord Cutler Beckett (Tom Hollander), Chairman of the British East India Trading Company, whose hatred for the pirates unites the normally fractious cutthroats of the world. Historians also wax prolific about how businesses and governments work together for profit, and here not only does Beckett rely on the vast British Navy for support, he also has command of the supernatural Davy Jones (Bill Nighy) and his ghostly ship, *the Flying Dutchman.*

To end piracy, Lord Beckett has imposed martial law and suspended habeas corpus wherever the long arm of Britain reaches, summarily hanging men, women, and children whom he even slightly suspects of fostering piracy. Stopping Lord Beckett requires that the Nine Lords of the Brethren Court—all pirate captains—gather together and pool their pieces of eight. Unfortunately for the Brethren, one of the Lords is Captain Jack Sparrow (Johnny Depp), who is trapped in Davy Jones'

Locker. So, in order to save the world of the pirates, they must first rescue Jack Sparrow.

This is the primary plot of the third installment of the *Pirates of the Caribbean* trilogy. After the second installment, *Pirates of the Caribbean: Dead Man's Chest* came out in 2006, it left so many loose threads that they had to be woven together in this latest endeavor, and critics have made counting the numerous subplots in *At World's End* an integral part of their reviews. The pirates must obtain a map from Captain Sao Feng (Chow Yun-Fat); save Will Turner's (Orlando Bloom) father Bootstrap Bill (Stellan Skarsgård) from his servitude on Jones' ship; and unite the Brethren's nine pieces of eight to free the sea goddess Calypso, who is currently captured in human form as Tia Dalma (Naomi Harris). Captain Barbossa (Geoffrey Rush) fights with Sparrow over the captaincy of the *Black Pearl,* and the on-again, off-again love story between Will and Elizabeth Swann (Keira Knightley) ensues. With so many characters changing their allegiances and following their own private agendas, writers Ted Elliott and Terry Rossio are often forced to halt the action in order to deliver explanations of the characters' actions and further create the mythology behind the *Pirates of the Caribbean* franchise.

The result of this sea of plotlines—the press kit contends that there are fifteen major plot lines—accompanying a vast amount of action is that director Gore Verbinski's film runs nearly three hours long. After all that, the audience is also expected to keep watching as the end credits roll or miss a touching piece of story epilogue.

At World's End was filmed concurrently with the second film *Pirates of the Caribbean: Dead Man's Chest,* which means that unlike the first installment, *The Curse of the Black Pearl,* parts two and three do not stand alone. *Dead Man's Chest* sets up the story for *At World's End,* which in turn completes the story offered in *Dead Man's Chest,* which requires the audience to see both to be fully satisfied. Despite this, *Dead Man's Chest,* as of this writing, was the third highest grossing movie in international box-office history, with earnings of $650 million worldwide. Until this enormously successful franchise based on an amusement park ride came about, pirate movies did not fare well at the box office, a fact that further underscores these films' remarkable achievement.

Labyrinthine plot aside, *At World's End* and its two predecessors are consistently quality products. All deliver high production values (courtesy of production designer Rick Heinrichs), gorgeous photography (cinematographer Dariusz Wolski), breathtaking action sequences with unbelievable stunts (stunt coordinator George Mar-

shall Ruge), awesome special effects (visual effects supervisors John Knoll and Charles Gibson) and rousing music (Hans Zimmer).

Adding most to the franchise's success, however, is the character of Jack Sparrow. The mincing, morally compromised, quirky cutthroat created by Johnny Depp carries the films. Although Captain Sparrow shows up late in this installment, he is given a choice opportunity to showcase his character by acting against an army of his own duplicates. It is well known that Depp was inspired by a combination of a Rastafarian, the cartoon skunk Pepe Le Pew, and Rolling Stones guitarist Keith Richards when he created the Sparrow character. So despite an arguably disappointing cameo, it is both amusing and rewarding to see Richards show up as Captain Teague, the Keeper of the Code and Sparrow's mentor and father, thus putting the final flourish on the *Pirates* series.

Beverley Bare Buehrer

CREDITS

Capt. Jack Sparrow: Johnny Depp
Elizabeth Swann: Keira Knightley
Will Turner: Orlando Bloom
Barbossa: Geoffrey Rush
Davy Jones: Bill Nighy
Sao Feng: Chow Yun-Fat
Admiral James Norrington: Jack Davenport
Bootstrap Bill Turner: Stellan Skarsgard
Gov. Weatherby Swann: Jonathan Pryce
Tia Dalma: Naomie Harris
Lord Cutler Beckett: Tom Hollander
Joshamee Gibbs: Kevin McNally
Ragetti: Mackenzie Crook
Marty: Martin Klebba
Pintel: Lee Arenberg
Sumbhajee Angria: Marshall Manesh
Origin: USA
Language: English
Released: 2007
Directed by: Gore Verbinski
Written by: Terry Rossio, Ted Elliott
Cinematography by: Dariusz Wolski
Music by: Hans Zimmer
MPAA rating: PG-13
Running time: 168 minutes

REVIEWS

Boston Globe Online. May 23, 2007.
Chicago Sun-Times Online. May 24, 2007.

Entertainment Weekly Online. May 23, 2007.
Hollywood Reporter Online. May 24, 2007.
Los Angeles Times Online. May 23, 2007.
New York Times Online. May 24, 2007.
Rolling Stone Online. May 22, 2007.
San Francisco Chronicle. May 24, 2007, p. E1.
Variety Online. May 22, 2007.
Washington Post. May 24, 2007, p. C1.

QUOTES

Barbossa: "The only way for a pirate to make a living these days is by betraying other pirates."

TRIVIA

Filming was started without a finished script.

AWARDS

Nomination:

Oscars 2007: Makeup, Visual FX
British Acad. 2007: Visual FX
Golden Raspberries 2007: Worst Support. Actor (Bloom)
Screen Actors Guild 2008: Outstanding Performance by a Stunt Ensemble in a Motion Picture.

PREMONITION

> *Reality is only a nightmare away.*
> —Movie tagline

> *It's not your imagination.*
> —Movie tagline

Box Office: $47.8 million

Time warp dramas have become a staple of Hollywood in the current millennia, beginning with films like *Memento* (2000) and continuing with *Donnie Darko* (2001), *Deja Vu* (2006), and another Sandra Bullock romance, *The Lake House* (2006). Although the once innovative idea of time travel with a twist is growing fusty, it can provide a suitably suspenseful framework for a psychological drama with a cohesive plot, something *Premonition* lacks.

A sweet opening prologue (filmed in de-saturated color to indicate it is not the present), finds protagonist Linda Hanson (Sandra Bullock) and her handsome husband Jim (Julian McMahon) newly ensconced in their first home. Ten years later, they have two daughters—ten-year-old Bridgette (Courtney Taylor Burness) and six-year-old Megan (Shyann McClure)—Linda is a stay-at-home mom, and their marriage has gone stale.

It is Thursday morning and Jim is expected home from a business trip. Linda does her usual routine: takes the girls to school, goes running, and cleans the house. She listens to an answering machine message but is confused when Jim says that he meant what he said in front of the girls. Then Sheriff Reilly (Marc Macaulay) comes to the door and tells her that Jim was killed in a car accident on Wednesday (there is no explanation as to why notification took so long)—a semi truck jack-knifed coming over the hill at Mile Marker 220. Linda's mother, Joanne (Kate Nelligan), comes over and Linda falls asleep on the couch in her clothes.

When she wakes up in bed in a nightgown to find that her mother is not in the house, it is Monday, and Jim and the girls are having breakfast, she believes she has had a nightmare. Linda goes through the same daily routine except she trips and falls in the backyard, where she puts her hand on a portentously bloody, dead crow that she throws in the garbage can. After falling asleep with Jim, Linda wakes up wearing one of Jim's shirts and finds the other side of the bed is empty. She also finds an empty bottle of lithium prescribed by a Dr. Norman Roth (Peter Stormare) and pills in her bathroom sink. She goes downstairs where Jim's wake is in progress. The girls are outside and Bridgette's face is covered with cuts and stitches but Linda has no idea what happened.

At the cemetery, Linda notices a mysterious blonde lurking around and she confronts her. The blonde says they talked yesterday—Linda does not remember. It is Saturday. That evening, Dr. Roth comes to the house; Joanne called him, thinking that Linda is having a breakdown and has her committed. At the hospital, Linda hears Roth tell the sheriff that Linda first came to see him on Tuesday, claiming that she knew her husband was going to die. The doctor gives her a sedative and when Linda wakes up, Jim is alive and taking a shower and Bridgette's face is fine (but the dead crow is still in the garbage can). Thoroughly confused and frightened, Linda goes to see Dr. Roth (it is Tuesday) and tells him, "I wake up and he's dead. I wake up and he's alive." He prescribes the lithium to help Linda cope. When she next goes to Jim's office and meets the new assistant manager—Claire (Amber Valletta), the mystery blonde, Linda is suspicious. At home, she starts to take a couple of pills but drops the bottle in the sink. It begins to rain and the girls rush to get inside; Bridgette is running and goes through the glass doorwall. After they get home from the hospital, Linda covers up the mirrors so Bridgette will not have to look at her marred face.

Frantic and afraid she may be losing her mind, Linda decides to make a chart of the days: Monday, Jim is at the office; Tuesday is Bridgette's accident and Linda sees Dr. Roth; Wednesday, Jim goes on his business trip and dies; Thursday, Linda is notified; Saturday is the funeral. That leaves Friday and the previous Sunday unaccounted for. Jim refuses to cancel his business trip but Linda makes him promise that he will wake her before he leaves. When Linda wakes up again she is on the couch, it is Friday, and Jim is dead. Linda goes to see Claire and discovers that she and Jim were supposed to meet in a hotel room. Linda also goes to the bank and learns that Jim went there on Wednesday morning and suddenly tripled his death benefits policy. Linda calmly makes funeral arrangements.

As expected, she wakes to find it is Sunday and Jim is lying next to her. Linda goes to church and talks to Father Kennedy (Jude Ciccolella), who tells her that premonitions are not uncommon. They talk about faith and how "faith is believing in something beyond yourself." Linda does not think she has any faith, although Father Kennedy replies, "It's never too late to realize what's important in your life. To fight for it." Linda drives out to Mile Marker 220 and tries to imagine what happened (or will happen).

When the family spends Sunday evening together, Linda is insistent that the girls give their father an extra hug and that Jim tell them how much he loves them. He also tells his daughters that he still loves their mother very much. Linda goes outside (a storm is starting) and she and Jim argue about their marriage. Lightning strikes the electric wires and Linda sees an electrocuted crow fall to the ground. Back in their bedroom, they are both subdued. Linda tells Jim that she had a dream that he is going to die. They are close for the first time in a long time.

The next day, Wednesday, Jim drives the girls to school while Linda gets into her car and follows. Jim gets a phone call: It is Claire calling from the hotel, but Jim says he cannot start an affair. Jim then leaves his message for Linda on the answering machine. Then Linda calls to say that she has following him. Jim pulls his car over and Linda notices he has just passed Mile Marker 220. She screams that he has to turn the car around; when he makes a U-turn, Jim nearly hits another car and stalls his own vehicle in the middle of the road. Linda sees the truck coming over the rise and begs Jim to get out of the car. In a rather nasty extended scene, she sees the truck jackknife and hit the car, which explodes. Linda wakes up for the last time to find the house is packed up and the movers are there and when she arises, it is obvious she is pregnant. She remembers what Father Kennedy told her about faith as the screen fades to black.

Considering the time-warp nature of *Premonition*, the plot is actually quite simple to follow, particularly after Linda makes her chart and the viewer can also start to surmise what happens when. The biggest change is

Linda's realization that she can only do so much. She calms after seemingly admitting that she cannot prevent Jim's death and thus stops her own odd and hysterical behavior, so Dr. Roth does not have her committed (this is implied). The film poses the question of whether or not is it Linda's fault that Jim dies. Perhaps if she did not drive after him and call his cellphone, he would not have turned around and stalled his car in the road. When the sheriff initially comes to the house, it seems Jim was fated to die in a car crash regardless of Linda's actions. The rather odd conversation Linda has with Father Kennedy implies that Linda can only realize what is important to her and what is worth fighting for if Jim dies. They achieved a tentative reconciliation first and now Linda will have the new baby.

Premonition is presented as moody and low-key with lots of silences, lingering glances, and brooding. Clichéd horror screeches are heard when Linda pulls open the shower curtain for instance—an intentional mood choice on director Mennan Yapo's part. The color palette is subdued—golden lighting and autumnal hues. Ultimately, the film rests on Bullock's capable shoulders since McMahon has little to do but look annoyed or worried. The two young actresses playing the daughters are suitably adorable. However, viewers are kept at a distance and cannot become emotionally invested. It is too bad that Jim dies, but how nice that Linda is not crazy after all.

Christine Tomassini

CREDITS

Linda Hanson: Sandra Bullock
Jim Hanson: Julian McMahon
Annie: Nia Long
Joanne: Kate Nelligan
Claire: Amber Valletta
Dr. Norman Roth: Peter Stormare
Bridgette: Courtney Taylor Burness
Megan: Shyann McClure
Origin: USA
Language: English
Released: 2007
Production: Ashok Amritraj, Jon Jashni, Adam Shankman, Jennifer Gibgot; Offspring Entertainment, Hyde Park Entertainment, TriStar Pictures; released by Sony Pictures Entertainment
Directed by: Mennan Yapo
Written by: Bill Kelly
Cinematography by: Torsten Lippstock
Music by: Klaus Badelt
Sound: Steve Aaron

Music Supervisor: Buck Damon
Editing: Neil Travis
Art Direction: Thomas T. Taylor
Costumes: Jill Ohanneson
Production Design: Dennis Washington
MPAA rating: PG-13
Running time: 97 minutes

REVIEWS

Boston Globe Online. March 16, 2007.
Chicago Sun-Times Online. March 16, 2007.
Detroit Free Press Online. March 16, 2007.
Detroit News Online. March 16, 2007, p. 1F.
Entertainment Weekly. March 23, 2007, p. 46.
Hollywood Reporter Online. March 12, 2007.
Los Angeles Times Online. March 16, 2007.
New York Times Online. March 16, 2007.
San Francisco Chronicle. March 16, 2007, p. E5.
Variety Online. March 11, 2007.
Washington Post Online. March 16, 2007.

QUOTES

Linda (muttering in reply to Jim's saying his overnight trip will be a good break for them): "Might be a bigger break than you bargained for."

TRIVIA

Turkish-German director Mennan Yapo makes his English-language feature debut with this film.

PRIDE

There are no shortcuts to a dream.
—Movie tagline

Reach for it with everything you've got.
—Movie tagline

Two can reach higher than one. Eight will touch a miracle.
—Movie tagline

Box Office: $7 million

Pride treads the familiar territory of the inspirational sports film. It contains the usual elements—a motivating coach, a pack of unruly underdogs, and an arrogant rival team to serve as their nemesis—interwoven with the theme of racism. Combining such elements could easily result in a film that is preachy and overdone, and the notable aspect of *Pride* is how it manages to avoid that fate. South African director Sunu Gonera, making his directorial debut, understands the sports movie genre and hits all the marks in the usual order and, for the

most part, with subtlety. Of course, it also helped that accomplished actor Terrence Howard is cast as the star and manages to project both power and a quiet grace throughout this not especially well-written film. As Sam Adams, writing in the *Los Angeles Times* put it, "Howard seems to be in an altogether and substantially more idiosyncratic film."

As many sports stories are, *Pride* was "inspired by a true story." Jim Ellis, the swim coach on whom the story was based, was asked by a *Philadelphia Inquirer* reporter what was true about the film. Ellis responded, "My name is." For the record, Ellis was indeed a swim coach who helped several children from the poor Nicetown section of Philadelphia make it to the Olympic trials in the 1970s.

The Jim Ellis (Terrence Howard) in this story is a college graduate who has been having trouble finding a job because he is black. He finally ends up with a low-level temporary job at the Marcus Foster Recreation Center. The center is staffed by a worn-out Elston (Bernie Mac), who has tried for years to keep the center from being shut down. The building is falling apart, and the only kids who go there are a small group of teenage boys who play basketball on the raggedy outdoor court.

While poking around the club, Ellis is excited to come upon a long-unused swimming pool. A former high-level swimmer, he cleans it up and is soon swimming laps on his own time. The teenagers, who include Andre (Kevin Phillips), Reggie (Evan Ross), and Hakim (Nate Parker), make fun of Ellis at first, but he entices them into the water and soon they are picking up tips on the finer points of how to hold one's hand while doing the freestyle stroke. The film is not much concerned with the specifics of how, exactly, as the teenagers go from non-swimmers to championship-winning athletes. Instead, the film focuses on the issues of race and the various ways it works on the teens.

For example, after the boys have been practicing for awhile, they feel that they are ready to take their team, PDR, to its first meet. They go to the rich, white section of town and proceed to get beaten badly. Instead of making them the noble victims, the film has them behave in a more human way. They react to their humiliation over the loss, their shame at wearing the wrong swimming attire, and the disdain directed toward them by the other teams and coaches who treat them as a joke. They cope with such feelings the only way they know how, physical violence, and they end up fighting against one another.

For some critics, the film's emotionally-charged moments were too heavy-handed. In the *Los Angeles Daily News,* Glenn Whipp called *Pride* "a collection of clichés that would be tiresome even if we hadn't seen them in the glut of inspirational sports movies released recently." Despite its retreaded plot and stock characters, the film has a genuine heart at its core. When the team gets approval to have a meet at its own recreation center, the swimmers immediately get to work cleaning. Even Elston joins in. On the day of the meet, hundreds of local townspeople show up to support the PDR. It is an important moment for a community that normally does not have much to be proud of. When the other team arrives, the swimmers take one look at the surroundings and their coach (Tom Arnold) announces that the whole team has suddenly taken sick and will be unable to compete. Yet even after this humiliation, the boys react with dignity. One by one, each of them jumps into the water, completing his race even without the other team. It is a noble, powerful, and heart-breaking moment.

Jill Hamilton

CREDITS

Jim Ellis: Terrence Howard
Elston: Bernie Mac
Sue Davis: Kimberly Elise
Bink: Tom Arnold
Walt: Alphonso McAuley
Hakim: Nathaniel Parker
Andre: Kevin Phillips
Jake: Scott Reeves
Puddin' Head: Brandon Fobbs
Willie: Regine Nehy
Reggie: Evan Ross
Franklin: Gary Sturgis
Origin: USA
Language: English
Released: 2007
Production: Michael Ohoven, Adam Rosenfelt, Brett Forbes, Patrick Rizzotti; Element Films, Fortress Features, Cinered, Paul Hall Productions; released by Lions Gate
Directed by: Sunu Gonera
Written by: J. Mills Goodloe, Norman Vance, Jr., Kevin Michael Smith, Michael Gozzard
Cinematography by: Matthew F. Leonetti
Music by: Aaron Zigman
Sound: Paul Ledford
Music Supervisor: Jay Faires
Editing: Billy Fox
Art Direction: Monroe Kelly
Costumes: Paul Simmons
Production Design: Steve Saklad
MPAA rating: PG
Running time: 108 minutes

REVIEWS

Boxoffice Online. March 23, 2007.
Chicago Sun-Times Online. March 23, 2007.
Entertainment Weekly. March 30, 2007, p. 52.
Hollywood Reporter Online. March 19, 2007.
Los Angeles Times Online. March 23, 2007.
New York Times Online. March 22, 2007.
San Francisco Chronicle. March 23, 2007, p. E5.
Variety Online. March 19, 2007.
Washington Post Online. March 23, 2007.

QUOTES

Jim Ellis: "My life is way too short for me to spend my time around people who don't care about nothin'."

TRIVIA

The journal that the character of Puddin' Head writes in is actor Brandon Fobbs's actual personal journal.

PRIVATE FEARS IN PUBLIC PLACES
(Coeurs)

For six strangers in search of love, the City of Lights can be a very lonely place.
—Movie tagline

Legendary French director Alain Resnais sets *Private Fears in Public Places* (*Coeurs*) in a rare snowstorm in Paris, an apt metaphor for the story of six lonely people desperately seeking love in the City of Light. Resnais draws his narrative from a play by Alan Ayckbourn, who also wrote the play that became Resnais' Cesar®-winning cinematic adaptation, *Smoking/No Smoking* (1993). The structure of *Private Fears in Public Places* is fairly theatrical and formal, consisting of some fifty distinct scenes usually involving two people. While the relationships the film portrays are in various stages of dissolution, the film itself is a perfect marriage of theater and cinema, with a cast of seasoned professionals and Resnais' expert craftsmanship. Separating each scene is a signature dissolve of snow falling, which is charming despite losing some of its effectiveness toward the end of the film.

With no formal plot, the movie seamlessly incorporates both poignant, heartfelt drama and light comedy with the aid of Ayckbourn's play and a wonderfully crafted script by Jean-Michel Ribes. An early scene shows Nicole (Laura Morante) looking at apartments for her and her fiancé Dan (Lambert Wilson), who was recently dishonorably discharged from the Army. When the real estate agent Thierry (André Dussollier) inquires about Dan's line of work with, "What's he in?", Nicole pithily but truthfully replies "Limbo." It feels as if we are dropped in the middle of the character's relationships, or in the case of Nicole and Dan, near the end. Frustrated by his increasingly alcoholic behavior and refusal to find work, Nicole constantly badgers Dan, which further increases the divide.

To further emphasize the separation that exists between all the main characters, Resnais literally creates divisions between them and in all of the chic, stylish interiors there are physical divisions expertly positioned. The main settings of the neon-hued hotel bar where the lonely aging Lionel (Pierre Arditi) works and Dan frequents features a beaded curtain divider. The placid, cool-toned real estate office where Thierry works with his devout Christian assistant Charlotte (Sabine Azéma) features a clear partition between them. In the home where Charlotte cares for Lionel's sickly father Arthur (voice of Claude Rich), the bedroom that serves as his infirmary is separated from the kitchen set by a doorway that the camera never enters; only Arthur's feet are visible to the audience. The first apartment Thierry shows Nicole has literally been cut in two, with one window serving two separate rooms. Dan demands their new apartment contain a separate room just for him—hard to come by in Paris real estate—and the unnecessary study is ultimately what causes an irreparable rift in their relationship. Resnais also employs overhead shots in several scenes, the increase in distance from the characters and inability to see their faces adding to the atmosphere of segregation.

Each character and situation is unique and wholly dimensional. One of the most tragic characters is Thierry's sister Gaëlle (Isabelle Carré), a pretty, blonde thirty-something luckless in love, who frequents cafés alone wearing a red flower pinned to her lapel in the hope of meeting someone. When she finally does meet someone she likes, it turns out to be Dan, who has agreed with Nicole that they should see other people. After one successful but extremely booze-soaked date, they agree to meet the next day, but she turns and runs off after seeing him with Nicole, who is actually at the bar to officially end things with Dan. Fatefully, Dan has no way of contacting Gaëlle to clear up the misunderstanding.

One of the most interesting characters is Charlotte, whose moral, pious exterior hides quite a different side that is revealed when she loans a videotape of her favorite Christian television program to Thierry. Dutifully watching the tape alone at home, Thierry finds that when the show has ended, a lingerie-clad woman dancing provocatively appears in a home video that was obviously meant to be taped over. When he borrows another tape with the same scenario, he is sure the woman is Charlotte and makes an awkward and extremely unwelcome advance toward Charlotte the next day at work. While initially there may be some doubt as to the identity of the woman on the tape, it becomes all too

clear in a later scene where Charlotte is tending to the extremely unpleasant Arthur. Alternately berating her and covering her with the food she prepares for him, Charlotte steps into the bathroom with a shopping bag and reemerges in black lingerie, and in one of the film's funniest scenes, enters Arthur's room for the last time before he is found in extremely bad condition but with a curious smile on his face.

Faith plays a role in the film mostly in the context of relationships. Charlotte explains to the weary Lionel that it is Satan who wants people to simply give up when "trials" are thrown at them, but that it is God who gives people obstacles in order that they may overcome them. While the characters certainly all have their share of relationship trials, they vary in their ability to overcome them.

The performances are uniformly excellent, with Arditi and Azéma standing out. The scene in which they clasp hands as a surreal snow falls in the tiny apartment, a highlight, showcases Eric Gautier's magical cinematography and Resnais' judicious use of symbolism.

Hilary White

CREDITS

Nicole: Laura Morante
Dan: Lambert Wilson
Lionel: Pierre Arditi
Gaëlle: Isabelle Carré
Thierry: André Dussollier
Charlotte: Sabine Azéma
Origin: France, Italy
Language: French
Released: 2006
Production: Bruno Pesery; Arena Films, France 2 Cinema, BIM Films, Soudaine Compagnie; released by IFC First Take
Directed by: Alain Resnais
Written by: Alain Resnais, Alan Ayckbourn, Jean-Michel Ribes
Cinematography by: Eric Gautier
Music by: Mark Snow
Sound: Jean-Marie Blondel
Editing: Herve De Luze
Costumes: Jackie Budin
Production Design: Jacques Saulnier
MPAA rating: Unrated
Running time: 120 minutes

REVIEWS

Chicago Sun-Times Online. June 8, 2007.
Entertainment Weekly Online. April 11, 2007.

Hollywood Reporter Online. September 15, 2006.
Los Angeles Times Online. May 4, 2007.
New York Times Online. April 13, 2007.
Premiere Online. April 13, 2007.
Variety Online. September 5, 2006.
Village Voice Online. April 10, 2007.

P.S. I LOVE YOU

Sometimes there's only one thing left to say.
—Movie tagline

His life ended. Now, a new one will begin.
—Movie tagline

Sometimes you have to live life one letter at a time.
—Movie tagline

Box Office: $53.6

Tackling the crowded romantic comedy genre in a vain attempt to rival *Ghost* (1990) and *The Notebook* (2004) is writer/director Richard LaGravenese's *P.S. I Love You.* The high-concept comedy/drama is based on Irish author Cecelia Ahern's best-selling novel about a newly widowed young woman forced to comes to terms with her husband's tragic demise.

The film is set in New York, eschewing the novel's Dublin locale, and opens with the couple bickering over a minor incident instead of Holly Kennedy (Hilary Swank) all ready grieving her husband's death, as she does in the novel. This drastic departure from the book serves to undermine his subsequent tragic demise and the selfless love shown by Gerry (Gerard Butler) from beyond the grave. It is perhaps the filmmakers' ham-handed attempt to establish that they are classic opposites: Holly is an uptight and unhappy American and Gerry is a lovable, near-saintly Irishman. Other issues cause tension: Gerry wants a baby right away, while the career-minded Holly would prefer to wait. Despite often showing the couple at odds, they are supposed to be very happily married. Then, jarringly, Gerry is diagnosed with a brain tumor and dies.

The conceit is the same as that of the novel: Gerry leaves ten letters for Holly, to be opened on the first of each month after his passing. LaGravenese and co-writer Steven Rogers update the notes from those of the book slightly but convey the same message and each contain the sentiment which is also the film's title, "P.S. I Love You." They are designed to force Holly to move on, have fun, and find someone new and are delivered to her by assorted strangers. While having various local businesses, including Holly's dry cleaners, "in" on the game is a somewhat quaint idea in our modern, indifferent world, it also comes across as contrived.

The notes are received either by Holly, or her friends Denise (Lisa Kudrow) and Sharon (Gina Gershon). The messages grow in difficulty level, beginning with relatively simple tasks, such as karaoke singing, and gradually work up to a trip to Ireland, where Holly and Gerry met. On her trip abroad, she meets William (Jeffrey Dean Morgan), a childhood friend of Gerry's, and the two sleep together. She also visits Gerry's parents and revisits the place she and Gerry first met, and the film indicates that this trip, as well as her tryst with William, has liberated her. The audience, however, must first suffer through another worn gimmick, a flashback scene showing how the couple first met. While the conceit allows Butler more screen time, we must also suffer through the ridiculous vision of Holly in her younger, more innocent days as a freshly-scrubbed art student.

LaGravenese also worked with Hilary Swank in the earlier drama, *Freedom Writers* (2007) playing a teacher in a role more to type and better suited to her talents. Rarely cast as a romantic lead, Swank exudes sincerity in the thinly written role that requires her, more than once, to act in her underwear. Butler is also called upon to disrobe, performing a schmaltzy strip tease during the extended opening credits segment. His participation in this tearjerker seems dubious, as he is called upon to feature in several, embarrassingly syrupy scenes. Writing in *Variety*, John Anderson, sympathized, opining, "LaGravenese…leaves no sentimental stone unturned in what for the charismatic Scotsman Butler is a painful exercise in Irish-accented emoting and manufactured charm."

The filmmakers have cast the movie in classic soap opera fashion, with three handsome, well-built men to appeal to what will surely be a primarily female audience. In addition to Butler, there is the striking Morgan, who conveys believable country charm, and the suitably attractive Harry Connick, Jr., delivering a limp performance as Daniel, another romantic interest of Holly's.

Supporting actors Kudrow and Gershon are miscast as Holly's friends, and the three lack the camaraderie crucial to the plot. Kathy Bates takes on a small, rather lifeless part as Holly's embittered mother Patricia, abandoned by Holly's father years ago, and who disapproved of her union with Gerry. Denise, Sharon, and Patricia are the film's much-needed voice of reason, as they, like the audience, begin to wonder if receiving these letters is unnaturally tying Holly to her deceased husband.

The film generally hews closely to the novel and suffers from the same problems, with characters and situations that strain believability and a saccharine tone. No stranger to sentiment, LaGravenese also wrote the

320

screenplays for *The Bridges of Madison County* (1995), *The Horse Whisperer* (1998), and *The Fisher King* (1991). It is difficult to tread the line between tragedy and comedy, and the post-mortem love story *P.S. I Love You* makes far too many melodramatic missteps along it.

James S. O'Neill

CREDITS

Holly: Hilary Swank
Gerry: Gerard Butler
Denise: Lisa Kudrow
Sharon: Gina Gershon
Daniel: Harry Connick, Jr.
William: Jeffrey Dean Morgan
Patricia: Kathy Bates
John: James Marsters
Origin: USA
Language: English
Released: 2007
Production: Wendy Finerman, Broderick Johnson, Andrew A. Kosove, Molly Smith; Grosvenor Park, Alcon Entertainment; released by Warner Bros.
Directed by: Richard LaGravenese
Written by: Richard LaGravenese, Steven Rogers
Cinematography by: Terry Stacey

Music by: John Powell
Sound: Douglas Huszti, Mark Stoeckinger
Music Supervisor: Mary Ramos
Editing: David Moritz
Art Direction: Kerry Dean Williams
Costumes: Cindy Evans
Production Design: Shepherd Frankel
MPAA rating: PG-13
Running time: 126 minutes

REVIEWS

Boston Globe Online. December 21, 2007.
Entertainment Weekly Online. December 12, 2007.
Hollywood Reporter Online. December 14, 2007.
Los Angeles Times Online. December 21, 2007.
New York Times Online. December 21, 2007.
San Francisco Chronicle. December 21, 2007, p. E1.
Variety Online. December 13, 2007.
Washington Post Online. December 21, 2007.

QUOTES

Sharon McCarthy: "You gotta be rich to be insane, Hol. Losing your mind is not a luxury for the middle class."

TRIVIA

During the filming of a strip sequence, Gerard Butler's suspenders hit Hilary Swank on the forehead. She received a cut and had to be brought to a hospital where she received several stitches.

R

RATATOUILLE

He's dying to become a chef.
—Movie tagline

A comedy with great taste.
—Movie tagline

Box Office: $206.4 million

Ratatouille, the latest computer-animated wonder from Pixar Studios, is predicated on a potentially dubious, even disgusting, premise—a rat who longs to be a gourmet chef. If the thought of rats roaming around a kitchen sounds unappealing, screenwriter/director Brad Bird dispels (or at least alleviates) such discomfort with an array of memorable characters, a complex plot, funny situations, and the nuanced animation we have come to expect from the Pixar wizards of Emeryville, California. Yet what elevates *Ratatouille* into the realm of the classic is that it also delivers a serious message about what it means to be an artist and to strive for excellence in a world that too often settles for mediocrity. It is not a theme we would ordinarily expect from a mainstream movie, let alone an animated one, but, coming from Bird, it may not be such a surprise after all. His previous feature, *The Incredibles* (2004), has the most adult sensibility of all the Pixar films, and *Ratatouille,* with its focus on French cuisine and the central paradox of a rat wanting to make his mark on the culinary arts, exhibits a sophistication lacking in most animated fare.

Inspired by famed chef Auguste Gusteau (voice of Brad Garrett), Remy (voice of Patton Oswalt) is a country rat with a sensitive palate and a taste for fine food, a quality that his father Django (voice of Brian Dennehy) and brother Émile (voice of Peter Sohn) can-

not fathom. Remy's acute sense of smell makes him an ideal poison checker for the rat colony, but, to his family, for whom a daily diet of garbage is adequate, Remy's fixation on zesty flavors and combining ingredients is incomprehensible. Remy, ultimately, is an artist who feels cooking is a calling and sees food not simply as a means to survival, but a path to self-expression. One is reminded of the cook Primo in *Big Night* (1996), who was constantly at war with the philistine customers surrounding him.

When Remy gets separated from his family and finds himself not only in Paris but in the sewers below Gusteau's, the gourmet restaurant he admires, it is a dream come true. He cannot help but make his way to the kitchen, where the new garbage boy, the gangly, awkward Linguini (voice of Lou Romano), has just ruined the soup, prompting Remy to scurry around and furiously add ingredients to correct the boy's mistake. Once the patrons begin raving about the soup, everyone ends up thinking that the neophyte Linguini has created something masterful, while Linguini himself quickly discovers that Remy is the one with talent. A rat, of course, cannot be seen in a kitchen, so they forge a friendship in which Remy hides under Linguini's toque and, by pulling his hair as if it were the strings on a marionette, guides him around the kitchen. Their teamwork produces great physical comedy as Linguini, attempting to do Remy's bidding, is tossed to and fro.

As in many Pixar features, the supporting characters are just as engaging. Linguini's antagonist is the apoplectic Skinner (voice of Ian Holm), the head chef, who always seems inches from catching Remy and who is itching to seize control of the restaurant in light of Gusteau's recent death. The rotund, jovial Gusteau appears as a ghost, or perhaps a figment of the imagination, to Remy and functions as a kind of fairy godfather, inspiring the little fellow with his book *Anyone Can Cook!*, whose title succinctly summarizes Gusteau's philosophy. Linguini is put under the tutelage of Colette (voice of Janeane Garofalo, doing a wonderful French accent), a no-nonsense chef who tries to instill the basics in Linguini but who also develops a soft spot for him. Peter O'Toole contributes great work as Anton Ego, the imperious, snobby restaurant critic known as "The Grim Eater," who was Gusteau's nemesis (it is believed that Ego's harsh criticism ultimately killed the great Gusteau) but who becomes, at the end, the surprise linchpin to the film's emotional payoff.

Even among Pixar's stellar lineup, Brad Bird's two films are special because there is a genuine philosophy underpinning the stories and one that goes against the cultural grain. It is a philosophy that champions excellence, what many might dismiss as elitism—some people are simply better at certain things than other people, and it is right to celebrate that reality. It is the principle that the family in *The Incredibles* championed, but *Ratatouille* changes the proposition to illustrate that one does not have to be born great to achieve greatness.

While sophisticated characters and ideas are at the heart of *Ratatouille,* it works on so many levels, exhibiting in its own way the dedication to craft and meticulous attention to detail that Remy himself believes in. The story moves along with a narrative flow and does not follow a predictable course. The animation is pristine, and the kitchen itself, where so much of the action takes place, feels like a genuine set. We get to know the minor workers, and, at those moments when chaos breaks out, there is a fluidity to the movements and the illusion that these computer-animated creatures are whizzing around and crashing into real surfaces.

As the restaurant flourishes, Skinner grows angrier. If Remy is the guardian of the highest culinary standards against a father and brother content to feast on garbage, Remy's true enemy in the kitchen is Skinner, whose idea to sell the Gusteau name and image for a line of frozen dinners is the antithesis of everything Remy believes in. In a way, Skinner's concept takes the "anyone can cook" ethos and reduces it to the lowest common denominator. When Skinner discovers that Linguini is Gusteau's son and thus the rightful heir to the restaurant, the hapless boy becomes even more of an annoyance. Yet the film does not take what would have been the easy route of building a plot around Skinner trying to thwart Linguini and steal what is rightfully his. Indeed, once Remy discovers Linguini's true heritage, Skinner is expelled

from the kitchen, and the story focuses more on the complex relationships between the central characters.

Remy becomes conflicted when his family and the whole rat colony reappear and he finds himself torn between stealing food for them and being true to his vocation as a chef. After all, Remy feels indebted to Linguini, who has allowed him to excel in the kitchen, and they share a close bond—Linguini playfully calls him "Little Chef"—but when Linguini and Colette fall in love and Linguini publicly gives her credit for his success, Remy grows jealous of her. Linguini cannot acknowledge that a rat is the true artist helping him in the kitchen and initiating the rebirth of Gusteau's. It is, to be sure, an odd kind of triangle, but its very unconventionality makes *Ratatouille* so different from other animated films.

The conclusion takes an already wonderful story and lifts it to a higher level when Ego, hearing so much about the recent success of Gusteau's, decides to review it again. Deserted by his human colleagues after telling the truth about Remy, Linguini must rely solely on Colette and Remy, who leads the rat colony in running the kitchen on Ego's big night. Remy decides to serve ratatouille, which Colette describes as a peasant dish, but which proves to be transcendent. In a dazzling and touching shot, as Ego eats the dinner, he flashes to a moment from his childhood when his mother cooked him the same meal. It is a brief but poignant scene and a tribute to the power of great art and the lasting attachment we feel for those creations that touched us in our youth. The universality is underscored by the fact that the seemingly coldest of men can feel this way and have his heart restored through a timeless artistic experience, which, *Ratatouille* suggests, is open to everyone.

Ego's stellar review, delivered as a monologue, also makes a profound statement. While the film's opening scene contrasts Gusteau's "anyone can cook" philosophy with Ego's repudiation of this point of view, Ego, at the end, undergoes a change that reveals a refined perspective on the late chef's thinking: "Not everyone can become a great artist, but a great artist can come from anywhere." It is one of the most mature and thoughtful ideas one can find about the artist in a popular film, upholding a democratic belief in everyone's potential regardless of background but clearheadedly seeing the reality that some will inevitably be better than others.

With just his third animated feature—the wonderful but underappreciated *The Iron Giant* (1999) was his first—Brad Bird has established himself at the front ranks of contemporary animators. One can only imagine where his gifts will take him next. With his mastery of story, characters, and mise-en-scène and his ability to direct outstanding vocal performances, all while imbuing his work with a keen emotional depth, there seems to be no limit to his talent.

Peter N. Chumo II

CREDITS

Remy: Patton Oswalt (Voice)
Django: Brian Dennehy (Voice)
Auguste Gusteau: Brad Garrett (Voice)
Collette: Janeane Garofalo (Voice)
Skinner: Ian Holm (Voice)
Anton Ego: Peter O'Toole (Voice)
Horst: Will Arnett (Voice)
Larousse: James Remar (Voice)
Linguini: Lou Romano (Voice)
Mustafa: John Ratzenberger (Voice)
Armbrister Minion: Brad Bird (Voice)
Emile: Peter Sohn (Voice)
Stephane Roux (Narrated)
Origin: USA
Language: English
Released: 2007
Production: Brad Lewis; Pixar, Walt Disney Pictures; released by Buena Vista
Directed by: Brad Bird
Written by: Brad Bird, Jan Pinkava, Jim Capobianco
Cinematography by: Sharon Calahan, Robert Anderson
Music by: Michael Giacchino
Sound: Randy Thom
Editing: Darren T. Holmes
Art Direction: Dominique Louis
Production Design: Harley Jessup
MPAA rating: G
Running time: 110 minutes

REVIEWS

Boston Globe Online. June 29, 2007.
Chicago Sun-Times Online. June 292007.
Entertainment Weekly. June 29, 2007, p. 113.
Hollywood Reporter Online. June 15, 2007.
Los Angeles Times Online. June 29, 2007.
New York Times Online. June 29, 2007.
Rolling Stone Online. June 25, 2007.
San Francisco Chronicle. June 29, 2007, p. E1.
Variety Online. June 15, 2007.
Washington Post. June 29, 2007, p. C1.

QUOTES

Remy: "If you are what you eat, I only want to eat good stuff."

Anton Ego: "Not everyone can be a great artist. But a great artist can come from anywhere."

TRIVIA

Remy has 1.15 million hairs rendered, whereas Colette has 115,000 hairs rendered. An average person has about 110,000 hairs.

AWARDS

Oscars 2007: Animated Film
British Acad. 2007: Animated Film
Golden Globes 2008: Animated Film

Nomination:

Oscars 2007: Orig. Screenplay, Sound, Sound FX Editing, Orig. Score.

THE REAPING

What Hath God Wrought?
—Movie tagline

The rivers ran red with blood. Darkness fell upon the earth. No one thought this could happen again. Until now.
—Movie tagline

Box Office: $25.1 million

Katherine Winter (Hilary Swank) is an ordained minister who has lost her faith. It happened far away in the Sudan. It was in that dry, sandy, hopeless place, while she was trying to help the helpless people, that her daughter and husband were murdered.

Now she spends her time teaching at Louisiana State University and gallivanting around the world debunking miracles—although how she manages to get the university to allow her to abandon her students mid-semester in order to do all this, or how she manages to grade papers while traveling, is never revealed. She is aided in her efforts by a graduate student, Ben (Idris Elba), an African American man with the stereotypical ghetto background (misspent youth, bullet-riddled body, tattoos, etc.) but who, unlike Katherine, has found his faith by the sheer fact that he has survived.

Together Ben and Katherine have just debunked the miracles that were taking place in Concepcion, Chile, where an earthquake had uncovered the corpse of a monk who had been dead four years and whose body was perfectly preserved. People began lining up to partake of the miracle and fell into some kind of otherworldly mental state. Ben and Katherine follow a tunnel also exposed by the quake and find at the end that toxic waste had been dropped into an old well and that is what has preserved the monk's body and drove people into hallucinogenic states. As Katherine proudly states at her next lecture, she has now investigated forty-eight miracles and explained all forty-eight of them scientifically. "The only miracle," she proclaims, "is that they keep on believing in miracles."

Meanwhile, Father Michael Costigan (Stephen Rea), who had been in the Sudan with Katherine, suddenly finds himself faced with a supernatural situation of his own. Photographs he has of Katherine are spontaneously combusting and when the photos are put side by side, the burn marks form the shape of an upside down sickle with a cross on its handle. He telephones Katherine in an attempt to warn her, but he is trapped in his own room and burned alive.

Katherine and Ben, however, are off on a new investigation. Initially, Katherine was not interested in Doug Blackwell's (David Morrissey) tale of how his little town of Haven's River was running red with blood, but when he tells her that a young boy had been found dead on the riverbank that morning and that the boy's twelve-year-old sister, Loren (AnnaSophia Robb), was being blamed for his death, Katherine's tender heart is moved.

While investigating the river, Katherine sees Loren among the cypress trees and runs after her, while poor Ben suddenly finds it raining frogs. That night, while Doug is barbequing a nice fish dinner for them at his antebellum mansion, when flies and maggots suddenly engulf their grill. A neighbor's cows have been struck by what looks like mad cow disease and his bull is running amuck. Other plagues follow, including, lice, boils, and locusts, while a flock of birds is casting darkness upon the land. The conclusion of everyone in town is that Satan is protecting Loren, which is why God is visiting these plagues upon them. Katherine, who has lost a daughter, does not agree with the townspeople and will not do anything to harm the child.

During the course of the investigation, Katherine has flashbacks to her experiences in the Sudan. In fact, one night she dreams of the Sudan so vividly that the next morning she finds her feet covered in sand and blood. For the first time, she begins to suspect Loren, wondering if the girl is part of the satanic cult with which her mother was involved.

Mixing elements of classic horror films such as *The Omen* (1976) and *The Exorcist* (1973), with references to a child "reborn with the eyes of Satan", *The Reaping* also mixes in a healthy dose of *Rosemary's Baby* (1968) but fails to add anything new or interesting to the genre.

The film is sufficiently atmospheric, but writers Carey W. Hayes and Chad Hayes failed to think the script all the way through. Working from a story by Brian Rousso, they give the audience the requisite plot twists and turns, but, except for the final twist, these convolutions are simply absurd. The Hayes writing team is also responsible for the dreadful *House of Wax* (2005) remake, whose only distinction is that it features Paris Hilton. This film, however, has two-time Oscar® winner Hilary Swank carrying the film's weight. She looks appropriately triumphant during a debunking and later puzzled when she cannot explain something scientifically, which significantly raises the film's profile.

The Reaping sat on Warner Bros. shelf for quite a while, and the fact that there was fairly heavy tinkering involved is obvious. The end result is a film that fails to engage the audience's intelligence with dialogue and plot, instead relying on computer-generated imagery.

Beverley Bare Buehrer

CREDITS

Katherine Winter: Hilary Swank
Doug Blackwell: David Morrissey
Ben: Idris Elba
Loren McConell: AnnaSophia Robb
Sheriff Cade: William Ragsdale
Father Costigan: Stephen Rea
Origin: USA
Language: English
Released: 2007
Production: Joel Silver, Robert Zemeckis, Herbert W. Gains, Susan Downey; Village Roadshow Pictures, Dark Castle Entertainment; released by Warner Bros.
Directed by: Stephen Hopkins
Written by: Carey Hayes, Chad Hayes, Brian Rousso
Cinematography by: Peter Levy
Music by: John Frizzell
Sound: Pud Cusack
Editing: Colby Parker, Jr.
Art Direction: Scott Ritenour
Costumes: Jeffrey Kurland
Production Design: Graham Walker
MPAA rating: R
Running time: 98 minutes

REVIEWS

Boxoffice Online. April 5, 2007.
Chicago Sun-Times Online. April 5, 2007.
Entertainment Weekly Online. April 4, 2007.
Hollywood Reporter Online. April 2, 2007.
New York Times Online. April 5, 2007.
Premiere Online. April 4, 2007.

San Francisco Chronicle. April 5, 2007, p. C1.
Variety Online. March 30, 2007.
Washington Post. April 5, 2007, p. C1.

RED ROAD

Andrea Arnold's *Red Road,* her startling debut feature, is also the first film of three in the Advance Party film series led by executive producers Lone Scherfig and Anders Thomas Jensen. Advance Party is a Danish-Scottish initiative modeled after the avant-garde Danish Dogma 95 film collective led by Lars von Trier and Thomas Vinterberg, who follow specific rules in an effort to bring authenticity to filmmaking. Arnold's *Red Road* is a perfect example of the group's effort to purify filmmaking. Its stripped-down but highly effective style is one of the hallmarks of collective.

The rules followed by Advance Party included that the three low-budget films would be helmed by neophyte directors, the films would all be set in Scotland, they would be shot digitally in six weeks, and each film would contain the same characters embodied by the same actors. Scherfig and Jensen created a rough draft of the characters with the story and character detail to be decided by the individual director.

Arnold's *Red Road* is a dramatic thriller played out against a stark, gray Glasgow background, which *Chicago Sun-Times* critic Jim Emerson described as "post-apocalyptic," and which echoes the emotional state of the film's main character, Jackie (Kate Dickie). From her post at the City Eye Control, Jackie sits sullenly and silently, vigilantly monitoring the grainy images on the closed-circuit television from surveillance cameras set up around crime-laden parts of the city. Near a seedy housing complex known as Red Road where many ex-convicts reside, Jackie makes a chilling discovery when she recognizes Clyde (Tony Curran), who has just been released from prison. She becomes obsessed with his every move and begins to stalk him. As he spies her in a diner, it is clear he does not recognize her. Suspense builds as the audience is left to wonder what Clyde's crime was and what Jackie's motivation might be for her following him everywhere.

The film is highly sexually charged. The red-haired Clyde is portrayed as having a lusty sexual appetite and the first shot of Clyde on the closed-circuit television shows him having sex with a woman in a field. He openly gropes the waitress at the diner and, when Jackie summons the courage to crash a party at his Red Road apartment, he develops a sexual interest in her as well. This leads the viewer to believe his crime may have been sexual in nature. Jackie, shown wearing a wedding ring

but living alone, has loveless sex with a married coworker from which she seemingly derives no pleasure. She is repulsed by Clyde but is passionate about him and leads him on sexually. Near the end of the film, Jackie and Clyde's flirtation culminates in an explicit and raw sexual encounter at his apartment. When she makes it look like a rape and the police arrest the parolee the following day, it is still unclear to viewers what her motivation may be.

Clyde has an ally in ex-con and petty thief Stevie (Martin Compston) who, with his girlfriend April (Nathalie Press) live with Clyde at Red Road. After he is arrested Clyde confronts Jackie at her apartment and the truth is revealed: While driving high on drugs, Clyde had accidentally killed Jackie's husband and daughter. He does not recognize her, she says, because he never looked at her once in court. This revelation strains credulity and does not fully account for Jackie's bizarre actions, and her vendetta seems a bit misplaced.

Arnold lets the viewer see Clyde through the mistrust and suspicion of Jackie while allowing him to have another side in reality. An earlier scene shows Jackie watching him on camera as he drives to a school and menacingly approaches a teenage girl who seems not to know him. It is later revealed that he has a teenage daughter who he never knew and he is merely trying to reconnect with her. When Jackie sees the girl at Red Road after her father has been taken away by police, she realizes she must drop the charges. As Jackie finally comes to accept her devastating loss, visually the film also brightens with some sunlight finally emerging on the perpetually dreary screen.

In addition to its low budget, lack of visual gimmickry, and digital quality images, Arnold's *Red Road* also employs a non-traditional narrative style that utilizes very little dialogue and no soundtrack, so the performances are of utmost importance. In her on-screen feature debut, Kate Dickie proves to be highly successful, with her restrained devastation apparent in her expressive face and thin, bone-weary body. Curran is at once menacing and vulnerable, though he shows a softer side after they have their sexual liaison. The two have a final encounter after the charges are dropped and he is released. The scene is cathartic for the characters and the audience, as Clyde speaks of his troubled past as an unloved child and how lucky her own child had been to know she was loved. Arnold's dark film ultimately concludes on a lighter note, with both characters finding some sort of redemption.

Arnold, who won an Oscar® for her short film *Wasp* (2003), expands on her acclaim with *Red Road,* which both won over critics and won awards, taking a Special Jury Prize at the 2006 Cannes Film Festival and sweeping the BAFTA Awards, Scotland. *Red Road* is also a triumph for the Advance Party, with Jim Emerson declaring that *Red Road* "distills the essence of Hitchcock ("Rear Window"), film noir, and Bertoluccian obsession into a new kind of thriller that feels distinctly Scottish (or Glaswegian)."

Hilary White

CREDITS

Clyde: Tony Curran
Stevie: Martin Compston
April: Nathalie Press
Jackie: Kate Dickie
Alfred: Andrew Armour
Origin: Great Britain, Czech Republic
Language: English
Released: 2006
Production: Carrie Comerford; Zentropa Entertainment, Sigma Film; released by Tartan USA
Directed by: Andrea Arnold
Written by: Andrea Arnold
Cinematography by: Robbie Ryan
Sound: Martin Belshaw
Editing: Nicolas Chaudeurge
Costumes: Carole K. Millar
Production Design: Helen Scott
MPAA rating: Unrated
Running time: 113 minutes

REVIEWS

Baltimore Sun Online. April 20, 2007.
Boston Globe Online. May 11, 2007.
Hollywood Reporter Online. May 21, 2006.
Los Angeles Times Online. April 13, 2007.
New York Times Online. April 13, 2007.
San Francisco Chronicle. May 4, 2007, p. E5.
Variety Online. May 20, 2006.

REIGN OVER ME

> *Let in the unexpected.*
> —Movie tagline

Box Office: $19.6

The tale of the lonely misfit in New York City has been told many times before—in iconic films like *Midnight Cowboy* (1969) and *Taxi Driver* (1976)—but Mike Binder has created a new twist on that image in *Reign Over Me*. Instead of Travis Bickle driving his taxi while

boiling over with Vietnam veteran-rage, there is a post-9/11 ghost full of grief and anger set loose on the streets. That this ghost is embodied by Adam Sandler on a motorized scooter is one of the most remarkable qualities of Binder's brave and unorthodox movie. The filmmaker takes an actor who stands for inane adolescent crudity, puts him on a ridiculous-looking transportation toy, and somehow turns him into a figure of such gravity that he becomes a metaphor for the mood of an entire city and nation.

Looking like a latter-day Bob Dylan, his hair a tangled mass of indifference, his face full of stubble and strange little blotches and pimples, Sandler's Charlie Fineman is a shell of a man, gliding down Manhattan streets on his Go-Ped, an over-aged child listening to music on huge headphones. In Binder's rendition, this orphan of the Age of Terror moves through a dark, indifferent streetscape full of vehicles and building facades but not bustling so much with pedestrians as the New York of movies usually does. The streets seem vaguely haunted by the memories of that tragic morning in 2001. Yet no one talks directly about it. Time has passed, lives have continued, and a pretense of normalcy reigns. This so-called normalcy is what makes Charlie's plight so painful as it seems that nearly everyone else has figured out how to cope with grief. He is a man alone as he moves through traffic, existing almost in another dimension as an alien in the midst of a city that pretends all is well again.

Charlie suddenly pops back up on the radar of his old dental school roommate, Alan Johnson (Don Cheadle), who sees him passing by on the street a couple times in the course of a few weeks, and corrals him the second time. Why it has taken five or more years for this chance encounter to occur is something rendered credible by the sheer size of New York and the conventions of Hollywood storytelling. A man can get lost in the city, and Charlie has been hiding in plain sight ever since his wife and three daughters were killed aboard one of the planes that crashed into the World Trade Center. As Alan rediscovers him, Charlie does not come close to speaking of the tragedy; Alan knows only because he had read about it in the newspapers, but he does not mention the words "September 11" or "World Trade Center" by name in referring to Charlie, and no one else does, either. The tragedy has taken on euphemisms, which is one of the script's many wonderful little ironies that suggest the whole city remains in denial, even though its "sane" inhabitants have found socially acceptable ways to grieve and move on. Charlie is insane because he has not. And that is his problem.

Coping becomes Alan's problem too because Alan is also a misfit. Although he moves through a life that seems solid and prosperous, with a beautiful wife, Janeane (Jada Pinkett Smith) and two daughters; a successful dental practice; and a spacious apartment full of books and prosperity, Alan has a troubled mind. He feels stifled and fenced in, and he has difficulty communicating and even more trouble standing up to his business partners and his wife. Yet all of his problems are as hidden as Charlie's are obvious. Alan is socially adept, expert at negotiating the encounters that make up life, but he is lying, even to himself. Charlie is broken, socially inept, off kilter, volatile, and unpredictable, but true to himself.

This is the brilliance of casting Sandler and Cheadle, which at first seems mainly a cynical ploy to boost box-office receipts by enticing Sandler fans to see a serious, slow-paced, emotional movie they otherwise would likely avoid. In a bizarre transformation, Sandler's usual monotone, mumbling delivery seems genuine for his character, rather than an contrived over-the-top comic persona. His Charlie, who lacks emotional effect and who seems to have reverted entirely to an adolescence of playing video games and listening to old rock songs, is believable as a hollowed-out man whose life has been reduced to reassuring security blankets. Moreover, Cheadle, one of the classiest actors on the planet, a man who oozes sincerity and genuineness, plays a man who seems lost and insincere.

Reign Over Me is keenly observant about social proprieties and about the many levels at which human communication operates. In a breathtakingly composed scene by cinematographer Russ Alsobrook that rips open ordinary family life to reveal the anguish of the compromises within it, Cheadle's Alan is sitting at a breakfast table in his spacious kitchen, reading the morning paper, his children off to the far right of the frame getting their lunches, while his wife is at the far left of the screen doing kitchen chores and telling him how she has signed them up for another photography class. The audience sees Cheadle's true demeanor, one of utter exasperation, as he glances at the camera, away from his wife's eyes, then turns and presents a strained happy face of acceptance to her—a lie to smooth out their relationship. This is the most remarkable of many scenes in the filmed in the Johnsons' apartment, in the dental office, in restaurants, and finally in courtrooms. These scenes offer viewers fascinating tableaux, as if modern life had somehow been captured in a Renaissance painting and was presented centuries later, preserved in all its contradictions.

In his script and directing, Binder also is daring and challenging. His film is thoroughly grounded in plot conventions, including a disappointing hackneyed suggestion that Charlie's woes, as is always the case in Hollywood, can be best resolved by bedding down with a glamorous woman who is inexplicably available to him.

Yet it toys with the expected revelations, slows down and tweaks the arcs of character development, and asks real questions about how society handles personal tragedy. It gently shines a spotlight on the prevalent unhappiness of society by raising the question about why Alan is so unhappy in his day-to-day life, so unable to appreciate the treasures that Charlie has lost.

In spite of himself, Binder somehow succeeds. He skates dangerously along the edge of a sea of clichés. Alan is the stifled husband in need of the freedom to just be a guy with no commitments again. Janeane, like all the women in this film, is thinly drawn. She seems to be both radiantly beautiful and superbly intelligent and sensitive, yet there is no mention of her having a career. It is difficult to believe she is a housewife who sits around at home all day doing jigsaw puzzles. It is difficult to accept the character of Donna (Saffron Burrows), who wants to perform oral sex on her dentist because her former husband had a long-running affair. Is this a revenge motif, power ploy, or unconventional therapy? No satisfactory explanation is offered. Angela (Liv Tyler), a therapist whom Alan enlists to help Charlie, is only a little more credible as the most beautiful psychiatrist world history.

Looked at superficially, the whole movie is a whopper, suggesting that if a man in the deepest sort of distress can only find his old college buddy to hang with, that he will be somehow drawn out of post-traumatic stress disorder by the sheer force of his friend's desire to help him. It also suggests, as many movies about mental turmoil do, that the borderline insane will show the sane the real path to wholeness and truth. Yet, because of how carefully and beautifully Binder observes and chronicles his two main characters' foibles, and how delicately and respectfully he treats their emotions and difficulties, he succeeds.

Some might observe that Binder does so in spite of Sandler, not because of him. Binder has certainly coaxed a best-ever performance from Sandler. Yet he has also demanded too much of him and has relied too much on the Sandler persona. Charlie gets crude and adolescent quite a few too many times, losing credibility with each occurrence. It is believable that Charlie has regressed emotionally because of the tragedy he suffered, but it is not clear why he has turned into a twelve-year-old sexually. Charlie's character arc is barely believable: It is unclear why he changes and how he holds himself together. Although he is more believable as an empty shell than as a healing human being, Sandler gives the role a fine effort.

In another sense, the very idiosyncratic nature of Sandler's character is its own best explanation. Charlie is who he is, and that is why he is so prickly and problematic. Although it draws out the movie in something of an anticlimactic fashion, Binder's insistence on not providing one big healing breakthrough is also laudable. At the end, Charlie is not fixed and Alan is still in some peril, though there is the strong suggestion that both are on their way back to health, with a judicial assist from a sage Judge Raines (Donald Sutherland).

Binder's rescued at least one other cliché, too: the way that men fall back on music and video games as a retreat from fearsome emotions. That Charlie finds refuge in battling artificial monsters and listening to the Who and Bruce Springsteen is an apt commentary on the social development of the American male. Sandler is very comfortable in this territory, and he is most believable when he goes into full retreat mode by donning headphones: He then becomes the scared little boy who does not want to grow up, and that is a familiar trope, extending from Charlie Chaplin through Peter Pan to Adam Sandler in every previous Sandler movie. Cheadle also manages to make Alan's enthusiasm for such escapes believable because Cheadle is a consummate actor who makes yet another difficult performance seem like a piece of cake. Not a glance, nor a word from Cheadle is unconvincing in this film. Never grandstanding with his character, he always understands that while his troubles are not grandiose, they are real.

What is most appealing about *Reign Over Me* is its willingness to confront an issue rarely addressed in public, that is, the social acceptability of mourning. Binder's story raises the question of why some methods of handling tragedy are more socially acceptable than others, and how someone who does not fit into the acceptable mode of public hand-wringing gets ostracized. What is to be done with the broken men and women who are casualties of the so-called war on terror, viewers may ask themselves. Binder asks these questions in courageous fashion by presenting viewers with the Templetons, Charlie's in-laws, who are both well-meaning and infuriatingly meddlesome. They too have suffered tragedy, but they know how to exist in ways that elicit comfortable responses in others, whereas Charlie cannot so easily negotiate that path. Their struggle, which intensifies in the movie's last half-hour, is emblematic of the larger struggle that Binder suggests is still being waged in New York and the country as a whole. There is no easy solution, however, about how to come to terms with tragedy and long-term peril once the official grieving period is over. It is not too much to suggest that, given the events since September 11, 2001, this is one of the key issues of our time, and that Charlie Fineman, playing video games, is a sad Everyman of the post-9/11 world and perhaps the first of many modern counterparts to Travis Bickle. Perhaps Binder is

saying we still need to discuss what really happened that morning, and all that has happened since.

Michael Betzold

CREDITS

Charlie Fineman: Adam Sandler
Alan Johnson: Don Cheadle
Janeane Johnson: Jada Pinkett Smith
Angela Oakhurst: Liv Tyler
Donna Remar: Saffron Burrows
Judge Raines: Donald Sutherland
Jonathan Timpleman: Robert Klein
Ginger Timpleman: Melinda Dillon
Stetler: Jonathan Banks
Bryan Sugarman: Mike Binder
Origin: USA
Language: English
Released: 2007
Production: Jack Binder, Michael Rotenberg; Mr. Madison, Sunlight, Relativity, Columbia Pictures; released by Sony Pictures Entertainment
Directed by: Mike Binder
Written by: Mike Binder
Cinematography by: Russ T. Alsobrook
Music by: Rolfe Kent
Sound: Elmo Weber, Carlos De Larious
Music Supervisor: Dave Jordan
Editing: Steve Edwards, Jeremy Roush
Art Direction: Gregory A. Berry
Costumes: Deborah L. Scott
Production Design: Pipo Winter
MPAA rating: R
Running time: 128 minutes

REVIEWS

Boxoffice Online. March 23, 2007.
Chicago Sun-Times Online. March 23, 2007.
Entertainment Weekly. March 30, 2007, p. 50.
Hollywood Reporter Online. March 16, 2007.
Los Angeles Times Online. March 23, 2007.
New York Times Online. March 23, 2007.
San Francisco Chronicle. March 23, 2007, p. E5.
Variety Online. March 15, 2007.
Washington Post Online. March 23, 2007.

QUOTES

Alan (to his wife): "I was stuck in Charlieworld. I couldn't leave."

TRIVIA

Title is taken from the Who song "Love, Reign O'er Me," which is also covered by Pearl Jam on the soundtrack.

RENDITION

What if someone you love...just disappeared?
  —Movie tagline

Box Office: $9.7 million

In *Rendition*, a man finds himself being purposefully conveyed to a predetermined destination of someone else's choosing, and, by the film's end, viewers will themselves have some idea of what that feels like. The title refers to a policy known as "extraordinary rendition," which allows the Unites States government to seize people suspected of terrorist ties and spirit them away to secret overseas prisons where others use the more down-and-dirty methods of truth extraction, while our country's hands remain seemingly clean and above reproach. Whether these individuals are actually monsters thwarted on the verge of committing nightmarish acts or merely wronged innocents is to be determined later. In the meantime, those who disappear are completely and indefinitely cut off from both loved ones and legal representation. Though initiated during the Clinton years as an extreme measure to be resorted to only in cases of absolute necessity, the succeeding administration has reportedly used it since the September 11, 2001 attacks with a frequency and zeal that sincerely alarms some but makes others sleep more soundly and securely. In making this highly topical film to explore the legitimate concerns swirling around the subject, director Gavin Hood and screenwriter Kelley Sane stressed that they "didn't want to...tell the audience what to think." While viewers may differ on questions regarding the morality, legality, and efficacy of outsourced torture, as well as whether the practice is being resorted to judiciously, most will agree that there is a definite opinion being expressed in *Rendition*. Hood and Sane make a concerted effort to elicit viewers' sympathies in favor of a specific viewpoint.

Before authorities swoop down and carry away Egyptian-born United States resident Anwar El-Ibrahimi (Omar Metwally), he is presented in a thoroughly positive light. Anwar is a well-dressed, well-mannered chemical engineer who thoughtfully takes time out during a hectic business trip to Cape Town, South Africa to touch base with his perky blond wife, Isabella (Reese Witherspoon), and their adorable little boy (Aramis Knight). Everything is lighthearted, a thoroughly pleasing and benign portrait of domestic tranquility between a foreigner happily assimilated into American society over the course of two decades and a loving wife who could not look more like the All-American girl- next-door. Thus, it gives viewers pause when this innocuous, contented family man gets unsettlingly snared—and then some—in a rather hastily thrown law enforcement

net. The plot highlights the possibility of egregious error during such government-sponsored fishing expeditions.

Also unnerving and rather repellent is the smug, steely surety of Corrine Whitman (Meryl Streep), the head of CIA counterterrorism, who gives a terse green light to Anwar's abduction based upon seemingly flimsy evidence. Her decisive actions are in part propelled by the fact that one of the Agency's own is among the victims of a bomb explosion somewhere in Northern Africa. After the order is given, viewers see the airplane upon which Anwar is coming home pass the vertical majesty of the Washington Monument in what seems like a visual representation of how time-honored lines are now being crossed.

A hallmark of numerous thrillers by Alfred Hitchcock was the terrifying predicament of needing to prove one's innocence but being unable to do so, the desperate struggle to correct the misapprehensions of others while caught in a vice that continuously, excruciatingly tightens. Here, it is viscerally disturbing to watch Anwar's seemingly sincere bafflement concerning cellphone records that purportedly connect him to people the authorities are determinedly hunting. Most of those watching will have sized the man up and tend to believe him, especially upon hearing that his assertions have been backed up by a polygraph test. Therefore, they will likely wish to put a brake on the proceedings as Anwar is hooded, shackled, and roughly transported to an African prison, where the agony will not let up until he provides information that he does not possess.

Director Hood also makes sure that those watching *Rendition* feel for Anwar's family by tugging at every heartstring he can. For example, there is the early scene in which Isabella and her young son forlornly scan the airport concourse in vain for any sign of their loved one, the camera at one point zeroing in to capture the concerned look in the endearing tyke's bewildered, searching eyes. To further enhance Isabella's burden and the audience's sympathy, she is not only pregnant but soon to give birth. The character cannot help but be admired as she sets out to discover what has happened to her husband. The script provides her with a stroke of convenient good luck, as it just so happens that Alan Smith (Peter Sarsgaard), an old college classmate (and, one gets the feeling, former boyfriend) now works for a United States senator (a right-on-target Alan Arkin) who would be in a position to ferret out what Isabella needs to know. While savvy senior Senator Hawkins has his own reservations about rendition, he points out how politically foolhardy it would be for him to take on the administration armed with anything less than crystal-clear proof of a horrific governmental misstep. He tells Isabella that he unfortunately has little help to offer, to which she cries, "Please don't be another one of those people who just turns away!" With her plea, the makers of the film seem to be talking directly to its viewers.

Witherspoon's role largely consists of oppressed, knitted-brow concern and plaintive outbursts, her character wearily but earnestly waddling around in vain for assistance amidst Washington's cold marble halls and stonewalls. In one of the film's more heavy-handed shots, Isabella doubles over in pain immediately after shuffling dejectedly past a view of the Capitol.

Rendition potently depicts Anwar's torment and humiliation. Stripped naked, he is repeatedly fetched from a cramped, black hellhole to be tortured before viewers' eyes using a variety of agonizing methods. Looking on is Douglas Freeman (an unremittingly-muted, miscast Jake Gyllenhaal), a CIA analyst who makes an uneasy, queasy transition from deskwork to the dungeons when called upon to observe the "interrogation" of Anwar conducted by local glowering heavy-torture specialist Abasi Fawal (Yigal Naor). As Fawal's men extract blood from a stone but none of the information they desire, an increasingly discomforted Douglas (and, it is obviously hoped, those watching) comes to recognize not just the futility but the folly of what is transpiring. If the truth will not be believed, then Anwar tries to satisfy them with lies, after which Douglas aptly quotes from Shakespeare about how men under unbearable duress are likely to say anything. "In all the years you've been doing this," Douglas asks those in charge, "how often can you say that we've produced truly legitimate intelligence? Give me anything that outweighs the fact that if you torture one person you create ten, a hundred, a thousand new enemies." It is certainly food for thought.

A point is made when Douglas is guided by conscience to circumvent strong opposition to freeing Anwar, bravely setting the situation to rights. The subsequent bittersweet scene showing the still-dazed former prisoner's reunification with his family may elicit some tears for one to dab at, but those behind *Rendition* want viewers to recognize that the consequences of government mistakes cannot be wiped away as easily.

Throughout the film, the main plot is interwoven with a disquieting (and somewhat distracting) one about the creation of enemies Douglas had spoken about, showing the rise of an exceedingly fresh-faced, fervent wave of new terrorists indoctrinated into believing that suicidal fanaticism against the United States and its allies is the surest way to curry God's favor. When Fawal's daughter Fatima (Zineb Oukach) is revealed to have tragically died in that earlier blast, crying over the ticking body of her bomb-encased boyfriend, Khalid (Moa Khouas), it is meant to be another miserable domino-fall set in motion by American hubris.

Like Isabella's exertions on behalf of her husband, *Rendition* also struggled to make much headway at the box-office. As a number of critics noted, the film's timely and valid argument is too passionately pressed. Writing in the *Hollywood Reporter*, Kirk Honeycutt called it "a contrived melodrama, emotionally jerry-rigged to ensure audiences arrive at the proper conclusion." The film's contents make the aforementioned assertions by its makers to the contrary seem disingenuous for their intentions starkly contrast the courage of their convictions as portrayed so clearly on screen.

David L. Boxerbaum

CREDITS

Corrinne Whitman: Meryl Streep
Isabella El-Ibrahimi: Reese Witherspoon
Douglas Freeman: Jake Gyllenhaal
Alan Smith: Peter Sarsgaard
Senator Hawkins: Alan Arkin
Anwar El-Ibrahimi: Omar Metwally
Abasi Fawal: Yigal Naor
Khalid: Moa Khouas
Fatima: Zineb Oukach
Origin: USA
Language: English
Released: 2007
Production: Steve Golin, Marcus Viscidi; Anonymous Content, Level 1 Entertainment; released by New Line Cinema
Directed by: Gavin Hood
Written by: Kelley Sane
Cinematography by: Dion Beebe
Music by: Paul Hepker, Mark Killian
Sound: Nico Louw
Editing: Megan Gill
Costumes: Michael Wilkinson
Production Design: Barry Robison
MPAA rating: R
Running time: 120 minutes

REVIEWS

Boston Globe Online. October 19, 2007.
Chicago Sun-Times Online. October 19, 2007.
Christian Science Monitor Online. October 19, 2007.
Entertainment Weekly Online. October 12, 2007.
Hollywood Reporter Online. September 7, 2007.
Los Angeles Times Online. October 19, 2007.
New York Times Online. October 19, 2007.
Rolling Stone Online. October 18, 2007.
San Francisco Chronicle. October 19, 2007, p. E9.

Variety Online. September 7, 2007.
Washington Post Online. October 19, 2007.

QUOTES

Douglas Freeman: "In all the years you've been doing this, how often can you say that we've produced truly legitimate intelligence? Once? Twice? Ten times? Give me a statistic; give me a number. Give me a pie chart, I love pie charts. Anything, anything that outweighs the fact that if you torture one person you create ten, a hundred, a thousand new enemies."

RENO 911!: MIAMI

Eight Cops, Not One Clue.
—Movie tagline

Box Office: $20.3 million

The basic formula of *Reno 911!: Miami* is fairly simple: cross the television show *COPS* with equal parts *Airplane!* (1980) and *Police Academy* (1984). Ever the intrepid comedy team, writer/director Robert Ben Garant and his co-writers and co-stars Thomas Lennon and Kerri Kenney-Silver, all former members of MTV's comedy ensemble series *The State*, head to Miami for the troupe's first big-screen outing.

The plot of *Reno 911!: Miami* is as simple as it is wonderfully ludicrous: The bungling Reno sheriff's department is the only law enforcement agency left in Miami when the national law enforcement convention is subjected to a bioterror attack, trapping police officers from all over the country (including, apparently, Miami's entire police force) in the convention center. It is up to the *Reno 911!* crew to maintain order on the streets. The film announces right away that it will not be bound to the strict *COPS*-like documentary (or mockumentary) style of Comedy Central's *Reno 911!* television show by opening with what turns out to be an elaborate dream sequence involving a high-pressure hostage situation and featuring Danny DeVito (one of several celebrity cameos) as the district attorney. The deputies are introduced in the several opening scenes that follow, including an incident response call involving a runaway chicken. Not too long into the film, the team is invited to the aforementioned law enforcement convention in Miami—they pack up a bus (of course) and head across country. Ever the victims of rotten luck (or, more often, their own hilarious incompetence), they are not to be found on the check-in list for the convention and opt to shack up in what is surely high in the running for the grimiest, most lurid motel in all of Miami. This has the unintended benefit of keeping them outside of the convention center when the bioterror attack occurs. This

entire setup exists primarily to allow the *Reno 911!* ensemble to have a new venue for their misadventures—it lends a certain fish-out-of-water quality to the proceedings.

The plot is extremely thin, serving mostly as a springboard for what is actually the meat of the film—the specific situations: Officers Jones (Cedric Yarbrough) and Garcia (Carlos Alazraqui) are continually captured by a mysterious drug lord (Paul Rudd); the crew has to contend with a dead beached whale on, of all things, a topless beach (simple solution: blow up the whale); Deputies Raineesha Williams (Niecy Nash) and Trudy Wiegel (Kerri Kenney-Silver) respond to a report of lewd behavior and are confronted by *Reno 911!* series regular Terry (Nick Swardson), on roller skates and dressed in short-shorts, who informs them that he is staying in Miami in one of his seventeen houses recording an album. In a particularly zany moment, officers Jones and Garcia are sent on a call to remove an alligator from a backyard pool and are given advice by a somewhat overzealous, shorts-wearing (shorts seem to be a running gag for this troupe) neighbor who shows them how to deal with the gator: "You got to come at him like a predator," he advises them, "not like a prey. Like a predator." He is then promptly eaten. Lieutenant Jim Dangle (Thomas Lennon) and Deputy Travis Junior (Robert Ben Garant) also go out on a particularly dangerous (and dangerously funny) call: they have to check out a disturbance at notorious hip-hop producer Shug Knight's house. When Dangle fires a shot in the air to get the attention of the partying crowd, he and Junior find themselves on the business ends of a few dozen pistols—they have to do a striptease in order to escape (apparently crazy trumps violence).

Eventually, the *Reno 911!* crew screw things up one too many times, and deputy mayor Jeff Spoder (Patton Oswalt) tells them to leave Miami. They try to make it up to him by bringing him an ice cream cake, but wind up instead catching him red-handed with the drug lord. It turns out that the biological attack on the convention center was, in fact, a conspiracy by Spoder and the drug lord to remove the government hierarchy and law enforcement from the scene, effectively putting the deputy mayor in charge of Miami and leaving the drug lord (who reveals his name to be Ethan) free to make Miami the largest "narco-empire" that the world has ever known. After a chuckle-inducing chase in golf carts, the team corners and captures Jeff (who also happens to have the antidote to the biotoxin). The gang return to the convention center with the antidote in hand, save their fellow officers, and are treated by their colleagues as heroes.

Many of the cameos and supporting performances lend *Reno 911!: Miami* much of its comedic punch.

Standouts include The Rock (also know as Dwayne Johnson) as Rick Smith, an overly self-confident SWAT officer, Patton Oswalt as deputy mayor Jeff Spoder, and Paul Reubens as Terry's dad. The two guest performers who steal absolutely every scene they are in, though, are Paul Rudd as Ethan the Drug Lord and Nick Swardson as Terry (who refers to himself as "Super Terry"). Ethan sports a Tony Montana from *Scarface* (1983) accent until he is forced to reveal that he is actually from Fort Collins, Colorado, but had to move to Miami because it was too hard to sell cocaine in Colorado. Terry is brilliant in all his over-the-top gay roller-skating glory. A walking punch line, Terry makes outlandish claims (all of which prove to be true by the end of the film) and generally drips with innuendo, apple martini lube, and hilarity.

The *Reno 911!* cast is easily the film's greatest strength—they are lovable, well-intentioned, and deadly funny. Just seeing Thomas Lennon in character as Lieutenant Jim Dangle with his trademark ultra-short shorts (so that he can be a "law enfacement cheetah") and moustache, even out of context, is pure comedy gold.

Oddly, relying so heavily on this wonderful ensemble to drive the film forward has its drawbacks as well—namely, to receive the full effect of the comedy requires some previous knowledge of and investment in the characters. Audience members familiar with the deputies' antics on the small screen will likely find more to enjoy in the film. The uninitiated will probably be left wondering what all the buzz is about.

John Boaz

CREDITS

Lt. Jim Dangle: Thomas Lennon
Deputy Travis Junior: Robert Ben Garant
Deputy Raineesha Williams: Niecy Nash
Terry: Nick Swardson
Deputy Trudy Wiegel: Kerri Kenney-Silver
Deputy James Garcia: Carlos Alazraqui
Deputy Cherisha Kimball: Mary Birdsong
Deputy Clementine Johnson: Wendi McLendon-Covey
Deputy S. Jones: Cedric Yarbrough
Ethan the drug lord: Paul Rudd
District Attorney: Danny DeVito (Cameo)
Head of Bomb Squad: Dwayne "The Rock" Johnson (Cameo)
Origin: USA
Language: English
Released: 2007
Production: Danny DeVito, Stacey Sher, Michael Shamberg, John Landgraf; Comedy Central, Jersey Films, Double Feature Films, High Sierra Carpeting; released by 20th Century-Fox

Directed by: Robert Ben Garant
Written by: Thomas Lennon, Robert Ben Garant, Kerri Kenney-Silver
Cinematography by: Joe Kessler
Music by: Craig (Shudder to Think) Wedren
Sound: Dennis Salcedo
Editing: John Refoua
Costumes: Mary Ann Bozek
MPAA rating: R
Running time: 84 minutes

REVIEWS

Chicago Sun-Times Online. February 23, 2007.
Detroit News. February 23, 2007, p. 4F.
Hollywood Reporter Online. February 23, 2007.
Los Angeles Times Online. February 23, 2007.
New York Times Online. February 23, 2007.
San Francisco Chronicle. February 23, 2007, p. E5.
Variety Online. February 22, 2007.
Washington Post. February 23, 2007, p. C5.

QUOTES

Deputy Travis Junior: "Reno is a lot like Mayberry on the TV except that everyone's on crystal meth and prostitution's legal."
Deputy Trudy Weigel: "I became a police officer because my doctor told me I needed to get out of the house more."

TRIVIA

The scene in which the officers blow up a whale is based on a actual incident that occurred in Florence, Oregon on November 12, 1970.

RESCUE DAWN

A true story of survival...declassified.
—Movie tagline

Box Office: $5.5 million

The true story of Vietnam-era prisoner-of-war (POW) Dieter Dengler is perfectly suited for Werner Herzog. The veteran German director loves stories of men overcoming nature to accomplish nearly impossible and often bizarre feats, such as the man who lugged a sailing vessel through the jungles and mountains of the Amazon rain forest in *Fitzcarraldo* (1982). Dengler's saga takes place in another jungle, in the mountains of Laos after he is shot down while flying secret bombing missions for the U.S. Navy in 1965, in the early days of America's involvement in Vietnam.

Shot down, captured, and held prisoner by the Vietcong, Dengler never loses his will to regain his freedom.

Herzog loves his story so much that he has made two separate films about it—the first a documentary called *Little Dieter Needs to Fly* (1997) and now this thinly fictionalized feature, *Rescue Dawn*, which hews very closely to Dengler's life story. It is easy to see what attracts Herzog to the saga: It features a character who refuses to give up his quest despite all odds, and who has become a political pariah because Americans were not even supposed to be in Laos at all. He is not completely abandoned by his country. While training for the mission, however, he is told not to use his radio so that the enemy cannot intercept the signal and counter-attack, so for all practical purposes he is on his own. Herzog has a soft spot for the rugged individual, the iconoclast whose motives are nonetheless laudable even if others believe he is crazy.

In a departure from the usual Herzog film, though, the protagonist of *Rescue Dawn* is not insane or a social misfit, such as the hero of his *Grizzly Man* (2005), who is both. So instead of feeling ambivalent about an antihero's quixotic pursuit of some crazed goal, audiences can root heartily for Dengler. What he wants to achieve—his escape and reunification with his fellow sailors—is what moviegoers love to see: the tale of a true hero, not to mention a patriot.

Christian Bale plays Dengler as an optimistic, resourceful, likable hero. He is the grown-up version of the little boy who has wanted to fly combat missions ever since he saw an Allied warplane on a bombing mission heading toward his apartment building when he was growing up in Germany during World War II. As Dengler recounts the story, the pilot looked him right in the eye and sparked in the boy an insatiable desire to take wing. But Dengler signed up thinking Vietnam would be a lark, not the beginnings of a protracted and unwinnable guerrilla war.

The story fits neatly into three acts. The prologue consists of a few scenes aboard Dengler's aircraft carrier. An officer swears the pilots to secrecy as he assigns them to fly over the mountainous North Vietnamese border into Laos, which the Vietcong guerrillas are using as a staging area. And the men poke fun at a military training film about how to survive in the jungle, a vignette that epitomizes the cocky, adolescent attitude of the Americans in general, including Dengler, who still believes in schoolyard rituals of comradeship.

Big-budget special effects are not within Herzog's financial reach, so the scenes of Dengler's mission might strike some audiences as a little clumsy. In fact, however, they fit nicely into the authentic time-period documentary feel of the film: in parts *Rescue Dawn*, with its slightly faded and fuzzy coloration, looks like a movie from the mid-1960s. Once Dengler is shot down,

moreover, his capture, mild torture by local village militia, and his interview with a Vietcong leader, where he refuses to sign a pledge renouncing his country and its values, play out like something from a period movie by Luis Buñuel—or by Herzog himself. Eschewing smooth dramatic buildup and scene transitions, Herzog presents *Rescue Dawn,* all the way to the end, as a series of sudden, unpredictable events, a dance between happenings that are out of Dengler's control and Dengler's continued efforts to get control of his situation.

Eventually Dengler is taken to a POW camp in a remote area of the jungle, the site of the prolonged and fascinating Act Two. He meets three (presumably) Vietnamese prisoners and two other Americans: Duane (Steve Zahn), a pilot shot down more than a year earlier, and Gene (Jeremy Davies), a prisoner whose grip on reality is tenuous, and who keeps insisting that the captives will be released very soon. The very first day he is in the camp and meets his fellow POWs, Dengler informs them he plans to escape. At first they scoff, with Duane telling him the real prison is outside the bamboo stakes, in the jungle. But soon Dengler demonstrates his resourcefulness, stealing a nail and fashioning it into a lock-picking device to free the other men of the handcuffs in which, along with leg shackles, they are made to sleep every night.

As POW dramas go, this is a taut and fascinating one. It includes tensions between the three Americans, with Gene's participation (and sanity) questionable. Davies, who looks so emaciated his ribs are sticking out, channels Dennis Hopper as a half-crazed hippie with a paranoid, conspiratorial worldview. It is a remarkable performance, and his character is much like the usual Herzog protagonist. Zahn quietly does an even more effective job shaping Duane into an intelligent, stubborn cynic gradually won over by Dengler's skills and attitude.

With these two wonderful supporting roles, Bale is given an opportunity to shine, and he does so, breathing a flexible but determined will into his every action and pronouncement. Bale makes Dengler's heroism into something very warm and human, something within reach of ordinary people, and when Herzog allows his plotters to show signs of fear and emotion (Duane vomits during the escape attempt), it only heightens viewers appreciation of their courage. Herzog's refusal to go Hollywood with the story, and to allow its awkward, confusing, sudden jolts and jerks to breathe freely without too much directorial manipulation, make *Rescue Dawn* mesmerizing. Its tone is very similar to some of the best World War II movies, and its attitude much like Clint Eastwood's pair of 2006 films about Iwo Jima: completely sympathetic for characters on both sides of the conflict, and utterly devoid of political messages. Even the message that war is hell is played down because the details of the situation make it unnecessary to do more than show what happens.

Bale is wonderful, but one cannot help but wonder why he did not try a dialect coach who would give him at least a hint of a German accent. He seems far too WASPish to be an immigrant American.

The third act of the film concerns what happens once Dengler makes good on his escape plans, though they do go a bit awry. This part is the closest to a typical Herzog film, as sanity fades away in the middle of an unforgiving, majestic, overwhelming natural world. It is a survivalist tale that ends as abruptly and inexplicably as it must have seemed to Dengler.

Herzog's documentary on Dengler shows us his entire life, and because this film concerns only his imprisonment and escape, it probably should have ended with his rescue. The epilogue scenes, with his Navy comrades spiriting him away from the hospital for a shipboard celebration complete with a microphone-wielding emcee, seem like something from another film, and are hard to digest after the beautiful solemnity, solitude, and courage of Dengler's jungle exile. At the end, Herzog seems to shy away a little in the realization that he has made what could be seen as a gung-ho, patriotic film. Dengler refuses to give the hordes of fellow sailors awaiting their missions some jingoistic rhetoric, settling instead for an off-the-cuff, homespun homily about how to survive. He seems uncomfortable, despite his shouts of joy, being out of the action, and so does Herzog.

Michael Betzold

CREDITS

Dieter Dengler: Christian Bale
Duane: Steve Zahn
Gene: Jeremy Davies
Lessard: Evan Jones
Admiral: Marshall Bell
Squad Leader: Zach Grenier
Spook: Toby Huss
Phisit: Abhijati Jusakul
Norman: Pat Healy
Y.C.: Galen Yuen
Procet: Lek Chaiyan Chunsuttiwat
Origin: USA
Language: English
Released: 2006
Production: Elton Brand, Steve Marlton, Harry Knapp; Gibraltar Entertainment; released by MGM
Directed by: Werner Herzog

Written by: Werner Herzog
Cinematography by: Peter Zeitlinger
Music by: Klaus Badelt
Sound: Paul Paragon
Editing: Joe Bini
Art Direction: Arin Pinijvararak
Costumes: Annie Dunn
MPAA rating: PG-13
Running time: 125 minutes

REVIEWS

Boxoffice Online. March 30, 2007.
Entertainment Weekly. July 13, 2007, p. 46.
Hollywood Reporter Online. July 3, 2007.
Los Angeles Times Online. July 4, 2007.
New York Times Online. July 4, 2007.
New Yorker Online. July 9, 2007.
Newsweek Online. June 28, 2007.
Premiere Online. July 5, 2007.
Variety Online. September 11, 2006.

QUOTES

Dieter: "When I was uh...five or something', I was looking out the window, with my brother...and we see this fighter plane coming right at us. I was not scared. I was mesmerized! Because for me, this pilot was this all-mighty being from the clouds. From that moment on, I knew I wanted to be him. I wanted to be one of them. I wanted to be a pilot."
Duane: "You're a strange bird, Dieter. A man tries to kill you and you want his job."

TRIVIA

Christian Bale lost 55 pounds for his role, Steve Zahn lost 40 pounds for his, and Jeremy Davies lost 33 pounds for his. In a show of solidarity, director Werner Herzog lost almost 30 pounds.

AWARDS

Nomination:
Ind. Spirit 2008: Support. Actor (Zahn).

RESERVATION ROAD

To find the truth, you have to find who's hiding it.
—Movie tagline

The sadistic revenge drama *Reservation Road* was directed by Terry George, who last helmed *Hotel Rwanda* (2004), but the film does not contain a hint of the political subtext that might have made it slightly more interesting or relevant. Instead, the perpetually dreary tragedy focuses on the personal plight of two men and one woman caught in a downward spiral of grief, revenge, and crisis of conscience without giving any special insight into either those involved or the topics touched upon.

Most critics found the film, about the aftermath of a child's death in a tragic accident, an excruciating, pointless exercise in misery and payback without any corresponding catharsis or meaning. Based on the well-received 1998 novel by John Burnham Schwartz, credited for the adaptation along with George, the drama is more suited to the page, where the emotions and characters are more fully explored and more precisely organized.

The pivotal event, a hit-and-run accident, happens in the first few minutes of the film. Ethan Learner (Joaquin Phoenix) and his wife Grace (Jennifer Connelly) have stopped for gas on Reservation Road after their ten-year-old son Josh's (Sean Curley) cello recital; a motorist strikes and kills the boy then drives off in front of a shocked Ethan. After attending a Boston Red Sox game at Fenway Park, Dwight (Mark Ruffalo) and his son Lucas (Eddie Alderson) are late in returning Lucas to the home of Dwight's ex-wife Ruth (Mira Sorvino); after Dwight hits something, he panics, and drives off in haste.

Soon, all of Connecticut knows of the tragedy, including Dwight who now knows exactly what he has done. Ethan, whose grief has turned to anger, turns to the Internet when the police investigation has stalled, and reads advice from other grieving parents in the same situation. In a ridiculously convenient plot twist, Ethan hires Dwight's law firm to suss out the killer and Dwight himself is assigned the job.

In the book, Dwight is a more complex, morally compromised character. Racked with guilt and agony, he is also selfish and a bit sly in his decision not to turn himself in. He wants to be a free man and spend time with his own son and family. The film has turned Dwight into a spineless shell of his literature self, merely too timid and frightened to speak up until the film's end when the inevitable confrontation with Ethan indeed comes to play out.

The film purports to be a study in grief, examining the different ways Ethan, Grace, and Dwight deal with the unbearable accident. Ethan becomes enraged and obsessed with tracking down the driver and exacting justice. Grace turns her anger inward, into depression, and quietly works on healing through time and acceptance. The different ways they deal with it drives a wedge between them, each not understanding the methods of the other. There is nothing too enlightening, however, about showing Ethan busily searching chat rooms for answers or Grace, alone, in silent contemplation. As Mahnola Dargis noted in the *New York Times,* "*Reservation Road* wants to say something about grief, wrath and vengeance, which suggests that it's angling for some kind of post-September 11 relevance. But its insistence on turning Ethan and Dwight into equals—both loving father, both racked with pain—flattens the story's ambitions."

As in *Hotel Rwanda,* George is graced with a highly gifted cast. Phoenix is one of the best at delivering deep-seated melancholy and rage. Ruffalo's demeanor is equally suited to his role, and he plays the hunted animal as if he were born to it. Connelly has inhabited numerous roles that require her to portray depression convincingly. They work well off one another but are given little to do but play a single emotion through the entire film until the end. For the audience, it becomes a tedious and predictable march to the finish, when viewers know something finally must happen.

George uses a number of hackneyed techniques to indicate parallels between the two men. Several jump cuts showing the men engaged in identical activities. It is already established that their sons were both around the same age and Ruth used to teach piano to the Learner's daughter Emma (Elle Fanning). They are both upscale professionals, Ethan a professor, Dwight a lawyer. Having Ethan engage Dwight's law firm is just one more forced plot device to drive home the point that they are two sides of the same coin.

The film was updated from the novel to 2004, the year the Boston Red Sox won their first World Series in a generation, and shot on location in Connecticut. This slice of reality, however, fails to provide a much needed upbeat backdrop and Dwight and Lucas watch the Red Sox games with seemingly little interest or fanfare, which is in itself a tragedy.

James S. O'Neill

CREDITS

Ethan Learner: Joaquin Phoenix
Dwight Arno: Mark Ruffalo
Grace Learner: Jennifer Connelly
Ruth Wheldon: Mira Sorvino
Emma Learner: Elle Fanning
Steve: John Slattery
Sergeant Burke: Antoni Corone
Josh Learner: Sean Curley
Lucas Arno: Eddie Alderson
Origin: USA
Language: English
Released: 2007

Resident Evil: Extinction

Production: Nick Wechsler, A. Kitman Ho; Random House, Inc., Miracle Pictures, Volume One Entertainment; released by Focus Features
Directed by: Terry George
Written by: John Burnham Schwartz, Terry George
Cinematography by: John Lindley
Music by: Mark Isham
Sound: Gary Alper
Music Supervisor: Budd Carr, Nora Felder
Editing: Naomi Geraghty
Art Direction: Kim Jennings
Costumes: Catherine George
Production Design: Ford Wheeler
MPAA rating: R
Running time: 102 minutes

REVIEWS

Boston Globe Online. October 19, 2007.
Chicago Sun-Times Online. October 19, 2007.
Christian Science Monitor Online. October 19, 2007.
Entertainment Weekly Online. October 17, 2007.
Hollywood Reporter Online. September 13, 2007.
Los Angeles Times Online. October 19, 2007.
New York Times Online. October 19, 2007.
Rolling Stone Online. October 18, 2007.
San Francisco Chronicle. October 19, 2007, p. E12.
Variety Online. September 13, 2007.
Washington Post Online. October 19, 2007.

TRIVIA

A portion of the production was filmed in Stamford, Connecticut.

RESIDENT EVIL: EXTINCTION

Experimentation...Evolution...Extinction.
—Movie tagline
We Have Witnessed the Beginning...We Have Seen the Apocalypse...Now We Face Extinction.
—Movie tagline

Box Office: $50.6 million

Resident Evil: Extinction, the third in the zombie-film trilogy that includes *Resident Evil* (2002) and *Resident Evil: Apocalypse* (2004), aspires to the cult-level of post-apocalyptic genres classics like the Mad Max trilogy (1979–1985) or even *Escape from New York* (1981), but falls far short and delivers only a tired retread of its predecessors. The pulp-entertainment pastiche and first-person narrative construct established in the opening chapter of the series is woefully absent as *Resident Evil: Extinction* careens down the path set by its immediate predecessor. Like *Apocalypse,* the latest entry in the series provides a diminishing amount of thrills, action, and narrative.

In the time that has passed since the events of *Apocalypse,* the world has been ravaged by the T-Virus (the side effects of which result in turning those infected with the virus into the living dead). Civilization has been reduced to pockets of survivors searching for areas unaffected by the virus. One such group, led by Claire Redfield (Ali Larter) and Carlos Olivera (Oded Fehr reprising his role from the second film), takes the form of a caravan headed west. Alice (Milla Jovovich), the heroine of the first two films, is also aimlessly wandering the wasteland (à la the Mad Max films). Meanwhile, the evil Umbrella Corporation is searching for a cure to the T-Virus, though for nefarious and not humanitarian reasons. It seems that the mad scientist Dr. Isaacs (Iain Glen) has designs on domesticating those afflicted with the T-Virus as a cheap labor force for the company. Eventually, these three groups converge on one another and computer-generated zombie carnage ensues.

As written by co-producer and series stalwart Paul W.S. Anderson (he also directed the first film and wrote the sequel), *Extinction* does little more than serve up a plodding version of its gaming forebears. The plot, as Erin Meister noted in the *Boston Globe,* does not move beyond poorly reproduced game play. "Alice faces and overcomes an obstacle," laments Meister, "continues to hightail it with the caravan [of survivors], is met by someone or something that provides information about the next leg of her journey, and [then] proceeds toward that end." Ultimately, the film is nothing more than another level to the game (and not a very engaging one at that). The fault here lies in the transition from a first-person narrative to multi-player carnage and the shifting of setting from the claustrophobic Hive to the entire world. In the first film, the story unraveled as the amnesiac Alice experienced it. Her character functioned as a surrogate for the viewer (or player to carry the gaming analogy to its conclusion). The thrills and dangers were immediate and entertaining. Subsequent installments in the series forgo the first-person tack and consist of chaotic group action sequences connected by ham-fisted storytelling.

There is nothing scary or thrilling about the proceedings. The film moves slowly from one action sequence to another. Whereas the first film embraced a kinetic tempo, *Extinction* is no more than a series of repetitive shoot-'em-ups (as was *Apocalypse*). In fact, the central conflict between Alice (and by proxy, the human race) and the constructs of evil corporate America, as

338

MAGILL'S CINEMA ANNUAL

well as the misuse of technology, are taken as a given in this installment and are neither further explored nor explained. Like *Apocalypse,* the climactic battle between Alice and a mutated T-Virus victim is a forced conclusion that is neither exciting nor satisfying.

These films have become nothing more than set pieces to showcase Jovovich as Alice. Supporting characters exist solely to move Alice from scene to scene and be the next victim of violence. The characters are also eerily interchangeable with those from the previous film. Again, had the franchise stuck with telling the story entirely from Alice's point of view, the shortcomings of these characters and the focus on Alice would not be as glaring or annoying. But, in trying to expand the Resident Evil universe, these films have only diminished it. Though the video-game vixen role has become second nature for Jovovich, she is, as Frank Scheck noted in the *Hollywood Reporter,* "a striking action heroine, though she's more convincing visually...than vocally."

Director Russell Mulcahy (*Highlander* [1986]) tries ably to steer the film out of the rut that the franchise finds itself in, but cannot overcome the tedious and unoriginal script by Anderson. Oscar®-winning production designer Eugenio Caballero (*Pan's Labyrinth* [2006]) manages to create a few impressive set pieces (notably a Las Vegas reclaimed by the desert), but they are quickly left behind in a flurry of forgettable action sequences.

Although billed as the "final" film in the Resident Evil trilogy, *Extinction* comes complete with a non-ending that practically begs for a fourth film. Had this film reestablished the kinetic style and claustrophobic mood of the original film, the promise of another entry in the saga might not seem like a threat. But, as Matt Zoller Seitz deftly observed in the *New York Times, Resident Evil: Extinction* is "not exactly dull [but it is] never interesting either."

Michael J. Tyrkus

CREDITS

Alice: Milla Jovovich
Carlos Olivera: Oded Fehr
Claire Redfield: Ali Larter
Dr. Isaacs: Iain Glen
Betty: Ashanti
Mikey: Christopher Egan
K-Mart: Spencer Locke
Slater: Matthew Marsden
Chase: Linden Ashby
L.J.: Mike Epps
Albert: Jason O'Mara

Origin: Canada, Great Britain
Language: English
Released: 2007
Production: Bernd Eichinger, Samuel Hadida, Robert Kulzer, Jeremy Bolt, Paul W.S. Anderson; Davis Films, Constantin Film, Impact Pictures; released by Sony Pictures
Directed by: Russell Mulcahy
Written by: Paul W.S. Anderson
Cinematography by: David Johnson
Music by: Charlie Clouser
Sound: Luciano Larobina
Editing: Niven Howie
Art Direction: Marco Niro
Costumes: Joseph Porro
Production Design: Eugenio Caballero
MPAA rating: R
Running time: 94 minutes

REVIEWS

Boston Globe Online. September 22, 2007.
Entertainment Weekly Online. September 26, 2007.
Hollywood Reporter Online. September 24, 2007.
Los Angeles Times Online. September 24, 2007.
New York Times Online. September 24, 2007.
Premiere Online. September 24, 2007.
Variety Online. September 21, 2007.

QUOTES

Alice (to the White Queen): "I knew your sister. She was a homicidal bitch."

TRIVIA

Alice's new costume was designed by Milla Jovovich's clothing line, Jovovich-Hawk.

TRIVIA

When filming the crow attack scene, only two actual crows were used. The rest were created using special effects.

RESURRECTING THE CHAMP

Based on a true story, that was based on a lie.
—Movie tagline

Box Office: $3.1 million

More than one film in 2007 addressed the theme of journalistic integrity and the news business. *Interview* was about a de-fanged writer willing to do anything to get on top again who was cleverly outmaneuvered by his young ingénue interviewee. *Resurrecting the Champ* is another cautionary tale in that vein, with a mediocre writer out to make a name for himself by exploiting a seemingly weaker, but undoubtedly more famous, subject.

The writer is Erik (Josh Hartnett) assigned to the sports beat and regularly insulted by his dismissive boss Metz (Alan Alda). The subject is former heavyweight boxer Bob "Champ" Satterfield (Samuel L. Jackson), now a homeless old alcoholic. The Champ, however, recalls his glory days in vivid detail to the eager scribe, including a match with Rocky Marciano, that has Erik salivating with journalistic possibility.

The film is based, in part, on fact. J. R. Moehringer's *Los Angeles Times Magazine* article about Battlin' Bob Satterfield, a homeless former boxer, was a Pulitzer Prize finalist. Director Rod Lurie's tale takes place in Denver, where fictional journalist Erik is separated from his wife Joyce (Kathryn Morris) and desperate for the respect of his six-year-old son Teddy (Dakota Goyo). He sees the Champ as his way to do that as well as prove himself to *Denver Times* editor Metz.

Erik first comes across Champ after he is beaten and ridiculed by three street punks. Erik invites Champ to a fight he is covering and Champ's keen insights work their way into Erik's article, which garners unusual praise. He is emboldened to go over his boss's head and approach Whitley (David Paymer), the editor of the paper's Sunday magazine, directly and pitches what will become a cover story about the rise and fall of the Champ.

Lurie, along with writers Michael Bortman and Allison Burnett, give the newsroom scenes a canny reality that even actual journalists of big-city papers have agreed are spot-on. There is a nice good cop/bad cop dichotomy between the hard-nosed Metz (who gets to berate Erik with such lines such as "A lot of typing, not much writing"), and the more expansive Whitley that ensures Erik is given a fair chance.

Though it is clear both Erik and the Champ have something to gain by their camaraderie, it begins to become less clear who is actually more manipulative. Clearly Erik has exploited the washed-up boxer for his own ends, but then it comes to light that perhaps this garrulous transient is not who he claims to be. Suddenly, Erik's stunning cover-story success is in jeopardy and the search begins to authenticate the Champ as Satterfield, using old fight footage and photographs. As in *Interview*, the tables have turned and the predator becomes the prey.

The filmmakers inject a superfluous subplot involving father-son relationships and here the film is much weaker than in its main narrative thrust. Erik's father

was a famous sportscaster but not, perhaps, the best father. The cringe-inducing, made-up stories Erik regales his own son with about all the famous people he has met are an attempt to be a better father, but are sadly misguided. Paralleling Erik, the Champ displays a scar on his lower back that he attributes to his bad father. And the Champ's son became a gang member who was killed.

A consummate actor, Samuel L. Jackson plays the Champ without a trace of pathos ("I'm not a bum; just homeless") and a healthy dose of his usual wisdom wrapped in humor. Jackson, however, would never simply play the good-natured has-been with a heart of gold, and injects him with realistic streetwise cunning. It is clear no one will get the better of him. Josh Hartnett has a plum role in Erik, who is alternately a conniving social climber and doting father, and shows more range than he has in the past. Supporting actors Alan Alda and David Paymer are seasoned professionals whose performances are crucial to the realistic feel of the newsroom.

When Erik becomes an overnight sensation he is summoned to Chicago to serve as an on-air commentator for prizefight. The cable network's casting director, Andrea (Teri Hatcher), attempts to seduce him, and though the role is a small one, it is doubtless one of Hatcher's career-best performances.

Although the film backs off from what could have been a more scorching reprisal, it at least has the audience, as well as Erik, anxious about what will unfold. The film veers off track in its familial message and during its excessively long-winded, emotional monologues, but ultimately delivers an original, well-acted, intelligent story.

James S. O'Neill

CREDITS

Champ: Samuel L. Jackson
Erik: Josh Hartnett
Andrea Flak: Teri Hatcher
Joyce: Kathryn Morris
Metz: Alan Alda
Whitley: David Paymer
Polly: Rachel Nichols
Teddy: Dakota Goyo
Satterfield Jr.: Harry J. Lennix
Epstein: Peter Coyote
Kenny: Ryan McDonald
Origin: USA
Language: English
Released: 2007

Production: Mike Medavoy, Bob Yari, Rod Lurie, Marc Frydman; released by Yari Film Group
Directed by: Rod Lurie
Written by: Michael Bortman, Allison Burnett
Cinematography by: Adam Kane
Music by: Lawrence Nash Groupé
Sound: Trevor Jolly
Music Supervisor: Kevin J. Edelman
Editing: Sarah Boyd
Art Direction: Bill Ives
Costumes: Wendy Partridge
Production Design: Ken Rempel
MPAA rating: PG-13
Running time: 111 minutes

REVIEWS

Boston Globe Online. August 24, 2007.
Chicago Sun-Times Online. August 24, 2007.
Christian Science Monitor Online. August 24, 2007.
Entertainment Weekly Online. August 22, 2007.
Hollywood Reporter Online. January 21, 2007.
Los Angeles Times Online. August 24, 2007.
New York Times Online. August 24, 2007.
Premiere Online. August 23, 2007.
San Francisco Chronicle. August 24, 2007, p. E1.
Variety Online. January 22, 2007.
Washington Post. August 24, 2007, p. C6.

QUOTES

Erik: "A writer, like a boxer, must stand alone."
Champ: "I'm not a bum, just homeless."

ROCKET SCIENCE

Hal Hefner had his whole life...on the tip of his tongue.
—Movie tagline

Rocket Science, written and directed by Jeffrey Blitz, revolves around Hal Hefner (Reece Daniel Thompson), a lonely, put-upon New Jersey teenager with a stutter that renders him nearly speechless most of the time and that makes normal social interaction, even ordering lunch at the school cafeteria, a challenge for him. If one could relate to his mind-set and struggles, it might be possible to find a way into this story. Unfortunately, Hal is not a very interesting protagonist on which to build a narrative, and the film itself is suffused with a quirky sensibility that is guaranteed to engender overwrought critical acclaim but is really pretentious and tedious.

Critics have made comparisons to cult favorite *Rushmore* (1998)—the spirit of Wes Anderson hangs over

Rocket Science—and the brilliant *Election* (1999), probably because these films set in high school have an idiosyncratic point of view and actually focus on school itself and overachievers rather than typically mindless teen-movie melodrama and high jinks. But *Rocket Science* taps into the milieu of sophisticated teen films without the benefit of a plot or central character to give it its own reason for being.

In addition to his speech impediment, Hal faces a tough home life. At the beginning of the film, his father (Denis O'Hare) walks out, and his mother (Lisbeth Bartlett) quickly takes up with a Korean-American man, Judge Pete (Stephen Park). It is supposed to be some kind of joke on clueless suburbanites when Judge Pete brings a tuna casserole for dinner and Hal's mom mistakes it for some exotic Korean dish. Hal's brother, Earl (Vincent Piazza), is a bully who nonetheless sees himself as a wise mentor to his troubled sibling.

It is little wonder Hal thinks that he has found a haven when Ginny Ryerson (Anna Kendrick), a bright, self-assured, pretty student recruits him for the debate team, the last thing in the world he would see for himself. But he is flattered to be noticed in this way, and he is instantly smitten by her. Given her intelligence, spunk, and overwhelming drive to be a winner, Ginny is the most intriguing character in the movie. Her determination immediately draws comparisons to Reese Witherspoon's Tracy Flick in *Election,* but Ginny never becomes fully developed enough to make viewers truly care about her.

Even when it seems as if the relationship between Hal and Ginny might go somewhere exciting (they do take the first steps in a tentative teenage romance), Blitz insists on layering the film with so many eccentricities that it becomes self-conscious in the extreme. Across the street from Ginny lives Lewis (Josh Kay), a geek common in independent films, who spies on Ginny from his window. Lewis's mom and dad play the cello and piano, respectively, engaging in what they call "music therapy" for the good of their marriage. But when they play the Violent Femmes' "Blister in the Sun," it is just one more incongruous detail meant to make the audience laugh at these kooky people. And the film's narrator (Dan Cashman), who sounds like Alec Baldwin from Wes Anderson's *The Royal Tenenbaums* (2001), feels like a device meant to impart a sense of deep meaning that does not flow naturally from the screenplay itself. Even the little touches quickly become more annoying and precious as the film inches along, with shots of the lonely Hal hiding in the janitor's closet at school, running alone in the school corridor, and riding his bicycle in the middle of a long suburban street. His alienation is accentuated repeatedly so that viewers cannot miss the point.

One bright spot is the appearance of Jonah Hill, who made such an impression in *Superbad* (2007). In just two short scenes as a philosophy enthusiast in *Rocket Science,* he generates some laughs while further reinforcing the dormancy of the rest of the film.

While Blitz ratchets up the angst, he does not develop a credible plot. Ginny claims to see potential in Hal, but no debate teacher, even one as seemingly oblivious as Coach Lumbly (Margo Martindale), would let a student who can barely talk enter such competitions. It would be like the baseball coach starting a pitcher who cannot reach home plate. The story is built on this absurd premise, yet everything hinges on it. When Ginny mysteriously disappears, only to reappear enrolled at a private school, viewers discover that she had a bigger scheme in mind all along—she wanted to back a poor debater to help her atone for the second-place finish she suffered in the previous year's state championships when her partner, Ben Wekselbaum (Nicholas D'Agosto), froze on the stage. Hal, of course, is hurt at being used, but even Ginny's betrayal is hard to care about because the plan itself is far-fetched and their relationship is so thin. To make matters worse, Ginny is such a firecracker that Hal seems even duller once she is largely gone from the movie.

Hal concocts his own plot for revenge, which ultimately goes nowhere. He tracks down Ben, who, in an implausible plot turn, dropped out of school and fled the suburbs after his disastrous debate performance, only to find work at a dry cleaners in Trenton. (We are supposed to think it is funny that the naïve Ben considers Trenton the big city.) They team up for the upcoming championships, and Ben improves Hal's technique slightly by getting him to sing his debating points to the tune of the "Battle Hymn of the Republic." It is yet one more goofy narrative tic that smacks of the arbitrary. Hal does not get to finish the debate, however, because his and Ben's application as a home-schooled team is declared invalid, rendering the final act just as pointless as everything that went before.

By the end of the film, it is not clear that Hal has learned anything. Every movie does not have to conclude with a great epiphany or even a character transformation and a story set in the world of high school debate does not have to finish with a decisive competition, but there should be some compelling reason for watching a boring, non-communicative character suffer while an assortment of oddballs orbit around him.

A would-be exercise in style rooted in the most obvious expressions of teen isolation and suburban ennui, *Rocket Science* is a chore to sit through. What is most surprising, perhaps, is that Blitz helmed the wonderful documentary about contestants in the National Spelling Bee, *Spellbound* (2003). In the real lives of these overachievers and their families, Blitz found all the drama, humanity, and suspense so sorely lacking in his feature narrative debut.

Peter N. Chumo II

CREDITS

Hal Hefner: Reece Daniel Thompson
Ginny Ryerson: Anna Kendrick
Coach Lumbly: Margo Martindale
Ben Wekselbaum: Nicholas D'Agosto
Earl Hefner: Vincent Piazza
Origin: USA
Language: English
Released: 2007
Production: Effie T. Brown, HBO Films, Sean Welch; Duly Noted, B&W Films; released by Picturehouse
Directed by: Jeffrey Blitz
Written by: Jeffrey Blitz
Cinematography by: Jo Willems
Music by: Eef Barzelay
Sound: Ken Ishii
Music Supervisor: Evyen J. Klean
Editing: Yana Gorskaya
Art Direction: Halina Gebarowicz
Costumes: Ernesto Martinez
Production Design: Rick Butler
MPAA rating: R
Running time: 98 minutes

REVIEWS

Boston Globe Online. August 17, 2007.
Chicago Sun-Times Online. August 16, 2007.
Entertainment Weekly Online. August 8, 2007.
Hollywood Reporter Online. January 20, 2007.
New York Times Online. August 10, 2007.
Premiere Online. August 9, 2007.
San Francisco Chronicle. August 10, 2007, p. E1.
Variety Online. January 21, 2007.
Washington Post. August 17, 2007, p. C6.

QUOTES

Ben Wekselbaum: "Man, it's a blessing to be squarely and dearly out of the goddamn suburbs."
Hal Hefner: "It's one of those two, love or revenge, I'm not really sure which one. But it's one of those two that made me throw a cello through somebody's window, so you figure it out."

TRIVIA

Like the film's main character, director Jeffrey Blitz also had a stammer as a teenager and joined his high school's debate team.

Nomination:

Ind. Spirit 2008: First Feature, Support. Actress (Kendrick), First Screenplay.

RUSH HOUR 3

> *This summer, they're kicking it in Paris.*
> —Movie tagline

> *The fastest mouth in the East and the loudest mouth in the West prepare for their finest hour!*
> —Movie tagline

Box Office: $140.1 million

The calendar of movie releases in 2007 will perhaps best be remembered for what has been termed "the summer of three-quels," a summer movie season filled with third chapters in previously successful film franchises, most notably, *Pirates of the Caribbean: At World's End, Shrek the Third, Spider-Man 3, The Bourne Ultimatum,* and *Ocean's Thirteen.* On the surface, this would seem to be an ideal situation for both Hollywood and moviegoers—one can see how releasing films with established pedigrees and built-in fan bases could be both crowd-pleasing (in the most populist sense of the word) and extremely profitable. And, indeed, all of these films grossed hundreds of millions of dollars internationally. However, far from being the "sure thing" Hollywood was counting on, these three-quels, for the most part, exhibited characteristics of the law of diminishing returns. With the exception of *The Bourne Ultimatum* (the only critical and popular hit of the three-quels), all of these films made less than their previous chapters and were largely considered creative and popular disappointments. Granted, *Spider-Man 3* was still the highest-grossing film of 2007—making the case that franchise filmmaking is still wildly profitable—but neither critics nor audiences embraced the film as they had the previous Spider-Man chapters. The 2007 summer movie season began with Hollywood feeling as if they had been given a license to print money, thanks to the continuing adventures of Jack Sparrow, Shrek, and Spider-Man, but the season ended with a general sense of unmet expectations.

Perhaps that end-of-summer malaise was the perfect time to release Brett Ratner's *Rush Hour 3,* one of the least successful of the 2007 three-quels and one of the most creatively bankrupt films to be released by Hollywood in some time. The best word to describe almost every aspect of *Rush Hour 3*'s production is "lazy." This is a film that was wholeheartedly expecting to rest on its laurels, a completely phoned-in sequel, in every way,

shape, and form, which was hoping that the goodwill engendered by *Rush Hour* (1998) and *Rush Hour 2* (2001) might make moviegoers more forgiving of this exercise in going through the motions. The main person to blame is director Ratner, a ham-fisted engineer of underwhelming Hollywood product, who previously directed two other half-hearted third chapters of once-popular film franchises (*Red Dragon* [2002] and *X-Men: The Last Stand* [2006]). Throughout *Rush Hour 3,* Ratner fails on multiple levels to inject the film with any sense of life or even the fun that cropped up in moments of the previous *Rush Hour* films.

That is not to say that the movie's stars, Jackie Chan and Chris Tucker, are entirely blameless. An enormous star in Asia, Chan has struggled to find his niche in the American film industry, and his increasingly juvenile U.S. releases have failed to attract much attention of late. Tucker, on the other hand, seems to have retired from filmmaking all together, aside from making *Rush Hour* movies. A bombastic comedian who won a huge fan following with his hilarious work in 1995's *Friday,* Tucker has devolved, career-wise, into the worst kind of paycheck player, emerging as a shadow of his former self who makes public appearances only to sleepwalk through familiar shtick.

While the first two *Rush Hour* films were built around fairly organic fish-out-of-water premises—placing Chan in urban Los Angeles and Tucker in Hong Kong—*Rush Hour 3* struggles constantly to find new water, retreading the Los Angeles scenes of the first *Rush Hour* until it unceremoniously dumps the stars in an insultingly caricatured version of France. The film is set three years after *Rush Hour 2,* and Inspector Lee (Jackie Chan) is now a bodyguard for the Chinese ambassador Han (Tzi Ma), whose daughter Lee and James Carter (Chris Tucker) saved in the first movie. After Han announces to the World Criminal Court (which has strangely convened in Los Angeles of all places) that he knows the identity of Shy Shen, the legendary head of the Chinese Triad mafia, Han is shot, an act that brings Carter and Lee back together in their attempt to find the would-be assassin. It turns out that the contract killer is Lee's long-lost brother Kenji (Hiroyuki Sanada), who, along with his Triad cohorts, makes another attempt on Han and his daughter Soo Yung (Zhang Jingchu), the now-grown damsel in distress of the original *Rush Hour.* Lee and Carter discover that the Triad baddies are based in Paris, so they leave Soo Yung in the care of the head of the World Criminal Court, French ambassador Reynard (Max von Sydow), and travel to France. (Of course, that it might be a mistake to leave Soo Yung in the custody of a powerful Frenchman—who is connected to both Han and the Triads—right after they discover that the bad guys are French, does not occur to either Carter or Lee.)

In France, the crime-fighting duo meet a variety of borderline racist French characters, including George (Yvan Attal), a snobby cab driver who soon learns to love American-style violence, and the over-the-top Detective Revi (played by legendary director Roman Polanski) who molests our heroes with violent cavity-searches before he lets them into the country. (One wonders how, given his sordid legal history, anyone was able to convince Polanski that watching him molest anyone on-screen could be even the slightest bit funny.) After Carter and Lee meet Geneviève (Noémie Lenoir), a mysterious woman with firsthand knowledge of Shy Shen's identity, they are soon drawn into a final confrontation at the Eiffel Tower between Kenji and the Triads, who are now holding Soo Yung hostage.

Beyond the implied racism, lazy screenwriting, and incoherent plot, the two most cardinal sins of *Rush Hour 3* are that it is neither particularly funny nor exciting. Big Hollywood blockbusters do not necessarily need to be politically correct or have well-plotted narratives, if they can deliver a crisp, fun sense of spectacle. Unfortunately, *Rush Hour 3* fails that goal in all regards. The best word to describe the action sequences in *Rush Hour 3* is "turgid." In the age of Michael Bay and of Paul Greengrass's Jason Bourne movies, modern audiences are intimately familiar with how pulse-pounding, slickly-produced action sequences should look and feel. Ratner, however, seems completely inept and unprepared when it comes to action, staging fight scenes that look less convincing than a community theater sword-fight. Chan is a legendary martial arts master, but in *Rush Hour 3,* he seems tired and listless, as if he feels the sequel's big budget will somehow hide his lack of commitment to the action scenes. In one scene Lee and Carter are inexplicably drawn into a fight with a seven-foot Chinese giant at a martial arts studio (the scene makes no sense on any level), and the whole sequence looks as if it was blocked and filmed in about ten minutes. There are fight scenes in 1970s Roger Moore James Bond movies that had more of a pulse and sense of danger. And the final battle, set on an unconvincing replica of the Eiffel Tower, looks like something one might see at an amusement park stunt show.

With such poor action, *Rush Hour 3* should have been able to fall back on Chan's and Tucker's comedic timing, but even that seems strangely absent. The duo retreat into their old routines, lamely trying to resurrect running jokes from the previous *Rush Hour* movies, and this is where it truly becomes apparent how dated the whole affair has become. *Rush Hour 3* would have been a very popular film back in 1997, because that is where its sensibilities reside. This is a movie that smugly as-

sumes that we all think Jackie Chan is the greatest martial arts guru ever, Chris Tucker is the funniest man alive, and big explosions are the be-all and end-all pinnacle of action filmmaking. The problem is, filmgoers have all seen Jet Li and *House of Flying Daggers* (2004), been introduced to Chris Rock and Dave Chappelle, and sat through actions movies ranging from *The Matrix* (1999) to *The Bourne Ultimatum*. We know there is something better out there and, as an audience, we resent Ratner for treating us like such ill-informed, easily impressed yokels. It has been said that good things come in threes. While the summer of three-quels might prove that adage wrong, at the very least, one can hope that the "good thing" that comes of *Rush Hour 3* is that it brings this limp franchise to a long-delayed and much-needed end.

Tom Burns

CREDITS

Chief Inspector Lee: Jackie Chan
Det. James Carter: Chris Tucker
Varden Reynard: Max von Sydow
Kenji: Hiroyuki Sanada
George: Yvan Attal
Isabella: Rosalyn Sanchez
Det. Jacques Revi: Roman Polanski
Geneviève: Noémie Lenoir
Consul Han: Tzi Ma
George's Wife: Julie Depardieu
Dragon Lady: Youki Kudoh
Sister Agnes: Dana Ivey
Soo Yung: Zhang Jingchu
Origin: USA
Language: English
Released: 2007
Production: Arthur Sarkissian, Roger Birnbaum, Jay Stern, Jonathan Glickman, Andrew Z. Davis; released by New Line Cinema
Directed by: Brett Ratner
Written by: Jeff Nathanson
Cinematography by: J. Michael Muro
Music by: Lalo Schifrin
Sound: Jeff Wexler, George A. Flores
Editing: Don Zimmerman, Mark Helfrich, Dean Zimmerman
Art Direction: Chad S. Frey
Costumes: Betsy Heimann
Production Design: Ed Verreaux
MPAA rating: PG-13
Running time: 91 minutes

REVIEWS

Boston Globe Online. August 9, 2007.
Chicago Sun-Times Online. August 10, 2007.
Entertainment Weekly Online. August 8, 2007.

Hollywood Reporter Online. August 3, 2007.
Los Angeles Times Online. August 10, 2007.
New York Times Online. August 10, 2007.
San Francisco Chronicle. August 9, 2007, p. E1.
Variety Online. August 2, 2007.
Wall Street Journal. August 10, 2007, p. W1.
Washington Post. August 10, 2007, p. C1.

QUOTES

Detective James Carter: "How do you say surrender in Chinese?"

Detective James Carter: "It's over Reynard, you know what it's like for old men in prison. They call you Pops, they make you work in the library, your best friend is gonna be a MOUSE."

TRIVIA

Both Steven Seagal and Jean-Claude Van Damme were considered for the role of the villain in the film, but the part eventually went to Hiroyuki Sanada after multiple script rewrites.

S

THE SAVAGES

Box Office: $6.2 million

Philip Seymour Hoffman has made a career out of playing unkempt, slovenly characters, which is why his portrayal of the fastidious, vivacious Truman Capote in *Capote* was Oscar®-worthy. But never has Hoffman been more of an unhappy slob than in his portrayal of Jon in Tamara Jenkins's acclaimed character study, *The Savages*.

The plot of *The Savages* is simple on the surface. Jon's younger sister, Wendy (Laura Linney), gets a phone call informing her that their estranged father, Lenny (Philip Bosco), has lapsed into some form of dementia at the home he shares in Sun City, Arizona, with his female companion of twenty years. By the time the two siblings fly out there, the woman has died, and her children greet them with the news that Lenny cannot live there anymore. And he has been hospitalized with a diagnosis of Parkinson's disease.

The father whom they have never been close to in the past has suddenly become their responsibility, and it is a huge challenge for Jon and Wendy. Their lives are a bit of a mess themselves as they approach middle age (Jon is forty-two, Wendy thirty-seven). Jon teaches theater at a college in Buffalo, New York (his specialty is Bertolt Brecht and the "theater of social unrest"), while Wendy is a freelance office temp and unsuccessful playwright in New York City. Their personal lives are miserable: Jon's girlfriend of three years is leaving to return to Poland because they cannot commit to marriage, and Wendy is having an affair with an older married man who stops by for quickies while he is walking his dog.

Neither of Lenny's children has a family because neither has worked out their own problematic childhood. It is revealed that their mother abandoned them while they were small and their father was abusive and neglectful. The nature of the abuse is not spelled out—Jenkins, who wrote the screenplay as well as directing, wisely steers clear of moralizing specifics. Instead of flashbacks that depict their unhappy childhoods, Jenkins gives us, in all their struggles and failures, the adult products of that childhood. It is a familiar, realistic, and depressing picture, and rarely has it been tackled so compellingly and entertainingly.

The great strength of *The Savages* is its perceptive portrayals of the siblings and the keen challenges they face in overcoming their emotional baggage. Hoffman, as Jon, is a slumping hulk of a man, almost hollowed out with grief. He is like a big dead weight on the earth, barely able to move or speak, having lived so many years with his sadness and grief. He functions professionally and socially, shuffling around and performing his teaching and his intellectual work, but he does so doggedly. And being in the presence of his father seems to make him retreat further into himself. When, in a comic turn of events, he strains his shoulder playing tennis and hoists himself up in a device that stretches his neck, he is trussed up like a man with a toothache in an old-fashioned film, and he can only barely articulate his words through his clenched jaw. It is funny, but the sad thing is that it is only a minor variation on his customary appearance. This role may be right up Hoffman's alley, but he is still brilliant in executing it.

Linney's Wendy is still looking for a Peter Pan to rescue her, but she is not looking very hard, because her expectations for herself are low. She has settled for the paltry affair and for a life of artistic rejection, and she medicates herself for depression and anxiety. She is easily flustered and prone to guilt: Though an adult, at times Wendy becomes like a child who is not in control of her emotions.

As the slow-paced film ripens, Jon and Wendy find plenty to fight about, both internally and with each other, as they struggle to become the family they never were. Jon plays the practical, hardheaded father of this new family, while Wendy plays the emotional, hopeful, fanciful mother. "We're taking better care of Dad than he ever did of us," Jon tells Wendy in a moment that makes their task seem noble, and it is true: They are trying to be the caring parent for their father, but it is tough. What is also true is what Jon later tells Wendy: that she is operating out of guilt and trying to make things right before it is too late. But it is too late to relive their childhoods, and they are stuck, and in fact Jon clearly is acting out of the same guilt, confusion, and mixed motives as Wendy.

Linney's performance, in the kind of role that is often played by Catherine Keener, is as compelling as Hoffman's, and that is no mean feat. They are both playing characters viewers want to cheer for but shrink away from, because they are so painfully real, and also because their plight is such a familiar, distasteful, and frightening one. The least believable character is Lenny, who seems much more accepting of the situation and much less troublesome than many older people with worsening dementia and anger management issues.

In fact, though *The Savages* is brave and frank, unafraid of issues like toilet functioning, it shrinks from the potentially more brutal realities of the situation it depicts. When Jon finds a nursing home for Lenny, and Wendy reluctantly agrees to move him in, they talk disparagingly of the stink and inhumanity of such places. Yet the home seems full of helpful workers, clean and uncluttered hallways, and reasonable if not bright and cheery living quarters. It is hardly a nightmare, other than a psychological one for Jon and Wendy, who cannot bear to see their father cooped up and dying. But this, too, is a bit of a cop-out. If Jon and Wendy were so ill-treated by their father that they choose to remain out of touch with him most of their adult lives, why would they suddenly become so caring? Too many Jons and Wendys in the real world would throw their father in the nursing home, walk out, and never come back to visit. Of course, that would not make a very watchable movie, but the Savage children do seem especially "un-savage" toward their father, though they can be savage with each other. For his part, Lenny, except for oc-

casional outbursts, seems so gentle that it is hard to believe he was ever a monster.

Jenkins has aspirations, clearly, for *The Savages* to be the kind of Brechtian drama that Jon tells his class demands a thinking and argumentative response from its audience. But after some satirical opening scenes in Sun City, the film lapses into melodrama—rather compelling and intelligent and restrained melodrama, to be sure. As it reaches its climax, the film loses its bite and becomes mushier. Lessons are learned, and Jon and Wendy find enough resolution to take tentative steps forward in their lives, rather than continuing to shuffle sideways. It is the kind of drama mainstream critics love, because it is not preachy and it is well written and performed. Yet in many ways, it merely dips its toe in the maelstrom of the issues it confronts, giving us comforting solutions to its disturbing confrontations. It shrinks back from real mania, leaving us two characters a lot of baby-boomer adults with aging parents can identify with. Jon and Wendy are just troubled enough to give us pause and a sense of recognition, but not so troubled that we cannot laugh at and enjoy their foibles. Most winningly of all, the story offers a measure of hope.

Jenkins is too good and thoughtful a writer and director not to recognize her story's own shortcomings, and that must be why Wendy, in discussing her autobiographical play about their abusive childhood, seeks assurance not once, but twice, that her tale is not too "middle-class and whiny." She is reassured it is not, but neither is it anything like Brecht. It is safe and sound, but sound is not a bad thing to be in a movie about this topic.

Michael Betzold

CREDITS

Wendy Savage: Laura Linney
Jon Savage: Philip Seymour Hoffman
Lenny Savage: Philip Bosco
Larry: Peter Friedman
Kasia: Cara Seymour
Origin: USA
Language: English
Released: 2007
Production: Ted Hope, Anne Carey, Erica Westheimer; This Is That, Cooper's Town Prods, Lone Star Film Group, Ad Hominem Enterprises; released by Fox Searchlight
Directed by: Tamara Jenkins
Written by: Tamara Jenkins
Cinematography by: W. Mott Hupfel III
Music by: Stephen Trask

Sound: Mathew Price

Editing: Brian A. Kates

Costumes: David C. Robinson

Production Design: Jane Ann Stewart

MPAA rating: R

Running time: 113 minutes

REVIEWS

Entertainment Weekly. November 30, 2007, p. 114.

Hollywood Reporter Online. January 20, 2007.

Los Angeles Times Online. November 28, 2007.

New York Times Online. November 28, 2007.

New Yorker Online. December 3, 2007.

Newsweek Online. December 3, 2007.

Premiere Online. November 27, 2007.

Rolling Stone Online. December 13, 2007.

Variety Online. January 21, 2007.

Village Voice Online. November 27, 2007.

Wall Street Journal. November 30, 2007, p. W1.

QUOTES

Wendy Savage (about her brother's house): "It looks like the Unabomber lives here."

Jon Savage: "We don't have to go after him Wendy, we're not in a Sam Shepard play."

Wendy Savage: "Maybe dad didn't abandon us. Maybe he just forgot who we were."

AWARDS

Ind. Spirit 2008: Actor (Hoffman), Screenplay

Nomination:

Oscars 2007: Actress (Linney), Orig. Screenplay

Golden Globes 2008: Actor—Mus./Comedy (Hoffman)

Ind. Spirit 2008: Cinematog., Director (Jenkins)

Writers Guild 2007: Orig. Screenplay.

SAW IV

> *It's a trap.*
> —Movie tagline

Box Office: $63.3 million

Each October, we see the gore-filled result of what the filmmakers of the *Saw* franchise have been busy brainstorming all year: fresh new, Machiavellian methods and medieval-looking devices for the series antihero Jigsaw (Tobin Bell) to use to torture his victims in his usual kill-or-be-killed fashion. Directed by series regular Darren Lynn Bousman, who helmed *Saw II* (2005) and *Saw III* (2006), *Saw IV* is also the first in the series not

written by creators/executive producers James Wan and Leigh Whannell. But screenwriters Patrick Melton and Marcus Dunstan do not fail to deliver the typical, convoluted plot. *Saw IV*'s time traveling story is so labyrinthine, it prompted Peter Hartlaub of the *San Francisco Chronicle* to warn viewers, "your only hope of understanding everything is to eat lots of fish the night before and then watch each of the previous films, in order, right before you enter the theater."

Although the film's numerous plot twists and timeline strain logic, it can be said of the *Saw* films that the filmmakers go to extraordinary lengths to achieve narrative continuity and valiantly attempt, in *Saw IV,* to tie together the many story threads and characters from the previous films. They also fill out the background of John Kramer, seen in numerous flashbacks before he became the Jigsaw Killer, in an effort to further explain the complex psychology driving this moralistic serial killer. And while Jigsaw lies dead on a mortuary slab in this installment, the door is left wide open for *Saw V* and *Saw VI,* reportedly already in the making.

The grotesque opening scene graphically depicts Jigsaw's autopsy in progress, with a gratuitous shot of his genitalia on full display. The dissection of his stomach yields a microcassette, which, when played by Detective Hoffman (Costas Mandylor), promises more "games" are afoot. *Saw IV* opens, in *Saw* tradition, where the last film left off, with Hoffman and SWAT Commander Rigg (Lyriq Bent) coming upon the remains of Detective Kerry (Dina Meyer), killed in one of Jigsaw's fatal traps set by his apprentice Amanda Young (Shawnee Smith), who like Jigsaw, is now dead. Federal Bureau of Investigation agents Perez (Athena Karkanis) and Strahm (Scott Patterson) are soon on the scene to investigate and deduce that Jigsaw must have another assistant still active.

The first of the new games promised involves Rigg's partner Eric Matthews (Donnie Wahlberg) who is shown on top of a block of ice, chained to a machine, his fate linked to that of Hoffman, who sits in an electric chair chained to the same trap. One's eyes are sewn shut while the other's mouth is similarly sealed. In *Saw II,* it turned out that all the victims' deaths had already taken place and were being viewed by police on videotape, and the feeling grows that what we are watching now may also have already occurred. And indeed, it has.

Meanwhile, Rigg is kidnapped by Jigsaw's new assistant and forced into an elaborate game in which he discovers torture victims and must decide whether to free them or let the victims do as they will to either free themselves or die. One female victim is a prostitute who nearly has her scalp ripped from her head. A motel owner, revealed to be a rapist, gets his comeuppance when his limbs are ripped from his body. A married couple, with whom Rigg has past ties, are strapped together with several giant spikes protruding from their bodies. With agents Perez and Strahm hot on his trail, the gruesome clues lead Rigg to his final test, discovering Hoffman and Matthews. As Jigsaw had predicted, Rigg's zeal to save people would be his downfall in the test, leading to the frustratingly unnecessary death of his partner who would have been momentarily freed if Rigg had not interfered.

Flashbacks show John, an engineer and developer, and his wife Jill (Betsy Russell), engaged in more noble efforts, including running a free clinic and attempting to find housing solutions for the inner-city poor. The couple is also happily expecting a child. Their pursuits, as well as Jill's pregnancy, end badly because of the inadvertent actions of depraved others, causing John to become Jigsaw, a puppet-master who doles out his unique brand of perverted justice. As well as flashbacks to a young John, there are also flashbacks involving Rigg that attempt to tie together plot threads and characters running through the other three films.

The reason for the continued expansion of this torture pornography series is that it has proved to be extremely lucrative. Although *Saw IV* made $63 million, significantly less than its predecessor's $80 million and *Saw II*'s impressive $87 million gross, it still turned a handsome profit and grossed more than the original's $55 million. And as long as the filmmakers continue dreaming up inventive new torture systems, Jigsaw may well give Freddy Kruger a run for his money.

James S. O'Neill

CREDITS

Jigsaw/John: Tobin Bell
Hoffman: Costas Mandylor
Agent Strahm: Scott Patterson
Jill: Betsy Russell
Rigg: Lyriq Bent
Agent Perez: Athena Karkanis
Cecil: Billy Otis
Origin: USA
Language: English
Released: 2007
Production: Gregg Hoffman, Oren Koules, Mark Burg; Twisted Pictures; released by Lionsgate
Directed by: Darren Lynn Bousman
Written by: Patrick Melton, Marcus Dunstan
Cinematography by: David A. Armstrong
Music by: Charlie Clouser
Sound: Richard Penn

Editing: Kevin Greutert, Brett Sullivan
Art Direction: Anthony Ianni
Costumes: Alex Kavanagh
Production Design: David Hackl
MPAA rating: R
Running time: 108 minutes

REVIEWS

Boston Globe Online. October 27, 2007.
Entertainment Weekly Online. October 31, 2007.
Hollywood Reporter Online. October 29, 2007.
Los Angeles Times Online. October 27, 2007.
New York Times Online. October 27, 2007.
San Francisco Chronicle. October 29, 2007, p. E1.
Variety Online. October 26, 2007.

QUOTES

Jigsaw: "You think it is over, but the games have just begun."

TRIVIA

The dog that Ivan is seen with is director Darren Lynn Bousman's dog Chance.

THE SEEKER: THE DARK IS RISING

Even the smallest of light...shines in the darkness.
—Movie tagline

Box Office: $8.8 million

Family-film specialists Walden Media, in their first collaboration with 20th Century-Fox, adapt yet another award-winning children's novel, this time with disappointing results. The second book in British author Susan Cooper's series *The Dark Is Rising,* the novel is a children's fantasy about an eleven-year-old British boy who finds he suddenly has extrasensory powers and learns that he is actually a member of the Light, one of a dying breed who battle to save the world from the ill-intentioned Dark. The film radically departs from the book, stripping the tale of its quaint, English charm and character-driven story and replacing it with chaotic action and jazzy, computer-generated effects producing cheap thrills.

Neither a critical nor box office success, the PG-rated *The Seeker: The Dark Is Rising* suffers from its Hollywoodization, exactly what Walden avoided with the charming children's story they also produced in 2007, *The Water Horse,* released in conjunction with Disney, suggesting theirs may be the more fruitful collaboration.

Perhaps in an effort to appeal to teenagers as well as children, John Hodge's script presents us with a fourteen-year-old American protagonist, Will Stanton (Alexander Ludwig), the seventh son of a seventh son who lives with his large family that has recently relocated to Britain. The onset of Will's puberty brings on his powers—including great strength, command of fire, telepathy, and telekinesis—as well as a burdensome responsibility. One of the film's main flaws is how quickly Will accepts his fate as the last combatant to try and overcome the Dark. Without a struggle to come to terms with a seemingly unthinkable fate, Will loses audience sympathy from the start. And director David L. Cunningham's disorienting and complicated shots and camera angles serve only to keep the audience at arm's length from its lackluster hero.

When Will is waylaid by a mysterious horseman known as the Rider (Christopher Eccleston), the Old Ones quickly come to his aid: Dawson (James Cosmo), George (Jim Piddock), Miss Greythorne (Frances Conroy) and their leader Merriman (Ian McShane). Will is told he is a Sign-Seeker, and they are, like him, guardians of the Light. The Rider is one of the Dark, who are growing stronger. So strong, in fact, that Will is told he has five days in which to overcome their evil forces. In that time, he must find the six magical signs that bear the special cross-marks, before Rider sniffs them out. The quest takes him back in time, where some of the signs are hidden, and back to the present again, which Will's power easily enables him to do.

Despite his designation as "The Seeker," there is so little effort on Will's part to find the signs that the film loses its main thrust as a quest movie. Gathering at the Old Ones' mystical Great Hall, Will learns the form the signs will take and finds the first one, conveniently, inside a pendant he bought at the mall for his sister Gwen. Will finds his Holy Grail, the final sign, discovering it is himself. He is then easily able to defeat Rider, who has unleashed a great blizzard, and defend the Light.

The script's clichéd dialogue, pat situations, and flat characterization of good versus evil hardly does justice to the source material. The rushed, overblown spectacle, which includes hordes of computer-generated snakes, men morphing into monsters, and a Viking war, may appeal to younger viewers. The *Los Angeles Times*'s Kevin Crust observes, "What made it to the screen is stripped down to its action essentials, skipping ahead from one effects-laden clash to the next. It feels as if entire reels have been dropped." Children may also delight that the adult characters are handled in rote, kid's film fashion, with little to do but encourage the young hero to succeed and give sage advice that is quickly disregarded. The talented and versatile McShane and Conroy are given nothing of significance to do and not much of

consequence to say, their years of experience condensed into such obvious utterances as "Find the signs!" Despite the time-constraint premise and frantic action, there is virtually no suspense and events unfold predictably.

With a teenage hero who possesses magical powers, the filmmakers' decision to court further comparisons with Harry Potter by making Will's family suspiciously close in resemblance to that of Ron Weasley's of that franchise, was probably not the wisest.

Hilary White

CREDITS

The Rider: Christopher Eccleston
Merriman Lyon: Ian McShane
Miss Greythorne: Frances Conroy
Mary Stanton: Wendy Crewson
Will Stanton: Alexander Ludwig
John Stanton: John Benjamin Hickey
Max Stanton: Gregory Edward Smith
Dawson: James Cosmo
Old George: Jim Piddock
Origin: USA
Language: English
Released: 2007
Production: Marc Platt; Walden Media; released by 20th Century-Fox
Directed by: David L. Cunningham
Written by: John Hodge
Cinematography by: Joel Ransom
Music by: Christophe Beck
Sound: Keith Garcia
Music Supervisor: Patrick Houlihan
Editing: Eric A. Sears, Geoffrey Rowland
Art Direction: Bill Crutcher
Costumes: Vinilla Burnham
Production Design: David Lee
MPAA rating: PG
Running time: 94 minutes

REVIEWS

Boston Globe Online. October 5, 2007.
Hollywood Reporter Online. October 5, 2007.
Los Angeles Times Online. October 5, 2007.
New York Times Online. October 5, 2007.
San Francisco Chronicle. October 5, 2007, p. E5.
Seattle Post-Intelligencer Online. October 4, 2007.
Variety Online. October 4, 2007.
Washington Post Online. October 5, 2007.

QUOTES

Will Stanton: "I'm supposed to save the world? I don't even know how to talk to a girl!"

SEPTEMBER DAWN

The untold story of an American tragedy.
    —Movie tagline

Box Office: $1.1 million

If a movie's successfulness strictly depends upon its cinematography, *September Dawn* would be considered one of the good ones. Unfortunately, everything else about this historical Western adventure is truly inferior.

Director-co-writer Christopher Cain (actor Dean Cain's father) has fashioned a dreary, old-fashioned "settlers" drama, set in 1857 Utah, in which the Mormons are the ruthless executioners of a wagon train of 120 Missouri Christians, who had been trying to get to the new frontier in California. Apart from being a poorly told story, it also seems unfair and one-sided.

Cain's screenplay (written with Carole Whang Schutter, based on her novel) leads up to the Mountain Meadows massacre (on the ominous day of September 11) by suggesting that Mormon leader Brigham Young (Terence Stamp) planned the whole thing and lied under oath in a follow-up trial. In addition, Young pins the blame on a deranged bishop in his order, Jacob Samuelson (Jon Voight).

In an extended flashback, the bulk of the narrative, the bishop and his henchmen cross paths with the Missouri Christians and form an uneasy alliance. Jacob is wary of these outsiders, but the bishop's oldest son, Jonathan (Trent Ford), falls for a settler girl, Emily (Tamara Hope), in what becomes a Romeo-and-Juliet romance, and he charms the other travelers with his horse-whispering skills.

Eventually, the two communities have a falling out when the bishop hears the voice of his late spiritual leader, Joseph Smith, who orders him to kill the "gentiles" he has encountered. This moment leads to the mass killing in which mercenary Native Americans help with the butchery and Jonathan finds himself caught between his new girlfriend and his fanatical father (who ends up shooting Emily in the heart). Jonathan's younger brother, Micah (Taylor Handley), becomes insane and joins the Indians (actually donning greasepaint). The entire incident ends bloodily and badly, but Christians will never forget this "September Dawn."

Juan Ruiz-Anchia does a commendable job photographing what amounts to an amateurish Christian high school play with actors wearing costumes, not clothes. Ruiz-Anchia is most proficient shooting the great outdoor scenes—and the Utah wilderness territory looks gorgeous in color and widescreen (a couple of shots are reminiscent of the spectacular cinematography of Terrence Malick's *Days of Heaven* [1978]).

But one's appreciation of *September Dawn*'s visual splendors wears thin after a while, particularly because the script is trite and clichéd and the acting is overdone. Jon Voight, the biggest name in the cast, is also the worst in the cast. Once again, Voight shamelessly hams it up as he has the last several years in other films. Trent Ford appears to be grooming himself to be the next Hollywood "hottie," but his performance is forced. Taylor Handley is particularly bad playing the younger brother who loses his mind and joins the Indians in the slaughter. And Tamara Hope is simpering and insipid as the young love interest.

At least Terence Stamp avoids being overly declamatory as Brigham Young, but he is on screen only very briefly in the framing story (and just what is the talented British actor doing in this film?). It is also disconcerting to see Lolita Davidovich in a very small and insignificant role.

Still, what is most egregious and disturbing about *September Dawn* is not the style but the content. Cain's film condemns the Mormons and deifies the other Christians so forcefully, it sends the message that Mormons are bad and non-Mormon Christians are good—period. Could the timing of this production's release have anything to do with the 2007–2008 presidential race, during which the Christian right tried to discredit Republican candidate Mitt Romney for his Mormon faith? Or is the film a good versus evil allegory about 9/11? Either way, *September Dawn* lacks insight, nuance, or even historical grounding (the moviemakers inadvertently acknowledge this by admitting Jacob Samuelson is a fictional character).

The critics were not kind to *September Dawn*. Matt Zoller Seitz in the *New York Times* said "The maudlin, grotesque western…apes *Schindler's List* in hopes of creating a Christian Holocaust picture." Roger Ebert in the *Chicago Sun-Times* declared it "strange, confused, unpleasant" and J. Hoberman in the *Village Voice* added, "*September Dawn* has the ham-fisted lyricism of political ads and pharmaceutical commercials." Finally, the *Austin Chronicle* simply called the film "a mess."

It is hard to imagine even fanatical, right-wing Christians would enjoy *September Dawn*, unless they happen to be bloodthirsty—the extended massacre scenes are quite brutal and filmed in slow-motion (the film was rated R in the theaters). It is also hard to believe anyone would be fooled by the propagandistic element. But you never know—lots of people voted for George W. Bush.

Eric Monder

CREDITS

Jacob Samuelson: Jon Voight
Jonathan Samuelson: Trent Ford

Micah Samuelson: Taylor Handley
Emily Hudson: Tamara Hope
John D. Lee: Jon(athan) Gries
Captain Fancher: Shaun Johnston
Nancy Dunlap: Lolita Davidovich
Joseph Smith: Dean Cain
Robert Humphries: Huntley Ritter
Brigham Young: Terence Stamp
Origin: USA, Canada
Language: English
Released: 2007
Production: Kevin Matossian, Scott Duthie, Christopher Cain; Voice Pictures; released by Black Diamond Pictures
Directed by: Christopher Cain
Written by: Christopher Cain, Carole Whang Schutter
Cinematography by: Juan Ruiz-Anchia
Music by: William Ross
Sound: George Tarrant
Editing: Jack Hofstra
Art Direction: Janet Lakeman
Costumes: Carol Case
Production Design: Rick Roberts
MPAA rating: R
Running time: 110 minutes

REVIEWS

Boston Globe Online. August 24, 2007.
Chicago Sun-Times Online. August 24, 2007.
Hollywood Reporter Online. August 24, 2007.
Los Angeles Times Online. August 24, 2007.
New York Times Online. August 24, 2007.
Seattle Post-Intelligencer Online. August 23, 2007.
Variety Online. August 21, 2007.
Washington Post Online. August 24, 2007.

TRIVIA

Dean Cain, the director's son, appears as Joseph Smith.

SERAPHIM FALLS

Never turn your back on the past.
—Movie tagline

Seraphim Falls is a minimalist Western, shot mainly in New Mexico, involving a revenge plot and an extended chase across the wilderness, from the "Ruby Mountains, 1868" into the desert far below. The backstory involves the destruction of a family and a farmhouse during the American Civil War. Gideon (Pierce Brosnan), a captain in the Union army, is in pursuit of a Confederate officer named Carver (Liam Neeson), whom he traces to the family farm in Seraphim Falls, Georgia. Gideon orders his soldiers to torch the barn; the flames spread to the farmhouse. Inside is an infant, whose mother and her son attempt to rescue, but die trying in the flames. The hideous irony is that the war is over, and these lives are senselessly wasted. This heartbreaking experience leads Carver to conclude, "Nobody can protect nobody in this world." Clearly, Carver has been seriously wronged, but initially he seems to be the villain of the piece, merely because the audience lacks context and understanding.

The film begins, however, several years later, in the Ruby Mountains of Nevada, with Gideon, now apparently a trapper, cooking game over a fire he built on the snowy mountainside. He senses that he is not alone, then he is shot in the left arm and goes tumbling down the mountainside. But the man is a survivor. His free fall ends on a riverbank. He attempts to shimmy over a tree that has fallen across the river. He loses his balance and plunges into the river rapids, then goes over a waterfall. But he finally extracts himself, builds a fire to dry his clothes, digs the bullet out of his arm with his Bowie knife, then uses the heated blade to cauterize his wound. There is hardly any dialogue through the first thirty minutes of action, and, as a matter of fact, very little dialogue thereafter in this sparse, laconic Western.

Gideon is being tracked by Carver and his four hired killers, who have come down the mountain to find Gideon's body, only to conclude that their prey is still alive. Hiding in a tree and then attacking, Gideon manages to kill one of his pursuers with his Bowie knife. He is now armed with a pistol. Gideon finds his way down the mountain to a rancher's cabin, where he attempts to steal a horse. He is stopped by the woman who lives in the cabin, who puts a rifle on him and keeps him captive until her husband comes home. But Gideon still escapes during the night and has gone by the time Carver arrives with his posse. This is the first of multiple escapes. Gideon rigs a trap and manages to kill another of Carver's men. Gideon then happens upon three desperadoes, who are wanted men fleeing bounty hunters; when one of them follows Gideon because he fears that Gideon may attempt to collect the reward money that is on his head, Gideon kills him with a knife to the throat. Taking the outlaw's horse, Gideon then rides into a railroad construction camp, and is taken captive there as a suspected horse thief. But, again, he manages to escape, just ahead of Carver's posse. One of the railroad workers at the camp seems to recognize Gideon from his legendary Civil War escapades. He tells his fellow workers that Gideon lost two sons by that bridge at Antietam in 1862: "They say he killed one hundred men." So Gideon seems to be a killing machine. Carver's attempt to capture him and wreak revenge would seem to be futile, but Carver is not prone to giving up, either.

And so the pursuit continues. A group of Mormon missionaries is encountered. After Carver and his men leave, they discover that the missionaries have emptied their weapons. But Carver has one bullet he has set aside "for him." Eventually, Carver has lost all of his hired guns, but the pursuit continues, one on one, into the desert, where the contest becomes hallucinatory. Both Gideon, then Carver, encounter an odd, metaphysical Indian (Wes Studi), who speaks in mythic riddles while wearing an absurd stovepipe hat. According to the end credits, this oddball is named "Charon" (for the boatman on the River Styx, because Westerns are supposed to be mythic, above all, and this one seems to involve a mythic quest). The Indian barters with Gideon for one of the two horses Gideon has (one of them belonging to Carver, left temporarily behind in the dust), and then the Indian gives the horse back to Carver, saying, cryptically, "That which is yours will always be returned to you; that which you take will always be taken from you." Even more bizarre is a later encounter with a peddler named Madame Louise (Anjelica Huston, unexpectedly), who seems to appear with a horse and wagon out of nowhere. Gideon trades her his horse for a bullet; Carver trades his canteen of water for a Colt revolver with one shell. She seems to be a metaphorical temptress, a metaphorical stand-in for the devil. Huston gets her picture on the jacket of the DVD, even though her performance is quite brief.

Director David Von Ancken is a novice, up from television, with experience directing the *Without a Trace* series. *Premiere* magazine idiotically suggested that "fans of last year's tense *The Proposition* (co-starring Anjelica's half-brother Danny Huston) will enjoy," but to say that *Seraphim Falls* co-stars Huston is to stretch her cameo absurdly. The screenplay, obviously in need of more thought and development, was written by Von Ancken and Abby Everett Jaques. In his *New York Times* review Stephen Holden accurately described the film as a "handsome, old-fashioned western of few words and heavy meanings that unfolds with the sanctimonious grandeur of a biblical allegory." Holden saw a resemblance to Clint Eastwood's *The Outlaw Josey Wales* (1976), believing it might have "inspired" Von Ancken, because his plot "follows that film's story closely enough to qualify as a self-conscious homage."

The conclusion of the film is abstract and metaphorical, in odd contrast to the utter realism of the first two-thirds of the film. In the DVD commentary Brosnan called *Seraphim Falls* an antiwar film. Neeson remarked about "the futility of mankind killing mankind over and over." Both actors seemed pleased to be included in this Western: "Can you believe it? Two lads from Ireland!" Brosnan says to Neeson. The main story line is elegant in its simplicity, yet oddly sparse, dramatically focused, but ultimately thin. Although the motive for the hatred and revenge is ultimately made clear, the explanation, first hinted through dream-sequence flashbacks, is a long time coming, requiring some patience on the part of the viewer. The cinematography by Academy Award®-winner John Toll shows both a respect and an affinity for the landscape and is effective. The final confrontation between Brosnan and Neeson in the desert recalls the stark cinematography in the Death Valley conclusion of Erich von Stroheim's epic *Greed* (1924), both in the way the two actors are framed against the desolation and in the poses struck.

In his DVD commentary director Von Ancken speaks of his admiration for John Ford and Eastwood, but the images of von Stroheim surely lingered in his mind, or in the mind of his cinematographer. The replication of shots at the end could not have been merely accidental. Unfortunately, however, writer/director Von Ancken is no von Stroheim, and this Western moved pretty quickly to video. The linear narrative is purposeful, but the backstory is initially enigmatic, and the hallucinatory ending merely peculiar, because it fractures the solemn tone that dominates most of the story, opting instead for "pretentious, surreal gimmickry," in the words of Holden. Unfortunately, this ruins the trajectory toward forgiveness and reconciliation that appears to be happening unexpectedly.

James M. Welsh

CREDITS

Carver: Liam Neeson
Gideon: Pierce Brosnan
Madame Louise: Anjelica Huston
Hayes: Michael Wincott
Pope: Robert Baker
Parsons: Ed Lauter
Kid: John Robinson
Abraham: Tom Noonan
Henry: Kevin J. O'Connor
Origin: USA
Language: English
Released: 2006
Production: Bruce Davey, David Flynn; Destination Films, Icon Entertainment Media; released by Samuel Goldwyn Films
Directed by: David Von Ancken
Written by: David Von Ancken, Abby Everett Jaques
Cinematography by: John Toll
Music by: Harry Gregson-Williams

Sound: William Sarokin
Editing: Conrad Buff
Art Direction: Guy Barnes
Costumes: Deborah L. Scott
Production Design: Michael Z. Hanan
MPAA rating: R
Running time: 115 minutes

REVIEWS

Austin Chronicle Online. January 26, 2007.
Boxoffice Online. January 26, 2007.
Chicago Sun-Times Online. January 26, 2007.
Hollywood Reporter Online. September 8, 2006.
Los Angeles Times Online. January 26, 2007.
New York Times Online. January 26, 2007.
Premiere Magazine Online. January 24, 2007.
USA Today Online. January 26, 2007.
Variety Online. September 18, 2006.

QUOTES

Carver: "Nobody can protect nobody in this world."
Madame Louise Fair: "You men, you always choosing a gun over a remedy."

SHOOT 'EM UP

No name, no past, nothing to lose.
    —Movie tagline

Box Office: $12.8 million

Whether writer/director Michael Davis intended *Shoot 'Em Up* to be a spoof of or tribute to American and Hong Kong action films is difficult to determine. The film veers wildly from tongue-in-cheek humor to more moronic jokes, from cartoonish violence to unpleasantly graphic killings. While Davis's intentions may have been honorable, the result is a mess.

Smith (Clive Owen) is waiting on a bench in an anonymous city, calmly eating a carrot, when a pregnant woman (Ramona Pringle) walks by, obviously in distress. When a gunman (Wiley M. Pickett) follows her into an abandoned building, Smith reluctantly rescues her. Taking the man's gun, he fights off a seemingly endless supply of gunmen while delivering the baby. To make certain that the audience knows all this is meant as lighthearted, Davis has Smith sever the umbilical cord by shooting it. When the mother dies in a subsequent shootout, Smith assumes responsibility for the infant. What follows offers variations on this opening scene as Smith protects the baby boy, whom he names Oliver after the orphan hero of Charles Dickens's

Oliver Twist, from his pursuers while trying to discover why they want the child. Smith enlists the assistance of prostitute Donna Quintano (Monica Bellucci), who slowly takes to baby Oliver.

Leading the bad guys is Hertz (Paul Giamatti), a wisecracking killer working for weapons manufacturer Hammerson (Stephen McHattie). The convoluted plot involves Hammerson's desire to railroad Senator Rutledge (Daniel Pilon), a presidential candidate supporting strong gun-control measures. Smith soon discovers that two groups of thugs are after Oliver. It turns out that Rutledge, dying of a rare disease, wants the baby's bone marrow. Davis obviously does not take any of this seriously, showing how insignificant his plot is by continuing Hertz's pursuit of Smith, Quintano, and Oliver when there is no longer any reason to do so.

Davis, who has written and directed several sex comedies, such as *100 Girls* (2000), as well as the horror film *Monster Man* (2003), is primarily interested in style. He is inspired by such films as *Die Hard* (1988), in which a resourceful lone man, played by Bruce Willis, fends off numerous villains with his ingenuity, as well as balletic Hong Kong action films, especially those directed by John Woo and Johnnie To. The major influence seems to be Woo's *Hard-Boiled* (1992), in which cop Chow Yun-Fat fights to protect babies from gangsters. *Hard-Boiled* features the hero sliding across floors, guns blazing. Davis has Smith do this several times, once on a conveyer belt.

The same week *Shoot 'Em Up* appeared in theaters, Woo released *Stranglehold,* a video-game spinoff of *Hard-Boiled.* This coincidence is notable because of the close resemblance of *Shoot 'Em Up* to a video game. "Shoot-'em-up" was once a popular term for Westerns, suggesting that such films are nothing but gunplay. The phrase also refers to a genre of video game in which one character shoots a considerable number of enemies, an apt description of the film.

Davis attempts to provide stylized fun. The violence should not offend because it is unrealistic, especially when Smith kills every time he shoots, while the opposition always misses him, even from a few feet away. Seeing Smith fly through the air in slow motion is entertaining, yet not all the killings are cartoonish. Hertz shoots two of his henchmen point-blank, and Oliver's mother is killed. Smith kills two hoodlums with his ever-present carrots. The first one is mildly amusing, the second overkill. Either the violence is a joke or it is not. In trying to have it both ways, Davis misfires in much the same way as *Lucky Number Slevin* (2006) and *Smokin' Aces* (2007) did before him.

In the tradition of Ursula Andress, Bellucci delivers her lines as if she has learned them phonetically. Giamatti gives his dialogue a comic spin, saying everything in a sinister whisper as if he is speaking in quotation marks. Clearly enjoying his offbeat casting as a gun-toting villain, Giamatti seems to be having a good time. Davis undermines Giamatti occasionally, as when Hertz utters "Nice tits" to a corpse. Too much of the humor in *Shoot 'Em Up* is on this adolescent level. Davis even stoops to making Smith say, "What's up, doc?"

Davis fares better with the corny one-liners Smith offers after dispatching a miscreant. As deliberately bad puns making fun of the punch lines in the James Bond films, these jokes are better than most of Davis's humor. Smith says, "So much for seat belts," after a particularly spectacular stunt involving two vehicles. The stunts are generally well done, aided by Peter Amundson's editing. The cinematography of Peter Pau, who shot Woo's *The Killer* (1989), is splendidly noirish, with grainy daytime shots, shadowy nights, lots of water reflections. Pau's painstaking work deserves a better project.

The same can be said for Owen, who emerges with his dignity intact. Owen plays Smith straight, never winking at the audience—except for the Bugs Bunny joke. That Owen gives Smith haunted eyes and a range of subtle emotions can, however, be said to work against Davis's intention. If Smith is real, then all these deaths are painful.

Shoot 'Em Up is full of references to other films. The baby lying in the middle of a road recalls the Coen brothers' *Raising Arizona* (1987). There is an attempted robbery of a restaurant at the end, as in Quentin Tarantino's *Pulp Fiction* (1994). Smith steals a BMW, a nod to *The Hire* (2001–2002), the eight short BMW promotional films starring Owen and directed by Woo, Wong Kar Wai, John Frankenheimer, and others. Spotting such allusions makes watching *Shoot 'Em Up* a bit less painful, though they call attention to how inferior it is to its sources. Tony Scott's "Beat the Devil" from *The Hire* displays more style and wit in eleven minutes than in the entirety of Davis's effort. While some films spoof genres with affection, as with the considerably better action comedy *Hot Fuzz* (2007), Davis seems to display contempt for the conventions as well as for his viewers.

The film received decidedly mixed responses from reviewers. While Owen Gleiberman of *Entertainment Weekly* praised its "silly, scuzzball joy," most critics were more in line with the assessment of A. O. Scott of the *New York Times,* who, repulsed by the grim onslaught of violence, called it "a worthless piece of garbage." Filmgoers apparently did not know what to make of *Shoot 'Em Up* from its advertisements, and the film made a dismal $5.2 million in its first weekend of release, drop-

ping to $2.6 million the following weekend, a likely indication of poor word of mouth.

Michael Adams

CREDITS

Smith: Clive Owen
Hertz: Paul Giamatti
Donna Quintano: Monica Bellucci
Senator Rutledge: Daniel Pilon
Hertz's Driver: Julian Richings
Origin: USA
Language: English
Released: 2007
Production: Don Murphy, Susan Montford, Rick Benattar; released by New Line Cinema
Directed by: Michael Davis
Written by: Michael Davis
Cinematography by: Peter Pau
Music by: Paul Haslinger
Sound: John J. Thomson
Music Supervisor: Dana Sano
Editing: Peter Amundson
Art Direction: Patrick Banister
Costumes: Denise Cronenberg
Production Design: Gary Frutkoff
MPAA rating: R
Running time: 87 minutes

REVIEWS

Chicago Sun-Times Online. September 6, 2007.
Entertainment Weekly Online. September 9, 2007.
Hollywood Reporter Online. August 22, 2007.
Los Angeles Times Online. September 7, 2007.
New York Times Online. September 7, 2007.
Rolling Stone Online. September 4, 2007.
San Francisco Chronicle. September 7, 2007, p. E7.
Variety Online. July 31, 2007.
Washington Post Online. September 7, 2007.

QUOTES

Mr. Hertz: "My god! Do we really suck or is this guy really that good?"
Mr. Smith: "I'm a British nanny, and I'm dangerous."

TRIVIA

"Baby Oliver" was cast before he was born as the producers found a pregnant woman scheduled to deliver around the time filming began, ensuring that the child would be a genuine newborn.

SHOOTER

Yesterday was about honor. Today is about justice.
—Movie tagline

Box Office: $47 million

Rambo has returned—in the person of Bob Lee Swagger. The aptly named marksman, the subject of novels by Stephen Hunter, is the protagonist of *Shooter*, a man bent on avenging the corruption of the U.S. government. Mark Wahlberg plays Swagger with his usual understated bluster. Wahlberg, an underrated actor who is finally getting his due, follows up his Oscar®-nominated performance in *The Departed* with another cynical, tough-guy role. Wahlberg is almost always a soft-spoken, hard-edged man with machismo and heart, and this is a perfect role for him.

He is allowed to show off his huge biceps, his buff body, and his contempt for all pretense. His mumbling swallows up some of his dialogue at times, but it is not that great a loss. Director Antoine Fuqua and scriptwriter Jonathan Lemkin are incapable of subtlety. *Shooter* is cartoonishly obvious in its concept, plot, and execution, gleefully trafficking in clichés and overwrought conspiracy theories. It is perfectly positioned for its time, however: It ought to appeal mainly to militia types, but it will draw in others of a quite different political bent, too, for whom the government is an easy target of suspicion and indictment.

Betrayal of patriotism is the theme. Swagger is a long-range sniper, a Marine scout specializing in top-secret assignments for clandestine U.S. government forces. In the opening scene, he covers operatives in Ethiopia, eliminating local forces that are intercepting them from his mountain hideout. But his spotter is killed and the military abandons him behind enemy lines so as not to risk exposure of their operation, which turns out to be corrupt.

Three years later, Swagger is a macho hermit in the high Rockies, living in a cabin with his dog, his guns, his copy of the 9/11 Commission report, and a remarkable mountaintop cable connection. "Let's see what lies they're telling us today," he tells his dog as he logs on to his computer. Soon he is visited by Colonel Isaac Johnson (Danny Glover), who has a mission for him: help his unidentified team of operatives prevent an assassination attempt on the president that the Secret Service cannot be trusted with because it is an "inside job." Swagger is apparently the only man in the universe with knowledge of long-distance sniping. After his obligatory initial refusal, he signs on—and finds out he is the designated patsy for the killing not of the president, but the man next to him on the podium, an Ethiopian bishop who is about to reveal the Americans' massacre of innocent civilians in Ethiopia who refused to give up their village so that a pipeline could go through.

Giving a nod to the conspiracy theories surrounding the John Kennedy assassination, Swagger is shot by

an Officer Timmons (Lee Harvey Oswald killed an Officer Tippet). But Timmons bungles the job, and Swagger, wounded, makes a remarkable escape. The object of a nationwide manhunt, he manages to find refuge in the home of his former spotter's ex-wife Sarah (Kate Mara), who wanted to enter nursing school and now gets to operate on Swagger's shoulder, exchange sultry glances with him, and help him launch his counterattack. Swagger soon returns to Philadelphia, the site of the shooting, wearing no disguise, in order to flush out the only Federal Bureau of Investigation agent, a rookie named Nick Memphis (Michael Peña), who is suspicious of what happened. The caper involves Sarah dressing like a hooker, for reasons unknown.

Swagger attempts to take down the enemy within the government, clear his name, and right all wrongs. In the process, he finds out the enemy includes not only Johnson and several sinister cohorts, but a wheelchair-bound former sharpshooter and a very corrupt U.S. senator (Ned Beatty). He cannot seek judicial recourse until he kills a few hundred members of this conspiracy and their foot soldiers because, he explains to Nick, "these people killed my dog!" He seeks advice from a sage of sharpshooting on how the conspirators might have duplicated his bullet in the assassination—a particularly arcane line of inquiry in a film where plotters do not even bother not to leave fingerprints on weapons. The backwoods font of wisdom fills Swagger's conspiracy cup, and it is eventually revealed that the government betrays its patriots for profit, that every politician is part of the conspiracy, and that the only way to break their murderous stranglehold on the country is to have long-range shootouts on mountaintops. When Swagger finally turns himself in and proves his innocence with a demonstration involving his weapon in a conference room, the attorney general tells him that there is no way of cleaning up the filth except by shooting up the streets, like in the Wild West.

Screenwriter Lemkin includes a few contemporary references—Abu Ghraib for instance—to make the message resonate that the United States is a nation betrayed, and that it needs an action hero to take revenge and then walk away from the inferno of his retribution in slow motion. This Wahlberg must do, several times, the slow-motion walk being the real cinematic badge of heroism.

It is senseless to point out all the plot weaknesses, ridiculous assumptions, and corny dialogue in a film like *Shooter*, because it is a comic book. What makes it particularly awful, however, is that it has pretensions. Fuqua wants his careless movie to be taken seriously. But as an indictment of the U.S. government's support of oil interests, it is certainly no *Syriana* (2005). Glover, for one, does not take it seriously: His villainy is so off-the-cuff that it is impossible to believe his character for one minute. Beatty is better: all puffed up and pompous, fittingly ridiculous, worthy of contempt. But the real problem is that most of the villains are interchangeable parts. The film does not make the effort to craft us a believable, nuanced conspiracy peopled with meaningful characters.

This is a film where sentiment is everything, where emotional resonance is key, and where the moviemakers count on connecting viscerally with fed-up Americans. It is pure exploitation of honorable values; cinematic manipulation in the long tradition of skimpy Hollywood nods to betrayed Middle America. But even in terms of its own action-hero genre, it falls short of making an impact. Its rugged individualist hero is impotent without his precision weaponry: He can blow things up but not bring coherence to the picture.

Michael Betzold

CREDITS

Bob Lee Swagger: Mark Wahlberg
Nick Memphis: Michael Peña
Col. Isaac Johnson: Danny Glover
Sarah Fenn: Kate Mara
Jack Payne: Elias Koteas
Alourdes Galindo: Rhona Mitra
Michael Sandor: Rade Serbedzija
Mr. Rate: Levon Helm
Senator Charles F. Meachum: Ned Beatty
Russ Turner: Tate Donovan
Howard Purnell: Justin Louis
Origin: USA
Language: English
Released: 2007
Production: Lorenzo di Bonaventura, Ric Kidney; di Bonaventura Pictures; released by Paramount
Directed by: Antoine Fuqua
Written by: Jonathan Lemkin
Cinematography by: Peter Menzies, Jr.
Music by: Mark Mancina
Sound: Rob Young, Bruce Litecky
Editing: Conrad Buff, Eric A. Sears
Art Direction: Jeremy Stanbridge, Denise Pizzini
Costumes: Ha Nguyen
Production Design: J. Dennis Washington
MPAA rating: R
Running time: 122 minutes

REVIEWS

Boxoffice Online. March 23, 2007.
Chicago Sun-Times Online. March 23, 2007.
Entertainment Weekly. March 30, 2007, p. 54.
Hollywood Reporter Online. March 23, 2007.
Los Angeles Times Online. March 23, 2007.
New York Times Online. March 23, 2007.
San Francisco Chronicle. March 23, 2007, p. E1.
Variety Online. March 22, 2007.
Washington Post. March 23, 2007, p. C1.

QUOTES

Bob Lee Swagger: "You don' understand how serious this is. They killed my dog."

TRIVIA

The portraits on the walls in the room where the conspirators meet in Langley, Virginia are all of Republican presidents.

SHREK THE THIRD

He's in for the royal treatment.
—Movie tagline
Who's ready for Thirds?
—Movie tagline

Box Office: $323 million

It did not take long for Shrek to go from radical to overcivilized. The yellowish-green ogre journeyed most of the way to respectability in his disappointing first sequel, and in *Shrek the Third* the transformation is complete—and completely disheartening.

The original *Shrek* (2001) was as innovative and shrewd as any animated feature in the history of cinema. It was at once an original fantasy, a delightful entertainment, and a devastating satire of the Disneyfication of traditional fairy tales and the crass commercialization of fairy-tale characters. With its acerbic take on the mainstream morality and values of the dominant mode of animated storytelling of the twentieth century, it was revolutionary in style, viewpoint, and language, and as anarchic in its approach to comedy as the Marx Brothers were in the 1930s.

Like some other forms of postmodernism, however, *Shrek* quickly fell prey to the temptations of popularity. Finding a huge audience for its parody, the creators of *Shrek* skipped even a nod at irony and went straight to the bank, commercializing their characters without any acknowledgment that their characters were predicated on anticommercialism, and counting on the less attentive members of Shrek fandom to go along. So complete was this transformation in *Shrek 2* in 2004 that it did not seem the perpetrators of the sequel had even watched, much less made, the original. Shamelessly,

Shrek and his beloved ogress, Fiona, and their sidekick, the scabrous donkey named only Donkey, became commercial pitchmen for all kinds of products, and in the sequel a *second* sidekick, Puss in Boots, was added, to provide another source of sidekick-style humor (instead of additional plot) and another character for use in endorsements.

This time around, there were no expectations to dash. Obviously now just another franchise in a world of media properties, *Shrek* launched a full assault on the beachheads of commercial enterprise, with the ogre and his cohorts hawking a huge array of products and even public-service-style causes, and spinning off games, toys, specially designed snack-food packages, and special offers at fast-food joints. So ubiquitous was the ogre on billboards and the airwaves that he was caught in a contradiction as the spokesman for both an antiobesity campaign and for fast-food products that contribute heavily to obesity in children.

After a first sequel that recycled the plot of the original, the creators of the franchise churned out a second that would touch familiar bases and bring back the characters from the first two films. Back to pick up their paychecks are Mike Myers as the voice of Shrek, Cameron Diaz as Fiona, Eddie Murphy as Donkey, and Antonio Banderas as Puss in Boots. The result is dull and ordinary. The original characters have acquired plenty of baggage, in the form of families and minor comrades milked desperately for laughs, the Gingerbread Man (voice of Conrad Vernon), Pinocchio (voice of Cody Cameron), and the Three Pigs (voice of Cody Cameron), among them. At the outset of the film, Fiona's father dies, leaving Shrek himself to assume the crown of the kingdom of Far Far Away (a defanged, satirical version of Hollywood) or find a proper heir. Fiona, waving goodbye from a dock crowded with the mutant offspring of Donkey and the dragon who swooned over him in the first episode, announces she is pregnant. This leads to a crisis of confidence for Shrek, who is not sure how an ogre can turn into a decent father—a plot point that seems designed for male moviegoers to visit their own anxieties about fatherhood.

For some reason, the heir apparent turns out to be Artie (voice of Justin Timberlake), otherwise known as Arthur of the Knights of the Round Table fame, whom the heroes find is the least popular kid in class at a high school called Worcestershire. The high school setting allows a few outdated linguistic salvos at teen-speak, presumably a sop to the fans of *Shrek* who have grown into teens as the franchise has aged. Later, there is a feminist uprising of sorts led by Fiona's mother, the Queen (voice of Julie Andrews), which includes some of the swooning princesses of fairy-tale lore—Snow White (voice of Amy Poehler), Sleeping Beauty (voice of Cheri

Oteri), and Cinderella (voice of Amy Sedaris)—bursting out of their passive mode and becoming revenge-seeking power-punk icons, an obvious bone thrown to young postfeminist mothers.

Having something for every demographic is one mark of a successful franchise. (The kids, as is too often the case, get a few fecal and vomit jokes and not much else.) A mark of a tired franchise is such desperation as having a New-Age Merlin (voice of Eric Idle) mix up a magic spell and switch the sidekicks into each other's bodies. It is actually one of the funnier things in a very unfunny movie. By all measures except the profitability assured by endorsement deals and worldwide video distribution, *Shrek the Third* is an enormous bomb.

The plot, simplistically, produces a gang of villainous fairy-tale characters, led by Prince Charming (voice of Rupert Everett), to battle the good guys over the rights to the throne. In the original *Shrek,* the fairy-tale characters who appeared had been disenfranchised by their commercial bosses (a.k.a. Disney), who had exploited and exiled them. In this sanitized installment, Prince Charming rallies his army by appealing to villains such as Captain Hook to seize the booty unjustly given to others. (It is a stretch, because Prince Charming was hardly a villain in the Cinderella story.) The false issue the scriptwriters propose is that the fairy-tale villains were unjustly victimized. Artie's solution is to encourage the villains to be their real, good selves, just like the no-longer-dangerous Shrek. Instead of blaming entertainment moguls for distorting old tales of morality, Shrek's creators now say it is unfair to have villains at all. Thus did Shrek and his tale turn from anarchic to cuddly. *Shrek the Third* is nothing more than exactly what *Shrek the First* so gloriously lampooned—a shameless piece of life-sapping merchandise. How the mightily mischievous have fallen into the swamp of franchising.

Michael Betzold

CREDITS

Shrek: Mike Myers (Voice)
Fiona: Cameron Diaz (Voice)
Donkey: Eddie Murphy (Voice)
Puss in Boots: Antonio Banderas (Voice)
King Harold: John Cleese (Voice)
Queen Lillian: Julie Andrews (Voice)
Artie: Justin Timberlake (Voice)
Prince Charming: Rupert Everett (Voice)
Cinderella: Amy Sedaris (Voice)
Rapunzel: Maya Rudolph (Voice)
Sleeping Beauty: Cheri Oteri (Voice)
Snow White: Amy Poehler (Voice)

Lancelot: John Krasinski (Voice)
Capt. Hook: Ian McShane (Voice)
Merlin: Eric Idle (Voice)
Mabel: Regis Philbin (Voice)
Doris: Larry King (Voice)
Gingerbread Man/Rumplestiltskin/Headless Horseman:
   Conrad Vernon (Voice)
Pinocchio/Three Pigs: Cody Cameron (Voice)
Ship Captain: Seth Rogen (Voice)
Origin: USA
Language: English
Released: 2007
Directed by: Chris Miller, Raman Hui
Written by: Jeffrey Price, Peter S. Seaman, Jon Zack
Music by: Harry Gregson-Williams
MPAA rating: PG
Running time: 92 minutes

REVIEWS

Boston Globe Online. May 17, 2007.
Chicago Sun-Times Online. May 17, 2007.
Entertainment Weekly. May 25, 2007, p. 61.
Hollywood Reporter Online. May 10, 2007.
Los Angeles Times Online. May 18, 2007.
New York Times Online. May 18, 2007.
Rolling Stone Online. May 17, 2007.
San Francisco Chronicle. May 17, 2007, p. E1.
Variety Online. May 9, 2007.
Washington Post. May 18, 2007, p. C1.

QUOTES

Donkey (after seeing Shrek naked): "You know, you really need
   to get yourself a pair of jammies!"

TRIVIA

Donkey and Dragon have five children: Coco, Debbie, Peanut,
   Parfait, and Bananas.

AWARDS

Nomination:

British Acad. 2007: Animated Film.

SICKO

> *This might hurt a little.*
> —Movie tagline
> *What seems to be the problem?*
> —Movie tagline

Box Office: $24.5 million

About the time Michael Moore was completing *Sicko,* his documentary exposé of the American health-care industry, Toronto filmmakers Rick Caine and Debbie Melnyk released an unauthorized documentary about Moore's "gotcha" tactics titled *Manufacturing Dissent* at the South by Southwest Film Festival in Austin, Texas. According to *New York Times* reporter John Anderson, the Melnyk-Caine documentary raised basic questions about nonfiction filmmaking, such as "Should all documentary-making be considered subjective and ultimately manipulative, or should the viewer be able to believe what he or she sees?" Moore's distributor, The Weinstein Company, had "no comment" concerning either the Melnyk-Caine documentary attack or concerning *Sicko,* the new Moore project, which was then being kept under wraps.

But this was only one of many attempts to discredit Moore and his tactics and his motives in anticipation of his latest controversial documentary. The right-wing *Washington Times* as well as the left-wing *New York Times* both ran stories about the U.S. government's investigation into Moore's trip to Cuba. According to the *Washington Times,* the Treasury Department's Office of Foreign Assets Control notified Moore by letter on May 2, 2007, that it was "conducting a civil investigation for possible violations of the U.S. trade embargo restricting travel to Cuba."

Why? As William Booth explained it in his "Letter from Cannes" to the *Washington Post,* the film had already "cranked up the anti-Moore blogosphere and conservative pundits (they need each other for this tango)," by asking, pointedly, why "one of the richest nations on Earth has a health-care system that leaves 50 million Americans without coverage?" Moore's thesis suggests that "the American health-care system is sick because the political system is unwell." Moore traces the cause back to the Nixon administration, which enabled the creation of a monstrous super-lobby including the American Medical Association, the pharmaceutical industry, and the insurance industry, all taking a combined stand against socialism in general and socialized medicine in particular. Moore attacks the failings of American health care by making comparisons to superior health care in France, England, and Canada. Moore told the AARP (formerly known as the American Association of Retired Persons) that his film was not partisan: "I started with the assumption that illness knows no political stripe." Moore visits hospitals outside the United States in order to demonstrate the ease of obtaining quality health care in Cuba, Canada, and Europe.

The film makes claims that some critics considered questionable. *USA Today* reporter Richard Wolf, for example, complained that *Sicko* "uses omission, exaggeration and cinematic sleight of hand to make its points." But the film's alleged inaccuracies would appear to be trivial. *Sicko* claims, for example, that "nearly 50 million Americans have no health insurance," but Wolf claims, in a fervor of nit-picking, that the true number for 2005 was only 44.8 million, and that U.S. health care costs $6,100 per person per year, whereas the film says the cost is $7,000 per person per year. On the other hand, Moore told Jeffrey Kluger of *Time* magazine, for example, that Cubans "live on average a month longer" than Americans do. Anthony DePalma of the *New York Times* confirmed that statistics from the World Health Organization and other sources indicate that "the people of Cuba and the United States have about the same life expectancy—seventy-seven years, give or take a few months—while infant mortality in Cuba is significantly lower than in the United States." The reason, apparently, is that the Cubans emphasize early intervention: "Clinic visits are free, and the focus is on preventing disease rather than treating it."

Reviews of the film were reasonably positive. Claudia Puig of *USA Today* considered *Sicko* Moore's "most ambitious project," defending it as his "biggest, best and most impassioned work." In the *New Yorker,* Atul Gawande first outlined "a few insufferable traits" of the director: "He is manipulative, smug, and self-righteous. He has no interest in complexity. And he mocks the weak as well as the powerful." Even so, the critic calls *Sicko* a "revelation," oddly enough, because "the movie brings to light nothing that the media haven't covered extensively for years." Stuart Klawans of the *Nation* doubted that Moore had "ever before relied so heavily on so many people. They help him make his argument about the failures of American medicine (or, rather, the successes of American insurance-gouging). But to Moore's great credit, the debating points never seem more important than the individuals who back them up."

New Yorker reviewer David Denby was not so favorably impressed, however. He wrote that Moore "has teased and bullied his way to some brilliant highs in his career as a political entertainer," but in *Sicko,* he "scrapes bottom." Denby objected to Moore's "silly stunts" and globetrotting escapades, and this critic has a point. Likewise, Stephen Hunter of the *Washington Post* claimed Moore "never goes for the big picture." For Hunter the film made two points: "The American health-care system is busted and Michael Moore is not the guy to fix it." But that charge was in part refuted by a story written by Kevin Sack for the *New York Times,* a campaign mounted by Moore for health-care reform: "a single-payer system, with the government as insurer, that would guarantee access to health care for all Americans and put the private insurance industry out of business."

In his *Time* review of *Sicko,* Richard Corliss pointed out that Moore was not the first to notice the "inequities and iniquities" of the American health-care system: "He's never the first to address a gut issue, whether it's corporate greed (*Roger & Me*), American violence (*Bowling for Columbine*), the politics of terror (*Fahrenheit 9/11*). But he's the one who does it the noisiest, with the highest entertainment value, mixing muckraking with showmanship, Ida Tarbell with P. T. Barnum." Moore has been more entertaining and clownish, but in this case the more potentially deadly topic deserves and gets a more subdued treatment.

For Moore, *Sicko* seems to represent a higher sense of purpose than his earlier work, as the director trades upon his reputation as the most insistent and notorious documentary filmmaker now working. "I think one movie can make a difference," Moore told a congressional hearing, adding, "I really want to make a contribution to the national debate on this issue." Given his celebrity status following the success of *Fahrenheit 9/11* (2004), many viewers will be inclined to believe Moore's extravagant claim. Meanwhile, skeptics will have to wait to see what kind of political action, if any, may follow Moore's exposé. But, regardless, the film deserves attention and respect, as it was bound to get, given Moore's reputation.

James M. Welsh

CREDITS

Origin: USA

Language: English

Released: 2007

Production: Michael Moore, Meghan O'Hara; Dog Eat Dog Productions; released by Weinstein Co.

Directed by: Michael Moore

Written by: Michael Moore

Music by: Erin O'Hara

Editing: Dan Swietlik, Geoffrey Richman, Christopher Seward

MPAA rating: PG-13

Running time: 113 minutes

REVIEWS

Austin Chronicle Online. June 29, 2007.
Boston Globe Online. June 29, 2007.
Chicago Sun-Times Online. June 29, 2007.
Christian Science Monitor. June 29, 2007.
Entertainment Weekly. July 13, 2007, p. 50.
Los Angeles Times Online. June 29, 2007.
New York Times Online. June 22, 2007.
Rolling Stone Online. June 13, 2007.

San Francisco Chronicle. June 29, 2007, p. E1.
Variety Online. May 19, 2007.
Washington Post. June 29, 2007, p. C1.

AWARDS

Nomination:

Oscars 2007: Feature Doc.
Writers Guild 2008: Screenplay.

THE SIMPSONS MOVIE

See our family and feel better about yours.
—Movie tagline

Box Office: $183 million

It is easy to say that, without indulging in any hyperbole, that *The Simpsons*—Fox's long-running animated sitcom from the minds of Matt Groening, James L. Brooks, and Sam Simon—is one of the most significant television programs in the history of the medium. While many popular television series experience periods of seemingly global popularity, few have ever penetrated so deeply and so permanently into pop culture and the world psyche as *The Simpsons*. The adventures of Homer Simpson and family have influenced (or, at the very least, been reflected in) almost every facet of modern American society—TV, merchandising, music, comic books, food products, toys, video games, Halloween costumes, clothing, vocabulary (Homer's catch phrase "D'oh!" made it into the *Oxford English Dictionary*)...the list goes on and on. In a 2003 BBC poll, British voters chose Homer Simpson as "the greatest American ever," besting his nearest competitor, Abraham Lincoln, by an enormous margin.

As a result, it might seem odd that the producers of *The Simpsons* waited almost eighteen years to attempt a film version of such a successful series. However, given the program's unprecedented fame, there have been nearly decades of admittedly unreasonable expectations surrounding the first family of Springfield's eventual move to the big screen. Rumors of a *Simpsons* movie have run rampant for years, ranging from fictionalized storylines about Bart losing his virginity to a live-action version starring John Goodman as Homer (Gary Oldman was Homer's first choice to play his movie doppelganger in the episode "I Am Furious Yellow"). However, the producers did not officially begin preproduction on the eventual *Simpsons* movie until 2001, gathering a writing staff that brought together an all-star team of *Simpsons* alumni, including James L. Brooks, Matt Groening, Al Jean, Mike Scully, Richard Sakai, George Meyer, David Mirkin, Mike Reiss, John Swartzwelder,

Jon Vitti, Ian Maxtone-Graham, and Matt Selman. After feverishly working on a script that was allegedly rewritten over one hundred times, *The Simpsons Movie* was finally sent to its animation team in 2006 and, after more post-test-screening revisions, was released to the public in July 2007. Despite fears that audiences would not flock to see a movie based on a television series that aired in syndication almost every day of the week—a fear Homer himself mocked in the film's opening—*The Simpsons Movie* was a major box office success, grossing over $180 million domestically and $340 million worldwide.

Despite the high expectations surrounding the release and frequent complaints from disgruntled fans lamenting the show's alleged decline in quality over the years, it is hard to argue that *The Simpsons Movie* is anything but, first and foremost, a very, very funny film. It may be true that the show has never recaptured the subversive spark of its fifth and sixth seasons—long held to be the best in the series' history—but, regardless, *The Simpsons Movie* acts as a widescreen representation of the best that the show has ever had to offer. The plot is simplistic, even by the show's standards, however, which seems to be a conscious act by the writing team. This is a film that very easily could have descended into a self-perpetuating spiral of self-referential in-jokes and smug fanboy sarcasm. Instead, the writing team has constructed a story that is somehow both welcoming and accessible while still paying off huge dividends to the invested longtime fans of the show. The writers accomplished this goal by focusing their attention almost entirely on the core Simpson family members—a decision that annoyed some whom expected that every supporting character in Springfield would be given a moment in the spotlight. And while, yes, it is a bit of a shame that Sideshow Bob, Mr. Burns, or Bumblebee Man were not given more to do, ultimately, the decision to restrict the movie to the Simpsons proper was a wise one, an act that gave the plot a surprisingly level of emotional depth and narrative pace.

The story revolves around an environmental catastrophe in Springfield, a topic long mined for humor by the *Simpsons* writers, dating back to 1990's Season Two episode "Two Cars in Every Garage and Three Eyes on Every Fish." After being treated to a sublimely violent opening "Itchy & Scratchy" cartoon, we join the residents of Springfield at a lakeside concert, headlined by the punk rockers Green Day (one of the film's two celebrity cameos), a rock show that ends in tragedy because of the almost critically toxic levels of pollution in Lake Springfield. Soon thereafter, Grampa Simpson (voice of Dan Castellaneta) speaks in tongues during a church service, prophesying dark days ahead for Springfield and warning the churchgoers of the mysterious "Eeepa." The majority of the Simpsons are unfazed by Grampa's "senior moment"—except for uber-mom and moral compass Marge (voice of Julie Kavner)—and the oblivious Homer (voice of Dan Castellaneta) and Bart (voice of Nancy Cartwright) are soon competing with each other in an ever-escalating dare contest. This leads to one of the film's most memorable scenes, Bart skateboarding naked through the streets of downtown Springfield, a hilariously choreographed sequence that ends with the first moment of on-screen full-frontal male nudity in *Simpsons* history. (The moment is strangely both innocent and shocking at the same time.) This event, and Homer's dismissal of Bart's morbid embarrassment, prompts one of the film's major B-stories—Bart's growing dissatisfaction with Homer as his father and his search for paternal comfort with his next-door neighbor, goody-goody Ned Flanders (voice of Harry Shearer).

The skateboarding montage also indirectly introduces Homer to his new pet pig, a relationship that spawns probably the film's funniest (and most publicized) gag, that is, "Spider-Pig" (Homer helps his porcine buddy [voice of Tress MacNeille] walk across the ceilings of his house to the tune of the old *Spider-Man* cartoon theme song). While Marge tries to decipher Grampa's portents of doom and Lisa (voice of Yeardley Smith) petitions for environmental action with her new Irish boyfriend Colin (voice of Tress MacNeille), Homer gathers his pig's "leavings" in an ever-growing silo of animal waste. When Lisa finally convinces the town that even one more pollutant in Lake Springfield could cause an apocalyptic toxic disaster, Mayor Quimby (voice of Dan Castellaneta) outlaws dumping in the distressed body of water, a law Homer breaks almost immediately. (He dumps his silo of pig waste into the lake to rush to the site of free donuts.) This turns the lake into a biohazard nightmare, prompting Russ Cargill (voice of Albert Brooks), the evil new head of the Environmental Protection Agency (EPA, or "Eeepa"), a former corporate CEO in the Enron and Halliburton tradition, to persuade President Arnold Schwarzenegger (voice of Harry Shearer) to enclose all of Springfield beneath a glass dome, ostensibly to protect the rest of America. (Though Cargill does, also, own the company that built the dome.) When the trapped residents of Springfield discover that Homer is responsible for their plight, an angry mob tries to lynch the Simpsons, but the family is able to escape the dome and start a new life in the pristine landscapes of Alaska. After the Springfield citizens become more and more unruly under their new dome-rule, Cargill persuades Schwarzenegger to blow up the town to cover their mistake. (In the film's second celebrity cameo, Tom Hanks is hired to promote the crater that Springfield will become as the "new Grand

Canyon.") When the Simpsons learn of Springfield's approaching doom, the family is split apart—with the selfish Homer on one side, and the rest of the Simpsons dead-set on saving their hometown.

As with any great episode of the TV show, you could spent hours simply recounting the one-liners from *The Simpsons Movie*. From Ralph Wiggum's (voice of Nancy Cartwright) declaration that he "likes men now" to Russ Cargill's claim that the residents of Springfield were not, in fact, trapped like rats—"Rats can't be trapped this easily, you're trapped like…carrots"—this might be one of the most quotable movies since *Fletch* (1985) or *Caddyshack* (1980). However, it is surprising how driven and plot-oriented the main story is, given the show's historical love of diversions and tangents. Every scene in *The Simpsons Movie* moves the plot forward, which is a welcome change from some of the flimsier B-stories that have been featured in some of the series' more recent seasons. Another surprise is how oddly emotional the final product ended up being. Bart's estrangement from Homer feels more real and tangible than it ever has in the show's history, and there is a truly heart-wrenching scene where Marge leaves Homer a "Dear John" videotape that should have won Julie Kavner some year-end best supporting actress nominations for her vocal work alone. *The Simpsons Movie* may not have delivered the wall-to-wall laughs that some fans were expecting, but it ended up being much more emotionally satisfying than any fan or critic could have anticipated.

The movie is not without its flaws. The laughs do drag in places (particularly in the Alaska scenes), the story turn with the Inuit healer seems forced, Homer's emotional epiphany is not particularly profound, and Flanders does seem strangely toothless as the ideal dad figure, especially because his character has become such a potent representation of the hypocrisies of the Religious Right over the years. The end credit jokes are also disappointingly lame, coming across like a brief encore set from an exhausted band that should have left the stage on a higher note. However, the rest of the movie is so legitimately charming, funny, brisk, irreverent, and eminently rewatchable that any of those smaller flaws can be easily forgiven. While the movie lacks the revolutionary spark of the show's earlier seasons, it does succeed in constructing a compelling, solid theatrical comedy. The critical response to *The Simpsons Movie* was largely positive, with most dissenters arguing that the movie, at its worst, simply failed to live up to the TV show's sterling reputation. *New York Times* reviewer A. O. Scott commented that, "Do I sound disappointed? I'm not, really. Or only a little. *The Simpsons Movie*, in the end, is as good as an average episode of *The Simpsons*. In other words, I'd be willing to watch it only—excuse me while I crunch some numbers here—20 or 30 more times." This may not be the mythical "Best. Movie. Ever." that some Simpson fans were hoping for, but there is little reason to say "D'oh!" after watching *The Simpsons Movie.*

Tom Burns

CREDITS

Homer/Barney/Grampa/Itchy/Krusty/Mayor Quimby/Sideshow Mel: Dan Castellaneta (Voice)

Marge/Patty/Selma: Julie Kavner (Voice)

Bart/Maggie/Ralph/Nelson/Todd Flanders: Nancy Cartwright (Voice)

Lisa: Yeardley Smith (Voice)

Seymour Skinner/Lenny/Dr. Hibbert/Ned Flanders/Mr. Burns/Smithers/Otto: Harry Shearer (Voice)

Moe/Apu/Sea Captain/Professor Frink/Comic Book Guy/Chief Wiggum/Lou/Carl: Hank Azaria (Voice)

Russ Cargill: Albert Brooks (Voice)

Fat Tony: Joe Mantegna (Voice)

Edna Krabappel: Marcia Wallace (Voice)

Milhouse/Jimbo Jones/Rod Flanders: Pamela Hayden (Voice)

Himself: Tom Hanks (Voice)

Origin: USA

Released: 2007

Production: James L. Brooks, Richard Sakai, Matt Groening, Al Jean, Mike Scully; Gracie Films; released by 20th Century-Fox Films

Directed by: David Silverman

Written by: James L. Brooks, David Mirkin, Matt Groening, Mike Reiss, Al Jean, Ian Maxtone-Graham, George Meyer, Mike Scully, Matt Selman, John Swartzwelder, Jon Vitti

Music by: Hans Zimmer

MPAA rating: PG-13

Running time: 87 minutes

REVIEWS

Boston Globe Online. July 26, 2007.
Chicago Sun-Times Online. July 26, 2007.
Entertainment Weekly Online. July 24, 2007.
Los Angeles Online. July 27, 2007.
New York Times Online. July 27, 2007.

QUOTES

Ned Flanders: "Look at that, you can see the four states that border Springfield: Ohio, Nevada, Maine, and Kentucky."

Homer Simpson (standing up and addressing the audience after watching the *Itchy and Scratchy* movie): "I can't believe we're paying to see something we get on TV for free! If you ask me, everybody in this theater is a giant sucker! Especially you!"

Tom Hanks (introducing a PSA): "Hello, I'm Tom Hanks. The U.S. government has lost its credibility so it's borrowing some of mine."

TRIVIA

Work on the film's script began in 2003 and 158 drafts were written.

AWARDS

Nomination:

British Acad. 2007: Animated Film
Golden Globes 2008: Animated Film.

SKINWALKERS

They live among us. They hunt us.
—Movie tagline

For Them to Live, We Must Die.
—Movie tagline

The Beast Waits Within.
—Movie tagline

Box Office: $1 million

Even the tagline for James Isaac's *Skinwalkers* hints at the confusion that so clearly marked the production of the entire film, "They Hunt Us." The odd thing about that line is that there is no "Us" in *Skinwalkers.* Supposedly using an old Navajo legend as a starting point, *Skinwalkers* is primarily about good werewolves versus bad werewolves, but the tagline probably sounded more appealing than "They Hunt Each Other." The clear confusion between product and marketing is only one of several signs that the concept behind *Skinwalkers* was severely muddied from conception to the final product. Isaac knows how to stage an interesting action sequence and there are some good ideas in his film, but the final product feels like one that has had too many cooks in its kitchen with sloppy editing, poorly developed characters, and clichéd dialogue. Even werewolf fans, who have come to forgive a few of those flaws, will be disappointed by a film that fails to pay off the typical strengths of the genre.

In the world of *Skinwalkers,* when the moon goes full, some of the afflicted turn into evil werewolves, the kind that like to kill innocent bystanders for food and pleasure, but others keep their lupine desires in check, usually with chains and shackles. Jonas (Elias Koteas) is the head of the good werewolves while Varek (Jason Behr) leads the pack of motorcycle-riding wicked creatures of the night. Clearly modeled after the biker chic creatures from Kathryn Bigelow's far-superior *Near Dark* (1987), the gang of blood-lusting vamps include Varek's girlfriend Sonja (Nastassia Malthe), Zo (Kim Coates), and Grenier (Rogue Johnston), who uses a hawk to chase his prey. The bad side embraces their deepest instincts, claiming that they are better than the human race, while the good side believes in protecting the innocent bystanders from being devoured.

Each side needs to find a boy who is something like the Harry Potter of the werewolf world. A prophecy dictates that a red moon will herald the coming of a just-turned thirteen-year-old boy who can stop the war. That boy, Timothy (Matthew Knight), has been guarded all of his life by the good werewolves, led by Jonas and his daughter Katherine (Sarah Carter), with the assistance of her boyfriend Adam (Shawn Roberts). Now that the moon has gone red, Jonas and his gang must stop Varek and the other werewolves in black from getting to Timothy by his thirteenth birthday. Timothy's mother, Rachel (Rhona Mitra), gets dragged along for the ride and learns that she too may be a crucial part of the battle between good and evil werewolves.

A vast majority of the script for *Skinwalkers* is consumed with dialogue about prophecies, red moons, and the beast inside. Viewers come to a film like *Skinwalkers,* especially considering the involvement of legendary effects man Stan Winston, whose studio produced the effects, hoping for action and transformation. Probably because of budgetary constraints, the film contains shockingly little of either. Writers James DeMonaco, Todd Harthan, and James Roday have essentially crafted a chase movie with people who only coincidentally turn into wolves under the full moon. The good wolves ride in a truck, the bad wolves drive choppers, and everyone inexplicably ends up in the same forest for a shootout. Most of the action in *Skinwalkers* consists of a few well-staged gunfights, not exactly what viewers looking for a creature feature will be expecting.

Like a lot of nearly straight-to-DVD horror films, *Skinwalkers* feels like a movie mangled by the long road of production. Some of the sloppy editing can probably be attributed to the attempt to trim the bloodletting and primal urges to land a PG-13 rating. The film was originally 110 minutes long (and the back of the DVD case even incorrectly still lists it as such), but was trimmed down to ninety-one minutes to land the more box office-friendly rating. The editing left plot holes and awkward transitions through out.

Editing can be blamed for part of the failure of *Skinwalkers,* but it also feels as if the writers, director, and producers may not have been on the same page, no matter the rating. By trying to be everything (family drama, horror film, action flick) *Skinwalkers* ends up being surprisingly little at all. The core of the idea is a good one, but the execution falls incredibly flat by placing emphasis on dialogue and shotguns instead of fanged teeth and hairy transformations. *Skinwalkers* never embraces its B-movie origins as it needed to in order to succeed. With its family melodrama and general lack of actual werewolves, *Skinwalkers* is a creature feature that will fail to get under the skin of even the most diehard wolfman fanatic.

Brian Tallerico

CREDITS

Varek: Jason Behr
Jonas: Elias Koteas
Rachel: Rhona Mitra
Timothy: Matthew Knight
Zo: Kim Coates
Will: Tom Jackson
Nana: Barbara Gordon
Origin: USA, Canada, Germany
Language: English
Released: 2007
Production: Don Carmody, Dennis Berardi, Red Moon Films; After Dark Films, Constantin Film, Stan Winston Prods.; released by Lionsgate
Directed by: James Isaac
Written by: James DeMonaco, James Roday, Todd Harthan
Cinematography by: Adam Kane, David A. Armstrong
Music by: Andrew Lockington
Sound: David Lee
Editing: Allan Lee
Costumes: Antoinette Messam
Production Design: David Hackl
MPAA rating: PG-13
Running time: 110 minutes

REVIEWS

Boston Globe Online. August 11, 2007.
Hollywood Reporter Online. August 13, 2007.
Los Angeles Times Online. August 13, 2007.
New York Times Online. August 11, 2007.
Variety Online. August 10, 2007.

QUOTES

Varek: "I am not human. And I will not risk spending the rest of my days as one. Diseased and flawed...we're better than that."

SLEUTH

Obey the rules.
—Movie tagline

Sleuth is director Kenneth Branagh's sparse, pared-down reinvention of the 1972 film by Joseph L. Mankiewicz that was based on Anthony Shaffer's long-running two-man play. The 2007 version loosely adheres to the theme of the original, a sadistic, psychological cat-and-mouse game between an aging cuckold and his wife's new lover, but it jettisons the original film's dialogue and has rewritten the third act. Replacing them are an in-your-face theme of morbid jealously and overly stylized dialogue, penned by British playwright and Nobel Prize for literature winner Harold Pinter.

There is an interesting symmetry at play in the casting of this version. In the original, the younger role of Milo Tindle was played by Michael Caine. Thirty-five years later, Caine takes on the role of the older society husband, Andrew Wyke, with Jude Law as the young suitor Milo. Law also starred in the 2004 remake of *Alfie* (1966) the film that propelled Caine to stardom.

Kenneth Branagh's reimagination goes against the current trend of supersizing a remake, in both style and length, the 2007 version trims almost forty-five minutes from the running time by reworking the entire third act and trimming much of the setup of the first two acts. Gone from the remake is the Bizarro Geppetto workshop-like atmosphere of Andrew's manse in the original and replaced with an extremely stark, cavernous, and nearly uninhabitable interior, overpopulated with security cameras and nary a stick of furniture. The stylization continues with the cinematography that features a palette of icy hues, extreme close-ups, and odd camera angles with action that is either off the screen or shown on grainy security monitors. These effects often fight with the actors and the action on screen.

The story is essentially a two-hander revolving around the struggling actor Milo Tindle (Jude Law) and Caine's extremely wealthy mystery writer Andrew Wyke. The story begins with the young Milo paying a visit to the estate of his lover's husband, Wyke, to request that the author grant his wife a divorce. The snobbish, self-proclaimed lover of games and gamesmanship is willing to grant Milo's wishes but points out that a woman of his wife's means could never be content with the lifestyle of a struggling actor. The creative and resourceful Wyke has a plan to alleviate Milo's financial plight. What ensues is an elaborate insurance scam involving Milo's theft of Wyke's family jewels valued at 800,000 pounds. What Law's character does not realize is that the heist is a trap designed for Andrew's amusement and ultimately, Milo's humiliation. Andrew severely underestimates the mettle of his rival and what ensues is a highly charged, homoerotic game of cat and mouse, with several plot twists, and more than a hint of the Michael Caine/ Christopher Reeve murder/mystery based on a play, *Deathtrap* (1982).

Caine inherits the role that was played by Laurence Olivier in the Mankiewicz film and Caine seamlessly steps into the part. Caine is an actor who completely commits to the character, regardless of situation or dialogue, and Pinter's script requires the utmost commitment. Caine's Wyke is not the man born into privilege as in the original, so much of the class conflict is missing, but his character is just as contemptuous. Law is one of the busiest young British actors in film today and he smoothly handles the various permutations of Milo, perhaps a little too smoothly, as it is not too hard to imagine him sliding into the world of Wyke's high society and he appears too sharp to fall for such a trap. This seems to undermine the storyline but the two are such strong performers they are able to rise above the film's many shortcoming.

The screenplay by the usually inspired Pinter is long on pretentiousness and overly literary dialogue. Pinter claims his goal is to avoid too much plot work and to develop character by layering atmosphere, insight, and philosophy within the actor's words. The dialogue seems more appropriate for the stage and is not as effective on film. The loss of the third act creates a plot that is so abbreviated it seems as though something was left on the cutting-room floor, prompting one critic to wonder if this shorter version was merely a reflection of modern society's seemingly shorter attention span.

Where Branagh's film succeeds is in the timing, taking a compelling story and a successful film that has since faded from memory and coupling it with the cinematic tour de force of Pinter, Caine, and Law. The result, however, falls well short of expectations.

Michael White

CREDITS

Andrew Wyke: Michael Caine
Milo Tindle: Jude Law
Origin: Great Britain, USA
Language: English
Released: 2007
Production: Jude Law, Kenneth Branagh, Tom Sternberg, Marion Pilowsky, Simon Halfon; Castle Rock Entertainment, Timnick Films, Riff Raff; released by Sony Pictures Classics
Directed by: Kenneth Branagh
Written by: Harold Pinter
Cinematography by: Haris Zambarloukos
Music by: Patrick Doyle
Sound: Peter Glossop
Editing: Neil Farrell
Art Direction: Iain White

Costumes: Alexandra Byrne
Production Design: Tim Harvey
MPAA rating: R
Running time: 86 minutes

REVIEWS

Entertainment Weekly Online. October 10, 2007.
Hollywood Reporter Online. August 31, 2007.
Los Angeles Times Online. October 12, 2007.
New York Times Online. October 12, 2007.
Variety Online. August 30, 2007.
Village Voice Online. October 9, 2007.

QUOTES

Andrew Wyke (on Milo being an actor): "Why have I never heard of you?"
Milo Tindle: "You will before long."

TRIVIA

The entire film was shot in sequence.

SLOW BURN

The truth is just a trick of light.
—Movie tagline
Tonight...Believe No One.
—Movie tagline

Box Office: $1.2 million

Slow Burn went through a long gestation before it was stillborn. This hard-boiled cops-and-gangsters movie, filmed in Montreal and completed in 2005, did not get a studio release until two years later. Originally scheduled for a June debut, it suddenly got pulled up to April and opened with no advance screenings or reviews. Without a major star or a decent publicity campaign, the opening was dreadful.

It deserved a better fate. Smart, clever, funny, and tense, this directorial debut from screenwriter Wayne Beach is low budget but does not suffer from it. It has the classy look, sassy dialogue, and condensed style of an old-school B-movie detective potboiler. It features nice acting from Ray Liotta and a host of supporting characters, a streetwise demeanor, and a quick-moving, well-edited script from Beach. In fact, clocking in at around ninety minutes, there is nothing slow about it—and barely is there a wasted moment. It is lean, mean, and dirty.

True to its genre, at the center of the film is a femme fatale who is deadly indeed—one Nora Timmer (Jolene Blalock). She is introduced by the narrator/protagonist, big-city district attorney Ford Cole (Ray Liotta), as the up-and-coming assistant prosecutor who has proved to be a big asset because she is smart, cunning, and beautiful. But, on a night when Cole, who is running for mayor, is being interviewed by a magazine reporter (Chiwetel Ejiofor) to be profiled as one of the city's most eligible bachelors and promising politicians, Nora shows up after midnight with a tragic story to tell. She tells Cole she has been raped by one of her informants, Isaac Duperde (Mekhi Phifer), and has had to kill him in self-defense. Needless to say, it is a potential embarrassment for Cole's campaign, a possibly fatal setback in his efforts to catch a shadowy gangster boss, and a personal problem too—because Nora has been bedding down with Cole.

The plot quickly thickens when a man shows up at the station with some information to share. Luther Pinks (James Todd Smith a.k.a. LL Cool J) is a cool character with a story to tell that contradicts Nora's completely. Nora first met Isaac in a record store where both Isaac and Luther were working. While Nora claims Isaac was stalking her, Luther claims Nora was roping in Isaac into a complicated entrapment scheme, and that Nora is actually working for the crime boss Cole is trying to catch.

Beach obviously knows standard screenwriting techniques—he adds a ticking clock in the form of evidence that something big is about to blow at five a.m. the next day, and Cole begs the chief of police, who hates him, to give him until dawn before he proceeds with the announcement of charges in Isaac's death. The plot deepens to involve the gang boss's possible big ambitions to take over a slum area of the city and profit by redeveloping it.

Slow Burn develops rather deliciously into an elaborate cat-and-mouse game that is made all the more delectable because it is not clear who is the cat, who is the mouse, and who is the cheese. Is Luther baiting the hook for Ford? Is Nora conniving or being betrayed? And what is the real role of another informant, Jeffrey Sykes (Taye Diggs) and of the reporter himself? These questions pose increasing ethical challenges for Cole, who is trapped between personal affairs, his political ambitions, his legal responsibilities, and his sense of ethics.

Beach winds his story tightly and blithely around cleverly building plot tensions and carefully parceled-out pieces of dialogue. He deftly portrays Cole's increasing bewilderment by mixing in passionate scenes of his lovemaking with Nora, and of Nora's seduction of Isaac. Both classy and sleazy, streetwise and sophisticated, *Slow Burn* a homage to Dashiell Hammett and others of his ilk. And it has an interesting cast—full of fine African American actors spinning the head of Liotta, a square-jawed, sweating but resourceful protagonist trying to keep his head about him.

Beach's only mistake may be in trying to do too much, especially with the question of whether Nora is a white woman trying to pose as black. She is, according to the dialogue, a "trick of light," a phantom who can move back and forth between two worlds divided by race, but also between the worlds of crime and law enforcement. Nora's uncertain race is perhaps the most preposterous element in a plot that piles on twists at the end, giving viewers a revolving door of red herrings and suspects. One problem is that, apart from Ford, none of the characters has aroused much sympathy, so the audience does not have much of a rooting interest in who the villains really are and who, if anyone, is on the side of justice.

If there is such a thing as creating too large a web of intrigue, so that a point of reference is lost, Beach is in danger of doing that in *Slow Burn*. But otherwise it is a finely crafted film, though it is so eager to inhabit its genre that it does not break any new ground. We have seen these characters, and this sort of plot, many times before, yet Beach seems to take a playful delight in spinning the tropes his way. Smith, that is, LL Cool J, gives an outstandingly entertaining performance as the lordly informant who says people and situations always smell like certain kinds of food to him. The underused Phifer and Ejiofor are splendid too, and Blalock is seductive in a pleasantly understated way—her expressions are pregnant with meaning. Liotta is a little more problematic: with his fat face and perpetually panicked, puzzled expression, he looks and acts too much like a piece of meat for the rest of the cast to chew on.

Beach strays dangerously close to cliché on many occasions, and sometimes crosses the line, but overall his film is both taut and tantalizing. One hopes it will revive its prospects on video, because it is certainly the kind of film that will work well on the small screen: Beach excels in close-ups and quick edits, and *Slow Burn* verges on claustrophobic. But it is wise and witty in its chatter, and moves along so quickly that it has not an ounce of flab.

Michael Betzold

CREDITS

Ford Cole: Ray Liotta
Nora Timmer: Jolene Blalock
Luther Pinks: LL Cool J (as James Todd Smith)
Isaac Duperde: Mekhi Phifer

Godfrey: Bruce McGill
Ty Trippin: Chiwetel Ejiofor
Jeffrey Sykes: Taye Diggs
Origin: USA
Language: English
Released: 2005
Production: Fisher Stevens, Sidney Kimmel, Bonnie Timmerman, Tim Williams; GreeneStreet Films; released by Lionsgate Films
Directed by: Wayne Beach
Written by: Wayne Beach
Cinematography by: Wally Pfister
Music by: Jeff Rona
Sound: Pierre Blain
Editing: Kristina Boden
Costumes: Nicoletta Massone
Production Design: Tim Galvin
MPAA rating: R
Running time: 93 minutes

REVIEWS

Boston Globe Online. April 14, 2007.
Boxoffice Online. April 13, 2007.
Hollywood Reporter Online. April 16, 2007.
Los Angeles Times Online. April 16, 2007.
New York Times Online. April 14, 2007.
Variety Online. September 26, 2005.

SMOKIN' ACES

May the best hitman win.
—Movie tagline

When you're worth $1 million dead, you don't have long to live.
—Movie tagline

The only way to even the score is to take Buddy Israel out of the game.
—Movie tagline

Box Office: $35.8 million

Films released during the first three months of any year are invariably dregs distributors want to unload on audiences sated or bored by the award-laden efforts released at year's end. Universal's decision to release Joe Carnahan's *Smokin' Aces* in January 2007 was clearly motivated by a perceived need of restless viewers for good, trashy fun. Unfortunately, releasing a film in January is also the same as pinning a "kick me" sign on it where critics are concerned, and, indeed, reviewers enjoyed pummeling *Smokin' Aces*.

Claudia Puig of *USA Today* called it a "pointless exercise with gaping plot holes as big as Vegas' MGM

Grand." In the *New Yorker,* David Denby derided Carnahan's "whorish insensitivity." A. O. Scott of the *New York Times* was even harsher, calling *Smokin' Aces* "a Viagra suppository for compulsive action fetishists and a movie that may not only be dumb in itself, but also the cause of dumbness in others. Watching it is like being smacked in the face for a hundred minutes with a raw sirloin steak." Nearly the only critic to speak up for *Smokin' Aces* was Owen Gleiberman of *Entertainment Weekly* who said it "has a catchy, pungent spirit, with an invention that seldom lets down."

The plot of *Smokin' Aces* concerns Las Vegas lounge entertainer and magician Buddy "Aces" Israel (Jeremy Piven). Attracted by the glamour of the Mafia, Buddy supplements his income from card tricks by becoming a mob insider, even surpassing Frank Sinatra by participating in an armed robbery at one point. Then, for some reason, he decides to become an informer. (Carnahan's script is annoyingly vague about several plot points and character motivations, hurling too much information at the viewer too fast.)

To prevent Buddy from cooperating with the Federal Bureau of Investigation (FBI), legendary mob boss Primo Sparazza (Joseph Ruskin) and his henchman Serna (Alex Rocco) send several assassins to kill him, hoping that one will be bound to get through the heavy security at the Lake Tahoe hotel where the entertainer occupies the penthouse. The hit persons include the truly disgusting Tremor brothers (Chris Pine, Kevin Durand, and Maury Sterling), smooth operator Pasquale Acosta (Nestor Carbonell), master-of-disguise Lazlo Soot (Tommy Flanagan), and, representing African American womanhood, Georgia Sykes (Alicia Keys) and Sharice Watters (Taraji P. Henson).

There is also a team of bail bondsmen (Ben Affleck, Peter Berg, and Martin Henderson) who somehow become involved, working for the very strange Rip Reed (Jason Bateman). Affleck and Berg are also the first to depart, obviously having more significant projects to move on to. Trying to prevent the hit are clean-cut FBI agents Donald Carruthers (Ray Liotta) and Richard Messner (Ryan Reynolds), operating under the instructions of the bureau's assistant director, Stanley Locke (Andy Garcia). Needless to say, mayhem ensues.

Smokin' Aces is the long-awaited follow-up to Carnahan's critically acclaimed *Narc* (2002). It is worlds away, however, in tone from that hard-boiled yet realistic look at undercover narcotics officers. If *Narc* is a serious, though violent drama, *Smokin' Aces* is essentially a cartoon. Most reviewers observed Carnahan's obvious debt to Quentin Tarantino's *Pulp Fiction* (1994), but while Tarantino delights at inverting the clichés of the genre, Carnahan's approach is more heavy-handed, constantly pounding his viewers over the head and in the stomach with dark comedy and violent images.

An equal debt is owed to Bryan Singer and Christopher McQuarrie's *The Usual Suspects* (1995), with Acosta and Soot variations on Kevin Spacey's immortal Keyser Söze. The twists at the end of *Smokin' Aces* are also similar to those in *The Usual Suspects,* though much less satisfying. Anyone half alert can see the revelation about Sparazza coming early on.

Carnahan's other model seems to be graphic novels, as his images of a loony psycho wielding a chain saw and a hot babe with a big gun can attest. The director, who created a comic to unveil his characters' back stories, wants to have fun, yet there is a big difference between drawings of gruesome gore and having the screen awash with blood. *Smokin' Aces* is deliberately unrealistic much of the time, as when two combatants fire away point-blank at each other in an elevator, with neither dying, only to inject serious notes, especially at the end, with an undeservedly moralistic denouement.

Smokin' Aces has plenty of good moments, including Affleck's smart-aleck background report about Buddy and Henson's hilarious lecture about female empowerment to a befuddled hotel receptionist (Lorna Scott). Then there are totally humorless bits, such as Henderson's seeking refuge in a trailer with a wacky nurse (Marianne Muellerleile) and her bizarrely hyperactive grandson (Zach Cumer). This extraneous interlude is much too long, not to mention Carnahan's lack of originality in making fun of trailer-park trash.

All the actors give fine performances. Carbonell gives his killer a sensitive intensity. Meant to suggest Pam Grier in her prime, pop singer Keys makes Georgia swagger without reducing her to a sexy cliché. Henson captures the insecurity within Sharice's cocky exterior. The rapper Common has smooth charisma as Buddy's suspicious flunky, though how he knows the magician plans to betray him is not at all clear. Believably over the top, the almost unrecognizable Bateman is a hoot. Adopting a soft Southern accent, Garcia gives one of his best performances ever as the bureaucratic FBI agent.

Reynolds and, especially, Liotta are good, but their characters' solemn earnestness is out of sync with the rest of the film, as is Buddy. Piven is a gifted comic actor, as he shows with his slimy agent Ari Gold on *Entourage* (begun in 2004) and with his George Costanza impersonation in episodes of *Seinfeld* (1990–1998). Yet his repulsive Buddy is not funny at all: a sleazy, whining, suicidal cokehead. The audience should have some reason for wanting Buddy to survive, but Carnahan provides none, offering nothing to root for outside the well-being of Carruthers and Messner.

With *Smokin' Aces,* one of the bloodiest Hollywood films ever, Carnahan tries to do too much without thinking through the thematic and stylistic implications and consequences of his actions. Rarely has a film been so equally funny and repugnant.

Michael Adams

CREDITS

Buddy "Aces" Israel: Jeremy Piven
Jack Dupree: Ben Affleck
Stanley Locke: Andy Garcia
Donald Carruthers: Ray Liotta
Georgia Sykes: Alicia Keys
Richard Messner: Ryan Reynolds
"Pistol" Pete Deeks: Peter Berg
Sharice Watters: Taraji P. Henson
Hollis Elmore: Martin Henderson
Darwin Tremor: Chris Pine
Rupert "Rip" Reed: Jason Bateman
Primo Sparazza: Joseph Ruskin
Loretta Wyman: Davenia McFadden
Acosta: Nestor Carbonell
Lazlo Soot: Tommy Flanagan
Serna: Alex Rocco
The Swede: Vladimir Kulich
Victor "Baby Buzz" Padiche: David Proval
Hugo Croop: Joel Edgerton
Bill: Matthew Fox
Sir Ivy: Common
Freeman Heller: Mike Falkow
Jeeves Tremor: Kevin Durand
Lestor Tremor: Maury Sterling
Morris Mecklen: Curtis Armstrong
Origin: USA
Language: English
Released: 2007
Production: Tim Bevan, Eric Fellner; Working Title Productions, Studio Canal Plus, Relativity, Scion Films; released by Universal Pictures
Directed by: Joe Carnahan
Written by: Joe Carnahan
Cinematography by: Mauro Fiore
Music by: Clint Mansell
Sound: Jim Stuebe
Music Supervisor: Nick Angel
Editing: Rob Frazen
Art Direction: Maria Baker
Costumes: Mary Zophres
Production Design: Martin Whist
MPAA rating: R
Running time: 109 minutes

REVIEWS

Boxoffice Online. January 26, 2007.
Chicago Sun-Times Online. January 26, 2007.
Hollywood Reporter Online. January 22, 2007.
Los Angeles Times Online. January 26, 2007.
New York Times Online. January 26, 2007.
San Francisco Chronicle. January 26, 2007, p. E1.
Variety Online. January 17, 2007.
Washington Post. January 26, 2007, p. C1.

QUOTES

Buddy "Aces": "You're looking at me like, like...I just asked you the f***ing square root of something."

TRIVIA

Director Joe Carnahan appears briefly during the scene in which Jack Dupree is talking about Buddy Israel. As the scene unfolds a bank robbery is shown and Carnahan can be seen leaning against a truck wearing sunglasses and sporting a beard.

SOUTHLAND TALES

Have a nice apocalypse.
  —Movie tagline
This is the way the world ends.
  —Movie tagline
The future is just like you imagined.
  —Movie tagline

A convoluted apocalyptic satire, *Southland Tales* finds a mantra in an inverted segment of T. S. Eliot's 1925 poem "The Hollow Men"—"This is the way the world ends...not with a whimper, but with a bang." Chronicling the intersecting lives of a group of political figures, media personalities, and Marxist anarchists in Los Angeles following a nuclear bombing on American soil, the film is bursting with ideas that never quite connect in any meaningful way. Though his ambition is visible on the screen, writer/director Richard Kelly—exploring similar themes to those in his popular debut *Donnie Darko* (1999)—unfortunately falls flat in his attempt to make the viewer feel anything for the myriad of cartoonish characters that people this overlong whimper of a film.

On July 4, 2005, terrorists detonate an atomic bomb in Abilene, Texas, throwing the United States into World War III and creating an oil crisis. Three years later, the country is living in a fascist state under a strict Republican regime in which all citizens are monitored by an organization called USIDent. Boxer Santaros (Dwayne Johnson), a Schwarzenegger-esque action star married to the daughter of Republican vice presidential candidate Bobby Frost (Holmes Osborne), resurfaces in Los Angeles after waking in the desert with amnesia. Paranoid that he has been used as a pawn by the current administration, he decides to go underground yet falls into a relationship with porn star Krysta Now (Sarah

Michelle Gellar). The two collaborate on a screenplay about the end of the world in which they will star together, with Santaros assuming the role of cop. In order to research his role, Santaros attempts to ride along with real cop Roland Taverner (Seann William Scott), but Santaros has unwittingly partnered up with Roland's twin brother, Ronald (also played by Scott), who is only masquerading as a cop to aid the work of the neo-Marxist group he is a part of. Ronald's motive is to perpetrate a crime with Santaros in tow, thus damaging the actor's public image and ultimately the chances of his father-in-law's Republican ticket of winning the impending election.

While Santaros struggles to escape his past and prepare for his new role, an elfin German scientist, Baron von Westphalen (Wallace Shawn), promises a solution to the diminishing oil supply in Fluid Karma, a clean, alternative-energy source that derives its power from the ocean. Unfortunately, Fluid Karma, which is also the name of an experimental hallucinogen used in experiments on Iraq War soldiers such as narrator Pilot Abilene (Justin Timberlake), has a few drawbacks. These disparate characters all collide during a Fourth of July celebration as a collection of powerful figures prepares to watch the fireworks from a state-of-the-art blimp over the city as it takes its maiden voyage.

While no one can say that Kelly suffers from a lack of vision, some may consider it a warning that he felt it necessary to write three graphic novels to act as a prologue to the film (which is actually divided into chapters IV, V, and VI), and planned to launch more than one Web site in order to help explain the film. Famously booed at Cannes when screened in a cut twenty minutes longer than the theatrical version—and which spurred Roger Ebert of the *Chicago Sun-Times* to suggest "that Kelly keep right on cutting until he whittles it down to a ukulele pick"—the film is never as clever as it believes, and its satirical targets (pornography, rampant consumerism, television news, and the Bush administration) are not shot through with any fresh arrows.

It is clear that Kelly wrote *Southland Tales* under the influence of Stanley Kubrick's *Dr. Strangelove* (1964) and the works of Philip K. Dick (in one scene, Jon Lovitz, portraying a murderous cop, says "Flow my tears..." after shooting a victim, literally acting out the title of Dick's novel *Flow My Tears, the Policeman Said* [1974]), but more than anything, it resembles the child of Kathryn Bigelow's millennial virtual-reality thriller *Strange Days* (1995) (as noted by Todd McCarthy in *Variety*) and Robert Altman's *Short Cuts* (1993). There are also elements of Kurt Vonnegut's novels present, such as the time-traveling aspect of *Slaughterhouse Five* (1969) or the zaniness of *Breakfast of Champions* (1973), but with little of the humanity of either of those works. One can

tell that Kelly has a sprawling and exciting narrative mapped out in his mind, but he cannot seem to transfer any of that energy to the screen. Something is certainly lost in translation, and the result is confusing and self-indulgent. In the director's defense, however, he has spoken openly about the difficulties with recutting it after its Cannes premiere, describing the reediting process as a "big game of Jenga." Ruthe Stein of the *San Francisco Chronicle* may have the key to enjoying the film when she advises "the best way to watch is not to try to make sense of this muddle but to appreciate the scattered moments of lucidity and striking visuals."

Southland Tales's casting is nothing if not inspired. Previously known for more standard action-oriented roles, Dwayne "The Rock" Johnson is given a chance to add a different type of role to his resume. Unfortunately, his wide-eyed, finger-twitching performance does not do anything to keep the film buoyant. At the same time, Gellar does all she can with the shrill Krysta Now and Seann William Scott gives the type of thoughtful, restrained performance that he has not been permitted to give in previous roles. Timberlake's Greek chorus character, Pilot Abilene, seems to exist only to explain the proceedings to a baffled audience, but is also given the film's most electrifying and purely cinematic moment—a drug-induced fantasy in which he lip-synchs to The Killers' song "All These Things I've Done" in a video arcade surrounded by latex-clad nurses. Kelly also reveals himself to be a fan of *Saturday Night Live,* placing former and present cast members Lovitz, Cheri Oteri, Amy Poehler, and Nora Dunn in supporting roles. A brief, non-speaking glimpse of Janeane Garofalo provides evidence of an excised subplot.

The critical drubbing received by *Southland Tales,* just the second film from a director barely in his thirties, can be attributable only to increased expectations following a debut as original and thrilling as *Donnie Darko*. In spite of its failures, adventurous filmgoers are likely to seek it out based on its reputation alone. Comparing the two films, one can even find a template for Kelly's possible obsessions—key characters receiving eye wounds in the denouement, choreographed dance sequences, and rips in the space-time continuum—for a start. For his follow-up, though, perhaps he would do best to try something completely different and make sure that audiences are not required to read a graphic novel or visit a Web site before beginning to even try and understand his film.

David Hodgson

CREDITS

Boxer Santaros: Dwayne Johnson
Krysta Now: Sarah Michelle Gellar

Roland/Ronald: Seann William Scott
Dr. Soberin Exx: Curtis Armstrong
Cyndi: Nora Dunn
Dion: Wood Harris
Vaughn: John Larroquette
Madeline Santaros: Mandy Moore
Sen. Bobby Frost: Holmes Osborne
Nana Mae Frost: Miranda Richardson
Pilot Abilene: Justin Timberlake
Origin: USA
Language: English
Released: 2006
Production: Sean McKittrick, Kendall Morgan, Matthew Rhodes, Bo Hyde; Cherry Road, Darko Entertainment; released by Samuel Goldwyn Films
Directed by: Richard Kelly
Written by: Richard Kelly
Cinematography by: Steven Poster
Music by: Moby
Sound: Peter J. Devlin
Editing: Sam Bauer
Costumes: April Ferry
Production Design: Alexander Hammond
MPAA rating: R
Running time: 144 minutes

REVIEWS

Boston Globe Online. November 16, 2007.
Chicago Sun-Times Online. November 16, 2007.
Entertainment Weekly Online. November 7, 2007.
Hollywood Reporter Online. May 22, 2006.
Los Angeles Times Online. November 14, 2007.
New York Times Online. November 14, 2007.
San Francisco Chronicle. November 16, 2007, p. E8.
Variety Online. May 21, 2006.
Village Voice Online. November 6, 2007.
Washington Post Online. November 16, 2007.

QUOTES

Starla Von Luft: "The information that I have uncovered could get me killed. But it was a risk I was willing to take. The fate of the Earth depends on you, Jericho."

TRIVIA

This is the first film in which Dwayne Johnson has not used "The Rock" in his name.

SPIDER-MAN 3

The greatest battle lies within.
—Movie tagline

How long can any man fight the darkness...before he finds it in himself?
—Movie tagline

Box Office: $336.5 million

In 2004 director Sam Raimi accomplished a rare feat: He transcended his 2002 work, *Spider-Man,* with its sequel in terms of visual ostentation that highlighted an innovative script. The computer-generated-imagery effects in this third installment of the series are state-of-the-art wizardry surpassing both of its predecessors, yet the plot is glutted with too many villains while devoting too much running time to an unbearable melodramatic romance. Unfortunately, Raimi failed to hit the trifecta with *Spider-Man 3.* The fragmented story lines do not complement the stunning aerial superhero battles taking place throughout the skyscrapers and concrete canyons of the web slinger's primary battlefield, Manhattan. Roger Ebert found *Spider-Man 2* the most compelling superhero epic since Christopher Reeve's debut as the Man of Steel in Richard Donner's 1978 classic, *Superman.* Ebert declared that the genre placed an overemphasis on the superpowers rather than the human component of a character. Of *Spider-Man 3* he wrote: "This time I desperately wanted Peter Parker to be shortchanged. If I argued earlier that Bruce Wayne and Clark Kent were boring human beings, I had no idea how Peter would begin to wear on my nerves." Sam Raimi, his brother Ivan Raimi, and Alvin Sargent also tamper with Spider-Man's genesis by inserting a retroactive continuity element that only attenuates the wall crawler's resolve by diluting the events of his Uncle Ben's murder in the origin story.

In the trilogy thus far, Raimi has used many characters and events from Spider-Man's rich source material spanning forty-five years in over sixteen comic book titles. The first villain introduced is actually the dark side of Peter Parker/Spider-Man (Tobey Maguire, reprising the role) residing within his psyche. This dark geek emerges when influenced by a mysterious black alien goop that hops from a meteor to the back of Parker's moped. Early in the story, it is learned that this spindly, obsidian organism is in fact a symbiote that covers its hosts with its tendrils in the process of merging with them. The first appearance of the alien symbiotic black costume was in a limited series by Marvel called *Marvel Superheroes Secret Wars* in 1984–1985. In it, Spider-Man, along with well over twenty main Marvel characters, is abducted by a godlike entity known as the Beyonder and transported to a planet composed of several worlds. After a battle in issue number eight, Spider-Man is introduced to an extraterrestrial booth, which harnesses an advanced technology that could instantaneously repair his torn costume. The result is a living symbiotic garment capable of resembling a whole wardrobe of civilian clothes that obeys Peter's mental commands. The design differed in that it was completely black except for a large white spider emblem emblazoned on the chest and back. In the movie, the costume retains its basic design but looks as though it was dipped in a tub of black ink.

Another vintage character from Spider-Man's gallery of diabolical villains is the Sandman (a.k.a. Flint Marko). Sandman arrived in the Marvel universe in 1963 in *The Amazing Spider-Man No. 4*. In his first clash with Sandman, Spider-Man defeated him by using a vacuum cleaner at his high school. Sandman never truly recovered from that travesty. Thomas Hayden Church fleshes out the film version by playing Marko as a sensitive, misunderstood loser rather than a nefarious rogue. Flint's career in crime resembles a ball and chain, one he reluctantly continues in order to procure medication for his gravely ill daughter. Having recently escaped from prison, Marko falls into an outdoor laboratory vat full of sand in his attempt at eluding capture from a posse of New York City's Finest. A group of scientists are conducting an experiment with a particle accelerator in which Marko's molecular structure is inadvertently destabilized and fused with the sand—resulting in his DNA being permanently altered. Marko takes on all the physical characteristics of sand. The transmutative properties Marko displays are a gold nugget in the film.

Parker is first attacked by Harry Osborn (James Franco), son of the late Norman Osborn who menaced New York as the pernicious Green Goblin on a bat-shaped jet glider. Harry, haunted by his father, injects himself with the same formula the senior Osborn developed in *Spider-Man* and immediately possesses the same superpowers (great strength, stamina and an impressive healing factor) as well as the cost: obsessive megalomaniacal insanity. Harry is armed with the same array of weapons as Norman, which includes explosive pumpkin grenades and razor-sharp bats, but he has altered the Goblin appearance. Credited as the New Goblin, Harry chases after Peter upon a flying board through narrow alleys at breakneck speed like an X-Games bad-boy poseur. During the course of the film, these two engage in battle only when Parker is out of costume. It is interesting that as the franchise grows, Spider-Man is seen either fighting sans mask or the mask is shredded beyond utility. Perhaps in *Spider-Man 4*, Raimi will dispense with it altogether.

Topher Grace plays Eddie Brock, a dishonest photographer who doctors a photograph in order to erroneously depict Spider-Man as a crook. Peter, realizing that the symbiote has transformed him into a Travolta-esque strutting goth, complete with matching black hair and eye shadow, finds his redemption at a Catholic church. The ear-splitting clamor of the cathedral bells provoke an allergic response from the alien and it drops down on Brock, who has been praying to God to kill Parker because of the dark Peter exposing his dirty photography and causing J. Jonah Jameson to terminate his employment at the *Daily Bugle*. (Once again, J. K. Simmons swallows every scene he is in as the contentious, flat-topped, cigar-chewing editor-in-chief).

In the first two films, Raimi wisely avoided a major pitfall of the original Batman franchise in that he limited the number of foes to one. With three antagonists in the mill, determining the direction of the plot grows uncertain.

Both of Parker's alter egos are at the top of their game. With Spider-Man's mounting success, Peter's inner narration is reminiscent of Sally Field's 1985 Oscar® acceptance speech, "People really like me!" Spider-Man's ascent to the status of revered icon in the film strays from his humble beginnings. Stan Lee and artist Steve Ditko presented a fresh character that was mistrusted by many New Yorkers who found him creepy and dangerous and admired by a minority of fans. In the films, he rivals Captain America's popularity. As the character evolved into Marvel's flagship hero, Spider-Man's public relations problem mirrored Parker's quotidian soap opera hang-ups. In his full Lycra suit, he had many run-ins with law enforcement, who often attempted to apprehend him by use of deadly force. Two new characters introduced in the third film, Captain George Stacy (James Cromwell) and his daughter, Gwen (Bryce Dallas Howard), a peer of Peter's, were killed in *The Amazing Spider-Man* No.'s 90 and 121, respectively, with the web slinger being listed as the top suspect. This resulted in Spider-Man's core fan base sympathizing with him. Although the preeminent figure for Marvel, he is ironically the most ambivalently viewed superhero in the universe he resides in.

During an overextended running time of 139 minutes, *Spider-Man 3* simply neutered the ongoing cinematic storyline. The trilogy's edge peaked with *Spider-Man 2*. The clichéd story lines and redundant plot scenarios nullify originality. One unique story thread involves Mary Jane (Kirsten Dunst), who was replaced in her first starring role in a Broadway musical for lack of vocal talent. She is jealous of Peter's growing fame as Spider-Man, which has eclipsed her acting career—a nice bit of realism and an unexpected character arc. Toward the movie's end however, Raimi plugs in the same utilitarian climax that he has used in each *Spider-Man* film, as Mary Jane, once again, is used as Spider-bait by a crazed villain obsessed with Spider-Man's demise. Once again, she is saved, once again, the two share a bittersweet moment at the film's ending.

From hero in his fictitious Manhattan to a soaring sales product in the real one, Spider-Man has dodged a lot of bullets. He has defied censorship from the Comics Code Authority (*The Amazing Spider-Man* No.'s 96-98 ran without the code's approval because of its storyline referring to drug use) as well as subduing a horde of his own clones. Can his cinematic incarnation do as well against two of his greatest threats yet: repetition and boredom?

David M. Roberts

CREDITS

Peter Parker/Spider-Man: Tobey Maguire
Mary Jane Watson: Kirsten Dunst
Harry Osborn/New Goblin: James Franco
Flint Marko/Sandman: Thomas Haden Church
Eddie Brock/Venom: Topher Grace
Gwen Stacy: Bryce Dallas Howard
Capt. George Stacy: James Cromwell
May Parker: Rosemary Harris
J. Jonah Jameson: J. K. Simmons
Dr. Curt Connors: Dylan Baker
Joseph "Robbie" Robertson: Bill Nunn
Emma Marko: Theresa Russell
Hoffman: Theodore (Ted) Raimi
Ben Parker: Cliff Robertson
Miss Brant: Elizabeth Banks
Penny Marko: Perla Haney-Jardine
Dennis Carradine/Carjacker: Michael (Mike) Papajohn
Flash Thompson: Joe Manganiello
Jennifer Dugan: Lucy Gordon
Maitre d': Bruce Campbell
John Jameson: Daniel Gillies
Origin: USA
Released: 2007
Production: Laura Ziskin, Avi Arad, Grant Curtis; Columbia Pictures, Marvel Studios; released by Sony Pictures
Directed by: Sam Raimi
Written by: Sam Raimi, Alvin Sargent, Ivan Raimi
Cinematography by: Bill Pope
Music by: Christopher Young
Sound: Joseph Geisinger
Editing: Bob Murawski
Art Direction: Chris Burian-Mohr, David Klassen
Costumes: James Acheson
Production Design: Neil Spisak, J. Michael Riva
MPAA rating: PG-13
Running time: 139 minutes

REVIEWS

Boston Globe Online. May 2, 2007.
Chicago Sun-Times Online. November 16, 2007.

Entertainment Weekly Online. May 1, 2007.
Los Angeles Times Online. May 2, 2007.
New York Times Online. May 4, 2007.

QUOTES

Aunt May: "Uncle Ben meant the world to us, but he wouldn't want us living one second with revenge in our hearts. It's like a poison. It can take you over, before you know it, turn you into something ugly."

TRIVIA

Elisha Cuthbert and Scarlett Johansson were both considered for the role of Gwen Stacy.

TRIVIA

Ground corn was used as sand in the film since it reflected well on camera.

AWARDS

Nomination:

British Acad. 2007: Visual FX.

STARDUST

This summer a star falls. The chase begins.
  —Movie tagline
The fairy tale that won't behave.
  —Movie tagline

Box Office: $38.6 million

Attempting to enumerate every film that has ever endeavored to intrigue through the use of highly sought after female stars—their faces so radiant they seem lit from within and their wondrous, heavenly forms covered in alluring, shimmering garb—would be almost as tiresome a task as counting all that twinkles in a night's sky. Just for the fact that it features the lovely Michelle Pfeiffer, lured back to the screen from contented domesticity for the first time in half a decade, *Stardust* would certainly make that first list. What makes this film uncommon, however, is that one of its central characters would qualify for that second tally, being an actual highly coveted star that has fallen from the heavens and assumes a walking, talking, and quite appealing form. The film is a delightful breath of cinematic fresh air, a whimsical, romantic, adventure-filled epic fantasy, winningly weaving together yarns concerning the star; a sincere young man's quest to impress his lady love; scheming princes attempting to gain the throne or kill each other trying; horrid crones endeavoring to achieve everlasting life by gobbling down still-beating hearts;

and a swishy swashbuckling pirate who steers his remarkable, floating vessel through the clouds.

Even before the film's title has materialized on-screen like a commercialized constellation, viewers have already ventured (with the help of narrator Ian McKellen) from the Victorian village of Wall to a realm lying mere footsteps away yet exceedingly far removed from earthly reality of any era. The cozy little hamlet is so named because of the stone structure that demarcates a transition from the mundane to the magical, its sole breach guarded around the clock to prevent any foolhardy forays by townspeople ill-prepared for all that lies beyond in the mystical kingdom of Stormhold. As the watchman is still dutiful but now decrepit, a young and curious Dunstan Thorn (Ben Barnes) is able to circumvent the codger and make his way to a dazzling sort of supernatural supermarket, where pint-sized elephants peek from tiny cages and bottles stuffed with attentive eyeballs peer at passersby. From a stunning and saucy witch's assistant named Una (Kate Magowan), Dunstan gets both a good-luck flower and, nine months later, a son named Tristan, who is delivered to a shocked Dunstan's door just before that celestial initial display of the movie's moniker.

Much of *Stardust* is the story of Tristan's (Charlie Cox) coming of age. Now eighteen, he is a mere shop boy but aiming high nonetheless. He thinks a great deal of beautiful and most likely out-of-reach Victoria (Sienna Miller), who thinks even more of herself than Tristan does. She accepts the young man's pathetically earnest attentions while openly planning to also accept an engagement ring from much more dapper and dashing Humphrey (Henry Cavill), which makes the lovesick Tristan feel frustrated and forlorn. However, Tristan sees his last, best chance to rise in her estimation when a falling star lands in Stormhold, and vows to make a risky, forbidden crossing into the unpredictable unknown to retrieve the extraordinary object for her upcoming birthday. As played by Cox, Tristan comes off as a likable, sweet-natured fellow, and many will feel a melancholic nostalgic pang or two as they empathize with the young man's arduous, ardor-fueled striving to prove himself worthy to someone who is eventually recognized to have been unworthy of all the trouble.

There are a couple of enjoyable, warmhearted scenes between the older Dunstan (Nathaniel Parker) and Tristan. In the first, Dunstan imparts fatherly wisdom in an attempt to bolster the confidence of a son feeling head and shoulders below Victoria's other, more polished suitor. Looking back, he tells Tristan that every man he ever envied ended up having "an unremarkable life," and while the lad still looks doubtful about his own, those watching wholly anticipate that time will prove him wrong. In the other scene, Tristan learns of his bi-realm, "unconventional heritage," and reads a touching note

written upon his birth by his absent mother. Using an accompanying magic candle, an astonished Tristan lands with a thud on top of the star at the bottom of an awesome crater.

The star's name is Yvaine (Claire Danes), and she has lain there resplendent if slightly gimpy since impact. She is humorously out-of-sorts, irritably bemoaning how being flattened by some "flying moron" has added insult to her injuries. Yvaine is not too keen about becoming anyone's birthday present/love offering, and as Tristan leads her off she lets him know about it. As the two make their way across Stormhold, viewers wait for these initial angry sparks to turn to those of a much different kind.

Yvaine would not gripe so much about Tristan's plans for her if she knew what others in the kingdom were plotting. A covetous coven comprised of the hideous and ancient Lamia (Michelle Pfeiffer) and her two equally appalling sisters are hell-bent on ripping out Yvaine's heart and slurping it down, which apparently for witches brings on immortality. Lamia is able to temporarily transform herself from frightening to fetching before venturing out on this mission, and pausing before a mirror, she coos with delight. Also desiring to get their hands on Yvaine are the infighting (and, judging by their behavior, perhaps inbred) surviving sons of the recently deceased King of Stormhold (Peter O'Toole). The monarch had sent an enchanted jewel up into the heavens, which will turn color when possessed by a worthy successor, and it was this all-important object, which Yvaine now wears around her neck, that had knocked her from the sky like some sort of cosmic cue ball. Obtain the precious stone and be king. Gulp down her heart, and that reign would never end.

As expected, Tristan gradually comes to have his own interest in Yvaine's heart, truly falling for the star and she for him. She makes him reconsider jumping through hoops to win Victoria's approval, asserting that real love does not require the offering-up of treasures in order to be treasured. Tristan comes to mature from his initial ineffectuality as a lover, fighter, and even shop boy into grateful Yvaine's flowing-haired, sword-wielding protector. While some critics did not quite buy Tristan's rather quick transformation, he would not be the first person to be emboldened by love.

It is a highly fanciful, eventful passage through exquisite, verdant terrain on the way back to prosaic Wall. (These scenes in *Stardust* were shot largely in Iceland and Scotland.) A unicorn shows up on two occasions at just the right time to lend a much-needed helping hoof. A man is turned into a goat, and vice versa. Tristan's mother shows up in the form of a bird, and her son spends part of his journey as a caged mouse.

Most will find themselves swallowing the curious ingredients in this brew with complete ease, finding the proceedings amusing and pleasantly absorbing. There is a waggishness in the air throughout, with especially humorous little touches like the male turned female who seems a tad too enamored with those new breasts and who talks in a wholly incongruous tone that can best be described as a manly burp. Thoroughly enjoyable is the otherworldly, ever-increasing lineup of deceased princes, who marvelously appear like a banged-up Greek Chorus commenting on (and often delighting in) their surviving siblings' travails. Then there is Captain Shakespeare (Robert De Niro), the pirate who scoops up Tristan and Yvaine as he passes them in the clouds, snarling mightily in an attempt to cover up the fact that he feels "oh, so pretty" inside. Watching De Niro portray a character who prances in front of a mirror, fluttering fan in hand and sporting a thoroughly feminine getup, few will blame Prince Septimus (Mark Strong) for his astonished, "What the hell is this?" There are also darker, unsettling moments of dramatic treachery and thunderous, seemingly insurmountable evil. An intense sense of urgency is created by crosscutting between an imperiled Yvaine, those closing in on her, and those racing to the rescue, quite suspenseful action that is suitably enhanced by ominous, anxiety-inducing music. Once love conquers all (and a twist lands Tristan and Yvaine on the thrones of Stormhold), there is an appropriate use of the customary "happily ever after."

Made on a budget that topped $70 million, *Stardust* had a less-than-hoped-for gross despite generally positive reviews. The film was based upon a story by Neil Gaiman and illustrator Charles Vess, which was originally told in a 1990's DC Comics miniseries before being subsequently published in novel form. Director Matthew Vaughn, in quite a turnaround from the subject matter of his first effort, *Layer Cake* (2005), gets fine performances from his entire cast, which also includes the comical Ricky Gervais as Ferdy the Fence. Few viewers should require a witch's spell to find themselves enchanted by such engaging fairy-tale fun, aimed particularly, like *The Princess Bride* (1987), at those whose pajamas no longer include a back flap and feet.

David L. Boxerbaum

CREDITS

Tristan: Charlie Cox
Yvaine: Claire Danes
Captain Shakespeare: Robert De Niro
Victoria: Sienna Miller
Lamia: Michelle Pfeiffer
King of Stormhold: Peter O'Toole

Primus: Jason Flemyng
Secondus: Rupert Everett
Septimus: Mark Strong
Humphrey: Henry Cavill
Ferdy the Fence: Ricky Gervais
Adult Dunstan Thorn: Nathaniel Parker
Young Dunstan Thorn: Ben Barnes
Sextus: David Walliams
Una: Kate Magowan
Old Guard: David Kelly
Empusa: Sarah Alexander
Narrator: Ian McKellen (Voice)
Origin: Great Britain, USA
Language: English
Released: 2007
Production: Lorenzo di Bonaventura, Michael Dreyer, Neil Gaiman, Matthew Vaughn; di Bonaventura Pictures; MARV Films; released by Paramount
Directed by: Matthew Vaughn
Written by: Matthew Vaughn, Jane Goldman
Cinematography by: Ben Davis
Music by: Ilan Eshkeri
Editing: Jon Harris
Production Design: Gavin Bocquet
Sound: Matthew Collinge
Costumes: Sammy Sheldon
MPAA rating: PG-13
Running time: 128 minutes

REVIEWS

Boston Globe Online. August 10, 2007.
Chicago Sun-Times Online. August 10, 2007.
Entertainment Weekly Online. August 8, 2007.
Los Angeles Times Online. August 10, 2007.
New York Times Online. August 10, 2007.

QUOTES

Young Dunstan Thorn: "Because, let's be honest, it's a field. Look, do you see another world out there? No, you see a field. Do you see anything non human? No, and you know why? Because it's a field!"

TRIVIA

All of the princes wear clothing sporting a pattern which spells out their number in Roman numerals, composed by smaller Arabic numerals.

STARTER FOR 10

Starter for 10 is a familiar reference for fans of the long-running British TV show *University Challenge*. The show pits university trivia teams against each other and the host, Bamber Gascoigne, opens each round with the phrase. For Brian Jackson (James McAvoy), appearing on the show has been a lifelong dream. One of his most memorable moments with his late father (James Gaddas) occurred when Brian was just a little boy. While the family was watching the show, little Brian answered one of the questions and his father was quite pleased. "Ever since I can remember," narrates Brian, "I've wanted to be clever. Some people are born clever, same way some people are born beautiful. I'm not one of those people." One of the first things Brian does when he arrives at Bristol University is to sign up for the quiz team.

But *Starter for 10* does not follow the sports-movie model where the all-important match is the climax of the film. Instead, this British comedy's more obvious forebears are the quirky, coming-of-age classics of John Hughes. The movie takes place in 1985 and the soundtrack is filled with songs by 1980s mainstays like The Cure, The Smiths, and Motorhead. The talented and appealing McAvoy showed more range as the beleaguered Scottish doctor in *The Last King of Scotland*, also released in 2006, but is thoroughly capable leading this decidedly more inconspicuous independent film directed by Tom Vaughan. Sam Adams of the *Los Angeles Times* wrote, "If the journey is familiar, at least the company is good."

At Bristol, Brian is instantly taken with his blond and bright fellow teammate, Alice Harbinson (Alice Eve). Brian, who hails from a working-class home in Essex, is also intrigued by Alice's wealthy upbringing and what he perceives as her sophistication. "Smoking is what I do best—second best, anyway," coos Alice when Brian visits her huge family home over a school holiday. Brian, who has the typically passionate nature of a college undergraduate, is wildly in love with Alice and is moved to write poetry about her. The audience will realize that Alice, although she likes Brian well enough, is just toying with him to pass the time.

Brian will also be the last to realize that the real recipient of his ardor should be his best friend, Rebecca Epstein (Rebecca Hall). Rebecca, who bears more than a passing resemblance to Hughes's muse Molly Ringwald, is a campus radical and very involved with various campus protests. Brian is intrigued by Rebecca's Jewishness, as well as by her wry sense of humor, but he is so focused on his pursuit of Alice that he does not realize that Rebecca is really the girl for him.

There are also some nice moments between Brian and the best friend, Spencer (Dominic Cooper), he left behind in Essex. Spencer fears that Brian is going to become, as he puts it, a "wanker." In fact, Brian does become a bit of one and starts viewing Spencer's poor job prospects as a broad social issue rather than something his friend is personally experiencing. Writer David Nicholls (who based the screenplay on his novel) portrays the issue in a refreshing manner, refusing to paint either the college boy or his working-class friend as having the obvious moral upper hand. When Spencer pays a surprise visit to Brian on campus, Brian is a little taken aback. Perhaps he does not want his old life to interfere with this new, improved version of himself. Spencer gets into a fight with the pompous quiz team leader, Patrick (Benedict Cumberbatch), and Brian is not immediately sure on which side he should be fighting.

With its capable but low-key performances and failure to deliver anything remotely novel to the genre, perhaps the main virtue of *Starter for 10* is the time machine it offers viewers of a certain age. It gives those who attended college in the 1980s ninety minutes to relive those days—when school provided a chance to create a more dashing version of oneself and romantic longing could be expressed by a Cure song.

Jill Hamilton

CREDITS

Brian Jackson: James McAvoy
Rebecca Epstein: Rebecca Hall
Spencer: Dominic Cooper
Michael Harbinson: Charles Dance
Alice Harbinson: Alice Eve
Julie Jackson: Catherine Tate
Patrick: Benedict Cumberbatch
Bamber Gascoigne: Mark Gatiss
Rose Harbinson: Lindsay Duncan
Origin: USA, Great Britain
Language: English
Released: 2006
Production: Tom Hanks, Gary Goetzman, Pippa Harris; Playtone Picture, Neal Street Productions; released by Picturehouse
Directed by: Tom Vaughan
Written by: David Nicholls
Cinematography by: Ashley Rowe
Music by: Blake Neely
Sound: Tony Dawe
Music Supervisor: Deva Anderson, Delphine Robertson
Editing: Jon Harris, Heather Persons
Art Direction: Nick Gottschalk
Costumes: Charlotte Morris
Production Design: Sarah Greenwood
MPAA rating: PG-13
Running time: 96 minutes

REVIEWS

Boxoffice Online. February 16, 2007.
Entertainment Weekly. March 2, 2007, p. 51.

Guardian Online. November 10, 2006.
Hollywood Reporter Online. September 15, 2006.
Los Angeles Times Online. February 23, 2007.
New York Times Online. February 22, 2007.
Rolling Stone Online. February 21, 2007.
USA Today Online. February 22, 2007.
Variety Online. September 21, 2006.

QUOTES

Brian: "Ever since I can remember, I've wanted to be clever. Some people are born clever, same way some people are born beautiful. I'm not one of those people."

STEPHANIE DALEY

The truth is what we believe.
—Movie tagline

What would you do...if it was yours?
—Movie tagline

The low-budget, independent *Stephanie Daley* won acclaim at several festivals, including winning the Waldo Salt Screenwriting Award at the 2006 Sundance Film Festival. Written and directed by Hilary Brougher, whose only previous directorial effort was the obscure *The Sticky Fingers of Time* (1997), *Stephanie Daley* tackles a difficult subject with an admirable combination of frankness and aplomb.

Its focus is on two females at different stages of life who in different ways have confronted the misery and mystery of giving birth prematurely to babies who did not survive. Tilda Swinton plays Lydie Crane, a forensic psychiatrist assigned to interview Stephanie Daley (Amber Tamblyn), a teenager who has become notorious as the "Ski Mom" for giving birth to, and then trying to dispose of, a premature fetus while on a high school ski club outing. Stephanie is facing criminal charges, and Lydie, who herself is twenty-nine weeks pregnant, is working for the prosecutor and trying to determine whether Stephanie is mentally competent to stand trial.

Brougher unfolds the story delicately and cautiously, allowing the audience at first to see only enough of what happened on the ski trip—a trail of blood in the snow as Stephanie walks down a hill—to help viewers piece together the story. And it is not long before viewers understand Lydie's tale too, as Lydie reveals to Stephanie that she gave birth to a stillborn child at twenty-one weeks gestation just before conceiving her current pregnancy.

Lydie is married to Paul (Timothy Hutton), an architect, and they live in a rustic house on the outskirts of a small town. They have a mutual friend, Frank (De-

nis O'Hare), who seems to share a special relationship with Lydie—they interact in a way that implies intimacy though they are not actually intimate.

Stephanie's story unfolds in flashbacks as she narrates to Lydie what happened. Stephanie is an insecure, inexperienced teenager who has never had a serious boyfriend. Her best friend does, however, and she is trying to get Stephanie to be more confident. The girls go to a party, and Stephanie wanders upstairs. There she is joined by an older boy named Casey (Kel O'Neill) who inexplicably seduces her, and they have sex, until a knock at the door interrupts them. The awkward seduction is scripted for maximum credibility but does not reveal much about Stephanie, and the audience is left a bit puzzled about the underlying reasons for her liaison. Was she merely bored, or overcome, or confused?

The middle of the film explores what happens afterward to Stephanie, who denies to Lydie that she knew she was pregnant (Casey informed her that he did not have an orgasm, so she thinks that what happened "didn't count" as real sex). She never sees Casey again, and is plunged back into the social shoals of high school. Though many of the high school scenes are highly realistic, they do not help much in elucidating the plot or character motivation. Stephanie is clearly unhappy both before and after her rendezvous with Casey, but she does not seem inordinately so. There are some troubles with her parents, but not terrible ones, and Stephanie does not seem especially disturbed or unusually awkward—she is just a typical girl struggling to fit into the treacherous high school social scene.

Interspersed with these flashbacks that lead up to Stephanie's tragedy, which unfold in a series of interviews that take place over several days, are scenes of Lydie's domestic life. She is worried about her pregnancy, largely because she is haunted by what happened with her previous attempt, though she denies there is much of a connection. Her relationship with Paul also seems strained, for reasons that are not well explained. She finds an earring in the bathroom; it is not hers, so she becomes suspicious that he is having an affair. But Paul's character is thinly drawn, and other than the stillbirth, viewers do not get any explanation for the tension between them.

This is the major failing of a script that is laudably restrained and credible: It fails to shed enough light on its characters. Not only do they lack a backstory, they seem to lack strong personalities, beliefs, or motivations. This is fine in the case of Stephanie Daley; after all, she is just a teenage still struggling to find her identity. But it is a fatal shortcoming for the characters of Lydie and Paul.

The script seems to have been written around the tragedies that befall the two pregnant females. The characters seem to be built around the infanticide and the stillbirth, rather than having strong features of their own. At least *Stephanie Daley* does not make the mistake of other "issue" films: It is never preachy. In fact, it is so devoid of moral judgments that its resolution is rather murky. It does not take a strong position, but it does do a fine job of exploring some largely uncharted territory.

The film's most important scenes are near the end. There is a harrowing and almost unforgettably painful depiction of what happens to Stephanie in the bathroom at the ski resort; it is restrained but still horrifying to watch. And there is a revelation by Lydie to her friend Frank about how she callously disposed of the ashes of her stillborn baby. Neither woman, it seems, had the needed opportunity to grieve over the loss of her child—Stephanie, because she panicked and then was immediately caught up in a scandal, and Lydie, because she chose not to mourn. They both, the film makes clear, discarded the being they created.

Both Swinton and Tamblyn give wonderfully poignant and believable performances as women at different stages of life experiencing anguish over events that are still nearly taboo to discuss, and for which American culture lacks rituals to mark. Swinton is, as always, masterful at portraying the coping but emotionally fragile woman beneath the surface of outward professionalism; in this sense, it is much like her breathtaking performance in *Michael Clayton* (2007). Tamblyn is incredibly moving and realistic as the teenager trapped in the terrifying silence and loneliness of adolescence. It is only too bad that Brougham has not fleshed out these characters; it almost seems as if she is afraid to give them more motivation or personality, as if doing so would detract from the universality of the emotions her brave film explores. But, of course, more depth would not have detracted, it would have made the emotions and the choices all the more vivid and compelling.

Michael Betzold

CREDITS

Stephanie Daley: Amber Tamblyn
Lydie Crane: Tilda Swinton
Paul: Timothy Hutton
Frank: Denis O'Hare
Joe: Jim Gaffigan
Jane: Deirdre O'Connell
Miri: Melissa Leo
Rhana: Halley Feiffer
Casey White: Kel O'Neill

Origin: USA
Language: English
Released: 2006
Production: Sean Costello, Lynette Howell, Samara Koffler, Jen Roskind; RedBone Films, Silverwood Films; released by Regent Releasing
Directed by: Hilary Brougher
Written by: Hilary Brougher
Cinematography by: David Rush Morrison
Music by: David Mansfield
Sound: Judy Karp
Music Supervisor: Liz Regan
Editing: Keith Reamer
Production Design: Sharon Lomofsky
MPAA rating: R
Running time: 91 minutes

REVIEWS

Boxoffice Online. April 20, 2007.
Entertainment Weekly. April 27, 2007, p. 120.
Hollywood Reporter Online. January 27, 2006.
New York Times Online. April 20, 2007.
Variety Online. January 23, 2006.
Village Voice Online. April 17, 2007.

QUOTES

Stephanie Daley: "What if what I believe turns out not to be true?"
Lydia Crane: "Then stop believing it."

TRIVIA

The teen party scene was filmed in the location manager's basement.

STOMP THE YARD

He will challenge their traditions. Their traditions will change his life.
—Movie tagline

Beyond the pride. Beyond the rivalry. Beyond the tradition.
—Movie tagline

Box Office: $61.4 million

Even though it boasts some of the most modern dance steps around, *Stomp the Yard* has an old, familiar feel to it. It is basically a by-the-numbers sports movie, with all the conventions of the genre. There are gang rivalries, young love, and a big competition at the finale. What makes *Stomp the Yard* better than many is that the sport it covers—stepping—is a very entertaining sport to watch. Stepping, which involves elaborate dance-offs, is a tradition on African American college campuses. Much stomping, hand clapping, and dramatic miming moves convey the message that the other teams are, to put it kindly, unworthy. The film's coming-of-age meets extended dance-video construction is what Rachel Saltz of the *New York Times* called "a strange and at times strangely compelling mix of black fraternity recruitment video and inspirational tale about a hip-hop boy in a stepping world."

DJ (Columbus Short) is a hip-hop dancer in Los Angeles. He and his posse spend their evenings in underground clubs engaging in dance-offs with other groups. While engaging and entertaining, these dance face-offs come off as contrived efforts at injecting more drama into the dance mix. Michael Ordoña of the *Los Angeles Times* found it hard to take the stepping contests seriously, writing, "It's hard not to laugh when the tough-guy dancers appear offended by their opponents' choreography." After beating one such dance team, a scuffle breaks out and DJ's little brother Duron (Chris Brown) is killed. DJ is sent to Atlanta to live with his stern, groundskeeper uncle, Nate (Harry J. Lennix), and loving aunt (Valarie Pettiford). Uncle Nate has pulled some strings and enrolled DJ in the prestigious (and fictitious) Truth University. DJ, who comes from a poor background, is not interested in mixing with the up-and-coming, rich young black students who populate the campus. That is, until he meets April (Meagan Good). April is the girlfriend of the arrogant Grant (Darrin Henson), who leads the Mu Gamma Xi fraternity championship stepping team. DJ wants April and, while he is cherry-picking Grant's life, he may as well take the stepping championship away, too. DJ joins rival fraternity, Theta Nu Theta, who are perennial runners-up in the annual stepping contest.

It is only a matter of time before DJ wins the girl and the championship and develops a new maturity, but the plot must give him a few requisite obstacles to overcome. One particularly convoluted hurdle involves the chancellor of the school, Dr. Palmer (Allan Louis), who also happens to be April's father. The chancellor was once a romantic rival of Uncle Nate. He still holds a grudge against Nate and is willing to take out his anger on DJ. A brief scuffle between old-school, traditional stepping and the newer, brasher moves that DJ has picked up from the streets is also easily solved. In addition, the film presents the weakly examined idea that by joining a fraternity, DJ is joining a long line of illustrious black leaders such as Martin Luther King, Jr.

It is clear from the beginning of the film that DJ will ultimately prevail. He is attractive, charming, and an innovative dancer; in movie terms, pretty much a guarantee of success. Although it is no mystery as to

how the film will end, it is fun to watch DJ's journey. DJ is charismatic and it is easy to root for him. And after director Sylvain White, a veteran of music videos, gets the bulk of his jittery camera moves out of his system at the beginning of the film, it is exciting to watch the stepping. The moves are percussive, dramatic and sometimes funny. When White calms down long enough to simply let the camera film the dance moves, the energy of the dancers is contagious.

In general, critics liked the dancing well enough but it was a rare reviewer who gave the film unadulterated praise. Mick LaSalle of the *San Francisco Chronicle* had mixed feelings about the film. He wrote, "The film...is in every way a completely flabby mess. But the charm of the actors and the intrinsic appeal of the subject matter make it possible to watch it without falling asleep or screaming." Wesley Morris of the *Boston Globe* enjoyed the film and wrote, "I'm a sucker for a movie that mixes suds with sweat." Apparently, audiences agreed. With a $14 million budget, *Stomp the Yard* brought in more than $61 million at the box office.

Jill Hamilton

CREDITS

DJ: Columbus Short
April: Meagan Good
Sylvester: Brian J. White
Zeke: Laz Alonso
Rich Brown: Ne-Yo
Grant: Darrin Henson
Jackie: Valarie Pettiford
Nate: Harry J. Lennix
Dr. Palmer: Allan Louis
Origin: USA
Language: English
Released: 2007
Production: Will Packer; Screen Gems, Rainforest Films; released by Sony Pictures
Directed by: Sylvain White
Written by: Robert Adetuyi
Cinematography by: Scott Kevan
Music by: Sam Retzer, Tim Boland
Sound: Shirley Libby
Music Supervisor: Ali Muhammad, Akinah Rahmaan
Editing: David Checel
Costumes: Keith Lewis
Production Design: Jonathan Carlson
MPAA rating: PG-13
Running time: 114 minutes

REVIEWS

Chicago Sun-Times Online. January 12, 2007.
Entertainment Weekly. January 19, 2007, p. 60.

Hollywood Reporter Online. January 8, 2007.
Los Angeles Times Online. January 12, 2007.
New York Times Online. January 12, 2007.
San Francisco Chronicle. January 12, 2007, p. E6.
Variety Online. January 7, 2007.
Washington Post. January 12, 2007, p. C4.

QUOTES

DJ: "I already schooled you once tonight homeboy. How many lessons you wanna learn?"

TRIVIA

Nearly 2,000 extras were used during the step tournament scenes. However, they weren't aware that they were filming a movie and they actually cheered and booed the dancers.

SUNSHINE

If the sun dies, so do we.
—Movie tagline

Dark days are coming.
—Movie tagline

Box Office: $3.7 million

When the Fox Searchlight logo fades out in the opening frames of director Danny Boyle's *Sunshine,* the viewer is left simply with a view of the blinding sun. The image is powerful: It simultaneously serves as a reminder to the audience of the power of cinema as a visual medium, and as a message that what is to follow will be both illuminating and confounding, both serious science fiction and outlandish spectacle. Often compared, fairly or unfairly, to Stanley Kubrick's *2001: A Space Odyssey* (1968), by both critics and science-fiction film enthusiasts, *Sunshine* may not live up to the legacy of Kubrick's masterpiece, but it certainly does what the best sci-fi films attempt to do: to comment on humanity's current state while also saying something about human nature, and the clash of ideologies that underlie human conflict.

The plot of *Sunshine* is fairly simple classic science-fiction fare, and it bears brief discussion because the story's content serves as a reflection of the film's form and function. In the first half of the movie, it is revealed that the sun is dying—Earth is freezing over in the subsequent solar winter. Seven years prior, the *Icarus I* had been launched in an attempt to restart the sun, but the ship vanished—the movie centers on the mission of the *Icarus II.* The crew of *Icarus II* has already been in space en route to the sun for sixteen months—as they pass Mercury, they discover the distress beacon of *Icarus I.* The crew has to decide whether to continue with the mission as planned or to attempt to rendezvous with

Icarus I. The decision is left to physicist Robert Capa (played by Irish actor Cillian Murphy), as he is the most well-equipped to weigh the consequences of a rescue mission. Reasoning that it would be better to have two nuclear payloads at their disposal rather than one, Capa persuades Captain Kaneda (Hiroyuki Sanada) to attempt a rescue mission. From this point on, the crew is beset by problems that threaten to derail the mission. When Trey, the navigator (Benedict Wong), plots *Icarus II*'s new course to intercept *Icarus I,* he neglects to account for the new angle of the heat shield, and a part of the ship is damaged by solar radiation, sending Trey into a guilt-fueled suicidal depression. When Capa and Kaneda go for a space walk to try to repair the damage, pilot Cassie (Rose Byrne) rotates the heat shield to give them as much cover as possible, not only causing expected damage to two communications towers, but also accidentally igniting a fire in the oxygen garden. *Icarus II*'s computer realigns the heat shield to minimize the damage, killing Kaneda, while Capa barely makes it to safety. The crew uses most of their oxygen putting out the fire, making a trip to *Icarus I* all the more imperative.

When the *Icarus II* is finally able to dock with *Icarus I,* Capa goes aboard with Harvey (Troy Garity), communications officer and acting captain (he is the highest-ranking officer after the late Kaneda), Mace (Chris Evans, best known for his role as Johnny Storm/The Human Torch in the *Fantastic Four* movies), and Searle (Cliff Curtis), the ship's psychiatrist, who has something of a sunlight obsession (he spends a lot of time on the *Icarus*'s observation deck viewing the sun at different intensities). They discover that *Icarus I* abandoned its mission at the behest of its captain, Pinbacker (Mark Strong), who has left a video message behind that says, "When He chooses for us to die, it is not our place to challenge God." They soon discover that the computer is not functioning (meaning that *Icarus I*'s payload is useless), and they find the remains of the *Icarus I* crew incinerated in the observation lounge. Things go from bad to worse when the airlocks between *Icarus I* and *II* mysteriously disengage, in the process destroying their means of getting back to *Icarus II.* The four men find one space suit, and it is decided that Capa, as the one who knows how to deliver the payload, is the person who absolutely must survive. Only Capa and Mace make it back to *Icarus II,* where it is discovered that the remaining crew does not have enough oxygen to survive long enough to deliver the payload, and they decide to kill Trey to make the oxygen last longer. Trey, however, is found dead, his veins opened with a scalpel, an apparent suicide. Thinking that they now have only four crew members on board, Capa is disconcerted when the computer later informs him that there is not enough oxygen to complete the mission and that five crew members are still aboard *Icarus II*. The computer is unable to identify the fifth, but Capa soon finds him on the observation deck—it is the hideously burned Captain Pinbacker from the *Icarus I*. Pinbacker slashes Capa with a scalpel (clearly, Pinbacker murdered Trey) and chases Capa into an airlock and seals him in. Pinbacker then proceeds to kill Corazon, the ship's botanist (Michelle Yeoh), sabotages the mainframe, and chases Cassie into the payload section of the ship. Mace dies trying to save the mainframe and Capa, realizing that the payload must be armed manually, dons a space suit once more, depressurizes *Icarus II* to escape the airlock, and scrambles inside the payload section as the rest of *Icarus II* explodes. Inside the payload, which is rocketing toward the sun, Capa is attacked by Pinbacker but manages to overcome him with Cassie's help and detonates the payload. The film cuts to a quick shot of Earth, showing Capa's sister and her children playing in the snow next to the iconic Sydney Opera House. The sun flashes briefly on the horizon, indicating that the mission was a success.

Sunshine is largely a movie of duality, of dialectics. This can be seen in several elements of the film, including in its imagery, in the structure of the film's plot, and the concepts it directly discusses. The most stark and constant visual example of contrast in the film is, of course, the blinding light of the sun set against the blackness of space—the persistent refrain of light and dark, brilliant and subdued, signal to the viewer that the subject under consideration is a dialogue between opposites. Also, the structure of the movie reflects this sense of opposing elements engaged in conflict. For the first half of the movie, the crew, and especially Capa, is fraught with the implacability and consequence of choice—and the crew does suffer for its own choices, but the results, negative or positive, are the work of the crew's own doing. The choice to rendezvous with *Icarus I* has many ultimately horrifying implications, including damage to the ship and the loss of crew members, but once the two *Icarus* ships dock and Pinbacker comes aboard, choice is in short supply. If Capa is choice—the choice to attempt to save humanity, the choice to try to do what is right—then Pinbacker is the absence of choice, and the film takes quite a drastic turn after the crew docks with *Icarus I*. No longer does the crew of the *Icarus II* struggle against itself and nature for survival— Pinbacker brings with him the zealotry of religious fundamentalism that seeks to supplant choice with the will of God. The collision of scientifically grounded secular humanism and extreme religious fundamentalism is, in fact, the overarching subject of *Sunshine*. The crew of the *Icarus II* is on a scientifically grounded mission to attempt to save all of humanity from certain extinction, whereas Pinbacker is driven solely by a belief that God

has told him that it is His will that humanity should die. To say, however, that *Sunshine* is simply an allegory for secular humanism or the scientific method versus religious fundamentalism is not entirely useful, and is also a bit limiting—it would reduce these concepts to black hat/white hat melodrama—but the clash of these ideas married to an excellent science-fiction opera in which the stakes are nothing more nor less than the fate of all of humanity makes for sublimely effective storytelling.

The comparison to *2001: A Space Odyssey* is inevitable not only because of the obvious parallels between the subject matter and the metaphysical concerns of the two films, but the association is also apt in one of *Sunshine*'s most striking features: its visuals. Like Kubrick, Boyle has a real talent for visual storytelling (well-showcased in *Trainspotting* [1996]), to the point that his rendering of life in space is as awe-inspiring and gripping today as Kubrick's was in the late 1960s. For example, a shot of Mercury passing over the surface of the sun is so incredible that it looks as if it were actually filmed rather than rendered in a computer. The most fascinating thing about Boyle's visual technique, however, is how it enhances the storytelling. When members of the *Icarus II* crew board the dark *Icarus I* with flashlights, Boyle has still images of various *Icarus I* crew members pop on the screen at the instant a flashlight's beam shines into the camera. The effect is haunting—it is both an invocation of what the *Icarus II* crew seeks, and confirmation that the crew of the failed mission can now be glimpsed only in the frozen instant captured by a photograph. Similarly, Pinbacker is given a unique, character-defining visual signature that distorts him—a reflection of his insanity and his obsession. Like the sun, he cannot be directly beheld, only glimpsed—he is both visible and obscured. Finally, the most compelling image comes at the end of the film when Capa must detonate the payload to restart the sun. As the chain reaction progresses, a wall of flame surrounds and approaches Capa, but seems to stop just as it reaches him. This is a moment foretold both by Capa and Pinbacker—early in the film, Capa notes that forces in the sun cause space and time to break down, and Pinbacker says that God tells him that the moment will come when one man remains, the last man alone with God. Given *Sunshine*'s dominant science versus religion conflict, the image serves almost as a synthesis of the two—Capa seems to exist in one continuous single moment, as if he has stepped into both a scientific and metaphysical manifestation of eternity. Whatever the comparisons to *2001: A Space Odyssey*, *Sunshine* packs a very powerful visual wallop of its own.

Sunshine, then, is nothing less than a potent meditation on choice—Capa is left to make many choices throughout the course of the film, and the movie challenges the audience to question its own choices. The effectiveness of the film is somewhat marred by the shift in the film's plot from a think-piece into a thriller, but the overall conceit of *Sunshine*—an argument between the secular and the religious—combined with its use of imagery makes for a challenging and compelling film.

John Boaz

CREDITS

Capa: Cillian Murphy
Mace: Chris Evans
Cassie: Rose Byrne
Corazon: Michelle Yeoh
Kaneda: Hiroyuki Sanada
Searle: Cliff Curtis
Harvey: Troy Garity
Trey: Benedict Wong
Pinbacker: Mark Strong
Origin: Great Britain, USA
Language: English
Released: 2007
Production: Andrew Macdonald; DNA Films Ltd., Dune Entertainment, Major Studio Partners; released by Fox Searchlight
Directed by: Danny Boyle
Written by: Alex Garland
Cinematography by: Alwin Küchler
Music by: John Murphy
Sound: Tim Fraser, Tom Sayers, John Hayward
Editing: Chris Gill
Art Direction: David Warren
Costumes: Suttirat Larlarb
Production Design: Mark Tildesley
MPAA rating: R
Running time: 107 minutes

REVIEWS

Boston Globe Online. July 20, 2007.
Chicago Sun-Times Online. July 20, 2007.
Entertainment Weekly. July 27, 2007, p. 51.
Guardian Online. April 4, 2007.
Los Angeles Times Online. July 20, 2007.
New York Times Online. July 20, 2007.
Observer Online. April 8, 2007.
San Francisco Chronicle. July 20, 2007, p. E5.
Variety Online. April 3, 2007.
Wall Street Journal Online. July 20, 2007.

QUOTES

Capa: "So, if you wake up one morning and it's a particularly beautiful day, you'll know we made it."

TRIVIA

The distinctive gold color used for the crew' spacesuits was chosen to make them more memorable to sci-fi fans.

SUPERBAD

Box Office: $121.5 million

Comedy producer du jour Judd Apatow (*The 40 Year Old Virgin* [2005], *Knocked Up,* [2007]) treads the well-worn trails blazed by the likes of *Porky's* (1982) and *American Pie* (1999), breaking no new comedic ground but putting his unique stamp of geek chic on the genre, his *Superbad* reminiscent of a savvier, sexed-up *Revenge of the Nerds* (1984). An extremely raunchy teen sex comedy with a heart, Roger Ebert waxed poetic in his *Chicago Sun-Times* review: "The movie is astonishingly foul-mouthed, but in a fluent, confident way where the point isn't the dirty words, but the flow and rhythm, and the deep, sad yearning they represent." While the coarse, sexually charged humor will go over well with adolescents, it is the embarrassing and humiliating situations the characters endure that literally define the teenage years that everyone will painfully relate to.

Co-executive producers and writers Seth Rogen and Evan Goldberg are childhood friends who devised this odyssey into sexual manhood as teenagers (and named the protagonists after themselves). Television's *Freaks and Geeks* (1999–2000) alumnus Rogen has since been a ubiquitous figure in recent comedies, particularly Apatow's, with roles in *Anchorman: The Legend of Ron Burgundy* (2004), *The 40 Year Old Virgin, You, Me & Dupree* (2006), and playing the lead in *Knocked Up.* Emmy®-nominated Goldberg became a writer for *Da Ali G Show.* Along with the director Greg Mottola (*The Daytrippers* [1996]), Rogen and Goldberg cast the film with an eye for talented young actors that they could also envision being friends with.

Set three weeks before the end of their senior year in high school, unpopular, virginal buddies Seth (Jonah Hill) and Evan (Michael Cera) see their chance to finally score when they are invited to one last senior fling. The crass, rotund Seth believes the way into a girl's pants is to ply her with copious amounts of liquor, which the boys are conveniently dispatched to procure by the party's host and Seth's object of lust, Jules (Emma Stone). The thin, neurotic Evan is less inclined to rush into bed with Becca (Martha MacIsaac) but when she asks him to bring her favorite alcoholic libation to the party, he is more than willing to comply to gain her favor. To accomplish their mission, the boys look to the even more unpopular Fogell (Christopher Mintz-Plasse), not so much a friend as a comic foil. The puny, bespectacled

Fogell has managed to buy a fake ID card rechristening him "McLovin" and the boys charge him with buying liquor for the entire party.

Seasoned thespian Hill (*Click* [2006], *Rocket Science* [2007], *Knocked Up*) is thoroughly believable and effective as the eternally horny senior with a weird childhood obsession with drawing phalluses. Cera, an old pro who showed such comic brilliance in television's *Arrested Development* and starred in the Internet comedy series *Clark and Michael*, uses his almost uncanny comic timing and trademark vulnerability mixed with a doggedly worried demeanor as the perfect foil to the obnoxious Seth. But it is Mintz-Plasse, a real-life high school student in his first acting role, that is the film's scene-stealer, his lisping line deliveries and overly confident mannerisms as McLovin are used to great comic effect and are a staple of the film's comedy.

Just as Fogell manages to persuade the blasé liquor-store clerk Mindy (Erica Vittina Phillips) he is McLovin, Hawaiian organ donor, and hands her the money, a hooded man knocks Fogell out and robs the store. Seth and Evan return to the store just in time to see the police interrogating Fogell and assume he was caught with his fake ID. Officer Slater (Bill Hader) and Officer Michaels (Seth Rogen) are the hilariously bizarre men in blue who proceed to take McLovin on the ride of his life, accompanying them on various calls where he shares a beer with them, stops a fleeing criminal, and later uses their police gun to play target-practice games.

Seth and Evan set off on an adventure of their own while trying to procure enough alcohol for the party but eventually meet up with the police and McLovin. The boys abscond with the liquor still in McLovin's possession, and finally make it to the party where things do not go quite as any of the boys' had expected.

During their journey, Seth and Evan learn some hard truths about each other and the nature of life. The more academic Evan and Fogell will be attending Dartmouth in the fall and, unbeknownst to the less scholarly Seth, will be sharing a room. When he learns the truth, Seth feels abandoned and betrayed by his best friend. Evan knows Seth is somewhat of a crude joke but realizes the value of his friendship in the end. While Fogell remains the butt of their jokes, he is the only one who manages to (almost) have sex with an actual female.

Set in the present time, the film has an intentionally retro, 1970s feel best evidenced in the soul-laden soundtrack that includes Curtis Mayfield, the Bar-Kays, Rick James, and The Four Tops, along with a few more recent hits such as Van Halen's "Panama," prominently featured in one key scene. The filmmakers end with a particularly creative touch, the final credits revealing the numerous and quite imaginative drawings of phalluses

of the childhood Seth, actually rendered by David Goldberg, brother of filmmaker Evan Goldberg.

Hilary White

CREDITS

Seth: Jonah Hill
Evan: Michael Cera
Officer Slater: Bill Hader
Officer Michaels: Seth Rogen
Fogell: Christopher Mintz-Plasse
Nicola: Aviva
Evan's Mom: Stacy Edwards
Mark: Kevin Corrigan
Jules: Emma Stone
Becca: Martha MacIsaac
Origin: USA
Language: English
Released: 2007
Production: Judd Apatow, Shauna Robertson; Columbia Pictures; released by Sony Pictures Entertainment
Directed by: Greg Mottola
Written by: Seth Rogen, Evan Goldberg
Cinematography by: Russ T. Alsobrook
Music by: Lyle Workman
Sound: Harrison D. Marsh
Music Supervisor: Jonathan Karp
Editing: William Kerr
Art Direction: Gerald Sullivan
Costumes: Debra McGuire
Production Design: Chris Spellman
MPAA rating: R
Running time: 118 minutes

REVIEWS

Boston Globe Online. August 17, 2007.
Chicago Sun-Times Online. August 16, 2007.
Entertainment Weekly Online. August 15, 2007.
Hollywood Reporter Online. August 7, 2007.
Los Angeles Times Online. August 17, 2007.
New York Times Online. August 17, 2007.
New Yorker Online. August 20, 2007.
Rolling Stone Online. August 7, 2007.
San Francisco Chronicle. August 17, 2007, p. E1.
Variety Online. August 7, 2007.
Washington Post. August 17, 2007, p. C1.

QUOTES

Seth: "When I was a little kid, I kinda had this problem. And it's not even that big of a deal, something like eight percent of kids do it. For some reason, I don't know why. I would just kinda…sit around all day…and draw pictures of dicks."

TRIVIA

The word "f**k" is used 186 times in the movie. The movie itself is only 118 minutes long. This averages to approximately 1.6 uses of the word per minute.

SURF'S UP

A major ocean picture.
—Movie tagline

The ocean just got cooler.
—Movie tagline

Box Office: $58.9 million

Like many sophisticated computer-animated films today, *Surf's Up* can appeal to both adults and children, but its clever faux-documentary style in the manner of a Christopher Guest comedy would likely draw in more adults, who can readily appreciate its unusual approach to the familiar story of a little guy battling the odds to live his dream. Ever since the penguins stole the show in *Madagascar* (2005), these creatures seem to be appearing everywhere in movies, from the documentary *March of the Penguins* (2005) to 2006's story of singing and dancing penguins, *Happy Feet*. The story of surfing penguins may feel a bit redundant at this point, but *Surf's Up*, directed by Ash Brannon and Chris Buck, has a soul of its own, with engaging characters, bright animation, and solid voice work from the cast.

The broad plotline revolves around a rockhopper penguin named Cody Maverick (voice of Shia LaBeouf), a teenager who wants to be a champion surfer. He is inspired by the larger-than-life Big Z, who revolutionized the sport and long ago visited Cody's hometown of Shiverpool, Antarctica. "You know, kid, you never give up. Find a way because that's what winners do," Z tells Cody when they first meet. It is a lesson we have seen played out in many animated features, but the fresh characters and sly sense of humor make the journey entertaining nonetheless.

The deadpan treatment of penguin surfing as a genuine sport broadcast on SPEN (Sports Penguin Entertainment Network) and the documentary framing device give *Surf's Up* its inspired moments. In the early scenes, Cody is interviewed about the history of surfing, which, humorously enough, we learn actually originated with penguins and goes back to caveman days; details such as the wall painting hieroglyphics are hilarious. We also see old footage of penguin surfing featuring Big Z on film stock that looks appropriately scratched and grainy to make it seem like it has just been pulled from

the archives. When Cody's mom, Edna (voice of Dana Belben), tells us that her son never knew his father and we are shown a photo of a shark about to eat a penguin, the screenplay flirts with an edginess and even a poignancy without ever becoming too dark. It also subtly sets up Cody as a boy in need of a mentor. These creative touches and character nuances may go over the heads of small children, but they make the movie a joy, as do the documentary interviews with the concerned Edna and Cody's jealous big brother, Glen (voice of Brian Posehn), which hilariously capture the rivalry and tension within the family.

Under the influence of a talent scout, a shorebird named Mikey Abromowitz (voice of a fast-talking Mario Cantone), Cody leaves his dead-end job at the fish factory and makes his way to the island of Pen Gu for the surfing competition named after the legend himself, The Big Z Memorial Surf Off, and meets a vain, slick promoter, an otter named Reggie Belafonte (voice of James Woods). Cody faces Tank "The Shredder" Evans (voice of Diedrich Bader), a cocky, bulked-up emperor penguin who defeated Big Z years ago, leaving him to what everyone believed was a watery grave. Cody also makes friends with Chicken Joe (voice of Jon Heder, doing yet another variation on his signature Napoleon Dynamite), a surfer from Sheboygan, Wisconsin, and falls in love with the warmhearted Lani (voice of Zooey Deschanel), a gentoo penguin who works as a lifeguard.

After Cody is injured in a matchup with Tank—in a humorous bit, the network cannot help but replay the wipeout over and over again—Lani takes Cody into the jungle and puts him under the care of Geek (voice of Jeff Bridges, doing a laid-back hippie voice that recalls his work as The Dude in *The Big Lebowski*, 1998). Geek, it turns out, is really Big Z, who, knowing that Tank was surpassing him in ability, faked his own death during a competition and went into hiding rather than return to shore as a loser/has-been. Without belaboring the point, the story touches on a real issue of middle-age discontent and a star having to own up to seeing his moment in the spotlight disappear—a theme that adults more than children can relate to.

Big Z mentors Cody to be a great surfer, starting with making a board (a very funny scene in which Z, hankering for the old days, cannot simply let Cody learn on his own but has to be involved every step of the way). Their interplay is the heart of the story, a father-son-like relationship that is funny and sometimes contentious yet moving nonetheless. It probably helped that Bridges and LaBeouf were in the studio together to record their lines—unlike the usual fashion in which voice actors work alone—and thus were able to develop a genuine rapport that carried over to their characters.

Meanwhile, because everyone but Lani thinks that Cody is missing, Chicken Joe embarks on a search that leads him to a tribe of penguins who eat chicken—poor Joe mistakes a boiling cauldron for a hot tub—although the threat is never so ominous that it destroys the film's overall good-heartedness. Because it really does not do anything for the central story, however, Chicken Joe's subplot feels a bit superfluous.

Nevertheless, the film moves along at a great pace, cutting between Cody and Joe while peppering the film with funny interviews with some small-fry penguins to keep the kiddies laughing and ensure that we do not lose track of the documentary framework. And ultimately the various strands come together at the big surfing tournament, which, in the final round, pits Cody, Joe, and Tank against each other. The message may be predictable; unlike the obnoxious Tank, who, in a comic, almost obscene, fashion, practically makes love to his trophies, Cody knows that winning is not everything and maneuvers against Tank to enable the clueless Joe to be the victor. Z emerges from seclusion to save Cody's life at a crucial moment, and his return is greeted with a hero's welcome.

Because *Surf's Up*'s screenplay weds a familiar coming-of-age tale and life lesson about perseverance to likable characters, it is easy to be delighted by these adorable penguins with spunk and attitude. Factor in the originality of the documentary conceit, and the film is just hip enough without losing its sense of innocence and belief that one more tale of an underdog proving his mettle can charm us and make us smile at the end.

Peter N. Chumo II

CREDITS

Cody Maverick: Shia LaBeouf (Voice)
The Geek: Jeff Bridges (Voice)
Lani: Zooey Deschanel (Voice)
Chicken Joe: Jon Heder (Voice)
Reggie Belafonte: James Woods (Voice)
Tank: Diedrich Bader (Voice)
Mikey Abromowitz: Mario Cantone (Voice)
Edna Maverick: Dana Belben (Voice)
Glen Maverick: Brian Posehn (Voice)
Origin: USA
Language: English
Released: 2007
Production: Christopher Jenkins; Columbia Pictures, Sony Pictures Animation; released by Sony Pictures
Directed by: Chris Buck, Ash Brannon
Written by: Lisa Addario, Joe Syracuse, Don Rhymer, Ash Brannon, Chris Buck, Christopher Jenkins

Music by: Mychael Danna
Music Supervisor: Liza Richardson
Editing: Ivan Bilancio
Art Direction: Sylvain Deboissy
Production Design: Paul Lasaine
MPAA rating: PG
Running time: 85 minutes

REVIEWS

Boston Globe Online. June 8, 2007.
Chicago Sun-Times Online. June 8, 2007.
Entertainment Weekly. June 15, 2007, p. 60.
Hollywood Reporter Online. June 4, 2007.
Los Angeles Times Online. June 8, 2007.
New York Times Online. June 7, 2007.
San Francisco Chronicle. June 8, 2007, p. E1.
Variety Online. June 1, 2007.
Washington Post. June 8, 2007, p. C1.

QUOTES

Cody Maverick (on his surfing hero): "Big Z is surfing. There may as well not have been an ocean before Z."
Cody Maverick: "My brother was the big egg. I was the little egg."

TRIVIA

All of the actors in the film got to record their lines together in the same room, which is unusual for an animated film.

AWARDS

Nomination:

Oscars 2007: Animated Film.

SWEENEY TODD: THE DEMON BARBER OF FLEET STREET

Never forget. Never forgive.
—Movie tagline

Box Office: $52.8 million

How appropriate that the Daniel Day-Lewis oil saga *There Will Be Blood* opened in theaters alongside *Sweeney Todd: The Demon Barber of Fleet Street* in the waning days of 2007, the former's title seeming like a helpful heads-up about all the gushing slit throats that make the latter such a sanguinary spectacle. There is certainly no paucity of plasma in *Sweeney Todd*. It seeps, spurts, and splashes, it voluminously cascades and spectacularly geysers like one of the other film's derricks. If that is not enough to slow down many viewers' popcorn consumption, there are also the accompanying gurgles, splashes, and sloshes, not to mention the sickening sound of skin and sinew being carved, the disturbing thud of the dying and dead as they plunge down through a trap door (often landing on their semi-detached heads), and the nauseating squish of fresh flesh as it is ground into a macabre meat-pie filling. Tim Burton, the film's fitting director and a devoted fan of the 1979 smashingly successful, weird and wonderful Stephen Sondheim stage musical upon which it is based, was always disappointed whenever the bleeding was too fleeting in the work's various stagings, vowing to enthusiastically go with the flow in his screen version. Mixed with all the disconcerting bright red blood is some truly enjoyable dark humor and gripping drama, thunderous, dread-inducing crashes of music intermingled with tender, melodic songs of deep devotion, and an oppressively grim grayness that is occasionally broken by delightful, colorful views of past and hoped-for happiness.

Although *Sweeney Todd* arrived in theaters for Christmas, it is certainly not a musical ending on a note of suitably seasonal uplift. There is definitely no warm-hearted, cheerful cry of "God bless us every one!" by a tiny tot here, only a young lad putting an end to the titular habitual throat-slitter with one of the demon barber's own treasured razors. There is something decidedly Dickensian, however, about the depiction here of nineteenth-century London, combined with the clear stylistic influence of old black-and-white horror films. The dark, stormy skies, periodically highlighted by ominous flashes of lightning, blanket the pasty white populace below as they scurry past the gloomy-looking edifices that line the shadowy, mazelike streets. The visuals have been so desaturated as to be nearly completely devoid of color, mirroring the vibrancy that fifteen years of wrongful imprisonment has drained from bitterly cynical haircutter Benjamin Barker (an excellent Johnny Depp, riveting throughout). His face is almost Kabuki-white, and his ordeal has created a colorless streak in his otherwise dark hair. Lost in what appears to be the most painfully unpleasant of thoughts, Benjamin could be mistaken for a cold corpse were it not for a burning yearning for vengeance that soon makes that deathly face come alive. Flashbacks, replete with vibrant flowers and bathed in a golden, glowing light, hark back to before his happiness was snuffed out. That was accomplished by smoothly crooked Judge Turpin (a wonderfully odious and creepy Alan Rickman) and his orthodontically-challenged, vicious sidekick, Beadle Bamford (Timothy Spall), banishing Benjamin to an Australian prison so that the judge could move in on the handsome, blameless barber's comely and virtuous wife (Laura Michelle Kelly) and little daughter, Johanna (Jayne Wisener). Back in the bleak present, Benjamin aims to settle the score.

The most comedic character in *Sweeney Todd* is the woefully unsuccessful baker, Mrs. Nellie Lovett (Helena Bonham Carter), who, like Benjamin, does not appear to be in the pink of health as her establishment slips further into the red. The curious creature sings quite amusingly about her admittedly wretch-inducing "Worst Pies in London," all the while using her rolling pin to squash encroaching roaches possessing less-discerning tastes. Times are tough, meat is high-priced and scarce, making it hard to keep up with the lady down the way who has stooped to filling her pies with stray cats. It is from Mrs. Lovett, Benjamin's long-ago landlady, that he learns the excruciating truth that transforms rage into madness: His wife poisoned herself after being raped by Turpin, and his daughter is now the fiend's ward. Benjamin has so greatly changed from the man he once was that he now wants to be known by a completely different name: Sweeney Todd. Mrs. Lovett is clearly smitten with Sweeney, but he only has eyes (and rather wild ones, too) for his shiny silver straight razors. Reunited with the tonsorial tools that will soon be slicing back toward numerous pairs of tonsils, the mesmerized, reenergized man fondles them rapturously as he sings a disturbing love song to "My Friends."

Until Sweeney can arrange his judgment day for the powerful, despicable judge, the seething, impatient man will vent his frustration by opening up the necks of anyone who fills his chair, misanthropically certain they must have done something along the way that is deserving of death. (In this way, he has become as heartless and unjust as his magisterial prey is shown to be.) It is then that Mrs. Lovett has her demented brainstorm, figuring that it would be not only foolish but shameful to waste what will be a bountiful, steady supply of meat. Soon there is a widespread, drooling clamoring for what people do not realize is a scrumptious but cannibalistic concoction, delightedly licking their fingers as they ravenously wolf down their neighbors. It is admittedly (if amorally) resourceful of Mrs. Lovett but exceedingly repulsive—and ghoulishly fun to watch. An especially dark, witty ditty is "A Little Priest," in which she and Sweeney peer out at passersby and size up their potential savoriness. Of special note in this lighter vein is the "By the Sea" sequence, in which Mrs. Lovett daydreams about a bright, picturesque future betrothed to Sweeney. The cheerfully colored, breath-of-fresh-air visuals seem especially vivid when bracketed by scene after drab scene accented only with red. While yearning to be on Sweeney's arm, it is quite comical to see that, even in the woman's wishful thinking, she cannot help but recognize how dauntingly difficult it would be to distract his one-track mind from glowering thoughts of payback.

Besides these amusing numbers, many of which give the actors' tongues a thorough workout as the clever lyrics scamper briskly forth, there are some truly lovely tunes welling up with sweet affection. "Johanna" is a beautiful standout that pops up more than once, sometimes sung by Anthony, the young sailor who arrived with Sweeney and has fallen in love at first sight with the man's flaxen-haired offspring. (Anthony is played by Jamie Campbell Bower, whose features and shoulder-length hair make him look every bit like Claire Danes's sister.) Perhaps even more memorable is "Not While I'm Around," sung to Mrs. Lovett with gratitude by Toby (Edward Sanders), the street urchin who comes to enjoy a stable home with the unstable lady. (Sanders is wonderful and adorable, his big eyes strongly resembling those of Angela Lansbury, winner of the Tony Award for her portrayal of Mrs. Lovett in the original Broadway production.)

These welcome additions of honey and humor give way completely to horror as the film approaches its climactic showdown between Sweeney and Judge Turpin (who is too late in recognizing the tormented man who himself admits that "the years no doubt have changed me"). Having already given fatally close shaves to a string of men, Sweeney is able to lure into his chair the one who stole everything from him (and who is currently in lecherous, twisted pursuit of Johanna). Both the razoring and then the judge himself are thoroughly and enthusiastically executed after the two men sing a duet. This time the blood is especially voluminous, covering a maniacally satisfied Sweeney and even gushing up to splatter the ceiling. This violent propulsion represents the powerful freeing of the barber's long-pent-up wrath.

At both the beginning and end of Sondheim's musical, audiences are urged to "Attend the tale of Sweeney Todd," to heed its message that revenge begets revenge and leads to disaster. The final image of Burton's film is a strikingly disturbing and haunting one that abundantly conveys that point. Sweeney has perceived too late that some colossal collateral damage has resulted on the way to his vengeful victory. It is painful to watch it slowly dawn on him that the half-crazed, too-intrusive beggar woman he had silenced so that his fevered plan could proceed unimpeded was actually his adored wife, a shattering realization that completes his descent into madness. Also now realizing that besotted Mrs. Lovett had selfishly withheld the truth about what happened to his spouse in order to hold onto him for herself, Sweeney flings her into her own fiery oven. As he cradles his wife's dead body, completely lost in his misery, Toby comes up from behind and avenges Mrs. Lovett. Sweeney's blood pools with his beloved's in a tragically tardy and ghastly reunification, the fatal gushing forth from his throat symbolizing his final release from torment.

"Depp sings!" may suffice as this generation's "Garbo talks!," as the actor's fans eagerly awaited to hear if what emanated from his mouth would meet with expectations. The risk-taking actor acquits himself quite nicely, as does the rest of Burton's troupe of untrained vocalists. (Only Kelly is a professional singer.) "I prefer actors who sing over singers who act," said Sondheim, who had final approval on all casting. He was pleased with the performers' ability to thoroughly convey character and emotion in a work where song lyrics predominate over the spoken word. Bonham Carter, though good, could have used more of the zesty, off-kilter twinkle that made Lansbury's memorable performance shine. Certainly not lacking in zest is the comedic turn by Sacha Baron Cohen of *Borat* (2006) fame, who portrays the flamboyant, faux-Italian con man/hair cutter whose attempt to blackmail Sweeney comes to an abrupt dead end. (The temporary and imperfect hiding of his corpse in a trunk is quite reminiscent of 1944's *Arsenic and Old Lace*.) *Sweeney Todd*, the sixth collaboration between Depp and the director, was critically acclaimed and rightly received numerous awards and nominations. Working closely with Sondheim, Burton has skillfully created a condensed but fairly faithful, visually striking, and thrilling adaptation, its viewers likely to enjoyably soak up what is a bloody-good telling of the tale.

David L. Boxerbaum

CREDITS

Sweeney Todd: Johnny Depp
Mrs. Nellie Lovett: Helena Bonham Carter
Judge Turpin: Alan Rickman
Beadle Bamford: Timothy Spall
Adolfo Pirelli: Sacha Baron Cohen
Johanna: Jayne Wisener
Anthony Hope: Jamie Campbell Bower
Toby: Edward Sanders
Origin: USA
Language: English
Released: 2007
Production: Richard D. Zanuck, Walter F. Parkes, Laurie MacDonald, John Logan; Zanuck Company, DreamWorks; released by Paramount
Directed by: Tim Burton
Written by: John Logan
Cinematography by: Dariusz Wolski
Music by: Stephen Sondheim

Sound: Tony Dawe
Editing: Chris Lebenzon
Art Direction: Gary Freeman
Costumes: Colleen Atwood
Production Design: Dante Ferretti
MPAA rating: R
Running time: 117 minutes

REVIEWS

Boston Globe Online. December 21, 2007.
Chicago Sun-Times Online. December 21, 2007.
Christian Science Monitor Online. December 21, 2007.
Entertainment Weekly Online. December 12, 2007.
Hollywood Reporter Online. December 4, 2007.
Los Angeles Times Online. December 21, 2007.
New York Times Online. December 21, 2007.
New Yorker Online. December 24, 2007.
Rolling Stone Online. December 13, 2007.
San Francisco Chronicle. December 21, 2007, p. E1.
Variety Online. December 3, 2007.
Washington Post. December 21, 2007, p. C1.

QUOTES

Sweeney Todd (holding up one of his razors): "At last! My arm is complete again!"

TRIVIA

Helena Bonham Carter rehearsed her songs while practicing baking techniques in order to perfect her timing.

AWARDS

Oscars 2007: Art Dir./Set Dec.
Golden Globes 2008: Actor—Mus./Comedy (Depp), Film—Mus./Comedy

Nomination:

Oscars 2007: Actor (Depp), Costume Des.
British Acad. 2007: Costume Des., Makeup
Golden Globes 2008: Actress—Mus./Comedy (Bonham Carter), Director (Burton).

SYDNEY WHITE

Freshman year is no fairy tale.
—Movie tagline

Box Office: $11.9 million

Sydney White is an affable, entertaining update of Disney's 1937 classic, *Snow White and the Seven Dwarfs,* transferred to a college campus and overlaid with plot conventions and character types reminiscent of *Mean*

Girls (2004). Amanda Bynes is adorable and winning in the title role of a tomboy heading off for her freshman year at Southern Atlantic University and finding herself doing battle with the sorority set she at first tries to embrace but is ultimately shunned by.

Sydney is most at home on construction sites where her widowed father (John Schneider) plies his trade as a plumber. Determined to follow in her late mother's footsteps and pledge her sorority, Kappa Phi Nu, Sydney finds that she does not fit in with the snobs who run not only the Greek system but the school as well. Rejected by the Kappas, especially their queen bee, Rachel Witchburn (Sara Paxton), Sydney ends up living in a house called the Vortex, a ramshackle dwelling populated by seven amiable but dorky guys.

The essential plot of *Sydney White* is very familiar—the outcasts banding together to make their voices heard and score a victory against the cool, beautiful kids who look down on everyone else. But what makes the movie a delight is the way it creatively weaves in elements of the *Snow White* story. The evil Rachel Witchburn, for example, does not have a traditional magic mirror but consults a "Hot or Not" poll on MySpace.com to monitor her social standing versus Sydney's. The seven dorks Sydney lives with are, of course, stand-ins for the dwarfs and share similar character traits. Led by a "Doc" figure, the intellectual Terrence (Jeremy Howard), who continues to take classes even though he graduated six years ago, the group also includes such archetypes as the "Sneezy" Lenny (Jack Carpenter), a poor fellow allergic to just about everything; the "Bashful" Jeremy (Adam Hendershott), who talks through a sock puppet; and the "Sleepy" Embele (Donté Bonner), a Nigerian immigrant who has been in America for three years but still suffers from constant jet lag. And, like the original dwarfs, these guys do not have much experience with women. What gives their relationship with Sydney such a kick is that she is a bit awkward socially and something of a dork herself—at least as much as the cute Amanda Bynes can be—and even shares their passion for comic books. And the love interest, desired by both Sydney and Rachel, is literally a prince, that is, his name is Tyler Prince (Matt Long). In this fairy-tale world in which only Rachel and her minions are truly bad, this frat boy not only prepares meals for the homeless but can even enjoy playing video games with the dorks.

Bynes is perky and charming and shows some gutsiness when Sydney leads the dorks in a campaign to challenge the Greeks in the student council election. Without Bynes's considerable appeal—her facial expressions alone are a great source of humor—the clichés might have been hard to swallow, but she makes Sydney so likable and endearing that one cannot help but root for her. And Crystal Hunt makes an impression with some cute moments as a Southern sorority pledge named Dinky, who eventually falls in love with a dork.

Some of the *Snow White* references are especially smart in Chad Gomez Creasey's screenplay. One line even harkens back to the tale's origins—when Rachel has the Vortex condemned so she can build a Greek center and the situation looks especially bleak, one of the dorks declares, "Things are looking grim, brothers." And the computer virus that Rachel sends to attack Sydney's hard drive and erase all of her files is a twist on the poisoned apple, forcing Sydney to pull an all-nighter to prepare her election speech. She falls asleep, and only a kiss from Tyler can wake her in time to rally just about the whole school to defeat the evil queen. Admittedly, the conclusion is an idealized vision of college life in which the whole student body comes together as outsiders, but it nicely fits the fairy-tale tone of the movie.

Serviceably directed by Joe Nussbaum, *Sydney White* has a reliable underdogs-versus-the-elites rousing finish and a positive message about fighting for what you believe in, but the plot itself is really secondary to the goodwill engendered by Bynes's comic skill and Gomez Creasey's imaginative *Snow White* conceit. And without ever becoming too heavy, the film also has just a touch of poignancy, with Sydney's close relationship with her father and the memory of her late mother inspiring her along the way. All of these elements prevent the movie from being another postmodern, tongue-in-cheek fairy tale and allow it to become that rarity in movies today—a wholesome, warmhearted, and clever teen comedy.

Peter N. Chumo II

CREDITS

Sydney White: Amanda Bynes
Tyler Prince: Matt Long
Rachel Witchburn: Sara Paxton
Paul White: John Schneider
Demetria "Dinky" Rosemead Hotchkiss: Crystal Hunt
Lenny: Jack Carpenter
Terrence: Jeremy Howard
Origin: USA
Language: English
Released: 2007
Production: David C. Robinson, Clifford Werber; Morgan Creek Productions; released by Universal
Directed by: Joe Nussbaum
Written by: Chad Gomez Creasey
Cinematography by: Mark Irwin
Music by: Deborah Lurie
Sound: Thomas E. Allen
Music Supervisor: JoJo Villanueva
Editing: Danny Saphire
Art Direction: Andrew White
Costumes: Beverly Safier
Production Design: Mark Garner
MPAA rating: PG-13
Running time: 105 minutes

REVIEWS

Baltimore Sun Online. September 21, 2007.
Boston Globe Online. September 21, 2007.
Entertainment Weekly Online. September 26, 2007.
Hollywood Reporter Online. September 21, 2007.
Los Angeles Times Online. September 21, 2007.
New York Times Online. September 21, 2007.
San Francisco Chronicle. September 21, 2007, p. E9.
Variety Online. September 21, 2007.

QUOTES

Sydney White: "I tried to eat a plastic flower once, kinda hurt."

TRIVIA

In the last scene of the film, Amanda Bynes can be seen wearing a short from her own Steve & Barry's clothing line.

T

TALK TO ME

Never underestimate a man with something to
say.
—Movie tagline
Inspired by a true story.
—Movie tagline

Box Office: $4.5 million

Talk to Me, the story of celebrity disc jockey Ralph Waldo "Petey" Greene, would have been considered a "race movie" if it had been made thirty years ago, but this film, directed by Kasi Lemmons, tells a story that goes far beyond a core African American audience, because it has a great deal to say about drive and ambition in mass media and the meaning of success and celebrity in America. Petey Greene, an ex-con with a gift of gab, wants more than anything else to work on radio after his release from prison, where he was serving a ten-year sentence for armed robbery when the film begins. He forces an introduction with Dewey Hughes, program manager for Washington, D.C., radio station WOL, when Hughes comes to Lorton Penitentiary to visit his brother, who is also serving time there. Dewey is everything Petey is not, all spit and polish and business suits, a black man trying to succeed within the white establishment.

The fact that Petey Greene is played by Don Cheadle is in itself a marker of the importance of this film. Don Cheadle is arguably the most gifted and charismatic actor of his generation now working in Hollywood, most recently defined by his starring roles in *Crash* (2004) and *Hotel Rwanda* (2004). As a result of his work on *Hotel Rwanda,* Cheadle has also become an activist, profoundly concerned about the genocide in Darfur. While in Washington, D.C., shooting this film, Cheadle spoke to a group at the U.S. Holocaust Memorial Museum and met with Sudanese rebel leader Minni Minnawi. Because *Talk to Me* makes similar claims for Petey Greene as a political activist, Cheadle would seem to be a natural match for the role.

Though Cheadle is the best-known actor in the cast, he is paired with another powerful actor, Chiwetel Ejiofor, who plays Dewey Hughes, the man who gives Petey his chance to go on air. Dewey functions as Petey's alter ego, who lacks Petey's brazenness and outspokenness. As he says to Petey midway through the picture, "You say the things I'm afraid to say and I do the things you're afraid to do." Petey goes on air and ultimately becomes the voice of black Washington. Essentially, Petey invents talk radio in Washington, D.C.; he is the right talent with the right message, and the response to him is overwhelming. But it takes some doing to convince station owner E. G. Sonderling (Martin Sheen) that Petey is the "right" talent to put on air, replacing "Sunny" Jim Kelsey, played by Vondie Curtis-Hall, who is married in real life to director Kasi Lemmons. Cedric the Entertainer plays another WOL on-air personality, "Nighthawk" Bob Terry, but this actor, true to his pseudonym, mainly offers comic relief. The astonishing Taraji P. Henson gives an especially lively and spirited performance as Petey's girlfriend, Vernell Watson.

Petey Greene is on duty at the station when the news comes over the wire that Martin Luther King, Jr.

has been murdered in Memphis, only thirty-nine years old. Petey makes the necessary announcement, adding "I don't know if I'm just sad or angry." It is clear that some of his listeners are more angry than sad, because riots begin breaking out immediately in the District of Columbia. Realizing what is happening, Petey goes back on air to calm his listeners, his people, saying: "Look out the window and tell me what you see." Petey tells his radio audience, "I went to prison because I was a knucklehead," whereas the Reverend King went to prison to achieve moral ends, and finally quoting Martin Luther King by saying "The ultimate measure of a man is where he stands in times of controversy." Petey speaks with the voice of reason while this crisis is in progress and earns the respect of his colleagues.

Petey is clearly presented as a courageous man of considerable talent. Dewey, who becomes his manager, wants to take Petey to the pinnacle of success, and launches a second career for Petey in television (*Petey Greene's Washington* aired on WDCA-TV) and then as a stand-up comedian. Dewey's greatest achievement comes when Petey is booked to appear with Johnny Carson on *The Tonight Show* in New York City. But Petey is not ready for that level of success. As his girlfriend Vernell tells Dewey, "He's just a badass n***er from D.C. who likes to run his mouth." That is an absurd understatement, but Petey purposefully blows his chance to go national on the Carson show, ruining his relationship with Dewey. "All I ever wanted to do was my own little thing on the radio," he tells Dewey to explain his behavior. "Quit trying to change me."

Dewey takes Petey's failure personally and breaks off his personal relationship with Petey. The action then springs forward in time to May 1982. In the intervening period, Dewey has gone back into radio, this time as an on-air personality himself. He is so successful that he eventually is able to buy radio station WOL. Vernell puts him in touch with Petey, and a reconciliation of sorts is accomplished. But the end is near, and Petey Greene dies in 1984, at the age of fifty-three. Dewey gives a eulogy at Petey's funeral, which begins as follows: "This is Petey Greene's Washington, Ladies and Gentlemen. This is P-Town." The real Dewey Hughes, living in Los Angeles, served as a consultant on the film project. Concerning their friendship, Lemmons expresses a key question: "Can you love somebody enough to let them be themselves?" The answer to that question is obviously rhetorical. The plot of the film is limited to the story of Petey's local success and the friendship between Petey and Dewey, but maybe that is enough. The film succeeds, modestly, thanks to the talents of Cheadle and Ejiofor.

James M. Welsh

CREDITS

Ralph Waldo "Petey" Greene: Don Cheadle
Dewey Hughes: Chiwetel Ejiofor
E. G. Sonderling: Martin Sheen
Vernell Watson: Taraji P. Henson
"Nighthawk" Bob Terry: Cedric the Entertainer
Peaches: Elle Downs
Milo Hughes: Mike Epps
Sunny Jim Kelsey: Vondie Curtis-Hall
Origin: USA
Language: English
Released: 2007
Production: Mark Gordon, Sidney Kimmel; Pelagius Film, Joe Fries, Josh McLaughlin; released by Focus Features
Directed by: Kasi Lemmons
Written by: Michael Genet, Rick Famuyiwa
Cinematography by: Stéphane Fontaine
Music by: Terence Blanchard
Sound: Glen Gauthier
Music Supervisor: Barry Cole
Editing: Terilyn Shropshire
Art Direction: Patrick Banister
Costumes: Gersha Phillips
Production Design: Warren Alan Young
MPAA rating: R
Running time: 118 minutes

REVIEWS

Chicago Sun-Times Online. July 13, 2007.
Entertainment Weekly. July 20, 2007, p. 57.
Hollywood Reporter Online. June 22, 2007.
Los Angeles Times Online. July 13, 2007.
New York Times Online. July 13, 2007.
Variety Online. June 21, 2007.
Washington Post. July 13, 2007, p. C1.

QUOTES

Dewey Hughes (to Petey Greene): "I need you to say the things I can't say, and you need me to do the things you can't do."

TRIVIA

An version of this film was in development in June 2000 with Martin Lawrence attached.

AWARDS

Ind. Spirit 2008: Support. Actor (Ejiofor)
Nomination:
Ind. Spirit 2008: Actor (Cheadle).

THERE WILL BE BLOOD

There Will Be Greed. There Will Be Vengeance.
　　—Movie tagline

When ambition meets faith.
    —Movie tagline

Box Office: $38.8 million

With such films as *Boogie Nights* (1997), Paul Thomas Anderson established himself as a major writer/director concerned with such themes as family, loyalty, and chance. Anderson also has a distinctively visual style, cramming lots of information into a frame, constantly moving his camera. Anderson's films are deeply personal visions of his native Southern California. *There Will Be Blood* represents a departure, loosely adapted from Upton Sinclair's *Oil!* (1927) and set during 1898–1927. Nevertheless, it encompasses Anderson's usual concerns and is even more cinematic than his previous four feature films. It is also a masterpiece, managing to be both an intimate character study and an epic vision of America.

There Will Be Blood opens with Daniel Plainview (Daniel Day-Lewis) prospecting for silver somewhere in California in 1898. When he discovers oil as well, he acquires a partner (Barry Del Sherman) and begins a drilling operation. The partner is killed in an accident, one of several such mishaps throughout the film, and Plainview adopts his infant son. *There Will Be Blood* follows Plainview as he slowly accumulates more potential wells. A stranger, Paul Sunday (Paul Dano), sells him information about the location of oil on his family's farm, and the film shifts to Plainview's acquisition of the oil rights on the Sunday farm and surrounding properties, as this enterprise becomes the center of his burgeoning empire. *There Will Be Blood* differs so much from Sinclair's novel, whose characters have different names and relationships and which concerns itself as much with radical politics as with business, that it is as much an original as Anderson's earlier screenplays.

Plainview fights off advances from powerful Standard Oil, makes deals with Union Oil, and finds an antagonist/moral conscience in Paul Sunday's brother, Eli (also played by Dano). Suspicious of the oilman's every move, Eli is a self-styled evangelical preacher in the manner of Tom Cruise's self-help guru in Anderson's *Magnolia* (1999). *There Will Be Blood* has a slow, meditative pace punctuated by bursts of energy, as when Eli, before his congregation, including a curious Plainview, claims to cure an elderly woman (Irene G. Hunter) of her arthritis by chasing the devil from her body. Similar explosive scenes include Eli's angry outburst against his father (David Willis) for allowing Plainview to exploit the family and Plainview's embarrassing himself, in a fancy restaurant, with a tirade against a Standard Oil man (David Warshofsky). Such scenes are indicative of Anderson's approach to film, with *Boogie Nights* and *Magnolia,* in particular, crammed with characters humiliating each other and themselves. Such emotional-

ity can be wearing, especially in *Magnolia,* but Anderson weaves his characters' passions and disappointments more smoothly into his adaptation of Sinclair's novel. *There Will Be Blood* remains fascinating from first to last shot, though even some of the admirers of one of the most enthusiastically reviewed films of 2007 feel Anderson goes a bit too far in the final sequence.

Plainview starts off as that American archetype, the would-be entrepreneur, but as he becomes more successful, he changes. Reviewers have seen *There Will Be Blood* as a portrait of greed, but Plainview is not after wealth so much as power, which corrupts him and drives him mad. That Anderson does not intend a didactic screed about capitalism or religion or where America went wrong is one of the qualities that makes *There Will Be Blood* a great film. It comments on the American dream and what Wright Morris, that most American of novelists, calls the American character, but Anderson does not spell out his themes. This quality represents a big advancement for a director not known for his subtlety.

Like most of his contemporaries, Anderson is strongly influenced by other filmmakers. An obvious influence on *There Will Be Blood* is Erich von Stroheim's *Greed* (1924), from Frank Norris's *McTeague* (1899). The two films are similar not only thematically but in the visual sweep of their western settings. *There Will Be Blood* is dedicated to Robert Altman and recalls *McCabe and Mrs. Miller* (1971), Altman's vision of the conflict between capitalism and individuality on the western frontier. An even bigger influence is Roman Polanski's *Chinatown* (1974), arguably the greatest American film about the corruption of wealth and power. As a portrait of obsession, *There Will Be Blood* resembles John Ford's *The Searchers* (1956). Ford uses the western landscape for its natural beauty tainted by the acts of humans, with his heroes tiny figures cast against an imposing backdrop. Anderson's California is more forbidding, a bleak, almost barren land challenging its settlers to conquer it. Plainview goes mad trying to be bigger than the land itself. *There Will Be Blood* has an austerity missing from most American films, a European sensibility. It is like a Ford film remade by Ingmar Bergman.

Perhaps to signal that *There Will Be Blood* is a departure, Anderson does not use any of the actors, such as Philip Baker Hall, Luis Guzmán, Philip Seymour Hoffman, and John C. Reilly, who have become part of his stock company. Dano, the sullen teenager in *Little Miss Sunshine* (2006), gives Eli a mixture of innocence and calculation. In many senses, Eli is Plainview's mirror image, both seeking control of their worlds and being twisted by the effort. Several scenes involve Eli's reactions to Plainview, as Dano shows his character assessing his circumstances and his possible courses of action. Dano relies a bit too much, perhaps, on pursing his lips and squinting. Ciarán Hinds appears as Plainview's assistant and, while he has little dialogue, uses his imposing presence to lend authority to his boss's actions. Kevin J. O'Connor, who has had a long career in mostly undistinguished films, provides a subtle desperation and vulnerability as a man who shows up claiming to be Plainview's half-brother. (Plainview has both a desire for and a resistance to familial ties.) Casting director Cassandra Kulukundis has done a splendid job by finding O'Connor, Willis, Warshofsky, and Hans Howes, as a small landowner who blackmails Plainview. All are excellent and even better is Dillon Freasier as H. W., Plainview's adoptive son. The young actor excels at conveying H. W.'s desperate need for affection from the man he believes to be his father and his resentment of Plainview's neglect. Such relationships between children and their fathers or surrogate fathers are endemic to Anderson's work.

The fine work of these actors is overshadowed by the towering performance of Day-Lewis. Already widely considered one of the greatest film actors, Day-Lewis solidifies his status with Plainview, advancing to the heights occupied by Marlon Brando and few others. He conveys Plainview's slowly encroaching madness primarily with his intense eyes and stiff body language. The performance is like his Bill the Butcher in *Gangs of New York* (2002), but without any of the cartoonish embellishments. Day-Lewis adopts a slow, almost hypnotic manner of speaking that suggests a man who knows what he wants and how to achieve it and who will not allow any emotional softness to interfere with the achievement of his goals. Plainview is the mythic American businessman who lives for work and nothing else. As many have observed, Day-Lewis adopts the voice of John Huston, who creates in *Chinatown* one of the cinema's most indelible villains. Huston's Noah Cross thinks his evil, manipulative behavior is justified, and so does Plainview. As evil as Plainview is, he is no monster, always remaining recognizably human. Day-Lewis stands out especially when circumstances lead to Plainview's being baptized by Eli against his will. As Eli forces Plainview to acknowledge his sins, Day-Lewis shows a man struggling against this humiliation, fighting against the truth of what he is being forced to say, and vowing revenge—all at the same time. At several key moments, Day-Lewis reveals glimpses of Plainview's awareness of what he has allowed himself to become. He says, "I hate most people" not as a statement of defiance but with a degree of regret.

There Will Be Blood is always visually striking. Cinematographer Robert Elswit, who has shot all of Anderson's previous films, as well as *Syriana* (2005) and *Michael Clayton* (2007), lights much of the film in a twilight gloom. The film opens with Plainview descending into and ascending from a mineshaft, and Elswit accentuates blacks, grays, and deep browns to create the impression that Plainview has never emerged from his pit. A shot of black figures silhouetted against a smoky sky while a derrick burns out of control suggests the hell into which Plainview has plunged. The opening scenes of Plainview and his men wallowing in their oily pits recall Thomas Sutpen and his slaves creating his plantation from the primeval mire in William Faulkner's *Absalom, Absalom!* (1936). In both instances the characters are creating an American empire from nothing without regard to the consequences of their acts.

Much has been made of the opening images, the film without dialogue, except for an exclamation when Plainview falls into a pit, for its first fifteen minutes. As with several tracking shots throughout *There Will Be Blood*, Anderson is not showing off stylistically but using cinematic language to establish tone and theme. Production designer Jack Fisk, who helped give a similar look to Terrence Malick's *The New World* (2005), has made ramshackle buildings and towers to demonstrate both the newness of Plainview's world and its precariousness. Neither humans nor their artifacts will endure. Fisk was also art director for Malick's *Days of Heaven* (1978), yet another influence on Anderson's treatment of innocence and deceit in the American west.

Underscoring the visual and dramatic flourishes of *There Will Be Blood* is the score by Jonny Greenwood, the lead guitarist for Radiohead. Greenwood, who has composed symphonic scores for the BBC, has created atonal, often repetitive music, reminiscent of the film work of Philip Glass, Michael Nyman, and Toru Takemitsu. While some admirers of the film have objected to Greenwood's insistent music, the distorted sounds, at times like shrieks, complement the danger and chaos of Plainview's world, his self-destructive impulse, and his tortured mental state. In *Entertainment Weekly*, Lisa Schwarzbaum rightly praised Greenwood's contribution as revolutionary. Anderson also uses pieces by Johannes Brahms and Arvo Pärt, and when Brahms's uplifting melody is heard again during the closing credits, it is as jarring as Greenwood's music because of the thundering irony of the context. This world will never be the same.

Nothing in Anderson's previous work, as fine as it is, especially *Boogie Nights,* has prepared for the scope of this look at ambition running off the rails. It is fitting that the first word heard in the film is "No" and that the last line is "I'm finished." In between comes a psychological, aesthetic, and mythic epic comparable to David Lean's *Lawrence of Arabia* (1962) in its complexity. *There Will Be Blood* is finally concerned with nothing less than the enigmatic nature of human behavior. In a key scene Plainview whispers something the audience cannot hear. The truth is elusive; much about life must remain a mystery.

Michael Adams

CREDITS

Daniel Plainview: Daniel Day-Lewis
Eli Sunday/Paul Sunday: Paul Dano
Henry: Kevin J. O'Connor
Fletcher: Ciarán Hinds
Abel Sunday: David Willis
H. W. Plainview: Dillon Freasier
Adult H. W.: Russell Harvard
Mary Sunday: Sydney McCallister
Adult Mary: Colleen Foy
Origin: USA
Language: English
Released: 2007
Production: Paul Thomas Anderson, JoAnne Sellar, Daniel Lupi; Ghoulardi Film Co.; released by Paramount Vantage
Directed by: Paul Thomas Anderson
Written by: Paul Thomas Anderson
Cinematography by: Robert Elswit
Music by: Jonny Greenwood
Sound: John Pritchett
Editing: Dylan Tichenor
Art Direction: David Crank
Costumes: Mark Bridges
Production Design: Jack Fisk
MPAA rating: R
Running time: 158 minutes

REVIEWS

Entertainment Weekly Online. December 26, 2007.
Hollywood Reporter Online. October 1, 2007.
Los Angeles Times Online. December 26, 2007.
New York Times Online. December 26, 2007.
New Yorker Online. December 17, 2007.
Newsweek Online. December 17, 2007.
Premiere Online. December 13, 2007.
Variety Online. November 1, 2007.
Wall Street Journal. December 28, 2007, p. W2.

QUOTES

Daniel Plainview: "I hate most people. I want to earn enough money so I can get away from everyone."
Eli Sunday: "Things go up, things go down, but at least the Lord is always around."

TRIVIA

The film's first line of dialogue is not spoken until 14 minutes and 30 seconds in.

AWARDS

Oscars 2007: Actor (Day-Lewis), Cinematog.
British Acad. 2007: Actor (Day-Lewis)

Golden Globes 2008: Actor—Drama (Day-Lewis)
Screen Actors Guild 2007: Actor (Day-Lewis)
Nomination:
Oscars 2007: Adapt. Screenplay, Art Dir./Set Dec., Director (Anderson), Film, Film Editing, Sound FX Editing
British Acad. 2007: Adapt. Screenplay, Cinematog., Director (Anderson), Film, Production Des., Sound, Support. Actor (Dano), Orig. Score
Directors Guild 2007: Director (Anderson)
Golden Globes 2008: Film—Drama
Writers Guild 2007: Adapt. Screenplay.

THINGS WE LOST IN THE FIRE

Hope comes with letting go.
—Movie tagline

Box Office: $3.3 million

Early on in *Things We Lost in the Fire*, when a morose moppet says she feels as if she is stuck in a sad movie, it would not be surprising if audiences emphatically nodded their agreement in unison. As she and her brother wait to delightedly gulp down the ice cream their father has run out to purchase, the children are instead handed the news that he has been gunned down and will never return. Their mother is set adrift in fathomless grief, desperately flailing to stay afloat when she is not exhaustedly, sullenly still. An intermittently heroin-addicted old pal of the decedent becomes a soothing pseudo-dad, but then the mom's pained prickliness leads her to selfishly rip him away from the children, shoving him out of the house and back into the arms of his addiction. These and other painful events do indeed make the film a lugubrious slog, although, in the end, it appears that hope may have finally, mercifully, gained an adequate foothold.

What makes all the dreariness and devastation of this slow and rather predictable weepie particularly worth watching, however, is the captivating performance of Benicio Del Toro as the aforementioned down-and-out addict, Jerry Sunborne. With his almost untamable shock of hair and eyes that tend to make him look perpetually sleep-deprived, Del Toro is convincing as a man whose life prospects and very person seem equally and eminently exhausted. However, often with an interesting delivery of a few words or slight deviation in his expression, the actor conveys a sense that there is always more going on below the surface, intriguing glimmers of thoughts and emotions that the engaging actor's magnetism continually draws viewers in to mine. There is a charming gentleness and a decency about his Jerry, an affecting example of how a good person can take an ill-advised narcotic detour and become horribly lost, struggling for years thereafter to get permanently back on track.

Ironically, Jerry gets his best opportunity to merge back into a better way of life upon the death of his cherished best friend, the one person who had never given up on him. Successful real estate developer Brian Burke (David Duchovny) had ventured for years to a seedier part of town to mark Jerry's birthdays and throw a little help his way, steadfastly maintaining a bond that had solidified back when both were kids. Brian's wife, Audrey (Halle Berry), cannot understand this loyalty to a junkie, the visits making her worried and, especially, peeved. Brian, however, unlike Audrey, has memories of the person before the poison.

Learning of Brian's long-standing allegiance, his pressing on through Jerry's apparently few ups and many downs and in spite of his wife's vociferous disapproval and growing resentment, convinces viewers of the junkie's worth. Further evidence is provided in early glimpses of Jerry's appealing, easygoing playfulness with the Burkes' young children, daughter Harper (Alexis Llewellyn) and son Dory (Micah Berry). As mourners mingle at the Burkes' beautiful home after Brian's funeral, one feels sympathy for Jerry as he remains on the periphery, his suit fitting him only slightly better than he fits in with the well-off strangers nearby. He smokes to help squelch his disease (in both senses of the word), and viewers will also notice that his underlying tension seems to manifest itself in the sideways twisting of his lips.

Despite the continued revelations of Jerry's attributes, he would certainly fall short as a candidate for sainthood, unlike Brian, who floats through the flashbacks with a serene beatified benevolence that some will find grating. That the man is shown being killed while chivalrously intervening during a couple's domestic dispute only enhances this halo effect. Those watching are given many scenes, which look back at his loving eleven-year marriage to Audrey, meant to illustrate and emphasize the magnitude of what has been lost. They will see that the couple was close but may not feel it, as Berry and Duchovny have too little palpable chemistry.

The main focus of the film is the ever-fluctuating, awkward affinity that develops between Jerry and Audrey once she asks him to come live with her and the children. Some might not be able to buy that this acutely overwhelmed woman would, in effect, ask for more trouble by inviting someone like Jerry into her presence, especially considering she has two young, impressionable kids. After all, Audrey had admitted to him after the funeral that she had hated him for years, and would, if she were Brian, have cut Jerry loose years ago. However,

one senses that she now feels a kinship with him, as both lost the person who meant the most to them when Brian died. In her despair, Audrey is desperately clawing for anything that might in some way reconnect her with him. She also seems to feel that she is doing what Brian would want her to do, keeping tabs on Jerry now that he can no longer do so. Lastly, guilt gnaws at Audrey as she remembers how she tore into her husband about money missing from their car, only recently realizing that she had incorrectly jumped to the conclusion that Brian's friend had helped himself. Thus, multiple reasons propel her past her misgivings to offer Jerry a pleasant and safe place to stay in exchange for a man's help around the house.

Viewers of *Things We Lost in the Fire* will surely foresee the problems ahead. It comes as no surprise that a sweet, consoling, mutually beneficial connection will soon form between Jerry and the fatherless children, and that an emotionally raw Audrey (who is still wistfully sniffing Brian's shirts) will balk as if the poor guy has gone from user to usurper, thoughtlessly supplanting her beloved husband and blotting out his memory. Audrey is heartbroken to watch Jerry succeed in getting Dory to dunk his head underwater, something that Brian had repeatedly been unable to persuade the boy to do. "That victory was not supposed to be yours," she feels the need to tell Jerry. He is taken aback and puzzled, having had no intention whatsoever of stealing anyone's thunder, but nonetheless feels the necessity to apologize. After another such situation, the profoundly sensitive, anguished woman goes so far as to push away the man she herself had chosen to pull into their midst, furiously ordering him to vacate the premises immediately. Berry is quite good in such scenes, a beautiful, fragile vessel of barely contained grief, showing signs of unattractive but wholly understandable stress fractures as she struggles not to shatter completely and have her bewilderment uncontrollably gush forth.

Jerry's subsequent, vividly depicted relapse, wholly expected by viewers for some time, covers familiar cinematic territory, yet Del Toro imbues these agonizing scenes with a poignancy that elicits concern for this particularly affecting afflicted man. Brought back from the brink by Audrey's bringing him back into her household, Jerry is therefore on hand to steady her as she finally releases her powerful, pent-up bereavement in a wailing torrent of tears. Each has now held the other one up—both literally and figuratively—when it was needed most, the compassion shared by these unlikely comrades making both now ripe for recovery. The script thankfully does not have their recuperative roads intersect romantically, especially after a thoroughly unbelievable early scene in which Audrey aims to cure her insomnia by having her hubby's buddy lie intertwined with her in bed, instructing him how to comfortingly stroke her ear the way Brian always had.

Things We Lost in the Fire failed to spark much interest, despite reviews that particularly praised Del Toro's engrossing work and even predicted his nomination for an Academy Award®. The production was the feature film debut for screenwriter Allan Loeb, and the English-language debut for promising Danish director Susanne Bier. A disciple of the Dogma movement, Bier likes to use a searching handheld camera, here with mixed results. She is particularly fond of zeroing in for extreme close-ups of characters' eyes, attempting to highlight telling emotional information that may be obtained there. After a while, however, it amounts to ocular overkill. Bier also offers up numerous shots of water, such as the gushing of a shower nozzle or rain flowing down windowpanes, which are apparently symbolic of a restorative cleansing, a clarifying rinsing-away of what ails or burdens one so that a fresh start might be possible. It appears, at the film's end, that new beginnings are indeed possible for both Audrey and Jerry, two people who have been through devastating metaphorical fires, helped each other to extinguish them, and now seem able to rise from the ashes.

David L. Boxerbaum

CREDITS

Audrey Burke: Halle Berry
Jerry Sunborne: Benicio Del Toro
Brian Burke: David Duchovny
Kelly: Alison Lohman
Neal: Omar Benson Miller
Howard Glassman: John Carroll Lynch
Brenda: Robin Weigert
Harper Burke: Alexis Llewellyn
Dory Burke: Micah Berry
Diane: Paula Newsome
Origin: USA
Language: English
Released: 2007
Production: Sam Mendes, Sam Mercer; Neal Street Productions; released by DreamWorks
Directed by: Susanne Bier
Written by: Allan Loeb
Cinematography by: Tom Stern
Music by: Johan Söderqvist
Sound: James Kusan
Music Supervisor: Susan Jacobs
Editing: Pernille Bech Christensen, Bruce Cannon
Art Direction: Geoff Wallace
Costumes: Karen Matthews

Production Design: Richard Sherman
MPAA rating: R
Running time: 118 minutes

REVIEWS

Boston Globe Online. October 19, 2007.
Chicago Sun-Times Online. October 19, 2007.
Entertainment Weekly Online. October 19, 2007.
Hollywood Reporter Online. October 9, 2007.
Los Angeles Times Online. October 19, 2007.
New York Times Online. October 19, 2007.
Rolling Stone Online. October 18, 2007.
San Francisco Chronicle. October 19, 2007, p. E9.
Variety Online. October 10, 2007.
Wall Street Journal. October 19, 2007, p. W1.
Washington Post. October 19, 2007, p. C1.

QUOTES

Audrey Burke: "What's heroin like?"
Jerry Sunborne: "Do you hear that expression being kissed by God?"

TRIVIA

Some prints were shipped to theaters using the fake title *Water*.

30 DAYS OF NIGHT

They're coming.
—Movie tagline

Box Office: $39.6 million

"We should have come to this place years ago," says one of the vampires to another in the horror film *30 Days of Night*. Indeed, what could make a better winter vacation spot than Barrow, Alaska, if you are undead? After all, for a whole month there is no sunlight at all, so you do not even need to bring your coffins along to hide in during the day.

The concept of a monthlong night during which vampires can terrorize a whole town is the one thing *30 Days of Night* has over other vampire movies. It is not the first story in which a group of villagers have had to hold off bloodsucking predators until morning—it is just the first time morning seems so far away. It is a great setup, and too bad director David Slade and screenwriters Steve Niles, Brian Nelson, and Stuart Beattie could not figure out enough clever ways to make use of all that time.

Slade made the splendidly horrifying and challenging psychological thriller *Hard Candy* (2005), the story of a predator's prey who turns the tables. If only Slade could have brought some of the nuanced cat-and-mouse game of that film to this material. Instead, this is a film that has few new ideas about vampires and their prey, or about the impact of terror on a captive town. It has very little to offer in terms of a study of violence except lots of blood, and even that gets a little tiring. It is a great idea that quickly runs out of smaller ideas to sustain it.

As the film opens, the sun is setting for the last day before winter's long night in the northernmost town of the United States. Everyone who is getting out of the village is trying to catch the last plane out before darkness descends for good. And the two members of the Alaska state police assigned to Barrow are investigating some strange occurrences, like a pile of burned cell phones. Apparently, they are unaware that is the first thing modern vampires do, cut off any possibility of calling for help.

All the familiar tropes of old vampire flicks and modern horror movies are present. A half-insane prophet of doom walks away from an icebound ship into town to serve as the vampires' advance man. The cop hero, Eben (Josh Hartnett), gets thrown back together with his former wife Stella (Melissa George). It seems she has stopped in town without telling him in order to do her year's last inspection as a state fire marshal and, sure enough, she misses the last plane out of town. And there is an unsurprising roster of potential victims, including Eben's younger brother, their grandmother, an addled old man, some innocent children, and many sled dogs just ready to be slaughtered.

The opening rounds of attacks by the vampires are vicious and unsparing, and the creatures seem to have superhuman powers that suck people away with an inexplicable vacuumlike force. The standard horror-flick fright tricks are employed. Then, fewer than thirty minutes into the film, there is a bloody massacre on the streets that leaves Barrow as little more than a town full of dismembered corpses flowing red into the snow. This is such a quick and near-total orgy of violence that it almost seems as if the filmmakers have quickly lost interest in their own setup. The townsfolk are so easily overcome, and the monsters so powerful and relentless, that it seems there is no story left.

But for the remaining hour of the film, a crew of survivors holds out, implausibly. Eben seems less interested in saving the townsfolk than in saving himself, his family, his girlfriend, and a few friends. First they hide out in an attic whose ladder is hidden. The film suddenly leaps to Day Seven, however, and only then do they make a run for supplies at the grocery store. How they have been feeding themselves until then is not explained. The film next jumps to Day Eighteen and

then to Day Twenty-Nine. There are various diversions (an ultraviolet lamp works as well as sunlight to stop the vampires) and several gruesome discoveries—it seems the remaining townsfolk have either changed into vampires themselves or have become suicidal. The vampires keep feasting, their mouths are always covered with blood, and their leader makes senseless scary pronouncements in some sort of Transylvanian tongue (subtitles are provided). The requisite amount of gore and mayhem is also provided, but the scriptwriters and director do not have enough ideas of how to build the tension over thirty days. The encounters with the vampires are episodic, and it is not clear how the holdouts have survived for weeks without being caught. The plot could have worked just as well over the course of three to seven nights, but then the title of the film would have had to have been changed.

30 Days of Night makes a stab at creating Barrow on a studio lot, but the town looks phony nonetheless and the filmmakers get a few basic things wrong. Above the Arctic Circle, for one thing, the sun does not shine one day and then suddenly stop shining—there is a week or two in which actual midday light turns gradually into fainter and fainter smudges of twilight. Also, the Alaska Pipeline does not end at Barrow; it ends at another North Slope town, Prudhoe Bay, many miles distant. And Barrow does not look like an Old West frontier town—the architecture tends more to Quonset huts than to ornate saloons. And finally, this Barrow seems to be inhabited almost entirely by white people, rather than the native peoples who live in the real Barrow.

Hartnett seems truly horrified that his career has descended to this role, but he plays it gamely, grieving while doing what needs to be done, even if it is chopping off the head of his former partner. A nifty ending saves the film, and for horror fans there is plenty of blood and violence to feast on. But the vampires are uninteresting—they look like mortals dressed up for a Halloween party. There is no depth or complexity to the survivors and little sense or consistency to their tactics. You just wait for them to be killed off, predictably, one by one. It is a shame there is only a couple minutes' worth of plot to fill up the thirty days of darkness.

Michael Betzold

CREDITS

Eben Oleson: Josh Hartnett
Stella Oleson: Melissa George
Marlow: Danny Huston
The Stranger: Ben Foster
Beau Brower: Mark Boone Junior

Jake Oleson: Mark Rendall
Origin: USA
Language: English
Released: 2007
Production: Sam Raimi, Robert Tapert; Ghost House Pictures, Dark Horse Entertainment, Columbia Pictures; released by Sony Pictures Entertainment
Directed by: David Slade
Written by: Stuart Beattie, Steve Niles, Brian Nelson
Cinematography by: Jo Willems
Music by: Brian Reitzell
Sound: Tim Prebble
Editing: Art Jones
Art Direction: Mark Robins, Nigel Churcher
Costumes: Jane Holland
Production Design: Paul Denham Austerberry
MPAA rating: R
Running time: 113 minutes

REVIEWS

Boston Globe Online. October 19, 2007.
Chicago Sun-Times Online. October 19, 2007.
Entertainment Weekly Online. October 17, 2007.
Hollywood Reporter Online. October 18, 2007.
Los Angeles Times Online. October 19, 2007.
New York Times Online. October 19, 2007.
San Francisco Chronicle. October 19, 2007, p. E9.
Variety Online. October 17, 2007.
Washington Post Online. October 19, 2007.

QUOTES

The Stranger: "That cold ain't the weather. That's Death approaching."

TRIVIA

At one time, producer Sam Raimi was set to direct the film.

THIS CHRISTMAS

You can't exchange family.
—Movie tagline

Box Office: $49 million

A vast majority of the success or failure of a family holiday movie can be attributed to how likable the characters or even the cast are sitting around that fictional Christmas dinner. Audiences repeatedly return to spend time with the Griswolds of *National Lampoon's Christmas Vacation* (1989) or the Parkers of *A Christmas Story* (1983) because they like spending time with those families. Too many holiday movies of recent years have given audiences mean-spirited characters who they would never invite to share their Christmas goose and the films have consequently failed. In the spirit of Christmas, audiences will forgive almost any cliché if they can even find a character or two with whom they would like to share a cup of eggnog. Preston A. Whitmore II's *This Christmas* wallows in holiday clichés and features some questionable stabs at humor, but is filled with such a quality ensemble and characters who are easy to root for that it works despite itself. The film may be a little naughty if analyzed too closely, but everyone involved is too nice for audiences to care.

The huge ensemble of *This Christmas* centers on a family headed by Ma'Dere Whitfield (Loretta Devine) in the days approaching December 25. Ma'Dere's husband left her years ago and she has grown romantically involved with family friend Joseph Black (Delroy Lindo), but the two still hide their relationship from her extensive family, especially the sensitive Quentin (Idris Elba). Quentin is the oldest and closest to the now-absent father and cannot bring himself to understand that his mother might have fallen for someone new. Quentin is also the unexpected guest at this year's Christmas dinner, having been absent for years, but forced home because he is on the run from some loan sharks (who will inevitably end up at the Whitfield household). The other members of the Whitfield clan start with the youngest, Michael "Baby" Whitfield (Chris Brown), who hides an incredible vocal talent from his mother because it was a love of music that drove her husband to run off and travel the world. His brother, Claude (Columbus Short) happens to be AWOL and hiding a marriage to a pregnant, white woman named Sandi (Jessica Stroup). His sister, Kelli (Sharon Leal) is the tough-as-nails member of the clan who meets a guy named Gerald (Mekhi Phifer) that might break her cool exterior. Kelli looks down on her sister Lisa (Regina King) because she kowtows to and even cuts the meat for her cheating husband Malcolm (Laz Alonso). Finally, Melanie (Lauren London) has brought home her new beau Devean (Keith D. Robinson), who ends up basically being along for the family ride.

With that many characters and plot threads, the biggest downfall of *This Christmas* is one not uncommon to a lot of households during the holiday season: overcrowding. The story of the downtrodden Lisa, as played by the always-great Regina King, could have been a movie unto itself. The same goes for the story of Quentin and his refusal to say goodbye to a father who left him years ago and recognize that the man currently with his mother could be the best paternal figure he will ever have. Every single plot thread in *This Christmas* feels as if it could have been developed into something more, which leads some of the film to feel abrupt. Just when a story is getting interesting, director Whitmore has to move on to another one to keep the film at a reasonable running time. At the same time, a few of the plotlines devolve into some awkward physical humor in the final act of *This Christmas,* and the decision to end one with a man being whipped while he lies on the bathroom floor unable to move was in poor taste, as much as viewers might agree that he deserves it.

Most holiday comedies feature a dearth of character or plotlines that could be developed further, much less an overabundance. That alone separates *This Christmas* from the pack and makes it a film that viewers are likely to return over the holiday season. *This Christmas* ends with one of the most bizarre scenes of the year—a dance line with the entire ensemble getting something like a curtain call in front of the camera. It goes on for much longer than one would expect and is something that most directors would have placed under the closing credits. The remarkable thing is that it works and it does so solely because of the goodwill built up by the film and its ensemble. Featuring warm, likable work by Lindo, King, Leal, Devine, and more, *This Christmas* could never be considered a film that breaks the mold of the holiday family comedy, but it fits into it much more enjoyably than many of the seasonal offerings of recent years.

Brian Tallerico

CREDITS

Joseph Black: Delroy Lindo
Quentin Whitfield: Idris Elba
Ma'Dere: Loretta Devine
Kelli Whitfield: Sharon Leal
Melanie Whitfield: Lauren London
Lisa Moore: Regina King
Michael "Baby" Whitfield: Chris Brown
Devean Brooks: Keith D. Robinson
Malcolm Moore: Laz Alonso
Claude Whitfield: Columbus Short
Gerald: Mekhi Phifer
Origin: USA
Language: English
Released: 2007
Production: Preston Whitmore II, Will Packer; Rainforest Films, Screen Gems, Facilitator Films; released by Sony Pictures Entertainment
Directed by: Preston A. Whitmore II
Written by: Preston A. Whitmore II
Cinematography by: Alexander Gruszynski
Sound: Willie Burton
Music Supervisor: Spring Aspers

Editing: Paul Seydor
Costumes: Francine Jamison-Tanchuck
Production Design: Dawn Snyder
MPAA rating: PG-13
Running time: 117 minutes

REVIEWS

Boston Globe Online. November 21, 2007.
Chicago Sun-Times Online. November 21, 2007.
Entertainment Weekly. November 30, 2007, p. 117.
Hollywood Reporter Online. October 26, 2007.
Los Angeles Times Online. November 21, 2007.
New York Times Online. November 21, 2007.
San Francisco Chronicle. November 21, 2007, p. E1.
Variety Online. October 25, 2007.
Washington Post. November 21, 2007, p. C9.

TRIVIA

The fake title *Another Gathering* was used on release prints.

300

Prepare for glory!
    —Movie tagline
Spartans, tonight, we dine in hell!
    —Movie tagline
This is where we fight, this is where they die!
    —Movie tagline

Box Office: $210.6 million

The Greek historian Herodotus is the primary source chronicling the Greco-Persian war, a battle that resulted in thwarting the expansive onslaught of the Persian Empire into Europe. The Battle of Thermopylae details the 480 B.C. account of 300 Spartans allied with approximately 2,000 other Greeks. This hoi polloi army prevented the Persian advance for three days by forming an impasse on the one narrow road into Greece. Led by King Leonidas of Sparta, this tiny force inflicted a loss on the great army of the emperor Xerxes I disproportionate to their size. After three days, the Persians prevailed and successfully laid siege to the pass but sustained an exorbitant casualty rate. It is believed that this Greek force bought the Athenian navy adequate time to prepare for the upcoming naval battle that would establish this alliance of the Greek city-states as the victors.

Adapted from the graphic novel of the same name, *300* was directed by Zack Snyder (whose first work was the 2004 remake of *Dawn of the Dead*). The film's backdrop is a digitally created setting that gives the production a surreal look with a color scheme that ranges from radiant green to sepia contrasted with burnt red. Remaining faithful to the 1998 work by comic guru Frank Miller and Lynn Varley, the computer graphics fail to replicate the ebullient mood as illustrated in Miller's artwork. Additionally, the Spartan troops resemble a male bondage choir bearing a wardrobe consisting of black leather briefs and flowing red capes. The soldiers display washboard abs and bare their chiseled pectorals as they battle their effete enemies, who are bedecked with glittering jewelry and heavy makeup. Xerxes (Brazilian actor Rodrigo Santoro) with his silver eye shadow and multiple piercings resembles a male model in a Frederick's of Hollywood catalog more than the Persian emperor.

While King Leonidas (solidly played by Scottish actor Gerard Butler) leads his Spartans to war by strategically holding back their greater numbers by executing the phalanx formation, his wife, Queen Gorgo (Lena Headey), is striving to garner support for the king. She does so by approaching Theron (Dominic West), a prominent politician who has a heavy influence on the Spartan council. He agrees to endorse her cause of bolstering Leonidas's forces if she agrees to submit to him sexually. Reluctantly she accepts his bribe and the political pandering among the upper echelons of Sparta mushrooms into a full-blown Thermopylae-gate.

An ironic component to the story could be viewed as a commentary on a cruel custom practiced in ancient Grecian culture. Prior to their initial battle with the Persians, Leonidas is approached by Ephialtes (Andrew Tiernan). Shunned as a hunchbacked pariah, Ephialtes seeks to restore his father's name by joining the Spartan garrison. In Greek society, infanticide was common if a newborn exhibited any physical deformity. Survival of the fittest was the institutional norm. Leonidas rejects his offer, stating that his disfigurement would prove to be a weak link in the phalanx. Spurned, Ephialtes betrays his countrymen by leading the Persians to a secret goat path that will cause the Spartans to be surrounded. His story is reminiscent of the Greek play, *Philoctetes*, by the classical playwright Sophocles. In that tragedy Philoctetes is a war hero who is betrayed and exiled on the Island of Lemnos by his brothers-in-arms because of a severe snakebite on his foot that has rendered him ineffective as a warrior. Similarly, Ephialtes is rejected by his own people, which serves to expedite their eventual demise.

Xerxes appeals to Leonidas by encouraging his surrender. In return, the emperor will allow the king to retain his title by pledging his allegiance and compliance solely to the emperor. Leonidas responds by pitching his spear at Xerxes, which slashes the Persian's cheek. Xerxes orders his men to deliver the coup de grâce and the Spartans are killed by a rain of arrows. Throughout the

story, a voice-over is delivered by the sole survivor of the 300, Dilios (David Wenham) who was told by Leonidas to return to Sparta in order to inform its citizens of their sacrifice. As he recounts his tale to his countrymen a year later, 40,000 Greeks are preparing to battle the Persian army at Plataea.

Although a box office hit, *300* was not without controversy. Criticized by Iranian officials for its negative portrayal of Persians, President Mahmoud Ahmadinejad officially reproached the film. Gene Seymour of *Newsday* addresses the debate as a misguided one and comments in his review: "the movie's just too darned silly to withstand any ideological theorizing." Warner Brothers played down the film's controversy by stating that the film "is a work of fiction inspired by the Frank Miller graphic novel and loosely based on a historical event. The studio developed this film purely as a fictional work with the sole purpose of entertaining audiences; it is not meant to disparage an ethnicity or culture or make any sort of political statement."

David M. Roberts

CREDITS

King Leonidas: Gerard Butler
Queen Gorgo: Lena Headey
Theron: Dominic West
Dilios: David Wenham
Xerxes: Rodrigo Santoro
Ephialtes: Andrew Tiernan
Origin: USA
Language: English
Released: 2007
Production: Mark Canton, Gianni Nunnari, Bernie Goldmann, Jeffrey Silver; Legendary Pictures, Virtual Studios; released by Warner Bros.
Directed by: Zack Snyder
Written by: Zack Snyder, Kurt Johnstad, Michael B. Gordon
Cinematography by: Larry Fong
Music by: Tyler Bates
Sound: Patrick Rousseau
Editing: William Hoy
Art Direction: Isabelle Guay
Costumes: Michael Wilkinson
Production Design: James Bissell
MPAA rating: R
Running time: 116 minutes

REVIEWS

Boston Globe Online. March 8, 2007.
Chicago Sun-Times Online. March 9, 2007.

Entertainment Weekly. March 15, 2007, p. 45.
Hollywood Reporter Online. February 15, 2007.
Los Angeles Times Online. March 9, 2007.
New York Times Online. March 9, 2007.
Rolling Stone Online. March 7, 2007.
San Francisco Chronicle. March 9, 2007, p. E1.
Variety Online. February 14, 2007.
Washington Post Online. March 9, 2007.

QUOTES

Dilios: "And so my king died, and my brothers died, barely a year ago. Long I pondered my king's cryptic talk of victory. But time has proven him wise, for from free Greek to free Greek, the word was spread that bold Leonidas and his three hundred, so far from home, laid down their lives. Not just for Sparta, but for all Greece and the promise this country holds."

Stelios: "Our ancestors built this wall using ancient stones from the bosom of Greece herself. And with a little Spartan help, your Persian scouts supplied the mortar."

TRIVIA

The film was shot on blue and green screens in Montreal, Canada and includes 1,523 cuts with 1,006 visual effects shots.

AWARDS

Nomination:

Screen Actors Guild 2008: Outstanding Performance by a Stunt Ensemble in a Motion Picture.

3:10 TO YUMA

Time waits for one man.
—Movie tagline

Box Office: $53.6 million

Trying to secure funding in Hollywood for a Western may not be quite as arduous a task as the search by yesteryear's settlers for life-sustaining water in desert-like frontier territory, but it is close. The Western was once a staple of Tinseltown's output that made both money and stars; interest in backing films of what has come to be considered an outmoded genre has long been about as lively as a dead gunslinger. One enthusiasm that has failed to dwindle is director James Mangold's long-standing passion for the 1957 film *3:10 to Yuma*, resulting in his morality play *Cop Land* (1997) having more than a Western whiff about it and a lead character sharing the last name of one of *Yuma*'s lead actors, Van Heflin. However, when Mangold decided he would like to try his hand at an actual retelling of the forty-year-

old film's tale (which began life as a short story by Elmore Leonard), studio after studio passed on the idea. Lucky for moviegoers, Mangold persevered to see his project to fruition, as his admirable and absorbing *3:10 to Yuma* makes the best attempt in years to puff resuscitative air into the Western. Made on a budget of $55 million, it opened modestly but in the number one spot, and garnered numerous favorable reviews.

Despite its bountiful exchanges of bullets, this action-packed *3:10 to Yuma* is still less about the gunplay and more about the interplay between two very different men—one a sober, hardworking, and thoroughly upstanding citizen in great need, and the other a notorious outlaw who, blithely and bloodily, takes what he wants. The first is snakebitten Dan Evans (Christian Bale), a drought-plagued Arizona rancher whose barn is torched at the outset by his debtors. The Transcontinental Railroad is coming, and it would be more lucrative for the holder of his mortgage to force the struggling man off the property and sell it to land-hungry executives with much deeper pockets. It is quickly made clear that there is a long, daunting list of pressures bearing down on Evans like the collapsing beams of the engulfed structure. Despite Evans's steady, stoic exterior, viewers need only look into the determined eyes burning out of his haggard, sun-scorched face to sense an underlying frustration and humiliating sense of impotency. Already having lost a leg in the Civil War, his heart is now being ripped out as his family loses faith in, and respect for, an unsuccessful provider who has yet to put his remaining foot down and take a powerful, stalwart stand against those grinding their own heels upon the Evanses' fortunes and future.

Especially critical of Evans is his teenaged son, William (Logan Lerman). (To further intensify the rancher's burden, Mangold's film also gives Evans a younger son in need of medicine for a respiratory condition that necessitated the family's move to such arid environs in the first place.) Feeling he is doing the best he can to eke out a satisfactory existence for his family, Evans says to William, "When you walk in my shoes you might understand." The young man replies with disdainful emphasis: "I'm not ever walkin' in your shoes." For hero-worship, William naively immerses himself in romanticized tales of gunslinging bandits, admiring the nerve and potency of larger-than-life figures who, unlike his father, men fear to cross.

That description certainly applies to *3:10 to Yuma*'s other main character, the brawny, smirking, and thoroughly lethal Ben Wade (Russell Crowe), with whom Evans and his sons have a fateful chance encounter during the outlaw and his fearsome gang's twenty-second robbing of a coach transporting railroad funds. Viewers are given multiple shots of William that convey an awed fascination at meeting this famous, formidable man in the flesh. When Evans and the boys are relieved of their horses, William is visible over his father's shoulder, emphasizing the man's humiliation at being trumped yet again with his offspring on hand to witness it.

Soon after, when Wade is captured while tarrying with a woman in a nearby town, Evans steps forward to join a small group of men sworn to transport the prisoner across miles of hazardous terrain and past Wade's looming, loyal followers to catch the train to Yuma, where a noose most likely awaits. Rising to the occasion, the desperate rancher grabs onto an opportunity to not only earn some much-needed money for his family but also rise in their estimation. It is an exceedingly hazardous proposition, but, as Evans tells his wife Alice (Gretchen Mol), "I'm tired of watching my boys go hungry. I'm tired of the way that they look at me, and I'm tired of the way that you don't."

While the original *3:10 to Yuma* quickly jumped to the end of the journey for an effective, claustrophobic juxtaposition of Evans and Wade as the clock ticked suspensefully toward the appointed hour à la *High Noon* (1952), Mangold has chosen to open up the proceedings (perhaps a bit too much) by showing how things transpired and how various characters expired along the way. A rip-roaring amount of sound and fury has been added as a result, with thunderously pounding horse hooves, booming explosions, chaotic and deadly violence, breakneck escapes, and cacophonous weapon discharges. During the trek, viewers see how an uneasy and unanticipated alliance is formed between Evans and Wade, working together to elude not only enraged Apache warriors but also railroad men who have their own unpleasant—as well as unlawful—plans for Wade. Through it all, the shackled man is able to maintain a cocksure upper hand, gradually picking off those transporting him with alarming ease, cunning, and brutality. (He repeatedly sticks a fork in one victim to be sure the man is done.)

While Bale's skilled, sympathetic portrayal of Evans is a remarkable, palpable mix of downtrodden woe and straight-arrowed nobility of purpose, emasculated and yet still thoroughly masculine, it is Crowe's multifaceted Wade who most intently intrigues. A volatile, violent man often exhibiting an immoral, blasé disregard for human lives that get in his way also quotes the Bible, sketches artistically, and both speaks tenderly and acts with gentility toward women. A grizzled old bounty hunter (Peter Fonda) who speaks ill of his own mother gets tossed off a cliff by the offended outlaw, who points out that even bad men have a soft spot for dear old mom. Wade's untamable power and ability to remain unbowed with an unshakable, cool command is what impresses William so, and those watching will find it

hard to avoid feeling similarly in spite of the man's less-attractive attributes. The character's curious composition of contradictory elements leaves the boy the way most viewers will be left, rather befuddled and unable to pigeonhole him.

Long before Wade has been successfully conveyed to the town of Contention, he has begun playing manipulative mind games with those around him, especially Evans. Wade tries to size up the beleaguered man, identifying all his buttons and then pushing them to his own advantage. This continues in earnest once he is holed up alone with Evans, the surviving other men having cowardly fallen away from their duty as the criminal's cohorts fill the streets with guns for hire. (William, who disobeyed his concerned father's wishes and showed up during the perilous undertaking with indispensable assistance, is ordered home to safety but, thankfully, fails once again to listen.) Wade tries to dissuade Evans from his word, attempting to entice him with monetary offers far in excess of what seeing his commitment through will be worth. All Evans has to do is shirk his responsibilities, look the other way—and let people think that someone has yet again got the best of him. The scene creates a profound sense of tension and dread, because one realizes that the man has no price, that Wade's tainted money and the easy, dishonorable way out might solve Evans's financial woes but not his aching, essential need to reclaim the respect of others and his own self-worth. It is here that the character fully comes into his own, pinched in a slowly closing vise while persevering to do what a good man, even though he is outmanned, must do.

The finale of Mangold's film is probably the most significant difference from the original. Less tidy and uplifting, here Evans is gunned down by Wade's adoring, maniacal righthand man, Charlie (Ben Foster), just as Evans has completed his task. Some viewers will have a problem forgetting about the war vet's amputation as he hurtles on and off roof peaks with Wade. Many more may find it hard to swallow that Wade not only decides to help Evans succeed in the end but also chooses to put a period at the end of his efforts by slaying Charlie and the rest of the gang before voluntarily boarding the train. However, there are definite glimpses of the complicated Wade's surprised appreciation for Evans's mettle and unswerving determination, a respect for the man with whom he happens to be at cross-purposes but against whom he has nothing personal. Both men learn something about what makes the other tick as the clock approaches 3:10, and Wade has apparently resolved that he wants to give the long-suffering man a well-deserved, heroic, uplifting triumph to bask in with his family. Wade could always escape down the line as he had done before and, it is hinted, intends to do again. His final actions, even the most stunning, can perhaps best be explained using a line his character uttered in the 1957 version: "I owed you that."

David L. Boxerbaum

CREDITS

Ben Wade: Russell Crowe
Dan Evans: Christian Bale
Charlie Prince: Ben Foster
William Evans: Logan Lerman
Byron McElroy: Peter Fonda
Alice Evans: Gretchen Mol
Grayson Butterfield: Dallas Roberts
Doc Potter: Alan Tudyk
Emmy Nelson: Vinessa Shaw
Tucker: Kevin Durand
Tommy Darden: Johnny Whitworth
Origin: USA
Language: English
Released: 2007
Production: Cathy Konrad; Tree Line Films, Relativity; released by Lionsgate
Directed by: James Mangold
Written by: Halsted Welles, Michael Brandt, Derek Haas
Cinematography by: Phedon Papamichael
Music by: Marco Beltrami
Sound: Jim Stuebe
Editing: Michael McCusker
Art Direction: Gregory A. Berry
Costumes: Arianne Phillips
Production Design: Andrew Menzies
MPAA rating: R
Running time: 120 minutes

REVIEWS

Boston Globe Online. September 7, 2007.
Chicago Sun-Times Online. September 6, 2007.
Entertainment Weekly Online. August 28, 2007.
Hollywood Reporter Online. August 17, 2007.
Los Angeles Times Online. September 7, 2007.
New York Times Online. September 7, 2007.
New Yorker Online. September 3, 2007.
Newsweek Online. September 10, 2007.
Rolling Stone Online. September 4, 2007.
San Francisco Chronicle. September 7, 2007, p. E1.
Variety Online. August 16, 2007.
Wall Street Journal. September 7, 2007, p. W1.
Washington Post. September 7, 2007, p. C1.

QUOTES

Ben Wade: "I've always liked you Byron, but you never know when to shut up."
Ben Wade: "Remind me never to play poker in this town."

TRIVIA

The weekend before the production was to wrap, a storm dumped nearly two feet of snow on what was supposed to be a drought-plagued town. Labourers shoveled the snow from the buildings' balconies and roofs and distributed eighty-nine dump trucks worth of soil across the set. Backhoes created an eight-foot-tall rampart of snow just beyond the sight line for the final six days of shooting.

AWARDS

Nomination:
Oscars 2007: Sound, Orig. Score
Screen Actors Guild 2007: Cast.

TMNT
(Teenage Mutant Ninja Turtles)

Raising Shell in 2007.
—Movie tagline

Box Office: $54.1 million

A franchise that started as a parody, or at least a commentary, on the superhero genre, has come full-circle and become too self-important. Odd, considering that it has been used to sell everything from action figures and beach towels to electric toothbrushes.

This incarnation picks up at least a few years after the events of the live-action Teenage Mutant Ninja Turtles movies of the 1990s, dropping the puppets and actors in rubber suits for computer-generated imagery (CGI) in the process. The task of making the turtles look as realistic as possible having been accomplished, the biggest problem becomes the writing and all that it entails, including pacing, character development, dialogue, and the story itself.

The film starts with an overly long sequence in which a narrator (voice of Laurence Fishburne) tells of a warrior who, 3,000 years ago in Central America, found a portal to another dimension that provided him with immortality, turned his four trusted generals to stone, and unleashed thirteen monsters on the world. While this is obviously important, and is a visual achievement of some merit, it probably could have been tighter, especially because it delays the audience's first glimpse of the eponymous heroes.

The ancient sequence leads into modern-day Central America, where a village is being terrorized by a group of military thugs, who run into a mysterious avenger. April O'Neil (voice of Sarah Michelle Gellar), the Turtles' erstwhile sidekick, is actually the first recognizable character encountered. Although she is there in her capacity as a shipping agent, transporting a stone statue, her suspicions are aroused by the shadowy figure that defended the village. Of course, she finds Leonardo (voice of James Arnold Taylor), whom Splinter (voice of Mako in his last role) has sent there to learn leadership. How he is supposed to learn leadership by himself is never adequately explained.

Leo has not returned, thinking he has failed in his training, but April tries to persuade him to come back. This scene tidily sets up the various conflicts to be played out back in New York, where the rest of the Turtles still reside in various states of development and employment. Michelangelo (voice of Mikey Kelley) has become a tech-support worker; Donatello (voice of Mitchell Whitfield) has a job as an entertainer who dresses up as a Teenage Mutant Ninja Turtle at children's birthday parties (in an apparent homage to the beginning of *Ghostbusters II* [1989]), and calls himself "Cowabunga Carl"; Raphael (voice of Nolan North) is secretly a nighttime vigilante called "The Nightwatcher" who partners with April's beau Casey Jones (voice of Chris Evans) on his nocturnal patrols. He misses and resents Leonardo the most, and his conflict with his brother gives the movie most of its perceived dramatic heft. Unfortunately, it also pushes the other two brothers to the background. While Donatello's anachronistic playfulness may or may not be needed, it might have helped to have some of the old winking humor acknowledging how ridiculous the premise is in the first place. The darker mood and brooding Raphael character does, however, allow for one of the film's better set pieces, as Raph and Leo battle each other during a rainstorm on a rooftop. The scene is beautifully rendered, and almost pulls off the emotional charge the filmmakers were presumably shooting for.

April and Casey deliver the last of the Stone Generals to Max Winters (voice of Patrick Stewart) to complete the plot triangle and present the Turtles with a villain to fight, as the Foot Clan, led by Karai (voice of Ziyi Zhang) comes into Winters's employ as hired help and the generals are brought to life. Max calls them his "brothers" and "sister," setting up an obvious parallel to the Turtles own dysfunction.

As the stone generals and the Foot go about collecting the monsters, it becomes clear that most of the focus of the story will be the internal family dynamic between the brothers, and the outside events will intersect with the boys only when it can highlight their conflict. This is fine for older fans looking for character development, but most likely detracts from the enjoyment of the audience the filmmakers were obviously targeting with the film's PG rating.

The external struggle finally hits home when the generals figure out that Winters wishes to banish the thirteen monsters to the dimension from whence they came. This act will end the curse, and with it, their immortality. When they encounter Leonardo after the rooftop battle with Raph, they decide to substitute him for the thirteenth monster, thereby closing the portal and ensuring their 3,000-year reign. This brings the Turtles out of hiding, back into action, and forges them into the family they need to be. The climactic battle brings all the disparate groups together, and also sets up the parallel confrontation between the reunited Turtle brothers and Winters's stone "brothers." It also shows the different observances of honor among the two ninja groups, as Karai keeps her word to Winters in the face of an offer to switch sides by the generals.

In addition to the weaknesses of plot, dialogue, pacing, and story, the biggest problem seems to be that the film attempts to provide something for everyone, and fails to deliver a cohesive whole. Old-school fans cannot be pleased with the dumbing-down and weakening of the wry "yeah, we know it's all a joke" humor of the source material, while younger fans, looking for spectacle and action, may feel cheated by the long gaps for exposition.

The CGI has finally given the Turtles a medium in which they can move about unfettered by the failings of 2-D animation or cumbersome live-action. Indeed, the cityscape, the textures, and the facial personalities of the Turtles themselves are evidence that these characters should have been computer generated long ago. It is a shame that it did not happen earlier, when there was still a reason to make this film besides the corporate need for product, and there was someone with a passion for the source material to do it. While there seems to be a lot going on, all it really adds up to is a studio's attempt to milk a few more merchandising and box office dollars from a familiar franchise. *TMNT* is a symbol, and a victim, of the fact that it is completely unnecessary.

Jim Craddock

CREDITS

Donatello: Mitchell Whitfield (Voice)
Leonardo: James Arnold Taylor (Voice)
Master Splinter: Mako (Voice)
Max J. Winters: Patrick Stewart (Voice)
Michelangelo: Mikey Kelley (Voice)
Raphael/Nightwatcher: Nolan North (Voice)
Casey Jones: Chris Evans (Voice)
April O'Neil: Sarah Michelle Gellar (Voice)
Origin: USA, Hong Kong

Language: English

Released: 2007

Production: Thomas K. Gray, H. Galen Walker, Paul Wang; Imagi Animation Studios; released by Warner Bros.

Directed by: Kevin Munroe

Written by: Kevin Munroe

Cinematography by: Steve Lumley

Music by: Klaus Badelt

Sound: Cameron Frankley

Music Supervisor: Julianne Jordan

Editing: John Damien Ryan

Art Direction: Mon Cheung, Ahtam Tam

Production Design: Simon Murton

MPAA rating: PG

Running time: 86 minutes

REVIEWS

Boxoffice Online. March 23, 2007.
Entertainment Weekly. March 30, 2007, p. 54.
Hollywood Reporter Online. March 19, 2007.
Los Angeles Times Online. March 23, 2007.
New York Times Online. March 22, 2007.
San Francisco Chronicle. March 23, 2007, p. E5.
Variety Online. March 18, 2007.
Washington Post Online. March 23, 2007.

QUOTES

Master Splinter: "We must return to the surface to take back what is ours."

TRIVIA

The very last line of the film, spoken by Raphael is: "Man, I love being a turtle!" which has been featured in every film based on the turtles.

TRIVIA

Despite the film being set in New York City, only the Brooklyn Bridge appears and most of the remaining cityscape in the film is fictional.

TRADE

You'll pay for this.
  —Movie tagline

Innocents lost…sometimes forever.
  —Movie tagline

Each year, more than 100,000 people are trafficked across international borders…against their will.
  —Movie tagline

Trade excels at bringing the plight of global sex trafficking to a wider audience but fails in turning the message into a viable film with its manipulative, exploitative tactics and too many glaring narrative missteps. The many, gratuitous scenes of graphic sexual assault and abuse of the young women that are kidnapped and later sold on the Internet are perhaps the most grievous of these missteps, milking their misery for the emotional manipulation of the audience.

The film is based on Peter Landesman's article, "The Girls Next Door," featured in the *New York Times Magazine.* The reality is that *Trade* is an independent film with a serious message but big-budget action sensibility, with breathless chase scenes and hokey action segments taking up far too much screen time. German director Marco Kreuzpaintner and writer Jose Rivera seem lost, whiplashing between an action road picture and crime thriller in a vain effort to "entertain" as well as educate. In the process, the message loses its potency and the film fails completely.

The film opens in Mexico City with a jarring scene of thirteen-year-old Adriana (Paulina Gaitan) being snatched off her new bike, kidnapped by a Russian sex-slave network. Adriana's brother Jorge (Cesar Ramos) is on the business end of a different crime, conning a foreign traveler, both incidents conveying the idea that Mexico City is certainly a dangerous place for anyone, native or foreign. As *Variety*'s Robert Koehler put more plainly, "A robbery of an absurdly naive white Yanqui tourist transmits the unambiguous message that Mexico is a crime-filled cesspool." An absurd plot turn has Jorge plying his trade in the city's main plaza when he manages to glean that his sister has been abducted, setting off a manhunt that stretches from Mexico City to New Jersey.

Rather than contacting the corrupt Mexican police, Jorge chases Adriana and her abductors Yochenko (Pavel Lychnikoff) and Manuelo (Marco Pérez) to the Texas border some 1,200 miles away without detection, where the slaves have been smuggled into the United States. In Juárez, Jorge joins forces with a federal insurance-fraud investigator Ray (Kevin Kline), who, again without police aid, improbably accompanies Jorge on the remainder of his quest. This extended road-trip segment, complete with the two unlikely allies bonding, seems like an altogether different movie. In an even more bizarre contrivance, it is revealed that Ray's illegitimate daughter was also kidnapped by the same sex-slave traders.

Instead of focusing on Adriana's plight, the film decides to concentrate on her fellow kidnap victim, Veronica (Alicja Bachleda-Curus), instead, essentially negating the payoff of Jorge's drawn-out chase from

Mexico to rescue his sister. While the kidnappers spare Adriana from rape—they intend to auction off her virginity online—the Polish teenager Veronica is sexually assaulted by the vile Manuelo. There are other victims, too, including a young Thai boy who is injected in the neck with drugs and delivered to an elderly pederast who "won" him at auction. This particularly graphic injection scene, shown in close-up, prompted Koehler to observe, "The feeling grows that the film has crossed the line from political thriller to sordid sensationalism." Many other critics agreed, *Chicago Sun-Times*' Roger Ebert among them, noting, "the movie seems to have an unwholesome determination to show us the victims being terrified and threatened. When I left the screening, I just didn't feel right." When the plot goes so far as to have the girls escape their captors, only to be horribly reabducted, any trust or goodwill from the audience has truly fled.

The film's most effective and most genuine, emotionally cathartic moment features Veronica, who has become Adriana's protector. In an unexpected, heartwrenching scene, punctuated by the moody strains of Rufus Wainwright's operatic "Agnus Dei," Veronica commits suicide after declaring she will make her kidnappers pay—literally, in fact, as they will not only lose her as a lucrative commodity but their lives will also be in jeopardy for not delivering the goods as promised. The act seems to actually shake the evil Manuelo, but, just as that sole scene is not enough to save the film, her suicide was not enough to turn Manuelo from the dark side.

The extremely disappointing end to the film, which involves a police raid of the genteel suburban New Jersey home where the victims are stashed, is unsurprising given the plot trajectory throughout but it is contrived to the point of insult to the viewer.

Like many contemporary social issues that have become the topics of films, the high-profile star promoting it is more interesting than the film. Kevin Kline held a press conference with a special screening of the film for the United Nations to help bring about awareness of the enormous extent of sex trafficking in the United States. That alone, perhaps, justifies this disappointing but topical film's existence.

Hilary White

CREDITS

Ray: Kevin Kline
Jorge: Cesar Ramos
Veronica: Alicja Bachleda-Curus
Adriana: Paulina Gaitan
Manuelo: Marco Pérez

Origin: USA
Language: English
Released: 2007
Production: Roland Emmerich, Rosilyn Heller; Centropolis Entertainment, VIP Medienfonds 4; released by Roadside Attractions
Directed by: Marco Kreuzpaintner
Written by: Jose Rivera
Cinematography by: Daniel Gottschalk
Music by: Jacobo Lieberman, Leonardo Heiblum
Sound: Pawel Wdowczak
Music Supervisor: Lynn Fainchtein
Editing: Hansjörg Weissbrich
Art Direction: Jim Oberlander
Costumes: Carol Oditz
Production Design: Bernt Capra
MPAA rating: R
Running time: 119 minutes

REVIEWS

Boston Globe Online. September 28, 2007.
Chicago Sun-Times Online. September 28, 2007.
Entertainment Weekly Online. September 26, 2007.
Hollywood Reporter Online. January 25, 2007.
Los Angeles Times Online. September 28, 2007.
New York Times Online. September 28, 2007.
San Francisco Chronicle. September 28,2007, p. E9.
Variety Online. January 25, 2007.
Washington Post Online. September 28, 2007.

TRIVIA

Milla Jovovich was originally set to play Veronica, but eventually withdrew from the film.

TRANSFORMERS

Their war. Our world.
—Movie tagline

Box Office: $319.2 million

In an era when *Pirates of the Caribbean: The Curse of the Black Pearl* (2003), a film based on a Walt Disney theme-park ride resulted in a multibillion-dollar franchise, unfathomable merchandising opportunities, and multiple Oscar® nominations—including a Best Actor nomination for Johnny Depp—it seems almost quaint to be surprised at the success of a movie based on a popular Japanese toy line/cartoon. And yet, Michael Bay's *Transformers* surprised both critics and box office pundits by becoming one of the most successful movies of 2007's crowded summer movie season, ranking among and outperforming some of the industry's most high-profile franchise sequels. (Only *Spider-Man 3* and *Shrek the Third* grossed more money at the domestic box office. *Transformers* ranked number three in box office totals for 2007, right above *Pirates of the Caribbean: At World's End*.)

There were multiple reasons to either expect or doubt *Transformers'* box office clout. On one hand, Michael Bay's post-*Armageddon* (1998) track record had been dubious (following the dual disappointments of *Pearl Harbor* [2001] and *The Island* [2005]) and the premise seemed, to some, to be flimsy at best. On the other hand, however, perhaps it was that simplicity of concept that made *Transformers* so irresistible to a certain segment of the moviegoing audience. Giant robots from outer space who have the ability to transform into a wide variety of vehicles—semitrucks, sports cars, helicopters, and jet planes, to name a few—sounds like a movie pitch written by an excitable thirteen-year-old boy. The producers of *Transformers* would probably make the argument that that is exactly the market they were trying to appeal to and that a sense of youthful wonder was exactly what made the movie appealing to an even broader cross-section of the public. While film scholars might cringe at the idea of a movie being constructed around a Japanese toy line from the 1980s, the premise itself—robots in disguise—has so much potential for popcorn thrills that it is surprising that it took so long for such a film to be greenlit. However, despite the film's perfect storm of a corporate-merchandizing-synergy concept, the final result is surprisingly lacking, which is saying something when all audiences were expecting was, at best, a big-screen version of Rock 'Em Sock 'Em Robots.

Transformers' main problem is that the film itself represents two conflicting schools of corporate Hollywood filmmaking. "School Number One" is the Jerry Bruckheimer School of Action (represented by Michael Bay), in which image is everything; nothing matters more than big, fast, shiny, expensive toys; and the more bombast the better. "School Number Two" is the Steven Spielberg School (he executive produced *Transformers*), in which wide-eyed wonder, sentimentality, and "heart" are always hard-wired into the sense of spectacle. The result of this thematic clash is a strange mish-mash of military jingoism, vehicle fetishism, and outsider teen comedy, which never quite coheres as a whole.

Possibly in an attempt to make the film feel more "epic," the storyline is spread thinly across several parallel plotlines. The core story, which can best be summed up by the *Transformers'* cartoon theme song, is: "The Autobots wage their battle to destroy the evil forces of the Decepticons." Two robotic alien races, with the ability to transform into different vehicles they "scan," have

battled for centuries over the Allspark, a legendary cube with almost limitless power. Centuries ago, the Allspark and Megatron, the leader of the Decepticons, crash-landed on Earth, where they both became frozen in the Arctic. Flash-forward to present day and the audience is introduced to a series of characters who all have some connection to the Allspark mystery. There's Sam Witwicky (Shia LaBeouf), a California teenager with a crush on the hottest girl in school (Megan Fox) and whose ancestor, Captain Archibald Witwicky, mounted an Arctic expedition that may have discovered the location of the Allspark, which makes Sam a person of interest to both the noble Autobots and the evil Decepticons. When Sam's dad takes his son to buy his first car, the boy is subtly coerced into buying a 1976 Chevrolet Camaro that is actually an Autobot named Bumblebee.

In addition to Sam's discovery of his ancestor's legacy and the existence of the Transformers, viewers also follow the story of a group of American soldiers in Qatar (led by Josh Duhamel) that find themselves under siege by the Decepticons and the struggles of the U.S. government—embodied by the strangely hands-on secretary of defense (Jon Voight), a group of federally employed computer hackers, and a mysterious covert agent/man-in-black (John Turturro)—to understand why so many giant robots are trying to break into military databases. As can be expected, the storylines soon merge together, as the good guys, that is, the Autobots and the Americans, team up to keep the Allspark out of the robotic hands of the bad guys, which leads to a massive robot-on-robot battle spanning from Hoover Dam to the streets of downtown Los Angeles.

The most engaging part of *Transformers* is LaBeouf's boy-and-his-robot storyline and, whenever the plot strays too far away from Sam Witwicky, the movie as whole begins to wane. Almost all of the military sequences seem as if Bay cut-and-pasted them out of the Jerry Bruckheimer playbook—Bruckheimer has a reputation for talking the military into letting his filmmakers have access to the most expensive toys in their coffers for, it has been rumored, positive portrayals in his films (see *Top Gun* [1986], *Crimson Tide* [1995], etc.). And while the Qatar scenes have an impressive scope, they have almost nothing to do with the core narrative, making them some of the most costly wastes of time ever filmed. The Voight/Turturro sequences make even less sense, suggesting some sort of deep government conspiracy—right out of the final scenes of *Raiders of the Lost Ark* (1981). But when the audience pays to see a *Transformers* movie, they do not want to see *The X-Files* (1998). They want to see giant robots doing things, preferably violent things. Perhaps Bay should have copied more from Spielberg's playbook and developed the Sam/

Bumblebee storyline into a much more high-octane version of *E.T.: The Extra-Terrestrial* (1982) instead.

While it is not surprising that the narrative in a *Transformers* movie is lacking, what is surprising is how ineffective the action scenes actually are. This sort of film is exactly why special-effects companies are created, but, after the initial thrill of watching a jet plane transform into a forty-foot-tall towering robot wears off, there is not much else to grab viewers' attentions. The transforming scenes are truly impressive, and the special-effects artists do deserve immense credit for making the robots look so natural and three-dimensional among their real-world settings. Unfortunately, because of a core design problem, once the Transformers change from their vehicle to robot forms, they look almost identical, particularly in fight scenes. During the film-ending massive robot throwdown in Los Angeles, once the Transformers lock arms and begin wrestling among the skyscrapers, viewers will be hard-pressed to distinguish an Autobot from a Decepticon. Thanks to this sense of anonymity, the Transformers themselves are barely able to individualize themselves as characters, making it both hard to care about them and tell them apart. The final fight becomes a simple cacophony of metal-on-metal clanging, rather than a life-or-death struggle between protagonist and antagonist. It is both a confusing (and headache-inducing) way to end a film that somehow finds a way to squander its inherent simplicity.

Hopefully, in future *Transformers* sequels (and, given the original's box office receipts, they are a foregone conclusion), Bay and Spielberg will ditch the keyed-up machismo and louder-is-better philosophies of Bruckheimer and embrace a simple story of good versus bad robots—because, frankly, the premise cannot support any more than that.

Tom Burns

CREDITS

Sam Witwicky: Shia LaBeouf
Mikaela Banes: Megan Fox
Capt. Lennox: Josh Duhamel
Master Sgt. Epps: Tyrese Gibson
Glen: Anthony Anderson
Agent Simmons: John Turturro
Keller: Jon Voight
Maggie: Rachael Taylor
Colonel: Glenn Morshower
Bobby Bolivia: Bernie Mac
Figueroa: Amaury Nolasco
Sparkplug Witwicky: Kevin Dunn
Donnelly: Zack (Zach) Ward

Banacheck: Michael O'Neill
Judy Witwicky: Julie White
Trent: Travis Van Winkle
Mr. Hosney: Peter Jacobson
Optimus Prime: Peter Cullen (Voice)
Megatron: Hugo Weaving (Voice)
Barricade: Jess Harnell (Voice)
Ratchet: Robert Foxworth (Voice)
Frenzy: Reno Wilson (Voice)
Jazz: Darius McCrary (Voice)
Bumblebee: Mark Ryan (Voice)
Origin: USA
Language: English
Released: 2007
Production: Lorenzo di Bonaventura, Don Murphy, Ian Bryce, Tom DeSanto; Hasbro, Inc., DreamWorks Pictures; released by Paramount Pictures
Directed by: Michael Bay
Written by: Alex Kurtzman, Roberto Orci
Cinematography by: Mitchell Amundsen
Music by: Steve Jablonsky
Sound: Erik Aadahl
Music Supervisor: Dave Jordan
Editing: Paul Rubell, Glen Scantlebury, Thomas A. Muldoon
Art Direction: Sean Haworth, Beat Frutiger, Kevin Kavanaugh
Costumes: Deborah L. Scott
Production Design: Jeff Mann
MPAA rating: PG-13
Running time: 140 minutes

REVIEWS

Boston Globe Online. July 2, 2007.
Chicago Sun-Times Online. July 2, 2007.
Entertainment Weekly. July 13, 2007, p. 48.
Hollywood Reporter Online. June 29, 2007.
Los Angeles Times Online. July 2, 2007.
New York Times Online. July 2, 2007.
New Yorker Online. July 9, 2007.
San Francisco Chronicle. July 2, 2007, p. E1.
Variety Online. June 22, 2007.
Washington Post. July 2, 2007, p. C1.

QUOTES

Optimus Prime (defending the virtue of the human race): "Were we so different? They're a young species. They have much to learn. But I've seen goodness in them. Freedom is the right of all sentient beings. You all know there's only one way to end this war."

TRIVIA

After originally calling the film a "stupid toy movie," director Michael Bay reconsidered, citing that he had had a similar reaction to *Raiders of the Lost Ark* when it was originally released, and thought that since he had been wrong about that film he might be wrong about this one as well.

AWARDS

Nomination:

Oscars 2007: Sound, Sound FX Editing, Visual FX.

THE TV SET

A place where dreams are canceled.
—Movie tagline

The TV Set is a viciously amusing satire on the television industry that does a fine job skewering the industry while making a serious statement about creativity and compromise. With the familiarity of an industry insider, the film finely details the slow and painful process from creative impulse to mediocre show. So slow and painful, at times *The TV Set* is uncomfortable to watch. Joe Morgenstern of the *Wall Street Journal* likened the comedy to films in another genre: "Most horror films these days are haplessly synthetic, but *The TV Set* is the real deal—smart, funny and authentically terrifying."

Director/writer Jake Kasdan, the son of director Lawrence Kasdan and actress and writer Meg Kasdan, can certainly rely on his vast store of experience with the inner workings of the entertainment industry that ranges from child actor in his father's film *The Big Chill* (1983) to one of the creators of the TV show *Freaks and Geeks*. Although the program had a vocal following of devotees, it was deemed too quirky for audiences and quickly pulled from the schedule. David Denby of the *New Yorker* wrote that Kasdan "appears to know, with an almost nauseated sense of familiarity, all the ways in which the TV industry can cheat, cozen, seduce, and buy even a halfway serious writer out of his convictions."

The TV Set concerns the fate of a pilot for a new show called "The Wexler Chronicles." Writer and creator Mike Klein (David Duchovny) is aiming to make a quality, semiautobiographical drama about a young man returning to his hometown after his brother's suicide. Lenny (Sigourney Weaver), an executive at The Panda Network, loves the idea and calls it her best script of the season. She thinks everything is great…except for the suicide angle. To prove her point, she cites statistics showing that viewers overwhelmingly find suicide to be depressing, ignoring the fact that the premise of the show is entirely formed around the suicide. A slave to focus groups and the opinion of her teenage daughter, Weaver's Lenny is a typically cold network executive who has no problem with radically changing a show so it will appeal to the widest demographic, as evidenced by the success of her latest reality series, "Slut Wars."

A recurring theme in the film is the way that one's integrity can slowly be compromised. Mike is horrified by the thought of the network changing his show and entertains the notion of quitting. His supportive wife (Justine Bateman) reminds him that she is eight months pregnant and would appreciate it if he could give it another try. Although the show is not as he originally envisioned, Mike decides he would like to preserve the shred of integrity that is left. Lenny comes up with the idea that they film two versions of the pilot—one with the suicide and one without. "Shoot it both ways—the bummer version and my version," commands Lenny, "And see which works." When Mike points out that changing the entire premise of the story is going to involve some heavy plot wrangling, Lenny breezily suggests that he need only jot down some new dialogue to patch into the script.

Mike complains to his manager Alice (a pitch-perfect Judy Greer), "If I don't worry about the content in my show, then I'm part of the problem. I'm making the world more mediocre!" Awash in industry-speak, Alice tells him he is "overstating the situation." "But you've never seen *Taxi Driver*!" Mike points out. "I am going to rent *The Taxi Driver*, okay?" she hilariously and incorrectly assures him.

As in Robert Altman's genre masterpiece, *The Player* (1992), much of the humor in *The TV Set* is of the insider variety but certainly can be appreciated by those less versed in entertainment jargon. What makes this comedy so painfully real are the constant manipulations and power struggles hidden behind the forced jocularity. No one ever comes right out and says that something needs to be changed. They constantly talk of loving the work, but having a few minor "concerns." Such concerns must be addressed or it is darkly hinted that the network will not be able to give the show the support it so richly deserves.

Just as bit by painful bit Mike's integrity is compromised, his show has slowly morphed from "The Wexler Chronicles," into "Call Me Crazy!" Minor injustices become major pitfalls: the network installs a new lead actor, Zach Harper (Fran Kranz), whose acting "style" includes imitating Robert De Niro in the aforementioned *Taxi Driver* (1976); the pilot must be screened by a focus group of senior citizens. *The TV Set* is not about a grand injustice, but rather about a hundred tiny ones that affect anyone so bold as to try to do something new in Hollywood.

Jill Hamilton

CREDITS

Mike Klein: David Duchovny
Lenny: Sigourney Weaver

Richard McCallister: Ioan Gruffudd

Alice: Judy Greer

Zach Harper: Fran Kranz

Laurel Simon: Lindsay Sloane

Natalie Klein: Justine Bateman

Chloe McCallister: Lucy Davis

Origin: USA

Language: English

Released: 2006

Production: Aaron Ryder, Jake Kasdan; Wexler Chronicles; released by ThinkFilm

Directed by: Jake Kasdan

Written by: Jake Kasdan

Cinematography by: Uta Briesewitz

Music by: Michael Andrews

Sound: Bob Grieve

Music Supervisor: Manish Raval, Tom Wolfe

Editing: Tara Timpone

Art Direction: Lauren E. Polizzi

Costumes: Debra McGuire

Production Design: Jefferson Sage

MPAA rating: R

Running time: 87 minutes

REVIEWS

Boxoffice Online. April 6, 2007.
Entertainment Weekly Online. April 4, 2007.
Hollywood Reporter Online. May 4, 2006.
Los Angeles Times Online. April 6, 2007.
New York Times Online. April 6, 2007.
Variety Online. April 1, 2006.
Village Voice Online. April 3, 2007.

QUOTES

Mike: "If I don't worry about the content in my show, then I'm part of the problem. I'm making the world more mediocre!"

Alice: "I think that you're overstating the situation just a little bit."

TRIVIA

Sigourney Weaver's character was originally conceived as a man and was changed late in pre-production.

28 WEEKS LATER

Week One: No Trace. Week Two: No Warning. Week Eight: No Control. Week Sixteen: No Cure. Week Twenty Eight: No Escape.
   —Movie tagline

It's Back.
   —Movie tagline
When days turn to weeks.
   —Movie tagline

Box Office: $28.6 million

The "rage" virus is back in England, just when the uninfected thought it was safe to return home, and that is the concept which drives this sequel to Danny Boyle's *28 Days Later* (2002), even though the original was not exactly a blockbuster, grossing $45 million at the box office. This time the action is focused on a family. The children, Andy (Mackintosh Muggleton) and Tammy (Imogen Poots), have been safely evacuated from England, while Alice, the mother (Catherine McCormack,) and Don (Robert Carlyle), the father, are survivors of the "rage" plague, hiding out with an elderly couple in a rural village, until they come under attack by crazed, blood-infected zombies. The couple is separated, and the husband elects to save himself, leaving his wife behind to the horrors of the invading zombies soon to follow. He breaks through an upstairs window and onto the tile roof, then falls to the ground. He is pursued in a mad dash to the river but somehow manages to escape downriver in a boat with an outboard motor. He will live to later hold a position of managerial authority in renewed London, where he will be reunited with his son and daughter.

In fact, twenty-eight weeks later (hence the title), a United Nations force, led by American troops with General Stone (Idris Elba) in command, attempts to recapture London, or at least part of the city, a Green Zone, now divided into three sectors, protected by military snipers. One of them, a soldier named Doyle (Jeremy Renner) later becomes the protector of the children, Andy and Tammy, and Scarlet (Rose Byrne), a medical officer who believes that one or both of the children may carry a blood defect that could be used as an antivirus that would make them immune to the plague. Seeking to rescue mementos from home, Andy and Tammy escape from the Green Zone to return to where they lived. This security breach is noted and they are followed and rescued, but not before they are reunited with their mother, who had not died as supposed, but was somehow immune to the effects of the "rage" virus. She is placed in medical isolation. When her husband Don visits her to ask her forgiveness for having abandoned her earlier, he kisses her, only to discover that she is a carrier of the virus, which turns him into a mad killer who then reinfects the whole colony. The situation quickly collapses out of control. General Stone gives the order for the mass extermination of Sector One. Trooper Doyle has fallen into the sector and then decides to rescue the medical officer and the children, with the help of his friend Flynn (Harold Perrineau, Jr.), who pilots a helicopter. After a horrendous fire-bombing of the sector and an awful (and also awfully coincidental) zombie encounter in the subway, the children somehow manage to escape to Wembley Stadium, where Doyle had arranged to have Flynn meet them with the helicopter, in order to transport them safely across the English Channel to France, but all is not well. The children were infected and not immune, after all, and the film ends with a coda, "28 days later," that shows Paris being overrun with bloodlusting zombies. This horror plot is programmed to operate on cycles of twenty-eight days or twenty-eight weeks.

Former director Danny Boyle and his collaborator Alex Garland were the executive producers behind director Juan Carlos Fresnadillo, who shares writing credits with Rowan Joffe, E. L. Lavigne, and Jesús Olmo for this horrific fable. This sequel is effectively directed and follows through on the satiric potential of Boyle's original picture. As *New York Times* reviewer A. O. Scott wrote, "the satire is biting, and so are the zombies." *USA Today* reviewer Claudia Puig found the film "powerfully creepy" rather than satirical, but also decidedly "bloody, gory and provocative." What is provocative is the way the armed forces attempt to "protect" the Green Zone by ultimately destroying it and attempting to annihilate everything in it, which would seem to be an allegory for the current American mission in the Iraq war, which also has a Green Zone in Baghdad, to protect, to kill, and to destroy. Puig thought the sequel was even more terrifying than the original, because this time the army is in charge: "As soldiers become indiscriminate snipers, [the film] raises the question of which is worse: zombies who devour passersby or the wrong-headed and inexplicably aggressive policy of the military called in to restore civilization." But *Washington Post* reviewer Desson Thomson was on to what this sleazy movie was at heart: "It's a B movie along the lines of *Night of the Living Dead*," he wrote, "that plays like a reality TV nightmare with no narrative beginning, middle or ending—just survival as an ongoing quest." Such a bloody awful spectacle can be neither pleasant nor uplifting, and only perversely entertaining. One reviewer warned that *28 Weeks Later* is not for the faint of heart or the weak of stomach—to which one might add, nor is it especially for the strong of mind or the intellectually demanding. It is a horror picture with an appetite for obvious political allegory, nothing more, nothing less, designed to leave zombie fans lusting for future, additional outrages to be found in the next sequel, which is sure to come,

because it is amply foreshadowed in the concluding moments of *28 Weeks Later.*

James M. Welsh

CREDITS

Don: Robert Carlyle
Scarlet: Rose Byrne
Sgt. Doyle: Jeremy Renner
Flynn: Harold Perrineau, Jr.
Alice: Catherine McCormack
Gen. Stone: Idris Elba
Origin: Great Britain, USA
Language: English
Released: 2007
Directed by: Juan Carlos Fresnadillo
Written by: Juan Carlos Fresnadillo, Rowan Joffe, Jesús Olmo, E. L. Lavigne
Cinematography by: Enrique Chediak
MPAA rating: R
Running time: 99 minutes

REVIEWS

Boston Globe Online. May 11, 2007.
Chicago Sun-Times Online. May 11, 2007.
Entertainment Weekly. May 18, 2007, p. 47.
Hollywood Reporter Online. May 9, 2007.
Los Angeles Times Online. May 11, 2007.
New York Times Online. May 11, 2007.
Premiere Online. May 10, 2007.
San Francisco Chronicle. May 11, 2007, p. C5.
Variety Online. May 8, 2007.
Washington Post. May 11, 2007, p. C1.

QUOTES

Donald Harris (describing the ordeal he and his wife lived through to their children): "Your mum and I were hiding in a house. A wee cottage. There was an old couple that owned it. And they were there, too. Three other people. And we were, uh…just trying to stay alive, I suppose. We were doing okay for a while. And then we were attacked. They came in through the kitchen window. They were really fast, you know? Chased us. Chased your mum. And we were trapped. Trapped in the bedroom. I…I seen them…biting. I couldn't do anything. I tried to go back. She was already gone."

TRIVIA

The Millennium Stadium in Cardiff was used as a stand-in for Wembley Stadium since, at the time of filming, the refurbished Wembley was still under construction.

2 DAYS IN PARIS

He knew Paris was for lovers. He just didn't think they were all hers.
—Movie tagline

Box Office: $4.4 million

Julie Delpy has been acting in films since 1978, when she was nine, but had never directed a feature-length film until *2 Days in Paris* (also known as *Deux jours à Paris*). Delpy, who previously made three short films, not only wrote, directed, and starred in *2 Days in Paris,* but edited it and composed the musical score as well. The delightful result indicates that she is as talented at filmmaking as she is at acting.

Marion (Julie Delpy) is a French photographer living in New York. Returning from a two-week vacation in Venice, she and her American boyfriend, Jack (Adam Goldberg), spend two days visiting her parents. Not knowing French and feeling bewildered by the eccentric Jeannot (Albert Delpy) and Anna (Marie Pillet), the director's real-life parents, Jack is at a loss. When he and Marion begin running into her old boyfriends, Jack becomes increasingly jealous and finally decides he does not know her at all.

Marion and Jack initially seem like variations on the characters played by Delpy and Ethan Hawke in Richard Linklater's *Before Sunrise* (1995) and *Before Sunset* (2004), the latter co-written by Delpy. While Linklater's characters are self-absorbed and sweet, Marion and Jack have a harder, more ironic edge. Jack thinks he is allergic to almost everything and is constantly repulsed by the French concept of hygiene. Marion feels strongly about everything and seems always to be looking for an argument: ridiculing her mother for feeding her cat foie gras, challenging a cab driver's racist views, accusing an ex-boyfriend of going to Thailand for underage sexual partners.

The pair are Woody Allen neurotics, with Delpy's film owing a considerable debt to Allen's, especially *Annie Hall* (1977) and *Manhattan* (1979). Delpy seems to be playing a variation on Diane Keaton's character in the latter film, alternating between being charming and bitter. She even sounds like Keaton at times. Marion and Jack resemble Allen's characters in their self-absorption, in their impatience with the foibles of others, and in their self-criticism. Marion is fully aware of her tendency to overreact to most situations but cannot control herself. While Delpy may share her character's views, she is poking fun at Marion's insistence upon voicing her opinion about any and all issues.

2 Days in Paris recalls Allen's films stylistically as well. Marion's voice-over narration comments ironically on the events. Instead of simply staging the argument in which Jack breaks up with Marion only to reconcile with her, Delpy shows the scene without dialogue while Marion summarizes it in her narration. The argument itself is not as important, Delpy knows, as the result. Beginning the dialogue of one scene while holding the image of the previous scene is also like Allen. Although most of Allen's films are comedies, they always look like serious dramas, never overlighted, with shadows and layers of gray. Likewise, the cinematography of Lubomir Bakchev in *2 Days in Paris* has a drabber, grainier look than in most comedies, helping to create some ironic distance from the characters. The film's visual style, including the composition of shots, with multiple characters in most of the frames, shows the influence of one of Delpy's mentors, Krzysztof Kieslowski.

The playful nature of *2 Days in Paris* can be seen in its many in-jokes. Not only do Delpy's parents play Marion's, but her cat also appears as her pet. While the cat's real name is Max, in the film, it is Jean-Luc, a nod to Jean-Luc Godard, who cast Delpy in *Détective* (1985). Trying on sunglasses in front of a mirror, Jack says he is going for a Godard look. The couple visit Jim Morrison's grave because American tourists are expected to do so. Jack says that while he is not a big Morrison fan, he likes Val Kilmer, who plays the singer in Oliver Stone's *The Doors* (1991), and Goldberg worked with Kilmer in *The Salton Sea* (2002).

While Delpy is excellent as usual, the big surprise in the cast is Goldberg, once the director's boyfriend, who has made little impression in most of his film work, which includes *A Beautiful Mind* (2001). Goldberg is equally adept at conveying Jack's exasperation and patience, as with his bemused look when a Frenchman explains Jack's Jewishness to him. Early in the film, the bearded, tattooed Jack encounters a group of American tourists looking for the Louvre and deliberately gives them incorrect directions because one is sporting a Bush-Cheney T-shirt. Much later, Jack runs into them again, looking tired and disheveled, they gaze at him with hostility, and he, after a lengthy, nervous pause, simply gives them a quiet greeting. The latter scene is one of several in which Delpy passes up the options of shouting and physical comedy, and tries for something different. It works here and elsewhere in the film, one of the best ever made by an actor making the transition to auteur.

Michael Adams

CREDITS

Marion: Julie Delpy
Jack: Adam Goldberg
Jeannot: Albert Delpy

Anna: Marie Pillet
Mathieu: Adan Jodorowsky
Lukas: Daniel Brühl
Rose: Alexia Landeau
Manu: Alex Nahon
Origin: France, Germany
Language: English, French
Released: 2007
Production: Julie Delpy, Christophe Mazodier, Thierry Potok; ThreeL Filmproduktion, Tempête Sous un Crâne Production; released by Samuel Goldwyn Films
Directed by: Julie Delpy
Written by: Julie Delpy
Cinematography by: Lubomir Bakchev
Sound: Nicolas Cantin, Jörg Höhne
Editing: Julie Delpy, Jeff Werner, Étienne Boussac
Art Direction: Barbara Marc
Costumes: Stéphane Rollot
MPAA rating: R
Running time: 96 minutes

REVIEWS

Boston Globe Online. August 24, 2007.
Chicago Sun-Times Online. August 24, 2007.
Entertainment Weekly Online. August 8, 2007.
Los Angeles Times Online. August 10, 2007.
New York Times Online. August 10, 2007.
San Francisco Chronicle. August 24, 2007, p. E7.
Variety Online. February 10, 2007.
Washington Post Online. August 24, 2007.

QUOTES

Jeannot (to his daughter about her American boyfriend): "He's not like the morons you usually bring home."

AWARDS

Nomination:

Ind. Spirit 2008: First Feature.

U~V

UNDERDOG

One nation…under dog.
—Movie tagline

Have no fear.
—Movie tagline

Box Office: $43.8 million

Like 2000's *The Adventures of Rocky & Bullwinkle* and 2007's *Alvin and the Chipmunks, Underdog* takes a beloved cartoon from the 1960s and uses a combination of live action and computer-generated animation to repackage baby-boomer brands for a new generation of moviegoers; and like those other films, perhaps *Underdog* should have been left a 1960s cartoon time capsule. Although the film almost certainly is entertaining for its intended audience (very young children), it lacks the ironic intelligence and tongue-in-cheek sensibility that seem to be the hallmarks of children's fare that can also be enjoyed by adults. Despite its reliance on hackneyed, lowest common denominator gags and a lackluster plot, however, the film does manage to say a few interesting things about abusing power. But if anything saves *Underdog* from simply being an attempt to cash in on a well-known and beloved character, it is the film's sheer heart, the vocal talent of Jason Lee as the lovable hound Shoeshine (who becomes the superhero Underdog), and the performance of the excellent Peter Dinklage of *The Station Agent* and *Elf* (both released in 2003) as Underdog's nemesis, Dr. Simon Barsinister.

Underdog opens with the voice-over narration of Jason Lee as Shoeshine, a lovable-looking beagle and police dog, described as "the worst dog on the force." After a bungled bomb-sniffing episode, Shoeshine is turned out onto the street where he is picked up by Cad (Patrick Warburton), a security guard in the building where Dr. Simon Barsinister has his lab. Barsinister is performing genetic experiments on strays. Just as Barsinister is about to experiment on Shoeshine, the dog is able to get free and wreak havoc in the lab. Shoeshine is coated in chemicals that obviously alter his body and give him powers, because the dog smashes through the walls to escape the lab. Once outside, Shoeshine is hit by a car but survives unscathed. Dan Unger, the driver of the car, a very hard-luck paternal James Belushi, decides to take Shoeshine home to his young son, Jack (Alex Neuberger). Jack does not take to Shoeshine at first—in fact, the very next day, Jack comes home to find the house completely trashed (because Shoeshine has not yet figured out how to control his powers). When Jack scolds Shoeshine, the beagle begins to explain himself to Jack—and Jack, naturally, reacts badly to the fact that the dog speaks. Eventually, Jack calms down and he and Shoeshine go to a park close by. There, they meet Molly (Taylor Momsen), a girl from Jack's school, and her dog, Polly Purebred (voice of Amy Adams). Shoeshine immediately falls for Polly—he even gets the opportunity to rescue Molly and Polly from a mugger surreptitiously.

Shoeshine gradually discovers the extent of his powers and realizes, with Jack's urging, that he can use them for fighting crime and helping people—in fact, it is Jack that encourages Shoeshine to create the superhero personal of Underdog (including an outfit) and to make "Shoeshine" his mild-mannered secret identity. Meanwhile, Barsinister manages to re-create his lab in the sewers and begins to search for Shoeshine when he realizes that he cannot duplicate the formula that created Underdog. Ultimately, Barsinister traces Underdog to Dan and Jack—he has Cad capture Dan and holds him hostage. Barsinister lures Underdog and Jack to his makeshift lab and threatens to harm Jack and Dan if Underdog does not give up his powers. Underdog acquiesces, and Barsinister drains Underdog's powers into little blue pills—Underdog is also forced to take a pill that turns him into a regular dog. Barsinister gives a few of the blue pills to three German shepherds, who become Underdog-like superdogs. With the German shepherds and a bomb in tow, Barsinister takes City Hall hostage. Jack, Dan, and Shoeshine escape the lab, Shoeshine gets into City Hall and, in the chaos, manages to get hold of one of Barsinister's blue pills, restoring his powers. Underdog turns the German shepherds against Barsinister (it helps that Barsinister is verbally abusive to the dogs), and convinces them to hold Barsinister down. Underdog grabs the bomb and buries it deep within the earth—it explodes, and blasts Underdog into space. He crashes back to Earth, leaving him shaken but unharmed. The German shepherds are restored to their normal selves, and Barsinister is made to share a prison cell with his bumbling henchman, Cad. With the city safe once more, Shoeshine returns to his life—and ends the film taking a triumphant and goofy flight over the city as Underdog.

It is undeniably true that *Underdog* is filmmaking at its silliest—perhaps even its lowest (there are several ridiculous animal-themed jokes and bodily-humor bits). This was almost certainly done in an attempt to appeal to small children and, though adults may wish to see a more witty and sophisticated application of the source material, it is clear that *Underdog* is meant to be good fun. The proof is largely in the casting and in the story itself. Jason Lee has established himself as a versatile comedic actor, and ably applies his talent to Shoeshine/Underdog. Peter Dinklage is a well-respected actor who here has an opportunity to marry his dramatic chops, showcased so brilliantly in *The Station Agent*, with his flair for manic comedy that he was able to show off briefly in *Elf*. Amy Adams is a rising star, and casting her to voice Polly Purebred shows a bit of savvy on the part of the filmmakers for recognizing and scooping up new talent. Also, the film's plot, though using the well-worn trappings of superhero lore in the context of what is, mostly, a boy-and-his-dog film, is all about having heart and constantly striving to help one another overcome obstacles, both external and self-imposed.

A major criticism of the film, in fact, is its stark lack of originality. This position is understandable, as *Underdog* does indeed recycle much from the superhero and various family-film genres. One positive thing that may be said of *Underdog* in this regard, however, is that

it includes many references to other films, tucked into the film's visual storytelling, that exist specifically to reward the diligent observer and the cinematic omnivore. The obvious references to specific scenes from other films are many: Underdog trying to figure out how to use his powers is similar to Peter Parker's discovery of his powers in *Spider-Man* (2002); a sequence in which Underdog confronts a thief climbing up the side of a building, as well as the scene in which Underdog and Polly Purebred go flying, are direct references to 1978's *Superman*; and when Underdog is launched into space by an exploding bomb, the sequence is certainly meant to be reminiscent of a comparable one in *Superman Returns* (2006). Many more less-obvious examples exist throughout the movie, ranging from the slightly analogous (the super German shepherds that Underdog fights recall the three Kryptonian villains Superman had to face in 1980's *Superman II*) to the very obscure (true pop-culture trivia buffs will recognize Warburton as the star of the short-lived live-action television series *The Tick*, based on the comic-book-spoof superhero). Although these scenes have a certain groan-inducing element about them in their attempt to equate *Underdog* with other films, they also place the movie in good, familiar company and, ultimately, help the audience smile and cheer for a cute beagle that becomes a superhero.

John Boaz

CREDITS

Simon Barsinister: Peter Dinklage
Cad: Patrick Warburton
Jack: Alex Neuberger
Molly: Taylor Momsen
Mayor: John Slattery
Riff Raff: Brad Garrett
Dan Unger: James Belushi
Underdog/Shoeshine Boy: Jason Lee (Voice)
Sweet Polly Purebred: Amy Adams (Voice)
Origin: USA
Language: English
Released: 2007
Production: Gary Barber, Roger Birnbaum, Jay Polstein, Jonathan Glickman; Walt Disney Company, Spyglass Entertainment; released by Buena Vista
Directed by: Frederik Du Chau
Written by: Adam Rifkin, Joe Piscatella, Craig A. Williams
Cinematography by: David Eggby
Music by: Randy Edelman
Sound: Tom Williams
Editing: Tom Finan

Art Direction: James F. Truesdale

Costumes: Gary Jones

Production Design: Garreth Stover

MPAA rating: PG

Running time: 84 minutes

REVIEWS

Boston Globe Online. August 4, 2007.
Entertainment Weekly Online. August 8, 2007.
Hollywood Reporter Online. August 4, 2007.
Los Angeles Times Online. August 6, 2007.
New York Times Online. August 4, 2007.
Premiere Online. August 6, 2007.
Variety Online. August 3, 2007.

QUOTES

Shoeshine Boy: "Y'know, you never see dogs hurting each other for money."
Jack: "You never see people sniffing each other's butts."
Shoeshine Boy: "Touché."

TRIVIA

General Mills breakfast cereal products are seen in the Unger household. The *Underdog* cartoon series was originally created to help promote their products.

AN UNREASONABLE MAN

Ralph Nader: How do you define a legacy?
—Movie tagline

To many partisan Democrats, Ralph Nader is regarded as more than an unreasonable man. In their opinion, he is an unredeemable man. After a lifetime of unparalleled public service as a consumer advocate, Nader became the favorite scapegoat for the Democratic Party's failure to win the 2000 presidential election and, as such, he is widely blamed by liberals for allowing the administration of George W. Bush to take office, start the war in Iraq, and roll back environmental and social welfare programs.

Whether blame for the 2000 electoral outcome can rightly be assigned to Nader, who ran for president on the Green Party ticket and garnered less than 5 percent of the vote, the fact is that Nader now constitutes a truly tragic figure—a man whose own principles have led him from a populist champion into a no-man's-land where he is a virtual pariah. How and why that happened is part of what is explored in *An Unreasonable Man,* written and directed by Henriette Mantel and

Steve Skrovan. It is a largely sympathetic documentary about Nader's life that does include several caustic critics of his foray into electoral politics.

The issue of his culpability in 2000 is raised at the film's outset but not fully explored until the end. In-between is a fairly straightforward account of Nader's life and career, hewing closely to the facts but largely based on interviews with his former staffers and colleagues. The fact that some of these friends turn against him after 2000 lends further credibility to their praise of his earlier efforts.

What emerges from this life story is a portrait of a gutsy, driven, and relentlessly hardworking citizen, a man who almost single-handedly defined what it means to be an American political activist in the late twentieth century. With the help of some wonderful archival footage, viewers are able to easily follow the inspiring tale of a little-known attorney who exposed the American auto companies' complicity in building and marketing unsafe cars as glamorous toys. Nader's landmark initial book, *Unsafe at Any Speed,* was such a lightning bolt that it inspired a vicious counterattack from General Motors (GM). The automaker stalked and tried to entrap Nader, but the scheme was exposed, and GM's chief executive had to apologize to Congress during hearings. Nader sued and won a huge settlement for invasion of privacy, and the filmmakers note the irony that the big automaker's court-ordered payment of more than $400,000 provided the seed money for Nader's larger crusade.

Nader turned from a lone wolf to the head of a group of young activists, dubbed Nader's Raiders, because a couple of college students approached him looking to join his efforts. In interviews with the initiators of this effort, you can still sense their enthusiasm. They took on a slew of consumer issues, writing many reports of high quality. But during the turmoil of the late 1960s and early 1970s, these efforts were considered tame rather than radical.

An Unreasonable Man points out that Nader has always believed in democracy and in working inside the system to make changes. He also believed that exposure of product defects and regulatory problems would lead to better laws and enlightened government oversight. In many cases it did, and Nader's legacy includes a slew of things Americans now take for granted, including the Clean Air Act, seat belts and air bags in cars, nutritional labels on food, protection from workplace hazards, and the Freedom of Information Act.

In terms of what he achieved for the public, some argue in this film, Nader's list of accomplishments exceeds that of any president of his lifetime. All the more ironic, then, given what the film shows the audience of his ascetic life with its eighteen-hour workdays and total dedication to his causes, that Nader could be accused of selfishness in his refusal to abandon his 2000 campaign.

The filmmakers try hard to give us a sense of Nader as a person, but because he seems so singularly dedicated to politics, there is little even his closest colleagues can tell us about him that is not already publicly known. We do not get any startlingly new insights about Nader, but we do get what seems to be a full picture of a man who has seemingly sacrificed any private life to public services. Not only are there no skeletons in Nader's closet, apparently there is not even a closet.

An Unreasonable Man culminates with a fairly full discussion of Nader's 2000 and 2004 presidential campaigns, which are already starting to fade into the myth of half-examined received truths. The film emphasizes what enthusiasm he precipitated in mass rallies in many cities, including one in Madison Square Garden that was organized in ten days and drew 20,000 people. On stage with him were celebrities (including Michael Moore), who four years later would beg him not to run, saying the exact opposite of what they had urged people to do in 2000.

A complete discussion of what happened in the 2000 election would require its own film, but here, there is a fair if not complete discussion of Nader's impact. *An Unreasonable Man,* though obviously on Nader's side, still gives plenty of critics room to denounce him, sometimes viciously, and shows how some of his former colleagues divided over his presidential campaign. It also makes clear that Nader came to his third-party run after twenty years of being disappointed by the Democratic Party, starting with Jimmy Carter's refusal to back his proposal for a Consumer Protection Agency in the federal government. In fact, the film shows that Nader actively worked for Walter Mondale in 1984.

Nader and his supporters debunk the idea that his campaign is what lost the White House for Al Gore, using some familiar arguments: that Gore did not carry his own home state of Tennessee, that Nader spent most of his time campaigning in states that were not swing states rather than intentionally trying to be a spoiler, that no candidate with that much support has ever dropped out of a presidential race, and that Gore lost Florida by fewer votes than even the least popular of all the minor party candidates garnered in that state. None of these arguments is likely to persuade the many voters who believe Nader sabotaged not just an election but altered the course of history profoundly. This is what makes the film a fully wrought tragedy and one that gives many insights into what has become of U.S. politics since the mid-twentieth century. But the movie has a futile tone to it, the feeling of a well-reasoned

argument that is doomed to remain unconvincing. No amount of reasoning is likely to resurrect the image of Ralph Nader, regardless of whether one believes it is unreasonable men who often make the most important changes in the world.

Michael Betzold

CREDITS

Himself: Ralph Nader
Origin: USA
Language: English
Released: 2006
Production: Kevin O'Donnell; Two Left Legs; released by IFC Films
Directed by: Henriette Mantel, Steve Skrovan
Written by: Henriette Mantel, Steve Skrovan
Cinematography by: Mark Raker
Music by: Joe Kraemer
Sound: Craig Clark
Editing: Alexis Provost, Beth Gallagher
MPAA rating: Unrated
Running time: 122 minutes

REVIEWS

Entertainment Weekly. February 16, 2007, p. 59.
Hollywood Reporter Online. January 26, 2006.
Los Angeles Times Online. February 9, 2007.
New York Times Online. January 31, 2007.
Premiere Magazine Online. January 25, 2007.
San Francisco Chronicle. March 9, 2007, p. E5.
Variety Online. January 31, 2006.
Village Voice Online. January 30, 2007.
Washington Post. February 23, 2007, p. C5.

QUOTES

Ralph Nader: "Let it not be said that this generation refused to give up so little in order to achieve so much."

VACANCY

How can you escape...if they can see everything?
    —Movie tagline
Once you've checked in...the terror begins.
    —Movie tagline

Box Office: $19.4 million

Very little about *Vacancy* makes sense, and this horror film does not even manage to do much with its new twist on a very routine horror-movie setup, the couple stranded in a strange motel in the middle of nowhere. It is stylish in some ways, though, and it looks as if director Nimród Antal, making his first film in English, is trying to evoke Alfred Hitchcock, using a spare lighting technique and kitschy opening credits.

Unlike Hitchcock, though, Antal does not have much of a story to work with, just an idea for a story, in the screenplay by Mark L. Smith. And Antal has an unlikely couple for the leads. Luke Wilson, normally a deadpan comic, plays David, who has driven off the interstate in the middle of the night to take a shortcut to somewhere. Kate Beckinsale, more at home in glamour roles and period costumes, plays David's wife Amy, who is upset to find that her husband has led them into deserted territory.

The pair are fighting bitterly anyway, and apparently their marriage has fallen apart since the unexplained death of their young son, Charlie. They are divorcing, and this is their last trip together, though the purpose of the trip is murky. Hopelessly lost, though David will not admit it, they stop at a remote gas station, after David narrowly avoids hitting an animal on the highway. There, a helpful attendant appears out of nowhere and looks under the hood. We have seen this setup before, however, and we know the guy is actually disabling, not fixing, the car. So there is no surprise when it breaks down a mile away and the couple has to walk back to the gas station to seek help in the motel.

Antal does all this set-up work rather deftly. David's and Amy's faces often appear disembodied as they drive in the car, or as they are reflecting off a rear-view or side mirror. Everything around them is dark, and they are like two actors in spotlights on a blank stage. It is done rather effectively, though a bit too frequently, but it gives *Vacancy* an intriguing look at first.

Once they get to the motel, however, all subtlety disappears. As soon as they get in the lobby, they hear screams from behind the manager's door. The manager, Mason (Frank Whaley), appears, holding a remote control and explaining that things can get boring out in the middle of nowhere. He is clearly a nutcase, but David and Amy, having no options for car repair, have to take a room.

At first the room is just disgusting: When Amy turns on the faucet, the water is rusty red, and there is a cockroach skittering across the floor. Then there is a loud knocking at the door, and at the door to the adjoining room. There is no one there, however, and the manager insists they are the only guests. Then David turns on the television, but there are no channels, so he puts in a cassette tape. It turns out to be a snuff film, and David and Amy soon recognize that the film has been shot in their very room.

This is the sole original idea in *Vacancy*, and it seems to afford promise as a plot device. David soon realizes there is a camera in what seems like a heating vent, and that they are being filmed. The promotional tagline for the movie asks: "How can you escape...if they can see everything?" The answer, disappointingly, seems to be that you can find a trap door under a rug in the bathroom and crawl through a tunnel that leads to the manager's office.

What viewers are hoping to see is an elaborate cat-and-mouse game between the manager, his minions, and the trapped lodgers, but the only mice are in the tunnel and the cats seem either stupid or largely disinterested. It is not clear why the evil ones knock loudly at the door when the manager could just let them all in with a key. Why David and Amy are able to fend them off just by continually retreating into their room is inexplicable. And if the manager has the elaborate surveillance system that is shown in his office, how can David and Amy go out of its range so easily?

So, instead of intrigue and slowly building tension, there is puzzlement. The captors are not very interesting: If David and Amy try to run away, they emerge from the bushes outside and chase them down, but they never enter the room. Instead of psychological torture that might fit the kind of demented mind that would show the captives their own prospective mutilation and death, viewers get only ridiculous chase scenes, including one through the tunnel that makes no sense at all. If the people who have been doing this at the motel do not even know the way to get through the tunnel system they have apparently designed, how are they successful? The pursuers are shadowy, ill-defined, uninteresting figures who also seem purposeless and the manager himself is ineffectual.

In the end, the resolution of the movie is itself a nonsensical spasm of violence in which the result seems more accidental than calculated. Of course, before that happens, David and Amy pledge to start their relationship over and renew their love. Viewers expect that, but Wilson is chubby and unappealing, and though Beckinsale throws her usual energy into the role, she has no choice but to succumb to the tedium of the plot.

Vacancy takes an old, overused horror setup and gives it the twist of the video surveillance. But it has absolutely no idea what to do with the plot it has set-up. Loud knocking at the door, mice in a tunnel, cars running people down: These are not things that would put anyone on the edge of his seat. The best that can be said for *Vacancy* is that there is not a lot of gratuitous violence and gruesome torture. There is just the promise of gruesome torture, and then the tedium of a movie with no ideas on how to build psychological tension. At least, it is mercifully short.

Michael Betzold

CREDITS

David Fox: Luke Wilson
Amy Fox: Kate Beckinsale
Mason: Frank Whaley
Mechanic: Ethan (Randall) Embry
Origin: USA
Language: English
Released: 2007
Production: Hal Lieberman; Screen Gems; released by Sony Pictures
Directed by: Nimród Antal
Written by: Mark L. Smith
Cinematography by: Andrzej Sekula
Music by: Paul Haslinger
Sound: Ed White
Editing: Armen Minasian
Art Direction: Chris Cornwell
Costumes: Maya Lieberman
Production Design: Jon Gary Steele
MPAA rating: R
Running time: 80 minutes

REVIEWS

Boxoffice Online. April 20, 2007.
Chicago Sun-Times Online. April 20, 2007.
Entertainment Weekly. April 27, 2007, p. 118.
Hollywood Reporter Online. April 18, 2007.
Los Angeles Times Online. April 20, 2007.
New York Times Online. April 20, 2007.
San Francisco Chronicle. April 20, 2007, p. E8.
Variety Online. April 15, 2007.
Washington Post Online. April 20, 2007.

QUOTES

Amy (on seeing their room): "I'm sleeping in my clothes."
David replies: "I'm going to sleep in my shoes."

TRIVIA

The film was shipped to theaters under the fake title *Temporary Arrangement.*

THE VALET
(La Doublure)

Box Office: $1.9 million

Francis Veber is the best known director of French comedies, almost all of them highly successful in his na-

tive country. All are farcical to some degree, but they also are often witty and occasionally even offer insights into such topics as love and friendship. *The Valet* is only a bland addition to the writer/director's oeuvre.

Pierre Levasseur (Daniel Auteuil) is a wealthy business executive having an affair with supermodel Elena Simonsen (Alice Taglioni). When a photograph of the two together is published in a newspaper, Levasseur tries to convince his wife, Christine (Kristin Scott Thomas), that Elena is a stranger and that she was actually in the company of the blurred image of the passerby next to her in the photo. Although Levasseur has promised Elena he will leave Christine, he cannot because she owns controlling interest in his corporation. Clever Christine is amused by the steps he undertakes to protect his lie and plots to counteract his deception.

Somehow—the film is not that concerned with credibility—Levasseur's lawyer (Richard Berry) tracks down François Pignon (Gad Elmaleh), a parking valet at a swanky restaurant near the Eiffel Tower, and persuades him to pose as Elena's boyfriend and live with her. (The character's name is an in-joke, having been used for the protagonists of six films written by Veber.) François is susceptible because he has just been dumped by his childhood sweetheart, Émilie (Virginie Ledoyen), a bookstore owner, who finds him too dull. Seeing François with Elena in a restaurant and in the tabloids makes Émilie reconsider her decision.

Upset that Levasseur wants to placate the wife he has been promising to leave, Elena agrees to the deception for twenty million euros to teach her lover a lesson. Honest François wants only the 32,450 euros Émilie needs to save her store. The farcical elements of *The Valet* come from the responses of François's friends and relatives, initially skeptical that a parking valet, and an ordinary-looking one at that, could attract such a woman, to his new love and the resulting misunderstandings. Throughout it all, the valet remains earthbound because the romance is a fake. "It's like when I park a great car," he explains. "Perfect, but not mine."

Veber keeps the audience on François's side by making the character humble and decent, as well as unnerved by the unexpected media attention. His loyalty to Émilie is touching. Elmaleh underplays the part, presenting François as a mistreated puppy who longs for affection and understanding. Elena could have been a clichéd spoiled beauty, but both Veber and Taglioni make her complex and likable. Taglioni excels when she conveys Elena's pain when the model finally realizes what kind of man Levasseur really is. This moment seems to point *The Valet* toward a bittersweet ending, but Veber undercuts the serious side of his material with a slapstick conclusion.

Auteuil is arguably France's greatest film actor. Best known for such serious fare as *The Widow of Saint-Pierre* (2000) and *Caché* (2005), he also displays considerable comic talent as a man pretending to be gay to protect his job in Veber's *The Closet* (2001). In *The Valet*, however, Veber requires him to make Levasseur a bombastic blowhard. It is all a bit unseemly for someone of Auteuil's talent, but the actor may have enjoyed breaking away from the repressed characters he specializes in. Scott Thomas elevates the clichéd part of the wronged wife through her typically cool grace. The best performance is by Dany Boon as François's roommate, Richard, providing slow-take comic responses to his friend's new status as a sex symbol.

Veber's films, while generally amusing, too often have underdeveloped situations and characters and hazy logic. They can be counted upon for mild chuckles but little more. A tiresome routine involves Émilie's father (Michel Aumont), a physician who constantly becomes ill while visiting his patients and ends up being treated by them. Veber is also not much of a stylist, putting most of the action at the center of the frame, letting many scenes run on a beat too long, and ending others abruptly. His best films, such as *The Dinner Game* (1998), have a thin layer of cynicism, but *Valet* is too soft around the edges and at its center. Levasseur is meant to represent the heartless rich but comes off as more of a buffoon than a true villain. In his screenplay for *La Cage aux folles* (1978), his work most familiar to Americans, Veber strikes a good balance between broad comedy and genuine emotions. Here, both the comedy and the emotions seem muted.

Michael Adams

CREDITS

Pierre Levasseur: Daniel Auteuil
Christine Levasseur: Kristin Scott Thomas
Émilie: Virginie Ledoyen
Foix: Richard Berry
François Pignon: Gad Elmaleh
Elena: Alice Taglioni
Richard: Dany Boon
Origin: France
Language: French
Released: 2006
Production: Patrice Ledoux; Gaumont, Efve Films, TF-1 Films, Kairos Films; released by Sony Pictures Classics
Directed by: Francis Veber
Written by: Francis Veber

Cinematography by: Robert Fraisse
Music by: Alexandre Desplat
Sound: Bernard Bats, Thomas Desjonquères
Editing: Georges Klotz
Costumes: Jacqueline Bouchard
Production Design: Dominique André
MPAA rating: PG-13
Running time: 85 minutes

REVIEWS

Boxoffice Online. April 20, 2007.
Chicago Sun-Times Online. April 27, 2007.
Entertainment Weekly Online. April 18, 2007.
Hollywood Reporter Online. April 5, 2006.
Los Angeles Times Online. April 20, 2007.
New York Times Online. April 20, 2007.
San Francisco Chronicle. April 27, 2007, p. E5.
Variety Online. March 30, 2006.
Village Voice Online. April 17, 2007.

TRIVIA

The French title translates to understudy or stand-in.

LA VIE EN ROSE
(La Môme)
(The Kid)

The extraordinary life of Edith Piaf.
—Movie tagline

Box Office: $10.1 million

The story behind this biopic is a familiar one: beloved but flawed popular singer as damaged goods, abused by a rough-and-tumble world, then somehow miraculously "discovered," but ultimately worn down by the bad habits of her youth, able to achieve just enough of her inner potential to make the world mourn the loss of her at the end of her days. In jazz, it is the story of Billie Holiday; in American popular music it is the story of Judy Garland; in France it is the story of Edith Piaf, once described as "the best-known and best-loved popular singer in French history." A tall order, perhaps, but like Judy Garland, her excesses and vulnerabilities were very public and widely acknowledged. Born Edith Giovanna Gassion in Paris, Piaf died at the age of forty-seven in 1963, after having achieved fame not only in her native France, but in the United States of America, where she not only played Carnegie Hall in New York City but appeared eight times on *The Ed Sullivan Show*. As Judith Thurman noted in the *New Yorker*, shortly before she died "ravaged by malnutrition, alcoholism, morphine addiction, ulcers, tuberculosis, pancreatitis, hepatitis, rheumatoid arthritis, and, ultimately, cancer," Piaf admitted that "I've had an irresistible need to destroy myself."

La Vie en Rose (also known as *La Môme* and *The Kid*) is a film about desperation and discovery, the story of an enormously talented singer who is heard, then "discovered" by those who are able to exploit her talent. It begins by revealing the miserable life of street urchin Edith (Marion Cotillard). She is abandoned by her irresponsible mother and taken in by her grandmother, who is Madame of a brothel. There little Edith is treated a bit more kindly than the other residents, especially by a prostitute who wants desperately to be her surrogate mother. Her father, taken away from her by the war, later returns to take Edith from the brothel. He is a contortionist who works with a circus, until he has a disagreement with the management and decides to go solo. Edith likes the circus, however, and is influenced by the performers and the atmosphere. While watching a fire-eater practice his act, Edith has a vision in which Saint Thérèse of Lisieux apparently speaks to her, which somehow seems to give her a sense of spiritual purpose and helps her to overcome a bout of temporary blindness. (The screenplay by director Olivier Dahan and Isabelle Sobelman, let it be said, is not always as coherent as one might have wished, but Dahan told the *New York Times* that he wanted the film's emphasis to fall on Piaf's music rather than her life.) Later, when Louis Gassion, (Jean-Paul Rouve) her contortionist father, performs alone at a village not long after they have departed the circus, the crowd wants more, and her father orders Edith to sing. So ordered, she sings "La Marseillaise" and immediately wins over the crowd. This unexpected success opens a new path for her, as a street singer, as her mother, Annetta Maillard (Clotilde Courau), had also been.

Edith is later "discovered" by Louis Leplée (Gérard Depardieu) an impresario and cabaret owner, who changes her name to "Piaf," French for "sparrow," and turns her into a marketable little songbird; but because of underworld connections and scandals, she later has to reinvent herself professionally after the murder of Louis Leplée. Therefore, she is more or less forced to take voice lessons, in order to become an accomplished music-hall performer, under the mentoring of Leplée's friend, Raymond Asso (Marc Barbé), a process that took two to three years. Through an act of determination and sheer will, she breaks through her vulnerability in order to find a new confidence in her talent when she sings "La Vie en Rose." At the very end of her career, Piaf "discovers" a new song, "Non, Je Ne Regrette Rien," which becomes her signature song and anthem at the end of her career when she sings it at the end of the film at the famous Olympia music hall, after nearly canceling because she is so infirm.

What is most remarkable about *La Vie en Rose* is the stellar performance by Cotillard as Piaf. Reviewing the film for *TLS,* Lucy Dallas called her impersonation "extraordinary: she has her look, posture, raspy speaking voice, bravado and charisma without even seeming to resort to impressionism." The flaws of the film are chiefly organizational and reside mainly in the screenplay. Discussing the film's unanswered questions and omissions, Dallas complains that the "Second World War is skated over, as are Piaf's two husbands, and the loss of her child is only referred to briefly right at the end." The constant switchback approach towards the two extremes of Piaf's career tends to be awkward and potentially incoherent, depending constantly on disorienting flashbacks and flash-forwards used far too frequently. The chronological confusion is augmented by geographical confusion as well, as the action jumps from Paris to New York to California. One major problem with this approach is that lacunae are obvious. Viewers know that Edith's father went to war, for example, but two world wars were fought in France during her lifetime, and, as already noted, World War II seems to have been ignored. The story is understandably existential and personal, but the film seems oddly out of touch with what is was taking place in the world at large.

In a *New York Times* profile, written in July of 2006 when the film was still in production, Kristin Hohenadel mentions Piaf's involvement with the French Resistance during the German occupation of France during World War II. On the other hand, Judith Thurman noted that Piaf entertained French prisoners of war in Nazi Germany, though one would never know that from watching the Dahan film, "which tacks back and forth from Piaf's death to her birth in 1915, docking like a cruise ship at various colorful destinations in between, but giving the war years a pass." So, the life story is incomplete, even though the legend is well covered and well defined. If Dahan's purpose was "to make the case for Piaf as an eternal artist with international appeal" (as the filmmaker asserted), then that purpose has been admirably achieved. If his purpose was to emphasize Piaf's music rather than her life, the film does not support that intention. As Lucy Dallas wrote in *Times Literary Supplement,* "Great emphasis is placed on Piaf's personal tribulations, but the film would have benefited from examining her career more closely." No mention is made of "Yves Montand (who became her lover)" or of "Charles Aznavour (who became her secretary), among others." According to Thurman, there were many other protégés, including Eddie Constantine, Gilbert Bécaud, and Georges Moustaki. Dahan's biographical picture is a work of strong performances, enchanting music, and seductive charm, but there may be reason to ask if it ultimately does justice to the career of a woman who was voted tenth out of one hundred historical figures and celebrities in order of significance in a French survey taken in 2005 to establish "The Greatest French Person of All Time." As Piaf was an artiste whose music tapped into the very essence of being French, it is easy to wonder if any film director could meet that challenge.

James M. Welsh

CREDITS

Edith Piaf: Marion Cotillard
Louis Leplée: Gérard Depardieu
Titine: Emmanuelle Seigner
Louis Barrier: Pascal Greggory
Mômone: Sylvie Testud
Anetta: Clotilde Courau
Louis: Jean-Paul Rouve
Louise: Catherine Allegret
Marcel Cerdan: Jean-Pierre Martins
Raymond Asso: Marc Barbé
Origin: France, Great Britain, Czech Republic
Language: French
Released: 2007
Production: Alain Goldman; TF-1 Films, Songbird Pictures, Okko Productions; released by Picturehouse
Directed by: Olivier Dahan
Written by: Olivier Dahan, Isabelle Sobelman
Cinematography by: Tetsuo Nagata
Music by: Christopher Gunning
Sound: Jean-Paul Hurier, Laurent Zeilig
Editing: Richard Marizy

Art Direction: Cecile Vatelot
Costumes: Marit Allen
Production Design: Olivier Raoux
MPAA rating: PG-13
Running time: 140 minutes

REVIEWS

Christian Science Monitor Online. June 8, 2007.
Entertainment Weekly. June 15 2007, p. 61.
Los Angeles Times Online. June 8, 2007.
New York Times Online. June 8, 2007.
San Francisco Chronicle. June 8, 2007, p. E5.
Variety Online. February 8, 2007.
Village Voice Online. June 6, 2007.

TRIVIA

Actress Marion Cotillard lip-synchs to the voice of Jil Aigrot as the adult Piaf.

To help portray Edith Piaf, Marion Cotillard shaved back her hairline and shaved off her eyebrows, which were later penciled in, to better resemble the singer.

Marion Cotillard is one of only five actors to have won an Academy Award for a part spoken mainly in a foreign language.

AWARDS

Oscars 2007: Actress (Cotillard), Makeup
British Acad. 2007: Actress (Cotillard), Costume Des., Makeup, Orig. Score
Golden Globes 2008: Actress—Mus./Comedy (Cotillard)
Nomination:
Oscars 2007: Costume Des.
British Acad. 2007: Foreign Film, Production Des., Sound
Screen Actors Guild 2007: Actress (Cotillard).

WAITRESS

If only life were as easy as pie.
—Movie tagline

Box Office: $19.1 million

Waitress is a concoction not unlike the exquisite pies dreamed up and baked into reality by its lead character as an escape from her troubles. The film mixes humor, melodrama, and romance with a generous helping of sweetener that rarely feels artificial.

Small-town waitress Jenna (Keri Russell) learns she is pregnant in the opening scene, and the rest of the film follows how she copes with this unwelcome surprise. Jenna is trapped in a loveless marriage to Earl (Jeremy Sisto), who breaks her spirit at every opportunity, even forbidding her to attend an out-of-town pie bake-off Jenna dreams of winning. Fellow waitresses Becky (Cheryl Hines) and Dawn (Adrienne Shelly) make misguided attempts to cheer her up, only to leave her more miserable. A ray of light shines into Jenna's life when her lifelong doctor retires and is replaced by the young and charmingly awkward Dr. Pomatter (Nathan Fillion). Despite every obstacle forbidding it, Jenna and Dr. Pomatter strike up an intense affair that fulfills not just her physical needs, but her desire to be listened to, to be admired, and to be understood. Cranky pie-shop owner Old Joe (Andy Griffith) appears throughout at just the right moments to dole out sage advice while barking his lunch orders, but it is left to Jenna to find a way to resolve her ambivalence toward her pregnancy, unhappy marriage, poorly timed yet just-in-time affair, and pie-baking dreams.

On paper, these ingredients suggest a recipe for an overbaked, empty-calorie mess, yet *Waitress* deftly straddles the fine line between oversentimentality and heartfelt charm. Russell is a marvel as Jenna, underplaying emotion during the early stretch of the film as her character sees no point in feeling or dreaming. Her life is all but over, and she bemusedly waits to find how it can get any worse. However, when the good doctor reveals his love for her and she knows for the first time how it feels to be worshipped, a montage of shots showing Jenna slowly emerging from a state of shock into one of pure bliss is simply magical. Russell and Fillion display true chemistry as the lonely waitress and smitten doctor, imbuing their scenes together with an authenticity rarely found in modern romances. Fillion, more typically known for wisecracking roles in science-fiction and action films and television, here displays real charisma as a romantic lead.

Any character study lives and dies by its script, and *Waitress* glows brightest in its one-on-one interactions between Jenna and the colorful inhabitants of her life. The dialogue is crisp and never obvious, favoring frank observations over pat cute-isms. Scenes showcasing the scenery-chewing Griffith come dangerously close to syrupy, and his presence as a wisdom-spewing, colorful relic with a predictable fate is unabashedly cliché. Still, the wordplay in the Old Joe moments is fun and refreshingly tart enough not to derail the entire production.

As with any fine pastry, the film is not without its visual flourishes. During Jenna's many personal trials, *Waitress* peers into her imagination to see how she copes with her mounting struggles. Each insight is a close-up of a pie crust as Jenna pours in ingredients that symbolize her feelings of the moment. As Jenna's voice-over shifts from feeling to feeling, so do the ingredients, and she names each new pie (e.g., "Bad Baby Pie") in case they actually make it onto the next day's menu. The film also employs a unique, deep focusing technique at the climax, blurring everything around the shot except Jenna and the thing that suddenly matters most, eclipsing all else. The effect is one of bravura, yet wholly effective.

Waitress was written and directed by Adrienne Shelly, who also played waitress Dawn. The film made headlines well before its release when Shelly was murdered while wrapping postproduction on *Waitress*. While this certainly drew more attention to the small film than it would have otherwise received, the significant critical praise and festival buzz heaped on Shelly's final work were well deserved on the film's own merits.

Chris Lamphear

CREDITS

Jenna: Keri Russell
Dr. Pomatter: Nathan Fillion
Becky: Cheryl Hines
Cal: Lew Temple
Earl: Jeremy Sisto
Ogie: Eddie Jemison
Old Joe: Andy Griffith
Francine Pomatter: Darby Stanchfield
Dawn: Adrienne Shelly
Origin: USA
Language: English
Released: 2007
Production: Michael Roiff; Night & Day Pictures; released by Fox Searchlight
Directed by: Adrienne Shelly
Written by: Adrienne Shelly
Cinematography by: Matthew Irving
Music by: Andrew Hollander
Sound: Fredrick Helm
Music Supervisor: Greg Danylyshyn, Gerry Cueller
Editing: Annette Davey
Production Design: Ramsey Avery
MPAA rating: PG-13
Running time: 107 minutes

REVIEWS

Entertainment Weekly. May 11, 2007, p. 58.
Los Angeles Times Online. May 2, 2007.
New York Times Online. May 2, 2007.
Newsweek Online. May 7, 2007.
Premiere Online. May 2, 2007.
Rolling Stone Online. April 18, 2007.
Variety Online. January 24, 2007.
Village Voice Online. May 1, 2007.

QUOTES

Old Joe (to Jenna): "What you do with food is unearthly."
Jenna: "When I get drunk I do stupid things, like sleep with my husband."

TRIVIA

Adrienne Shelly's daughter Sophie has a cameo at the end of the film.

AWARDS

Nomination:

Ind. Spirit 2008: Screenplay.

WALK HARD: THE DEWEY COX STORY

Life made him tough. Love made him strong.
Music made him hard.
—Movie tagline

Box Office: $18.3 million

Spoofing music and the way it has been mawkishly reflected in recent biopics (*Ray* [2004], *Walk the Line* [2005]) is clearly not the most challenging target for satire but the team behind *Walk Hard: The Dewey Cox Story* display such a consistent commitment to their subject that their willingness to do nearly anything to provoke laughter is infectious. Like a lot of the biopics it spoofs, *Walk Hard* falls into the trap of believing that being repetitive is effective, which leads to the largely one-joke film feeling much longer than its actual running time, but the performances are funny enough to keep the paper-thin concept from wearing out its welcome. *Walk Hard* may play the same comedic tune at least once too often, but it remains undeniably catchy.

John C. Reilly plays the title character, Dewey Cox, in what is, for at least the first two acts, primarily a note-for-note parody of James Mangold's *Walk the Line*. Like the original "Man in Black," Johnny Cash, Dewey's brother, his father's favorite son, passed away in a horrible accident (the film should serve as a warning to kids interested in playing "machete fight"). Cox tries to escape the shadow of his brother's death through music and starts recording his own songs, including the hilarious title track and several others. He marries an unsupportive wife who he leaves to take care of his ever-expanding family while he goes on tour and falls for a regular stage partner. Dewey Cox dabbles in drugs, goes to jail, falls to the bottom of the musical ladder and eventually stages a late-career comeback. The script for *Walk Hard* is incredibly loyal to all of the major beats of *Walk the Line* with new music and more below-the-belt humor thrown in.

Like the biopics it parodies, the music drives the action in *Walk Hard: The Dewey Cox Story*. Reilly and his team wrote and recorded dozens of new tracks for the movie and while they did it with their tongues firmly in their cheeks, what is most astonishing is that a few of the Cox tunes are shockingly catchy, while not forgetting to be hilariously dirty at the same time. "Let's Duet" (with the emphasis strong enough on the last two syllables that the *e* sounds more like an *i*), the title track, and "Beautiful Ride" are some of the best movie tunes of the last few years, comedy or otherwise. The clear devotion to the creation of material that could be both funny and musically well written lends an air of authenticity to the entirety of *Walk Hard* that cannot be underestimated. The songs could have just been filler for the physical comedy in between, but they were clearly just as important a part of the production of *Walk Hard* as any element of the film.

The best songs on paper still need a great band to make them work on camera and the perfectly cast ensemble hit almost all the right notes. Reilly has long been one of the most consistent actors in comedy or drama and he is completely fearless as Dewey Cox, selling every ridiculous note of the story without ever winking at the camera as a lot of lesser actors would. A supporting team that includes Jenna Fischer, Kristen Wiig, Tim Meadows, and cameos by Paul Rudd, Jack Black, and more, provide the perfect backing band for Reilly. There is not an unlikable or off performance in *Walk Hard: The Dewey Cox Story*.

All that holds *Walk Hard* back from pure musical comedy genius is the sense that the joke has worn treacherously thin before the final act has begun. Even the most talented and devoted ensemble can fall into the deadly trap of "third act comedy," where the audience has heard most of the jokes before and can see all of the new ones coming from a mile away. For example, when the "wrong son died" beat is hit for the sixth and seventh time, it produces more eye-rolling than laughter, even if the source (that the beat was hit at least that many times in *Walk the Line* for dramatic purpose) may be true. Parodies, especially of stories as well known as that of Johnny Cash, are particularly prone to the pitfalls of predictability and *Walk Hard* definitely grows stale before the final tune is played. It may be very well made and consistently enjoyable, but when the credits roll it is

hard to kick the feeling that the creators told only one joke—a funny joke, but one joke nonetheless.

Brian Tallerico

CREDITS

Dewey Cox: John C. Reilly
Darlene Madison: Jenna Fischer
Pa Cox: Raymond J. Barry
Edith: Kristen Wiig
Sam: Tim Meadows
L'Chai'm: Harold Ramis
Ma Cox: Margo Martindale
Theo: Chris Parnell
Dave: Matt Besser
Schwartzberg: David Krumholtz
Buddy Holly: Frankie Muniz
Elvis: Jack White
George Harrison: Justin Long
John Lennon: Paul Rudd
Ringo Starr: Jason Schwartzman
Origin: USA
Language: English
Released: 2007
Production: Judd Apatow, Jake Kasdan, Clayton Townsend; Columbia Pictures, Relativity, Charlie Lyons; released by Sony Pictures Entertainment
Directed by: Jake Kasdan
Written by: Jake Kasdan, Judd Apatow
Cinematography by: Uta Briesewitz
Music by: Michael Andrews
Sound: Tateum Kohut
Music Supervisor: Manish Raval, Tom Wolfe
Editing: Tara Timpone, Steven Welch
Art Direction: Domenic Silvestri
Costumes: Debra McGuire
Production Design: Jefferson Sage
MPAA rating: R
Running time: 96 minutes

REVIEWS

Boston Globe Online. December 21, 2007.
Chicago Sun-Times Online. December 21, 2007.
Entertainment Weekly Online. December 12, 2007.
Hollywood Reporter Online. December 17, 2007.
Los Angeles Times Online. December 21, 2007.
New York Times Online. December 21, 2007.
Rolling Stone Online. December 13, 2007.
San Francisco Chronicle. December 20, 2007, p. E1.
Variety Online. December 14, 2007.
Washington Post. December 21, 2007, p. C7.

QUOTES

Nate: "Let's go play machete fight. Ain't no terrible tragedy's gonna happen today!"

TRIVIA

During the scene with the orchestra, a Sabian cymbal can be seen in the background. However, since Sabian Cymbals was founded in 1981 there is no way they could have been in use in 1966 (when the scene is set).

AWARDS

Nomination:

Golden Globes 2008: Actor—Mus./Comedy (Reilly), Song ("Walk Hard").

WAR

Vengeance is the ultimate weapon.
—Movie tagline

One wants justice, the other wants revenge.
—Movie tagline

Box Office: $22.5 million

War is an attempt to combine the martial arts genre, the Asian urban action genre associated with such directors as Johnnie To and John Woo, the chase film, and the plot twists of American crime films such as *Pulp Fiction* (1994) and *The Usual Suspects* (1995). While the film is moderately entertaining, director Philip G. Atwell and screenwriters Gregory J. Bradley and Lee Anthony Smith perhaps try to cram in too much and end up treating the genres they are trying to honor too superficially.

The film opens with Federal Bureau of Investigation agents Jack Crawford (Jason Statham) and Tom Lone (Terry Chen) tracking a former Central Intelligence Agency agent turned assassin known only as Rogue. (The film's original, better title was *Rogue*.) Lone shoots the fleeing Rogue in the face before he falls into San Francisco Bay, and the agents assume (hope) he is dead. Then a masked figure arrives at Lone's home to shoot him, his wife (Steph Song), and daughter (Annika Foo), leaving Crawford devastated.

A few years later, Rogue (Jet Li) appears to be resurrected with a new face. A San Francisco turf war has developed between a triad headed by Li Chang (John Lone) and the local yakusa run by Shiro Yanagawa (Ryo Ishibashi). Rogue, using the name Victor Shaw, appears to be a henchman for both sides. *War* leaves the viewer wondering if Rogue is a double agent or a ruthless opportunist or whether something else is going on.

Crawford, joined by agents Wick (Mathew St. Patrick) and Goi (Sung Kang), try to stop the war and find Rogue. The assassin is unusually elusive, seeming to have an almost mystical ability to appear and disappear at will. *War* builds toward a surprise plot twist, clearly influenced by *The Usual Suspects,* and to a confrontation between Rogue and Crawford.

Along the way are car and motorcycle chases, several shootouts, and fights with other weapons, including an automobile wheel tossed through a glass door. All the action sequences are well staged by Atwell, stunt coordinator Rocky Capella, and martial arts choreographer Casey Yuen, who has worked with Li and Statham several times. The best scene is a shootout in a Japanese restaurant, well edited by Scott Richter and reminiscent of the nightclub scene in Michael Mann's *Collateral* (2004). The grisliest scene is a bloody, realistic swordfight between Rogue and Shiro.

While these action sequences may lack originality, except for a nifty chase through enormous drainage pipes, they are quite effective. Cinematographer Pierre Morel gives San Francisco a noirish glimmer, with deep shades of black, green, and red. To make *War* something more than a popcorn film, it needs some thematic complexity and an emotional payoff, as with Andrew Lau and Alan Mak's *Infernal Affairs* (2002) and Mann's *Heat* (1995), which Atwell has cited as an influence and whose repetitive score composer Brian Tyler emulates. The film makes tentative steps toward some depth but never articulates its existential potential.

Despite his martial arts background, Li occasionally displays some acting skill, especially in *Hero* (2002), but here he mostly provides a satisfied smirk. Statham, who worked with Li in *The One* (2001), tries to inject a degree of depth into Crawford, helping make him a conflicted, tortured soul. Speaking in a gruff whisper, Statham strives to hide his British accent, but it sneaks in from time to time. Devon Aoki brings some offbeat spunkiness to the role of Shiro's daughter and heir apparent. She seems to be having the most fun in the cast. Also good in small roles are Luis Guzmán as a shady friend of Crawford and Saul Rubinek as the disgraced plastic surgeon who transforms Rogue's appearance.

Atwell, a music-video director making his feature debut, shows considerable affinity for action, though the dialogue scenes drag a bit. *War* is reasonably entertaining and avoids the cynical treatment of violence that makes some films in this genre repellant. The most serious flaw is a too abrupt resolution to the central conflict, followed by a clumsily anticlimactic shot that undercuts the emotional resonance the filmmakers think they have achieved.

Michael Adams

CREDITS

Rogue/Victor Shaw: Jet Li
Jack Crawford: Jason Statham
Chang: John Lone
Kira: Devon Aoki
Benny: Luis Guzmán
Dr. Sherman: Saul Rubinek
Shiro: Ryo Ishibashi
Goi: Sung Kang
Wick: Mathew St. Patrick
Maria: Nadine Velazquez
Origin: USA
Language: English
Released: 2007
Production: Steve Chasman, Christopher Petzel, Jim Thompson; Mosaic Media Group, Fierce Entertainment; released by Lionsgate Films
Directed by: Philip G. Atwell
Written by: Lee Anthony Smith, Gregory J. Bradley
Cinematography by: Pierre Morel
Music by: Brian Tyler
Sound: Michael Williamson
Editing: Scott Richter
Art Direction: Catherine Ircha
Costumes: Cynthia Ann Summers
Production Design: Chris August
MPAA rating: R
Running time: 103 minutes

REVIEWS

Boston Globe Online. August 25, 2007.
Eye Weekly Online. August 23, 2007.
Hollywood Reporter Online. August 27, 2007.
Los Angeles Times Online. August 27, 2007.
New York Times Online. August 25, 2007.
San Francisco Chronicle. August 27, 2007, p. E1.
Variety Online. August 24, 2007.

QUOTES

Jack Crawford: "Get ready for a war."
Goi: "My gun's bigger than yours."

TRIVIA

Jet Li drives a Spyker C8 Spyder, which costs approximately $287,000.

THE WATER HORSE: LEGEND OF THE DEEP

Every big secret starts small.
—Movie tagline

How do you keep a secret this big?
—Movie tagline

Box Office: $40.4 million

The myth of the Loch Ness monster is playfully explored against a backdrop of World War II Scotland in the charming, earnest family film, *The Water Horse: Legend of the Deep.* Although the key to the film's success lies in the time-tested children's story of a boy who adopts an orphaned mythological creature, based on the book by Dick King-Smith, director Jay Russell makes the most of an immensely talented British cast, breathtaking scenery, and judicious use of computer-generated-imagery (CGI) effects.

Best known for their *The Chronicles of Narnia* series, producer Walden Media is also responsible for other films based on classic children's literature, including *Charlotte's Web* (2006), *Bridge to Terabithia* (2007), and *Nim's Island* (2008). *The Water Horse: Legend of the Deep* is a further example of their commitment to tasteful, high-brow, family-friendly films—the characters are rich and complex and sophisticated, psychological drama easily mixes with good-natured comedy. The filmmakers refuse to pander to an underage audience, making it ideal entertainment for adults and children.

Written by Robert Nelson Jacobs, *The Water Horse* is updated from the 1930s of King-Smith's book, when the Loch Ness monster originally came to the world's attention. The film takes place in wartime 1940s, lending more gravitas, and given a modern framing device. In modern-day Scotland, two young tourists enter a pub and encounter a grizzled local (Brian Cox) who tells them the "real," tale of the Loch Ness monster. Used in the *The Princess Bride* (1987), the same type of framing device was used to purposefully disrupt the story; here it also pulls the viewer out of the story, although either not intentionally or perhaps as some type of visual comedy. It works well as a bookend but it is jarring when the camera cuts to a close-up of Cox midway through the engrossing tale.

The tale that Cox relates concerns a lonely, sullen boy named Angus MacMorrow (Alex Etel), who, while his father Charlie (Craig Hall) is away in the Royal Navy, lives with his mother Anne (Emily Watson) and his older sister Kirstie (Priyanka Xi) in a house near Loch Ness, Scotland. The gorgeous, Scottish scenery is one of the film's chief attractions, thought most of the filming took place in New Zealand.

Although afraid of the water, Angus loves roaming around the loch, finding a giant, ancient-looking, rock-like orb one day that he carries home and hides in his father's workshop. Angus is surprised the following day when his "rock" cracks open, producing an adorable sea creature of unknown species. This early incarnation of the Loch Ness monster has been widely compared to E. T. and Shrek in appearance, with smooth skin, large, expressive eyes, tiny hornlike protrusions on his head, and a playful demeanor. The creature quickly bonds with Angus who feeds potatoes to his newly hatched sidekick and builds it a miniature swimming pool in a trashcan.

Adding to Angus's angst over keeping the newly-christened Crusoe hidden from his mother (who is sure to disapprove) is the fact that the MacMorrow home has been commandeered by the army, led by the staid Captain Hamilton (David Morrissey), who believes that the next Nazi invasion on British soil will be through Loch Ness while others, possibly more informed, simply believe he was gifted a post that would be far from the actual front lines of battle. Soldiers are posted throughout the home, including one commanding the kitchen with his watchful bulldog, delightfully named Churchill.

Viewers learn that the cause of Angus's aquaphobia may be rooted in the fact that his father has actually died aboard ship, a fact Anne tells the mysterious, handsome handyman Lewis Mowbray (Ben Chaplin) who has recently come to work on the MacMorrow estate. It becomes more difficult for Angus to hide Crusoe as Mowbray is dispatched to clean out the shed. Crusoe is moved inside to a guest bathroom bathtub, where a startled Kirstie first learns of the creature. Angus is again thwarted when Mowbray is sent to fix the bathroom's plumbing. Unable to conceal Crusoe, the surprised but pleased Mowbray eagerly launches into a history of the magical, mythical "water horse," a creature that is the sole of its kind, laying a single egg which hatches only after its death. Mowbray allows the children to have their secret, eventually helping Angus transport the hyper-expanding creature to the loch when it reaches the size of a large horse, without Anne suspecting a thing.

Much of the film's early humor comes from Crusoe waddling around the house looking for food and finding trouble instead. Several elaborate, mildly distressing chase scenes involving Churchill and Crusoe are staged for laughs. The pub-going locals are also employed for subplot comedy, as well. Two fishing buddies come upon the now fearsomely large Crusoe and, incorporating fact into fiction, humorously stage a fake photograph of the monster, which they believe will make them rich and famous. The photo used in the film is identical to the iconic photograph of "Nessie," later revealed as a hoax in 1992.

The story is also rich with psychological drama as Angus has refused to accept the fact of his father's death. In this way the film is, essentially, a coming-of-age story, with Angus working through his grief and fear with the

help of Crusoe and, in the end, being able to accept the fact that his father will never return. With both the captain and Mowbray showing an interest in Anne, the filmmakers slyly have her return interest in both. She eventually loses respect for the captain while gaining more for Mowbray, who turns out to be a decorated war hero but who, more importantly to her, is able to finally make her children laugh again.

The film certainly echoes *E.T. the Extra-Terrestrial* (1982), the story of a boy and his alien friend having adventures, and a few scenes are nearly lifted straight from Steven Spielberg's classic, but this film's point of departure comes as the creature reaches skyscraper heights and grows "wild," in the loch, at one point even turning on Angus. The computer-generated monstrosity blends well with the excellent live actors and background and is animated enough to be sympathetic without looking too artificial. The lively, engaging action scene showing Angus riding on Crusoe's back through the loch is one of the film's emotional as well as CGI highlights.

As viewers will have already guessed, Cox turns out to be the Angus of the tale and the film ends with another young boy finding another egg near Loch Ness. While such clichéd plot turns are occasionally used in *The Water Horse: Legend of the Deep,* the effect of the film as a whole more than forgives the use of the more well-worn storytelling devices.

Hilary White

CREDITS

Angus MacMorrow: Alex Etel
Anne MacMorrow: Emily Watson
Lewis Mowbray: Ben Chaplin
Capt. Hamilton: David Morrissey
Kirstie MacMorrow: Priyanka Xi
Old Angus: Brian Cox
Origin: Great Britain, USA
Language: English
Released: 2007
Production: Robert Bernstein, Douglas Rae, Barrie M. Osborne, Charlie Lyons; Walden Media, Beacon Pictures, Ecosse Films, Revolution Studios; released by Sony Pictures Entertainment
Directed by: Jay Russell
Written by: Robert Nelson Jacobs
Cinematography by: Oliver Stapleton
Music by: James Newton Howard
Sound: Tony Johnson
Music Supervisor: Denise Luiso
Editing: Mark Warner
Art Direction: Dan Hennah

Costumes: John Bloomfield
Production Design: Tony Burrough
MPAA rating: PG
Running time: 111 minutes

REVIEWS

Boston Globe Online. December 25, 2007.
Chicago Sun-Times Online. December 24, 2007.
Entertainment Weekly Online. December 12, 2007.
Hollywood Reporter Online. December 14, 2007.
Los Angeles Times Online. December 25, 2007.
New York Times Online. December 25, 2007.
San Francisco Chronicle. December 25, 2007, p. D1.
Variety Online. December 13, 2007.
Washington Post. December 25, 2007, p. C1.

TRIVIA

The title *Discovery* was used when the film was shipped to theaters.

WE OWN THE NIGHT

*Two brothers on opposite sides of the law. Beyond
their differences lies loyalty.*
—Movie tagline

Box Office: $28.6 million

As murder and other major felony crime rates in the city of New York continue to decline, *We Own the Night* takes the audience back to the violent, drug-riddled Big Apple of the late 1980s. On a par with *The Departed* (2006) and *Eastern Promises* (2007)—though not as compelling or controlled as either—the film charts the reconciliation of two brothers as they attempt to subvert Brooklyn's ruthless Russian mafia. Writer/director James Gray elicits believable performances from his stars, effectively ratchets up the suspense, and deftly orchestrates two standout action sequences. Unfortunately, plot contrivances in the final act cause the movie to founder, and the conclusion does not achieve the catharsis for which it was aiming.

As the story begins in 1988, Brighton Beach nightclub manager Bobby Green (Joaquin Phoenix) is moving up. He has a gorgeous, adoring girlfriend, Amada (Eva Mendes), and his boss, Buzhayev (Moni Moshonov), has offered him a chance to manage a spinoff of his El Caribe club in Manhattan. Unbeknownst to his employer and colleagues, Bobby (having forsaken his father's surname, Grusinsky) comes from a family of New York Police Department (NYPD) officers. His brother, Joseph (Mark Wahlberg), has just been

commended by the force and heads up an antinarcotics team, and his father, Bert (Robert Duvall), is the deputy chief of police. When Joseph and Bert ask Bobby to observe Buzhayev's nephew Vadim (Alex Veadov), a brutal drug dealer operating from inside the El Caribe, Bobby initially demurs. But after Vadim's thugs gun down Joseph in front of his home, Bobby decides to help the police catch his brother's attackers, eventually becoming an officer himself.

Although its story and characters are not especially novel, the film's four lead performers deliver fine turns here. As Bert, the father attempting to protect his sons from circling assassins, Duvall is a solid, reassuring presence. Wahlberg makes Joseph's descent from super-cop to traumatized survivor sympathetic, and Phoenix particularly shines when depicting a fearful Bobby caught in the crossfire between the cops and the mob. Phoenix's scenes with Mendes in the film's first half are another highlight; for this genre, they convey a surprising degree of warmth and intimacy.

What Phoenix is unable to make believable is Bobby's quick acceptance into the NYPD in the film's last act. In light of Bobby's ties to Vadim, it is not "untenable" that his father and brother would ask him to be an informant; that he is handed a badge and a gun so soon afterward seems utterly preposterous. As *Empire* critic Kim Newman remarked, "If the New York Police Department really worked like this, they'd be as terrifying as the mob they're supposed to be taking down." (That Phoenix looks somewhat ridiculous in an ill-fitting police cap does not help matters.) Because the details of earlier scenes are painstakingly specific and ring of verisimilitude—like the foil tins of homemade deviled eggs and macaroni and cheese served at Joseph's NYPD reception—glaring plot problems like these are all the more disappointing.

While *We Own the Night* will not be hailed for its credibility, it will likely be remembered for two stunningly executed action scenes. The first is when Bobby, wired by the police, infiltrates Vadim's drug warehouse. Sweating and woozy, Bobby betrays his nerves, arousing Vadim's suspicions. After the dealer discovers a microphone concealed in Bobby's lighter, a disorienting gunfight ensues, with bullets, blood, and bodies everywhere. Gray's depiction of the chaos is as skillful as it is frightening. The second scene is a virtuoso car chase on a rainy Queens highway. Driving in separate vehicles, Bert and Bobby are hunted by Vadim and his cronies. After his driver is shot, Bobby struggles to maintain control of the car, all the while watching in horror as Vadim's vehicle rushes toward his dad's. The driving rain and careening cars are depicted with a shaky handheld camera, creating a sickening sense of immediacy; heightening the tension are the pounding industrial sound effects, Mendes's screams, and Phoenix's labored breathing. Gray summons the stuff of nightmares to fashion the most memorable car chase in recent memory.

Considering Gray's flair for building suspense—and with a cast like this at his disposal—*We Own the Night* had the potential to be a much tighter, more potent film. While Gray demonstrates his chops as a director in several key scenes, his screenwriting still needs honing. But once he has (or pens himself) a better script, there is no telling what he might achieve.

Marisa Carroll

CREDITS

Bobby Green: Joaquin Phoenix
Joseph Grusinsky: Mark Wahlberg
Bert Grusinsky: Robert Duvall
Amada Juarez: Eva Mendes
Marat Buzhayev: Moni Moshonov
Vadim: Alex Veadov
Jumbo: Danny Hoch
Jack Shapiro: Tony Musante
Michael Solo: Antoni Corone
Origin: USA
Language: English
Released: 2007
Production: Nick Wechsler, Marc Butan, Joaquin Phoenix, Mark Wahlberg; Twenty9Twenty9 Productions; released by Sony Pictures
Directed by: James Gray
Written by: James Gray
Cinematography by: Joaquin Baca-Asay
Music by: Wojciech Kilar
Sound: Thomas Varga
Music Supervisor: Dana Sano
Editing: John Axelrad
Art Direction: James Feng
Costumes: Michael Clancy
Production Design: Ford Wheeler
MPAA rating: R
Running time: 117 minutes

REVIEWS

Boston Globe Online. October 12, 2007.
Chicago Sun-Times Online. October 12, 2007.
Entertainment Weekly Online. October 10, 2007.
Hollywood Reporter Online. June 1, 2007.
Los Angeles Times Online. October 12, 2007.
New York Times Online. October 12, 2007.
Rolling Stone Online. October 19, 2007.
San Francisco Chronicle. October 12, 2007, p. E1.

Variety Online. May 27, 2007.
Washington Post. October 12, 2007, p. C1.

QUOTES

Joseph Grusinsky (after giving his brother a gun): "Better to be judged by 12 than carried by six."

TRIVIA

Mark Wahlberg and Joaquin Phoenix previously worked with director James Gray on *The Yards* (2000).

WHY DID I GET MARRIED?

(Tyler Perry's Why Did I Get Married?)

Because we complete each other's sentences.
—Movie tagline

Because two are stronger than one.
—Movie tagline

Because every moment we share is better than the last.
—Movie tagline

Because no one inspires me more.
—Movie tagline

Box Office: $55.2 million

Tyler Perry adapts another of his highly successful plays to film in *Why Did I Get Married?* (also known as *Tyler Perry's Why Did I Get Married?*), his most refined work to date. Earlier in 2007, Perry did away with his female drag persona Madea and produced the likable comedy *Daddy's Little Girls*. The writer/director continues to evolve in *Why Did I Get Married?*, which strays even further from his usual, hysteria-filled slapstick humor and uses his most talented African American cast yet to dip his toe into the psychological drama of dysfunctional marriage. The Perry franchise mainstays are still apparent and the drama mingles, sometimes uneasily, with his usual interesting, atypical characters; religious fervor; loud, over-the-top dialogue; melodrama; and farce.

Perry hits a nerve with his loyal audience, who continue to see his films in droves without prior press screenings and, usually, despite lack of critical acclaim. The concept of *Why Did I Get Married?* is certainly nothing new—four couples meet in a snowy Colorado resort to dissect their marital issues—its middle-age, middle-class, navel-gazing reminiscent of *The Big Chill* (1983). An able cast, however, fleshes out the generally well-written characters and gains the audience sympathy crucial to pave over the occasional plot pitfalls and telegraphed action.

Among the couples, all friends since college, by far the most sympathetic character is Sheila (Jill Scott), the sweet, pious, overweight wife of the cruel Mike (Richard T. Jones), who taunts her so mercilessly while blatantly flaunting his sexy mistress that it is difficult to watch. When Sheila is ejected from the flight west for being unable to fit into one seat, Mike proceeds with his mistress, Trina (Denise Boutte) while he instructs Sheila to either drive or take the bus. Perry courageously resists the urge to couch the situation in humor, letting Sheila's pathos touch the audience unvarnished. Better known as a singer, it is Scott's first film role and though her naturally fuller figure is also heavily padded, her natural likability shines through.

Sheila's counterpoint is feisty, opinionated Angela (Tasha Smith), who regards her husband Marcus (Michael Jai White), a former professional football player who now works at her salon, as a failure, and she constantly and publicly berates him. Marcus deals with his frustration by having an affair and ends up with a venereal disease. Terry (Tyler Perry) is a put-upon pediatrician whose wife Diane (Sharon Leal) puts her career as a lawyer before her husband and young daughter.

In what may be termed a comeback, Janet Jackson is featured as Patricia, a best-selling author and psychologist who draws upon her real-life relationships and experiences for her books. Her husband Gavin (Malik Yoba), is an architect trying to help his wife overcome her grief over their lost son. Also along for the bumpy ride is the local sheriff, Troy (Lamman Rucker), who persuades Sheila, arriving later than the rest in a rental car, to avoid the snowy roads and stay the night with him in the sheriff's office.

During the course of their tempestuous annual retreat, a number of secrets are revealed as the couples wrestle with a lengthy and thorny list of problems that include, but are not limited to, infidelity, paternity, humiliation, emasculation, and grief. Ultimately, these issues will be resolved all too neatly in the end with some, naturally, also mined for too-obvious comedy. One glaring example—one of the film's set pieces—is a scene that culminates with Sheila hitting Mike over the head with a wine bottle after learning of his affair.

After a meaty lead role in *Poetic Justice* (1993), Jackson next appeared on the big screen in *Nutty Professor II: The Klumps* (2000). While the role of Patricia is certainly Jackson's best since her debut and her performance is acclaimed, she is nonetheless overshadowed by her talented castmates, especially Scott and the scene-stealing Smith, who, in addition to her shrewishness,

also has the irresistible appeal of telling it exactly like it is.

Although on the surface they are liars and adulterers, Perry paints his men, who exhibit typically ascribed male behaviors such as failure to communicate, heavy drinking, and workaholism, more flatteringly than his women. The dialogue is of the mainstream, comedy variety with the usual colloquialisms trotted out, and in some cases, walked around the block a few times. Perry has purged the film of the play's musical numbers, odd considering the casting of singers Scott and Jackson, instead utilizing original compositions by Jay Weigel, who also scored Perry's *Madea's Family Reunion* (2006).

While the issues explored are too numerous and resolved too patly and easily in this morality play, the beautifully shot, energetic, and involving film certainly qualifies as solid, mainstream entertainment and another crowd-pleasing triumph for a more restrained Perry.

Hilary White

CREDITS

Terry: Tyler Perry
Patricia: Janet Jackson
Sheila: Jill Scott
Gavin: Malik Yoba
Mike: Richard T. Jones
Marcus: Michael Jai White
Troy: Lamman Rucker
Diane: Sharon Leal
Angela: Tasha Smith
Trina: Denise Boutte
Origin: USA
Language: English
Released: 2007
Production: Tyler Perry, Reuben Cannon; released by Lionsgate
Directed by: Tyler Perry
Written by: Tyler Perry
Cinematography by: Toyomichi Kurita
Music by: Aaron Zigman
Music Supervisor: Joel High
Editing: Maysie Hoy
Art Direction: Lauren Fitzsimmons
Sound: Shirley Libby
Costumes: Keith Lewis
Production Design: Ina Mayhew
MPAA rating: PG-13
Running time: 113 minutes

REVIEWS

Boston Globe Online. October 13, 2007.
Boxoffice Online. October 12, 2007.

Entertainment Weekly Online. October 17, 2007.
Hollywood Reporter Online. October 15, 2007.
Los Angeles Times Online. October 15, 2007.
New York Times Online. October 13, 2007.
Variety Online. October 12, 2007.

QUOTES

Trina: "You belong in the kitchen."
Angela: "And you belong on the corner. Need a pimp?"

WILD HOGS

Four guys from the suburbs hit the road...and the road hit back.
—Movie tagline

A lot can happen on the road to nowhere.
—Movie tagline

Ride hard...or stay home!
—Movie tagline

Box Office: $168.3 million

The gulf in taste between professional movie critics and casual moviegoers became apparent yet again with the release of Walt Becker's action comedy *Wild Hogs*. While critics generally gave *Wild Hogs* a hearty trouncing, Ty Burr of the *Boston Globe* was one of the kinder reviewers, writing, "*Wild Hogs* wants to be as dumb as they come, but there are smart people involved no matter how they try to hide it." Regardless, moviegoers flocked to the film, which debuted at number one and grossed more than $168 million in the United States.

At a screening at a Los Angeles-area theater, the demographics of the theatergoers mirrored those of the actors on screen. Baby boomers went to see *Wild Hogs* for several reasons. The film featured familiar stars Tim Allen, John Travolta, William H. Macy, and Martin Lawrence. With such veterans on board, it was pretty much guaranteed that however terrible the script was, the actors would bring a certain professionalism to the proceedings. Secondly, in 2007 there was such a dearth of films aimed at audiences beyond adolescent age, older viewers were likely willing to see just about anything aimed at their demographic. And finally, the film is about suburban people experiencing a midlife crisis—a topic familiar to many of the intended viewers.

The aforementioned stars and their winning performances are what makes *Wild Hogs* watchable. This quartet collectively combines comedic talent and powerful acting chops and are able to cover all the bases without breaking a sweat. If there is a silly reaction shot that must be made, rest assured that Lawrence will execute it perfectly. Macy has no trouble nailing the role

of a nervous, nerdy guy who never gets the girl. Allen waltzes through the film with his usual sarcastic swagger. And Travolta, with his sometimes high-pitched voice and nervous fidgeting, seems to be having a fine time hamming it up. The male-bonding/road-movie premise, however, and predictable testosterone-infused humor is shockingly banal, especially for an actor of Macy's stature, but Allen, Travolta, and Lawrence have all had their share of hackneyed material. Gene Seymour of *Newsday* complained that all of the actors "are shoehorned into every threadbare gag about bodily waste, property damage and haphazard homoeroticism that can withstand a PG-13 rating."

The "Wild Hogs" of the title are a group of four settled suburban men who ride motorcycles. In recent years, most of their road trips have only been to the local bar to have a weekly beer. When Woody Stevens (John Travolta), the alpha-male of the group, tells them that he wants to go on a real cross-country road trip, it makes the others nervous. Doug Madsen (Tim Allen), a former wild man, is now a settled dentist who fears he cannot get away from work. Bobby Davis (Martin Lawrence), a plumber who dreams of writing a book, knows his overbearing wife will never stand for such a trip. Dudley Frank (William H. Macy), a shy computer geek who can never get a date, is the only one who is willing to go. (Dudley's name is indicative of the movie's subtlety.) What Woody fails to mention is the real reason he wants to get out of town: His supermodel wife is leaving him and he has just lost his considerable fortune.

Woody eventually sells his friends on the trip and the men set out for adventure. They find it in the form of Jack (Ray Liotta), who heads a group of "real" bikers. His gang takes an instant dislike to the Wild Hogs and he promptly steal Dudley's bike. When Woody secretly goes back for revenge, his plans go awry and he ends up torching Jack's beloved biker bar. Woody does not reveal to his buddies the real reason he suddenly and urgently wants to get back on the road but, in actuality, it is so the film may chronicle more musty, retreaded escapades.

Along the way, predictable hilarity ensues. Dudley eats some overly hot chili and his eyes comically bug out, the Wild Hogs' tent burns down, and Woody gets hit in the face with a large bird. The jokes that land with the biggest thud are the frequent homosexual cracks. In one instance, the four men wake up tentless in the morning and are forced to huddle together to stay warm. A stern highway patrolman (John C. McGinley) finds them and immediately wants to join what he assumes is a big gay party. The many gay jokes are not only offensive, but they show a deplorable immaturity from screenwriter Brad Copeland, better remembered from his Emmy-nominated work on the television series *Arrested Development* (2003–2006).

Jill Hamilton

CREDITS

Woody Stevens: John Travolta
Doug Madsen: Tim Allen
Bobby Davis: Martin Lawrence
Dudley Frank: William H. Macy
Jack: Ray Liotta
Maggie: Marisa Tomei
Red: Kevin Durand
Murdock: M. C. Gainey
Kelly Madsen: Jill Hennessy
Karen Davis: Tichina Arnold
Charley: Stephen Tobolowsky
Highway Patrolman: John C. McGinley
Origin: USA
Language: English
Released: 2007
Production: Mike Tollin, Brian Robbins, Todd Lieberman; Touchstone Pictures; released by Buena Vista
Directed by: Walt Becker
Written by: Brad Copeland
Cinematography by: Robbie Greenberg
Music by: Teddy Castellucci
Sound: Steve Cantamessa
Editing: Christopher Greenbury, Stuart Pappé
Art Direction: Gregory Van Horn
Costumes: Penny Rose
Production Design: Michael Corenblith
MPAA rating: PG-13
Running time: 99 minutes

REVIEWS

Chicago Sun-Times Online. March 2, 2007.
Entertainment Weekly. March 9, 2007, p. 85.
Hollywood Reporter Online. February 27, 2007.
Los Angeles Times Online. March 2, 2007.
New York Times Online. March 2, 2007.
San Francisco Chronicle. March 2, 2007, p. E4.
Variety Online. February 24, 2007.
Washington Post Online. March 2, 2007.

QUOTES

Doug Madsen: "Woody, sorry I said you had ego issues."
Woody Stevens: "Sorry I said you were a pussy."
Doug Madsen: "You didn't call me a pussy."

Woody Stevens: "Well, not to your face, but that's what I was thinking."

TRIVIA

The script originally identified the bad guys as Hell's Angels until the motorcycle gang sued Disney.

THE WIND THAT SHAKES THE BARLEY

Box Office: $1.8 million

British director Ken Loach's uncompromising historical drama, *The Wind That Shakes the Barley,* immediately thrusts the viewer into the chaotic world of British-occupied 1920s Ireland. After a rousing hurling match surrounded by lush green fields, the Irish players return to their modest cottage only to be attacked by the thuggish "Black and Tan" squads patrolling the countryside who quickly dispatch a seventeen-year-old in front of his friends and family. His crime: refusing to give his name in English. The contrast between the bucolic sporting match and the brutal bloody aftermath is immediate and its impact as forceful as the tactics used by the British. The injustice faced by the Irish immediately draws the audience in to their plight. But Loach's period piece takes an even darker turn after the Irish have unified to vanquish their common enemy and obtain Irish independence and political in-fighting have split them into factions that cause civil war and literally pits brother against brother.

The film's title refers to the song of the same name by Robert Dwyer Joyce about the 1798 Irish Rebellion and is beautifully sung by Peggy Lynch at seventeen-year-old Micheail's (Laurence Barry) funeral and its lyrics sadly echo the trajectory of the film's protagonist. The song speaks of a man who chooses the cause of his country over his own life and love. Despite the attacks and the murder of his young friend, Damien O'Donovan (Cillian Murphy) is a medical student determined to leave Ireland to pursue his career as a doctor in London. Another run-in with the British, who attack the driver at the train station where Damien is to depart, causes him to rethink his decision and embark upon a war that will forever alter the course of his life.

Damien's brother Teddy (Pádraic Delaney) is one of leaders of the Irish Republican Army (IRA) and the relationship of the brothers frames the film's political drama. Initially, Teddy, a former seminary student, is painted as the idealist whose belief in a free Ireland drives his every move. Damien follows in his footsteps and becomes as committed to the cause as Teddy, causing him to commit heinous acts he never would have believed himself capable of. A particularly harrowing scene shows the extent of his dedication when he is forced to shoot a childhood friend who informed the British of the IRA's whereabouts on one occasion. As he loads his revolver, a rueful Damien says, "I studied anatomy for five years, Dan. And now I'm going to shoot this man in the head. I've known Chris Reilly since he was a child. I hope this Ireland we're fighting for is worth it." By the time a truce with the British results in the Anglo-Irish Treaty of 1921—creating the Irish Free State with Northern Ireland remaining within the British Commonwealth—Damien has become the idealist, refusing, along with a number of Irish, to accept the compromised terms of Irish freedom and continues the hopeless fight for complete independence. Teddy is now on the other side, enforcing the treaty, and the film concludes as he personally oversees his brother's execution.

Although the British are clearly put in an oppressive light, Loach and his frequent collaborator, screenwriter Paul Laverty, make clear and logical arguments for both sides of the Irish civil conflict, and each side has a valid point of view. It is merely a question of choosing which side and soon it becomes brother against brother. The use of the personal to illustrate the political works especially well in this low-budget, independent film, for which Loach received the Palme d'Or at the 2006 Cannes Film Festival. Critical acclaim for the film was widespread with the exception of the British press, which attacked the filmmaker and the film's controversial subject matter.

Criticism was also leveled against the film's violence. Of course, in a war film violence is inevitable, but it is used economically and with restraint to great effect by Loach. The scene in which Teddy and the other members of the IRA are imprisoned and Teddy is tortured by the British using pliers to pull out his fingernails is an early example. Damien's love interest, the strong-willed Sinead (Orla Fitzgerald), has her long red hair cruelly shorn by the Black and Tans. Obvious budget constraints also limited the extent of the conflicts, with the British occupation looking decidedly like the same half dozen soldiers in each scene; when the IRA take out an equal number of officers, the conflict is ended and a truce is reached.

Murphy, who is best known in the United States for his role as the villain Scarecrow in *Batman Begins* (2005), makes use of his native Irish accent and turns in a nuanced and highly believable performance as the reluctant rebel turned committed revolutionary. Delaney has the more true to life but thankless role of idealist turned realist and lends authenticity to each scene he is in. The two brothers share a pragmatic approach to the war and their parts in it, and the actors bring the warring siblings to life with engrossing realism.

Hilary White

CREDITS

Damien O'Donovan: Cillian Murphy
Dan: Liam Cunningham
Bernadette: Mary Murphy
Teddy O'Donovan: Pádraic Delaney
Sinead: Orla Fitzgerald
Peggy: Mary Riordan
Micheail: Laurence Barry
Origin: Spain, Italy, Germany, Ireland, Great Britain
Language: English
Released: 2006
Production: Rebecca O'Brien; Sixteen Films, Matador Films; released by IFC Films
Directed by: Ken Loach
Written by: Paul Laverty
Cinematography by: Barry Ackroyd
Music by: George Fenton
Sound: Ray Beckett, Kevin Brazier
Editing: Jonathan Morris
Art Direction: Michael Higgins, Mark Lowry
Costumes: Eimer Ni Mhaoldomhnaigh
Production Design: Fergus Clegg
MPAA rating: Unrated
Running time: 127 minutes

REVIEWS

Boston Globe Online. March 16, 2007.
Boxoffice Online. March 16, 2007.
Entertainment Weekly. March 23, 2007, p. 44.
Hollywood Reporter Online. May 19, 2006.
Los Angeles Times Online. March 16, 2007.
New York Times Online. March 16, 2007.
New Yorker Online. March 19, 2007.
Observer Online. June 25, 2006.
Premiere Magazine Online. March 15, 2007.
Variety Online. May 18, 2006.
Village Voice Online. March 13, 2007.

QUOTES

Finbar: "Mercenaries! That were paid to come over here to make us crawl, and to wipe us out. We've just sent a message to the British cabinet that will echo and reverberate around the world! If they bring their savagery over here, we will meet it with a savagery of our own!"

TRIVIA

The man playing the piano in the cinema scene is Neil Brand, one of Britain's foremost silent cinema accompanists.

WRISTCUTTERS: A LOVE STORY

There is love after death.
—Movie tagline

Life is a trip, but the afterlife is one hell of a ride.
—Movie tagline

Wristcutters: A Love Story is an imaginative indie film that posits an afterlife inhabited solely by suicides. It is a depressing but not a horrible existence, a desolate landscape where, as the protagonist observes, everything is like our world, "just a little worse." Based on a novella by Israeli writer Etgar Keret called "Kneller's Happy Campers" (from the collection *The Bus Driver Who Wanted to Be God and Other Stories*), the movie, helmed by Croatian director Goran Dukic, is a bit long and rambling even at eighty-eight minutes. But the appealing lead actors lend the story an offbeat charm and poignancy, and the vision of this particular afterlife is, to say the least, original.

Patrick Fugit stars as Zia, who thoroughly cleans his shabby apartment before slashing his wrists in his bathroom sink over the breakup with his beautiful girlfriend, Desiree (Leslie Bibb). The next time we see him, he is in the netherworld and working at a dingy restaurant called Kamikaze Pizza. Zia makes friends with Eugene (Shea Whigham), a Russian who lives with his parents and brother, all suicides. When Zia learns that Desiree is also in this world, he persuades Eugene to join him on a road trip to find her. They pick up a pretty hitchhiker, Mikal (Shannyn Sossamon), who believes that she does not belong here and wants to talk to whoever is in charge. Zia's quest to find Desiree and Mikal's quest to find some authority figure become the narrative spine of the film.

As the road trip progresses, both Zia and Eugene fall a bit for Mikal, and a low-key rivalry develops. In one funny scene, when Mikal wants to drive, Eugene sits cramped in the front seat between her and Zia so that they will not be together; even in the afterlife, jealousy, it seems, is a constant. But Dukic seems more interested in conveying a certain mood than in telling a conventional love story (although Zia and Mikal's growing attraction is persuasive). The desert highway feels forsaken, and cinematographer Vanja Cernjul's washed-out colors set just the right mood for a spiritual limbo.

Certain details not found in the original story are clever, such as the bottom of Eugene's old jalopy being a

kind of black hole where, if someone drops something, it is lost forever. While many of the episodes do not go anywhere in particular or serve a narrative arc, they show the characters developing a rapport, as when Mikal vandalizes a sign and then Zia pleads with a policeman on her behalf. And then, as with many characters, we see the wound from the cop's suicide—a darkly comic touch.

The movie takes a turn when the threesome literally run into the loopy Kneller (Tom Waits) asleep in the middle of the road and taking a break from searching for his lost dog. Kneller runs a camp where small miracles such as levitation occur. The centerpiece of this section of the movie is the meeting of a cult where the messianic leader called King (Will Arnett) kills himself in a failed attempt to separate his body from his soul. Unfortunately, this narrative detour is murky and unsatisfying. Zia finally finds Desiree, who, it turns out, killed herself in the wake of King's first suicide and became his acolyte. By now, however, because Zia and Mikal have fallen for each other, the loss of Desiree is no longer important. Perhaps the presence of a self-proclaimed messiah inherently has more resonance in a novella set in Israel and does not translate easily to an American setting, where it is simply not apparent what we are supposed to think of this crazy figure who ends up killing himself twice. Evacuating everyone in the aftermath of King's ceremony, Kneller is revealed to be not a suicide but rather an undercover agent of the people in charge. But what this sequence is supposed to say about false messiahs, religious fervor of the masses, or the exact role of the authorities in this world is not clear. It is a muddled climax to an otherwise enjoyable, off-kilter film.

What is perhaps most surprising about *Wristcutters* is its unabashedly hopeful final scene, a stark departure from Keret's story. In both the novella and the movie, Mikal gets to return to her life, but, in the film, Kneller gives Zia a second chance at life as well, and both Mikal and Zia wake up in the same hospital room. The happy ending pleasantly defies our expectations, and the smiles that close the film are well earned.

Wristcutters: A Love Story is a shaggy-dog of a story. While the road trip is compelling only intermittently and the treatment of religion in the final act is more confusing than enlightening, the likable actors have a nice, easygoing chemistry and breathe life into a story whose overall conception is, given the downbeat subject matter, surprisingly refreshing. The film's absurd moments, eccentric point of view on a bleak afterlife, and ultimately life-affirming message about getting a second chance to appreciate one's time on Earth are all magical in their own strange way and compensate for the film's narrative shortcomings.

Peter N. Chumo II

CREDITS

Zia: Patrick Fugit
Mikal: Shannyn Sossamon
Eugene: Shea Whigham
Desiree: Leslie Bibb
Kneller: Tom Waits
Mike: Mark Boone Junior
Eugene's Mother: Mary Pat Gleason
Erik: Abraham Benrubi
King: Will Arnett
Jim: Clayne Crawford
Origin: USA
Language: English
Released: 2006
Production: Adam Sherman, Chris Coen, Tatiana Kelly, Mikal P. Lazarev; Halcyon Productions, Crispy Films, No Matter Pictures; released by Autonomous Films
Directed by: Goran Dukic
Written by: Goran Dukic

Cinematography by: Vanja Cernjul
Music by: Bobby Johnston
Sound: Lee Ascher
Music Supervisor: Robin Urdang
Editing: Jonathan Alberts
Production Design: Linda Sena
Costumes: Carla Biggert
MPAA rating: R
Running time: 88 minutes

REVIEWS

Entertainment Weekly Online. October 17, 2007.
Hollywood Reporter Online. January 25, 2006.
New York Times Online. October 19, 2007.
Variety Online. January 25, 2006.
Village Voice Online. October 16, 2007.

QUOTES

Mikal: "Who the hell wants to be stuck in a place where you can't even smile?"

TRIVIA

Eugene kills himself by pouring "Dead Guy Ale" onto his guitar and electrocuting himself.

Y-Z

YEAR OF THE DOG

Has the world left you a stray?
—Movie tagline

Box Office: $1.5 million

As a screenwriter, Mike White has proven that he can write for the mainstream in such films as *School of Rock* (2003) and *Nacho Libre* (2006). But it is clear his heart is in quirkier fare, such as *The Good Girl* (2002) and, especially, the peculiar *Chuck & Buck* (2000), which he also appeared in. *Year of the Dog* is the first film White has both written and directed and it definitely leans toward the offbeat. Manohla Dargis wrote in the *New York Times* that "*Year of the Dog* is exactly the kind of story you would expect Mr. White to make for his directing debut. It's funny ha-ha but firmly in touch with its downer side, which means it's also funny in a kind of existential way."

White wrote the starring role in the film specifically for *Saturday Night Live* (*SNL*) alumnus Molly Shannon. The two are well matched as both thrive in uncomfortable, awkward situations: White's Buck in *Chuck & Buck* and Shannon's Mary Catherine from *SNL* were both grotesque characters that challenged audiences. In *Year of the Dog*, Shannon's performance as Peggy is much more subtle, but the film is still filled with awkward, uncomfortable moments. Kevin Crust of the *Los Angeles Times* wrote: "With pathos competing equally against the often pungent laughs for the audience's attention, it's a movie that is both unsettling and amusing, most comparable to *Chuck & Buck* in tone."

Peggy is a forty-something frump who works in a bland cubicle-filled office where some ill-defined, uninteresting business is conducted. Robin (Josh Pais), is her money-grubbing, sullen boss who constantly complains about real or imagined slights from his higher-ups. Her vivacious coworker, Layla (Regina King), regales Peggy endlessly with the ups-and-downs of her relationship with her straying boyfriend. If only she could get him to propose, Layla tells Peggy, she could stop worrying. Her brother Pier (Tom McCarthy) and his wife, Bret (Laura Dern), are the sort of modern, hyper-protective parents who must carefully inspect all new toys before allowing them to be played with. They pity poor, lonely Peggy.

In the film's early scenes, Peggy does not say much, but the audience can glean a good deal about her character simply by watching her reactions to those around her. She murmurs sympathetically to Layla, assuages Robin's ego and dutifully listens while her sister-in-law gives excessive details about the lice breakout in the first grade and its ensuing political consequences. Peggy is content with her mundane life, finding happiness and comfort in her precious puppy, Pencil. When Pencil wanders out one night, accidentally ingests something toxic and dies the next day, Peggy's life is thrown completely off-track. She meets a sweet fellow animal lover, Newt (Peter Sarsgaard), a volunteer at the A.S.P.C.A. Newt introduces her to the idea of being a vegan and gets her interested in animal rights issues. She begins falling in love with Newt and starts thinking that they might be able to have a satisfying relationship. Her hopes are dashed when Newt announces that he is incapable of such a relationship and is basically celibate.

Pencil's death, Newt's rejection, and her newfound passion for animal rights issues all mix together in Peggy's brain in an unhealthy fashion and she starts becoming unhinged. After her boss refuses to sign an animal rights petition, she forges his signature. Soon, she starts signing office checks in his name and sends them to animal rights organizations. She gets drunk and ruins her sister-in-law's fur coats. She rescues fifteen dogs from the pound and lets them run wild in her house. At her lowest point, she lies in bed, jobless and surrounded by dogs who seem intent on chewing her entire house apart.

Shannon's startling performance as Peggy, sweet and sad, carries the film. As Dargis observed, "so much of the performance willfully goes against the grain, pushing at us with naked, frenzied need that can feel embarrassing and, at times, almost grotesque." Peggy does not always make intelligent choices and is not even particularly likable, but she is endearingly human. Although focusing on animal rights, White's film carries a more subtle and human message: Peggy's passion for the cause and her love of animals is where she finds her true self. Although she becomes overzealous and strident, struggling to maintain her sanity, her heart is in the right place.

Jill Hamilton

CREDITS

Peggy: Molly Shannon
Newt: Peter Sarsgaard
Bret: Laura Dern
Pier: Tom McCarthy
Layla: Regina King
Al: John C. Reilly
Robin: Josh Pais
Origin: USA
Language: English
Released: 2007
Production: Dede Gardner, Mike White, Ben LeClair; Plan B Entertainment, Rip Cord; released by Paramount Vantage
Directed by: Mike White
Written by: Mike White
Cinematography by: Tim Orr
Music by: Christophe Beck
Sound: Aaron Glascock, Curt Schulkey
Editing: Dody Dorn
Art Direction: Macie Vener
Costumes: Nancy Steiner
Production Design: Daniel Bradford
MPAA rating: PG-13
Running time: 98 minutes

REVIEWS

Entertainment Weekly Online. April 11, 2007.
Hollywood Reporter Online. January 21, 2007.
Los Angeles Times Online. April 13, 2007.
New York Times Online. April 13, 2007.
Variety Online. January 21, 2007.
Village Voice Online. April 10, 2007.

QUOTES

Layla: "Even retarded, crippled people get married."

TRIVIA

Molly Shannon is actually allergic to dogs.

AWARDS

Nomination:

Ind. Spirit 2008: Screenplay.

YOU KILL ME

Love is always worth another shot.
    —Movie tagline

"Hi, my name is Frank. I'm an alcoholic. I kill people for a living…This is anonymous, right?"
    —Movie tagline

Box Office: $2.4 million

Ben Kingsley has played many distinguished roles, not to mention saintly ones, so when he attempts to portray a small-time gangster in John Dahl's *You Kill Me,* it is a stretch. But then the whole movie is a reach, a deadpan satire of the rehabilitation of an alcoholic hit man. Kingsley plays Frank, the hit man with the drinking problem, as a guy who seems not to understand that what he does for a living is unusual or disturbing; he is ridiculously parochial in his view, and the character has little resonance either as a comic foil or an antihero.

That is certainly not all Kingsley's fault, for his protagonist is saddled with a conceit that seems like something Dahl himself might have thought up when he had one too many. Dahl has already proven himself a master of absurdist black comedy (in such masterfully infuriating films as *Red Rock West* [1992]); here, however, he stumbles over his own inability to keep the film's one-note joke going. Playing the story straight does not yield enough laughs, so it ends up being an off-kilter character study, and as that it fails badly.

The opening scene deftly establishes Frank's milieu and problem. It shows him opening his front door, taking a swig of whiskey, throwing the bottle down his snow-covered front walk, shoveling his way to it, taking another swig, and by these successive steps getting the walk cleared. It is a metaphor for his life, which proceeds only from one drink to the next. Frank is assigned by his mob family to make a hit on a rival gangster, O'Leary (Dennis Farina), to keep him from getting on a train bound for New York, where he is about to make a deal with Chinese businessmen that will upset the balance of gangland power in Buffalo. But Frank falls into a drunken stupor while he is waiting in his car at the train station, and he misses his hit.

The repercussions are severe. The boss of the local Polish crime family (Philip Baker Hall) reprimands him and tells him he cannot work any more until he gets straight. He sends him to San Francisco to get sober, because he does not want him around any longer to mess things up. There, he is watched over by a family friend, Dave (Bill Pullman), who is a real estate agent. He sends Frank to an Alcoholics Anonymous (AA) meeting and gets him a job as a mortuary assistant at a local funeral home. Frank is not happy about either of these developments. In fact, he is morose.

Then, as happens only in Hollywood movies, Frank meets Laurel (Téa Leoni), a sassy younger woman whose hated stepfather has died (she brings some shoes to the morgue for him to be buried in). No amount of screen-writing acumen can make us believe Leoni's character is so desperate for a relationship that she takes a shine to Kingsley's Frank—who is not only old but rather unattractive, with a lumpy, bald head and a dour demeanor. Dahl makes a passing nod to the credibility problem by having Laurel declare that she likes older men because they are confident and no longer experimenting, and they will not tell her they are gay. Apparently there are no straight men under sixty in San Francisco.

Not only does the acid-tongued Laurel take a shine to Frank, for reasons unknown, she falls for him even harder after he reveals that he has a drinking problem and after he relapses a couple times and misses a couple dates. And after he reveals—at an AA meeting—that his job is killing people.

Back in Buffalo, Frank's Polish crime family is being muscled out of their territory by O'Leary's Irish mob. Without Frank, their hit man, they present no threat. In San Francisco, Dave uses Frank's services to threaten a city supervisor so he will not tear down a house that Dave wants to turn a tidy profit on. The film sputters along with such subplots.

Luke Wilson is along for the ride as Frank's AA sponsor. His character has a job collecting tolls and does not have much else to do in the film. Wilson has no comic lines and his character does not progress at all—he is completely static and uninteresting.

Dahl clearly wants his audiences to enjoy the absurdity of his setup. It feels like a satire of twelve-step programs when Frank announces to the group that he needs to get sober so he can get on with his livelihood of murdering people. But it is really not; in fact, the AA meetings seem to be the film's one nod to credibility, with real, believable people. In the end, we are supposed to root for Frank to overcome all odds, solve his problem, save the day, and win the girl—a pretty standard outcome that fails to fulfill the movie's absurd-ist premise.

Along the way, there are a few laughs that stem from Frank's deadpan descriptions of his profession. But those wear rather thin quite quickly, and the script by Christopher Markus and Stephen McFeely seems to be reaching rather desperately for laughs. Walking down San Francisco's steep hills backward, as Laurel advises Frank to do, does not really provide the missing comedy. With only the one-note joke—the hit man trying to get sober—to sustain it, *You Kill Me* ends up seeking refuge in some pretty ordinary plot devices.

Neither Kingsley nor Leoni is particularly believable. Kingsley makes Frank seem not so much a man battling demons as a rather dim-witted soul seeking refuge somewhere. Kingsley's Polish American working-class accent comes and goes, and it is hard to distinguish his mannerisms and speech patterns from a simple lack of brains. It is certainly the polar opposite of Gandhi, Kingsley's greatest role, and Kingsley does not seem to be able to play this role without stumbling into near-incoherence. Leoni does the best she can with an odd-ball character, but there is no way she could make any audience believe she would fall in love with Frank.

You Kill Me is passable entertainment, clever enough to occupy an hour or so, but it drags even at a slim ninety minutes. It is an original but thin comic premise that does not sustain itself as a feature-length movie.

Michael Betzold

CREDITS

Frank Falenczyk: Ben Kingsley
Lauren Pearson: Téa Leoni
Edward O'Leary: Dennis Farina
Roman Krzeminski: Philip Baker Hall
Dave: Bill Pullman
Tom: Luke Wilson
Kathleen Fitzgerald: Jayne Eastwood
Stef: Marcus Thomas
Doris: Alison Sealy-Smith
Origin: USA
Language: English
Released: 2007
Production: Al Corley, Bart Rosenblatt, Eugene Musso, Carol Baum, Zvi Howard Rosenman; Code Entertainment; released by IFC Films

Directed by: John Dahl
Written by: Christopher Markus, Stephen McFeely
Cinematography by: Jeffrey Jur
Music by: Marcelo Zarvos
Sound: Louis Marion, Jon Johnson
Music Supervisor: John Bissell
Editing: Scott Chestnut
Production Design: John Dondertman
Costumes: Linda Madden
MPAA rating: R
Running time: 92 minutes

REVIEWS

Chicago Sun-Times Online. June 22, 2007.
Entertainment Weekly. June 29, 2007, p. 117.
Hollywood Reporter Online. June 21, 2007.
Los Angeles Times Online. June 22, 2007.
New York Times Online. June 22, 2007.
San Francisco Chronicle. June 22, 2007, p. E7.
Variety Online. April 28, 2007.
Washington Post Online. June 22, 2007.

QUOTES

Frank Falenczyk: "It isn't that I'm sorry I killed them; it's that I'm sorry I killed them badly."

TRIVIA

The entire film was shot in a modest 26 days.

YOUTH WITHOUT YOUTH

When distinctively original American filmmakers were flourishing in the 1970s, no one, not even Woody Allen, Robert Altman, or Martin Scorsese, had a better decade than Francis Ford Coppola. With four acclaimed masterpieces, *The Godfather* (1972), *The Godfather, Part II* (1974), *The Conversation* (1974), and *Apocalypse Now* (1979), Coppola seemed the most talented director of them all. Then a sharp decline set in, with none of his subsequent work being as well received by critics and the public, though *Bram Stoker's Dracula* (1992) has been severely underrated. In the years since his last film, *The Rainmaker* (1997), Coppola seemed to settle into retirement, becoming better known for his increasingly successful vineyard and as the father of writer/director Sofia Coppola. Then he began a comeback with *Youth without Youth,* a smaller, more personal film than the large-scale efforts for which he is best known. *Youth without Youth* is clearly the work of an artist, but it,

unfortunately, lacks the sharp focus and energy of Coppola's best films.

Based on a novella by the Romanian philosopher Mircea Eliade (1907–1986), *Youth without Youth* tells the story of Dominic (Tim Roth), a Romanian academic who has devoted his life to the seemingly endless pursuit of the origin of language. Then one day in Bucharest in 1938, the seventy-year-old is struck by lightning. Though most of his body is burned, he not only survives, but finds himself thirty years younger, astonishing a medical professor (Bruno Ganz) and the world's press. When the Nazis then taking control of Romania want to study him for signs of something they can use as part of their master-race plan, Dominic flees to Switzerland. (Eliade himself was exiled from Romania after World War II for his support of the fascist Iron Guard.)

Dominic never seems to age and will seemingly have all the time he needs to complete his study. Then in 1955 he meets and falls in love with the twenty-five-year-old Veronica (Alexandra Maria Lara), a dead ringer for the lost love who spurned him in his youth. Then following a motoring accident, Veronica finds herself possessed by the spirit of Rupini, an Indian woman from fourteen centuries earlier. Dominic takes Veronica to India where she is apparently released from her spell. When they go to Malta, she is taken over at night by the spirits of a series of women, each speaking different ancient languages, each from an increasingly distant past. Veronica seems to be helping Dominic achieve his dream, yet the toll of being possessed doubles her age. Dominic must choose between his intellectual pursuit and his love of Veronica.

It is easy to see what attracted Coppola to *Youth without Youth,* with its theme of an elderly man getting a second chance to realize his dream, as well as showing the dangers of sacrificing a personal life for one's work. It is a deeply intellectual film dealing with language, communication, redemption, escape, and the nature of love, yet Coppola, who also adapted Eliade's novella, first published in 1988, seems merely to touch briefly upon each of his themes. Though based on a short work of fiction, the film has the sketchy quality that often results from reducing a long novel to its highlights. Coppola never finds the right balance between ideas and emotions, does not build toward a satisfying resolution.

Mihai Malaimare, Jr. provides some striking images, finding a different color palette for each of the settings, from the dank gloom of Romania to the diffused brightness of India. The cinematographer is partial to the kind of shots of late-afternoon light almost exclusively seen in films set in Europe, giving the material a melancholy glow. Coppola and Malaimare offer an unusual number of overhead shots, as if the gods are looking down on the actions of these foolish mortals. Much odder are the horizontal and even upside-down shots that appear almost like projection errors. Such stylized visuals, however, cannot provide the necessary energy missing from *Youth without Youth*. To complain that a film is too slow is unfair when such a tempo serves the filmmaker's goals. *Youth without Youth* has, however, a distractingly leaden pace, with lengthy scenes reminiscent of adaptations of plays.

Roth can be an excellent actor when playing characters with an edge, as with his Van Gogh in Robert Altman's *Vincent & Theo* (1990) and his undercover cop in Quentin Tarantino's *Reservoir Dogs* (1992). He does not do as well with ordinary men, as Dominic, despite his age reversal, essentially is. Much of *Youth without Youth* shows the protagonist thinking, as he struggles to find the truth about his circumstances, and Roth just seems to be blank at these moments. The actor does much better when Dominic is confronted by his goading doppelganger. As the double, Roth finds just the right degree of malice simply by raising his eyebrows or baring his teeth. As she has shown in *Control* (2007), Lara has surprising presence for someone with pleasant but ordinary looks. When she and Roth are on screen together, all eyes are on her. She has the star quality Roth lacks.

With the exception of a timid endorsement by Manohla Dargis in the *New York Times, Youth without Youth* got an especially hostile reception from reviewers who were not to be swayed by goodwill toward Coppola's comeback attempt. Owen Gleiberman of *Entertainment Weekly* even went so far as to name it the worst film of 2007, labeling it a "sodden, bloated, and incomprehensible disaster." Such negativity is a bit harsh. *Youth without Youth* is hardly an embarrassing vanity project like the Bill Murray version of *The Razor's Edge* (1984), which it resembles thematically. Coppola shows flashes of his old talent and treats his themes with respect, if without sufficient insight. As with François Truffaut's misguided *Fahrenheit 451* (1966), which *Youth without Youth* also resembles, Coppola's film is a failure but an admirable one. An artist of his stature has earned the right to blunder.

Michael Adams

CREDITS

Dominic: Tim Roth
Laura/Veronica/Rupini: Alexandra Maria Lara
Professor Stanciulescu: Bruno Ganz
Dr. Josef Rudolf: André Hennicke
Woman in Room 6: Alexandra Pirici

Origin: USA
Language: English
Released: 2007
Production: Francis Ford Coppola; American Zoetrope; released by Sony Pictures Classics
Directed by: Francis Ford Coppola
Written by: Francis Ford Coppola
Cinematography by: Mihai Malaimare, Jr.
Music by: Osvaldo Golijov
Sound: Mihai Bogos
Editing: Walter Murch
Art Direction: Ruxandra Ionica, Mircea Onisoru
Costumes: Gloria Papura
Production Design: Calin Papura
MPAA rating: R
Running time: 124 minutes

REVIEWS

Entertainment Weekly Online. December 12, 2007.
Hollywood Reporter Online. October 22, 2007.
Los Angeles Times Online. December 14, 2007.
New York Times Online. December 14, 2007.
Premiere Online. December 13, 2007.
San Francisco Chronicle. December 14, 2007, p. E12.
Variety Online. October 20, 2007.
Village Voice Online. December 11, 2007.
Wall Street Journal. December 14, 2007, p. W1.

TRIVIA

More than 170 hours of footage were originally shot for the film.

AWARDS

Nomination:
Ind. Spirit 2006: Cinematog.

ZODIAC

There's more than one way to lose your life to a killer.
—Movie tagline

Box Office: $33.1 million

Zodiac is based on the books *Zodiac* and *Zodiac Unmasked* by Robert Graysmith, a former cartoonist who worked at the *San Francisco Chronicle* during the height of the Zodiac killer scare in the San Francisco Bay Area during the late 1960s and early 1970s. While not the first film to tackle the Zodiac phenomenon, with *Dirty Harry* (1971) probably being the most well-known and sensational treatment, *Zodiac* is as maddening and as engrossing as the unsolved crime it dramatizes, and therein lies its brilliance: It manages to make palpable for the audience the obsession and paranoia of the main characters, to the point that the audience becomes vicariously drawn into the desire to know the truth and the suspense of wondering where the search might lead next.

The plot of *Zodiac* seems, at a glance, to be fairly straightforward: A psychotic killer stalks and murders people (mostly young couples) in the San Francisco Bay Area in the late 1960s, and two newspapermen and a San Francisco police inspector become obsessed with solving the crime. After killing a couple in Vallejo, the killer sends letters to several Bay Area newspapers, including the *San Francisco Chronicle,* where cartoonist Robert Graysmith (Jake Gyllenhaal) and frenetic crime-beat reporter Paul Avery (Robert Downey, Jr.) work. The letter contains a code, a cipher, which the killer claims contains his identity (this penchant for sending letters to newspapers detailing his crimes and containing ciphers is Zodiac's trademark)—and Graysmith becomes obsessed with the Zodiac and his codes. When the code is cracked, it does not reveal Zodiac's identity, but a disturbed and obsessive mind. Two more murders follow in short order, including that of a cab driver in San Francisco, which triggers the involvement of San Francisco police inspector David Toschi (Mark Ruffalo). These three men—Graysmith, Avery, and Toschi—all pursue the Zodiac relentlessly, and their personal lives and careers all suffer for it. (This notion of obsession to the detriment of all else feeds one of the film's central themes: Pursuit of the truth is difficult and costly, it often produces dubious results, and yet is a necessary human drive.)

Zodiac has all the trappings of the police procedural: it is heavily detail-oriented, its main characters are driven and intelligent (and refreshing saddled with very human, and not outlandish, characteristics and flaws), and the action follows from crime to leads to near breakthroughs to failures in a predominantly linear way. By sticking rigidly to so familiar a structure, director David Fincher is able to capitalize upon and undercut audience expectation, and the integrity of the characters and performances ensures that this is not done in a way that feels like a cheat. Again, one of the potential problems with *Zodiac,* especially in the context of the police procedural, which usually demands eventual resolution, is that the crimes upon which it is based remain unsolved. What Fincher achieves via this unrelenting investigative approach, however, is quite interesting and perhaps unique. Without committing to a definite answer regarding the question of the Zodiac killer's identity, Fincher is still able to deliver to the audience a reasonable degree of certainty and some measure of closure. By making his characters intelligent, relentless seekers, Fincher dodges

the potentially dissatisfying effect of leaving the film largely unresolved, and arrives at something like courtroom truth—events need not be proven to have (or have not) occurred, but the evidence must be sufficient to eradicate reasonable doubt. After nearly three hours of watching Graysmith and others attempt to track down and identify the Zodiac, knowing full well that the case was never actually solved, it is almost impossible not to side with Graysmith (and Fincher) in guessing at the identity of the Zodiac. In fact, the sheer quantity of details involved in the case as discussed in the film, including the many false leads, are so overwhelming that not only is it amazing that the film is only 158 minutes long, but also that it feels much, much shorter.

In keeping with the notion of procedures and how they help or hinder the investigative process, a particularly fascinating aspect of *Zodiac* is its focus on how the human systems of institutions and bureaucracies often thwart progress. The Zodiac kills across county lines—the San Francisco, Napa, Vallejo, and Riverside police departments all hold evidence in the murders linked to the Zodiac, which individually mean very little, but which together could lead directly to Zodiac. Yet, the inability of these various agencies to coordinate their information effectively results in incomplete information as well as lost leads and time. For Fincher and his cast of investigators, the law enforcement infrastructure itself is often the real enemy—it takes on the dimensions of another character, actively thwarting the efforts of the police to catch the killer. The indictment runs deep—the same society that helps create a psychopathic killer also creates a leviathan bureaucracy that renders the pursuit of truth and justice next to impossible.

Story and plot elements are not the only storytelling tools that Fincher wields to great effect. Fincher goes so far as to imbue the casting and depiction of the Zodiac with import. The Zodiac was never captured—only varying descriptions of him exist. Thus, three different actors portray the Zodiac killer at various points in the movie: Richmond Arquette, Bob Stephenson, and John Lacy. This adds both a level of theatricality as well as a certain emotional reality to the film: The device not only underscores the point that the crimes are unsolved, but it also prevents the audience from settling into any sense of smug certainty about what it might be seeing and hearing (just as multiple witnesses to an accident seldom give the same account of the accident, so the audience is made to feel unsure of who the Zodiac is from scene to scene). Most interestingly, the actor who plays Arthur Leigh Allen (John Carroll Lynch), the suspect posited by Graysmith (and Fincher) to be the most likely Zodiac killer suspect, never plays the Zodiac (at least according to the credits), though the other actors who play the Zodiac all have builds similar to Lynch.

Also, the simple treatment of the pop music of the 1960s and 1970s in *Zodiac* is endowed with a care that, in turn, greatly enhances the power of the film. The most notable example of this is the song "Hurdy Gurdy Man" (1968) performed by Donovan, which is used to score both the first murder and end credits. Clearly a student of Martin Scorsese's use of popular music in cinematic storytelling, Fincher punches up the powerful guitars and drums as the first couple is shot, and the lyrics work brilliantly against the action taking place on screen: "'Tis then when the hurdy gurdy man/ comes singing songs of love…Here comes the roly-poly man/ He's singing songs of love." What is striking about this is not only how the song cuts across and enhances the action, but also how it describes the situation so well: The music itself is foreboding and speaks to a powerful release, and the lyrics expressly mention a roly-poly man who comes along singing songs of love. The actors who portray the Zodiac killer could all certainly be described as roly-poly (they are all a bit large and lumbering), and the Zodiac liked to attack couples in secluded places, especially "lover's lanes." That the song is intended to be the Zodiac's theme is enforced by its reappearance during the end credits. The song becomes entangled with the memory of the first murder, and Fincher uses it to invoke, chillingly, the fear of witnessing the killing.

Fincher deftly employs another bit of minutiae in *Zodiac* to stunning effect. He opts to show only three actual murders throughout the entire 158-minute running time of the film. The murders are: Michael Mageau (Jimmi Simpson) and Darlene Ferrin (Ciara Hughes) in their car in Vallejo, California (July 1969); Bryan Hartnell (Patrick Scott Lewis) and Cecelia Ann Shepherd (Pell James) by a lake in Napa, California (September 1969); and taxi driver Paul Lee Stine (Charles Schneider) in San Francisco (October 1969). The film, in fact, opens with the Mageau/Ferrin murder, and Stine is killed before the film's first hour is over. These murders, along with the earlier killing of David Faraday and Betty Lou Jensen in December 1968 (which takes place prior to the action of the film, but is referenced by the Zodiac killer both in his telephone confession to the police just after the Mageau/Ferrin killing and in his note to the *San Francisco Chronicle*) are the only murders ever definitively linked to the Zodiac. By depicting only these essential crimes so early in the film and not the other subsequent murders for which the Zodiac claimed credit over the years (as many as thirty-seven, but which could never be officially attributed to the Zodiac, a fact mentioned in the film), Fincher achieves a haunting effect: The horror of the murders is bolstered by their credibility, and the fact that they occur so closely together at the beginning of the movie gives an early sense that what follows will be a bloodbath. It is a device designed to keep the audience on the edge of its seat, waiting for the next act of violence. When no murder is forthcoming, the suspense, paranoia, and obsession build in the viewer, just as they do in the central characters of Robert Graysmith, Paul Avery, and Inspector Toschi, and carry through to the final scene.

Zodiac is a well-wrought piece of cinematic art, one that argues very strongly in favor of the notion that God, or the Devil, is in the details. All of the performances are top-notch, with ensemble acting emphasized over star power. This is easily Fincher's most cogent, ambitious, and satisfying piece.

John Boaz

CREDITS

Inspector David Toschi: Mark Ruffalo
Robert Graysmith: Jake Gyllenhaal
Paul Avery: Robert Downey, Jr.
Melvin Belli: Brian Cox
Melanie: Chloë Sevigny
Arthur Leigh Allen: John Carroll Lynch
Bob Vaughn: Charles Fleischer
Mel Nicolai: Zach Grenier
Sherwood Morrill: Philip Baker Hall
Sgt. Jack Mulanax: Elias Koteas
Ken Narlow: Donal Logue
Captain Marty Lee: Dermot Mulroney
Charles Thieriot: John Terry
Templeton Peck: John Getz
Duffy Jennings: Adam Goldberg
Carol Fisher: Candy Clark
Zodiac 4: John Lacy
Officer George Bawart: James Le Gros
Origin: USA
Language: English
Released: 2007
Production: Mike Medavoy, Arnold W. Messer, Bradley J. Fischer; Phoenix Pictures; released by Paramount Pictures
Directed by: David Fincher
Written by: James Vanderbilt
Cinematography by: Harris Savides
Music by: David Shire
Sound: Drew Kunin
Music Supervisor: George Drakoulias, Randall Poster
Editing: Angus Wall
Art Direction: Keith Cunningham
Costumes: Casey Storm
Production Design: Donald Graham Burt
MPAA rating: R
Running time: 158 minutes

REVIEWS

Boxoffice Online. March 2, 2007.

Chicago Sun-Times Online. March 2, 2007.

Entertainment Weekly. March 9, 2007, p. 83.

Hollywood Reporter Online. February 23, 2007.

Los Angeles Times Online. March 2, 2007.

New York Times Online. March 2, 2007.

Rolling Stone Online. February 28, 2007.

San Francisco Chronicle. March 2, 2007, p. E1.

Variety Online. February 22, 2007.

Washington Post. March 2, 2007, p. C1.

QUOTES

Robert Graysmith: "I…I need to know who he is. I…I need to stand there, I need to look him in the eye and I need to know that it's him."

TRIVIA

Inspector David Toschi served as the inspiration for Steve McQueen's character in *Bullitt* and for Clint Eastwood's "Dirty Harry," among others.

AWARDS

Nomination:

Writers Guild 2007: Adapt. Screenplay.

List of Awards

Academy Awards

Film: *No Country for Old Men*
Animated Film: *Ratatouille*
Director: Ethan Coen, Joel Coen (*No Country for Old Men*)
Actor: Daniel Day-Lewis (*There Will Be Blood*)
Actress: Marion Cotillard (*La Vie en Rose*)
Supporting Actor: Javier Bardem (*No Country for Old Men*)
Supporting Actress: Tilda Swinton (*Michael Clayton*)
Original Screenplay: Diablo Cody (*Juno*)
Adapted Screenplay: Joel Coen, Ethan Coen (*No Country for Old Men*)
Cinematography: Robert Elswit (*There Will Be Blood*)
Editing: Christopher Rouse (*The Bourne Ultimatum*)
Art Direction: Dante Ferretti, Francesca Lo Schiavo (*Sweeney Todd: The Demon Barber of Fleet Street*)
Visual Effects: Michael L. Fink, Bill Westenhofer, Ben Morris, Trevor Wood (*The Golden Compass*)
Sound: Scott Millan, David Parker, Kirk Francis (*The Bourne Ultimatum*)
Sound Editing: Karen M. Baker, Per Hallberg (*The Bourne Ultimatum*)
Makeup: Didier Lavergne, Jan Archibald (*La Vien en Rose*)

Costume Design: Alexandra Byrne (*Elizabeth: The Golden Age*)
Original Score: Dario Marianelli (*Atonement*)
Original Song: "Falling Slowly" (Glen Hansard and Markéta Irglová, *Once*)
Foreign Language Film: *The Counterfeiters*
Documentary, Feature: *Taxi to the Dark Side*
Best Documentary, Short Subject: *Freeheld*
Best Short Film, Animated: *Peter & the Wolf*
Best Short Film, Live Action: *Le Mozart des pickpockets*

British Academy of Film & Television Arts Awards

Animated Film: *Ratatouille*
Film: *Atonement*
Director: Joel Coen, Ethan Coen (*No Country for Old Men*)
Original Screenplay: Diablo Cody (*Juno*)
Adapted Screenplay: Ronald Harwood (*The Diving Bell and the Butterfly*)
Actor: Daniel Day-Lewis (*There Will Be Blood*)
Actress: Marion Cotillard (*La Vie en Rose*)
Supporting Actor: Javier Bardem (*No Country for Old Men*)
Supporting Actress: Tilda Swinton (*Michael Clayton*)

Editing: Christopher Rouse (*The Bourne Ultimatum*)
Cinematography: Roger Deakins (*No Country for Old Men*)
Production Design: Sarah Greenwood, Katie Spencer (*Atonement*)
Costume Design: Marit Allen (*La Vie en Rose*)
Makeup: Jean Archibald, Didier Lavergne (*La Vie en Rose*)
Sound: Kirk Francis, Scott Millan, David Parker, Karen M. Baker, Per Hallberg (*The Bourne Ultimatum*)
Visual Effects: Michael L. Fink, Bill Westenhofer, Ben Morris, Trevor Wood (*The Golden Compass*)
Music: Christopher Gunning (*La Vie en Rose*)
Foreign Film: *The Lives of Others*
Short Animation: *The Pearce Sisters*
Short Film: *Dog Altogether*

Directors Guild of America Awards

Outstanding Directorial Achievement in Motion Pictures: Joel Coen, Ethan Coen (*No Country for Old Men*)
Outstanding Directorial Achievement in Documentary: Asger Leth (*Ghosts of Cité Soleil*)

Golden Globes

Film, Drama: *Atonement*

Film, Musical or Comedy: *Sweeney Todd: The Demon Barber of Fleet Street*

Animated Film: *Ratatouille*

Director: Julian Schnabel (*The Diving Bell and the Butterfly*)

Actor, Drama: Daniel Day-Lewis (*There Will Be Blood*)

Actor, Musical or Comedy: Johnny Depp (*Sweeney Todd: The Demon Barber of Fleet Street*)

Actress, Drama: Julie Christie (*Away from Her*)

Actress, Musical or Comedy: Marion Cotillard (*La Vie en Rose*)

Supporting Actor: Javier Bardem (*No Country for Old Men*)

Supporting Actress: Cate Blanchett (*I'm Not There*)

Screenplay: Joel Coen, Ethan Coen (*No Country for Old Men*)

Score: Dario Marianelli (*Atonement*)

Song: "Guaranteed" (Eddie Vedder, *Into the Wild*)

Foreign Language Film: *The Diving Bell and the Butterfly*

Golden Raspberry Awards

Worst Picture: *I Know Who Killed Me*

Worst Director: Chris Sivertson (*I Know Who Killed Me*)

Worst Actor: Eddie Murphy (*Norbit*)

Worst Actress: Lindsay Lohan (*I Know Who Killed Me*)

Worst Supporting Actor: Eddie Murphy (*Norbit*)

Worst Supporting Actress: Eddie Murphy (*Norbit*)

Worst Screenplay: Jeff Hammond (*I Know Who Killed Me*)

Worst Screen Couple: Lindsay Lohan (*I Know Who Killed Me*)

Worst Excuse for a Horror Movie: *I Know Who Killed Me*

Worst Prequel or Sequel: *Daddy Day Camp*

Worst Remake or Rip-Off: *I Know Who Killed Me*

Independent Spirit Awards

Film: *Juno*

First Film: Scott Frank, *The Lookout*

Director: Julian Schnabel (*The Diving Bell and the Butterfly*)

Actor: Philip Seymour Hoffman (*The Savages*)

Actress: Ellen Page (*Juno*)

Supporting Actor: Chiwetel Ejiofor (*Talk to Me*)

Supporting Actress: Cate Blanchett (*I'm Not There*)

Screenplay: Tamara Jenkins (*The Savages*)

First Screenplay: Diablo Cody (*Juno*)

Cinematography: Janusz Kaminski (*The Diving Bell and the Butterfly*)

Foreign Language Film: *Once*

Documentary: *Crazy Love*

Screen Actors Guild Awards

Actor: Daniel Day-Lewis (*There Will Be Blood*)

Actress: Julie Christie (*Away from Her*)

Supporting Actor: Javier Bardem (*No Country for Old Men*)

Supporting Actress: Ruby Dee (*American Gangster*)

Ensemble Cast: *No Country for Old Men*

Stunt Ensemble: *The Bourne Ultimatum*

Writers Guild of America Awards

Original Screenplay: Diablo Cody (*Juno*)

Adapted Screenplay: Ethan Coen, Joel Coen (*No Country for Old Men*)

Documentary Screenplay Award: Alex Gibney (*Taxi to the Dark Side*)

Obituaries

Marit Allen (September 17, 1941–November 26, 2007). The fashion editor and costume designer was born in Cheshire, England and studied briefly at the University of Grenoble. Allen worked at the society magazine *Queen* and was the fashion editor at *Vogue* from 1964 to 1973. Through her (then) marriage to film producer Sandy Lieberson, Allen met a number of film directors, first working as a fashion consultant on *Kaleidoscope* (1966) and designing Julie Christie's costumes for director Nicolas Roeg's *Don't Look Now* (1973). Roeg also gave Allen her first full credit as a costume designer on 1980's *Bad Timing*. Credits include *Eureka* (1984), *The Hit* (1984), *Little Shop of Horrors* (1986), *White Mischief* (1987), *Dirty Rotten Scoundrels* (1988), *The Witches* (1990), *Stalin* (1992), *Mrs. Doubtfire* (1993), *The Secret Garden* (1993), *Dead Man* (1995), *Eyes Wide Shut* (1999), *Ride with the Devil* (1999), *Hulk* (2003), *Thunderbirds* (2004), *Brokeback Mountain* (2005), *La Vie en Rose* (2007), and *Love in the Time of Cholera* (2007).

Hollis Alpert (September 24, 1916–November 18, 2007). Born in Herkimer, New York, the film critic was the co-founder of the National Society of Film Critics in 1966, along with Pauline Kael. Alpert served in World War II as a combat historian and worked at the *New Yorker* from 1950 to 1956 while also writing freelance book and film reviews, which led to his work as a movie critic for the weekly magazine, *Saturday Review*. The Society was founded in counterpoint to the New York Film Critics Circle, which favored newspaper critics. Alpert left the *Saturday Review* in 1975 and then served as the editor of *American Film Magazine* for six years. He also wrote a number of books, including *The Barrymores* (1964), *Fellini: A Life* (1986), and *Broadway!: 125 Years of Musical Theatre* (1991).

Tige Andrews (March 19, 1920–January 27, 2007). The actor was born Tiger Andrews in Brooklyn, New York and he graduated from the American Academy of Dramatic Arts, beginning his career on stage. Andrews appeared on Broadway in *Mister Roberts* and then in the 1955 film

version. Other screen credits include *The Wings of Eagles* (1957), *China Doll* (1958), *Imitation General* (1958), *Onionhead* (1958), *A Private's Affair* (1959), *The Last Tycoon* (1976), *Raid on Entebbe* (1977), and *Gypsy Angels* (1980). Andrews had a recurring role on the television series *The Detectives Starring Robert Taylor* (1959–62) and played Captain Adam Greer on *The Mod Squad* (1968–72).

Michelangelo Antonioni (September 29, 1912–July 30, 2007). The film director was born in Ferrara, Italy to a family of landowners; he attended the University of Bologna, earning an economics and commerce degree in 1935. He also founded the university's theatrical troupe, where he wrote and directed plays, and also wrote film reviews for the local newspaper. In 1940, Antonioni took classes at the Institute of Experimental Filmmaking and, in 1943, made his first film, the short documentary *Gente del Po/People of the Po Valley*. He continued to write and make short documentaries until his first narrative feature, 1950's *Cronaca di un Amore/Story of a Love Affair*. Credits include *Le Amiche/The Girlfriends* (1955), *Il Grido/The Outcry* (1957), *L'Avventura/The Adventure* (1959), *La Notte/The Night* (1960), *L'Eclisse/The Eclipse* (1962), *Il Deserto Rosso/The Red Desert* (1964), *Blow-Up* (1966, Oscar® nominations for best director and screenplay), *Zabriskie Point* (1970), *The Passenger* (1975), *Il Mistery di Oberwald/The Mystery of Oberwald* (1980), and *Identificazaione di una Donna/The Identification of a Woman* (1982). In 1985, Antonioni suffered a stroke that severely limited his ability to speak and he retired until 1995 when he directed (with Wim Wenders assisting) *Beyond the Clouds*, based on a book of his own stories; he also collaborated with Steven Soderbergh and Wong Kar-Wai on *Eros* (2004). The director received the Life Achievement Award from the Academy of Motion Pictures Arts and Sciences in 1995.

Jeanne Bates (May 21, 1918–November 28, 2007). The supporting actress was born in Berkeley, California and began her career on radio soap operas while attending San

Mateo Junior College. Bates was the lead on the radio mystery series *Whodunit* and married the show's writer, Lew X. Lansworth. She was a contract player with Columbia Pictures and made her film debut in 1943's *The Chance of a Lifetime*. Among Bates' television roles were Nurse Willis on *Ben Casey* (1961–66). Film credits include *The Phantom* (1943), *The Mask of Diijion* (1946), *Sabaka* (1955), *The Strangler* (1964), *Eraserhead* (1978), and *Mom* (1989).

Marc Behm (January 12, 1925–July 12, 2007). Born in Trenton, New Jersey, the screenwriter and novelist stayed in Europe after his military service. Behm's first success came with Peter Stone for their 1961 story "The Unsuspecting Wife," which was adapted (by Stone) as 1963's *Charade*. Films include *Help!* (1965), *Twelve Plus One* (1969), *Someone Behind the Door* (1971), *Piaf* (1974), and *Lady Chatterley's Lover* (1981). Behm's novel, *The Eye of the Beholder*, was filmed in 1983 and 1999.

Ingmar Bergman (July 14, 1918–July 30, 2007). Born in Uppsala, Sweden, Bergman directed for film, theatre, and television. His father was a Lutheran clergyman and Bergman often wrote about his parents and childhood. He began working in the theater in the early 1940s and also began writing scripts, including 1944's *Torment*. The director made more than fifty films, including *Summer Interlude* (1950), *Waiting Women* (1952), *A Lesson in Love* (1953), *Sawdust and Tinsel* (1953), *Smiles of a Summer Night* (1955), *The Seventh Seal* (1956), *Wild Strawberries* (1957), *The Magician* (1959), *Winter Light* (1963), *Persona* (1966), *The Passion of Anna* (1970), *Cries and Whispers* (1972), *Scenes from a Marriage* (1973), *Autumn Sonata* (1978), and *From the Life of the Marionettes* (1980). Bergman won best foreign film Oscar®s for *The Virgin Spring* (1960), *Through a Glass Darkly* (1961), and *Fanny and Alexander* (1983). He announced his retirement from theatrical film-making with *Fanny and Alexander* but continued to make television films, including *After the Rehearsal* (1984) and *Saraband* (2003). The novels Bergman wrote about his parents, *The Best Intentions, Sunday's Children,* and *Private Confessions* were all filmed by other directors, and he published a memoir, *The Magic Lantern*, in 1987.

A(lbert) I(saac) Bezzerides (August 9, 1908–January 1, 2007). The novelist and screenwriter was born in Samsun, Turkey but grew up in Fresno, California. He began writing stories while studying at the University of California Berkeley and was first published in 1935. His 1938 novel *Long Haul* was filmed as the 1940 melodrama *They Drive By Night*. Bezzerides, known as "Buzz," became a contract screenwriter for Warner Bros. and his first film credit was 1942's *Juke Joint*. Film credits include *Action in the North Atlantic* (1943), *Desert Fury* (1947), *Thieves' Highway* (1949, from his novel), *Sirocco* (1951), *On Dangerous Ground* (1952), *Beneath the 12-Mile Reef* (1953), *Track of the Cat* (1954), and *Kiss Me Deadly* (1955). Later, Bezzerides worked in television; he was also the co-creator of the 1960s western series, *The Big Valley.*

Joey Bishop (February 3, 1918–October 17, 2007). The last surviving member of Frank Sinatra's "Rat Pack" was born Joseph Abraham Gottlieb in the Bronx, New York and the comedian grew up in Philadelphia. Dropping out of high school, Bishop formed a comedy trio with two friends and worked the club circuit. After serving in World War II,

Bishop developed a solo act and also began appearing on television. Sinatra first saw Bishop perform at the Latin Quarter in 1952 and asked the comedian to open for him; he appeared in *Ocean's 11* (1960) and *Sergeants Three* (1962) and with Dean Martin in *Texas Across the River* (1966). Other film credits include *The Naked and the Dead* (1958), *Johnny Cool* (1963), *Valley of the Dolls* (1967), *Who's Minding the Mint?* (1967), *The Delta Force* (1986), *Betsey's Wedding* (1990), and *Trigger Happy* (1996). Bishop also had his own television comedy series and a late night talk-show, both in the 1960s.

Janet Blair (April 23, 1921–February 19, 2007). Born Martha Janet Lafferty in Altoona, Pennsylvania, the actress took her last name from a county in the state. She was spotted by a talent scout for Columbia Pictures while singing at the Cocoanut Grove in 1941 and was given a contract. Films include *Broadway* (1942), *My Sister Eileen* (1942), *Something to Shout About* (1943), *Once Upon a Time* (1944), *The Fabulous Dorseys* (1947), *The Black Arrow* (1948), and *The Fuller Brush Man* (1948). When Columbia dropped her contract, Blair moved into theater and television, making an occasional movie, including *Public Pigeon No. 1* (1957), *Boys Night Out* (1962), and *The One and Only, Genuine, Original Family Band* (1968).

Jean-Claude Brialy (March 30, 1933–May 30, 2007). The actor was born in Aumale, Algeria and studied at the Strasbourg Centre of Dramatic Art before coming to Paris in 1954. Brialy started his career by appearing in several short films and bit parts for friends Jacques Rivette, Jean-Luc Godard, and Claude Chabrol. Credits include *Le Beau Serge* (1958), *Les Cousins* (1959), *Une Femme est Une Femme* (1961), *Paris Belongs to Us* (1961), *Le Ronde* (1964), *The Bride Wore Black* (1967), *Claire's Knee* (1970), *Inspector Lavardin* (1986), *Les Innocents* (1988), *Queen Margot* (1994), *Beaumarchais the Scoundrel* (1996), *The Count of Monte Cristo* (1999), and *Monsieur Max* (2006). Brialy also wrote and directed some ten films, wrote two memoirs in 2000 and 2004, and continued to appear on stage, also serving as the artistic director of several theatrical companies.

Herman Brix (May 19, 1906–February 24, 2007). Born in Tacoma, Washington, the actor appeared under the name Bruce Bennett for most of his career. A college football player, Brix won a silver medal in shot-put at the 1928 Olympics. He was chosen by writer Edgar Rice Burroughs to appear as Tarzan in 1935's *The New Adventures of Tarzan* and 1938's *Tarzan and the Green Goddess* but the actor then changed his name to avoid typecasting. After his film career ended in the 1960s, Brix was involved in various business interests. Credits include *Sahara* (1943), *Mildred Pierce* (1945), *The Man I Love* (1946), *A Stolen Life* (1946), *Dark Passage* (1947), *Nora Prentiss* (1947), *The Treasure of Sierra Madre* (1948), *Angels in the Outfield* (1951), *Sudden Fear* (1952), *Hidden Guns* (1956), and *The Cosmic Man* (1959).

Roscoe Lee Browne (May 2, 1925–April 11, 2007). The actor with the notable baritone voice was born in Woodbury, New Jersey and graduated from Lincoln University, an historically black college, in 1946. Browne returned to the university to teach and became a track star in the early 1950s, later working as a sales representative until 1956 when he decided to audition for the New York Shakespeare

Festival. He appeared in a number of stage roles and on television, with a recurring role on *Soap*. Screen credits include *The Connection* (1962), *Topaz* (1969), *The Liberation of L.B. Jones* (1970), *The Cowboys* (1972), *Superfly T.N.T.* (1973), *Uptown Saturday Night* (1974), *King* (1978), *Jumpin' Jack Flash* (1986), *The Mambo Kings* (1992), *Babe* (1995), *Babe: Pig in the City* (1998), *Hamlet* (2001), and *Garfield: A Tale of Two Kitties* (2006).

Carol Bruce (November 15, 1919–October 9, 2007). Born Shirley Levy in Great Neck, New York, the actress began her career as a nightclub singer and was best known for her stage roles, including 1940's *Louisiana Purchase*, the 1946 revival of *Show Boat*, and the 1952 London production of *Pal Joey*. Bruce signed a contract with Universal Pictures, but the studio didn't make much use of her and she returned to the stage. Bruce also worked on television, notably as radio station owner Mama Carlson in *WKRP in Cincinnati* (1978–82). Film credits include *This Woman Is Mine* (1941), *Keep 'Em Flying* (1941), *Behind the Eight Ball* (1942), *American Gigolo* (1980), and *Planes, Trains and Automobiles* (1987).

Ron Carey (December 11, 1935–January 16, 2007). Born Ronald Cicenia in Newark, New Jersey, the short character actor and comedian played the role of Officer Carl Levitt on television's *Barney Miller* (1976–82). Carey did standup comedy and got his first television break with his 1966 appearance on *The Merv Griffin Show*. Screen credits include *The Out of Towners* (1970), *High Anxiety* (1977), *Fatso* (1980), *History of the World: Part I* (1981), and *Lucky Luke* (1994).

Kitty Carlisle Hart (September 3, 1910–April 17, 2007). The actress and performing arts advocate was born Catherine Conn in New Orleans, Louisiana. She was educated in Europe and trained at the Royal Academy of Dramatic Arts in London and the Theatre de l'Atelier in Paris. Carlisle picked her stage name from the phone book and, in 1932, she was hired for the title role in the operetta *Rio Rita*. Paramount Pictures offered her a film contract and she made her film debut in 1934's *Murder at the Vanities* as well as *She Loves Me* and *Here Is My Heart*. On loan to MGM, Carlisle played the part of the opera singer in the Marx Brothers' hit *A Night at the Opera* (1935). Paramount then bought out her contract and Carlisle returned to New York where she sang at supper clubs and appeared in operettas as well as in the occasional film role. In 1946, Carlisle married playwright Moss Hart. Carlisle was a panelist on the television game shows *To Tell the Truth* and *What's My Line?* and continued to perform on stage, including a one-woman show, *My Life on the Wicked Stage*. She also served as the chairperson of the New York State Council of the Arts for 20 years. Her memoir, *Kitty: An Autobiography*, was published in 1988. Additional film credits include *Larceny With Music* (1943), *Hollywood Canteen* (1944), *Radio Days* (1987), and *Six Degrees of Separation* (1993).

A.J. Carothers (October 22, 1931–April 9, 2007). Born in Houston, Texas, the screenwriter began his career as a story editor on such television programs as *Studio One*, *Playhouse 90*, and *GE Theater*. Carothers also worked with Walt Disney for seven years, writing *Miracle of the White Stallion* (1963), *Emil and the Detectives* (1964), and *The Happiest Millionaire* (1968). Other works include *Goldilocks* (1971),

Topper Returns (1973), *Forever* (1978), *Hero at Large* (1980), *Making of a Male Model* (1983), and *The Secret of My Succe$s* (1987).

Anthony Carras (November 23, 1920–August 15, 2007). The film editor was born in Detroit, Michigan and graduated from the Pasadena Playhouse College of Theater Arts. He directed 1963's *Operation Bikini* and 1971's *House of Fear* (which he also wrote). Carras served as film editor on *Beast from the Haunted Cave* (1959), *A Bucket of Blood* (1959), *Blood and Steel* (1959), *The House of Usher* (1960), *Last Woman on Earth* (1960), *The Pit and the Pendulum* (1961), *Tales of Terror* (1962), *X* (1963), *The Comedy of Terrors* (1964), and *Tarzan and the Great River* (1967).

Jean-Pierre Cassel (October 27, 1932–April 19, 2007). The debonair actor, known for his roles in romantic comedies, was born Jean-Pierre Crochon in Paris. He worked as a movie extra and nightclub dancer before Gene Kelly, in Paris to direct 1957's *The Happy Road*, offered him a small role. Cassel's breakthrough came in 1960's *Les Jeux de l'Amour/Playing at Love* for director Philippe de Broca. He also worked with de Broca in *Le Farceur/The Joker* (1960), *L'Amant de Cinq Jours/Infidelity* (1961), and *Chouans!* (1988). Other credits include *Le Caporal Epingle/The Vanishing Corporal* (1962), *Cyrano et D'Artagnan* (1963), *Les Fetes Galantes/The Lace Wars* (1965), *Those Magnificent Men in Their Flying Machines* (1965), *Is Paris Burning?* (1966), *L'Armee des Ombres/The Army of Shadows* (1969), *La Rupture/The Break-Up* (1970), *The Discreet Charm of the Bourgoisie* (1972), *The Three Musketeers* (1973), *The Four Musketeers* (1974), *Murder on the Orient Express* (1974), *Vincent and Theo* (1990), *Pret-a-Porter* (1994), *Le Ceremonie/A Judgment in Stone* (1995), *The Crimson Rivers* (2000), and *Le Scaphandre et le Papillon/The Diving Bell and the Butterfly* (2007). Cassel's autobiography *A Mes Amours (To My Loves)* was published in 2004.

Bob Clark (August 5, 1941–April 4, 2007). Born Benjamin Clark in New Orleans, Louisiana, the director grew up in Alabama and Florida, eventually studying theater at the University of Miami. He began his career with low-budget exploitation and horror films, include *She-Man* (1967), *Children Shouldn't Play With Dead Things* (1972), *Deathdream* (1974), and *Black Christmas* (1974). Clark's biggest hit was the teen sex comedy *Porky's* (1982) and its sequel, *Porky's II: The Next Day* (1983) as well as the holiday perennial, *A Christmas Story* (1983). Other credits include *Murder by Decree* (1979), *Tribute* (1980), *Rhinestone* (1984), *Turk 182!* (1985), *Loose Cannons* (1990), *Baby Geniuses* (1999), and *Superbabies: Baby Geniuses 2* (2004).

Luigi Comencini (June 8, 1916–April 6, 2007). The director was born in Salo, Italy, and started his career as a film critic before helming the documentary *Bambini in Citta/Children in the City* (1946). This brought him to the attention of producer Carlo Ponti, who hired Comencini to direct 1948's *Proibito Rubate/Stealing Forbidden*. Credits include *L'Imperatore di Capri/The Emperor of Capri* (1949), *La Valigia dei Sogni/The Suitcase of Dreams* (1953), *Pane, Amore e Fantasia/Bread, Love and Dreams* (1953), *Pane, Amore e Gelosia/Bread, Love and Jealousy* (1954), *La Finestra sul Luna Park/Window on the Fairground* (1956), *Tutti e Casa/Everybody Home* (1960), *Incompreso/Misunderstood* (1966), *The Millionairess* (1972), and *Un Ragazzo di*

Calabria/A Boy from Calabria (1987) as well as several miniseries for television, including *The Adventures of Pinocchio* (1972), *Heart* (1984), and *History* (1986). Comencini retired in 1989.

Laraine Day (October 13, 1917–November 10, 2007). Born La Raine Johnson in Roosevelt, Utah, the actress moved with her family to Long Beach, California as a child. She studied under Elias Day (whose surname she took as a stage name) at the Long Beach Players' Guild and did several bit parts in such films as *Tough to Handle* (1937) and *Stella Dallas* (1937). Although signed as a contract player with MGM, the studio regarded her as ordinary and Day found her best roles on loan-outs, including Alfred Hitchcock's *Foreign Correspondent* (1940) and Charles Vidor's *My Son, My Son* (1940). Day played Nurse Mary Lamont in seven of the Dr. Kildare series, beginning with *Calling Dr. Kildare* (1939) and ending with *Dr. Kildare's Wedding Day* (1941). Other credits include *I Take This Woman* (1939), *Sergeant Madden* (1939), *Tarzan Finds a Son* (1939), *And One Was Beautiful* (1940), *Kathleen* (1941), *The Trial of Mary Dugan* (1941), *Unholy Partners* (1941), *Journey for Margaret* (1942), *A Yank on the Burma Road* (1942), *Mr. Lucky* (1943), *The Story of Dr. Wassell* (1944), *Keep Your Powder Dry* (1945), *The Locket* (1946), *Tycoon* (1947), *My Dear Secretary* (1948), *I Married a Communist* (1949), *The High and the Mighty* (1954), and *The Third Voice* (1960). Day essentially retired from acting after her marriage to baseball manager Leo Durocher in 1947 (they divorced in 1960) though she hosted a sports interview program and frequently appeared on television.

Yvonne De Carlo (September 1, 1922–January 8, 2007). Born Margaret Yvonne Middleton in Vancouver, British Columbia, the glamorous actress later gained famed as vampire wife and mother Lily Munster in the television series, *The Munsters* (1964–66) and subsequent made-for-television movies. De Carlo (the last name was her mother's maiden name) made some 100 films beginning with extra work as a teenager and was signed by Paramount Pictures and later by Universal. Credits include *Salome, Where She Danced* (1945), *Frontier Gal* (1945), *Song of Scheherazade* (1947), *Casbah* (1948), *Criss Cross* (1949), *Tomahawk* (1951), *The San Francisco Story* (1952), *The Captain's Paradise* (1953), *Sea Devils* (1953), *Sombrero* (1953), *Tonight's the Night* (1954), *Death of a Scoundrel* (1956), *Flame of the Islands* (1956), *Raw Edge* (1956), *The Ten Commandments* (1956), *Band of Angels* (1957), *McLintock!* (1963), *Munster Go Home!* (1966), *Satan's Cheerleaders* (1977), *Silent Scream* (1980), and *American Gothic* (1988). Her memoir, *Yvonne: An Autobiography,* was published in 1987.

Solveig Dommartin (May 16, 1961–January 11, 2007). The actress was born in Paris and worked in the theater before making her film debut as trapeze artist Marion in Wim Wenders' *Wings of Desire* (1988), reprising her role in *Faraway, So Close!* (1993). Dommartin also edited Wenders' film *Tokyo-Ga* (1985) and co-wrote and acted in the director's *Until the End of the World* (1991). Other credits include *No Fear, No Die* (1990), *The Prisoner of St. Petersburg* (1990), and *I Can't Sleep* (1994).

Donfeld (July 3, 1934–February 3, 2007). The costume designer was born Donald Lee Feld in Los Angeles and attended the Chouinard Art Institute. He was a four-time

Academy Award® nominee for *Days of Wine and Roses* (1962), *They Shoot Horses, Don't They?* (1969), *Tom Sawyer* (1973), and *Prizzi's Honor* (1985). Donfeld began his career in the 1950s, designing costumes for Academy Award® production numbers; his first screen credit came in *Sanctuary* (1961). Other credits include *Dead Ringer* (1964), *Robin and the Seven Hoods* (1964), *Viva Las Vegas* (1964), *The Great Race* (1965), *Walk in the Spring Rain* (1970), *Diamonds Are Forever* (1971), and *Fun With Dick and Jane* (1977).

Peter Ellenshaw (May 24, 1913–February 12, 2007). The visual effects pioneer and matte artist was born in Essex, England and began his career in the 1930s. In 1947, Ellenshaw's work caught the attention of an art director for Walt Disney Studios and he was hired to work on *Treasure Island* (1950), beginning a collaboration that included 34 films. He also worked on Disney television shows, including *Davy Crockett* and *Zorro,* and painted the first map of Disneyland, which was featured in souvenir booklets; he officially retired from the studio in 1979. Ellenshaw won an Oscar® for *Mary Poppins* (1964) and was nominated for *Bedknobs and Broomsticks* (1971), *The Island at the Top of the World* (1974), and *The Black Hole* (1979). Other credits include *The Story of Robin Hood and His Merrie Men* (1952), *20,000 Leagues Under the Sea* (1954), *Darby O'Gill and the Little People* (1959), *Swiss Family Robinson* (1960), and *The Love Bug* (1969).

Robert Enders (1923–September 7, 2007). The director, writer, and producer was born in Pennsylvania and began his career in advertising, later producing live television and industrial films. Enders moved to England in 1972, writing and producing *Voices.* He formed Bowden Prods. with actress Glenda Jackson, producing the films *Hedda* (1975) and *Nasty Habits* (1977), writing and producing *The Maids* (1975) and *Stevie* (1978), and also did some television productions starring Jackson in the 1980s. Enders later taught screenwriting at the University of Southern California and the University of California Los Angeles.

Ray Evans (February 4, 1915–February 15, 2007). Born in Salmanca, New York, the songwriter met his writing partner Jay Livingston while attending the University of Pennsylvania in the 1930s. After working in New York, they moved to Los Angeles in 1944 and worked under contract for Paramount from 1945 to 1955. The duo won Oscar®s for the songs "Buttons and Bows" (*The Paleface,* 1948), "Mona Lisa" (*Captain Carey, USA,* 1950), and "Whatever Will Be, Will Be (Que Sera, Sera)" (*The Man Who Knew Too Much,* 1956). They were nominated for "The Cat and the Canary" (*Why Girls Leave Home,* 1945), "Tammy" (*Tammy and the Doctor,* 1957), "Almost in Your Arms" (*Houseboat,* 1958), and "Dear Heart" (*Dear Heart,* 1964). Evans and Livingston also wrote "Silver Bells" for Bob Hope, which was featured in 1951's *The Lemon Drop Kid* and the television themes for *Bonanza* and *Mister Ed* among many other works. The duo were named to the Songwriters Hall of Fame in 1977; Jay Livingston died in 2001.

Clive Exton (April 11, 1930–August 16, 2007). Born Clive Jack Montague Brooks in London, England, the screenwriter began as an actor but decided he could write better lines. His first work was the television play *No Fixed Abode*

(1959) and Exton signed a contract with ABC Television for a series of dramas in the 1960s; he later continued his work with a number of series, including *Jeeves and Wooster, Poirot,* and *Rosemary & Thyme.* Screen credits include *No Place to Go* (1963), *Night Must Fall* (1964), *Isadora* (1968), *Entertaining Mr. Sloane* (1969), *10 Rillington Place* (1971), *The House in Nightmare Park* (1973), and *Red Sonja* (1985).

Fernando Fernan-Gonzalez (August 28, 1921–November 21, 2007). The actor, writer, and director was born in Lima, Peru while his actress mother was on tour. They returned to Spain when he was three and Fernan-Gonzalez joined a school theater troupe as a boy, turning professional at seventeen. Eventually abandoning the theater because of stage fright, he made some 200 films and directed 20, including *The Madhouse* (1953), *Life Ahead* (1958), *Life Around Us* (1959), *The Strange Journey* (1963), *Life Goes On* (1964), and *Journey to Nowhere* (1986). Film credits include *The Spirit of the Beehive* (1973), *Maravillas* (1980), *Belle Epoque* (1994), *All About My Mother* (1999), and *Butterfly* (1999).

Freddie Fields (July 12, 1923–December 11, 2007). The Hollywood talent agent and producer was born Fred Feldman in Ferndale, New York and began his career working for a small, independent New York agency until he joined Music Corporation of America (MCA) in 1946. Fields stayed with the agency until 1960 when he and partner David Begelman formed Creative Management Associates (CMA), which represented such stars as Steve McQueen, Robert Redford, Barbra Streisand, Paul Newman, Sidney Poitier, and Dustin Hoffman. CMA was sold in 1974; from 1980 to 1984, Fields was the head of production at MGM/UA Entertainment. Among Fields' films as an independent producer were *Lipstick* (1976), *Looking for Mr. Goodbar* (1977), *American Gigolo* (1980), *Crimes of the Heart* (1986), and *Glory* (1989).

John Flynn (March 14, 1932–April 4, 2007). Born in Chicago, Illinois, the action director studied at the University of California Los Angeles and began his career as a script supervisor. Credits include *The Sergeant* (1968), *The Outfit* (1973), *Rolling Thunder* (1977), *Marilyn: The Untold Story* (1980), *Best Seller* (1987), *Lock Up* (1989), *Out for Justice* (1981), *Brainscan* (1994), and *Protection* (2001).

Freddie Francis (December 22, 1917–March 17, 2007). The award-winning cinematographer and director was born in London and first studied engineering before pursuing his interests in photography. Francis worked in the army film unit during World War II and later at Denham and Elstree studios as a camera operator. His first credit as a director of photography came with 1956's *A Hill in Korea.* Credits include *Time Without Pity* (1957), *Room at the Top* (1958), *Saturday Night and Sunday Morning* (1960), *Sons and Lovers* (1960, for which he won an Oscar®), *The Innocents* (1961), and *Night Must Fall* (1964). Francis turned his attention to directing and did not return to cinematography until 1980 with *The Elephant Man* as well as *The French Lieutenant's Woman* (1981), *The Executioner's Song* (1982), *Dune* (1984), *Glory* (1989, his second Oscar®), *Cape Fear* (1991), and *The Straight Story* (1999). After directing the 1962 comedy *Two and Two Make Six,* Francis worked with British cult studios Hammer and Amicus on such films as *Paranoiac* (1962), *Nightmare* (1963), *Dr.*

Terror's House of Horrors (1964), *The Evil of Frankenstein* (1964), *The Psychopath* (1965), *The Skull* (1965), *Dracula Has Risen from the Grave* (1968), *Tales from the Crypt* (1971), *The Creeping Flesh* (1972), *The Ghoul* (1975), *The Doctor and the Devils* (1985), and *Dark Tower* (1986).

Richard Franklin (July 15, 1948–July 11, 2007). The director was born in Melbourne, Australia; there being no film schools in Australia at the time, Franklin went to the University of Southern California in 1967. He returned to Australia and began directing for television in 1970. His first film credit was 1975's *The True Story of Eskimo Nell.* Credits include *Fantasm* (1976), *Patrick* (1978), *Road Games* (1981), *Psycho 2* (1983), *Cloak & Dagger* (1984), *F/X 2* (1991), *Sorrento Beach* (1995), *Brilliant Lies* (1996), and *Visitors* (2003).

Alice Ghostley (August 14, 1926–September 21, 2007). Born in Eve, Missouri, the character actress grew up in Oklahoma and quit college to move to New York, working a series of odd jobs before making her Broadway debut in the revue *Leonard Stillman's New Faces of 1952.* Ghostley received a Tony nomination in 1963 for the comedy *The Beauty Part* and won the award in 1965 as best featured actress for *The Sign in Sidney Brustein's Window.* She played good witch Esmeralda on the television series *Bewitched* from 1969 to 1972 and Bernice Clifton on *Designing Women* from 1987 to 1993. Ghostley's film credits include *To Kill a Mockingbird* (1962), *The Graduate* (1967), *With Six You Get Eggroll* (1968), *Gator* (1976), *Grease* (1978), *Not for Publication* (1984), *Neil Simon's The Odd Couple 2* (1998), and *Whispers: An Elephant's Tale* (2000).

Bernard Gordon (October 29, 1918–May 11, 2007). Born in New Britain, Connecticut, the screenwriter studied English and film at City College of New York. After moving to Los Angeles, Gordon got a job as a script reader at Paramount, later moving to Warner Bros. Gordon was subpoenaed during the McCarthy hearings and, though he was not called on to testify, the studio fired him and he did freelance work from 1947 to 1952. During the blacklist, Gordon wrote under pseudonyms, including John T. Williams and Raymond T. Marcus. He met film producer Philip Yordan and moved to France and Spain to work for him from 1960 to 1973 with Yordan taking onscreen credit though some of the screenwriter's credits were later restored. Gordon entitled his memoir, published in 2000, *Hollywood Exile, or How I Learned to Love the Blacklist.* Credits include *The Law vs. Billy the Kid* (1954), *Earth vs. Flying Saucers* (1956), *Chicago Confidential* (1957), *Escape from San Quentin* (1957), *Hellcats of the Navy* (1957), *The Man Who Turned to Stone* (1957), *Zombies of Mora Tau* (1957), *The Case Against Brooklyn* (1958), *El Cid* (1961), *The Day of the Triffids* (1962), *55 Days of Peking* (1963), *The Thin Red Line* (1964), *Battle of the Bulge* (1965), and *Horror Express* (1973).

Robert Goulet (November 26, 1933–October 30, 2007). Born in Lawrence, Massachusetts the singer and actor was raised in Edmonton, Alberta and began to work in radio as a teenager. Goulet studied singing at the Royal Conservatory of Music in Toronto and made his concert debut in 1951. He played leading roles in musical productions in Canada but was virtually unknown when he was cast as Lancelot in the original Broadway production of *Camelot* in

1961; the show ran for over two years and Goulet later played King Arthur in the 1993 revival. He also received a Tony award in 1968 as best actor in a musical for *The Happy Time*. Goulet was signed by Columbia Records in 1962 and had over 20 bestselling albums. He had a sporadic film career, including *Gay Purr-ee* (1962), *Honeymoon Hotel* (1964), *I'd Rather Be Rich* (1964), *I Deal in Danger* (1966), *Underground* (1970), *Atlantic City* (1980), *Beetlejuice* (1988), and *The Naked Gun 2½* (1991).

Pierre Granier-Deferre (July 22, 1927–November 16, 2007). The writer/director was born in Paris and studied at L'Institut des Hautes Etudes Cinematographiques before beginning his career as an assistant in the 1950s. Credits include *Paris in August* (1966), *The Cat* (1971), *The Widow Couderc* (1971), *The Last Train* (1973), *The French Detective* (1975), *The Trap* (1975), *A Woman at Her Window* (1977), *A Strange Affair* (1981), *The Northern Star* (1982), *Cours Prive* (1986), *Widow's Walk* (1987), and *The Voice* (1992). After making his last feature film, *Le Petit Garcon*, in 1995, Granier-Deferre wrote and occasionally directed episodes of the television series *Inspector Maigret*.

Dabbs Greer (April 2, 1917–April 28, 2007). The character actor was born Robert William Greer in Fairview, Missouri and began acting in children's theater productions at the age of eight. Greer made his film debut as an extra in 1938's *Jesse James*. He moved to Pasadena in 1943 and taught at the Pasadena Playhouse where he began using his mother's maiden name as his first name professionally. Greer appeared in more than 100 film and television roles, including having recurring roles on *Gunsmoke*, *Little House on the Prairie*, *Hank*, *Picket Fences*, and *Maybe It's Me*. Screen credits include *Invasion of the Body Snatchers* (1956), *I Want to Live!* (1958), *It! The Terror from Beyond Space* (1958), *Roustabout* (1964), *The Cheyenne Social Club* (1970), *Pacific Heights* (1990), and *The Green Mile* (1999).

Charles B. Griffith (September 23, 1930–September 28, 2007). The screenwriter and director was born in Chicago, Illinois, the grandson of vaudeville and radio performer Myrtle Vail. Griffith first came to Hollywood in a failed attempt to help Vail move into television. Griffith was known for the low-budget films he did with Roger Corman, whom he met in 1954. Films include *Gunslinger* (1956), *It Conquered the World* (1956), *Attack of the Crab Monsters* (1957), *Rock All Night* (1957), *Teenage Doll* (1957), *A Bucket of Blood* (1959), *Beast from Haunted Cave* (1960), *Little Shop of Horrors* (1960), *Creature from the Haunted Sea* (1961), *The Wild Angels* (1966), *The Devil's Angels* (1967), *Death Race 2000* (1975), *Eat My Dust* (1976), *Up from the Depths* (1979), *Dr. Heckyl and Mr. Hype* (1980), and *Not of This Earth* (1988).

George Grizzard (April 1, 1928–October 2, 2007). Born in Roanoke Rapids, North Carolina, the actor grew up in Washington, D.C. and briefly worked in advertising before starting his career at the Arena Stage. After moving to New York in 1954, Grizzard made his Broadway debut opposite Paul Newman in 1955's *The Desperate Hours* and he appeared in several plays by Edward Albee, including *Who's Afraid of Virginia Woolf?*, *A Delicate Balance* (for which he won a Tony Award in 1996), and *Seascape*. He also frequently guest-starred on television and won Emmys for his roles in *The Adams Chronicles* (1976) and *The Oldest*

Living Graduate (1980). Film credits include *From the Terrace* (1960), *Advise & Consent* (1962), *Happy Birthday, Wanda June* (1971), *Comes a Horseman* (1978), *Seems Like Old Times* (1980), *Bachelor Party* (1984), *Small Time Crooks* (2000), *Wonder Boys* (2000), and *Flags of Our Fathers* (2006).

Curtis Harrington (September 17, 1928–May 6, 2007). Born in Los Angeles, the director maintained a cult following for his horror films. He began directing shorts in his teens and graduated with a film studies degree from the University of California Los Angeles. Harrington worked with producer Jerry Wald and received production credits on the films *Mardi Gras* (1958), *Hound Dog Man* (1959), *Return to Peyton Place* (1961), and *The Stripper* (1963). His first directorial credit was 1961's *Night Tide*. Harrington also used the pseudonym John Sebastian for some films. Credits include *Voyage to the Prehistoric Planet* (1965), *Queen of Blood* (1966), *Games* (1967), *Whoever Slew Auntie Roo?* (1971), *What's the Matter with Helen?* (1971), *Cat Creature* (1973), *The Killing Kind* (1973), *Killer Bees (1974)*, *The Dead Don't Die* (1975), *Ruby* (1977), *Devil Dog, Hound of Hell* (1978), and *Mata Hari* (1985). His last work, which he wrote, directed, and starred in, was the 2002 short *Usher*, based on the Edgar Allan Poe story.

Betty Hutton (February 26, 1921–March 11, 2007). The singer and actress was born Elizabeth June Thornburg in Battle Creek, Michigan. Hutton started her singing career as a teenager and it was bandleader Vincent Lopez who changed her last name. She appeared in the Broadway revue *Two for the Show* in 1940 and *Panama Hattie* in 1941, which lead to a role in the 1941 Paramount film, *The Fleet's In*, and a studio contract. Credits include *Let's Face it* (1943), *Here Come the Waves* (1944), *The Miracle of Morgan's Creek* (1944), *Incendiary Blonde* (1945), *The Stork Club* (1945), *The Perils of Pauline* (1947), *Dream Girl* (1948), *Annie Get Your Gun* (1950), *The Greatest Show on Earth* (1952), and *Somebody Loves Me* (1952), after which Hutton walked out on her Paramount contract. Her last film was the low-budget *Spring Reunion* (1957). Hutton later developed an addiction to pills and alcohol and, after converting to Catholicism, worked briefly as an housekeeper at a Rhode Island rectory. Hutton occasionally appeared on stage in the 1980s and later received an education degree and taught classes on film and television.

George Jenkins (November 19, 1908–April 6, 2007). The set designer was born in Baltimore, Maryland and he left his architectural studies at the University of Pennsylvania to design sets. His award-winning work with the Philadelphia Plays and Players theater led to Jenkins' move to Broadway in the late 1930s. His work on the 1944 comedy *I Remember Mama* was seen by film producer Samuel Goldwyn, who brought Jenkins to Hollywood to work on *The Best Years of Our Lives* (1946). Jenkins shared an Academy Award® for best art direction/set decoration with George Gaines for 1976's *All the President's Men*. Other screen credits include *The Bishop's Wife* (1947), *The Secret Life of Walter Mitty* (1947), *The Miracle Worker* (1962), *Mickey One* (1965), *Wait Until Dark* (1967), *The Subject Was Roses* (1968), *Klute* (1971), *The Paper Chase* (1973), *The Parallax View* (1974), *Night Moves* (1975), *Comes a Horseman*

(1978), *The China Syndrome* (1979), *Sophie's Choice* (1982), and *Presumed Innocent* (1990).

Roy Jenson (February 9, 1927–April 24, 2007). Born in Calgary, Alberta, the character actor was usually typecast as a bad guy in numerous film and television roles. Jenson graduated from the University of Southern California Los Angeles and, while playing professional football in Canada, was recruited to work as a stunt double on the 1954 film *River of No Return*. Jenson continued doing stunt work before appearing in the film *Harper* (1966). Other screen credits include *The Great Escape* (1963), *The Getaway* (1972), *The Way We Were* (1973), *Chinatown* (1974), and *Every Which Way But Loose* (1978).

Marcia Mae Jones (August 1, 1924–September 2, 2007). A prolific child actress, Jones was born in Los Angeles and it was her actress mother Freda who took her to the studio as a baby. She received her first screen credit for 1931's *The Champ* but her career declined in the 1940s and Jones retired after 1952's *The Star,* though she later worked in television. Credits include *Night Nurse* (1931), *Bombshell* (1933), *The Garden of Allah* (1936), *Heidi* (1937), *The Life of Emile Zola* (1937), *Mountain Justice* (1937), *These Three* (1937), *The Adventures of Tom Sawyer* (1938), *Mad About Music* (1938), *First Love* (1939), *The Little Princess* (1939), *Anne of Windy Poplars* (1940), *Let's Go Collegiate* (1941), *Nice Girl?* (1941), *Secrets of a Co-Ed* (1942), *Top Man* (1943), *Lady in the Deathhouse* (1944), and *The Daughter of Rosie O'Grady* (1950).

Deborah Kerr (September 30, 1921–October 16, 2007). Born Deborah Jane Kerr Trimmer in Helensburgh, Scotland, the actress did some radio work in her teens and moved to London to study at the Sadler's Wells ballet school, making her debut in 1939 before deciding she was more interested in acting. Kerr's role in 1940's *Contraband* was cut but she was finally seen on screen in 1941's *Major Barbara,* which was rapidly followed by *Love on the Dole, Penn of Pennsylvania,* and *Hatter's Castle.* Although Kerr received six Oscar® nominations (for *Edward, My Son* , *From Here to Eternity* , *The King and I* , *Heaven Knows, Mr. Allison* , *Separate Tables* , *The Sundowners*), she only received a statuette in 1994 for lifetime achievement. Early roles included *The Day Will Dawn* (1942), *The Life and Death of Colonel Blimp* (1943), *Perfect Strangers* (1944), *I See a Dark Stranger* (1945), and *Black Narcissus* (1946) before Kerr became a contract player for MGM. Her MGM films include *The Hucksters* (1947), *If Winter Comes* (1947), *King Solomon's Mines* (1950), *Quo Vadis* (1951), *Julius Caesar* (1952), *The Prisoner of Zenda* (1952), and *Young Bess* (1953); she then left the studio. Later credits include *The End of the Affair* (1954), *Tea and Sympathy* (1956), *The Proud and the Profane* (1956), *An Affair to Remember* (1957), *Bonjour Tristesse* (1957), *The Grass is Greener* (1960), *The Naked Edge* (1961), *The Innocents* (1961), *The Chalk Garden* (1963), *The Night of the Iguana* (1964), *Marriage on the Rocks* (1965), *Eye of the Devil* (1966), *Casino Royale* (1967), *Prudence and the Pill* (1968), *The Arrangement* (1968), and *The Gypsy Moths* (1969). She first left screen acting in 1969, tired of lackluster roles, though Kerr made several television movies and appeared on stage, and then retired from acting in the late 1980s due to

Parkinson's disease. The actress' husband, writer Peter Viertel, died some three weeks after Kerr.

Michael Kidd (August 12, 1915–December 23, 2007). Born Michael Greenwald in Brooklyn, New York, the choreographer became interested in dance in high school although he first studied chemical engineering at City College of New York. Deciding to study dance instead, Kidd won a scholarship to the School of American Ballet in 1937, eventually joining American Ballet Theatre where he danced leading roles and staged his only ballet, *On Stage!* in 1945. Kidd left to work on Broadway, where he received Tony awards for *Finian's Rainbow* (1947), *Guys and Dolls* (1951), *Can-Can* (1954), *L'il Abner* (1957), and *Destry Rides Again* (1960). His first film choreography was 1952's *Where's Charley?* Other screen credits include *The Band Wagon* (1953), *Knock on Wood* (1954), *Seven Brides for Seven Brothers* (1954), *Guys and Dolls* (1955), *It's Always Fair Weather* (1955), *Merry Andrew* (1958), *L'il Abner* (1959), *Star!* (1968) and *Hello, Dolly!* (1969). Kidd received an Oscar® for lifetime achievement in 1997.

Laszlo Kovacs (May 14, 1933–July 22, 2007). The cinematographer was born in Cece, Hungary, and studied at the Academy of Drama and Film Art. Kovacs and fellow cinematographer Vilmos Zsigmond secretly filmed the 1956 Hungarian revolution in Budapest and came to the United States in 1957 as political refugees. Some of their original footage was included in the documentary *Torn from the Flag* (2006). Kovacs began his career working on a number of low-budget features (often for Roger Corman). Credits include *The Notorious Daughter of Fanny Hill* (1966), *Hells Angels on Wheels* (1967), *A Man Called Dagger* (1967), *Psych-Out* (1968), *The Savage Seven* (1968), *Targets* (1968), *Easy Rider* (1969), *Five Easy Pieces* (1970), *That Cold Day in the Park* (1970), *The Last Movie* (1971), *The King of Marvin Gardens* (1972), *The Last Picture Show* (1972), *What's Up, Doc?* (1972), *Paper Moon* (1974), *At Long Last Love* (1975), *Shampoo* (1975), *Nickelodeon* (1976), *New York, New York* (1977), *The Last Waltz* (1978), *Paradise Alley* (1978), *Frances* (1982), *Ghostbusters* (1984), *Little Nikita* (1988), *Say Anything* (1989), *Shattered* (1991), *The Next Karate Kid* (1994), *My Best Friend's Wedding* (1997), *Miss Congeniality* (2000), and *Two Weeks Notice* (2002). Kovacs received a lifetime achievement award from the American Society of Cinematographers in 2002.

Charles Lane (January 26, 1905–July 9, 2007). Born Charles Gerstle Levison in San Francisco, California, the prolific character actor played in hundreds of film and television roles, often cast as mean-spirited or cantankerous, including his role as the rent collector in 1946's *It's a Wonderful Life.* Lane began his career with a bit in *Smart Money* (1931) and was first credited as Charles Levison in such films as *Blondie Johnson* (1933), *Broadway Bill* (1934), *Mr. Deeds Goes to Town* (1936), *You Can't Take It With You* (1938), *Mr. Smith Goes to Washington* (1939), and *Arsenic and Old Lace* (1944). Lane also had recurring television roles on such shows as *Petticoat Junction, The Beverly Hillbillies,* and *I Love Lucy.* His last role was in the television movie *The Computer Wore Tennis Shoes* (1995) but he appeared via satellite at the 2005 Emmy awards, honored as one of the first members of the Screen Actors Guild, which he had joined in 1933.

Moira Lister (August 6, 1923–October 27, 2007). Born in Cape Town, South Africa, the actress took acting lessons as a child and debuted on stage at the age of six. In 1944, Lister moved to London and worked in the theater while making her film debut in *The Shipbuilders*. Other film credits include *Wanted for Murder* (1946), *Pool of London* (1950), *A Run for Your Money* (1950), *White Corridors* (1951), *The Cruel Sea* (1953), *Trouble in Store* (1953), *The Wicked Wife* (1953), *The Deep Blue Sea* (1955), *Abandon Ship* (1956), and *The Yellow Rolls-Royce* (1965). Lister continued to appear on stage and on various radio programs and television. Her autobiography, *A Very Merry Moira*, was published in 1969.

Calvin Lockhart (September 18, 1934–March 29, 2007). The actor was born Bert Cooper in Nassau, Bahamas. Lockhart came to New York at 18 and eventually studied acting with Uta Hagen; he later moved to Italy, Germany, and England where he found work in the theater, on television, and in films. Credits include *Joanna* (1968), *Cotton Comes to Harlem* (1970), *Halls of Anger* (1970), *Melinda* (1972), *The Beast Must Die* (1974), *Uptown Saturday Night* (1974), *Let's Do It Again* (1975), *The Baron* (1977), *Coming to America* (1988), *Predator 2* (1990), and *Wild at Heart* (1990).

Al Mancini (November 13, 1932–November 12, 2007). The character actor was born in Steubenville, Ohio and began acting while studying commercial art at Kent State University before moving to New York where he worked on stage and in television. While working in London on the satirical revue *The Premise*, Mancini became part of the BBC's *That Was the Week That Was* in 1962 and he later worked on a number of other series in Britain and the United States, including *Rhoda*, *All in the Family*, and *NYPD Blue*. Film credits include *The Dirty Game* (1965), *The Dirty Dozen* (1967), *Don't Raise the Bridge, Lower the River* (1967), *Madame Sin* (1972), *Miller's Crossing* (1990), and *Babe: Pig in the City* (1998).

Delbert Mann (January 30, 1920–November 11, 2007). The director was born in Lawrence, Kansas and grew up in Nashville, Tennessee where he attended Vanderbilt University and became involved in community theater. After serving in World War II, Mann earned a master's degree from the Yale School of Drama. In 1949, Mann joined NBC as a floor manager and assistant director, directing live original dramas, including 1953's *Marty*; Mann also directed the 1955 screen version, which won him an Oscar®. Other credits include *The Bachelor Party* (1957), *Desire Under the Elms* (1957), *Separate Tables* (1958), *Middle of the Night* (1959), *The Dark at the Top of the Stairs* (1960), *Lover Come Back* (1961), *The Outsider* (1961), *That Touch of Mink* (1962), *A Gathering of Eagles* (1963), *Dear Heart* (1964), *Mister Buddwing* (1966), *Fitzwilly* (1967), *Kidnapped* (1971), *Night Crossing* (1982), and *Bronte* (1983). Television credits include *Heidi* (1968), *David Copperfield* (1970), *Jane Eyre* (1971), *The Man Without a Country* (1973), *A Girl Named Sooner* (1975), *All Quiet on the Western Front* (1979), *The Last Days of Patton* (1986), *Incident in a Small Town* (1994), and *Lily in Winter* (1994). Mann published his memoirs, *Looking Back...at Live Television and Other Matters*, in 1998.

Kerwin Mathews (January 8, 1926–July 5, 2007). The actor, known for his action and fantasy roles, was born in Seattle, Washington and raised in Wisconsin where he attended Benoit College. Mathews moved to Hollywood in 1954 and became a contract player with Columbia Pictures, making his screen debut in 1955's *Five Against the House*. Credits include *The Garment Jungle* (1957), *The Seventh Voyage of Sinbad* (1958), *Tarawa Beachhead* (1958), *The Last Blitzkrieg* (1959), *Man on a String* (1960), *The Three Worlds of Gulliver* (1960), *The Warrior Empress* (1960), *The Devil at Four O'Clock* (1961), *Jack the Giant Killer* (1962), *Pirates of Blood River* (1962), *Maniac* (1963), *The Waltz King* (1963), and *Nightmare in Blood* (1976). Mathews retired in 1978 and became an antiques dealer.

Bobby Mauch (July 6, 1921–October 15, 2007). Actor and film editor Robert Joseph Mauch was born in Peoria, Illinois along with identical twin Billy (William). They began acting as children and made their debut in *Anthony Adverse* (1936); they confessed to director Mervyn LeRoy that although Billy was hired with Bobby as his stand-in, they both took turns with their role as they did in *The White Angel* (1936). Their mother then insisted that Warner Bros. would have to offer both sons contracts and they were cast in 1937's *The Prince and the Pauper*. The twins also played together in *Penrod and His Twin Brother* (1938), *Penrod's Double Take* (1938), and *I'll Tell the World* (1939). After serving in World War II, Bobby became a film editor while Billy (who died in 2006) joined Warner Bros. as a sound editor.

Lois Maxwell (February 14, 1927–September 29, 2007). The actress was born Lois Hooker in Kitchener, Ontario and played M's secretary, Miss Moneypenny, in fourteen of the James Bond films. Maxwell began her career in radio and came to Britain as part of the Entertainment Corps of the Canadian army before attending the Royal Academy of Dramatic Arts where she met future Bond, Roger Moore. Maxwell had small parts in the films *A Matter of Life and Death* and *Spring Song* (both 1946) and then moved to Hollywood, becoming a contract player with Warner Bros. She appeared in the films *That Hagen Girl* (1947), *The Big Punch* and *The Decision of Christopher Blake* (both 1948). When Warner failed to promote her career, Maxwell returned to Britain, appearing in a number of films, including *The Woman's Angle* (1951), *Lady in the Fog* (1952), *Women of Twilight* (1952), *Mantrap* (1953), *Passport to Treason* (1956), *Satellite in the Sky* (1956), *Kill Me Tomorrow* (1957), *Lolita* (1962), and *The Haunting* (1963). Her first Bond film was 1962's *Dr. No* and her last, 1985's *A View to a Kill*.

Barbara McNair (March 4, 1934–February 4, 2007). Born in Racine, Wisconsin, the singer and actress moved to New York in the mid-1950s and sang at the Village Vanguard, which lead to a role in the musical *The Body Beautiful* in 1958. Screen credits include *If He Hollers, Let Him Go* (1968), *Change of Habit* (1969), *They Call Me MISTER Tibbs!* (1970), and *The Organization* (1971). McNair also hosted her own variety series, *The Barbara McNair Show*, from 1969 to 1971, and continued to work on television and in nightclubs.

Lynn Merrick (November 19, 1919–March 25, 2007). Born Marilyn Merrick Llewelling in Fort Worth, Texas, the actress began her career as a model before signing with Republic, appearing opposite Don "Red" Barry in sixteen "B" westerns, beginning with 1940's *Two Gun Sheriff*. Merrick moved to Columbia Pictures in 1943, appearing in such films as *Meet Miss Bobby Socks* (1944), *A Guy, A Gal and a Pal* (1945), *Boston Blackie Booked on Suspicion* (1945), *A Close Call for Boston Blackie* (1946), and *I Love Trouble* (1948). She left acting in the 1950s and later worked in the fashion and modeling industries.

Jim Mitchell (November 30, 1943–July 12, 2007). James Lowell Mitchell was born in Stockton, California and, along with his younger brother Artie, produced a number of adult films in the 1960s and 1970s, including *Behind the Green Door* (1972), *Resurrection of Eve* (1973), and *Sodom & Gomorrah* (1975). Mitchell first became involved in peep-show films and longer "nudies" and the brothers owned a number of theaters as well as movie and video production services. In 1991, Mitchell was convicted of voluntary manslaughter in the death of his brother; after his release from prison, Mitchell turned to raising horses.

Kieron Moore (October 5, 1924–July 15, 2007). The actor was born Kieron O'Hanrahan in Skibbereen, Ireland where his journalist father was a fervent promoter of Irish nationalism. Moore began studying medicine in Dublin but he acted as a hobby and was offered a movie contract by Alexander Korda after working on the London stage, making his screen debut in 1945's *The Voice Within*. Other credits included *Man About the House* (1947), *Mine Own Executioner* (1947), *Anna Karenina* (1948), *Saints and Sinners* (1949), *David and Bathsheba* (1951), *Ten Tall Men* (1951), *Mantrap* (1953), *Recoil* (1953), *The Blue Peter* (1954), *The Green Scarf* (1954), *Satellite in the Sky* (1956), *The Steel Bayonet* (1957), *Dr. Blood's Coffin* (1960), *The League of Gentlemen* (1960), *The Day of the Triffids* (1962), *Arabesque* (1966), and *Custer of the West* (1966). After leaving acting, Moore worked for a Catholic relief agency and the Catholic newspaper, *The Universe*.

Ulrich Muehe (June 20, 1953–July 22, 2007). The actor was born in Grimma, East Germany and began his theater studies in 1975, joining the Berlin's Volksbuehne theater and later the Deutsches Theater. Muehe also worked on television, starring as pathologist Robert Kolmaar in the crime serial *Last Witness* (1998–2007). Films include *Schtonk!* (1991), *The Castle* (1996), *Funny Games* (1997), *The Lives of Others* (2006), and *My Fuhrer: The Absolutely Truest Truth About Adolf Hitler* (2007).

Barry Nelson (April 16, 1920–April 7, 2007). Born Robert Haakon Nielsen in San Francisco, the actor graduated from the University of California Berkeley in 1941 and was soon signed to a contract by MGM. Films include *Shadow of the Thin Man* (1941), *Dr. Kildare's Victory* (1942), *Johnny Eager* (1942), *A Yank on the Burma Road* (1942), *Bataan* (1943), *Winged Victory* (1944), *Mary, Mary* (1963), *Airport* (1970), *Pete 'n' Tillie* (1972), and *The Shining* (1980). Nelson also starred on stage and had a number of television roles, including co-starring in the situation comedy *My Favorite Husband* (1953–57). Nelson was also the first actor to play a version of James Bond—starring as the Americanized Jimmy Bond in 1954's *Casino Royale*, filmed as part of the CBS anthology series *Climax!*

Carlo Ponti (December 11, 1912–January 9, 2007). The film producer, who discovered and later married Sophia Loren, was born in Magenta, Italy and worked as a lawyer before moving into film in the late 1930s. Ponti produced *Two Women*, which won Loren the best actress Oscar® in 1962. Among his other films were *Piccolo Mondo Antico* (1941), *La Strada* (1954), *War and Peace* (1956), *The Black Orchid* (1959), *Heller in Pink Tights* (1960), *Contempt* (1963), *Yesterday, Today and Tomorrow* (1963), *Marriage Italian Style* (1964), *Dr. Zhivago* (1965), *Lady L* (1965), *Blowup* (1966), *Zabriskie Point* (1970), *The Passenger* (1975), and *A Special Day* (1977).

Tom Poston (October 17, 1921–April 30, 2007). The comedic actor was born in Columbus, Ohio and, after serving in World War II, studied at the American Academy of Dramatic Arts, making his Broadway debut in 1947. Poston was also featured on television on *The Steve Allen Show*, *To Tell the Truth*, *Mork and Mindy*, *The Bob Newhart Show*, *Newhart*, *Grace Under Fire*, and *Bob*. Films include *Soldier in the Rain* (1963), *Cold Turkey* (1971), *Rabbit Test* (1978), *Up the Academy* (1980), *Krippendorf's Tribe* (1998), *Beethoven's 5th* (2003), *Christmas with the Kranks* (2004), and *The Princess Diaries 2* (2004).

Mala Powers (December 20, 1931–June 11, 2007). Born Mary Ellen Powers in San Francisco, the actress made her debut at eleven in the Bowery Boys movie, *Tough as They Come* (1942). At nineteen, Powers appeared in *Cyrano de Bergerac* and *The Outrage* (both 1950) and was signed to a contract at RKO by Howard Hughes. But after a promising start, most of Powers' roles were in "B" films, including *Edge of Doom* (1950), *City Beneath the Sea* (1953), *City That Never Sleeps* (1953), *The Yellow Mountain* (1954), *Rage of Dawn* (1955), *Bengazi* (1955), *Storm Rider* (1957), *The Unknown Terror* (1957), *The Colossus of New York* (1958), *Escape from Planet Earth* (1967), and *Doomsday Machine* (1972).

Fons Rademakers (September 5, 1920–February 22, 2007). The director was born Alphonse Marie Rademakers in Roosendaal, the Netherlands. He studied acting at Amsterdam's Academy of Dramatic Arts and, after World War II, studied film in Paris under Jean Renoir and in Rome under Vittorio de Sica. Rademakers first film, *Village on the River*, was nominated for a best foreign language film Oscar® in 1959 and his 1986 film, *The Assault*, won the award in 1986. Other films include *Max Havelaar* (1976) and *The Rose Garden* (1989).

Charles Nelson Reilly (January 13, 1931–May 25, 2007). The comedic actor and stage director was born in the Bronx, New York and was most familiar for his television appearances as a panelist on *Match Game* and *The Hollywood Squares* and a guest on *The Tonight Show* as well as such programs as *The Ghost and Mrs. Muir* and *The X-Files*. Reilly won a Tony in 1962 for his role in the original Broadway production of *How to Succeed in Business Without Really Trying*. Film work includes *Cannonball Run 2* (1984), *All Dogs Go to Heaven* (1989), *Rock-a-Doodle* (1992), and *Boys Will Be Boys* (1997). His one-man stage show, *Save it for the Stage: The Life of Reilly*, was made into the 2006 film, *The Life of Reilly*.

Ian Richardson (April 7, 1934–February 9, 2007). The actor was born in Edinburgh, Scotland and trained at the College of Dramatic Arts in Glasgow. Richardson joined the Birmingham Repertory Theatre Company in the late 1950s but then became a member of the Royal Shakespeare Company from 1960 to 1975. Credits include *Tinker, Tailor, Soldier, Spy* (1979), *Private Schulz* (1981), *The Hound of the Baskervilles* (1983), *The Last Viceroy* (1984), *Brazil* (1985), *The Fourth Protocol* (1987), *Porterhouse Blue* (1987), *The Winslow Boy* (1989), *House of Cards* (1990), *Rosencrantz & Guildenstern Are Dead* (1990), *An Ungentlemanly Act* (1992), *To Play the King* (1993), *The Final Cut* (1995), *BAPS* (1997), *Dark City* (1998), *102 Dalmatians* (2000), *Murder Rooms: The Dark Beginnings of Sherlock Holmes* (2001), *Bleak House* (2005), and *Becoming Jane* (2007).

Anton Rodgers (January 10, 1933–December 1, 2007). The actor was born in Wisbech, England, working as a child actor in stage productions of *Great Expectations* (1948) and *The Winslow Boy* (1949); Rodgers continued to have a long stage career. He also starred in the television series *Fresh Fields* (1984–86) and *May to December* (1989–94). Screen credits include *Rotten to the Core* (1956), *Crash Dive* (1959), *The Iron Maiden* (1962), *Carry on Jack* (1963), *The Day of the Jackal* (1973), *Lillie* (1978), *The Fourth Protocol* (1987), *Dirty Rotten Scoundrels* (1988), *Son of the Pink Panther* (1993), *The Merchant of Venice* (2004), and *Longford* (2006).

Stuart Rosenberg (August 11, 1927–March 15, 2007). Born in Brooklyn, New York, the director studied at New York University and, in the early 1950s, took a television job as an apprentice film editor before directing such series as *The Defenders, Naked City, The Twilight Zone,* and *The Untouchables.* Rosenberg's first feature film was 1967's *Cool Hand Luke* and he would also direct Paul Newman in *WUSA* (1970), *Pocket Money* (1972), and *The Drowning Pool* (1975). Other credits include *The April Fools* (1969), *Move* (1970), *The Laughing Policeman* (1973), *Voyage of the Damned* (1976), *The Amityville Horror* (1979), *Brubaker* (1980), *The Pope of Greenwich Village* (1984), and *My Heroes Have Always Been Cowboys* (1991). Rosenberg also taught directing at the American Film Institute.

Frank Rosenfelt (November 15, 1921–August 2, 2007). Born in Peabody, Massachusetts, the studio executive graduated from Cornell Law School and worked as a lawyer for RKO from 1950 to 1955. He then joined Metro-Goldwyn-Mayer and became its president and chief executive in 1973, overseeing MGM's purchase of United Artists in 1981. Rosenfelt stepped down in 1982 and later opened a consulting business.

Gordon Scott (August 3, 1926–April 30, 2007). The actor was born Gordon M. Werschkull in Portland, Oregon and took up bodybuilding in his teens. While working as a lifeguard at the Sahara Hotel in Las Vegas, Scott was spotted by Hollywood producer Sol Lesser who offered him a contract (and changed his last name), making him the eleventh actor to play Tarzan in 1954's *Tarzan's Hidden Jungle.* This was followed by *Tarzan and the Lost Safari* (1957), *Tarzan Fight for Life* (1958), *Tarzan and the Trappers* (1958), *Tarzan's Greatest Adventure* (1959), and *Tarzan the Magnificent* (1960). Tired of the role, Scott moved to Italy and worked on such genre muscle films as *Samson and the Seven Miracles of the World* (1962), *Hero of*

Rome (1963), *Gladiator of Rome* (1963), *Conquest of Mycene* (1963), and *Hercules and the Princess of Troy* (1965). Scott's last film was 1966's *Death Ray Tramplers* and he later supported himself with residuals and by attending autograph shows and film conventions but he lived his later years as a semi-recluse.

Ousmane Sembene (January 1, 1923–June 9, 2007). The writer/director was born in the village of Ziguinchor in Senegal, then a French colony. Sembene went to Marseilles, France and was a dock worker until Senegal's independence in 1960. He published his first novel in 1956 and continued writing while studying film at the Gorky Film Institute in Moscow. Sembene began his career with the shorts *Borom Sarett* (1963) and *Niaye* (1964) and his first feature was 1966's *La Noire de.../Black Girl.* Credits include *Mandabi/The Money Order* (1968), *Emitai* (1972), *Xala* (1974), *Ceddo* (1976), *Camp de Thiaroye* (1988), *Guelwaar* (1992), *Faat Kine* (2000), and *Moolaade* (2002).

Michel Serrault (January 24, 1928–July 29, 2007). Born in Brunoy, France, Serrault was best known to most filmgoers for his role as Albin in 1978's *La Caux aux Folles/The Birdcage* and its two sequels (1981, 1986). He had played the role onstage for five years, beginning in 1973, opposite Jean Poiret, with whom he also did a cabaret act. The two had met in the 1950s and appeared together in 18 films, from 1956 to 1984, and a number of plays. Serrault made his stage debut in 1948 and his film debut in 1954's *Peek-a-boo.* Credits include *Les Diaboliques* (1955), *Mam'zelle Pigalle* (1956), *Assassins et Voleurs* (1957), *La Belle Americaine* (1961), *Warrior's Rest* (1962), *King of Hearts* (1966), *The Life Annuity* (1972), *Garde a Vue* (1981), *The Hatter's Ghost* (1982), *The Old Lady Who Walked in the Sea* (1991), *Nelly and Monsieur Arnaud* (1995), *Beaumarchais the Scoundrel* (1996), *Artemisia* (1997), *Rien ne va Plus* (1998), *The Butterfly* (2002), *Joyeux Noel* (2003), and *Hometown Boys* (2006). Serrault published his memoirs, *Did You Say Serrault?,* in 2001.

Melville Shavelson (April 1, 1917–August 8, 2007). The writer, producer, and director was born in Brooklyn, New York and graduated from Cornell University in 1937. Shavelson began his career in radio in 1938, hired by Bob Hope as a gag writer. He wrote the Hope films *The Princess and the Pirate* (1944), *The Great Lover* (1949), *Sorrowful Jones* (1949), *The Seven Little Foys* (1955, Oscar® nomination), and *Beau James* (1956). Other credits include *Wonder Man* (1945), *The Kid from Brooklyn* (1946), *I'll See You in My Dreams* (1951), *On Moonlight Bay* (1951), *April in Paris* (1952), *Houseboat* (1958, Oscar® nomination), *The Five Pennies* (1959), *It Started in Naples* (1960), *A New Kind of Love* (1963), *Cast a Giant Shadow* (1966), *Yours, Mine and Ours* (1968), *The War Between Men and Women* (1972), and *Mixed Company* (1974). He also worked on television and created the Danny Thomas series *Make Room for Daddy* and the 1969 series *My World, and Welcome to It.* Shavelson published his autobiography, *How to Succeed in Hollywood Without Really Trying: PS—You Can't!,* in 2007.

David Shaw (August 27, 1916–July 27, 2007). Born Samuel David Shamforoff in Brooklyn, New York, the writer began his career in radio after World War II and followed his older brother, writer Irwin Shaw, to Los Angeles in the late 1940s. Shaw wrote for a number of television series, including *The Defenders, Playhouse 90, Studio One,* and *The Philco TV Playhouse.* Film credits include *A Foreign Affair* (1948), *The Man Inside* (1958), and *If It's Tuesday, This Must Be Belgium* (1969). Shaw retired in the early 1980s and began a second career as a painter.

Sidney Sheldon (February 11, 1917–January 30, 2007). The writer was born Sidney Schechtel in Chicago, Illinois. He moved to Los Angeles in the late 1930s and was hired as a script reader for Universal. His first writing credits (along with Ben Roberts) were for the films *Borrowed Hero, Gambling Daughters,* and *South of Panama* (all 1941). In 1947, Sheldon won an Oscar® for best original screenplay for *The Bachelor and the Bobby Soxer,* which lead to a contract with MGM. Credits include *Easter Parade* (1948), *The Barkleys of Broadway* (1949), *Annie Get Your Gun* (1950), *Nancy Goes to Rio* (1950), *Rich, Young and Pretty* (1951), *Three Guys Named Mike* (1951), *You're Never Too Young* (1955), *Anything Goes* (1956), *Birds & the Bees* (1956), *Pardners* (1956), *All in a Night's Work* (1961), and *Billy Rose's Jumbo* (1962). Sheldon also directed *Dream Wife* (1953) and *The Buster Keaton Story* (1957, also wrote). He segued into television in the 1960s with *The Patty Duke Show* and *I Dream of Jeannie,* and later *Hart to Hart.* Sheldon published his first novel in 1970; many were adapted for film and television, including *The Other Side of Midnight* (1977), *Bloodline* (1979), *Rage of Angels* (1980), *The Naked Face* (1984), *If Tomorrow Comes* (1986), *Windmill of the Gods* (1988), *Memories of Midnight* (1991), *The Sands of Time* (1992), *A Stranger in the Mirror* (1993), and *Nothing Lasts Forever* (1995). Sheldon's memoir, *The Other Side of Me,* was published in 2005.

Joel Siegel (July 7, 1943–June 29, 2007). The film critic was born in Los Angeles and graduated from the University of California Los Angeles with a degree in history. Siegel reviewed books for the *Los Angeles Times* and, after moving to New York, worked on radio and the local ABC affiliate as their entertainment critic. In 1981, Siegel joined *Good Morning America* and continued to work on the show until shortly before his death from cancer. In 1991, Siegel and Gene Wilder founded Gilda's Club, a nonprofit organization for cancer patients and their family and friends.

Art Stevens (May 1, 1915–May 22, 2007). Born in Roy, Montana, the animator applied for a job at the Disney Studios in 1939 and first worked on 1940's *Fantasia;* he remained with the studio until his retirement in 1983. Stevens co-directed *The Rescuers* (1977) and *The Fox and the Hound* (1981). Animation credits include *Peter Pan* (1953), *101 Dalmatians* (1961), *Mary Poppins* (1964), *Bedknobs and Broomsticks* (1971), and *Robin Hood* (1973).

Herman Stein (August 19, 1915–March 15, 2007). Born in Philadelphia, Pennsylvania, the composer wrote and arranged for radio programs and jazz orchestras before becoming a staff composer at Universal from 1951 to 1958. However, since several composers usually worked on a single picture, Stein frequently did not receive on-screen credit. Films include *Here Come the Nelsons* (1952), *Abbott and Costello Go to Mars* (1953), *City Beneath the Sea* (1953), *Girls in the Night* (1953), *It Came from Outer Space* (1953), *Ma and Pa Kettle on Vacation* (1953), *The Black Shield of Falworth* (1954), *The Creature from the Black Lagoon* (1954), *Drums Across the River* (1954), *The Far Country*

(1954), *This Island Earth* (1955), *Tarantula* (1955), *Backlash* (1956), *The Great Man* (1956), *The Mole People* (1956), and *The Incredible Shrinking Man* (1957). Stein later freelanced on such films as *The Intruder* (1962) and *Let's Kill Uncle* (1966) and he scored a number of television shows, including *Gunsmoke, Wagon Train, Daniel Boone, Lost in Space,* and *Voyage to the Bottom of the Sea.*

Burt Topper (July 31, 1928–April 3, 2007). Born in Coney Island, New York, he grew up in Los Angeles. Topper wrote, directed, and produced a number of low-budget features for American International Pictures, eventually becoming the head of production for the studio. Credits include *Hell Squad* (1958), *Tank Commandos* (1958), *Diary of a High School Bride* (1959), *War Is Hell* (1963), *The Strangler* (1964), *The Devil's 8* (1969), *The Hard Ride* (1971), and *The Day the Lord Got Busted* (1976).

William J. Tuttle (April 13, 1912–July 27, 2007). The makeup artist was born in Jacksonville, Florida. After moving to Los Angeles at eighteen, Tuttle took art classes at the University of Southern California and became an apprentice of Jack Dawn, then the head of the Twentieth Century Pictures makeup department. When Dawn left for MGM, Tuttle followed and after Dawn retired, Tuttle was the head at MGM from 1960 to 1969. Credits include *Summer Stock* (1950), *An American in Paris* (1951), *Royal Wedding* (1951), *Show Boat* (1951), *The Bad and the Beautiful* (1952), *Million Dollar Mermaid* (1952), *Pat and Mike* (1952), *Singin' in the Rain (1952), The Band Wagon* (1953), *Brigadoon* (1954), *Blackboard Jungle* (1955), *Cat on a Hot Tin Roof* (1958), *Lust for Life* (1956), *Gigi* (1958), *Some Came Running* (1958), *North by Northwest* (1959), *Bells Are Ringing* (1960), *The Time Machine* (1960), *The Courtship of Eddie's Father* (1963), and *Viva Las Vegas* (1964). Tuttle developed his own makeup line, Custom Color Cosmetics, and worked independently on such films as *Young Frankenstein* (1974), *Logan's Run* (1976), and *Zorro, the Gay Blade* (1981). He also taught at USC from 1970 to 1995. Tuttle received an honorary Oscar® in 1965 for his work on *The 7 Faces of Dr. Lao;* the Academy did not have an official category for makeup until 1981.

Miyoshi Umeki (May 8, 1929–August 28, 2007). The actress was born in Otaru, Japan and began her career singing in nightclubs and on the radio and television. She moved to the United States in 1955 and her work on the variety show *Arthur Godfrey and His Friends* brought Umeki to the attention of Joshua Logan, who hired her for 1957's *Sayonara.* She was the first Asian performer to win an Oscar® for her work. Umeki was nominated for a Tony award for the Broadway musical *Flower Drum Song,* repeating her role in the 1961 movie version. Other credits include *Cry for Happy* (1961), *The Horizontal Lieutenant* (1962), and *A Girl Named Tamiko* (1962); she also played housekeeper Mrs. Livingston on the ABC series, *The Courtship of Eddie's Father,* from 1969 to 1972. Umeki then retired from acting.

Jack Valenti (September 5, 1921–April 26, 2007). Born in Houston, Texas, Valenti was the public face of the Motion Picture Association of America (MPAA) and the creator of its voluntary ratings code in 1968. After serving in World War II, he attended Harvard Business School and worked in Humble Oil's advertising department before meeting

Senator Lyndon B. Johnson in 1956. Valenti became a political consultant during John F. Kennedy's presidential campaign and was later hired by Johnson as a special assistant. He took over as head of the MPAA in 1966 and retired in 2004. Valenti's memoir, *This Time, This Place: My Life in War, the White House, and Hollywood,* was published in 2007.

Peter Viertel (November 16, 1920–November 4, 2007). Born in Dresden, Germany, the writer was the son of poet/director Berthold and screenwriter Salka Viertel. Growing up in Santa Monica, California, Viertel was surrounded by the émigré Hollywood community. He wrote novels and screenplays as well as a 1992 memoir, *Dangerous Friends: At Large with Huston and Hemingway in the Fifties.* Credits include *Saboteur* (1942), *The Hard Way* (1943), *We Were Strangers* (1949), *Decision Before Dawn* (1951), *The Sun Also Rises* (1957), *The Old Man and the Sea* (1958), and *White Hunter, Black Heart* (1990), which was based on his novel. Viertel married actress Deborah Kerr in 1960; she predeceased him by some three weeks.

Floyd Red Crow Westerman (August 17, 1936–December 13, 2007). Born on the Sisseton-Wahpeton Dakota Sioux reservation in South Dakota, Westerman was an actor, singer, and political activist. Orphaned as a child, Westerman was sent to a government boarding school and studied theater and education at Northern State College. He sang in coffeehouses and his 1970 debut album was *Custer Died for Your Sins.* Westerman made his film debut in 1989's *Renegade.* Other credits include *Dances with Wolves* (1990), *The Doors* (1991), *Son of the Morning Star* (1991), *Buffalo Girls* (1995), *Grey Owl* (1999), *Hidalgo* (2004), and *The Tillamook Treasure* (2006). Westerman was also featured on such television shows as *Walker, Texas Ranger, Dharma & Greg, Northern Exposure,* and *The X-Files.*

Monty Westmore (June 12, 1923–November 13, 2007). Born Montague George Westmore in Los Angeles, he was a third-generation member of Hollywood makeup artists. Westmore began his career in 1943, working as an apprentice for his uncle, Perc Westmore, at Warner Bros. and later moved to Universal. Westmore amassed more than 100 screen credits, including *What Ever Happened to Baby Jane?* (1962), *Strait-Jacket* (1964), *The Life and Times of Judge Roy Bean* (1972), *The Towering Inferno* (1974), *Fort Apache, the Bronx* (1981), *The Verdict* (1982), *The Color of Money* (1986), *Stand by Me* (1986), *Chaplin* (1992), *Hook* (1992), *Jurassic Park* (1993), *The Shawshank Redemption* (1994), *Message in a Bottle* (1998), and *How the Grinch Stole Christmas* (2000).

Nicholas Worth (September 4, 1937–May 7, 2007). Born in St. Louis, Mississippi, the character actor often played the

villain in numerous pictures. Worth moved to Los Angeles in 1965 and studied at the Pasadena Playhouse, making his film debut in *For Pete's Sake* (1966). Other credits include *Don't Answer the Phone* (1980), *Swamp Thing* (1982), *The Rape of Richard Beck* (1985), *The Naked Gun: From the Files of Police Squad!* (1988), and *Darkman* (1990).

Jane Wyman (January 5, 1917–September 10, 2007). The actress was born Sarah Jane Mayfield Fulks in St. Joseph, Missouri and started as a chorus girl in films in the early 1930s. Wyman changed her name when she was offered a contract with Warner Bros. in 1936. She received Oscar® nominations for *The Yearling* (1946), *The Glass Menagerie* (1950), *The Blue Veil* (1951), and *Magnificent Obsession* (1954); she won for *Johnny Belinda* (1948). Credits include *Brother Rat* (1938), *Brother Rat and a Baby* (1940), *The Lost Weekend* (1945), *Stage Fright* (1950), *Here Comes the Groom* (1951), *The Story of Will Rogers* (1952), *So Big* (1953), *All That Heaven Allows* (1955), *Miracle in the Rain* (1956), *Pollyanna* (1960), and *How to Commit Marriage* (1969). Wyman played matriarch Angela Channing on the CBS series *Falcon Crest* from 1981 to 1990. Wyman was married to Ronald Reagan from 1940 to 1948 and always maintained a decorous silence about her ex-husband during his later political career.

Edward Yang (November 6, 1947–June 29, 2007). The director was born in Shanghai, China but grew up in Taiwan. He first studied engineering and came to the United States in the 1970s to do graduate work, later working as a computer engineer. Yang, who always had an interest in film, switched careers when he was given a chance to write the script for 1981's *The Winter of 1905.* Credits include *That Day, on the Beach* (1983), *Taipei Story* (1985), *The Terrorizer* (1986), *A Brighter Summer Day* (1991), *A Confucian Confusion* (1994), *Mahjong* (1996), and *Yi Yi* (2000).

Peter Zinner (July 24, 1919–November 13, 2007). The film editor was born in Vienna, Austria and studied music and composition, but his family fled the Nazis in 1938. Zinner came to Los Angeles in 1940 and became an apprentice music and film editor at 20th Century-Fox in 1943; he later worked at Universal and MGM as well as independently. Zinner received Oscar® nominations for *The Godfather* (1972) and *An Officer and a Gentleman* (1982) and he won for *The Deer Hunter* (1978). Other credits include *The Professionals* (1966), *In Cold Blood* (1967), *Gunn* (1967), *The Red Tent* (1969), *Darling Lili* (1970), *The Godfather, Part 2* (1974), *Mahogany* (1975), *A Star is Born* (1976), *The Winds of War* (1983), *War and Remembrance* (1988), and *Citizen Cohn* (1992). Zinner also directed one film, 1981's *The Salamander.*

Selected Film Books of 2007

Abbott, Stacey. *Celluloid Vampires: Life After Death in the Modern World.* University of Texas Press, 2007. Traces the evolution of the American vampire film and the vampire archetype.

Alda, Alan. *Things I Overheard While Talking to Myself.* Random House, 2007. After recovering from a near-fatal health crisis, the actor examines the meaningful moments in his life and shares his inspirational philosophy.

Alter, Stephen. *Fantasies of a Bollywood Love Thief: Inside the World of Indian Moviemaking.* Harcourt/Harvest, 2007. A look at the Hindi-language films produced in Mumbai that focuses on the production of the film *Omkara*, an updated take on Shakespeare's *Othello*.

Armstrong, Stephen B. *Pictures about Extremes: The Films of John Frankenheimer.* McFarland & Co., 2007. Offers an overview of the director's life and career as well as an analysis of his films' thematic and stylistic elements.

Atkinson, Michael and Laurel Shifrin. *Flickipedia: Perfect Films for Every Occasion, Holiday, Mood, Ordeal, and Whim.* Chicago Review Press, 2007. Provides more than 1,300 movie suggestions, organized by such categories as holidays, life phases, and emotional upheavals.

Bach, Steven. *Leni: The Life and Work of Leni Riefenstahl.* Knopf, 2007. Explores the filmmaker's private life, ambitions, her opportunistic courting of Nazi sponsorship, and her revisionist personal history.

Barrier, Michael. *The Animated Man: A Life of Walt Disney.* University of California Press, 2007. Animation historian Barrier's biography of Disney and his impact on animated film.

Basinger, Jeanine. *The Star Machine.* Knopf, 2007. Looks at Hollywood from the 1930s to the 1950s and how the studios manufactured and promoted their stars, including Errol Flynn, Lana Turner, Veronica Lake, Clark Gable, and many others.

Berry, S. Torriano and Venise T. Berry. *Historical Dictionary of African American Cinema.* Scarecrow Press, 2007. Looks at the role African Americans played in the film industry.

Blakesley, David. *The Terministic Screen: Rhetorical Perspectives on Film.* Southern Illinois University Press, 2007. Fifteen essays examine the importance of rhetoric in film and film theory studies.

Blottner, Gene. *Wild Bill Elliott: A Complete Filmography.* McFarland & Co., 2007. Study of the career of the western star, including his 78 lead roles and more than 130 supporting parts.

Boswell, Parley Ann. *Edith Wharton on Film.* Southern Illinois University Press, 2007. Explores both the texts where Wharton referenced film and Hollywood culture and film adaptation of the author's works.

Bourne, Stephen. *Ethel Waters: Stormy Weather.* Scarecrow Press, 2007. Biography of the African American actress and singer from her vaudeville and Broadway career to her work in films.

Boyar, Burt. *Photo by Sammy Davis, Jr.* Regan, 2007. Collection of photographs, beginning in the early 1950s, that Davis took of his family and friends, including Jerry Lewis, Dean Martin, and Frank Sinatra.

Branaghan, Sim, and Steve Chibnall. *British Film Posters: An Illustrated History.* British Film Institute, 2007. Covers design, printing, and display as well as biographies of major artists.

Bret, David. *Joan Crawford: Hollywood Martyr.* Carroll & Graf, 2007. Rags-to-riches celebrity biography of the actress, including the scandals that plagued her personal life.

Carroll, Noel. *Comedy Incarnate: Buster Keaton, Physical Humor, and Bodily Coping.* Blackwell Publishing, 2007. Surveys the characteristics of Keaton's visual style and the philosophies behind it.

Casper, Drew. *Postwar Hollywood: 1946–1962.* Blackwell Publishing, 2007. Comprehensive history of the post-

World War II film industry, including emerging genres, censorship, new technologies, and business practices.

Cavallaro, Dani. *Anime Intersections: Traditions and Innovation in Theme and Technique.* McFarland & Co., 2007. Explores the technical and thematic developments of anime from its origins as a subset of Japanese film to its worldwide popularity.

Ceplair, Larry. *The Marxist and the Movies: A Biography of Paul Jarrico.* University Press of Kentucky, 2007. Considers the life, career, and political activism of the screenwriter and his problems with the Hollywood blacklist.

Chandler, Charlotte. *Ingrid: Ingrid Bergman, a Personal Biography.* Simon & Schuster, 2007. Straightforward accounting of the life and career of the actress, who died in 1982.

Chibnall, Steve. *Quota Quickies: The Birth of the British "B" Film.* British Film Institute, 2007. Traces the development of the low-budget indigenous supporting features, beginning in 1927, including genres, studios, producers, distributors, and stars.

Chopra, Anupama. *King of Bollywood: Shah Rukh Khan and the Seductive World of Indian Cinema.* Warner Books, 2007. A biography of the New Delhi-born superstar as well as a concise history of the Indian film industry.

Clayton, Alex. *The Body in Hollywood Slapstick.* McFarland & Co., 2007. Examines how physical comedy worked in slapstick films, including those of Laurel & Hardy, Harold Lloyd, Charlie Chaplin, and Buster Keaton.

Cook, Bernie, editor. *Thelma & Louise Live!: The Cultural Afterlife of an American Film.* University of Texas Press, 2007. Six film scholars consider the initial reception and ongoing impact of the film.

Cornea, Christine. *Science Fiction Cinema: Between Fantasy and Reality.* Rutgers University Press, 2007. Explores the development of the science fiction film through an historical and theoretical reassessment of the genre.

Craig, Rob. *The Films of Larry Buchanan: A Critical Examination.* McFarland & Co., 2007. Looks at the themes in more than twenty of the filmmaker's work, including their political subtext.

Curry, Christopher Wayne. *Film Alchemy: The Independent Cinema of Ted V. Mickels.* McFarland & Co., 2007. Examines nineteen of the exploitation filmmaker's movie or video productions.

Cusic, Don. *Gene Autry: His Life and Career.* McFarland & Co., 2007. Biography of the actor/singer who also found success in business and sports.

De La Hoz, Cindy. *Lucy at the Movies.* Running Press, 2007. Overview of actress Lucille Ball's film career with a synopsis, cast and credits, and behind the scenes notes and critical reception of each movie.

De Winter, Helen. *"What I Really Want to Do Is Produce\PO": Top Producers Talk About Movies and Money.* Faber and Faber, 2007. Twenty-one film producers, working in Hollywood, New York, and England, describe their job functions, including developing material, budgeting, financing, and distribution.

Deracy, Christopher, and Gaye Williams Ortiz. *Theology and Film: Challenging the Sacred/Secular Divide.* Blackwell Publishing, 2007. Explores the debate between theology and contemporary culture and how film can enrich the study of theology.

Dern, Bruce. *Things I've Said, But Probably Shouldn't Have.* John Wiley & Sons, 2007. Primarily serves as a memoir of Dern's acting career rather than his personal life.

Dherbier, Yann-Brice, and Pierre-Henri Verlhac, editors. *Grace Kelly: A Life in Pictures.* Pavilion Books, 2007. A photographical tribute to the actress on the 25th anniversary of her death.

Dixon, Wheeler Winston. *Film Talk: Directors at Work.* Rutgers University Press, 2007. Interviews with eleven filmmakers, including Monte Hellman, Albert Maysles, Robert Downey Sr., Bennett Miller, and Jamie Babbit.

Doherty, Thomas. *Hollywood's Censor: Joseph I. Breen & the Production Code Administration.* Columbia University Press, 2007. A comprehensive study of film censorship that focuses on Breen, the head of the puritanical Production Code Administration from 1934 to 1954.

Douglas, Kirk. *Let's Face It: 90 Years of Living, Loving, and Learning.* John Wiley & Sons, 2007. The actor reminisces about his childhood, marriage, family, friends, and long career.

Edwards, Matthew, editor. *Film Out of Bounds: Essays and Interviews on Non-Mainstream Cinema Worldwide.* McFarland & Co., 2007. Essays on fringe films and filmmakers.

Farrell, Mike. *Just Call Me Mike: A Journey to Actor and Activist.* Akashic, 2007. In this autobiography, the actor and producer recalls both his career and personal interest in politics and human rights activities.

Flesher, Paul V.M., and Robert Torry. *Film & Religion: An Introduction.* Abingdon, 2007. Essays that focus on the religious themes and historical context of American films released since World War II.

Flinn, Caryl. *Brass Diva: The Life and Legends of Ethel Merman.* University of California Press, 2007. Complex portrait uses more than fifty of Merman's own scrapbooks to document her career from the 1930s through the 1970s.

Flynn, Roderick, and Pat Brereton. *Historical Dictionary of Irish Cinema.* Scarecrow Press, 2007. A history of the film industry in Ireland from the late 1910s to the present, including its actors, directors, and films about the country.

Garrett, Greg. *The Gospel According to Hollywood.* Westminster John Knox, 2007. Offers an analysis of dozens of mainstream Hollywood films from the past five decades to extract their religious and spiritual themes.

Gemunden, Gerd, and Mary R. Desjardins, editors. *Dietrich Icon.* Duke University Press, 2007. A collection of essays on the career and persona of Marlene Dietrich.

Glut, Don. *I Was a Teenage Movie Maker: The Book.* McFarland & Co., 2007. A first-hand account of Glut's career and his filmmaking experiences at the University of Southern California.

Goldmark, Daniel, Lawrence Kramer, and Richard Leppert, editors. *Beyond the Soundtrack: Representing Music in*

Cinema. University of California Press, 2007. A collection of essays by musicologists and film scholars that posits music as equal to image in shaping a film.

Granger, Farley, and Robert Calhoun. *Include Me Out: My Life from Goldwyn to Broadway.* St. Martin's, 2007. Memoir of the actor's career from his time as a contract player for Samuel Goldwyn to his work in the theater and on television.

Green, Bill, and Will Russell. *I'm a Lebowski, You're a Lebowski: Life, the Big Lebowski, and What Have You.* Bloba Books, 2007. A look at the 1998 Joel and Ethan Coen film (a failure upon its release), which has developed a cult following.

Greene, Doyle. *The Mexican Cinema of Darkness: A Critical Study of Sex, Landmark Horror and Exploitation Films, 1969–1988.* McFarland & Co., 2007. Looks at six critical films of Mexican horror cinema, including *El Topo* and *Santa Sangre.*

Harness, Kyp. *The Art of Charlie Chaplin: A Film-by-Film Analysis.* McFarland & Co., 2007. Frames the biographical details of Chaplin's life within the context of his career as actor, director, and producer.

Harris, Mark. *Pictures at a Revolution: Five Movies and the Birth of the New Hollywood.* Penguin Press, 2007. Harris examines the five films nominated for Best Picture at the 1968 Academy Awards® and the wider changes they signaled in Hollywood.

Harvey, Adam. *The Soundtracks of Woody Allen: A Complete Guide to the Songs and Music in Every Film, 1969–2005.* McFarland & Co., 2007. Focuses on how Allen utilizes music within his films.

Hays, Matthew. *The View from Here: Conversations with Gay and Lesbian Filmmakers.* Arsenal Pulp Press, 2007. Interviews with writers, directors, and producers, including John Waters, Kenneth Anger, Monika Treut, Don Roos, Lea Pool, Pedro Almodovar, and others.

Hirsch, Foster. *Otto Preminger: The Man Who Would Be King.* Knopf, 2007. Biography of the Viennese-born filmmaker that offers some 100 new interviews with family and co-workers as well as a reappraisal of Preminger's films.

Holm, D.K. *Independent Cinema.* Kamera Books, 2007. Assessments of independent films and interviews with filmmakers.

Jewell, Richard. *The Golden Age of Cinema: Hollywood, 1929–1945.* Black Publishing, 2007. A history of the peak of the studio system, including an analysis of seminal films of the period.

Jones, Kent. *Physical Evidence: Selected Film Criticism.* Wesleyan University Press, 2007. The editor-at-large of *Film Comment* balances academia with pop culture as he looks at films and the filmmaking process.

Kalinak, Kathryn. *How the West Was Sung: Music in the Westerns of John Ford.* University of California Press, 2007. Analyzes the director's use of music, including folk and period music.

Kane, Jim. *Western Movie Wit and Wisdom.* Bright Sky Press, 2007. Compilations of quotes from western films from the silent era to the present, including serials, miniseries, and documentaries.

Keenan, Richard. *The Films of Robert Wise.* Scarecrow Press, 2007. Examines the director's career and his 40 feature films, from 1944's *Curse of the Cat People* to 2001's *A Storm in Summer.*

Kellow, Brian. *Ethel Merman: A Life.* Viking, 2007. Includes more than 100 interviews with Merman's family, friends, and co-workers to showcase her life on Broadway and in films and television.

Kennedy, Matthew. *Joan Blondell: A Life Between Takes.* University Press of Mississippi, 2007. A biography of the actress from her work in vaudeville to her Hollywood career and television roles.

Kobel, Peter, and the Library of Congress. *Silent Movies: The Birth of Film and the Triumph of Movie Culture.* Little, Brown, 2007. Using stills, posters, and promotional materials from the Library of Congress's collection, Kobel examines the international movie industry from 1893 to 1927.

Lanza, Joseph. *Phallic Frenzy: Ken Russell and His Films.* Chicago Review Press, 2007. Biography of the eccentric filmmaker, including his problems with censorship.

Lee, Anna, with Barbara Roisman Cooper. *Anna Lee: Memoir of a Career on General Hospital and in Film.* McFarland & Co., 2007. Memoir of the actress's career in England and Hollywood, completed by Cooper after Lee's death in 2004.

Leigh, Wendy. *True Grace: The Life and Death of an American Princess.* St. Martin's, 2007. Biography of Grace Kelly, whose career effectively ended with her marriage to Prince Rainier of Monaco that also covers her later charitable work.

Lichtenfeld, Eric. *Action Speaks Louder: Violence, Spectacle, and the American Action Movie.* Wesleyan University Press, 2007. Study of the action genre from vigilante films of the 1970s through superhero films.

Lisanti, Tom. *Glamour Girls of Sixties Hollywood: Seventy-Four Profiles.* McFarland & Co., 2007. Biographical profiles and interviews with the models, showgirls, centerfolds, and beauty queens who appeared onscreen in the 1960s.

Lowe, Barry. *Atomic Blonde: The Films of Mamie Van Doren.* McFarland & Co., 2007. Biography of the bombshell blonde who began her career at Universal Pictures in 1953.

Mainon, Dominique, and James Ursini. *Cinema of Obsession: Erotic Fixation and Love Gone Wrong in the Movies.* Limelight Editions, 2007. Explores obsessive love and erotic fixation in films, including fugitive lovers, male masochism, and female obsession.

Malone, Peter, editor. *Through a Catholic Lens: Religious Perspectives of 19 Film Directors from Around the World.* Scarecrow Press, 2007. Examines the Catholic subtext in the works of such directors as Kevin Smith, Mel Gibson, Neil Jordan, Roberto Benigni, Pedro Almodovar, and others.

Mamet, David. *Bambi vs. Godzilla: On the Nature, Purpose, and Practice of the Movie Business.* Pantheon, 2007. A veteran screenwriter and director, Mamet offers his insider's view on the movie industry.

Massood, Paula J., editor. *The Spike Lee Reader.* Temple University Press, 2007. Sixteen essays explore the impact of the African American director's films on race, gender, and sexuality.

McDonald, Paul, and Janet Wasko, editors. *The Contemporary Hollywood Film Industry.* Blackwell Publishing, 2007. Essays examine the state of the U.S. film industry from the 1980s to the present, including the star system, the global marketplace, and new media.

McGilligan, Patrick *Oscar Micheaux: The Great and Only: The Life of America's First Great Black Filmmaker.* Harper-Collins, 2007. A biography of the independent filmmaker who offered an uncompromising look at African American society through his work in the "race picture" market.

Miyao, Daisuke. *Sessue Hayakawa: Silent Cinema and Transnational Stardom.* Duke University Press, 2007. Critical study of the Japanese actor's international silent film career.

Muir, John Kenneth. *The Rock and Roll Film Encyclopedia.* Applause Books, 2007. Offers 230 film entries covering 1956–2005, including documentaries and films starring rock stars as well as interviews and biographical entries on musicians.

Nochimson, Martha. *Dying to Belong: Gangster Movies in Hollywood and Hong Kong.* Blackwell Publishing, 2007. Explores and contrasts the screen traditions of American and Hong Kong gangster films.

Nollen, Scott Allen. *Warners Wiseguys: All 112 Films That Robinson, Cagney and Bogart Made for the Studio.* McFarland & Co., 2007. Provides commentary and other information on the films of Edward G. Robinson, James Cagney, and Humphrey Bogart.

Norman, Marc. *What Happens Next: A History of American Screenwriting.* Harmony, 2007. Norman, an award-winning screenwriter, looks at the history of his profession from silent films to the present, including censorship, the blacklist, and the rise of the writer-director.

Nourmand, Tony. *Audrey Hepburn: The Paramount Years.* Chronicle Books, 2007. Collection of more than 200 photographs and illustrations of the actress's career at the Paramount studio in such films as *Roman Holiday, Sabrina, Funny Face,* and *Breakfast at Tiffany's.*

Oscherwitz, Dayna, and MaryEllen Higgins. *Historical Dictionary of French Cinema.* Scarecrow Press, 2007. Looks at the film industry in France from the silent era to the present day and the major theoretical and cultural issues relating to it.

Ostin, Joyce. *Hollywood Dads.* Chronicle Books, 2007. Intimate portraits of fifty famous fathers and their children.

Overstreet, Jeffrey. *Through a Screen Darkly: Looking Closer at Beauty, Truth and Evil in the Movies.* Regal, 2007. The cultural commentator and film critic of *Christianity Today* examines cinema as an art form and experience to be shared between Christian culture and secular society.

Paietta, Ann C. *Teachers in the Movies.* McFarland & Co., 2007. A filmography of more than 800 titles that feature educators as primary characters from the 1890s to the present.

Paik, Karen. *To Infinity and Beyond!: The Story of Pixar Animation Studios.* Chronicle Books, 2007. A history of the studio from its founding in 1986 to the merger with Disney.

Parish, James Robert. *Fiasco: A History of Hollywood's Icon Flops.* Wiley, 2007. Parish looks at fifteen costly flops, including 1969's *Paint Your Wagon,* 1987's *Ishtar,* and 2001's *Town and Country.*

Parish, James Robert. *It's Good to Be the King: The Seriously Funny Life of Mel Brooks.* Wiley, 2007. The life and career of Mel Brooks as comedian, writer, and filmmaker, as well as his marriage to actress Anne Bancroft.

Paul, Louis. *Tales from the Cult Film Trenches.* McFarland & Co., 2007. Offers interviews with thirty-six actors of sixties and seventies horror, science fiction, and exploitation cinema.

Polan, Dana. *Scenes of Instruction: The Beginnings of the U.S. Study of Film.* University of California Press, 2007. Chronicles the beginnings of film study courses in the American university system prior to World War II.

Rankin, Walter. *Grimm Pictures: Fairy Tale Archetypes in Eight Horror and Suspense Films.* McFarland & Co., 2007. Looks at how films have explored images, themes, and symbols that originated in the Grimm brothers' fairy tales.

Reinhartz, Adele. *Jesus of Hollywood.* Oxford, 2007. Reinhartz, a New Testament scholar, provides an analysis of the depictions of Jesus from silent films through *The Passion of the Christ,* including biographies and satires.

Rhodes, Gary D., editor. *Stanley Kubrick: Essays on His Films and Legacy.* McFarland & Co., 2007. Includes seventeen critical essays on the director's career and films.

Rickitt, Richard. *Special Effects: The History and Technique.* Billboard Books, 2007. A history of special effects from miniature photography and animation to pyrotechnics, animatronics, and CGI.

Robinson, Harlow. *Russians in Hollywood, Hollywood's Russians: Biography of an Image.* Northeastern University Press, 2007. Looks at Russian émigrés who worked in the American film industry as well as representations of Russia and the Soviet Union onscreen.

Rode, Alan K. *Charles McGraw: Biography of a Film Noir Tough Guy.* McFarland & Co., 2007. Looks at the life and career of the actor, including his film and television appearances.

Rodowick, D.N. *The Virtual Life of Film.* Harvard University Press, 2007. Examines the emergence of digital technologies in the culture of moviemaking and viewing.

Rosenthal, Daniel. *100 Shakespeare Films.* British Film Institute, 2007. Alphabetical listing (by play) of Shakespeare films and genre adaptations from 1907's *Tempest* to 2006's *As You Like It.*

Ross, Lawrence C. *Money Shot: The Wild Nights and Lonely Days Inside the Black Porn Industry.* Thunder's Mouth Press, 2007. A look at, and interviews with, black porn actors and the industry they work in.

Rowell, Erica. *The Brothers Grim: The Films of Ethan and Joel Coen.* Scarecrow Press, 2007. Examines the recurring themes and relationships in the filmmakers' work.

Sanders, Steven M., editor. *The Philosophy of the Science Fiction Film.* University Press of Kentucky, 2007. Essays explore philosophical themes and concepts of the genre.

Sandler, Kevin S. *The Naked Truth: Why Hollywood Doesn't Make X-Rated Movies.* Rutgers University Press, 2007. Considers the MPAA's rating system and how it's used by the mainstream Hollywood film industry.

Santopietro, Tom. *Considering Doris Day.* St. Martin's, 2007. Offers an evaluation of Day's recording and acting careers, including her thirty-nine films.

Schmenner, Will, and Corinne Granof, editors. *Casting a Shadow: Creating the Alfred Hitchcock Film.* Northwestern University Press, 2007. Examines Hitchcock's collaborative filmmaking process through sketches and storyboards.

Schneider, Steven Jay, editor. *501 Movie Actors.* Barron's Educational Series, 2007. Comprehensive guide to film stars throughout cinema history, including filmography, influences, and collaborations.

Schneider, Steven Jay, editor. *501 Movie Directors.* Barron's Educational Series, 2007. Chronological compendium of directors worldwide over the past 100 years, including their work and influences, filmography, and awards.

Schubart, Rikke. *Super Bitches and Action Babes: The Female Hero in Popular Cinema, 1970–2006.* McFarland & Co., 2007. Provides a critical analysis of five female archetypes: the dominatrix, Amazon, daughter, mother, and rape-avenger.

Seagrave, Kerry. *Actors Organize: A History of Union Formation Efforts in America, 1880–1919.* McFarland & Co., 2007. Focuses on the era's two main unions: Actors' Equity Association and the White Rats Actors' Union.

Senn, Bryan. *A Year of Fear: A Day-by-Day Guide to 366 Horror Films.* McFarland & Co., 2007. Offers a collection of horror films to suit any occasion and why the film fits a particular day's history.

Shargel, Raphael, editor. *Ingmar Bergman: Interviews.* University Press of Mississippi, 2007. Includes interviews with the filmmaker from 1957 to 2002.

Shaw, Deborah *Contemporary Latin American Cinema: Breaking Into the Global Market.* Scarecrow Press, 2007. Explores significant films that came out of Latin America since 2000.

Shimizu, Celine Parrenas. *The Hypersexuality of Race: Performing Asian/American Women on Screen and Scene.* Duke University Press, 2007. Takes a nuanced approach to the sexual depictions of Asian/American women in film, video, and theatrical productions.

Shindler, Colin. *Garbo & Gilbert in Love: Hollywood's First Great Celebrity Couple.* Orion, 2007. Story of the ill-fated and turbulent romance between silent screen stars John Gilbert and Greta Garbo.

Sikov, Ed. *Dark Victory: The Life of Bette Davis.* Holt, 2007. Biography of the volatile actress that primarily focuses on her eighteen-year career at Warner Bros. and the fifty-two films Davis made for the studio.

Singer, Irving. *Ingmar Bergman, Cinematic Philosopher.* MIT Press, 2007. Looks at the development of themes, motifs, and techniques in Bergman's films.

Slide, Anthony, Jane Burman Powell, and Lori Goldman Berthelsen. *Now Playing: Hand-Painted Poster Art from the 1950s Through the 1950s.* Angel City Press, 2007. Showcases original movie posters commissioned by regional theater owners to advertise new films.

Sloan, Jane. *Reel Women: An International Directory of Contemporary Feature Films about Women.* Scarecrow Press, 2007. Provides information on more than 2,400 films from some 100 countries that feature female protagonists.

Spadoni, Robert. *Uncanny Bodies: The Coming of Sound Film and the Origins of the Horror Genre.* University of California Press, 2007. Examines how the transition to sound enhanced the horror genre and the reception of the first sound horror films, including *Dracula* and *Frankenstein.*

Stacy, Jim, editor. *Reading Brokeback Mountain: Essays on the Story and the Film.* McFarland & Co., 2007. A collection of fifteen essays on Annie Proulx's story and the 2005 Ang Lee-directed film adaptation.

Stoehr, Kevin L, and Michael C. Connolly, editors. *John Ford in Focus: Essays on the Filmmaker's Life and Work.* McFarland & Co., 2007. Looks at the director's personal life and artistic vision and places Ford's films within a broader cultural context.

Stokes, Lisa Odham. *Historical Dictionary of Hong Kong Cinema.* Scarecrow Press, 2007. An evaluation of Hong Kong cinema and its filmmaking community.

Stone, Alan A. *Movies and the Moral Adventures of Life.* MIT Press, 2007. Essays that see films—both arthouse and blockbusters—from the viewpoint of life lessons.

Stratyner, Leslie, and James R. Keller, editors. *Fantasy Fiction into Film.* McFarland & Co., 2007. Essays on movies adapted from various types of fantasy fiction and the differences between page and screen.

Thompson, Dave. *Black and White and Blue: Adult Cinema from the Victorian Age to the VCR.* ECW Press, 2007. Surveys more than 300 films from the kineoscopes of the 1880s to the late 1970s and the popularity of the home VCR on the adult film industry.

Thompson, Kristin. *The Frodo Franchise: The Lord of the Rings and Modern Hollywood.* University of California Press, 2007. Interviews with seventy-six people that address the trilogy's impact on the fantasy genre, new technologies, working in New Zealand, and independent film.

Thornton, S.A. *The Japanese Period Film: A Critical Analysis, to 1970.* McFarland & Co., 2007. Describes the iconography and characteristics of Japanese period film.

Tichler, Rosemarie, and Barry Jay Kaplan. *Actors at Work.* Faber and Faber, 2007. Interviews with fourteen actors, including Estelle Parsons, Meryl Streep, Dianne Wiest, Kevin Kline, John Lithgow, Kevin Spacey, and others, who discuss their different working methods.

Tonguette, Peter Prescott. *Orson Welles Remembered: Interviews with His Actors, Editors, Cinematographers, and Magicians.* McFarland & Co., 2007. Interviews with thirty individuals who worked with Welles, conducted between 2003 and 2005.

Trimborn, Jurgen. *Leni Riefenstahl: A Life.* Faber & Faber, 2007. Critical biography by a film historian of the German filmmaker and propagandist of the Third Reich.

Valenti, Jack. *This Time, This Place: My Life in War, the White House, and Hollywood.* Harmony, 2007. Memoir includes Valenti's World War II service, his work as an assistant to Lyndon B. Johnson, and his thirty-eight years as CEO of the Motion Pictures Association of America.

Vogel, Michelle. *Olive Thomas: The Life and Death of a Silent Film Beauty.* McFarland & Co., 2007. Biography of the actress who died at the age of twenty-five.

Weisenfeld, Judith. *Hollywood Be Thy Name: African American Religion in American Film, 1929–1949.* University of California Press, 2007. Examines how both studio and independent producers created stories that featured black religious practices and how they reflected race and society.

Xu, Gary. *Sinascape: Contemporary Chinese Cinema.* Scarecrow Press, 2007. Examines the films and film industry of China, Taiwan, and Hong Kong.

Yeatter, Bryan L. *Cinema of the Philippines: A History and Filmography, 1897–2005.* McFarland & Co., 2007. A chronological arrangement covers the history of Filipino cinema.

Zhang, Zhen, editor. *The Urban Generation: Chinese Cinema and Society at the Turn of the Twenty-First Century.* Duke University Press, 2007. Looks at the alternative cinema of China's young filmmakers after 1989.

Director Index

Ben Affleck (1972-)
  Gone Baby Gone *149*

Paul Thomas Anderson (1970-)
  There Will Be Blood *392*

Stephen John Anderson
  Meet the Robinsons *258*

Wes Anderson (1970-)
  The Darjeeling Limited *91*

Peter Andrews
  See Steven Soderbergh

Nimród Antal
  Vacancy *418*

Judd Apatow (1968-)
  Knocked Up *231*

Michael Apted (1941-)
  Amazing Grace *10*

Andrea Arnold
  Red Road *327*

Olivier Assayas (1955-)
  Paris, je t'aime *306*

Philip G. Atwell
  War *428*

Noah Baumbach (1969-)
  Margot at the Wedding *255*

Michael Bay (1965-)
  Transformers *407*

Wayne Beach
  Slow Burn *367*

Walt Becker
  Wild Hogs *434*

Steve Bendelack
  Mr. Bean's Holiday *268*

Robert Benton (1932-)
  Feast of Love *124*

Peter Berg (1964-)
  The Kingdom *227*

Shari Springer Berman
  The Nanny Diaries *282*

Luc Besson (1959-)
  Angel-A *15*
  Arthur and the Invisibles *18*

Susanne Bier (1960-)
  Things We Lost in the
    Fire *395*

Mike Binder (1958-)
  Reign Over Me *328*

Brad Bird (1957-)
  Ratatouille *323*

Jeffrey Blitz (1969-)
  Rocket Science *341*

Paul J. Bolger
  Happily N'Ever After *170*

Joon-ho Bong
  The Host *183*

Rachid Bouchareb
  Days of Glory *93*

Darren Lynn Bousman (1979-)
  Saw IV *349*

Danny Boyle (1956-)
  Sunshine *381*

Tom Brady
  The Comebacks *79*

Kenneth Branagh (1960-)
  Sleuth *365*

Ash Brannon
  Surf's Up *385*

Theodore Braun
  Darfur Now *90*

Craig Brewer
  Black Snake Moan *47*

Hilary Brougher
  Stephanie Daley *378*

Chris Buck
  Surf's Up *385*

Charles Burnett (1944-)
  Killer of Sheep *224*

Tim Burton (1960-)
  Sweeney Todd: The Demon Bar-
    ber of Fleet Street *386*

Steve Buscemi (1957-)
  Interview *208*

Christopher Cain (1943-)
  September Dawn *352*

Joe Carnahan (1969-)
  Smokin' Aces *368*

John Carney
  Once *300*

Steve Carr
  Are We Done Yet? *16*

D.J. Caruso (1965-)
  Disturbia *99*

Nick Cassavetes (1959-)
  Alpha Dog *7*

Michael Caton-Jones (1958-)
  Beyond the Gates *44*

Claude Chabrol (1930-)
  Comedy of Power *80*

Gurinder Chadha
  Paris, je t'aime *306*

Christian Charles
  Full of It *138*

Gregory Hoblit (1944-)
Fracture *132*

Gavin Hood
Rendition *331*

Stephen Hopkins
The Reaping *325*

Raman Hui
Shrek the Third *358*

Leon Ichaso
El Cantante *69*

James Isaac (1960-)
Skinwalkers *364*

Julian Jarrold
Becoming Jane *36*

Tamara Jenkins
The Savages *347*

Roland Joffé (1945-)
Captivity *70*

Mark Steven Johnson
Ghost Rider *144*

Neil Jordan (1950-)
The Brave One *56*

Shekhar Kapur (1945-)
Elizabeth: The Golden
Age *108*

Jake Kasdan (1975-)
The TV Set *410*
Walk Hard: The Dewey Cox
Story *426*

Jonathan Kasdan
In the Land of Women *202*

Richard Kelly
Southland Tales *370*

Dan Klores
Crazy Love *83*

Lajos Koltai (1946-)
Evening *115*

Sue Kramer
Gray Matters *156*

Marco Kreuzpaintner
Trade *406*

Ken Kwapis
License to Wed *241*

Richard LaGravenese (1959-)
Freedom Writers *136*
Paris, je t'aime *306*
P.S. I Love You *320*

Francis Lawrence
I Am Legend *193*

Marc Lawrence (1959-)
Music and Lyrics *275*

Ray Lawrence (1948-)
Jindabyne *216*

Patrice Leconte (1947-)
My Best Friend *277*

Ang Lee (1954-)
Lust, Caution *252*

Doug Lefler
The Last Legion *238*

Michael Lehmann (1957-)
Because I Said So *34*

Kasi Lemmons (1961-)
Talk to Me *391*

Kevin Lima
Enchanted *110*

Alexandra Lipsitz
Air Guitar Nation *3*

Ken Loach (1936-)
The Wind That Shakes the Barley *435*

Sidney Lumet (1924-)
Before the Devil Knows You're
Dead *40*

Rod Lurie (1962-)
Resurrecting the Champ *339*

Douglas Mackinnon
The Flying Scotsman *129*

Guy Maddin (1956-)
Brand Upon the Brain! *54*

James Mangold (1964-)
3:10 to Yuma *402*

Henriette Mantel
An Unreasonable Man *417*

Garry Marshall (1934-)
Georgia Rule *142*

Les Mayfield
Code Name: The Cleaner *76*

Sean McNamara (1963-)
Bratz *55*

Dave Meyers
The Hitcher *176*

Menno Meyjes
Martian Child *256*

Chris Miller
Shrek the Third *358*

Seishi Minakimi
Paprika *305*

Anthony Minghella (1954-2008)
Breaking and Entering *61*

Michael Moore (1954-)
Sicko *360*

Greg Mottola (1964-)
Superbad *383*

Russell Mulcahy (1953-)
Resident Evil: Extinction *338*

Kevin Munroe
TMNT *404*

Mira Nair (1957-)
The Namesake *279*

Vincenzo Natali
Paris, je t'aime *306*

Mike Newell (1942-)
Love in the Time of Chol-
era *249*

Eric Nicholas
Alone With Her *6*

Mike Nichols (1931-)
Charlie Wilson's War *74*

Marcus Nispel
Pathfinder *308*

Chris Noonan
Miss Potter *265*

Joe Nussbaum
Sydney White *389*

Bob Odenkirk (1962-)
The Brothers Solomon *64*

Frank Oz (1944-)
Death at a Funeral *95*

Danny Pang
The Messengers *259*

Oxide Pang Chun
The Messengers *259*

Alexander Payne (1961-)
Paris, je t'aime *306*

Sean Penn (1960-)
Into the Wild *209*

Tyler Perry (1969-)
Daddy's Little Girls *86*
Why Did I Get Married? *432*

Michael Polish (1972-)
The Astronaut Farmer *21*

Sarah Polley (1979-)
Away From Her *31*

Christopher Quinn
God Grew Tired of Us *146*

Sam Raimi (1959-)
Spider-Man 3 *372*

George Ratliff
Joshua *218*

Brett Ratner (1970-)
Rush Hour 3 *343*

Billy Ray
Breach *59*

Robert Redford (1937-)
Lions for Lambs *243*

Jason Reitman
Juno *220*

Alain Resnais (1922-)
Private Fears in Public
Places *318*

Brian Robbins (1964-)
Norbit *294*

Chris Rock (1966-)
  I Think I Love My Wife *198*

Robert Rodriguez (1968-)
  Grindhouse *159*

Eli Roth (1972-)
  Hostel: Part II *185*

Jay Russell (1960-)
  The Water Horse: Legend of the
    Deep *429*

Walter Salles (1956-)
  Paris, je t'aime *306*

Fred Savage (1976-)
  Daddy Day Camp *85*

John Sayles (1950-)
  Honeydripper *181*

Oliver Schmitz
  Paris, je t'aime *306*

Julian Schnabel (1951-)
  The Diving Bell and the Butter-
    fly *101*

Joel Schumacher (1942-)
  The Number 23 *295*

Ridley Scott (1939-)
  American Gangster *13*

Aaron Seltzer
  Epic Movie *112*

Tom Shadyac (1960-)
  Evan Almighty *114*

Akiva Shaffer (1977-)
  Hot Rod *188*

Adam Shankman
  Hairspray *165*

Robert Shaye
  The Last Mimzy *240*

Adrienne Shelly (1966-2006)
  Waitress *425*

Richard Shepard
  The Hunting Party *191*

Kristen Sheridan
  August Rush *26*

David Silverman (1957-)
  The Simpsons Movie *362*

David Sington
  In the Shadow of the
    Moon *204*

Chris Sivertson
  I Know Who Killed Me *194*

Steve Skrovan
  An Unreasonable Man *417*

David Slade
  30 Days of Night *397*

Simon J. Smith
  Bee Movie *38*

Zack Snyder
  300 *400*

Steven Soderbergh (1963-)
  Ocean's Thirteen *299*

Will Speck
  Blades of Glory *49*

Tim Story
  Fantastic Four: Rise of the Silver
    Surfer *121*

Colin Strause
  Aliens vs. Predator: Requiem *4*

Greg Strause
  Aliens vs. Predator: Requiem *4*

James C. Strouse
  Grace Is Gone *153*

Noburhiro Suwa
  Paris, je t'aime *306*

Robin Swicord
  The Jane Austen Book
    Club *215*

Lee Tamahori (1950-)
  Next *286*

Quentin Tarantino (1963-)
  Grindhouse *159*

Julie Taymor (1952-)
  Across the Universe *1*

Daniela Thomas
  Paris, je t'aime *306*

Daniéle Thompson
  Avenue Montaigne *28*

Jon Turteltaub
  National Treasure: Book of Se-
    crets *284*

Tom Tykwer (1965-)
  Paris, je t'aime *306*
  Perfume: The Story of a Mur-
    derer *312*

Gus Van Sant (1952-)
  Paris, je t'aime *306*

Tom Vaughan
  Starter for 10 *376*

Matthew Vaughn
  Stardust *374*

Francis Veber (1937-)
  The Valet *420*

Gore Verbinski
  Pirates of the Caribbean: At
    World's End *313*

Paul Verhoeven (1938-)
  Black Book *46*

David Von Ancken
  Seraphim Falls *353*

Florian Henskel von Donnersmarck
  The Lives of Others *246*

Katja von Garnier
  Blood and Chocolate *50*

Taika Waititi
  Eagle vs. Shark *105*

James Wan
  Dead Silence *94*
  Death Sentence *97*

Denzel Washington (1954-)
  The Great Debaters *157*

Peter Webber
  Hannibal Rising *168*

Martin Weisz
  The Hills Have Eyes II *175*

Chris Weitz (1970-)
  The Golden Compass *147*

Mike White (1970-)
  Year of the Dog *439*

Sylvain White
  Stomp the Yard *379*

Preston A. Whitmore, II
  This Christmas *399*

Michael Winterbottom (1961-)
  A Mighty Heart *263*

Len Wiseman
  Live Free or Die Hard *244*

Edgar Wright
  Hot Fuzz *186*

Joe Wright
  Atonement *23*

Mennan Yapo
  Premonition *315*

David Yates
  Harry Potter and the Order of
    the Phoenix *171*

Corey Yuen (1951-)
  DOA: Dead or Alive *103*

Robert Zemeckis (1952-)
  Beowulf *42*

Rob Zombie (1966-)
  Halloween *167*

Screenwriter Index

Hilary Brougher
     Stephanie Daley *378*

John Brown
     The Flying Scotsman *129*

Chris Buck
     Surf's Up *385*

Allison Burnett
     Feast of Love *124*
     Resurrecting the Champ *339*

Charles Burnett (1944-)
     Killer of Sheep *224*

John Burnham Schwartz
     Reservation Road *336*

Scott Burns
     The Bourne Ultimatum *52*

Steve Buscemi (1957-)
     Interview *208*

Jez Butterworth (1969-)
     The Last Legion *238*

Tom Butterworth (1967-)
     The Last Legion *238*

Christopher Cain (1943-)
     September Dawn *352*

Jim Capobianco
     Ratatouille *323*

Joe Carnahan (1969-)
     Smokin' Aces *368*

Matthew Carnahan
     The Kingdom *227*
     Lions for Lambs *243*

Michael Carnes
     Mr. Woodcock *273*

John Carney
     Once *300*

Nick Cassavetes (1959-)
     Alpha Dog *7*

Nick Castle (1947-)
     August Rush *26*

Claude Chabrol (1930-)
     Comedy of Power *80*

Gurinder Chadha
     Paris, je t'aime *306*

Sylvain Chomet (1963-)
     Paris, je t'aime *306*

Robert Chomiak
     Fido *126*

Beatrix Christian
     Jindabyne *216*

Louis C. K. (1967-)
     I Think I Love My Wife *198*

Dick Clement (1937-)
     Across the Universe *1*

Diablo Cody
     Juno *220*

Ethan Coen (1957-)
     No Country for Old Men *288*
     Paris, je t'aime *306*

Joel Coen (1954-)
     No Country for Old Men *288*
     Paris, je t'aime *306*

Joel Cohen
     Evan Almighty *114*

Larry Cohen (1947-)
     Captivity *70*

Isabel Coixet
     Paris, je t'aime *306*

Brad Copeland
     Wild Hogs *434*

Francis Ford Coppola (1939-)
     Youth Without Youth *442*

Roman Coppola (1965-)
     The Darjeeling Limited *91*

Laurence Coriat
     A Mighty Heart *263*

Craig Cox
     Blades of Glory *49*

Jeff Cox
     Blades of Glory *49*

Dean Craig
     Death at a Funeral *95*

Jonathan Craven
     The Hills Have Eyes II *175*

Wes Craven (1939-)
     The Hills Have Eyes II *175*
     Paris, je t'aime *306*

Chad Gomez Creasey
     Sydney White *389*

Alfonso Cuaron (1961-)
     Paris, je t'aime *306*

Michael Cunningham
     Evening *115*

Andrew Currie
     Fido *126*

Deborah Curtis
     Control *81*

Olivier Dahan
     La Vie en Rose *421*

Art D'Alessandro
     The Final Season *128*

Frank Darabont (1959-)
     The Mist *267*

David Darmstaedter
     El Cantante *69*

Michael Davis (1961-)
     Shoot 'Em Up *355*

Mick Davis
     The Invisible *212*

Julie Delpy (1969-)
     2 Days in Paris *413*

Vince DeMeglio
     License to Wed *241*

James DeMonaco (1968-)
     Skinwalkers *364*

Leslie Dixon
     Hairspray *165*
     The Heartbreak Kid *174*

Andrew Dominik
     The Assassination of Jesse James
          by the Coward Robert
          Ford *19*

Christopher Doyle (1952-)
     Paris, je t'aime *306*

Robin Driscoll
     Mr. Bean's Holiday *268*

Goran Dukic
     Wristcutters: A Love Story *437*

Marcus Dunstan
     Saw IV *349*

Bernd Eichinger
     Perfume: The Story of a Mur-
          derer *312*

Robert Eisele
     The Great Debaters *157*

Ted Elliott
     Pirates of the Caribbean: At
          World's End *313*

Carl Ellsworth
     Disturbia *99*

Toby Emmerich
     The Last Mimzy *240*

Bruce A. Evans
     Mr. Brooks *270*

Rick Famuyiwa (1973-)
     Talk to Me *391*

Barry Fanaro
     I Now Pronounce You Chuck and
          Larry *196*

Bobby Farrelly (1958-)
     The Heartbreak Kid *174*

Peter Farrelly (1957-)
     The Heartbreak Kid *174*

Spike Feresten
     Bee Movie *38*

Charles Ferguson
     No End in Sight *290*

Pascale Ferran
     Lady Chatterley *235*

Andrew Fleming (1964-)
     Nancy Drew *281*

Dan Fogelman
     Fred Claus *134*

Will Forte (1970-)
The Brothers Solomon *64*

Scott Frank (1960-)
The Lookout *248*

Juan Carlos Fresnadillo
28 Weeks Later *411*

Anthony Frewin
Color Me Kubrick *77*

Jason Friedberg
Epic Movie *112*

Mark Frost
Fantastic Four: Rise of the Silver
Surfer *121*

Carol Fuchs
No Reservations *292*

Neil Gaiman
Beowulf *42*

George Gallo (1956-)
Code Name: The Cleaner *76*

Robert Ben Garant
Balls of Fury *33*
Reno 911!: Miami *333*

Celine Garcia
Arthur and the Invisibles *18*

Pierce Gardner
Dan in Real Life *88*

Alex Garland
Sunshine *381*

Jeff Garlin (1962-)
I Want Someone to Eat Cheese
With *199*

Michael Genet
Talk to Me *391*

Terry George
Reservation Road *336*

Glenn Gers
Fracture *132*

Raynold Gideon
Mr. Brooks *270*

David Gilbert
Joshua *218*

Josh Gilbert
Mr. Woodcock *273*

Tony Gilroy
The Bourne Ultimatum *52*
Michael Clayton *260*

Evan Goldberg
Superbad *383*

Michael Goldberg
Harry Potter and the Order of
the Phoenix *171*

Gary Goldman (1944-)
Next *286*

Jane Goldman
Stardust *374*

Akiva Goldsman (1963-)
I Am Legend *193*

J. Mills Goodloe
Pride *317*

Michael B. Gordon
300 *400*

Michael Gozzard
Pride *317*

Susannah Grant (1963-)
Catch and Release *73*

James Gray
We Own the Night *431*

James Grayford
The Final Season *128*

Matt Greenberg
1408 *131*

Matt Greenhalgh
Control *81*

Nathan Greno
Meet the Robinsons *258*

Matt Groening (1954-)
The Simpsons Movie *362*

Adam Gross
DOA: Dead or Alive *103*

Seth Gross
DOA: Dead or Alive *103*

Joey Gutierrez
The Comebacks *79*

Jun-won Ha
The Host *183*

Derek Haas
3:10 to Yuma *402*

Paul Haggis
In the Valley of Elah *205*

Donald Hall
Meet the Robinsons *258*

Jeffrey Hammond
I Know Who Killed Me *194*

Christopher Hampton (1946-)
Atonement *23*

Curtis Hanson (1945-)
Lucky You *251*

Joby Harold
Awake *29*

Thomas Harris
Hannibal Rising *168*

James V. Hart
August Rush *26*

Todd Harthan
Skinwalkers *364*

Hal Hartley (1959-)
Fay Grim *123*

Ronald Harwood (1934-)
The Diving Bell and the Butterfly *101*

Love in the Time of Chol-
era *249*

Ethan Hawke (1971-)
The Hottest State *189*

Carey Hayes
The Reaping *325*

Chad Hayes
The Reaping *325*

Todd Haynes (1961-)
I'm Not There *200*

Denis Heaton
Fido *126*

Peter Hedges (1962-)
Dan in Real Life *88*

Zach Helm
Mr. Magorium's Wonder Emporium *272*

Jonathan Hensleigh
Next *286*

Werner Herzog (1942-)
Rescue Dawn *334*

Michael Hirst
Elizabeth: The Golden
Age *108*

John Hodge
The Seeker: The Dark Is Rising *350*

Kevin Hood
Becoming Jane *36*

Karen Leigh Hopkins
Because I Said So *34*

Declan Hughes
The Flying Scotsman *129*

Wang Hui-ling
Lust, Caution *252*

Leon Ichaso
El Cantante *69*

Robert Nelson Jacobs
The Water Horse: Legend of the
Deep *429*

Susan Estelle Jansen
Bratz *55*

Karen Janszen
Gracie *154*

Abby Everett Jaques
Seraphim Falls *353*

Al Jean
The Simpsons Movie *362*

Ian Mackenzie Jeffers
Death Sentence *97*

Christopher Jenkins
Surf's Up *385*

Steve Oedekerk (1961-)
Evan Almighty *114*

Nancy Oliver
Lars and the Real Girl *237*

Jesús Olmo
28 Weeks Later *411*

Roberto Orci
Transformers *407*

John Orloff
A Mighty Heart *263*

David Paterson
Bridge to Terabithia *62*

Tiffany Paulsen
Nancy Drew *281*

Alexander Payne (1961-)
I Now Pronounce You Chuck and
Larry *196*
Paris, je t'aime *306*

Don Payne
Fantastic Four: Rise of the Silver
Surfer *121*

Simon Pegg (1970-)
Hot Fuzz *186*

Sean Penn (1960-)
Into the Wild *209*

Tyler Perry (1969-)
Daddy's Little Girls *86*
Why Did I Get Married? *432*

Fernley Phillips
The Number 23 *295*

Jan Pinkava (1963-)
Ratatouille *323*

Harold Pinter (1930-)
Sleuth *365*

Joe Piscatella
Underdog *415*

Mark Polish (1972-)
The Astronaut Farmer *21*

Michael Polish (1972-)
The Astronaut Farmer *21*

Sarah Polley (1979-)
Away From Her *31*

Jeffrey Price
Shrek the Third *358*

Kathryn Price
The Game Plan *141*

Mark Protosevich
I Am Legend *193*

Robert Pulcini
The Nanny Diaries *282*

Daniel Pyne
Fracture *132*

Ivan Raimi (1956-)
Spider-Man 3 *372*

Sam Raimi (1959-)
Spider-Man 3 *372*

Tim Rasmussen
License to Wed *241*

George Ratliff
Joshua *218*

Billy Ray
Breach *59*

Eric Red
The Hitcher *176*

Aurian Redson
Meet the Robinsons *258*

Mike Reiss
The Simpsons Movie *362*

Jeff Rendell
Grindhouse *159*

Alain Resnais (1922-)
Private Fears in Public
Places *318*

Don Rhymer
Surf's Up *385*

Jean-Michel Ribes
Private Fears in Public
Places *318*

Adam Rifkin (1966-)
Underdog *415*

Jose Rivera
Trade *406*

Andy Robin
Bee Movie *38*

Chris Rock (1966-)
I Think I Love My Wife *198*

James Roday (1976-)
Skinwalkers *364*

Geoff Rodkey
Daddy Day Camp *85*

Robert Rodriguez (1968-)
Grindhouse *159*

Seth Rogen (1982-)
Superbad *383*

Steven Rogers
P.S. I Love You *320*

David Ronn
Norbit *294*

Simon Rose
The Flying Scotsman *129*

Terry Rossio (1960-)
Pirates of the Caribbean: At
World's End *313*

Eli Roth (1972-)
Grindhouse *159*
Hostel: Part II *185*

Eric Roth
Lucky You *251*

William Rotko
Breach *59*

Christine Roum
The Invisible *212*

Brian Rousso
The Reaping *325*

Bruce Joel Rubin
The Last Mimzy *240*

Shane Salerno
Aliens vs. Predator: Requiem *4*

Walter Salles (1956-)
Paris, je t'aime *306*

Kelley Sane
Rendition *331*

Alvin Sargent
Spider-Man 3 *372*

John Sayles (1950-)
Honeydripper *181*

James Schamus
Lust, Caution *252*

David Schechter
Interview *208*

Jay Scherick
Norbit *294*

Oliver Schmitz
Paris, je t'aime *306*

Jason Schwartzman (1980-)
The Darjeeling Limited *91*

Mike Scully
The Simpsons Movie *362*

Peter S. Seaman
Shrek the Third *358*

Jerry Seinfeld (1954-)
Bee Movie *38*

Matt Selman
The Simpsons Movie *362*

Aaron Seltzer
Epic Movie *112*

Adrienne Shelly (1966-2006)
Waitress *425*

Richard Shepard
The Hunting Party *191*

Josh Siegal
Kickin' It Old Skool *223*

Steve Skrovan
An Unreasonable Man *417*

Trace Slobotkin
Kickin' It Old Skool *223*

Kevin Michael Smith
Pride *317*

Lee Anthony Smith
War *428*

Mark L. Smith
Vacancy *418*

Cinematographer Index

Reuben Aaronson
  The Ground Truth *162*

Thomas Ackerman
  Balls of Fury *33*

Barry Ackroyd
  The Wind That Shakes the Barley *435*

Remi Adefarasin
  Amazing Grace *10*
  Elizabeth: The Golden Age *108*
  Fred Claus *134*

Pierre Aim
  Paris, je t'aime *306*

Russ T. Alsobrook
  Reign Over Me *328*
  Superbad *383*

Michel Amathieu
  Paris, je t'aime *306*

Mitchell Amundsen
  Transformers *407*

Robert Anderson (1923-)
  Ratatouille *323*

Peter Andrews
  See Steven Soderbergh

Thierry Arbogast
  Angel-A *15*
  Arthur and the Invisibles *18*

David A. Armstrong
  Saw IV *349*
  Skinwalkers *364*

Howard Atherton
  Color Me Kubrick *77*

Joaquin Baca-Asay
  We Own the Night *431*

John Bailey (1942-)
  License to Wed *241*

Lubomir Bakchev
  2 Days in Paris *413*

Ian Baker
  Evan Almighty *114*

Laurent Bares
  Hitman *178*

John Bartley
  Gray Matters *156*

Bojan Bazelli
  Hairspray *165*

Alfonso Beato
  Love in the Time of Cholera *249*

Dion Beebe
  Rendition *331*

Gabriel Beristain
  The Invisible *212*

Pete Biagi
  I Want Someone to Eat Cheese With *199*

Larry Blanford
  Fantastic Four: Rise of the Silver Surfer *121*

Patrick Blossier
  Days of Glory *93*

Hagen Bogdanski
  The Lives of Others *246*

Jean-Louis Bompoint
  Grace Is Gone *153*

Russell Boyd
  Ghost Rider *144*

Henry Braham
  The Golden Compass *147*

Uta Briesewitz
  The TV Set *410*
  Walk Hard: The Dewey Cox Story *426*

Eigil Bryld
  Becoming Jane *36*

Don Burgess
  Enchanted *110*

Charles Burnett (1944-)
  Killer of Sheep *224*

Sarah Crawley Cabiya
  Fay Grim *123*

Sharon Calahan
  Ratatouille *323*

Paul Cameron
  In the Land of Women *202*

Russell Carpenter
  Awake *29*

Vanja Cernjul (1968-)
  Wristcutters: A Love Story *437*

Milan Chadima
  Grindhouse *159*
  Hostel: Part II *185*

Chi Ying Chan
  DOA: Dead or Alive *103*

Michael Chapman (1935-)
  Bridge to Terabithia *62*

Claudio Chea
  El Cantante *69*

Enrique Chediak
  28 Weeks Later *411*

Adam Clark
  Eagle vs. Shark *105*

Alar Kivilo
   The Lookout *248*

Rainer Klausmann
   The Invasion *210*

Alwin Küchler
   Sunshine *381*

Toyomichi Kurita
   Why Did I Get Married? *432*

Edward Lachman (1948-)
   I'm Not There *200*

Jean-Claude Larrieu
   Paris, je t'aime *306*

John R. Leonetti
   Dead Silence *94*
   Death Sentence *97*
   I Know Who Killed Me *194*

Matthew F. Leonetti (1941-)
   The Heartbreak Kid *174*
   Pride *317*

Andrew Lesnie
   I Am Legend *193*

Peter Levy
   The Reaping *325*

Matthew Libatique (1969-)
   The Number 23 *295*

Karl Walter Lindenlaub
   Black Book *46*
   Georgia Rule *142*

John Lindley
   Catch and Release *73*
   Mr. Brooks *270*
   Reservation Road *336*

Torsten Lippstock
   Premonition *315*

Steve Lumley
   TMNT *404*

Julio Macat
   Because I Said So *34*

Mihai Malaimare, Jr.
   Youth Without Youth *442*

Chris Manley
   Gracie *154*

Pascal Marti
   Paris, je t'aime *306*

John Mathieson
   August Rush *26*

Clark Mathis
   Norbit *294*

Shawn Maurer
   Epic Movie *112*

Sam McCurdy
   The Hills Have Eyes II *175*

Seamus McGarvey
   Atonement *23*

Peter Menzies, Jr.
   Shooter *356*

Anastas Michos
   Perfect Stranger *310*

Amir M. Mokri
   National Treasure: Book of Secrets *284*

Pierre Morel
   War *428*

Kramer Morgenthau
   Feast of Love *124*
   Fracture *132*
   Full of It *138*

David Rush Morrison
   Stephanie Daley *378*

M. David Mullen (1962-)
   The Astronaut Farmer *21*

J. Michael Muro
   The Last Mimzy *240*
   Rush Hour 3 *343*

Tetsuo Nagata
   Paris, je t'aime *306*
   La Vie en Rose *421*

Christopher Norr
   The Hottest State *189*

Clive North
   In the Shadow of the Moon *204*

Tim Orr
   Year of the Dog *439*

Roman Osin
   Mr. Magorium's Wonder Emporium *272*

Gyula Pados
   Evening *115*

Phedon Papamichael (1962-)
   3:10 to Yuma *402*

Phil Parmet
   Grindhouse *159*
   Halloween *167*

Peter Pau
   Shoot 'Em Up *355*

Daniel Pearl
   Aliens vs. Predator: Requiem *4*
   Captivity *70*
   Pathfinder *308*

J. Eddie Peck (1958-)
   Paris, je t'aime *306*

Wally Pfister
   Slow Burn *367*

Mathieu Poirot-Delpech
   Paris, je t'aime *306*

Marco Pontecorvo
   The Last Legion *238*

Luc Pontpellier
   Away From Her *31*

Bill Pope
   Spider-Man 3 *372*

Dick Pope
   Honeydripper *181*

Steven Poster (1944-)
   Southland Tales *370*

Robert Presley
   Beowulf *42*

Tom Priestley
   Delta Farce *98*

Rodrigo Prieto
   Lust, Caution *252*

David Quesemand
   Paris, je t'aime *306*

Pascal Rabaud
   Paris, je t'aime *306*

Mark Raker
   An Unreasonable Man *417*

Joel Ransom
   The Seeker: The Dark Is Rising *350*

Tami Reiker
   Mr. Woodcock *273*

William Rexer
   I Think I Love My Wife *198*

Anthony B. Richmond (1942-)
   The Comebacks *79*
   Good Luck Chuck *151*

Robert Rodriguez (1968-)
   Grindhouse *159*

Antonio Rossi
   No End in Sight *290*

Philippe Rousselot (1945-)
   The Brave One *56*
   The Great Debaters *157*
   Lions for Lambs *243*

Ashley Rowe
   Starter for 10 *376*

Martin Ruhe
   Control *81*

Juan Ruiz-Anchia (1949-)
   September Dawn *352*

Robbie Ryan
   Red Road *327*

Anthony Sacco
   Air Guitar Nation *3*

Geno Salvatori
   Daddy Day Camp *85*

Harris Savides
   American Gangster *13*
   Margot at the Wedding *255*
   Zodiac *443*

Roberto Schaefer
   The Kite Runner *229*

Editor Index

Jonathan Alberts
    Wristcutters: A Love Story *437*
Michael Aller
    Daddy Day Camp *85*
Peter Amundson
    Shoot 'Em Up *355*
Mick Audsley
    Love in the Time of Chol-
        era *249*
John Axelrad
    The Messengers *259*
    We Own the Night *431*
Luc Barnier
    Paris, je t'aime *306*
Ned Bastille
    Norbit *294*
Sam Bauer
    Southland Tales *370*
Alan Baumgarten
    The Heartbreak Kid *174*
    Mr. Woodcock *273*
Chad Beck
    No End in Sight *290*
Alan Edward Bell
    The Comebacks *79*
Peter E. Berger
    Alvin and the Chipmunks *9*
Alexander Berner
    Perfume: The Story of a Mur-
        derer *312*
Ivan Bilancio
    Surf's Up *385*
Jill Bilcock
    Elizabeth: The Golden
        Age *108*

Joe Bini
    Rescue Dawn *334*
Sue Blainey
    The Hills Have Eyes II *175*
John Bloom
    Charlie Wilson's War *74*
Kristina Boden
    Slow Burn *367*
Valerio Bonelli
    Hannibal Rising *168*
Matthias Bonnefoy
    Paris, je t'aime *306*
Francoise Bonnot
    Across the Universe *1*
Étienne Boussac
    2 Days in Paris *413*
Sarah Boyd
    Resurrecting the Champ *339*
Peter Boyle
    1408 *131*
Maryanne Brandon
    The Jane Austen Book
        Club *215*
Wendy Greene Bricmont
    I Think I Love My Wife *198*
Conrad Buff
    Seraphim Falls *353*
    Shooter *356*
Edgar Burcken
    Darfur Now *90*
Jobter Burg
    Black Book *46*
Charles Burnett (1944-)
    Killer of Sheep *224*

Malcolm Campbell
    Hot Rod *188*
Jeff W. Canavan
    Bratz *55*
Bruce Cannon
    Things We Lost in the
        Fire *395*
Jay Cassidy
    Into the Wild *209*
Nicolas Chaudeurge
    Red Road *327*
David Checel
    Stomp the Yard *379*
Matt Chesse
    The Kite Runner *229*
Scott Chestnut
    You Kill Me *440*
Ka-Fai Cheung
    DOA: Dead or Alive *103*
Peter Christelis
    A Mighty Heart *263*
Pernille Bech Christensen
    Things We Lost in the
        Fire *395*
Curtiss Clayton
    The Assassination of Jesse James
        by the Coward Robert
        Ford *19*
Anne V. Coates
    Catch and Release *73*
    The Golden Compass *147*
Mark Conte
    Delta Farce *98*
Cari Coughlin
    Alone With Her *6*

Michael Jablow
The Game Plan *141*

Simon Jacquet
Paris, je t'aime *306*

Roderick Jaynes
No Country for Old Men *288*

Allyson C. Johnson
Evening *115*
The Namesake *279*

Art Jones
30 Days of Night *397*

Lawrence Jordan
I Know Who Killed Me *194*

Pip Karmel
No Reservations *292*

Brian A. Kates
The Savages *347*

Ellen Keneshea
Meet the Robinsons *258*

Harry Keramidas
The Final Season *128*

Yannick Kergoat
Days of Glory *93*

William Kerr
Superbad *383*

Seon Min Kim
The Host *183*

Elizabeth King
Gracie *154*

Anne Klotz
Paris, je t'aime *306*

Georges Klotz
The Valet *420*

Joe Klotz
Grace Is Gone *153*

Michael N. Knue
Dead Silence *94*
Death Sentence *97*

Carole Kravetz
The Hunting Party *191*

Angie Lam
DOA: Dead or Alive *103*

Sylvie Landra
Avenue Montaigne *28*

Tony Lawson
The Brave One *56*

Chris Lebenzon
Sweeney Todd: The Demon Barber of Fleet Street *386*

Allan Lee
Skinwalkers *364*

Cindy Lee
No End in Sight *290*

Marty Levenstein
In the Land of Women *202*

Michael A. Levine
Factory Girl *119*

Carol Littleton
In the Land of Women *202*
Margot at the Wedding *255*

Mark Livolsi
Fred Claus *134*

Christian Lonk
Beyond the Gates *44*

Ethan Maniquis
Grindhouse *159*

Richard Marizy
La Vie en Rose *421*

Roger Mattiussi
Fido *126*

Jim May
The Hitcher *176*

Michael McCusker
3:10 to Yuma *402*

Craig McKay
Awake *29*

Isabel Meier
Paris, je t'aime *306*

Sally Menke
Grindhouse *159*

Beverley Mills
Death at a Funeral *95*

Armen Minasian
The Messengers *259*
Vacancy *418*

Stephen Mirrione
Ocean's Thirteen *299*

Andrew Mondshein
Feast of Love *124*
The Hoax *179*

Colin Monie
The Flying Scotsman *129*

David Moritz
Freedom Writers *136*
P.S. I Love You *320*

Kirk Morri
The Hills Have Eyes II *175*

Jonathan Morris
The Wind That Shakes the Barley *435*

Susan E. Morse
Music and Lyrics *275*

Thomas A. Muldoon
Transformers *407*

Paul Mullen
Once *300*

Bob Murawski (1964-)
Spider-Man 3 *372*

Walter Murch
Youth Without Youth *442*

Mathilde Muyard
Lady Chatterley *235*

Darrin Navarro
Bug *66*

Joel Negron
The Invasion *210*

Richard Nord
Captivity *70*

Jeremiah O'Driscoll
Beowulf *42*

Conor O'Neil
Air Guitar Nation *3*

Adriana Pacheco
The Hottest State *189*

Jim Page
Disturbia *99*

Stuart Pappé
Wild Hogs *434*

Colby Parker, Jr.
The Kingdom *227*
The Reaping *325*

Richard Pearson
Blades of Glory *49*

Gregory Perer
Enchanted *110*

Heather Persons
Starter for 10 *376*

Sabrina Plisco
Mr. Magorium's Wonder Emporium *272*

Peck Prior
Epic Movie *112*

Alexis Provost
An Unreasonable Man *417*

Jay Rabinowitz
I'm Not There *200*

Steve Rasch
I Want Someone to Eat Cheese With *199*

Keith Reamer
Stephanie Daley *378*

John Refoua
Balls of Fury *33*
Reno 911!: Miami *333*

David Rennie
National Treasure: Book of Secrets *284*

Geoffrey Richman
God Grew Tired of Us *146*
Sicko *360*

Scott Richter
War *428*

Dan Zimmerman
  Aliens vs. Predator: Requiem *4*

Dean Zimmerman
  Rush Hour 3 *343*

Don Zimmerman
  Rush Hour 3 *343*

Art Director Index

David Allday
  Amazing Grace *10*

Grant Armstrong
  Miss Potter *265*

Steve Arnold
  Balls of Fury *33*

Alan Au
  I Now Pronounce You Chuck and
    Larry *196*

Francois Audouy
  Lions for Lambs *243*

Chris August
  Hot Rod *188*

Ian Bailie
  Atonement *23*

Maria Baker
  Smokin' Aces *368*

Patrick Banister
  Shoot 'Em Up *355*
  Talk to Me *391*

Guy Barnes
  Seraphim Falls *353*

Ben Barraud
  Awake *29*
  The Nanny Diaries *282*

Toni Barton
  I Think I Love My Wife *198*

David Baxa
  Hostel: Part II *185*

Charley Beal
  Perfect Stranger *310*

Gregory A. Berry
  Reign Over Me *328*
  3:10 to Yuma *402*

Jon Billington
  The Number 23 *295*

Roberto Bonelli
  Love in the Time of Chol-
    era *249*

Peter Borck
  Freedom Writers *136*

Drew Boughton
  National Treasure: Book of Se-
    crets *284*

Clay Brown
  Michael Clayton *260*

David Bryan
  A Mighty Heart *263*

Silke Buhr
  The Lives of Others *246*

Chris Burian-Mohr
  Spider-Man 3 *372*

Roberto Caruso
  The Last Legion *238*

Todd Cherniawsky
  Nancy Drew *281*

Mon Cheung
  TMNT *404*

John Chichester
  Feast of Love *124*

Wong Ching
  DOA: Dead or Alive *103*

Nigel Churcher
  30 Days of Night *397*

Ursula Cleary
  The Flying Scotsman *129*

Laia Colet
  Perfume: The Story of a Mur-
    derer *312*

Chris Cornwell
  Gone Baby Gone *149*
  Vacancy *418*

Robert Cowper
  The Bourne Ultimatum *52*

David Crank
  There Will Be Blood *392*

Bill Crutcher
  The Seeker: The Dark Is Ris-
    ing *350*

Douglas Cumming
  The Comebacks *79*
  Disturbia *99*

Howard Cummings
  I Am Legend *193*

Keith Cunningham
  Zodiac *443*

Marc Dabe
  The Brothers Solomon *64*

Charlie Daboub
  Alvin and the Chipmunks *9*

Liba Daniels
  Black Snake Moan *47*

Dins W.W. Danielsen
  Delta Farce *98*

Dennis Davenport
  Hairspray *165*
  The Lookout *248*

Joshu de Cartier
  Lars and the Real Girl *237*

Katya DeBear
  Joshua *218*

Ivan Maussion
My Best Friend *277*

Caty Maxey
The Invasion *210*

David McHenry
Becoming Jane *36*

Natalja Meier
Fay Grim *123*

Mark J. Mullins
Daddy Day Camp *85*

Karen Murphy
The Kite Runner *229*

Jim Nedza
Evan Almighty *114*

Norman Newberry
Beowulf *42*
Georgia Rule *142*

Andy Nicholson
The Bourne Ultimatum *52*
Breaking and Entering *61*
The Golden Compass *147*

Marco Niro
Resident Evil: Extinction *338*

Jim Oberlander
The Astronaut Farmer *21*
Trade *406*

Adam O'Neill
Blood and Chocolate *50*

Micrea Onisoru
Youth Without Youth *442*

Rosa Palomo
Death Sentence *97*

Greg Papalia
Beowulf *42*

Nenad Pecur
Hannibal Rising *168*

Jay Pelissier
Norbit *294*

Pierre Perrault
I'm Not There *200*

Alan Petherick
Alpha Dog *7*

Catherine Pierrat
Comedy of Power *80*

Arin Pinijvararak
Rescue Dawn *334*

Denise Pizzini
Shooter *356*

Lauren E. Polizzi
The TV Set *410*

Margot Ready
In the Land of Women *202*

Seth Reed
Blades of Glory *49*

John Richardson (1936-)
Into the Wild *209*

Bradford Ricker
Charlie Wilson's War *74*

Scott Ritenour
The Reaping *325*

Mark Robins
30 Days of Night *397*

Mindy Roffman
Fracture *132*

Peter Rogness
Across the Universe *1*

Philippe Rouchier
Arthur and the Invisibles *18*

Robh Ruppel
Meet the Robinsons *258*

Peter Russell
Ghost Rider *144*

David Sandefur
The Number 23 *295*

Adam Scher
I Think I Love My Wife *198*

Lissette Schettini
Grace Is Gone *153*

Sebastian Schroeder
The Jane Austen Book
Club *215*

Catherine Schroer
Juno *220*

Astrid Sieben
Beyond the Gates *44*

Domenic Silvestri
Into the Wild *209*
Walk Hard: The Dewey Cox
Story *426*

Troy Sizemore
The Assassination of Jesse James
by the Coward Robert
Ford *19*
Live Free or Die Hard *244*

Bill Skinner
I Am Legend *193*

William Ladd (Bill) Skinner
Mr. Brooks *270*

Eloise Stammerjohn
Honeydripper *181*

Jeremy Stanbridge
Shooter *356*

Andrew Stearn
Breach *59*

Adam Stockhausen
The Darjeeling Limited *91*
Margot at the Wedding *255*

Gerald Sullivan
Superbad *383*

David Swayze
I Now Pronounce You Chuck and
Larry *196*

Ahtam Tam
TMNT *404*

Sandra Tanaka
Fantastic Four: Rise of the Silver
Surfer *121*

Christopher Tandon
Because I Said So *34*

Thomas T. Taylor
Premonition *315*

Marco Trentini
Charlie Wilson's War *74*

James F. Truesdale
The Invasion *210*
Mr. Woodcock *273*
Underdog *415*

Benno Tutter
Away From Her *31*

Gregory Van Horn
Wild Hogs *434*

Cecile Vatelot
La Vie en Rose *421*

Macie Vener
Year of the Dog *439*

Mario R. Ventenilla
August Rush *26*

Geoff Wallace
Things We Lost in the
Fire *395*

Frank Walsh
Elizabeth: The Golden
Age *108*

Jennifer Ward
Bridge to Terabithia *62*

David Warren
Sunshine *381*

Ken Watkins
The Messengers *259*

Andrew White
Sydney White *389*

Iain White
Sleuth *365*

Kerry Dean Williams
P.S. I Love You *320*

Tony Wohlgemuth
Good Luck Chuck *151*

Michael Norman Wong
Fido *126*

Patricia Woodbridge
I Am Legend *193*
Music and Lyrics *275*

Tu Xinran
The Painted Veil *303*

Chelsea Yusep
    Kickin' It Old Skool *223*
Frank Zito
    Bug *66*

Music Director Index

Bryan Adams
    Color Me Kubrick *77*

Armand Amar
    Days of Glory *93*

Michael Andrews
    Paris, je t'aime *306*
    The TV Set *410*
    Walk Hard: The Dewey Cox
       Story *426*

Craig Armstrong
    Elizabeth: The Golden
       Age *108*

David Arnold (1962-)
    Amazing Grace *10*
    Grindhouse *159*
    Hot Fuzz *186*

Klaus Badelt
    Premonition *315*
    Rescue Dawn *334*
    TMNT *404*

Nathan Barr
    Grindhouse *159*
    Hostel: Part II *185*

Eef Barzelay
    Rocket Science *341*

Tyler Bates
    Grindhouse *159*
    Halloween *167*
    300 *400*

Christophe Beck
    Fred Claus *134*
    License to Wed *241*
    The Seeker: The Dark Is Ris-
       ing *350*
    Year of the Dog *439*

Marco Beltrami
    Captivity *70*
    The Invisible *212*
    Live Free or Die Hard *244*
    3:10 to Yuma *402*

Terence Blanchard (1962-)
    Talk to Me *391*

Tim Boland
    Stomp the Yard *379*

Scott Bomar
    Black Snake Moan *47*

Michael Brook
    Into the Wild *209*

BT (Brian Transeau) (1971-)
    Catch and Release *73*

Paul Buckley
    Happily N'Ever After *170*

Carter Burwell (1955-)
    Before the Devil Knows You're
       Dead *40*
    The Hoax *179*
    No Country for Old Men *288*

Teddy Castellucci
    Are We Done Yet? *16*
    Wild Hogs *434*

Nick Cave
    The Assassination of Jesse James
       by the Coward Robert
       Ford *19*

Matthieu Chabrol
    Comedy of Power *80*

George S. Clinton (1947-)
    Code Name: The Cleaner *76*

Charlie Clouser
    Dead Silence *94*

Death Sentence *97*
    Resident Evil: Extinction *338*
    Saw IV *349*

John Coda
    Bratz *55*

Dan Crane
    Air Guitar Nation *3*

Douglas J. Cuomo
    Crazy Love *83*

Jeff Danna (1964-)
    Fracture *132*

Mychael Danna (1958-)
    Breach *59*
    Fracture *132*
    Surf's Up *385*

Mason Daring (1949-)
    Honeydripper *181*

John Debney (1957-)
    Evan Almighty *114*
    Georgia Rule *142*

Xavier Demerliac
    My Best Friend *277*

Alexandre Desplat
    The Golden Compass *147*
    Lust, Caution *252*
    Mr. Magorium's Wonder Empo-
       rium *272*
    The Painted Veil *303*
    The Valet *420*

Ramin Djawadi
    Mr. Brooks *270*

James Dooley
    Daddy Day Camp *85*

Patrick Doyle (1953-)
    The Last Legion *238*
    Sleuth *365*

Mark Mancina (1957-)
August Rush *26*
Shooter *356*

Clint Mansell
Smokin' Aces *368*

David Mansfield (1956-)
Stephanie Daley *378*

Dario Marianelli
Atonement *23*
Beyond the Gates *44*
The Brave One *56*

Stuart Matthewman
The Astronaut Farmer *21*

Brian McKnight
Daddy's Little Girls *86*

Joel McNeely
I Know Who Killed Me *194*

Alan Menken (1949-)
Enchanted *110*

Mateo Messina
Juno *220*

Marcus Miller (1959-)
I Think I Love My Wife *198*

Moby (1965-)
Southland Tales *370*

Trevor Morris
The Hills Have Eyes II *175*

Stephane Moucha
The Lives of Others *246*

Nico Muhly
Joshua *218*

John Murphy
Sunshine *381*

Peter Nashel
No End in Sight *290*

Blake Neely
Starter for 10 *376*

New Order
Control *81*

David Newman (1954-)
Norbit *294*

Molly Nyman
A Mighty Heart *263*

Erin O'Hara
Sicko *360*

John Ottman (1964-)
Fantastic Four: Rise of the Silver Surfer *121*
The Invasion *210*

Martin Phipps
The Flying Scotsman *129*

Phoenix Foundation
Eagle vs. Shark *105*

Antonio Pinto
Love in the Time of Cholera *249*
Perfect Stranger *310*

Nicola Piovani
Avenue Montaigne *28*

John Powell
The Bourne Ultimatum *52*
P.S. I Love You *320*

Trevor Rabin (1954-)
Hot Rod *188*
National Treasure: Book of Secrets *284*

Brian Reitzell
30 Days of Night *397*

Sam Retzer
Stomp the Yard *379*

Graeme Revell (1955-)
Awake *29*
Darfur Now *90*
Grindhouse *159*

Craig Richey
The King of Kong: A Fistful of Quarters *226*

Robert Rodriguez (1968-)
Grindhouse *159*

Jeff Rona (1957-)
Slow Burn *367*

William Ross
September Dawn *352*

David E. Russo
Alone With Her *6*

Bill Ryan
The Heartbreak Kid *174*

Brendan Ryan
The Heartbreak Kid *174*

Jamie Saft
God Grew Tired of Us *146*

Ralph Sall
Nancy Drew *281*

Nitin Sawhney
The Namesake *279*

Lalo Schifrin (1932-)
Rush Hour 3 *343*

Adam Schlesinger
Music and Lyrics *275*

Eric Serra
Arthur and the Invisibles *18*

Marc Shaiman (1959-)
Hairspray *165*

Theodore Shapiro
Blades of Glory *49*
Mr. Woodcock *273*

Ed Shearmur (1966-)
Epic Movie *112*
Factory Girl *119*

Philip Sheppard
In the Shadow of the Moon *204*

David Shire (1937-)
Zodiac *443*

Howard Shore (1946-)
Eastern Promises *106*
The Last Mimzy *240*

Alan Silvestri (1950-)
Beowulf *42*

Mark Snow (1946-)
Private Fears in Public Places *318*

Johan Söderqvist
Things We Lost in the Fire *395*

Stephen Sondheim (1930-)
Sweeney Todd: The Demon Barber of Fleet Street *386*

Jason Staczek
Brand Upon the Brain! *54*

Tommy Stinson
Catch and Release *73*

Marc Streitenfeld
American Gangster *13*

Mark Suozzo (1953-)
The Nanny Diaries *282*

John Swihart
The Brothers Solomon *64*
Full of It *138*

Carl Thiel
Grindhouse *159*

Béeatrice Thiriet
Lady Chatterley *235*

David Torn
Lars and the Real Girl *237*

Stephen Trask
Feast of Love *124*
In the Land of Women *202*
The Savages *347*

Tom Tykwer (1965-)
Paris, je t'aime *306*
Perfume: The Story of a Murderer *312*

Brian Tyler
Aliens vs. Predator: Requiem *4*
Bug *66*
War *428*

Shigeru Umebayashi
Hannibal Rising *168*

Edward Vedder
Into the Wild *209*

James A. Venable
Kickin' It Old Skool *223*

Loudon Wainwright, III
Knocked Up *231*

Nathan Wang
The Final Season *128*
The Game Plan *141*

Craig (Shudder to Think) Wedren
  Reno 911!: Miami *333*
Nigel Westlake
  Miss Potter *265*
Lyle Workman
  Superbad *383*
Gabriel Yared (1949-)
  Breaking and Entering *61*
  1408 *131*
  The Lives of Others *246*
Christopher Young (1954-)
  Ghost Rider *144*

Lucky You *251*
Spider-Man 3 *372*
Geoff Zanelli
  Disturbia *99*
  Hitman *178*
Marcelo Zarvos
  You Kill Me *440*
Aaron Zigman
  Alpha Dog *7*
  Bridge to Terabithia *62*
  Good Luck Chuck *151*

The Jane Austen Book
  Club *215*
Martian Child *256*
Mr. Magorium's Wonder Empo-
  rium *272*
Pride *317*
Why Did I Get Married? *432*
Hans Zimmer (1957-)
  August Rush *26*
  Pirates of the Caribbean: At
    World's End *313*
  The Simpsons Movie *362*

Performer Index

Caroline Aaron (1952-)
Nancy Drew *281*

Bonnie Aarons
I Know Who Killed Me *194*

Khalid Abdalla
The Kite Runner *229*

Talon G. Ackerman
Daddy Day Camp *85*

Amy Adams (1974-)
Charlie Wilson's War *74*
Enchanted *110*
Underdog (V) *415*

Ben Affleck (1972-)
Smokin' Aces *368*

Casey Affleck (1975-)
The Assassination of Jesse James
by the Coward Robert
Ford *19*
Gone Baby Gone *149*
Ocean's Thirteen *299*

Liam Aiken (1990-)
Fay Grim *123*

Malin Akerman (1978-)
The Brothers Solomon *64*
The Heartbreak Kid *174*
The Invasion *210*

Carlos Alazraqui
Reno 911!: Miami *333*

Jessica Alba (1981-)
Awake *29*
Fantastic Four: Rise of the Silver
Surfer *121*
Good Luck Chuck *151*

Alan Alda (1936-)
Resurrecting the Champ *339*

Eddie Alderson
Reservation Road *336*

Tom Aldredge (1928-)
The Assassination of Jesse James
by the Coward Robert
Ford *19*

Raquel Alessi
Ghost Rider *144*

Flex Alexander (1970-)
The Hills Have Eyes II *175*

Jane Alexander (1939-)
Feast of Love *124*

Sarah Alexander (1971-)
Stardust *374*

Héelèene Alexandridis
Lady Chatterley *235*

Catherine Allegret (1946-)
La Vie en Rose *421*

Aleisha Allen (1991-)
Are We Done Yet? *16*

Joan Allen (1956-)
The Bourne Ultimatum *52*

Tim Allen (1953-)
Wild Hogs *434*

Daniella Alonso
The Hills Have Eyes II *175*

Laz Alonso
Captivity *70*
Stomp the Yard *379*
This Christmas *399*

Aris Alvarado
Kickin' It Old Skool *223*

Mathieu Amalric (1965-)
The Diving Bell and the Butterfly *101*

Elena Anaya (1975-)
In the Land of Women *202*

Anthony Anderson (1970-)
Arthur and the Invisibles
(V) *18*
Transformers *407*

Christopher Anderson
The Flying Scotsman *129*

Joe Anderson
Across the Universe *1*
Becoming Jane *36*
Control *81*

Stephen John Anderson
Meet the Robinsons (V) *258*

Julie Andrews (1935-)
Enchanted (N) *110*
Shrek the Third (V) *358*

Naveen Andrews (1971-)
The Brave One *56*
Grindhouse *159*

Michael Angarano (1987-)
The Final Season *128*

Joey Ansah (1982-)
The Bourne Ultimatum *52*

Jasmine Jessica Anthony
1408 *131*

Marc Anthony (1969-)
El Cantante *69*

Devon Aoki (1982-)
DOA: Dead or Alive *103*
War *428*

Melissa Arcaro
Grindhouse *159*

Fanny Ardant (1949-)
Paris, je t'aime *306*

Pierre Arditti (1944-)
Private Fears in Public
Places *318*

Lee Arenberg (1962-)
Pirates of the Caribbean: At
World's End *313*

Niels Arestrup (1949-)
The Diving Bell and the Butterfly *101*

Yancey Arias (1971-)
Live Free or Die Hard *244*

Alan Arkin (1934-)
Rendition *331*

Andrew Armour
Red Road *327*

Curtis Armstrong (1953-)
Smokin' Aces *368*
Southland Tales *370*

Will Arnett (1970-)
Blades of Glory *49*
The Brothers Solomon *64*
The Comebacks *79*
Hot Rod *188*
Ratatouille (V) *323*
Wristcutters: A Love Story *437*

Tichina Arnold (1971-)
Wild Hogs *434*

Tom Arnold (1959-)
The Final Season *128*
Pride *317*

Nicholas Reese Art
The Nanny Diaries *282*

Ashanti (1980-)
Resident Evil: Extinction *338*

Linden Ashby (1960-)
Resident Evil: Extinction *338*

Jane Asher (1946-)
Death at a Funeral *95*

John Ashton (1948-)
Gone Baby Gone *149*

Armand Assante (1949-)
American Gangster *13*

Sean Astin (1971-)
The Final Season *128*

Eileen Atkins (1934-)
Evening *115*

Rowan Atkinson (1955-)
Mr. Bean's Holiday *268*

Yvan Attal (1965-)
Rush Hour 3 *343*

Julie Austin
The Flying Scotsman *129*

Daniel Auteuil (1950-)
My Best Friend *277*
The Valet *420*

Aviva (1984-)
Superbad *383*

Nicki Aycox (1975-)
Perfect Stranger *310*

Dan Aykroyd (1952-)
I Now Pronounce You Chuck and
Larry *196*

Reiko Aylesworth (1972-)
Aliens vs. Predator: Requiem *4*
Mr. Brooks *270*

Hank Azaria (1964-)
The Simpsons Movie (V) *362*

Sabine Azéma
Private Fears in Public
Places *318*

Michael Bacall
Grindhouse *159*

Alicja Bachleda-Curus
Trade *406*

George Back
The Comebacks *79*

Kevin Bacon (1958-)
Death Sentence *97*

Diedrich Bader (1966-)
Balls of Fury *33*
Surf's Up (V) *385*

Du-na Bae
The Host *183*

Tim Bagley
Knocked Up *231*

Dylan Baker (1958-)
The Hunting Party *191*
Fido *126*
Spider-Man 3 *372*

Kathy Baker (1950-)
The Jane Austen Book
Club *215*

Robert Baker (1979-)
Seraphim Falls *353*

Bob Balaban (1945-)
No Reservations *292*

Kyley Baldridge
Mr. Woodcock *273*

Max Baldry
Mr. Bean's Holiday *268*

Christian Bale (1974-)
I'm Not There *200*
Rescue Dawn *334*
3:10 to Yuma *402*

Penny Balfour
Arthur and the Invisibles *18*

Jean-François Balmer
Comedy of Power *80*

David Bamber (1954-)
Miss Potter *265*

Eric Bana (1968-)
Lucky You *251*

Antonio Banderas (1960-)
Shrek the Third (V) *358*

Elizabeth Banks (1974-)
Fred Claus *134*
Spider-Man 3 *372*

Jonathan Banks (1947-)
Reign Over Me *328*

David Banner
Black Snake Moan *47*

Marc Barbé
La Vie en Rose *421*

Javier Bardem (1969-)
Love in the Time of Chol-
era *249*
No Country for Old Men *288*

Ashraf Barhoum
The Kingdom *227*

Ellen Barkin (1954-)
Ocean's Thirteen *299*

Ben Barnes
Stardust *374*

Jacinda Barrett (1972-)
The Namesake *279*

Laurence Barry
The Wind That Shakes the Barley *435*

Raymond J. Barry (1939-)
Walk Hard: The Dewey Cox
Story *426*

Stephanie Barry
No Reservations *292*

Drew Barrymore (1975-)
Lucky You *251*
Music and Lyrics *275*

Roger Bart (1962-)
American Gangster *13*
Hostel: Part II *185*

Justin Bartha (1978-)
National Treasure: Book of Secrets *284*

Jay Baruchel (1982-)
Knocked Up *231*

Angela Bassett (1958-)
Meet the Robinsons (V) *258*

Julie Bataille
Paris, je t'aime *306*

Jason Bateman (1969-)
Arthur and the Invisibles
(V) *18*
Juno *220*
The Kingdom *227*

Mr. Magorium's Wonder Emporium *272*
Smokin' Aces *368*

Justine Bateman (1966-)
The TV Set *410*

Kathy Bates (1948-)
Bee Movie *(V)* *38*
Fred Claus *134*
The Golden Compass (V) *147*
P.S. I Love You *320*

Brian Baumgartner (1972-)
License to Wed *241*

Sean Bean (1959-)
The Hitcher *176*

Nancy Beatty
Lars and the Real Girl *237*

Ned Beatty (1937-)
Charlie Wilson's War *74*
Shooter *356*

Garcelle Beauvais (1966-)
I Know Who Killed Me *194*

Jim Beaver (1950-)
Next *286*

Kate Beckinsale (1974-)
Vacancy *418*

Grace Bednarczyk
Grace Is Gone *153*

Jason Behr (1973-)
Skinwalkers *364*

Leila Bekhti
Paris, je t'aime *306*

Dana Belben
Surf's Up *(V)* *385*

Marshall Bell (1944-)
The Final Season *128*
Nancy Drew *281*
Rescue Dawn *334*

Tobin Bell (1942-)
Saw IV *349*

Zoë Bell (1978-)
Grindhouse *159*

Maria Bello (1967-)
The Jane Austen Book
Club *215*

Monica Bellucci (1968-)
Shoot 'Em Up *355*

James Belushi (1954-)
Underdog *415*

Haley Bennett
Music and Lyrics *275*

Jimmy Bennett (1996-)
Evan Almighty *114*

Sonja Bennett
Fido *126*

Abraham Benrubi (1969-)
Wristcutters: A Love Story *437*

Lyriq Bent
Saw IV *349*

Wes Bentley (1978-)
Ghost Rider *144*

Peter Berg (1964-)
Lions for Lambs *243*
Smokin' Aces *368*

Christian Berkel (1957-)
Black Book *46*

Xander Berkeley (1958-)
Fracture *132*

Steven Berkoff (1937-)
The Flying Scotsman *129*

François Berléand (1952-)
Comedy of Power *80*

Elizabeth Berrington (1970-)
Fred Claus *134*

Halle Berry (1968-)
Perfect Stranger *310*
Things We Lost in the
Fire *395*

Micah Berry
Things We Lost in the
Fire *395*

Richard Berry (1950-)
The Valet *420*

Melchior Beslon
Paris, je t'aime *306*

Matt Besser
Walk Hard: The Dewey Cox
Story *426*

Leslie Bibb (1974-)
Wristcutters: A Love Story *437*

Michael Biehn (1956-)
Grindhouse *159*

Jessica Biel (1982-)
I Now Pronounce You Chuck and
Larry *196*
Next *286*

Leo Bill
Becoming Jane *36*

Mike Binder (1958-)
Reign Over Me *328*

Juliette Binoche (1964-)
Breaking and Entering *61*
Dan in Real Life *88*
Paris, je t'aime *306*

Panther Bior
God Grew Tired of Us *146*

Brad Bird (1957-)
Ratatouille *(V)* *323*

Mary Birdsong
Reno 911!: Miami *333*

Jack Black (1969-)
Margot at the Wedding *255*

Selma Blair (1972-)
Feast of Love *124*

Jolene Blalock
Slow Burn *367*

Bernard Blancan
Days of Glory *93*

Cate Blanchett (1969-)
Elizabeth: The Golden
Age *108*
Hot Fuzz *186*
I'm Not There *200*

Brenda Blethyn (1946-)
Atonement *23*

Peter Blok
Black Book *46*

Nikki Blonsky
Hairspray *165*

Moon Bloodgood (1975-)
Pathfinder *308*

Orlando Bloom (1977-)
Pirates of the Caribbean: At
World's End *313*

Marc Blucas (1972-)
The Jane Austen Book
Club *215*

Emily Blunt (1983-)
Charlie Wilson's War *74*
Dan in Real Life *88*
The Jane Austen Book
Club *215*

Philip Daniel Bolden (1995-)
Are We Done Yet? *16*

Jackson Bond
The Invasion *210*

Helena Bonham Carter (1966-)
Harry Potter and the Order of
the Phoenix *171*
Sweeney Todd: The Demon Barber of Fleet Street *386*

Bono (1960-)
Across the Universe *1*

Dany Boon (1966-)
My Best Friend *277*
The Valet *420*

Powers Boothe (1949-)
The Final Season *128*

Seydou Boro
Paris, je t'aime *306*

Alex Borstein (1972-)
The Lookout *248*

Philip Bosco (1930-)
The Savages *347*

Barry Bostwick (1945-)
Evening *115*
Nancy Drew *281*

Sami Bouajila (1966-)
Days of Glory *93*

Denise Boutte (1982-)
Why Did I Get Married? *432*

Jamie Campbell Bower
Sweeney Todd: The Demon Barber of Fleet Street *386*

David Bowie (1947-)
Arthur and the Invisibles (V) *18*

Peter Bowles (1936-)
Color Me Kubrick *77*

Billy Boyd (1968-)
The Flying Scotsman *129*

Derek Boyer (1969-)
DOA: Dead or Alive *103*

Charles Bracy
Killer of Sheep *224*

David Bradley (1942-)
Harry Potter and the Order of the Phoenix *171*

Alice Braga
I Am Legend *193*

Sonia Braga (1951-)
The Hottest State *189*

Claude Brasseur (1936-)
Avenue Montaigne *28*

Benjamin Bratt (1963-)
Love in the Time of Cholera *249*

Andre Braugher (1962-)
Fantastic Four: Rise of the Silver Surfer *121*
The Mist *267*

Ewen Bremner (1971-)
Death at a Funeral *95*

Amy Brenneman (1964-)
The Jane Austen Book Club *215*

Abigail Breslin (1996-)
No Reservations *292*

Chris "Ludacris" Bridges
Fred Claus *134*

Jeff Bridges (1949-)
Surf's Up (V) *385*

Spencir Bridges (1998-)
Daddy Day Camp *85*

Jim Broadbent (1949-)
Hot Fuzz *186*

Matthew Broderick (1962-)
Bee Movie (V) *38*

Adam Brody (1980-)
In the Land of Women *202*

Adrien Brody (1973-)
The Darjeeling Limited *91*

James Brolin (1940-)
The Hunting Party *191*

Josh Brolin (1968-)
American Gangster *13*
Grindhouse *159*
In the Valley of Elah *205*
No Country for Old Men *288*

Albert Brooks (1947-)
The Simpsons Movie (V) *362*

Pierce Brosnan (1953-)
Seraphim Falls *353*

Chris Brown
This Christmas *399*

Clancy Brown (1959-)
Pathfinder *308*

Sean Brown
The Flying Scotsman *129*

Sullivan Brown
Brand Upon the Brain! *54*

Roscoe Lee Browne
Epic Movie (N) *112*

Logan Browning
Bratz *55*

Agnes Bruckner (1985-)
Blood and Chocolate *50*

Amy Bruckner (1991-)
Nancy Drew *281*

Daniel Brühl
2 Days in Paris *413*

Patrick Bruel (1959-)
Comedy of Power *80*

Daniel Bruhl (1978-)
The Bourne Ultimatum *52*

Sandra Bullock (1964-)
Premonition *315*

Richard Burgi (1958-)
Hostel: Part II *185*

Billy Burke (1966-)
Feast of Love *124*
Fracture *132*

Courtney Taylor Burness
Premonition *315*

Saffron Burrows (1973-)
Fay Grim *123*
Reign Over Me *328*

Steve Buscemi (1957-)
I Now Pronounce You Chuck and Larry *196*
I Think I Love My Wife *198*
Interview *208*
Paris, je t'aime *306*

Sophia Bush (1982-)
The Hitcher *176*

Gerard Butler (1969-)
P.S. I Love You *320*
300 *400*

Kate Butler
Bridge to Terabithia *62*

Norbert Lee Butz
Dan in Real Life *88*

Hie-bong Byeon
The Host *183*

Amanda Bynes (1986-)
Hairspray *165*
Sydney White *389*

Gabriel Byrne (1950-)
Jindabyne *216*

Rose Byrne (1979-)
Sunshine *381*
28 Weeks Later *411*

Scott Caan (1976-)
Ocean's Thirteen *299*

Nicolas Cage (1964-)
Ghost Rider *144*
Grindhouse *159*
National Treasure: Book of Secrets *284*
Next *286*

Dean Cain (1966-)
September Dawn *352*

Michael Caine (1933-)
Sleuth *365*

Muzaffer Cakar
The Flying Scotsman *129*

Frank Caliendo (1974-)
The Comebacks *79*

Alexander Calvert
Kickin' It Old Skool *223*

Cody Cameron
Shrek the Third (V) *358*

Adam Campbell
Epic Movie *112*

Bruce Campbell (1958-)
Spider-Man 3 *372*

Jose Pablo Cantillo (1979-)
Disturbia *99*

Marilyne Canto (1963-)
Comedy of Power *80*

Mario Cantone (1959-)
Surf's Up (V) *385*

Joshua Caras
Gracie *154*

Nestor Carbonell (1967-)
Smokin' Aces *368*

Steve Carell (1963-)
Dan in Real Life *88*
Evan Almighty *114*

Billy Connolly (1942-)
Fido *126*

Frances Conroy (1953-)
The Seeker: The Dark Is Rising *350*

Paddy Considine (1974-)
The Bourne Ultimatum *52*
Hot Fuzz *186*

Anne Consigny
The Diving Bell and the Butterfly *101*

Yorgo Constantine
Live Free or Die Hard *244*

Steve Coogan (1965-)
Hot Fuzz *186*

Dane Cook (1972-)
Dan in Real Life *88*
Good Luck Chuck *151*
Mr. Brooks *270*

Rachael Leigh Cook (1979-)
The Final Season *128*
Nancy Drew *281*

Jennifer Coolidge (1963-)
Epic Movie *112*

Bradley Cooper (1975-)
The Comebacks *79*

Chris Cooper (1951-)
Breach *59*
The Kingdom *227*

Dominic Cooper (1978-)
Starter for 10 *376*

Alicia Coppola (1968-)
National Treasure: Book of Secrets *284*

John Corbett (1962-)
The Messengers *259*

Barry Corbin (1940-)
In the Valley of Elah *205*
No Country for Old Men *288*

Nathan Corddry
The Nanny Diaries *282*

Rob Corddry (1971-)
The Heartbreak Kid *174*
I Now Pronounce You Chuck and Larry *196*

Abbie Cornish (1982-)
Elizabeth: The Golden Age *108*

Antoni Corone
Reservation Road *336*
We Own the Night *431*

Kevin Corrigan (1969-)
American Gangster *13*
Superbad *383*

James Cosmo (1948-)
The Last Legion *238*

The Seeker: The Dark Is Rising *350*

Kevin Costner (1955-)
Mr. Brooks *270*

John Cothran, Jr. (1947-)
Black Snake Moan *47*

Marion Cotillard (1975-)
La Vie en Rose *421*

Jean-Louis Coulloc'h
Lady Chatterley *235*

Clotilde Courau (1969-)
La Vie en Rose *421*

Tom Courtenay (1937-)
The Golden Compass *147*

Allen Covert (1964-)
I Now Pronounce You Chuck and Larry *196*

Rachel Covey
Enchanted *110*

Brian Cox (1946-)
The Flying Scotsman *129*
The Water Horse: Legend of the Deep *429*
Zodiac *443*

Charlie Cox (1982-)
Stardust *374*

Peter Coyote (1942-)
Resurrecting the Champ *339*

Daniel Craig (1968-)
The Golden Compass *147*
The Invasion *210*

Clayne Crawford (1978-)
Wristcutters: A Love Story *437*

Terry Crews (1968-)
Balls of Fury *33*
Norbit *294*

Wendy Crewson (1956-)
Away From Her *31*
The Seeker: The Dark Is Rising *350*

James Cromwell (1940-)
Becoming Jane *36*
Spider-Man 3 *372*

Mackenzie Crook (1971-)
Pirates of the Caribbean: At World's End *313*

David Cross (1964-)
Alvin and the Chipmunks *9*
I'm Not There *200*

Flora Cross
Margot at the Wedding *255*

Lindsay Crouse (1948-)
Mr. Brooks *270*

Russell Crowe (1964-)
American Gangster *13*
3:10 to Yuma *402*

Marie-Josée Croze (1970-)
The Diving Bell and the Butterfly *101*

Tom Cruise (1962-)
Lions for Lambs *243*

Brett Cullen (1956-)
Ghost Rider *144*

Peter Cullen (1944-)
Transformers (V) *407*

Benedict Cumberbatch (1977-)
Amazing Grace *10*
Atonement *23*
Starter for 10 *376*

Alan Cumming (1965-)
Gray Matters *156*

Liam Cunningham (1961-)
The Wind That Shakes the Barley *435*

Sean Curley
Reservation Road *336*

Tony Curran (1969-)
Red Road *327*

Cliff Curtis (1968-)
Fracture *132*
Live Free or Die Hard *244*
Sunshine *381*

Vondie Curtis-Hall (1956-)
Honeydripper *181*
Talk to Me *391*

Joan Cusack (1962-)
Martian Child *256*

John Cusack (1966-)
1408 *131*
Grace Is Gone *153*
Martian Child *256*

Sinead Cusack (1948-)
Eastern Promises *106*

Henry Ian Cusick
Hitman *178*

Elisha Cuthbert (1982-)
Captivity *70*

Henry Czerny (1959-)
Fido *126*

Mark Dacascos (1964-)
Code Name: The Cleaner *76*

Yaya DaCosta
Honeydripper *181*

Willem Dafoe (1955-)
Mr. Bean's Holiday *268*
Paris, je t'aime *306*

Nicholas D'Agosto
Rocket Science *341*

Timothy Dalton (1944-)
Hot Fuzz *186*

Matt Damon (1970-)
The Bourne Ultimatum *52*
Ocean's Thirteen *299*

Charles Dance (1946-)
    Starter for 10 *376*

Hugh Dancy (1975-)
    Beyond the Gates *44*
    Blood and Chocolate *50*
    Evening *115*
    The Jane Austen Book
      Club *215*

Claire Danes (1979-)
    Evening *115*
    Stardust *374*

Dani (1947-)
    Avenue Montaigne *28*

Jeff Daniels (1955-)
    The Lookout *248*

Sybil Danning (1952-)
    Grindhouse *159*

Paul Dano (1984-)
    There Will Be Blood *392*

John Bul Dau
    God Grew Tired of Us *146*

Alexa Davalos (1982-)
    Feast of Love *124*
    The Mist *267*

Jack Davenport (1973-)
    Pirates of the Caribbean: At
      World's End *313*

DeRay David
    Code Name: The Cleaner *76*

Keith David (1954-)
    Delta Farce *98*

Lolita Davidovich (1961-)
    September Dawn *352*

James Davidson
    Color Me Kubrick *77*

Embeth Davidtz (1966-)
    Fracture *132*

Jeremy Davies (1969-)
    Rescue Dawn *334*

DeRay Davis
    License to Wed *241*

Hope Davis (1964-)
    The Hoax *179*

Lucy Davis (1973-)
    The TV Set *410*

Warwick Davis (1970-)
    Harry Potter and the Order of
      the Phoenix *171*

William B. Davis
    The Messengers *259*

Bruce Davison (1946-)
    Breach *59*

Rosario Dawson (1979-)
    Grindhouse *159*

Daniel Day-Lewis (1957-)
    There Will Be Blood *392*

Isaach de Bankolé (1957-)
    The Diving Bell and the Butter-
      fly *101*

Emma de Caunes (1976-)
    Mr. Bean's Holiday *268*

Cécile de France (1975-)
    Avenue Montaigne *28*

Derek de Lint (1950-)
    Black Book *46*

Robert De Niro (1943-)
    Arthur and the Invisibles
      (V) *18*
    Stardust *374*

Jamel Debbouze (1975-)
    Angel-A *15*
    Days of Glory *93*

Ruby Dee (1924-)
    American Gangster *13*

Benicio Del Toro (1967-)
    Things We Lost in the
      Fire *395*

Pádraic Delaney
    The Wind That Shakes the Bar-
      ley *435*

Albert Delpy
    2 Days in Paris *413*

Julie Delpy (1969-)
    The Hoax *179*
    2 Days in Paris *413*

Patrick Dempsey (1966-)
    Enchanted *110*
    Freedom Writers *136*

Jeffrey DeMunn (1947-)
    The Mist *267*

Brian Dennehy (1939-)
    Ratatouille (V) *323*

Géerard Depardieu (1948-)
    Paris, je t'aime *306*
    La Vie en Rose *421*

Julie Depardieu (1973-)
    Rush Hour 3 *343*

Johnny Depp (1963-)
    Pirates of the Caribbean: At
      World's End *313*
    Sweeney Todd: The Demon Bar-
      ber of Fleet Street *386*

Bruce Dern (1936-)
    The Astronaut Farmer *21*

Laura Dern (1966-)
    Year of the Dog *439*

Zooey Deschanel (1980-)
    The Assassination of Jesse James
      by the Coward Robert
      Ford *19*

Bridge to Terabithia *62*
    Surf's Up (V) *385*

Cyril Descours
    Paris, je t'aime *306*

Loretta Devine (1949-)
    This Christmas *399*

Danny DeVito (1944-)
    Reno 911!: Miami *333*

Noureen DeWulf (1984-)
    The Comebacks *79*
    Ocean's Thirteen *299*

Caroline Dhavernas (1978-)
    Breach *59*

Sergio Di Zio
    The Lookout *248*

Cameron Diaz (1972-)
    Shrek the Third (V) *358*

Andy Dick (1965-)
    The Comebacks *79*
    Happily N'Ever After (V) *170*

Bryan Dick (1978-)
    Blood and Chocolate *50*

Eric Dickerson
    The Comebacks *79*

Kate Dickie
    Red Road *327*

Felipe Dieppa
    Evan Almighty *114*

Brian Dierker
    Into the Wild *209*

Taye Diggs (1972-)
    Slow Burn *367*

Garret Dillahunt
    The Assassination of Jesse James
      by the Coward Robert
      Ford *19*
    No Country for Old Men *288*

Melinda Dillon (1939-)
    Reign Over Me *328*

Peter Dinklage (1969-)
    Death at a Funeral *95*
    Underdog *415*

Snoop Dogg
    Arthur and the Invisibles
      (V) *18*

John Doman (1945-)
    Gracie *154*

Ron Donachie
    The Flying Scotsman *129*

Daisy Donovan (1975-)
    Death at a Funeral *95*

Tate Donovan (1963-)
    Nancy Drew *281*
    Shooter *356*

Paul Dooley (1928-)
Hairspray *165*

Omar Doom (1976-)
Grindhouse *159*

David Doty
Nancy Drew *281*

Illeana Douglas (1965-)
Factory Girl *119*

Gary Dourdan (1966-)
Perfect Stranger *310*

Brad Dourif (1950-)
Halloween *167*

Robert Downey, Jr. (1965-)
Lucky You *251*
Zodiac *443*

Elle Downs (1973-)
Talk to Me *391*

Brian Doyle-Murray (1945-)
Daddy Day Camp *85*

Rachel Dratch
I Now Pronounce You Chuck and
Larry *196*

Lionel Dray
Paris, je t'aime *306*

James Dreyfus (1968-)
Color Me Kubrick *77*

David Duchovny (1960-)
Things We Lost in the
Fire *395*
The TV Set *410*

Jamal Duff
The Game Plan *141*

Dennis Dugan (1946-)
I Now Pronounce You Chuck and
Larry *196*

Josh Duhamel (1972-)
Transformers *407*

Olympia Dukakis (1931-)
Away From Her *31*
In the Land of Women *202*

Lindsay Duncan (1950-)
Starter for 10 *376*

Michael Clarke Duncan (1957-)
The Last Mimzy *240*

Greg Dunham
The Lookout *248*

Kevin Dunn (1956-)
Lions for Lambs *243*
Transformers *407*

Nora Dunn (1952-)
Southland Tales *370*

Kirsten Dunst (1982-)
Spider-Man 3 *372*

Albert Dupontel (1964-)
Avenue Montaigne *28*

Julie Durand
My Best Friend *277*

Kevin Durand (1974-)
Smokin' Aces *368*
3:10 to Yuma *402*
Wild Hogs *434*

André Dussollier (1946-)
Private Fears in Public
Places *318*

Charles S. Dutton (1951-)
Honeydripper *181*

Robert Duvall (1931-)
Lucky You *251*
We Own the Night *431*

Jayne Eastwood (1946-)
You Kill Me *440*

Zekiria Ebrahimi
The Kite Runner *229*

Christopher Eccleston (1964-)
The Seeker: The Dark Is Rising *350*

Aaron Eckhart (1968-)
No Reservations *292*

Eric Edelstein
The Hills Have Eyes II *175*

Joel Edgerton (1974-)
Smokin' Aces *368*

Stacy Edwards (1965-)
Superbad *383*

Zac Efron (1987-)
Hairspray *165*

Christopher Egan (1984-)
Resident Evil: Extinction *338*
Smokin' Aces *368*

Peter Egan (1946-)
Death at a Funeral *95*

Elham Ehsas
The Kite Runner *229*

Bob Einstein (1940-)
Ocean's Thirteen *299*

Jesse Eisenberg (1983-)
The Hunting Party *191*

Chiwetel Ejiofor (1976-)
American Gangster *13*
Slow Burn *367*
Talk to Me *391*

Carmen Ejogo (1975-)
The Brave One *56*

Idris Elba (1972-)
American Gangster *13*
Daddy's Little Girls *86*
The Reaping *325*
This Christmas *399*
28 Weeks Later *411*

Kevin Eldon (1960-)
Hot Fuzz *186*

Carmen Electra (1972-)
Epic Movie *112*
Full of It *138*

Kimberly Elise (1971-)
The Great Debaters *157*
Pride *317*

Hector Elizondo (1936-)
Georgia Rule *142*
Love in the Time of Chol-
era *249*

Alison Elliott (1970-)
The Assassination of Jesse James
by the Coward Robert
Ford *19*

Sam Elliott (1944-)
Ghost Rider *144*
The Golden Compass *147*

Gad Elmaleh (1971-)
The Valet *420*

Cary Elwes (1962-)
Georgia Rule *142*

Ethan (Randall) Embry (1978-)
Vacancy *418*

Ellia English
Good Luck Chuck *151*

Bill Engvall
Delta Farce *98*

Mike Epps (1970-)
Resident Evil: Extinction *338*
Talk to Me *391*

Homayoun Ershadi
The Kite Runner *229*

Emilio Estevez (1962-)
Arthur and the Invisibles
(V) *18*

Erik Estrada (1949-)
Kickin' It Old Skool *223*

Alex Etel
The Water Horse: Legend of the
Deep *429*

Chris Evans (1981-)
Fantastic Four: Rise of the Silver
Surfer *121*
The Nanny Diaries *282*
Sunshine *381*
TMNT (V) *404*

Alice Eve
Starter for 10 *376*

Rupert Everett (1959-)
Shrek the Third (V) *358*
Stardust *374*

Jeff Fahey (1954-)
Grindhouse *159*

Michael Fairman (1934-)
Dead Silence *94*

Marianne Faithfull (1946-)
Paris, je t'aime *306*

Peter Falk (1927-)
Next *286*

Mike Falkow
Smokin' Aces *368*

Jimmy Fallon (1974-)
Arthur and the Invisibles
(V) *18*
Factory Girl *119*

David Fane
Eagle vs. Shark *105*

Elle Fanning (1998-)
Reservation Road *336*

Dennis Farina (1944-)
You Kill Me *440*

Vera Farmiga (1973-)
Breaking and Entering *61*
Joshua *218*

Nicholas Farrell (1955-)
Amazing Grace *10*

Mia Farrow (1945-)
Arthur and the Invisibles *18*

Alexia Fast
Kickin' It Old Skool *223*

Oded Fehr (1970-)
Resident Evil: Extinction *338*

Halley Feiffer
Margot at the Wedding *255*
Stephanie Daley *378*

Tom Felton (1987-)
Harry Potter and the Order of
the Phoenix *171*

Edwige Fenech (1948-)
Hostel: Part II *185*

Colin Ferguson (1972-)
Because I Said So *34*

Stacy Ferguson (1975-)
Grindhouse *159*

Vanessa Ferlito (1970-)
Grindhouse *159*

Will Ferrell (1968-)
Blades of Glory *49*

William Fichtner (1956-)
Blades of Glory *49*

Ralph Fiennes (1962-)
Harry Potter and the Order of
the Phoenix *171*

David Figlioli
I Know Who Killed Me *194*

Nathan Fillion (1971-)
Waitress *425*

Albert Finney (1936-)
Amazing Grace *10*

Before the Devil Knows You're
Dead *40*
The Bourne Ultimatum *52*

Colin Firth (1961-)
The Last Legion *238*

Jenna Fischer (1974-)
Blades of Glory *49*
The Brothers Solomon *64*
Walk Hard: The Dewey Cox
Story *426*

Laurence Fishburne (1963-)
Fantastic Four: Rise of the Silver
Surfer (V) *121*

Frances Fisher (1952-)
In the Valley of Elah *205*

Isla Fisher (1976-)
Hot Rod *188*
The Lookout *248*

Parisa Fitz-Henley
The Jane Austen Book
Club *215*

Orla Fitzgerald
The Wind That Shakes the Barley *435*

Leo Fitzpatrick (1978-)
Fay Grim *123*

Tommy Flanagan (1965-)
Smokin' Aces *368*

Charles Fleischer (1950-)
Zodiac *443*

Jason Flemyng (1966-)
Stardust *374*

Josh Flitter (1994-)
License to Wed *241*
Nancy Drew *281*

Suzanne Flon (1918-2005)
Avenue Montaigne *28*

Barbara Flynn (1948-)
Miss Potter *265*

Jackie Flynn
The Game Plan *141*

Brandon Fobbs
Pride *317*

Dan Fogler
Balls of Fury *33*
Good Luck Chuck *151*

Jane Fonda (1937-)
Georgia Rule *142*

Peter Fonda (1939-)
Ghost Rider *144*
3:10 to Yuma *402*

Trent Ford
September Dawn *352*

William Forsythe (1955-)
Halloween *167*

Will Forte (1970-)
The Brothers Solomon *64*

Ben Foster (1980-)
Alpha Dog *7*
30 Days of Night *397*
3:10 to Yuma *402*

Jodie Foster (1963-)
The Brave One *56*

Laurence Fox (1978-)
Becoming Jane *36*

Matthew Fox (1966-)
Smokin' Aces *368*

Megan Fox (1986-)
Transformers *407*

Vivica A. Fox (1964-)
Kickin' It Old Skool *223*

Robert Foxworth (1941-)
Transformers (V) *407*

Jamie Foxx (1967-)
The Kingdom *227*

Colleen Foy
There Will Be Blood *392*

Jon Francis
See Jon(athan) Gries

James Franco (1978-)
In the Valley of Elah *205*
Spider-Man 3 *372*

Marcus Carl Franklin
I'm Not There *200*

Laura Fraser (1976-)
The Flying Scotsman *129*

Dillon Freasier
There Will Be Blood *392*

Cassandra Freeman
I Think I Love My Wife *198*

Martin Freeman (1971-)
Breaking and Entering *61*
Hot Fuzz *186*

Morgan Freeman (1937-)
Evan Almighty *114*
Feast of Love *124*
Gone Baby Gone *149*

Paul Freeman (1943-)
Hot Fuzz *186*

Andrew Friedman
Live Free or Die Hard *244*

Peter Friedman (1949-)
The Savages *347*

Rupert Friend (1981-)
The Last Legion *238*

Joshua Friesen
Catch and Release *73*

Nick Frost (1972-)
Hot Fuzz *186*

Jordan Fry (1993-)
  Meet the Robinsons *(V)* *258*

Dana Fuchs
  Across the Universe *1*

Patrick Fugit (1982-)
  Wristcutters: A Love Story *437*

Niall Greig Fulton
  The Flying Scotsman *129*

Deborra-Lee Furness (1960-)
  Jindabyne *216*

Toru Furuya
  Paprika *(V)* *305*

Dan Futterman (1967-)
  A Mighty Heart *263*

Ariel Gade (1997-)
  Aliens vs. Predator: Requiem *4*

Jim Gaffigan (1966-)
  Stephanie Daley *378*

M.C. Gainey (1948-)
  Wild Hogs *434*

Charlotte Gainsbourg (1972-)
  I'm Not There *200*

Paulina Gaitan
  Trade *406*

Carlos Gallardo
  Grindhouse *159*

Tom Gallop
  The Bourne Ultimatum *52*

Nathan Gamble
  The Mist *267*

Michael Gambon (1940-)
  Amazing Grace *10*
  Harry Potter and the Order of
    the Phoenix *171*

James Gammon (1940-)
  The Final Season *128*

Richard Gant (1940-)
  Daddy Day Camp *85*

Bruno Ganz (1941-)
  Youth Without Youth *442*

Romola Garai (1982-)
  Amazing Grace *10*
  Atonement *23*

Robert Ben Garant
  Reno 911!: Miami *333*

Andy Garcia (1956-)
  Ocean's Thirteen *299*
  Smokin' Aces *368*

Jesse Garcia
  The Comebacks *79*

Andrew Garfield
  Lions for Lambs *243*

Troy Garity (1973-)
  Sunshine *381*

Jeff Garlin (1962-)
  I Want Someone to Eat Cheese
    With *199*

Olatz López Garmendia
  The Diving Bell and the Butter-
    fly *101*

Alice Garner (1969-)
  Jindabyne *216*

Jennifer Garner (1972-)
  Catch and Release *73*
  Juno *220*
  The Kingdom *227*

Kelli Garner (1984-)
  Lars and the Real Girl *237*

Janeane Garofalo (1964-)
  Ratatouille *(V)* *323*

Brad Garrett (1960-)
  Music and Lyrics *275*
  Ratatouille *(V)* *323*
  Underdog *415*

Jordan Garrett (1992-)
  Death Sentence *97*

Spencer Garrett (1963-)
  I Know Who Killed Me *194*

Julia Garro
  Gracie *154*

Edi Gathegi
  Gone Baby Gone *149*

Mark Gatiss
  Starter for 10 *376*

Rafi Gavron
  Breaking and Entering *61*

Julie Gayet (1972-)
  My Best Friend *277*

Gloria Gaynor
  Gray Matters *156*

Ben Gazzara (1930-)
  Paris, je t'aime *306*

Martina Gedeck (1961-)
  The Lives of Others *246*

Sarah Michelle Gellar (1977-)
  Happily N'Ever After *(V)* *170*
  Southland Tales *370*
  TMNT *(V)* *404*

Melissa George (1976-)
  30 Days of Night *397*

Brian Geraghty (1974-)
  I Know Who Killed Me *194*

Richard Gere (1949-)
  I'm Not There *200*
  The Hoax *179*
  The Hunting Party *191*

Peter Gerety (1940-)
  Charlie Wilson's War *74*

Lauren German (1978-)
  Hostel: Part II *185*

Gina Gershon (1962-)
  P.S. I Love You *320*
  I Want Someone to Eat Cheese
    With *199*

Ricky Gervais (1961-)
  Stardust *374*

John Getz (1947-)
  Zodiac *443*

Paul Giamatti (1967-)
  Fred Claus *134*
  The Nanny Diaries *282*
  Shoot 'Em Up *355*

Matyclock Gibbs
  Miss Potter *265*

Tyrese Gibson (1978-)
  Transformers *407*

Dana Gilhooley
  Grace Is Gone *153*

Daniel Gillies (1976-)
  Captivity *70*
  Spider-Man 3 *372*

Hippolyte Girardot (1955-)
  Lady Chatterley *235*
  Paris, je t'aime *306*

Benoit Giros
  Days of Glory *93*

Mary Pat Gleason
  I Now Pronounce You Chuck and
    Larry *196*
  Wristcutters: A Love Story *437*

Brendan Gleeson (1954-)
  Harry Potter and the Order of
    the Phoenix *171*

Iain Glen (1961-)
  The Last Legion *238*
  Resident Evil: Extinction *338*

Scott Glenn (1942-)
  The Bourne Ultimatum *52*
  Freedom Writers *136*

Crispin Glover (1964-)
  Beowulf *(V)* *42*
  Epic Movie *112*

Danny Glover (1947-)
  Honeydripper *181*
  Shooter *356*

Adam Goldberg (1970-)
  2 Days in Paris *413*
  Zodiac *443*

Jeff Goldblum (1952-)
  Fay Grim *123*

Meagan Good (1981-)
  Stomp the Yard *379*

Danielle Harris (1977-)
Halloween *167*

Ed Harris (1949-)
Gone Baby Gone *149*
National Treasure: Book of Secrets *284*

Jesse Harris
The Hottest State *189*

Naomie Harris (1976-)
Pirates of the Caribbean: At World's End *313*

Rachael Harris (1968-)
License to Wed *241*

Rosemary Harris (1930-)
Before the Devil Knows You're Dead *40*
Spider-Man 3 *372*

Wood Harris (1969-)
Southland Tales *370*

Michelle Harrison
The Invisible *212*

Jess Harnell
Transformers (V) *407*

Josh Hartnett (1978-)
Resurrecting the Champ *339*
30 Days of Night *397*

Russell Harvard
There Will Be Blood *392*

Sajid Hasan
A Mighty Heart *263*

David Hasselhoff (1952-)
Kickin' It Old Skool *223*

Teri Hatcher (1964-)
Resurrecting the Champ *339*

Anne Hathaway (1982-)
Becoming Jane *36*

Shawn Hatosy (1975-)
Alpha Dog *7*
Factory Girl *119*

Keeley Hawes (1977-)
Death at a Funeral *95*

Ethan Hawke (1971-)
Before the Devil Knows You're Dead *40*
The Hottest State *189*

Pamela Hayden
The Simpsons Movie (V) *362*

Dennis Haysbert (1955-)
Breach *59*

Chris Haywood (1949-)
Jindabyne *216*

Lena Headey (1976-)
300 *400*

Pat Healy (1971-)
Rescue Dawn *334*

John Heard (1946-)
The Great Debaters *157*

Jon Heder (1977-)
Blades of Glory *49*
Surf's Up (V) *385*

Garrett Hedlund (1984-)
Death Sentence *97*
Georgia Rule *142*

Katherine Heigl (1978-)
Knocked Up *231*

Marg Helgenberger (1958-)
Mr. Brooks *270*

Levon Helm (1943-)
Shooter *356*

Toby Hemingway
Feast of Love *124*

Martin Henderson (1974-)
Smokin' Aces *368*

Joan Heney
Dead Silence *94*

Jill Hennessy (1969-)
Wild Hogs *434*

André Hennicke
Youth Without Youth *442*

Darrin Henson
Stomp the Yard *379*

Taraji P. Henson (1970-)
Smokin' Aces *368*
Talk to Me *391*

April Lee Hernandez
Freedom Writers *136*

Jay Hernandez (1978-)
Grindhouse *159*
Hostel: Part II *185*

Edward Herrmann (1943-)
I Think I Love My Wife *198*

Annelise Hesme (1976-)
Avenue Montaigne *28*

John Benjamin Hickey (1963-)
Freedom Writers *136*
The Seeker: The Dark Is Rising *350*

John Michael Higgins (1962-)
Evan Almighty *114*
Fred Claus *134*

Freddie Highmore (1992-)
Arthur and the Invisibles *18*
August Rush *26*
The Golden Compass (V) *147*

Jonah Hill (1983-)
Evan Almighty *114*
Knocked Up *231*
Superbad *383*

Aisha Hinds (1975-)
Mr. Brooks *270*

Ciarán Hinds (1953-)
Amazing Grace *10*
Margot at the Wedding *255*
There Will Be Blood *392*

Cheryl Hines (1965-)
Waitress *425*

Emile Hirsch (1985-)
Alpha Dog *7*
Into the Wild *209*

Danny Hoch (1970-)
We Own the Night *431*

Dustin Hoffman (1937-)
Mr. Magorium's Wonder Emporium *272*
Perfume: The Story of a Murderer *312*

Philip Seymour Hoffman (1967-)
Before the Devil Knows You're Dead *40*
Charlie Wilson's War *74*
The Savages *347*

Thom Hoffman (1957-)
Black Book *46*

Hal Holbrook (1925-)
Into the Wild *209*

Laurie Holden (1972-)
The Mist *267*

Tom Hollander (1969-)
Elizabeth: The Golden Age *108*
Pirates of the Caribbean: At World's End *313*

Ian Holm (1931-)
Ratatouille (V) *323*

James Hong (1929-)
Balls of Fury *33*

William Hootkins
Color Me Kubrick *77*

Tamara Hope (1984-)
September Dawn *352*

Anthony Hopkins (1937-)
Beowulf (V) *42*
Fracture *132*

Loren Horsley
Eagle vs. Shark *105*

Dominique Horwitz
Beyond the Gates *44*

Bob Hoskins (1942-)
Paris, je t'aime *306*

Serge Houde (1953-)
The Invisible *212*

Rachel House
Eagle vs. Shark *105*

Arliss Howard (1955-)
Awake *29*

Bryce Dallas Howard (1981-)
Spider-Man 3 *372*

Jeremy Howard
Sydney White *389*

John Howard (1952-)
Jindabyne *216*

Ken Howard (1944-)
Michael Clayton *260*

Terrence Howard (1969-)
August Rush *26*
Awake *29*
The Brave One *56*
The Hunting Party *191*
Pride *317*

Steve Howey (1977-)
DOA: Dead or Alive *103*

Felicity Huffman (1962-)
Georgia Rule *142*

Bonnie Hunt (1964-)
I Want Someone to Eat Cheese
With *199*

Crystal Hunt
Sydney White *389*

Moray Hunter
The Flying Scotsman *129*

Isabelle Huppert (1955-)
Comedy of Power *80*

Rachel Hurd-Wood (1990-)
Perfume: The Story of a Murderer *312*

John Hurt (1940-)
Beyond the Gates *44*
Perfume: The Story of a Murderer
(N) *312*

William Hurt (1950-)
Into the Wild *209*
Mr. Brooks *270*

Toby Huss (1966-)
Rescue Dawn *334*

Anjelica Huston (1951-)
The Darjeeling Limited *91*
Martian Child *256*
Seraphim Falls *353*

Danny Huston (1962-)
The Number 23 *295*
30 Days of Night *397*

Jack Huston
Factory Girl *119*

Josh Hutcherson (1992-)
Bridge to Terabithia *62*

Timothy Hutton (1960-)
The Last Mimzy *240*
Stephanie Daley *378*

Stanislav Ianevski (1985-)
Hostel: Part II *185*

Ice Cube (1969-)
Are We Done Yet? *16*

Eric Idle (1943-)
Shrek the Third (V) *358*

Rhys Ifans (1968-)
Elizabeth: The Golden
Age *108*
Hannibal Rising *168*

Markeéta IrglovaIrglová
Once *300*

Brittney Irvin (1984-)
Hot Rod *188*

Michael Irvin (1966-)
The Comebacks *79*

Jason Isaacs (1963-)
Harry Potter and the Order of
the Phoenix *171*

Ryo Ishibashi (1956-)
War *428*

Gregory Itzin (1948-)
I Know Who Killed Me *194*

Dana Ivey (1942-)
Rush Hour 3 *343*

Eddie Izzard (1962-)
Ocean's Thirteen *299*

Janet Jackson (1966-)
Why Did I Get Married? *432*

John M. Jackson (1950-)
The Invasion *210*

Peter Jackson (1961-)
Hot Fuzz *186*

Samuel L. Jackson (1948-)
Black Snake Moan *47*
1408 *131*
Resurrecting the Champ *339*

Tom Jackson (1948-)
Skinwalkers *364*

Derek Jacobi (1938-)
The Golden Compass *147*

Peter Jacobson (1965-)
Transformers *407*

Sam Jaeger
Catch and Release *73*

Kevin James (1965-)
I Now Pronounce You Chuck and
Larry *196*

Thomas Jane (1969-)
The Mist *267*

Allison Janney (1960-)
Hairspray *165*
Juno *220*

Eddie Jemison
Ocean's Thirteen *299*
Waitress *425*

Héctor Jiménez (1973-)
Epic Movie *112*

Zhang Jingchu
Rush Hour 3 *343*

Adan Jodorowsky
2 Days in Paris *413*

Scarlett Johansson (1984-)
The Nanny Diaries *282*

Mable John
Honeydripper *181*

Corey Johnson (1961-)
The Bourne Ultimatum *52*

Dwayne "The Rock" Johnson (1972-)
The Game Plan *141*
Reno 911!: Miami *333*
Southland Tales *370*

Kristen Johnston (1967-)
Music and Lyrics *275*

Shaun Johnston
September Dawn *352*

Angelina Jolie (1975-)
Beowulf (V) *42*
A Mighty Heart *263*

Doug Jones (1960-)
Fantastic Four: Rise of the Silver
Surfer *121*

Evan Jones
Lucky You *251*
Rescue Dawn *334*

Richard T. Jones (1972-)
Why Did I Get Married? *432*

Tamala Jones (1974-)
Daddy Day Camp *85*

Toby Jones (1967-)
Amazing Grace *10*
The Mist *267*
The Painted Veil *303*

Tommy Lee Jones (1946-)
In the Valley of Elah *205*
No Country for Old Men *288*

Vera Jordanova (1975-)
Hostel: Part II *185*

Milla Jovovich (1975-)
Resident Evil: Extinction *338*

Robert Joy (1951-)
Aliens vs. Predator: Requiem *4*

Ashley Judd (1968-)
Bug *66*

Mark Boone Junior
30 Days of Night *397*
Wristcutters: A Love Story *437*

Abhijati Jusakul
Rescue Dawn *334*

Mindy Kaling (1979-)
License to Wed *241*

Sung Kang (1972-)
War *428*

Lisa Kaplan
Happily N'Ever After *170*

Amara Karan
The Darjeeling Limited *91*

Athena Karkanis
Saw IV *349*

Vincent Kartheiser (1979-)
Alpha Dog *7*

Stana Katic
Feast of Love *124*

Nicky Katt (1970-)
The Brave One *56*
Grindhouse *159*

Julie Kavner (1951-)
The Simpsons Movie (V) *362*

Lainie Kazan (1942-)
Bratz *55*

Zoe Kazan
Fracture *132*

Stacy Keach (1941-)
Honeydripper *181*

Diane Keaton (1946-)
Because I Said So *34*

Toby Kebbell
Control *81*

Catherine Keener (1961-)
Into the Wild *209*

Harvey Keitel (1947-)
Arthur and the Invisibles
(V) *18*
National Treasure: Book of Se-
crets *284*

Elijah Kelley
Hairspray *165*

Mikey Kelley
TMNT (V) *404*

David Kelly (1929-)
Stardust *374*

Anna Kendrick
Rocket Science *341*

Jamie Kennedy (1970-)
Kickin' It Old Skool *223*

Patrick Kennedy (1977-)
Atonement *23*

Ryan Kennedy (1982-)
The Invisible *212*

Kerri Kenney
The Comebacks *79*

Kerri Kenney-Silver
Reno 911!: Miami *333*

Ljubomir Kerekes
The Hunting Party *191*

Alicia Keys
The Nanny Diaries *282*
Smokin' Aces *368*

Irrfan Khan
A Mighty Heart *263*
The Namesake *279*

Moa Khouas
Rendition *331*

Nicole Kidman (1966-)
The Golden Compass *147*
The Invasion *210*
Margot at the Wedding *255*

Axel Kiener
Paris, je t'aime *306*

Udo Kier (1944-)
Grindhouse *159*

Craig Kilborn (1962-)
Full of It *138*

Larry King (1933-)
Bee Movie (V) *38*
Shrek the Third (V) *358*

Regina King (1971-)
This Christmas *399*
Year of the Dog *439*

Richard King
I Want Someone to Eat Cheese
With *199*

Ben Kingsley (1943-)
The Last Legion *238*
You Kill Me *440*

Alex Kingston (1963-)
Alpha Dog *7*

Greg Kinnear (1963-)
Feast of Love *124*

Angela Kinsey (1971-)
License to Wed *241*

Tory Kittles
Next *286*

Martin Klebba (1969-)
Pirates of the Caribbean: At
World's End *313*

Robert Klein (1942-)
Reign Over Me *328*

Volkmar Kleinert
The Lives of Others *246*

Kevin Kline (1947-)
Trade *406*

Richard Kline (1944-)
I Now Pronounce You Chuck and
Larry *196*

Milan Knazko (1945-)
Hostel: Part II *185*

Robert Knepper (1959-)
Hitman *178*

Matthew Knight
Skinwalkers *364*

Keira Knightley (1985-)
Atonement *23*
Pirates of the Caribbean: At
World's End *313*

Zachary Knighton (1978-)
The Hitcher *176*

Ah-sung Ko
The Host *183*

Waldemar Kobus
Black Book *46*

Sebastian Koch (1962-)
Black Book *46*
The Lives of Others *246*

David Koechner (1962-)
The Comebacks *79*

Jacob Kogan
Joshua *218*

Mina Kolb
I Want Someone to Eat Cheese
With *199*

Satoshi Kon
Paprika (V) *305*

Kane (Takeshi) Kosugi (1973-)
DOA: Dead or Alive *103*

Elias Koteas (1961-)
Shooter *356*
Skinwalkers *364*
Zodiac *443*

Fran Kranz
The TV Set *410*

John Krasinski (1979-)
License to Wed *241*
Shrek the Third (V) *358*

Lenny Kravitz
The Brave One *56*

Thomas Kretschmann (1962-)
Next *286*

Gretchen Krich
Brand Upon the Brain! *54*

Diane Kruger (1976-)
The Hunting Party *191*
National Treasure: Book of Se-
crets *284*

David Krumholtz (1978-)
Walk Hard: The Dewey Cox
Story *426*

Youki Kudoh (1971-)
Rush Hour 3 *343*

Lisa Kudrow (1963-)
P.S. I Love You *320*

Vladimir Kulich (1956-)
Smokin' Aces *368*

Olga Kurylenko
Hitman *178*
Paris, je t'aime *306*

Ryan Kwanten (1976-)
Dead Silence *94*

Shia LaBeouf (1986-)
Disturbia *99*
Surf's Up (V) *385*
Transformers *407*

John Lacy (1965-)
Zodiac *443*

Jordan Ladd (1975-)
Grindhouse *159*
Hostel: Part II *185*

Stuart Lafferty
Death Sentence *97*

Lisa Lampanelli
Delta Farce *98*

Alexia Landeau
2 Days in Paris *413*

Wallace Langham (1965-)
I Want Someone to Eat Cheese
With *199*

Alexandra Maria Lara (1978-)
Control *81*
Youth Without Youth *442*

Vincent Laresca (1974-)
El Cantante *69*

John Larroquette (1947-)
Southland Tales *370*

Larry the Cable Guy (1963-)
Delta Farce *98*

Ali Larter (1976-)
Resident Evil: Extinction *338*

Ed Lauter (1940-)
The Number 23 *295*
Seraphim Falls *353*

Jude Law (1972-)
Breaking and Entering *61*
Sleuth *365*

Phyllida Law (1932-)
Miss Potter *265*

Martin Lawrence (1965-)
Wild Hogs *434*

Matthew Lawrence (1980-)
The Comebacks *79*

Maya Lawson
Brand Upon the Brain! *54*

Marlene Lawston
Dan in Real Life *88*

Eva Lazzaro (1995-)
Jindabyne *216*

Sylvestria Le Touzel
Amazing Grace *10*

Sharon Leal (1972-)
This Christmas *399*
Why Did I Get Married? *432*

Heath Ledger (1979-2008)
I'm Not There *200*

Virginie Ledoyen (1976-)
The Valet *420*

Bobby Lee (1972-)
Kickin' It Old Skool *223*

Christopher Lee (1922-)
The Golden Compass *147*

Jason Lee (1971-)
Alvin and the Chipmunks *9*
Underdog (V) *415*

Adam LeFevre
Arthur and the Invisibles *18*

John Leguizamo (1964-)
Love in the Time of Chol-
era *249*

Jennifer Jason Leigh (1963-)
Margot at the Wedding *255*

Valérie Lemercier (1964-)
Avenue Montaigne *28*

Harry J. Lennix (1964-)
Resurrecting the Champ *339*
Stomp the Yard *379*

Thomas Lennon (1969-)
Balls of Fury *33*
Reno 911!: Miami *333*

Noémie Lenoir (1979-)
Rush Hour 3 *343*

Melissa Leo (1960-)
Mr. Woodcock *273*
Stephanie Daley *378*

Téa Leoni (1966-)
You Kill Me *440*

Logan Lerman (1992-)
The Number 23 *295*
3:10 to Yuma *402*

Anton Lesser (1952-)
Miss Potter *265*

Katie Leung (1987-)
Harry Potter and the Order of
the Phoenix *171*

Tony Leung Chiu-Wai (1962-)
Lust, Caution *252*

Margarita Levieva (1985-)
The Invisible *212*

Ted Levine (1958-)
American Gangster *13*
The Assassination of Jesse James
by the Coward Robert
Ford *19*

Barry Levinson (1942-)
Bee Movie (V) *38*

Jason Lewis
Mr. Brooks *270*

Johnny Lewis
Aliens vs. Predator: Requiem *4*

Juliette Lewis (1973-)
Catch and Release *73*

Gong Li (1965-)
Hannibal Rising *168*

Jet Li (1963-)
War *428*

Delroy Lindo (1952-)
This Christmas *399*

Laura Linney (1964-)
Breach *59*
The Hottest State *189*
Jindabyne *216*
The Nanny Diaries *282*
The Savages *347*

Ray Liotta (1955-)
Bee Movie (V) *38*
Slow Burn *367*
Smokin' Aces *368*
Wild Hogs *434*

Lucy Liu (1968-)
Code Name: The Cleaner *76*

LL Cool J (1968-)
Slow Burn *367*

Alexis Llewellyn
Things We Lost in the
Fire *395*

Spencer Locke (1991-)
Resident Evil: Extinction *338*

Donal Logue (1966-)
Ghost Rider *144*
Zodiac *443*

Lindsay Lohan (1986-)
Georgia Rule *142*
I Know Who Killed Me *194*

Alison Lohman (1979-)
Beowulf (V) *42*
Things We Lost in the
Fire *395*

Lauren London
This Christmas *399*

John Lone (1952-)
War *428*

Jackie Long
The Comebacks *79*

Justin Long (1978-)
Alvin and the Chipmunks
(V) *9*
Live Free or Die Hard *244*
Walk Hard: The Dewey Cox
Story *426*

Matt Long
   Ghost Rider *144*
   Sydney White *389*

Nia Long (1970-)
   Are We Done Yet? *16*
   Premonition *315*

George Lopez (1961-)
   Balls of Fury *33*

Jennifer Lopez (1970-)
   El Cantante *69*

Jonathan Loughran (1966-)
   Grindhouse *159*
   I Now Pronounce You Chuck and
      Larry *196*

Allan Louis
   Stomp the Yard *379*

Justin Louis (1967-)
   Shooter *356*

Elina Löwensohn (1967-)
   Fay Grim *123*

Florencia Lozano
   Perfect Stranger *310*

Alexander Ludwig
   The Seeker: The Dark Is Ris-
      ing *350*

Derek Luke (1974-)
   Lions for Lambs *243*

Stephen Lunsford
   Bratz *55*

Evanna Lynch
   Harry Potter and the Order of
      the Phoenix *171*

Jane Lynch (1960-)
   Alvin and the Chipmunks *9*

John Carroll Lynch (1963-)
   Full of It *138*
   Things We Lost in the
      Fire *395*
   Zodiac *443*

Tzi Ma
   Rush Hour 3 *343*

Erik Steffen Maahs
   Brand Upon the Brain! *54*

Luke Mably (1976-)
   Color Me Kubrick *77*

Bernie Mac (1958-)
   Ocean's Thirteen *299*
   Pride *317*
   Transformers *407*

Hayes MacArthur
   The Game Plan *141*

Kelly Macdonald (1977-)
   No Country for Old Men *288*

Matthew Macfayden
   Death at a Funeral *95*

Niall Macgregor
   The Flying Scotsman *129*

Gabriel Macht (1972-)
   Because I Said So *34*

Martha MacIsaac (1984-)
   Superbad *383*

Bill Macy (1922-)
   Mr. Woodcock *273*

William H. Macy (1950-)
   Wild Hogs *434*

Amy Madigan (1957-)
   Gone Baby Gone *149*

Bailee Madison
   Bridge to Terabithia *62*

Madonna (1959-)
   Arthur and the Invisibles
      (V) *18*

Virginia Madsen (1963-)
   The Astronaut Farmer *21*
   The Number 23 *295*

Maggie Q
   Balls of Fury *33*

Kate Magowan
   Stardust *374*

Tobey Maguire (1975-)
   Spider-Man 3 *372*

Ahmad Khan Mahmoodzada
   The Kite Runner *229*

John Mahoney (1940-)
   Dan in Real Life *88*

Louis Mahoney
   Beyond the Gates *44*

Aissa Maiga (1975-)
   Paris, je t'aime *306*

Michael Maize
   National Treasure: Book of Se-
      crets *284*

Lee Majors (1940-)
   The Brothers Solomon *64*

Mako (1933-2006)
   TMNT (V) *404*

John Malkovich (1953-)
   Beowulf (V) *42*
   Color Me Kubrick *77*

Jena Malone (1984-)
   Into the Wild *209*

Natassia Malthe (1974-)
   DOA: Dead or Alive *103*

Aasif Mandvi
   Music and Lyrics *275*

Costas Mandylor (1965-)
   Saw IV *349*

Tyler Mane (1966-)
   Halloween *167*

Marshall Manesh (1950-)
   Pirates of the Caribbean: At
      World's End *313*

Joe Manganiello (1976-)
   Spider-Man 3 *372*

Gudrun Mangel
   The Flying Scotsman *129*

Leslie Mann (1972-)
   Knocked Up *231*

J.P. Manoux (1969-)
   Knocked Up *231*

Gina Mantegna (1990-)
   In the Land of Women *202*

Joe Mantegna (1947-)
   The Simpsons Movie (V) *362*

Michael Mantell
   Ocean's Thirteen *299*

Kate Mara (1983-)
   Full of It *138*
   Shooter *356*

Richard "Cheech" Marin (1946-)
   Grindhouse *159*

Mario
   Freedom Writers *136*

Brian Markinson
   Charlie Wilson's War *74*

Christopher Marquette (1984-)
   The Invisible *212*

James Marsden (1973-)
   Enchanted *110*
   Hairspray *165*

Matthew Marsden (1972-)
   DOA: Dead or Alive *103*
   Resident Evil: Extinction *338*

Kris Marshall (1973-)
   Death at a Funeral *95*

Paula Marshall (1964-)
   I Know Who Killed Me *194*

James Marsters
   P.S. I Love You *320*

Anna Maxwell Martin
   Becoming Jane *36*

Margo Martindale (1951-)
   Paris, je t'aime *306*
   Rocket Science *341*
   Walk Hard: The Dewey Cox
      Story *426*

Olivier Martinez (1966-)
   Blood and Chocolate *50*

Jean-Pierre Martins
   La Vie en Rose *421*

Heather Matarazzo (1982-)
   Hostel: Part II *185*

Jayma Mays
   Epic Movie *112*

Alphonso McAuley
    Pride *317*

James McAvoy (1979-)
    Atonement *23*
    Becoming Jane *36*
    Starter for 10 *376*

Chi McBride (1961-)
    The Brothers Solomon *64*

Danny McBride
    The Heartbreak Kid *174*
    Hot Rod *188*

Sydney McCallister
    There Will Be Blood *392*

Tom McCarthy
    Year of the Dog *439*

Jesse McCartney (1987-)
    Alvin and the Chipmunks
      (V) *9*

China Anne McClain
    Daddy's Little Girls *86*

Lauryn Alisa McClain
    Daddy's Little Girls *86*

Sierra Aylina McClain
    Daddy's Little Girls *86*

Shyann McClure
    Premonition *315*

Elias McConnell
    Paris, je t'aime *306*

Catherine McCormack (1972-)
    28 Weeks Later *411*

Mary McCormack (1969-)
    1408 *131*

Martin Luther McCoy
    Across the Universe *1*

Darius McCrary (1976-)
    Transformers (V) *407*

Helen McCrory (1968-)
    Becoming Jane *36*

Dylan McDermott (1962-)
    The Messengers *259*

Christopher McDonald (1955-)
    Awake *29*
    Kickin' It Old Skool *223*

Ryan McDonald (1984-)
    Resurrecting the Champ *339*

Neal McDonough (1966-)
    The Hitcher *176*
    I Know Who Killed Me *194*

Malcolm McDowell (1943-)
    Halloween *167*

Davenia McFadden (1961-)
    Smokin' Aces *368*

Bruce McGill (1950-)
    The Lookout *248*
    Slow Burn *367*

John C. McGinley (1959-)
    Are We Done Yet? *16*
    Wild Hogs *434*

Rose McGowan (1975-)
    Grindhouse *159*

Derek McGrath (1951-)
    Full of It *138*

Ewan McGregor (1971-)
    Miss Potter *265*

Michael McKean (1947-)
    Joshua *218*

Gina McKee (1964-)
    Atonement *23*

Ian McKellen (1939-)
    The Golden Compass (V) *147*
    Stardust (N) *374*

Kevin McKidd (1973-)
    Hannibal Rising *168*
    The Last Legion *238*

Jake McLaughlin
    In the Valley of Elah *205*

Wendi McLendon-Covey
    Reno 911!: Miami *333*

Josh McLerran
    Daddy Day Camp *85*

Julian McMahon (1968-)
    Fantastic Four: Rise of the Silver
      Surfer *121*
    Premonition *315*

John McMartin (1929-)
    No Reservations *292*

Michael McMillian
    The Hills Have Eyes II *175*

Kevin McNally (1956-)
    Pirates of the Caribbean: At
      World's End *313*

Ian McShane (1942-)
    The Golden Compass (V) *147*
    Hot Rod *188*
    The Seeker: The Dark Is Ris-
      ing *350*
    Shrek the Third (V) *358*

Michael McShane (1957-)
    Happily N'Ever After (V) *170*

Tim Meadows (1961-)
    Walk Hard: The Dewey Cox
      Story *426*

Russell Means (1939-)
    Pathfinder *308*

Julio Oscar Mechoso (1955-)
    Grindhouse *159*

Gilbert Melki (1958-)
    Angel-A *15*

Carlos Mencia
    The Heartbreak Kid *174*

Eva Mendes (1978-)
    Ghost Rider *144*
    We Own the Night *431*

Gonzalo Menendez (1971-)
    Fantastic Four: Rise of the Silver
      Surfer *121*

Maria Menounos (1978-)
    Kickin' It Old Skool *223*

Idina Menzel (1971-)
    Enchanted *110*

S. Epatha Merkerson (1952-)
    Black Snake Moan *47*

Debra Messing (1968-)
    Lucky You *251*

Laurie Metcalf (1955-)
    Georgia Rule *142*
    Meet the Robinsons (V) *258*

Omar Metwally
    Rendition *331*

Jonathan Rhys Meyers
    August Rush *26*

Giovanna Mezzogiorno (1974-)
    Love in the Time of Chol-
      era *249*

Dash Mihok (1974-)
    I Am Legend *193*

Johnny Lee Miller
    The Flying Scotsman *129*

Larry Miller (1953-)
    Bee Movie (V) *38*
    The Final Season *128*

Omar Benson Miller (1978-)
    Things We Lost in the
      Fire *395*

Penelope Ann Miller (1964-)
    The Messengers *259*

Sienna Miller (1981-)
    Factory Girl *119*
    Interview *208*
    Stardust *374*

Dustin Milligan
    In the Land of Women *202*
    The Messengers *259*

Zach Mills
    Mr. Magorium's Wonder Empo-
      rium *272*

Mina E. Mina
    Eastern Promises *106*

Christopher Mintz-Plasse
    Superbad *383*

Helen Mirren (1946-)
    National Treasure: Book of Se-
      crets *284*

Finesse Mitchell (1972-)
    The Comebacks *79*

Alex Neuberger (1992-)
Underdog *415*

Brooke Nevin (1982-)
The Comebacks *79*

Paula Newsome
Things We Lost in the
Fire *395*

Thandie Newton (1972-)
Norbit *294*

Sing Ngai (1967-)
DOA: Dead or Alive *103*

Marisol Nichols (1973-)
Delta Farce *98*

Rachel Nichols (1980-)
Resurrecting the Champ *339*

Bill Nighy (1949-)
Hot Fuzz *186*
Pirates of the Caribbean: At
World's End *313*

Alessandro Nivola (1972-)
Grace Is Gone *153*

Amaury Nolasco (1970-)
Transformers *407*

Nick Nolte (1941-)
Paris, je t'aime *306*

Tom Noonan (1951-)
Seraphim Falls *353*

Nolan North
TMNT (V) *404*

Jeremy Northam (1961-)
The Invasion *210*

Edward Norton (1969-)
The Painted Veil *303*

B.J. Novak
Knocked Up *231*

Miguel A. Núñez, Jr. (1964-)
Kickin' It Old Skool *223*

Bill Nunn (1953-)
Spider-Man 3 *372*

Andy Nyman
Death at a Funeral *95*

Brian F. O'Byrne (1967-)
Before the Devil Knows You're
Dead *40*
Bug *66*
No Reservations *292*

Deirdre O'Connell
Stephanie Daley *378*

Kevin J. O'Connor (1964-)
Seraphim Falls *353*
There Will Be Blood *392*

Michael Offei
Hitman *178*

Denis O'Hare (1962-)
Charlie Wilson's War *74*

A Mighty Heart *263*
Stephanie Daley *378*

Akio Ohtsuka
Paprika (V) *305*

Michael O'Keefe (1955-)
Michael Clayton *260*

Shélan O'Keefe
Grace Is Gone *153*

Sophie Okonedo (1969-)
Martian Child *256*

Gary Oldman (1958-)
Harry Potter and the Order of
the Phoenix *171*

Matt O'Leary (1987-)
Death Sentence *97*

Lena Olin (1955-)
Awake *29*

Alex O'Loughlin (1977-)
The Invisible *212*

Eric Christian Olsen (1977-)
The Comebacks *79*
License to Wed *241*

Timothy Olyphant (1968-)
Catch and Release *73*
Hitman *178*
Live Free or Die Hard *244*

Jason O'Mara
Resident Evil: Extinction *338*

Kel O'Neill
Stephanie Daley *378*

Michael O'Neill
Transformers *407*

Julia Ormond (1965-)
I Know Who Killed Me *194*

Ed O'Ross (1949-)
Delta Farce *98*

John Ortiz
Aliens vs. Predator: Requiem *4*
American Gangster *13*
El Cantante *69*

Holmes Osborne (1952-)
Southland Tales *370*

Patton Oswalt (1969-)
Ratatouille (V) *323*

Cheri Oteri (1962-)
Shrek the Third (V) *358*

Billy Otis
Saw IV *349*

Peter O'Toole (1932-)
Ratatouille (V) *323*
Stardust *374*

Zineb Oukach
Rendition *331*

Clive Owen (1965-)
Elizabeth: The Golden
Age *108*
Shoot 'Em Up *355*

Lloyd Owen (1966-)
Miss Potter *265*

Daniel Abol Pach
God Grew Tired of Us *146*

Al Pacino (1940-)
Ocean's Thirteen *299*

Ellen Page (1987-)
Juno *220*

Michelle Page (1987-)
I Know Who Killed Me *194*

Daniel André Pageon
The Flying Scotsman *129*

Josh Pais (1964-)
Year of the Dog *439*

Zane Pais
Margot at the Wedding *255*

Aleksa Palladino (1980-)
Before the Devil Knows You're
Dead *40*

Chazz Palminteri (1952-)
Arthur and the Invisibles
(V) *18*

Danielle Panabaker (1987-)
Mr. Brooks *270*

Kay Panabaker (1990-)
Nancy Drew *281*

Ty Panitz (1999-)
Because I Said So *34*

Archie Panjabi (1972-)
A Mighty Heart *263*

Michael Papajohn (1964-)
I Know Who Killed Me *194*
Spider-Man 3 *372*

Hae-il Park
The Host *183*

Mary-Louise Parker (1964-)
The Assassination of Jesse James
by the Coward Robert
Ford *19*

Nate Parker (1963-)
The Great Debaters *157*
Pride *317*
Stardust *374*

Craig Parkinson
Control *81*

James Parks (1968-)
Grindhouse *159*

Michael Parks (1938-)
The Assassination of Jesse James
by the Coward Robert
Ford *19*
Grindhouse *159*

Taylor Parks
Hairspray *165*

Chris Parnell (1967-)
Hot Rod *188*

Walk Hard: The Dewey Cox
Story *426*

Janel Parrish
Bratz *55*

Steven Pasquale
Aliens vs. Predator: Requiem *4*

David Pasquesi
I Want Someone to Eat Cheese
With *199*

Bill Paterson (1945-)
Miss Potter *265*

Angela Paton
The Final Season *128*

Jason Patric
In the Valley of Elah *205*

Robert Patrick (1959-)
Balls of Fury *33*
Bridge to Terabithia *62*

Scott Patterson (1958-)
Saw IV *349*

Will Patton (1954-)
Code Name: The Cleaner *76*
A Mighty Heart *263*

Sara Paxton (1988-)
Sydney White *389*

David Paymer (1954-)
Ocean's Thirteen *299*
Resurrecting the Champ *339*

Trevor Peacock (1931-)
Fred Claus *134*

Guy Pearce (1967-)
Factory Girl *119*

James Anthony Pearson
Control *81*

Amanda Peet (1972-)
Martian Child *256*

Simon Pegg (1970-)
Hot Fuzz *186*

Mark Pellegrino (1965-)
The Number 23 *295*

Steve Pemberton
Mr. Bean's Holiday *268*

Michael Peña (1976-)
Lions for Lambs *243*
Shooter *356*

Kal Penn (1977-)
Epic Movie *112*
The Namesake *279*

Piper Perabo (1977-)
Because I Said So *34*

Manny Perez
El Cantante *69*

Marco Pérez
Trade *406*

Harold Perrineau, Jr. (1963-)
28 Weeks Later *411*

Tyler Perry (1969-)
Why Did I Get Married? *432*

Valarie Pettiford (1960-)
Stomp the Yard *379*

Madison Pettis
The Game Plan *141*

Michelle Pfeiffer (1957-)
Hairspray *165*
Stardust *374*

Mekhi Phifer (1975-)
This Christmas *399*
Slow Burn *367*

Regis Philbin (1934-)
Shrek the Third (V) *358*

Ryan Phillippe (1974-)
Breach *59*

Bijou Phillips (1980-)
Hostel: Part II *185*

Graham Phillips
Evan Almighty *114*

Kevin Phillips
Pride *317*

Leslie Phillips (1924-)
Color Me Kubrick *77*

Joaquin Phoenix (1974-)
Reservation Road *336*
We Own the Night *431*

Vincent Piazza
Rocket Science *341*

Jim Piddock (1956-)
The Seeker: The Dark Is Rising *350*

Wendell Pierce (1962-)
I Think I Love My Wife *198*

Rosamund Pike (1979-)
Fracture *132*

Alison Pill (1985-)
Dan in Real Life *88*

Marie Pillet
2 Days in Paris *413*

Daniel Pilon (1940-)
Shoot 'Em Up *355*

Chris Pine (1980-)
Smokin' Aces *368*

Jada Pinkett Smith (1971-)
Reign Over Me *328*

Ryan Pinkston
Full of It *138*

Gordon Pinsent (1930-)
Away From Her *31*

Roddy Piper (1951-)
Kickin' It Old Skool *223*

Alexandra Pirici
Youth Without Youth *442*

Brad Pitt (1963-)
The Assassination of Jesse James
by the Coward Robert
Ford *19*
Ocean's Thirteen *299*

Jeremy Piven (1965-)
The Kingdom *227*
Smokin' Aces *368*

Oliver Platt (1960-)
Martian Child *256*

Bruno Podalydes
Paris, je t'aime *306*

Amy Poehler (1971-)
Blades of Glory *49*
Mr. Woodcock *273*
Shrek the Third (V) *358*

Sydney Tamiia Poitier (1973-)
Grindhouse *159*

Roman Polanski (1933-)
Rush Hour 3 *343*

Jasper Polish
The Astronaut Farmer *21*

Logan Polish
The Astronaut Farmer *21*

Mark Polish (1972-)
The Astronaut Farmer *21*

Jon Polito (1950-)
American Gangster *13*

Sydney Pollack (1934-)
Avenue Montaigne *28*
Michael Clayton *260*

Teri Polo (1969-)
Full of It *138*

Scott Porter
Music and Lyrics *275*

Natalie Portman (1981-)
Mr. Magorium's Wonder Empo-
rium *272*
Paris, je t'aime *306*

Richard Portnow (1950-)
Perfect Stranger *310*

Brian Posehn
Surf's Up (V) *385*

Parker Posey (1968-)
Fay Grim *123*

Clifton Powell (1956-)
Norbit *294*

Robert Prescott
Michael Clayton *260*

Nathalie Press
Red Road *327*

Jaime Pressly (1977-)
DOA: Dead or Alive *103*

Kelly Preston (1963-)
Death Sentence *97*

Freddie Prinze, Jr. (1976-)
Happily N'Ever After (V) *170*

David Proval (1942-)
Smokin' Aces *368*

Jonathan Pryce (1947-)
Pirates of the Caribbean: At
World's End *313*

Robert Pugh (1950-)
The Last Legion *238*

Bill Pullman (1953-)
You Kill Me *440*

Leah Purcell (1970-)
Jindabyne *216*

Om Puri (1950-)
Charlie Wilson's War *74*

Paul Putner (1967-)
Paris, je t'aime *306*

Maggie Q (1979-)
Live Free or Die Hard *244*

Shaobo Qin (1982-)
Ocean's Thirteen *299*

DJ Qualls (1978-)
Delta Farce *98*

Queen Latifah (1970-)
Hairspray *165*

Jill Quigg
Gone Baby Gone *149*

Kathleen Quinlan (1952-)
Breach *59*

Lily Rabe (1982-)
No Reservations *292*

Alexis Raben
The Invasion *210*

Daniel Radcliffe (1989-)
Harry Potter and the Order of
the Phoenix *171*

Paul Rae
Daddy Day Camp *85*

Cyril Raffaelli (1974-)
Live Free or Die Hard *244*

William Ragsdale (1961-)
The Reaping *325*

Aishwarya Rai (1973-)
The Last Legion *238*

Theodore (Ted) Raimi (1965-)
Spider-Man 3 *372*

Edgar Ramirez (1977-)
The Bourne Ultimatum *52*

Harold Ramis (1944-)
Knocked Up *231*

Walk Hard: The Dewey Cox
Story *426*

Cesar Ramos
Trade *406*

Nathalia Ramos
Bratz *55*

Douglas Rand
Arthur and the Invisibles *18*

Rie Rasmussen
Angel-A *15*

John Ratzenberger (1947-)
Ratatouille (V) *323*

Gina Ravera (1968-)
The Great Debaters *157*

K'Sun Ray
Fido *126*

Stephen Rea (1946-)
The Reaping *325*

Robert Redford (1937-)
Lions for Lambs *243*

Lynn Redgrave (1943-)
The Jane Austen Book
Club *215*

Vanessa Redgrave (1937-)
Atonement *23*
Evening *115*

Eddie Redmayne
Elizabeth: The Golden
Age *108*

Roger Rees (1944-)
The Invasion *210*

Sean Rees-Memyss
Jindabyne *216*

Scott Reeves (1966-)
Pride *317*

Laura Regan (1977-)
Dead Silence *94*

Halina Reijn (1975-)
Black Book *46*

John C. Reilly (1965-)
Walk Hard: The Dewey Cox
Story *426*
Year of the Dog *439*

Tatea Reilly
Jindabyne *216*

Carl Reiner (1922-)
Ocean's Thirteen *299*

James Remar (1953-)
Ratatouille (V) *323*

Mark Rendall (1988-)
30 Days of Night *397*

Jeremy Renner (1971-)
The Assassination of Jesse James
by the Coward Robert
Ford *19*
28 Weeks Later *411*

Callum Keith Rennie (1960-)
Code Name: The Cleaner *76*
The Invisible *212*

Robin Renucci (1956-)
Comedy of Power *80*

Ryan Reynolds (1976-)
Smokin' Aces *368*

Ving Rhames (1961-)
I Now Pronounce You Chuck and
Larry *196*

Serge Riaboukine
Angel-A *15*

Giovanni Ribisi (1974-)
Perfect Stranger *310*

Christina Ricci (1980-)
Black Snake Moan *47*

Robert Ri'chard (1983-)
The Comebacks *79*

Dakota Blue Richards
The Golden Compass *147*

Kim Richards (1964-)
Black Snake Moan *47*

Michael Richards (1948-)
Bee Movie (V) *38*

Cameron Richardson
Alvin and the Chipmunks *9*

Ian Richardson (1934-2007)
Becoming Jane *36*

Joely Richardson (1965-)
The Last Mimzy *240*

Miranda Richardson (1958-)
Fred Claus *134*
Paris, je t'aime *306*
Southland Tales *370*

Natasha Richardson (1963-)
Evening *115*

Salli Richardson (1967-)
I Am Legend *193*

Julian Richings (1955-)
Shoot 'Em Up *355*

Alan Rickman (1946-)
Harry Potter and the Order of
the Phoenix *171*
Perfume: The Story of a Murderer *312*
Sweeney Todd: The Demon Barber of Fleet Street *386*

Katja Riemann (1963-)
Blood and Chocolate *50*

Terence Rigby (1937-)
Color Me Kubrick *77*

Diana Rigg (1938-)
The Painted Veil *303*

Sam Riley
Control *81*

Mary Riordan
The Wind That Shakes the Barley *435*

Huntley Ritter
September Dawn *352*

Sam Robards (1961-)
Awake *29*

AnnaSophia Robb (1993-)
Bridge to Terabithia *62*
The Reaping *325*

Dallas Roberts (1970-)
Joshua *218*
3:10 to Yuma *402*

Emma Roberts (1991-)
Nancy Drew *281*

Eric Roberts (1956-)
DOA: Dead or Alive *103*

Judith Roberts
Dead Silence *94*
The Nanny Diaries *282*

Julia Roberts (1967-)
Charlie Wilson's War *74*

Brittany Robertson
Dan in Real Life *88*

Cliff Robertson (1925-)
Spider-Man 3 *372*

John Robinson
Seraphim Falls *353*

Karen Robinson
Lars and the Real Girl *237*

Keith D. Robinson
This Christmas *399*

Zuleikha Robinson (1977-)
The Namesake *279*

Alex Rocco (1936-)
Smokin' Aces *368*

Jean Rochefort (1930-)
Mr. Bean's Holiday *268*

Chris Rock (1966-)
Bee Movie (V) *38*
I Think I Love My Wife *198*

Rock, The
See Dwayne "The Rock" Johnson

Sam Rockwell (1968-)
The Assassination of Jesse James by the Coward Robert Ford *19*
Joshua *218*

Karel Roden (1962-)
Mr. Bean's Holiday *268*

Dennis Rodman (1961-)
The Comebacks *79*

Freddy Rodríguez (1975-)
Grindhouse *159*

Sarah Roemer
Disturbia *99*

Seth Rogen (1982-)
Knocked Up *231*
Shrek the Third (V) *358*
Superbad *383*

Poppy Rogers
Breaking and Entering *61*

Lou Romano (1972-)
Ratatouille (V) *323*

Saoirse Ronan (1994-)
Atonement *23*

Michael Rosenbaum (1972-)
Kickin' It Old Skool *223*

Evan Ross (1988-)
Pride *317*

Hugh Ross
The Assassination of Jesse James by the Coward Robert Ford (N) *19*

Lonny Ross
Good Luck Chuck *151*

Tracee Ellis Ross (1972-)
Daddy's Little Girls *86*

Isabella Rossellini (1952-)
Brand Upon the Brain! (N) *54*

Eli Roth (1972-)
Grindhouse *159*

Tim Roth (1961-)
Youth Without Youth *442*

Jean-Paul Rouve
La Vie en Rose *421*

Stephane Roux
Ratatouille (N) *323*

Rodney Rowland (1964-)
I Know Who Killed Me *194*

Gena Rowlands (1934-)
Paris, je t'aime *306*

Saul Rubinek (1949-)
War *428*

Alan Ruck (1960-)
Kickin' It Old Skool *223*

Lamman Rucker
Why Did I Get Married? *432*

Paul Rudd (1969-)
Knocked Up *231*
Reno 911!: Miami *333*
Walk Hard: The Dewey Cox Story *426*

Maya Rudolph (1972-)
Shrek the Third (V) *358*

Mark Ruffalo (1967-)
Reservation Road *336*
Zodiac *443*

Debra Jo Rupp (1951-)
Kickin' It Old Skool *223*

Geoffrey Rush (1951-)
Elizabeth: The Golden Age *108*
Pirates of the Caribbean: At World's End *313*

Joseph Ruskin (1925-)
Smokin' Aces *368*

Tim Russ (1956-)
Live Free or Die Hard *244*

Betsy Russell (1964-)
Saw IV *349*

Keri Russell (1976-)
August Rush *26*
Waitress *425*

Kurt Russell (1951-)
Grindhouse *159*

Theresa Russell (1957-)
Spider-Man 3 *372*

Camilla Rutherford
The Darjeeling Limited *91*

Amy Ryan (1970-)
Before the Devil Knows You're Dead *40*
Dan in Real Life *88*
Gone Baby Gone *149*

Mark Ryan
Transformers (V) *407*

Meg Ryan (1961-)
In the Land of Women *202*

Thomas Jay Ryan (1962-)
Fay Grim *123*

RZA
American Gangster *13*

William Sadler (1950-)
August Rush *26*
The Mist *267*

Melissa Sagemiller (1974-)
Mr. Woodcock *273*

Ludivine Sagnier (1979-)
Paris, je t'aime *306*

Mathew St. Patrick
War *428*

John Salley (1964-)
The Comebacks *79*

Andy Samberg (1978-)
Hot Rod *188*

Hiroyuki Sanada (1960-)
Rush Hour 3 *343*
Sunshine *381*

Roselyn Sanchez (1973-)
The Game Plan *141*
Rush Hour 3 *343*

Edward Sanders
    Sweeney Todd: The Demon Bar-
        ber of Fleet Street *386*

Henry Sanders (1942-)
    Killer of Sheep *224*

Adam Sandler (1966-)
    I Now Pronounce You Chuck and
        Larry *196*
    Reign Over Me *328*

Julian Sands (1958-)
    Ocean's Thirteen *299*

Thomas Sangster (1990-)
    The Last Legion *238*

Ruben Santiago-Hudson (1956-)
    American Gangster *13*
    Mr. Brooks *270*

Rodrigo Santoro (1975-)
    300 *400*

Horatio Sanz (1969-)
    Lucky You *251*

Susan Sarandon (1946-)
    Enchanted *110*
    In the Valley of Elah *205*
    Mr. Woodcock *273*

Peter Sarsgaard (1971-)
    Rendition *331*
    Year of the Dog *439*

Tom Savini (1946-)
    Grindhouse *159*

Katherine E. Scharhon
    Brand Upon the Brain! *54*

John Schneider (1960-)
    Sydney White *389*

Paul Schneider (1973-)
    The Assassination of Jesse James
        by the Coward Robert
        Ford *19*
    Lars and the Real Girl *237*

Rob Schneider (1963-)
    I Now Pronounce You Chuck and
        Larry *196*

Liev Schreiber (1967-)
    Love in the Time of Chol-
        era *249*
    The Painted Veil *303*

Barbet Schroeder (1941-)
    Paris, je t'aime *306*

Carly Schroeder (1990-)
    Gracie *154*

Matt Schulze (1972-)
    Mr. Brooks *270*

Jason Schwartzman (1980-)
    The Darjeeling Limited *91*
    Walk Hard: The Dewey Cox
        Story *426*

Campbell Scott (1962-)
    Music and Lyrics *275*

Donovan Scott (1946-)
    I Know Who Killed Me *194*

Dougray Scott
    Hitman *178*

Jill Scott
    Why Did I Get Married? *432*

Seann William Scott (1976-)
    Mr. Woodcock *273*
    Southland Tales *370*

Tom Everett Scott (1970-)
    Because I Said So *34*

Kristin Scott Thomas (1960-)
    The Golden Compass (V) *147*
    The Valet *420*

Alison Sealy-Smith
    You Kill Me *440*

Nick Searcy (1959-)
    The Comebacks *79*

Amy Sedaris (1961-)
    Shrek the Third (V) *358*
    I Want Someone to Eat Cheese
        With *199*

Kyra Sedgwick (1965-)
    The Game Plan *141*

Jason Segal
    Knocked Up *231*

Emmanuelle Seigner (1966-)
    The Diving Bell and the Butter-
        fly *101*
    La Vie en Rose *421*

Jerry Seinfeld (1954-)
    Bee Movie (V) *38*

Tom Selleck (1945-)
    Meet the Robinsons (V) *258*

Rade Serbedzija (1946-)
    Shooter *356*

Brian Sergent
    Eagle vs. Shark *105*

Chloë Sevigny (1975-)
    Zodiac *443*

Rufus Sewell (1967-)
    Amazing Grace *10*
    Paris, je t'aime *306*

Amanda Seyfried (1985-)
    Alpha Dog *7*

Cara Seymour
    The Savages *347*

Christopher Shand
    Gracie *154*

Michael Shannon (1974-)
    Before the Devil Knows You're
        Dead *40*
    Bug *66*

Molly Shannon (1964-)
    Evan Almighty *114*
    Gray Matters *156*
    Year of the Dog *439*

Fiona Shaw (1958-)
    Catch and Release *73*
    Fracture *132*
    Harry Potter and the Order of
        the Phoenix *171*

Vinessa Shaw (1976-)
    3:10 to Yuma *402*

Wallace Shawn (1943-)
    Happily N'Ever After (V) *170*

Skyler Shaye
    Bratz *55*

Harry Shearer (1943-)
    The Simpsons Movie (V) *362*

Martin Sheen (1940-)
    Talk to Me *391*

Rachel Shelley (1969-)
    Gray Matters *156*

Adrienne Shelly (1966-2006)
    Waitress *425*

Robert Shelly
    Control *81*

Marley Shelton (1974-)
    Grindhouse *159*

Dax Shepard (1975-)
    The Comebacks *79*

Sam Shepard (1943-)
    The Assassination of Jesse James
        by the Coward Robert
        Ford *19*

Rade Sherbedgia
    See Rade Serbedzija

Andrew Sheridan
    Control *81*

Nicolette Sheridan (1963-)
    Code Name: The Cleaner *76*

Columbus Short (1982-)
    Stomp the Yard *379*
    This Christmas *399*

Robin Shou (1960-)
    DOA: Dead or Alive *103*

John Shrapnel (1942-)
    Elizabeth: The Golden
        Age *108*

Andrew Shue (1967-)
    Gracie *154*

Elisabeth Shue (1963-)
    Gracie *154*

Alexander Siddig (1965-)
    The Last Legion *238*

Sarah Silverman (1970-)
    I Want Someone to Eat Cheese
        With *199*

Silvio Simac (1973-)
DOA: Dead or Alive *103*

Chelan Simmons (1982-)
Good Luck Chuck *151*

J.K. Simmons (1955-)
The Astronaut Farmer *21*
Juno *220*
Spider-Man 3 *372*

Johnny (John W.) Simmons
Evan Almighty *114*

Mathieu Simonet (1975-)
Days of Glory *93*

Wesley Singerman
Meet the Robinsons *(V)* *258*

Jeremy Sisto (1974-)
Waitress *425*

Stellan Skarsgard (1951-)
Pirates of the Caribbean: At
World's End *313*

Jerzy Skolimowski (1938-)
Eastern Promises *106*

John Slattery (1963-)
Charlie Wilson's War *74*
Reservation Road *336*
Underdog *415*

Lindsay Sloane (1977-)
The TV Set *410*

Joey Slotnick (1968-)
I Want Someone to Eat Cheese
With *199*

Jean Smart (1959-)
Lucky You *251*

Adrian Smith
The Flying Scotsman *129*

Charles Martin Smith (1953-)
Lucky You *251*

Gregory Edward Smith (1983-)
The Seeker: The Dark Is Rising *350*

James Todd Smith
See LL Cool J

Kevin Smith (1970-)
Catch and Release *73*
Live Free or Die Hard *244*

Maggie Smith (1934-)
Becoming Jane *36*
Harry Potter and the Order of
the Phoenix *171*

Michael Bailey Smith (1957-)
The Hills Have Eyes II *175*

Tasha Smith (1971-)
Daddy's Little Girls *86*
Why Did I Get Married? *432*

Vanetta Smith
Freedom Writers *136*

Will Smith (1968-)
I Am Legend *193*

Willow Smith
I Am Legend *193*

Yeardley Smith (1964-)
The Simpsons Movie *(V)* *362*

Jimmy Smits (1956-)
The Jane Austen Book
Club *215*

Jurnee Smollett (1986-)
The Great Debaters *157*

Brittany Snow (1986-)
Hairspray *165*

Peter Sohn
Ratatouille *(V)* *323*

Josef Sommer (1934-)
The Invasion *210*

Kang-ho Song
The Host *183*

Mira Sorvino
Reservation Road *336*

Shannyn Sossamon (1979-)
Wristcutters: A Love Story *437*

Kath Soucie (1967-)
Happily N'Ever After *(V)* *170*

Sissy Spacek (1949-)
Gray Matters *156*
Hot Rod *188*

Kevin Spacey (1959-)
Fred Claus *134*

Rafe Spall (1983-)
Hot Fuzz *186*

Timothy Spall (1957-)
Enchanted *110*
Sweeney Todd: The Demon Bar-
ber of Fleet Street *386*

Martin Spanjers
The Comebacks *79*

Lester "Rasta" Speight
Norbit *294*

Jordana Spiro (1977-)
Alone With Her *6*

Josh Stamberg
Fracture *132*

Terence Stamp (1940-)
September Dawn *352*

Darby Stanchfield
Waitress *425*

Harry Dean Stanton (1926-)
Alpha Dog *7*

Martin Starr
Knocked Up *231*

Jason Statham (1972-)
War *428*

Chelsea Staub
Bratz *55*

Imelda Staunton (1956-)
Freedom Writers *136*
Harry Potter and the Order of
the Phoenix *171*

Mary Steenburgen (1952-)
The Brave One *56*

Eddie Steeples
I Know Who Killed Me *194*

Maury Sterling
Smokin' Aces *368*

Fisher Stevens (1963-)
Awake *29*

Cynthia Stevenson (1963-)
Full of It *138*

Juliet Stevenson (1956-)
Breaking and Entering *61*

Kristen Stewart (1990-)
In the Land of Women *202*
Into the Wild *209*
The Messengers *259*

Patrick Stewart (1940-)
TMNT *(V)* *404*

Julia Stiles (1981-)
The Bourne Ultimatum *52*

Ben Stiller (1965-)
The Heartbreak Kid *174*

Jerry Stiller (1927-)
Hairspray *165*
The Heartbreak Kid *174*

Sting (1951-)
Bee Movie *(V)* *38*

Colin Stinton (1947-)
The Bourne Ultimatum *52*

Jesse Lee Stoffer
Gracie *154*

Emma Stone (1988-)
Superbad *383*

Sharon Stone (1958-)
Alpha Dog *7*

Simon Stone
Jindabyne *216*

Peter Stormare (1953-)
Premonition *315*

Ken Stott (1955-)
Charlie Wilson's War *74*

David Strathairn (1949-)
The Bourne Ultimatum *52*
Fracture *132*

Peter Strauss (1947-)
License to Wed *241*

Meryl Streep (1949-)
    Evening *115*
    Lions for Lambs *243*
    Rendition *331*

KaDee Strickland (1975-)
    American Gangster *13*

Mark Strong (1963-)
    Stardust *374*
    Sunshine *381*

Jessica Stroup
    The Hills Have Eyes II *175*

Jim Sturgess
    Across the Universe *1*

Gary Sturgis (1966-)
    Daddy's Little Girls *86*
    Pride *317*

Ali Suliman
    The Kingdom *227*

Nicole Sullivan (1970-)
    Meet the Robinsons *(V)* *258*

Donald (Don) Sumpter (1943-)
    Eastern Promises *106*

Ethan Suplee
    Mr. Woodcock *273*

Donald Sutherland (1934-)
    Reign Over Me *328*

Mena Suvari (1979-)
    Factory Girl *119*

Dominique Swain (1980-)
    Alpha Dog *7*

Hilary Swank (1974-)
    Freedom Writers *136*
    P.S. I Love You *320*
    The Reaping *325*

Nick Swardson (1976-)
    Blades of Glory *49*
    I Now Pronounce You Chuck and
        Larry *196*
    Reno 911!: Miami *333*

Jeremy Swift
    Fred Claus *134*

Tilda Swinton (1961-)
    Michael Clayton *260*
    Stephanie Daley *378*

Wanda Sykes (1964-)
    Evan Almighty *114*

Tabu
    The Namesake *279*

Jorma Taccone (1977-)
    Hot Rod *188*

Helena-Lia Tachovská
    Hannibal Rising *168*

Alice Taglioni (1977-)
    The Valet *420*

Charlie Tahan
    I Am Legend *193*

Ana Claudia Talancón (1980-)
    Alone With Her *6*
    Love in the Time of Chol-
        era *249*

Amber Tamblyn (1983-)
    Stephanie Daley *378*

Nabi Tanha
    The Kite Runner *229*

Quentin Tarantino (1963-)
    Grindhouse *159*

Catherine Tate
    Starter for 10 *376*

Jay Tavare
    Pathfinder *308*

Christine Taylor (1971-)
    License to Wed *241*

James Arnold Taylor (1948-)
    TMNT *(V)* *404*

Lawrence Taylor (1959-)
    The Comebacks *79*

Rachael Taylor (1984-)
    Transformers *407*

Scout Taylor-Compton (1989-)
    Halloween *167*

Owen Teale (1961-)
    The Last Legion *238*

Juno Temple
    Atonement *23*

Lew Temple
    Waitress *425*

John Terry (1944-)
    Zodiac *443*

Sylvie Testud (1971-)
    La Vie en Rose *421*

Charlize Theron (1975-)
    In the Valley of Elah *205*

David Thewlis (1963-)
    Harry Potter and the Order of
        the Phoenix *171*

Max Thieriot (1988-)
    The Astronaut Farmer *21*
    Nancy Drew *281*

Olivia Thirlby
    Juno *220*

Aaran Thomas
    Hannibal Rising *168*

Leon G. Thomas, III
    August Rush *26*

Marcus Thomas
    You Kill Me *440*

Emma Thompson (1959-)
    Harry Potter and the Order of
        the Phoenix *171*

Reece Daniel Thompson (1988-)
    Rocket Science *341*

Tracie Thoms (1975-)
    Grindhouse *159*

Ulrich Thomsen (1963-)
    Hitman *178*

Kristen Thomson
    Away From Her *31*

Billy Bob Thornton (1955-)
    The Astronaut Farmer *21*
    Mr. Woodcock *273*

David Thornton (1953-)
    Alpha Dog *7*

David Threlfall (1953-)
    Elizabeth: The Golden
        Age *108*

Andrew Tiernan (1965-)
    300 *400*

Justin Timberlake (1981-)
    Alpha Dog *7*
    Black Snake Moan *47*
    Shrek the Third *(V)* *358*
    Southland Tales *370*

Joel Tobeck (1971-)
    Eagle vs. Shark *105*

Stephen Tobolowsky (1951-)
    Wild Hogs *434*

Thomas Tofel
    I Know Who Killed Me *194*

Marisa Tomei (1964-)
    Before the Devil Knows You're
        Dead *40*
    Wild Hogs *434*

Rip Torn (1931-)
    Bee Movie *(V)* *38*

Gina Torres (1969-)
    I Think I Love My Wife *198*

Shaun Toub
    The Kite Runner *229*

Steve Toussaint
    Beyond the Gates *44*

Michelle Trachtenberg (1985-)
    Kickin' It Old Skool *223*

Sam Trammell (1971-)
    Aliens vs. Predator: Requiem *4*

Nancy Travis (1961-)
    The Jane Austen Book
        Club *215*

John Travolta (1954-)
    Hairspray *165*
    Wild Hogs *434*

Harry Treadway
    Control *81*

Danny Trejo (1944-)
    Delta Farce *98*
    Grindhouse *159*
    Halloween *167*

John Trent (-1983)
Alone With Her *6*

Michael Trucco (1970-)
Next *286*

Stanley Tucci (1960-)
The Hoax *179*

Chris Tucker (1972-)
Rush Hour 3 *343*

Jonathan Tucker (1982-)
In the Valley of Elah *205*

Alan Tudyk (1971-)
Death at a Funeral *95*
Knocked Up *231*
3:10 to Yuma *402*

Ulrich Tukur (1957-)
The Lives of Others *246*

Paige Turco (1965-)
The Game Plan *141*

Evan Turner
The Messengers *259*

Theodore Turner
The Messengers *259*

John Turturro (1957-)
Margot at the Wedding *255*
Transformers *407*

Nicholas Turturro (1962-)
I Now Pronounce You Chuck and
Larry *196*

Aisha Tyler (1970-)
Balls of Fury *33*
Death Sentence *97*

Liv Tyler (1977-)
Reign Over Me *328*

Tyrese
See Tyrese Gibson

Gaspard Ulliel (1984-)
Hannibal Rising *168*
Paris, je t'aime *306*

Gabrielle Union (1973-)
Daddy's Little Girls *86*

Karl Urban (1972-)
Pathfinder *308*

James Urbaniak (1963-)
Fay Grim *123*

Holly Valance (1983-)
DOA: Dead or Alive *103*

Amber Valletta (1974-)
Dead Silence *94*
Premonition *315*

Anneliese van der Pol
Bratz *55*

Jennifer Van Dyck (1962-)
Michael Clayton *260*

Carice van Houten
Black Book *46*

Travis Van Winkle (1982-)
Transformers *407*

Fernando Vargas
Alpha Dog *7*

Jacob Vargas
The Hills Have Eyes II *175*

Nelson Vasquez
El Cantante *69*

Peter Vaughan (1923-)
Death at a Funeral *95*

Vince Vaughn (1970-)
Fred Claus *134*
Into the Wild *209*

Alex Veadov
We Own the Night *431*

Makenzie Vega (1994-)
In the Land of Women *202*

Nadine Velazquez
War *428*

Lenny Venito
The Brave One *56*

Conrad Vernon
Shrek the Third (V) *358*

Pruitt Taylor Vince (1960-)
Captivity *70*

Kelly Vitz
Nancy Drew *281*

Jon Voight (1938-)
Bratz *55*
National Treasure: Book of Secrets *284*
September Dawn *352*
Transformers *407*

Max von Sydow (1929-)
The Diving Bell and the Butterfly *101*
Rush Hour 3 *343*

Jenny Wade
No Reservations *292*

Donnie Wahlberg (1969-)
Dead Silence *94*

Mark Wahlberg (1971-)
Shooter *356*
We Own the Night *431*

Heather Wahlquist
Alpha Dog *7*

Tom Waits (1949-)
Wristcutters: A Love Story *437*

Christopher Walken (1943-)
Balls of Fury *33*
Hairspray *165*

Ben Walker
The Golden Compass *147*

Nicola Walker
Beyond the Gates *44*

Marcia Wallace (1942-)
The Simpsons Movie (V) *362*

David Walliams
Stardust *374*

Amanda Walsh
Full of It *138*

Harriet Walter (1951-)
Atonement *23*

Julie Walters (1950-)
Becoming Jane *36*
Harry Potter and the Order of
the Phoenix *171*

Lee-Hom Wang
Lust, Caution *252*

Patrick Warburton (1964-)
Bee Movie (V) *38*
Happily N'Ever After (V) *170*
Underdog *415*

Fred Ward (1943-)
Feast of Love *124*

Wally Ward
See Wallace Langham

Zack (Zach) Ward (1973-)
Transformers *407*

Denzel Washington (1954-)
American Gangster *13*
The Great Debaters *157*

Kerry Washington (1977-)
Fantastic Four: Rise of the Silver
Surfer *121*
I Think I Love My Wife *198*

Leonor Watling
Paris, je t'aime *306*

Alberta Watson (1955-)
Away From Her *31*
The Lookout *248*

Emily Watson (1967-)
Miss Potter *265*
The Water Horse: Legend of the
Deep *429*

Emma Watson (1990-)
Harry Potter and the Order of
the Phoenix *171*

Naomi Watts (1968-)
Eastern Promises *106*
The Painted Veil *303*

Marlon Wayans (1972-)
Norbit *294*

Carl Weathers (1948-)
The Comebacks *79*

Sigourney Weaver (1949-)
Happily N'Ever After (V) *170*
The TV Set *410*

Hugo Weaving (1959-)
  Transformers *(V)* *407*

Mark Webber (1980-)
  The Hottest State *189*

Tang Wei
  Lust, Caution *252*

Robin Weigert
  Things We Lost in the
    Fire *395*

Rachel Weisz (1971-)
  Fred Claus *134*

Titus Welliver (1961-)
  Gone Baby Gone *149*

David Wenham (1965-)
  300 *400*

Adam West (1928-)
  Meet the Robinsons *(V)* *258*

Chandra West (1970-)
  I Now Pronounce You Chuck and
    Larry *196*

Dominic West
  Hannibal Rising *168*
  300 *400*

Celia Weston
  The Invasion *210*
  Joshua *218*
  No Reservations *292*

Frank Whaley (1963-)
  Vacancy *418*

Shea Whigham
  Wristcutters: A Love Story *437*

Ben Whishaw
  I'm Not There *200*
  Perfume: The Story of a Mur-
    derer *312*

Denzel Whitaker
  The Great Debaters *157*

Forest Whitaker (1961-)
  The Great Debaters *157*

Brian J. White
  DOA: Dead or Alive *103*
  The Game Plan *141*
  Stomp the Yard *379*

Jack White
  Walk Hard: The Dewey Cox
    Story *426*

Julie White
  Transformers *407*

Michael Jai White (1967-)
  Why Did I Get Married? *432*

Welker White
  I Think I Love My Wife *198*

Billie Whitelaw (1932-)
  Hot Fuzz *186*

Mitchell Whitfield (1968-)
  TMNT *(V)* *404*

Daniel Lawrence Whitney
  See Larry the Cable Guy

Johnny Whitworth (1975-)
  3:10 to Yuma *402*

Dianne Wiest (1948-)
  Dan in Real Life *88*

Kristen Wiig
  The Brothers Solomon *64*
  Knocked Up *231*
  Walk Hard: The Dewey Cox
    Story *426*

Olivia Wilde
  Alpha Dog *7*

Noah Wilder
  The Last Mimzy *240*

Tom Wilkinson (1948-)
  Michael Clayton *260*

Fred Willard (1939-)
  Epic Movie *112*

Clarence Williams, III (1939-)
  American Gangster *13*

Harland Williams (1967-)
  Meet the Robinsons *(V)* *258*

Jermaine Williams
  The Comebacks *79*
  The Great Debaters *157*

JoBeth Williams (1953-)
  In the Land of Women *202*

Katt Micah Williams
  Norbit *294*

Malinda Williams (1975-)
  Daddy's Little Girls *86*

Mark Williams (1959-)
  Harry Potter and the Order of
    the Phoenix *171*

Michael K. Williams
  Gone Baby Gone *149*
  I Think I Love My Wife *198*

Michelle Williams (1980-)
  The Hottest State *189*
  I'm Not There *200*

Robin Williams (1952-)
  August Rush *26*
  License to Wed *241*

Bruce Willis (1955-)
  Alpha Dog *7*
  The Astronaut Farmer *21*
  Grindhouse *159*
  Live Free or Die Hard *244*
  Perfect Stranger *310*

David Willis
  There Will Be Blood *392*

Gary Wilmes
  A Mighty Heart *263*

Lambert Wilson (1959-)
  Private Fears in Public
    Places *318*

Luke Wilson (1971-)
  Vacancy *418*
  You Kill Me *440*

Owen Wilson (1968-)
  The Darjeeling Limited *91*

Patrick Wilson (1973-)
  Evening *115*

Rainn Wilson (1968-)
  The Last Mimzy *240*

Reno Wilson
  Transformers *(V)* *407*

Scott Wilson (1942-)
  The Heartbreak Kid *174*

Stuart Wilson (1946-)
  Hot Fuzz *186*

Jeff Wincott (1957-)
  The Invasion *210*

Michael Wincott (1959-)
  Seraphim Falls *353*

Oprah Winfrey (1954-)
  Bee Movie *(V)* *38*

Mary Elizabeth Winstead (1984-)
  Grindhouse *159*
  Live Free or Die Hard *244*

Ray Winstone (1957-)
  Beowulf *(V)* *42*
  Breaking and Entering *61*

Jayne Wisener
  Sweeney Todd: The Demon Bar-
    ber of Fleet Street *386*

Reese Witherspoon (1976-)
  Rendition *331*

Victor Wolf
  In the Valley of Elah *205*

Wallace Wolodarsky
  The Darjeeling Limited *91*

Anthony Wong (1961-)
  The Painted Veil *303*

Benedict Wong
  Sunshine *381*

Elijah Wood (1981-)
  Paris, je t'aime *306*

Evan Rachel Wood (1987-)
  Across the Universe *1*

James Woods (1947-)
  Surf's Up *(V)* *385*

Edward Woodward (1930-)
  Hot Fuzz *186*

Bonnie Wright
  Harry Potter and the Order of
    the Phoenix *171*

Jeffrey Wright (1965-)
  The Invasion *210*
  Live Free or Die Hard *244*

Philip Wright
  The Flying Scotsman *129*

Robin Wright Penn (1966-)
  Beowulf *(V)* *42*
  Breaking and Entering *61*

Deance Wyatt
  Freedom Writers *136*

Rhiannon Leigh Wyn
  The Last Mimzy *240*

Priyanka Xi
  The Water Horse: Legend of the
    Deep *429*

Li Xin
  Paris, je t'aime *306*

Cedric Yarbrough
  Reno 911!: Miami *333*

Kelvin Han Yee
  Lucky You *251*

Anton Yelchin (1989-)
  Alpha Dog *7*

Michelle Yeoh (1962-)
  Sunshine *381*

Stelios Yiakmis
  Jindabyne *216*

Malik Yoba (1967-)
  Why Did I Get Married? *432*

Aaron Yoo
  Disturbia *99*

Lee Thompson Young
  The Hills Have Eyes II *175*

Galen Yuen
  Rescue Dawn *334*

Chow Yun-Fat (1955-)
  Pirates of the Caribbean: At
    World's End *313*

Steve Zahn (1968-)
  Rescue Dawn *334*

Kevin Zegers (1984-)
  The Jane Austen Book
    Club *215*

Renée Zellweger (1969-)
  Bee Movie *(V)* *38*
  Miss Potter *265*

Roschdy Zem
  Days of Glory *93*

Catherine Zeta-Jones (1969-)
  No Reservations *292*

José Zúñiga
  Next *286*

Subject Index

Title Index

This cumulative index is an alphabetical list of all films covered in the volumes of the *Magill's Cinema Annual*. Film titles are indexed on a word-by-word basis, including articles and prepositions. English leading articles (A, An, The) are ignored, as are foreign leading articles (El, Il, La, Las, Le, Les, Los). Acronyms appear alphabetically as if regular words. Common abbreviations in titles file as if they are spelled out. Proper names in titles are alphabetized beginning with the individual's first name. Titles with numbers are alphabetized as if the numbers were spelled out. When numeric titles gather in close proximity to each other, the titles will be arranged in a low-to-high numeric sequence. Films reviewed in this volume are cited in bold with an Arabic number indicating the page number on which the review begins; films reviewed in past volumes are cited with the *Annual* year in which the review was published. Original and alternate titles are cross-referenced to the American release title. Titles of retrospective films are followed by the year, in brackets, of their original release.

A

A corps perdu. *See* Straight for the Heart.

A. I.: Artificial Intelligence 2002

A la Mode (Fausto) 1995

A Lot Like Love 2006

A Ma Soeur. *See* Fat Girl.

A nos amours 1984

Abandon 2003

ABCD 2002

Abgeschminkt! *See* Making Up!.

About a Boy 2003

About Adam 2002

About Last Night... 1986

About Schmidt 2003

Above the Law 1988

Above the Rim 1995

Abre Los Ojos. *See* Open Your Eyes.

Abril Despedacado. *See* Behind the Sun.

Absence of Malice 1981

Absolute Beginners 1986

Absolute Power 1997

Absolution 1988

Abyss, The 1989

Accepted 2007

Accidental Tourist, The 1988

Accompanist, The 1993

Accordeur de tremblements de terre, L'. *See* Piano Tuner of Earthquakes, The.

Accused, The 1988

Ace in the Hole 1986, 1991

Ace Ventura: Pet Detective 1995

Ace Ventura: When Nature Calls 1996

Aces: Iron Eagle III 1992

Acid House, The 2000

Acqua e sapone. *See* Water and Soap.

Across the Tracks 1991

Across the Universe pg. 1

Acting on Impulse 1995

Action Jackson 1988

Actress 1988

Adam Sandler's 8 Crazy Nights 2003

Adam's Rib 1992

Adaptation 2003

Addams Family, The 1991

Addams Family Values 1993

Addicted to Love 1997

Addiction, The 1995

Addition, L'. *See* Patsy, The.

Adjo, Solidaritet. *See* Farewell Illusion.

Adjuster, The 1992

Adolescente, L' 1982

Adventure of Huck Finn, The 1993

Adventures in Babysitting 1987

Adventures of Baron Munchausen, The 1989

Adventures of Buckaroo Banzai, The 1984

Adventures of Elmo in Grouchland, The 2000

Adventures of Felix, The 2002

Adventures of Ford Fairlane, The 1990

Adventures of Mark Twain, The 1986

Adventures of Milo and Otis, The 1989

Adventures of Pinocchio, The 1996

Adventures of Pluto Nash, The 2003

Adventures of Priscilla, Queen of the Desert, The 1995

Adventures of Rocky and Bullwinkle, The 2001

Adventures of Sebastian Cole, The, 2000

Adventures of Sharkboy and Lavagirl in 3-D, The 2006

Adventures of the American Rabbit, The 1986

Advocate 1995

Aelita 1995

Aeon Flux 2006

Affair of Love, An 2001

Affair of the Necklace, The 2002

Affaire de Femmes, Une. *See* Story of Women.

Affaire de Gout, Un. *See* Matter of Taste, A.

Affengeil 1992

Affliction 1999

Afraid of the Dark 1992

Africa the Serengeti 1995

After Dark, My Sweet 1990

After Hours 1985

After Life 2000

After Midnight 1989

After the Rehearsal 1984

After the Sunset 2005

Afterglow 1979

Against All Odds 1983

Against the Ropes 2005

Age Isn't Everything (Life in the Food Chain) 1995

Age of Innocence, The 1993

Agent Cody Banks 2004

Agent Cody Banks 2: Destination London 2005

Agent on Ice 1986

Agnes Browne 2001

Agnes of God 1985

Aid 1988

Aileen: Life and Death of a Serial Killer 2005

Aileen Wuornos: The Selling of a Serial Killer 1995

Air America 1990

Air Bud 1997

Air Bud: Golden Receiver 1999

Air Force One 1997

Air Guitar Nation pg. 3

Air Up There, The 1995

Airborne 1993

Airheads 1995

Airplane II: The Sequel 1982

Akai Hashi no Shita no Nurui Mizo. *See* Warm Water Under a Red Bridge.

Akeelah and the Bee 2007

Akira Kurosawa's Dreams 1990

Al-Jenna-An. *See* Paradise Now.

Aladdin (Corbucci) 1987

Aladdin (Musker & Clements) 1992

Alamo, The 2005

Alamo Bay 1985

Alan and Naomi 1992

Alan Smithee Film, An 1999

Alarmist, The 1999

Alaska 1996

Alberto Express 1992

Albino Alligator 1997

Alchemist, The 1986

Alex & Emma 2004

Alexander 2005

Alfie 2005

Alfred Hitchcock's Bon Voyage & Aventure Malgache. *See* Aventure Malgache.

Ali 2002

Alias Betty 2004

Alice (Allen) 1990

Alice (Svankmajer) 1988

Alice et Martin 2001

Alien Nation 1988

Alien Predator 1987

Alien Resurrection 1997

Alien vs. Predator 2005

Aliens 1986

Alien3 1992

Aliens vs. Predator: Requiem pg. 4

Alive 1993

Alive and Kicking 1997

All About My Mother 2000

All About the Benjamins 2003

All Dogs Go to Heaven 1989

All Dogs Go to Heaven II 1996

All I Desire 1987

All I Want for Christmas 1991

All of Me 1984

All or Nothing 2003

All Over Me 1997

All Quiet on the Western Front 1985

All the King's Men 2007

All the Little Animals 2000

All the Pretty Horses 2001

All the Rage. *See* It's the Rage.

All the Real Girls 2004

All the Right Moves 1983

All the Vermeers in New York 1992

All's Fair 1989

All-American High 1987

Allan Quatermain and the Lost City of Gold 1987

Alley Cat 1984

Alligator Eyes 1990

Allnighter, The 1987

Almost an Angel 1990

Almost Famous 2001

Almost Heroes 1999

Almost You 1985

Aloha Summer 1988

Alone. *See* Solas.

Alone in the Dark 2006

Alone with Her pg. 6

Along Came a Spider 2002

Along Came Polly 2005

Alpha Dog pg. 7

Alphabet City 1983

Alpine Fire 1987

Altars of the World 1985

Alvin and the Chipmunks pg. 9

Always (Jaglom) 1985

Always (Spielberg) 1989

Amadeus 1984, 1985

Amanda 1989

Amantes. *See* Lovers.

Amantes del Circulo Polar, Los. *See* Lovers of the Arctic Circle, The.

Amants du Pont Neuf, Les 1995

Amateur 1995

Amateur, The 1982

Amazing Grace pg. 10

Amazing Grace and Chuck 1987

Amazing Panda Adventure, The 1995

Amazon Women on the Moon 1987

Ambition 1991

Amelie 2002

Amen 2004

America 1986

American Anthem 1986

American Beauty 2000

American Blue Note 1991

American Buffalo 1996

American Chai 2003

American Cyborg: Steel Warrior 1995

American Desi 2002

American Dream 1992

American Dreamer 1984

American Dreamz 2007

American Fabulous 1992

American Flyers 1985

American Friends 1993

American Gangster pg. 13

American Gothic 1988

American Haunting, An 2007

American Heart 1993

American History X 1999

American in Paris, An 1985

American Justice 1986

American Me 1992

American Movie 2000

American Ninja 1984, 1991

American Ninja 1985

American Ninja II 1987

American Ninja III 1989

American Outlaws 2002

American Pie 2000

American Pie 2 2002

American Pop 1981

American President, The 1995

American Psycho 2001

American Rhapsody, An 2002

American Stories 1989

American Splendor 2004

American Summer, An 1991

American Taboo 1984, 1991

American Tail, An 1986

American Tail: Fievel Goes West, An 1991

American Wedding 2004

American Werewolf in London, An 1981

American Werewolf in Paris, An 1997

American Women. *See* The Closer You Get.

America's Sweethearts 2002

Ami de mon amie, L'. *See* Boyfriends and Girlfriends.

Amin: The Rise and Fall 1983

Amistad 1997

Amityville Horror, The 2006

Amityville II: The Possession 1981

Amityville 3-D 1983

Among Giants 2000

Among People 1988

Amongst Friends 1993

Amor brujo, El 1986

Amores Perros 2002

Amos and Andrew 1993

Amour de Swann, Un. *See* Swann in Love.

Anaconda 1997

Analyze That 2003

Analyze This 2000

Anastasia 1997

Anchorman: The Legend of Ron Burgundy 2005

Anchors Aweigh 1985

And God Created Woman 1988

…And God Spoke 1995

And Life Goes On (Zebdegi Edame Darad) 1995

And Nothing but the Truth 1984

And Now Ladies and Gentlemen 2004

And the Ship Sails On 1984

And You Thought Your Parents Were Weird 1991

And Your Mother Too. *See* Y tu mama tambien.

Andre 1995

Android 1984

Ane qui a bu la lune, L'. *See* Donkey Who Drank the Moon, The.

Angel at My Table, An 1991

Angel Baby 1997

Angel Dust 1987

Angel Dust (Ishii) 1997

Angel Eyes 2002

Angel Heart 1987

Angel 1984

Angel III 1988

Angel Town 1990

Angel-A pg. 15

Angela's Ashes 2000

Angelo My Love 1983

Angels and Insects 1996

Angels in the Outfield 1995

Anger Management 2004

Angie 1995

Angry Harvest 1986

Anguish 1987

Angus 1995

Angustia. *See* Anguish.

Anima Mundi 1995

Animal, The 2002

Animal Behavior 1989

Animal Factory 2001

Animal Kingdom, The 1985

Anna 1987

Anna and the King 2000

Anna Karamazova 1995

Annapolis 2007

Anne Frank Remembered 1996

Annee des meduses, L' 1987

Annees sandwiches, Les. *See* Sandwich Years, The.

Annie 1982

Annihilators, The 1986

Between the Teeth 1995

Beverly Hillbillies, The 1993

Beverly Hills Brats 1989

Beverly Hills Cop 1984

Beverly Hills Cop II 1987

Beverly Hills Cop III 1995

Beverly Hills Ninja 1997

Bewitched 2006

Beyond Borders 2004

Beyond Rangoon 1995

Beyond Reasonable Doubt 1983

Beyond Silence 1999

Beyond the Gates pg. 44

Beyond the Limit 1983

Beyond the Mat 2001

Beyond the Rocks 2006

Beyond the Sea 2005

Beyond Therapy 1987

Bhaji on the Beach 1995

Bian Lian. *See* The King of Masks.

Bicentennial Man 2000

Big 1988

Big Bad Mama II 1988

Big Bang, The 1990

Big Blue, The (Besson) 1988

Big Blue, The (Horn) 1988

Big Bounce, The 2005

Big Bully 1996

Big Business 1988

Big Chill, The 1983

Big Daddy 2000

Big Easy, The 1987

Big Fat Liar 2003

Big Fish 2004

Big Girls Don't Cry, They Get Even 1992

Big Green, The 1995

Big Hit, The 1999

Big Kahuna, The 2001

Big Lebowski, The 1999

Big Man on Campus 1989

Big Momma's House 2001

Big Momma's House 2 2007

Big Night 1996

Big One, The 1999

Big Picture, The 1989

Big Shots 1987

Big Squeeze, The 1996

Big Tease, The 2001

Big Time 1988

Big Top Pee-Wee 1988

Big Town, The 1987

Big Trouble (Cassavetes) 1986

Big Trouble (Sonnenfeld) 2003

Big Trouble in Little China 1986

Biker Boyz 2004

Bill and Ted's Bogus Journey 1991

Bill and Ted's Excellent Adventure 1989

Billy Bathgate 1991

Billy Budd 1981

Billy Elliot 2001

Billy Madison 1995

Billy's Hollywood Screen Kiss 1999

Biloxi Blues 1988

Bin-jip. *See* 3-Iron.

Bingo 1991

BINGO 2000

Bio-Dome 1996

Bird 1988

Bird on a Wire 1990

Birdcage, The 1996

Birdy 1984

Birth 2005

Birth of a Nation, The 1982, 1992

Birthday Girl 2003

Bitter Moon 1995

Bittere Ernte. *See* Angry Harvest.

Bix (1990) 1995

Bix (1991) 1995

Bizet's Carmen 1984

Black and White 2001

Black Beauty 1995

Black Book pg. 46

Black Cat, The (Fulci) 1984

Black Cat (Shin) 1993

Black Cat, White Cat 2000

Black Cauldron, The 1985

Black Christmas 2007

Black Dahlia, The 2007

Black Dog 1999

Black Harvest 1995

Black Hawk Down 2002

Black Joy 1986

Black Knight 2002

Black Lizard 1995

Black Mask 2000

Black Moon Rising 1986

Black Peter 1985

Black Rain (Imamura) 1990

Black Rain (Scott) 1989

Black Robe 1991

Black Sheep 1996

Black Snake Moan pg. 47

Black Stallion Returns, The 1983

Black Widow 1987

Blackboard Jungle 1986, 1992

Blackout 1988

Blackout. *See* I Like It Like That.

Blade 1999

Blade II 2003

Blade Runner 1982

Blade: Trinity 2005

Blades of Glory pg. 49

Blair Witch Project, The 2000

Blame It on Night 1984

Blame It on Rio 1984

Blame It on the Bellboy 1992

Blank Check 1995

Blankman 1995

Blassblaue Frauenschrift, Eine. *See* Woman's Pale Blue Handwriting, A.

Blast 'em 1995

Blast from the Past 2000

Blaze 1989

Bless the Child 2001

Bless Their Little Hearts 1991

Blessures Assassines, Les. *See* Murderous Maids.

Blind Date 1987

Blind Fairies *See* Ignorant Fairies

Blind Fury 1990

Blind Swordsman: Zatoichi, The. *See* Zatoichi.

Blink 1995

Bliss 1986

Bliss 1997

Blob, The 1988

Blood and Chocolate pg. 50

Blood and Concrete 1991

Blood and Wine 1997

Blood Diamond 2007

Blood Diner 1987

Blood in Blood Out 1995

Blood, Guts, Bullets and Octane 2001

Blood Money 1988

Blood of Heroes, The 1990

Blood Salvage 1990

Blood Simple 1985

Blood Wedding 1982

Blood Work 2003

Bloodfist 1989

Bloodhounds of Broadway 1989

BloodRayne 2007

Bloodsport 1988

Bloody Sunday 2003

Blow 2002

Blow Dry 2002

Blow Out 1981

Blown Away 1995

Blue (Jarman) 1995

Blue (Kieslowski) 1993

Blue Car 2004

Blue Chips 1995

Blue City 1986

Blue Crush 2003

Blue Desert 1991

Blue Ice 1995

Blue Iguana, The 1988

Blue in the Face 1995

Blue Kite, The 1995

Blue Monkey 1987

Blue Skies Again 1983

Blue Sky 1995

Blue Steel 1990

Blue Streak 2000

Blue Thunder 1983

Blue Velvet 1986

Blue Villa, The 1995

Bluebeard's Eighth Wife 1986

Blues Brothers 2000 1999

Blues Lahofesh Hagadol. *See* Late Summer Blues.

Boat, The. *See* Boot, Das.

Boat is Full, The 1982

Boat Trip 2004

Bob le Flambeur 1983

Bob Marley: Time Will Tell. *See* Time Will Tell.

Bob Roberts 1992

Bobby 2007

Bobby Jones: Stroke of Genius 2005

Bodies, Rest, and Motion 1993

Body, The 2002

Body and Soul 1982

Body Chemistry 1990

Body Double 1984

Body Heat 1981

Body Melt 1995

Body of Evidence 1993

Body Parts 1991

Body Rock 1984

Body Shots 2000

Body Slam 1987

Body Snatchers 1995

Bodyguard, The 1992

Bodyguards, The. *See* La Scorta.

Boesman & Lena 2001

Bogus 1996

Boheme, La 1982

Boiler Room 2001

Boiling Point 1993

Bolero (Derek) 1984

Bolero (Lelouch) 1982

Bollywood/Hollywood 2003

Bom Yeorum Gaeul Gyeoul Geurigo…Bom. *See* Spring, Summer, Autumn, Winter…And Spring.

Bon Plaisir, Le 1984

Bon Voyage 1995

Bon Voyage (Rappenaeau) 2005

Bone Collector, The 2000

Bonfire of the Vanities, The 1990

Bongwater 1999

Bonne Route. *See* Latcho Drom.

Boogeyman 2006

Boogie Nights 1997

Book of Love 1991

Book of Shadows: Blair Witch 2 2001

Boomerang 1992

Boost, The 1988

Boot, Das 1982

Boot Ist Voll, Das. *See* Boat Is Full, The.

Bootmen 2001

Booty Call 1997

Booye Kafoor, Atre Yas. *See* Smell of Camphor, Fragrance of Jasmine.

Bopha! 1993

Borat: Cultural Learnings of America for Make Benefit Glorious Nation of Kazakhstan 2007

Border, The 1982

Boricua's Bond 2001

Born American 1986

Born in East L.A. 1987

Born Into Brothels: Calcutta's Red Light Kids 2006

Born on the Fourth of July 1989

Born Romantic 2002

Born to Be Wild 1996

Born to Race 1988

Born Yesterday 1993

Borrowers, The 1999

Borstal Boy 2003

Bose Zellen. *See* Free Radicals.

Bossa Nova 2001

Bostonians, The 1984

Bottle Rocket 1996

Boum, La 1983

Bounce 2001

Bound 1996

Bound and Gagged 1993

Bound by Honor 1993

Bounty, The 1984

Bourne Identity, The 2003

Bourne Supremacy, The 2005

Bourne Ultimatum, The pg. 52

Bowfinger 2000

Box of Moonlight 1997

Boxer, The 1997

Boxer and Death, The 1988

Boxing Helena 1993

Boy in Blue, The 1986

Boy Who Could Fly, The 1986

Boy Who Cried Bitch, The 1991

Boyfriend School, The. *See* Don't Tell Her It's Me.

Boyfriends 1997

Boyfriends and Girlfriends 1988

Boynton Beach Bereavement Club, The. *See* Boynton Beach Club, The.

Boynton Beach Club, The 2007

Boys 1996

Boys, The 1985

Boys and Girls 2001

Boys Don't Cry 2000

Boys from Brazil, The 1985

Boys Next Door, The 1986

Boys on the Side 1995

Boyz N the Hood 1991

Braddock 1988

Brady Bunch Movie, The 1995

Brady's Escape 1984

Brain Damage 1988

Brain Dead 1990

Brain Donors 1995

Brainstorm 1983

Bram Stoker's Dracula 1992

Branches of the Tree, The 1995

Brand Upon the Brain! pg. 54

Brandon Teena Story, The 2000

Brassed Off 1997

Brat. *See* Brother.

Bratz pg. 55

Brave One, The pg. 56

Brave Little Toaster, The 1987

Braveheart 1995

Brazil 1985

Breach pg. 59

Bread and Roses 2002

Bread and Salt 1995

Bread and Tulips 2002

Bread, My Sweet, The 2004

Break of Dawn 1988

Break-Up, The 2007

Breakdown 1997

Breakfast Club, The 1985

Breakfast of Champions 2000

Breakfast on Pluto 2006

Breakin' 1984

Breakin' All the Rules 2005

Breaking and Entering pg. 61

Breaking In 1989

Breaking the Rules 1992

Breaking the Sound Barrier. *See* Sound Barrier, The.

Breaking the Waves 1996

Breakin' II: Electric Boogaloo 1984

Breaking Up 1997

Breath of Life, A 1993

Breathing Room 1996

Breathless 1983

Brenda Starr 1992

Brewster McCloud 1985

Brewster's Millions 1985

Brian Wilson: I Just Wasn't Made for These Times 1995

Brick 2007

Bride, The 1985

Bride and Prejudice 2006

Bride of Chucky 1999

Bride of Re-Animator 1991

Bride of the Wind 2002

Bride with White Hair, The 1995

Bridesmaid, The 2007

Bridge of San Luis Rey, The 1981

Bridge of San Luis Rey, The 2006

Bridge on the River Kwai, The 1990

Bridge to Terabithia pg. 62

Bridges of Madison County, The 1995

Bridget Jones: The Edge of Reason 2005

Bridget Jones's Diary 2002

Brief Encounter 1990

Brief History of Time, A 1992

Bright Angel 1991

Bright Lights, Big City 1988

Bright Young Things 2005

Brighton Beach Memoirs 1986

Brimstone and Treacle 1982

Bring It On 2001

Bring on the Night 1985

Bringing Down the House 2004

Bringing Out the Dead 2000

Brittania Hospital 1983

Broadcast News 1987

Broadway Damage 1999

Broadway Danny Rose 1984

Brodre. *See* Brothers.

Brokeback Mountain 2006

Brokedown Palace 2000

Broken April. *See* Behind the Sun.

Broken Arrow 1996

Broken Blossoms 1984

Broken English 1997

Broken Flowers 2006

Broken Hearts Club, The 2001

Broken Lizard's Club Dread. *See* Club Dread.

Broken Rainbow 1985

Broken Vessels 1999

Broken Wings 2005

Bronx Tale, A 1993

Brother (Balabanov) 1999

Brother (Kitano) 2001

Brother Bear 2004

Brother from Another Planet, The 1984

Brother of Sleep 1996

Brotherhood of the Wolf 2003

Brothers 2006

Brothers, The 2002

Brothers Grimm, The 2006

Brother's Keeper 1993

Brother's Kiss, A 1997

Brothers McMullen, The 1995

Brothers Solomon, The pg. 64

Brown Bunny, The 2005

Brown Sugar 2003

Browning Version, The 1995

Bruce Almighty 2004

Bruce Lee Story, The. *See* Dragon.

Bu-Su 1988

Carried Away 1996

Carriers Are Waiting, The 2001

Carrington 1995

Cars 2007

Casa de los Babys 2004

Casa in bilico, Una. *See* Tottering Lives.

Casanova 2006

Casino 1995

Casino Royale 2007

Casper 1995

Cast Away 2001

Castle, The 2000

Casual Sex? 1988

Casualties of War 1989

Cat on a Hot Tin Roof 1993

Cat People 1981, 1982

Catacombs 1988

Catch a Fire 2007

Catch and Release pg. 73

Catch Me If You Can 1989

Catch Me If You Can (Spielberg) 2003

Catch That Kid 2005

Catfish in Black Bean Sauce 2001

Cats & Dogs 2002

Cats Don't Dance 1997

Cat's Meow, The 2003

Cattle Annie and Little Britches 1981

Catwoman 2005

Caught 1996

Caught Up 1999

Cave, The 2006

Cave Girl 1985

Caveman's Valentine, The 2002

CB4 1993

Cease Fire 1985

Cecil B. Demented 2001

Celebrity 1999

Celeste 1982

Celestial Clockwork 1996

Cell, The 2001

Cellular 2005

Celluloid Closet, The 1996

Celtic Pride 1996

Cement Garden, The 1995

Cemetery Club, The 1993

Cemetery Man 1996

Center of the Web 1992

Center of the World, The 2002

Center Stage 2001

Central do Brasil. *See* Central Station.

Central Station 1999

Century 1995

Ceravani tanto Amati. *See* We All Loved Each Other So Much.

Cercle Rouge, Le 2004

Ceremonie, La 1996

Certain Fury 1985

Certain Regard, Un. *See* Hotel Terminus.

C'est la vie 1990

Ceux qui m'aiment predont le train. *See* Those Who Love Me Can Take the Train.

Chac 2001

Chain of Desire 1993

Chain Reaction 1996

Chaindance. *See* Common Bonds.

Chained Heat 1983

Chairman of the Board 1999

Challenge, The 1982

Chamber, The 1996

Chambermaid of the Titanic, The 1999

Chameleon Street 1991

Champion 1991

Champions 1984

Chan Is Missing 1982

Chances Are 1989

Changing Lanes 2003

Changing Times 2007

Chantilly Lace 1995

Chaos 2004

Chaos. *See* Ran.

Chaplin 1992

Character 1999

Chariots of Fire 1981

Charlie and the Chocolate Factory 2006

Charlie's Angels 2001

Charlie's Angels: Full Throttle 2004

Charlie Wilson's War pg. 74

Charlotte Gray 2003

Charlotte's Web 2007

Charm Discret de la Bourgeoisie, Le. *See* The Discreet Charm of the Bourgeoisie.

Chase, The 1995

Chasers 1995

Chasing Amy 1988

Chasing Liberty 2005

Chasing Papi 2004

Chateau, The 2003

Chateau de ma mere, Le. *See* My Mother's Castle.

Chattahoochee 1990

Chattanooga Choo Choo 1984

Cheap Shots 1991

Cheaper by the Dozen 2004

Cheaper by the Dozen 2 2006

Cheatin' Hearts 1993

Check Is in the Mail, The 1986

Checking Out 1989

Cheech & Chong Still Smokin' 1983

Cheech & Chong's The Corsican Brothers 1984

Cheetah 1989

Chef in Love, A 1997

Chelsea Walls 2003

Chere Inconnue. *See* I Sent a Letter to My Love.

Cherish 2003

Cherry Orchard, The 2003

Cherry Pink. *See* Just Looking.

Chevre, La. *See* Goat, The.

Chicago 2003

Chicago Joe and the Showgirl 1990

Chicken Hawk: Men Who Love Boys 1995

Chicken Little 2006

Chicken Run 2001

Chief Zabu 1988

Chihwaseon: Painted Fire 2003

Child, The 2007

Child's Play 1988

Child's Play II 1990

Dickie Roberts: Former Child Star 2004

Die Another Day 2003

Die Fetten Jahre sind vorbei. *See* Edukators, The.

Die Hard 1988

Die Hard II 1990

Die Hard with a Vengeance 1995

Die Mommie Die! 2004

Die Story Von Monty Spinneratz. *See* A Rat's Story.

Dieu Est Grand, Je Suis Tout Petite. *See* God Is Great, I'm Not.

Different for Girls 1997

DIG! 2005

Digging to China 1999

Diggstown 1992

Dim Sum 1985

Dimanche a la Campagne, Un. *See* A Sunday in the Country.

Diner 1982

Dinner Game, The 2000

Dinner Rush 2002

Dinosaur 2001

Dinosaur's Story, A. *See* We're Back.

Dirty Cop No Donut 2003

Dirty Dancing 1987

Dirty Dancing: Havana Nights 2005

Dirty Dishes 1983

Dirty Harry 1982

Dirty Love 2006

Dirty Pretty Things 2004

Dirty Rotten Scoundrels 1988

Dirty Shame, A 2005

Dirty Work 1999

Disappearance of Garcia Lorca, The 1997

Disclosure 1995

Discreet Charm of the Bourgeoisie, The 2001

Discrete, La 1992

Dish, The 2002

Disney's Teacher's Pet 2005

Disney's The Kid 2001

Disorderlies 1987

Disorganized Crime 1989

Disraeli 1981

Distant Harmony 1988

Distant Thunder 1988

Distant Voices, Still Lives 1988

Distinguished Gentleman, The 1992

Distribution of Lead, The 1989

Disturbed 1990

Disturbia pg. 99

Disturbing Behavior 1999

Diva 1982

Divan 2005

Divided Love. *See* Maneuvers.

Divided We Fall 2002

Divine Intervention: A Chronicle of Love and Pain 2004

Divine Secrets of the Ya-Ya Sisterhood, The 2003

Diving Bell and the Butterfly, The pg. 101

Diving In 1990

Divorce, Le 2004

Divorcee, The 1981

Djomeh 2002

Do or Die 1995

Do the Right Thing 1989

D.O.A. 1988

DOA: Dead or Alive pg. 103

Doc Hollywood 1991

Doc's Kingdom 1988

Docteur Petiot 1995

Doctor, The 1991

Dr. Agaki 2000

Doctor and the Devils, The 1985

Dr. Bethune 1995

Dr. Butcher, M.D. 1982

Doctor Detroit 1983

Dr. Dolittle 1999

Dr. Dolittle 2 2002

Dr. Giggles 1992

Dr. Jekyll and Ms. Hyde 1995

Dr. Petiot. *See* Docteur Petiot.

Dr. Seuss' How the Grinch Stole Christmas 2001

Dr. Seuss" The Cat in the Hat 2004

Dr. Sleep. *See* Close Your Eyes.

Dr. T and the Women 2001

Doctor Zhivago 1990

Dodgeball: A True Underdog Story 2005

Dog of Flanders, A 2000

Dog Park 2000

Dogfight 1991

Dogma 2000

Dogville 2005

Doin' Time on Planet Earth 1988

Dolls 1987

Dolls 2006

Dolly Dearest 1992

Dolly In. *See* Travelling Avant.

Dolores Claiborne 1995

Domestic Disturbance 2002

Dominick and Eugene 1988

Dominion: Prequel to the Exorcist 2006

Domino 2006

Don Juan DeMarco 1995

Don Juan, My Love 1991

Dona Herlinda and Her Son 1986

Donkey Who Drank the Moon, The 1988

Donna della luna, La. *See* Woman in the Moon.

Donnie Brasco 1997

Donnie Darko 2003

Don't Be a Menace to South Central While Drinking Your Juice in the Hood 1996

Don't Come Knocking 2007

Don't Cry, It's Only Thunder 1982

Don't Move 2006

Don't Say a Word 2002

Don't Tell 2007

Don't Tell Her It's Me 1990

Don't Tell Mom the Babysitter's Dead 1991

Don't Tempt Me! *See* No News from God.

Doom 2006

Doom Generation, The 1995

Door in the Floor, The 2005

Door to Door 1984

Doors, The 1991

Dopamine 2004

Dorm That Dripped Blood, The 1983

Edes Emma, Draga Bobe: Vazlatok, Aktok. *See* Sweet Emma, Dear Bobe: Sketches, Nudes.

Edge, The 1997

Edge of Sanity 1989

Edge of Seventeen 2000

Edith and Marcel 1984

Edith's Diary 1986

Ed's Next Move 1996

Edtv 2000

Educating Rita 1983

Education of Little Tree, The 1997

Edukators, The 2006

Edward Scissorhands 1990

Edward II 1992

Efficiency Expert, The 1992

Efter Repetitionen. *See* After the Rehearsal.

Egares, Les. *See* Strayed.

Eiga Joyu. *See* Actress.

8 1/2 Women 2001

Eight Below 2007

Eight Days a Week 2000

Eight Heads in a Duffle Bag 1997

Eight Legged Freaks 2003

Eight Men Out 1988

8 Mile 2003

Eight Million Ways to Die 1986

8MM 2000

8 Seconds 1995

8 Women 2003

Eighteen Again 1988

Eighth Day, The 1997

Eighty-Four Charing Cross Road 1987

Eighty-Four Charlie MoPic 1989

Eine Liebe in Deutchland. *See* Love in Germany, A.

Election 2000

Electric Dreams 1984

Elektra 2006

Elephant 2004

Elegant Criminel, L' 1992

Elementary School, The 1995

Eleni 1985

Eleni (2005). *See* Weeping Meadow.

Elf 2004

Eliminators 1986

Elizabeth 1999

Elizabeth: The Golden Age pg. 108

Elizabethtown 2006

Ella Enchanted 2005

Elling 2003

Elliot Fauman, Ph.D. 1990

Eloge de l'Amour. *See* In Praise of Love.

Elvira, Mistress of the Dark 1988

Embalmer, The 2004

Emerald Forest, The 1985

Emile 2006

Eminent Domain 1991

Emma 1996

Emmanuelle 5 1987

Emperor Waltz, The 1986

Emperor's Club, The 2003

Emperor's New Clothes, The 1987

Emperor's New Clothes, The (Taylor) 2003

Emperor's New Groove, The 2001

Emperor's Shadow 2000

Empire of the Sun 1987

Empire Records 1995

Empire Strikes Back, The 1997

Emploi du Temps, L. *See* Time Out.

Employee of the Month 2007

Emporte-Moi. *See* Set Me Free.

Empty Mirror, The 2000

Enchanted pg. 110

Enchanted April 1992

Enchanted Cottage, The 1981

Encino Man 1992

Encore. *See* One More.

End of Days 2000

End of Innocence, The 1990

End of Old Times, The 1992

End of the Affair 2000

End of the Line (Glenn) 1987

End of the Line (Russell) 1988

End of the Spear 2007

End of Violence, The 1997

Endangered Species 1982

Endurance 2000

Enduring Love 2005

Endgame 1986

Endless Summer II, The 1995

Enemies, A Love Story 1989

Enemy at the Gates 2002

Enemy Mine 1985

Enemy of the State 1999

Enemy Territory 1987

Enfant, L'. *See* Child, The.

English Patient, The 1996

Englishman Who Went Up a Hill But Came Down a Mountain, The 1995

Enid Is Sleeping. *See* Over Her Dead Body.

Enigma (Szwarc) 1983

Enigma (Apted) 2003

Enough 2003

Enron: The Smartest Guys in the Room 2006

Enter the Ninja 1982

Entity, The 1983

Entrapment 2000

Entre nous 1984

Envy 2005

Epic Movie pg. 112

Equilibrium 2003

Equinox 1993

Eragon 2007

Eraser 1996

Erendira 1984

Erik the Viking 1989

Erin Brockovich 2001

Ermo 1995

Ernest Goes to Camp 1987

Ernest Goes to Jail 1990

Ernest Rides Again 1993

Ernest Saves Christmas 1988

Ernest Scared Stupid 1991

Eros 2006

Erotique 1995

Escanaba in da Moonlight 2002

Escape Artist, The 1982

Escape from Alcatraz 1982

Escape from L.A. 1996

Far from Heaven 2003

Far from Home 1989

Far From Home: The Adventures of Yellow Dog 1995

Far North 1988

Far Off Place, A 1993

Far Out Man 1990

Faraway, So Close 1993

Farewell Illusion 1986

Farewell My Concubine 1993

Farewell to the King 1989

Fargo 1996

Farinelli 1995

Farmer and Chase 1997

Fast and the Furious, The 2002

Fast and the Furious: Tokyo Drift, The 2007

Fast, Cheap & Out of Control 1997

Fast Food 1989

Fast Food, Fast Women 2002

Fast Forward 1985

Fast Talking 1986

Fast Times at Ridgemont High 1982

Fat Albert 2005

Fat City 1983

Fat Girl 2002

Fat Guy Goes Nutzoid 1987

Fat Man and Little Boy 1989

Fatal Attraction 1987

Fatal Beauty 1987

Fatal Instinct 1993

Fate Ignoranti. *See* Ignorant Fairies.

Father 1995

Father Hood 1993

Father of the Bride (Minnelli) 1993

Father of the Bride (Shyer) 1991

Father of the Bride Part II 1995

Fathers and Sons 1992

Father's Day 1997

Fausto. *See* A la Mode.

Fauteuils d'orchestre. *See* Avenue Montaigne.

Favor, The 1995

Favour, the Watch, and the Very Big Fish, The 1992

Fay Grim pg. 123

Fear 1988

Fear 1996

Fear and Loathing in Las Vegas 1999

Fear, Anxiety and Depression 1989

Fear of a Black Hat 1995

Feardotcom 2003

Fearless 1993

Fearless. *See* Jet Li's Fearless.

Feast of July 1995

Feast of Love pg. 124

Federal Hill 1995

Fedora 1986

Feds 1988

Feed 1992

Feel the Heat 1987

Feeling Minnesota 1996

Felicia's Journey 2000

Felix 1988

Fellini: I'm a Born Liar 2004

Female Perversions 1997

Femme d'a Cote, La. *See* Woman Next Door, The.

Femme de Chambre du Titanic, La. *See* Chambermaid of the Titanic.

Femme de mon pote, La. *See* My Best Friend's Girl.

Femme Fatale 2003

Femme Nikita, La 1991

Femmes de personne 1986

FernGully: The Last Rainforest 1992

Ferris Bueller's Day Off 1986

Festival Express 2005

Festival in Cannes 2003

Feud, The 1990

Fever 1988

Fever Pitch 1985

Fever Pitch 2000

Fever Pitch 2006

Few Days with Me, A 1988

Few Good Men, A 1992

Fido pg. 126

Field, The 1990

Field of Dreams 1989

Fierce Creatures 1997

15 Minutes 2002

Fifth Element, The 1997

50 First Dates 2005

51st State, The. *See* Formula 51.

54 1999

Fifty-Fifty 1993

Fifty-two Pick-up 1986

Fight Club 2000

Fighter 2002

Fighting Back 1982

Fighting Temptations, The 2004

Filles ne Savent pas Nager, Les. *See* Girls Can't Swim.

Fils, Le. *See* Son, The.

Filth and the Fury, The 2001

Fin aout debut septembre. *See* Late August, Early September.

Final Analysis 1992

Final Approach 1991

Final Cut 2005

Final Destination 2001

Final Destination 2 2004

Final Destination 3 2007

Final Fantasy: The Spirits Within 2002

Final Friday, The. *See* Jason Goes to Hell.

Final Option, The 1983

Final Sacrifice, The. *See* Children of the Corn II.

Final Season 1988

Final Season, The pg. 128

Find Me Guilty 2007

Finders Keepers 1984

Finding Forrester 2001

Finding Nemo 2004

Finding Neverland 2005

Fine Mess, A 1986

Fine Romance, A 1992

Finestra di Fronte, La. *See* Facing Windows.

Finzan 1995

Fiorile 1995

Fire and Ice (Bakshi) 1983

Fire and Ice (Bogner) 1987

Fire Birds 1990

Fire Down Below 1997

Fire from the Mountain 1987

Fortune Cookie, The 1986

40 Days and 40 Nights 2003

40 Year Old Virgin, The 2006

48 Hrs. 1982

Foster Daddy, Tora! 1981

Fountain, The 2007

Four Adventures of Reinette and
 Mirabelle 1989

Four Brothers 2006

Four Days in September 1999

Four Feathers, The 2003

Four Friends 1981

4 Little Girls 1997

Four Rooms 1995

Four Seasons, The 1981

Four Weddings and a Funeral 1995

1492: Conquest of Paradise 1992

1408 pg. 131

4th Man, The 1984

Fourth Protocol, The 1987

Fourth War, The 1990

Fox and the Hound, The 1981

Foxfire 1996

Foxtrap 1986

Fracture pg. 132

Frailty 2003

Frances 1982

Frank and Ollie 1995

Frank Miller's Sin City. *See* Sin City.

Frankenhooker 1990

Frankenstein. *See* Mary Shelley's Frankenstein.

Frankenstein Unbound. *See* Roger
 Corman's Frankenstein Unbound.

Frankie and Johnny 1991

Frankie Starlight 1995

Frantic 1988

Fraternity Vacation 1985

Frauds 1995

Freaked 1993

Freaky Friday 2004

Fred Claus pg. 134

Freddie as F.R.O.7 1992

Freddy Got Fingered 2002

Freddy vs. Jason 2004

Freddy's Dead 1991

Free and Easy 1989

Free Enterprise 2000

Free Radicals 2005

Free Ride 1986

Free Willy 1993

Free Willy II: The Adventure Home
 1995

Free Willy III: The Rescue 1997

Freedom On My Mind 1995

Freedom Writers pg. 136

Freedomland 2007

Freejack 1992

Freeway 1988

Freeway 1996

Freeze—Die—Come to Life 1995

French Connection, The 1982

French Kiss 1995

French Lesson 1986

French Lieutenant's Woman, The
 1981

French Twist 1996

Frequency 2001

Fresh 1995

Fresh Horses 1988

Freshman, The 1990

Freud 1983

Frida 2003

Friday 1995

Friday After Next 2003

Friday Night 2004

Friday Night Lights 2005

Friday the 13th, Part III 1982

Friday the 13th, Part IV 1984

Friday the 13th, Part VI 1986

Friday the 13th Part VII 1988

Friday the 13th Part VIII 1989

Fried Green Tomatoes 1991

Friend of the Deceased, A 1999

Friends & Lovers 2000

Friends with Money 2007

Fright Night 1985

Frighteners, The 1996

Fringe Dwellers, The 1987

From Beyond 1986

From Dusk Till Dawn 1996

From Hell 2002

From Hollywood to Deadwood 1988

From Swastikas to Jim Crow 2001

From the Hip 1987

Front, The 1985

Frosh: Nine Months in a Freshman
 Dorm 1995

Frozen Assets 1992

Fruhlingssinfonie. *See* Spring Symphony.

Fruit Machine, The 1988

Fu-zung cen. *See* Hibiscus Town.

Fucking Amal. *See* Show Me Love.

Fugitive, The 1993

Full Blast 2001

Full Frontal 2003

Full Metal Jacket 1987

Full Monty, The 1997

Full Moon in Paris 1984

Full Moon in the Blue Water 1988

Full of It pg. 138

Fun Down There 1989

Fun With Dick and Jane 2006

Funeral, The 1987

Funeral, The (Ferrara) 1996

Funny About Love 1990

Funny Bones 1995

Funny Farm (Clark) 1983

Funny Farm (Hill) 1988

Further Adventures of Tennessee
 Buck, The 1988

G

Gabbeh 1997

Gabriela 1984

Gabrielle 2007

Gaby—A True Story 1987

Gadjo Dilo 1999

Galactic Gigolo 1988

Galaxy Quest 2000

Gallipoli 1981

Gambler, The 2000

Game, The 1989

Game, The 1997

Game Plan, The pg. 141

Game 6 2007

Go Now 1999

Goal! The Dream Begins 2007

Goat, The 1985

Gobots 1986

God Doesn't Believe in Us Anymore 1988

God Grew Tired of Us pg. 146

God Is Great, I'm Not 2003

God Is My Witness 1993

God Said "Ha"! 2000

Goddess of 1967, The 2003

Godfather, Part III, The 1990

Gods and Generals 2004

Gods and Monsters 1999

Gods Must Be Crazy, The 1984

Gods Must Be Crazy II, The 1990

God's Will 1989

Godsend 2005

Godzilla 1985 1985

Godzilla 1997

Godzilla 2000 2001

Gohatto. *See* Taboo.

Goin' to Chicago 1991

Going All the Way 1997

Going Berserk 1983

Going Undercover 1988

Goin' South 1978

Gold Diggers: The Secret of Bear Mountain 1995

Golden Bowl, The 2002

Golden Child, The 1986

Golden Compass, The pg. 147

Golden Gate 1995

Golden Seal 1983

Goldeneye 1995

Gone Baby Gone pg. 149

Gone Fishin' 1997

Gone in Sixty Seconds 2001

Gone With the Wind 1981, 1982, 1997

Gong fu. *See* Kung Fu Hustle.

Gonza the Spearman 1988

Good Boy! 2004

Good Burger 1997

Good Bye Cruel World 1984

Good Bye, Lenin! 2005

Good Evening, Mr. Wallenberg 1995

Good German, The 2007

Good Girl, The 2003

Good Luck Chuck pg. 151

Good Man in Africa, A 1995

Good Marriage, A. *See* Beau Mariage, Le.

Good Morning, Babylon 1987

Good Morning, Vietnam 1987

Good Mother, The 1988

Good Night, and Good Luck 2006

Good Shepherd, The 2007

Good Son, The 1993

Good Thief, The 2004

Good Weather, But Stormy Late This Afternoon 1987

Good Will Hunting 1997

Good Woman, A 2007

Good Woman of Bangkok, The 1992

Good Work. *See* Beau Travail.

Good Year, A 2007

Goodbye, Children. *See* Au Revoir les Enfants.

Goodbye Lover 2000

Goodbye, New York 1985

Goodbye People, The 1986

GoodFellas 1990

Goofy Movie, A 1995

Goonies, The 1985

Gordy 1995

Gorillas in the Mist 1988

Gorky Park 1983

Gorky Triology, The. *See* Among People.

Gosford Park 2002

Gospel 1984

Gospel According to Vic 1986

Gossip 2001

Gossip (Nutley) 2003

Gost 1988

Gotcha! 1985

Gothic 1987

Gothika 2004

Gout des Autres, Le. *See* Taste of Others, The.

Gouttes d'Eau sur Pierres Brulantes. *See* Water Drops on Burning Rocks.

Governess 1999

Goya in Bordeaux 2001

Grace Is Gone pg. 153

Grace of My Heart 1996

Grace Quigley 1985

Gracie pg. 154

Graffiti Bridge 1990

Gran Fiesta, La 1987

Grand Bleu, Le. *See* Big Blue, The (Besson).

Grand Canyon 1991

Grand Canyon: The Hidden Secrets 1987

Grand Chemin, Le. *See* Grand Highway, The.

Grand Highway, The 1988

Grand Illusion, The 2000

Grand Isle 1995

Grande Cocomero, Il. *See* Great Pumpkin, The.

Grandfather, The 2000

Grandma's Boy 2007

Grandview, U.S.A. 1984

Grass Harp, The 1996

Gravesend 1997

Graveyard Shift. *See* Stephen King's Graveyard Shift.

Gray Matters pg. 156

Gray's Anatomy 1997

Grease 1997

Grease II 1982

Great Balls of Fire! 1989

Great Barrier Reef, The 1990

Great Day In Harlem, A 1995

Great Debaters, The pg. 157

Great Expectations 1999

Great Mouse Detective, The 1986

Great Muppet Caper, The 1981

Great Outdoors, The 1988

Great Pumpkin, The 1993

Great Raid, The 2006

Great Wall, A 1986

Great White Hype, The 1996

Greatest Game Ever Played, The 2006

Greedy 1995

Happy Together 1990

Happy Together 1997

Hard Candy 2007

Hard Choices 1986

Hard Core Logo 1999

Hard Eight 1997

Hard Hunted 1995

Hard Promises 1992

Hard Rain 1999

Hard Target 1993

Hard Ticket to Hawaii 1987

Hard Times 1988

Hard to Hold 1984

Hard to Kill 1990

Hard Traveling 1986

Hard Way, The (Badham) 1991

Hard Way, The (Sherman) 1984

Hard Word, The 2004

Hardball 2002

Hardbodies 1984

Hardbodies II 1986

Hardware 1990

Harlem Nights 1989

Harley Davidson and the Marlboro Man 1991

Harmonists, The 2000

Harold & Kumar Go to White Castle 2005

Harriet Craig 1984

Harriet the Spy 1996

Harrison's Flowers 2003

Harry and Son 1984

Harry and the Hendersons 1987

Harry, He's Here to Help. *See* With a Friend Like Harry.

Harry Potter and the Chamber of Secrets 2003

Harry Potter and the Goblet of Fire 2006

Harry Potter and the Order of the Phoenix pg. 171

Harry Potter and the Prisoner of Azkaban 2005

Harry Potter and the Sorcerer's Stone 2002

Harry, Un Ami Qui Vous Veut du Bien. *See* With a Friend Like Harry.

Hart's War 2003

Harvard Man 2003

Harvest, The 1995

Hasty Heart, The 1987

Hatchet Man, The 1982

Hatouna Mehuheret. *See* Late Marriage.

Haunted Honeymoon 1986

Haunted Mansion, The 2004

Haunted Summer 1988

Haunting, The 2000

Hauru no ugoku shiro. *See* Howl's Moving Castle.

Haute tension. *See* High Tension.

Hav Plenty 1999

Havana 1990

Hawk, The 1995

Hawks 1988

He Got Game 1999

He Liu. *See* River, The.

He Loves Me…He Loves Me Not 2004

He Said, She Said 1991

Head Above Water 1997

Head in the Clouds 2005

Head Office 1986

Head of State 2004

Head On 2000

Head-On 2006

Head Over Heels 2002

Heads or Tails 1983

Hear My Song 1991

Hear No Evil 1993

Hearing Voices 1991

Heart 1987

Heart and Souls 1993

Heart Condition 1990

Heart in Winter, A. *See* Coeur en hiver, Un.

Heart Like a Wheel 1983

Heart of a Stag 1984

Heart of Dixie 1989

Heart of Midnight 1989

Heart of the Game, The 2007

Heartaches 1982

Heartbreak Hotel 1988

Heartbreak Kid, The 1986

Heartbreak Kid, The (Farrelly/Farrelly) pg. 174

Heartbreak Ridge 1986

Heartbreaker 1983

Heartbreakers 2002

Heartburn 1986

Heartland 1981

Hearts in Atlantis 2002

Hearts of Darkness: A Filmmaker's Apocalypse 1992

Hearts of Fire 1987

Heat 1987

Heat (Mann) 1995

Heat and Dust 1984

Heat of Desire 1984

Heathcliff 1986

Heathers 1989

Heatwave 1983

Heaven (Keaton) 1987

Heaven (Tykwer) 2003

Heaven and Earth (Kadokawa) 1991

Heaven and Earth (Stone) 1993

Heaven Help Us 1985

Heaven's Gate 1981

Heaven's Prisoners 1996

Heavenly Bodies 1984

Heavenly Creatures 1995

Heavenly Kid, The 1985

Heavy 1996

Heavyweights 1995

Hecate 1984

Hedwig and the Angry Inch 2002

Heidi Fleiss: Hollywood Madame 1996

Heights 2006

Heist, The 2002

Helas Pour Moi 1995

Held Up 2001

Hell High 1989

Hellbent 1989

Hellbound 1988

Hellboy 2005

Heller Wahn. *See* Sheer Madness.

Hello Again 1987

Hello, Dolly! 1986

Homme et une femme, Un. *See* Man and a Woman, A.

Hondo 1982

Honey 2004

Honey, I Blew Up the Kid 1992

Honey, I Shrunk the Kids 1989

Honeybunch 1988

Honeydripper pg. 181

Honeymoon Academy 1990

Honeymoon in Vegas 1992

Honeymooners, The 2006

Hong Gaoliang. *See* Red Sorghum.

Honky Tonk Freeway 1981

Honkytonk Man 1982

Honneponnetge. *See* Honeybunch.

Honor Betrayed. *See* Fear.

Honorable Mr. Wong, The. *See* Hatchet Man, The.

Honour of the House 2001

Hoodlum 1997

Hoodwinked 2007

Hook 1991

Hoop Dreams 1995

Hoosiers 1986

Hoot 2007

Hope and Glory 1987

Hope and Pain 1988

Hope Floats 1999

Horror Show, The 1989

Hors la Vie 1995

Horse of Pride, The 1985

Horse Whisperer, The 1999

Horseman on the Roof, The 1996

Host, The pg. 183

Hostage 2006

Hostel 2007

Hostel: Part II pg. 185

Hot Chick, The 2003

Hot Dog...The Movie 1984

Hot Fuzz pg. 186

Hot Pursuit 1987

Hot Rod pg. 188

Hot Shots! 1991

Hot Shots! Part Deux 1993

Hot Spot, The 1990

Hot to Trot 1988

Hotel Colonial 1987

Hotel De Love 1997

Hotel New Hampshire, The 1984

Hotel Rwanda 2005

Hotel Terminus 1988

Hotshot 1987

Hottest State, The pg. 189

Hound of the Baskervilles, The 1981

Hours, The 2003

Hours and Times, The 1992

House 1986

House II 1987

House Arrest 1996

House of Cards 1993

House of D 2006

House of Flying Daggers 2005

House of Fools 2004

House of Games 1987

House of Luk 2001

House of Mirth 2002

House of 1,000 Corpses 2004

House of Sand and Fog 2004

House of the Spirits, The 1995

House of Wax 2006

House of Yes, The 1997

House on Carroll Street, The 1988

House on Haunted Hill 2000

House on Limb, A. *See* Tottering Lives.

House Party 1990

House Party II 1991

House Party III 1995

House Where Evil Dwells, The 1982

Houseboat 1986

Houseguest 1995

Household Saints 1993

Householder, The 1984

Housekeeper, A 2004

Housekeeper, The 1987

Housekeeping 1987

Housesitter 1992

How I Got into College 1989

How I Killed My Father 2004

How Stella Got Her Groove Back 1999

How to Deal 2004

How to Eat Fried Worms 2007

How to Get Ahead in Advertising 1989

How to Get the Man's Foot Outta Your Ass. *See* Baadasssss!

How to Lose a Guy in 10 Days 2004

How to Make an American Quilt 1995

How to Make Love to a Negro Without Getting Tired 1990

Howard the Duck 1986

Howard's End 1992

Howling, The 1981

Howling III, The. *See* Marsupials, The.

Howl's Moving Castle 2006

Hsi Yen. *See* Wedding Banquet, The.

Hsimeng Jensheng. *See* Puppetmaster, The.

Hudson Hawk 1991

Hudsucker Proxy, The 1995

Hugh Hefner: Once Upon a Time 1992

Hugo Pool 1997

Huit Femmes. *See* 8 Women.

Hulk 2004

Human Nature 2003

Human Resources 2002

Human Shield, The 1992

Human Stain, The 2004

Humongous 1982

Hunchback of Notre Dame, The 1996

Hungarian Fairy Tale, A 1989

Hunger, The 1983

Hungry Feeling, A 1988

Hunk 1987

Hunt for Red October, The 1990

Hunted, The 1995

Hunted, The 2004

Hunters of the Golden Cobra, The 1984

Hunting Party, The pg. 191

Huo Yuan Jia. *See* Jet Li's Fearless.

Hurlyburly 1999

Hurricane, The 2000

In the Company of Men 1997

In the Cut 2004

In the Heat of Passion 1992

In the Heat of the Night 1992

In the Land of the Deaf 1995

In the Land of Women pg. 202

In the Line of Fire 1993

In the Mirror of Maya Deren 2004

In the Mood 1987

In the Mood for Love 2002

In the Mouth of Madness 1995

In the Name of the Father 1993

In the Realms of the Unreal 2006

In the Shadow of Kilimanjaro 1986

In the Shadow of the Moon pg. 204

In the Shadow of the Stars 1992

In the Soup 1992

In the Spirit 1990

In the Valley of Elah pg. 205

In This World 2004

In Too Deep 2000

In Weiter Ferne, So Nah! *See* Faraway, So Close.

Inchon 1982

Incident at Oglala 1992

Incident at Raven's Gate 1988

Incognito 1999

Inconvenient Truth, An 2007

Incredible Journey, The. *See* Homeward Bound.

Incredibles, The 2005

Incredibly True Adventures of Two Girls in Love, The 1995

Incubus, The 1982

Indecent Proposal 1993

Indigènes. *See* Days of Glory.

Independence Day 1996

Indian in the Cupboard, The 1995

Indian Runner, The 1991

Indian Summer 1993

Indiana Jones and the Last Crusade 1989

Indiana Jones and the Temple of Doom 1984

Indochine 1992

Inevitable Grace 1995

Infamous 2007

Infernal Affairs 2005

Infinity 1991

Infinity (Broderick) 1996

Informer, The 1986

Inkwell, The 1995

Inland Empire 2007

Inland Sea, The 1995

Inner Circle, The 1991

Innerspace 1987

Innocent, The 1988

Innocent, The 1995

Innocent Blood 1992

Innocent Man, An 1989

Innocent Sleep, The 1997

Innocents Abroad 1992

Inside I'm Dancing. *See* Rory O'Shea Was Here.

Inside Man 2007

Inside Monkey Zetterland 1993

Insider, The 2000

Insignificance 1985

Insomnia (Skjoldbjaerg) 1999

Insomnia (Nolan) 2003

Inspector Gadget 2000

Instant Karma 1990

Instinct 2000

Intacto 2004

Intermission 2005

Internal Affairs 1990

Interpreter, The 2006

Interrogation, The 1990

Intersection 1995

Interview pg. 208

Interview with the Vampire 1995

Intervista 1993

Intimacy 2002

Intimate Relations 1997

Intimate Strangers 2005

Into the Blue 2006

Into the Night 1985

Into the Sun 1992

Into the West 1993

Into the Wild pg. 209

Intolerable Cruelty 2004

Invaders from Mars 1986

Invasion! *See* Top of the Food Chain.

Invasion, The pg. 210

Invasion of the Body Snatchers 1982

Invasion U.S.A. 1985

Inventing the Abbotts 1997

Invention of Love 2001

Invincible 2003

Invincible 2007

Invisible, The pg. 212

Invisible Circus 2002

Invisible Kid, The 1988

Invitation au voyage 1983

Invitation to the Dance 1985

I.Q. 1995

Iris 2002

Irma la Douce 1986

Irma Vep 1997

Iron Eagle 1986

Iron Eagle II 1988

Iron Giant, The 2000

Iron Maze 1991

Iron Triangle, The 1989

Iron Will 1995

Ironweed 1987

Irreconcilable Differences 1984

Irreversible 2004

Ishtar 1987

Island, The 2006

Island of Dr. Moreau, The 1996

Isn't She Great 2001

Istoriya As-Klyachimol. *See* Asya's Happiness.

It Could Happen to You 1995

It Couldn't Happen Here 1988

It Had to Be You 1989

It Happened One Night 1982

It Happened Tomorrow 1983

It Runs in the Family 2004

It Takes Two 1988

It Takes Two 1995

Italian for Beginners 2002

Italian Job, The 2004

Italiensk for Begyndere. *See* Italian for Beginners.

It's a Wonderful Life 1982
It's Alive III 1987
It's All About Love 2005
It's All Gone Pete Tong 2006
It's All True 1993
It's My Party 1996
It's Pat 1995
It's the Rage 2001
Ivan and Abraham 1995
I've Heard the Mermaids Singing 1987

J

Jack 1996
Jack and His Friends 1993
Jack and Sarah 1996
Jack Frost 1999
Jack the Bear 1993
Jackal, The 1997
Jackass Number Two 2007
Jacket, The 2006
Jackie Brown 1997
Jackie Chan's First Strike 1997
Jacknife 1989
Jackpot 2002
Jack's Back 1988
Jacob 1988
Jacob's Ladder 1990
Jacquot of Nantes 1993
Jade 1995
Jagged Edge 1985
J'ai epouse une ombre. *See* I Married a Shadow.
Jailhouse Rock 1986
Jake Speed 1986
Jakob the Liar 2000
James and the Giant Peach 1996
James' Journey to Jerusalem 2005
James Joyce's Women 1985
Jamon, Jamon 1993
Jane Austen Book Club, The pg. 215
Jane Eyre 1996
January Man, The 1989
Japanese Story 2005
Jarhead 2006

Jason Goes to Hell 1993
Jason X 2003
Jason's Lyric 1995
Jawbreaker 2000
Jaws: The Revenge 1987
Jaws 3-D 1983
Jay and Silent Bob Strike Back 2002
Jazzman 1984
Je Rentre a la Maison. *See* I'm Going Home.
Je tu il elle 1985
Je vous salue, Marie. *See* Hail Mary.
Jean de Florette 1987
Jeanne Dielman, 23 Quai du Commerce, 1080 Bruxelles 1981
Jeepers Creepers 2002
Jeepers Creepers 2 2004
Jefferson in Paris 1995
Jeffrey 1995
Jekyll and Hyde…Together Again 1982
Jennifer Eight 1992
Jerky Boys 1995
Jerome 2001
Jerry Maguire 1996
Jersey Girl 2005
Jerusalem 1996
Jesus of Montreal 1989
Jesus' Son 2000
Jet Lag 2004
Jet Li's Fearless 2007
Jetsons 1990
Jewel of the Nile, The 1985
JFK 1991
Jigsaw Man, The 1984
Jim and Piraterna Blom. *See* Jim and the Pirates.
Jim and the Pirates 1987
Jiminy Glick in Lalawood 2006
Jimmy Hollywood 1995
Jimmy Neutron: Boy Genius 2002
Jimmy the Kid 1983
Jindabyne pg. 216
Jingle All the Way 1996
Jinxed 1982
Jit 1995

Jo-Jo at the Gate of Lions 1995
Jo Jo Dancer, Your Life Is Calling 1986
Joan the Mad. *See* Mad Love.
Jocks 1987
Joe Dirt 2002
Joe Gould's Secret 2001
Joe Somebody 2002
Joe the King 2000
Joe Versus the Volcano 1990
Joe's Apartment 1996
Joey 1985
Joey Takes a Cab 1991
John and the Missus 1987
John Carpenter's Ghosts of Mars 2002
John Carpenter's Vampires 1999
John Grisham's the Rainmaker 1998
John Huston 1988
John Huston and the Dubliners 1987
John Q 2003
John Tucker Must Die 2007
Johnny Be Good 1988
Johnny Dangerously 1984
Johnny English 2004
Johnny Handsome 1989
Johnny Mnemonic 1995
Johnny Stecchino 1992
Johnny Suede 1992
johns 1997
Johnson Family Vacation 2005
Joke of Destiny, A 1984
Joseph Conrad's the Secret Agent 1996
Josh and S.A.M. 1993
Joshua pg. 218
Joshua Then and Now 1985
Josie and the Pussycats 2002
Journey into Fear 1985
Journey of August King 1995
Journey of Hope 1991
Journey of Love 1990
Journey of Natty Gann, The 1985
Journey to Spirit Island 1988
Joy Luck Club, The 1993
Joy of Sex 1984

Joy Ride 2002

Joyeux Noel 2007

Joysticks 1983

Ju Dou 1991

Juana la Loca. *See* Mad Love.

Judas Kiss 2000

Judas Project, The 1995

Jude 1996

Judge Dredd 1995

Judgement in Berlin 1988

Judgement Night 1993

Judy Berlin 2001

Juice 1992

Julia Has Two Lovers 1991

Julian Po 1997

Julien Donkey-Boy 2000

Jumanji 1995

Jument vapeur, La. *See* Dirty Dishes.

Jump Tomorrow 2002

Jumpin' at the Boneyard 1992

Jumpin' Jack Flash 1986

Jumpin' Night in the Garden of Eden, A 1988

Junebug 2006

Jungle Book, The 1995

Jungle Book 2, The 2004

Jungle Fever 1991

Jungle2Jungle 1997

Junior 1995

Juno pg. 220

Jurassic Park 1993

Jurassic Park III 2002

Juror, The 1996

Jury Duty 1995

Just a Kiss 2003

Just a Little Harmless Sex 2000

Just Another Girl on the I.R.T. 1993

Just Between Friends 1986

Just Cause 1995

Just Friends 2006

Just Like a Woman 1995

Just Like Heaven 2006

Just Looking 2002

Just Married 2004

Just My Luck 2007

Just One of the Guys 1985

Just One Time 2002

Just the Ticket 2000

Just the Way You Are 1984

Just Visiting 2002

Just Write 1999

Justice in the Coalfields 1996

Juwanna Mann 2003

K

K-9 1989

K-19: The Widowmaker 2003

K-PAX 2002

Kadisbellan. *See* Slingshot, The.

Kadosh 2001

Kaena: The Prophecy 2005

Kafka 1991

Kalifornia 1993

Kama Sutra: A Tale of Love 1997

Kamikaze Hearts 1995

Kamilla and the Thief 1988

Kandahar 2002

Kandyland 1988

Kangaroo 1987

Kangaroo Jack 2004

Kansas 1988

Kansas City 1996

Karakter. *See* Character.

Karate Kid, The 1984

Karate Kid: Part II, The 1986

Karate Kid: Part III, The 1989

Kate & Leopold 2002

Kazaam 1996

Kazoku. *See* Where Spring Comes Late.

Keep, The 1983

Keep the River On Your Right: A Modern Cannibal Tale 2002

Keeping Mum 2007

Keeping the Faith 2001

Keeping Up with the Steins 2007

Kerouac, the Movie 1985

Key Exchange 1985

Keys of the Kingdom, The 1989

Keys to Tulsa 1997

Khuda Gawah. *See* God Is My Witness.

Kickboxer 1989

Kickboxer II 1991

Kicked in the Head 1997

Kickin' It Old Skool pg. 223

Kicking and Screaming (Baumbach) 1995

Kicking & Screaming 2006

Kid, The. *See* Vie en Rose, La.

Kid & I, The 2006

Kid Brother, The 1987

Kid Colter 1985

Kid in King Arthur's Court, A 1995

Kid Stays in the Picture, The 2003

Kidnapped 1987

Kids 1995

Kids in the Hall: Brain Candy, The 1996

Kika 1995

Kikujiro 2001

Kill Bill: Vol. 1 2004

Kill Bill: Vol. 2 2005

Kill Me Again 1989

Kill Me Later 2002

Kill-Off, The 1990

Killer Image 1992

Killer Instinct 1995

Killer Klowns from Outer Space 1988

Killer of Sheep pg. 224

Killer Party 1986

Killing Affair, A 1988

Klling Fields, The 1984

Killing Floor, The 1995

Killing of a Chinese Bookie, The 1986

Killing Time 1999

Killing Time, The, 1987

Killing Zoe 1995

Killpoint 1984

Kindergarten Cop 1990

Kindred, The 1987

King, The 2007

King Arthur 2005

King and I, The 2000

King David 1985

Laserman, The 1988, 1990

Lassie 1995

Lassie 2007

Lassie Come Home 1993

Lassiter 1984

Last Act, The 1992

Last Action Hero 1993

Last American Virgin, The 1982

Last Boy Scout, The 1991

Last Call at Maud's 1993

Last Castle, The 2002

Last Cigarette, The 2000

Last Dance, The 1996

Last Day of Winter, The 1987

Last Days 2006

Last Days of Disco, The 1999

Last Emperor, The 1987

Last Exit to Brooklyn 1990

Last Holiday 2007

Last Hunter, The 1984

Last King of Scotland, The 2007

Last Kiss, The 2003

Last Kiss, The 2007

Last Legion, The pg. 239

Last Man Standing 1996

Last Mimzy, The pg. 240

Last Night 1999

Last of England, The 1988

Last of the Dogmen 1995

Last of the Finest, The 1990

Last of the Mohicans, The 1992

Last Orders 2003

Last Party, The 1993

Last Resort 1986

Last Resort 2002

Last Rites 1988

Last Samurai, The 2004

Last Seduction, The 1995

Last September, The 2001

Last Shot, The 2005

Last Starfighter, The 1984

Last Straw, The 1987

Last Supper 1996

Last Temptation of Christ, The 1988

Last Time I Committed Suicide, The 1997

Last Time I Saw Paris, The 1993

Last Summer in the Hamptons 1995

Last Wedding 2003

Latcho Drom 1995

Late August, Early September 2000

Late Chrysanthemums 1985

Late for Dinner 1991

Late Marriage 2003

Late Summer Blues 1987

Latin Boys Go to Hell 1997

Latter Days 2005

L' Auberge Espagnole 2004

Laurel Canyon 2004

Law of Desire, The 1987

Law of Enclosures, The 2002

Lawn Dogs 1999

Lawless Heart 2004

Lawnmower Man, The 1992

Lawnmower Man 2: Beyond Cyberspace 1996

Lawrence of Arabia 1990

Laws of Attraction 2005

Laws of Gravity 1992

Layer Cake 2006

L' Ecole de la chair. *See* School of Flesh, The.

Leading Man, The 1999

League of Extraordinary Gentlemen, The 2004

League of Their Own, A 1992

Lean on Me 1989

Leap of Faith 1992

Leatherface 1990

Leave It to Beaver 1997

Leave to Remain 1988

Leaving Las Vegas 1995

Leaving Normal 1992

Lebedyne ozero. *See* Swan Lake.

Leben der Anderen, Das. *See* Lives of Others, The.

Lectrice, La. *See* Reader, The.

Leela 2003

Left Hand Side of the Fridge, The 2002

Legal Eagles 1986

Legally Blonde 2002

Legally Blonde 2: Red, White & Blonde 2004

Legend 1986

Legend of Bagger Vance, The 2001

Legend of Billie Jean, The 1985

Legend of 1900 2000

Legend of Rita, The 2002

Legend of Wolf Mountain, The 1995

Legend of Zorro, The 2006

Legends 1995

Legends of the Fall 1995

Leggenda del Pianista Sull'oceano, La. *See* Legend of 1900.

Lemon Sisters, The 1990

Lemon Sky 1987

Lemony Snicket's A Series of Unfortunate Events 2005

Leo Tolstoy's Anna Karenina 1997

Leolo 1993

Leon the Pig Farmer 1995

Leonard Part VI 1987

Leopard Son, The 1996

Leprechaun 1993

Leprechaun II 1995

Les Patterson Saves the World 1987

Less Than Zero 1987

Let Him Have It 1991

Let It Come Down: The Life of Paul Bowles 2000

Let It Ride 1989

Let's Fall in Love. *See* New York in Short: The Shvitz and Let's Fall in Love.

Let's Get Lost 1988

Let's Spend the Night Together 1983

Lethal Weapon 1987

Lethal Weapon 2 1989

Lethal Weapon 3 1992

Lethal Weapon 4 1999

Letter to Brezhnev 1986

Letters from Iwo Jima 2007

Leviathan 1989

Levity 2004

Levy and Goliath 1988

Local Hero 1983

Lock, Stock, and Two Smoking Barrels 2000

Lock Up 1989

Locusts, The 1997

Lodz Ghetto 1989

Lola 1982

Lola La Loca 1988

Lola Rennt. *See* Run, Lola, Run.

Lolita 1999

London Kills Me 1992

Lone Runner, The 1988

Lone Star 1996

Lone Wolf McQuade 1983

Lonely Guy, The 1984

Lonely Hearts (Cox) 1983

Lonely Hearts (Lane) 1995

Lonely in America 1991

Lonely Lady, The 1983

Lonely Passion of Judith Hearne, The 1987

Lonesome Jim 2007

Long Day Closes, The 1993

Long Dimanche de Fiancailles, Un. *See* Very Long Engagement, A.

Long Good Friday, The 1982

Long Gray Line, The 1981

Long Kiss Goodnight, The 1996

Long Live the Lady! 1988

Long, Long Trailer, The 1986

Long Lost Friend, The. *See* Apprentice to Murder.

Long Walk Home, The 1990

Long Way Home, The 1999

Long Weekend, The 1990

Longest Yard, The 2006

Longshot, The 1986

Longtime Companion 1990

Look at Me 2006

Look Who's Talking 1989

Look Who's Talking Now 1993

Look Who's Talking Too 1990

Lookin' to Get Out 1982

Looking for Comedy in the Muslim World 2007

Looking for Richard 1996

Lookout, The pg. 248

Looney Tunes: Back in Action 2004

Loophole 1986

Loose Cannons 1990

Loose Connections 1988

Loose Screws 1986

L'ora di religione: Il sorriso di mia madre. *See* My Mother's Smile.

Lord of Illusions 1995

Lord of the Flies 1990

Lord of the Rings: The Fellowship of the Rings 2002

Lord of the Rings: The Return of the King 2004

Lord of the Rings: The Two Towers 2003

Lord of War 2006

Lords of Discipline, The 1983

Lords of Dogtown 2006

Lords of the Deep 1989

Lorenzo's Oil 1992

Loser 2001

Losin' It 1983

Losing Isaiah 1995

Loss of Sexual Innocence 2000

Lost and Delirious 2002

Lost and Found 2000

Lost Angels 1989

Lost Boys, The 1987

Lost City, The 2007

Lost Highway 1997

Lost in America 1985

Lost in La Mancha 2004

Lost in Siberia 1991

Lost in Space 1999

Lost in Translation 2004

Lost in Yonkers. *See* Neil Simon's Lost in Yonkers.

Lost Moment, The 1982

Lost Prophet 1995

Lost Souls 2001

Lost Weekend, The 1986

Lost Words, The 1995

Lost World, The 1997

Lou, Pat, and Joe D 1988

Louis Bluie 1985

Louis Prima: The Wildest 2001

Loulou 1981

Love Actually 2004

Love Affair 1995

Love After Love 1995

Love Always 1997

Love and a .45 1995

Love and Basketball 2001

Love and Death in Long Island 1999

Love and Human Remains 1995

Love and Murder 1991

Love and Other Catastrophes 1997

Love & Sex 2001

Love at Large 1990

Love Child, The 1988

Love Child: A True Story 1982

Love Come Down 2002

Love Crimes 1992

Love Don't Cost a Thing 2004

Love Field 1992

Love in Germany, A 1984

Love in the Afternoon 1986

Love in the Time of Cholera pg. 249

Love in the Time of Money 2003

Love Is a Dog from Hell 1988

Love Is the Devil 1999

love jones 1997

Love/Juice 2001

Love Letter, The 2000

Love Letters 1984

Love Liza 2004

Love Potion #9 1992

Love Serenade 1997

Love Song for Bobby Long, A 2006

Love Stinks 2000

Love Story, A. *See* Bound and Gagged.

Love Streams 1984

Love the Hard Way 2004

Love, the Magician. *See* Amor brujo, El.

Love! Valour! Compassion! 1997

Love Walked In 1999

Love Without Pity 1991

Loveless, The 1984, 1986

No Retreat, No Surrender 1986

No Retreat, No Surrender II 1989

No Secrets 1991

No Small Affair 1984

No Such Thing 2003

No Way Out 1987, 1992

Nobody Loves Me 1996

Nobody's Fool (Benton) 1995

Nobody's Fool (Purcell) 1986

Nobody's Perfect 1990

Noce en Galilee. *See* Wedding in Galilee, A.

Noche de los lapices, La. *See* Night of the Pencils, The.

Nochnoi Dozor. *See* Night Watch.

Noel 2005

Noises Off 1992

Nomads 1986

Non ti muovere. *See* Don't Move.

Nora 2002

Norbit pg. 294

Normal Life 1996

Norte, El 1983

North 1995

North Country 2006

North Shore 1987

North Star, The 1982

Northfork 2004

Nostalgia 1984

Nostradamus 1995

Not Another Teen Movie 2002

Not for Publication 1984

Not of This Earth 1988

Not Quite Paradise 1986

Not Since Casanova 1988

Not Without My Daughter 1991

Notebook, The 2005

Notebook on Cities and Clothes 1992

Notes on a Scandal 2007

Nothing but Trouble 1991

Nothing in Common 1986

Nothing Personal 1997

Nothing to Lose 1997

Notorious Bettie Page, The 2007

Notte di San Lorenzo, La. *See* Night of the Shooting Stars, The.

Notting Hill 2000

Nouvelle Eve, The. *See* New Eve, The.

November 2006

Novocaine 2002

Now and Then 1995

Nowhere 1997

Nowhere in Africa 2004

Nowhere to Hide 1987

Nowhere to Run 1993

Nueve Reinas. *See* Nine Queens.

Nuit de Varennes, La 1983, 1984

Nuits Fauves, Les. *See* Savage Nights.

Nuits de la pleine lune, Les. *See* Full Moon In Paris.

Number One with a Bullet 1987

Number 23, The pg. 295

Nuns on the Run 1990

Nurse Betty 2001

Nutcracker Prince, The 1990

Nutcracker, The 1986

Nutcracker, The. *See* George Balanchine's the Nutcracker.

Nuts 1987

Nutty Professor, The 1996

Nutty Professor 2: The Klumps 2001

O

O 2002

O Brother, Where Art Thou? 2001

O' Despair. *See* Long Weekend, The.

Oak, The 1995

Oasis, The 1984

Obecna Skola. *See* Elementary School, The.

Oberst Redl. *See* Colonel Redl.

Object of Beauty, The 1991

Object of My Affection, The 1999

Oblivion 1995

Obsessed 1988

O.C. and Stiggs 1987

Ocean's Eleven 2002

Ocean's Thirteen pg. 299

Ocean's Twelve 2005

Oci Ciornie. *See* Dark Eyes.

October Sky 2000

Octopussy 1983

Odd Man Out 1985

Oedipus Rex 1995

Oedipus Rex 1984

Oedipus Wrecks. *See* New York Stories.

Of Human Bondage 1986

Of Love and Shadows 1996

Of Mice and Men 1992

Of Unknown Origin 1983

Off Beat 1986

Off Limits 1988

Off the Menu: The Last Days of Chasen's 1999

Office Killer 1997

Office Party 1989

Office Space 2000

Officer and a Gentleman, An 1982

Official Story, The 1985

Offret. *See* Sacrifice, The.

Oh God, You Devil 1984

O'Hara's Wife 1982

Old Explorers 1991

Old Gringo 1989

Old Joy 2007

Old Lady Who Walked in the Sea, The 1995

Old School 2004

Oldboy 2006

Oleanna 1995

Oliver and Company 1988

Oliver Twist 2006

Olivier Olivier 1993

Omen, The 2007

On Deadly Ground 1995

On Golden Pond 1981

On Guard! 2004

On the Edge 1986

On the Line 2002

On the Town 1985

On Valentine's Day 1986

Once pg. 300

Once Around 1991

Once Bitten 1985

Once More 1988

Once Were Warriors 1995

Once Upon a Crime 1992

Once Upon A Forest 1993

Once Upon a Time in America 1984

Once Upon a Time in Mexico 2004

Once Upon a Time in the Midlands 2004

Once Upon a Time...When We Were Colored 1996

Once We Were Dreamers 1987

One 2001

One, The 2002

One and a Two, A. *See* Yi Yi.

One Crazy Summer 1986

One Day in September 2001

One False Move 1992

One Fine Day 1996

One Flew over the Cuckoo's Nest 1985, 1991

One from the Heart 1982

One Good Cop 1991

One Hour Photo 2003

101 Dalmatians 1996

101 Reykjavik 2002

102 Dalmatians 2001

187 1997

112th and Central 1993

One Magic Christmas 1985

One More Saturday 1986

One More Tomorrow 1986

One Nation Under God 1995

One Night at McCool's 2002

One Night Stand 1997

One Tough Cop 1999

One True Thing 1999

Onegin 2000

Onimaru. *See* Arashi Ga Oka.

Only Emptiness Remains 1985

Only the Lonely 1991

Only the Strong 1993

Only the Strong Survive 2004

Only Thrill, The 1999

Only When I Laugh 1981

Only You 1995

Open Doors 1991

Open Range 2004

Open Season 2007

Open Water 2005

Open Your Eyes 2000

Opening Night 1988

Opera 1987

Operation Condor 1997

Operation Dumbo Drop 1995

Opportunists, The 2001

Opportunity Knocks 1990

Opposite of Sex, The 1999

Opposite Sex, The 1993

Orange County 2003

Orchestra Seats. *See* Avenue Montaigne.

Ordeal by Innocence 1985

Order, The 2004

Orgazmo 1999

Original Gangstas 1996

Original Kings of Comedy, The 2001

Original Sin 2002

Orlando 1993

Orphan Muses, The 2002

Orphans 1987

Orphans of the Storm 1984

Osama 2005

Oscar 1991

Oscar & Lucinda 1997

Osmosis Jones 2002

Ososhiki. *See* Funeral, The.

Osterman Weekend, The 1983

Otac Na Sluzbenom Putu. *See* When Father Was Away on Business.

Otello 1986

Othello 1995

Other People's Money 1991

Other Side of Heaven, The 2003

Other Sister, The 2000

Other Voices, Other Rooms 1997

Others, The 2002

Our Lady of the Assassins 2002

Our Relations 1985

Our Song 2002

Out Cold 1989

Out for Justice 1991

Out in the World. *See* Among People.

Out of Africa 1985

Out of Bounds 1986

Out of Control 1985

Out of Life. *See* Hors la Vie.

Out of Order 1985

Out of Sight 1999

Out of Sync 1995

Out of the Dark 1989

Out of the Past 1991

Out of Time 2004

Out-of-Towners, The 2000

Out on a Limb 1992

Out to Sea 1997

Outbreak 1995

Outfoxed: Rupert Murdoch's War on Journalism 2005

Outing, The 1987

Outland 1981

Outrageous Fortune 1987

Outside Providence 2000

Outsiders, The 1983

Over Her Dead Body 1995

Over the Edge 1987

Over the Hedge 2007

Over the Hill 1995

Over the Ocean 1995

Over the Top 1987

Overboard 1987

Overexposed 1990

Overseas 1991

Owning Mahowny 2004

Ox, The 1992

Oxford, Blues 1984

Oxygen 2000

P

P.O.W. the Escape 1986

P.S. 2005

Pacific Heights 1990

Pacifier, The 2006

Package, The 1989

Pacte des Loups, Le. *See* Brotherhood of the Wolf.

Pagemaster, The 1995

Paint Job, The 1995

Painted Desert, The 1995

Painted Veil, The pg. 303

Palais Royale 1988

Pale Rider 1985

Palindromes 2006

Pallbearer, The 1996

Palmetto 1999

Palombella Rossa. *See* Redwood Pigeon.

Palookaville 1996

Panama Deception, The 1992

Pane e Tulipani. *See* Bread and Tulips.

Panic 2001

Panic Room, The 2003

Pan's Labyrinth 2007

Panther 1995

Papa's Song 2001

Paparazzi 2005

Paper, The 1995

Paper Hearts 1995

Paper Mask 1991

Paper Wedding, A 1991

Paperback Romance 1997

Paperhouse 1988

Paprika pg. 305

Paradise (Donoghue) 1991

Paradise (Gillard) 1982

Paradise Lost 1996

Paradise Now 2006

Paradise Road 1997

Parasite 1982

Parde-ye akhar. *See* Last Act, The.

Parent Trap, The 1999

Parenthood 1989

Parents 1989

Paris, I Love You. *See* Paris, je t'aime.

Paris, Texas 1984

Paris Blues 1992

Paris Is Burning 1991

Paris je t'aime pg. 306

Parsifal 1983

Parsley Days 2001

Parting Glances 1986

Partisans of Vilna 1986

Partners 1982

Party Animal 1985

Party Girl 1995

Party Line 1988

Party Monster 2004

Pascali's Island 1988

Pass the Ammo 1988

Passage, The 1988

Passage to India, A 1984, 1990

Passages 1995

Passed Away 1992

Passenger 57 1992

Passion (Duncan) 2001

Passion (Godard) 1983

Passion d'amore 1984

Passion Fish 1992

Passion in the Desert 1999

Passion of Martin, The 1991

Passion of Mind 2001

Passion of the Christ, The 2005

Passion to Kill, A 1995

Passionada 2003

Pastime 1991

Patch Adams 1999

Patch of Blue, A 1986

Pathfinder 1990

Pathfinder pg. 308

Paths of Glory 1991

Patinoire, La. *See* Ice Rink, The.

Patriot, The 2001

Patriot Games 1992

Patsy, The 1985

Patti Rocks 1987

Patty Hearst 1988

Paul Bowles: The Complete Outsider 1995

Paulie 1999

Pauline a la plage. *See* Pauline at the Beach.

Pauline and Paulette 2003

Pauline at the Beach 1983

Paura e amore. *See* Three Sisters.

Pavilion of Women 2002

Pay It Forward 2001

Payback 2000

Paycheck 2004

PCU 1995

Peace, Propaganda & The Promised Land 2006

Peaceful Air of the West 1995

Peacemaker, The 1997

Pearl Harbor 2002

Pebble and the Penguin, The 1995

Pecker 1999

Pee-wee's Big Adventure 1985

Peggy Sue Got Married 1986

Pelican Brief, The 1993

Pelle Erobreren. *See* Pelle the Conqueror.

Pelle the Conquered 1988

Pelle the Conqueror 1987

Penitent, The 1988

Penitentiary II 1982

Penitentiary III 1987

Penn and Teller Get Killed 1989

Pennies from Heaven 1981

People I Know 2004

People on Sunday 1986

People Under the Stairs, The 1991

People vs. Larry Flynt, The 1996

Pepi, Luci, Bom 1992

Perez Family, The 1995

Perfect 1985

Perfect Candidate, A 1996

Perfect Man, The 2006

Perfect Match, The 1987

Perfect Model, The 1989

Perfect Murder, A 1999

Perfect Murder, The 1988

Perfect Score, The 2005

Perfect Son, The 2002

Perfect Storm, The 2001

Perfect Stranger pg. 310

Perfect Weapon, The 1991

Perfect World, A 1993

Perfectly Normal 1991

Perfume: The Story of a Murderer pg. 312

Perhaps Some Other Time 1992

Peril 1985

Peril en la demeure. *See* Peril.

Permanent Midnight 1999

Rapture, The 1991

Raspad 1992

Rasputin 1985

Rat Race 2002

Ratatouille pg. 323

Ratboy 1986

Rat's Tale, A 1999

Ratcatcher 2001

Rate It X 1986

Ravenous 2000

Raw Deal 1986

Rawhead Rex 1987

Ray 2005

Rayon vert, Le. *See* Summer.

Razorback 1985

Razor's Edge, The 1984

Re-Animator 1985

Read My Lips 2003

Reader, The 1988, 1989

Ready to Rumble 2001

Ready to Wear 1995

Real Blonde, The 1999

Real Genius 1985

Real McCoy, The 1993

Real Men 1987

Real Women Have Curves 2003

Reality Bites 1995

Reaping, The pg. 325

Rear Window 2001

Reason to Believe, A 1995

Rebel 1986

Rebound 2006

Reckless 1984

Reckless 1995

Reckless Kelly 1995

Reckoning, The 2005

Recruit, The 2004

Recruits 1986

Red 1995

Red Corner 1997

Red Dawn 1984

Red Dragon 2003

Red Eye 2006

Red Firecracker, Green Firecracker 1995

Red Heat 1988

Red Planet 2001

Red Road pg. 327

Red Rock West 1995

Red Scorpion 1989

Red Sonja 1985

Red Sorghum 1988

Red Surf 1990

Red Violin, The 1999

Redl Ezredes. *See* Colonel Redl.

Reds 1981

Redwood Pigeon 1995

Reefer and the Model 1988

Ref, The 1995

Reflecting Skin, The 1991

Reform School Girls 1986

Regarding Henry 1991

Regeneration 1999

Reign of Fire 2003

Reign Over Me pg. 328

Reindeer Games 2001

Reine Margot, La. *See* Queen Margot.

Rejuvenator, The 1988

Relax, It's Just Sex 2000

Relentless 1989

Relic, The 1997

Religion Hour, The. *See* My Mother's Smile.

Remains of the Day, The 1993

Remember the Titans 2001

Remo Williams 1985

Renaissance Man 1995

Rendez-vous 1988

Rendezvous in Paris 1996

Rendition pg. 331

Renegades 1989

Reno 911!: Miami pg. 333

Rent 2006

Rent-a-Cop 1988

Rent Control 1984

Rented Lips 1988

Repentance 1987

Replacement Killers, The 1999

Replacements, The 2001

Repo Man 1984

Repossessed 1990

Requiem for a Dream 2001

Requiem for Dominic 1991

Rescue, The 1988

Rescue Dawn pg. 334

Rescuers Down Under, The 1990

Reservation Road pg. 336

Reservoir Dogs 1992

Resident Alien: Quentin Crisp in America 1992

Resident Evil 2003

Resident Evil: Apocalypse 2005

Resident Evil: Extinction pg. 338

Respiro 2004

Ressources Humaines. *See* Human Resources.

Restless Natives 1986

Restoration 1995

Resurrected, The 1995

Resurrecting the Champ pg. 339

Retour de Martin Guerre, Le. *See* Return of Martin Guerre, The.

Return, The 2007

Return of Horror High 1987

Return of Martin Guerre, The 1983

Return of Superfly, The 1990

Return of the Jedi 1983, 1997

Return of the Living Dead, The 1985

Return of the Living Dead II 1988

Return of the Living Dead III 1993

Return of the Musketeers, The 1989

Return of the Secaucus 7 1982

Return of the Soldier, The 1983

Return of the Swamp Thing, The 1989

Return to Me 2001

Return to Never Land 2003

Return to Oz 1985

Return to Paradise 1999

Return to Snowy River 1988

Return to the Blue Lagoon 1991

Reuben, Reuben 1983

Revenge 1990

Revenge of the Nerds 1984

Revenge of the Nerds II 1987

Revenge of the Ninja 1983

Reversal of Fortune 1990

Revolution 1985

Revolution! 1995

Revolution #9 2004

Rhapsody in August 1991

Rhinestone 1984

Rhyme & Reason 1998

Rhythm Thief 1995

Rich and Famous 1981

Rich Girl 1991

Rich in Love 1993

Rich Man's Wife 1996

Richard III 1995

Richard Pryor Here and Now 1983

Richard's Things 1981

Richie Rich 1995

Ricochet 1991

Riddle of the Sands, The 1984

Ride 1999

Ride in the Whirlwind 1966

Ride to Wounded Knee 1995

Ride with the Devil 2000

Ridicule 1996

Riding Giants 2005

Riding in Cars with Boys 2002

Riding the Edge 1989

Rien ne va plus. *See* Swindle, The.

Riff-Raff 1993

Right Hand Man, The 1987

Right Stuff, The 1983

Rikky and Pete 1988

Rimini Rimini 1987

Ring, The 2003

Ring Two, The 2006

Ringer, The 2006

Ringmaster 1999

Riot in Cell Block 11 1982

Ripe 1997

Ripoux, Les. *See* My New Partner.

Rising Sun 1993

Risk 1995

Risky Business 1983

Rita, Sue and Bob Too 1987

River, The (Rydell) 1984

River, The (Tsai) 2002

River of Death 1993

River Rat, The 1984

River Runs Through It, A 1992

River Wild, The 1995

Riverbend 1989

River's Edge 1987

Road Home, The 2002

Road House 1989

Road to El Dorado, The 2001

Road to Perdition 2003

Road to Wellville, The 1995

Road Trip 2001

Road Warrior, The 1982

Roadside Prophets 1992

Rob Roy 1995

Robert A. Heinlein's The Puppet Masters. *See* Puppet Masters, The.

Robin Hood 1991

Robin Hood: Men In Tights 1993

Robocop 1987

Robocop II 1990

Robocop III 1993

Robot Jox 1990

Robot Stories 2005

Robots 2006

Rock, The 1996

Rock-a-Doodle 1992

Rock 'n Roll Meller. *See* Hellbent.

Rock Hudson's Home Movies 1995

Rock School 2006

Rock Star 2002

Rock the Boat 2000

Rocket Gibraltar 1988

Rocket Man 1997

Rocket Science pg. 341

Rocketeer, The 1991

Rocky III 1982

Rocky IV 1985

Rocky V 1990

Rocky Balboa 2007

Roger and Me 1989

Roger Corman's Frankenstein Unbound 1990

Roger Dodger 2003

Roi Danse, Le. *See* King Is Dancing, The.

Rois et reine. *See* Kings and Queen.

Rok spokojnego slonca. *See* Year of the Quiet Sun, A.

Roll Bounce 2006

Rollerball 2003

Rollercoaster 2001

Rolling Stones at the Max 1991

Roman Holiday 1989

Romance 2000

Romance of Book and Sword, The 1987

Romancing the Stone 1984

Romantic Comedy 1983

Romeo 1989

Romeo and Julia 1992

Romeo is Bleeding 1995

Romeo Must Die 2001

Romper Stomper 1993

Romuald et Juliette. *See* Mama, There's a Man in Your Bed.

Romy & Michelle's High School Reunion 1997

Ronin 1999

Rooftops 1989

Rookie, The 1990

Rookie, The 2003

Rookie of the Year 1993

Room with a View, A 1986

Roommates 1995

Rory O'Shea Was Here 2006

Rosa Luxemburg 1987

Rosalie Goes Shopping 1990

Rosary Murders, The 1987

Rose Garden, The 1989

Rosencrantz and Guildenstern Are Dead 1991

Rosewood 1997

Rosie 2000

Rouge of the North 1988

Rough Cut 1982

Rough Magic

Roughly Speaking 1982

'Round Midnight 1986

Rounders 1999

Rover Dangerfield 1991

Row of Crows, A. *See* Climate for Killing, A.

Seven Men from Now 1987

Seven Minutes in Heaven 1986

Seven Women, Seven Sins 1987

Seven Year Itch, The 1986

Seven Years in Tibet 1998

Seventh Coin, The 1993

Seventh Sign, The 1988

Severance 1989

Sex and Lucia 2003

Sex, Drugs, and Democracy 1995

Sex, Drugs, Rock and Roll 1991

sex, lies and videotape 1989

Sex: The Annabel Chong Story 2001

Sexbomb 1989

Sexy Beast 2002

Shades of Doubt 1995

Shadey 1987

Shadow, The 1995

Shadow Army, The. *See* Army of Shadows.

Shadow Conspiracy, The

Shadow Dancing 1988

Shadow Magic 2002

Shadow of the Raven 1990

Shadow of the Vampire 2001

Shadow of the Wolf 1993

Shadowboxer 2007

Shadowlands 1993

Shadows and Fog 1992

Shadrach 1999

Shaft 2001

Shag 1988

Shaggy Dog, The 2007

Shakedown 1988

Shakes the Clown 1992

Shakespeare in Love 1999

Shaking the Tree 1992

Shall We Dance? 1997

Shall We Dance? 2005

Shallow Grave 1995

Shallow Hal 2002

Shame 1988

Shanghai Knights 2004

Shanghai Noon 2001

Shanghai Surprise 1986

Shanghai Triad 1995

Shaolin Soccer 2005

Shape of Things, The 2004

Shark Tale 2005

Sharky's Machine 1981

Sharma and Beyond 1986

Shatterbrain. *See* Resurrected, The.

Shattered 1991

Shattered Glass 2004

Shaun of the Dead 2005

Shaunglong Hui. *See* Twin Dragons.

Shawshank Redemption, The 1995

She Hate Me 2005

She Must Be Seeing Things 1987

Sherrybaby 2007

She-Devil 1989

Sheena 1984

Sheer Madness 1985

Shelf Life 1995

Sheltering Sky, The 1990

Sherlock Holmes 1982

Sherman's March 1986

She's All That 2000

She's De Lovely. *See* De-Lovely.

She's Gotta Have It 1986

She's Having a Baby 1988

She's Out of Control 1989

She's So Lovely 1997

She's the Man 2007

She's the One 1996

Shiloh 2: Shiloh Season 2000

Shimian Maifu. *See* House of Flying Daggers.

Shine 1996

Shining, The

Shining Through 1992

Shipping News, The 2002

Shipwrecked 1991

Shiqisuide Danche. *See* Beijing Bicycle.

Shirley Valentine 1989

Shiza. *See* Shizo.

Shoah 1985

Shock to the System, A 1990

Shocker 1989

Shoot 'Em Up pg. 355

Shoot the Moon 1982

Shoot to Kill 1988

Shooter pg. 356

Shooting, The 1995

Shooting Dogs. *See* Beyond the Gates.

Shooting Fish 1999

Shooting Party, The 1985

Shootist, The 1982

Shopgirl 2006

Short Circuit 1986

Short Circuit II 1988

Short Cuts 1993

Short Film About Love, A 1995

Short Time 1990

Shot, The 1996

Shout 1991

Show, The 1995

Show Me Love 2000

Show of Force, A 1990

Showdown in Little Tokyo 1991

Shower, The 2001

Showgirls 1995

Showtime 2003

Shrek 2002

Shrek the Third pg. 358

Shrek 2 2005

Shrimp on the Barbie, The 1990

Shvitz, The. *See* New York in Short: The Shvitz and Let's Fall in Love.

Shy People 1987

Siberiade 1982

Sibling Rivalry 1990

Sicilian, The 1987

Sick: The Life and Death of Bob Flanagan, Supermasochist 1997

Sicko pg. 360

Sid and Nancy 1986

Side Out 1990

Sidekicks 1993

Sidewalk Stories 1989

Sidewalks of New York, The 2002

Sideways 2005

Siege, The 1999

Siesta 1987

Smilla's Sense of Snow 1997

Smithereens 1982, 1985

Smoke 1995

Smoke Signals 1999

Smokey and the Bandit, Part 3 1983

Smokin' Aces pg. 368

Smoking/No Smoking 2001

Smooth Talk 1985

Smurfs and the Magic Flute, The 1983

Snake Eyes 1999

Snake Eyes. *See* Dangerous Game.

Snakes on a Plane 2007

Snapper, The 1993

Snatch 2002

Sneakers 1992

Sniper 1993

Snow Day 2001

Snow Dogs 2003

Snow Falling in Cedars 2000

Snows of Kilimanjaro, The 1982

S.O.B. 1981

So I Married an Axe Murderer 1993

Soapdish 1991

Sobibor, October 14, 1943, 4 p.m. 2002

Society 1992

Sofie 1993

Soft Fruit 2001

Soft Shell Man 2003

Softly Softly 1985

Sokhout. *See* Silence, The.

Sol del Membrillo, El. *See* Dream of Light.

Solarbabies 1986

Solaris 2003

Solas 2001

Soldier 1999

Soldier, The 1982

Soldier's Daughter Never Cries, A 1999

Soldier's Story, A 1984

Soldier's Tale, A 1988

Solid Gold Cadillac, The 1984

Solo 1996

Solomon and Gaenor 2001

Some Girls 1988

Some Kind of Hero 1982

Some Kind of Wonderful 1987

Some Like It Hot 1986, 1988

Some Mother's Son 1996

Someone Else's America 1996

Someone Like You 2002

Someone to Love 1987, 1988

Someone to Watch Over Me 1987

Somersault 2007

Something New 2007

Something to Do with the Wall 1995

Something to Talk About 1995

Something Wicked This Way Comes 1983

Something Wild 1986

Something Within Me 1995

Something's Gotta Give 2004

Sommersby 1993

Son, The 2003

Son of Darkness: To Die For II 1995

Son of the Bride 2003

Son of the Mask 2006

Son of the Pink Panther 1993

Son-in-Law 1993

Sonatine 1999

Song for Martin 2003

Songcatcher 2001

Songwriter 1984

Sonny 2003

Sonny Boy 1990

Sons 1989

Sons of Steel 1988

Son's Room, The 2002

Sontagsbarn. *See* Sunday's Children.

Sophie's Choice 1982

Sorority Babes in the Slimeball Bowl-o-Rama 1988

Sorority Boys 2003

Sorority House Massacre 1987

Sotto Sotto. *See* Softly Softly.

Soul Food 1997

Soul Man 1986

Soul Plane 2005

Soul Survivors 2002

Sound Barrier, The 1984, 1990

Sound of Thunder, A 2006

Sour Grapes 1999

Source, The 2000

Soursweet 1988

Sous le Sable. *See* Under the Sand.

Sous le Soleil de Satan. *See* Under the Sun of Satan.

Sous Sol 1997

South Central 1992

South of Reno 1987

South Park: Bigger, Longer & Uncut 2000

Southern Comfort 1981

Southland Tales pg. 370

Souvenir 1988

Space Cowboys 2001

Space Jam 1996

Spaceballs 1987

Spacecamp 1986

Spaced Invaders 1990

Spacehunter: Adventures in the Forbidden Zone 1983

Spalding Gray's Monster in a Box. *See* Monster in a Box.

Spanglish 2005

Spanish Prisoner, The 1999

Spanking the Monkey 1995

Spartacus 1991

Spartan 2005

Spawn 1997

Speaking in Strings 2000

Speaking Parts 1990

Special Day, A 1984

Special Effects 1986

Specialist, The 1995

Species 1995

Species 2 1999

Specter of the Rose 1982

Speechless 1995

Speed 1995

Speed 2: Cruise Control 1997

Speed Zone 1989

Spellbinder 1988

Spellbound 1989

Sphere 1999

Tapeheads 1988

Taps 1981

Target 1985

Target 1996

Tarnation 2005

Tarzan 2000

Tarzan and the Lost City 1999

Tasogare Seibei. *See* Twilight Samurai, The.

Taste of Others, The 2002

Tatie Danielle 1991

Taxi 2005

Taxi Blues 1991

Taxi nach Kairo. *See* Taxi to Cairo.

Taxi to Cairo 1988

Taxi to the Toilet. *See* Taxi Zum Klo.

Taxi Zum Klo 1981

Taxing Woman, A 1988

Taxing Woman's Return, A 1989

Tea in the Harem 1986

Tea With Mussolini 2000

Teachers 1984

Teacher's Pet: The Movie. *See* Disney's Teacher's Pet.

Teaching Mrs. Tingle 2000

Team America: World Police 2005

Tears of the Sun 2004

Ted and Venus 1991

Teen Witch 1989

Teen Wolf 1985

Teenage Mutant Ninja Turtles 1990

Teenage Mutant Ninja Turtles (2007). *See* TMNT.

Teenage Mutant Ninja Turtles II 1991

Teenage Mutant Ninja Turtles III 1993

Telephone, The 1988

Telling Lies in America 1997

Temp, The 1993

Tempest 1982

Temporada de patos. *See* Duck Season.

Temps qui changent, Les. *See* Changing Times.

Temps qui reste, Les. *See* Time to Leave.

Temps Retrouve. *See* Time Regained.

Temptress Moon 1997

Ten 2004

Ten Things I Hate About You 2000

10 to Midnight 1983

Tenacious D in the Pick of Destiny 2007

Tender Mercies 1983

Tenebrae. *See* Unsane.

Tenue de soiree. *See* Menage.

Tequila Sunrise 1988

Terminal, The 2005

Terminal Bliss 1992

Terminal Velocity 1995

Terminator, The 1984

Terminator 2 1991

Terminator 3: Rise of the Machines 2004

Termini Station 1991

Terminus. *See* End of the Line.

Terms of Endearment 1983

Terror Within, The 1989

Terrorvision 1986

Tess 1981

Test of Love 1985

Testament 1983

Testimony 1987

Tetsuo: The Iron Man 1992

Tex 1982, 1987

Texas Chainsaw Massacre, The (Nispel) 2004

Texas Chainsaw Massacre, Part II, The 1986

Texas Chainsaw Massacre: The Beginning, The 2007

Texas Comedy Massacre, The 1988

Texas Rangers 2003

Texas Tenor: The Illinois Jacquet Story 1995

Texasville 1990

Thank You and Good Night 1992

Thank You for Smoking 2007

That Championship Season 1982

That Darn Cat 1997

That Night 1993

That Old Feeling 1997

That Sinking Feeling 1984

That Thing You Do! 1996

That Was Then...This Is Now 1985

That's Entertainment! III 1995

That's Life! 1986, 1988

The au harem d'Archi Ahmed, Le. *See* Tea in the Harem.

Thelma and Louise 1991

Thelonious Monk 1988

Theory of Flight, The 1999

There Goes My Baby 1995

There Goes the Neighborhood 1995

There Will Be Blood pg. 392

There's Nothing Out There 1992

There's Something About Mary 1999

Theremin: An Electronic Odyssey 1995

They All Laughed 1981

They Call Me Bruce 1982

They Drive by Night 1982

They Live 1988

They Live by Night 1981

They Might Be Giants 1982

They Still Call Me Bruce 1987

They Won't Believe Me 1987

They're Playing with Fire 1984

Thiassos, O. *See* Traveling Players, The.

Thief 1981

Thief, The 1999

Thief of Hearts 1984

Thieves 1996

Thin Blue Line, The 1988

Thin Line Between Love and Hate, A 1996

Thin Red Line, The 1999

Thing, The 1982

Thing Called Love, The 1995

Things Are Tough All Over 1982

Things Change 1988

Things to Do in Denver When You're Dead 1995

Things We Lost in the Fire pg. 395

Think Big 1990

Third World Cop 2001

Thirteen 2004

To Return. *See* Volver.

To Sir with Love 1992

To Sleep with Anger 1990

To Wong Foo, Thanks for Everything! Julie Newmar 1995

Todo Sobre Mi Madre. *See* All About My Mother.

Together 2002

Together 2004

Tokyo Pop 1988

Tokyo-Ga 1985

Tom and Huck 1995

Tom and Jerry 1993

Tom & Viv 1995

Tomb Raider. *See* Lara Croft: Tomb Raider.

Tomboy 1985

Tombstone 1993

Tomcats 2002

Tommy Boy 1995

Tomorrow 1983

Tomorrow Never Dies 1997

Tomorrow's a Killer. *See* Prettykill.

Too Beautiful for You 1990

Too Hot to Handle 1983

Too Much 1987

Too Much Sleep 2002

Too Much Sun 1991

Too Outrageous! 1987

Too Scared to Scream 1985

Too Soon to Love

Tootsie 1982

Top Dog 1995

Top Gun 1986

Top of the Food Chain 2002

Top Secret 1984

Topio stin omichi. *See* Landscape in the Mist.

Topsy-Turvy 2000

Tora-San Goes to Viena 1989

Torajiro Kamone Uta. *See* Foster Daddy, Tora!

Torch Song Trilogy 1988

Torment 1986

Torn Apart 1990

Torn Curtain 1984

Torque 2005

Torrents of Spring 1990

Tortilla Soup 2002

Total Eclipse 1995

Total Recall 1990

Totally F***ed Up 1995

Toto le heros. *See* Toto the Hero.

Toto the Hero 1992

Tottering Lives 1988

Touch 1997

Touch and Go 1986

Touch of a Stranger 1990

Touch of Evil 1999

Touch of Larceny, A 1986

Touch the Sound 2006

Touching the Void 2005

Tough Enough 1983

Tough Guys 1986

Tough Guys Don't Dance 1987

Tougher than Leather 1988

Touki-Bouki 1995

Tous les matins du monde 1992

Toward the Within 1995

Town and Country 2002

Town is Quiet, The 2002

Toxic Avenger, The 1986

Toxic Avenger, Part II, The 1989

Toxic Avenger, Part III, The 1989

Toy, The 1982

Toy Soldiers (Fisher) 1984

Toy Soldiers (Petrie) 1991

Toy Story 1995

Toy Story 2 2000

Toys 1992

Trace, The 1984

Traces of Red 1992

Track 1988

Tracks in the Snow 1986

Trade pg. 406

Trade Winds 1982

Trading Hearts 1988

Trading Mom 1995

Trading Places 1983

Traffic 2001

Tragedia di un umo ridiculo. *See* Tragedy of a Ridiculous Man.

Tragedy of a Ridiculous Man 1982

Trail of the Lonesome Pine, The. *See* Waiting for the Moon.

Trail of the Pink Panther 1982

Train de Vie. *See* Train of Life.

Train of Life 2000

Training Day 2002

Trainspotting 1996

Trancers 1985

Transamerica 2006

Transformers pg. 407

Transformers, The 1986

Transporter 2 2006

Transylvania 6-5000 1985

Trapped 2003

Trapped in Paradise 1995

Traps 1995

Traveling Players, The 1990

Traveller 1997

Travelling Avant 1987

Travelling North 1987

Traviata, La 1982

Tre fratelli. *See* Three Brothers.

Treasure Island 2001

Treasure of the Four Crowns 1983

Treasure of the Sierra Madre, The 1983

Treasure Planet 2003

Trees Lounge 1996

Trekkies 2000

Tremors 1990

Trenchcoat 1983

Trespass 1992

Trial, The 1995

Trial and Error 1997

Trial by Jury 1995

Tribulations of Balthasar Kober, The 1988

Trick 2000

Trick or Treat 1986

Trigger Effect, The 1996

Trilogia: To Livadi pou dakryzei. *See* Weeping Meadow.

Trilogy: After the Life, The 2005